# Principles of Marketing

**The European Edition**

PHILIP KOTLER   GARY ARMSTRONG

JOHN SAUNDERS   VERONICA WONG

PRENTICE HALL

*London   New York   Toronto   Sydney   Tokyo   Singapore*
*Madrid   Mexico City   Munich*

First published 1996 by
Prentice Hall Europe
Campus 400, Maylands Avenue
Hemel Hempstead
Hertfordshire, HP2 7EZ
A division of
Simon & Schuster International Group

Text design by Claire Brodmann, Burton on Trent

Cover design by Designers & Partners Ltd, Oxford

Typeset in Melior and Gill by Goodfellow & Egan Ltd, Cambridge

Colour origination by Create Publishing Services Limited, Bath

Printed and bound in Great Britain by Bath Press Colour Books, Glasgow

A Library of Congress Cataloging-in-Publication Data catalog record for this book is available from the publisher

A British Library Cataloguing in Publication Data catalogue record for this book is available from the British Library

ISBN: 0-13-165903-0

1 2 3 4 5 00 99 98 97 96

# To Wong and Bridget

# Supplements

A successful marketing course requires more than a well-written book. Today's classroom requires a dedicated teacher and a fully integrated teaching system. *Principles of Marketing* is supported by an extensive system of supplemental learning and teaching aids:

**Instructor's Resource Manual**. This helpful teaching resource, prepared by T. C. Melewar, contains chapter overviews that follow the full-colour transparencies and teaching tips, class exercises, stories, quotations and anecdotes to help in class preparation, discussion notes for all cases and answers to end-of-chapter questions and exercises. A **computerised test item file** is included. (ISBN: 0-13-239328-X).

**Full-Colour Transparencies**. The transparencies package includes full-colour transparencies of tables and figures prepared to ensure clear classroom presentation (ISBN: 0-13-239336-0).

**The European Casebook on Principles of Marketing** by Jim Saker and Gareth Smith is a collection of new and comprehensive marketing cases for use with *Principles of Marketing: The European Edition*. (ISBN: 0-13-227653-4, £19.95/$36.95). An instructor's manual is available with this book.

**Interactive Marketing Software** Innovative and challenging software is available to assist teaching and learning on introductory marketing courses and is ideal for classroom sessions or self-study. Mixing animation graphics and images, the software provides 10 modules of interactive problem-solving activities and practical exercises, enabling students to work at their own pace in a supportive and structured environment. The exercises are underpinned by tutorial material which defines and explains the concepts and terminology used. Topics covered by the software are identified by the computer icon reproduced here and in the contents of this book. The number on screen relates to the software module.

The package also includes a sophisticated assessment builder of 250 questions for selecting and compiling assessments and tests (ISBN: 0-13-254982-3 (demonstration disks). Available to teaching institutions on a site licence basis at £850/$1500. For further information about the software please contact your local representative or Chris Bunting (email: christopher-bunting@prenhall.co.uk) at the address below.

All the above items can be ordered from our inspection copy department at Prentice Hall Europe, Campus 400, Maylands Avenue, Hemel Hempstead, Herts HP2 7EZ, UK. Tel: +1442 881900, Fax: +1442 882265

# Contents

**Preface**   xiii

**About the authors**   xviii

**Ecu conversion table**   xx

PART ONE   **Marketing and the Marketing Process**   1

1   **Marketing in a changing world: satisfying human needs**   3

Chapter objectives   3
Chapter preview   Marketing touches our daily life   3
Introduction   4
What is marketing?   6
Marketing management   12
Marketing management philosophies   14
The goals of the marketing system   20
Marketing challenges in the 1990s   22
Summary   27
Discussing the issues   28
Applying the concepts   29
References   29
CASE 1   Amphitrion: your ultimate host in Greece   *Alkis S. Magdalinos*   30

2   **Marketing and society: social responsibility and marketing ethics**   33

Chapter objectives   33
Chapter preview   Brown & Williamson Tobacco: 'Keeping smokers addicted'   33
Introduction   35
Social criticisms of marketing   36
Citizen and public actions to regulate marketing   49

Business actions towards socially responsible marketing    52
Principles for public policy towards marketing    60
Summary    62
Discussing the issues    63
Applying the concepts    64
References    64

CASE 2    Nestlé: singled out again and again    65

## 3    Strategic marketing planning    68

Chapter objectives    68
Chapter preview    Levi's strategic marketing and planning    68
Introduction    70
Strategic planning    70
The strategic plan    73
The marketing process    91
The brand plan    97
Marketing organization    102
Marketing control    104
Summary    108
Discussing the issues    110
Applying the concepts    110
References    110

CASE 3    Trap-Ease: the big cheese of mousetraps    112

OVERVIEW CASE I    **KitKat: have a break ...**    *Sylvie Laforet*    115

PART TWO    **The Marketing Setting**    127

## 4    The marketing environment    129

Chapter objectives    129
Chapter preview    Unilever: Power?    129
Introduction    134
The company's microenvironment    134
The company's macroenvironment    140
Responding to the marketing environment    159
Summary    160
Discussing the issues    160
Applying the concepts    161
References    161

CASE 4    Angelou's restaurant (and snack bar?)    *Alkis S. Magdalinos*    163

## 5    The global marketplace    165

Chapter objectives    165
Chapter preview    Danone taps the Japanese yoghurt market    165
The importance of internationalization    166
Risks in international marketing    171
Analysis of international market opportunity    173
Deciding which markets to enter    186
Establishing market entry mode    187

Making a firm commitment    191
Allocating necessary resources    191
Identifying technical issues    192
Developing a strategic marketing plan    192
Organizing an operational team and implementing a marketing strategy    199
Evaluate and control operations    200
Summary    200
Discussing the issues    201
Applying the concepts    202
References    202
CASE 5    Procter & Gamble: going global in cosmetics    203

## 6 Market information and marketing research    208

Chapter objectives    208
Chapter preview    Qantas: taking off in tomorrow's market    208
Introduction    210
The marketing information system    211
Developing information    211
Defining the market    231
Measuring current market demand    233
Forecasting future demand    237
Distributing information    243
Summary    247
Discussing the issues    248
Applying the concepts    248
References    248
CASE 6    Ballygowan springs into new age Kisqua    *Brenda Cullen*    250

OVERVIEW CASE 2    **Mitsui & Company**    *Colin Egan and Peter McKiernan*    261

### PART THREE    Buyer Behaviour    265

## 7 Consumer markets    267

Chapter objectives    267
Chapter preview    Porsche: a special car for the special few    267
Models of consumer behaviour    269
Characteristics affecting consumer behaviour    270
Consumer decision process    288
Types of buying decision behaviour    289
The buyer decision process    291
The buyer decision process for new products    297
Summary    300
Discussing the issues    301
Applying the concepts    301
References    302
CASE 7    Bic versus Gillette: the disposable wars    304

## 8 Business markets and business buyer behaviour    307

Chapter objectives    307

Chapter preview    Selling business jets: the ultimate executive toy    307
Business markets    309
Business buyer behaviour    315
Institutional and government markets    329
Summary    333
Discussing the issues    333
Applying the concepts    334
References    334
CASE 8    Troll-AEG    Javier Sarda, Franscesc Parés and Lluís G. Renart    335

OVERVIEW CASE 3    **Jacobs Kaffee Wien: spreading a golden light**    345

PART FOUR    **Core Strategy**    349

9    **Market segmentation and targeting**    351

Chapter objectives    351
Chapter preview    Procter & Gamble: how many is too many?    351
Markets    353
Market segmentation    354
Market targeting    380
Summary    387
Discussing the issues    388
Applying the concepts    388
References    388
CASE 9    Coffee-Mate    389

10    **Positioning**    398

Chapter objectives    398
Chapter preview    Castrol: liquid engineering    398
Core strategy    400
Differentiation    401
What is market positioning?    409
Perceptual mapping    412
Positioning strategies    414
Choosing and implementing a positional strategy    421
Summary    427
Discussing the issues    428
Applying the concepts    428
References    428
CASE 10    Cadbury's TimeOut: choc around the clock    Damien McLoughlin and Benoit Heilbrunn    429

11    **Building customer satisfaction through quality, value and service**    435

Chapter objectives    435
Chapter preview    Rubbermaid: Want to buy an expensive rubber dustpan?    435
Satisfying customer needs    438
Defining customer value and satisfaction    439
Delivering customer value and satisfaction    445
Retaining customers    449
Implementing total quality marketing    456

Summary        457
Discussing the issues        460
Applying the concepts        461
References        461
CASE 11        Feinschmecker Sauce: pricey n' spicy        *Verena M. Priemer*        462

## 12 Creating competitive advantage: competitor analysis and competitive marketing strategies        465

Chapter objectives        465
Chapter preview        Federal Express: losing a packet in Europe        465
Gaining a competitive advantage        468
Competitor analysis        468
Competitive strategies        477
Balancing customer and competitor orientations        494
Summary        495
Discussing the issues        496
Applying the concepts        497
References        497
CASE 12        BMW: putting the 'brrrrum' back in Brum        499

OVERVIEW CASE 4        **A cola challenge: cola with breakfast**        505

PART FIVE        **Product**        507

## 13 Designing products: new-product development and  product life-cycle strategies        509

Chapter objectives        509
Chapter preview        Aerostructures Hamble        509
Introduction        510
Innovation and new-product development        511
New-product development process        514
Product life-cycle strategies        531
Summary        538
Discussing the issues        540
Applying the concepts        540
References        540
CASE 13        The Swatchmobile: any colour combination, including black        541

## 14 Designing products: products, brands, packaging and services        544

Chapter objectives        544
Chapter preview        Revlon        544
Introduction        545
What is a product?        545
Product classifications        547
Individual product decisions        551
Product line decisions        574
Product mix decisions        578
International product decisions        579
Summary        580

Discussing the issues    581
Applying the concepts    581
References    582
CASE 14    Colgate: one squeeze too many?    583

15    **Marketing services**    586

Chapter objectives    586
Chapter preview    Lufthansa: listening to customers    586
Services marketing    588
Summary    605
Discussing the issues    606
Applying the concepts    606
References    606
CASE 15    Tibigarden: is there life after EuroDisney?    607

OVERVIEW CASE 5    **Mapanza Breweries**    *Hapenga M. Kabeta*    611

PART SIX    **Price**    617

16    **Pricing products: pricing considerations and approaches**    619

Chapter objectives    619
Chapter preview    *The Times:* for a change    619
Naming the price    621
Factors to consider when setting prices    622
General pricing approaches    635
Summary    645
Discussing the issues    646
Applying the concepts    647
References    647
CASE 16    Proton MPi: Malaysian styling, Japanese engineering, and European pricing    *Richard Lynch*    648

17    **Pricing products: pricing strategies**    654

Chapter objectives    654
Chapter preview    Mobile phones: even more mobile customers    654
Pricing strategies    655
New-product pricing strategies    656
Product-mix pricing strategies    658
Price-adjustment strategies    660
Price changes    668
Summary    673
Discussing the issues    674
Applying the concepts    675
References    675
CASE 17    Stena Sealink versus Le Shuttle, Eurostar and the rest    676

OVERVIEW CASE 6    **Amaizer: It tastes awful, but we're working on it**    681

**PART SEVEN**   **Promotions**   683

**18**   **Promoting products: communication and promotion strategy**   685

Chapter objectives   685
Chapter preview   British Home Stores   685
Steps in developing effective communication   687
Summary   709
Discussing the issues   710
Applying the concepts   710
References   710

CASE 18   Absolut Vodka: absolutely successful   *Pontus Alenroth, Robert Björnström, Joakim Eriksson and Thomas Helgesson*   711

**19**   **Promoting products: advertising, sales promotion and public relations**   714

Chapter objectives   714
Chapter preview   Promotions medley!   714
Advertising   715
Important decisions in advertising   716
Sales promotion   738
Public relations   750
Summary   754
Discussing the issues   755
Applying the concepts   755
References   756

CASE 19   Diesel Jeans & Workwear: 'We're all different, but aren't we all different in the same way?'   *Malin Nilsson, Anki Sjöström, Anneli Zell and Thomas Helgesson*   757

**20**   **Promoting products: personal selling and sales management**   760

Chapter objectives   760
Chapter preview   Airbus   760
Setting salesforce objectives   763
Designing salesforce strategy   764
Recruiting and selecting salespeople   767
Training salespeople   768
Supervising salespeople   769
Evaluating salespeople   774
Principles of personal selling   777
Summary   785
Discussing the issues   785
Applying the concepts   787
References   788

CASE 20   Britcraft Jetprop: Whose sale is it anyhow?   788

OVERVIEW CASE 7   **Bang & Olufsen: different by design**   *Anton Hartmann-Olesen*   797

PART EIGHT   **Place**   803

**21**   **Placing products: distribution channels and logistics management**   805

Chapter objectives   805
Chapter preview   Economos   805
Introduction   807
The nature of distribution channels   808
Channel behaviour and organization   812
Channel design decisions   821
Channel management decisions   829
Physical distribution and logistics management   831
Summary   842
Discussing the issues   844
Applying the concepts   844
References   844
CASE 21   Freixenet *Cava*: bubbles down a new way   *Roberto Alvarez del Blanco and Jeff Rapaport*   845

**22**   **Placing products: retailing and wholesaling**   853

Chapter objectives   853
Chapter preview   IKEA   853
Retailing   856
Store retailing   856
Nonstore retailing   877
Retailer marketing decisions   887
Retailing trends   893
Wholesaling   895
Types of wholesalers   896
Wholesaler marketing decisions   900
Trends in wholesaling   901
Summary   904
Discussing the issues   905
Applying the concepts   905
References   905
CASE 22   Pieta luxury chocolates   907

OVERVIEW CASE 8   **GTE: competition comes calling**   911

**Glossary**   915

**Subject index**   940

**Company/brand index**   946

**Name index**   949

**Copyright acknowledgements**   956

# *Preface*

Marketing is the business function that identifies an organization's customer needs and wants, determines which target markets it can serve best and designs appropriate products, services and programmes to serve these markets. However, marketing is much more than just an isolated business function – it is a philosophy that guides the entire organization. The goal of marketing is to create customer satisfaction profitably by building valued relationships with customers. The marketing people cannot accomplish this goal by themselves. They must work closely with other people in their company and with other organizations in their value-chain, to provide superior value to customers. Thus, marketing calls upon everyone in the organization to 'think customer' and to do all that they can to help create and deliver superior customer value and satisfaction. As Professor Stephen Burnett says, 'In a truly great marketing organization, you can't tell who's in the marketing department. Everyone in the organization has to make decisions based on the impact on the cosumer.'

Many people see marketing as advertising or selling. They are wrong. Real marketing is less about selling and more about knowing what to make! Organizations gain market leadership by understanding consumer needs and finding solutions that delight customers through superior value, quality and service. No amount of advertising or selling can compensate for a lack of customer satisfaction.

Marketing is all around us. 'We are all customers now', notes the author Peter Mullen, 'in every area of customer inter-relationship from the supply and consumption of education and health care to the queue in the Post Office and the ride in the Intercity express, and in every financial transaction from the buying of biscuits to the purchase of a shroud.' Marketing is not only for manufacturing companies, wholesalers and retailers but for all kinds of individuals and organizations. Lawyers, accountants and doctors use marketing to manage demand for their services. So do hospitals, museums and performing arts groups. No politician can get the needed votes and no resort the needed tourists, without developing and carrying out marketing plans. *Principles of Marketing* helps students learn and apply the basic concepts and practices of modern marketing as used in a wide variety of settings: in product and service firms, consumer and business markets, profit and non-profit organizations, domestic and global companies and small and large businesses.

People in these organizations need to know how to define and segment markets and how to position themselves by developing need-satisfying products and services for their chosen target segments. They must know how to price their offerings attractively and affordably, and how to choose and manage the marketing channel that delivers products to customers. They need to know how to advertise and promote products so that customers will know about and want them. All of these demand a broad range of skills to sense, serve and satisfy consumers.

People need to understand marketing from the point of view of consumers and citizens. Someone is always trying to sell us something, so we need to recognize the methods they use. When they are seeking jobs people have to market themselves. Many will start their careers within a salesforce, in retailing, in advertising, in research or in one of the many other marketing areas.

## APPROACH AND OBJECTIVES

*Principles of Marketing* takes a practical, managerial approach to marketing. It is rich in practical examples and applications, showing the major decisions that marketing managers face in their efforts to balance the organization's objectives and resources against needs and opportunities in the global marketplace. Each chapter opens with a preview, a major example describing a market situation. Boxed Marketing Highlights, short examples, company cases and colour illustrations highlight high-interest ideas, stories and marketing strategies.

*Principles of Marketing* tells the stories that reveal the drama of modern marketing: BMW's entry into the off-the-road market; the Swatchmobile; Levi Strauss Co.'s startling success in finding new ways to grow globally; Apple Computers' and KFC's invasion of Japan; Qantas's struggle in the Southeast Asian airline market; 3M's legendary emphasis on new product development; MTV's segmentation of the European music market, Virgin's lifestyle marketing: B&O's Euro-segmentation; LVMH's focus on luxury products; EuroDisney's disastrous adventure; Nestlé's difficulty with pressure groups and adverse publicity; Stena Sealink's quest for cross-channel passengers against le Shuttle and Eurostar. These and dozens of other examples and illustrations throughout each chapter reinforce key concepts and bring marketing to life.

*Principles of Marketing* gives a comprehensive and innovative managerial and practical introduction to marketing. Its style and extensive use of examples and illustrations make the book straightforward, easy to read, lively and enjoyable.

## THE EUROPEAN EDITION

The European edition of Principles of Marketing offers significant changes in perspective in organization, content and style. Recognizing Europe's internationalism, examples and cases are not from Europe alone but from Europe, the US, Japan, other countries in Southeast Asia and Africa. Some examples and cases concentrate on national issues but many pan-European and global cases have an exciting international appeal. Although they cover many markets and products, the brands and customers used are close to the experience or aspiration of readers. Some examples are about global brands, such as KitKat, Calvin Klein and Mercedes, while others cover interesting markets such as those for jeans and beer to executive jets and mine sweepers.

The book is in eight parts that first cover marketing concepts and strategy and then the marketing mix.

**Part 1**, *The Marketing Process*, introduces marketing in a changing world then immediately addresses the important issues of marketing and society, social responsibility and marketing ethics. Chapter 3, Strategic Marketing Planning, then provides an early framework for marketing thinking and sets the stage for the remainder of the text.

**Part 2**, *The Marketing Setting*, examines the environment in which modern firms compete and how to gather information on the markets. It first covers the dimensions of the marketing environment and then the global marketplace. Chapter 6 considers marketing information and marketing research.

**Part 3**, *Buyer Behaviour*, contains one chapter on consumer marketing and one on industrial marketing that includes selling to international government agencies.

**Part 4**, *Core Strategy*, begins with a chapter on market segmentation and targeting and is followed by a separate chapter on positioning. The next two chapters then show how to build customer satisfaction through quality, value and service, ways of creating competitive advantage and how to compete.

The final four parts are about the marketing mix.

**Part 5**, *Product*, has two chapters on designing the product: new-product development, product life cycle, products, brands, packaging and service. The final chapter focuses on the increasingly important area of marketing services.

**Part 6**, *Price*, has two chapters: one on pricing consideration and approaches and the other on pricing strategies.

**Part 7**, *Promotions,* has a chapter on communication and promotional strategy and two more on parts of the communications mix: advertising, sales promotion and public relations, then personal selling and sales management.

**Part 8**, *Place*, represents the last stage in getting products or services to the buyer: distribution channels and logistics management, and retailing and wholesaling.

## LEARNING AIDS

Many aids to student learning come within this book. The main ones are:

**Chapter Objectives** say what students will be able to do after completing each chapter.

**Chapter Previews**. Each chapter begins with a preview that gives an appropriate example of marketing in practice.

**Full-colour** coded figures, photographs, advertisements and illustrations appear throughout the text. In each chapter key concepts and applications are illustrated with strong, full-colour visual materials.

**Marketing Highlights**. Additional examples and important information appear in Marketing Highlight exhibits throughout the text.

**Summaries**. Each chapter ends with a summary that wraps up the main points and concepts.

**Discussing the Issues**. At the end of each chapter the discussion issues are presented as questions for use in lectures, seminars or tutorials.

**Applying the Concepts**. These exercises are for use in seminars or as practical assignments.

**Cases**. Case studies for class or written discussion are provided at the end of each chapter. These cases challenge students to apply marketing principles to real companies in real situations.

**Overview Cases**. These are integrative comprehensive cases following each major part of the text. These cases allow students to apply and integrate concepts from each chapter within a larger business context.

**Glossary**. An extensive glossary provides quick reference to the key terms in the book. These terms are printed in bold at their first or key reference.

**Indexes**. Subject, company and author indexes reference all information and examples in the book.

## ACKNOWLEDGEMENTS

No book is the work only of its authors. We owe much to the pioneers of marketing who first identified its major issues and developed its concepts and techniques. Our thanks also go to our colleagues at the J. L. Kellogg Graduate School of Management, Northwestern University, the Kenan-Flagler Business School, University of North Carolina at Chapel Hill; Loughborough University Business School and Warwick Business School for ideas, encouragement and suggestions. Also thanks to all our friends in MEG, EMAC and the AMA who have stimulated and advised us over the years. Special thanks go to T.C. of De Montfort University for his patience and work on the Instructor's Manual, Gareth Smith and Jim Saker for their enthusiasm and energy with the European Casebook and to Mark Smalley, Fatimah Moran, Stephen Cleary, Alan Hawley and Ken Randall at Staffordshire University for their pioneering work on the interactive marketing training software. We also owe a particular thanks to our many colleagues who share our international vision and have contributed such an outstanding set of international cases to this book: Pontus Alenroth, Roberto Alvarez del Blanco, Robert Björnström, Brenda Cullen, Peter Doyle, Colin Egan, Joakim Eriksson, Anton Hartmann-Olesen, Benoit Heilbrunn, Thomas Helgesson, Hapenga M. Kabeta, Sylvie Laforet, Richard Lynch, Peter McKiernan, Damien McLoughlin, Alkis Magdalinos, Malin Nilsson, Franscesc Parés, Verena A. Priemer, Jeff Rapaport, Lluís G. Renart, Javier Sarda, Anki Sjöström and Anneli Zell.

Many reviewers at other colleges provided valuable comments and suggestions. We are indebted to the following colleagues: Chris Blackburn, Oxford Brookes University, D. Brownlie, University of Stirling, Drs H. D. H. A. Cabooter, Hogeschool Venlo, Auorey Gilmore, University of Ulster at Jordanstown, Dr Constantine S. Katsikeas, Cardiff Business School, University of Wales, Tore Kristensen, IOA – Copenhagen Business School, Damien McLoughlin, Dublin City University, Professor M. T. G. Meulenberg, Agricultural University, Blain Meyrick, Coventry University, Elaine O'Brien, University of Strathclyde, Adrian Palmer, De Montfort University, David Shipley, Trinity College, Dublin, Chris Simango, University of Northumbria at Newcastle, M. van den Bosch, HEAO – Arnhem, Richard Varey, Sheffield Hallam University, and Helen R. Woodruffe, University of Salford.

Thanks are also due to the teachers listed here whose suggestions contributed at the development stage of the book: Sally L. Andrews, Hanzehogeschool, Jeanette Baker, Sheffield Hallam University, William Barlow, Dundee Institute of Technology, Mrs Margaret Barnes, South Bank University, Grete Birtwistle, Glasgow Caledonian University, Gordon Bolt, University of the West of England, Bristol, Humphrey Bourne, City University, Dr U. B. Bradley, London Guildhall University, D. R. Brennan, Middlesex University, Chris Corbridge, University of the West of England, Bristol, J. W. Cross, Southampton Institute of Higher Education, Paul Custance, Harper Adams Agricultural College, Linda Danielis, University of Northumbria at Newcastle, Sallie Davies, Leeds Metropolitan University, Dr Leslie de Chernatony, The Open University,

Jeanine B. Delaney, University of Dundee, Charles Dennis, West London Institute of Higher Education, Mr S. Dhat, West Suffolk College, Gillian Dowling, Carlow Regional Technical College, K. Edward, Dundee Institute of Technology, B. A. Evans, University of Sunderland, Jenny Evans, University of Hertfordshire, Jörg Finsinger, University of Vienna, Brenda Flaherty, Regional Technical College, Athlone, P. Gardner, Peterborough Regional College, Ms S. Graham-Hill, Oxford Brookes University, Stuart M. Haddock, University of Central Lancashire, Stephen Halliday, Buckinghamshire College of Higher Education, Viviane Hamon, Groupe EIA, Toni Hilton, University of the West of England, Bristol, Abigail Hind, Harper Adams Agricultural College, Stephen P. Hogan, University of Brighton, Peter Hyde, University of Birmingham, Warwick Jones, University of the West of England, Bristol, Brian Jones, Wirral Metropolitan College, Nik Joshi, Mid-Kent College of Higher and Further Education, P. J. Kitchen, Keele University, G. Lindsay, Milton Keynes College, Wendy Lomax, Kingston University, S. Lowe, Kings College, London, Stephen Paul Ludlow, University of North London, Colin P. B. Madill, University of East London, Professor R. Mann, Berufsakademie Villingen-Schwenningen, R. L. Marshall, Warrington Collegiate Institute, Danielle McCartan-Quinn, University of Ulster, Kenneth McClement, Dundee College of Further Education, Dr J. Paul McDonald, Waterford Regional Technical College, Phil McKeown, Belfast Institute of Further and Higher Education, Mr P. G. McMorrow, Swindon College, Derek S. C. Milward, Dudley College of Technology, Dr R. S. Minhas, University of Sheffield, Dr S. O. Monye, South Bank University, Gerry O'Donnell, Regional Technical College, Tallaght, Kevin O'Sullivan, Regional Technical College, Athlone, Naomi Pattisson, Harper Adams Agricultural College, Veronica G. Payne, Manchester Metropolitan University, Michael Pole, University of Salford, Ariane Portegies, Netherlands Institute for Tourism and Transport Studies, Gert-Jan C. Ransijn, Haagse Hogeschool, Lluis G. Renart, IESE, Ruth Rettie, Kingston University, Kevin Robins, Kingston University, Donal Rogan, Regional Technical College, Tallaght, R. K. Rosen, University of Portsmouth, Gelareh Roshan, Bournemouth University, Patrick F. Scanlon, Sligo Regional Technical College, Anj Schaefer, University of Buckingham, F. Simons, HEAO – Arnhem, John Sisk, Regional Technical College, Richard W. Smith, Stroud College of Further Education, J. Southan, University of Salford, Mrs Marilyn A. Stone, Heriot-Watt University, Mr L. W. Stops, Bournemouth University, Gill Thwaites, Bournemouth University, K. Tomlinson, Canterbury Christ Church College of Higher Education, Thomas O. Toole, Waterford Regional Technical College, Ann M. Torres, University College Galway, L. B. Trustrum, Staffordshire University, Gervase Tyson, Dundee Institute of Technology, Dr Udo Wagner, University of Vienna, Michael Walsh, Cork Regional Technical College, Michael Ward, University College, Salford, Gary Warnaby, Manchester Metropolitan University, Mr J. Watkinson, Tresham Institute, Hildegard Wiesehöfer, University of Derby, S. H. Wilson, Manchester Metropolitan University, G. A. Wootten, University of the West of England, Bristol, Sheila Wright, De Montfort University, G. Wright, University of Bradford, and Michael Yorke, Barnes College.

We also owe a great deal to the people at Prentice Hall who helped develop this book: marketing editor Julia Helmsley provided encouragement, sound advice and championed our cause; Ann Greenwood, production editor, did a very fine job of guiding the book smoothly through production and Malcolm Forbes was our very patient and professional copy editor. Additional thanks go to Amanda Graseman, Moira Graves, Nicola Horton, Michelle Long, Stuart Macfarlane, Laura Miller, Mary Ann Page, Allison Pearson, Susan Richards, and John Yates, and also to Paul Barrett at Goodfellow & Egan.

Philip Kotler    Gary Armstrong    John Saunders    Veronica Wong

# About the authors

**Philip Kotler** is S. C. Johnson & Son Distinguished Professor of International Marketing at the J. L. Kellogg Graduate School of Management, Northwestern University. He received his master's degree at the University of Chicago and his PhD at MIT, both in Economics. Dr Kotler is author of *Marketing Management: Analysis, Planning, Implementation and Control* (Prentice Hall). He has authored several other successful books and he has written over 100 articles for leading journals. He is the only three-time winner of the Alpha Kappa Psi award for the best annual article in the *Journal of Marketing*. Dr Kotler's numerous major honours include the Paul D. Converse Award given by the American Marketing Association to honour 'outstanding contributions to the science of marketing' and the Stuart Henderson Britt Award as Marketer of the Year. In 1985, he was named the first recipient of two major awards: the Distinguished Marketing Educator of the Year Award, given by the American Marketing Association and the Philip Kotler Award for Excellence in Health Care Marketing. Dr Kotler has served as a director of the American Marketing Association. He has consulted with many major US and foreign companies on marketing strategy.

**Gary Armstrong** is Professor and Chair of Marketing in the Kenan-Flagler Business School at the University of North Carolina at Chapel Hill. He received his PhD in marketing from Northwestern University. Dr Armstrong has contributed numerous articles to leading research journals and consulted with many companies on marketing strategy. But Dr Armstrong's first love is teaching. He has been very active in Kenan-Flagler's undergraduate business programme and he has received several campus-wide and business schools teaching awards. He is the only repeat recipient of the School's highly regarded Award for Excellence in Undergraduate Teaching, which he won for the third time in 1993.

**John Saunders**, BSc (Loughborough), MBA (Cranfield), PhD (Bradford), FBAM, FCIM, FRSA is Director of Loughborough University Business School and National Westminster Bank Professor of Marketing. Previously, he worked for the Universities of Warwick, Bradford, Huddersfield and Hawaii, Hawker-Siddeley Group and British Aerospace. He edits the *International Journal of Research in Marketing*, is an assistant editor of the British Journal of Management's Fellowship committee and Chartered Institute of Marketing's senate. His publications include *The Marketing Initiative, Competitive Positioning*, with Dr Graham Hooley, and over sixty refereed journal articles. As a consultant and trainer, he has worked with many multinational organizations.

**Veronica Wong**, BSc, MBA (Bradford), PhD (CNAA) is a senior lecturer in marketing at Warwick Business School. Dr Wong was born in Malaysia where she studied until her first degree. She has also taught in Malaysia and worked for Ciba Geigy. She was Economic and Social Research Council (ESRC) research assistant at Bradford, held an ESRC research fellowship at Loughborough and, with Dr Paul Stoneman, currently holds an ESRC grant on Green marketing. Dr Wong wrote Warwick's distance learning MBA *Marketing Management* module and the Department of Trade and Industry's manual on *Identifying and Exploiting New Market Opportunities*. She has published over forty papers in refereed conferences and journals.

# Ecu conversion table

The value of one ecu at the time of going to press is given in the following list.

A$ 1.71 (Australian dollars)
BF 38.8 (Belgian francs)
C$ 1.72 (Canadian dollars)
DFl 2.12 (Dutch guilders)
DKr 7.33 (Danish kroner)
DM 1.89 (Deutschmarks)
Dr 302 (Greek drachmas)
Esc 195 (Portuguese escudos)
FFr 6.47 (French francs)
Fmk 5.53 (Finnish markka)
I£ 0.81 (Irish punt)
L 2,066 (Italian lire)
NKr 8.20 (Norwegian kroner)
Pta 161 (Spanish pesetas)
Sch 13.2 (Austrian schillings)
SFr 1.56 (Swiss francs)
SKr 9.29 (Swedish kronor)
UK£ 0.83 (Sterling)
US$ 1.26 (US dollars)
¥ 122 (Japanese yen)

# PART ONE

# Marketing and the marketing process

# Marketing in a changing world

## Satisfying human needs

## CHAPTER OBJECTIVES

After reading this chapter, you should be able to:

- Define *marketing* and discuss its role in the economy.

- Compare the five marketing management philosophies.

- Identify the goals of the marketing system.

- Explain the primary forces that are now changing the world marketing landscape and challenging marketing strategy.

## CHAPTER PREVIEW

### Marketing touches our daily life

Marketing touches all of us every day of our lives. We wake up to the bleep of a Sanyo radio alarm clock. It plays a track from a Chris Rea album and then a commercial advertising ZZ Top concert tickets. Then we brush our teeth with Colgate, some of us shave with a Gillette Sensor razor, gargle with Scope and use a range of toiletries and appliances produced by manufacturers around the world. We put on our Levi jeans and Nike shoes and head for the kitchen, where we have a pot of Danone breakfast yoghurt and wash down a bowl of Kellogg's Fruit n' Fibre with a mug of Kenco coffee.

We consume oranges grown in Spain and tea imported from Sri Lanka, read a newspaper made of Canadian wood pulp and tune in to international news coming from as far away as America. We fetch our mail to find an Air Miles handbook, direct mail from the RSPCA inviting donations to help save animals' lives, a letter from a Prudential insurance agent and coupons offering discounts on our favourite branded items in our local grocery superstore. We step out of the door and drive our made-in-Genk Ford to the IKEA superstore to fetch some do-it-yourself shelves for the apartment. We may stop at a Marks & Spencer to fetch some special St Michael fresh tropical fruits and gourmet party food. We buy Madonna's latest album at Virgin Megastore, grab a Big Mac at McDonald's and book a trip to EuroDisney at a Thomas Cook travel agency.

The *marketing system* has made all this possible with little effort on our part. It has given us a standard of living that our ancestors could not have imagined.

## INTRODUCTION

The marketing system that delivers our high standard of living consists of many large and small companies, all seeking success. Many factors contribute to making a business successful – great strategy, dedicated employees, good information systems, excellent implementation. However, today's successful companies at all levels have one thing in common – they are strongly customer-focused and heavily committed to marketing. These companies share an absolute dedication to sensing, serving and satisfying the needs of customers in well-understood markets. They motivate everyone in the organization to deliver high quality and value for their customers.

Many people think that only large companies operating in highly developed economies use marketing, but marketing actually occurs both inside and outside the business sector, in small and large organizations and in all kinds of countries. In the business sector, marketing first spread most rapidly in consumer packaged-goods companies, consumer durables companies and industrial equipment companies. Within the past few decades, however, consumer service firms, especially airline, insurance and financial services companies, have also adopted modern marketing practices. The latest business groups to take an interest in marketing are professionals such as lawyers, accountants, physicians and architects, who now have begun to advertise and to price their services aggressively.

Marketing also has become a vital component in the strategies of many *non-profit* organizations, such as schools, churches, hospitals, museums, performing arts groups and even police departments. Consider the following developments:

> Many universities, facing declining enrolments and rising competition and costs, are using marketing to compete for students and funds. They are defining target markets, improving their communication and promotion, and responding better to student needs and wants.

> To stem the falling number of church-goers, many of Britain's church groups are seeking more effective ways to attract members and maintain financial support. Increasingly, and despite the controversy, preachers are using the press, television and radio to advertise religion to the general public. They are conducting marketing research to better understand member needs and are redesigning their 'service offerings' accordingly. Some evangelical groups are even starting their own radio and television stations. The Vatican has been known to have appointed the advertising agency, Saatchi and Saatchi, to run a £2.5m television campaign.[1]

1 ecu = UK£0.83

> Cuts in funding for the performing arts are forcing museum and gallery managers to be more customer-oriented. To attract customers and boost income, many are taking steps to employ marketing techniques, ranging from sponsorships, advertising and direct mail to more aggressive shop merchandising and catering for corporate hospitality.[2]

> Finally, many longstanding non-profit organisations – the YMCA, the Red Cross, the Salvation Army, the Girl Scouts – are striving to modernise their missions and 'products' to attract more members and donors.[3]

Even government agencies have shown an increased interest in marketing. For example, various government agencies are now designing *social marketing campaigns* to

Government agencies such as England's Health Education Authority have successfully used marketing tools to reach target audiences.

encourage energy conservation and concern for the environment, or to discourage smoking, excessive drinking and drug use.[4]

Finally, marketing is practised widely all over the world. Most countries in North and South America, Western Europe and the Far East have well-developed marketing systems. Even in Eastern Europe and the former Soviet republics, where marketing has long had a bad name, long-endured economic stagnation has caused nations to move towards market-oriented economies. Dramatic political and social changes have created new market opportunities and left business and government leaders in most of these nations eager to learn everything they can about modern marketing practices.

Sound marketing is critical to the success of every organization – whether large or small, for profit or non-profit, domestic or global. In this chapter, we define marketing and its core concepts, describe the central philosophies of marketing thinking and practice, explain the goals of the marketing system, and discuss some of the significant new challenges that marketers now face.

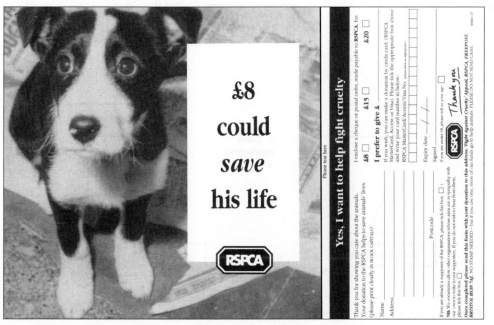

Non-profit organizations such as the Royal Society for the Prevention of Cruelty to Animals (RSPCA) also use marketing techniques to attract donors.

## WHAT IS MARKETING?

What does the term *marketing* mean? Marketing must be understood not in the old sense of making a sale – 'selling' – but in the new sense of *satisfying customer needs*. Many people mistakenly think of marketing only as selling and promotion. And no wonder, for every day we are bombarded with television commercials, newspaper ads, direct mail and sales calls. Someone is always trying to sell us something. It seems that we cannot escape death, taxes or selling!

Therefore, many students are surprised to learn that selling is only the tip of the marketing iceberg; it is but one of several marketing functions, and often, not the most important one. If the marketer does a good job of identifying customer needs, develops good products and prices, distributes and promotes them effectively, these goods will sell very easily.

Everyone knows something about 'hot' products. When Sony designed its first Walkman cassette and disc players, when Nintendo first offered its improved video game console, and when The Body Shop introduced animal-cruelty-free cosmetics and toiletries, these manufacturers were swamped with orders. They had designed the 'right' products: not 'me-too' products, but ones offering new benefits. Peter Drucker, a leading management thinker, has put it this way: 'The aim of marketing is to make selling superfluous. The aim is to know and understand the customer so well that the product or service fits … and sells itself.'[5]

This does not mean that selling and promotion are unimportant. Rather, it means that they are part of a larger **marketing mix** – a set of marketing tools that work together to affect the marketplace. We define **marketing** as: *a social and managerial process by which individuals and groups obtain what they need and want through creating and exchanging products and value with others.*[6] To explain this definition, we examine the following important terms: *needs, wants, and demands; products; value and satisfaction; exchange, transactions and relationships;* and *markets.* Figure 1.1 shows that these core marketing concepts are linked, with each concept building on the one before it.

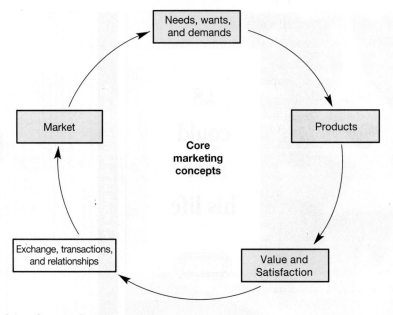

**Figure 1.1**   Core marketing concepts.

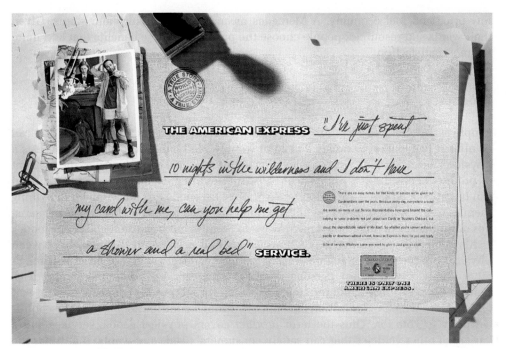

This ad assures card members that American Express World Service representatives go beyond the call of duty to solve their unexpected problems.

## Needs, wants, and demands

The most basic concept underlying marketing is that of human needs. A **human need** is a state of felt deprivation. Humans have many complex needs. These include basic *physical* needs for food, clothing, warmth and safety; *social* needs for belonging and affection; and *individual* needs for knowledge and self-expression. These needs are not invented by marketers, they are a basic part of the human make-up. When a need is not satisfied, a person will do one of two things:

1. look for an object that will satisfy it; or
2. try to reduce the need.

People in industrial societies may try to find or develop objects that will satisfy their desires. People in less-developed societies may try to reduce their desires and satisfy them with what is available.

**Human wants** are the form taken by human needs as they are shaped by culture and individual personality. A hungry person in Bahrain may want a vegetable curry, mango chutney and lassi. A hungry person in Eindhoven may want a ham and cheese roll, salad and a beer. A hungry person in Hong Kong may want a bowl of noodles, char siu pork and jasmine tea. Wants are described in terms of objects that will satisfy needs. As a society evolves, the wants of its members expand. As people are exposed to more objects that arouse their interest and desire, producers try to provide more want-satisfying products and services.

People have narrow, basic needs (e.g. for food or shelter), but almost unlimited wants. However, they also have limited resources. They therefore want to choose products that provide the most satisfaction for their money. When backed by an ability to pay – that is, buying power – wants become **demands**.

Consumers view products as bundles of benefits and choose products that give them the best bundle for their money. Thus a Ford Fiesta means basic transportation, low price and fuel economy. A Mercedes means comfort, luxury and status. Given their wants and resources, people choose the product with the benefits that add up to the most satisfaction.

## Products

People satisfy their needs and wants with products. A **product** is anything that can be offered to a market to satisfy a need or want. Usually, the word *product* suggests a physical object, such as a car, a television set or a bar of soap. However, the concept of product is not limited to physical objects – anything capable of satisfying a need can be called a product. The importance of physical goods lies not so much in owning them as in the benefits they provide. We don't buy food to look at, but because it satisfies our hunger. We don't buy a microwave to admire, but because it cooks our food.

Marketers often use the expressions *goods* and *services* to distinguish between physical products and intangible ones. Moreover, consumers obtain benefits through other vehicles, such as *persons, places, organizations, activities* and *ideas*. Consumers decide which entertainers to watch on television, which places to visit on vacation, which organizations to support through contributions and which political party to vote for. Thus the term *product* covers physical goods, services and a variety of other vehicles that can satisfy consumers' needs and wants. It at times the term *product* does not seem to fit, we could substitute other terms such as *satisfier, resource* or *offer*.

Many sellers make the mistake of paying more attention to the physical products they offer than to the benefits produced by these products. They see themselves as selling a product rather than providing a *solution* to a need. A manufacturer of drill bits may think that the customer needs a drill bit, but what the customer *really* needs is a hole. These sellers may suffer from 'marketing myopia'.[7] They are so taken with their products that they focus only on existing wants and lose sight of underlying customer needs. They forget that a physical product is only a tool to solve a consumer problem. These sellers have trouble if a new product comes along that serves the need better or less expensively. The customer with the same *need* will *want* the new product.

## Value and satisfaction

Consumers usually face a broad array of products that might satisfy a given need. How do they choose among these many products? Consumers make buying choices based on their perceptions of a product's value.

Suppose you need to travel three miles each day to work. A variety of products could satisfy this need, ranging from roller skates, a bicycle or motocycle to a car, taxi or bus. Besides simply getting to work, you also have several additional needs: you want to get there easily, quickly, safely and economically. Each product has a different capacity to satisfy these various needs. The bicycle would require more effort, and is slower and less safe, although more economical, than the car. You must decide which product delivers the most total satisfaction.

The guiding concept is **customer value**. You will estimate the capacity of each product to satisfy your total needs. You might rank the products from the most need-satisfying to the least need-satisfying. If you were to imagine the *ideal* product for this task, you might answer that it would get you to work in a split second with complete safety, no effort and zero cost. Of course, no such product exists. Still, you will value each existing product according to how close it comes to your ideal product. Suppose you are mostly interested in the speed and ease of getting to work. If all of the products were free, we would predict that you would choose the car. But therein lies the rub. Because each product does involve a cost, and because the car costs much more than any of the other products, you will not necessarily buy the car. You will end up choosing the product that gives the most benefit for the money spent – the greatest *value*.

Today, consumer-behaviourists have gone far beyond narrow economic assumptions about how consumers form value judgements and make product choices. We will look at modern theories of consumer-choice behaviour in Chapter 7.

## Exchange, transactions and relationships

Marketing occurs when people decide to satisfy needs and wants through exchange. **Exchange** is the act of obtaining a desired object from someone by offering something in return. Exchange is only one of many ways people can obtain a desired object. For example, hungry people can find food by hunting, fishing or gathering fruit. They could beg for food or take food from someone else. Finally, they could offer money, another good or a service in return for food.

As a means of satisfying needs, exchange has much in its favour. People do not have to prey on others or depend on donations. Nor must they possess the skills to produce every necessity for themselves. They can concentrate on making things they are good at making and trade them for needed items made by others. Thus exchange allows a society to produce much more than it would with any alternative system.

Exchange is the core concept of marketing. For an exchange to take place, several conditions must be satisfied. Of course, at least two parties must participate and each must have something of value to offer to the other. Each party also must want to deal with the other party and each must be free to accept or reject the other's offer. Finally, each party must be able to communicate and deliver.

These conditions simply make exchange *possible*. Whether exchange actually *takes place* depends on the parties' coming to an agreement. If they agree, we must conclude that the act of exchange has left both of them better off or, at least, not worse off. After all, each was free to reject or accept the offer. In this sense, exchange creates value just as production creates value. It gives people more consumption choices or possibilities.

Whereas exchange is the core concept of marketing, a transaction is marketing's unit of measurement. A **transaction** consists of a trading of values between two parties. In a transaction, we must be able to say that one party gives $X$ to another party and gets $Y$ in return. For example, you pay a retailer £300 for a television set or the hotel £90 a night for a room. This is a classic **monetary transaction**, but not all transactions involve money. In a barter transaction, you might trade your old refrigerator in return for a neighbour's secondhand television set. A **barter transaction** also can involve services as well as goods: for example, when a lawyer writes a will for a doctor in return for a medical examination (see Marketing Highlight 1.1). A transaction involves at least two things of value, conditions that are agreed upon, a time of agreement and a place of agreement.

In the broadest sense, the market tries to bring about a response to some offer. The response may be more than simply 'buying' or 'trading' goods and services. A political candidate, for instance, wants a response called 'votes', a church wants 'membership', and a social-action group wants 'idea acceptance'. Marketing consists of

## MARKETING HIGHLIGHT 1.1

### Going back to barter

With today's high prices, many companies are returning to the primitive but time-honoured practice of barter – trading goods and services that they make or provide for other goods and services that they need. The European barter market is estimated to be worth up to $200 million* a year and forecasts put the value at nearly $1 billion by the end of this decade. On a global scale, companies barter more than $275 billion worth of goods and services a year, and the practice is growing rapidly.

Companies use barter to increase sales, unload extra goods, and save cash. For example, companies are offering television programmes to broadcasters in exchange for air-time: Unilever owns the European rights to the TV game shows, 'Wheel of Fortune' and 'Jeopardy', which it barters to stations all over Europe. Others like PepsiCo traded Pepsi-Cola and pizza parlours to the Russians for ships and Stolichnaya vodka, while Pierre Cardin served as a consultant to China in exchange for silks and cashmeres, and Turnkey Contracts and Consultancy, a Singapore company, was paid in Burmese logs for the construction of an International Business Centre in Burma's capital city, Rangoon.

* 1 ecu = US$1.26.

Sources: 'TV barters for the future', *The European* (25–31 March 1994); Victor Mallet, 'Barter proves best for business, Burma style', *Financial Times* (8 February 1994), 8; Quote from Cyndee Miller, 'Worldwide money crunch fuels more international barter', *Marketing News* (2 March,

As a result of this increase in barter activity, many kinds of specialty companies have appeared to help other companies with their bartering. Retail-trade exchanges and trade clubs arrange barter for small retailers. Larger corporations use trade consultants and brokerage firms. Media brokerage houses provide advertising in exchange for products, and international barter is often handled by counter-trade organizations.

Barter has become especially important in today's global markets, where it now accounts for as much as 40 per cent of all world trade. The present world currency shortage means that more and more companies are being forced to trade for goods and services rather than cold, hard cash. International barter transactions can be very complex. For example, a trader for SGD International, a New York-based bartering company, arranged the following series of exchanges:

[The trader] supplied a load of latex rubber to a Czech company in exchange for 9,000 metres of finished carpeting. He then traded the carpeting for hotel room credits. The rooms were traded to a Japanese company for electronic equipment, which [the trader] bartered away for convention space. The final [exchange] came when he swapped the convention space for ad space that his company used.

1992), 5; also see Arthur Bragg, 'Bartering comes of age', *Sales & Marketing Management* (January 1988), 61–3; Joe Mandese, 'Marketers swap old product for ad time, space', *Advertising Age* (14 October 1991), 3.

actions taken to obtain a desired response from a target audience towards some product, service, idea or other object.

Transaction marketing is part of the larger idea of **relationship marketing**. Smart marketers work at building long-term relationships with valued customers, distributors, dealers and suppliers. They build strong economic and social ties by promising and consistently delivering high-quality products, good service and fair prices. Increasingly, marketing is shifting from trying to maximize the profit on each individual transaction to maximizing mutually beneficial relationships with consumers and other parties. The operating assumption is: *build good relationships and profitable transactions will follow*.

### Markets

The concept of transactions leads to the concept of a market. A **market** is the set of actual and potential buyers of a product. To understand the nature of a market,

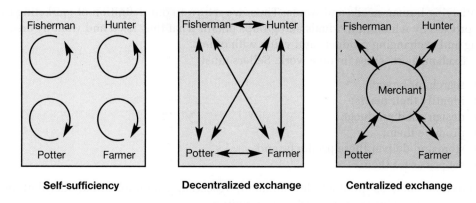

| | | |
|---|---|---|
| **Self-sufficiency** | **Decentralized exchange** | **Centralized exchange** |

**Figure 1.2** Evolution towards centralized exchange.

imagine a primitive economy consisting of only four people: a fisherman, a hunter, a potter and a farmer. Figure 1.2 shows the three different ways in which these traders could meet their needs:

1. *Self-sufficiency* They gather the needed goods for themselves. Thus, the hunter spends most of the time hunting, but also must take time to fish, make pottery, and farm to obtain the other goods. The hunter is thereby less efficient at hunting and the same is true of the other traders.
2. *Decentralized exchange* Each person sees the other three as potential 'buyers' who make up a market. Thus, the hunter may make separate trips to trade meat for the goods of the fisherman, the potter and the farmer.
3. *Centralized exchange* A new person called a *merchant* appears and locates in a central area called a *marketplace*. Each trader brings goods to the merchant and trades for other needed goods. Thus, rather than transacting with the other providers, the hunter transacts with one 'market' to obtain all the needed goods. Merchants and central marketplaces greatly reduce the total number of transactions needed to accomplish a given volume of exchange.[8]

As the number of persons and transactions increases in a society, the number of merchants and marketplaces also increases. In advanced societies, markets need not be physical locations where buyers and sellers interact. With modern communications and transportation, a merchant easily can advertise a product on a late evening television programme, take orders from thousands of customers over the phone, and mail the goods to the buyers on the following day without having had any physical contact with them.

A market can grow up around a product, a service or anything else of value. For example, a *labour market* consists of people who are willing to offer their work in return for wages or products. In fact, various institutions, such as employment agencies and job-counselling firms, will grow up around a labour market to help it function better. The *money market* is another important market that emerges to meet the needs of people so that they can borrow, lend, save and protect money. The *donor market* has emerged to meet the financial needs of non-profit organizations.

## Marketing

The concept of markets finally brings us full circle to the concept of marketing. **Marketing** means working with markets to bring about exchanges for the purpose of satisfying human needs and wants. Thus, we return to our definition of marketing as a process by which individuals and groups obtain what they need and want by creating and exchanging products and value with others.

Exchange processes involve work. Sellers must:

- search for buyers;
- identify their needs;
- design good products;
- promote them;
- store and deliver these products; and
- set prices for them.

Activities such as product development, research, communication, distribution, pricing and service are core marketing activities.

Although we normally think of marketing as being carried on by sellers, buyers also carry on marketing activities. Consumers do 'marketing' when they search for the goods they need at prices they can afford. Company purchasing agents do 'marketing' when they track down sellers and bargain for good terms. A *sellers' market* is one in which sellers have more power and buyers must be the more active 'marketers'. In a *buyers' market*, buyers have more power and sellers have to be more active 'marketers'.

In recent decades, the supply of goods has grown faster than the demand for them. Today, most markets have become buyers' markets, and marketing has become identified with sellers seeking out buyers. This book acknowledges that trend and examines marketing problems facing sellers in a buyers' market.

## MARKETING MANAGEMENT

Most people think of marketing management as finding enough customers for the company's current output, but this is too limited a view. The organization has a desired level of demand for its products. At any point in time, there may be no demand, adequate demand, irregular demand, or too much demand, and marketing management must find ways to deal with these different demand states. Marketing management is concerned not only with finding and increasing demand, but also with changing or even reducing it. Thus marketing management seeks to affect the level, timing and nature of demand in a way that helps the organization achieve its objectives. Simply put, marketing management is *demand management*. Marketing managers in different organizations might face any of the following states of demand. The marketing task is to manage demand states effectively.

### Negative demand

A large part of the market dislikes the product and may even pay to avoid it. Examples are vaccinations, dental work, cancer screenings and seat belts. Marketers must analyse why the market dislikes the product, and whether product redesign, lower prices or more positive promotion can change the consumer attitudes.

### No demand

Target consumers may be uninterested in the product. Thus farmers may not care about a new farming method and consumers may not be interested in three-wheeled electric cars. The marketer must find ways to connect the product's benefits with the market's needs and interests.

### Latent demand

Consumers have a want that is not satisfied by any existing product or service. There is strong latent demand for nonharmful cigarettes, safer neighbourhoods, biodegradable packages and more fuel-efficient cars. The marketing task is to measure the size of the potential market and develop effective goods and services that will satisfy the demand.

### Falling demand

Sooner or later, every organization faces falling demand for one of its products. Churches have seen their membership decline and dairy farmers have seen consumption of full-cream milk fall. The marketer must find the cause of market decline and restimulate demand by finding new markets, changing product features or creating more effective communications.

### Irregular demand

Demand varies on a seasonal, daily or even hourly basis, causing problems of idle or overworked capacity. In mass transit, much equipment is idle during slow travel hours and too little is available during peak hours. Museums are undervisited during weekdays and overcrowded during weekends. Marketers must find ways to change the time pattern of demand through flexible pricing, promotion and other incentives.

### Full demand

The organization has just the amount of demand it wants and can handle. The marketer works to maintain the current level of demand in the face of changing consumer preferences and increasing competition. The organization maintains quality and continually measures consumer satisfaction to make sure it is doing a good job.

### Overfull demand

Demand is higher than the company can or wants to handle. For example, many motorways carry more traffic than they are built for and Disney World is overcrowded in the summertime. Utilities, bus companies, restaurants and other businesses often face overfull demand at peak times. The marketing task, called *demarketing*, is to find ways to reduce the demand temporarily or permanently. Demarketing involves actions such as raising prices and reducing promotion and service. Demarketing does not aim to destroy demand, but selectively to reduce it.

We define **marketing management** as the analysis, planning, implementation and control of programmes designed to create, build and maintain beneficial exchanges with target buyers for the purpose of achieving organizational objectives. Marketing managers include sales managers and salespeople, advertising executives, sales-promotion people, marketing researchers, product managers, pricing specialists and others.

## MARKETING MANAGEMENT PHILOSOPHIES

We describe marketing management as carrying out tasks to achieve desired exchanges with target markets. What *philosophy* should guide these marketing efforts? What weight should be given to the interests of the organization, customers and society? Very often these interests conflict. Invariably, the organization's marketing management philosophy influences the way it approaches its buyers.

There are five alternative concepts under which organizations conduct their marketing activities: the production, product, selling, marketing, and societal marketing concepts.

### The production concept

The **production concept** holds that consumers will favour products that are available and highly affordable and that management therefore should focus on improving production and distribution efficiency. This concept is one of the oldest philosophies that guides sellers.

The production concept is a useful philosophy in two types of situations. The first occurs when the demand for a product exceeds the supply. Here, management should look for ways to increase production. The second situation occurs when the product's cost is too high and improved productivity is needed to bring it down. For example, Henry Ford's whole philosophy was to perfect the production of the Model T so that its cost could be reduced and more people could afford it. He joked about offering people a car of any colour as long as it was black. Today, Texas Instruments (TI) follows this philosophy of increased production and lower costs in order to bring down prices. The company won a big share of the hand-calculator market with this philosophy. But when it used the same strategy in the digital watch market, TI failed. Although TI's watches were priced low, customers did not find them very attractive. In its drive to bring down prices, TI lost sight of something else that its customers wanted – namely, *attractive*, affordable digital watches.

### The product concept

Another important concept guiding sellers, the **product concept**, holds that consumers will favour products that offer the most quality, performance and innovative features, and that an organization should thus devote energy to making continuous product improvements. Some manufacturers believe that if they can build a better mousetrap, the world will beat a path to their door.[9] But they are often rudely shocked. Buyers may well be looking for a better solution to a mouse problem, but not necessarily for a better mousetrap. The solution might be a chemical spray, an exterminating service or something that works better than a mousetrap. Furthermore a better mousetrap will not sell unless the manufacturer designs, packages and prices it attractively; places it in convenient distribution channels; and brings it to the attention of people who need it and convinces them that it is a better product. A product orientation leads to obsession with technology because managers believe that technical superiority is the key to business success.

The product concept also can lead to 'marketing myopia'. For instance, railway management once thought that users wanted *trains* rather than *transportation* and overlooked the growing challenge of airlines, buses, trucks and cars. Building bigger and better trains would not solve consumers' demand for transportation, but creating other forms of transportation and extending choice would.

## The selling concept

Many organizations follow the **selling concept**, which holds that consumers will not buy enough of the organization's products unless it undertakes a large-scale selling and promotion effort. The concept is typically practised with **unsought goods** – those that buyers do not normally think of buying, such as encyclopaedias and funeral plots. These industries must be good at tracking down prospects and selling them on product benefits.

The selling concept is also practised in the non-profit area. A political party, for example, will vigorously sell its candidate to voters as a fantastic person for the job. The candidate works hard at selling himself – shaking hands, kissing babies, meeting donors and making speeches. Much money also has to be spent on radio and television advertising, posters and mailings. Candidate flaws are often hidden from the public because the aim is to get the sale, not to worry about consumer satisfaction afterwards.

A selling-oriented organization thus focuses on short-term results – profits via sales now – rather than on longer-term market and financial benefits created by satisfied customers who want more of the goods or services offered by the organization.

## The marketing concept

The **marketing concept** holds that achieving organizational goals depends on determining the needs and wants of target markets and delivering the desired satisfactions more effectively and efficiently than competitors do. Surprisingly, this concept is a relatively recent business philosophy. The marketing concept has been stated in colourful ways such as 'Find a need and fill it' (Kaiser Sand & Gravel); 'To fly, to serve' (British Airways); and 'We're not satisfied until you are' (GE).

The selling concept and the marketing concept are frequently confused. Figure 1.3 compares the two concepts. The selling concept takes an *inside-out* perspective. It

**Figure 1.3**   The selling and marketing concepts contrasted.

## McDonald's applies the marketing concept

McDonald's Corporation, the American fast-food hamburger retailer, is a master global marketer. With 11,000 outlets in 50 countries and more than $18.7 billion in annual worldwide sales, McDonald's doubles the sales of its nearest rival, Burger King. Nineteen million customers pass through the famous golden arches each day. McDonald's now serves 145 hamburgers per second. Credit for this performance belongs to a strong marketing orientation: McDonald's knows how to serve people and adapt to changing consumer wants.

Before McDonald's appeared, Americans could get hamburgers in restaurants or diners. But consumers often encountered poor-quality hamburgers, slow and unfriendly service, unattractive decor, unclean conditions and a noisy atmosphere. In 1955, Ray Kroc, a 52-year-old salesman of milkshake-mixing machines, became excited about a string of seven restaurants owned by Richard and Maurice McDonald. Kroc liked their fast-food restaurant concept and bought the chain for $2.7 million. He decided to expand the chain by selling franchises and the number of restaurants rapidly grew. As times changed, so did McDonald's. It expanded its sit-down sections, improved the decor, launched a breakfast menu, added new food items and opened new outlets in busy, high-traffic areas.

Kroc's marketing philosophy is captured in McDonald's motto of 'Q.S.C. & V.', which stands for quality, service, cleanliness and value. Customers enter a spotlessly clean restaurant, walk up to a friendly counter-person, quickly receive a good-tasting meal, and eat it there or take it out. There are no jukeboxes or telephones to create a teenage hangout. Nor are there any cigarette machines – McDonald's is a family affair, appealing strongly to children.

McDonald's has mastered the art of serving consumers and it carefully teaches the basics to its employees and franchisees. All franchisees take training courses at McDonald's 'Hamburger University' in Elk Grove Village, Illinois. They emerge with a degree in 'Hamburgerology' and a minor in French fries. McDonald's monitors product and service quality through continuous customer surveys and puts great energy into improving hamburger production methods in order to simplify operations, bring down costs, speed up service and bring greater value to customers. Beyond these efforts, each McDonald's restaurant works to become a part of its neighbourhood through community involvement and service projects.

In its 2,700 restaurants outside the United States, McDonald's carefully customizes its menu and service to local tastes and customs. It serves corn soup and teriyaki burgers in Japan, pasta salads in Rome, and wine and live piano music with its McNuggets in Paris. When McDonald's opened its first restaurant in

starts with the factory, focuses on the company's existing products and calls for heavy selling and promotion to obtain profitable sales. In contrast, the marketing concept takes an *outside-in* perspective. It starts with a well-defined market, focuses on customer needs, coordinates all the marketing activities affecting customers and makes profits by creating customer satisfaction. Under the marketing concept, companies produce what consumers want, thereby satisfying consumers and making profits.

Many successful and well-known global companies have adopted the marketing concept. IKEA, Marks & Spencer, Procter & Gamble, Marriott, Nordström and McDonald's follow it faithfully (see Marketing Highlight 1.2). Toyota, the highly successful Japanese car manufacturer, is also a prime example of an organization that takes a customer- and marketing-oriented view of its business.

Toyota openly publicizes its intent on getting deep into the hearts and minds of its customers, to establish precisely what they want and subsequently find ways to fulfil their wishes. In Japan, Toyota has built the Amlux, a 14-storey building resembling a blue and black striped rocket, which it uses to attract millions of visitors. These could be potential customers or people with ideas on how the company should

Moscow, it quickly won the hearts of Russian consumers. However, the company had to overcome some monstrous hurdles in order to meet its high standards for consumer satisfaction in this new market. It had to educate suppliers, employees and even consumers about the time-tested, McDonald's way of doing things. Technical experts with special strains of disease-resistant seed were brought in from Canada to teach Russian farmers how to grow russet Burbank potatoes for French fries, and the company built its own pasteurizing plant to ensure a plentiful supply of fresh milk. It trained Russian managers at Hamburger University and subjected each of 630 new employees (most of whom didn't know a Chicken McNugget from an Egg McMuffin) to 16 to 20 hours of training on such essentials as cooking meat patties, assembling Filet-O-Fish sandwiches and giving service with a smile. McDonald's even had to train consumers – most Muscovites had never seen a fast-food restaurant. Customers waiting in line were shown videos telling them everything from how to order and pay at the counter to how to handle a Big Mac. And in its usual way, McDonald's began immediately to build community involvement. On opening day, it held a kick-off party for 700 Muscovite orphans, and it donated all opening-day proceeds to the Moscow Children's Fund. As a result, the new Moscow restaurant got off to a very successful start. About 50,000 customers swarmed through the restaurant during its first day of business.

Riding on its success in Moscow, McDonald's continues to pursue opportunities to serve new customers around the globe. It recently opened its largest restaurant anywhere, in Beijing, China. The 28,000-square-foot restaurant has 29 cash registers and seats 700 people. Through this huge Beijing outlet, McDonald's expects to treat more than ten thousand customers each day to its special brand of customer care.

Thus, McDonald's focus on consumers has made it the world's largest food-service organization. It remains the market leader in its home country, while rapidly expanding its worldwide presence. The company's huge success has been reflected in the increased value of its stock over the years: 250 shares of McDonald's stock purchased for less than $6,000 in 1965 would be worth well over a million dollars today!

Sources: Penny Moser, 'The McDonald's mystique', *Fortune* (4 July 1988), 112–16; Scott Hume, 'McDonald's Fred Turner: making all the right moves', *Advertising Age* (1 January 1990), 6, 17; Gail McKnight, 'Here comes Bolshoi Mac', *USA Today Weekend*, (26–28 January 1990), 4–5; Rosemarie Boyle, 'McDonald's gives Soviets something worth waiting for', *Advertising Age* (19 March 1990), 61; and 'Food draws raves, prices don't at Beijing McDonald's opening', *Durham Herald-Sun* (12 April 1992), B12.

respond to consumers' vehicle requirements. These visitors are allowed to spend as much time as they want designing their own vehicles on computer/TV screen in the vehicle-design studio. There is a two-way information centre where visitors obtain specific information about the company, its dealers or products. The visitors are also allowed to expound, at length, on what they think Toyota should be doing or making. Meanwhile, Toyota's attentive note-taking staff ensure that the entire Amlux complex is dedicated to involving potential customers who can give them close insights into how their car needs can be satisfied.

In marketing-led organizations, the entire workforce share the belief that the customer is all-important and that building lasting relationships is the key to customer retention. The following quotes reflect the level of dedication successful marketing organizations devote to customers:

We believe that real customer focus has to start from the top down and the bottom up, and it has to be totally accepted by the whole workforce. Otherwise, the lines of communication will fail. (Divisional Director of the adventure park, Alton Towers, UK)

> We put the same amount of energy into attracting existing customers as we do attracting new customers. Within the mentality of each store is the realisation that the existing customer is all-important to today's business. (Chris Moore, Domino's Pizza)

> We don't rely on buying customer loyalty, we believe we have to earn customer loyalty, and we do that by making sure that the products we offer and the service ... meet exactly what the customer requires from us. (Peter Whinney, Operations Manager, Land Rover)

Many companies claim to practise the marketing concept, but do not. They have the *forms* of marketing – such as a marketing director, product managers, marketing plans and marketing research – but this does not mean that they are *market-focused* and *customer-driven* companies. The question is whether they are finely tuned to changing customer needs and competitor strategies. Formerly great Western companies – Philips, General Motors, IBM, General Electric Company – all lost substantial market share because they failed to adjust their marketing strategies to the changing marketplace. Several years of hard work are needed to turn a sales-oriented company into a marketing-oriented company. The goal is to build customer satisfaction into the very fabric of the firm. Customer satisfaction is no longer a fad. As one marketing analyst notes: 'It's becoming a way of life ... as embedded into corporate cultures as information technology and strategic planning.'[10]

Why is it supremely important to satisfy customers? A company's sales come from two groups: *new* customers and *repeat* customers. It usually costs more to attract new customers than to retain current customers. Therefore, customer *retention* is often more critical than customer *attraction*. The key to customer retention is *customer satisfaction*. A satisfied customer buys more, stays 'loyal' longer, talks favourably to others, pays less attention to competing brands and advertising, is less price sensitive and costs less to serve than a first-time customer.

However, the marketing concept does not mean that a company should try to give *all* consumers *everything* they want. Marketers must balance creating more value for customers against making profits for the company:

> The purpose of marketing is not to *maximise* customer satisfaction. The shortest definition of marketing I know is 'meeting needs profitably'. The purpose of marketing is to generate customer value [at a profit]. The truth is [that the relationship with a customer] will break up if value evaporates. You've got to continue to generate more value for the consumer but not give away the house. It's a very delicate balance.[11]

## The societal marketing concept

The **societal marketing concept** holds that the organization should determine the needs, wants and interests of target markets. It should then deliver the desired satisfactions more effectively and efficiently than competitors in a way that maintains or improves the consumer's *and the society*'s well-being. The societal marketing concept is the newest of the five marketing management philosophies.

The societal marketing concept questions whether the pure marketing concept is adequate in an age of environmental problems, resource shortages, worldwide economic problems and neglected social services. It asks if the firm that senses, serves and satisfies individual wants is always doing what's best for consumers and society in the long run. According to the societal marketing concept, the pure marketing concept overlooks possible conflicts between short-run consumer *wants* and long-run consumer *welfare*.

Consider the Coca-Cola Company. Most people see it as a highly responsible corporation producing fine soft drinks that satisfy consumer tastes. Yet certain

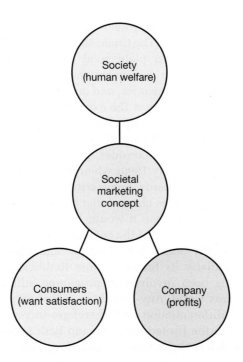

**Figure 1.4**   Three considerations underlying the societal marketing concept.

consumer and environmental groups have voiced concerns that Coke has little nutritional value, can harm people's teeth, contains caffeine and adds to the litter problem with disposable bottles and cans.

Such concerns and conflicts led to the societal marketing concept. As Figure 1.4 shows, the societal marketing concept calls upon marketers to balance three considerations in setting their marketing policies: company profits, consumer wants, and society's interests. Originally, most companies based their marketing decisions largely on short-run company profit. Eventually, they began to recognize the long-run importance of satisfying consumer wants and the marketing concept emerged. Now many companies are beginning to think of society's interests when making their marketing decisions.

One such company is the international corporation, Johnson & Johnson, that stresses community and environmental responsibility. J&J's concern for societal interests is summarized in a company document called 'Our Credo', which stresses honesty, integrity and putting people before profits. Under this credo, Johnson & Johnson would rather take a big loss than ship a bad batch of one of its products. And the company supports many community and employee programmes that benefit its consumers and workers, and the environment. J&J's chief executive puts it this way: 'If we keep trying to do what's right, at the end of the day we believe the marketplace will reward us.'[12]

The company backs these words with actions. Consider the tragic tampering case in which eight people died from swallowing cyanide-laced capsules of Tylenol, a Johnson & Johnson brand. Although J&J believed that the pills had been altered in only a few stores, not in the factory, it quickly recalled all of its product. The recall cost the company $240 million in earnings. In the long run, however, the company's swift recall of Tylenol strengthened consumer confidence and loyalty, and Tylenol remains the leading brand of pain reliever in the US market. In this and other cases,

J&J management has found that doing what's right benefits both consumers and the company. Says the chief executive: 'The Credo should not be viewed as some kind of social welfare program … it's just plain good business.'[13] Thus over the years, Johnson & Johnson's dedication to consumers and community service has made it one of America's most admired companies, *and* one of the most profitable.

Increasingly, firms also have to meet the expectations of society as a whole. For example, society expects businesses to uphold basic ethical and environmental standards. Not only should they have ethics and environmental policies, they must also genuinely uphold these standards. Consider, for instance, the bad publicity The Body Shop received during the early 1990s when the company came under attack in 1992 over its environmental standards. Some critics who researched the company's ethical and environmental practices charged that the high standards which it claims to uphold might be less genuine than it would like the world to think. The critics also expressed a broader concern – that the company persistently appears to exaggerate its involvement in worthy causes. Such charges cannot be ignored by the company's management, particularly its founder, Anita Roddick, and chairman, Gordon Roddick, who have long been involved in promoting ethical and environmental causes within the business world. Any tarnishing of Body Shop's image removes the organization's point of differentiation and, therefore, increases its vulnerability to competition, like Boots in the United Kingdom and Bath & Body Works, the US natural toiletries group, which is expanding into global markets.[14]

## THE GOALS OF THE MARKETING SYSTEM

Our marketing system consists of the collective marketing activities of tens of thousands of profit and non-profit organizations at home and around the globe. This marketing system affects everyone – buyers, sellers and many public groups with common characteristics. The goals of these groups may conflict.

*Buyers* want good-quality products at reasonable prices in convenient locations. They want: wide brand and feature assortments; helpful, pleasant and honest salespeople; and strong warranties backed by good follow-up service. The marketing system can greatly affect buyer satisfaction.

*Sellers* face many challenging decisions when preparing an offer for the market. What consumer groups should be targeted? What do target consumers need and how should products be designed and priced to give the greatest value? What wholesalers and retailers should be used? What advertising, personal selling and sales promotion would help sell the product? The market demands a lot. Sellers must apply modern marketing thinking in order to develop an offer that attracts and satisfies customers.

Legislators, public interest groups and other *publics* have a strong interest in the marketing activities of business. Do manufacturers make safe and reliable products? Do they describe their products accurately in ads and packaging? Is competition working in the market to provide a reasonable range of quality and price choice? Are manufacturing and packaging activities hurting the environment? The marketing system has a significant impact on the quality of life, and various groups of citizens want to make the system work as well as possible. They act as watchdogs of consumer interests and favour consumer education, information and protection.

The marketing system affects so many people in so many ways that it inevitably stirs controversy. Some people intensely dislike modern marketing activity, charging it with ruining the environment, bombarding the public with senseless ads, creating unnecessary wants, teaching greed to youngsters and committing several other 'sins'.

Consider the following:

> For the past 6,000 years the field of marketing has been thought of as made up of fast-buck artists, con-men, wheeler-dealers, and shoddy-goods distributors. Too many of us have been 'taken' by the touts or con-men; and all of us at times have been prodded into buying all sorts of 'things' we really did not need, and which we found later on we did not even want.[15]

Others vigorously defend marketing:

> Aggressive marketing policies and practices have been largely responsible for the high material standard of living in the west. Today through mass, low-cost marketing we enjoy products which once were considered luxuries, and which still are so classified in many foreign countries.[16]

What should a society seek from its marketing system? Four goals have been suggested: maximize consumption, maximize consumer satisfaction, maximize choice, and maximize quality of life.

## Maximize consumption

Many business executives believe that marketing's job should be to stimulate maximum consumption, which in turn will create maximum production, employment and wealth. This view has been promoted by slogans such as 'Who says you can't have it all?' (Michelob); or 'The costliest perfume in the world' (Joy); or 'Greed is good' (from the movie *Wall Street*). The assumption is that the more people spend, buy, and consume the happier they are. 'More is better' is the war cry. Yet some people doubt that increased material goods mean more happiness. They see too many affluent people leading unhappy lives. Their philosophy is 'less is more' and 'small is beautiful'.

## Maximize consumer satisfaction

Another view holds that the goal of the marketing system is to maximize consumer satisfaction, not simply the quantity of consumption. Buying a new car or owning more clothes counts only if this adds to the buyer's satisfaction.

Unfortunately, consumer satisfaction is difficult to measure. First, nobody has discovered how to measure the total satisfaction created by a particular product or marketing activity. Second, the satisfaction that some individual consumers get from the 'goods' of a product or service must be offset by the 'evils', such as pollution and environmental damage. Third, the satisfaction that some people get from consuming certain goods, such as status goods, depends on the fact that few other people have these goods. Thus, evaluating the marketing system in terms of how much satisfaction it delivers is difficult. Companies, however, can develop ways to evaluate the level of satisfaction offered to customers. Consider the following example:

> The international courier company, Federal Express, tried to rate not only the quality of their existing services, but also what it could be delivering. In both the US and European markets, FedEx went beyond its customer satisfaction index to improve its basic offering, while growing its customer base. FedEx discovered from its customer satisfaction surveys that it had been providing customers with a 'more than satisfactory' level of service. The firm decided that 'good enough' was not good enough. It examined its entire package delivery and billing process, charting the costs and activities at each step from the customer's

perspective. It offers to its 20,000 or so key customers 'Powership', a computer terminal which generates address labels with routing instructions and automatic billing in the form of an invoice that hits the computer screen when the package arrives. FedEx uses its customer knowledge to upgrade and improve its core services. It claims that its employees understand their customers' needs better than the customers themselves. As a result, customer loyalty is strengthened, with customers forming an even closer relationship with the company. Customer satisfaction levels have soared, so has customer spending.[17]

## Maximize choice

Some marketers believe that the goal of a marketing system should be to maximize product variety and consumer choice. This system would enable consumers to find goods that satisfy their tastes exactly. Consumers would be able to realize their lifestyle fully, and could therefore maximize their overall satisfaction.

Unfortunately, maximizing consumer choice comes at a cost. First, the price of goods and services rises because producing great variety increases production and inventory costs. In turn, higher prices reduce consumers' real income and consumption. Second, the increase in product variety will require greater consumer search and effort: consumers have to spend more time learning about and evaluating the different products. Third, the existence of more products will not necessarily increase the consumer's real choice. For example, hundreds of brands of beer are sold worldwide, but most of them taste about the same. So when a product category contains many brands with few differences, consumers face a choice that is really no choice at all. Finally, not all consumers welcome great product variety. For some consumers, too much choice leads to confusion and frustration.

## Maximize life quality

Many people believe that the goal of a marketing system should be to improve the *quality of life*. This includes not only the quality, quantity, availability and cost of goods, but also the quality of the physical and cultural environments. Advocates of this view would judge marketing systems not only by the amount of direct consumer satisfaction, but also by the impact of marketing on the quality of the environment. Most people would agree that quality of life is a worthwhile goal for the marketing system. But they might also agree that quality is hard to measure and that it means different things to different people.

## MARKETING CHALLENGES IN THE 1990S

Marketing operates within a dynamic global environment. Every decade calls upon marketing managers to think freshly about their marketing objectives and practices. Rapid changes can quickly make yesterday's winning strategies out of date. As management thought-leader Peter Drucker once observed, a company's winning formula for the last decade will probably be its undoing in the next decade.

What are the marketing challenges of the 1990s? Today's companies are wrestling with increased global competition, environmental decline, economic stagnation, and a host of other economic, political and social problems. In the European Union (EU),

Many US companies are finding new global opportunities. Looking for growth, MTV tries to repeat its phenomenal American success abroad, here in Hungary.

as the concept of nationally separate markets vaporizes, competition among sellers will further intensify. There is increasing pressure on individual firms within member countries to adjust to evolving deregulation and advancement of universal trading standards within the single market. However, these problems also provide marketing opportunities.

We now look more deeply into three key forces that are changing the marketing landscape and challenging marketing strategy: rapid globalization, the changing world economy, and the call for more socially responsible actions.

## Rapid globalization

The world economy has undergone radical change during the past two decades. Geographical and cultural distances have shrunk with the advent of jet planes, fax machines, global computer and telephone hook-ups, world television satellite and cable broadcasts, and other technical advances. This has allowed companies to greatly expand their geographical market coverage, purchasing, and manufacturing. Many companies are trying to create a global structure to move ideas swiftly around the world. The picture is one of a vastly more complex marketing environment for both companies and consumers.

Today, almost every company, large or small, is touched in some way by global competition. European and US firms, for example, are being challenged at home by the skilful marketing of Japanese and other Asian multinationals. Companies like Toyota, Honda, Fujitsu, Sony and Samsung have often outperformed their Western competitors in overseas markets. Similarly, Western companies in a wide range of industries have found new opportunities abroad. Glaxo, Asea Brown Boveri, Coca-Cola, IKEA, Toys 'R' Us, Club Mediterranean and many others have developed global operations, making and selling their products worldwide. The following are just a few of the countless examples of Western companies taking advantage of international marketing opportunities:

> IKEA, the Swedish home furnishings retailer, grew from one store in 1958 to more than 100 stores, stretched over 22 countries, by the early 1990s. IKEA's European expansion has hit the fortunes of traditional furniture retailers and manufacturers in supposedly staid furniture markets. Some have not survived the onslaught. [The UK's Habitat] was later acquired by IKEA. IKEA has successfully spread into the North American, Far Eastern and Australian markets. It practises its four-pronged philosophy – attention to product quality, value (low prices and 'more for your money'), innovative style and service – which it has successfully transferred to markets world-wide. Over the years, IKEA has built, and capitalised on, its

## Tomorrow the world

Ford, the world's second largest vehicle manufacturer, is seeking to become a truly global car company. It wants to break down national and regional barriers that have blocked its drive to build common vehicles for the world market. Ford has embarked on a massive worldwide reorganization programme to streamline operations – successful restructuring underpins its ambitions to become a global company.

All the world's car makers have to meet similar challenges: to improve the efficiency of their enormous investment programmes, while generating a greater diversity of products, and they must increase the speed of new product introduction. Many have to squeeze their massive materials purchasing bills by using global sourcing for parts and systems. Companies can no longer afford the luxury of duplication in a global market characterized by overcapacity and shrinking margins. This has been the case with Ford Europe, which traditionally duplicated, rather than complemented, its US parent's product design, development and engineering efforts. The European operation produced vehicles solely for the European market, with some exports to the rest of the world.

Ford's recent corporate revolution creates a single operating unit through merging its European and North American operations as well as its automotive components group. Four vehicle programme centres (VPCs) in North America and one VPC in Europe now replace previously independent regional companies. The European VPC has worldwide responsibility for small and medium front-wheel drive cars, built in manufacturing plants in Europe, the US and Mexico. The other four VPCs are responsible for large front-wheel drive cars, such as the Ford Taurus, rear-wheel drive cars, including Jaguar lines (though Jaguar will continue to maintain its resources in the United Kingdom), personal-use trucks and commercial vehicles, such as the highly successful European Ford Transit van.

Ford's new way of doing business will provide customers with a broader range of products and reduce the cost of operations. It would also ensure that the group remains competitive in quality and value against their keenest global competitors.

'affordable style' mass market positioning. IKEA's international expansion has raised its fortunes in what competition claims to be a traditionally dull and fragmented market. IKEA has proven that, with the right marketing approach, fortunes can be grown even in staid, old markets.

Coca-Cola and Pepsi, fierce competitors in the global soft drinks market, recently have watched the domestic (US) soft-drink market go flat, growing at only about 1 percent per year. Thus, both now have created new marketing strategies to attack Western Europe, a market growing at an 8 percent clip. Coca-Cola invested millions of dollars in marketing at the Barcelona Olympics and in the opening of EuroDisney. Coke makes about 80 percent of its profits outside of America and it has always led Pepsi abroad. Still, Pepsi thinks that it can compete successfully with Coke in Europe. It is investing almost $500 million in European businesses during the mid-nineties in what both companies view as their new big battleground.

Toys 'R' Us spent several years slogging through the swamps of Japanese bureaucracy before it was allowed to open the very first large US discount store in Japan, the world's No. 2 toy market behind the United States. The entry of this foreign giant has Japanese toymakers and retailers edgy. The typical small Japanese toy store stocks only 1,000 to 2,000 items, whereas Toys 'R' Us stores carry as many as 15,000. And the discounter will likely offer toys at prices 10 percent to 15 percent below those of competitors. The opening of the first Japanese store was 'astonishing', attracting more than 60,000 visitors in the first three days. Toys 'R' Us plans to open ten new Japanese stores each year from now through the end of the decade. If the company's invasion of Japan succeeds as well as its recent entry into Europe, Japanese retailers will have their hands full. Toys 'R' Us began with just five European stores in 1985 but now has over 76 and growing. European sales, now about $800 million, are growing at triple the rate of total sales.

Mondeo: the European version of Ford's 'world car'.

The move towards globalization is already partly paying off, as shown in Ford's recent success with its first global car – the Mondeo. This was a $6bn 6-year programme aimed at developing a common car to replace the Ford Sierra in Europe and the Ford Tempo/Mercury Topaz in North America. The Mondeo was launched in Europe in 1993 and in the United States a year later. The Mondeo/Ford Contour/Mercury Mystique is assembled at Ford's Genk plant in Belgium, at Kansas City in the US and in Mexico. The same family of four-cylinder engines is made at plants at Bridgend (United Kingdom) and at Cologne (Germany) for Europe and at Chihuahua in Mexico for the North American market. A top-of-the-range aluminium V6 engine is made at Cleveland, Ohio for both the US and European-produced vehicles. Manual transmissions are made in Europe at Halewood (United Kingdom) and at Cologne.

After a worldwide search, common component producers have been chosen to supply both the European and North American assembly plants. The lessons from the Mondeo programme are used to show the way forward for the company. Product development in the United States and Europe becomes fully integrated with the five VPCs. They have specific worldwide responsibilities and all report to one product-development executive. Furthermore manufacturing, purchasing, marketing and sales operations are integrated worldwide with one strategy office coordinating strategic planning. Ford has learnt to adapt to a globalizing world at last.

Source: This study has been heavily drawn from Kevin Done, 'Tomorrow the world', *Financial Times* (22 April 1994), 17. See also, 'The world car: enter the McFord', *The Economist* (23 July 1994), 77.

After ten years of relentless growth in America, Music Television's (MTV) home market has become saturated. Now the company is looking abroad for growth. It recently set up MTV Europe, which reaches 27 countries and 25 million homes. It is 'aggressively pan-European' – its programming and advertising are the same throughout Europe, and they are all in English. Initially, MTV has to convince advertisers that a true 'Euro-consumer' exists.[18]

Today, companies are not only trying to sell more of their locally produced goods in international markets, they are also buying or making more components and obtaining supplies abroad. Increasingly, international firms have to coordinate more and more functional operations across borders and to increase efficiency (see Marketing Highlight 1.3). Consequently, many domestically purchased goods and services are 'hybrids', with design, material purchases, manufacturing, and marketing taking place in several countries. British consumers who decide to 'buy British' might reasonably decide to avoid Sony televisions and purchase Amstrad's. Imagine their surprise when they learn that the Amstrad TV was actually made from parts and components imported from the Far East, whereas the Sony product was assembled in the United Kingdom from British-made parts.

Thus managers in countries around the world are asking: Just what is global marketing? How does it differ from domestic marketing? How do global competitors and forces affect our business? To what extent should we 'go global'? Many companies are forming strategic alliances with foreign companies, even competitors, who serve as suppliers or marketing partners. The past few years have produced some surprising alliances between competitors such as Mazda and Ford, Rover and Honda,

General Electric and Matsushita, Philips and Siemens, and Daimler Benz and United Technologies of the United States. Winning companies in the 1990s may well be those that have built the best global networks.[19]

## The changing world economy

A sluggish world economy has resulted in more difficult times for both consumers and marketers. Around the world, people's needs are greater than ever, but in many areas, people lack the means to pay for needed goods. Markets, after all, consist of people with needs *and* purchasing power. In many cases, the latter currently is lacking. In the developed Western and Asian economies, although wages have risen, real buying power has declined, especially for the less skilled members of the workforce. Many households have managed to maintain their buying power only because both spouses work. However, many workers have lost their jobs as manufacturers have automated to improve productivity or 'downsized' to cut costs.

Current economic conditions create both problems and opportunities for marketers. Some companies are facing declining demand and see few opportunities for growth. Others, however, are developing new solutions to changing consumer problems. Stronger businesses have recognized and taken advantage of recent developments in communications and related technologies. These developments have raised customers' expectations of product quality, performance and durability. They no longer accept or tolerate shoddy products. Power and control also have shifted from brand manufacturers to channel members who have become as sophisticated at marketing and exploiting technology as producers themselves. Many are finding ways to offer consumers 'more for less', like Sweden's IKEA and America's Toys 'R' Us. Heavy discounters are emerging to offer consumers quality merchandise at everyday low prices. These days, customers want value and more value. Increasingly, marketers must deliver offerings that delight, not merely satisfy, customers. Toyota has succeeded in doing that: its highly acclaimed Lexus luxury line offers consumers all the technology (gadgetry) and comfort they can ever dream of, and, at about £44,000, is considered exceptionally good value for money, compared to rival offerings in its class.

## The call for more ethics and social responsibility

A third factor in today's marketing environment is the increased call for companies to take responsibility for the social and environmental impact of their actions. Corporate ethics has become a hot topic in almost every business arena, from the corporate boardroom to the business school classroom. And few companies can ignore the renewed and very demanding environmental movement.

The ethics and environmental movements will place even stricter demands on companies in the future. Consider recent environmental developments. The West was shocked, after the fall of communism, to find out about the massive environmental negligence of the former Eastern bloc governments. In these and many Asian countries, air, water and soil pollution has added to our environmental concerns. These concerns led to representatives from more than one hundred countries attending the Earth Summit in Rio de Janeiro in 1992 to consider how to handle such problems as the destruction of rain forests, global warming, endangered species and other environmental threats. The pressure is on to 'clean up' our environment. Clearly, in the future, companies will be held to an increasingly higher standard of environmental responsibility in their marketing and manufacturing activities.

More specifically, in the EU, the toughening up of environmental rules should drive nonconformers out of business, while others who are committed to 'cleaning up' or 'greening' their practices and operations will emerge the stronger. Specialist industries for environmental goods and services (e.g. paper, bottle and tyre recyclers) have expanded quickly in recent years. As they say, 'there is money in Europe's muck'.[20]

## The new marketing landscape

The past decade taught business firms everywhere a humbling lesson. Domestic companies learned that they can no longer ignore global markets and competitors. Successful firms in mature industries learned that they cannot overlook emerging markets, technologies and management approaches. Companies of every sort learned that they cannot remain inwardly focused, ignoring the needs of their customers.

Prominent Western multinationals of the 1970s, including Philips, Volvo, General Motors and RCA, that floundered at marketing are all struggling to revive their fortunes today. They failed to understand their changing marketplace, their customers and the need to provide value. Today, General Motors is still trying to figure out why so many consumers around the world have switched to Japanese and European cars. In the consumer electronics industry, Philips has lost its way, losing share to Japanese competitors that have been more successful in turning expensive technologies into mass consumer products. Volvo, which has long capitalized on its safety positioning, has, of late, lost this unique selling point to other car manufacturers who have turned the safety benefit into a universal feature: many large European and Japanese car producers now offer, as standard features, driver and passenger airbags, antilock braking system and other safety devices. RCA, inventor of so many new products, never quite mastered the art of marketing and now puts its name on products largely imported from Asia.

Today, companies must become customer-oriented and market driven in all that they do. It's not enough to be product or technology driven – too many companies still design their products without customer input, only to find them rejected in the marketplace. It is not enough to be good at winning new customers – too many companies forget about customers after the sale, only to lose their future business. Not surprisingly, we have seen a flood of books with titles such as *The Customer Driven Company, Keep the Customer, Customers for Life, Total Customer Service: The ultimate weapon*, and *The Only Thing that Matters: Bringing the customer into the center of your business*.[21] These books emphasize that for the 1990s and beyond, the key to success will be a strong focus on the marketplace and a total marketing commitment to providing value to customers.

## SUMMARY

*Marketing* touches everyone's life. It is the means by which a standard of living is developed and delivered to a people. Many people confuse marketing with *selling*, but in fact, marketing occurs both before and after the selling event. Marketing actually combines many activities – marketing research, product development, distribution, pricing, advertising, personal selling and others – designed to sense, serve and satisfy consumer needs while meeting the organization's goals.

Marketing is human activity directed at satisfying needs and wants through *exchange processes*. The core concepts of marketing are *needs, wants, demands, products, exchange, transactions* and *markets*.

*Marketing management* is the analysis, planning, implementation and control of programmes designed to create, build and maintain beneficial exchanges with target markets in order to achieve organizational objectives. Marketers must be good at managing the level, timing, and composition of demand because actual demand can be different from what the organization wants.

Marketing management can be guided by five different philosophies. The *production concept* holds that consumers favour products which are available at low cost and that management's task is to improve production efficiency and bring down prices. The *product concept* holds that consumers favour quality products and that little promotional effort is thus required. The *selling concept* holds that consumers will not buy enough of the company's products unless stimulated through heavy selling and promotion. The *marketing concept* holds that a company should research the needs and wants of a well-defined target market and deliver the desired satisfactions. The *societal marketing concept* holds that the company should generate customer satisfaction and long-run societal well-being as the key to achieving both its goals and its responsibilities.

Marketing practices have a considerable impact on people in our society. Different goals have been proposed for a marketing system, such as maximizing *consumption, consumer satisfaction, consumer choice*, or *quality of life*. Marketing operates within a dynamic global environment. Rapid changes can quickly make yesterday's winning strategies obsolete. Marketers are facing many new challenges and opportunities in the 1990s. With the end of the Cold War, today's companies are wrestling with increased global competition, a sluggish world economy, a call for greater social responsibility, and a host of other economic, political and social problems. However, these problems also offer marketing opportunities. The future for adaptive organizations will always look bright. To be successful, they will have to be strongly market focused.

## ■ DISCUSSING THE ISSUES

1. Why should you study marketing?

2. Historian Arnold Toynbee and economist John Kenneth Galbraith have argued that the desires stimulated by marketing efforts are not genuine: 'A man who is hungry need never be told of his need for food.' Is this a valid criticism of marketing? Why or why not?

3. Many people dislike or fear certain products and would not 'demand' them at any price. How might a health-care marketer manage the *negative* demand for such products as colon-cancer screenings?

4. Changes in the world's political structure and balance of power are leading to cuts in Western nations' military budgets. Before these changes were made, defence contractors followed the product concept and focused on high technology. Will military suppliers now need to change to the marketing concept? Who are their customers?

5. What is the single biggest difference between the marketing concept and the production, product and selling concepts? Which concepts are easiest to apply in the short run? Which concept can offer the best long-term success?

6. According to economist Milton Friedman: 'Few trends could so thoroughly undermine the very foundations of our free society as the acceptance by corporate officials of a social responsibility other than to make as much money for their stockholders as possible.' Do you agree or disagree with Friedman's statement? What are some drawbacks of the societal marketing concept?

# ■ APPLYING THE CONCEPTS

**1.** Go to McDonald's and order a meal. Note the questions you are asked, and observe how special orders are handled. Next go to a restaurant on your college or university campus and order a meal. Note the questions you are asked here, and observe whether special orders are handled the same way as they are at McDonald's.

- Did you observe any significant differences in how orders are handled?
- Consider the differences you saw. Do you think the restaurants have different marketing management philosophies? Which is closest to the marketing concept? Is one closer to the selling or production concept?
- What are the advantages of closely following the marketing concept? Are there any disadvantages?

**2.** Take a trip to a shopping mall. Find the directory sign. Make a list of five main categories of stores, such as department stores, shoe stores, bookstores, women's clothing shops and restaurants. List the competing stores in each category, and take a walk past them and quickly observe their merchandise and style. Take a look at the public spaces of the mall, and note how they are decorated. Watch the shoppers in the mall.

- Four basic goals for the marketing system have been suggested: maximizing consumption, consumer satisfaction, consumer choice or quality of life. Do you think the mall serves some of these goals more, or better, than others?
- Are the competing stores really unique, or could one pretty much substitute for another? What does this say about the overall goals that the mall is fulfilling?
- Consider the attitudes of the shoppers you saw. Did some apparently find shopping a pleasure, while others found it a bother?

# ■ REFERENCES

1. Martin Wroe, 'Ministries, missions and markets', *Marketing Business* (October 1993), 8–11.
2. 'Balancing act', *Marketing Business* (October 1991), 41–3.
3. For more examples, see Philip Kotler and Karen Fox, *Strategic Marketing for Educational Institutions* (Englewood Cliffs, NJ: Prentice Hall, 1985); Bradley G. Morrison and Julie Gordon Dalgleish, *Waiting in the Wings: A larger audience for the arts and how to develop it* (New York: ACA Books, 1987); and Norman Shawchuck, Philip Kotler, Bruce Wren and Gustav Rath, *Marketing for Congregations: Choosing to serve people more effectively* (Nashville, TN: Abingdon Press, 1993).
4. Philip Kotler and Eduardo Roberto, *Social Marketing: Strategies for changing public behaviour* (New York: Free Press, 1990).
5. Peter F. Drucker, *Management: Tasks, responsibilities, practices* (New York: Harper & Row, 1973), 64–5.
6. Here are some other definitions: 'Marketing is the performance of business activities that direct the flow of goods and services from producer to consumer or user'. 'Marketing is selling goods that don't come back to people that do'. 'Marketing is getting the right goods and services to the right people at the right place at the right time at the right price with the right communication and promotion'. 'Marketing is the creation and delivery of a standard of living'. 'Marketing is the creation of time, place and possession utilities'. The American Marketing Association approved the definition: 'Marketing is the process of planning and executing the conception, pricing, promotion, and distribution of ideas, goods, and services to create exchanges that satisfy individual and organizational objectives'. As you can see, there is no single, universally agreed definition of marketing. There are definitions that emphasize marketing as a process, a concept or philosophy of business, or an orientation. The diversity of views adopted by authors is reflected in the wide selection of marketing definitions in common use. See Michael J. Baker, *Macmillan Dictionary of Marketing & Advertising*, 2nd edn (London: Macmillan, 1990), 148–9.
7. See Theodore Levitt's classic article, 'Marketing myopia', *Harvard Business Review* (July–August 1960), 45–56.
8. The number of transactions in a decentralized exchange system is given by $N(N-1)/2$. With four persons, this means $4(4-1)/2 = 6$ transactions. In a centralized exchange system, the number of transactions is given by $N$, here 4. Thus a centralized exchange system reduces the number of transactions needed for exchange.
9. Ralph Waldo Emerson offered this advice: 'If a man … makes a better mousetrap … the world will beat a path to his door'. Several companies, however, have built better mousetraps yet failed. One was a laser mousetrap costing $1,500. Contrary to popular assumptions, people do not automatically learn about new products,

believe product claims, or willingly pay higher prices.

10. Howard Schlossberg, 'Customer satisfaction: not a fad, but a way of life', *Marketing News* (10 June 1991), 18.

11. Thomas E. Caruso, 'Kotler: future marketers will focus on customer data base to compete globally', *Marketing News* (8 June 1992), 21–2.

12. See 'Leaders of the Most Admired', *Fortune* (29 January 1990), 40–54.

13. Ibid. 54.

14. Andrew Jack and Neil Buckley, 'Halo slips on the raspberry bubbles', *Financial Times* (27–28 August 1994), 8.

15. Richard N. Farmer, 'Would you want your daughter to marry a marketing man?', *Journal of Marketing* (January 1967), 1.

16. William J. Stanton and Charles Futrell, *Fundamentals of Marketing*, 8th edn (New York: McGraw-Hill, 1987), 7.

17. The Boston Consulting Group, 'Discovering how to maximise customer share', *Marketing Business* (September 1993), 13.

18. For these and other examples, see J. Reynolds, 'IKEA: a competitive company with style', *Retail and Distribution Management*, **16**, 3 (1988); B. Saporito, 'IKEA's got 'em lining up', *Fortune*, **123**, 5 (1991); 'Soda-pop celebrity', *The Economist* (14 September 1991), 75–6; 'MTV: rock on', *The Economist* (3 August 1991), 66; Robert Neff, 'Guess who's selling barbies in Japan now?', *Business Week* (9 December 1991), 72–6; Patrick Oster, 'Toys "R" Us making Europe its playpen', *Business Week* (20 January 1992), 88–91; Julie Skur Hill, 'Toys "R" Us seeks global growth', *Advertising Age* (30 March 1992), 33; and Kevin Cote, 'Toys "R" Us grows in Europe', *Advertising Age* (27 April 1992), 1–16.

19. For more on strategic alliances, see Jordan D. Lewis, *Partnerships for Profit: Structuring and managing strategic alliances* (New York: Free Press, 1990); Peter Lorange and Johan Roos, *Strategic Alliances: Formation, implementation and evolution* (Cambridge, MA: Blackwell, 1992); and Frederick E. Webster, Jr., 'The changing role of marketing in the corporation', *Journal of Marketing* (October 1992), 1–17.

20. 'The money in Europe's muck', *The Economist* (20 November 1993), 109–10.

21. Richard C. Whitely, *The Customer Driven Company* (Reading, MA: Addison-Wesley, 1991); Robert L. Desanick, *Keep the Customer* (Boston: Houghton Mifflin, 1990); Charles Sewell, *Customers for Life: How to turn the one-time buyer into a lifetime customer* (New York: Pocket Books, 1990); William H. Davidow and Bro Uttal, *Total Customer Service: The ultimate weapon* (New York: Harper & Row, 1989); and Karl Albrecht, *The Only Thing that Matters: Bringing the customer into the center of your business* (New York: Harper Business, 1992).

## CASE 1

## Amphitrion: your ultimate host in Greece    *Alkis S. Magdalinos**

Around the end of October 1993 Constantinos Mitsiou, owner and manager of the Greek Amphitrion Group of Companies, was wondering if he should launch a special tour for teenagers. What he had in mind was a tour lasting fourteen days that would incorporate most of the natural beauty spots of Greece, as well as numerous historic and archaeological sites. He had already concluded a tentative agreement with a couple of professors who would act as guides and worked out a preliminary itinerary, but he was now not sure if he should continue with the idea.

Amphitrion, which started as a travel agency in 1957, was now a large travel and shipping business – 'your ultimate hosts in Greece'. The head office of Amphitrion is in Constitution Square, a prestigious business area in the centre of Athens. It also has branches in Tokyo, Washington, DC, and Toronto as well as other Greek offices in Athens, Crete and

* University of La Verne, Greece.

Piraeus. The largest part of the touring business was for executives and employees of businesses who bought their tickets from the agency branch of the business. These clients also bought family holidays and travel. In 1993, the biggest part of the clientele was middle and senior executives and, sometimes, their secretaries and assistants. Only some 10 per cent of sales come from 'drop-ins', people who casually dropped in at one of Amphitrion's travel offices.

Mr Mitsiou had first started thinking about his teenager tour after a meeting with other agents at an International Convention, in Milan, in September 1993. He had had a discussion with a travel agent from Rome who told him about a similar exercise he had organized successfully during the last holiday season. He was already thinking of repeating the tour in Greece. He also told Mr Mitsiou that both parents and teenagers looked forward to such tours since it allowed them to have separate vacations. The best time for the tours was between July and August when schools were on holiday. Parents accepted the idea of the tour if the agent could guarantee the proper supervision and the calibre of the people acting as guides.

When Mr Mitsiou came back to Athens he repeated the idea to Joan and George Lykidis, friends of his, and asked them whether they wanted to act as guides for the tour. Mr Lykidis was the head teacher of one of Athens's largest schools and a professor of history. Both Mr and Mrs Lykidis were enthusiastic about the idea and were eager to take it on.

Mr Mitsiou did not know if anyone else in Greece had started such a tour. However, he knew that for some years a professor at a well-known school had organized tours of Europe for students from private schools. The activity had developed into a profitable summer business. As far as Mr Mitsiou knew, the tours were always successful and sold out each year. The teacher used no special advertising for his tours, getting most of his business from old students who had been on the tour themselves and now sent their children.

The tours Mr Mitsiou had in mind would focus on Greece, including its local colour as well as the important historic and archaeological sites around the country. Characteristically, Mr Mitsiou said the nature of the tour had occurred to him after reading letters from parents and professors in the daily press. These complained about the theoretical way Greek history was taught at school. To Mr Mitsiou, it was obvious from the letters that parents and students wanted a tour visiting the sites they had studied so dryly in their history classes. Parents definitely looked forward to giving their children a well-organized tour in which they would visit all these places and where, with proper guidance, the entire history of their ancestry would be revealed to them.

Mr Mitsiou also knew very well that teenagers would not like it if the whole of the itinerary comprised only visits to museums, and to historic and archaeological sites. He would therefore give them a chance to enjoy the beautiful seashores and beaches; to go into towns and villages; and to have fun at tavernas and discos and enjoy some dancing and entertainment.

After some considerable thought he developed the following itinerary:

Day 1    Departure from Athens – Thermopylae – Tempi – Mount Olympus – Thessaloniki overnight.

Day 2    Morning free. Afternoon visit Eptapyrgio, Old City, St Demetrious Church, International Fairgrounds, night at a disco, stay overnight at Eptapyrgio.

Day 3    Depart for Philippi, visit sites of interest at Kavala, stay overnight on Thasos Island.

Day 4    Swimming at Golden Beach – Makrynammos, visit Necropolis Museum, return to Kavala, stay overnight.

Day 5    Depart for Polygyros, Agion Oros, swimming at Chalkidiki Beach, overnight in Thessaloniki, go to a disco.

Day 6    Leave for ancient Pella, Vergina, Tomb of Philippos, Grevena, Metsovo, stay overnight.

Day 7    Ioannina, visit Vella Monastery, Ali Pasha Island in Ioannina lake, old town, stay overnight.

Day 8    Dodoni, Arta, Agrinio, Messolonghi, visit sites, Aetolikon, the lagoon, fishing ponds at Tholi, overnight in Messolonghi.

Day 9    Depart for Patras, visit sites, leave for Kyllini, swimming, stay overnight.

Day 10    Leave for Olympia, visit archaeological grounds, overnight in Vityna.

Day 11    Leave for Tripolis, Sparta, visit the museum, Mystras, Gythio, Diros caves, Gerolimena for swimming, overnight in Areopolis.

Day 12    Departure for Kalamata, Pylos, Methoni, swimming, return to Kalamata, afternoon free, disco, stay overnight.

Day 13    Leave for Tripolis, Nafplio, Tolo, swimming, Tyrins, Argos, Mycenae, Nemea, overnight in Korinth.

Day 14    Ancient Korinth, Sykion, Kiato, Nerantza for swimming, return to Athens.

Mr Mitsiou knew that tours of this type could be cancelled at the last moment, which would mean that money would have to be refunded. If that happened, the total spending on the promotion of the tour would amount to a loss of about Dr 266,000.* In addition, money had to be paid two months in advance to secure good rooms, especially at places with only one hotel, and this would be a significant sum that would have to be written off if the tour did not go ahead. By Mr Mitsiou's calculation advertising and other expenses would bring the loss to about Dr 1,000,000 if the whole tour was cancelled.

*1 ecu = US$1.26 = Dr 302 (Greek drachmas).

## CASE I (cont)

With a group of forty participants on tour, his total cost came to Dr 2,260,000. From this he expected to clear 7 per cent profit. If he had more people on the tour the profits would be greater but George Lykidis had already said that more than forty teenagers would be impossible to supervise properly.

It was important not to cancel the tour in the first year once it had been advertised. Word of mouth was the best way of attracting tour members, particularly as a result of previous members telling their friends. So he decided he would go ahead with as few as twenty participants, even though that meant he would make a loss. By charging more he could make money with only twenty participants, but he did not think that he could charge more than Dr 60,450 per person in the first year. When he had organized tours in the past he had used subagents who required a 5 per cent commission. In this project, however, his margins were so small that he would not use subagents.

Soon after he had finished working out the plans for the tour, Mr Mitsiou met a friend, a very renowned lawyer, who had two sons in their teens. The lawyer said that he would never let his sons go on such a tour. He added that such tours treated teenagers like sheep. Anyhow teenagers had no interest in history, no matter what newspapers said to the contrary. His idea was to give his boys some money and a couple of tickets, and to allow them to travel for as long as the money lasted. For that age group, guides were not important, and it was best to give such teenagers the chance to prove that they were responsible and could travel on their own. This worried Mr Mitsiou since he always trusted his friend's opinions. He started to reconsider his planned tour and to think of other ways to make the tour look more attractive.

### Questions

1. Has Mr Mitsiou taken a marketing-oriented approach to developing his teenage tour idea? What elements of marketing orientation, if any, are missing?
2. Is the teenage tour idea financially attractive? Does it fit the strengths of the Amphitrion Group? Is it a market that the company naturally understands?
3. Would the tour have been attractive to you as a teenager? Would this Greek tour be attractive to teenagers in your country? Would you have found a similar tour of your own country attractive? Would your parents find it attractive? Who is the customer in this case and what do they want?
4. Is running a tour the only way to see if it would be successful or not? How else do you think its appeal could be tested? How could the tour be changed to be more appealing and less risky?

## CHAPTER TWO

# Marketing and society

## Social responsibility and marketing ethics

## CHAPTER OBJECTIVES

After reading this chapter, you should be able to:

■ List and respond to the social criticisms of marketing.

■ Define *consumerism* and *environmentalism* and explain how they affect marketing strategies.

■ Describe the principles of socially responsible marketing.

■ Explain the role of ethics in marketing.

## CHAPTER PREVIEW

### Brown & Williamson Tobacco: 'Keeping smokers addicted'

It has long been known that tobacco companies controlled nicotine levels in their cigarettes. In the 1940s, nicotine and tar levels in cigarettes were more than three times today's levels. Manufacturers have gradually reduced them through refinements in the processing technique to satisfy demand for smoother and lighter cigarettes. A new battle started between the US Food and Drug Administration (FDA) and tobacco companies in June 1994. At the centre of the debate was damning evidence presented to Congress which suggested that US tobacco companies had been deliberately manipulating the amount of nicotine in cigarettes to keep the nation's 46 million smokers addicted.

On 21 June 1994, a House of Representatives subcommittee heard allegations that Brown & Williamson (B&W) Tobacco, a US subsidiary of Britain's BAT Industries, had secretly developed a genetically engineered tobacco called Y-1 that contained more than twice the amount of nicotine found in normal tobacco plants. Mr David Kessler, head of the US FDA, informed the committee that B&W had earlier denied breeding tobacco plants for high or low nicotine content. Yet the company had several million pounds of Y-1 tobacco stored in US warehouses and had been using it in five local brands of cigarettes.

Kessler has recently backed off from earlier suggestions that US tobacco manufacturers had deliberately 'spiked' their products to keep smokers addicted, but has more recently said it is sufficient to show that cigarette companies have the ability to control nicotine levels in their products, allowing them to remain at addictive levels. Kessler hoped to use the evidence implicating B&W in the Y-1 row to push his case for bringing tobacco under his agency's control. He has previously threatened to regulate cigarettes as drugs if he could show that manufacturers intend consumers to buy them to satisfy an addiction. The discovery of the Y-1 high-nicotine tobacco proved beyond doubt that tobacco firms were manipulating and controlling nicotine concentration in their products.

B&W defended the allegations. First, it accused Kessler of blowing the issue out of proportion. Second, it stressed the fact that Y-1 is nothing secret and just one of a variety of local and foreign tobaccos it used to give the unique 'recipe' of ingredients that went into each brand. 'Y-1 was a blending tool for flavour', B&W said. In any case, according to parent BAT Industries, the Y-1 strain had been largely withdrawn after proving unpopular with consumers. Interestingly, ASH, an anti-smoking lobby, said that it had no evidence to contradict BAT's assertion.

Tobacco companies argue that they cannot eliminate nicotine altogether from their products as it is an essential contributor to cigarette flavour. Smokers no longer enjoy cigarettes when the nicotine level falls below a certain point. So, it is important to adjust the level of nicotine and other flavour-enhancers to provide what cigarettes consumers like. Mr Walker Merriman, vice-president of the Tobacco Institute, said that 'consumer preference' was the specific reason for having any particular level of nicotine and tar in any particular cigarette. Low-nicotine brands have commanded very low market share, while no-nicotine brands had failed through lack of demand.

In reality, Kessler is more concerned now with two issues: whether cigarettes are addictive, and if manufacturers intend them to be addictive. If so on either issue, the FDA may be able to bring them under its jurisdiction as a drug. He can then force the tobacco industry gradually to reduce nicotine levels in their products and so wean smokers away from the habit. The industry position is that cigarettes are *not* a drug, as defined in the 1938 Federal Food, Drug and Cosmetic Act, because they 'do not intend to affect the structure or any function of the body'. Furthermore, manufacturers argue that smoking cannot be addictive because 50 per cent or more of American citizens today who have ever smoked have quit – over 90 per cent of them without professional help. Critics of Kessler's policy say that there is a risk that smokers would smoke even more cigarettes to compensate for the loss of nicotine intake, which raises smokers' exposure to another serious health risk – the carcinogenic ingredients of cigarettes. Besides, this policy would boost industry profits.

One debate is whether tobacco companies like B&W are knowingly manipulating nicotine levels in their products with intent to cause addiction. If so, such socially irresponsible behaviour must arguably be controlled. On past record, it will take a long time to reach the point at which the FDA will bring the tobacco industry under its control. Things are stirring up fast though. The race is already on to sue America's tobacco giants. In February 1995, a New Orleans court ruled, in effect, that every American ever addicted to nicotine – or the relations of any nicotine-dependent-but-now-dead American – could sue the tobacco companies. Four American states also are to sue for the cost of treating smokers!

These recent events in the United States must now surely trivialize the tobacco advertising debate in Europe. The emergence of medical evidence suggesting that smoking is a health hazard has triggered reactions from antismoking groups who argue that smoking should be at least discouraged, if not banned outright. Over the 1980s, lobbying by antismoking campaigners throughout Europe brought about the enforcement of tighter restrictions, notably on tobacco advertising.

Those who rage against the evil of cigarette advertising assume that it is creating droves of new smokers. Tobacco firms, to their annoyance, argue that the assumption is doubtful. They claim that there is no brand evidence that advertising has much effect on total consumption. It is true that, according to a recent study, advertising bans in Norway, Finland, Canada and New Zealand helped to reduce cigarette consumption. But studies in other countries, such as Italy and Sweden, have shown that bans were followed by increases in smoking. Ironically, some argue that a ban would have one drawback: it would end the health warnings that now accompany tobacco advertising.

Tobacco firms claim that they advertise not to expand demand for cigarettes, but merely to maintain their market share against competitors' brands. Is this a bogus or friendly argument? In the interest of consumer safety and well-being, should tobacco firms even bother to circumvent current rules? Indeed, current restrictions are already tight. Cigarette companies are prohibited from advertising on television in many European markets. To stave off more draconian legislation, they have agreed: to stop advertising in the cinema or on posters near schools; to reduce advertising on shop fronts; to stop using celebrities in their advertising; and to avoid any hint that smoking brings social or sexual success. Yet, tobacco adverts are not quite dead! Advertisers often resort to the use of cryptic pictures, like *red* motorcycles – the clue that told consumers to rush out and buy 'Marlboro' (red is the Marlboro brand colour).

Worse, tobacco firms are preying on children. Their aggressive campaigns in the less developed and affluent Far Eastern countries, with fewer consumer protection laws, are also cause for concern. Should tobacco firms take greater responsibility for communicating the health hazards of smoking, and discouraging the habit, which clearly will hurt the industry? Can society expect the industry to regulate its own actions and practise socially responsible marketing? Is advertising of hazardous products ethical? Can customers and society, at large, be left to develop their own sense of personal responsibility – to avoid harmful products – even if firms don't? Or are legislators the ultimate force that protects innocent consumers from unsavoury marketing?[1]

Marketers face difficult decisions when choosing to serve customers profitably on the one hand, and seeking to maintain a close fit between consumers' wants or desires and societal welfare on the other. In this chapter, we discuss marketing in the context of society, the need for integrity, social responsibility and sound ethics, and the dilemmas that marketing people face. We begin with a look at criticisms of marketing's impact on individual consumers and society as a whole. Next, we discuss consumerism, environmentalism and regulation, and the way they affect marketing strategies. This leads to an overview of responsible or enlightened marketing and marketing ethics. Finally, we conclude with a set of principles for public policy towards marketing: consumer and producer freedom, avoiding harm, meeting basic needs, economic efficiency, innovation, and consumer education, information and protection.

## INTRODUCTION

Responsible marketers discover what consumers want and respond with the right products, priced to give good value to buyers and profit to the producer. The **marketing concept** is a philosophy of service and mutual gain. Its practice leads the economy by an invisible hand to satisfy the many and changing needs of millions of consumers. But does social responsibility and morality have any role to play? Or is it incompatible with commercial survival in a competitive global marketplace?

Those are the sort of questions that used to be asked only in classrooms and communes. But, in an era when the consumer is wiser to much more of a company's practice, together with increasingly wider concerns about environmental issues, animal testing and human rights, the need for social responsibility and sound ethics in marketing has become crucial if customers' demands are to be fulfilled. How companies behave in the broadest sense is beginning to have an impact on how people view their products and services. Johnson & Johnson's very speedy recall of contaminated Tylenol capsules from store shelves to prevent further possibilities of consumer injury was a socially responsible act. The 'Tylenol scares' was a serious public issue and caused great consumer concern in markets where the drug was sold. However, in taking responsible action, the brand value remained undamaged in the long run and sales revived when the problem was resolved.

Not all marketers follow the marketing concept, however. In fact, some companies use questionable marketing practices, and some marketing actions that seem innocent in themselves strongly affect the larger society. Consider, again, the sale of sensitive products such as cigarettes. Ordinarily, companies should be free to sell cigarettes, and smokers should be free to buy them. But this transaction affects the public interest. First, the smoker may be shortening his or her own life. Second, smoking places a burden on the smoker's family and on society at large. Third, other people around the smoker may have to inhale the smoke and may suffer discomfort and harm. This is not to say that cigarettes should be banned, although the antismoking lobbyists would welcome that. Rather, it shows that private transactions may involve larger questions of public policy. In practice, the answers are by no means always clear cut. It may be ethical for tobacco firms to stop peddling cigarettes altogether, but this, while seen by absolute moralists as 'the right thing' to do, will lead to companies' demise, job losses and their repercussions on the wider community.

This chapter examines the social effects of private marketing practices. We examine several questions: What are the most frequent social criticisms of marketing? What steps have private citizens taken to curb marketing ills? What steps have legislators and government agencies taken to curb marketing ills? What steps have enlightened companies taken to carry out socially responsible and ethical marketing? We examine how marketing affects and is affected by each of these issues.

## SOCIAL CRITICISMS OF MARKETING

Marketing receives much criticism. Some of this criticism is justified; much is not.[2] Social critics claim that certain marketing practices hurt individual consumers, society as a whole and other business firms.

### Marketing's impact on individual consumers

Consumers have many concerns about how well marketing and businesses, as a whole, serve their interests. Surveys usually show that consumers hold slightly unfavourable attitudes towards marketing practices.[3] One consumer survey found that consumers are most worried about high prices, poor-quality and dangerous products, misleading advertising claims, and several other marketing-related problems (see Figure 2.1). Consumer advocates, government agencies, and other critics have accused marketing of harming consumers through high prices, deceptive practices, high-pressure selling, shoddy or unsafe products, planned obsolescence and poor service to disadvantaged consumers.

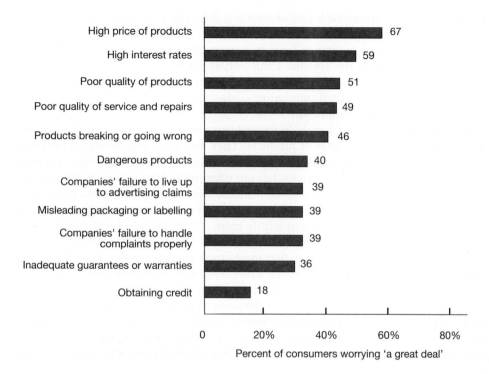

High price of products — 67
High interest rates — 59
Poor quality of products — 51
Poor quality of service and repairs — 49
Products breaking or going wrong — 46
Dangerous products — 40
Companies' failure to live up to advertising claims — 39
Misleading packaging or labelling — 39
Companies' failure to handle complaints properly — 39
Inadequate guarantees or warranties — 36
Obtaining credit — 18

0    20%    40%    60%    80%

Percent of consumers worrying 'a great deal'

**Figure 2.1** Survey of consumer concerns (Source: Myrlie Evers, 'Consumerism in the Eighties', *Public Relations Journal* (August 1983), 24–6. Reprinted with permission. © 1983. See also 'The public is willing to take on business', *Business Week* (29 May 1989), 29.)

## High prices

Many critics charge that marketing practices raise the cost of goods and cause prices to be higher than they would be if clever marketing was not applied. They point to three factors: *high costs of distribution, high advertising and promotion costs*, and *excessive mark-ups.*

*High costs of distribution*    A long-standing charge is that greedy middlemen mark up prices beyond the value of their services. Critics charge either that there are too many middlemen, or that middlemen are inefficient and poorly run, provide unnecessary or duplicate services, and practise poor management and planning. As a result, distribution costs too much and consumers pay for these excessive costs in the form of higher prices.

How do retailers answer these charges? They argue, first, that middlemen do work which would otherwise have to be done by manufacturers or consumers. Second, the rising mark-up reflects improved services that consumers themselves want – more convenience, larger stores and assortment, longer store opening hours, return privileges and others. Third, the costs of operating stores keep rising, forcing retailers to raise their prices. Fourth, retail competition is so intense that margins are actually quite low; for example, after taxes, supermarket chains are typically left with barely 1 per cent profit on their sales.

*High advertising and promotion costs*    Modern marketing is also accused of pushing up prices because of heavy advertising and sales promotion. For example, a dozen tablets of a heavily promoted brand of aspirin sell for the same price as do 100 tablets of less promoted brands. Differentiated products – cosmetics, detergents, toiletries – include promotion and packaging costs that can amount to 40 per cent or more of the manufacturer's price to the retailer. Critics charge that much of the packaging and promotion adds only psychological value to the product rather than real functional value. Retailers use additional promotion – advertising, displays and competitions – that add even more to retail prices.

Marketers answer these charges in several ways. First, consumers *want* more than the merely functional qualities of products. They also want psychological benefits – they want to feel wealthy, beautiful or special. Consumers can usually buy functional versions of products at lower prices, but are often willing to pay more for products that also provide desired psychological benefits. Second, branding gives buyers confidence. A brand name implies a certain quality and consumers are willing to pay for well-known brands even if they cost a little more. Third, heavy advertising is needed to inform millions of potential buyers of the merits of a brand. If consumers want to know what is available on the market, they must expect manufacturers to spend large sums of money on advertising. Fourth, heavy advertising and promotion may be necessary for a firm to match competitors' efforts. The business would lose 'share of mind' if it did not match competitive spending. At the same time, companies are cost conscious about promotion and try to spend their money wisely. Finally, heavy sales promotion is needed from time to time because goods are produced ahead of demand in a mass-production economy. Special incentives have to be offered in order to sell inventories.

*Excessive mark-ups*   Critics also charge that some companies mark up goods excessively. They point to the drug industry, where a pill costing 5 pence to make may cost the consumer 40 pence to buy. Or to the pricing tactics of perfume manufacturers, who take advantage of customers' ignorance of the true worth of a 50 gram bottle of Joy perfume, whilst preying on their desire to fulfil emotional needs.

1 ecu = UK£0.83
= 83 pence

Marketers argue that most businesses try to deal fairly with consumers because they want repeat business. Most consumer abuses are unintentional. When shady marketers do take advantage of consumers, they should be reported to industry watchdogs and to other consumer-interest or consumer-protection groups. Marketers also stress that consumers often don't understand the reason for high mark-ups. For example, pharmaceutical mark-ups must cover the costs of purchasing, promoting and distributing existing medicines plus the high research and development costs of finding new medicines.

### Deceptive practices

Marketers are sometimes accused of deceptive practices that lead consumers to believe they will get more value than they actually do. Deceptive practices fall into three groups: *deceptive pricing, promotion* and *packaging*.

Deceptive pricing includes practices such as falsely advertising 'factory' or 'wholesale' prices or a large price reduction from a phony high list price. Deceptive promotion includes practices such as overstating the product's features or performance, luring the customer to the store for a bargain that is out of stock, or running rigged contests. Deceptive packaging includes exaggerating package contents through subtle design, not filling the package to the top, using misleading labelling, or describing size in misleading terms.

Deceptive practices have led to legislation and other consumer-protection actions. Positive changes have already taken place, for example, with regard to European directives aimed at the cosmetic industry. The Council Directive 93/35/EEC of 14 June 1993 brings far-reaching changes to cosmetic laws. The legislation controls the constituents of cosmetic products and their associated instructions and warnings about use, and specifies requirements relating to the marketing of cosmetic products, which cover product claims, labelling, information on packaging and details on the product's intended function. Where a product claims to remove 'unsightly cellulite' or make the user look '20 years younger', proofs must be documented and made available to the enforcement authorities. These laws will also require clear details specifying where animal testing has been carried out on both the finished product and/or its ingredients. The EU has recognized increased public resistance to animal testing and is proposing a limited ban on animal testing for cosmetic ingredients from 1 January 1998. Similar directives are found to regulate industry practices in the United States. In 1938, the Wheeler-Lea Act gave the FTC the power to regulate 'unfair or deceptive acts or practices'. The FTC has published several guidelines listing deceptive practices. The toughest problem is defining what is 'deceptive'. For example, some years ago, Shell Oil advertised that Super Shell petrol with platformate gave more mileage than did the same fuel without platformate. Now this was true, but what Shell did not say is that almost *all* petrol includes platformate. Its defence was that it had never claimed that platformate was found only in Shell petroleum fuel. But even though the message was literally true, the FTC felt that the ad's *intent* was to deceive.

Marketers argue that most companies avoid deceptive practices because such practices harm their business in the long run. If consumers do not get what they expect, they will switch to more reliable products. In addition, consumers usually protect themselves from deception. Most consumers recognize a marketer's selling intent and are careful when they buy, sometimes to the point of not believing completely true product claims. Theodore Levitt claims that some advertising puffery is bound to occur – and that it may even be desirable:

> There is hardly a company that would not go down in ruin if it refused to provide fluff, because nobody will buy pure functionality ... Worse, it denies ... man's honest needs and values. ... Without distortion, embellishment and elaboration, life would be drab, dull, anguished and at its existential worst ...[4]

### High-pressure selling

Salespeople are sometimes accused of high-pressure selling that persuades people to buy goods they had no thought of buying. It is often said that encyclopaedias, insurance, property and jewellery are *sold*, not *bought*. Salespeople are trained to deliver smooth, canned talks to entice purchase. They sell hard because commissions and sales contests promise big prizes to those who sell the most.

Marketers know that buyers can often be talked into buying unwanted or unneeded things. A key question is whether industry self-regulatory or trading standards bodies, consumer-protection laws, and consumer-interest groups are sufficiently effective in checking and curbing unsavoury sales practices. In this modern era, it is encouraging to note that one or more of these can work to the advantage of consumers. Or, where malpractices are pervasive, regulators will catch out wrongdoers, who will invariably pay the penalties for irresponsible marketing. This is evident in the case of the mis-selling of life assurance policies in the UK market (see Marketing Highlight 2.1).

# We have ways of making you buy!

Britain's life assurance industry was severely criticized for mis-selling, offering poor value to customers who surrender their policies early, for exploiting customers' ignorance – in short, for breaking the rules!

Since May 1992 LAUTRO, the body that regulates the selling of life-insurance, has fined at least a dozen life assurance companies a total of nearly £1m. for failing to ensure potential customers were fully informed about different policies. Those singled out included Scottish Widows, which was fined £120,000, Guardian Royal Exchange (£100,000), and General Accident, Commercial Union and Norwich Union (£50,000 each). Norwich Union also paid a record £300,000 fine for professional misconduct. It even temporarily suspended its entire salesforce of 800, including 200 sales agents, so that they could be retrained to give proper financial advice.

In June 1994, the Office of Fair Trading (OFT), a government watchdog, published its report on 60 of the United Kingdom's largest life insurers. It criticized firms for poor 'surrender values' – many household names, the symbols of probity and financial solidity, were short-changing customers who cashed in long-term policies early. London & Manchester, London Life, MGM, Refuge, Royal Life, Tunbridge Wells, Abbey Life, Allied Dunbar, Confederation Life, Cornhill Insurance, Irish Life, Midland Life and Reliance Mutual were all found to offer zero surrender value at the end of the first year for two types of policies investigated by the OFT. So, if a customer cancelled a £100 a month, 10-year savings plan after only one year, she got no money back from the insurer. There were also wide disparities in the surrender values of life insurance policies, although such information was seldom disclosed to buyers.

What is all the fuss about, though? Why should companies be penalized because their investors want to cash in earlier on long-term savings plans? Regulators believe that life insurers had exploited customers' ignorance, selling them products that generated big profits for the sellers but were unsuited to the buyer. In many cases, insurers were accused of filling the pockets of salespeople, senior managers and, in the case of limited companies, the shareholders, by extracting fat commission from the high-pressure selling schemes that customers did not really want or need (one reason why they cancel the policy prematurely). In tens of thousands of cases, policies have been against the best interests of customers. Salespeople exploited the vulnerability of potential customers to get a sale. Sales 'tricks' were not unusual in the industry. For example, some salespeople sent letters to married women, talking about their company and appending a blank form with a piece of paper telling the woman: 'This is what you get when your husband dies.'

Although the surrender values offered by the insurers in later years were reasonable, the OFT suggested that more people stopped paying their premiums in the first year than in any later year. This drop-out or lapse rate is estimated to be in the 17 to 23 per cent range. Indeed, data prepared for the Securities and Investments Board in 1992 suggested that one-quarter to one-third of all policies were cashed in during the first two years alone. The OFT also found that a number of companies actually profited from early lapse rates and that many people holding policies with companies which have relatively high lapse rates were actually worse off than if they had no policy at all. Insurers benefit because most customers are unlikely to hold their policies to maturity. Lapses are their profits!

The insurance companies' response is that customers have the product literature to help them assess their policies. The OFT argues that the idea that customers could understand readily the surrender values of their policies simply by reading the product literature is quite false. 'These things are not only obscure to the average consumer but to the informed consumer as well,' says John Mills, head of the OFT's consumer policy division.

Regulators blame the unacceptably high level of policy cancellation on mis-selling. So, what fuels this pervasive practice in the industry? How could an industry with such a strong position in British society become accused of such a breach of trust? Nearly 70 per cent of UK families have some form of life insurance, with the industry paying out about £10bn a year in benefits.

One answer is that not nearly as many people would have bought life insurance if the products had not been actively sold to them. Another is that few consumers have the expertise to compare the costs and benefits of different policies. What consumers buy is all about how quickly the sales rep gets to them and how persuasive he or she is. Vigorous selling works.

Then, from the mid-1980s, there was the surge in interest by cash-rich consumers in financial investment, including individually tailored pension products. It was an exciting period, where successful salespeople, usually self-employed, could earn commissions of £500,000 a year up to £1m.

Although many independent financial advisors ensure that clients get good value for money from respectable insurers, there are many others who are forced to sell poor-quality products, because they are trapped in a commission structure that requires them to sell or starve.

One insurance sales representative says: 'You would see that some prospective clients might have to struggle to pay the premiums, but because your livelihood depended on it, you would play on their emotions to try to sell them something.' Another salesman commented: 'We were licensed to give best advice, but it wasn't. A superior product offered by another company would not be mentioned. This is standard practice; under LAUTRO rules, direct salesmen need not discuss competing products.' Sales people argue that they were often put under increasing pressure and encouraged by a range of incentives, some of them fairly obvious, such as bottles of whisky and holidays in the Bahamas. In one life office,

the manager would lend his Rolex watch for a day to the agent who topped the sales league that week. There were bizarre punishments for those that do badly: at one branch of a big insurer, the worst performer over the previous month would be told to walk around the building for a day dressed in ladies' underwear.

Two key issues are now addressed by regulators and watchdogs: what customers are told about products and the people selling them; and self-regulation versus government (statutory) regulation. The OFT wants independent financial advisors (IFAs), who are supposed to offer a full range of policies and independent advice, to tell customers their commission for selling a given policy. Predictably, IFAs protest that disclosure will force many of them out of business. Life assurance salespeople and tied agents, who sell only one firm's products, are now self-regulated. Some, however, want tougher regulation by government rather than a strengthened self-regulatory system. Life insurers should disclose far more detail about their policies to customers. Britain's biggest insurer, Prudential, a strong proponent of statutory control, has pledged its support for greater transparency. Other insurers would be wise to follow suit. The regulators are getting keener.

The moral of the story is clear. Using trickery or vigorous sales approaches to pressure customers unfairly into buying financial products (or any product or service) that they either do not need or would do better to buy elsewhere, does not make sound marketing sense. Consumers become disenchanted or disillusioned or withdraw consumption altogether, as in the early cancellation of long-term insurance policies. High-pressure selling usually backfires on the aggressive sellers. You cannot sell something nobody wants, no matter how you push it!

Sources: Alison Smith, 'Standard Life's surrender bonus', *Financial Times* (21 November 1994), 22; Alison Smith, 'OFT names insurers offering zero first year surrender value', *Financial Times* (9–10 July 1994), 1; Alison Smith, 'Back from the brink', *Financial Times* (23 June 1994), 16; Norma Cohen, 'Life insurers criticised for poor surrender values', 'Your lapses are their profits', *Financial Times* (18–19 June 1994), I, III; Peter Marsh, 'We have ways of making you buy', *Financial Times* (14 June 1994), 18; Peter Marsh, 'When he dies, my dear, all this will be yours', *Financial Times* (11–12 June 1994), I, XII; 'All life's troubles', *The Economist* (17 July 1993), 76–7; John Authers and Norma Cohen, 'Increased share of premiums for life salesmen', *Financial Times* (26 February 1992), 1.

### Shoddy or unsafe products

Another criticism is that products lack the quality they should have. One complaint is that products are not made well. Some European car makers still bear the brunt of many such complaints. Quality problems used to plague the Rover car company, formerly a subsidiary of British Aerospace. There also was a long-standing joke about Jaguar cars – that you must be very rich to own a Jaguar, the reason being that you have to have two, in case one doesn't start in the morning! In recent years, however, both Jaguar and Rover have adopted modern quality control techniques and dramatically improved product quality.

A second complaint is that some products deliver little benefit. In an attempt to persuade customers to buy their brand rather than any other, manufacturers sometimes make claims that are not fully substantiated. In the United Kingdom, for example, the Independent Television Commission (ITC) recently introduced new rules covering the advertising of medicines and treatments, health claims, and nutrition and dietary supplements, including slimming products. The move brings the ITC in line with public- and private-sector opinion, and followed the publication of new advertising rules by the Advertising Standards Authority in January 1995, while also accommodating recent European Union legislation governing the advertising and sales of these products. Health claims for food, for example, must now be fully substantiated. Creative ads must guard against encouraging overindulgence in products such as confectionery, so, advertisers must pay responsible attention to health implications.[5]

In fragmented markets where many brands are promising a wide array of product benefits, consumers are often left confused. In fact, consumers often end up paying more for product benefits that do not exist (see Marketing Highlight 2.2).

A third complaint concerns product safety. Product safety has been a problem for several reasons, including manufacturer indifference, increased production complexity, poorly trained labour and poor quality control. For years now, consumer protection groups or associations in many countries have regularly tested products for safety and reported hazards found in tested products, such as electrical dangers in appliances, injury risks from lawn mowers and faulty car design. The testing and reporting activities of these organizations have helped consumers make better buying decisions and have encouraged businesses to eliminate product flaws. Lever Brothers' problem with its notorious Persil Power clearly shows the risks to firms when product safety is not thoroughly checked out:

> Persil Power was launched in 1993. It was to be Lever's new, wonder laundry soap. It contained an ingredient called the manganese accelerator, which gave the powder its exceptional cleaning performance and environmental credentials. However, the accelerator had been found to damage clothes. The Consumers' Association took on the task of testing consumers' claims (and that of arch rival Procter & Gamble) that the manganese accelerator damaged clothes. The Consumers' Association test results were positive and the company was branded guilty. Lever Brothers was forced to reformulate the powder and reduce the manganese accelerator content of Persil Power by 80% after admitting that Persil Power could damage clothes. The Consumers' Association investigated the effects of the manganese accelerator in the reformulated Persil Power, and expected to find that the accelerator, even at reduced levels, causes damage to clothes. As the investigations proceeded, Lever stopped buying further stocks of the accelerator from its supplier, the specialist chemical company Hickson International. Lever finally dropped the 'accelerator' formulation.[6]

However, most manufacturers *want* to produce quality goods. Consumers who are unhappy with a firm's products may avoid its other products and talk other

Responsible marketers take appropriate actions when product safety problems occur. Here, a company recalls faulty Sapona Foam Cleaners and sets up a Helpline and collection service for customers.

consumers into doing the same. The way a company deals with product quality and safety problems can damage or help its reputation. Companies selling poor-quality or unsafe products risk damaging conflicts with consumer groups. Moreover unsafe products can result in product liability suits and large awards for damages.

### Planned obsolescence

Critics have also charged that some producers follow a programme of **planned obsolescence**, causing their products to become obsolete before they should actually need replacement. In many cases, producers have been accused of continually changing consumer concepts of acceptable styles in order to encourage more and earlier buying. An obvious example is constantly changing clothing fashions. Critics claim that this practice is frequently found in the consumer electronics industry. The Japanese camera, watch and consumer electronics companies frustrate consumers because rapid and frequent model replacement has created difficulties in obtaining spare parts for old models; dealers refuse to repair outdated models and planned obsolescence rapidly erodes basic product values. Producers have also been accused of holding back attractive functional features, then introducing them later to make older models obsolete. Finally, producers have been accused of using materials and components that will break, wear, rust or rot sooner than they should. For example, many drapery manufacturers are using a higher percentage of rayon in their curtains. They argue that rayon reduces the price of the curtains and has better holding power.

**MARKETING HIGHLIGHT 2.2**

## 'Shopper's friend' offers proofs on brand benefit claims

The Consumers' Association (CA) in the United Kingdom is an independent, self-appointed organization, that seeks to police the goods and services offered by consumer-products manufacturers and business sectors. It was set up, back in 1957, because of the poor quality of manufactured products. Since then, the CA – and its public face, *Which?* magazine – has played an important role in providing consumers a counterpoint to the persuasive marketing of consumer goods and services. The CA is committed to improving the quality of people's purchasing decisions. It tests all sorts of consumer goods and services, ranging from soap powders, kettles and motor cars to free-range turkeys, holidays and insurance policies. The CA's work is financed by its 803,000 members with more than 1 million subscriptions across its range of publications from the original *Which?* to *Holiday Which?* and *Which? way to Health*, including other publications on wine and gardening. The magazines do not take advertisements, thus reinforcing the CA's impartiality. The CA carries out independent research or tests on products and services and then rates these based on 'value for money' and effectiveness criteria. Its range of *Which?* magazines is the 'mouthpiece' of the Association, these playing the role of 'shopper's friend' by offering unbiased views on brand features, quality and/or performance, and advice on 'best buy' and 'good value' purchases. Investigations are triggered in several ways, but there is no formal complaints procedure for the consumer to follow. Generally, the criteria for any investigation are: How many people will it affect? How important an issue is it? Can the CA do anything about it?

Here is an example of a toothpaste test reported in one recent issue of the CA's *Which?* magazine. The test sought to substantiate the oral health, including medicinal (e.g. relief from the pain of sensitive teeth), claims made in toothpaste advertising. The report gives the facts, figures and test results. It guides the reader through the main claims made for toothpastes and picks out the brands the test team believes can substantiate their claims and those which cannot.

It first explains the dental problems which manufacturers' claims promise to tackle, and then looks for evidence to substantiate these claims. Three main types of 'claims' are: (1) prevention of gum disease/antiplaque property; (2) protection of sensitive teeth; and (3) tartar control. To substantiate claims, the test team turns to (a) evidence from clinical trials and (b) evidence of 'availability of actives', that is, that the effective ingredient has not been inactivated by any of the other chemicals in the toothpaste. Unsubstantiated claims are ones where the manufacturer did not provide the test team with evidence either of suitable clinical trials on the particular toothpaste or of 'availability of actives'. This does not mean the toothpaste is not effective, but that the test panel has not seen enough proof that the manufacturer can substantiate its dental health claim(s).

The results for some of the 60 manufacturers' and own-label brands of toothpaste tested are summarized in Table 1.

The CA asserts that no manufacturer should make claims for its products, on packaging or in advertising, unless it can be substantiated by evidence of a reasonable standard. Its test results provide assurance for the beneficial effect of fluoride in reducing tooth decay and sensitivity. In addition, the report advises consumers on how to keep their teeth healthy – for example, cut down on sugary food and drinks, brush teeth thoroughly and properly with a fluoride toothpaste, pursue with good brushing and flossing to keep plaque and tartar off the teeth. It draws attention to recommended toothpaste brands, but highlights the fact that many expensive toothpastes marked for sensitive teeth do not contain fluoride, so will not offer protection against decay. Again, those that *can* substantiate their claims are clearly singled out.

The services of consumer-interest bodies like the CA and similar bodies (e.g. the Consumer Union in America) are invaluable as they offer impartial information and guidance on all kinds of purchasing decisions. The CA relies on expert panels and professionals, together with its own teams of testers and evaluators, to conduct product evaluations. Testing criteria for products and services are always described in full. Where appropriate, accreditation bodies' results are also consulted and compared with its own test results. Not surprisingly, the CA has made many enemies of manufacturers and businesses

| Table 1 | Claim versus performance of toothpaste |

**Is claim substantiated by toothpaste performance?**

| Claims made | Yes | No |
|---|---|---|
| Prevention of gum disease | Colgate Gum Protection Formula<br>Mentadent P | Aqua Fresh Triple Protection<br>Asda Anti-Plaque<br>Boots Anti-Plaque<br>Boots Total Care<br>Co-Op Anti-Plaque<br>Gateway Fresh Breath Anti-Plaque<br>Gibbs SR<br>Macleans Anti-Plaque<br>Oral B Zendium<br>Tesco Dental Care Minty Blue Gel<br>Waitrose Plaque-Control<br>Superdrug Oral Health Gum Health Formula |
| Protection of sensitive teeth | Asda Sensitive<br>Boots Formula<br>Gateway Fresh Breath Formula<br>Macleans Sensitive<br>Mentadent S<br>Safeway Sensitive<br>Sainsbury's Oral Health Sensitive Teeth<br>Tesco Sensitive Teeth Formula<br>Sensodyne Original and Mint<br>Sensodyne F<br>Waitrose Sensitive | Boots Formula F |
| Tartar control | Colgate Tartar Control Formula<br>Crest Tartar Control<br>Crest Ultra Protection<br>Mentadent P<br>Sainsbury's Oral Health Tartar Control<br>Tesco Dental Care Anti-Tartar | Safeway Tartar Control<br>Superdrug Oral Health Tartar Control |

that fail to deliver good value to customers. Questions about the CA's impartiality and accountability are often raised by aggrieved companies.

Access to unbiased information remains important if consumers' buying decisions are to be improved. Manufacturers that achieve poor product ratings are invariably given the option to challenge the test results. Many use these findings to direct product-improvement efforts and make positive changes in their products. The CA's printed mission is to 'empower people to make informed consumer decisions' and improve the quality of goods and services. If these goals are truly achieved, then the role of consumer bodies who have the consumer at heart is more important now – in the era of consumerism – than ever before. Brand owners beware! Friend or foe, 'shopper's friend', vigilant as ever, is here to stay.

Sources: Consumers' Association, 'Toothpaste', *Which?* (July 1992), 372–5; Tom O'Sullivan, 'Shopper's friend counters enemies', *Marketing Week* (10 February 1995), 22–3.

Critics claim that using more rayon causes the curtains to fall apart sooner. European consumers have also found, to their annoyance, how rapidly certain local brands of toasters rust – for an appliance that hardly gets into contact with water, this is an amazing technological feat!

Marketers respond that consumers *like* style changes; they get tired of the old goods and want a new look in fashion or a new design in cars. No one has to buy the new look, and if too few people like it, it will simply fail. Companies frequently withhold new features when they are not fully tested, when they add more cost to the product than consumers are willing to pay, and for other good reasons. But they do so at the risk that a competitor will introduce the new feature and steal the market. Moreover companies often put in new materials to lower their costs and prices. They do not design their products to break down earlier, because they do not want to lose their customers to other brands. Thus much so-called planned obsolescence is the working of the competitive and technological forces in a free society – forces that lead to ever-improving goods and services.

### Poor service to disadvantaged consumers

Finally, marketing has been accused of poorly serving disadvantaged consumers. Critics claim that the urban poor often have to shop in smaller stores that carry inferior goods and charge higher prices. Marketing's eye on profits also means that disadvantaged consumers are not viable segments to target. The high-income consumer is the preferred target.

Clearly, better marketing systems must be built in low-income areas – one hope is to get large retailers to open outlets in low-income areas. Moreover low-income people clearly need consumer protection. Consumer protection agencies should take action against suppliers who advertise false values, sell old merchandise as new, or charge too much for credit.

## Marketing's impact on society as a whole

The marketing system as we – in Europe and other developed economies outside North America – are experiencing it, has been accused of adding to several 'evils' in our society at large. Advertising has been a special target. It has been blamed for creating false wants, nurturing greedy aspirations and inculcating too much materialism in our society.

### False wants and too much materialism

Critics have charged that the marketing system urges too much interest in material possessions. People are judged by what they *own* rather than by what they *are*. To be considered successful, personal possessions such as a smart-looking house or apartment in a prime residential site, expensive cars and the latest clothes and consumer electronics are sought. In the United States, reports have us believe that this yearning for wealth, possessions and status appears to have hit its peak in recent years:

> Money, money, money is the incantation of today. Bewitched by an epidemic of money enchantment, Americans wriggle in a St. Vitus's dance of materialism unseen since the Gilded Age of the Roaring Twenties. Under the blazing sun of money, all other values shine palely. ... The evidence is everywhere. Open the scarlet covers of the Saks Fifth Avenue Christmas catalog, for starters, and look at what Santa Claus offers today's young family,

from Dad's $1,650 ostrich-skin briefcase and Mom's $39,500 fur coat to Junior's $4,000, 15-     1 ecu = US$1.26
mph miniature Mercedes.[7]

Is there a similar enchantment with money in Europe? Asia? The rest of the world? It is neither feasible nor appropriate for this chapter to indulge readers in an extensive debate on cross-cultural similarities and dissimilarities in materialistic tendencies and behaviour, and whether marketing is the root cause of these desires. Rather, we acknowledge the phenomenon of the 'yuppy generation' that emerged in the 1980s, symbolizing a new materialistic culture which looked certain to stay. In the 1990s, many social scientists are noting a reaction against the opulence and waste of the 1980s and a return to more basic values and social commitment. For example, when asked in a recent poll what they value most in their lives, subjects listed enjoyable work (86 per cent), happy children (84 per cent), a good marriage (69 per cent), and contributions to society (66 per cent). However, when asked what most symbolizes success, 85 per cent said money and the things it will buy. Thus our infatuation with material things continues.[8]

Critics do not view this interest in material things as a natural state of mind but rather as a matter of false wants created by marketing. Businesses stimulate people's desires for goods through the force of advertising, and advertisers use the mass media to create materialistic models of the good life. People work harder to earn the necessary money. Their purchases increase the output of the nation's industry, and industry, in turn, uses the advertising media to stimulate more desire for their industrial output. Thus marketing is seen as creating false wants that benefit industry more than they benefit consumers.

These criticisms overstate the power of business to create needs, however. People have strong defences against advertising and other marketing tools. Marketers are most effective when they appeal to existing wants rather than when they attempt to create new ones. Furthermore people seek information when making important purchases and often do not rely on single sources. Even minor purchases that may be affected by advertising messages lead to repeat purchases only if the product performs as promised. Finally, the high failure rate of new products shows that companies are not always able to control demand.

On a deeper level, our wants and values are influenced not only by marketers, but also by family, peer groups, religion, ethnic background and education. If societies become highly materialistic, these values will have arisen out of basic socialization processes that go much deeper than business and mass media could produce alone. The importance of wealth and material possessions to the overseas Chinese, for example, is explained more by cultural and socialization factors than by sustained exposure to Western advertising influences.

## Too few social goods

Business has been accused of overselling private goods at the expense of public goods. As private goods increase, they require more public services that are usually not forthcoming. For example, an increase in car ownership (private good) requires more highways, traffic control, parking spaces and police services (public goods). The overselling of private goods results in 'social costs'. For cars, the social costs include excessive traffic congestion, air pollution, and deaths and injuries from car accidents.

A way must be found to restore a balance between private and public goods. One option is to make producers bear the full social costs of their operations. For example, the government could require car manufacturers to build cars with additional safety features and better pollution-control systems. Automotive makers would then raise their prices to cover extra costs. If buyers found the price of some cars too high, however, the producers of these cars would disappear, and demand would move to those producers that could support both the private and social costs.

### Cultural pollution

Critics charge the marketing system with creating *cultural pollution*. Our senses are being assaulted constantly by advertising. Commercials interrupt serious programmes; pages of ads obscure printed matter; billboards mar beautiful scenery. These interruptions continuously pollute people's minds with messages of materialism, sex, power or status. Although most people do not find advertising overly annoying (some even think it is the best part of television programming), some critics call for sweeping changes.

Marketers answer the charges of 'commercial noise' with the following arguments. First, they hope that their ads reach primarily the target audience. But because of mass-communication channels, some ads are bound to reach people who have no interest in the product and are therefore bored or annoyed. People who buy magazines slanted towards their interests – such as *Vogue* or *Fortune* – rarely complain about the ads because the magazines advertise products of interest. Second, ads make television and radio free media and keep down the costs of magazines and newspapers. Most people think commercials are a small price to pay.

### Too much political power

Another criticism is that business wields too much political power. 'Oil', 'tobacco', and 'alcohol' have the support of important politicians and civil servants who look after an industry's interests against the public interest. Advertisers are accused of holding too much power over the mass media, limiting their freedom to report independently and objectively.

The setting up of citizens' charters and greater concern for consumer rights and protection in the 1990s will see improvements, not regression, in business accountability. Fortunately, many powerful business interests once thought to be untouchable have been tamed in the public interest. For example, in the United States, Ralph Nader, consumerism campaigner, caused legislation that forced the car industry to build more safety into its cars, and the Surgeon General's Report resulted in cigarette companies putting health warnings on their packages. Moreover, because the media receive advertising revenues from many different advertisers, it is easier to resist the influence of one or a few of them. Too much business power tends to result in counterforces that check and offset these powerful interests.

## Marketing's impact on other businesses

Critics also charge that a company's marketing practices can harm other companies and reduce competition. Three problems are involved: acquisition of competitors, marketing practices that create barriers to entry, and unfair competitive marketing practices.

Critics claim that firms are harmed and competition reduced when companies expand by acquiring competitors rather than by developing their own new products. In the car industry alone there has been a spate of acquisitions over the past decade: General Motors bought the British sports-car maker, Lotus, in 1986; Ford acquired 75 per cent of Britain's Aston Martin, which makes hand-built, high-performance cars, and Jaguar in 1987 and 1989 respectively; the US Chrysler bought Lamborghini in the late 1980s but sold the marque to a consortium of Malaysian and Indonesian businesses in 1994; Fiat owns Ferrari; BMW has taken over the Rover Group; Volkswagen controls Skoda.[9] These and many large international acquisitions in other industries, such as food and pharmaceuticals, have caused concern that more and more competitors will be absorbed and that competition will be reduced.

Acquisition is a complex subject. Acquisitions can sometimes be good for society. The acquiring company may gain economies of scale that lead to lower costs and lower prices. A well-managed company may take over a poorly managed company and improve its efficiency. An industry that was not very competitive might become more competitive after the acquisition. But acquisitions can also be harmful and are therefore closely regulated by the government.

Critics have also claimed that marketing practices bar new companies from entering an industry. Large marketing companies can use patents and heavy promotion spending and can tie up suppliers or dealers to keep out or drive out competitors. People concerned with antitrust regulation recognize that some barriers are the natural result of the economic advantages of doing business on a large scale. Other barriers could be challenged by existing and new laws. For example, some critics have proposed a progressive tax on advertising spending to reduce the role of selling costs as a substantial barrier to entry.

Finally, some firms have in fact used unfair competitive marketing practices with the intention of hurting or destroying other firms. They may set their prices below costs, threaten to cut off business with suppliers, or discourage the buying of a competitor's products. Various laws work to prevent such predatory competition. It is difficult, however, to prove that the intent or action was really predatory. When Laker Airlines first attacked British Airways' most profitable routes, the latter delayed its counterattack. Laker began to borrow huge sums of money to expand its fleet. It was laden with vast debt and interest obligations on its huge dollar loans when the American dollar appreciated against other currencies. British Airways then aggressively cut prices on Laker's most lucrative routes, restoring these to normal levels only after driving Laker into bankruptcy and out of the competitive arena altogether.[10] The question is whether this was unfair competition or the healthy competition of a more efficient carrier against the less efficient.

## CITIZEN AND PUBLIC ACTIONS TO REGULATE MARKETING

Because some people view business as the cause of many economic and social ills, grass-roots movements have arisen from time to time to keep business in line. The two main movements have been consumerism and environmentalism.

### Consumerism

Western business firms have been the target of organized consumer movements on three occasions. Consumerism has its origins in the United States. The first consumer movement took place in the early 1900s. It was fuelled by rising prices, Upton Sinclair's writings on conditions in the meat industry, and scandals in the drug industry. The second consumer movement, in the mid-1930s, was sparked by an upturn in consumer prices during the Great Depression and another drug scandal.

The third movement began in the 1960s. Consumers had become better educated, products had become more complex and hazardous, and people were unhappy with American institutions. Ralph Nader appeared on the scene in the 1960s to force many issues, and other well-known writers accused big business of wasteful and unethical practices. President John F. Kennedy declared that consumers have the right to safety and to be informed, to choose and to be heard. American Congress investigated certain industries and proposed consumer-protection legislation. Since then, many consumer groups have been organized and several consumer laws have been passed. The consumer movement has spread internationally and has become very strong in Europe.[11]

But what is the consumer movement? **Consumerism** is an organized movement of citizens and government agencies to improve the rights and power of buyers in relation to sellers. Traditional sellers' rights include:

- The right to introduce any product in any size and style, provided it is not hazardous to personal health or safety; or, if it is, to include proper warnings and controls.
- The right to charge any price for the product, provided no discrimination exists among similar kinds of buyers.
- The right to spend any amount to promote the product, provided it is not defined as unfair competition.
- The right to use any product message, provided it is not misleading or dishonest in content or execution.
- The right to use any buying incentive schemes, provided they are not unfair or misleading.

Traditional buyers' rights include:

- The right not to buy a product that is offered for sale.
- The right to expect the product to be safe.
- The right to expect the product to perform as claimed.

Comparing these rights, many believe that the balance of power lies on the sellers' side. True, the buyer can refuse to buy. But critics feel that the buyer has too little information, education and protection to make wise decisions when facing sophisticated sellers. Consumer advocates call for the following additional consumer rights:

- The right to be well informed about important aspects of the product.
- The right to be protected against questionable products and marketing practices.
- The right to influence products and marketing practices in ways that will improve the 'quality of life'.

Each proposed right has led to more specific proposals by consumerists. The right to be informed includes the right to know the true interest on a loan (truth in lending), the true cost per unit of a brand (unit pricing), the ingredients in a product (ingredient labelling), the nutrition in foods (nutritional labelling), product freshness (open dating), and the true benefits of a product (truth in advertising). Proposals related to consumer protection include strengthening consumer rights in cases of business fraud, requiring greater product safety and giving more power to government agencies. Proposals relating to quality of life include controlling the ingredients that go into certain products (detergents) and packaging (soft-drink containers), reducing the level of advertising 'noise' and putting consumer representatives on company boards to protect consumer interests.

Consumers have not only the *right* but also the *responsibility* to protect themselves instead of leaving this function to someone else. Consumers who believe that they got a bad deal have several remedies available, including: writing to the company heads or to the media; contacting government or private consumer-interest/protection initiatives or agencies; and going to small-claims courts.

## Environmentalism

Whereas consumerists consider whether the marketing system is efficiently serving consumer wants, environmentalists are concerned with marketing's effects on the environment and with the costs of serving consumer needs and wants. They are concerned with damage to the ecosystem caused by strip mining, forest depletion, acid rain, loss of the atmosphere's ozone layer, toxic wastes and litter. They are also concerned with the loss of recreational areas and with the increase in health problems caused by bad air, polluted water and chemically treated food. These concerns are the basis for **environmentalism** – an organized movement of concerned citizens and government agencies to protect and improve people's living environment.

Environmentalists are not against marketing and consumption; they simply want people and organizations to operate with more care for the environment. The marketing system's goal should not be to maximize consumption, consumer choice or consumer satisfaction, but rather to maximize life quality. And 'life quality' means not only the quantity and quality of consumer goods and services, but also the quality of the environment. Environmentalists want environmental costs included in both producer and consumer decision making.

Environmentalism has hit some industries hard. Heavy industry, public utilities, and chemical and steel companies have to spend heavily on clean-up technology, waste management and other pollution-control equipment. The car industry has had to introduce expensive emission controls in cars. In some countries, governments have introduced tough regulations to deal with environmental problems, as in the case of Germany. Take, for example, legislation imposed on carmakers:

> Stimulated by German legislation, BMW and Volkswagen led the way in establishing dismantling plants to enable them to take back cars and recycle many of the materials used. More recently, the German environment industry has backed plans by the car-makers' association, including companies making steel, glass and plastic, to make cars 85 per cent reusable by 2002. By 2015, only 5 per cent of the car's weight will be left on rubbish dumps according to this plan. The car industry, together with the environment and economics ministries, are creating a network of dealers which will recover the 2.5 million cars taken out of service in Germany every year. Many cars are already recyclable. BMW, for example, prides itself on its new 7 series BMW which is 85 per cent re-usable. The German plans are being extended across Europe. BMW has signed an agreement with Renault and Fiat which obliges all three companies to take and recycle their partners' cars abroad. Mr. Martin Waldhausen, a spokesman for the environment ministry, however, stresses that 'There have been a lot of fine words but little of it is actual substance' when referring to the car-makers' plans. He warns that if too much remains just talk, the environment ministry has vowed to force through laws to create a car recycling system. The outcome will have implications across the European Union.[12]

Many other industries are affected by environmental regulations. The packaging industry has had to find ways to reduce waste and energy consumption. The petroleum industry has had to create new low-lead and unleaded petrols. These industries often resent environmental regulations, especially when they are imposed too rapidly to allow companies to make proper adjustments. These companies have absorbed large costs and have passed them on to buyers.

A raft of directives on environment issues are continuing to make their way through the European Commission. Thus marketers' lives have, and will continue to, become more complicated. Marketers must check into the ecological properties of their products and packaging. They must raise prices to cover environmental costs, knowing that the product will be harder to sell. Yet environmental issues have become so important in our society that there is no turning back to the time when few managers worried about the effects of product and marketing decisions on environmental quality.[13]

Many analysts view the 1990s as the 'Earth Decade', in which protection of the natural environment will be the most important issue facing people around the world. Companies have responded with 'green marketing' – developing ecologically safer products, recyclable and biodegradable packaging, better pollution controls, and more energy-efficient operations. It will be essential to recognize that environmental marketing is part of overall environment management. It should not be treated in isolation. Sound practice in 'green marketing' calls for:

- A comprehensive assessment of current environment performance of the company.
- A genuine commitment to monitoring, auditing, reporting and measuring improvements in performance.
- Development of an achievable environment policy with clear goals and an action programme.
- Monitoring the evolution of the green agenda (don't become out of date as the laws are constantly changing).
- Investment in staff training and education, environmental science and technology.
- Consumer assistance and education programmes to increase consumers' environmental responsibility through information provision, product take-back services and helplines.
- Supplier education programmes.
- Building coalitions or bridges between the various interests.
- Contribution to environmental programmes.
- Greater adherence to marketing values: selling benefits, not products, and preservation of corporate, not just product values.[14]

### Public actions to regulate marketing

Citizen concerns about marketing practices will usually lead to public attention and legislative proposals. New bills will be debated – many will be defeated, others will be modified, and a few will become workable laws.

Figure 2.2 illustrates the principal legal issues facing marketing management. Individual country laws exist which affect marketing. The task is to translate these laws into the language that marketing executives understand as they make decisions about competitive relations, products, price, promotion and channels of distribution.

## BUSINESS ACTIONS TOWARDS SOCIALLY RESPONSIBLE MARKETING

At first, many companies opposed consumerism and environmentalism. They thought the criticisms were either unfair or unimportant. But by now, most companies have grown to accept the new consumer rights, at least in principle. They might oppose certain pieces of legislation as inappropriate ways to solve certain consumer problems, but they recognize the consumer's right to information and protection.

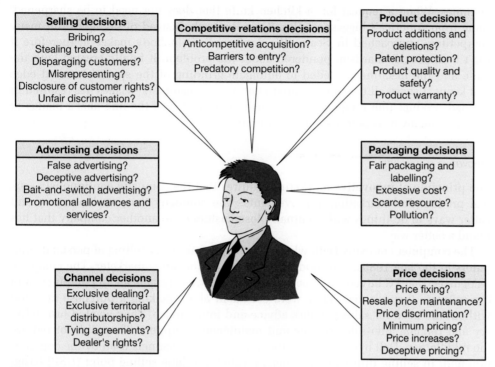

**Figure 2.2**    Legal issues facing marketing management.

Many of these companies have responded positively to consumerism and environmentalism in order to serve consumer needs better.


## Enlightened marketing

The philosophy of **enlightened marketing** holds that a company's marketing should support the best long-run performance of the marketing system. Enlightened marketers ensure that their marketing approach reflects corporate ethics. Enlightened marketing consists of five principles: consumer-oriented marketing, innovative marketing, value marketing, sense-of-mission marketing and societal marketing.


### *Consumer-oriented marketing*

**Consumer-oriented marketing** means that the company should view and organize its marketing activities from the consumer's point of view. It should work hard to sense, serve and satisfy the needs of a defined group of customers. Consider the following example.

Richardson Sheffield, a British cutlery maker, has fought off tough competition in a stagnant cutlery market in Britain in the 1980s, largely by making the customer happy. Its chairman, Mr Bryon Upton, claims that the most important ingredient in Richardson's recipe for success is the great stress the company puts on customer satisfaction and relationships. Attention to the needs of customers is consistently upheld throughout the firm, as seen in its speed in responding to customer enquiries and requests (letters are answered the same day, telexes the same hour and samples are provided within two days) through to its customer-led product development programmes. When a request for 'a kitchen knife that does not need to be sharpened' came from America's biggest retailer, Sears Roebuck, instead of saying as did many competitors approached by Sears, 'We don't make it; nobody makes it; therefore it can't be made', Richardson pondered about the problem. It finally created both the knife and the machinery needed to automate grinding of the special serrated edge that keeps it sharp all the time. Similar attention to customers' wishes has resulted in a broad product line ranging from a range of thirty top-of-the-line chef's blades to knives given away as petrol-station promotions.[15]

### Innovative marketing

The principle of **innovative marketing** requires that the company continuously seek real product and marketing improvements. The company that overlooks new and better ways to do things will eventually lose customers to another company that has found a better way.

The computer company Dell, which pioneered mail-order selling of personal computers in the late 1980s, is a good example of an innovative marketer. The company recognized that PC buyers were becoming more knowledgeable about computers and the software they wanted. They were confident about making a purchase decision without the need for sales people's advice and interference. They wanted fast delivery and reliable after-sales service and maintenance support. They did not require the middleman. Dell bypassed traditional distribution channels used by the competition and, in selling direct to customers, created a unique selling point (USP) based on its innovative distribution arrangements. The approach was so successful that many competitors followed suit. Today, Dell continues to maintain a direct relationship with consumers that enables the company to listen better, learn faster and become more agile in responding to their changing and differing needs.[16]

### Value marketing

According to the principle of **value marketing**, the company should put most of its resources into value-building marketing investments. Many things marketers do – one-shot sales promotions, minor packaging changes, advertising puffery – may raise sales in the short run but add less *value* than would actual improvements in the product's quality, features or convenience. Enlightened marketing calls for building long-run consumer loyalty by continually improving the value consumers receive from the firm's marketing offer.

### Sense-of-mission marketing

**Sense-of-mission-marketing** means that the company should define its mission in broad *social* terms rather than narrow *product* terms. When a company defines a social mission, employees feel better about their work and have a clearer sense of direction. For example, defined in narrow product terms, Johnson & Johnson's mission might be 'to sell Band-Aids and baby oil'. But the company states its mission more broadly:

> We believe that our first responsibility is to the doctors, nurses and patients, to mothers and all others who use our products and services. In meeting their needs everything we do must be of high quality. We must constantly strive to reduce our costs in order to maintain reasonable prices. Customers' orders must be serviced promptly and accurately. Our suppliers and distributors must have an opportunity to make a fair profit. We are responsible to our

employees, the men and women who work for us throughout the world. Everyone must be considered as an individual. We must respect their dignity and recognize their merit ... We are responsible to the communities in which we live and work and to the world community as well. We must be good citizens, support good works and charities and bear our fair share of taxes. We must encourage civic improvements and better health and education. We must maintain in good order the property we are privileged to use, protecting the environment and natural resources.[17]

Reshaping the basic task of selling consumer products into the larger mission of serving the interests of consumers, employees, suppliers, and others in the 'world community' gives a new sense of purpose to Johnson & Johnson employees.

### Societal marketing

Following the principle of **societal marketing**, an enlightened company makes marketing decisions by considering consumers' wants and long-run interests, the company's requirements, and society's long-run interests. The company is aware that neglecting consumer and societal long-term interests is a disservice to consumers and society. A crucial problem is this. In many cases customer needs, customer wants and customer long-run interests are the same thing, and customers are the best judges of what is good for them. However, customers do not invariably make decisions that are good for them. People want to eat fatty food, which is bad for their health; some people want to smoke cigarettes knowing that smoking can kill them and damage the environment for others; many enjoy drinking alcohol despite its ill effects. To control some of the potential evils of marketing there has to be access to the media for the counterargument – the counterargument against smoking, against fatty foods, against alcohol. There is also a need for regulation – self if not statutory – to check unsavoury demand.

A second problem is that what consumers want is sometimes at odds with societal welfare. If marketing's job is to fulfil customers' wants, unsavoury desires leave marketers with a dilemma. Consumers want the convenience and prestige of hardwood window frames, doors and furniture, but society would also like to keep the Amazon rainforest; consumers want the comfort of air-conditioning, yet we need the ozone layer; consumers worldwide should be using lead-free petrol, yet not all bother. Marketing has to be more alert to the inconsistencies between consumer wants and society's welfare. Where there is insufficient drive from within the consumer movement and consumers' own sense of responsibility, marketers would do better to control or regulate their own behaviour in providing goods or services that are undesirable for society at large. If not, legislation is likely to do that for them.

A societally oriented marketer should design products that are not only pleasing but also beneficial. The difference is shown in Figure 2.3. Products can be classified according to their degree of immediate consumer satisfaction and long-run consumer benefit. **Desirable products** give both high immediate satisfaction and high long-run benefits. A desirable product with immediate satisfaction and long-run benefit would be a tasty *and* nutritious breakfast food. **Pleasing products** give high immediate satisfaction but may hurt consumers in the long run. Examples are indulgence goods like confectionery, alcohol and cigarettes. **Salutary products** have low appeal but benefit consumers in the long run. Seat belts and air bags in cars are salutary products. Finally, **deficient products**, such as bad-tasting and ineffective medicines, have neither immediate appeal nor long-run benefits.

The challenge posed by pleasing products is that they sell very well but may end up hurting the consumer. The product opportunity, therefore, is to add long-run ben-

In this ad, consumers are assured that
there is no extra charge to own a
'green' Audi, and that the price does
not compromise on performance.

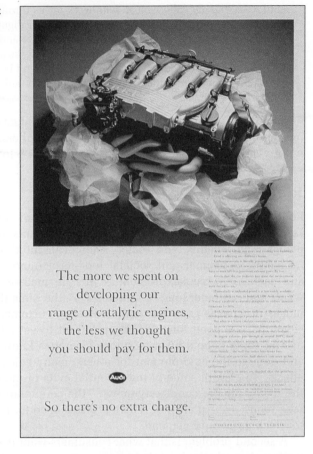

The more we spent on
developing our
range of catalytic engines,
the less we thought
you should pay for them.

So there's no extra charge.

efits without reducing the product's pleasing qualities. For example, the British drug
and household product manufacturer, Reckitt & Coleman developed a phosphate-free
laundry detergent that was relatively more effective than existing 'green' detergents.
The challenge posed by salutary products is to add some pleasing qualities so that
they will become more desirable in the consumers' minds. For example, synthetic
fats and fat substitutes, such as NutraSweet's Simplesse, promise to improve the
appeal of low-calorie and low-fat foods.

## Marketing ethics

Conscientious marketers face many moral dilemmas. The best thing to do is often unclear.
Because not all managers have fine moral sensitivity, companies need to develop *corporate marketing ethics policies*. Such policies offer broad guidelines that everyone
in the organization must follow. They cover distributor relations, advertising standards, customer service, pricing, product development and general ethical standards.

The finest guidelines cannot resolve all the difficult ethical situations the marketer
faces. Table 2.1 lists some difficult ethical situations marketers could face during
their careers. If marketers choose immediate sales-producing actions in all these
cases, their marketing behaviour might well be described as immoral or even amoral.
If they refuse to go along with *any* of the actions, they might be ineffective as market-

**TABLE 2.1**

1. You work for a cigarette company and up to now have not been convinced that cigarettes cause cancer. A report comes across your desk that clearly shows the link between smoking and cancer. What would you do?
2. Your R&D department has changed one of your products slightly. It is not really 'new and improved', but you know that putting this statement on the package and in advertising will increase sales. What would you do?
3. You have been asked to add a stripped-down model to your line that could be advertised to pull customers into the store. The product won't be very good, but salespeople will be able to switch buyers up to higher-priced units. You are asked to give the green light for this stripped-down version. What would you do?
4. You are thinking of hiring a product manager who has just left a competitor's company. She would be more than happy to tell you all the competitor's plans for the coming year. What would you do?
5. One of your top dealers in an important territory has had recent family troubles and his sales have slipped. It looks like it will take him a while to straighten out his family trouble. Meanwhile you are losing many sales. Legally, you can terminate the dealer's franchise and replace him. What would you do?
6. You have a chance to win a big account that will mean a lot to you and your company. The purchasing agent hints that a 'gift' would influence the decision. Your assistant recommends sending a fine colour television set to the buyer's home. What would you do?
7. You have heard that a competitor has a new product feature that will make a big difference in sales. The competitor will demonstrate the feature in a private dealer meeting at the annual trade show. You can easily send a snooper to this meeting to learn about the new feature. What would you do?
8. You have to choose between three ad campaigns outlined by your agency. The first (A) is a soft-sell, honest information campaign. The second (B) uses sex-loaded emotional appeals and exaggerates the product's benefits. The third (C) involves a noisy, irritating commercial that is sure to gain audience attention. Pretests show that the campaigns are effective in the following order: C, B and A. What would you do?
9. You are interviewing a capable woman applicant for a job as salesperson. She is better qualified than the men just interviewed. Nevertheless, you know that some of your important customers prefer dealing with men, and you will lose some sales if you hire her. What would you do?
10. You are a sales manager in an encyclopedia company. Your competitor's salespeople are getting into homes by pretending to take a research survey. After they finish the survey, they switch to their sales pitch. This technique seems to be very effective. What would you do?

**Figure 2.3**   Societal classification of new products.

ing managers and unhappy because of the constant moral tension. Managers need a set of principles that will help them figure out the moral importance of each situation and decide how far they can go in good conscience.

But *what* principle should guide companies and marketing managers on issues of ethics and social responsibility? One philosophy is that such issues are decided by the free market and legal system. Under this principle, companies and their managers are not responsible for making moral judgements. Companies can in good conscience do whatever the system allows.

A second philosophy puts responsibility not in the system, but in the hands of individual companies and managers. This more enlightened philosophy suggests that a company should have a 'social conscience'. Companies and managers should apply high standards of ethics and morality when making corporate decisions, regardless of 'what the system allows'. History provides an endless list of examples

---

**MARKETING HIGHLIGHT 2.3**

## In search of universal ethics

In July 1994, The Caux Round Table (CRT) launched an *international ethics code* – a seven-point *Principles for Business* – that stresses the need for moral values in business decision making. It is thought that the document is the first of its kind to attract affluent supporters from Europe, Japan and the United States. Signatories include Ryuzaburo Kaku, chairman of Japan's Canon, John Charlton, managing director of New York's Chase Manhattan Bank, and a group of senior executives from the twin cities Minneapolis/St Paul.

CRT was formed in 1968 by Frederik Philips, former president of the Dutch electronics giant, Philips, and Olivier Giscard D'Estaing, vice-chairman of the Insead business school at Fontainebleau, France, in an attempt to reduce the then escalating trade tensions with Japan. The group meets annually in the Swiss village of Caux-sur-Montreux. It is concerned with 'the development of constructive economic and social relationships between the participants' countries and with their joint responsibilities towards the rest of the world'.

The *Principles* epitomize the group's intention to set 'a world standard against which business behaviour can be measured', that is, a benchmark to help more companies devise their own codes. The authors of the initiative seek to 'begin a process that identifies shared values, reconciles differing values, and thereby develops a shared perspective on business behaviour acceptable to and honoured by all'.

The CRT's *Principles* affirm the responsibilities of business towards a range of stakeholders (e.g. customers, employees and shareholders) and to the countries in which they operate. Suppliers and competitors should expect businesses to 'honour their obligations in a spirit of honesty and fairness'. Business behaviour should be governed by a spirit of trust which goes beyond the letter of the law, while domestic and international rules should be respected. The principles also require companies to promote 'the progressive and judicious liberalisation of trade', 'to protect and, where possible, improve the environment' and to avoid illicit operations.

The *Principles* are supposedly drawn from two ethical traditions: the Japanese philosophy of *kyosei*, which calls for 'living and working together for the common good of mankind' and 'human dignity', which refers to the sacredness or value of each person as an end and not a means to the fulfilment of others' purposes or even majority prescription. Neville Cooper, chairman of the Top Management Partnership and a founder of the UK Institute of Business Ethics, noted that, at the beginning, the CRT group did not know if it was possible to reconcile three different approaches. The Americans tend to emphasize company rather than state responsibility for community affairs. The Japanese place more importance on the team rather than on the individual. In Europe, there is a strong tradition of individual rights. Although it seems idealistic to expect to amalgate differing cultural tendencies and preferences, Cooper insists that statements of practice, in the first instance, are an important way to clarify the ambiguities for people in an organization.

The case for corporate ethics is more widely accepted today than it was a decade ago. For example, in the United Kingdom, one in three leading companies now has its own code. Sceptics, however, say that an ethics code cannot make a business or employees' behaviour ethical. But then, supporters believe that it is a good start, and that it is only a tool, just as a hammer does not build a house. Enlightened companies would agree.

Sources: Tim Dickson, 'The search for universal ethics', *Financial Times* (22 July 1994), 11. Also, copies of the *Principles for Business* can be obtained from Caux Round Table Secretariat, Amaliastraat 10, 2514JC, The Hague, The Netherlands.

of company actions that were legal and allowed but were highly irresponsible. Consider the following example of a diet pill marketed in the United States:

> Prior to the Pure Food and Drug Act, the advertising for a diet pill promised that a person taking this pill could eat virtually anything at any time and still lose weight. Too good to be true? Actually the claim was quite true; the product lived up to its billing with frightening efficiency. It seems that the primary active ingredient in this 'diet supplement' was tapeworm larvae. These larvae would develop in the intestinal tract and, of course, be well fed; the pill taker would in time, quite literally, starve to death.[18]

Each company and marketing manager must work out a philosophy of socially responsible and ethical behaviour. Under the societal marketing concept, each manager must look beyond what is legal and allowed and develop standards based on personal integrity, corporate conscience and long-run consumer welfare. A clear and responsible philosophy will help the marketing manager deal with the many knotty questions posed by marketing and other human activities.

Many industrial and professional associations have suggested codes of ethics, and many companies are now adopting their own codes of ethics. About half of European firms (a moderate sum) compared to something like over 90 per cent of America's biggest 2,000 companies have established 'ethical codes of practice' for their employees. More recently, efforts are being made to establish a general international ethics code (see Marketing Highlight 2.3). Firms also have 'ethics education' programmes to teach managers about important ethics issues and help them find the proper responses.[19]

The current interest in ethics has its roots in high publicity scandals, which made international news. These ranged from the mid-1980s defence contracting misdemeanours (notably, General Dynamics, the US company that deliberately overcharged the Pentagon) to pollution (the case of Union Carbide's plant in Bhopal, India, which negligently released toxic fumes killing over 2,500 people).

Written codes do not, however, assure ethical behaviour. The code of the Prudential Corporation, a life insurance-to-property group, pledges to work for the good of its shareholders, customers and staff. It notes that 'in providing its business, the Prudential aims are ... to abide by the spirit of laws as well as their letter and to be a significant contributor to the development and well-being of the wider community in which we operate'. The guidelines are well-meaning but too abstract to direct action when the interests of the company diverge sharply from those of its employees, customers or the local community. There has to be the small print to tell employees what to do in specific dilemmas, such as when being offered, or asked for, a bribe. There should also be sanctions to enforce the code, so that ethical pledges are more than mere PR 'puff'.

Companies are urged to provide detailed policy on issues such as conflicts of interest, bribes, gift-giving, relations with competitors and shareholders' and other stakeholders' rights. Each function of the business should also have ethics policy tailored for them. For example, how is the export division which deals with Saudi Arabia, where bribes are routine business practice, to act? Some companies may set tougher standards than others. The ethical code of Levi Strauss, a jeans manufacturer, forbids bribes, whether or not prevalent or legal in the foreign country involved. Across Europe, national cultures naturally impose different standards of behaviour on individuals and organizations. In the European Union, each market sector in each country is still characterized by a mixture of accepted commercial practices, codes of practice and formalized legislation. The EU may eventually move towards a pan-European business ethics policy and codes of conduct, but that day is still some way off.[20]

Ethics and social responsibility require a total corporate commitment. They must be a component of the overall corporate culture. Ethics programmes or seminars for

In this innovative ad, the Co-operative Bank reflects its unspoken and unwritten culture – it professes that it will not do business with organizations that are environmentally or politically unsound.

This is the pony | The Watsons bought

Using money they kept in their bank | Who'd lent their money | To a company that tests

The cosmetics it makes | On animals.

It happens.

But not at the Co-operative Bank.

Our customers know there are some things we will never invest in.

Such as companies that test the cosmetics they make on animals.

Our policy is to lend only to companies we believe to be as sound ethically as they are financially.

Of course, we still provide all the normal services you'd expect from a clearing bank with assets of £2.5 billion, 5,000 'Link' cash machines and a full telephone banking service.

The difference is that along with financial peace of mind our customers receive one other important benefit.

More peace of mind.

*The* CO-OPERATIVE BANK

employees help to imbue corporate ethics and codes of conduct among staff, while ethical audits may be used to monitor and evaluate business conduct and to use the lessons to guide both policy and behaviour:

> In the final analysis, 'ethical behavior' must be an integral part of the organization, a way of life that is deeply ingrained in the collective corporate body … In any business enterprise, ethical behavior must be a tradition, a way of conducting one's affairs that is passed from generation to generation of employees at all levels of the organization. It is the responsibility of management, starting at the very top, to both set the example by personal conduct and create an environment that not only encourages and rewards ethical behavior, but which also makes anything less totally unacceptable.[21]

Marketing executives of the 1990s face many challenges. Technological advances in solar energy, home computers, cable television, modern medicine and new forms of transportation, recreation and communication provide abundant marketing opportunities. However, forces in the socioeconomic, cultural and natural environments increase the limits under which marketing can be carried out. Companies that are able to create new values and to practise societally responsible marketing will have a world to conquer.

## PRINCIPLES FOR PUBLIC POLICY TOWARDS MARKETING

Finally, we want to propose several principles that might guide the formulation of public policy towards marketing. These principles reflect assumptions underlying much of modern marketing theory and practice.

## The principle of consumer and producer freedom

As much as possible, marketing decisions should be made by consumers and producers under relative freedom. Marketing freedom is important if a marketing system is to deliver a high standard of living. People can achieve satisfaction in their own terms rather than in terms defined by someone else. This leads to greater fulfilment through a closer matching of products to desires. Freedom for producers and consumers is the cornerstone of a dynamic marketing system. But more principles are needed to implement this freedom and prevent abuses.

## The principle of curbing potential harm

As much as possible, transactions freely entered into by producers and consumers are their private business. The political system curbs producer or consumer freedom only to prevent transactions that harm or threaten to harm the producer, consumer or third parties. Transactional harm is widely recognized as grounds for government intervention. The central issue is whether there is sufficient actual or potential harm to justify the intervention.

## The principle of meeting basic needs

The marketing system should serve disadvantaged consumers as well as affluent ones. In a free-enterprise system, producers maker goods for markets that are willing and able to buy. Certain groups who lack purchasing power may go without needed goods and services, causing harm to their physical or psychological well-being. While preserving the principle of producer and consumer freedom, the marketing system should support economic and political actions to solve this problem. It should strive to meet the basic needs of all people, and all people should share to some extent in the standard of living it creates.

## The principle of economic efficiency

The marketing system strives to supply goods and services efficiently. The extent to which a society's needs and wants can be satisfied depends on how efficiently its scarce resources are used. For marketing to work efficiently, the system needs competition. An open market allows for competition, free flow of goods, freedom of information and informed buyers. These make a market efficient. To make profits, competitors must watch their costs carefully while developing products, prices and marketing programmes that serve buyer needs. Buyers get the most satisfaction by finding out about different competing products, prices and qualities and choosing carefully. The presence of active competition and well-informed buyers keeps quality high and prices low. But, more importantly, competition brings out the best in products and services. Producers that strive to offer the best value can expect to thrive.

## The principle of innovation

The marketing system encourages authentic innovation to bring down production and distribution costs and to develop new products to meet changing consumer needs. Much innovation is really imitation of other brands, with a slight difference to provide a selling point. The consumer may face ten very similar brands in a product class. But an effective marketing system encourages real product innovation and sustainable differentiation to meet the wants of different market segments.

## The principle of consumer education and information

An effective marketing system invests heavily in consumer education and information to increase long-run consumer satisfaction and welfare. The principle of economic efficiency requires this investment, especially in cases where products are confusing because of their numbers and conflicting claims. Ideally, companies will provide enough information about their products. But consumer groups, regulatory agencies and government can also give out information and ratings. They should encourage more access to the media for the counterarguments for or against consumption of goods or services, where neither businesses nor customers are behaving responsibly.

## The principle of consumer protection

Consumer education and information cannot do the whole job of protecting consumers. The marketing system also must provide consumer protection. Modern products are so complex that even trained consumers cannot evaluate them with confidence. Consumers do not know whether a mobile phone gives off cancer-causing radiation, whether a new car has safety flaws, or whether a new drug product has dangerous side effects. A government agency has to review and judge the safety levels of various foods, drugs, toys, appliances, fabrics, cars and housing. Similarly, it has to assess the integrity or professionalism of service providers like banks, insurance companies, doctors and police forces. Consumers may buy products but fail to understand the environmental consequences, so consumer protection also covers production and marketing activities that might harm the environment. Finally, consumer protection prevents deceptive practices and high-pressure selling techniques where consumers would be defenceless.

These seven principles are based on the assumption that marketing's goal is not just to maximize company profits or total consumption or consumer choice, but rather to balance that with maximization of life quality. Life quality means meeting basic needs, having available many good products, and enjoying the natural and cultural environment. Properly managed, the marketing system can help to create and deliver a higher quality of life to people around the world. The very implementation of the marketing philosophy can therefore be seen as a productive activity, not a destructive evil. Responsible marketing works.

## SUMMARY

A marketing system should sense, serve and satisfy consumer needs and improve the quality of consumers' lives. In working to meet consumer needs, marketers may take some actions that are not to everyone's liking or benefit. Marketing managers should be aware of the main *criticisms of marketing*.

Marketing's *impact on individual consumer welfare* has been criticized for its high prices, deceptive practices, high-pressure selling, shoddy or unsafe products, planned obsolescence and poor service to disadvantaged consumers. Marketing's *impact on society* has been criticized for creating false wants and too much material-ism, too few social goods, cultural pollution and too much political power. Critics have also criticized marketing's *impact on other businesses* for harming competitors and reducing competition through acquisitions, practices that create barriers to entry, and unfair competitive marketing practices.

Concerns about the marketing system have led to *citizen-action movements*. **Consumerism** is an organized social movement intended to strengthen the rights and power of consumers relative to sellers. Alert marketers view it as an opportunity to serve consumers better by providing more consumer information, education and protection.

**Environmentalism** is an organized social movement seeking to minimize the harm done to the environment and quality of life by marketing practices. It calls for curbing consumer wants when their satisfaction would create too much environ-mental cost. Citizen action has led to the passage of many laws to protect consumers in the area of product safety, truth in packaging, truth in lending and truth in advertising.

Many companies originally opposed these social movements and laws, but most of them now recognize a need for positive consumer information, education and pro-tection. Some companies have followed a policy of **enlightened marketing** based on the principles of *consumer orientation, innovation, value creation, social mission* and *societal orientation*. Increasingly, companies are responding to the need to pro-vide company policies and guidelines to help their employees deal with questions of *marketing ethics*. Companies are urged to consider seven principles for public policy towards modern, responsible marketing: *consumer and producer freedom*; *curbing potential harm*; *meeting basic needs*; *economic efficiency*; *innovation*; *consumer education and information*; and *consumer protection*.

---

# ■ DISCUSSING THE ISSUES

1. Consider the situation facing a manufacturer of baby food in which consumers complained of find-ing glass fragments in bottles. What action would you recommend to the firm? Is it right or wrong to recall its baby food?

2. Does marketing *create* barriers to entry or *reduce* them? Describe how a small local manufacturer of household cleaning products could use advertising to compete with the market leader which holds a dominant share of the product sector.

3. If you were a marketing manager at a chemical company, which would you prefer: government regulations on acceptable levels of air and water pollution, or a voluntary industry code suggesting target levels of emissions? Why?

4. Select a multinational company which you think practises the principles of enlightened marketing. Does your school? Give examples to support your answers.

5. Compare the marketing concept with the princi-ple of societal marketing. Do you think marketers should adopt the societal marketing concept? Why or why not?

6. If you had the power to change our marketing system in any way feasible, what improvements would you make? What improvements can you make as a consumer or entry-level marketing practitioner?

## ■ APPLYING THE CONCEPTS

1. Changes in consumer attitudes, especially the growth of consumerism and environmentalism, have led to more societal marketing – and to more marketing that is *supposedly* good for society, but is actually close to deception.

   ■ List three examples of marketing campaigns that you feel are genuine societal marketing. If possible, find examples of advertising or packaging that supports these campaigns.
   ■ Find three examples of deceptive or borderline imitations of societal marketing. How are you able to tell which campaigns are genuine and which are not?
   ■ What remedies, if any, would you recommend for this problem?

2. Consider our modern society. As a society, we have many things to be proud of – and many areas where there is more work to be done.

   ■ Make a list of ten important things that need to be done. Your list may include economic issues or education, health care, environment, politics or any other significant sphere.
   ■ Pick one issue that is especially important to you from this list. Using what you have learned so far from this course, make a list of ways in which marketing principles and tools could be used to help on your issue.

## ■ REFERENCES

1. See Richard Tomkins, 'Addiction or taste in battle for smokers' allegiance', *Financial Times* (23 June 1994), 6; 'The race is on to sue America's tobacco giants', *The Economist* (25 February 1995), 7; 'Tobacco adverts', *The Economist* (5 February 1994), 33–4. For more discussion about the gains and losses in a total ban on tobacco advertising, see David Short, 'Winners and losers in the tobacco advertising war', *The European* (24–30 June 1994), 25.

2. See Steven H. Star, 'Marketing and its discontents', *Harvard Business Review* (Nov.–Dec. 1989), 148–54.

3. See John F. Gaski and Michael Etzel, 'The index of consumer sentiment toward marketing', *Journal of Marketing* (July 1986), 71–81; 'The public is willing to take business on', *Business Week* (29 May 1989), 29; and Faye Rice, 'How to deal with tougher customers', *Fortune* (3 December 1990), 38–48.

4. Excerpts from Theodore Levitt, 'The morality (?) of advertising', *Harvard Business Review* (July–Aug. 1970), 84–92.

5. 'ITC unveils new rules on food, drugs', *Marketing Week* (3 February 1995), 9.

6. Sean Brierley, 'Lever drops "accelerator" formulation', *Marketing Week* (20 January 1994), 5; Sean Brierley and Tom O'Sullivan, 'Bubble bursts for Persil Power', *Marketing Week* (20 January 1994), 7; 'Lever rejects Persil Power pack flashes', *Marketing Week* (10 February 1995), 11, 22.

7. Myron Magnet, 'The money society', *Fortune* (6 July 1987), 26.

8. See Anne B. Fisher, 'A brewing revolt against the rich', *Fortune* (17 December 1990), 89–94; and Norval D. Glenn, 'What does family mean?', *American Demographics* (June 1992), 30–7.

9. 'America's new king of Europe's roads', *The Economist* (9 March 1991), 79–81; Kieren Cooke, 'Suharto family a driving force at Lamborghini', *Financial Times* (11 February 1994), 28.

10. Peter Doyle, *Marketing Management and Strategy*, 1st edn (New York: Prentice Hall, 1994), 148.

11. For more details, see Paul N. Bloom and Stephen A. Greyser, 'The maturing of consumerism', *Harvard Business Review* (Nov.–Dec. 1981), 130–9; Robert J. Samualson, 'The aging of Ralph Nader', *Newsweek* (16 Dec. 1985), 57; and Douglas A. Harbrecht, 'The second coming of Ralph Nader', *Business Week* (6 March 1989), 28.

12. Michael Lindemann, 'Green light begins to flash for recyclable cars in Germany', *Financial Times* (3 August 1994), 2.

13. For more details on the 'green' debate see INRA, *Europeans and the Environment in 1992*, report produced for the Commission of the European Communities Directorate General XVII Energy Bruxelles (1992); R. Schuster, *Environmentally Oriented Consumer Behaviour in Europe*, Hamburg: Kovac, 1992; R. Worcester, *Public and Elite Attitudes to Environmental Issues* (London: MORI, 1993); 'A survey of the global environment', *The Economist* (30 May 1992); Paul Abrahams, 'Chemicals and the environment', survey *Financial Times* (18 June 1993); Ian Hamilton Fazey, 'Paints and the environment', survey, *Financial Times* (8 April 1994).

14. Dorothy Mackenzie, 'Greener than thou', *Marketing Business* (April 1992), 10–13; Roland Rowell and Jane Hancock, 'Legal make-up', *Marketing Business* (November 1993), 42–3; 'Putting a price on being green', *Marketing*

Business (December 1989), 18–19; W. Hopfenbeck, *The Green Management Revolution* (New York: Prentice-Hall, 1992); K. Peattie, *Green Marketing* (London: Pitman, 1992).

15. 'Richardson Sheffield, a very British success', *The Economist* (4 March 1989), 86.

16. Alan Mitchell, 'Changing Channels', *Marketing Business* (February 1995), 10–13.

17. Quoted from 'Our credo', Johnson & Johnson, New Brunswick, NJ.

18. Dan R. Dalton and Richard A. Cosier, 'The four faces of social responsibility', *Business Horizons* (May–June 1982), 19–27.

19. 'Good takes on Greed', *The Economist* (17 February 1990), 87–9.

20. See Susan Norgan, *Marketing Management: A European perspective* (Wokingham, Berks: Addison-Wesley, 1994), 49.

21. From 'Ethics as a practical matter', a message from David R. Whitman, chairman of the board of Whirlpool Corporation, as reprinted in Ricky E. Griffin and Ronald J. Ebert, *Business* (Englewood Cliffs, NJ: Prentice Hall, 1989), 578–9. For more discussion, see Shelby D. Hunt, Van R. Wood, and Lawrence B. Chonko, 'Corporate ethical values and organizational commitment in marketing', *Journal of Marketing* (July 1989), 79–90.

## CASE 2

## Nestlé: singled out again and again

*during the first few months, the mother's milk will always be the most natural nutriment, and every mother able to do so, should herself suckle her children.*

Henri Nestlé, 1869

In July 1994 the corporate affairs department at Nestlé UK's headquarters in Croydon were bracing themselves for another burst of adverse publicity. At the forthcoming General Synod of the Church of England to take place at York University, an Oxford diocesan motion would call for a continued ban on Nescafé by the Church. They also wanted the Church Commissioners to disinvest their £1.1 million* in Nestlé. The Church's much publicized boycott of Nescafé occurred, amid much ridicule, in 1991, as a protest against the use of breast milk substitutes in the Third World countries. In the aftermath of the 1991 vote, Nescafé claimed their sales increased although many churchgoers said they stopped using the brand-leading coffee. The 1994 protest would be one of many the company had faced from activist protesters in the last twenty years although, according to Nestlé, the protesters' complaints had no foundation.

Nestlé SA, whose headquarters are in Vevey, Switzerland, is the world's largest food company, with annual worldwide sales of SFr 57.5 billion.* The company produces in 494 factories operating in 69 countries. Numerous Nestlé brands are quite familiar:

*1 ecu = US$1.26 = UK£0.83 = SFr 1.56 (Swiss francs).

Nestlé's chocolates, Nesquik, Nescafé, Crosse & Blackwell, Libby, Perrier, Friskies and many others. Over 100 years ago Henri Nestlé invented manufactured baby food 'to save a child's life' and the company have been suppliers ever since. Then, in the late 1970s and early 1980s, Nestlé came under heavy fire from health professionals who charged the company with encouraging Third World mothers to give up breast feeding and use a company-prepared formula. In 1974, the British charity, War on Want, published a pamphlet, *The Baby Killer*, that criticized Unigate and Nestlé's ill-advised marketing efforts in Africa. While War on Want criticized the entire infant formula industry, the German-based Third World Action Group issued a German 'translation' of the original pamphlet retitled *Nestlé Kills Babies*, which singled out Nestlé for 'unethical and immoral behaviour'. The pamphlets generated much publicity; the general public became both aware and concerned about the issue. Enraged at the protest, Nestlé sued the activists for defamation. The two-year long case kept media attention on the issue. 'We won the legal case, but it was a public-relations disaster', commented a Nestlé executive.

In 1977, two American social-interest groups, the Interfaith Center on Corporate Responsibility and the Infant Formula Action Coalition (INFACT), spearheaded a worldwide boycott against Nestlé. The campaign continued despite the fact that many organizations rejected the boycott. The US United Methodist

Church concluded that the activists were guilty of 'substantial and sometimes gross misrepresentation', of 'inflammatory rhetoric', and of using 'wildly exaggerated figures'. The boycott was called off in 1984 when the activists accepted that the company was complying with an infant formula marketing code adopted by the World Health Organization (WHO). Since then, church, university, local government and other action groups periodically rediscover the controversy and create publicity by calling for a boycott. Nestlé have not shrunk from the controversy. They continue to sell infant formula and display the Nestlé name on almost all their brands. This contrasts with some companies using furtive branding to hide common ownership.

The main accusation was the use of sophisticated promotional techniques to persuade hundreds of thousands of poverty-stricken, poorly educated mothers that formula feeding was better for their children. One issue predominates: the donation of free or low-cost supplies of infant formula to maternity wards and hospitals in developing countries. Formula feeding is not usually a wise practice in such countries. Because of poor living conditions and habits, people cannot or do not clean bottles properly and often mix formula with impure water. Furthermore income level does not permit many families to buy sufficient quantities of formula. Protesters particularly hit out at several industry practices, keeping Nestlé as their target:

- Promotional baby booklets ignoring or de-emphasizing breast feeding.
- Misleading advertising encouraging mothers to bottle feed their babies and showing breast feeding to be old-fashioned and inconvenient.
- Gifts and samples inducing mothers to bottle feed their infants.
- Posters and pamphlets in hospitals.
- Endorsements of bottle feeding by milk nurses.
- Formula is so expensive that poor customers dilute it to nonnutritious levels.

The WHO code eliminates all promotional efforts, requiring companies to serve primarily as passive 'order takers'. It prohibits advertising, samples and direct contact with consumers. Contacts with professionals (such as doctors) occur only if professionals

seek such contact. Manufacturers can package products with some form of visual corporate identity, but they cannot picture babies. The WHO code effectively allows almost no marketing. However, the code contains only *recommended* guidelines. They become *mandatory* only if individual governments adopt national codes through their own regulatory mechanisms.

In 1991, the controversy centred on the donation of free or low-cost supplies of infant formulas to maternity wards and hospitals in developing countries – a practice that WHO allows for infants who cannot be breast-fed. However, because of protests the International Association of Infant Food Manufacturers (IFM) are working with WHO and UNICEF to secure country-by-country agreements with countries to end free and low-cost supplies. By the end of 1994, only one small developing country had not agreed to the change.

Nestlé also have a policy on low-cost supplies in developing countries, as follows:

- Where there is government agreement, Nestlé will strictly apply the terms of that agreement.
- Where there have been no free or low-cost supplies up to now, Nestlé will not initiate the practice.
- Where there is no agreement Nestlé, in cooperation with others, will be active in trying to secure early government action.
- Where other companies break an agreement, Nestlé will work with IFM and governments to stop the breach.
- Nestlé will take disciplinary measures against any Nestlé personnel or distributors who deliberately violate Nestlé policy.

Given the repeated public relations problems that Nestlé faces, why do they not take unilateral action in ending free supplies? Since the Third World infant formula market is so small compared with Nestlé's worldwide interests, why bother with it? Part of the answer is in Henri Nestlé's desire 'to save a child's life'. The European Commission's directive on baby food concludes that infant formula is: 'the only processed foodstuff that wholly satisfies the nutritional requirements of infants' first four to six months of life'.

Few mothers in countries with very high infant mortality rates use anything other than breast milk. However, Kenya is probably typical of what happens when mothers do supplement breast milk with something else:

## CASE 2 *(cont)*

- 33 per cent use uji, a local food made from maize.
- 33 per cent use cow's milk.
- 28 per cent use water.
- 14 per cent use glucose.
- 11 per cent use milk powder, of which some is infant formula.
- 3 per cent use tea.

A study in the Ivory Coast shows the sort of problems that arise when Nestlé withdraws unilaterally. Other companies replaced the supplies to the affluent private nurseries but supplies for mothers in need collapsed. As a result, two premature babies fed on ordinary powdered milk did not survive, and the main hospital was not able to 'afford to buy enough to feed abandoned babies or those whose mothers are ill'.

### Questions

1. Was and is Nestlé's and the other IFM members' marketing of infant formula 'unethical and immoral'? Is it the case that ethical standards should be the responsibility of organizations such as WHO and UNESCO, and that the sole responsibility of firms is to work within the bounds set?
2. The WHO code is a *recommendation* to government. Is it Nestlé's responsibility to operate according to the *national legislation* of any given country, or to follow WHO's recommendations to that country? Who is sovereign? Do international bodies setting international standards, such as WHO and UNICEF, have a moral responsibility to make those standards

clearly understood by all parties and to demand action by national governments to enact them?
3. Are Nestlé just unlucky or did their actions precipitate their being singled out by activists? Is the activists' focus on Nestlé unjust and itself dangerous? What accounts for Nestlé's continuing in the infant formula market despite the protests?
4. Did Nestlé benefit from confronting the activists directly in court and winning? Should firms ever confront activists directly? What other forms of action are available to the company? Should firms withdraw from legitimate markets because of the justified or unjustified actions of pressure groups?
5. How should Nestlé respond to the threats from the General Synod in 1994? Since Nestlé claimed sales increased after the Nescafé boycott in 1991, should they just ignore the problem?

Sources: 'A boycott over infant formula', *Business Week* (23 April 1979), 137–40; John Sparks, 'The Nestlé controversy – anatomy of a boycott', Public Policy Education Fund, Inc. (June 1981); 'Infant formula protest teaches Nestlé a tactical lesson', *Marketing News* (10 June 1983), 1; Robert F. Hartley, *Marketing Mistakes* (Chichester, UK: Wiley, 1986); European Commission, Commission Directive on Infant Formula and Follow-on Formula, 91/321/EEC; The Associated Press, Abidjan, Ivory Coast (16 April 1991); UNICEF, *The State of the World's Children* (1992); RBL, Survey of Baby Feeding in Kenya (1992); Philip Kotler and Gary Armstrong, 'Nestlé: under fire again', in id. *Principles of Marketing* (London: Prentice Hall, 1994); Nestlé, *Nestlé and Baby Milk* (1994); Andrew Brown, 'Synod votes to end Nestlé boycott after passionate debate', *Independent* (12 July 1994), 'Church boycott of Nescafé ends', *The Times* (12 July 1994); Damion Thompson, 'Synod rejects disestablishment move', *The Daily Telegraph* (12 July 1994); 'Clear conscience for Nescafé drinkers', *Church Times* (17 July 1994); Sylvie Laforet and John Saunders, 'The management of brand portfolios: how the pros do it', *Journal of Advertising Research*, **34**, 5 (Sept.–Oct. 1994), 64–76.

## CHAPTER THREE

# Strategic marketing planning

## CHAPTER OBJECTIVES

After reading this chapter, you should be able to:

■ Explain companywide strategic planning and its principal steps.

■ Describe how companies develop mission statements and objectives.

■ Explain how companies evaluate and develop their 'business portfolios'.

■ Explain marketing's role in strategic planning.

■ Describe the marketing management process and the brand plan.

■ Show how marketing organizations are changing.

## CHAPTER PREVIEW

### Levi's strategic marketing and planning

Bavarian immigrant to America, Levi Strauss, carted a load of heavy fabric to California to make tents during the gold rush. He found that the gold seekers needed pants more than tents, so he used the fabric to make canvas pants. His blue jeans are now a worldwide institution. Levi Strauss & Co. still dominates the jeans industry. From the 1950s through the 1970s, as the baby boom caused an explosion in the number of young people, Levi Strauss & Co. and other jeans makers experienced heady 10 to 15 per cent annual sales growth, with little or no strategic or marketing planning effort. Selling jeans was easy – Levi concentrated on simply trying to make enough jeans to satisfy a seemingly insatiable market. However, by the early 1980s, demographics had caught up with the jeans industry. Its best customers, the baby-boomers, were ageing, and their tastes were changing with their waistlines – they bought fewer jeans and wore them longer. Meanwhile, the 18- to 24-

year-old segment, the group traditionally most likely to buy jeans, was shrinking. Thus Levi found itself fighting for share in a fading jeans market.

At first, despite the declining market, Levi Strauss & Co. stuck closely to its basic jeans business. It sought growth through mass-marketing strategies, substantially increasing its advertising and selling through mass retailers like Sears and J. C. Penney. When these tactics failed and profits continued to plummet, Levi tried diversification into faster-growing fashion and speciality apparel businesses. It had hastily added more than 75 new lines, including Ralph Lauren's Polo line (high fashion); the David Hunter line (classic men's sportswear); the Perry Ellis Collection (men's, women's, and children's casual sportswear); Tourage SSE (fashionable men's wear); Frank Shorter Sportswear (athletic wear); and many others. By 1984, Levi had diversified into a muddled array of businesses ranging from its true blue jeans to men's hats, ski-wear, and even denim maternity wear. As one analyst reported at the time in *Inc.* magazine:

> For years, Levi prospered with one strategy: chase the demand for blue jeans. Then came the designer jeans craze – and Levi became unstitched. The company diversified into fashion. It slapped its famous name on everything from running suits to women's polyester pants. The results were disastrous: profits collapsed by 79 per cent last year, and the company slashed about 5,000 jobs.

In 1985, in an effort to turn around an ailing Levi Strauss & Co., new management implemented a bold new strategic plan, beginning with a drastic reorganization. It sold most of the ill-fated fashion and speciality apparel businesses and took the company back to what it had always done best – making and selling jeans. For starters, Levi rejuvenated its flagship product, the classic button-fly, shrink-to-fit 501 jeans. It invested $38 million in the now-classic '501 blues' advertising campaign, a series of hip, documentary-style 'reality ads'. Never before had a company spent so much on a single item of clothing. At the time, many analysts questioned this strategy. As one put it: 'That's just too much to spend on one lousy pair of jeans.' However, the 501 blues campaign spoke for all of the company's products. It reminded consumers of Levi's strong tradition and refocused the company on its basic, blue jeans heritage. During the next six years, the campaign would more than double the sales of 501s.

1 ecu = US$1.26

Building on this solid-blue base, Levi began to add new products. For example, it successfully added prewashed, stonewashed, and brightly coloured jeans to its basic line. In late 1986, Levi introduced Dockers, casual and comfortable cotton pants targeted toward the ageing male baby-boomers. A natural extension of the jeans business, the new line had even broader appeal than anticipated. Not only did adults buy Dockers, so did their children. In the few years since its introduction, the Dockers line has become a one-billion-dollar-a-year success. Levi's has continued to develop new products for the ageing boomers. In 1992, it introduced 550 and 560 loose-fitting jeans – 'a loose interpretation of the original' – for men who've outgrown the company's slimmer-cut 501s.

In addition to introducing new products, Levi Strauss & Co. also stepped up its efforts to develop new markets. In 1991, for example, it developed jeans designed especially for women and launched an innovative five-month, $12 million 'Jeans for Women' advertising campaign, featuring renderings of the female form in blue jeans by four female artists.

But Levi's most dramatic turnaround has been in its international markets. In 1985, Levi almost sold its then stumbling and unprofitable foreign operations. Since then, however, the company has turned what was a patchwork of foreign licensees into a well coordinated team of worldwide subsidiaries. Levi is now a truly global apparel maker. Its strategy is to 'think globally, act locally'. It operates a closely coordinated worldwide marketing, manufacturing, and distribution system. Twice each year, Levi brings together managers from around the world to share product and advertising ideas and to search for those that have global appeal. For example, the Dockers line originated in Argentina, but has now become a worldwide best seller. However, within its global strategy, Levi encourages local units to tailor products and programmes to their home markets. For example, in Brazil, it developed the Feminina line of curvaceously cut jeans that provide the ultratight fit that

Brazilian women favour. Levi's European Docker division now plans to conquer Europe from its Swedish base. In doing so it has created the world's biggest advertisement, a 480 square metre banner hung on Stockholm's up-market NK department store.

In most markets abroad, Levi Strauss & Co. boldly plays up its deep American roots. For example, James Dean is a central figure in almost all Levi advertising in Japan. Indonesian ads show Levi-clad teenagers driving around Dubuque, Iowa, in 1960s convertibles. And almost all foreign ads feature English-language dialogue. However, whereas Americans usually think of their Levis as basic knockaround wear, most European and Asian consumers view them as up-market fashion statements. The prices match the snob appeal — a pair of Levi 501 jeans selling for $30 in the United States costs $63 in Tokyo and $88 in Paris, creating lush profit margins.

Levi's aggressive and innovative global marketing efforts have produced stunning results. As the domestic market continues to shrink, foreign sales have accounted for most of Levi's growth. Overseas markets now yield 39 per cent of the company's total revenues and 60 per cent of its profits. Perhaps more impressive, its foreign business is growing at 32 per cent per year, five times the growth rate of its domestic business. Levi continues to look for new international market opportunities. For example, the first Romanian shop to officially sell Levi's jeans recently opened to large crowds, and Levi is now racing competitors to reach jeans-starved consumers in Eastern Europe and the former Soviet republics. Dramatic strategic and marketing planning actions have transformed Levi Strauss into a vigorous and profitable company, one better matched to its changing market opportunities. Since its 1985 turnaround, Levi's sales have grown more than 31 per cent and profits have increased fivefold. Thus, by building a strong base in its core jeans business, coupled with well-planned product and market development, Levi has found ways to grow profitably despite the decline in the domestic jeans market. As one company observer suggests, Levi has learned that 'with the right mix of persistence and smarts, [planning new products and] cracking new markets can seem as effortless as breaking in a new pair of Levi's stone-washed jeans'.[1]

## INTRODUCTION

All companies need strategies to meet changing markets. No one strategy is best for all companies. Each company must find the way that makes most sense given its situation, opportunities, objectives and resources. Marketing plays an important role in **strategic planning**. It provides information and other inputs to help prepare the strategic plan. Strategic planning is also the first stage of marketing planning and defines marketing's role in the organization. The strategic plan guides marketing, which must work with other departments in the organization to achieve strategic objectives.

Here we look at the three stages of strategic market planning: first, the strategic plan and its implications for marketing; second, the marketing process; and thirdly, ways of putting the plan into action.

## STRATEGIC PLANNING

### Overview of planning

Many companies operate without formal plans. In new companies, managers are sometimes too busy for planning. In small companies, managers may think that only large corporations need planning. In mature companies, many managers argue that they have done well without formal planning, so it cannot be very important. They may resist taking the time to prepare a written plan. They may argue that the marketplace changes too fast for a plan to be useful – that it would end up collecting dust.[2]

Yet formal planning can yield many benefits for all types of companies, large and small, new and mature. It encourages systematic thinking. It forces the company to sharpen its objectives and policies, leads to better coordination of company efforts, and provides clearer performance standards for control. The argument that planning is less useful in a fast-changing environment makes little sense. The opposite is true: sound planning helps the company to anticipate and respond quickly to environmental changes, and to better prepare for sudden developments. The best-performing companies plan, but plan in a way that does not suppress entrepreneurship.[3]

Companies usually prepare annual plans, long-range plans, and strategic plans:

- The **annual plan** is a short-term plan that describes the current situation, company objectives, the strategy for the year, the action programme, budgets, and controls.
- The **long-range plan** describes the primary factors and forces affecting the organization during the next several years. It includes the long-term objectives, the main marketing strategies used to attain them and the resources required. This long-range plan is reviewed and updated each year so that the company always has a current long-range plan. The company's annual and long-range plans deal with current businesses and how to keep them going.
- The **strategic plan** involves adapting the firm to take advantage of opportunities in its constantly changing environment. It is the process of developing and maintaining a strategic fit between the organization's goals and capabilities and its changing marketing opportunities.

Strategic planning sets the stage for the marketing plan. It starts with its overall purpose and mission. These guide the formation of measurable corporate objectives. A corporate audit then gathers information on the company, its competitors, its market and the general environment in which the firm competes. A **SWOT analysis** gives a summary of the strengths and weaknesses of the company together with the opportunities and threats it faces. Next, headquarters decides what portfolio of businesses and products are best for the company and how much support to give each one. This helps to provide the strategic objectives that guide the company's various activities. Then each business and product unit develops detailed marketing and other functional plans to support the companywide plan. Thus marketing planning occurs at the business-unit, product and market levels. It supports company strategic planning with more detailed planning for specific marketing opportunities. For instance Nestlé, the world's largest food manufacturer, develops an overall strategic plan at its headquarters in Vevey, Switzerland. Below that, each strategic group, such as confectionery, develops subordinate strategic plans. These feed into the strategic plan's national operations. At each level, marketing and other functional plans will exist. At the final level, brand plans cover the marketing of brands such as Kit Kat, Lion and Quality Street in national markets.

## Planning functional strategies

The company's strategic plan establishes what kinds of businesses the company will be in and its objectives for each. Then, within each business unit more detailed planning takes place. The main functional departments in each unit – marketing, finance, accounting, buying, manufacturing, personnel and others – must work together to accomplish strategic objectives.

Each functional department deals with different publics to obtain resources such as cash, labour, raw materials, research ideas and manufacturing processes. For example, marketing brings in revenues by negotiating exchanges with consumers. Finance arranges exchanges with lenders and stockholders to obtain cash. Thus the marketing and finance departments must work together to obtain needed funds. Similarly, the personnel department supplies labour, and the buying department obtains materials needed for operations and manufacturing.

## Marketing's role in strategic planning

There is much overlap between overall company strategy and marketing strategy. Marketing looks at consumer needs and the company's ability to satisfy them; these factors guide the company mission and objectives. Most company strategy planning deals with marketing variables — market share, market development, growth — and it is sometimes hard to separate strategic planning from marketing planning. Some companies refer to their strategic planning as 'strategic marketing planning'.

Marketing plays a key role in the company's strategic planning in several ways. First, marketing provides a guiding *philosophy* – company strategy should revolve around serving the needs of important consumer groups. Second, marketing provides *inputs* to strategic planners by helping to identify attractive market opportunities and by assessing the firm's potential to take advantage of them. Finally, within individual business units, marketing designs *strategies* for reaching the unit's objectives.

Within each business unit, marketing management determines how to help achieve strategic objectives. Some marketing managers will find that their objective is not to build sales. Rather, it may be to hold existing sales with a smaller marketing budget, or even to reduce demand. Thus marketing management must manage demand to the level decided upon by the strategic planning prepared at headquarters. Marketing helps to assess each business unit's potential, set objectives for it, and then helps it to achieve those objectives.

## Marketing and the other business functions

In some firms marketing is just another function – all functions count in the company and none takes leadership. At the other extreme, some marketers claim that marketing is the *principal* function of the firm. They quote Drucker's statement: 'The aim of the business is to create customers.' They say it is marketing's job to define the company's mission, products, and markets and to direct the other functions in the task of serving customers.

More enlightened marketers prefer to put the *customer* at the centre of the company. These marketers argue that the firm cannot succeed without customers, so the crucial task is to attract and hold them. Customers are attracted by promises and held by satisfaction. Marketing defines the promise and ensures its delivery. However, because actual consumer satisfaction is affected by the performance of other departments, *all* functions should work together to sense, serve and satisfy customer needs. Marketing plays an integrative role in ensuring that all departments work together towards consumer satisfaction.

## Conflict between departments

Each business function has a different view of which publics and activities are most important. Manufacturing focuses on suppliers and production; finance addresses stockholders and sound investment; marketing emphasizes consumers and products, pricing, promotion, and distribution. Ideally, all the different functions should blend to achieve consumer satisfaction. In practice, departmental relations are full of conflicts and misunderstandings. The marketing department takes the consumer's point of view. But, when marketing tries to develop customer satisfaction, it often causes other departments to do a poorer job *in their terms*. Marketing department actions can increase buying costs, disrupt production schedules, increase inventories and create budget headaches. Thus the other departments may resist bending their efforts to the will of the marketing department.

Despite the resistance, marketers must get all departments to 'think consumer' and to put the consumer at the centre of company activity. Customer satisfaction requires a total company effort to deliver superior value to target customers.

Creating value for buyers is much more than a 'marketing function'; rather, '[it is] analogous to a symphony orchestra in which the contribution of each subgroup is tailored and integrated by a conductor – with a synergistic effect. A seller must draw upon and integrate effectively ... its entire human and other capital resources. ... [Creating superior value for buyers] is the proper focus of the entire business and not merely of a single department in it.'[4]

> ABB Asea Brown Boveri, formed in 1987 by the merger of Sweden's Asea and Switzerland's Brown Boveri, shows the benefits of customer focus. ABB launched a customer focus programme in 1990. It was initially a regional effort stressing time-based management to quicken response to customers by cutting total customer order to delivery time. The customer focus programme has since extended to all its operations. It encourages people in all its 5,000 plus profit centres to 'think customer', track customer satisfaction and to find ways to continually improve customer service.
>
> The company keeps 'close to the customer' by extreme decentralisation and a flat, team driven organisation. Sune Karlsson, who is responsible for the customer focus programme, says: 'the people in our many small groups are close to the customer, are more sensitive to their needs, and are more able to respond to those needs.' The role of keeping the customer satisfied and happy is not just the role of marketing people. Employees work together to develop a system of functional plans and then use cross-border co-ordination to accomplish the company's overall objectives. Furthermore, Karlsson suggests, 'We have learned that the customer focus programme reduces the optimal size of an operation (that is, improves efficiency). It ensures that the customer is better served and brings us closer to the ultimate goal of partnering (that is, long-term relationships).'[5]

## THE STRATEGIC PLAN

The strategic plan contains several components: the mission, the strategic imperatives, the strategic audit, SWOT analysis, portfolio analysis, objectives and strategies. All of these feed from and feed into marketing plans.

## The mission

A mission states the purpose of a company. Often firms start with a clear mission held within the mind of its founder. Then, over time, the mission fades as the company acquires new products and markets. A mission may be clear but forgotten by some managers. An extreme case of this was the Anglican Church Commissioners who thought they had the 'Midas touch' when they started speculating on the international property market. They found out that markets go down as well as up and lost a third of the church's ancient wealth in the process. Other problems can occur when the mission may remain clear but no longer fits the environment. The Levi preview shows them struggling with this problem.

When an organization is drifting, the management must renew its search for purpose. They must ask: What business are we in? What do consumers value? What are we in business for? What sort of business are we? What makes us special? These simple-sounding questions are among the most difficult the company will ever have to answer. Successful companies continuously raise these questions and answer them. Asking these basic questions is a sign of strength, not uncertainty.

Many organizations develop formal mission statements that answer these questions. A **mission statement** is a statement of the organization's purpose – what it wants to accomplish in the larger environment. A clear mission statement acts as an 'invisible hand' that guides people in the organization so that they can work independently and yet collectively towards overall organizational goals.

Traditionally, companies have defined their business in product terms ('We manufacture furniture'), or in technological terms ('We are a chemical-processing firm'). But mission statements should be *market-oriented*.

*What business are we in?* Asking this question helps. Market definitions of a business are better than product or technological definitions. Products and technologies eventually become outdated, but basic market needs may last forever. A market-oriented mission statement defines the business based on satisfying basic customer needs. Thus Rolls-Royce is in the power business, not the aero engine business. Visa's business is not credit cards, but is that of allowing customers to exchange value – to exchange assets, such as cash on deposit or equity in a home, for virtually anything, anywhere in the world. Creative 3M does more than just make adhesives, scientific equipment, and healthcare products; it solves people's problems by putting innovation to work for them.

*Who are our customers?* This is a probing question. Who are the customers of Rolls-Royce's new Trent aero engine? At one level it is the airframers, like Boeing or European Airbus. If they can get an airframer to launch a new aircraft with a Rolls-Royce engine, this saves development costs and early orders are likely. Is it the airline or leasing companies who eventually buy the engines? They will certainly have to sell to them as well. Is it the pilot, the service crew or even the passenger? Unlike the competition, Rolls-Royce have a brand name that is synonymous with prestige and luxury.

*What are we in business for?* This is a hard question for non-profit-making organizations. Do universities exist to educate students or to train them for industry? Is the pursuit of knowledge by the faculty the main reason for their existence? If so, is good research of economic value or is pure research better?

*What sort of business are we?* This question guides the strategy and structure of organizations. A company aiming at *cost leadership* seeks efficiency. These firms, like Aldi or KwikSave, run simple efficient organizations with careful cost control. These contrast with *differentiators*, like Sony, who aim to make profits by inventing products, such as the Walkman, whose uniqueness gives a competitive edge. *Focused* companies concentrate upon being the best at serving a well-defined target market. They succeed by tailoring their products or services to customers they know

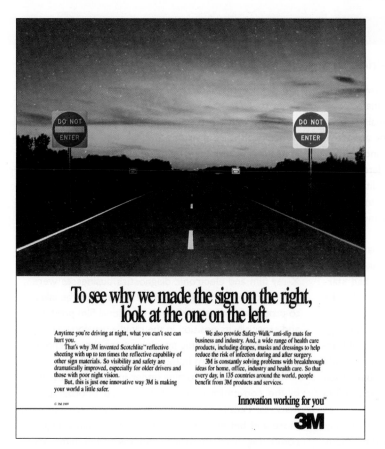

Company mission: 3M sees its mission not as making adhesives, scientific equipment and healthcare products, but as 'constantly solving [people's] problems with breakthrough ideas for home, office, industry and health care. So that every day, in 135 countries around the world, people benefit from 3M products and services.'

well. In Britain, Coutts & Co., a National Westminster Bank subsidiary, do this in providing their 'personal banking' to the very wealthy. Michael Porter[6] describes a fourth option that occurs if firms do not define how they are to do business: *stuck in the middle*.

Management should avoid making its mission too narrow or too broad. A lead pencil manufacturer that says it is in the communication equipment business is stating its mission too broadly. A mission should be:

- *Realistic*. Singapore International Airlines is excellent but it would be deluding itself if its mission was to become the world's largest airline.
- *Specific*. It should fit the company and no other. Many mission statements exist for public relations purposes so lack specific, workable guidelines. The statement 'We want to become the leading company in this industry by producing the highest-quality products with the best service at the lowest prices' sounds good but is full of generalities and contradictions. Such motherhood statements will not help the company make tough decisions.
- Based on *distinctive competences*. Bang & Olufsen have the technology to build microcomputers but an entry into that market would not take advantage of their core competences in style, hi-fi and exclusive distribution.
- *Motivating*. It should give people something to believe in. It should get a 'Yeah!', not a yawn or a 'Yuck!'. A company's mission should not say 'making more sales or profits' – profits are only a reward for undertaking a useful activity. A company's employees need to feel that their work is significant and that it contributes

## Eastman Kodak asks: 'What business are we in?'

Eastman Kodak is one of many firms now asking: 'What business are we in?' It is one of many companies that diversified in the 1980s. Originally a photographic products company, it entered the attractive pharmaceuticals and consumer healthcare industry by acquisition and alliances. Then, in the late 1980s, tough competition and tight economic conditions saw its fortunes decline. Its debt burden went up and its imaging business lacked money for investment. Like IBM, the company was a troubled giant.

In early 1994 George Fisher, the company's new chair, launched a new plan that would take Kodak back to its imaging roots. George Eastman had started the company in 1880 and it had grown to be the world's biggest photographic company using silver-halide technology. This time the proposed technology was digital imaging – a business that was a small fraction of current sales and a loss maker. Silver-halide offered little opportunity for development but digital imaging was on track for the much discussed 'information highway'. It offers the chance to take images from any source, manipulate them electronically, store them digitally (on PCs or CDs), transmit them,

and display them on everything from photographic paper to TVs.

Kodak wanted to sell its pharmaceuticals and consumer healthcare divisions and reinvest the proceeds in its imaging business. The move would also lighten the groups $7bn debt. Three divisions went up for sale: Stirling Winthrop (drugs and consumer health care), L&F products (personal care and household products), and the Clinical Diagnostics division. The sales raised $16.4bn, almost a quarter of Kodak's 1993 revenue.

After the sale, Kodak was left with its imaging business and Health Sciences division. Health Science's X-ray film and electronic diagnostics businesses were central to Kodak's imaging strategy. Steps would be taken to protect and develop Kodak's traditional film products and especially its position in the rapidly developing market for digital electronic imaging where their technology was the standard in multimedia applications.

Kodak is already coming under increasing pressure in the conventional silver-halide-based photographic markets. People in the developed world are buying more and better cameras but not more films. Fuji is competing hard on price, and own-label films are

to people's lives. Contrast the missions of the two computer giants IBM and Apple. When IBM sales were $50bn, president John Akers said that IBM's goal was to become a $100bn company by the end of the century. Meanwhile, Apple's long-term goal has been to put computer power into the hands of every person. Apple's mission is much more motivating than IBM's.

*Visions* guide the best missions. A vision is a contagious dream. Sony's president, Akio Morita, wanted everyone to have access to 'personal portable sound', and his company created the Walkman. Richard Branson thought 'flying should be fun' so founded Virgin Airlines. Thomas Monaghan wanted to deliver hot pizza to any home within 30 minutes, and he created Domino's Pizza.

The company's mission statement should provide a vision and direction for the company for the next ten to twenty years. They do not change every few years in response to each new turn in the environment. Still, a company must redefine its mission if that mission has lost credibility or no longer defines an optimal course for the company.[7] Marketing Highlight 3.1 describes how recent events have caused Eastman Kodak to think carefully about its mission. The hostile environment in the early 1990s caused Siemens, the German electronic giant, to review their strategy. Their seven core statements (Figure 3.1) provided strong communications and drove their strategy, structure and style of management.

undercutting Kodak's prices by 40 per cent. Unlike many market leaders, Kodak has joined the price cutters and launched Funtime priced 20 per cent lower than Kodak Gold. New markets in the East are growing fast but these are very price sensitive and bootlegging abounds.

The move into digital imaging is a gamble. So far Kodak has little to show for the millions of dollars it has invested in digital-imaging technology. Its Photo-CD system, that uses CDs to store images, was a flop in the consumer market. Only a few hundred were sold in 1993. Kodak's digital camera also has problems: the black-and-white model costs over $8,000 and produces poorer pictures than a 35mm camera.

Joint ventures make Kodak's prospects look better. A new digital camera from Apple Computer using Kodak technology may be on the market soon. It will cost a tenth of Kodak's product. Microsoft and Silicon Graphics are already using Kodak's digital-imaging

technology. Fisher says he is talking to several potential partners about longer-term ventures: 'We have to work with companies that are much stronger in software and telecoms than we are.' With these ventures, the digital imaging group expects to move into profit in two to three years. Will they? The 'electronic highways' to carry the digital pictures of little Jimmy do not exist yet. Also, there is still a price and quality gulf between silver-halide and digital imaging. The gap will eventually narrow, but expect it to close only slowly. Whenever a new technology takes on an old one, competition usually finds ways of squeezing unexpected performance out of the old dog.

Kodak missed out on video technology by concentrating on conventional films. They dominated the 16mm video film market that almost disappeared overnight when video cameras arrived. Their effort in digital imaging recognizes that their business is imaging, not silver-halide film.

Sources: Patrick Harveson, 'Eastman Kodak prepare for a new image', *Financial Times* (4 May 1993), 29; Patrick Harveson, 'Kodak to return to core with drug sale', *Financial Times* (4 May 1994), 23; Chris Butler and

Tony Patey, 'Drug firms on the trail of US partners', *The European* (6–12 May 1994), 15; 'Picture imperfect', *The Economist* (28 May 1994), 87–8.

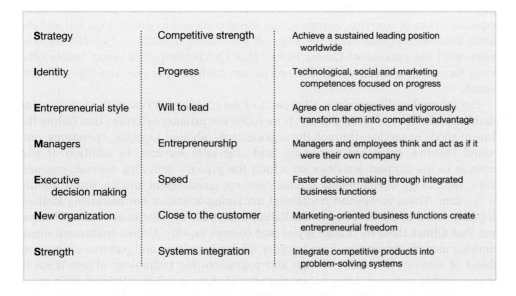

| Strategy | Competitive strength | Achieve a sustained leading position worldwide |
| --- | --- | --- |
| Identity | Progress | Technological, social and marketing competences focused on progress |
| Entrepreneurial style | Will to lead | Agree on clear objectives and vigorously transform them into competitive advantage |
| Managers | Entrepreneurship | Managers and employees think and act as if it were their own company |
| Executive decision making | Speed | Faster decision making through integrated business functions |
| New organization | Close to the customer | Marketing-oriented business functions create entrepreneurial freedom |
| Strength | Systems integration | Integrate competitive products into problem-solving systems |

**Figure 3.1**    Siemens' seven core statements.

## From mission to strategic objectives

The company's mission needs to be turned into strategic objectives to guide management. Each manager should have objectives and be responsible for reaching them. For example, their fertilizer business unit is one of International Minerals & Chemical Corporation's many activities. The fertilizer division does not say that its mission is to produce fertilizer. Instead, it says that its mission is to 'increase agricultural productivity'. This mission leads to a hierarchy of objectives, including business objectives and marketing objectives. The mission of increasing agricultural productivity leads to the company's business objective of researching new fertilizers that promise higher yields. Unfortunately, research is expensive and requires improved profits to plough back into research programmes. So improving profits becomes another key business objective. Profits are improved by increasing sales or reducing costs. Sales increase by improving the company's share of the domestic market, by entering new foreign markets, or both. These goals then become the company's current marketing objectives. The objective to 'increase our market share' is not as useful as the objective to 'increase our market share to 15 per cent in two years'. The mission states the philosophy and direction of a company whereas the strategic objectives are measurable goals.

## Strategic audit

'Knowledge is power': so stated Francis Bacon, the sixteenth-century philosopher, while according to the ancient Chinese strategist Sun Zi, 'The leader who does not want to buy information is inconsiderate and can never win'. The strategic audit covers the gathering of this vital information. It is the intelligence used to build the detailed objectives and strategy of a business. It has two parts: the external and internal audit.

The **external audit** or marketing environment audit examines the macroenvironment and task environment of a company. EuroDisney's problems can be partly explained by an excessive faith in company strengths and too little attention being paid to the macroenvironment. French labour costs make the park much more expensive than in America, Europe's high travel costs add to guests' total bill and the north European climate takes the edge off year-round operations. EuroDisney contrasts with the success of Center Parcs. This Dutch company's resort hotels offer north Europeans undercover health and leisure facilities that they can enjoy all year round.

The **internal audit** examines all aspects of the company. It covers the whole **value chain** described by Michael Porter.[8] It includes the primary activities that follow the flow of goods or services through the organization: inbound logistics, operations, outbound logistics, sales and marketing, and after-sales services. In addition, it also extends to the support activities on which the primary activities depend: procurement, technology development, human resource management and the infrastructure of the firm. These go beyond traditional marketing activities but marketing strategy depends on all of them. A key to the Italian Benetton's international success is a system that allows them to change styles and colours rapidly. Unlike traditional mass-clothing manufacturers who have to order fabrics in colours and patterns over a year ahead of seasons, Benetton's design and manufacturing technology allows them to change within a season. Long before the idea of close supplier relationships was re-imported from Japan, Marks & Spencer and C&A made supplier relations and human resource management central strategies.

Reading financial statements is basic to understanding the state of a company and seeing how it is developing. The operating statement and the balance sheet are the two main financial statements used. The **balance sheet** shows the assets, liabilities, and net worth of a company at a given time. The **operating statement** (also called profit-and-loss statement or income statement) is the more important of the two for marketing information. It shows company sales, cost of goods sold, and expenses during a specified time period. By comparing the operating statement from one time period to the next, the firm can spot favourable or unfavourable trends and take appropriate action. Marketing Highlight 3.2 describes these statements in more detail and explains their construction.

## SWOT analysis

The SWOT analysis draws the critical strengths, weaknesses, opportunities and threats (SWOT) from the strategic audit. The audit contains a wealth of data of differing importance and reliability. The SWOT analysis distils these data to show the critical items from the internal and external audit. The number of items is small for forceful communications and they show where a business should focus its attention.

### Opportunities and threats

Managers need to identify the main threats and opportunities that their company faces. The purpose of the analysis is to make the manager anticipate important developments that can have an impact on the firm. A large pet food division of a multinational company could list the following:

### Opportunities

- *Economic climate.* Because of improved economic conditions, pet ownership is increasing in almost all segments of the population.
- *Demographic changes.* (i) Increasing single parenthood, dual-income families and ageing will increase the trend towards convenient pet foods (from wet to dry); and (ii) the aged population will grow and increasingly keep pets as company.
- *Market.* The pet food market will follow the human market in the concern for healthy eating and preprepared luxury foods.
- *Technology.* New forms of pet food that are low in fat and calories, yet highly nutritious and tasty, will soon emerge. These products will appeal strongly to many of today's pet food buyers, whose health concerns extend to their pets.

### Threats

- *Competitive activity.* A large competitor has just announced that it will introduce a new premium pet food line, backed by a huge advertising and sales promotion blitz.
- *Channel pressure.* Industry analysts predict that supermarket chain buyers will face more than 10,000 new grocery product introductions next year. The buyers accept only 38 per cent of these new products and give each one only five months to prove itself.
- *Demographic changes.* (i) Increasing single parenthood and dual-income families will encourage the trend towards pets that need little care (cats rather than dogs), and (ii) will encourage the trend towards smaller pets who eat less.

■ *Politics.* European Union legislation will force manufacturers to disclose the content of their pet food. This will adversely affect the attractiveness of some ingredients like kangaroo and horse meat.

Not all threats call for the same attention or concern – the manager should assess the likelihood of each threat and the potential damage each could cause. The man-

## MARKETING HIGHLIGHT 3.2

### Financial statements: are we making money?

Table 1 shows the 1995 operating statement for a speciality store, Dale Parsons Men's Wear. This statement is for a retailer; the operating statement for a manufacturer would be somewhat different. Specifically, the section on purchases within the 'cost of goods sold' area would be replaced by 'Cost of goods manufactured'.

Table 1   Operating statement for Dale Parsons Men's Wear for year ending 31 December 1995 ($)

| | | | |
|---|---|---|---|
| Gross sales | | | 325,000 |
| less: Sales returns and allowances | | | 25,000 |
| Net sales | | | 300,000 |
| Cost of goods sold | | | |
| Beginning inventory, 1 January 1995, at cost | | 60,000 | |
| Gross purchases | 165,000 | | |
| less: Purchase discounts | 15,000 | | |
| Net purchases | 150,000 | | |
| plus: Freight-in | 10,000 | | |
| Net cost of delivered purchases | | 160,000 | |
| Cost of goods available for sale | | 220,000 | |
| less: Ending inventory, 31 December 1995, at cost | | 45,000 | |
| Total cost of goods sold | | | 175,000 |
| Gross margin | | | 125,000 |
| Expenses | | | |
| Selling expenses: | | | |
| Sales, salaries, and commissions | | 40,000 | |
| Advertising | | 5,000 | |
| Delivery | | 5,000 | |
| Total selling expenses | | | 50,000 |
| Administrative expenses: | | | |
| Office salaries | | 20,000 | |
| Office supplies | | 5,000 | |
| Miscellaneous (outside consultant) | | 5,000 | |
| Total administrative expenses | | | 30,000 |
| General expenses: | | | |
| Rent | | 10,000 | |
| Heat, light, telephone | | 5,000 | |
| Miscellaneous (insurance, depreciation) | | 5,000 | |
| Total general expenses | | | 20,000 |
| Total expenses | | | 100,000 |
| Net profit | | | 25,000 |

ager should then focus on the most probable and harmful threats and prepare plans in advance to meet them.

Opportunities occur when an environmental trend plays to a company's strength. The manager should assess each opportunity according to its potential attractiveness and the company's probability of success. Companies can rarely find ideal

---

The outline of the operating statement follows a logical series of steps to arrive at the firm's $25,000 net profit figure:

| | |
|---|---|
| Net sales | $300,000 |
| Cost of goods sold | −175,000 |
| Gross margin | $125,000 |
| Expenses | −100,000 |
| Net profit | $25,000 |

The first part details the amount that Parsons received for the goods sold during the year. The sales figures consist of three items: gross sales, returns or allowances, and net sales. **Gross sales** is the total amount charged to customers during the year for merchandise purchased in Parsons's store. As expected, some customers returned merchandise because of damage or a change of mind. If the customer gets a full refund or full credit on another purchase, we call this a return. Other customers may decide to keep the item if Parsons will reduce the price. This is called an allowance. By subtracting returns and allowances from gross sales, we arrive at net sales – what Parsons earned in revenue from a year of selling merchandise:

| | |
|---|---|
| Gross sales | $325,000 |
| Returns and allowances | −25,000 |
| Net sales | $300,000 |

The second part of the operating statement calculates the amount of sales revenue Dale Parsons retains after paying the costs of the merchandise. We start with the inventory in the store at the beginning of the year. During the year, Parsons bought $165,000 worth of suits, slacks, shirts, ties, jeans and other goods. Suppliers gave the store discounts totalling $15,000, so that net purchases were $150,000. Because the store is located away from regular shipping routes, Parsons had to pay an additional $10,000 to get the products delivered, giving

the firm a net cost of $160,000. Adding the beginning inventory, the cost of goods available for sale amounted to $220,000. The $45,000 ending inventory of clothes in the store on December 31 is then subtracted to come up with the $175,000 **cost of goods sold**. Here again we have followed a logical series of steps to figure out the cost of goods sold:

| | |
|---|---|
| Amount Parsons started with (beginning inventory) | $60,000 |
| Net amount purchased | +150,000 |
| Any added costs to obtain these purchases | +10,000 |
| Total cost of goods Parsons had available for sale during year | $220,000 |
| Amount Parsons had left over (ending inventory) | −45,000 |
| Cost of goods actually sold | $175,000 |

The difference between what Parsons paid for the merchandise ($175,000) and what he sold it for ($300,000) is called the **gross margin** ($125,000).

In order to show the profit Parsons 'cleared' at the end of the year, we must subtract from the gross margin the expenses incurred while doing business. *Selling expenses* included two sales employees, local newspaper and radio advertising, and the cost of delivering merchandise to customers after alterations. Selling expenses totalled $50,000 for the year. *Administrative expenses* included the salary for an office manager, office supplies such as stationery and business cards, and miscellaneous expenses including an administrative audit conducted by an outside consultant. Administrative expenses totalled $30,000 in 1995. Finally, the *general expenses* of rent, utilities, insurance, and depreciation came to $20,000. Total expenses were therefore $100,000 for the year. By subtracting expenses ($100,000) from the gross margin ($125,000), we arrive at the **net profit** of $25,000 for Parsons during 1995.

opportunities that exactly fit their objectives and resources. The development of opportunities involves risks. When evaluating opportunities, the manager must decide whether the expected returns justify these risks. A trend or development can be a threat or an opportunity depending on a company's strengths. The development of the steel-braced radial tyre was an opportunity for Michelin, who used their technological lead to gain market share. To the rest of the industry the new technology was a threat since the tyre's longer life reduced total demand and the new technology made their plant obsolete.

### Strengths and weaknesses

The strengths and weaknesses in the SWOT analysis do not list all features of a company but only those relating to **critical success factors**. A list that is too long betrays a lack of focus and an inability to discriminate what is important. The strengths or weaknesses are *relative*, not absolute. It is nice to be good at something, but it can be a weakness if the competition is stronger. Mercedes is good at making reliable luxury cars with low depreciation but this stopped being a strength when Honda's Acura and Toyota's Lexus beat them on all three fronts in the American market. The Japanese products were not cheap but they were styled for the American market and came with all the extras that buyers of German luxury cars had to pay for. Finally, the strengths should be *based on fact*. In buying Skoda, VW have acquired a well-known brand name, but is the name a strength? A failure to understand true strengths can be dangerous. A well-known aircraft manufacturer for years promoted the quality of its after-sales service. Only after it was acquired by another company did it find out that its reputation was the worst in the industry.

A major pet food manufacturer could pitch these strengths and weaknesses against the opportunities and threats:

### Strengths
- Market leader in the dry cat food market.
- Access to the group's leading world position in food technology.
- Market leader in luxury pet foods.
- The group's excellent worldwide grocery distribution.
- Pet food market leader in several big markets including France, Italy, Spain and South America.

### Weaknesses
- A number three in the wet pet food market.
- Excessive product range with several low-volume brands.
- Most brand names are little known, and are cluttered following acquisitions.
- Relatively low advertising and promotions budget.
- Product range needs many manufacturing skills.
- Poor store presence in several large markets: Germany, UK, US and Canada.
- Overall poor profits performance.

The pet food company shows how some parts of the SWOT *balance*. The strengths in dry and luxury pet foods match demographic trends, so this looks like an opportunity for growth. Access to food technology should also help them face changing consumer tastes and legislation. The weaknesses suggest a need for more focus. Dropping some uneconomic lines in the mass wet pet food market, simplifying the brand structure, and concentrating on fewer manufacturing processes, could release resources for developing the dry and luxury markets. By using their access to the worldwide grocery distribution the company could become a profitable focused company.

## The business portfolio

The **business portfolio** is the collection of businesses and products that make up the company. It is a link between the overall strategy of a company and those of its parts. The best business portfolio is the one that fits the company's strengths and weaknesses to opportunities in the environment. The company must (1) analyse its *current* business portfolio and decide which businesses should receive more, less, or no investment, and (2) develop growth strategies for adding *new* products or businesses to the portfolio.

### Analysing the current business portfolio

**Portfolio analysis** helps managers evaluate the businesses making up the company. The company will want to put strong resources into its more profitable businesses and phase down or drop its weaker ones. Recently, Sweden's Volvo has started disposing of its noncore businesses to strengthen its portfolio. It plans to sell its interests in consumer products (holdings in BCP), pharmaceuticals (28 per cent of Pharmacia), stock-brokering, property and investment. The tighter portfolio will allow Volvo to concentrate on revitalizing its vital passenger car, truck and bus operations.

Management's first step is to identify the key businesses making up the company. These are strategic business units. A **strategic business unit (SBU)** is a unit of the company that has a separate mission and objectives and that can be planned independently from other company businesses. An SBU can be a company division, a product line within a division, or sometimes a single product or brand.

The next step in business portfolio analysis calls for management to assess the attractiveness of its various SBUs and decide how much support each deserves. In some companies, this occurs informally. Management looks at the company's collection of businesses or products and uses judgement to decide how much each SBU should contribute and receive. Other companies use formal portfolio-planning methods.

The purpose of strategic planning is to find ways in which the company can best use its strengths to take advantage of attractive opportunities in the environment. So most standard portfolio-analysis methods evaluate SBUs on two important dimensions: the attractiveness of the SBU's market or industry; and the strength of the SBU's position in that market or industry. The best-known portfolio-planning methods are from the Boston Consulting Group, a leading management consulting firm, and by General Electric and Shell.

*The Boston Consulting Group box*     Using the Boston Consulting Group (BCG) approach, a company classifies all its SBUs according to the **growth-share matrix** shown in Figure 3.2. On the vertical axis, *market growth rate* provides a measure of market attractiveness. On the horizontal axis, *relative market share* serves as a measure of company strength in the market. By dividing the growth-share matrix as indicated, four types of SBUs can be distinguished:

1. **Stars**. Stars are high-growth, high-share businesses or products. They often need heavy investment to finance their rapid growth. Eventually their growth will slow down, and they will turn into cash cows.

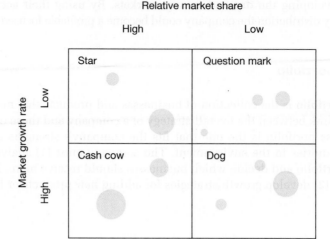

**Figure 3.2**   The BCG growth share matrix.

2. **Cash cows**. Cash cows are low-growth, high-share businesses or products. These established and successful SBUs need less investment to hold their market share. Thus they produce cash that the company uses to pay its bills and to support other SBUs that need investment.
3. **Question marks**. Question marks are low-share business units in high-growth markets. They require cash to hold their share, let alone increase it. Management has to think hard about question marks – which ones they should build into stars and which ones they should phase out.
4. **Dogs**. Dogs are low-growth, low-share businesses and products. They may generate enough cash to maintain themselves, but do not promise to be large sources of cash.

The ten circles in the growth-share matrix represent a company's ten current SBUs. The company has two stars, two cash cows, three question marks, and three dogs. The areas of the circles are proportional to the SBU's sales value. This company is in fair shape, although not in good shape. It wants to invest in the more promising question marks to make them stars, and to maintain the stars so that they will become cash cows as their markets mature. Fortunately, it has two good-sized cash cows whose income helps finance the company's question marks, stars, and dogs. The company should take some decisive action concerning its dogs and its question marks. The picture would be worse if the company had no stars, or had too many dogs, or had only one weak cash cow.

Once it has classified its SBUs, the company must determine what role each will play in the future. There are four alternative strategies for each SBU. The company can invest more in the business unit to *build* its share. It can invest just enough to *hold* the SBU's share at the current level. It can *harvest* the SBU, milking its short-term cash flow regardless of the long-term effect. Finally, the company can *divest* the SBU by selling it or phasing it out and using the resources elsewhere.

As time passes, SBUs change their positions in the growth-share matrix. Each SBU has a life cycle. Many SBUs start out as question marks and move into the star category if they succeed. They later become cash cows as market growth falls, then finally die off or turn into dogs towards the end of their life cycle. The company needs to add new products and units continuously, so that some of them will become stars and, eventually, cash cows that will help finance other SBUs.

*The General Electric grid*   General Electric introduced a comprehensive portfolio planning tool called a **strategic business-planning grid** (see Figure 3.3). It is similar to Shell's *directional policy matrix*. Like the BCG approach, it uses a matrix with two dimensions – one representing industry attractiveness (the vertical axis) and one representing company strength in the industry (the horizontal axis). The best businesses are those located in highly attractive industries where the company has high business strength.

The GE approach considers many factors besides market growth rate as part of industry attractiveness. It uses an industry attractiveness index made up of market size, market growth rate, industry profit margin, amount of competition, seasonality and cycle of demand, and industry cost structure. Each of these factors is rated and combined in an index of industry attractiveness. For our purposes, an industry's attractiveness is high, medium, or low. As an example, the Kraft subsidiary of Philip Morris has identified numerous highly attractive industries – natural foods, speciality frozen foods, physical fitness products, and others. It has withdrawn from less attractive industries such as bulk oils and cardboard packaging. The Dutch chemical giant Akzo Nobel has identified speciality chemicals, coatings and pharmaceuticals as attractive. Its less attractive bulk chemical and fibre businesses are being sold.

For *business strength*, the GE approach again uses an index rather than a simple measure of relative market share. The business strength index includes factors such as the company's relative market share, price competitiveness, product quality, customer and market knowledge, sales effectiveness, and geographic advantages. These factors are rated and combined in an index of business strengths described as strong, average, or weak. Thus, Kraft has substantial business strength in food and related industries, but is relatively weak in the home appliances industry.

The grid has three zones. The green cells at the upper left include the strong SBUs in which the company should invest and grow. The amber diagonal cells contain SBUs that are medium in overall attractiveness. The company should maintain its level of investment in these SBUs. The three red cells at the lower right indicate SBUs that are low in overall attractiveness. The company should give serious thought to harvesting or divesting these SBUs.

The circles represent four company SBUs; the areas of the circles are proportional to the relative sizes of the industries in which these SBUs compete. The pie slices

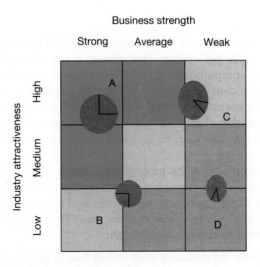

**Figure 3.3**   GE's strategic business-planning grid.

## MARKETING HIGHLIGHT 3.3

### Back to the basics

During the 1970s and early 1980s, strategic planners in Europe, the United States and Japan caught expansion fever. Big was beautiful and it seemed that everyone wanted to get bigger and grow faster by broadening their business portfolios. Companies milked their stodgy but profitable core businesses to get the cash needed to acquire glamorous, faster-growing businesses in more attractive industries. It did not seem to matter that many of the acquired businesses fitted poorly with old ones or that they operated in markets unfamiliar to company management.

Thus many firms exploded into huge conglomerates, sometimes containing hundreds of unrelated products and businesses in a dozen diverse industries. Managing these 'smorgasbord' portfolios often proved difficult. The conglomerate managers soon learned that it was tough to run businesses in industries they knew little about. Many newly acquired businesses bogged down under added layers of corporate management and increased administrative costs. Meanwhile the profitable core businesses that had financed the acquisitions withered from lack of investment and management attention.

By the mid-1980s, as attempt after attempt at scatter-gun diversification foundered, acquisition fever gave way to a new philosophy – getting back to the basics. The new trend had many names: 'narrowing the focus', 'sticking to your knitting', 'the contrac-

tion craze', 'the urge to purge'. They all mean narrowing the company's market focus and returning to the idea of serving one or a few core industries that the firm knows. The company sheds businesses that do not fit its narrowed focus and rebuilds by concentrating resources on other businesses that do. The result is a smaller, but more focused company; a stronger firm serving fewer markets, but serving them much better.

Since the mid-1980s, companies in all industries have worked at getting back in focus and shedding unrelated operations. Some companies have taken drastic steps. For example, during the 1970s Gulf & Western acquired businesses in dozens of diverse sectors: from auto parts and industrial equipment to apparel and furniture, from cement and cigars to racetracks and video games. Then, in 1983 and 1984, to regain focus and direction, the company purged itself of over 50 business units that made up nearly half of its $8bn in sales. In 1989, the company changed its name to Paramount Communications, to better reflect its narrower focus on entertainment and communications. It now concentrates its energies and resources on a leaner, tighter portfolio of entertainment and publishing units: Paramount Pictures, Simon & Schuster/Prentice Hall publishers, USA Cable Network, Pocket Books, Cinamerica Theatres and other related companies.

within the circles represent each SBU's market share. Thus circle A represents a company SBU with a 75 per cent market share in a good-sized, highly attractive industry in which the company has strong business strength. Circle B represents an SBU that has a 50 per cent market share, but the industry is not very attractive. Circles C and D represent two other company SBUs in industries where the company has small market shares and not much business strength. Altogether, the company should build A, maintain B, and make some hard decisions on what to do with C and D.

Management also would plot the projected positions of the SBUs with and without changes in strategies. By comparing current and projected business grids, management can identify the primary strategic issues and opportunities it faces. One of the aims of portfolio analysis is to direct firms away from investing in markets that look attractive but where they have no strength:

> In their rush away from the declining steel market four of Japan's 'famous five' big steel makers (Nippon, NKK, Kawasaki, Sumitomo and Kobe) diversified into the micro-chip busi-

Food companies are building strength by going back to their bread-and-butter basics. Quaker Oats sold its speciality retailing businesses – Jos. A. Bank (clothing), Brookstone (tools), and Eyelab (optical) – and will probably sell its profitable Fisher-Price toy operation. It used the proceeds to strengthen current food brands and to acquire the Golden Grain Macaroni Company (Rice-a-Roni and Noodle-Roni) and Gaines Foods (pet foods), whose products strongly complement Quaker's. General Mills ended 20 years of diversification by lopping off most of its nonfood businesses and moving back to the kitchen. It sold Izod (fashions), Monet (jewellery), Parker Brothers (games), Kenner (toys), and Eddie Bauer and Talbots (speciality retailers), while increasing investment in its basic consumer food brands (Wheaties and other cereals, Betty Crocker cake mixes, Gorton's seafoods, Gold Medal flour) and restaurants (Red Lobster, Darryl's).

Some food companies are still growing by acquisitions and mergers, but the new expansion fever differs notably from that of the last decade. The growth is not through broad diversification into attractive but unrelated new businesses. Instead, most are acquiring or merging with *related* companies, often competitors, in an attempt to build market power *within* their core businesses. Philip Morris has acquired General Foods and Kraft to become the United States' number one food company and in Europe Nestlé, the world's largest food company, has acquired Rowntree, Perrier, Carnation, Cereal Partners and others. As Nestlé has found, big shareholders dislike activities away from the core. Fund managers want them to liquidate their minority shareholding in L'Oréal, the French cosmetics multinational, and channel the proceeds into further strengthening their food interests.

These and other companies have concluded that fast-growing businesses in attractive industries are not good investments if they spread the company's resources too thin or if the company's managers cannot run them properly. They have learned that a company without market focus – one that tries to serve too many diverse markets – might end up serving few markets well.

Sources: See Thomas Moore, 'Old-line industry shapes up', *Fortune* (27 April 1987), 23–32; Walter Kiechel III, 'Corporate strategy for the 1990s', *Fortune* (29 February 1988), 34–42; 'G&W plans to expand in entertainment and publishing', press release, Paramount Communications (9 April 1990); and Brian Bremner, 'The age of consolidation', *Business Week* (14 October 1991), 86–94; Christopher Lorenz, 'Sugar daddy', *Financial Times* (20 April 1994), 19; Ian Verchère, Nestlé told to sell stake in L'Oréal', *The European* (22–28 April 1994), 17.

ness. They had the misplaced belief that chips would be to the 1980s what steel had been to the 1950s and that they, naturally, had to be part of it. The market was attractive but it did not fit their strengths. So far, none have made money from chips. The misadventure also distracted them from attending to their core business. In 1987 they said they would reduce fixed costs by 30 per cent but their 'salary-men' stayed in place. By 1993, their costs were up by 3.6 per cent and their losses huge.

The 'famous five's' failure contrasts with Eramet, a focused French company who are the world's biggest producer of ferro-nickel and high speed steels. They owe their number one position to their decision to invest their profits in a 'second leg' that would be a logical industrial and geographical diversification for them. They bought French Commentryene and Swedish Kloster Speedsteel. They quickly integrated them and, according to Yves Rambert, their chairman and chief executive, 'found that the French and the Swedes can work together'. The unified international marketing team is doing better than when the companies were separate. Eramat are now looking for a 'third industrial leg' that will have customers and technologies with which the group's management are familiar but does not compete for their present customers.[9]

*Problems with matrix approaches*

The BCG, GE, Shell and other formal methods revolutionized strategic planning. However, such approaches have limitations. They can be difficult, time-consuming, and costly to implement. Management may find it difficult to define SBUs and measure market share and growth. In addition, these approaches focus on classifying *current* businesses but provide little advice for *future* planning. Management must still rely on its judgement to set the business objectives for each SBU, to determine what resources to give to each and to work out which new businesses to add.

Formal planning approaches also can lead the company to place too much emphasis on market-share growth or growth through entry into attractive new markets. Using these approaches, many companies plunged into unrelated and new high-growth businesses that they did not know how to manage – with very bad results. At the same time, these companies were often too quick to abandon, sell, or milk to death their healthy mature businesses. As a result, many companies that diversified in the past are now narrowing their focus and getting back to the industries that they know best (see Marketing Highlight 3.3).

Despite these and other problems, and although many companies have dropped formal matrix methods in favour of customized approaches better suited to their situations, most companies remain firmly committed to strategic planning. Roughly 75 per cent of the *Fortune 500* companies practice some form of portfolio planning.[10]

Such analysis is no cure-all for finding the best strategy. Conversely, it can help management to understand the company's overall situation, to see how each business or product contributes, to assign resources to its businesses, and to orient the company for future success. When used properly, strategic planning is just one important aspect of overall strategic management, a way of thinking about how to manage a business.[11]

## Developing growth strategies

The **strategic focus** identifies ways of achieving sales and profit growth. This shows two routes to profitability: productivity increases and volume growth (Figure 3.4).

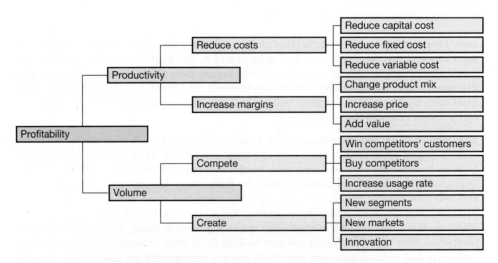

**Figure 3.4**    Growth strategy: strategic focus.

We use strategic focus to explain how Mercedes-Benz, the luxury car division of German Daimler-Benz industrial group, hopes to turn the group's DM 1.8bn 1993 loss into a satisfactory return by 1995.[12]

1 ecu = US$1.26
= DM 1.89
(Deutschmarks)

*Increasing market productivity*

*Reduce capital cost*   Firms reduce their capital cost by doing less or doing things quickly. Just-in-time (JIT) methods mean firms have less capital tied up in raw materials, work in progress on the shop floor and finished goods. By accelerating their product development Mercedes will increase their market responsiveness and accumulated development costs. They will also reduce capital costs by doing less themselves. Component manufacturers will provide more preassembled parts and a joint venture with a Romanian company will make car-interior parts.

*Reduce fixed costs*   Cost cutting is critical. Mercedes acknowledge that Japan's manufacturers have an average 35 per cent cost advantage over their German competitors. Japan's lower capital cost and longer working hours explain only 10 per cent of the difference. Mercedes responded by cutting 18,000 jobs in 1993 to save DM 5bn. Forced redundancies are almost unknown in Germany so the deduction is by the 'social measures' of the nonreplacement of people, early retirement and retraining.

*Reduce variable cost*   The company is sticking to its unconventional production methods where 10 to 15 'group workers' operate round cradles holding body shells. Meanwhile its new car plant at Rastatt will pioneer methods of 'lean production', logistics, total quality and workforce management. Other plants will adopt the proven methods. Car design will also change. It will be quicker, and future cars will be designed to a target price, rather than making the best car and then pricing it. The lessons will be passed on to their suppliers. In future they will work closer to Mercedes' research and development. The aim is to reduce the number of parts fitted at the works. The company is also changing its 'Made in Germany' policy, to produce where labour costs are lower. In 1996 it will launch a US-made sports utility vehicle.

*Change product mix*   The aim here is to sell more high-margin vehicles. Mercedes' current range does not cover luxury off-road vehicles, people movers, or small sports cars – all growth areas commanding premium prices. Moving into these markets will reduce Mercedes' dependence on their 'lower priced' models.

*Increase prices*   It is hard for Mercedes to increase prices. In the past they have sold basic models that are poorly equipped by modern standards. Customers then paid extra to have a car custom made for them with the features they wanted. The 'Made in Germany' label that has served them so long is no longer enough to command a premium price. The aim is to maintain a price premium by the brand's strength and superior quality across a broad range of products. This contrasts with the Japanese whose well-equipped luxury Lexus (Toyota), Acura (Honda) and Infiniti (Nissan) brands have tightly targeted small ranges.

*Add value*   Mercedes make and sell cars, but their customers want prestige and transport. Mercedes can add value by offering long-term service contracts, leasing deals or other financial packages that make buying easier and less risky for customers.

*Increasing volume*

The product/market expansion grid,[13] shown in Figure 3.5, is a useful device for identifying growth opportunities. This shows four routes to growth: market development, new markets, new products and diversification.

*Market penetration: win competitors' customers*     The new C class model (replacing the ageing 190) helped the company increase its sales by 23 per cent in 1994. Sales were up 40 per cent in Western Europe (excluding Germany), 34 per cent in the United States and 30 per cent in Japan. In Germany the 38 per cent growth gave a 2 per cent rise in market share.

*Market penetration: buy competitors*     So far Mercedes have not bought any competitors but other luxury car makers have: BMW have bought Rover, Ford has Jaguar, and GM part of Saab.

*Market penetration: increase usage rate*     The launch of a wider range of vehicles will increase the chance of customers having a second or third Mercedes. An unexpected outlet is a US dealer who gives away a mid-range Mercedes with every Rolls-Royce Silver Cloud.

*Market development: new segments*     Their original 190 launched Mercedes into the executive saloon market for the first time. Their 'even smaller car' produced at Rastatt will enter the family saloon market. New off-the-road vehicles and people carriers will also enter segments new to the company. In northern Europe the product is also now being promoted as a hire car.

*Market development: new markets*     German reunification gave the company an immediate sales boost. In Eastern Europe and China the brand's image and reputation for reliability and quality have made it *the* transport for the new rich.

*Product development: innovation*     Mercedes' deal with Swatch is an innovation. The size, style, motive power and target market are all new.

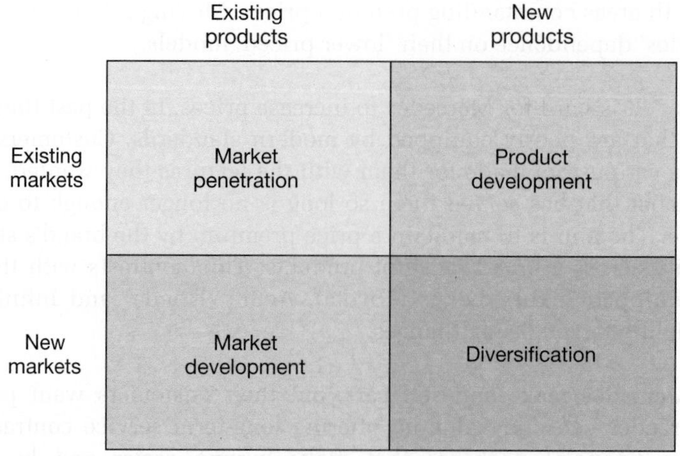

|  | Existing products | New products |
|---|---|---|
| Existing markets | Market penetration | Product development |
| New markets | Market development | Diversification |

**Figure 3.5**     Product/market expansion grid.

*Diversification*    **Diversification** is an option taken by Mercedes' parent company Daimler Benz. They have rapidly moved into aerospace by buying Dornier, Motoren Turbinen Union (MTU) and a 51 per cent stake in Messerschmitt Böelkow-Blohm (MBB). Their new Deutsche Aerospace (DASA) is now Germany's biggest aerospace and defence group. The motives behind the strategy were to offset stagnating vehicle sales and to use high technology from the acquisitions in cars and trucks. Like many other firms, Daimler Benz are finding diversification a difficult route. Shortly after consolidating the acquisitions, the 'peace dividend' damaged the defence sector and the international airline industry was in recession. Observers now question the logic of the acquisitions and doubt whether even a company with Daimler's management and financial strength can handle such a radical diversification.

## THE MARKETING PROCESS

The strategic plan defines the company's overall mission and objectives. Within each business unit, marketing plays a role in helping to accomplish the overall strategic objectives. Marketing's role and activities in the organization are shown in Figure 3.6. It summarizes the **marketing process** and the forces influencing marketing strategy.

### Marketing management

The company wants to design and put into action the marketing mix that will best achieve its objectives in its target markets. This involves four marketing management functions: analysis, planning, implementation, and control. Figure 3.7 shows the relationship between these functions. The company first develops overall strategic plans. These companywide strategic plans translate into marketing and other plans for each division, product and brand.

*Market analysis*    Managing the marketing function begins with a complete analysis of the company's situation. The company must analyse its markets and marketing

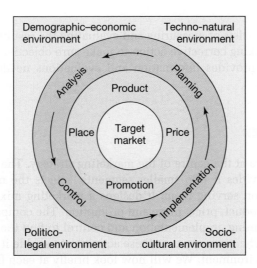

**Figure 3.6**    Influences on marketing strategy.

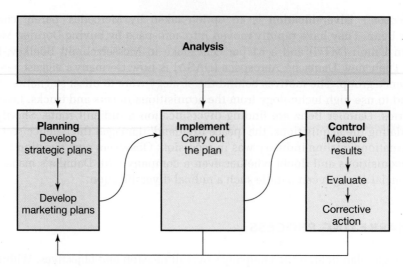

**Figure 3.7**   Market analysis, planning, implementation and control.

environment to find attractive opportunities and to avoid environmental threats. It must analyse company strengths and weaknesses, as well as current and possible marketing actions, to determine which opportunities it can best pursue. Marketing analysis feeds information and other inputs to each of the other marketing management functions.

*Marketing planning*   Through strategic planning, the company decides what it wants to do with each business unit. Marketing planning involves deciding marketing strategies that will help the company attain its overall strategic objectives. Marketing, product or brand plans are at the centre of this.

*Implementation*   Implementation turns strategic and marketing plans into actions that will achieve the company's objectives. Marketing plans are implemented by people in the marketing organization who work with others both inside and outside the company.

*Control*   Control consists of measuring and evaluating the results of marketing plans and activities and taking corrective action to make sure objectives are being reached. Marketing analysis provides information and evaluations needed for all the other marketing activities.

## Marketing strategy

Target consumers are at the centre of the marketing strategy. The company identifies the total market, divides it into smaller segments, selects the most promising segments and focuses on serving them. It designs a marketing mix using mechanisms under its control: product, price, place and promotion. The company engages in marketing analysis, planning, implementation and control to find the best marketing mix and to take action. The company uses these activities to enable it to watch and adapt to the marketing environment. We will now look briefly at each factor in the marketing process.

## Target consumers

To succeed in today's competitive marketplace, companies must be customer centred – winning customers from competitors by delivering greater value. However, before it can satisfy consumers, a company must first understand their needs and wants. So, sound marketing requires a careful analysis of consumers. Companies know that they cannot satisfy all consumers in a given market – at least not all consumers in the same way. There are too many kinds of consumers with too many kinds of needs and some companies are in a better position to serve certain segments of the market. As a consequence, each company must divide the total market, choose the best segments, and design strategies for profitably serving chosen segments better than its competitors do. This process involves five steps: demand measurement and forecasting, market segmentation, finding a differential advantage, market targeting and positioning.

## Demand measurement and forecasting

Suppose a company is looking at possible markets for a potential new product. First, the company needs to estimate the current and future size of the market and its segments. To estimate current market size, the company would identify all competing products, estimate the current sales of these products, and determine whether the market is large enough to profitably support another product.

Equally important is future market growth. Companies want to enter markets that show strong growth prospects. Growth potential may depend on the growth rate of certain age, income, and nationality groups that use the product. Growth may also relate to larger developments in the environment, such as economic conditions, the crime rate, and lifestyle changes. For example, the future markets for quality children's toys and clothing relate to current birth rates, trends in consumer affluence and projected family lifestyles. Forecasting the effect of these environmental forces is difficult, but it is necessary in order to make decisions about the market. The company's marketing information specialists probably will use complex techniques to measure and forecast demand.

## Market segmentation

If the demand forecast looks good, the company next decides how to enter the market. The market consists of many types of customers, products and needs. The marketer has to determine which segments offer the best opportunity for achieving company objectives. Consumers are grouped in various ways based on geographic factors (countries, regions, cities); demographic factors (sex, age, income, education); psychographic factors (social classes, lifestyles); and behavioural factors (purchase occasions, benefits sought, usage rates). The process of dividing a market into groups of buyers with different needs, characteristics, or behaviour who might require separate products or marketing mixes is **market segmentation**.

Every market has market segments, but not all ways of segmenting a market are equally useful. For example, Panadol would gain little by distinguishing between male and female users of pain relievers if both respond the same way to marketing stimuli. A **market segment** consists of consumers who respond in a similar way to a given set of marketing stimuli. In the car market, for example, consumers who choose the biggest, most comfortable car regardless of price make up one market segment. Another market segment would be customers who care mainly about price and operating economy. It would be difficult to make one model of car that was the first choice of every consumer. Companies are wise to focus their efforts on meeting the distinct needs of one or more market segments.

### Differential advantage

Companies perform best in markets where they have a differential advantage. A **differential advantage** is a sustainable internal or external strength it has over its competitors. There are five chief sources of differential advantage.

1 ecu = UK£0.83

*Product*   In 1994, Anglo-Dutch Unilever launched Omo Power (Persil Power in the UK) in a failed attempt to increase their European market share. It cost over £200m to develop the 'revolutionary' new washing powder that used a manganese-technique to give it superior performance. Quality, design, uniqueness and newness are other product-based differential advantages.

*Position*   The Bartle Bogle Hegarty's *risqué* advertising of Häagen-Dazs positioned it as a premium ice for young people. The brand is being attacked by Unilever's Ranieri and Ben & Jerry's but advertising is being doubled and below-the-line effort used to hold the position. Media coverage has extended to *Face*, a young style magazine, and gay titles *Phase* and *Attitude*.

*Value chain*   A company can gain a differential advantage from any stage in the value chain. Unilever's Walls ice-cream has strengths at the end of the chain. Their ownership of freezers in some outlets has blocked Mars' sales of their new ice-cream confectionery. At the other end of the chain, de Beers' control of diamond supplies mean they dominate that trade.

*Organization*   The speed and flexibility of America's young electronics companies like Apple, Microsoft, Intel and Compaq have given them a great advantage over industrial giants in America, Europe and Japan. Philips, Olivetti, Bull, Siemens and IBM threw resources at the microcomputer market but have fared poorly against the American 'gazelles'.

*Finance*   The financial reserves and breadth of America's General Electric (GE) means they are a tough competitor for Britain's Rolls-Royce aero engines. GE is more able than Rolls-Royce to absorb the cash flow during the fifteen years it takes to develop a new aero engine. GE's wealth also enabled them to buy Ireland's troubled Guinness Peat Aviation, the world's leading aircraft-leasing company.

### Market targeting

After a company has defined market segments, it can enter one or many segments of a given market. **Market targeting** involves evaluating each market segment's attractiveness and selecting one or more segments to enter. A company should target segments in which it has a differential advantage over its competitors; where it can generate the greatest customer value and sustain it over time. A company with limited resources might decide to serve only one or a few special segments; this strategy limits sales, but can be very profitable. Alternatively, a company might choose to serve several related segments – perhaps those with different kinds of customers but with the same basic wants. Or perhaps a large company might decide to offer a complete range of products to serve all market segments.

Most companies enter a new market by serving a single segment, and if this proves successful, they add segments. Large companies eventually seek full market coverage. They want to be the 'General Motors' (GM) of their industry. America's GM says that it makes a car for every 'person, purse, and personality'. Similarly, Japan's Seiko are proud of their range of 2,500 watches designed to cover consumer segments across the world. The leading company normally has different products designed to meet the special needs of each segment.

### Positioning

After a company has decided which market segments to enter, it must decide what 'position' it wants to occupy in those segments. A **product's position** is the place the product occupies in consumers' minds. If a product were perceived to be exactly like another product on the market, consumers would have no reason to buy it.

**Market positioning** gives a product a clear, distinctive, and desirable place in the minds of target consumers compared with competing products. Marketers plan positions that distinguish their products from competing brands and give them the greatest strategic advantage in their target markets. For example, Ford says, 'Everything we do is driven by you'. Renault builds cars that 'take your breath away'. Mitsubishi's are 'designed to be driven'. 'You can't go wrong' with a Volvo, while GM's Vauxhall and Opel promise that, 'Once driven, forever smitten'. Jaguar is positioned as 'A blending of art and machine', whereas Saab is 'The most intelligent car ever built'. Mercedes is 'Engineered like no other car in the world'. BMW is 'the ultimate driving machine'. Rolls-Royce cars are 'Strictly for the wealthy arrived individual', while their equally luxurious Bentley is 'The closest a car can come to having wings'. Such simple statements are the backbone of a product's marketing strategy.

In positioning its product, the company first identifies possible competitive advantages upon which to build the position. To gain competitive advantage, the company must offer greater value to chosen target segments, either by charging lower prices than competitors or by offering more benefits to justify higher prices. However, if the company positions the product as *offering* greater value, it must *deliver* greater value. Effective positioning begins with actually *differentiating* the company's marketing offer so that it gives consumers more value than offered by the competition.

The company can position a product on only one important differentiating factor or on several. However, positioning on too many factors can result in consumer confusion or disbelief. Once the company has chosen a desired position, it must take steps to deliver and communicate that position to target consumers. The company's entire marketing programme should support the chosen positioning strategy.

## Marketing strategies for competitive advantage

To be successful, the company must do a better job than its competitors of satisfying target consumers. Thus marketing strategies embrace the needs of consumers and the strategies of competitors. The company must consider its size and industry position, then decide how to position itself to gain the strongest possible competitive advantage.

The design of competitive marketing strategies begins with competitor analysis. The company constantly compares the value and customer satisfaction delivered by its products, prices, channels, and promotion with that of its close competitors. In this way it can discern areas of potential advantage and disadvantage. The company must formally or informally monitor the competitive environment to answer these and other important questions such as: Who are our competitors? What are their objectives and strategies? What are their strengths and weaknesses? How will they react to different competitive strategies we might use?

Which competitive marketing strategy a company adopts depends on its industry position. A firm that dominates a market can adopt one or more of several **market leader** strategies. Well-known leaders include Chanel (fragrances), Coca-Cola (soft drinks), McDonald's (fast food), Komatsu (large construction equipment), Kodak (photographic film), Lego (construction toys) and Boeing (civil aircraft).

**Market challengers** are runner-up companies that aggressively attack competitors to get more market share. For example, Pepsi challenges Coke and Airbus challenges Boeing. The challenger might attack the market leader, other firms of its own size, or smaller local and regional competitors. Some runner-up firms will choose to follow rather than challenge the market leader. Firms using **market follower** strategies seek stable market shares and profit by following competitors' product offers, prices and marketing programmes.[14] Smaller firms in a market, or even larger firms that lack established positions, often adopt **market nicher** strategies. They specialize in serving market niches that large competitors overlook or ignore. Market nichers avoid direct confrontations with the big companies by specializing along market, customer, product or marketing-mix lines. Through smart niching, low-share firms in an industry can be as profitable as their large competitors.

## Developing the marketing mix

Once the company has chosen its overall competitive marketing strategy, it is ready to begin planning the details of the marketing mix. The marketing mix is one of the dominant ideas in modern marketing. We define **marketing mix** as the set of controllable tactical marketing tools that the firm blends to produce the response it wants in the target market. The marketing mix consists of everything the firm can do to influence the demand for its product. The many possibilities gather into four groups of variables known as the 'four Ps': *product*, *price*, *place*, and *promotion*.[15] Figure 3.8 shows the particular marketing tools under each P.

**Product** means the totality 'goods-and-service' that the company offers the target market. The Honda Civic 'product' is nuts, bolts, spark plugs, pistons, headlights and many other parts. Honda offers several Civic styles and dozens of optional features. The car comes fully serviced, with a comprehensive warranty and financing that is as much a part of the product as the exhaust-pipe. Increasingly the most profitable part of the business for car companies is the loan that they offer to car buyers.

**Price** is what customers pay to get the product. Honda suggests retail prices that its dealers might charge for each car but dealers rarely charge the full sticker price. Instead, they negotiate the price with each customer. They offer discounts, trade-in allowances and credit terms to adjust for the current competitive situation and to bring the price into line with the buyer's perception of the car's value.

**Place** includes company activities that make the product available to target consumers. Honda maintains a body of independently owned dealerships that sell the company's cars. They select dealers carefully and support them strongly. The main dealers keep a stock of Hondas, demonstrate them to potential buyers, negotiate prices, close sales, arrange finance, and service the cars after the sale.

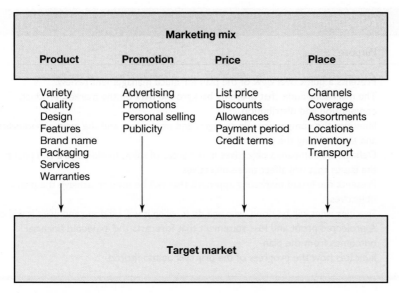

**Figure 3.8** The four Ps: the marketing mix.

**Promotion** means activities that communicate the merits of the product and persuade target customers to buy it. Honda spends millions on advertising each year to tell consumers about the company and its products. Dealership salespeople assist potential buyers and persuade them that a Honda is the car for them. Honda and its dealers offer special promotions – sales, cash rebates, low financing rates – as added purchase incentives.

An effective marketing programme blends the marketing mix elements into a co-ordinated programme designed to achieve the company's marketing objectives. The marketing mix constitutes the company's tactical tool kit for establishing strong positioning in target markets. However, note that the four Ps represent the sellers' view of the marketing tools available for influencing buyers. From a consumer viewpoint, each marketing tool must deliver a customer benefit. One marketing expert suggests that companies should view the four Ps as the customer's four Cs:[16]

| *Four Ps* | *Four Cs* |
| --- | --- |
| Product | Customer needs and wants |
| Price | Cost to the customer |
| Place | Convenience |
| Promotion | Communication |

Winning companies are those that meet customer needs economically and conveniently and with effective communication.

## THE BRAND PLAN

Each business, product or brand needs a detailed marketing plan. What does a marketing plan look like? Our discussion focuses on product or brand plans. A product or brand plan should contain the following sections: executive summary, current marketing situation, threats and opportunities, objectives and issues, marketing strategies, action programmes, budgets, and controls (see Table 3.1).

| TABLE 3.1 | *Contents of a marketing plan* |
|---|---|
| **Section** | **Purpose** |
| Executive summary | Presents a quick overview of the plan for quick management review. |
| Current marketing situation | The marketing audit that presents background data on the market, product, competition and distribution. |
| SWOT analysis | Identifies the company's main *strengths* and *weaknesses* and the main *opportunities* and *threats* facing the product. |
| Objectives and issues | Defines the company's objectives in the areas of sales, market share and profits, and the issues that will affect these objectives. |
| Marketing strategy | Presents the broad marketing approach that will be used to achieve the plan's objectives. |
| Action programmes | Specifies *what* will be done, *who* will do it, *when* it will be done and *what* it will cost. |
| Budgets | A projected profit and loss statement that forecasts the expected financial outcomes from the plan. |
| Controls | Indicates how the progress of the plan will be monitored. |

## Executive summary

The marketing plan should open with a short summary of the main goals and recommendations in the plan. Here is a short example:

> The 1996 Marketing Plan outlines an approach to attaining a significant increase in company sales and profits over the preceding year. The sales target is $240 million – a planned 20 per cent sales gain. We think this increase is attainable because of the improved economic, competitive, and distribution picture. The target operating margin is $25 million, a 25 per cent increase over last year. To achieve these goals, the sales promotion budget will be $4.8 million, or 2 per cent of projected sales. The advertising budget will be $7.2 million, or 3 per cent of projected sales. ... [more details follow]

The **executive summary** helps top management to find the plan's central points quickly. A table of contents should follow the executive summary.

## Marketing audit

The first main section of the plan describes the target market and the company's position in it (Table 3.2 gives the questions asked). It should start with the strategic imperatives: the pertinent objectives, policies and elements of strategy passed down from broader plans. In the **current marketing situation** section, the planner provides information about the market, product performance, competition, and distribution. It includes a *market description* that defines the market, including chief market segments. The planner shows market size, in total and by segment, for several past years, and then reviews customer needs together with factors in the marketing environment that may affect customer purchasing. Next, the *product review* shows sales, prices, and gross margins of the principal products in the product line. A section on *competition* identifies big competitors and their individual strategies for product quality, pricing, distribution, and promotion. It also shows the market shares held by the company and each competitor. Finally, a section on *distribution* describes recent sales trends and developments in the primary distribution channels.

Managing the marketing function would be hard enough if the marketer had to deal only with the controllable marketing-mix variables. Reality is harder. The company is in a complex marketing environment consisting of uncontrollable forces to which the company must adapt. The *environment* produces both threats and opportunities. The company must carefully analyse its environment so that it can avoid the threats and take advantage of the opportunities.

The company's marketing environment includes forces close to the company that affect its ability to serve its consumers, such as other company *departments*, *channel members*, *suppliers*, *competitors* and other *publics*. It also includes broader *demographic* and *economic* forces, *political* and *legal* forces, *technological* and *ecological* forces, and *social* and *cultural* forces. The company must consider all of these forces when developing and positioning its offer to the target market.

## SWOT analysis

This section draws from the market audit. It is a brief list of the *critical success factors* in the market, and rates strengths and weaknesses against the competition. The SWOT analysis should include costs and other nonmarketing variables. The outstanding opportunities and threats should be given. If plans depend upon assumption about the market, the economy or the competition, they need to be explicit.

## Objectives and issues

Having studied the strengths, weaknesses, opportunities and threats, the company sets objectives and considers issues that will affect them. The objectives are goals the company would like to attain during the plan's term. For example, the manager might want to achieve a 15 per cent market share, a 20 per cent pre-tax profit on sales, and a 25 per cent pre-tax profit on investment. If current market share is only 10 per cent, the question needs answering: Where are the extra sales to come from? From the competition, by increasing usage rate, by adding, and so on?

## Marketing strategy

In this section of the marketing plan, the manager outlines the broad marketing strategy or 'game plan' for attaining the objectives. **Marketing strategy** is the marketing logic by which the business unit hopes to achieve its marketing objectives. It shows how strategies for target markets and positioning build upon the firm's differential advantages. It should detail the market segments on which the company will focus. These segments differ in their needs and wants, responses to marketing, and profitability. The company should put its effort into those market segments it can best serve from a competitive point of view. It should develop a marketing strategy for each targeted segment.

## Marketing mix

The manager should also outline specific strategies for such marketing mix elements in each target market: new products, field sales, advertising, sales promotion, prices

**TABLE 3.2**    *Marketing audit questions*

# Marketing environment audit

## The macro-environment

1. *Demographic.* What primary demographic trends pose threats and opportunities for this company?
2. *Economic.* What developments in income, prices, savings, and credit will impact the company?
3. *Natural.* What is the outlook for costs and availability of natural resources and energy? Is the company environmentally responsible?
4. *Technology.* What technological changes are occurring? What is the company's position on technology?
5. *Political.* What current and proposed laws will affect company strategy?
6. *Cultural.* What is the public's attitude towards business and the company's products? What changes in consumer lifestyles might have an impact?

## The task environment

1. *Markets.* What is happening to market size, growth, geographic distribution and profits? What are the large market segments?
2. *Customers.* How do customers rate the company on product quality, service and price? How do they make their buying decisions?
3. *Competitors.* Who are the chief competitors? What are their strategies, market shares, and strengths and weaknesses?
4. *Channels.* What main channels does the company use to distribute products to customers? How are they performing?
5. *Suppliers.* What trends are affecting suppliers? What is the outlook for the availability of key production resources?
6. *Publics.* What key publics provide problems or opportunities? How should the company deal with these publics?

# Marketing strategy audit

1. *Mission.* Is the mission clearly defined and market-oriented?
2. *Objectives.* Has the company set clear objectives to guide marketing planning and performance? Do these objectives fit with the company's opportunities and strengths?
3. *Strategy.* Does the company have a sound marketing strategy for achieving its objectives?
4. *Budgets.* Has the company budgeted sufficient resources to segments, products, territories and marketing-mix elements?

# Marketing organization audit

1. *Formal structure.* Does the chief marketing officer have adequate authority over activities affecting customer satisfaction? Are activities optimally structured along functional, product, market and territory lines?
2. *Functional efficiency.* Do marketing, sales and other staff communicate effectively? Are the staff well trained, supervised, motivated and evaluated?
3. *Interface efficiency.* Do staff work well across functions: marketing with manufacturing, R&D, buying, personnel, etc.?

# Marketing systems audit

1. *Marketing information system.* Is the marketing intelligence system providing accurate and timely information about developments? Are decision makers using marketing research effectively?
2. *Planning system.* Does the company prepare annual, long-term and strategic plans? Are they used?
3. *Marketing control system.* Are annual plan objectives being achieved? Does management periodically analyse the sales and profitability of products, markets, territories and channels?
4. *New-product development.* Is the company well organized to gather, generate and screen new-product ideas? Does it carry out adequate product and market testing? Has the company succeeded with new products?

| Table 3.2 (cont) |
| --- |

**Productivity audit**

1. *Profitability analysis.* How profitable are the company's different products, markets, territories and channels? Should the company enter, expand or withdraw from any business segments? What would be the consequences?
2. *Cost-effectiveness analysis.* Do any activities have excessive costs? How can costs be reduced?

**Marketing function audit**

1. *Products.* Has the company developed sound product-line objectives? Should some products be phased out? Should some new products be added? Would some products benefit from quality, style, or feature changes?
2. *Price.* What are the company's pricing objectives, policies, strategies and procedures? Are the company's prices in line with customers' perceived value? Are price promotions used properly?
3. *Distribution.* What are the distribution objectives and strategies? Does the company have adequate market coverage and service? Should existing channels be changed or new ones added?
4. *Advertising, sales promotion and publicity.* What are the company's promotion objectives? How is the budget determined? Is it sufficient? Are advertising messages and media well developed and received? Does the company have well-developed sales promotion and public relations programmes?
5. *Salesforce.* What are the company's salesforce objectives? Is the salesforce large enough? Is it properly organized? Is it well trained, supervised, and motivated? How is the salesforce rated relative to those of competitors?

and distribution. The manager should explain how each strategy responds to the threats, opportunities, and critical issues described earlier in the plan.

## Action programmes

Marketing strategies become specific action programmes that answer the following questions: *What* will be done? *When* will it be done? *Who* is responsible for doing it? *How much* will it cost? For example, the manager may want to increase sales promotion as a key strategy for winning market share. A sales promotion action plan should outline special offers and their dates, trade shows entered, new point-of-purchase displays and other promotions. The action plan shows when activities will start, be reviewed, and be completed.

## Budgets

Action plans allow the manager to make a supporting **marketing budget** that is essentially a projected profit and loss statement. For revenues, it shows the forecast unit sales and the average net price. On the expense side, it shows the cost of production, physical distribution, and marketing. The difference is the projected profit. Higher management will review the budget and either approve or modify it. Once approved, the budget is the basis for materials buying, production scheduling, personnel planning, and marketing operations. Budgeting can be very difficult, and budgeting methods range from simple 'rules of thumb' to complex computer models.[17]

## Controls

The last section of the plan outlines the controls that will monitor progress. Typically, there are goals and budgets for each month or quarter. This practice allows higher management to review the results each period and to spot businesses or products that are not meeting their goals. The managers of these businesses and products have to explain these problems and the corrective actions they will take.

## Implementation

Planning good strategies is only a start towards successful marketing. A brilliant marketing strategy counts for little if the company fails to implement it properly. **Marketing implementation** is the process that turns marketing strategies and *plans* into marketing *actions* to accomplish strategic marketing objectives. Implementation involves day-to-day, month-to-month activities that effectively put the marketing plan to work. Whereas marketing planning addresses the *what* and *why* of marketing activities, implementation addresses the *who*, *where*, *when*, and *how*.

## MARKETING ORGANIZATION

The company must have people that can carry out marketing analysis, planning, implementation and control. If the company is very small, one person might do all the marketing work – research, selling, advertising, customer service, and other activities. As the company expands, organizations emerge to plan and carry out marketing activities. In large companies there can be many specialists: brand managers, salespeople and sales managers, market researchers, advertising experts, and other specialists.

Modern marketing activities occur in several forms. The most common form is the *functional organization* in which functional specialists head different marketing activities – a sales manager, advertising manager, marketing research manager, customer service manager, new-product manager. A company that sells across the country or internationally often uses a *geographic organization* in which its sales and marketing people run specific countries, regions, and districts. A geographic organization allows salespeople to settle into a territory, get to know their customers, and work with a minimum of travel time and cost.

Companies with many, very different products or brands often create a *product management* or *brand management* organization. Using this approach, a manager develops and implements a complete strategy and marketing programme for a specific product or brand. Product management first appeared in Procter & Gamble in 1929. A new soap, Camay, was not doing well, and a young P&G executive was assigned to give his exclusive attention to developing and promoting this brand. He was successful, and the company soon added other product managers. Since then, many organizations, especially in the food, soap, toiletries, and chemical industries, have introduced the brand management system, which is in widespread use today.

Recent dramatic changes in the marketing environment have caused many companies to rethink the role of the product manager. Today's consumers face an ever-growing set of brands and are now more deal-prone than brand-prone. As a result, companies are shifting away from national advertising in favour of pricing and other point-of-sale promotions. Brand managers have traditionally focused on long-term, brand-building strategies targeting a mass audience, but today's marketplace realities demand shorter-term, sales-building strategies designed for local markets.

A second significant force affecting brand management is the growing power of retailers. Larger, more powerful, and better-informed retailers are now demanding and getting more trade promotions in exchange for their scarce shelf space. The increase in trade promotion spending leaves fewer dollars for national advertising, the brand manager's primary marketing tool.

To cope with this change Campbell Soups created *brand sales managers*. These combine product manager and sales roles charged with handling brands in the field, working with the trade, and designing more localized brand strategies. The managers spend more time in the field working with salespeople, learning what is happening in stores, and getting closer to the customer.

Other companies, including Colgate-Palmolive, Procter & Gamble, Kraft and Lever Bros., have adopted *category management*. Under this system, brand managers report to a category manager who has total responsibility for an entire product line. For example, at Procter & Gamble, the brand manager for Dawn liquid dishwashing detergent reports to a manager who is responsible for Dawn, Ivory, Joy, and all other light-duty liquid detergents. The light-duty liquids manager, in turn, reports to a manager who is responsible for all of P&G's packaged soaps and detergents, including dishwashing detergents, and liquid and dry laundry detergents. This offers many advantages. First, the category managers have broader planning perspectives than brand managers do. Rather than focusing on specific brands, they shape the company's entire category offering. Second, it better matches the buying processes of retailers. Recently, retailers have begun making their individual buyers responsible for working with all suppliers of a specific product category. A category management system links up better with this new retailer 'category buying' system.

Some companies, including Nabisco, have started combining category management with another idea: *brand teams* or *category teams*. Instead of having several brand managers, Nabisco has three teams covering biscuits – one each for adult rich, nutritional biscuits, and children's biscuits. Headed by a category manager, each category team includes several marketing people-brand managers, a sales planning manager and a marketing information specialist handling brand strategy, advertising, and sales promotion. Each team also includes specialists from other company departments: a finance manager, a research and development specialist, and representatives from manufacturing, engineering, and distribution. Thus category managers act as a small business, with complete responsibility for the performance of the category and with a full complement of people to help them plan and implement category marketing strategies.

For companies that sell one product line to many different types of markets that have different needs and preferences, a *market management organization* might be best. Many companies are organized along market lines. A market management organization is similar to the product management organization. Market managers are responsible for developing long-range and annual plans for the sales and profits in their markets. This system's main advantage is that the company is organized around the needs of specific customer segments.

In 1992 Elida Gibbs, Unilever's personal care products division, scrapped both brand manager and sales development roles. They had many strong brands, including Pears, Fabergé Brut, Signal and Timotei, but sought to improve their service to retailers and pay more attention to developing the brands. To do this they created two new roles: brand development managers and customer development managers. *Customer development managers* work closely with customers and have also taken over many of the old responsibilities of brand management. This provides an opportunity for better coordination of sales, operations and marketing campaigns. The change leaves *brand development managers* with more time to spend on the strategic development of brands and innovation. They have the authority to pull together technical and managerial resources to see projects through to their completion.

Elida Gibbs' reorganization goes beyond sales and marketing. Cross-functional teamwork is central to the approach and this extends to the shop floor. The company is already benefiting from the change. Customer development managers have increased the number of correctly completed orders from 72 per cent to 90 per cent. In addition, brand development managers developed Aquatonic – an aerosol deodorant – in six months, less than half the usual time.[18]

## MARKETING CONTROL

Because many surprises occur during the implementation of marketing plans, the marketing department must engage in constant marketing control. **Marketing control** is the process of measuring and evaluating the results of marketing strategies and plans and taking corrective action to ensure the achievement of marketing objectives. It involves the four steps shown in Figure 3.9. Management first sets specific marketing goals. It then measures its performance in the marketplace and evaluates the causes of any differences between expected and actual performance. Finally, management takes corrective action to close the gaps between its goals and its performance. This may require changing the action programmes or even changing the goals.

**Operating control** involves checking ongoing performance against the annual plan and taking corrective action when necessary. Its purpose is to ensure that the company achieves the sales, profits, and other goals set out in its annual plan. It also involves determining the profitability of different products, territories, markets, and channels. **Strategic control** involves looking at whether the company's basic strategies match its opportunities and strengths. Marketing strategies and programmes can

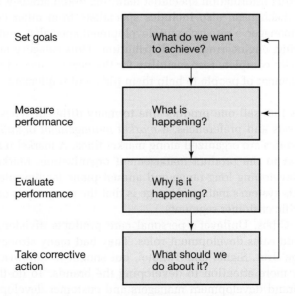

**Figure 3.9**    The control process.

quickly become outdated and each company should periodically reassess its overall approach to the marketplace. Besides providing the background for marketing planning, a **marketing audit** can also be a positive tool for strategic control. Sometimes it is conducted by an objective and experienced outside party who is independent of the marketing department. Table 3.2 shows the kind of questions the marketing auditor might ask. The findings may come as a surprise – and sometimes as a shock – to management. Management then decides which actions make sense and how and when to implement them.

## Implementing marketing

Many managers think that 'doing things right' (implementation) is as important, or even more important, than 'doing the right things' (strategy):

> A surprisingly large number of very successful large companies … don't have long-term strategic plans with an obsessive preoccupation on rivalry. They concentrate on operating details and doing things well. Hustle is their style and their strategy. They move fast and they get it right. … Countless companies in all industries, young or old, mature or booming, are finally learning the limits of strategy and concentrating on tactics and execution.[19]

Implementation is difficult – it is easier to think up good marketing strategies than it is to carry them out.

People at all levels of the marketing system must work together to implement marketing plans and strategies. Marketing implementation requires day-to-day decisions and actions by thousands of people both inside and outside the organization. Marketing managers make decisions about target segments, branding, packaging, pricing, promoting, and distributing. They work with people elsewhere in the company to get support for their products and programmes. They talk to engineering about product design, with manufacturing about production and inventory levels, and with finance about funding and cash flows. They also work with outside people. They meet with advertising agencies to plan ad campaigns and with the media to obtain publicity support. The salesforce urges retailers to advertise, say, Nestlé's products, provide ample shelf space and use company displays.

Successful implementation depends on several key elements. First, it requires an *action programme* that pulls all the people and activities together. The action programme shows what must be done, who will do it, and how decisions and actions will be coordinated. Second, the company's formal *organization structure* plays an important role in implementing marketing strategy. In their study of successful companies, Peters and Waterman found that these firms tended to have simple, flexible structures that allowed them to adapt quickly to changing conditions.[20] Their structures also tended to be more informal – Hewlett-Packard's MBWA (management by walking around), 3M's 'clubs' to create small-group interaction, and Nokia's youthful, egalitarian culture.[21] However, the structures used by these companies may not be right for other types of firms, and many of the study's excellent companies have had to change their structures as their strategies and situations changed. For example, the same informal structure that made Hewlett-Packard so successful caused problems later. The company has since moved towards a more formal structure (see Marketing Highlight 3.4).

Another factor affecting successful implementation is the company's **decision-and-reward systems** – formal and informal operating procedures that guide planning, budgeting, compensation, and other activities. For example, if a company

**MARKETING HIGHLIGHT 3.4**

## Hewlett-Packard's structure evolves

In 1939, two engineers, Bill Hewlett and David Packard, started Hewlett-Packard in a Palo Alto garage to build test equipment. At the start, Bill and Dave did everything themselves, from designing and building their equipment to marketing it. As the firm grew out of the garage and began to offer more and different types of test equipment, Hewlett and Packard could no longer make all the necessary operating decisions themselves. They hired functional managers to run various company activities. These managers were relatively autonomous, but they were still closely tied to the owners.

By the mid-1970s, Hewlett-Packard's forty-two divisions employed more than 30,000 people. The company's structure evolved to support its heavy emphasis on innovation and autonomy. Each division operated as an autonomous unit and was responsible for its own strategic planning, product development, marketing programmes, and implementation.

In 1982, Peters and Waterman, in their book *In Search of Excellence*, cited HP's structure as an important reason for the company's continued excellence. They praised HP's nonrestrictive structure and high degree of informal communication (its MBWA style – management by wandering around) that fostered autonomy by decentralizing decision-making responsibility and authority. The approach became known as the 'HP Way', a structure that encouraged innovation by abolishing rigid chains of command and putting managers and employees on a first-name basis.

But by the mid-1980s, although still profitable, Hewlett-Packard had begun to encounter problems in the fast-changing microcomputer and minicomputer markets. According to *Business Week*:

> Hewlett-Packard's famed innovative culture and decentralization [had] spawned such enormously

successful products as its 3000 minicomputer, the hand-held scientific calculator, and the ThinkJet non-impact printer. But when a new climate required its fiercely autonomous divisions to co-operate in product development and marketing, HP's passionate devotion to 'autonomy and entrepreneurship' that Peters and Waterman advocate became a hindrance.

Thus Hewlett-Packard moved to change its structure and culture in order to bring them in line with its changing situation. It established a system of committees to foster communication within and across its many and varied divisions and to coordinate product development, marketing, and other activities.

The new structure seemed to work well, for a while. However, the move towards centralization soon got out of hand:

> The committees kept multiplying, like a virus. [Soon] everything was by committee ... no one could make a decision. ... By the late 1980s, an unwieldy bureaucracy had bogged down the HP Way. A web of committees, originally designed to foster communication ... had pushed costs up and slowed down development.

Entering the 1990s, HP had no fewer than 38 in-house committees that made decisions on everything from technical specifications for new products to the best cities for staging product launches. This suffocating structure dramatically increased HP's decision-making and market-reaction time. For example, in one case, it took almost 100 people over seven weeks just to come up with a name for the company's New Wave Computing software.

In the fast-paced workstation and personal computer markets, HP's sluggish decision making put it at a serious disadvantage against such nimble competi-

---

compensates managers for short-run results, they will have little incentive to work towards long-run objectives. Companies recognizing this are broadening their incentive systems to include more than sales volume. For instance, Xerox rewards include customer satisfaction and Ferrero's the freshness of their chocolates in stores. Effective implementation also requires careful planning. At all levels, the company must fill its structure and systems with people who have the necessary skills, motivation, and personal characteristics. In recent years, more and more companies have

Hewlett-Packard began in this garage in 1939; now it operates around the world from this headquarters complex. Structure and culture changed with growth.

tors as Compaq Computer Corporation and Sun Microsystems. In 1990, when one of HP's most important projects, a series of high-speed workstations, slipped a year behind schedule as a result of seemingly endless meetings about technical decisions, top management finally took action. It removed the project's 200 engineers from the formal management structure so that they could continue work on the project free of the usual committee red tape. The workstation crisis convinced HP management that it must make similar changes throughout the company.

The cure was the company's most drastic reorganisation in 10 years. [Top management] wiped out

HP's committee structure and flattened the organisation. 'The results are incredible,' says [HP executive Bob] Frankenberg, who now deals with three committees instead of 38. 'We are doing more business and getting product out quicker with fewer people.'

Thus, in less than a decade, Hewlett-Packard's structure has evolved from the highly decentralized and informal 'HP Way' to a highly centralized committee system and back again to a point in between. HP is not likely to find a single best structure that will satisfy all of its future needs. Rather, it must continue adapting its structure to suit the requirements of its ever-changing environment.

Sources:     See Donald F. Harvey, *Business Policy and Strategic Management* (Columbus, OH: Merrill, 1982), 269–70; and Thomas J. Peters and Robert H. Waterman, *In Search of Excellence: Lessons from America's best-run companies* (New York: Harper & Row, 1982). Excerpts from 'Who's excel-

lent now?' *Business Week* (5 November 1984), 76–8; Barbara Buell, Robert D. Hof, and Gary McWilliams, 'Hewlett-Packard rethinks itself', *Business Week* (1 April 1991), 76–9; and Robert D. Hof, 'Suddenly, Hewlett-Packard is doing everything right', *Business Week* (23 March 1992), 88–9.

recognized that long-run human resources planning can give the company a strong competitive advantage.

Finally, for successful implementation, the firm's marketing strategies must fit with its culture. *Company culture* is a system of values and beliefs shared by people in an organization. It is the company's collective identity and meaning. The culture informally guides the behaviour of people at all company levels. Marketing strategies that do not fit the company's style and culture will be difficult to implement.

Because managerial style and culture are so hard to change, companies usually design strategies that fit their current cultures rather than trying to change their styles and cultures to fit new strategies.[22]

Thus successful marketing implementation depends on how well the company blends the five elements – action programmes, organization structure, decision-and-reward systems, human resources, and company culture – into a cohesive programme that supports its strategies.

## SUMMARY

*Strategic planning* involves developing a strategy for long-run survival and growth. Marketing helps in strategic planning, and the overall strategic plan defines marketing's role in the company. Not all companies use formal planning or use it well, yet formal planning offers several benefits. Companies develop three kinds of plans: *annual plans*, *long-range plans*, and *strategic plans*.

Each of the company's *functional departments* provides inputs for strategic planning. Each department has a different idea about which objectives and activities are most important. The marketing department stresses the consumer's point of view. Marketing managers must understand the point of view of the company's other functions and work with other functional managers to develop a system of plans that will best accomplish the firm's overall strategic objectives.

Strategic planning sets the stage for the rest of company planning. The strategic planning process consists of developing the company's mission, understanding a company's strengths and weaknesses, its environment, business portfolio, objectives and goals, and functional plans. Developing a sound *mission statement* is a challenging undertaking. The mission statement should be market-oriented, feasible, motivating, and specific, if it is to direct the firm to its best opportunities.

Companies have plans at many levels: global, regional, national, and so forth. The higher-level plans contain objectives and strategies that become part of subordinate plans. These *strategic imperatives* are objectives or defined practices. At each level a *strategic audit* reviews the company and its environment. A *SWOT analysis* summarizes the main elements of this audit into a statement of the company's strengths and weaknesses and the chief threats and opportunities that exist.

From here, strategic planning calls for analysing the company's *business portfolio* and deciding which businesses should receive more or fewer resources. The company might use a formal portfolio-planning method like the *BCG growth-share matrix* or the *General Electric grid*. However, most companies are now designing more customized portfolio-planning approaches that better suit their unique situations.

This analysis and mission lead to strategic objectives and goals. Management must decide how to achieve growth and profits objectives. The *strategic focus* shows how this depends upon increasing either productivity or volume. The *product/market expansion grid* shows four avenues for market growth: *market penetration*, *market development*, *product development*, and *diversification*.

Once strategic objectives and strategies are defined, management must prepare a set of *functional plans* that coordinates the activities of the marketing, finance, manufacturing, and other departments.

To fulfil their role in the organization, marketers engage in the *marketing process*. Consumers are at the centre of the marketing process. The company divides the total market into smaller segments and selects the segments it can best serve. It then designs its *marketing mix* in order to differentiate its marketing offer and to position this offer in selected target segments. To find the best mix and put it into action, the company engages in marketing analysis, marketing planning, marketing implementation, and marketing control.

Each business must prepare marketing plans for its products, brands, and markets. The main components of a *marketing plan* are the executive summary, current marketing situation, threats and opportunities, objectives and issues, marketing strategies, action programmes, budgets, and controls. To plan good strategies is often easier than to carry them out. To be successful, companies must implement the strategies effectively. *Implementation* is the process that turns marketing strategies into marketing actions. The process consists of five key elements.

1. The *action programme* identifies crucial tasks and decisions needed to implement the marketing plan, assigns them to specific people, and establishes a timetable.
2. The *organization structure* defines tasks and assignments and coordinates the efforts of the company's people and units.
3. The company's *decision-and-reward systems* guide activities like planning, information, budgeting, training, control and personnel evaluation and rewards. Well-designed action programmes, organization structures, and decision-and-reward systems can encourage good implementation.
4. Successful implementation also requires careful *human resources planning*. The company must recruit, allocate, develop, and maintain good people.
5. The firm's *company culture* can also make or break implementation. Company culture guides people in the company; good implementation relies on strong, clearly defined cultures that fit the chosen strategy.

Most of the responsibility for implementation goes to the company's marketing department. Modern marketing activities occur in a number of ways. The most common form is the *functional marketing organization*, in which marketing functions are directed by separate managers who report to the marketing director. The company might also use a *geographic organization* in which its sales force or other functions specialize by geographic area. The company may also use the *product management organization*, in which products are assigned to product managers who work with functional specialists to develop and achieve their plans. Another form is the *market management organization*, in which main markets are assigned to market managers who work with functional specialists.

Marketing organizations carry out marketing control. *Operating control* involves monitoring results to secure the achievement of annual sales and profit goals. It also calls for determining the profitability of the firm's products, territories, market segments, and channels. *Strategic control* makes sure that the company's marketing objectives, strategies, and systems fit with the current and forecast marketing environment. It uses the *marketing audit* to determine marketing opportunities and problems, and to recommend short-run and long-run actions to improve overall marketing performance. The company uses these resources to watch and adapt to the marketing environment.

# ■ DISCUSSING THE ISSUES

1. What are the benefits of a long-range plan? Why should managers take time to develop a long-term plan that will be changed every year?

2. Many companies undertake a marketing audit to identify the firm's strengths and weaknesses relative to competitors, and in relation to the opportunities and threats in the external environment. Why is it important that such an analysis should address relative, not absolute, company strengths and weaknesses?

3. An electronics manufacturer obtains the semiconductors it uses in production from a company-owned subsidiary that also sells to other manufacturers. The subsidiary is smaller and less profitable than are the competing products. Its growth rate has been below the industry average during the past five years. Into what cell of the BCG growth-share matrix does this strategic business unit fall? What should the parent company do with this SBU?

4. A consumer electronics company finds that sales in its main product line – video cassette recorders – are beginning to stabilize. The market is reaching maturity. What growth strategies might the firm pursue for this product line? How might the strategic-focus tool help managers examine the growth opportunities for this line?

5. The General Electric strategic business-planning grid gives a broad overview that can be helpful in strategic decision making. For what types of decisions would this grid be helpful? For what types of strategic decisions would it be less useful?

6. Sony is the market leader in audio-hifi systems, offering a wide range of equipment at moderately high prices. Discuss how a competitor would use market-challenger, market-follower and market-nicher strategies to compete effectively with Sony.

# ■ APPLYING THE CONCEPTS

1. Think about the shopping area near where you live. Assume that you wish to start a business here and are looking for a promising opportunity for a restaurant, a clothing store or a music store.

   ■ Is there an opportunity to open a distinctive and promising business? Describe your target market and how you will serve it differently than current businesses do.
   ■ What sort of marketing mix would you use for your business?

2. Take a product or service organization you are familiar with (you may refer to your college or university).

   ■ List the key external environmental opportunities or threats that face the organization.
   ■ What do you think are the organization's main strengths and weaknesses?
   ■ Suggest ways in which the organization might respond to the external forces.
   ■ Recommend a possible marketing strategy which will ensure that the organization matches its internal capabilities with external opportunities.

# ■ REFERENCES

1. See 'Dockers muscle in on Sweden with the world's biggest advertisement', *The European* (1–7 April 1994), 21; 'Levi's: the jeans giant slipped as the market shifted', *Business Week* (5 November 1984), 79–80; Miriam Rozen, 'The 501 blues', *Madison Avenue* (November 1984), 22–6; Marc Beauchamp, 'Tight fit', *Forbes* (11 August 1986); Joshua Hyatt, 'Levi Strauss learns a fitting lesson', *Inc.* (August 1985), 17; Brenton R. Schlender, 'How Levi Strauss did an LBO right', *Fortune* (7 May 1990), 105–7; Maria Shao, 'For Levi's, a flattering fit overseas', *Business Week* (5 November 1990),

76–7; 'A comfortable fit', *The Economist* (22 June 1991), 67–8; Marcy Magiera and Pat Sloan, 'Levi's, Lee loosen up for baby boomers', *Advertising Age* (3 August 1992), 9; and Marcy Magiera, 'Levi's Dockers looks for younger, upscale men with authentics', *Advertising Age* (18 January 1993), 4.
2. Malcolm MacDonald investigates the barriers to marketing planning in his article 'Ten barriers to marketing planning', *Journal of Marketing Management*, 5, 1 (1989), 1–18.
3. To see how planning and entrepreneurship exist side by side and how the best-performing companies have

balanced orientation towards marketing and technology, see Veronica Wong and John Saunders, 'Business orientation and corporate success', *Journal of Strategic Marketing*, 1, 1 (1993), 20–40.

4. John C. Narver and Stanley F. Slater, 'The effect of a market orientation on business profitability', *Journal of Marketing* (October 1990), 20–35.

5. 'Quality '93: empowering people with technology', advertising supplement, *Fortune* (20 September 1993). For more reading, see Yoram Wind, 'Marketing and the other business function', in Jagdish N. Sheth (ed.), *Research in Marketing*, vol. 5 (Greenwich, CT: JAI Press, 1981), 237–56: Robert W. Ruekert and Orville C. Walker, Jr., 'Marketing's interaction with other functional units: a conceptual framework and empirical evidence', *Journal of Marketing* (January 1987), 1–19.

6. Michael E. Porter, *Competitive Advantage: Creating and sustaining competitive performance* (New York: Free Press, 1985).

7. For more on mission statements, see G. Hooley and Laura Nash, 'Mission statements – mirrors and windows', *Harvard Business Review* (Mar.–Apr. 1988), 155–6; and Fred R. David, 'How companies define their missions statements', *Long Range Planning*, 22, 1 (1989), 90–7.

8. Michael Porter popularized his view of value chains through his book *Competitive Advantage*, *op. cit.*

9. Kenneth Goading, 'High speed steel group rolls towards floatation', *Financial Times* (24 June 1994), 27.

10. See Daniel H. Gray, 'Uses and misuses of strategic planning', *Harvard Business Review* (Jan.–Feb. 1986), 89–96; and Roger A. Kerin, Vijay Mahajan, and P. Rajan Varadarajan, *Contemporary Perspectives on Strategic Planning* (Boston: Allyn & Bacon, 1990).

11. Richard G. Hamermesh, 'Making planning strategic', *Harvard Business Review* (July–Aug. 1986), 115–20.

12. Information taken from: Guy de Jonquières, 'Pell-mell expansion has sparked controversy', *Financial Times* (11 June 1991), 8; and Christopher Parkes, 'New car plant will be test for "lean production"', *Financial Times* (25 June 1992), 4.

13. H. Igor Ansoff, 'Strategies for diversification', *Harvard Business Review* (Sept.–Oct. 1957), 113–24.

14. For more on follower strategies, see Daniel W. Haines, Rajan Chandran, and Arvind Parkhe, 'Winning by being

first to market…or second?', *Journal of Consumer Marketing* (winter 1989), 63–9.

15. The four-P classification was first suggested by E. Jerome McCarthy, *Basic Marketing: A managerial approach* (Homewood, IL: Irwin, 1960). For more discussion of this classification scheme, see Walter van Waterschoot and Christophe Van den Bulte, 'The 4P classification of the marketing mix revisited', *Journal of Marketing* (October 1992), 83–93.

16. Robert Lauterborn, 'New marketing litany: four P's passé; C-words take over', *Advertising Age* (1 October 1990), 26.

17. For an interesting discussion of marketing budgeting methods and processes, see Nigel F. Piercy, 'The marketing budgeting process: marketing management implications', *Journal of Marketing* (October 1987), 45–59.

18. See Robert Dewar and Don Schultz, 'The product manager: an idea whose time has gone', *Marketing Communications* (May 1989), 28–35; Kevin T. Higgins, 'Category management: new tool changing life for manufacturers and retailers', *Marketing News* (25 September 1989), 2, 19; Ira Teinowitz, 'Brand managers: 90s dinosaurs?', *Advertising Age* (19 December 1988); Betsey Spethman, 'Category management multiplies', *Advertising Age* (11 May 1992), 42; Guy de Jonquières, 'A clean break with tradition', *Financial Times* (12 July 1993), 12.

19. Amar Bhide, 'Hustle as strategy', *Harvard Business Review* (Sept.–Oct. 1986), 59.

20. See Thomas J. Peters and Robert H. Waterman, *In Search of Excellence: Lessons from America's best-run companies* (New York: Harper & Row, 1982). For an excellent summary of the study's findings on structure, see David A. Aaker, *Strategic Market Management*, 2nd edn (New York: Wiley, 1988), 154–7.

21. Greg McIvor, 'Nokia becomes a world leader', *The European* (26 Aug.–6 Sept. 1994), 28.

22. For more on company cultures, see Rohit Deshpande and Frederick E. Webster, Jr., 'Organizational culture and marketing: defining the research agenda', *Journal of Marketing* (January 1989), 3–15; Brian Dumaine, 'Creating a new company culture', *Fortune* (15 January 1990), 127–31; and John P. Kotter and James L. Heskett, *Corporate Culture and Performance* (New York: Free Press, 1992).

## Trap-Ease: the big cheese of mousetraps

One April morning, Martha House, president of Trap-Ease, entered her office. She paused for a moment to contemplate the Ralph Waldo Emerson quote which she had framed and hung near her desk: 'If a man [can]… make a better mousetrap than his neighbour… the world will make a beaten path to his door.' Perhaps, she mused, Emerson knew something that she did not. She *had* a better mouse-trap – Trap-Ease – but the world was not all that excited about it.

Martha had just returned from the National Hardware Show. Standing in the trade show display booth for long hours and answering the same questions hundreds of times had been tiring. Yet this show had excited her. Each year, National Hardware Show officials hold a contest to select the best new product introduced at the show. Of the more than 300 new products introduced at that year's show, her mousetrap had won first place. Such notoriety was not new for the Trap-Ease mousetrap. It had featured in *People* magazine and had been the subject of numerous talk shows and articles in various popular press and trade publications. Despite all this atten-tion, however, the expected demand for the trap had not materialized. Martha hoped that this award might stimulate increased interest and sales.

A group of investors who had obtained worldwide rights to market the innovative mousetrap had formed Trap-Ease in January. In return for marketing rights, the group agreed to pay the inventor and patent holder, a retired rancher, a royalty fee for each trap sold. The group then hired Martha to serve as president and to develop and manage the Trap-Ease organization.

The Trap-Ease is a simple yet clever device made by a plastics firm under contract for Trap-Ease. It consists of a square, plastic tube measuring about 15 cm long and 4 cm square. The tube bends in the mid-dle at a 30-degree angle, so that when the front part of the tube rests on a flat surface, the other end is elevated. The elevated end holds a removable cap for the bait (cheese, dog food or some other titbit). A hinged door is at the front end of the tube. When the trap is 'open', this door rests on two narrow 'stilts' attached to the two bottom corners of the door.

The trap works with simple efficiency. A mouse, smelling the bait, enters the tube through the open end. As it walks up the angled bottom towards the bait, its weight makes the elevated end of the trap drop downward. This elevates the open end, allowing the hinged door to swing closed, trapping the mouse. Small teeth on the ends of the stilts catch in a groove on the bottom of the trap, locking the door closed. The mouse is disposed of live or left alone for a few hours to suffocate in the trap.

Martha felt the trap had many advantages for the consumer when compared with traditional spring-loaded traps or poisons. Consumers can use it safely and easily with no risk of catching their fingers while loading it. It poses no injury or poisoning threat to children or pets. Furthermore, with Trap-Ease, con-sumers can avoid the unpleasant 'mess' with the vio-lent spring-loaded traps – it creates no 'clean-up' problem. Finally, consumers can reuse or throw away the trap.

Martha's early research suggested that women are the best target market for the Trap-Ease. Men are more willing to buy and use the traditional, spring-loaded trap. The targeted women, however, do not like the traditional trap. They often stay at home and take care of their children. Thus they want a means of dealing with the mouse problem that avoids the unpleasantness and risks that the standard trap cre-ates in the home.

To reach this target market, Martha decided to distribute Trap-Ease through national grocery, hard-ware and drug chains such as Safeway and CB Drug. She sold the trap directly to these large retailers, avoiding any wholesalers or other go-betweens. The traps sold in packages of two, with a suggested retail price of $2.49.* Although this price made the Trap-Ease five to ten times more expensive than smaller, standard traps, consumers appeared to offer little in-itial price resistance. The manufacturing cost for the Trap-Ease, including freight and packaging costs, was about 31 cents per unit. The company paid an addi-tional 8.2 cents per unit in royalty fees. Martha priced the traps to retailers at 99 cents per unit and esti-mated that, after sales and volume discounts, Trap-

*1 ecu = US$1.26.

**CASE 3 (cont)**

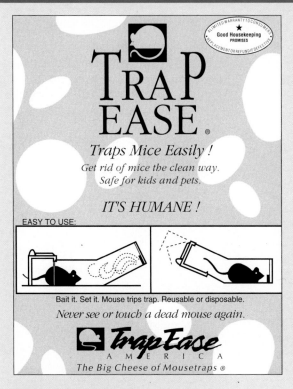

Exhibit 3.1   Trap-Ease advertisement

Ease would realize net revenues from retailers of 75 cents per unit.

To promote the product, Martha had budgeted approximately $60,000 for the first year. She planned to use $50,000 of this amount for travel costs to visit trade shows and to make sales calls on retailers. She would use the remaining $10,000 for advertising. So far, however, because the mousetrap had generated so much publicity, she had not felt that she needed to do much advertising. Still, she had placed advertising in *Good Housekeeping* and in other 'home and shelter' magazines (Exhibit 3.1). Martha was the company's only 'salesperson', but she intended to hire more salespeople soon.

Martha had initially forecasted Trap-Ease's first year's sales at five million units. Through April, however, the company had sold only several hundred thousand units. Martha wondered if most new products got off to such a slow start or if she was doing something wrong. She had detected some problems, although none seemed too serious. For one, there had not been enough repeat buying. For another, she

had noted that many of the retailers kept their sample mousetraps on their desks as conversation pieces, whereas she wanted the traps used and demonstrated. Martha wondered if consumers were also buying the traps as novelties rather than as solutions to their mouse problems.

Martha knew that the investor group believed that Trap-Ease had a 'once-in-a-lifetime' with its innovative mousetrap. She sensed the group's impatience. She had budgeted approximately $250,000 in administrative and fixed costs for the first year (not including marketing costs). To keep the investors happy, the company needed to sell enough traps to cover those costs and make a reasonable profit.

In these first few months, Martha had learned that marketing new products is not an easy task. For example, one national retailer had placed a large order with instructions for delivery to the loading dock at one of its warehouses between 1 p.m. and 3 p.m. on a specified day. When the truck delivering the order had arrived late, the retailer had refused to accept the shipment. The retailer told Martha it would be a year before she got another chance. Perhaps, Martha thought, she should send the retailer and other customers a copy of Emerson's famous quotation.

### Questions

1. Martha and the Trap-Ease investors feel they face a 'once-in-a-lifetime' opportunity. What information do they need to evaluate this opportunity? How do you think the group would write its mission statement? How would you write it?

2. Has Martha identified the best target market for Trap-Ease? What other market segments might the firm target?

3. How has the company positioned the Trap-Ease in its chosen target market? Could it position the product in other ways?

4. Describe the current marketing mix for Trap-Ease. Do you see any problems with this mix?

5. Who is Trap-Ease's competition?

6. How would you change Trap-Ease's marketing strategy? What kinds of control procedures would you establish for this strategy?

# KitKat

## Have a break …

*Sylvie Laforet*[*]

## INTRODUCTION

Sonia Ng sat down to have a cup of tea with her friend, Diane Crate, in the company's dimly lit canteen at York, in the North of England. She unwrapped the bright red paper band from a KitKat, then ran a finger down the foil between the two biscuits. She snapped the biscuits apart, handed one to Diane and sighed: 'This KitKat is not going to be like any I have eaten before.'

As a new assistant brand manager Sonia had to prepare the 1993 brand plan for KitKat. It was a great break for her as KitKat was Nestlé's top confectionery brand. Her first action was to gather what information she could about the brand, then talk to managers who knew about it.

**Exhibit 1.1** KitKat 2-finger: market performance

(a) KitKat 2-finger (tonnes)

| Year | KitKat 2-finger multipacks | CBCL multi-packs and minis | Chocolate confectionery |
|------|---------------------------|----------------------------|--------------------------|
| 1988 | 19,239 | 97,700 | 470,570 |
| 1989 | 22,224 | 106,000 | 472,405 |
| 1990 | 20,789 | 110,000 | 490,605 |
| 1991 | 20,792 | 114,500 | 484,000 |
| 1992 | 21,310 | 116,500 | 476,000 |

(b) KitKat 2-finger in consumer value (£m*.)

| Year | KitKat 2-finger multipacks | CBCL multi-packs and minis |
|------|---------------------------|----------------------------|
| 1988 | 78.3 | 395.8 |
| 1989 | 88.3 | 436.5 |
| 1990 | 91.1 | 463.6 |
| 1991 | 95.2 | 502.0 |
| 1992 | 104.0 | 540.0 |

*1 ecu = UK£0.83 = 83p

(c) KitKat 2-finger: competing brands' consumer value (£m.)

| Year | Penguin multipacks | Club multipacks |
|------|--------------------|-----------------|
| 1988 | 36.5 | 37.0 |
| 1989 | 38.0 | 34.0 |
| 1990 | 40.0 | 33.0 |
| 1991 | 44.0 | 32.0 |
| 1992 | 46.0 | 32.0 |

Sources: BCCCA, Nielson and despatches.

[*]South Bank University, London.

For the UK confectionery industry, 1991 had been a difficult year. Most manufacturers felt the effects of the economic recession. The confectionery market was hit by a VAT increase to 17.5 per cent that April. The market was down after several years of growth (Exhibits 1.1 and 1.2). Nevertheless, consumer spending on confectionery had been rising faster than on food, helped by a trend towards snacking. Business had been good for KitKat, and it had kept its position as the United Kingdom's number one confectionery brand. Its sales volume was at an all-time high (Exhibit 1.3). In consumer values, KitKat was worth over £190m. in 1990 – 3.5bn KitKat fingers.

## NESTLÉ ROWNTREE

Rowntree launched KitKat in August 1935 as 'Chocolate Crisp'. Renamed twice – in 1937 as 'KitKat Chocolate Crisp' and in 1949 as 'KitKat' – by 1950 it was Rowntree's biggest brand and it has remained so ever since. The origin of KitKat's name is uncertain. Some believe the name came from the eighteenth-century political 'KitKat Club', itself named after one Christopher (or Kit) Cat, who kept a pie house where the club met. The name KitKat has favourable onomatopoeic qualities that help the association of the wafer biscuit with a dry, soft snapping or cracking, as of the biscuit being broken or bitten. Other Rowntree brands include Rowntree's Fruit Pastilles (launched 1881), Rowntree's Fruit Gums (1893), Black Magic (1933), Aero (1935), Dairy Box (1936), Smarties (1937), Polo (1948) and After Eight (1962).

**Exhibit 1.2**   KitKat 4-finger: market performance

(a)   KitKat 4-finger (tonnes)

| Year | KitKat 4-finger | Countlines |
|---|---|---|
| 1988 | 22,253 | 215,300 |
| 1989 | 19,816 | 215,700 |
| 1990 | 18,919 | 228,600 |
| 1991 | 20,839 | 235,200 |
| 1992 | 21,670 | 236,000 |

(b)   KitKat 4-finger in consumer value (£m.)

| Year | KitKat 4-finger | Countlines |
|---|---|---|
| 1988 | 80.7 | 830.4 |
| 1989 | 75.6 | 845.5 |
| 1990 | 76.4 | 927.5 |
| 1991 | 86.0 | 1,017.0 |
| 1992 | 87.6 | 1,081.0 |

(c)   KitKat 4-finger: competing brands' consumer value (£m.)

| Year | Mars bars |
|---|---|
| 1988 | 128.6 |
| 1989 | 129.3 |
| 1990 | 134.0 |
| 1991 | 140.7 |
| 1992 | 145.6 |

Sources: BCCCA, Nielson and despatches.

**Exhibit 1.3**   KitKat sales history.

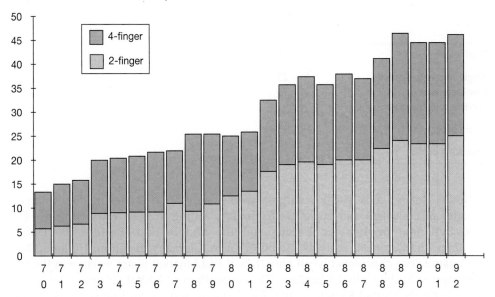

Rowntree merged with Mackintosh in 1969. Mackintosh's was another Yorkshire company whose brands included Quality Street – the world's top-selling confectionery assortment. During the 1970s and 1980s, Rowntree Mackintosh bought other businesses in Europe, Canada and the United States. In June 1988 Swiss-owned Nestlé SA bought Rowntree Mackintosh after a much publicized takeover battle. They said the brands justified the high price they paid for the company. Nestlé Rowntree became a division of Nestlé UK Ltd. Nestlé Rowntree reports to Nestlé UK Ltd in Croydon. Roger Hill is the chairman and chief executive of Nestlé UK Ltd and Richard West (who reports to Roger Hill) the managing director of Nestlé Rowntree.

The factory where KitKat is made is on the north side of the ancient walled town of York. Nestlé Rowntree's site includes sports grounds, a theatre, staff shops, a bank, library and other facilities. Just north of the site is New Earswick – a village created by the Rowntrees. Since the family were Quakers, the 'model village' has no pubs! Five thousand people work at the York site. Recent investments include a new £15.5m. Polo mint plant, a £14m. cocoa processing plant, £6m. for a Reco (research laboratory) extension and a new KitKat line. A chocolate-making plant costing £50m. will open in 1993–94 (see Exhibits 1.4 and 1.5).

**Exhibit 1.4**   Rowntree Nestlé operating performance

| Year | Total sales* | Operating profit (% of sales) | Capital investment (% of sales) | Productivity improvement** |
|------|-------------|-------------------------------|---------------------------------|----------------------------|
| 1987 | 100 | 3.0 | 5.0 | 108 |
| 1988 | 108 | 5.0 | 4.0 | 122 |
| 1989 | 116 | 5.0 | 6.0 | 132 |
| 1990 | 128 | 6.0 | 8.0 | 141 |
| 1991 | 134 | 5.0 | 8.0 | 147 |

Note: *1987 = 100; **1986 = 100.

**Exhibit 1.5**   Rowntree Nestlé results, 1991

|                              | % of sales |
|------------------------------|-----------|
| Total sales                  | 100       |
| Wages and employment         | 23        |
| Raw materials                | 35        |
| Services and finance costs   | 37        |
| Total costs                  | 95        |
| Operating profit             | 5         |

Nestlé Rowntree is Nestlé's largest works and the United Kingdom's largest exporter of chocolate and sugar confectionery, selling to over 120 countries. The most important markets are Europe and the Middle East. Besides the United Kingdom, the European markets include France, Germany, Belgium, Holland, Italy and Ireland. The chocolate biscuit countline (CBCL) market is not as large in the rest of Europe as in the United Kingdom. The proportions of KitKat volume sales are 67 per cent for the United Kingdom, 10.6 for Germany and 5.6 for France. During 1991 there was a 40 per cent increase in overseas sales.

## MANAGEMENT

Nestlé Rowntree has a functional structure.

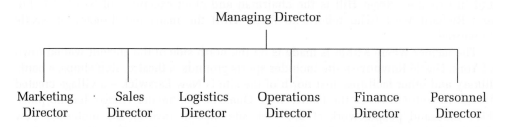

**Nestlé Rowntree Division**

Managing Director

Marketing Director — Sales Director — Logistics Director — Operations Director — Finance Director — Personnel Director

Apart from Finance and Personnel, there are two main units: operational and commercial. The commercial unit comprises sales and marketing. Cliff Robertson, Nestlé Rowntree's marketing director, explained the company's organization: 'It is a classic pyramidal management system, but within the commercial function we have a flat pyramid. The UK company is not decentralized. However, as a business unit within Nestlé worldwide we have much autonomy.' Robertson believes in coordinating the company's UK confectionery activities with those in the rest of Europe, but does not believe in the business being managed globally. According to Robertson, decentralization means being able to take decisions rapidly. The local company is highly responsive to the marketplace because their system reduces hierarchies and bureaucracy.

The company's management style is 'open' – 'team-work' based rather than 'boss–employee'. The marketing department and the marketing team are the team leaders within the division. The management style and values are 'not necessarily consistent across the company'. However, the company has pushed responsibility down the system, making people accountable for what they do. Employees know where specific responsibilities start and finish. 'We went through a very difficult period four years ago, in terms of redefining jobs,' says Robertson. 'We tried to provide very specific job descriptions. Those jobs were then put on a grading scheme from 1 to 15. We also have a self-appraisal system, so that individuals are given feedback on their performance.' Within the marketing department, the training takes two and a half years. The training is very specific and is identified during appraisals.

## STRATEGIC OBJECTIVES

Net operating profits, return on capital employed (ROCE) and market shares drive the company. Each product group has objectives. The company has a cascade system so that each brand has its objectives as well. Each has a brand plan – business plans for each brand. 'The marketing managers are not always able to put in capital to supply across the European markets,' says Robertson. 'We don't actually make the margins that we would make on our UK sales. They have a depressing effect on our group's ROCE. Nevertheless, it is one of the objectives we set.' (See Exhibit 1.6.)

The company's long-term aims are to become the clear leader in the UK confectionery industry and to generate real growth in the profitability and productivity of their confectionery business (Exhibits 1.7 and 1.8). They also aim to increase the efficiency of their supply chain and so improve customer service.

**Exhibit 1.6**   KitKat profit indicators

| Year | Division | KitKat 2-finger | KitKat 4-finger |
|------|----------|-----------------|-----------------|
| 1987 | 100 | 100 | 100 |
| 1988 | 151 | 116 | 144 |
| 1989 | 168 | 161 | 141 |
| 1990 | 193 | 186 | 173 |
| 1991 | 186 | 164 | 191 |

Note: 1987 = 100.

**Exhibit 1.7**   Chocolate confectionery market shares, 1991

| Company | Market share (%) |
|---------|------------------|
| Cadbury | 28.0 |
| Nestlé | 22.0 |
| Mars | 18.0 |
| Terry | 4.0 |
| Other | 28.0 |

**Exhibit 1.8**   CBCL manufacturer performance (1991 expenditure)

| | % share | % change year on year |
|---|---|---|
| Rowntree | 28.2 | 8.0 |
| United Biscuits | 23.2 | −1.0 |
| Jacobs | 13.0 | 27.0 |
| Mars | 8.0 | −19.0 |
| Burtons | 5.7 | 30.0 |
| Tunnocks | 3.9 | 22.0 |
| Fox's | 3.6 | −4.0 |
| Other | 3.4 | n/a |
| Private label | 11.0 | 26.0 |
| Total market | | 6.0 |

Source: AGB Superpanel.

## BUSINESS STRATEGY

The company's strategy is to pursue the company's objectives rather than to defend its position against competitors. For example, some countlines are 'below threshold size'. The objective for these is to improve the performance up to the threshold level. Rod Flint, the director of J. Walter Thompson who are responsible for Nestlé Rowntree's advertising, comments: 'Their objective is not always driven by the stock market. That gives Nestlé a long-term perspective. They are into world brand domination and they are highly global in their approach now, since they are also organizing their European marketing department.'

Basic principles drive the company's brand strategy. They believe in offering the consumer as good value for money as they can possibly afford. They also believe in long-term brands. They believe in differentiated products, one from another within their brand portfolio, which they think will offer a competitive advantage over those of their competitors. Part of the company's brand policy is also to dedicate significant sums of money to advertising and promotions to build customer loyalty and block the entrance of new competitors. On average, 10 per cent of the sales value of the brand goes on advertising and promotions.

The company works to ensure that its brands maintain clear positions in order to prevent cannibalization. Up to now, the best way to achieve this has been stand-alone product brands, as opposed to umbrella brands. More recently, however, the cost of establishing new brands has increased very dramatically. The company is now looking, therefore, for brand leverage across the confectionery business and across Nestlé's other product categories. Nestlé also wishes to improve its corporate image by associating its name more closely with successful brands. For example, KitKat becomes Nestlé KitKat.

## INVESTMENT

Recently, there have been major changes to fit the European market. The company's view is that they need to move towards more efficient manufacturing units – large plants with large runs of single products – which will increasingly compromise serving national consumers. Robertson's view is that they will be consumer-driven, but by European consumers, not British ones.

Capital investment is limited by the profits the company generates. The company is investing 'at record levels'. It spent £60m. in 1991 and planned to spend a further £69m. in 1992 (see Exhibit 1.4). Nestlé Rowntree manages its capital expenditure well. The company is reducing its working capital through a sophisticated supply-chain management system. They have a 'reverse marketing partnership' with their packaging suppliers. As a result, the company does not carry stocks of packs. They call off packaging and print through the company's suppliers 'just-in-time'.

The company has computerized warehouses and its own trucks, so it can control the stocks needed to serve the market. 'Improving productivity is one of the easiest ways of improving profitability,' says Robertson. 'But normally, improving productivity is associated with two factors. One is, if you are currently producing below your capacity, you are not using your assets base efficiently. As you improve your volume through purchases, you improve your efficiency and, therefore, you improve your productivity. The other factor is based upon investment. As we increase our investment in new capital, computerization and more sophisticated lines, then we increase our productivity.' The company has clear productivity objectives that are part of their annual plan. In 1991, however, the 4.5 per cent productivity gain was below target (see Exhibit 1.4). Also capacity limitations stopped them achieving the high customer services levels desired.

The company has introduced three new brands (Baci, Vice Versa and Milkybar Raisins) during 1991. Other new product developments will appear in 1992. Because of the tough economic environment and the competition in the confectionery industry, the company's total sales of confectionery are significantly lower than planned for (see Exhibit 1.4). This, combined with very high operating costs and low price increases, pressurizes Nestlé Rowntree's profits. The company's operating profit in 1991 was £36.8m., £1.4m. down on the previous year, and £3.2m. below target (see Exhibit 1.6).

## KITKAT

When launched in 1935, KitKat entered a market already dominated by Cadbury's Dairy Milk. From its beginning, KitKat was positioned as both a confectionery and a snack. It is now positioned half-way between a snack and an indulgence. In the consumers' eyes, however, KitKat is essentially a snack product and its 1957 slogan 'Have a break, have a KitKat' is widely known through long-running ads on TV and in other media.

The KitKat brand has two formats in the UK. The two-finger format is bought in a multipack (packs of 7 or more) at large grocers by housewives for their children. In contrast, the four-finger format is bought individually by 16–24 year olds for their consumption. The two-finger format is part of the CBCL sector, which implies specific usage, non-personal and 'family' consumption, as well as snack and lunch boxes for kids' consumption. The four-finger format is part of the general chocolate countline sector, which implies personal consumption, broad usage and the 'adults' and 'self-eats' categories. The four-finger format was the volume format but was overtaken by the two-finger format (Exhibits 1.9 and 1.10) as the grocery sector rose at the expense of the CTNs (confectioner/tobacconist/newsagent). About 18 per cent of KitKat two-finger's volume go through cash-and-carry to CTN, compared with 80 per cent of the four-finger format.

Nestlé Rowntree divides the chocolate market into three categories: chocolate box assortments (a gift-oriented marketplace); the countline market (a 'self-eat' market) –

a consumer-product category (i.e. KitKat four-finger); and CBCL – a sector that the company created. Thus Nestlé Rowntree has developed the KitKat business by marketing it as a countline product in its four-finger format, and by developing it as a CBCL in its two-finger format. This helped KitKat cover two sections in their stores, one selling confectionery and the other selling biscuits.

**Exhibit 1.9**    KitKat sales by pack and sector (tonnes)

| Year | 2-finger | | | 4-finger | | |
| | Singles | Multi-packs | Other | Singles | Multi-packs | Other |
|---|---|---|---|---|---|---|
| *All customers* | | | | | | |
| 1988 | 1,233 | 19,238 | 326 | 19,718 | 2,500 | 35 |
| 1989 | 1,140 | 22,224 | 324 | 17,248 | 2,567 | 1 |
| 1990 | 1,166 | 20,800 | 264 | 15,888 | 3,051 | 0 |
| 1991 | 1,188 | 21,070 | 264 | 17,148 | 3,691 | 0 |
| 1992 | 1,158 | 22,424 | 248 | 17,515 | 4,155 | 0 |
| *Multiple retail* | | | | | | |
| 1988 | 61 | 17,533 | 32 | 2,218 | 2,260 | 22 |
| 1989 | 58 | 20,410 | 206 | 1,866 | 2,575 | 0 |
| 1990 | 52 | 18,890 | 64 | 1,715 | 2,858 | 0 |
| 1991 | 53 | 19,136 | 64 | 1,812 | 3,433 | 0 |
| 1992 | 52 | 20,365 | 60 | 1,812 | 3,864 | 0 |
| *Wholesale/independent* | | | | | | |
| 1988 | 1,171 | 1,705 | 275 | 17,500 | 240 | 13 |
| 1989 | 1,081 | 1,813 | 219 | 15,384 | 192 | 1 |
| 1990 | 1,114 | 1,909 | 200 | 14,173 | 213 | 0 |
| 1991 | 1,134 | 1,933 | 200 | 15,296 | 258 | 0 |
| 1992 | 1,106 | 2,058 | 188 | 15,623 | 291 | 0 |

Sources: Internal.

**Exhibit 1.10**    KitKat volume distribution

(a)   Distribution (%)

| Year | Independent grocers covered | | Independent CTNs covered | |
| | KitKat 2-finger | Penguin | KitKat 4-finger | Mars bar |
|---|---|---|---|---|
| 1988 | 54.0 | 74.0 | 99.0 | 99.0 |
| 1989 | 54.0 | 68.0 | 99.0 | 99.0 |
| 1990 | 47.0 | 69.0 | 99.0 | 99.0 |
| 1991 | 52.0 | 74.0 | 99.0 | 99.0 |
| 1992 | 55.0 | 74.0 | 99.0 | 99.0 |

(b)   KitKat 2-finger share of CBCL forward stocks (%)

| Year | Multiple grocers | | Multiple CTNs | | Independent grocers | |
| | KitKat | Penguin | KitKat | Penguin | KitKat | Penguin |
|---|---|---|---|---|---|---|
| 1988 | 18.4 | 11.3 | n/a | n/a | 11.1 | 15.2 |
| 1989 | 18.6 | 11.0 | 17.6 | 2.4 | 15.0 | 10.3 |
| 1990 | 15.0 | 10.5 | 34.5 | 4.7 | 10.4 | 12.9 |
| 1991 | 11.2 | 10.9 | 41.5 | 4.7 | 11.6 | 13.5 |
| 1992 | 10.0 | 10.9 | 43.0 | 5.0 | 12.0 | 13.5 |

(c)  KitKat 4-finger share countline of forward stocks (%)

| Year | Multiple grocers | Multiple CTNs | Independent CTNs | Independent grocers |
|---|---|---|---|---|
| 1989 | 4.3 | 5.7 | 6.0 | 6.5 |
| 1990 | 5.4 | 4.5 | 4.9 | 6.0 |
| 1991 | 5.0 | 3.8 | 5.0 | 6.2 |
| 1992 | 5.0 | 3.6 | 5.0 | 6.2 |

Sources: Nielson and CR estimates.

Another reason for promoting KitKat as a CBCL is the growing power of the multiple grocers. There is a shift from a less structured retail sector into multiple businesses that are sophisticated and powerful. The company produced different packs for the multiple grocers and the independent sector. This avoids direct price and value comparison by the consumer and, therefore, restricts the power of the multiple retailers in their negotiations to increase their profitability to the company's detriment.

**Exhibit 1.11**  Brand shares

| | Value | | Volume | |
|---|---|---|---|---|
| Brand | % 1991 | % points change | % 1991 | % points change |
| KitKat 4-finger | 7.0 | 0.1 | 7.4 | 0.2 |
| Mars Bar | 12.8 | −1.2 | 17.2 | −1.5 |
| Snickers | 6.3 | 0.5 | 7.4 | 0.6 |
| Twix | 4.9 | −0.3 | 6.5 | −0.3 |
| Twirl | 4.0 | 1.3 | 3.7 | 1.7 |
| Drifter | 1.2 | 0.2 | 1.3 | 0.1 |

Source: Nielson.

**Exhibit 1.12**  CBCL brand performance

| Brand | % share (expenditure) | % change (year on year) |
|---|---|---|
| KitKat 2-finger | 21.2 | 4.0 |
| Penguin | 10.5 | 4.0 |
| Club | 8.0 | 3.0 |
| Twix | 6.7 | −15.0 |
| Blue Riband | 3.4 | 18.0 |
| Breakaway | 3.4 | 19.0 |
| Wagon Wheel | 3.1 | 39.0 |
| Tunnocks CW | 3.4 | 39.0 |
| Classic | 3.6 | −4.0 |
| Gold | 3.3 | −14.0 |
| Hob Nob Bars | 2.3 | 7.0 |
| Club Class | 2.5 | |
| Variety Pack | 0.5 | |
| Digestive Bars | 0.6 | |
| Private label | 11.0 | 26.0 |
| Total market | | 6.0 |

Source: AGB Superpanel.

The market share for KitKat two-finger was 22 per cent of the CBCL market in 1991 – the number one seller (see Exhibit 1.8). KitKat's nearest competitors are Mars Bars and Twix, both Mars products (see Exhibits 1.11 and 1.12). Twix was launched as a countline product but is now marketed as single fingers in the multipack format in the CBCL category. Two-finger KitKat's main CBCL competitors are United Biscuit and Mars; in the general chocolate countline category KitKat four-finger's main competitors are Mars and Cadbury.

## THE MARKET

Chocolate confectionery market is concentrated, stable and very competitive. Cadburys, Nestlé Rowntree and Mars are the United Kingdom's leaders (see Exhibit 1.7). Competition is fierce in the countline sector. Around £40m. went on advertising in the 1980s, making confectionery the most highly advertised of all product groups. KitKat has the biggest advertising expenditure in the UK confectionery market: £5.8m. in 1991.

Consumer spending in the confectionery market rose from £3.7bn to £3.9bn in 1991. The £1.5bn confectionery snack market, including countlines and chocolate blocks, is 38 per cent of the confectionery market. This market has grown by 20 per cent over the past five years, following the rise in popularity of snacking. Growth in both the countline market and the CBCL sector is expected to continue at a slower rate in 1992.

The CBCL market's growth up to 1991 was fuelled by new product launches, increased one-bar activity, relatively good value for money, and the growth of superstores. The poor start to 1991 signalled a shrinking market, brought on by price rises above inflation rates. The market only recovered slowly in mid-1991. In 1992 CBCL sales will be influenced by relative value for money, the success of bumper packs and retailer pricing policy. Value for money, competitive price cutting, 'one bar free' activity, bumper packs, new variants and the trading up to an 8-pack will pressurize two-finger KitKat's sales in the future. Due to the limited production capacity of two-finger KitKat, the brand is badly placed to cope with any increased price sensitivity or reduced price discipline within the market. Other factors restricting market growth are the reduced display space available to CBCL, reduced off-shelf activity due to its prohibitive costs, and lack of significant new product innovations.

As market leader, KitKat must retain a premium price and lead the market up. There is a risk to volume if the market does not follow. The market share for four-finger KitKat was 7 per cent within the general countline market, which leaves the brand as number two, after the Mars Bar. Four-finger KitKat had lost some of its market share to Mars Bar in 1990, but regained it in 1991. However, it still remains a weak number two, closely followed by two other Mars products, Twix and Snickers.

New product development, which fuelled countline growth in 1990, has slowed. Pressure will continue to be on the countline market as the population of 15–24 year-olds declines (1.3 per cent in 1991). The two-finger KitKat sales are biased towards C1, C2 socioeconomic and the 35–44 age groups. There is also a high penetration of very young consumers, particularly in the 12–15 age group. The four-finger format has a smarter image, inclines more towards 'chocolate occasions' consumption, and is consumed on the street. Consumption is heavily biased towards female buyers.

The two-finger format ads aim at the 30–44 year olds through morning television. Children are not specifically targeted. The four-finger format ads target the 16–24 year olds through TV and youth press. The ad strategy for this format is different from that of the two-finger. The company puts an emphasis on updating KitKat's brand image by making it appeal to the younger generation through advertising in trendy and young people's magazines and Independent Radio.

The promotions for the two-finger format are value- and grocery-trade-oriented (for example, 'one bar free' activity, or 10p off the next purchase). For the four-finger format, the promotions are different because of the different segments targeted (for example, 1p off). However, there is an annual pan-promotion for KitKat as a whole that consists of big promotions, price, and emphasis on brand awareness.

There is a price differentiation between the two formats. KitKat four-finger is 'twin-priced' in parallel with Twix, and 2p below the Mars Bar (see Exhibit 1.12). This is because KitKat is 'snacky' and not as hunger-satisfying as the Mars Bar. If the company deviated from that, its volume would drop. The two-finger format is not as price-sensitive as the four-finger. As a market leader within the CBCL category, it can more or less dictate price. Thus its competitor Penguin is priced 2p below two-finger KitKat. 'The objective for KitKat is to maintain customer loyalty by being innovative, and to remain *the* number one UK confectionery brand,' says brand manager Diane Crate. There is evidence of relative brand loyalty for KitKat. However, people who buy two-finger KitKat will also be likely to buy other brands, such as Classic, Club Orange, Penguin, Twix, Blue Riband and Gold. According to Brian Ford, the brand manager for the KitKat two-finger: 'Although Nestlé has tried to differentiate the two formats of KitKat in its segmentation and positioning strategies, the consumer sees no difference in the total brand.'

## COMPETITION

Competition is likely to come from small brands, grocery retailers' own labels and other lines coming into this country. There is also a cross-over between the chocolate countline and the CBCL sector. Cadbury has recently encroached into KitKat 'Have a break' territory with Time Out – a bar aimed at the CBCL sector. Time Out aims to bridge the gap between chocolate snack bars, such as Twirl, and wafer-based snacks, such as KitKat. It will compete with KitKat and Twix and should take sales away from brands with a 'heavy sweet' product image, like Spiro and Twix.

Competition from other European confectioners has intensified with the growth of discounters such as Aldi and Netto. This might lead to a price-cutting war in the multiple grocery sector, especially among Kwik Save, Lo-Cost and Asda. Aldi is a particular concern because they are importing bags of KitKat minis from Germany. Although Nestlé Rowntree sell many of their countlines as minis, they do not make or sell KitKat in that format. Besides losing them revenue, Aldi's KitKat minis cause other problems: first, large grocers, like Sainsbury and Tesco, now want supplies of minis like Aldi's. Second, the biscuit and chocolate used to make the German KitKat are unlike those used in Britain and distinctly different.

Outside the United Kingdom, the four-finger format sells more abroad than the two-finger format. European retailers outside the United Kingdom also emphasize minis (Aldi only imports that form). Nestlé Rowntree do not believe in selling minis in the United Kingdom, Ireland or Italy, because it might cannibalize its existing two-finger KitKat.

The company is producing to capacity. The problem is managing demand in the marketplace. 'We can't give them any more, so we use price to limit demand and to get maximum profit return on the amount we produce,' explains Ford. In his opinion, this is easier for the two-finger format because it is the market leader in the CBCL category, but is less easy in the four-finger case. 'It is not the market leader in the chocolate countline sector, therefore we cannot dictate price.'

## PAN-EUROPEAN MARKETING

To fit the regulations across Europe, some KitKats produced by Nestlé Rowntree have different chocolate to others. Although they taste different, unlike the German-made ones, consumers cannot tell the difference. The management of so many internationally important brands limited Nestlé Rowntree's freedom of action outside the United Kingdom. The pricing relationships between, say, France, Germany and the United Kingdom need careful controlling. At the same time, the company needs to achieve its UK business objectives. The marketing of brands will be different because these brands are at different product life-cycle states in different markets. 'The United Kingdom is probably the most sophisticated confectionery market in Europe,' claims Robertson. 'Therefore, for example, the company's advertising style for KitKat is not directly transferable to Germany. The German consumer does not understand the British sense of humour,' explains Robertson. 'So, from the business perspective, there is a pulling together in Europe, while from the consumer perspective, there are still marked differences between different types of consumers, and that is the biggest problem.'

The packing used for KitKat in the United Kingdom is different from that used elsewhere. So KitKat exported to Germany does not have UK packaging and vice versa. Germany's KitKat is flow-wrapped, whereas the United Kingdom has a foil and band. This relatively expensive format appeared because of the early competition with Cadbury. Their market-leading milk chocolate bars had blue foil and a blue wrapper. To differentiate it from Cadburys, the KitKat pack is a silver foil with a visually strong red band wrapped end to end.

Standardization to less expensive flow wrap is resisted in the United Kingdom because of the ritualistic way that UK consumers eat KitKat. Often they eat KitKat socially over a cup of tea. When eating KitKat, many consumers first take off the red wrapper, then run a finger down the foil between two biscuits. With the top of the foil broken, the KitKat fingers are snapped off and then eaten one by one, just as KitKat's new assistant brand manager, Sonia Ng, did. Her job was to develop a brand plan for KitKat. For her it was a great break; but not an easy one.

### QUESTIONS

1. What is the situation facing KitKat: the strengths and weaknesses of the brand and the opportunities and threats it faces?
2. Why are the two-finger and four-finger KitKats marketed differently? How do the customers for the four-finger KitKat differ from those for the two-finger KitKat? What are the differences in the way the company addresses the two target markets?
3. What is the effect of European integration on the marketing of KitKat? What are the barriers to the brand's standardization across Europe? Should the company now move towards standardizing its brand and packaging across Europe?
4. How would you describe the organizational structure of the company and its marketing department? In what alternative ways could the company organize the management of its wide range of confectionery? What structure would you recommend?
5. Prepare a brand plan for KitKat.

Sources: Prepared in conjunction with Sylvie Laforet of South Bank University, London, and with assistance from: the advertising agency J. Walter Thompson, London; Nestlé Rowntree, York; and Nestec, Vevey, Switzerland. Names, statistics and some details have been changed for commercial reasons.

# The marketing setting

## CHAPTER FOUR

# The marketing environment

## CHAPTER OBJECTIVES

After reading this chapter, you should be able to:

- Describe the environmental forces that affect the company's ability to serve its customers.

- Explain how changes in the demographic and economic environments affect marketing decisions.

- Identify the main trends in the firm's natural and technological environments.

- Explain the key changes that occur in the political and cultural environments.

## CHAPTER PREVIEW

### Unilever: Power?

'My God! They're really going to use it!' Nabil Sakkab, Procter & Gamble's European head of laundry products development, exclaimed to colleagues as his scientist's eye looked closely at the myriad, tiny pink crystals scattered among a heap of detergent he'd just poured on to his desk. It was mid-March 1994 – a memorable day. For Unilever this was the beginning of a protracted nightmare; for P&G, it was revelation day – they'd discovered the secret ingredient in rival Unilever's super-concentrated Power, a new, revolutionary washing powder. The new powder was called Omo Power in the Netherlands and Persil Power in the United Kingdom. In France, it appeared as Skip Power. Other brand names were used in various countries. Power was the biggest advance in fabric detergents in fifteen years, so Unilever claimed. Sales of Omo Power were leaping in the three European countries where it had been launched a month earlier. It worried P&G, not just because the rivals were doing one better than they, but that Power had a fatal flaw. It contained crystals of manganese, a catalyst – known as the 'accelerator'. Although the manganese catalyst dramatically increases the cleansing power of a detergent by allowing it to wash at much lower temperatures as well as speeding the bleaching process, it is 'unkind' to clothes – it attacks fabrics! P&G had dropped it as a possible ingredient ten years ago for that reason. Now they were astounded that Unilever would use the defective manganese.

The question P&G posed was 'WHY?' With that the Great Soap War over Unilever's Power detergent began.

### The push behind Power

1 ecu = UK£0.83

Power lay behind Unilever's strategy to salvage its market position in the £6bn European fabric detergent market, in which P&G had long overtaken it. In the past, Unilever had been slow to develop concentrated versions of the product, thus widening the gap between itself and its US rival. Power was the company's second entry into the concentrated fabric detergent market. It was not just another new product. It was to be the trailblazer in the industry, a quantum leap in detergent effectiveness. To win back a lead, Power had to be very different – in the lab and to consumers. This was made possible as a result of combining advanced product technology and innovative pan-European marketing techniques. It was the culmination of five years of developmental work. Unilever planned to launch Power in eleven countries in short order – a marketing blitzkrieg without precedent in Europe. Then there was Niall Fitzgerald, Unilever's global coordinator of detergents and a man of ability, drive and persuasive charm – much was riding on Power's success for him. Turning round Unilever's ailing detergents business could mean eventual ascent to the joint chairmanship of the group. The stakes were high. The sheer enthusiasm at top levels about Power products had Fitzgerald and his team in its grip.

### Alarm bells ring

With Sakkab's discovery, no one was awaiting it more eagerly than Ed Artzt, P&G's famously domineering chairman. Nicknamed the Prince of Darkness, he had a well-earned reputation for responding rapidly and ruthlessly when he felt P&G's interests were threatened. P&G was also working on a new detergent – Ariel Future – due for launch in late 1994. Power's success posed a significant threat to the company's current and imminent future products. However, the Power detergent was claiming a technological lead based on what he knew was a fundamentally flawed formula. Sakkab and his colleagues at P&G's European Technology Centre not only found that some dark dyes in cotton and viscose fabrics reacted badly to the detergent, they also discovered holes in clothes washed in Power. They also believed there were 'carry over' effects – the catalyst lingered in the clothes and continued to damage them when washed in other detergents – although this claim subsequently won little support from independent tests.

Artzt was ready for his next move. On 31 March 1994, he called on Fitzgerald and other top executives at Unilever House, London, and demanded that they withdrew their new detergent. This was a private warning.

### Unilever's response

There was a long tradition of collaboration between P&G and Unilever on technical issues, and, for all the aggression in the market, the two have been known in private to alert one another to product flaws and work together to solve problems. Unilever executives' suspicion had been aroused – Artzt was on a spoiling mission to undermine Power. Fitzgerald saw no need to take the costly and humiliating step of withdrawing Power, which had already been tested by scientists and consumers (over 60,000 of them) for two years without incident. A senior Unilever executive said: 'We got

Procter & Gamble strikes back: these campaigns draw attention to the damaging effects of Persil Power's manganese 'accelerator'.

very positive consumer responses and got nothing suggesting there was a problem. Unilever ignored P&G's private warning.

### P&G's public vilification campaign

The first public sign of trouble for Unilever was a story in the Dutch press on 27 April 1994. It quoted a spokesman for P&G alluding to fabric damage caused by Power. The Unilever response was to hold a press conference on 29 April denying P&G's claims, while also issuing two writs for product defamation and trademark infringement. Unilever also sought an injunction to stop P&G using the term 'Power' for its own detergents – a confusing twist, but, yes, things were getting 'grubbier' by this time!

Neither Unilever nor P&G was skilled in the art of corporate public relations. P&G hired for the first time the help of PR firm, The Rowland Company (a Saatchi & Saatchi subsidiary). They now had the upper-hand in their campaign of public vilification. Unilever was left ill-equipped to handle the onslaught. P&G started a ruthlessly well-organized knocking-copy campaign – literally running around Europe to consumers' associations, washing machine manufacturers, retailers and anybody else who would listen, giving them very extensive technical briefings with lots of lurid pictures of Power-damaged clothes.

### Unilever on the defensive

Until the end of May, Unilever just about managed to hold its own with consumers. Although Power sales fell after every P&G onslaught, Unilever was able to rebuild them with advertising and special offers.

Fitzgerald knew, however, that this defence could not hold out for long. Apart from anything else, Fitzgerald and his team knew that they had to address P&G's criticism about Power's effect on some dark dyes – which was true, although Unilever considered the circumstances extreme and irrelevant to consumers. Leading supermarket chains in various countries were considering emptying their shelves of Power, even though Unilever stood firmly behind its products, denying that there was a problem.

### The battle transforms

On 3 June 1994 Unilever conceded to the opposition:

- The company dropped the lawsuits against P&G, after P&G assured Unilever that its spokesman had been misquoted.
- It announced that it would reformulate Power, and reduce the level of the accelerator in the powder by 80 per cent.
- P&G released to the press a set of colour pictures of clothes damaged by Power, including shots of tattered boxer shorts, plus results from six test institutes, all of which were dutifully reproduced by the press all over Europe.

All hell broke loose with these announcements. Power became front-page news in several European countries; consumers' associations levelled a stream of reports damning Power detergents; environmental campaigners in Sweden accused Power of putting the nation's clothes in imminent jeopardy!

Unilever remained defensive with both the press and the public. It failed to find an effective counter to criticisms from all sides.

### Unilever's climbdown

Unilever revamped and relaunched Power products, while also retreating from its original broad market positioning to a more specialized niche – the package was changed to concentrate use of the product in lower temperatures and on white fabrics. The old products were, however, left on the shelves and the company attempted to reassure consumers through advertisements that guaranteed the safety of its revamped product. But then the Dutch consumers' union later confirmed the damaging effects of the upgraded Power.

By the summer of 1994, Power had become an obsession for top management in both companies. At Unilever, Sir Michael Perry and Morris Tabaksblat, the British and Dutch co-chairmen, started to take a more active role, with their questioning of the detergents team becoming more pointed.

At the end of July 1994, a series of newspaper ads were taken out in the United Kingdom by P&G which criticized Unilever's product. One version of the ad states that 'Only Ariel [Procter's rival product] washes so clean yet so safe', stressing that Ariel does not contain the accelerator. Another ad made similarly unfavourable comparisons between another Procter brand, Fairy, and Persil Power. Ironically, Lever complained to the Advertising Standards Association (ASA) about the advertisements. (Surprisingly, the ASA later, in December 1994, slammed P&G's ads for attacking Lever's Persil Power, and then, in January 1995, diluted its criticism of Procter's knocking campaign.)

In September 1994, Unilever management at last spoke up. Tabaksblat stated: 'We made a mistake. We launched a product which had a defect which we had not detected.' He also admitted that there had been a lack of appropriate safeguards in tests before the launch. Other executives also spoke up between September and December 1994: 'I think we were very enthusiastic about an exciting new product and did not look closely enough at the negatives. Somewhere between research and marketing something went wrong – under the normal pressure to be first to the market. With a quantum leap in technology, we may have to re-examine all our test regimes.'

Unilever finally admitted it was aware throughout that Power would damage fabrics more so than did earlier detergents. But it accepted that as the price of more effective stain removal. Also its detergent team got carried away and pushed the product harder than usual. Unilever obviously failed to anticipate how violently its arch rival would react. By the end of the year, independent tests, including the UK Consumers' Association *Which?* investigation, confirmed everybody's suspicions – that Power, even the reformulated version, with reduced manganese, was defective.

### The costs

After spending more than £200m. on developing, manufacturing and marketing Omo and Persil Power products, Lever remains a poor second to P&G in the European detergent market – no better than a year before Power's launch. A heavy price was exacted on reputations – the company's and the Persil and Omo brands. Unilever's image as a shrewd marketer and innovator was undermined. The whole affair has exacerbated consumers' scepticism towards manufacturers; as one retailer said, 'the whole (detergents) sector is drowning in over-claiming and publicity which leaves consumers confused'.

P&G, for its part, may have stopped Power in its tracks. It was the most effective watchdog in this case, thanks to its persistence in proving its point (also, thank goodness for competition). However, in 'picking a street fight' with Unilever, it reinforced its widespread image as a ruthless, self-seeking organization.

### The lessons

Many soap war observers would conclude that, with Power products, Unilever had practised socially irresponsible marketing – and deservedly paid heavily for it. However, the case has much broader lessons for businesses. First, the marketing environment for goods and services is getting fiercer. Firms must prepare for this. Second, the global marketing environment also is uniquely challenging. Simultaneous new product launch is risky. If something goes wrong in one national market, the chances are that the problems will spread quickly. The firm must attain a flexibility to redress matters rapidly. Third, firms must be alert to opportunities arising in the technological environment, capitalizing on these as rapidly as possible. Technology, however, can be a marketing curse as well as a blessing. Firms that seize on technical innovations as a unique selling point must subject their products to the most rigorous testing to uncover fatal flaws. If not, the invention could blow up in their faces. Fourth, communications with publics – other players in the marketing environment – are important. Companies can no longer hide behind brands, but have to explain themselves and their activities more effectively to consumers and the wider public. Fifth, consumers are more demanding than ever before – and competitors more ruthless. Their attitudes and behaviour will impact on firms as much as the latter's own marketing actions will evoke responses from customers and competitors. Providers that fail to appreciate how these and other environmental forces impact on their organizations will go to the wall. Unilever's soap war with P&G provides data not only to question marketers' social responsibilities and behaviour, but also to teach broader lessons about survival in today's tough marketing environment.

### Epilogue

'Soap wars force delay in Unilever board changes', the press reports. Unilever delayed Fitzgerald's ascent to its special committee by a year to 1996 – on the grounds that he still had much to do in detergents. Unilever finally dropped the 'accelerator' formulation and launched an accelerator-free New Persil Generation in the United Kingdom in February 1995.[1]

## INTRODUCTION

A company's **marketing environment** consists of the actors and forces outside marketing that affect marketing management's ability to develop and maintain successful transactions with its target customers. The marketing environment offers both opportunities and threats. Companies must use their marketing research and intelligence systems to watch the changing environment and must adapt their marketing strategies to environmental trends and developments.

The marketing environment consist of a microenvironment and a macroenvironment. The **microenvironment** consists of the forces close to the company that affect its ability to serve its customers – the company, suppliers, marketing channel firms, customer markets, competitors and publics. The **macroenvironment** consists of the larger societal forces that affect the whole microenvironment – demographic, economic, natural, technological, political and cultural forces. We look first at the company's microenvironment and then at its macroenvironment.

## THE COMPANY'S MICROENVIRONMENT

Marketing management's job is to create attractive offers for target markets. However, marketing managers cannot simply focus on the target market's needs. Their success also will be affected by actors in the company's microenvironment. These actors include other company departments, suppliers, marketing intermediaries, customers, competitors and various publics (see Figure 4.1).

### The company

In designing marketing plans, marketing management should take other company groups, such as top management, finance, research and development (R&D), purchasing, manufacturing and accounting, into consideration. All these interrelated groups form the internal environment (see Figure 4.2). Top management sets the company's mission, objectives, broad strategies and policies. Marketing managers must make decisions consistent with the plans made by top management, and marketing plans must be approved by top management before they can be implemented.

Marketing managers also must work closely with other company departments. Finance is concerned with finding and using funds to carry out the marketing plan.

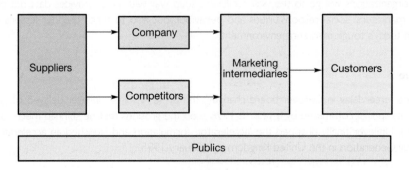

**Figure 4.1**  Principal actors in the company's microenvironment.

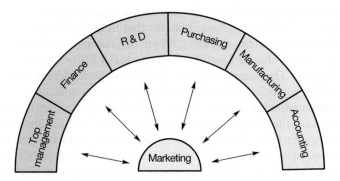

**Figure 4.2**   The company's internal environment.

The R&D department focuses on the problems of designing safe and attractive products. Purchasing worries about getting supplies and materials, whereas manufacturing is responsible for producing the desired quality and quantity of products. Accounting has to measure revenues and costs to help marketing know how well it is achieving its objectives. Therefore, all of these departments have an impact on the marketing department's plans and actions and its ability effectively to satisfy target customers' needs profitably.

## Suppliers

**Suppliers** are firms and individuals that provide the resources needed by the company to produce its goods and services. Supplier developments can seriously affect marketing. Marketing managers must therefore watch supply availability. Supply shortages or delays, labour strikes, and other events can cost sales in the short run and damage customer goodwill in the long run. Marketing managers must also monitor the price trends of their key inputs. Rising supply costs may force price increases that can harm the company's sales volume.

## Marketing intermediaries

**Marketing intermediaries** are firms that help the company to promote, sell, and distribute its goods to final buyers. They include middlemen, physical distribution firms, marketing services agencies, and financial intermediaries. **Middlemen** are distribution channel firms that help the company find customers or make sales to them. These include wholesalers and retailers who buy and resell merchandise (they are often called *resellers*). Selecting and working with middlemen is not easy. No longer do manufacturers have many small, independent middlemen from which to choose. They now face large and growing middlemen organizations who frequently have enough power to dictate terms or even shut the manufacturer out of large markets.

   **Physical distribution firms** help the company to stock and move goods from their points of origin to their destinations. Warehousing firms store and protect goods before they move to the next destination. Transportation firms include railroads, trucking companies, airlines, shipping companies and others that specialize in moving goods from one location to another. A company must determine the best ways to store and ship goods, balancing such factors as cost, delivery, speed and safety.

**Marketing services agencies** are the marketing research firms, advertising agencies, media firms and marketing consultancies that help the company target and promote its products to the right markets. When the company decides to use one of these agencies, it must choose carefully because these firms vary in creativity, quality, service and price. The company has to review the performance of these firms regularly and consider replacing those that no longer perform well.

**Financial intermediaries** include banks, credit companies, insurance companies and other businesses that help finance transactions or insure against the risks associated with the buying and selling of goods. Most firms and customers depend on financial intermediaries to finance their transactions. The company's marketing performance can be seriously affected by rising credit costs and limited credit. For example, small and medium-sized businesses in Britain have often found difficulty in obtaining finance for market and product development activities. Many such businesses blame this on the insupportive financial system in the United Kingdom. In marked contrast, the Japanese *kieretsu* system favours lower cost financing for both large and small companies that form part of the informal network of banking, trading and commercial organizations within the *kieretsu*. Whether or not businesses enjoy the support of a favourable financial system, individual businesses must be aware of financial organizations' impact on marketing effectiveness. For this reason, the company has to develop strong relationships with the most important financial institutions.

## Customers

The company must study its customer markets closely. Figure 4.3 shows six types of customer markets. **Consumer markets** consist of individuals and households that buy goods and services for personal consumption. **Business markets** buy goods and services for further processing or for use in their production process, whereas **reseller markets** buy goods and services to resell at a profit. **Institutional markets** are made up of schools, hospitals, nursing homes, prisons and other institutions that provide goods and services to people in their care. **Government markets** are made up of government agencies that buy goods and services in order to produce public services or transfer the goods and services to others who need them. Finally, **international markets** consist of buyers in other countries, including consumers, producers, resellers and governments. Each market type has special characteristics that call for careful study by the seller. At any point in time, the firm may deal with one or more

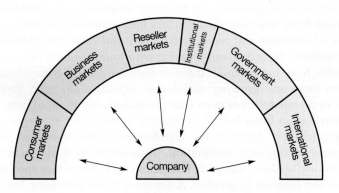

**Figure 4.3**    Types of customer markets.

customer markets: for example, Unilever has to communicate detergent brand bene-fits to consumers as well as maintaining a dialogue with retailers who stock and resell its branded products.

## Competitors

The marketing concept states that to be successful, a company must satisfy the needs and wants of consumers better than its competitors do. Thus, marketers must do more than simply adapt to the needs of target consumers. They must also gain strate-gic advantage by positioning their offerings strongly against competitors' offerings in the minds of consumers.

No single competitive marketing strategy is best for all companies. Each firm should consider its own size and industry position compared to those of its competi-tors. Large firms with dominant positions in an industry can use certain strategies that smaller firms cannot afford. But being large is not enough. There are winning strategies for large firms, but there are also losing ones. And small firms can develop strategies that give them better rates of return than large firms enjoy.

## Publics

The company's marketing environment also includes various publics. A **public** is any group that has an actual or potential interest in or impact on an organization's ability to achieve its objectives. Figure 4.4 shows seven types of publics:

1. *Financial publics.* Financial publics influence the company's ability to obtain funds. Banks, investment houses, and stockholders are the principal financial publics.
2. *Media publics.* Media publics are those that carry news, features and editorial opinion. They include newspapers, magazines and radio and television stations.
3. *Government publics.* Management must take government developments into account. Marketers must often consult the company's lawyers on issues of prod-uct safety, truth-in-advertising, and other matters.
4. *Citizen-action publics.* A company's marketing decisions may be questioned by consumer organizations, environmental groups, minority groups and other pres-sure groups. Its public relations department can help it stay in touch with con-sumer and citizen groups.

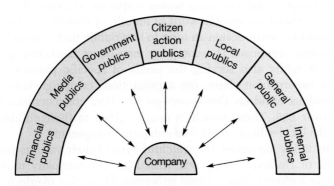

**Figure 4.4**  Types of publics.

Communicating with publics: Unilever's Uniview is a newsletter which communicates news and information to employees.

The Kemira Group uses this ad to communicate to both national and international customers, public and institutional investors. Its 'super-league' feels great about working for the firm; its customers feel they are in safe hands.

5. *Local publics.* Every company has local publics, such as neighbourhood residents and community organizations. Large companies usually appoint a community-relations officer to deal with the community, attend meetings, answer questions and contribute to worthwhile causes.

6. *General public.* A company needs to be concerned about the general public's attitude toward its products and activities. The public's image of the company affects its buying. Thus, many large corporations invest huge sums of money to promote and build a healthy corporate image.

7. *Internal publics.* A company's internal publics include its workers, managers, volunteers and the board of directors. Large companies use newsletters and other means to inform and motivate their internal publics. When employees feel good about their company, this positive attitude spills over to their external publics.

A company can prepare marketing plans for these publics as well as for its customer markets. Suppose the company wants a specific response from a particular public, such as goodwill, favourable word of mouth, or donations of time or money. The company would have to design an offer to this public that is attractive enough to produce the desired response. The company may target marketing programmes at customer markets while also serving the needs of specific publics. For example, Tesco, a British supermarket chain, ran a promotions campaign targeted at households with school-age children. Consumers get to collect vouchers issued at the store for purchases over £25. These vouchers can be given to their children to take to school to help the local school obtain free computer equipment.

Organizations today are under the watchful eyes of their various publics. As we saw in the case of Unilever's soap war with P&G, the company must explain its actions to a wider audience when things go wrong. Those that overlook the power of serious interest groups often learnt painful lessons (see Marketing Highlight 4.1).

## Speaking for Herman the Bull

Nutricia, a Dutch producer of baby foods and powders, is a leading investor in biotechnology research. It recently entered into a joint venture with the Dutch subsidiary of US biotechnology firm, GenPharm International, to carry out research which attempts to genetically engineer cows' milk. Trouble started after a human gene was inserted into the genetic material of a bull, Herman. The two companies hoped that the milk produced by Herman's female descendants would contain large amounts of lactoferrine, a substance normally found in human milk. The Dutch Society for the Protection of Animals launched an anti-Herman campaign. A first series of shock posters showed a starry-eyed cow with the question posed: 'Soon to be marketed with blonde hair and blue eyes?' A second depicted a woman's naked chest

The power of interest groups: the 'anti-Herman' campaign led by the Dutch Society for the Protection of Animals forced Nutricia and GenPharm International to abandon the controversial biotechnology research

with two neat rows of udders. The groups threatened to call an all-out boycott of Nutricia products.

The Dutch government, which has introduced 'never unless' rules to regulate genetic manipulation of animals, exceptionally permitted the Nutricia project to go ahead as scientists argued that large scale production of lactoferrine serves unique medical goals. The DSPA, however, stressed that the Nutricia project's motives were purely commercial, which was to manufacture the equivalent of mother's milk on an agribusiness scale at potential cost to animal welfare. Jasper Franse, a Nutricia spokesman, said, 'When the project was presented to us four years ago, it didn't seem likely to cause controversy. There is great pressure on us to keep investing in technology. But in the current climate, if a similar offer came up, the company would probably prefer to decline it.'

The project had to be abandoned. Nutricia has since admitted a loss of some DFl 4m.* and said it would handle such pioneering efforts more carefully in the future. Pressure groups in Holland declare that they have effectively scared investors from venturing into the most delicate and controversial fields of modern biotechnology – the genetic modification of an animal, which the Nutricia case exemplified. According to a spokesman for NIABA, a group representing the Dutch food industry for biotechnology matters, food companies in the country would invest between two and three times more in such research if they did not fear damaging upheavals. He added, 'The animal rights and environmental pressure groups may not represent a very large section of opinion but their blackmailing tactics have been known to work in the past. Any company that ignores their signals takes a very big chance.'

Dutch 'novel foods' laws now dictate that firms which want to market an entirely new product must first present their plans to the authorities and let them undergo a long series of safety tests. On top of national and European rules, some large companies in the Netherlands have adopted their own corporate policy statement to clarify their views on biotechnology development to avoid damaging controversy. In the light of the Nutricia affair, both investors and companies urge for an update of ethical rules at European levels.

* 1 ecu = US$1.26 = DFl 2.12 (Dutch guilders).

Source: Adapted from Barbara Smit, 'Herman the Bull scares off Dutch research pioneers', *The European* (22–28 July 1994), 25.

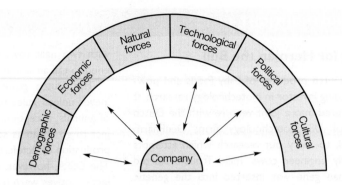

**Figure 4.5**    Influential forces in the company's macroenvironment.

## THE COMPANY'S MACROENVIRONMENT

The company and all the other actors operate in a larger macroenvironment of forces that shape opportunities and pose threats to the company. Figure 4.5 shows the six most influential forces in the company's macroenvironment. The remaining sections of this chapter examine these forces and show how they affect marketing plans.

### Demographic environment

**Demography** is the study of human populations in terms of size, density, location, age, gender, race, occupation and other statistics. The demographic environment is of considerable interest to marketers because it involves people, and people make up markets. Here, we discuss the most important demographic characteristics and trends in the largest world markets.

*Population size and growth trends*

In any geographic market, population size and growth trends can be used to gauge its broad potential for a wide range of goods and services. We often refer to the United States, Japan and Europe as the 'triad' markets. The European Union (EU), together with members in the European Free Trade Area (EFTA), has a population of around 370 million. With another 120 million from Eastern Europe and 280 million from the former USSR, the overall European market will be significantly larger than the North America Free Trade Area – the United States, Canada and Mexico – with a population of 370 million and Japan with 128 million. Marketers also view China, with 1.2 billion people, as a potentially lucrative growth market.

Population growth trends are important because they can offer marketers an indication of demand for certain goods and services. A 'baby boom' would suggest growing demand for infant foods, nursery appliances, maternity services, baby clothings, toys and so forth, in the short to medium term, with rising demand for family-size accommodation, larger cars, schools and educational services over the longer term. Differences in population growth patterns between country markets may also suggest different international marketing opportunities for firms operating abroad. The European population is growing on average by 0.6 per cent a year, well below the world average of 1.8 per cent. However, whereas growth is lowest in Germany and Hungary, it has risen by 30 per cent, between

1977 and 1990, in Turkey and Albania.[2] It is important to look, not just at broad regional population distribution, but also at individual country forecasts. A baby food, toy or children's apparel manufacturer, for example, may want to study these trends more closely.

## Changing age structure of a population

The most noticeable demographic shift in Europe, the United States and affluent Asian countries is the changing age structure of the population. In all three groups, the national populations are getting older, and the situation is forecast to worsen over the next fifty years. The population is ageing for two main reasons. First, there is a long-term slowdown in birth rate, so there are fewer young people to pull the population's average age down. Western European countries, with the exception of Ireland, rank below the 2.1 children per woman (fertility) level found in the United States, and well below the 3.3 world average. Italy, reporting 1.3 children per woman, has the lowest fertility level in the world. This 'birth-dearth' linked to smaller family sizes is due to people's desire to improve personal living standards, women's desire to work outside the home, and from effective birth control practices. These reasons apply to Asia's rich economies: rising female employment, mobility opportunities and widely available contraception have kept birth rates down. Fertility rates

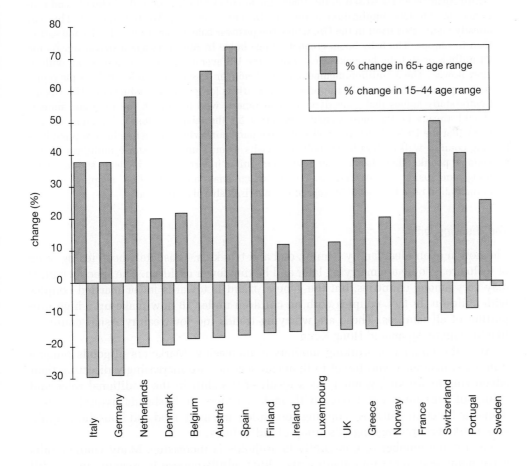

Source: National statistical offices.

**Figure 4.6**    Europe's ageing population: forecast growth rates to the year 2020.

in Japan, Singapore, South Korea and Hong Kong have declined steadily over the last two decades, and all lie below America's 2.1 average. The sharp fall in Singapore's birth rate during the 1970s even resulted in the government running special campaigns to persuade the country's professional women to bear children!

Secondly, as longevity increases there are more elderly people (see Figure 4.6) to pull the average age of the population up. By 2031, 38 per cent of the UK population will be over 50 years old. Compare this with 32 per cent in 1991 and only 28 per cent in 1951. In Germany, the balance of people over 65 years of age to persons of working age (or the *dependency ratio*) is expected to exceed 1:1 by 2031. Put more colourfully by historian and demographer, Peter Laslett, 'Europe and the West are growing older and will never be young again'. The picture is repeated in affluent Asian countries. The rapid ageing of the Japanese population is one of the government's biggest long-term worries.[3] This demographic shift has important implications for marketing managers:

> For example, the Henley Centre, a UK forecasting organisation, draws attention to the emerging 'Third Agers'. They will be 50–75 years old, have more free time, money and higher expectations than their predecessors. They are brought up to value aspirations and self-fulfilment. They are now in their forties, but will represent the first mass leisure class. Unlike their preceding generations whose upbringing gave them a more frugal outlook, 'Third Agers' were socialised in the 1960s, the era of expanding individual choices and economic growth. One implication is the rise in 'grey power' in Western Europe. This has already manifested itself in the US, where the postwar baby boom occurred a decade earlier than in Europe. The baby boom created a huge bulge in America's age distribution. As the 75 million or so baby boomers age, so does the US average age climb, and, along with it, 'grey power'. The 37 million members of the American Association of Retired People represents a powerful lobby – and, important new markets for leisure and education. The Henley Centre study argues that such dynamic consumers, who have both the time and money, should already be the most sought-after target for the leisure industry. Time-use studies show that the UK's 'Third Agers' already take part more widely in active leisure pursuits – long country walks, short-break holidays, visits to museums or historic buildings – than younger people. They also are 'catching' their juniors in terms of playing team sports, swimming and using sports centres, visits to cinemas and attending evening classes. Participation rates for the 45–59 year olds have risen sharply since 1986.[4]

## The changing family

The notion of an ideal family – mum, dad and two kids – has lately been losing some of its lustre. People are marrying later and having fewer children. The specific figures may vary among countries, but the general trend is towards fewer married couples with children. In fact, couples with no children under 18 now make up a high proportion of all families. These are worrying trends too for wealthy Asian countries like Singapore, Japan and Hong Kong.

Also, the number of working mothers is increasing. Marketers of goods ranging from cars, insurance and travel to financial services are increasingly directing their advertising to working women. As a result of the shift in the traditional roles and values of husbands and wives, with male partners or husbands assuming more domestic functions such as shopping and child care, more food and household appliance marketers are targeting this group of individuals.

Finally, the number of non-family households is increasing. Many young adults leave home and move into apartments. Other adults choose to remain single. Still others are divorced or widowed people living alone. By the year 2000, one-person/non-family and single-parent households – the fastest growing category of

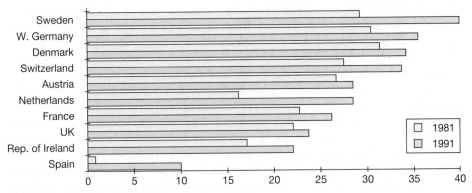

**Figure 4.7**    The rise of the one-person household.

households – will represent a sizeable proportion of all households. In Sweden, for example, one-person households now account for over 40 per cent of all homes. Between 1981 and 1991, there has been an upward trend towards single-person households (see Figure 4.7). In the United States, figures are comparable, with estimates putting the number at 47 per cent by the year 2000. These groups have their own special needs. For example, they need smaller apartments, inexpensive and smaller appliances, furniture and furnishings, and food that is packaged in smaller sizes.[5]

### Rising number of educated people

As economies in Eastern Europe and Asia develop, one hopes that more money will be spent on education. The proportion of the population that is educated will rise and the population, as a whole, will become better educated. The rising number of educated people will increase the demand for quality products, books, magazines and travel.

In many developed and industrializing countries, the workforce is also becoming more white collar. The most growth comes in the following occupational categories: computers, engineering, science, medicine, social service, buying, selling, secretarial, construction, refrigeration, health service, personal service and protection.[6]

### Increasing diversity

In the late 1980s and early 1990s, moves towards European integration have escalated. The EU now comprises fifteen member states – France, Luxembourg, Italy, Germany, with East Germany on unification, Netherlands, Belgium, Denmark, Ireland, United Kingdom, Greece, Spain, Portugal, and since January 1995, Sweden, Austria and Finland. The EU's enlargement programme is still high on politicians' agendas. Eastern and Central European countries, including former Soviet bloc states, are seeking to participate in the EU, which, in the longer term, could become a reality.

The EU, in its present state, and in a potentially enlarged form, presents huge challenges for domestic and international marketers. We will discuss international marketing issues in more detail in Chapter 5. In general, marketers operating in the vastly expanded EU must recognize the great diversity across member states. Unification strives to achieve harmonization of rules and regulations which will affect business practices across the Union. Many marketers believe the single European market will lead to convergence in consumer tastes. Global advertising agencies like Saatchi & Saatchi and Young and Rubicam were strong supporters of the idea of the 'Euro-consumer'. However, consumer needs, values, beliefs, habits and lifestyles differ across individual country markets, just as spending power and consumption patterns are likely to vary. Businesses will do well to identify national and regional differences and develop appropriate marketing strategies that take on board this diversity. Where there are European consumers, who display similar cultural values and tastes for particular goods and services, then pan-European strategies may be more cost-effective. For example, the internationalism of snob items, such as Rolex watches or Cartier jewellery, which appeal to a small number of like-minded consumers, or high-fashion purchases like Swatch watches and Benetton clothes, which pander to the younger generation of dedicated fashion followers, lend themselves to pan-European marketing or advertising. In most markets, however, firms have found that the 'one sight, one sound, one sell' dictum loses out to the more effective strategy of customization. Even Coca-Cola, arch-exponent of globalism, tailors the marketing of its drinks to suit different markets. Kronenbourg, France's most popular beer, is sold to a mass market with the eternal images of France, like cafés, boules and Citroen 2CVs. In Britain, Kronenbourg is presented as a drink for 'yuppies'. Unilever customizes its advertisements for Impulse, a body spray. In Britain, the handsome young fellow, who gets a whiff of Impulse from the lady nearby, presents her with a bunch of flowers. In the Italian version, Romeo offers the lady a rose. Whether the Euroconsumer is a myth or reality is widely debated today. Marketers must address a marketing basic: identify consumer needs and respond to them. Converging lifestyles, habits and tastes often may not mean converging needs. Europe remains a potpourri of cultures and systems, which present immense marketing opportunities for sellers. Although social and demographic factors and the marketing strategies of multinational consumer goods companies may combine to make lifestyles of different European (and rising wealthy Asian) nations more alike, companies that overlook diversity in favour of pan-European strategies must carefully develop and execute their standardized approaches.[7] We discuss pan-European versus standardized marketing practices in greater depth in the next chapter.

An analogy is made with the United States, which has often been called a 'melting pot' in which diverse groups from many nations and cultures have melted into a single, more homogeneous whole. But there are increasing signs that such melting did not occur. Rather, the United States seems to have become more of a 'salad bowl' in which various groups have mixed together but have maintained their diversity by retaining and valuing important ethnic and cultural differences.

Marketers now view America as a heterogeneous, not homogeneous, market. Many firms are turning to micromarketing – breaking down the market along geographic, ethnic and other lines and more finely targeting specific customer groups. For example, Cadbury Schweppes distributes its Schweppes drinks through 150 franchisees in America, each of which uses a different promotional strategy reflecting differences in target customer groups. America's 23 million Hispanic consumers are also receiving special attention from marketers and their ad agencies.[8]

## Economic environment

Markets require buying power as well as people. The **economic environment** consists of factors that affect consumer purchasing power and spending patterns. Marketers should be aware of the following predominant economic trends.

### Income distribution and changes in purchasing power

Recent global upheavals in technology and communications have brought about a shift in the balance of economic power from the west (mainly North American,

Canadian and Western European nations) towards the rapidly expanding economies of the Pacific Rim. Official statistics suggest that, by 2010, purchasing power income per head in countries like Singapore and South Korea will exceed that of the United States. Incomes in Singapore are close to the Western European average. Economic growth projections suggest that Europe will drop down the economic rankings. Assuming annual growth in Western Europe and the United States of 2.5 per cent, and 6 per cent in Asia as a whole, the share of world gross domestic product (GDP) taken by Asian developing countries, including China and India, could rise to 28 per cent in 2010 from 18 per cent in 1990. Western Europe's share will fall to 17 per cent from 22 per cent, while the United States will drop to 18 per cent from 23 per cent.[9] A narrowing of the wealth and living standards gap between the developed Western and rising Asian economies has important implications for international marketers. They must determine how rising incomes translate into increased purchasing power. Consumers with the greatest purchasing power are likely to belong to the higher socioeconomic groups, whose rising incomes mean that their spending patterns are less susceptible to economic downturns than lower income groups. So, marketers must determine a population's *income distribution*. The *upper* economic strata of a society become primary targets for expensive luxury goods, the *middle* income groups are more careful about spending, but can usually afford some luxuries sometimes, while the *lower* strata will afford only basic food, clothing and shelter needs. In some countries, an *underclass* exists – people permanently living on state welfare and/or below the poverty line – which has little purchasing power, often struggling to make even the most basic purchases.

Where consumer purchasing power is reduced, as in an economic recession, *value-for-money* becomes a key purchasing criterion. Marketers must pursue *value-based marketing* to capture and retain price conscious customers during lean economic times, unlike boom periods when consumers become literally addicted to personal consumption.[10] Rather than offering high quality at a high price, or lesser quality at very low prices, marketers have to look for ways to offer the more financially cautious buyers greater value – just the right combination of product quality and good service at a fair price.[11]

### Changing consumer spending patterns

Table 4.1 shows how European consumer expenditure on different products varies. Generally, for all countries, the total expenditures made by households tend to vary for essential categories of goods and services, with food, housing and transportation often using up most household income. Marketers also want to identify how spending patterns of consumers at different income levels vary. Some of these differences were noted over a century ago by Ernst Engel, who studied how people shifted their spending as their income rose. He found that as family income rises, the percentage spent on food declines, the percentage spent on housing remains constant (except for such utilities as gas, electricity and public services, which decrease), and both the percentage spent on other categories and that devoted to savings increase. **Engel's laws** generally have been supported by later studies.

Changes in chief economic variables such as income, cost of living, interest rates, and savings and borrowing patterns have a large impact on the marketplace. Companies watch these variables by using economic forecasting. Businesses do not have to be wiped out by an economic downturn or caught short in a boom. With adequate warning, they can take advantage of changes in the economic environment.

## Natural environment

The **natural environment** involves the natural resources that are needed as inputs by marketers or that are affected by marketing activities. Environmental concerns have grown steadily during the past two decades. Protection of the natural environment

| TABLE 4.1 | European consumer expenditure by product, 1990 (% of total expenditure) | | | | | | |
|---|---|---|---|---|---|---|---|
| | Food | Alcoholic drink | Non-alcoholic drink | Tobacco | Clothing | Footwear | Housing |
| *EU members* | | | | | | | |
| Austria | 16.8 | 2.3 | 0.7 | 1.9 | 8.8 | 2.3 | 17.8 |
| Belgium | 16.0 | 2.8 | 1.0 | 1.4 | 4.9 | 1.0 | 12.1 |
| Denmark | 14.8 | 3.1 | 0.6 | 2.9 | 4.7 | 0.7 | 19.7 |
| Finland | 16.6 | 3.3 | 0.5 | 1.7 | 4.1 | 0.8 | 14.3 |
| France | 15.1 | 1.9 | 0.5 | 1.0 | 5.5 | 1.1 | 12.2 |
| Germany E | 25.4 | 10.0 | 1.5 | 3.8 | 10.2 | 2.3 | 1.5 |
| Germany W | 17.3 | 2.3 | 0.6 | 1.7 | 7.5 | 1.6 | 15.6 |
| Greece | 41.8 | 2.2 | 1.0 | 2.5 | 6.4 | 0.8 | 10.3 |
| Ireland | 22.3 | 12.1 | 1.5 | 4.9 | 5.1 | 1.3 | 5.3 |
| Italy | 18.8 | 1.2 | 0.4 | 1.6 | 6.8 | 2.0 | 10.6 |
| Luxembourg | 13.7 | 1.4 | 0.6 | 4.7 | 5.6 | 0.6 | 11.9 |
| Netherlands | 15.1 | 1.1 | 0.4 | 1.8 | 5.0 | 1.7 | 11.7 |
| Portugal | 34.6 | 1.5 | 0.2 | 1.3 | 4.9 | 1.5 | 8.9 |
| Spain | 24.4 | 1.1 | 0.4 | 1.3 | 5.3 | 1.5 | 12.6 |
| Sweden | 15.2 | 2.7 | 0.4 | 1.9 | 5.4 | 1.0 | 17.6 |
| United Kingdom | 11.1 | 6.3 | 1.0 | 2.6 | 4.9 | 1.0 | 10.2 |
| *EFTA members* | | | | | | | |
| Iceland | 29.0 | 2.1 | 0.5 | 2.4 | 8.5 | | 10.9 |
| Liechtenstein | 11.5 | 6.0 | 1.1 | 2.0 | 6.1 | 1.0 | 18.3 |
| Norway | 18.4 | 3.4 | 1.1 | 2.3 | 6.2 | 1.3 | 12.2 |
| Switzerland | 19.2 | 4.7 | 0.8 | 1.6 | 3.9 | 0.9 | 13.5 |
| *Eastern Europe* | | | | | | | |
| Albania | 24.0 | 5.0 | 1.8 | 2.2 | 12.4 | 1.4 | 4.8 |
| Bulgaria | 18.7 | 11.6 | 1.0 | 2.6 | 7.4 | 2.6 | 2.0 |
| Czechoslovakia | 29.9 | 9.5 | 1.9 | 5.8 | 6.3 | 1.4 | 3.1 |
| Hungary | 26.2 | 9.5 | 2.5 | 2.1 | 6.9 | 1.2 | 4.8 |
| Poland | 25.1 | 11.2 | | 1.7 | 8.1 | 1.6 | 16.3 |
| Romania | 22.7 | 6.4 | 1.8 | 2.3 | 7.9 | 2.1 | 2.0 |
| USSR | 27.8 | 12.2 | 0.9 | 2.4 | 15.6 | 3.6 | 3.2 |
| Yugoslavia | 47.2 | 3.6 | 1.0 | 2.0 | 8.5 | 2.0 | 2.4 |
| *Others* | | | | | | | |
| Cyprus | 19.7 | 1.4 | 1.3 | 1.3 | 14.8 | 1.1 | 6.2 |
| Gibraltar | 31.0 | 1.1 | | 1.0 | 9.8 | 2.0 | 13.5 |
| Malta | 26.1 | 4.5 | 3.7 | 3.4 | 8.1 | 2.2 | 4.3 |
| Monaco | 17.7 | 2.3 | 0.5 | 1.3 | 7.2 | 1.6 | 12.5 |
| Turkey | 32.9 | 1.2 | 2.7 | 9.5 | 4.7 | 1.8 | 9.0 |

Source:    National Accounts/Euromonitor estimates.

will remain a crucial worldwide issue facing business and the public. In many cities around the world, air and water pollution have reached dangerous levels. Concern continues to mount about the depletion of the earth's ozone layer and the resulting 'greenhouse effect', a dangerous warming of the earth. And many of us fear that we soon will be buried in our own trash. Marketers should be aware of four trends in the natural environment.

| Household fuels | Household goods & services | Health | Transport | Communications | Leisure | Others | Total |
|---|---|---|---|---|---|---|---|
| 5.8 | 7.5 | 5.2 | 14.5 | 1.9 | 5.9 | 8.8 | 100.0 |
| 4.2 | 12.4 | 11.2 | 11.8 | 1.0 | 10.2 | 10.0 | 100.0 |
| 6.3 | 6.7 | 1.7 | 13.8 | 1.3 | 9.3 | 14.4 | 100.0 |
| 3.4 | 7.1 | 3.6 | 15.9 | | 9.5 | 19.2 | 100.0 |
| 6.8 | 8.2 | 9.3 | 14.8 | 2.1 | 7.4 | 14.1 | 100.0 |
| 0.8 | 12.1 | 4.0 | 2.0 | | 6.2 | 20.2 | 100.0 |
| 4.1 | 9.8 | 5.2 | 15.0 | 1.7 | 10.5 | 7.2 | 100.0 |
| 3.2 | 8.3 | 3.1 | 9.9 | 1.7 | 4.0 | 4.7 | 100.0 |
| 5.4 | 7.1 | 1.5 | 10.0 | 1.3 | 9.9 | 12.3 | 100.0 |
| 3.8 | 8.9 | 6.4 | 11.9 | 1.1 | 9.2 | 17.2 | 100.0 |
| 7.5 | 8.5 | 6.7 | 16.4 | | 3.0 | 19.5 | 100.0 |
| 5.5 | 8.0 | 12.2 | 9.7 | 1.3 | 9.9 | 16.6 | 100.0 |
| | 6.2 | 3.0 | 11.0 | 3.0 | 2.4 | 21.5 | 100.0 |
| 3.1 | 6.8 | 3.8 | 12.5 | 1.0 | 5.7 | 20.6 | 100.0 |
| 4.0 | 6.3 | 1.6 | 16.8 | | 7.2 | 19.8 | 100.0 |
| 3.2 | 5.3 | 1.2 | 12.8 | 1.5 | 8.4 | 30.4 | 100.0 |
| | 11.4 | 6.7 | 8.8 | | 9.0 | 10.8 | 100.0 |
| 3.6 | 6.0 | 12.6 | 11.8 | | 14.0 | 5.9 | 100.0 |
| 7.0 | 7.0 | 4.1 | 12.5 | 1.8 | 9.2 | 13.5 | 100.0 |
| 4.5 | 5.0 | 11.2 | 11.3 | | 9.9 | 13.4 | 100.0 |
| 4.0 | 9.8 | 3.6 | 6.9 | | 5.2 | 18.9 | 100.0 |
| 2.6 | 14.1 | 3.0 | 8.3 | | 6.9 | 19.2 | 100.0 |
| 3.2 | 16.2 | 6.7 | 8.6 | | 4.6 | 2.7 | 100.0 |
| 2.6 | 6.8 | 6.1 | 9.0 | | 13.5 | 8.7 | 100.0 |
| 2.5 | 6.6 | 7.7 | 8.4 | 0.3 | 8.6 | 2.0 | 100.0 |
| 0.9 | 5.5 | 4.0 | 4.1 | | 6.4 | 33.9 | 100.0 |
| 3.8 | 8.0 | 2.7 | 2.9 | | 8.3 | 8.6 | 100.0 |
| 9.0 | 4.4 | 4.1 | 8.6 | | 4.8 | 2.4 | 100.0 |
| 2.0 | 11.1 | 2.4 | 17.1 | | 5.4 | 16.2 | 100.0 |
| | 9.1 | 8.3 | 9.7 | | 9.1 | 5.0 | 100.0 |
| 2.4 | 10.2 | 3.8 | 17.0 | | 7.0 | 7.5 | 100.0 |
| 6.9 | 13.9 | 15.3 | 10.6 | | 7.3 | 3.0 | 100.0 |
| 5.7 | 10.6 | 11.1 | 6.0 | | 1.6 | 3.1 | 100.0 |

### Shortages of raw materials

Air and water may seem to be infinite resources, but some groups see long-run dangers. They warn of the potential dangers that propellants used in aerosol cans pose to the ozone layer. Water shortage is already a big problem in some parts of the world. Renewable resources, such as forests and food, also have to be used wisely. Companies in the forestry business are required to reforest timberlands in order to protect the soil and to ensure enough wood supplies to meet future demand. Food supply can be a critical problem because more and more of our limited farmable land is being developed for urban areas.

Nonrenewable resources, such as oil, coal and various minerals, pose a serious problem. Firms making products that require these increasingly scarce resources face large cost increases, even if the materials do remain available. They may not find it easy to pass these costs on to the consumer. However, firms engaged in research and development and in exploration can help by developing new sources and materials.

### Increased cost of energy

One nonrenewable resource – oil – has created the most serious problem for future economic growth. The large industrial economies of the world depend heavily on oil, and until economical energy substitutes can be developed, oil will continue to dominate the world political and economic picture. Big increases in the price of oil during the 1970s, and dramatic events like the 1991 Gulf War that affect oil availability, have spurred the search for alternative forms of energy. Many companies are

Environmental marketing: here Hewlett Packard attempts to market its high quality technology while promoting a good cause – the protection of endangered wildlife.

The versatile HP LaserJet 4 Plus.
Saves money. Saves paper. Saves wildlife.

searching for practical ways to harness solar, nuclear, wind and other forms of energy. For example, hundreds of firms already offer products that use solar energy for heating homes and other uses. Others are directing their research and development efforts to produce high energy-efficient technologies to meet customers' needs.

### Increased pollution

Industry has been largely blamed for damaging the quality of the natural environment. The 'green' movement draws attention to industry's 'dirty work': the disposal of chemical and nuclear wastes, the dangerous mercury levels in the ocean, the quantity of chemical pollutants in the soil and food supply, and the littering of the environment with nonbiodegradable bottles, plastics and other packaging materials.

Many companies, especially those at the 'grubbier' ends of manufacturing, often complain about the cost of fulfilling their obligations to 'clean up' regulations or to produce new greener technologies. On the other hand, more alert managers have adapted quickly to rising public environmental concerns, which have created marketing opportunities for firms. For example, Western Europe's environmental industry has seen tremendous growth since the mid-1980s: the market for environmental goods and services, such as antipollution equipment, scrubbers, recycling centres and landfill systems, is worth some $94 billion in 1993, only $40 billion less than the market in the United States (see Marketing Highlight 4.2).

1 ecu = US$1.26

Both public environmental interests and recent environmental regulations have forced many firms to search for new ways to produce more ecologically sensitive goods, recyclable or biodegradable packaging, improved pollution controls and energy-efficient operations. Niche green markets, where environmentally sensitive consumers are prepared to pay a premium price for green benefits, have emerged in sectors ranging from cosmetics, toiletries and detergents to passenger cars. However, most consumers worldwide are more likely to make trade-offs between green advantages and product quality and performance benefits in their purchasing decision. So, although environmental pressures upon businesses over the 1990s are expected to escalate, firms must seek to balance both the ecological and performance benefit expectations of the mass of consumers.[12]

### Government intervention in natural resource management

In most countries, industry has been pressured rather than persuaded into 'going green'. Environmental legislation has toughened up in recent years and businesses can expect this to continue in the foreseeable future. Recession in leading world economies over the early 1990s, however, forced governments to look at the potential of voluntary agreements with industry. The idea is to help industry meet environmental standards cost-effectively.

> A successful case is Holland's National Environmental Policy Plan (NEPP), which was first introduced in 1989 and set tight targets for pollution reduction. Some industries agreed to tougher pollution controls in return for greater government flexibility over their implementation. Although firms knew that failure to co-operate meant harsher laws would follow, the NEPP did provide a channel for government–industry dialogue and co-operation. Detailed plans were agreed with sectors accounting for 60–70 per cent of Holland's environmental pollution. Deals with oil refineries in Rotterdam helped to cut smog and sulphur dioxide emissions. Agreements with packaging firms led to a decline in the volume of municipal waste in 1992, the first time since 1945. Ammonia output also declined sharply.[13]

## Filthy lucre

Some firms complain that Europe's tough environmental regulations are driving them out of business. Many others, however, are cleaning up. Environmental pressures are one firm's expensive obligation, but another's chance for profit. The San Diego (US)-based *Environmental Business Journal* recently reported that the market in Western Europe for environmental goods and services was worth around $94bn* in 1992, only $40bn less than the market in the United States. Europe's environmental industry is reckoned to be growing at 7 per cent a year, according to the journal. Estimates put the number of environmental firms in Europe at around 16,000. The industry is attracting big players, including America's Waste Management, Asea Brown Boveri's Flakt, and Lurgi, which is part of Germany's Metallgesellschaft.

Germany is Europe's largest and toughest 'environmental state'. Germany's environmental laws have often ended up as the EU's environmental policy. Germany spends 1.55 per cent of its GDP on environmental investment. It also is the world's leading exporter of environmental technology, with sales of DM 35bn* in 1992. America comes a close second. Every time the EU adopts a German-sponsored 'green' law, it creates export opportunities for both German and their rival environmental firms elsewhere in Europe. For example, a European directive will force Europe's big towns to have sewage treatment plants by 2000, with its small towns to follow by 2005. The primitive state of sewage treatment in some parts of Europe means that there are now lots of orders for new plants. Some big operators like France's Générales des Eaux, Lyonnaise des Eaux Dumez and Saur, Bouygues's subsidiary, have successfully expanded abroad, including the tough German market, by giving public authorities in European countries a one-stop shop: that is, they finance, build and operate water-treatment plants.

Waste management – collecting, transporting and disposal of solid rubbish – accounts for just under 33 per cent of the total Western Europe environment market, and is the biggest single market for environmental firms in the European Union. New recycling laws, particularly in Germany, are creating fresh new opportunities for many companies.

The complexity of EU green directives and national laws also makes for a booming business in environmental consultancy, particularly in the areas of environmental auditing and risk management.

As recession bites in the early 1990s, the cost of applying environmental standards has been felt by governments and industries across the European Union. Complaints from European firms about the high cost of conforming to green standards may see fewer new laws passed. However, the existing ones will feed the environmental industry for some time. Chances are that the green business will keep growing over the remaining decade. With it will grow clever companies that have learnt to turn trash into cash!

*1 ecu = US$1.26 = DM 1.89 (Deutschmarks).

Source: Adapted from 'Pollution: the money in Europe's muck', *The Economist* (20 November 1993), 109–10.

In most developed Western nations, well-organized sectors, such as oils, chemicals, pharmaceuticals and food, are more likely to reach common agreements with government agencies and their plans for environmental control. The job, many argue, is still incomplete. Smaller firms and the least organized sector – households – are generally a long way away from signing up to total 'greenery'. For businesses and industries, environmental issues and government intervention are unlikely to vanish. Clever marketers should remain alert and proactive in the search for new green solutions to meet the world's environmental and natural resource dilemmas. Instead of opposing regulation, marketers should help develop solutions to the material and energy problems facing the world.

## Technological environment

The **technological environment** is perhaps the most dramatic force now shaping our destiny. Technology has released such wonders as penicillin, organ transplants and notebook computers. It has also released such horrors as the nuclear bomb, nerve gas and the machine gun, and such mixed blessings as cars, televisions and credit cards. Our attitude towards technology depends on whether we are more impressed with its wonders or its blunders.

Every new technology replaces an older technology. Transistors decimated the vacuum-tube industry, xerography killed the carbon-paper business, autos and highways hurt the railroads, and television hurt the movies. When old industries fought or ignored new technologies, their businesses declined.

New technologies create new markets and opportunities. The marketer should watch the following trends in technology.

### Fast pace of technological change

Many of today's common products were not available a hundred years ago: televisions, home freezers, automatic dishwashers, electronic computers, contraceptives, earth satellites, personal computers, compact disc players, video cassette recorders, facsimile machines, mobile phones. The list is unending! Companies that fail to anticipate and keep up with technological change soon find their products outdated. But, keeping pace with technological change is becoming more challenging for firms today. Technology life cycles are getting shorter. Take the typewriter. The first generation modern mechanical typewriter dominated the market for twenty-five years. Subsequent generations had shorter lives – fifteen years for electro-mechanical models, seven years for electronic versions and five years for first-generation microprocessor-based ones. Other examples of fast technological change are found. The average life of some computer software products, for example, is now well under one year.

Firms must track technological trends and determine whether or not these changes will affect their products' continued ability to solve customers' needs. Technologies arising in unrelated industries can also affect the firm's fortunes. The mechanical watch industry was overtaken by manufacturers of electronic components seeking new applications and growth opportunities for their quartz technology. Businesses must assiduously monitor their technological environment to avoid missing new product and market opportunities.

### High R&D budgets

Technology and innovations require heavy investments in research and development. It is not uncommon for pharmaceuticals companies, for example, to spend £150m. to £200m. to develop a new drug. High R&D spending also is a feature of many industries including cars, communications, computers, aerospace, engineering, entertainment and consumer electronics. Some companies spend billions on R&D each year. A recent study showed that the international top 200 companies devoted an average 4.85 per cent of 1993 sales to R&D. General Motors of the United States was the world's biggest spender with a budget of more than $4bn (£2.6bn). It is followed by German engineering group Daimler Benz, Ford Motor of the United States and Japan's Hitachi. These three nations dominate the world's top 20, which contains just one representative each from France (Alcatel Alsthom Compagnie Générale) and the Netherlands (Philips), as well as the Swiss–Swedish Asea Brown Boveri.[14]

In recent years, there has been a marked increase in collaborative technological research efforts between Western governments and industries. In Europe, this mood spawned subsidized programmes, such as Esprit, Eureka and Jessi, and in the US schemes such as Sematech, MCC and a HDTV (high-density television) consortium. These programmes stemmed from two main concerns: first, the soaring cost of R&D and the difficulty, even for big companies, of mastering an ever wider range of technologies; second, the increasing international competition, mainly from Japan, in electronics and related industries. There are mixed views on the success of these programmes, although collaboration has helped break down barriers between rival firms and stimulated the dissemination of know-how.[15]

### Concentration on minor improvements

As a result of the high cost of developing and introducing new technologies, many companies are tinkering – making minor product improvements – instead of gambling on substantial innovations. The high costs and risks of commercialization failure make firms take this cautious approach to their R&D investment. Most companies are content to put their money into copying competitors' products, making minor feature and style improvements, or offering simple extensions of current brands. Thus much research is in danger of being defensive rather than offensive.

### Increased regulation

As products become more complex, people need to know that they are safe. Thus, government agencies investigate and ban potentially unsafe products. In the EU and America, complex regulations exist for testing new drugs. The US Federal Food and Drug administration, for example, is notorious for its strict enforcement of drug testing and safety rules. Statutory and industry regulatory bodies exist to set safety standards for consumer products and penalize companies that fail to meet them. Stringent regulations have resulted in much higher research costs and in longer times between new product ideas and their introductions. Marketers should be aware of these regulations when seeking and developing new products.

Marketers need to understand the changing technological environment and the ways that new technologies can serve customer and human needs. They need to work closely with R&D people to encourage more market-oriented research. They also must be alert to the possible negative aspects of any innovation that might harm users or arouse opposition.

## Political environment

Marketing decisions are strongly affected by developments in the political environment. The **political environment** consists of laws, government agencies and pressure groups that influence and limit various organizations and individuals in a given society.

### Legislation regulating business

Even the most liberal advocates of free market economies agree that the system works best with at least some regulation. Well-conceived regulation can encourage competition and ensure fair markets for goods and services. Thus governments develop *public policy* to guide commerce – sets of laws and regulations that limit business for the good of society as a whole. Almost every marketing activity is subject to a wide range of laws and regulations.

Understanding the public policy implications of a particular marketing activity is not a simple matter. First, there are many laws created at different levels: in the EU, business operators are subject to European Commission, individual member state and specific local regulations; in the US, laws are created at the federal, state and local levels, and these regulations often overlap.

Second, the regulations are constantly changing – what was allowed last year may now be prohibited. In the single European market, deregulation and current moves towards harmonization are expected to take time, creating a state of flux, which challenges and confuses both domestic and international marketers. They must therefore work hard to keep up with these changes in the regulations and their interpretations.

In many developed economies, legislation affecting business has increased steadily over the years. This legislation has been enacted for a number of reasons. The first is to *protect companies* from each other. Although business executives may praise competition, they sometimes try to neutralize it when it threatens them. So laws are passed to define and prevent unfair competition. Antitrust agencies and monopolies and mergers commissions exist to enforce these laws.

The second purpose of government regulation is to *protect consumers* from unfair business practices. Some firms, if left alone, would make poor products, tell lies in their advertising and deceive consumers through their packaging and pricing. Unfair business practices have been defined and are enforced by various agencies.

The third purpose of government regulation is to *protect the interests of society* against unrestrained business behaviour. Profitable business activity does not always create a better quality of life. Regulation arises to ensure that firms take responsibility for the social costs of their production or products.

Managers sometimes argue that regulations and directives which are not pro-industry hamper, not help companies. For example, many pharmaceutical companies operating in Europe expressed disappointment over a recent policy document published by the European Commission. They argued that the policy propounded is unhelpful while optimists within the Commission believed it could still serve a useful purpose by stimulating an informed discussion in the European Parliament and among the Council of Industry Ministers of member states. The debate over whether the EU should be helping the European drug industry, and, if so, how, continues (see Marketing Highlight 4.3).

New laws and their enforcement will continue or increase. Business executives must watch these developments when planning their products and marketing programmes. Marketers need to know about the main laws protecting competition, consumers and society. International marketers should additionally be aware of regional, country and local laws that affect their international marketing activity.

## Growth of public interest groups

The number and power of public interest groups have increased during the past two decades. In Chapter 2 we discussed a broad range of societal marketing issues. The successful efforts of Ralph Nader's Public Citizen group in the United States raised the importance of the role of public interest groups as watchdogs on consumer interests. Nader lifted consumerism, an organized movement of citizens and government to strengthen the rights and powers of buyers in relation to sellers, into a powerful social force. Consumerism has spilled over to countries in Western Europe and other developed market economies such as Australia. Hundreds of other consumer interest

## MARKETING HIGHLIGHT 4.3

## The European Union and Europe's pharmaceutical industry: help or hindrance?

A policy document finalized in early March 1994 by the European Commission aims to achieve a more favourable environment for the European drug industry. Initial responses to the Commission's paper suggest that the echoes around European capitals may be a little muted to the question: Is the EU helping European drug companies or not? Many in the industry felt disappointed that the policy document contained much less than they had hoped for, that 'this is unlikely to have any influence or produce any change', 'a wasted opportunity', 'so vague it goes nowhere'.

So, what does the European Union aim to achieve for Europe's drug industry?

- The European Medicines Evaluation Agency, which comes into operation in 1995 and provides rapid access to the single market via new product authorization procedures.
- A centralized procedure leading to a single authorization for the whole of the European Union reserved for certain new drugs and mandatory for those derived from biotechnology.
- A decentralized procedure for most medicinal products based on mutual recognition of national marketing authorizations, disputes being settled by binding EU arbitration.

The procedure is supposed to speed authorizations – 300 days instead of several years – and limit cost increases in authorization processing. It should increase consumer confidence and improve public health protection. It will eventually reduce market-to-market diversity in information about therapeutic indications, side effects, presentation and package size.

### Recent legislation

Recent legislation includes the following directives:

- A directive on wholesale distribution of medicines which will facilitate and stimulate intra-community trade whilst ensuring the integrity of transactions, regulating recall of defective products and deterring counterfeit products.
- Directives on medicines advertising, labelling and leaflets which will improve information for patients, limit waste and impose requirements on promotion to health professionals.

groups, private and governmental, operate at all levels – regional, national, state/county and local levels. Other groups that marketers need to consider are those seeking to protect the environment and to advance the rights of various groups such as women, children, ethnic minorities, senior citizens, the handicapped and others.

### Increased emphasis on ethics and socially responsible actions

Written regulations cannot possibly cover all potential marketing abuses and existing laws are often difficult to enforce. However, beyond written laws and regulations, business is also governed by social codes and rules of professional ethics. Enlightened companies encourage their managers to look beyond what the regulatory system allows and simply to 'do the right thing'. These socially responsible firms actively seek out ways to protect the long-run interests of their consumers and the environment.

Increased concerns about the environment have created fresh interest in the issues of ethics and social responsibility. Almost every aspect of marketing involves such issues. Unfortunately, because these issues usually involve conflicting interests, well-meaning people can disagree honestly about the right course of action in a particular situation. Thus many industrial and professional trade associations have suggested codes of ethics, and many companies now are developing policies and guidelines to deal with complex social responsibility issues.

### Patent protection

Patent protection includes:

- A new regulation which ensures protection of intellectual property for up to fifteen years from the date of first marketing of the medicine in the European Union.
- A universal position being adopted in February 1994 on a revised draft directive on legal protection of biotechnological inventions, which opens the way for definite adoption in 1994.

### A stable and safe environment for new biotechnology projects

- Improved cooperation between the European Union and member states would avoid duplication of R&D efforts.
- The necessity to bring greater attention to ethical questions related to certain applications of biotechnology and to improve public understanding.

Source: Adapted from Peter O'Donnell, 'Disappointment over policy document', and 'What the European Union aims to achieve', in

- A review of the regulatory framework in the light of scientific knowledge.

### Programmes better suited to pharmaceutical R&D

Such programmes:

- Encourage multidisciplinary research and industry–university interaction.
- Promote integration and cooperation between prenormative research and R&D.
- Evolve research priorities in pharmaceutical research through pilot programmes.

These are very broad statements of intent. No wonder industry and consumers are not terribly impressed. Optimists within the Commission, however, believe that the policy document can still serve a useful purpose by stimulating an informed discussion in the European Parliament and in the Council of Industry Ministers.

'Pharmaceuticals: Research and Development', *Financial Times* (23 March 1994), VI.

In Chapter 2, we discussed in greater depth public and social responsibility issues surrounding key marketing decisions, the legal issues that marketers should understand, and the common ethical and societal concerns that marketers face.

## Cultural environment

The **cultural environment** is made up of institutions and other forces that affect society's basic values, perceptions, preferences and behaviours. People grow up in a particular society that shapes their basic beliefs and values. They absorb a world view that defines their relationships to themselves and others. The following cultural characteristics can affect marketing decision making. Marketers must be aware of these cultural influences and how they vary across societies within the markets served by the firm.

### Persistence of cultural values

People in a given society hold many beliefs and values. Their core beliefs and values have a high degree of persistence. For example, most of us believe in working, getting married, giving to charity and being honest. These beliefs shape more specific

# Ronald McDonald Children's Charities: playing a role in local communities

Ronald McDonald Children's Charities (RMCC) was founded in 1984 in the United States. It was established in memory of Ray Kroc, founder of McDonald's Corporation. He believed that 'It was important to have an involvement in the life and spirit of a community and the people around you'. This belief lives on in the McDonald's system and is evident in a variety of community programmes practised by McDonald's the world over. In 1989, for example, RMCC was set up in the United Kingdom, and through the efforts of McDonald's Restaurants Limited, its staff, customers and suppliers, over £3m. has since been raised for a wide variety of charitable causes that help children.

RMCC grants have been awarded to programmes which help young people reach their fullest potential and make a real difference for children and their well-being. The 'Ronald McDonald House' is a cornerstone of RMCC. The first was built at Philadelphia in the United States in 1974, close to the Philadelphia Children's Hospital. When a child is taken seriously ill and has to spend some time in hospital, families are usually faced with the problem of where to stay to be close at hand. The Ronald McDonald House has a set number of beds for parents to stay overnight and a family accommodation block. This means that the family can be together again as a unit while also providing a brief respite in a family environment.

There are now over 160 Ronald McDonald Houses in the United States, Canada, Australia, Japan and Europe. Each House is a 'home away from home' with the feel, aesthetics and comfort for family living. Families are able to prepare their own meals, relax and rest in privacy or enjoy the company of others living in when they so desire. The House is the result of a team effort between the hospital doctors and staff, the parents of the children and McDonalds. Each House is run by a separate charitable trust set up to oversee fund-raising and to manage the house. The boards of these trusts are made up of parents, hospital representatives and senior management of McDonald's. The trusts initiate their own fund-raising events. Throughout the year, McDonald's own restaurant staff are involved in local events to raise money for RMCC, and collecting boxes for donations from customers are placed in every restaurant. McDonald's Restaurants Limited, its franchisees, and also its suppliers, all donate to RMCC. Other recipients of money raised by RMCC include children's charities – such as hospitals, youth organizations, schools and many more worthy causes.

McDonald's restaurants not only display posters and collecting boxes for the RMCC programme, but also provide customers with information leaflets to disseminate information about their community involvement. These leaflets also sometimes contain requests for funds and/or volunteers who may be interested in helping in specific campaigns. This type of communication effort is also designed to raise customers' as well as other local and general publics'

attitudes and behaviours found in everyday life. *Core* beliefs and values are passed on from parents to children and are reinforced by schools, religious groups, business and government.

*Secondary* beliefs and values are more open to change. Believing in marriage is a core belief; believing that people should get married early in life is a secondary belief. Marketers have some chance of changing secondary values, but little chance of changing core values. For example, family-planning marketers could argue more effectively that people should get married later than that they should not get married at all.

## Shifts in secondary cultural values

Although core values are fairly persistent, cultural swings do take place. Consider the impact of popular music groups, movie personalities and other celebrities on young people's hair styling, clothing and sexual norms. Marketers want to predict

*"It is
important
to have an
involvement
in the life
and spirit of
a community
and the people
around you."*

Ray A Kroc
Founder
McDonald's Corporation

### What is McDonald's Involvement?

As well as their generous £1 million donation, McDonald's has lent expertise in setting up the House along with legal, design and construction advice. McDonald's is totally committed to working with representatives of the hospital and parents through the Alder Hey Family House Trust Ltd, a registered charity, which is responsible for raising funds and running the House now it is open.

Paul Preston, McDonald's UK President, explains: "With diminishing public-sector resources, it is vital that private enterprise plays a role in developing concepts such as the Ronald McDonald House where, at long last, parents can live in home-like surroundings whilst their child undergoes treatment. Hopefully the days in which parents have to camp out in the hospital are numbered.

"Ronald McDonald House is the result of team effort; a caring partnership between McDonald's, the Hospital staff and the families of the children."

*The Tree of Life*

The "Tree of Life" which is on display at the house. A visible thank-you to those who support the Trust.

McDonald's plays its role in the life and spirit of the surrounding local communities

awareness of Ray Kroc's philosophy of 'giving something back to the communities that give so much to us [McDonald's Corporation]'.

Source: 'Your questions answered', Ronald McDonald Children's Charities, London; The Public Relations Department, McDonald's Restaurants Limited, London.

cultural shifts in order to spot new opportunities or threats. Several firms offer 'futures' forecasts in this connection. For example, the Yankelovich marketing research firm tracks forty-one cultural values, such as 'anti-bigness', 'mysticism', 'living for today', 'away from possessions' and 'sensuousness'. The firm describes the percentage of the population who share the attitude as well as the percentage who go against the trend. For instance, the percentage of people who value physical fitness and well-being has risen steadily over the years. Such information helps marketers cater to trends with appropriate products and communication appeals.

The principal cultural values of a society are expressed in people's views of themselves and others, as well as in their views of organizations, society, nature and the universe.

*People's views of themselves*   People vary in their emphasis on serving themselves versus serving others. Some people seek personal pleasure, wanting fun, change and escape. Others seek self-realization through religion, recreation or the avid pursuit of careers or other life goals. People use products, brands and services as a means of self-expression and buy products and services that match their views of themselves.

In the 1980s, personal ambition and materialism increased dramatically, with significant marketing implications. In a 'me-society', people buy their 'dream cars' and take their 'dream vacations'. They spend more time in outdoor health activities (jogging, tennis), in thought, and on arts and crafts. The leisure industry (camping, skiing, boating, arts and crafts, and sports) faces good growth prospects in a society where people seek self-fulfilment.

*People's views of others*     More recently, observers have noted a shift from a 'me-society' to a 'we-society' in which more people want to be with and serve others. Flashy spending and self-indulgence appear to be on the way out, whereas saving, family concerns and helping others are on the rise. A recent survey showed that more people are becoming involved in charity, volunteer work and social service activities.[16] This suggests a bright future for 'social support' products and services that improve direct communication between people, such as health clubs, family vacations and games. It also suggests a growing market for 'social substitutes' – things like VCRs and computers that allow people who are alone to feel that they are not.

*People's views of organizations*     People vary in their attitudes towards corporations, government agencies, trade unions, universities and other organizations. By and large, people are willing to work for big organizations and expect them, in turn, to carry out society's work. There has been a decline in organizational loyalty, however. People are giving a little less to their organizations and are trusting them less.

This trend suggests that organizations need to find new ways to win consumer confidence. They need to review their advertising communications to make sure their messages are honest. Also, they need to review their various activities to make sure that they are coming across as 'good corporate citizens'. More companies are linking themselves to worthwhile causes, measuring their images with important publics and using public relations to build more positive images (see Marketing Highlight 4.4).

*People's views of society*     People vary in their attitudes toward their society – from patriots who defend it, to reformers who want to change it, to malcontents who want to leave it. People's orientation to their society influences their consumption patterns, levels of savings and attitudes toward the marketplace.

In the affluent and industrializing Asian nations, consumers aspire to achieve the high living standards and lifestyles of people in the more advanced Western countries. The display of conspicuous consumption and fondness for expensive Western brands – the common label for achievement and Westernisation – are highly acceptable behaviour. Consumer patriotism, for example, is not an issue, since locally made goods are often viewed as inferior or less desirable than foreign imported brands. By contrast, in the Western developed countries, the late 1980s and early 1990s saw an increase in consumer patriotism. European consumers reckoned that sticking to locally produced goods would save and protect jobs. Many US companies also responded to American patriotism with 'made in America' themes and flag-waving promotions, such as Chevrolet is 'the heartbeat of America', Black & Decker's flag-like symbol on its tools and the textile industry's 'Crafted with Pride in the USA' advertising campaign, which insisted that 'made in the USA' matters.[17]

*People's views of nature*     People vary in their attitudes toward the natural world. Some feel ruled by it, others feel in harmony with it and still others seek to master it.

A long-term trend has been people's growing mastery over nature through technology and the belief that nature is bountiful. More recently, however, people have recognized that nature is finite and fragile – that it can be destroyed or spoiled by human activities.

Love of nature is leading to more camping, hiking, boating, fishing and other outdoor activities. Business has responded by offering more hiking gear, camping equipment, better insect repellents and other products for nature enthusiasts. Tour operators are offering more tours to wilderness areas. Food producers have found growing markets for 'natural' products like natural cereal, natural ice cream, organically farmed produce and a variety of health foods. Marketing communicators are using appealing natural backgrounds in advertising their products.

*People's views of the universe*   Finally, people vary in their beliefs about the origin of the universe and their place in it. While the practice of religion remains strong in many parts of the world, religious conviction and practice have been dropping off through the years in certain countries, notably in the United States and Europe where, for example, church attendance has fallen gradually. As people lose their religious orientation, they seek goods and experiences with more immediate satisfactions. During the 1980s, people increasingly measured success in terms of career achievement, wealth, and worldly possessions. Some futurists, however, have noted an emerging renewal of interest in religion, perhaps as part of a broader search for a new inner purpose. In the 1990s, they believe, people are moving away from materialism and dog-eat-dog ambition to seek more permanent values and a more certain grasp of right and wrong. However, in many parts of the world that lie outside Western Europe and North America, where societies' value systems place great importance on economic ascendance and possession, such materialism and dog-eat-dog mentalities are unlikely to wane quickly in the near future. Nonetheless, there remains a vision of things to come:

> The Nineties will see a marked change in the way society defines success, with achievements such as a happy family life and service to one's community replacing money as the measure of one's worth.[18]

> The Nineties will be a far less cynical decade than the Eighties. Yes, we will still care what things cost. But we will seek to value only those things – family, community, earth, faith – that will endure.[19]

## RESPONDING TO THE MARKETING ENVIRONMENT

Many companies view the marketing environment as an 'uncontrollable' element to which they must adapt. They passively accept the marketing environment and do not try to change it. They analyse the environmental forces and design strategies that will help the company avoid the threats and take advantage of the opportunities the environment provides.

Other companies take an **environmental management perspective**.[20] Rather than simply watching and reacting, these firms take aggressive actions to affect the publics and forces in their marketing environment. Such companies hire lobbyists to influence legislation affecting their industries and stage media events to gain favourable press coverage. They run 'advertorials' (ads expressing editorial points of view) to shape public opinion. They press law suits and file complaints with regulators to keep competitors in line. They also form contractual agreements to better control their distribution channels.

Marketing management cannot always affect environmental forces. In many cases, it must settle for simply watching and reacting to the environment. For example, a company would have little success trying to influence geographic population shifts, the economic environment or important cultural values. But whenever possible, smart marketing managers will take a *proactive* rather than *reactive* approach to the marketing environment.

## SUMMARY

The company must start with the *marketing environment* in searching for opportunities and monitoring threats. The marketing environment consists of all the actors and forces that affect the company's ability to transact effectively with its target market. The company's marketing environment can be divided into the microenvironment and the macroenvironment.

The *microenvironment* consists of five components. First, the company's *internal environment* – its several departments and management levels – as it affects marketing management's decision making. Second, the *marketing channel firms* that cooperate to create value: the suppliers and marketing intermediaries (middlemen, physical distribution firms, marketing services agencies, financial intermediaries). Third, the five types of *markets* in which the company can sell: the consumer, producer, reseller, government and international markets. Fourth, the *competitors* facing the company. Fifth, the *publics* that have an actual or potential interest in or impact on the organization's ability to achieve its objectives. The seven types of public include the financial, media, government, citizen action, local, general, and internal publics.

The company's *macroenvironment* consists of primary forces that shape opportunities and pose threats to the company. These forces include demographic, economic, natural, technological, political and cultural forces.

The *demographic environment* must be studied. In many developed Western and Asian countries, trends in population growth, changes in age structure, the family and education levels, and increasing diversity, have important implications for marketing people. The *economic environment* shows changing real income and changing consumer spending patterns. The *natural environment* shows coming shortages of certain raw materials, increased energy costs, increased pollution levels and increasing government intervention in natural resource management. The *technological environment* shows rapid technological change, unlimited innovational opportunities, high R&D budgets, concentration on minor improvements rather than big discoveries, and increased regulation of technological change. The *political environment* shows increasing business regulation, the rising importance of public interest groups and increased emphasis on ethics and socially responsible actions. The *cultural environment* suggests long-run trends towards a 'we-society', decreasing organizational loyalty, increasing patriotism, an increasing appreciation for nature and a search for more meaningful and enduring values.

## ■ DISCUSSING THE ISSUES

1. In the 1950s and 1960s, politicians, celebrities and public figures did not usually think twice about being seen smoking. Would a president or prime minister be seen smoking today? How has the cultural environment changed? How might a cigarette manufacturer market its products differently to meet this new environment?

2. Select an adventure theme park. What environmental trends will affect the success of the park throughout the 1990s? If you were in charge of marketing at this organization, what plans would you make to deal with these trends?

3. Pressure groups, lobbyists, public interest groups play an important role in defending society's interests. Select one such group you are familiar with and describe its cause. Suggest ways in which goods or services providers targeted by the group might satisfactorily address the demands or pressures imposed by the group.

4. Younger customers are becoming more concerned about the natural environment. How would this trend affect a company that markets plastic sandwich bags? Discuss some effective responses to this trend.

5. A large alcoholic beverage marketer is planning to introduce an 'adult soft drink' – a socially acceptable substitute for stronger drinks that would be cheaper and lower in alcohol than wine. What cultural and other factors might affect the success of this product?

6. Some marketing goals, such as improved quality, require strong support from an internal public – a company's own employees. But surveys show that employees increasingly distrust management and company loyalty is eroding. How can a company market internally to help meet its goals?

## ■ APPLYING THE CONCEPTS

1. Changes in the marketing environment mean that marketers must meet new consumer needs that may be quite different – even directly opposite – from those in the past. You can track changes in the marketing environment by looking at how companies modify their products.

   - Make a list of the products you encounter in one day that claim to be 'low' or 'high' in some ingredient, such as low-tar cigarettes, or high-fibre cereal.
   - Write down similar products that seem to offer the opposite characteristics.
   - In each case, which product do you think came first? Do you think that this is an effective response to a changing marketing environment?

2. The political environment can have a direct impact on marketers and their plans. Thinking about a recent major political environmental change in a country of your choice, consider the following:

   - Name three industries that will probably have their marketing plans and strategies affected by the political changes.
   - For each of the industries that you named, list three potential strategies to help adapt to the coming changes in the political environment.
   - Although environmental changes appear likely, are they *certain*? How should companies plan for unsettled conditions?

## ■ REFERENCES

1. Tom O'Sullivan, 'ASA retreats on P&G ad attack', *Marketing Week* (27 January 1995), 9; 'Soap and chips', *Financial Times* (27 December 1994), 15; Roderick Oram, 'Washing whiter proves a murky business', *Financial Times* (21 December 1994), 8; Roderick Oram, 'Soap wars force delay in Unilever board changes', *Financial Times* (20 December 1994), 1; Sean Brierley, 'ASA document slams P&G ads', *Marketing Week* (2 December 1994), 7; Diane Summers, 'Procter set for rap on soap advert', *Financial Times* (1 December 1994), 9; Roderick Oram, 'P&G, Unilever soap wars leave market spinning', *Financial Times* (1 November 1994), 29; 'Persil Power "no better than others"', *Financial Times* (6 October 1994), 11; Barbara Smit, 'Unilever comes clean over detergent', *The European* (30 Sept.–6 Oct. 1994), 18; Tom O'Sullivan, 'Lever condemns new Ariel launch', *Marketing Week* (4 November 1994), 11; Diane Summers, 'Unilever detergent comes under renewed criticism', *Financial Times* (24–25 September 1994), 26;

Roderick Oram, 'Unilever concedes detergent damaged clothing', *Financial Times* (23 September 1994), 1; Diane Summers, 'Persil wars go to advert watchdog', *Financial Times* (2 August 1994), 7; 'Tale from the washroom', *The Economist* (11 June 1994), 89; David Short, 'Dirty fighting in soap wars', *The European* (5–11 August 1994), 17; Diane Summers, 'Procter steps up attack on Unilever's Persil Power', *Financial Times* (30–31 July 1994), 24; Diane Summers and Ronald van de Krol, 'Tests prove new soap powder safe, says Unilever', *Financial Times* (20 July 1994), 24; Tony Jackson, 'Unilever hit by new allegations in its soap war with Procter', *Financial Times* (28 June 1994), 20; Barbara Smit, 'Unilever sticks by Omo', *The European* (10–16 June 1994), 17; Helen Jones, 'Lever shoots down P&G claim', *Marketing Week* (10 June 1994), 9; Tony Jackson, 'Dirty tricks alleged in soap war', *Financial Times* (3 May 1994), 9, and 'Unilever takes Procter to court in row over "super" detergent', *Financial Times* (30 Apr.–1 May

1994), 1; Maggie Urry and Ronald van de Krol, 'Rival soaps in lather over "rotted" clothes claim', *Financial Times* (28 April 1994), 1; 'Lever claims upper hand in "green detergent" war', *ENDS Report 231* (April 1994), 27.

2. The *UN World Population Prospects* gives population details for individual countries.

3. 'Fings ain't wot they used to be', *The Economist* (28 May 1994), 77–8; see also Joe Schwartz, 'Is the baby boomlet ending?', *American Demographics* (May 1992), 9; European Commission, *Demographic Statistics*, and OECD are further sources of population statistics and projections.

4. David Nicholson-Lord, 'Mass leisure class is on the way, say forecasters', *Independent* (18 April 1994), 4; see also *Leisure Futures*, vol. 1, Henley Centre, London (1994), provides more details on the emerging leisure class; for more discussion about America's 'echo boom'/'baby boomlet' and the 'gray market', see Horst H. Stipp, 'Boomlet market', *American Demographics* (March 1989), 14–15; James U. McNeal, 'Growing up in the market', *American Demographics* (October 1992), 46–50; Walecia Konrad and Gail DeGeorge, 'US companies go for the gray', *Business Week* (3 April 1989), 64–7; Diane Crispell and William H. Frey, 'American maturity', *American Demographics* (March 1993), 31–42; Melinder Beck, 'The geezer boom', in 'The 21st century family', a special issue of *Newsweek* (winter/spring 1990), 62–7.

5. David Short, 'A different taste of things to come', *The European* (14–20 October 1994), 21; for an outstanding discussion of the changing nature of American households, see *American Households*, American Demographics Desk Reference Series, no. 3 (July 1992).

6. See Fabian Linden, 'In the rearview mirror', *American Demographics* (April 1984), 4–5. For more reading, see Bryant Robey and Cheryl Russell, 'A portrait of the American worker', *American Demographics* (March 1984), 17–21.

7. See 'The myth of the Euro-consumer', *The Economist* (4 November 1989), 107–8.

8. See Judith Waldrop and Thomas Exter, 'What the 1990 census will show', *American Demographics* (January 1990), 25; *American Diversity*, American Demographic Desk Reference Series, no. 1 (July 1991); and Brian Bremner, 'A spicier stew in the melting pot', *Business Week* (21 December 1992), 29–30.

9. See 'Can Europe compete? Balance of economic power begins to shift', *Financial Times* (9 March 1994), 14; 'Can Europe compete?', *Financial Times* (7 March 1994), 14; 'Can Europe compete? An elusive corporate consensus', and 'Can Europe compete? A relapse into Eurosclerosis', *Financial Times* (24 February 1994), 20, 21.

10. James W. Hughes, 'Understanding the squeezed consumer', *American Demographics* (July 1991), 44–50; see also Patricia Sellers, 'Winning over the new consumer', *Fortune* (29 July 1991), 113–25; and Brian O'Reilly, 'Preparing for leaner times', *Fortune* (27 January 1992), 40–7.

11. For more on value marketing, see Christopher Power, 'Value marketing', *Business Week* (11 November 1991), 132–40.

12. For more discussion about consumers' environmental consciousness and consumers' environmental decisions, see Sabine Dembkowski and Stuart Hanmer-Lloyd, 'The environmental value–attitude–system model: a framework to guide the understanding of environmentally-conscious consumer behaviour', *Journal of Marketing Management*, **10**, 7 (October 1994), 593–603; W. Adlwarth and F. Wimmer, 'Umweltbewusstsein und Kaufverhalten – Ergebnisse einer Verbraucherpanel – Studie' (Environmental consciousness and purchase behaviour: results of a consumer panel study), *Jahrbuch der Absatz- und Verbraucherforschung*, no. 2, Nuerenberg, Gesellschaft fuer Konsumforschung (1986), 166–92; see also Joe Schwartz, 'Earth day today', *American Demographics* (April 1990), 40–1; Jennifer Lawrence, 'Marketers drop "Recycled"', *Advertising Age* (9 March 1992), 1, 48; and Carl Frankel, 'Blueprint for green marketing', *American Demographics* (April 1992), 34–8.

13. 'Going Dutch', *The Economist* (20 November 1993), 110.

14. See 'R&D Scoreboard', *Financial Times* (17 June 1994), 14–15; *The UK R&D Scoreboard 1994*, Company Reporting Limited, Edinburgh, UK; Robert Buderi, 'R&D scoreboard: on a clear day you can see progress', *Business Week* (29 June 1992), 104–6.

15. Guy de Jonquières, 'Shortcomings of joint research', *Financial Times* (16 October 1990), 18.

16. See Bill Barol, 'The eighties are gone', *Newsweek* (14 January 1988), 48; Natalie de Combray, 'Volunteering in America', *American Demographics* (March 1987), 50–2; Annetta Miller, 'The new volunteerism', *Newsweek* (8 February 1988), 42–3; and Ronald Henkoff, 'Is greed dead?', *Fortune* (14 August 1989), 40–1.

17. See Kenneth Dreyfack, 'Draping Old Glory around just about everything', *Business Week* (27 October 1986), 66–7; Pat Sloan, 'Ads go all-American', *Advertising Age* (28 July 1986), 3, 52; 'Retailers rallying round the flag', *Advertising Age* (11 February 1991), 4; and Gary Levin, 'BASH, BASH, BASH: U.S. marketers turn red, white, and blue against Japan', *Advertising Age* (3 February 1992), 1, 44.

18. Anne B. Fisher, 'A brewing revolt against the rich', *Fortune* (17 December 1990), 89–94.

19. Anne B. Fisher, 'What consumers want in the 1990s', *Fortune* (21 January 1990), 112; see also Joseph M. Winski, 'Who we are, how we live, what we think', *Advertising Age* (20 January 1992), 16–18; and John Huey, 'Finding new heroes for a new era', *Fortune* (25 January 1993), 62–9.

20. See Carl P. Zeithaml and Valerie A. Zeithaml, 'Environmental management: revising the marketing perspective', *Journal of Marketing* (spring 1984), 46–53.

## CASE 4

### Angelou's restaurant (and snack bar?)   *Alkis S. Magdalinos**

John Angelou was trying to work out whether he should sell his traditional restaurant business that he had run in an Athens suburb for nearly twenty years. His restaurant had 20 tables, which meant that he could serve about 80 customers at a time. However, he rarely had more than 40–50 guests at a time and then only during peak hours on Friday or Saturday. His business's results were from fair to good but he and other family members worked very long hours to keep the business going.

The change in lifestyles and the proliferation of fast-food restaurants had him thinking very seriously about the long-run viability of his business. In particular, several foreign chains had moved in and were growing very fast. There were some well-known international names, such as Wendy's, McDonald's and KFC, as well as several Greek franchise chains, including Goody's and Lebel, and many new independent operations (see Exhibit 4.1). In addition, there were local and international pizzerias, such as Pizza Hut, many with home delivery services. Finally, sandwich bars were cropping up everywhere.

The previous week, a business friend of his had offered to buy Angelou's restaurant for what Mr Angelou thought was a shade less than a fair price. He had also obtained information about franchise fees. The price he could get for his current restaurant would only cover the rights to buy another restaurant and equipment in a new shopping centre that interested him. He would then need extra money to cover the franchise charge. The restaurant he was interested in would have space for 12 tables seating 48 guests in total and a bar that could accommodate 5–6 guests. Mr Angelou made some preliminary estimates. With 50 per cent capacity utilization, and charging depreciation for the equipment and salaries for his employees and himself, he came to the conclusion that he would just about break even after six months. However, it would take him two years operating at 80 per cent capacity to recover the value of his investment and the franchise fee.

Mr Angelou visited the shopping centre where his proposed new restaurant would be. The centre was

*University of La Verne, Greece.

**Exhibit 4.1**   Outlets in Greece selling food for consumption on the premises

| Type of outlets | 1980 | 1985 | 1990 |
|---|---|---|---|
| Traditional restaurants and tavernas | 15,000 | 16,500 | 16,450 |
| Fast-food (FF) restaurants | 27 | 752 | 10,585 |
| Local FF chains: number of outlets | 3 | 37 | 672 |
| International FF chains: number of outlets | 0 | 3 | 93 |

not ready yet but the manager took him round the premises. As they passed by a supermarket, Mr Angelou noticed a snack bar being built inside. He asked about it and the manager told him that this snack bar would operate as part of the supermarket during shopping hours – 8.00 a.m. to 8.00 p.m. Restaurants in Greece usually stay open until well after midnight. He also found out that the snack bar area could cater for about 10 persons at a time and that it would carry light foods, toasts, sandwiches, hot-dogs, light drinks, and so forth. The news upset Mr Angelou since he had expected to have the only place serving meals and drinks in the shopping centre.

He had been considering using the front part of his establishment as a cafeteria, serving light meals and snacks while operating a regular restaurant at the back. Angelou had great hopes for the cafeteria, assuming that clients and employees of the supermarket would become regular customers and that the revenue from the cafeteria would cover much of his general expenses. Now he was afraid that these customers would use the supermarket snack bar. The supermarket owners could operate the snack bar at very competitive prices. Since they could recover their overhead costs from the supermarket sales, they did not have to charge high prices in the snack bar to break even. He also knew that some supermarkets used their snack bars as loss leaders to attract customers. If Angelou reduced prices to gain customers from the supermarket snack bar he would soon run out of money.

At this point Mr Angelou started rethinking the whole plan. The shopping centre was in a rapidly developing suburb of Athens. Most of the area's 200,000 inhabitants had high incomes. Typical apartments in their range cost Dr 50 million but sometimes cost as much as Dr 60 to 80 million.* The centre had 20 stores, among which was a second, larger, supermarket without a snack bar. The centre also had a large department store, two shoe shops, three boutiques, two banks, a bookstore, a menswear store and some still unoccupied areas. Next to the centre, there was a small office building that was owned by the same people as the shopping centre. Two of the offices were used by construction firms, one by an architect, two by civil engineers, three by doctors and one by a dentist.

Mr Angelou estimated that between 40 and 50 people worked in this building. A local representative also told him that a branch of an insurance agency would soon be moving in, as well as a sales office of a large mechanical equipment and machinery firm. These two new offices would bring in a further 15 employees. Two blocks down the road a new secondary school was soon to open with an estimated enrolment of 1,500 students.

Angelou was happy with the people running the shop and office complex. The manager had already organized a shop-owner's association and invited Mr Angelou to one of their first meetings. He liked the people he met there. The meeting agreed that the association would start operating officially in three months and that the occasion would be celebrated by an official opening and meal at Mr Angelou's restaurant. Twice-monthly meetings of the association members would also take the form of a dinner party at Mr Angelou's restaurant. Also, at this meeting, the director of one of the banks had asked Mr Angelou to become a member of another association starting in the same area soon.

Mr Angelou had only one week to finalize his plans for the restaurant, otherwise he would not have enough time to prepare for the official opening of the centre. He had three alternative floor plans for the restaurant. First, he could have one large dining area, with kitchen and other facilities at the back. Second, he could place the kitchen facilities in the middle and divide the restaurant into two indepen-

dent dining room areas with separate entrances. His third choice had the kitchen and other facilities at the side, creating a corridor and a bar, and allowing the two dining rooms to communicate while, at the same time, keeping them separate.

Mr Angelou had also to decide whether or not to include a snack bar. He felt that this would serve those who would come to have a light snack. They would be mainly young people and students who would eat standing. On the other hand, a snack bar did not usually go hand-in-hand with a proper restaurant. Snack bars tended to be noisy and gave the impression of preparing food on the spot, an idea contrary to a restaurant where meals are prepared with care. He also had to make up his mind whether he wanted to open a traditional Greek restaurant or take out a franchise. If he did the latter, he would have less freedom in choosing a layout and the food it served. All these decisions had to be made soon, or Mr Angelou would not be ready for the official opening of the shopping centre. Whatever he decided to do, he had to act quickly.

## Questions

1. What are the strongest influences on Mr Angelou's decision to set up a new restaurant? Will moving to a new location change the balance of favourable and unfavourable influences?
2. What markets can Mr Angelou serve with his new restaurant? Does he need to choose between them or can he serve them all? Is it the right time to open another traditional Greek restaurant?
3. Mr Angelou computed the cost of a franchise, but what are the benefits? Why pay for a franchise from one of the national or international chains when a restaurateur, like Mr Angelou, already knows about food and how to serve it? What do large chains gain from having franchisees rather than running outlets themselves? If you were a franchiser, what would you control most carefully?
4. Should Mr Angelou go ahead and open the new restaurant? What will be the influence of the supermarket's snack bar and the other businesses and people in the area? Which floor plan should he adopt?

*1 ecu = US$1.26 = Dr 302 (Greek drachmas).

## CHAPTER FIVE

# The global marketplace

## CHAPTER OBJECTIVES

After reading this chapter, you should be able to:

- Discuss how foreign trade, economic, political–legal and cultural environments affect a company's international marketing decisions.

- Describe three key approaches to entering international markets.

- Explain how companies might adapt their marketing mixes for international markets.

- Identify the three main forms of international marketing organization.

## CHAPTER PREVIEW

### Danone taps the Japanese yoghurt market

To Western businesses, Japan, with its protected markets, daunting efficiency and alien culture, has long been seen as the ultimate challenge. Opportunity and profit are there, nonetheless, and as never before. But Western companies must learn to crack the market barriers. Those which have done so have learnt that Japan is not so alien a market as to be inaccessible to Western goods. These companies have also learnt to be astute international marketers.

    The French-based food multinational, Danone (previously known as BSN Gervais Danone) learnt a salutary lesson about the difficulties of imposing global tastes when it suffered losses, amounting to more than ¥ 2.5billion – the initial capital investment made in the 1970s to enter the Japanese yoghurt market. The irony of the situation was that the company seemed to be doing everything right: lots of market research, entering the market slowly, careful selection of a partner for a joint venture. After a market survey that lasted six months, Danone was convinced that annual sales growth as high as 100 per cent was imminent. Unfortunately, actual

1 ecu = US$1.26
= ¥122
(Japanese yen)

sales fell short of even the most conservative estimates. The company was forced to reassess its approach.

There seemed to be two main problems. First, Danone marketing professionals had not been prepared for the extreme politeness of the Japanese, who may say a product is good even if they do not like it. Secondly, Japanese consumers do not distinguish between Western health food and junk food. In their eyes, it is all Western food and they switch readily between products, not just brands. Sales remain strong as long as the products are heavily promoted, and drop off when advertising falls.

In retrospect, it is clear that the market had not been as open as the company initially thought. Consumers' tastes were actually well developed. But Danone had to bring their products closer to Japanese tastes: with less sugar, milder, and with less acid in the fruit flavours. The popularity of yoghurt drinks was not disputed. Japanese eat fewer meals at home, and it is hard to eat solid yoghurt with chopsticks. The company also found that Japanese consumers preferred smaller packages than their American and European counterparts. The company learnt that turning a profit in Japan tends to take much longer than in Europe or the United States, where it may average two to three years. In addition, Japan is the most expensive market in the world in terms of advertising costs. This, together with the expense of setting up shop (Japan has a very complicated distribution system), means that companies intending to break into the Japanese market should expect to take seven to ten years before they begin to make any money at all.

International marketing is more than exporting a firm's product or services to a foreign market. It requires huge investment and long-term commitment to the target market, cultural sensitivity, and a willingness to adapt one's product and marketing strategies. Tailoring the firm's offering to suit target customer needs cannot be overemphasized. Once the firm learns to do this, overseas markets can be lucrative and a recipe for success.

## THE IMPORTANCE OF INTERNATIONALIZATION

Companies pay little attention to international trade when the home market is big and teeming with opportunities. The home market is also much safer. Managers do not need to learn other languages, deal with strange and changing currencies, face political and legal uncertainties or adapt their products to different customer needs and expectations. This has been the attitude of many Western companies, which saw little need to sell in overseas markets because their domestic market alone seemed to offer attractive opportunities for growth.

Today, however, the business environment is changing and firms cannot afford to ignore international markets. The increasing dependency of nations around the world on each other's goods and services has raised awareness among companies of the need for a more international outlook in their approach to business. International markets are important because most firms are geared towards growth and so must seek new opportunities in foreign countries as their domestic markets mature. As international trade becomes more liberalized, firms are facing tougher foreign competition in the domestic market. They must develop the abilities to fight off competitors on their own home ground, or exploit business opportunities in foreign markets. For companies already selling in global industries, however, they have few options but to internationalize their operations.

Furthermore time and distance are shrinking rapidly with the advent of faster communication, transportation and financial flows. Products developed in one country are finding enthusiastic acceptance in other countries. Across Western Europe and North America, names such as Toyota, Sony and Toshiba have become household words in the same way McDonald's and Toys 'R' Us are familiar names to most young consumers in Asian countries like Japan, Singapore and Hong Kong.

Thus, as global competition intensifies, local companies that never thought about foreign competitors suddenly find these competitors in their own backyards. The firm that stays at home to play it safe not only misses the opportunity to enter other markets, but also risks losing its home market.

Consider, for example, Japanese victories over Western producers in many sectors – motorcycles, cars, cameras, consumer electronics, machine tools, photocopiers. Each of these markets used to be the stronghold of US, German and British companies in the 1970s, but are now dominated by Japanese manufacturers (see Marketing Highlight 5.1). The latter are not insulated from foreign competitors either. Increasing competition from lower-cost newly industrializing countries (NICs) in the Far East, notably South Korea and Taiwan, are posing a big threat to established Japanese firms in traditional industries like steel, chemicals and heavy machinery.

There have been victories for European firms in some overseas markets, nonetheless. In the United States, for example, American firms are fighting off aggressive assaults by international European companies: Bic's successful attacks on Gillette and Nestlé's gains in the coffee and candy markets are a reflection of the growing level of international competition in 'safe' home markets. In the European Union (EU) foreign firms' direct investment is on the increase and intra-Union flows of investment in all kinds of business sectors – cars, clothing, retailing, financial services – are particularly active. Many sophisticated and aggressive foreign, notably Japanese and Far Eastern, companies have increased their investment in the EU and see the emerging Eastern European economies as longer-term opportunities. So, more than ever, firms must strive to build **differential advantage** in both the domestic and overseas markets they serve.

Although some companies would like to stem the tide of foreign imports through protectionism, this response would be only a temporary and foolhardy solution. Suppressing a free-flow of foreign imports would lead to fewer choices for the consumer and higher prices for indigenously produced goods. In the long run, it would raise the cost of living and protect inefficient domestic firms. It also means that consumers' needs and wants would not be met effectively and efficiently. A better solution is to encourage more firms to learn to enter foreign markets and increase their global competitiveness. Danish brewer, Carlsberg, for example, have found that overseas sales are a recipe for success. It is small compared to competitors like Heineken, but has learnt to compete on equal footing with its global rivals:

> Carlsberg is probably one of the best international business success stories in the world. Jacob Christian Jacobsen, a brewer's son, apparently climbed a slope outside polluted, mid-19th century Copenhagen and decided to build a new factory to tap its fresh, clean waters. His original recipe was adapted from Bavaria. It caught on quickly and, by 1868, within just 20 years, the first kegs were being shipped overseas to Scotland. Today as many as 15 million people drink a Carlsberg each day in locations as diverse as Ireland, Malawi, Singapore and South America. The group brews in 40 countries, sells to 100 more and is smart in pandering to the idiosyncratic needs of local consumers. It has worked hard to secure a dominant position across Europe, which accounts for 80% of its sales. But, in the early 1990s, the group has had to work hard to reposition itself in Europe. Profits were showing a moderate increase but growth was slowing. The recession of the late eighties–early nineties was blamed for these difficulties but the real problem is more complex. The lion's share of profits came from mature northern markets such as Denmark and Britain, where consumption appeared to have peaked in the early nineties. There was also fiercer competition from cheaper brands. Carlsberg also saw a decline in domestic Danish beer sales, which formed almost a fifth of its total global sales. As part of a sweeping rationalisation programme, it

# The world's champion marketers: the Japanese

Few dispute that the Japanese have performed an economic miracle since World War II. In a very short time, they have achieved global market leadership in many industries: automotives, motorcycles, watches, cameras, optical instruments, steel, shipbuilding, computers, and consumer electronics. They have made strong inroads into tyres, chemicals, machine tools, financial services and even designer clothes, cosmetics, and food. Some credit the global success of Japanese companies to their unique business and management practices. Others point to the help they get from Japan's government, powerful trading companies, and banks. Still others say Japan's success was based on low wage rates and unfair dumping policies.

In any case, one of the main keys to Japan's success is certainly its skilful use of marketing. The Japanese came to the United States to study marketing and went home understanding it better than many US companies do. They know how to select a market, enter it in the right way, build market share, and protect that share against competitors. Having practised and seen how well it works in the US market, the Japanese came to Europe with the same game plan.

*Selecting markets.* The Japanese work hard to identify attractive global markets. First, they look for industries that require high skills and high labour intensity, but few natural resources. These include consumer electronics, cameras, watches, motorcycles, and pharmaceuticals. Second, they prefer markets in which consumers around the world would be willing to buy the same product designs. Finally, they look for industries in which the market leaders are weak or complacent.

*Entering markets.* Japanese study teams spend several months evaluating a target market and searching for market niches that are not being satisfied. Sometimes they start with a low-priced, stripped-down version of a product, like cameras and radio receivers. At other times, they start with a product that is as good as the competition's but priced lower, such as radios and televisions, or with a product of higher quality or incorporating new features, as in the case of cars and photocopiers.

The Japanese line up good distribution channels in order to provide quick service. They also use effective advertising to bring their products to the consumers' attention. Their basic entry strategy is to build market share rather than early profits, and they are often willing to wait as long as a decade before realizing their profits.

*Building market share.* Once Japanese firms gain a market foothold, they begin to expand their market share. Money is poured into product improvements and new models so that they can offer more and better products than the competition does. They spot new opportunities through market segmentation, develop markets in new countries, and work to build a network of world markets and production locations.

*Protecting market share.* Once the Japanese achieve market leadership, they become defenders rather than attackers. Their defence strategy is continuous product development and refined market segmentation. Their philosophy is to make 'tiny improvements in a thousand places'.

Recently, some experts have questioned whether Japanese companies can sustain their push towards global marketing dominance. They suggest that the Japanese emphasis on the long-term market share over short-term profits and their ability to market high-quality products at low prices have come at the expense of their employees, stockholders, and communities. They note that, compared to Western firms, Japanese companies work their employees longer hours for lower wages, pay their stockholders lower dividends, and contribute less to community and environmental causes. Other analysts, however, predict that Japan's marketing success is likely to continue.

In America and Europe, Western firms that have survived the Japanese onslaught are fighting back by adding new product lines, pricing more aggressively, streamlining production, buying or making components abroad, and forming strategic partnerships with foreign, including Japanese, companies. The British car company, Rover, formed a strategic alliance with Honda back in the 1980s in order to learn how to build good quality cars, and also benefited from adopting Japanese-style work practices. The firm became profitable again in the early 1990s, and was eventually sold off to BMW. Other companies, such as Ford, have also restructured and revamped their entire worldwide operations during the early 1990s to prepare for intensified global competition in the remaining years of the century. These companies are now leaner and fitter, and now look more set to survive in the longer term in their increasingly competitive international environment.

Looking at another aspect, it is clear that many Western companies are well able to compete successfully in Japan. US firms, for example, hold leading market shares: Coke leads in soft drinks (60 per cent share), Schick in razors (71 per cent), Polaroid in instant cameras (66 per cent), and McDonald's in fast food. Procter & Gamble markets the leading brand in several categories, ranging from disposable nappies and liquid laundry detergents to acne treatments. Apple, Motorola, Levi Strauss, Dow, and scores of other US companies have found that Japan offers large and profitable market opportunities.

While prominent American companies campaign for a bigger slice of the Japanese market, a growing number of European companies are also proving that they can penetrate the daunting Japanese market. Nor is success limited to large companies like Glaxo or those with well-established marques. For example, Teknek Electronics, a small British company that makes a precision machine which cleans sheet materials in the printed circuit industry, successfully entered the Japanese market despite its chief competitor in the market being a Japanese machine. Solid State Logic, a relatively young British company that makes professional audio equipment, has made significant progress within 20 months of setting up its subsidiary in Japan. Again, success is being achieved despite the prominence of Japanese firms in this field. In the consumer market, Scholl, the footwear and healthcare products group, in 1993, sold 2.8 million pairs of its 'healthy' support tights in the first year it introduced the product to the Japanese market. This was achieved despite Scholl not being recognized as much in Japan as a brand name as in other markets. Foseco, the specialty chemicals maker, now part of Burmah Castrol, sold its Sedex filters at a loss for one year in Japan while it set up local production to meet intense domestic price competition. It emerged from the trauma with 55 per cent of the Japanese market, and a reduction in production costs that enabled it to bring its own sales price down by 30 per cent. Foseco Japan now sells three times as many different types and sizes of Sedex filters as any Foseco company.

The success of Western companies in Japan stems largely from the firms' willingness to meet the Japanese market on its own, highly competitive terms. The key ingredients for success are: not treating the Japanese market as any other market; a high-quality or latest technology product; a high level of commitment to – invariably meaning a high level of investment in – the market; an ability to respond efficiently to specific market segment needs; and an understanding of the specific business culture. For most consumer products, tying up with a local distributor or partner is critical. Understanding the complex distribution system with its layers of wholesalers, and having the patience to handle it, are crucial in Japan, because it is difficult to get products on the shelves by directly approaching the retailer. A strong marketing plan, encompassing intensive and aggressive advertising, and close cooperation with wholesalers and retailers, are also essential, not only to reach and impress the consumer, but also to convince the wholesaler and the retail buyers that the firm is serious about its product.

In fact, very similar ingredients are found in Western and Japanese overseas marketing success recipes. These all point to one outstanding dimension, that is, superior marketing, as reflected in the firms' focus on market needs, sustained commitment to product and market development, and environmental, particularly cultural, sensitivity.

The Japanese are hailed 'the world's champion marketers'. They had probably read the American marketing textbooks that they had assiduously translated! And applied the lessons equally forcefully in the international marketing arena. This suggests that the broad principles for success are transferable to other national players. The question is: Have Western managers read the textbooks?

Sources: See Peter Doyle, John Saunders and Veronica Wong, 'Competition in global markets: a case study of American and Japanese competition in the British market', Journal of International Business Studies, 23, 3 (1992), 419–42; Michiyo Nakamoto, 'British companies reap benefits of Japanese markets', Financial Times (8 May 1991), 6; Michiyo Nakamoto, 'Use the system, win shelf space', Financial Times (16 February 1994), 19; Philip Kotler, Liam Fahey, and Somkid Jatusripitak, The New Competition (Englewood Cliffs, NJ: Prentice Hall, 1985); Vernon R. Alden, 'Who says you can't crack Japanese markets?', Harvard Business Review (Jan.–Feb. 1987), 52–6; Howard Schlossberg, 'Japan market hardly closed to US firms', Marketing News (9 July 1990), 1, 12; Ford S. Worthy, 'Keys to Japanese success in Asia', Fortune (7 October 1991), 157–60; and 'Why Japan must change', Fortune (9 March 1992), 66–7.

closed one of its two major Copenhagen breweries, the Tuborg plant which even had its own harbour. The company also acquired small Danish breweries, cut prices and introduced its own discount lines in supermarkets where the majority of Danish beer is sold. In Britain, in 1992, Carlsberg, merged with Allied-Lyons, food and drinks giant, to form Carlsberg-Tetley. Although some of the six breweries inherited from Allied-Lyons were closed eventually, the deal helped to lift overseas sales by 25 percent in 1993. In Britain, which accounts for almost a third of Carlsberg total sales, the merger was expected to improve its position greatly in a country where most beer is sold in pubs. Distribution and marketing have been re-structured to improve efficiency. Over the nineties, Carlsberg is posed to strengthen its position in southern Europe and the Far East. Its most promising foothold lies in countries such as Spain, where it is collaborating with Guinness, and Portugal, which has a more youthful population and where a shift is taking place from wine to beer. In the Far East, Carlsberg is already well established. Using its long standing presence in the region, it has started new ventures in Thailand and China. It anticipated an end to US sanctions against Vietnam and has taken a stake in a brewery there early in 1993. The Far East is currently the fastest growing contributor to group profits and Carlsberg expects this share to double over the mid nineties. As for tapping the potential of Eastern European markets, Carlsberg is taking a more cautious approach. The region, especially Poland, Hungary and Russia, is a very substantial export market, but with investment in a brewery costing close to £100 million, it has to be more certain of political and economic stability to safeguard its shareholders' money. Carlsberg is a quality brew facing increasingly intense competition from cheaper brands in the global market. It realises that the smoothing of prices within the European Union over the mid to late nineties has important implications for marketing. It has to keep its own prices down, but without sacrificing quality. It also recognises the increasing need to maintain a strong global brand image which requires considerable investment and managerial commitment at a time where global cost efficiencies are also under pressure. Carlsberg sees that its future lies in its ability to sustain global competitiveness and to continually exploit growth opportunities in fast growing foreign markets.[1]

1 ecu = UK£0.83

The importance of internationalization is also reflected by the fact that most governments run an export promotion programme, which tries to persuade local companies to export. Denmark pays more than half the salary of marketing consultants who help small and medium-size Danish companies get into exports. Many countries go even further and subsidize their companies by granting preferential land and energy costs – they even supply cash outright so that their companies can charge lower prices than do their foreign competitors.

On a global level, the General Agreement on Tariffs and Trade (GATT) acts as a vehicle by means of which national governments negotiate, and seek agreements, to secure freer trading of goods and services between countries. Free trade underpins global marketing by ensuring goods and services providers can make their offerings available to customers and compete on fair terms.

Today the pressure on firms operating in global industries is not just to export to other countries, but to strive to be a global firm. A **global industry** is one in which the strategic positions of competitors in given geographic or national markets are affected by their overall global positions. A **global firm**, therefore, is one that, by operating in more than one country, gains research and development, production, marketing and financial advantages in its costs and reputation that are not available to purely domestic competitors.[2] The global company sees the world as one market. It minimizes the importance of national boundaries, and raises capital, sources materials and components, and manufactures and markets its goods wherever it can do the best job. For example, Ford's 'world truck' sports a cab made in Europe and a chassis built in North America. It is assembled in Brazil and imported to the United States for sale. Thus global firms gain advantages by planning, operating and coordinating their activities on a worldwide basis. These gains are a key reason behind recent global restructuring programmes undertaken by leading German car producers, BMW and Mercedes Benz. **Global marketing** is concerned with integrating or standardizing marketing actions across a number of geographic markets. This does not rule out forceful adaptation of the marketing mix to individual countries, but suggests that firms, where possible, ignore traditional market boundaries and capitalize on similarities between markets to build competitive advantage.

Because firms around the world are globalizing at a rapid rate, domestic firms in global industries must act quickly before the window closes on them. This does not mean that small and medium-size firms must operate in a dozen countries to succeed. These firms can practise global nichemanship. The world, however, is becoming smaller and every company operating in a global industry – whether large or small – must assess and establish its place in world markets.

Firms that confront international competitors in their existing markets must ask the following basic questions:

1. What market position should we try to establish in our country, in the geographic region (e.g. Europe, North America, Asia, Australasia), and globally?
2. Who will our global competitors be and what are their strategies and resources?
3. Where should we produce or source our products?
4. What strategic alliances should we form with other firms around the world?

This chapter surveys the global marketplace and addresses the important decisions that firms have to make in international marketing planning. Each decision will be discussed in detail. First, however, let us take a look at the risks in doing business abroad.

## RISKS IN INTERNATIONAL MARKETING

Although the need for companies to go abroad is greater today than in the past, so are the risks. Managers must anticipate the risks and obstacles in doing business in foreign markets. Several complex problems confront companies that go global.

### High foreign country debt

High debt, inflation and unemployment in several countries have resulted in highly unstable governments and currencies, which limit trade and expose firms to many risks. Debt-laden and/or currency-starved countries are often not able to pay despite their willingness to purchase. The inability of poorer countries to pay by normal (cash) methods becomes a serious obstacle for supplying companies. In Eastern Europe and Russia, there has been a big growth in the use of **countertrade** to deal with this problem (we address countertrade later in this chapter).

### Exchange rate volatility

The level of a country's exchange rate affects the company's competitiveness in the foreign market. A weak pound will favour exports of British goods. A strong exchange rate intensifies the level of competition the firm faces at home. For European companies whose countries are members of the Exchange Rate Mechanism (ERM), much of the uncertainty is removed from fluctuating exchange rates. On the one hand, this is favourable for companies doing a great portion of their international business in the EU. On the other, however, the ERM does impose constraints on company decisions, such as productivity levels and government policy, as in their flexibility to reduce interest rates.

### Foreign government entry requirements

Companies often face constraints imposed by the foreign or 'host' country government. Some of these market entry conditions relate to a variety of working practices including: degree of control (ownership) allowed; the hiring of local nationals; local content rules; the percentage of output exported; and the amount of profits that can be taken from the country. India, China, Mexico, Brazil and many African countries maintain formal, and often strict, entry conditions, while more advanced countries, such as Japan and the United States, impose strict 'quality' criteria. The latter criteria, together with a range of factors, are collectively called nontariff barriers by economists, and have been used by many governments to protect local industries. In addition to nontariff barriers, foreign governments often impose high tariffs or direct trade barriers, such as excessive import duties, in order to protect their own industries (e.g. automotives in Malaysia and whiskey and rice in Japan). Tariffs and nontariff barriers are dealt with in more detail below (see 'The international trade system').

### Costs of marketing mix adaptation

Although the international firm gains from economies of scale in production, these must be weighed against the higher costs of product modification, distribution and communication expenditures in overseas markets. For example, the complex, multilayered distribution system traditionally used in Japan, together with Japanese high product quality expectations and expensive media costs, is a considerable barrier to market entry for many foreign firms.

### Other problems

War, terrorism and corruption are other dangers that confront international businesses. The number of localized conflicts in Eastern Europe is predicted to increase as a result of the resurgence in nationalism and ethnic rivalries in the post-cold war 'new world order'. A sector severely hit by the Persian Gulf War was the world airline industry which, in the first six months of 1991, lost more money than it had made in the previous ten years. Previous hostage-taking episodes in the Middle East and the widely publicized murders of Western businessmen in Turkey highlight a problem international companies have long been aware of. The problem of widespread corruption in some countries, where officials often award contracts to the highest briber, not the lowest bidder, presents a dilemma to many Western business people, particularly where anticorruption principles are well laid down in their firm's own business charter. The firm must therefore establish clear guidelines for their staff who have to do business in countries where corruption is an increasing problem. These guidelines should help them decide whether or not to bid for business, in the first instance, and, if so, where and when to draw the line.

The difficulties associated with doing business in foreign markets should not be used as excuses for avoiding international marketing. These risks and problems must be identified by managers and planned for. Like all marketing activities, the chance of success is far higher when obstacles are anticipated rather than reacted to.

The rest of this chapter is devoted to examining the important international marketing decisions firms make. Figure 5.1 presents a framework for analysis, planning,

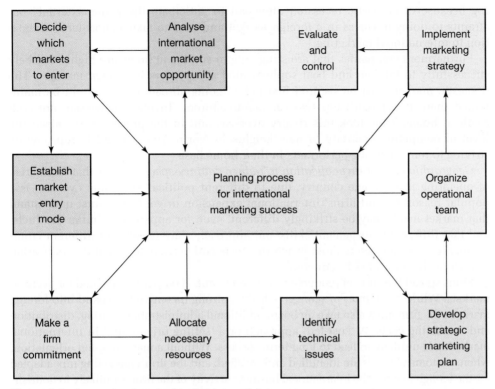

**Figure 5.1**    International marketing planning model.

implementation and control in relation to international marketing. The ten dimensions shown are useful for identifying the keys to foreign market success. Each dimension will be discussed in turn.

## ANALYSIS OF INTERNATIONAL MARKET OPPORTUNITY

### Deciding whether or not to go abroad

Doing international business successfully requires firms to take a market-led approach. A critical evaluation of why firms enter foreign markets shows that, in many cases, the practice of international business falls short of the market-led approach essential for long-term success. Firms must consider the factors that draw them into the international arena.

A surprisingly large proportion of sales to foreign markets are made in response to *chance orders* coming either from customers who are international players or from other sources like foreign buyers attending a domestic exhibition. Such 'passive exporting' is not international marketing although it contributes to international trade. It does not associate with the central principle of creating customer value and market targeting, there is little assessment of critical factors for competitive success, and it is unlikely to build a long-term market position.

*Limited domestic growth and/or intense domestic competition* is a key reason why firms enter foreign markets and has been a prime motivator behind the Japanese companies' overseas expansion programme over the 1970s and 1980s. In practice, many firms quickly suspend foreign market activity when the domestic economy improves or when they fail to make money in the overseas operation. Firms driven to exporting because of domestic recession often fail to anticipate the wider external constraints to doing business in a foreign market and tend to take a short-term orientation to international marketing.[3]

Furthermore companies that are struggling to survive at home are highly unlikely successfully to take on and beat sophisticated competitors in foreign markets. The domestic market must be secured first before going abroad and it should be maintained thereafter. Japan's top two car manufacturers, Toyota and Nissan, are arch rivals at home. They took this rivalry overseas and in the process have raised the level of competitive activity to new heights in North America and Europe, while striving to remain strong performers in their home base.

*Geographic market diversification to reduce country-specific risk* – that is, the risk of operating in only one country, due to different political–economic cycles – is a popular reason behind firms' international expansion drive. Firms must understand that market needs may be strikingly different, even for apparently similar products, and that different management skills and approaches are needed for different country markets. So, managers must weigh the costs and barriers to global diversification against the benefits of risk-reduction.

Firms spread the costs of production over more units if output is expanded for overseas markets. While *economies of scale* give firms a strong incentive to expand into foreign markets, the firm must also take on board additional administration, selling, distribution and marketing costs. A 'cost-led' approach or a 'selling orientation' in international marketing is unlikely to lead to long-term success. Without a marketing-led orientation, where customers' needs are identified and satisfied, and the firm's marketing mix adapted for the foreign market, the international business activity of the firm is unlikely to flourish.

International marketing is really about exploiting market opportunities based upon sound environment and specific market analyses. The exercise must be guided by strategic marketing planning together with management's firm commitment to the international operation. Opportunistic behaviour may be insufficient without a truly market-led approach to tackling foreign markets.

In summary, firms enter overseas markets for profits and/or survival. But firms must not confuse exporting with international marketing. The latter is about taking a long-term perspective of foreign market potential and relentlessly adopting a market-led approach to identifying, anticipating and satisfying the needs of customers in target international markets. Before going abroad, the firm must weigh the risks and question its ability to operate globally. Can the company learn to understand the preferences and buying behaviour of customers in other country markets? Can it offer competitively attractive products? Will it be able to adapt to other countries' business cultures and to deal effectively with foreign nationals? Do the company's managers have the requisite international experience? Has management considered the impact of foreign regulations and political environments?

Successful international marketing occurs when the firm identifies international market opportunities, anticipates potential obstacles, and develops and implements carefully planned strategies that match the firm's resources to customers needs and wants in the foreign market. The odds of success are raised when the firm is proactive as opposed to reactive in its approach to international markets.

## Understanding the global environment

Before deciding whether to sell abroad, a company must understand the international marketing environment thoroughly. That environment has changed a great deal in

There are 3 billion people in Asia. Half of them are under 25. Consider it a growing market.

You meet their needs. We meet yours. In the last two years alone, we've opened new offices in Bandung, Bangalore, Batam, Hanoi, Ho Chi Minh City, Kandy, Labuan, Qingdao and Taichung. If it's in Asia, to us, it's just around the corner. HongkongBank *Member HSBC Group*

Asia: a growing market. This Hongkong-Bank ad reinforces the region's potential, and illustrates how the bank can meet the needs of its international customers.

the last two decades, creating both new opportunities and new problems. The world economy has globalized. First, world trade and investment have grown rapidly, with many attractive markets opening up in Western Europe, Eastern Europe, Russia, China and elsewhere. There has been a growth of global brands in automotives, food, clothing, electronics and many other categories. The number of global companies has grown dramatically. While the United States' dominant position in world trade has declined, other countries, such as Japan and Germany, have increased their economic power in world markets. The international financial system has become more complex and fragile. In some countries' markets, Western companies face increasing trade barriers, erected to protect domestic markets against outside competition. There has also been increasing concern among members outside the European Union that 'Fortress Europe' presents greater barriers to penetrating the EU markets. This has been one of the factors behind Japanese multinationals' aggressive direct investment activities in the EU over the late 1980s and early 1990s – to become 'insiders' before it is too late.

## The international trade system

The company looking abroad must develop an understanding of the international trade system. When selling to another country, the firm faces various trade restrictions. The most common is the **tariff**, which is a tax levied by a foreign government against certain imported products. The tariff may be designed either to raise revenue or to protect domestic firms. The exporter also may face a **quota**, which sets limits on the amount of goods the importing country will accept in certain product categories. The purpose of the quota is to conserve on foreign exchange and to protect local

Many companies have made the world their market: opening the megastore in Milan (top left) and Virgin megastores in London, Los Angeles, Vienna and Tokyo.

industry and employment. An **embargo** is the strongest form of quota, which totally bans some kinds of imports.

Firms may face **exchange controls** that limit the amount of foreign exchange and the exchange rate against other currencies. The company may also face **nontariff trade barriers**, such as biases against company bids or restrictive product standards that favour or go against product features:

> One of the cleverest ways the Japanese have found to keep foreign manufacturers out of their domestic market is to plead 'uniqueness'. Japanese skin is different, the government argues, so foreign cosmetics companies must test their products in Japan before selling there. The Japanese say their stomachs are small and have room for only the mikan, the local tangerine, so imports of oranges are limited. Now the Japanese have come up with what may be the flakiest argument yet: Their snow is different, so ski equipment should be too.[4]

At the same time, certain forces help trade between nations – or at least between some nations. Certain countries have formed free-trade zones or economic communities – groups of nations organized to work towards common goals in the regulation of international trade. The most important such community is the European Union. The EU aims to create a single European market by reducing physical, financial and technical barriers to trade among member nations. It has yet to achieve the true 'common market' originally envisioned, although member nations continue to push to integrate economically (see Marketing Highlight 5.2). Other economic communities exist, such as the European Free Trade Association (EFTA), the Latin American Integration Association (LAIA), the Central American Common Market (CACM) and the Council for Mutual Economic Assistance (CMEA) in Eastern Europe. In the northern

American zone, the United States and Canada phased out trade barriers in 1989, and, with free-trade agreements with Mexico, they created a North American free-trade zone stretching from the Yukon to the Yucatán. A similar free-trade zone has been proposed which would include all the nations of South America.[5]

Although the recent trend towards free-trade zones has caused great excitement and new market opportunities, this trend also raises some concerns. For example, groups of countries that trade freely among themselves may tend to increase barriers to outsiders in the same way as 'Fortress Europe' is feared to block non-EU members. Stricter local-content rules may add a new kind of bureaucracy and will once again limit international trade. Furthermore environmentalists worry that companies that are unwilling to play by the strict rules of the West will relocate elsewhere, where pollution regulations are more lax.

Each nation has unique features that must be understood. A nation's readiness for different products and services and its attractiveness as a market to foreign firms depend on its economic, political–legal and cultural environments. These criteria are also useful for grouping countries which share common characteristics but can be discriminated from other groups of countries.

## Economic environment

The international marketer must study each country's economy. Two economic factors reflect the country's attractiveness as a market: the country's *industrial structure* and its *income distribution*.

The country's industrial structure shapes its product and service needs, income levels, and employment levels. Four types of industrial structures should be considered:

1. *Subsistence economies.* In a subsistence economy, the vast majority of people engage in simple agriculture. They consume most of their output and barter the rest for simple goods and services. They offer few market opportunities.
2. *Raw-material-exporting economies.* These economies are rich in one or more natural resources, but poor in other ways. Much of their revenue comes from exporting these resources. Examples are Malaysia (rubber and palm oil); Zaïre (copper, cobalt, and coffee); and Saudi Arabia (oil). These countries are good markets for large equipment, tools and supplies, and trucks. If there are many foreign residents and a wealthy upper class, they are also a market for luxury goods.
3. *Industrializing economies.* In an industrializing economy, manufacturing accounts for 10 per cent to 20 per cent of the country's economy. Examples include Egypt, the Philippines, India, and Brazil. As manufacturing increases, the country needs more imports of raw textile materials, steel and heavy machinery, and fewer imports of finished textiles, paper products and automotives. Industrialization typically creates a new rich class and a small but growing middle class, both demanding new types of imported goods.
4. *Industrial economies.* Industrial economies are large exporters of manufactured goods and investment funds. They trade goods among themselves and also export them to other types of economies for raw materials and semifinished goods. The varied manufacturing activities of these industrial nations and their large middle class make them rich markets for all sorts of goods. Asia's newly industrialized economies, such as Taiwan, Singapore, South Korea and Malaysia, fall under this category.

**MARKETING HIGHLIGHT 5.2**

## The European Union: threat or opportunity?

A rapidly changing European market is one of this decade's most significant developments that will impact on international marketing. Looking back at history, the European Economic Community (EEC), now evolved to the European Union (EU), was formed in 1957. It set out to create a single European market by reducing trade barriers among its member nations by developing Europeanwide policies on trade with nonmember nations. However, the dream of a true 'common market' was buried quickly under heaps of regulations and nationalistic squabbling. Different standards and norms continued to hinder companies, especially small and medium ones, in setting up abroad. Despite early common-market initiatives, Europe remained a fragmented maze of isolated and protected national markets, making it a difficult and confusing place to do business. Companies selling to or operating in Europe faced a hodgepodge of trade restrictions, economic conditions, and political tensions that varied widely by country. As a result, in the late 1970s and early 1980s, the European Community's performance deteriorated relative to the United States, Japan and other Far Eastern countries in economic growth and technological innovation.

The feeling that the original impetus had faded away led to new initiatives in 1985 to spearhead European development and completion of the internal market. The EC members jointly enacted the Single European Act of 1986, which set 31 December 1992 as the target date for completing the European economic unification process. Increasing international competition had forced the realization that pan-European scale was needed to compete with the United States and the Pacific Rim countries. National policies would no longer suffice. The Act called for sweeping deregulation to eliminate barriers to the free flow of products, services, finances, and labour among member countries, and '1992' came to symbolize the complete transformation of the European economy. This time the Act laid down concrete and detailed measures (300 initially, later reduced to 286), explicitly prescribed and linked to the beginning of 1993 for completion of the task.

The situation just after 1 January 1993 suggests that the initiative was, overall, a success, with all 286 measures proposed, but nevertheless, some serious obstacles remain and transformation of some proposals into national legislation has been slow in some countries. Meanwhile 1989 saw the fall of the Berlin Wall, followed soon by the crumbling of the USSR. The present situation – nationalism, war, economic chaos, criminality and immigration – in the former socialist countries is not promising, although 1989 represents a turning point for Europe. The EU is faced with the fact that a number of states from Eastern Europe now want to join the community. The enlargement towards northern countries (Finland, Austria and Sweden joined in January 1995) and southern Europe, together with the potential entry of former socialist countries, would reinforce the heterogeneity in the EU.

The EU, with over 370 million consumers (another 120 million more if Eastern Europeans are added and 280 million from the former USSR), arguably constitutes one of the world's single largest markets. It accounts for a quarter of the world's exports, compared to 14 per cent for the United States and 12 per cent for Japan. By the year 2000, the EU could contain as many as 450 million people in twenty-five countries, as more European nations seek admission to the free-trade area. Thus European economic unification promises tremendous opportunities for all European member states, as well as international firms – as trade barriers drop, lower costs will result in greater operating efficiency and productivity. European markets will grow and become more accessible. This invigorated European market should offer tremendous business opportunities to astute marketers.

However, many outsiders have mixed reactions. Just as 1992 has created many opportunities, so it also poses threats. As a result of increased unification, European companies will grow bigger and more competitive. Thus many companies from the United States, Japan, and other non-European countries are bracing themselves for an onslaught of new European competition, both in Western Europe and in other world markets. Perhaps an even bigger concern, however, is that lower barriers inside Europe will only create thicker outside walls. Some observers envision a 'Fortress Europe' that heaps favours on firms from European Union member states but hinders outsiders by imposing obstacles such as stiffer import quotas, local content requirements, and other nontariff barriers. Companies that already operate in Europe will be shielded from such protectionist moves. For this reason, companies that sell to Europe but are not now operating there are rushing to become insiders before the unification initiative threatens to close them out. They are building their own operations in Europe, acquiring existing businesses there, or forming strategic alliances with established European firms.

Renewed unification efforts since the crumbling of the Eastern Bloc countries have created much excitement within the European Community, but they have also drawn criticism. There is still confusion and disagreement among European politicians as to the scope and nature of the changes they want. Consequently, Europe fell far short of its goal of complete unification by 1992 – many doubt that the goal will ever be achieved. By mid-1992, fewer than half of the 279 provisions in the original 1992 plan had been ratified. The most difficult issues – those involving the free flow of money, people, and goods – were still unresolved. For example, in December 1991, European Community leaders approved the Maastricht Treaty, an amendment to the original EC charter, which calls for the establishment of the European Monetary System (a single European currency and central bank) by 1999. Before the treaty can become law, however, all twelve member states must approve it by legislative vote or by referendum. To date, there is still a big question mark over the Maastricht Treaty. Limited success has been achieved with preliminary steps towards the European Monetary System and, to a lesser extent, with the European Social Chapter.

Beyond these currency issues, actions such as standardizing taxes, abolishing border checks, and forging other Europeanwide efforts will require changing the entire economic make-up of Europe. There is also the question of overall acceptance of the planned integration process by the people of Europe. Individual countries will have to give up some of their independence for the common good, pushing aside the nationalism that has ruled European history

for centuries. For these reasons, the odds are low that Europe ever will realize the full unification vision.

Even if the EU does manage to standardize its general trade regulations, creating an economic community will not create a homogeneous market. With over a dozen different languages and distinctive national customs, Europe will be anything but a 'common market'. Although economic and political boundaries may fall, social and cultural differences will remain. And, though the unification effort may create common general standards, companies marketing in Europe still will face a daunting mass of local rules. Take advertising for example. One large advertising agency has prepared a 52-page book containing dense statistics on country-by-country restrictions. Ireland, for example, forbids ads for liquor but allows them for beer and wine – as long as they run after 7 p.m.; Spain allows ads only for drinks with less than 23 per cent alcohol, and they can run only after 9.30 p.m. In Holland, ads for sweets have to show a toothbrush in the corner of the television screen. The goals of 1992 have had little effect on such local rules.

Thus the European market will remain diverse, and more so than either the US or Japanese markets. Marketers must look upon this diversity as an opportunity to create differentiated product and service offerings to satisfy varying target markets.

To summarize, great changes are occurring in Europe. The prospects of a very much enlarged European Union are accelerating. Many more Eastern and southern European nations, together with the former Soviet republics, could eventually join the 'club'. Even if only partly successful, European unification will make a more efficient and competitive Europe a global force to be reckoned with. The best prepared companies will benefit most. Whether they like it or fear it, therefore, all companies must adapt their strategies to take advantage of developments in the 'New (and evolving) Europe', or risk losing out altogether.

Sources: Chris Halliburton and Reinhard Hunerberg, 'Marketing in a European environment', in id., *European Marketing: Readings and cases* (Wokingham, Berks: Addison-Wesley, 1993), 3–22; Colin Egan and Peter McKiernan, *Inside Fortress Europe: Strategies for the single market*, the EIU series (Wokingham, Berks: Addison-Wesley, 1994); John Rossant, Richard A. Melcher, and Steward Toy, 'Is Europe's express train to unity slowing down?', *Business Week* (3 February 1992), 46; Cyndee Miller, 'Marketers optimistic about EC despite monetary muddle', *Marketing News* (26 October 1992), 2; Shawn Tully, 'Europe 1992: more unity than you think', *Fortune* (24 August 1992), 136–42; and Andrew Hilton, 'Mythology, markets and the emerging Europe', *Harvard Business Review* (Nov.–Dec. 1992), 50–4; Brian Rothery, *What Maastricht Means for Business* (Aldershot: Gower, 1993).

The second economic factor is the country's income distribution. The international marketer might find countries with one of five different income distribution patterns:

1. very low family incomes;
2. mostly low family incomes;
3. very low/very high family incomes;
4. low/medium/high family incomes; and
5. mostly medium family incomes.

Consider the market for Lamborghinis, a car costing over £100,000. The market would be very small in countries with the first or second income patterns. Therefore, most Lamborghinis are sold in large markets like the United States, Europe and Japan, which have large segments of high-income consumers, or in small but wealthy countries like Saudi Arabia.

### Political–legal environment

Nations differ greatly in their political–legal environments. At least four political–legal factors should be considered in deciding whether to do business in a given country: attitudes towards international buying, political stability, monetary regulations, and government bureaucracy.

*Attitudes towards international buying*    Some nations are quite receptive to foreign firms, and others are quite hostile. Western firms have found newly industrialized countries in the Far East attractive overseas investment locations. In contrast, others like India are bothersome with its import quotas, currency restrictions and limits on the percentage of the management team that can be non-nationals (see Marketing Highlight 5.3).

*Political stability*    Stability is another issue. Governments change hands, sometimes violently. Even without a change, a government may decide to respond to new popular feelings. The foreign company's property may be taken, its currency holdings may be blocked, or import quotas or new duties may be set. International marketers may find it profitable to do business in an unstable country, but the unsteady situation will affect how they handle business and financial matters.

*Monetary regulations*    Sellers want to take their profits in a currency of value to them. Ideally, the buyer can pay in the seller's currency or in other world currencies. Short of this, sellers might accept a blocked currency – one whose removal from the country is restricted by the buyer's government – if they can buy other goods in that country that they need themselves or can sell elsewhere for a needed currency. Besides currency limits, a changing exchange rate, as mentioned earlier, creates high risks for the seller.

Most international trade involves cash transactions. Many Third World and former Eastern bloc nations do not have access to hard currency or credit terms to pay for their purchases from other countries. So Western companies, rather than lose the opportunity of a good deal, will accept payment in kind, which has led to a growing practice called countertrade. **Countertrade** is nothing new and was the way of doing

**MARKETING HIGHLIGHT 5.3**

## Breaking into an unreceptive market

It's one thing to want to do business in a particular country; it's quite another to be allowed into the country on reasonable terms. The problem of entering an unreceptive or blocked country calls for mega-marketing using economic, psychological, political, and public relations skills to gain the cooperation of several parties in the country.

For example, Pepsi-Cola used megamarketing in its attempt to enter the huge India market. Pepsi worked with an Indian business group to seek government approval for its entry. Both domestic soft-drink companies and antimultinational legislators objected to letting Pepsi into India, so Pepsi had to make an offer that the Indian government would find hard to refuse. Therefore, Pepsi offered to help India export enough of its agricultural products to more than offset the outlay for importing soft-drink syrup. Pepsi also promised to focus a good deal of selling effort on rural areas to help in their economic development. The company further offered to construct an agricultural research centre and to give food processing, packaging, and water-treatment technology

to India. After three years of haggling, the Indian bureaucracy finally approved Pepsi's extensive proposal.

Clearly, Pepsi's strategy was to bundle a set of benefits that would win the support of the various interest groups influencing the entry decision. Pepsi's marketing problem was not one of simply applying the 4 Ps in a new market, but rather one of just getting into the market in the first place. In trying to win over the government and public groups — and to maintain a reasonable relationship once admitted — Pepsi had to add two more Ps: 'politics' and 'public opinion'.

Many other large companies have learned that it pays to build good relations with host governments. Olivetti, for example, enters new markets by building housing for workers, supporting local arts and charities, and hiring and training local managers. IBM sponsors nutrition programmes for Latin American children and gives agricultural advice to the Mexican government. And Polaroid is helping Italy restore Leonardo da Vinci's *Last Supper*.

Sources: See Philip Kotler, 'Megamarketing', *Harvard Business Review* (Mar.–Apr. 1986), 117–24; Sheila Tefft, 'The mouse that roared at Pepsi', *Business Week* (7 September 1987), 42; and Anthony Spaeth, 'India beckons – and frustrates', *Wall Street Journal* (22 September 1989), R23–5.

business before money was invented. Today it still accounts for as much as 25 per cent of world trade.

Countertrade takes several forms. *Barter* involves the direct exchange of goods or services. For example, British coal mining equipment has been 'sold' for Indonesian plywood; Volkswagen cars were swapped for Bulgarian dried apricots; and Boeing 747s, fitted with Rolls-Royce engines, were exchanged for Saudi oil. Another form is *compensation* (or *buyback*), whereby the seller sells a plant, equipment, or technology to another country and agrees to take payment in the resulting products. Thus, Goodyear provided China with materials and training for a printing plant in exchange for finished labels. Another form is *counterpurchase*. Here, the seller receives full payment in cash but agrees to spend some portion of the money in the other country within a stated time period. For example, Pepsi sold $3 billion worth of cola-making equipment and know-how to Russia in 1990 for roubles, and agreed to buy Russian vodka, tankers and ships for reselling in the United States.

1 ecu = US$1.26

Countertrade deals can be very complex. For example, Daimler-Benz recently agreed to sell 30 trucks to Romania in exchange for 150 Romanian jeeps, which it then sold to Ecuador for bananas, which were in turn sold to a German supermarket chain for German currency. Through this roundabout process, Daimler-Benz finally obtained payment in German money.[6]

For some firms the bartering system has worked. However, companies must be aware of the complexities and/or the limits: Rank Xerox, trying to sell high technology to Russia, not surprisingly drew the line at accepting payment in racing camels and goat horns!

*Government bureaucracy*    A fourth factor is the extent to which the host government runs an efficient system for helping foreign companies: efficient customs handling, good market information and other factors that aid in doing business. A common shock to Western business people is how quickly barriers to trade disappear if a suitable payment (bribe) is made to some official (see Marketing Highlight 5.4).

### Cultural environment

Each country has its own folkways, norms and taboos. The seller must examine the way consumers in different countries think about and use certain products before planning a marketing programme. Cultural barriers must be identified. **Culture** is defined simply as *the learned distinctive way of life of a society*. The dimensions of culture include:

- The social organization of society (e.g. the class system in the United Kingdom, the caste system in India, the heavy reliance on social welfare in Sweden or the lack of it in Japan).
- Religion (ranging from the Islamic fundamentalism of Iran to the secular approaches of Western countries such as the United Kingdom).
- Customs and rituals.
- Values and attitudes towards domestic and international life.
- Education provision and literacy levels.
- Political system.
- Aesthetic systems (e.g. folklore, music, arts, literature).
- Language.

Culture permeates the lifestyles of customer targets and is manifested through the behavioural patterns of these customers. Culture and people's general behaviour influence the customer's action in the marketplace which, in turn, impact upon the firm's marketing decisions. There are often surprises. For example, the average Frenchman uses almost twice as many cosmetics and beauty aids as does his wife. The Germans and the French eat more packaged, branded spaghetti than do Italians. Italian children like to eat chocolate bars between slices of bread as a snack. Women in Tanzania will not give their children eggs for fear of making them bald or impotent. A good example of cultural differences is the case of a Scandinavian company wishing to sell baby clothes in Belgium. It discovered its clothes were virtually unsaleable because in most regions, clothes for baby girls are trimmed with blue and those for baby boys with pink.

Business norms and behaviour also vary from country to country. The unwary business executive needs to be briefed on these factors before conducting business in another country. Mistakes due to lack of understanding of foreign business behaviour affect business relations greatly. Here are some examples of different global business behaviour:

- In face-to-face communications, Japanese business executives rarely say no to the Western business executive. Thus Westerners tend to be frustrated and may not know where they stand. Where Westerners come to the point quickly, Japanese business executives may find this behaviour offensive.

- In France, wholesalers don't want to promote a product. They ask their retailers what they want and deliver it. If a foreign company builds its strategy around the French wholesaler's cooperation in promotions, it is likely to fail.
- When British executives exchange business cards, each usually gives the other's card a cursory glance and stuffs it in a pocket for later reference. In Japan, however,

---

**MARKETING HIGHLIGHT 5.4**

## To bribe or not?

Indeed, in Germany, the tax man gives tacit approval to backhanders: bribes are tax-deductible. The exact extent of the corruption is not known, but experts reckon that in the German public-sector contracts alone, the volume is at least DM 20 billion* a year. Such corruption is rarely exposed to the public, of course, but in Germany it is by all accounts a widespread and profitable affair. It starts out at local council level and goes on up the chain.

There have been a few sensational cases in the past twenty years. The Flick affair revealed in the 1980s substantial payments an industrialist made to Germany's main political parties. In another more recent case, Eduard Swick, a Bavarian businessman, was alleged to have paid leading members of the Bavarian government, including the late president Franz Josef Strauss, in return for help in his battle with tax collectors. Outside government circles, the most spectacular corruption case has been the Herzklappen affair whereby doctors were alleged to have colluded with manufacturers in overcharging health insurers for heart valves.

In Germany, a company can offset any bribes it makes as a necessary business expense. All the finance authorities ask for is the name of the recipient of the bribe. The information is not used specifically to track down the corrupt official – who, by taking the bribe, is actually breaking the law – but simply to ensure that he or she declares the money received on his or her tax return.

Unlike domestic corruption, the bribery of people in a foreign country is not an offence in Germany. Only in the United States, which passed the Foreign Corrupt Practices Act in 1977, are such payments illegal. Not surprisingly the US Department of Trade complains of unfair competition when confronted with these modes of working by European companies, especially in developing countries. (Note:

*1 ecu = US$1.26 = DM 1.89 (Deutschmarks).

Bribery of government and political officials in developing nations is a practice which German companies are not alone in adopting.)

Naturally, there are German parliamentary members who want to see changes, and the debate as to whether bribes should be offset against taxes continues.

Ingomar Hanchler, a Social Democratic member of parliament, argued in 1994 that it was not just a question of morality, but also an economic one: corruption damages free competition and subverts the market economy while also encouraging monopolies which can pay most. The counterargument is that bribery is a necessary vehicle for business. Outlawing it would 'damage German firms in the international market and threaten jobs', according to Joachim Grünewald, a state secretary in the finance ministry in Bonn. The federation of German industry, the BDI, also challenges the view that bribes should be considered corrupt, maintaining that unusual payments are not bribes at all but an essential expense and marketing cost.

What would a keen British business person hoping to invest in a deprived east German town do to get fast entry into this market? Well, in 1992, one such British businessman hoping to invest in the town of Potsdam, near Berlin, did the unthinkable (by German standards!):

> The British businessman was confronted with an unusual offer from a local politician. Pay DM 25,000 consultancy fee to a law company, the politician told him, and your case will be dealt with quickly and to your satisfaction. Needless to say, the British executive knew the official had connections with the law firm in question and what the money was for and where it was going. He chose not to pay the 'consultancy fee'. In refusing, he was probably an exception. He also did not get to invest in the town of Potsdam.

Source: Frederick Stüdemann, 'A land where bribes are tax-deductible', *The European* (17–23 June 1994), 3.

executives dutifully study each other's cards during a greeting, carefully noting company affiliation and rank. They hand their card to the most important person first.

- In the United Kingdom and the United States, business meals are common. In Germany, these are strictly social. Foreigners are rarely invited to dinner and such an invitation suggests a very advanced association. The opposite applies in Italy where entertaining is an essential part of business life (... guests should offer to pay but, in the end, should defer to their Italian host.). In France, watch out. There are two kinds of business lunch – one for building up relations, without expecting anything in return, and the other to discuss a deal in the making or to celebrate a deal afterwards. Deals, however, should be concluded in the office, never over a lunch table.
- Shaking hands on meeting and on parting is common in Germany, Belgium, France and Italy. Ignoring this custom, especially in France, causes offence. In France, it is advisable to shake hands with everyone in a crowded room.

The key to success for the international firm lies in assiduously researching and understanding each country's culture and proactively building **cultural empathy** with a view to establishing a long-term market position.

*Building cultural empathy*    Cultural empathy is achieved in a number of ways:

- *Acquire in-company knowledge and experience.* This is a slow and arduous approach but it does provide a lasting solution to understanding foreign culture.
- *Continuous market research.* The firm should undertake market research for general background information as well as commission more specific research for individual projects.
- *Visit foreign country and customers.* This is invaluable for developing first-hand knowledge of customers and markets. Such activities also build goodwill, clearly show the firm's commitment to the markets served and yield valuable feedback to the company's home base.
- *Hire local personnel.* Local personnel may be employed to speed up information gathering. This has been the approach used by many Japanese multinational firms in overseas markets. Sound local market knowledge helps to develop marketing strategies that are better geared to local requirements and conditions.
- *Use distributors/agents.* Firms may use local distributors or agents who are familiar with the marketplace. Honda's early market entry success in the United States and Europe was underpinned by using independent distributors to share the heavy investment in building market position and to provide market understanding, not just coverage. Cooperative relationships or partnerships with local companies also help to provide 'inside' information about national characteristics and local market conditions.
- *Joint ventures and strategic alliances.* The firm is able to accelerate the process of building cultural sensitivity through a joint venture or alliance with a host country company. Market entry is made easier and penetration faster. This is especially true for countries such as China and Japan. The Japanese market, as mentioned earlier, is noted for its complex distribution system. To succeed foreign firms are advised to form strategic partnerships with local Japanese firms. The firm should also get to grips with the 'chosen people' problem.[7] The typical Japanese businessman, like many of his European and American counterparts, regards his

own culture as the world's most nearly perfect. Thus, when a foreigner is on Japanese turf, he would do well to learn, respect and observe as many local customs as possible. The important point is that the firm builds cultural empathy with both the customers they serve and the intermediaries they have to work with.

■ *Build language skills*. Language is an essential part of a country's culture. It must be addressed by the company. British business people have often claimed that English is a world business language and therefore there is no need for them to develop language proficiencies. However, as the former German Chancellor, Willy Brandt, stated: 'If I am selling to you I will speak English, but if you are selling to me, dann mussen Sie Deutsch sprechen!' It is also important to distinguish the cultural and technical aspects of language. The technical characteristics are easily learnt and readily available in translation dictionaries and language courses. The cultural empathy derives from a deep understanding of the language and its use in both the verbal and nonverbal forms.[8] A lack of cultural understanding of language leads to errors in translation which can be, at best, embarrassing to both parties and, at worst, offensive to the host client/customer (see Marketing Highlight 5.5).

---

**MARKETING HIGHLIGHT 5.5**

## Avoiding errors in international marketing due to lack of cultural understanding

Here are some examples of careless translations which make an international marketer look downright foolish to foreign customers:

■ African men were upset by an advertisement for a men's deodorant that showed a happy man being chased by women. They thought the deodorant would make them weak and overrun by women.

■ Pepsodent's early foray into Southeast Asia failed because it advertised white teeth to a culture where yellow teeth are symbols of prestige.

■ When Coca-Cola first entered China, it provided shopkeepers with point-of-sale signs printed in *English*. This error was exacerbated when the shopkeepers translated the signs into their own calligraphy as 'Bite the wax tadpole'. Today the characters on Chinese Coke bottles translate as 'happiness in the mouth', which is an improvement on the 'Coke adds life' theme in the Japanese market, which translates into 'Coke brings your ancestors back from the dead'.

■ A television commercial in Lithuania for Wrigley's spearmint chewing gum backfired. Its key message came within a diphthong or two of urging the consumption of shark sperm.

■ Rolls-Royce avoided the name Silver Mist in German markets, where *mist* means 'manure'. Sunbeam, an electrical appliances manufacturer, entered the German market with its Mist-Stick hair-curling iron. Not surprisingly, the Germans had little use for a 'manure wand'.

■ A Taiwanese toy firm offers this intriguing set of instructions to children on how to install a ramp on a garage for toy cars. When translated into English it reads: 'Before you play with, please fix the waiting plate by yourself as per below diagram. But after you once fixed it, you can play with as is and no necessary to fix off again.'

Careless blunders are soon discovered and amended. They may result in little more than embarrassment for the marketer. Countless other more subtle errors may go undetected and damage the brand's performance in less obvious ways. As such, the international company must carefully screen its brand names and advertising messages to avoid those that might hurt sales, make the product look silly, or, worse, offend consumers in specific markets.

Sources: Some of these language blunders are found in David A. Ricks, 'Products that crashed into the language barrier', *Business and Society* (spring 1983), 46–50.

## DECIDING WHICH MARKETS TO ENTER

### Defining international marketing objectives and policies

The company should define its international marketing objectives and policies. First, it should decide what volume of foreign sales it wants. Most companies start small when they go abroad. Some plan to stay small, seeing foreign sales as a small part of their business. Other companies have bigger plans, seeing foreign business as equal to or even more important than their domestic business. Second, the company must choose how many countries it wants to market in. Generally, it makes better sense to operate in fewer countries with deeper penetration in each. Third, the company must decide on the types of countries to enter. A country's attractiveness depends on the product, geographical factors, income and population, political climate and other factors. The seller may prefer certain country groups or parts of the world.

After listing possible international markets, the company must screen and rank each one. Consider the following example:

> Many mass marketers dream of selling to China's 1 billion people. Some think of the market less elegantly as 2 billion armpits. To European brewers, though, the market is mouths, and the People's Republic is especially enticing. America's Anheuser-Busch, the largest brewery in the world, does not yet dominate it. But the Dutch Heineken certainly has its eyes on this potentially lucrative market.
>
> The China market already accounts for 100 million hectolitres of beer on an annual basis. The growth in 1993 alone amounted to the same volume as the French market. Industry observers believe that the potential of the market is impressive. The beer market there is already the third largest in the world behind the US and Germany, and still growing. Although the Chinese drink less than ten litres of beer per head a year, compared with Germany's record 144 litres per head, the actual size of the population guarantees attractive prospects. The Dutch brewing giant Heineken, is tapping into what has been dubbed the world's emerging beer market. The company, a 'Goliath' compared to Germany's Beck's and the Danish Carlsberg, is by far the most international brewery in the world. It enjoys an outstanding cash position, and has remained extremely profitable despite the recession in Europe. In 1994, Heineken's chairman, Karel Vuursteen, said that over the latter half of the nineties, Heineken would invest 800 million guilders into China. This overshadows the 220 million guilders the company had pumped into the Chinese market in the early nineties.
>
> Its main route into this vast market has been through acquiring stakes in local companies. In the early nineties, it also opened its own production plant in Vietnam. Additionally, it is building its own breweries in China. All this reflects an aggressive investment programme to tap the Far Eastern market. But, Heineken is going slowly and steadily. According to Roel Gooskens, a Heineken analyst at Van Meer James Capel, the company will build up its capacity and distribution network through cheap local brands, such as Rong Cheng in China, given that the Chinese cannot afford premium priced products like Heineken lager yet. But, expensive brands will be introduced gradually and will pay off in the longer term. The potential is there as the standard of living in China is rising to attractive levels for Western food and beverages.
>
> Heineken believes its unrivalled track record in countries, such as Africa, gives it more knowledge about brewing abroad than any of its competitors. Anheuser-Busch is primarily operating in the American market. Others, like Carlsberg and Beck's are too small to rival Heineken in a big place like China. With a foothold gained in Asia's largest market, Heineken looks set to conquer other promising markets in the region – Cambodia, India and Thailand, which have seen a 250 per cent growth over the early nineties.[9]

1 ecu = US$1.26
= DFl 2.12
(Dutch guilders)

Although Heineken's decision to exploit the Chinese beer market was straightforward – the sheer size of her population – we still can question whether market size alone is reason enough for selecting China. The company also must consider other

| TABLE 5.1 | *Indicators of market potential* |
|---|---|

| | |
|---|---|
| 1. *Demographic characteristics*<br>   Size of population<br>   Rate of population growth<br>   Degree of urbanization<br>   Population density<br>   Age structure and composition of the population | 4. *Technological factors*<br>   Level of technological skill<br>   Existing production technology<br>   Existing consumption technology<br>   Education levels |
| 2. *Geographic characteristics*<br>   Physical size of a country<br>   Topographical characteristics<br>   Climate conditions | 5. *Sociocultural factors*<br>   Dominant values<br>   Lifestyle patterns<br>   Ethnic groups<br>   Linguistic fragmentation |
| 3. *Economic factors*<br>   GNP per capita<br>   Income distribution<br>   Rate of growth of GNP<br>   Ratio of investment to GNP | 6. *National goals and plans*<br>   Industry priorities<br>   Infrastructure investment plans |

Source:   Susan P. Douglas, C. Samuel Craig, and Warren Keegan, 'Approaches to assessing international marketing opportunities for small and medium-sized business', *Columbia Journal of World Business* (Fall 1982), 26–32.

factors: Will the Chinese government be stable and supportive? Does China provide for the production and distribution technologies needed to produce and market Heineken products profitably? Will their products fit Chinese tastes, means and lifestyles?

Possible global markets should be ranked on several factors, including market size, market growth, cost of doing business, competitive advantage, and risk level. The goal is to determine the potential of each market, using indicators like those shown in Table 5.1. Then the marketer must decide which markets offer the greatest long-run return on investment.

## Assessing product potential

All aspects of the product concept should be considered in relation to the preceding analyses. Managers should consider if there is a good 'fit' between the product potential (that is, the benefits it offers) and market opportunity. The key determinant is whether or not the product is accepted in the proposed country's markets and the investment is profitable.

## ESTABLISHING MARKET ENTRY MODE

Once a company has decided to market in a foreign country, it must determine the best mode of entry. Its choices are exporting, joint venturing and direct investment. Figure 5.2 shows these routes to servicing foreign markets, along with the options each one offers. As we can see, each succeeding strategy involves more commitment and risk, but also more control and potential profits.

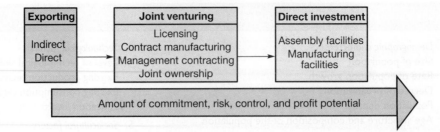

**Figure 5.2**  Market entry strategies.

## Exporting

The simplest way to enter a foreign market is through **exporting**. The company may passively export its surpluses from time to time, or it may make an active commitment to expand exports to a particular market. In either case, the company produces all its goods in its home country. It may or may not modify them for the export market. Exporting involves the least change in the company's product lines, organization, investments, or mission.

### Indirect exporting

Companies typically start with indirect exporting, working through independent home-based international marketing intermediaries. Indirect exporting involves less investment because the firm does not require an overseas salesforce or set of contacts. It also involves less risk. These home-based intermediaries – export merchants or agents, cooperative organizations, government export agencies and export-management companies – bring know-how and services to the relationship, so the seller normally makes fewer mistakes.

### Direct exporting

Sellers may eventually move into direct exporting, whereby they handle their own exports. The investment and risk are somewhat greater in this strategy, but so is the potential return. A company can conduct direct exporting in several ways. It can set up a domestic export department that carries out export activities. Or it can set up an overseas sales branch that handles sales, distribution, and perhaps promotion. The sales branch gives the seller more presence and programme control in the foreign market and often serves as a display centre and customer service centre. Or the company can send home-based salespeople abroad at certain times in order to find business. Finally, the company can do its exporting either through foreign-based distributors who buy and own the goods or through foreign-based agents who sell the goods on behalf of the company in exchange for an agreed fee or commission.

## Joint venturing

A second method of entering a foreign market is **joint venturing** – joining with foreign companies to produce or market the products or services. Joint venturing differs from exporting in that the company joins with a partner to sell or market abroad. It differs from direct investment in that an association is formed with someone in the foreign country. There are four types of joint ventures: licensing, contract manufacturing, management contracting and joint ownership.

## Licensing

**Licensing** is a simple way for a manufacturer to enter international marketing. The company enters into an agreement with a *licensee* in the foreign market. For a fee or royalty, the licensee buys the right to use the company's manufacturing process, trademark, patent, trade secret or other item of value. The company thus gains entry into the market at little risk; the licensee gains production expertise or a well-known product or brand name without having to start from scratch.

Coca-Cola markets internationally by licensing bottlers around the world and supplying them with the syrup needed to produce the product. Licensing has potential disadvantages, however. The firm has less control over the licensee than it would over its own production facilities. Furthermore, if the licensee is very successful, the firm has given up these profits, and if and when the contract ends, it may find it has created a competitor.

## Contract manufacturing

Another option is **contract manufacturing**. The company contracts with manufacturers in the foreign market to produce its product or provide its service. Many Western firms have used this mode for entering Taiwanese and South Korean markets.

The drawbacks of contract manufacturing are the decreased control over the manufacturing process and the loss of potential profits on manufacturing. The benefits are the chance to start faster, with less risk, and the later opportunity either to form a partnership with or to buy out the local manufacturer.

## Management contracting

Under **management contracting**, the domestic firm supplies management know-how to a foreign company that supplies the capital. The domestic firm exports management services rather than products. Hilton uses this arrangement in managing hotels around the world. Management contracting is a low-risk method of getting into a foreign market, and it yields income from the beginning. The arrangement is even more attractive if the contracting firm has an option to buy a share in the managed company later on. The arrangement is not sensible, however, if the company can put its scarce management talent to better uses or if it can make greater profits by undertaking the whole venture. Management contracting also prevents the company from setting up its own operations for a period of time. However, companies like McDonald's have deployed franchising where convenient to do so, while setting up its own restaurants (direct investment) where appropriate.

## Joint ownership

**Joint-ownership** ventures consist of one company joining forces with foreign investors to create a local business in which they share joint ownership and control. A company may buy an interest in a local firm, or the two parties may form a new business venture. Joint ownership may be needed for economic or political reasons.

A foreign government may require joint ownership as a condition for entry. Or the firm may lack the financial, physical, or managerial resources to undertake the venture alone. British Telecom's joint venture with MCI, America's number two long-distance carrier, is a case in point. Similarly, France Télécom and Deutsche Bundespost Telekom joined forces with Sprint, the third largest US long-distance telephone company, which paved the way for the two European telephone operators into the deregulated US market, as well as expanding the collaborators' opportunity to run a global telecommunications network.

Joint ownership has certain drawbacks. The partners may disagree over investment, marketing, or other policies. To enjoy partnership benefits, collaborators must clarify their expectations and objectives and work hard to secure a win-win outcome for all parties concerned.

### Direct investment

The biggest involvement in a foreign market comes through **direct investment** – the development of foreign-based assembly or manufacturing facilities. If a company has gained experience in exporting, and if the foreign market is large enough, foreign production facilities offer many advantages:

1. The firm may have lower costs in the form of cheaper labour or raw materials, foreign government investment incentives, and freight savings.
2. The firm may improve its image in the host country because it creates jobs.
3. Generally, a firm develops a deeper relationship with government, customers, local suppliers and distributors, allowing it to better adapt its products to the local market.
4. Finally, the firm keeps full control over the investment and therefore can develop manufacturing and marketing policies that serve its long-term international objectives.

The main disadvantage of direct investment is that the firm faces many risks, such as restricted or devalued currencies, declining markets or government takeovers. In some cases, a firm has no choice but to accept these risks if it wants to operate in the host country.

There are therefore direct and indirect ways of entering a foreign market. The important point is to note that entry mode decisions are dependent on market conditions and the firm's product characteristics, objectives and capabilities. The British construction machinery maker, JCB, initially faced severe problems in the French market. It recognized that these stemmed from using manufacturers' agents (that is, independent intermediaries) who sold the product but did not provide the service support needed for competitive success in this market. Fortunately, it responded in time. It set up a company-owned, full service distribution network and was rewarded by a large increase in market share and healthy profits.

To summarize, there are three alternative routes for entering foreign markets. It is useful to note that these are not mutually exclusive options. Neither should a linear progression – from engaging in exporting, through setting up joint ventures to direct investment – be assumed. Firms seeking to market goods and services in a foreign market should evaluate the alternative modes of entry and decide upon the most cost-effective path that would ensure long-term performance in that market.

## MAKING A FIRM COMMITMENT

Exploiting international marketing opportunities requires firm commitment from the company. It took European dairy products producers a good twenty years to build up a market for their products in Japan. A lack of commitment to a foreign market is a significant reason for poor exporting performance.[10] The persistence of Japanese multinationals in the US and European markets is particularly noteworthy.

Honda was prepared to sustain their motorcycle operations in the United States despite not making any money in the first five years of entry. Meanwhile they invested in continuous product improvement and market development to meet target customers' needs. The British car company, Rover, withdrew from the US market in 1991 following declining car sales and a failed entry with the 'Sterling', a luxury executive saloon. The company retreated after less than four years' presence in the American market. The problem was a culmination of poor quality cars on market entry, rapid model obsolescence and large unsalable stocks.[11] This early withdrawal is contrasted with Japan's Mazda who very successfully launched their Miata roadster in the United States. The Miata was a high-quality product which was aggressively promoted to an unserved segment – consumers who desired to own a Lotus Elan, but wanted to pay only a third of the cost! Mazda announced plans to introduce a whole range of innovative vehicles, including the 'Amati', a luxury car positioned against Toyota's luxury Lexus and Nissan's Infiniti brands. The difference in commitment levels shown by Rover and Mazda is illustrative of the broader malaise afflicting many British companies' performance in overseas markets. The French Peugeot also announced its withdrawal from the entrenched US market at the same time as Rover, offering yet another example of European entrenchment in the face of Japanese persistence in longer-term expansion in Western markets.

Mr Carl Hahn, management board chairman of Volkswagen, rationalizes the need for the European car manufacturing industry to accept the challenges of the North American market if the industry is to survive in the long term:

> The US market is important in particular because it sets the benchmark for competition in the world market. ... it shapes social demands on the car, in exhaust emissions, for example. We simply cannot afford to give up either the opportunities offered by the US market or the learning processes and experience it imposes.[12]

The demonstrable commitment to the foreign market cannot be overstated. It must come from the senior levels of management and be communicated throughout the company. Target customers in foreign countries must also be convinced that this commitment is lasting. Buyers of capital goods or expensive durable items feel more secure and happier to adopt a brand that is here to stay and enjoys strong service and after-sales support.

## ALLOCATING NECESSARY RESOURCES

To successfully build a strong market position in a foreign country, the firm must be prepared to allocate necessary resources to the planned expansion. Building a strong brand image and channel networks is difficult and highly expensive for any company to undertake. The investment needed to achieve international brand recognition, even in Europe alone, is enormous. When the Japanese firm, Canon, launched its first photocopier in the United States, it spent $15 million on TV advertising, a third of its R&D budget for the year. It has been calculated that to create 20 per cent brand awareness across Japan, the United States and West Germany costs $1 billion. The ratio between investment in product development, manufacturing or service delivery and worldwide marketing is often 1:10:100. Too many companies get this ratio reversed, and so often underestimate the costs of doing business abroad. This, together with their expectation of early high returns on investment, which is often unlikely, explains why firms all too readily withdraw from foreign markets before establishing a firm market presence.[13]

## IDENTIFYING TECHNICAL ISSUES

The firm has to address a range of factors from simple issues, such as voltage requirements, to important complex characteristics like disparate legal systems, which significantly impact on market entry mode and product acceptance. It is important for the firm to ensure early on that its product meets the foreign country's technical requirements. In Germany, for example, a DIN certificate proves the product conforms with technical requirements. The firm, in this case, should consult the Deutsche Institut für Normung for details on specifications.

The legal considerations range from strategic, such as the constraints on market entry mode, to operational issues, including advertising regulations or the types of sales promotion allowed in different markets entered. In France, the Toubon Law bans the use of foreign words in all walks of French life. With regard to advertising, the law prohibits the use of all foreign languages without a French translation of the same size, if in print, or without a French soundtrack, if on television or radio. When Unilever introduced Healthy Options, a British line of ready meals, to other European countries in 1989, it learned, too late, that many prohibit the use of the word 'healthy' in a product's name! Yet another example of the need for international firms to develop a sensitivity for domestic laws is given by Yves Rocher, a French cosmetics company:

> EU member states still regulate price promotions through their own local laws. This sometimes causes problems to firms when structuring promotions that cross boundaries. For Yves Rocher, the issue was that under German law, there was a ban of any price comparisons that were 'eye catching'. Yves Rocher sold cosmetics by mail order in Germany. The products were advertised in a uniform fashion for the various Member States and was spread by means of catalogues and brochures. Yves Rocher had distributed a brochure which showed, beside the former crossed out price, the new, lower price of those products in bold red characters. These were eye catching and therefore broke German law. The German law was, however, held to breach the European Treaty by creating a barrier to trade and effectively banning the promotion.

The Yves Rocher case was an important victory for cross-boundary price promotion exponents. It also showed that marketing professionals, targeting EU markets, must take account of developments related to European law to ensure legality of promotions throughout the Union.[14]

## DEVELOPING A STRATEGIC MARKETING PLAN

Managers, by this stage, should have a clear idea of the characteristics, profit potential and the risks associated with alternative entry modes for target foreign markets. Without the preceding analysis, international marketing is unlikely to be successful. Product policy, pricing, promotion and distribution decisions must also be based on sound market analysis. Firms have little influence over the external environmental factors, so must try to maximize the effectiveness of those decisions over which they can exercise control. The marketing programme for each foreign market must be carefully planned. Managers must first decide on the precise customer target or targets to be served. Then managers have to decide how, if at all, to modify the firm's marketing mix to local conditions. To do this requires a good understanding of country market conditions as well as cultural characteristics of customers in that market. We have already addressed the need for cultural sensitivity. This section will discuss reasons for standardization versus adaptation for the global market before highlighting specific international marketing-mix decisions.

### Standardization or adaptation for international markets?

At one extreme are companies that use a **standardized marketing mix** worldwide. Proponents highlight several reasons for global standardization.

*Homogeneous needs and preferences*    The presence of homogeneous needs among customers permits the building of global brands such as Levi jeans and Beatles records. In these cases, the 'home culture' has been successfully exported to mass markets abroad, where consumers show similar preferences for the cult image Levi portrays or the music and legend the Beatles developed.

The success of Häagen-Dazs is another case in point. The product has a long history in North America. Under a new, aggressive management team, it was successfully launched in Japan and Europe. Throughout these markets, Häagen-Dazs uses a standard marketing approach: high quality, high price, selective distribution outlets and sexual imagery. Similar examples can be found for niche products, especially luxury goods: Cartier jewellery, Rolex watches, Royal Doulton fine china, Mikimoto pearls and Louis Vuitton luggage are all marketed in the same way across the globe.

*Consumer mobility*    A larger number of people are travelling more widely, thus allowing more products to be marketed to them on a global basis. Kodak film, for example, is sold worldwide in its distinctive yellow box and the emphasis upon wide availability is similar across markets. Travellers can expect to find Novotel hotels across Europe to offer similar standards of service and food.

*Economies of scale/experience*    In many industries, cost advantages are essential for competitive success when operating on a global scale. Economies are derived from discounts from bulk purchases, sharing R&D, marketing, production and managerial resources among different markets. A standardized marketing programme reduces costs even further, letting companies offer consumers higher-quality and more reliable products at lower prices. Gillette Sensor's worldwide launch is a good case of how the firm derived scale economies from a standardized global approach. The Sensor took ten years to develop. It represented a breakthrough in wet-shave technology. It was essentially a niche product. To recuperate funds already spent on the product's development and launch, it needed high unit sales, so had to be marketed globally. Gillette identified three **cultural universals** (attributes that transcend national cultures) associated with wet shaving: comfort, closeness of shave, and safety. The company exploited these in a common communications campaign – 'the best a man can get'. The worldwide launch was a phenomenal success. So successful was the Sensor campaign that its effects spilled over into a new, complementary product – the Shaving Gel – which enjoyed raised awareness and sales!

*Technological feasibility*   In product sectors where the technological processes are becoming more homogeneous, adherence to these through standardization is a pre-requisite for market success. For simple technologies like the production of mould-ings, toys, paint, hand tools and so forth, it might make sense to standardize the product as much as possible to keep costs down. This is also the thinking behind Coca-Cola's decision that Coke should taste about the same around the world.

At the other extreme is an **adapted marketing mix**. In this case, the producer adjusts the marketing mix elements to each target, bearing more costs but hoping for a larger market share and return. Nestlé, for example, varies its product line and its advertis-ing in different countries. The rationale for marketing-mix adaptation is the reverse of the reasons given for standardization. Most important are the disparities among different country markets.

*Diversity*   Exponents of adaptation argue that consumers in different countries vary greatly in their geographic, demographic, economic, and cultural characteristics. Differences in the following factors suggest the need to adapt the firm's product offer-ing for international markets: product preferences; uses and conditions of product use; customer needs, perceptions and attitudes; consumers' shopping patterns; income levels and spending power; the country's laws and regulations; user/cus-tomer skills or education; competitive conditions; advertising laws; and media avail-ability. In the Single European Market, many argue that the 'Euroconsumer' is a myth. Marketers are advised to identify carefully differences that do exist across national markets and tailor products and services to suit local tastes and preferences. The dictum, 'different strokes for different folks', is still very much the way of busi-ness in international marketing.

The decision about which aspects of the marketing mix to standardize and which to adapt should be taken on the basis of target market conditions. Firms are often unwilling to modify their product offering for foreign markets because of 'cultural arrogance'. German and American machine-tool manufacturers, for example, have seen their world market shares dive over the 1980s due, in part, to their reluctance to adapt products and marketing approaches in the face of changing customer needs in their home and foreign markets. 'What's good for Germany is good enough for the world market' was the view typifying a large proportion of German machine-tool producers who formed the focus of a study into international marketing strategies in the UK market. This cultural arrogance has been termed the 'self-reference criterion' and has been a significant factor in accounting for the poor export performance of British firms.[15]

The question of whether to adapt or standardize the marketing mix has been much debated in recent years. However, global standardization is not an all-or-nothing proposition, but rather a matter of degree. Companies should look for more standard-ization to help keep down costs and prices and to build greater global brand power. But they must not replace long-run marketing thinking with short-run financial thinking. Although standardization saves money, marketers must make certain that they offer what consumers in each country want.[16]

Many possibilities exist between the extremes of standardization and complete adaptation. For example, Coca-Cola sells the same beverage worldwide, and in most markets it uses television spots showing 1,000 children singing the praises of Coke. For different local markets, however, it edits the commercials to include close-ups of children from those markets – there were at least 21 different versions of the spot.

Let us now examine marketing-mix decisions with regard to global marketing planning.

## Product

Five strategies allow for adapting product and promotion to a foreign market (see Figure 5.3).[17] We first discuss the three product strategies and then turn to the two promotion strategies.

**Straight product extension** means marketing a product in a foreign market without any change. Top management tells its marketing people: 'Take the product as it is and find customers for it.' The first step, however, should be to find out whether foreign consumers use that product and what form they prefer.

Straight extension has been successful in some cases and disastrous in others. Coca-Cola, Kellogg cereals, Heineken beer, and Black & Decker tools are all sold successfully in about the same form around the world. Philips began to make a profit in Japan only after it reduced the size of its coffee makers to fit into smaller Japanese kitchens and its shavers to fit smaller Japanese hands. The Japanese construction machinery maker, Komatsu, had to alter the design of the door handles of earth movers sold in Finland: drivers wearing thick gloves in winter found it impossible to grasp the door handles which were too small (obviously designed to fit the fingers of the average Japanese, but not the double-cladded ones of larger European users!). Straight extension is tempting because it involves no additional product-development costs, manufacturing changes, or new promotion. But it can be costly in the long run if products fail to satisfy foreign consumers.

**Product adaptation** involves changing the product to meet local conditions or wants. For example, McDonald's serves beer in Germany and coconut, mango, and tropical mint shakes in Hong Kong. In Japan, Mister Donut serves coffee in smaller and lighter cups that better fit the fingers of the average Japanese consumer; even the doughnuts are a little smaller. Campbell serves up soups that match unique tastes of consumers in different countries. For example, it sells duck-gizzard soup in the Guangdong Province of China; in Poland, it features flaki, a peppery tripe soup. And IBM adapts its worldwide product line to meet local needs. For example, IBM must make dozens of different keyboards – twenty for Europe alone – to match different languages.[18]

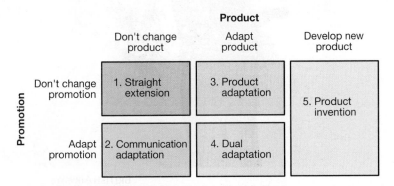

**Figure 5.3** Five international product and promotion strategies.

**Product invention** consists of creating something new for the foreign market. This strategy can take two forms. It might mean reintroducing earlier product forms that happen to be well adapted to the needs of a given country. For example, the National Cash Register Company reintroduced its crank-operated cash register at half the price of a modern cash register and sold large numbers in the Orient, Latin America, and Spain. Or a company might create a new product to meet a need in another country. For example, an enormous need exists for low-cost, high-protein foods in less developed countries. Companies such as Quaker Oats, Swift and Monsanto are researching the nutrition needs of these countries, creating new foods, and developing advertising campaigns to gain product trial and acceptance. Product invention can be costly, but the pay-offs are worthwhile.

## Promotion

Companies can either adopt the same promotion strategy they used in the home market or change it for each local market.

Consider the message. Some global companies use a standardized advertising theme around the world. Esso used 'Put a tiger in your tank', which gained international recognition. Of course, the copy may be varied in minor ways to adjust for language differences. In Japan, for instance, where consumers have trouble pronouncing 'snap, crackle, pop', the little Rice Krispies critters say 'patchy, pitchy, putchy'. Colours also are changed sometimes to avoid taboos in other countries. Black is an unlucky colour for the Chinese, white is a mourning colour in Japan, and green is associated with jungle sickness in Malaysia.

Even names must be changed. In Sweden, Helene Curtis changed the name of its 'Every Night Shampoo' to 'Every Day' because Swedish consumers usually wash their hair in the morning. Kellogg also had to rename 'Bran Buds' cereal in Sweden, where the name roughly translates as 'burned farmer'.

Global companies like British Airways are at the forefront in finding common threads among the world's consumers.

Other companies fully adapt their advertising messages to local markets. The Schwinn Bicycle Company might use a pleasure theme in the United States and a safety theme in Scandinavia. Kellogg ads in the United States promote the taste and nutrition of Kellogg's cereals versus competitors' brands. In France, where consumers drink little milk and eat little for breakfast, Kellogg's ads must convince consumers that cereals are a tasty and healthful breakfast.

Media also need to be adapted internationally because media availability varies from country to country. TV advertising time is very limited in Europe, for instance, ranging from four hours a day in France to none in Scandinavian countries. Advertisers must buy time months in advance, and they have little control over air times. Magazines also vary in effectiveness. For example, magazines are a popular medium in Italy and a minor one in Austria. Newspapers are national in the United Kingdom but are only local in Spain.

## Price

Companies also face many problems in setting their international prices.

Regardless of how companies go about pricing their products, their foreign prices will probably be higher than their domestic prices. A Gucci handbag may sell for £80 in Italy and £160 in Singapore. Why? Gucci faces a price escalation problem. It must add the cost of transportation, tariffs, importer margin, wholesaler margin and retailer margin to its factory price. Depending on these added costs, the product may have to sell for two to five times as much in another country to make the same profit. For example, a pair of Levi's jeans that sells for $30 in the United States typically fetches $63 in Tokyo and $88 in Paris. A Chrysler car priced at $10,000 in the United States sells for more than $47,000 in South Korea.[19]

Another problem involves setting a price for goods that a company ships to its foreign subsidiaries. If the company charges a foreign subsidiary too much, it may end up paying higher tariff duties even while paying lower income taxes in that country. If the company charges its subsidiary too little, it can be charged with *dumping* – that is, charging less than its costs or less than it charges in its home market. In the 1980s, Honda and Kawasaki were accused by their US counterparts of dumping motorcycles on the US market. The US International Trade Commission agreed and responded with a special five-year tariff on Japanese heavy motorcycles. The commission also ruled in the late 1980s that Japan was dumping computer memory chips in the US and laid stiff duties on future imports. In Europe, Japanese firms have also been accused of dumping products by their European counterparts. Dumping duties were imposed by the UK government on imports of Japanese photocopiers, microwave ovens and scientific instruments back in the 1980s. More recently, the EU imposed antidumping duties of as much as 96.8 per cent on imports of broadcasting cameras made by some Japanese companies. The duties were levied after an investigation by the European Commission, following complaints by BTS, part of Philips, and Thomson Broadcast of France (Europe's only makers of studio video cameras), found that Japanese exporters had, through unfair pricing, increased their share of the EU studio market from 52 per cent in 1989 to 70 per cent in 1992. The share of European producers had fallen from 48 per cent to 30 per cent over this same period of time.[20]

Last but not least, many global companies face a *grey* market. For example, Minolta sold its cameras to Hong Kong distributors for less than it charged German distributors because of lower transportation costs and tariffs. Minolta cameras ended up selling at retail for £80 in Hong Kong and £170 in Germany. Some Hong Kong wholesalers noticed this price difference and shipped Minolta cameras to German dealers for less than the dealers were paying their German distributor. The German distributor couldn't sell its stock and complained to Minolta. Thus a company often finds some enterprising distributors buying more than they can sell in their own country, then shipping goods to another country to take advantage of price differences. International companies try to prevent grey markets by raising their prices to lower cost distributors, dropping those who cheat, or altering the product for different countries.

## Distribution channels

The international company must take a whole-channel view of the problem of distributing products to final consumers. Figure 5.4 shows the three main links between the *seller* and the *final buyer*. The first link, the *seller's headquarters organization*, supervises the channels and is part of the channel itself. The second link, *channels between nations*, moves the products to the borders of the foreign nations. The third link, *channels within nations*, moves the products from their foreign entry point to the final consumers. Some manufacturers may think their job is done once the product leaves their hands, but they would do well to pay more attention to its handling within foreign countries.

Channels of distribution within countries vary greatly from nation to nation. First there are the large differences in the numbers and types of middlemen serving each foreign market. For example, a foreign company marketing in China must operate through a frustrating maze of state-controlled wholesalers and retailers. Chinese distributors often carry competitors' products and frequently refuse to share even basic sales and marketing information with their suppliers. Hustling for sales is an alien concept to Chinese distributors, who are used to selling all they can obtain. Working with or getting around this system sometimes requires substantial time and investment. When Coke and Pepsi first entered China, for example, customers bicycled up to bottling plants to get their soft drinks. Now, both companies have set up direct-distribution channels, investing heavily in trucks and refrigeration units for retailers.[21]

Another difference lies in the size and character of retail units abroad. Whereas large-scale retail chains dominate the British and US markets, most retailing in the rest of Europe and other countries is done by many small independent retailers. As the variety of anecdotes that we have offered, in relation to the penetration of Japanese markets by Western firms, suggests, getting to grips with a country's distribution structure is often crucial to achieving effective market access. The firm must therefore invest in acquiring knowledge about each foreign market's channel features and decide on how best to break into complex or entrenched distribution systems.

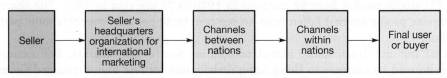

**Figure 5.4**  Whole-channel concept for international marketing.

## ORGANIZING AN OPERATIONAL TEAM AND IMPLEMENTING A MARKETING STRATEGY

The key to success in any marketing strategy is the firm's ability to implement the chosen strategy. Because of the firm's distance from its foreign markets, international marketing strategy implementation is particularly difficult. The firm must have an organization structure that fits with the international environment. It has to be flexible to implement different strategies for the various markets it operates in.

Companies manage their international marketing activities in at least three different ways. Most companies first organize an export department, then create an international division, and finally become a global organization.

### Export department

A firm normally gets into international marketing by simply shipping out its goods. If its international sales expand, the company organizes an **export department** with a sales manager and a few assistants. As sales increase, the export department can then expand to include various marketing services so that it can actively go after business. If the firm moves into joint ventures or direct investment, the export department will no longer be adequate.

### International division

Many companies get involved in several international markets and ventures. A company may export to one country, license to another, have a joint-ownership venture in a third, and own a subsidiary in a fourth. Sooner or later it will create an **international division** or subsidiary to handle all its international activities.

International divisions are organized in a variety of ways. The international division's corporate staff consists of marketing, manufacturing, research, finance, planning, and personnel specialists. They plan for and provide services to various operating units. Operating units may be organized in one of three ways. They may be *geographical* organizations, with country managers who are responsible for salespeople, sales branches, distributors, and licensees in their respective countries. Or the operating units may be *world product groups*, each responsible for worldwide sales of different product groups. Finally, operating units may be *international subsidiaries*, each responsible for its own sales and profits.

### Global organization

Several firms have passed beyond the international division stage and become truly **global organizations**. They stop thinking of themselves as national marketers who sell abroad and start thinking of themselves as global marketers. The top corporate management and staff plan worldwide manufacturing facilities, marketing policies, financial flows, and logistical systems. The global operating units report directly to the chief executive or executive committee of the organization, not to the head of an international division. Executives are trained in worldwide operations, not just domestic or international. The company recruits management from many countries, buys components and supplies where they cost the least, and invests where the expected returns are greatest.

Large companies must become more global in the 1990s if they hope to compete. As foreign companies successfully invade the domestic market, domestic companies must move more aggressively into foreign markets. They will have to change from companies that treat their foreign operations as secondary, to companies that view the entire world as a single borderless market.[22]

More intensely competitive international markets suggest that global firms must place a premium on organizational flexibility. GFT, the Italian firm, is the world's biggest manufacturer of designer clothes. Its product portfolio comprises expensive 'labels' such as Emanuel Ungaro, Giorgio Armani, Valentino and Baulmer. The company's international expansion required extreme flexibility in managing organizational change. The paradox the firm faced mirrors the dilemma confronting most global firms today:

> For GFT, globalisation is not about standardisation; it is about a quantum increase in complexity. The more the company has penetrated global markets, the more sustaining its growth depends on responding to myriad local differences in its key markets around the world.[23]

Organizing for effective international marketing is a considerable challenge that besets multinational firms of any size. The tension between *centralization* and *decentralization* is a very tight one. On the one hand, managers must agree upon the key strategic decisions and activities to centralize. On the other, they must give as much autonomy as possible to local staff who are close to market conditions. There is no one correct combination of centralized–decentralized organization. It is important to heed the maxim, '*Think global, act local*'. The organizational structure varies according to the firm's circumstances and over time. The firm must ensure that its structure fits with its international environment, while at the same time have the internal flexibility required to implement its strategic goal.[24]

Percy Barnevik, chief executive officer of the Swiss–Swedish group, Asea Brown Boveri, best sums up the real complexity of international business organizations. He describes the need to have a structure that leverages the firm's core technologies, gains scale economies and still maintains local market position and responsiveness:

> ABB is an organization with three internal contradictions. We want to be global and local, big and small, radically decentralized with centralized reporting and control. If we can resolve those contradictions we create real organizational advantage.

## EVALUATE AND CONTROL OPERATIONS

Any number of problems can beset the marketing plan, from unexpected competition to outbreak of war. The firm must be sensitive to such occurrences. Its flexibility to respond to environmental shocks determines long-term success. As such, the firm must evaluate the outcome of its marketing plans, analyse progress and variances from target goals and objectives, and take control actions where needed.

It is important to note that the model of planning decisions taken by international marketing managers, as discussed above, is an iterative process. The activities are continuous and must be undertaken continually to ensure environmental sensitivity and effective strategy implementation.

## SUMMARY

Companies today can no longer afford to pay attention only to their domestic market, no matter how large it is. Many industries are global industries, and those firms that operate globally achieve lower costs and higher brand awareness. At the same time, *global marketing* is risky because of variable exchange rates, unstable governments, protectionist tariffs and trade barriers, and several other factors. Given the potential gains and *risks* of international marketing, companies need a systematic way to make their international marketing decisions.

First, a company must *analyse* the *international market opportunity* open to it. To do this managers must understand the *global marketing environment*, especially the *international trade system*. It must assess each foreign market's *economic, political–legal*, and *cultural characteristics*. The company decides whether to go abroad based on a consideration of the potential risks and benefits. Second, it has to *decide which country markets* it wants *to enter*. It must determine the volume of foreign sales – assuming there is high *product potential* – and how many countries to market in, having weighed the probable rate of return on investment against the level of risk. Third, the company must *decide how to enter* each chosen market – whether through *exporting, joint venturing*, or *direct investment*. Many companies start as exporters, move to joint ventures, and finally make a direct investment in foreign markets. Increasingly, however, firms – domestic or international – use joint ventures and even direct investments to enter a new country market for the first time.

Fourth, the firm must *make a* wholehearted *commitment* to its overseas customers and markets. Fifth, it must be prepared to *allocate necessary resources* to initially secure a foothold, and then to build a strong position in the market. A sixth dimension is the consideration for country-specific *technical issues*, which, if overlooked, could cause the firm problems. The firm is then in a position to develop its *strategic marketing plan*, which must take stock of the level of *adaptation* or *standardization* appropriate for all elements of the marketing mix – *product, promotion, price* and *distribution channels*. The company has to also organize its operational team to achieve effective strategy implementation. The firm may adopt different organizational structures for managing international operations. Most firms start with an *export department* and graduate to an *international division*. A few become *global organizations*, with worldwide marketing planned and managed by the top officers of the company, who view the entire world as a single borderless market. Finally, managers should continually *evaluate* their international marketing programmes. Plans should be monitored and *control* procedures applied, when needed, to secure desired performance.

■ **DISCUSSING THE ISSUES**

1. With all the problems facing companies that 'go global', why are so many companies choosing to expand internationally? What are the advantages of expanding beyond the domestic market?

2. When exporting goods to a foreign country, a marketer may be faced with various trade restrictions. Discuss the effects these restrictions might have on an exporter's marketing mix: (a) tariffs; (b) quotas; and (c) embargoes.

3. When Honda first introduced its luxury executive car – the Legend – into the European market in

the mid-1980s, other European luxury car producers (e.g. Jaguar, Mercedes, BMW) were 'not impressed'. Some even went so far as to declare that: 'Honda's mass market appeal is no comparison; we are operating in the premium sector'. In 1990, Toyota, another established mass-market car producer, launched its luxury brand – the Lexus – which seized leadership from rival, Honda, and outcompetes the Legend. The Lexus is also becoming a noteworthy marque amongst prestigious labels like Mercedes and BMW. Discuss the Japanese strategy of long-term commitment to international markets. What are the key lessons for European companies seeking to internationalize?

4. Imported products are usually more expensive, but not always: a Nikon camera is cheaper in London than in Tokyo. Why are foreign prices sometimes higher and sometimes lower than domestic prices for exports?

5. 'Dumping' leads to price savings to the consumer. Why do EU and US governments make dumping illegal? What are the disadvantages to the consumer of dumping by foreign firms?

6. Which type of international marketing organization would you suggest for the following companies: (a) Raleigh Bicycles selling three models in the Far East; (b) a US manufacturer of toys, marketing its products in Europe; and (c) Rover, planning to sell its full line of cars and trucks in Kuwait.

## ■ APPLYING THE CONCEPTS

1. Go to a large electronics and appliance store that sells products such as televisions, stereos, hairdryers and microwave ovens. Pick one or two product categories to examine.

   ■ Make a list of brand names in the category and classify each name as being either 'your home country' or 'foreign'. How did you decide whether a brand was 'home' or 'foreign'?
   ■ Look at where these different brands were manufactured. Are any of the 'home' brands manufactured abroad and are any of the 'foreign' brands made locally? What does this tell you about how much international marketing is being done? Is 'global' a better term to describe some of these brands?

2. Entertainment, including movies, television programmes and music recordings, is America's second largest export category – only aircraft is larger.

   ■ Go to your college library and find several foreign magazines, local pictures, stories or ads featuring American entertainers. Study what you find. Look at the size and layout of the stories, and see if you can understand basically what is being said. Does American entertainment seem to be interesting or important to people in Europe or the rest of the world? What, if anything, do you think is appealing to them?
   ■ India has the largest movie industry in the world, yet few Indian films are ever shown in Europe. Why do you think this is so? Suggest some ways that Indian movie companies might make a bigger impact in Europe.

## ■ REFERENCES

1. Margaret Dolley, 'Carlsberg taps a universal taste for Danish Beer', The European (1–7 April 1994), 28.
2. For a good discussion of the differences between international, multinational, and global marketing, see Warren J. Keegan, Global Marketing Management, 4th edn (Englewood Cliffs, NJ: Prentice Hall, 1989), 6–11.
3. C. P. Rao, M. K. Erramilli, and G. K. Ganesh, 'Impact of domestic recession on export marketing behaviour', International Marketing Review, 7, 2 (1990), 54–65.
4. 'The unique Japanese', Fortune (24 November 1986), 8. For more on nontariff and other barriers, see Rahul Jacob, 'Export barriers the US hates most', Fortune (27 February 1989), 88–9; Carla Rapoport, 'The big split', Fortune (6 May 1991), 38–48: and Mark Maremont,

'Protectionism is king of the road', Business Week (13 May 1991), 57–8.
5. For more reading on free-trade zones, see Cyndee Miller, 'Nationalism endangers smooth transition to unified EC market', Marketing News (17 February 1992), 1, 10; Blayne Cutler, 'North American demographics', American Demographics (March 1992), 38–42; Paul Magnusson, '"Free trade" They can hardly wait', Business Week (14 September 1992), 24–5; Andrew Hilton, 'Mythology, markets, and the emerging Europe', Harvard Business Review (Nov.–Dec. 1992), 50–4; and Larry Armstrong, 'NAFTA isn't out, but it sure is down', Business Week (22 March 1993), 30–1.
6. For further reading, see Leo G. B. Welt, Trade Without

*Money: Barter and countertrade* (New York: Harcourt Brace Jovanovic, 1984); Demos Vardiabasis, '"Countertrade" New ways of doing business', *Business to Business* (December 1985), 67–71; Louis Kraar, 'How to sell to cashless buyers', *Fortune* (7 November 1988), 147–54; 'Pepsi to get ships, vodka in $3 billion deal', *Durham Morning Herald* (10 May 1990), B5; and Cyndee Miller, 'Worldwide money crunch fuels more international barter', *Marketing News* (2 March 1992), 5.

7. F. Reinstine, 'Selling to Japan: we did it their way', *Export Today*, **3**, 3, pp. 19–24.

8. For more insight into the custom clash in Europe, see John Mole, *Mind Your Manners: Culture clash in the European single market* (London: The Industrial Society Press, 1990).

9. Barbara Smit, 'Heineken sets out to quench China's thirst', *The European* (22–28 April 1994), 20.

10. G. J. Hooley and J. R. Newcombe, 'Ailing British exports: systems, causes and cures', *Quarterly Review of Marketing* (Summer 1983).

11. K. Done, 'Rover to quit US market after decline in car sales', *Financial Times* (10 August 1991).

12. See K. Done, 'Bold assault on the highway', *Financial Times* (10 August 1991); also Hooley and Newcombe, op. cit., and Done, 'Rover to quit', op. cit.

13. '1992: what are we fighting for?', *Marketing Business* (October 1988), 14–15.

14. Rolan Rowell, 'Marketing laws: a European flavour', *Marketing Business* (February 1994), 34–5.

15. See Peter Doyle, Veronica Wong and Vivienne Shaw, 'Marketing strategies of international competitors in the UK machine tool market', *Journal of Global Marketing*, **8**, 2 (1994), 75–96; and Hooley and Newcombe, op. cit.

16. See George S. Yip, 'Global strategy ... in a world of nations?', *Sloan Management Review* (Fall 1989), 29–41; Kamran Kashani, 'Beware the pitfalls of global marketing', *Harvard Business Review* (Sept.–Oct. 1989), 91–8; and Saeed Saminee and Kendall Roth, 'The influence of global marketing standardization on performance', *Journal of Marketing* (April 1992), 1–17.

17. See Keegan, *Global Marketing Management*, 378–81. Also see Peter G. P. Walters and Brian Toyne, 'Product modification and standardization in international markets: strategic options and facilitating policies', *Columbia Journal of World Business* (Winter 1989), 37–44.

18. For these and other examples, see Andrew Kupfer, 'How to be a global manager', *Fortune* (14 March 1988), 52–8; Maria Shao, 'For Levi's: a flattering fit overseas', *Business Week* (5 November 1990), 76–7; and Joseph Weber, 'Campbell: now it's M-M-global', *Business Week* (15 March 1993), 52–3.

19. Dori Jones Yang, 'Can Asia's four tigers be tamed?', *Business Week* (15 February 1988), 47; and Shao, 'For Levi's', op. cit., 78.

20. See Michael Oneal, 'Harley-Davidson: ready to hit the road again', *Business Week* (21 July 1986), 70. Also Guy de Jonquières, 'High duties against Japan', *Financial Times* (4 May 1994), 7.

21. See Maria Shao, 'Laying the foundation for the great mall of China', *Business Week* (25 January 1988), 68–9.

22. See Kenichi Ohmae, 'Managing in a borderless world', *Harvard Business Review* (May–June 1989), 152–61; and William J. Holstein, 'The stateless corporation', *Business Week* (14 May 1990), 98–105.

23. R. Howard, 'The designer organisation: Italy's GFT goes global', *Harvard Business Review* (Sept.–Oct. 1991), 28–44.

24. W. Taylor, 'The logic of global business', *Harvard Business Review* (Mar.–Apr. 1991), 90–105.

## CASE 5

## Procter & Gamble: going global in cosmetics

Procter & Gamble, the multinational company known for its household products Daz, Fairy, and so forth, has decided to expand its cosmetics business. The question is, can the firm that has got us to Pamper-away our babies' wetness, Crest-away our cavities and Tide-away the grime in our clothes now get us to make up our faces?

### Step 1   Diversifying

P&G's aggressive chairman, Edwin L. Artzt, thinks it can. The company tiptoed into the skin-care business

in 1985 when it bought the Oil of Ulay skin-care line. Under Artzt's leadership, P&G then drove headlong into the cosmetics business. In 1989, it bought Noxell Corporation and its Cover Girl and Clarion brand cosmetics lines for $1.3bn.[*]

A Baltimore pharmacist had founded Noxell in 1917 to sell little blue jars of a sunburn remedy he later named Noxzema skin cream. In the early 1960s, Noxell launched the Cover Girl line with a

[*]1 ecu = US$1.26.

foundation cream designed to conceal acne. It used famous models to advertise the product and eventually became the best-selling mass-market cosmetics brand in the United States, overtaking Maybelline in 1986. Noxell had also been successful with its 1987 launch of Clarion, a line of moderately priced, mass-market cosmetics for sensitive skin. However, to develop its new businesses, as with its expensive Clarion introduction, Noxell had to take money from its Cover Girl and Noxzema marketing budgets. Consequently, in the late 1980s, these established brands were in danger of fading.

Artzt saw the opportunity to strengthen Noxell's marketing support with P&G's considerable resources while at the same time providing P&G with new growth opportunities outside its stable of mature products. Artzt also recognized that cosmetics carried high gross margins and resisted recessions. In 1990, P&G obtained 47.7 per cent of its $24.08bn in total sales from personal-care products. About one-half of these sales came from paper products, including diapers. Another 32.2 per cent of its total sales came from laundry and cleaning products; 13.4 per cent from food and drinks and 6.7 per cent from pulp and chemicals.

After acquiring Noxell, Artzt turned P&G's marketers loose. They quickly redesigned Cover Girl's packaging, giving it an elegant look, but retained the brand's budget pricing strategy. P&G also sped up new product development. It backed these changes with a 58 per cent increase in advertising, spending $47.5 million on Cover Girl in the first nine months of 1990 alone. Ads spotlighted famous models of various ages who featured a more natural look. By 1991, Cover Girl's market share had increased to 23 per cent, up from 21 per cent in 1986. Meanwhile Maybelline's share had fallen to 17 per cent, down from 19 per cent in 1986.

### Step 2   Going international

P&G realized that it could not rest on its success. The cosmetics industry was changing, and P&G would have to change if it wanted to become a serious contender. Consumers were deserting department stores in droves, looking for distinctive brands offered by speciality clothing chains and cosmetics boutiques, such as the Body Shop. Analysts believed that women were tired of being assaulted as they entered department stores' cosmetics sections. Women wanted to buy cosmetics where they bought other items, which was increasingly in speciality shops. As a result, department store cosmetics sales were declining and mass merchandiser shares were increasing. The Cover Girl brand also faced problems. For example, the Cover Girl name suggested that the brand was for young, glamorous women, giving the line a built-in problem when appealing to career women, homemakers, and older women. In addition, Cover Girl generated 90 per cent of its sales in the United States, whereas the rest of the industry was increasingly going global. For these reasons, Artzt went shopping again.

At the same time, New York financier Ronald Perelman had decided that he might need to sell Revlon, his beauty-products company. Perelman had bought Revlon in 1985 for $1.83bn, following a bitter hostile takeover. However, Perelman had used junk bonds to finance this and other deals and found himself facing large debt repayments that caused a cash squeeze. As a result, Perelman considered selling some or all of Revlon's brands, including Max Factor and Almay cosmetics, Charlie and Jontou perfumes, and Flex shampoo.

Several big firms besides P&G expressed an interest in Revlon. Like P&G, these other companies wanted to expand their cosmetics businesses through acquisitions. Unilever, the Anglo-Dutch multinational, began buying US personal-care brands in 1989. As a result of its Fabergé and Elizabeth Arden acquisitions, Unilever held the number-three spot behind Estée Lauder and L'Oréal in sales at US department store cosmetics counters. Unilever had worldwide personal-care sales of $4.7bn in 1990. Gesparal, S.A. owned the majority of Cosmair's L'Oréal, which had 1989 worldwide revenues of $5.3bn. In turn, Nestlé, the Swiss food conglomerate, owned 49 per cent of Gesparal.

P&G was especially interested in Revlon's Max Factor and Betrix lines, because 80 per cent of their sales were outside the United States. These two brands would fit well with P&G's other lines and give the company a good basis to compete for a bigger share of the $16bn worldwide cosmetics and fragrance business. In April 1991, Artzt announced that P&G would pay $1.1bn for the two Revlon lines, which together captured $800 million in sales. Artzt decided not to buy Revlon's other big brands, which sold at higher prices in department stores.

It turned out, however, that Artzt had more in mind than simply buying lines that would give P&G an international presence. He also saw opportunities to use the new brands' distribution and marketing networks to speed Cover Girl's transition from a US brand to an international brand. Max Factor and Betrix gave P&G immediate access to Europe and Japan. Before the acquisitions, P&G had no cosmetics or fragrance sales in Japan and only $28 million in Europe. After the acquisition, P&G had annual sales of $237 million in Japan and $340 million in Europe. About 75 per cent of Max Factor's $600 million sales came from outside the United States, whereas all of Betrix's $200 million came from other countries. One analyst estimated that P&G had shortened by three years the time it would have taken to go global with its US brands.

Just as the Max Factor and Betrix lines helped P&G, so acquisition by P&G helped those two brands immensely. Betrix, especially, had learned that it took deep pockets to compete in the international cosmetics business. It achieved about 62.5 per cent of its sales in its home market, Germany, with the remainder coming from Switzerland, Spain, Italy, and Sweden. Betrix wanted to crack the French market but had not been successful against powerful L'Oréal, the dominant market leader, and P&G's marketing muscle could not help Betrix to force its way into the French market. Betrix's main brands were the mid-pricèd Ellen Betrix women's skin-care products and cosmetics and Henry M. Betrix men's toiletries. Its Eurocos Cosmetic subsidiary marketed upscale cosmetics under the Hugo Boss and Laura Biagiotti brand names.

### Step 3 Reviving Max Factor in the US market

P&G felt that it could make Max Factor more competitive in the US now that it was not under Revlon's umbrella. As it had done with Cover Girl, P&G quickly learned Max Factor's business and plotted strategies to improve its performance. P&G's man-

agers questioned Max Factor's use of actress Jaclyn Smith as a spokesperson. They revamped Max Factor with new products and technological improvements and strengthened the brand's promotion and advertising support.

Revlon, however, did not stand still after selling Max Factor to P&G. It hired a new management team for its Revlon brand, cut its manufacturing costs, and introduced a $200 million advertising barrage that featured a jazzy 'Shake Your Body' message.

Both firms realized that they had to find ways to attract younger women, including teenagers, without alienating older customers. Mass-market sales, such as sales through drugstores and discounters, grew only 2 per cent in 1991, compared with 6 per cent in 1990. Changing consumer demographics and shopping habits seemed to account for this slowdown. Ageing baby boomers had decided to invest in skin-care products and were buying fewer cosmetics like mascara, nail polish and lipstick.

These changes meant that attracting younger women had become even more important if the cosmetics companies were to revive sales growth. One college student suggested that she could understand the companies' interest in younger consumers. She felt that younger women often wanted to look older and might even use more cosmetics than they needed. 'Putting on make-up', she added, 'is a big part of growing up.' An industry consultant noted that: 'Younger women are constantly changing and reapplying their nail polish, something older women don't do.'

Yet the companies faced problems in attracting younger customers. First, there were fewer younger women than baby boomers. Second, all cosmetics manufacturers were fighting for shelf space and the attention of younger buyers. One analyst noted: 'There are simply too many manufacturers and too many products chasing too few customers. Competition was intense.' The analyst continued: 'Even at the prestige end of the mass market, L'Oréal had dropped its emphasis on quality and had begun emphasising having fun to lure more young customers.' Additional competition was coming from department store product lines, speciality shops, direct marketers such as Avon and home shopping networks.

As a result, P&G's cosmetics sales remained flat in 1991 at $722 million; and its market share slipped slightly to 34 per cent, down from 34.4 per cent in 1990. Revlon's share increased to 22.5 per cent, up from 20.4 per cent in 1990. Even with the slowdown, however, P&G remained the nation's largest seller of cosmetics sold through drug and mass merchandise stores. P&G admitted that it was still learning the cosmetics business. It faced distribution problems, being slow to fill orders and slow to deliver promised new products. In addition, the company had consolidated its cosmetics salesforce. Its salespeople now sold all three lines – Cover Girl, Clarion and Max Factor. Some distributors argued that P&G was expecting too much from a single salesperson. The product lines were simply too wide to expect one person to know much about all the products. P&G countered that the new system would reduce the number of salespeople with whom retailers had to deal.

## Step 4    Going global

Most recently, P&G has decided to overhaul the Max Factor line and launch its first simultaneous worldwide product introduction. The company introduced the new Max Factor line during the spring of 1993. The new products feature more elegant styling and more colours. The initial range was eye shadows, blushes and lipsticks. In 1994, it will introduce foundations, face powders and mascaras.

All of these products will be the same, no matter where in the world P&G sells them. Previously, P&G had used different products and strategies in different markets, often using local manufacturers. In Japan, for example, the Max Factor line had consisted primarily of skin-care products sold at high prices in department stores. Max Factor had accounted for 28 per cent of Revlon's Japanese sales of $507 million in 1990. However, the brand had not kept up with changing Japanese lifestyles and tastes, and it was steadily losing market share. Kao Corporation and Shiseido Company were emerging as powerful competitors in the Japanese market. In Europe, P&G sold Max Factor products in chain stores and pharmacies at lower prices.

The new line would feature similar styles, colours and images across all international markets. Packages

are a deep blue colour with gold trim. The products come in a variety of colours to meet the needs of women with differing skin tones. P&G has also revised its in-store displays. To support such changes, it will increase prices to between 8 and 10 per cent above previous Max Factor prices.

P&G is following the successful strategies of Estée Lauder's Clinique and Chanel, which have both been successful with standardized global marketing. Consumers around the globe recognize Clinique's blue-green packaging and Chanel's classic black compacts. P&G hopes that the standardized strategy will allow it to save money by unifying and consolidating many of its marketing efforts.

## Step 5    Watching the competition

Despite Artzt's perpetual optimism, however, P&G knows it is making a bold move. No other company has tried to develop a worldwide, mass-market cosmetics brand. The company has already learned from its experiences in the US market that the cosmetics business is complicated. P&G also knows that Revlon will be right behind with its own global strategy. Revlon already receives between 30 and 35 per cent of its revenue from 126 foreign countries and P&G expects that Revlon will try to take more of its regional brands global.

P&G also knows that it must watch its home market. Noting all the attention being paid to younger women, Maybelline is now focusing on ageing baby boomers. It plans to introduce a new line called Maybelline Revitalizing, which targets women of 35 and older. Maybelline claims that these products will help mature women look younger and it plans to sell the products through mass-market outlets. To stay ahead of the competitors in cosmetics, P&G will have to find some new marketing wrinkles.

## Questions

1. Who are Procter & Gamble's competitors, from an industry point of view and from a market point of view? Are there strategic groups in the industry? Why are these questions important for P&G?
2. What trends are shaping competitors' objectives in the cosmetics industry?

**CASE 5 (cont)**

3. Based on information in the case, which of Michael Porter's competitive positions have the various cosmetics competitors pursued to gain competitive advantage?

4. What actions should P&G take in order to expand the total cosmetics market and to protect and expand its market share?

5. What competitive strategies would you recommend for P&G's competitors?

Sources: Randall Smith, Kathleen Deveny, and Alecia Swasy, 'Sale of Revlon beauty line is considered by Perelman', *Wall Street Journal* (1 March 1991), B4; Alecia Swasy, 'Cover Girl is growing up and moving out as its new parent, P&G, takes charge', *Wall Street Journal* (28 March 1991), B1; Pat Sloan and Jennifer Lawrence, 'What P&G plans for cosmetics', *Advertising Age* (15 April 1991), 3, 46; Zachary Schiller and Larry Light, 'Procter & Gamble is following its nose', *Business Week* (22 April 1991), 28; Valerie Reitman and Jeffrey A. Trachenberg, 'Battle to make up the younger woman pits Revlon against its new rival, P&G', *Wall Street Journal* (10 July 1992); Valerie Reitman, 'P&G planning a fresh face for Max Factor', *Wall Street Journal* (29 December 1992), B1; Marilyn Much, 'Cosmetic war gets ugly as front moves abroad', *Investor's Business Daily* (14 January 1993), 4; and Gabriella Stern, 'Aging boomers are new target for Maybelline', *Wall Street Journal* (13 April 1993), B1.

## CHAPTER SIX

# Market information and marketing research

## CHAPTER OBJECTIVES

After reading this chapter, you should be able to:

- Explain the importance of information to the company.

- Define the marketing information system and discuss its parts.

- Describe the four steps in the marketing research process.

- Compare the advantages and disadvantages of various methods of collecting information.

- Discuss the main methods for estimating current market demand.

- Explain specific techniques that companies use to forecast future demand.

## CHAPTER PREVIEW

### Qantas: taking off in tomorrow's market

Qantas, Australia's international airline, is experiencing a demand bonanza. Its market area in the Pacific Basin contains some of the fastest-growing economies in the world – including Australia, China, Japan and the newly industrializing countries of Hong Kong, Malaysia, Singapore, South Korea, Taiwan and Thailand. The area's growth in air travel far exceeds world averages. Industry forecasts suggest that Pacific Basin air travel will grow at 10 per cent to 14 per cent per year through 1995. By the year 2000 the area will have a 40 per cent share of all international air passenger traffic.

Such explosive growth presents a huge opportunity for Qantas and the other airlines serving the Pacific Basin. However, it also presents some serious headaches. To take *advantage* of the growing demand, Qantas must first *forecast* it accurately and prepare to *meet* it. Air-travel demand has

many dimensions. Qantas must forecast how many and what kinds of people will be travelling, where they will want to go and when. It must project total demand as well as demand in each specific market it intends to serve. And Qantas must estimate what share of this total demand it can capture under alternative marketing strategies and in various competitive circumstances. Moreover it must forecast demand not just for next year, but also for the next two years, five years, and even further into the future.

Forecasting air-travel demand is no easy task. A host of factors affect how often people will travel and where they will go. To make accurate demand forecasts, Qantas must first anticipate changes in the factors that influence demand: worldwide and country-by-country economic conditions, demographic characteristics, population growth, political developments, technological advances, competitive activity and many other factors. Qantas has little control over many of these factors.

Demand can shift quickly and dramatically. For example, relative economic growth and political stability in Japan, Australia and the other Pacific Basin countries have caused a virtual explosion of demand for air travel there. Ever-increasing numbers of tourists from around the world are visiting these areas. In Australia, for instance, foreign tourism more than doubled between 1984 and 1988 and could triple between 1988 and the year 2000. Also, people from the Pacific Basin countries are themselves travelling more. For example, almost 12 million Japanese took holidays abroad last year, a 10 per cent increase over the previous year. Pampered business travellers bolstered the profitability of airlines in the region but most new travellers are nonbusiness people. By the turn of the century fewer than one in five passengers worldwide will be flying for business reasons – and many of those will be sitting in the economy section. Forecasting demand in the face of such drastic shifts can be difficult.

To make things even more complicated, Qantas must forecast more than just demand. The airline must also anticipate the many factors that can affect its ability to meet that demand. For example, what airport facilities will be available and how will this affect Qantas? Will there be enough skilled labour to staff and maintain its aircraft? In the Pacific Basin, as demand has skyrocketed, the support system has not. A shortage of runways and airport terminal space already limits the number of flights Qantas can schedule. As a result, Qantas may decide to buy fewer but larger planes. Fewer planes would require fewer crews and larger planes can hold more passengers at one time, which can make flights more profitable.

Competition in the region is hotting up too. Efficient non-Asian carriers, such as American Airlines, British Airways, United and Virgin, are attacking the region's markets and slashing fares in the process. Meanwhile, new local competitors, such as Taiwan's EVA Airways and Malaysia's Air Asia, are cutting into the market. Singapore Airlines and Cathay Pacific are two of the world's most profitable airlines and are fighting to hold on to their strong positions in the market. Singapore Airlines already has sixty-two aircraft including forty-two Boeing 747 jumbos. It plans to buy at least fifty more jets – all 747s or large wide-body Airbuses.

Qantas bases many important decisions on its forecasts. Perhaps the most important decision involves aircraft purchases. To meet burgeoning demand, Qantas knows that it will need more planes. But how many more planes? At about A$200 million for each new Boeing 747-400, ordering even a few too many planes can be very costly. On the other hand, if Qantas buys too few planes, it has few short-run solutions. It usually takes about two years to get delivery of a new plane. If Qantas overestimates demand by even a few percentage points, it will have costly overcapacity. If it underestimates demand, it could miss out on profit opportunities and disappoint customers who prefer to fly Qantas, resulting in long-term losses of sales and goodwill. Airlines have got these numbers badly wrong in the past, resulting in thousands of redundant jets parked in the deserts of America.

1 ecu = US$1.26 = A$1.71 (Australian dollars)

Besides rapid growth Qantas need to know about the changing nature of demand in the region. The declining proportion of business passengers means airlines are fighting harder for them, not just by offering cheaper fares but by extra service. In Europe, where the battle for the business traveller is well developed, Lufthansa has completed a huge study to find out what their business traveller wants. More leg and elbow room, said most travellers, but others want separate check-ins and passport controls. Fine, but all these options cost money, so what is the best set of benefits to offer and are the needs to be standardized across the region? There are even more unknowns about the needs of the hugely growing nonbusiness market. What do these new flyers want and what is the best way to look after them economically?

Ultimately, for Qantas, the forecasting problem is more than a matter of temporary gains or losses of customer satisfaction and sales – it's a matter of survival. Thus Qantas has a lot flying on the accuracy of its forecasts.[1]

## INTRODUCTION

To carry out marketing analysis, planning, implementation and control, managers need information. They need information about market demand, customers, competitors, dealers and other forces in the marketplace. One marketing executive put it this way: 'To manage a business well is to manage its future; and to manage the future is to manage information.'[2] Increasingly, marketers are viewing information as not just an input for making better decisions, but also a marketing asset that gives competitive advantage.[3]

During the past century, most companies were small and knew their customers at first hand. Managers picked up marketing information by being around people, observing them and asking questions. During this century, however, many factors have increased the need for more and better information. As companies become national or international in scope, they need more information on larger, more distant markets. As incomes increase and buyers become more selective, sellers need better information about how buyers respond to different products and appeals. As sellers use more complex marketing approaches and face more competition, they need information on the effectiveness of their marketing tools. Finally, in today's rapidly changing environments, managers need up-to-date information to make timely decisions.

The supply of information has also increased greatly. John Neisbitt suggests that the world is undergoing a 'mega-shift' from an industrial to an information-based economy.[4] He found that more than 65 per cent of the US workforce now work at producing or processing information, compared to only 17 per cent in 1950. Using improved computer systems and other technologies, companies can now provide information in great quantities. Many of today's managers sometimes receive too much information. For example, one study found that with companies offering all the information now available through supermarket scanners, a brand manager gets one million to one *billion* new numbers each week.[5] As Neisbitt points out: 'Running out of information is not a problem, but drowning in it is.'[6]

Marketers frequently complain that they lack enough information of the *right* kind or have too much of the *wrong* kind. Regarding the spread of information throughout the company, they say that it takes great effort to locate even simple facts. Subordinates may withhold information that they believe will reflect badly on their performance. Often, important information arrives too late to be useful, or on-time information is not accurate. So marketing managers need more and better information. Companies have greater capacity to provide managers with information, but have often not made good use of it. Many companies are now studying their managers' information needs and designing information systems to meet those needs.

## THE MARKETING INFORMATION SYSTEM

A **marketing information system (MIS)** consists of people, equipment and procedures to gather, sort, analyse, evaluate and distribute needed, timely and accurate information to marketing decision makers. Figure 6.1 illustrates the marketing information system concept. The MIS begins and ends with marketing managers. First, it interacts with these managers to assess their information needs. Next, it develops the needed information from internal company records, marketing intelligence activities and the marketing research process. Information analysis processes the information to make it more useful. Finally, the MIS distributes information to managers in the right form at the right time to help them in marketing planning, implementation and control.

## DEVELOPING INFORMATION

The information needed by marketing managers comes from *internal company records*, *marketing intelligence* and *marketing research*. The information analysis system then processes this information to make it more useful for managers.

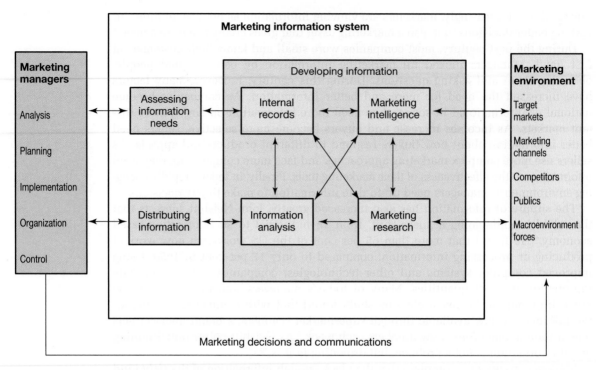

**Figure 6.1**    The marketing information system.

## Internal records

Most marketing managers use internal records and reports regularly, especially for making day-to-day planning, implementation and control decisions. **Internal records information** consists of information gathered from sources within the company to evaluate marketing performance and to detect marketing problems and opportunities. The company's accounting department prepares financial statements and keeps detailed records of sales, orders, costs and cash flows. Manufacturing reports on production schedules, shipments and inventories. The salesforce reports on reseller reactions and competitor activities. The customer service department provides information on customer satisfaction or service problems. Research studies done for one department may provide useful information for several others. Managers can use information gathered from these and other sources within the company to evaluate performance and to detect problems and opportunities.

Here are examples of how companies use internal records information in making better marketing decisions:[7]

*Office World* offers shoppers a free membership card when they make their first purchase at their store. The card entitles shoppers to discounts on selected items but also provides valuable information to the chain. Since Office World encourages customers to use their card with each purchase, Office World can track what customers buy, where and when. Using this information they can track the effectiveness of promotions, they can trace customers who have defected to other stores and keep in touch with them if they relocate.

*Istel* is a cross-fertilization scheme set up by AT&T in Europe. The system helps retailers share information about customers. Under the programme customers join the Istel club that gives them discounts when buying a range of products from member stores. AT&T estimate their card will save the average customer £180 a year. The retailers then use the information to build databases and to target incentives to valuable customers. 'The grocer may like to know who is a high spender in the scheme but is not shopping with them,' says Ruth Kemp of Istel. 'Then they can offer incentive to use their store.'

1 ecu = UK£0.83

Information from internal records is usually quicker and cheaper to get than information from other sources, but it also presents some problems. Because internal information was for other purposes, it may be incomplete or in the wrong form for making marketing decisions. For example, accounting department sales and cost data used for preparing financial statements need adapting for use in evaluating product, salesforce, or channel performance. In addition, the many different areas of a large company produce great amounts of information, and keeping track of it all is difficult. The marketing information system must gather, organize, process and index this mountain of information so that managers can find it easily and get it quickly.

## Marketing intelligence

**Marketing intelligence** is everyday information about developments in the marketing environment that helps managers prepare and adjust marketing plans. The marketing intelligence system determines the intelligence needed, collects it by searching the environment and delivers it to marketing managers who need it.

Marketing intelligence comes from many sources. Much intelligence is from the company's personnel – executives, engineers and scientists, purchasing agents and the salesforce. But company people are often busy and fail to pass on important information. The company must 'sell' its people on their importance as intelligence gatherers, train them to spot new developments and urge them to report intelligence back to the company.

The company must also persuade suppliers, resellers and customers to pass along important intelligence. Some information on competitors comes from what they say about themselves in annual reports, speeches, press releases and advertisements. The company can also learn about competitors from what others say about them in business publications and at trade shows. Or the company can watch what competitors do – buying and analysing competitors' products, monitoring their sales and checking for new patents.

Companies also buy intelligence information from outside suppliers. Dun & Bradstreet is the world's largest research company with branches in forty countries and a turnover of $1.26bn. Its largest subsidiary is Nielsen who sells data on brand shares, retail prices and percentages of stores stocking different brands. Its Info*Act Workstation offers companies the chance to analyse data from three sources on the PCs: Retail Index that monitors consumer sales and in-store conditions; Key Account Scantrack, a weekly analysis of sales, price elasticity and promotional effectiveness, and Homescan, a new consumer panel. Alliances between marketing research companies allow access to pan-European research. Other big international research companies are WPP, Taylor Nelson who owns AGB, GfK, MAI who owns NOP, and Infratest. The globalization of markets has led both large and small firms to form alliances in order to gain better international coverage and wider services. Taylor Nelson's AGB have joined with Information Resources Inc. of the United States to strengthen their position as international suppliers of retail audit and scanner data.[8] The services of these, and other agencies, now provide over 500 accessible computer databases:

1 ecu = US$1.26

Doing business in Germany? Check out CompuServe's German Company Library of financial and product information on over 48,000 German-owned firms. Want biographical sketches of key executives? Punch up Dun & Bradstreet Financial Profiles and Company Reports. Demographic data? Today's Associated Press news wire reports? A list of active trademarks? It's all available from on-line databases.[9]

Marketing intelligence can work not only for, but also against a company. Companies must sometimes take steps to protect themselves from the snooping of competitors. For example, Kellogg had treated the public to tours of its plants since 1906, but recently closed its newly upgraded plant to outsiders to prevent competitors from getting intelligence on its high-tech equipment. In Japan corporate intelligence is part of the industrial culture. Everyone from assembly-line workers to top executives considers it their duty to filter intelligence about the competition back to management. Western companies are less active, although most of America's Fortune 500 now have in-house corporate intelligence units. Businesses are getting increasingly aware of the need both to gather information and to protect what they have. In its Bangkok offices one European organization has a huge poster outside its lavatory saying: 'Wash and hush up! You never know who's listening! Keep our secrets secret.'[10]

Some companies set up an office to collect and circulate marketing intelligence. The staff scans relevant publications, summarizes important news and sends news bulletins to marketing managers. It develops a file of intelligence information and helps managers evaluate new information. These services greatly improve the quality of information available to marketing managers. The methods used to gather competitive information range from the ridiculous to the illegal. Managers routinely shred documents because trash cans can be an information source. Other firms have uncovered more sinister devices such as Spycatcher's TPR recording system that 'automatically interrogates telephones and faxes. Also a range of tiny microphones.' These, and other methods, appear in Marketing Highlight 6.1.[11]

## Marketing research

Managers cannot always wait for information to arrive in bits and pieces from the marketing intelligence system. They often require formal studies of specific situations. For example, Apple Computer wants to know how many and what kinds of people or companies will buy its new ultralight personal computer. Or a Dutch pet product firm needs to know the potential market for slimming tablets for dogs. What percentage of dogs are overweight, do their owners worry about it, and will they give the pill to their podgy pooches?[12] In these situations, the marketing intelligence system will not provide the detailed information needed. Because managers normally do not have the skills or time to obtain the information on their own, they need formal marketing research.

**Marketing research** is the function linking the consumer, customer and public to the marketer through information – information used: to identify and define marketing opportunities and problems; to generate, refine and evaluate marketing actions; to monitor marketing performance; and to improve understanding of the marketing process.[13] Marketing researchers specify the information needed to address marketing issues, design the method for collecting information, manage and implement the data collection process, analyse the results and communicate the findings and their implications.

Marketing researchers engage in a wide variety of activities, ranging from analyses of market potential and market shares to studies of customer satisfaction and purchase intentions. Every marketer needs research. A company can conduct marketing research in its research department or have some or all of it done outside. Although most large companies have their own marketing research departments, they often use outside firms to do special research tasks or special studies. A company with no research department will have to buy the services of research firms.

Many people think of marketing research as a lengthy, formal process carried out by large marketing companies. But many small businesses and non-profit organizations also use marketing research. Almost any organization can find informal, low-cost alternatives to the formal and complex marketing research techniques used by research experts in large firms (see Marketing Highlight 6.2).

## The marketing research process

The marketing research process (see Figure 6.2) consists of four steps: defining the problem and research objectives; developing the research plan; implementing the research plan; and interpreting and reporting the findings.

### Defining the problem and research objectives

The marketing manager and the researcher must work closely together to define the problem carefully and must agree on the research objectives. The manager understands the decision for which information is needed; the researcher understands marketing research and how to obtain the information.

Managers must know enough about marketing research to help in the planning and in the interpretation of research results. If they know little about marketing research, they may obtain the wrong information, accept wrong conclusions, or ask for information that costs too much. Experienced marketing researchers who understand the manager's problem also need involvement at this stage. The researcher must be able to help the manager define the problem and to suggest ways that research can help the manager make better decisions.

Defining the problem and research objectives is often the hardest step in the research process. The manager may know that something is wrong, without knowing the specific causes. For example, managers of a discount retail store chain hastily decided that poor advertising caused falling sales, and so they ordered research to test the company's advertising. It puzzled the managers when the research showed that current advertising was reaching the right people with the right message. It turned out that the chain's stores were not delivering what the advertising promised. Careful problem definition would have avoided the cost and delay of doing advertising research. It would have suggested research on the real problem of consumer reactions to the products, service and prices offered in the chain's stores.

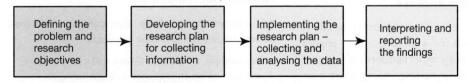

**Figure 6.2** The marketing research process.

# Snooping on competitors

European firms lag behind their Japanese and American competitors in gathering competitive intelligence. In Japanese companies it is a long-established practice, for, as Mitsui's corporate motto says: 'Information is the life blood of the company'. American firms are catching up. In the US competitive intelligence gathering has grown dramatically as more and more companies need to know what their competitors are doing. Such well-known companies as CIGNA, Ford, Motorola, Kodak, Gillette, Avon, Del Monte, Kraft, Mitsubishi and the 'Big Six' accounting firms are known to be busy snooping on their competitors. The Marketing Audit (TMA), Fuld and Company Inc. (FCI) and Kirk Tyson International are some of the new firms specializing in this sort of business. The techniques they use to collect intelligence fall into four main groups.

## *Getting information from published materials and public documents*

Keeping track of seemingly meaningless published information can provide competitor intelligence. For instance, the types of people sought in help-wanted ads can indicate something about a competitor's new strategies and products. Government agencies are another good source. For example, according to *Fortune*:

> Although it is often illegal for a company to photograph a competitor's plant from the air, there are legitimate ways to get the photos ... Aerial photos often are on file with geological survey or environmental protection agencies. These are public documents, available for a nominal fee.

According to Leonard Fuld, founder of FCI: 'in some countries the government is a rare font of information ... France has the Minitel, in the US we have an opus of information databases and networks.'

## *Getting information by observing competitors or analysing physical evidence*

Companies can get to know competitors better by buying their products or examining other physical evidence. An increasingly important form of competitive intelligence is benchmarking, taking apart competitors' products and imitating or improving upon their best features. Popular since the early 1980s, benchmarking has helped JCB keep ahead in earthmoving equipment. The company takes apart its international competitors' products, dissecting and examining them in detail. JCB also probed the manufacturing operations, the types of machine tools used, their speeds, manning levels, labour costs, quality control and testing procedures, and raw material. It built up a profile of all its main competitors' operations and performance ratios against which to benchmark. In this way, the company knew the extent to which competitors could vary their prices, what their strengths and weaknesses were, and how JCB could exploit these data to its advantage.

Beyond looking at competitors' products, companies can examine many other types of physical evidence:

> In the absence of better information on market share and the volume of product competitors are shipping, companies have measured the rust on rails of railroad sidings to their competitors' plant or have counted the tractor-trailers leaving loading bays.

Some companies even rifle their competitors' garbage:

> Once it has left the competitors' premises, refuse is legally considered abandoned property. While some companies now shred the paper coming out of their design labs, they often neglect to do this for all most revealing refuse from the marketing or public relations departments.

In a recent example of garbage snatching, Avon admitted that it had hired private detectives to paw through Mary Kay Cosmetics' garbage skips. Although an outraged Mary Kay sued to get its garbage back, Avon claimed that it had done nothing illegal. The skips had been located in a public car park and Avon had videotapes to prove it.

## *Getting information from people who do business with competitors*

Key customers can keep the company informed about competitors and their products:

> For example, a while back Gillette told a large account the date on which it planned to begin selling its new

Good News disposable razor. The distributor promptly called Bic and told it about the impending product launch. Bic put on a crash program and was able to start selling its razor shortly after Gillette did.

Intelligence can also be gathered by infiltrating customers' business operations:

> Companies may provide their engineers free of charge to customers ... The close, cooperative relationship that the engineers on loan cultivate with the customers' design staff often enables them to learn what new products competitors are pitching.

### Getting information from recruits and competitors' employees

Companies can obtain intelligence through job interviews or from conversations with competitors' employees.

> When they interview people for jobs, some companies pay special attention to those who have worked for competitors, even temporarily. Job seekers are eager to impress and often have not been warned about divulging what is proprietary. They sometimes volunteer valuable information.

> Companies send engineers to conferences and trade shows to question competitors' technical people. Often conversations start innocently – just a few fellow technicians discussing processes and problems ... [yet competitors'] engineers and scientists often brag about surmounting technical challenges, in the process divulging sensitive information.

> Companies sometimes advertise and hold interviews for jobs that don't exist in order to entice competitors' employees to spill the beans ... Often applicants have toiled in obscurity or feel that their careers have stalled. They're dying to impress somebody.

In the United States one of the most common ploys is to telephone competitors' employees and ask direct and indirect questions. 'The rule of thumb', says Jonathan Lax, founder of TMA, 'is to target employees a level below where you think you should start, because that person often knows just as much as his or her senior, and they are not as frequently asked or wary.' Secretaries, receptionists and switchboard operators regularly give away information inadvertently.

One European company is now being accused of beating the Americans at their own game. When Spanish born José Ignacio Lopez de Arriotua defected from General Motors to Volkswagen to be their new purchasing and production chief, he took seven GM executives with him. He also allegedly attempted to poach another forty. GM were angry and, through their Opel subsidiary, accused him of taking industrial secrets as well. VW and Lopez deny the allegations but German prosecutors launched an investigation.

### Why Europe is different

Niame Fine is founder of Protec Data, a firm specializing in protecting companies against competitive intelligence gatherers. She believes there are two main differences between US and European companies. Language and cultural blocks limit cross-border intelligence gathering. Approaching competitors' employees is subtle business and people are often put on their guard if approached by someone from a different country. She also says Europeans have greater loyalty than their job-hopping American counterparts.

Although most of these techniques are legal and some are considered to be shrewdly competitive, many involve questionable ethics. The company should take advantage of publicly available information, but avoid practices that might be considered illegal or unethical. A company does not have to break the law or accepted codes of ethics to get good intelligence. So far European businesses 'do as they would be done by' and linger at the ethical end of the spectrum of competitive intelligence. Will they be able to stay there?

Sources: Excerpts from Steven Flax, 'How to snoop on your competitors', *Fortune* (14 May 1984), 29–33; Brian Dumaine, 'Corporate spies snoop to conquer', *Fortune* (7 November 1988), 68–76; and Jeremy Main, 'How to steal the best ideas around', *Fortune* (19 October 1992), 102–6. Copyright © 1984, 1988, and 1992, Time Inc. All rights reserved. Also see Wendy Zellner and Bruce Hager, 'Dumpster raids? That's not very ladylike, Avon', *Business Week* (1 April 1991), 32; Michele Galen, 'These guys aren't spooks, they're "competitive analysts"', *Business Week* (14 October 1991), 97; and Richard S. Teitalbaum, 'The new race for intelligence', *Fortune* (2 November 1992), 104–8; 'Mr Lopez's many parts', *The Economist* (23 May 1993), 89; Tony McBurnie and David Clutterbuck, *The Marketing Edge* (London: Penguin, 1988); Kate Button, 'Spies like us', *Marketing Business* (March 1994), 7–9.

## Marketing research in small businesses and non-profit organizations

Managers of small businesses and non-profit organizations often think that marketing research is only for experts in large companies with big research budgets. However, smaller organizations can use many of the marketing research techniques in this chapter. They can also work in a less formal way and at little expense.

Managers of small businesses and non-profit organizations can obtain good marketing information simply by *observing* things around them. For example, retailers can evaluate new locations by observing vehicle and pedestrian traffic. They can visit competing stores to check on facilities and prices. They can evaluate their customer mix by recording how many and what kinds of customers shop in the store at different times. To monitor competitor advertising they can collect advertisements from local media.

Managers can conduct informal *surveys* using small convenience samples. The director of a local museum can learn what patrons think about new exhibits by conducting informal 'focus groups' – inviting small groups to lunch and having discussions on topics of interest. Retailers can talk to customers visiting the store; hospital workers can interview patients. Restaurant managers might make random phone calls during slack hours to interview consumers about where they eat out and what they think of various restaurants in the area.

Managers also can conduct *experiments*. For example, by changing the themes in regular fund-raising mailings and watching the results, a non-profit manager can find out much about which marketing strategies work best. By varying newspaper advertisements, a store manager can learn the effects of things such as ad size and position, price coupons and media used.

Small organizations can obtain most of the secondary data available to large businesses. In addition, many associations, local media, chambers of commerce, and government agencies provide special help to small organizations. The small-business bureaux offer free publications giving advice on topics ranging from planning to advertising. Local newspapers often provide information on local shoppers and their buying patterns.

Sometimes volunteers and colleges are willing to help carry out research. Non-profit organizations can often use volunteers from local service clubs and other sources. Many colleges are seeking small businesses and non-profit organizations to serve as cases for projects in marketing research classes.

In summary, secondary data collection, observation, surveys, and experiments work effectively for small organizations with small budgets. Although these informal research methods are less complex and less costly, they still need doing carefully. Managers must think carefully about the objectives of the research, formulate questions in advance, recognize the biases introduced by smaller samples and less skilled researchers, and conduct the research systematically. If carefully planned and implemented, low-cost research can provide reliable information for improving marketing decision making.

---

After the problem has been defined carefully, the manager and researcher must set the research objectives. A marketing research project might have one of three types of objectives. The objective of **exploratory research** is to gather preliminary information that will help define the problem and suggest hypotheses. The objective of **descriptive research** is to describe things such as the market potential for a product or the demographics and attitudes of consumers who buy the product. The objective of **causal research** is to test hypotheses about cause-and-effect relationships. For example, would a 10 per cent cut in CD prices increase sales sufficiently to offset the lost margin? Managers often start with exploratory research and later follow with descriptive or causal research.

The statement of the problem and research objectives guides the entire research process. The manager and researcher should put the statement in writing to be certain that they agree on the purpose and expected results of the research.

*Developing the research plan*

The second step of the marketing research process calls for determining the information needed, developing a plan for gathering it efficiently and presenting the plan to marketing management. The plan outlines sources of existing data and explains the specific research approaches, contact methods, sampling plans and instruments that researchers will use to gather new data.

*Determining information needs*    Research objectives need translating into specific information needs.

> Bolswessanen, the Dutch food and drinks company, decide to conduct research to find out how consumers would react to a new breakfast cereal aimed at the adult market. Across Europe young health-conscious people are abandoning croissants in France, rolls in Belgium and lonely expresso in Italy. Since Nestlé and General Mills set up Cereal Partners Worldwide as a joint venture, they have been very active in the market and the project has started to develop. The European breakfast cereal market has been growing fast but own labels dominate the adult sector.[14] Can Bolswessanen successfully compete with Kellogg's, the market leader, and the aggressive new competitor, Cereal Partners Worldwide? Their research might call for the following specific information:
>
> - The demographic, economic and lifestyle characteristics of current breakfast cereal users. (How do social and demographic trends affect the breakfast cereal market?)
> - Consumer-usage patterns for cereals: how much do they eat, where and when? (Will all the family eat the cereal or does each family member have their favourite?)
> - Retailer reactions to the new product. (Failure to get retailer support could hurt its sales.)
> - Consumer attitudes towards the new product. (Will consumers switch from own brands and is the product attractive enough to compete with Kellogg's?)
> - Forecasts of sales of the new product. (Will the new packaging increase Bolswessanen's profits?)
>
> Bolswessanen's managers will need this and many other types of information to decide whether to introduce the new product.

*Gathering secondary information*    To meet the manager's information needs, the researcher can gather secondary data, primary data, or both. **Secondary data** consist of information that already exists somewhere, having been collected for another purpose. **Primary data** consist of information collected for the specific purpose at hand.

Researchers usually start by gathering secondary data. Table 6.1 shows the many secondary data sources, including *internal* and *external* sources.[15] Secondary data are usually quicker and cheaper than primary data. For example, a visit to the library might provide all the information Bolswessanen needs on cereal usage, at almost no cost. A study to collect primary information might take weeks or months and cost a lot. Also, secondary sources can sometimes provide data an individual company cannot collect on its own – information that either is not directly available or would be too expensive to collect. For example, it would be too expensive for Bolswessanen to conduct a continuing retail store audit to find out about the market shares, prices and displays of competitors' brands. But it can buy Neilsen's Scantrack service.

Secondary data also have problems. The needed information may not exist – researchers can rarely obtain all the data they need from secondary sources. For example, Bolswessanen will not find existing information about consumer reactions to a new product that it has not yet placed on the market. Even when data are found, they might not be very usable. The researcher must evaluate secondary information carefully to make certain it is *relevant* (fits research project needs), *accurate* (reliably

| TABLE 6.1 | *Sources of secondary data* |
|---|---|

**Internal sources**

Internal sources include company profit and loss statements, balance sheets, sales figures, sales call reports, invoices, inventory records, and prior research reports.

**Government publications**

*Statistical Abstract,* usually updated annually, provides summary data on demographic, economic, social, and other aspects of the economy and society.

*Industrial Outlook* provides projections of industrial activity by industry and includes data on production, sales, shipments, employment, etc.

*Marketing Information Guide* provides a monthly annotated bibliography of marketing information. Other government publications include the *Annual Survey of Manufacturers; Business Statistics; Census of Manufacturers; Census of Population; Census of Retail Trade, Wholesale Trade,* and *Selected Service Industries; Census of Transportation; Federal Reserve Bulletin; Monthly Labor Review; Survey of Current Business;* and *Vital Statistics Report.*

**Periodicals and books**

*Business Periodicals Index,* a monthly, lists business articles appearing in a wide variety of business publications.

*Standard & Poor's Industry Surveys* provide updated statistics and analyses of industries.

*Moody's Manuals* provide financial data and names of executives in big companies.

*Encyclopedia of Associations* provides information on every large trade and professional association in the United States.

Marketing journals include the *Journal of Marketing, Journal of Marketing Research, Journal of Consumer Research,* and *International Journal of Research in Marketing.*

Useful trade magazines include *Advertising Age, Chain Store Age, Progressive Grocer, Sales & Marketing Management, Stores, Marketing Week,* and *Campaign.*

Useful general business magazines include *Business Week, Fortune, Forbes, The Economist,* and *Harvard Business Review.*

**Commercial data**

Here are just a few of the dozens of commercial research houses selling data to subscribers:

*A.C. Nielsen Company* provides supermarket scanner data on sales, market share, and retail prices (Scantrack), data on household purchasing (Scantrack National Electronic Household Panel), data on television audiences (Nielsen National Television Index), and others.

*IMS International* provides reports on the movement of pharmaceuticals, hospital laboratory supplies, animal health products, and personal care products.

*Information Resources, Inc.* provides supermarket scanner data for tracking grocery product movement (InfoScan) and single-source data collection (BehaviorScan).

*MRB Group (Simmons Market Research Bureau)* provides annual reports covering television markets, sporting goods, and proprietary drugs. The reports give lifestyle and geodemographic data by sex, income, age, and brand preferences (selective markets and media reaching them).

*NFO Research* provides data for the beverage industry (SIPS), for mail order businesses (MOMS), and for carpet and rug industries (CARS). It also provides a mail panel for concept and product testing, attitude and usage studies, and tracking and segmentation (Analycor).

**International data**

Here are only a few of the many sources providing international information:

*United Nations* publications include the *Statistical Yearbook,* a comprehensive source of international data for socioeconomic indicators; *Demographic Yearbook,* a collection of demographics data and vital statistics for 220 countries; and the *International Trade Statistics Yearbook,* which provides information on foreign trade for specific countries and commodities.

*Europa Yearbook* provides surveys on history, politics, population, economy, and natural resources for most countries of the world, along with information on the chief international organizations.

*Political Risk Yearbook* contains information on political situations in foreign countries, with reference to US investment. It predicts the political climate in each country.

*Foreign Economic Trends and Their Implications for the United States* provides reports on recent business, economic, and political developments in specific countries.

*International Marketing Data and Statistics* provides marketing statistics by country, including data on consumer product markets for countries outside the United States and Europe.

Other sources include *Country Studies, OECD Economic Surveys, Economic Survey of Europe, Asian Economic Handbook,* and *International Financial Statistics.*

collected and reported), *current* (sufficiently up to date for current decisions) and *impartial* (objectively collected and reported).

Secondary data provide a good starting point for research and often help to define problems and research objectives. In most cases, however, secondary sources cannot provide all the needed information and the company must collect primary data.

*Planning primary data collection*   Good decisions require good data. Just as researchers must carefully evaluate the quality of secondary information they obtain, they must also take great care in collecting primary data to ensure that they provide marketing decision makers with relevant, accurate, current and unbiased information. This could be **qualitative research** that measures a small sample of customers' views, or **quantitative research** that provides statistics from a large sample of consumers. Table 6.2 shows that designing a plan for primary data collection calls for a number of decisions on research approaches, contact methods, sampling plan and research instruments.

*Research approaches*   **Observational research** is the gathering of primary data by observing relevant people, actions and situations. For example:

- A food-products manufacturer sends researchers into supermarkets to find out the prices of competing brands or how much shelf space and display support retailers give its brands.
- A bank evaluates possible new branch locations by checking traffic patterns, neighbourhood conditions and the locations of competing branches.
- A maker of personal-care products pretests its ads by showing them to people and measuring eye movements, pulse rates and other physical reactions.
- A department store chain sends observers who pose as customers into its stores to check on store conditions and customer service.
- A museum checks the popularity of various exhibits by noting the amount of floor wear around them.

Several companies sell information collected through *mechanical observation*. For example, the Nielsen and AGB attach 'people meters' to television sets in selected homes to record who watches which programmes. They provide summaries of the size and demographic make-up of audiences for different television programmes. The television networks use these ratings to judge programme popularity and to set charges for advertising time. Advertisers use the ratings when selecting programmes for their commercials. *Checkout scanners* in retail stores also provide mechanical observation data. These laser scanners record consumer purchases in detail. Consumer products companies and retailers use scanner information to assess and improve product sales and store performance.[16] Some marketing research firms now offer **single-source data systems** that electronically monitor both consumers'

| TABLE 6.2 *Planning primary data collection* | | | |
|---|---|---|---|
| Research approaches | Contact methods | Sampling plan | Research instruments |
| Observation | Mail | Sampling unit | Questionnaire |
| Survey | Telephone | Sample size | Mechanical instruments |
| Experiment | Personal | Sampling procedure | |

purchases and consumers' exposure to various marketing activities to better evaluate the link between the two.[17]

Observational research can obtain information that people are unwilling or unable to provide. In some cases, observation is the only way to obtain the needed information. In contrast, some things are simply not observable, such as feelings, attitudes and motives, or private behaviour. Long-term or infrequent behaviour is also difficult to observe. Because of these limitations, researchers often use observation along with other data collection methods.

**Survey research** is the approach best suited for gathering *descriptive* information. A company that wants to know about people's knowledge, attitudes, preferences, or buying behaviour can often find out by asking them directly. Survey research is structured or unstructured. *Structured* surveys use formal lists of questions asked of all respondents in the same way. *Unstructured* surveys let the interviewer probe respondents and guide the interview according to their answers.

Survey research may be direct or indirect. In the *direct* approach, the researcher asks direct questions about behaviour or thoughts: for example, 'Why don't you buy clothes at C&A?' In contrast, the researcher might use the *indirect* approach by asking, 'What kinds of people buy clothes at C&A?' From the response to this indirect question, the researcher may be able to discover why the consumer avoids C&A clothing and why it attracts others. It may suggest reasons the consumer is not consciously aware of.

Survey research is the most widely used method for primary data collection and it is often the only method used in a research study. The principal advantage of survey research is its flexibility. It can obtain many different kinds of information in many different marketing situations. Depending on the survey design, it may also provide information more quickly and at lower cost than observational or experimental research.

However, survey research also presents some problems. Sometimes people are unable to answer survey questions because they do not remember, or never thought about, what they did and why they did it. Or people may be unwilling to respond to unknown interviewers or about things they consider private. Respondents may answer survey questions even when they do not know the answer, simply in order to appear smarter or more informed than they are. Or they may try to help the interviewer by giving pleasing answers. Finally, busy people may not take the time, or they might resent the intrusion into their privacy. Careful survey design can help to minimize these problems.

**Experimental research** gathers *causal* information. Experiments involve selecting matched groups of subjects, giving them different treatments, controlling unrelated factors and checking for differences in group responses. Thus experimental research tries to explain cause-and-effect relationships. Observation and surveys can collect information in experimental research.

Before extending their product range to include fragrances, researchers at Virgin Megastores might use experiments to answer questions such as the following:

- How much will the fragrances increase Virgin's sales?
- How will the fragrances affect the sales of other menu items?
- Which advertising approach would have the greatest effect on sales of their fragrances?
- How would different prices affect the sales of the product?
- How will the product affect the stores' overall image?

For example, to test the effects of two prices, Virgin could set up a simple experiment. It could introduce fragrances at one price in one city and at another price in

| **TABLE 6.3** | *Strengths and weaknesses of the three contact methods* | | |
| --- | --- | --- | --- |
| | Mail | Telephone | Personal |
| 1. Flexibility | Poor | Good | Excellent |
| 2. Quantity of data that can be collected | Good | Fair | Excellent |
| 3. Control of interviewer effects | Excellent | Fair | Poor |
| 4. Control of sample | Fair | Excellent | Fair |
| 5. Speed of data collection | Poor | Excellent | Good |
| 6. Response rate | Poor | Good | Good |
| 7. Cost | Good | Fair | Poor |

Source:  Adapted with permission of Macmillan Publishing Company from *Marketing Research: Measurement and Method*, 6th ed., by Donald S. Tull and Del I. Hawkins. Copyright © 1993 by Macmillan Publishing Company.

another city. If the cities are similar and if all other marketing efforts for the fragrances are the same, then differences in the price charged could explain the sales in the two cities. More complex experimental designs could include other variables and other locations.

*Contact methods*    Mail, telephone or personal interviews can collect data. Table 6.3 shows the strengths and weaknesses of each of these contact methods.

*Mail questionnaires* have many advantages. They can collect large amounts of information at a low cost per respondent. Respondents may give more honest answers to more personal questions on a mail questionnaire than to an unknown interviewer in person or over the phone, since there is no interviewer to bias the respondent's answers.

However, mail questionnaires also have disadvantages. They are not very flexible: they require simple and clearly worded questions; all respondents answer the same questions in a fixed order; and the researcher cannot adapt the questionnaire based on earlier answers. Mail surveys usually take longer to complete and the response rate – the number of people returning completed questionnaires – is often very low. Finally, the researcher often has little control over the mail questionnaire sample. Even with a good mailing list, it is often hard to control *who* at the mailing address fills out the questionnaire.

*Telephone interviewing* is the best method for gathering information quickly and it provides greater flexibility than mail questionnaires. Interviewers can explain questions that are not understood. Depending on the respondent's answers, they can skip some questions or probe further on others. Telephone interviewing also allows greater sample control. Interviewers can ask to speak to respondents with the desired characteristics, or even by name. Response rates tend to be higher than with mail questionnaires.[18]

However, telephone interviewing also has drawbacks. The cost per respondent is higher than with mail questionnaires and people may not want to discuss personal questions with an interviewer. Using an interviewer increases flexibility but also introduces interviewer bias. The way interviewers talk, small differences in how they ask questions and other differences may affect respondents' answers. Finally, different interviewers may interpret and record responses differently and under time pressures some interviewers might even cheat by recording answers without asking questions.

Researchers watch
a focus group
session.

Photograph: Mary Ann Page

*Personal interviewing* takes two forms – individual and group interviewing. *Individual interviewing* involves talking with people in their homes or offices, in the street, or in shopping malls. The interviewer must gain their cooperation and the time involved can range from a few minutes to several hours. Sometimes people get a small payment in return for their time.[19]

*Group interviewing* consists of inviting six to ten people to gather for a few hours with a trained moderator to talk about a product, service, or organization. The moderator needs objectivity, knowledge of the subject and industry and some understanding of group and consumer behaviour. The participants are normally paid a small sum for attending. The meeting is usually in a pleasant place and refreshments are served to foster an informal setting. The moderator starts with broad questions before moving to more specific issues and encourages easy-going discussion, hoping that group interactions will bring out actual feelings and thoughts. At the same time, the moderator 'focuses' the discussion – hence the name **focus-group** interviewing. The comments are recorded by written notes or on videotapes for study later. Focus-group interviewing has become one of the key marketing research tools for gaining insight into consumer thoughts and feelings.[20]

Personal interviewing is quite flexible and can collect large amounts of information. Trained interviewers can hold a respondent's attention for a long time and can explain difficult questions. They can guide interviews, explore issues and probe as the situation requires. Personal interviews can utilize any type of questionnaire. Interviewers can show subjects actual products, advertisements, or packages and observe reactions and behaviour. In most cases, personal interviews can be conducted fairly quickly.

The main drawbacks of personal interviewing are costs and sampling problems. Personal interviews may cost three to four times as much as telephone interviews. Group interview studies usually employ small sample sizes to keep time and costs down and it may be hard to generalize from the results. Because interviewers have more freedom in personal interviews, the problem of interviewer bias is greater.

Which contact method is best depends on what information the researcher wants and on the number and types of respondents needed. Advances in computers and communications have had an impact on methods of obtaining information. For example, most research firms now do Computer Assisted Telephone Interviewing (CATI). Professional interviewers call respondents, often using phone numbers drawn at random. When the respondent answers, the interviewer reads a set of questions from a video screen and types the respondent's answers directly into the computer. Although this procedure requires a large investment in computer equipment and interviewer training, it eliminates data editing and coding, reduces errors and saves time. Other research firms set up terminals in shopping centres – respondents sit down at a terminal, read questions from a screen and type their answers into the computer.[21]

There is no best contact method to use. The one chosen depends on the information needs, cost, speed and other issues. Table 6.4 shows the data collection methods used across Europe. Rational reasons may only account for part of the variation shown. Face-to-face interviews account for half the number but these figures are particularly high in southern Europe and the British Isles. The low penetration of telephones in some of these countries may be an influence but it may also reflect cultures who like socializing. Ireland's high use of group discussions may show that land's love of conversation. The Scandinavians' use of telephone interviews is partly explained by their being large countries with small populations. Their mobile phone use also shows their telephone orientation: 10 per cent are mobile phone users compared with 6 per cent in the United States and about 3 per cent in Germany and Japan.[22] In some countries, mail surveys do not work because of low literacy, but

**TABLE 6.4** *Data collection methods: quantitative and qualitative (% of expenditure for 1991)*

| | Mail survey (%) | Telephone (%) | Face-to-face (%) | Group discussions (%) | In-depth interviews (%) |
|---|---|---|---|---|---|
| Austria | na | na | na | na | na |
| Belgium | 7 | 15 | 57 | 10 | 8 |
| Britain | 8 | 15 | 67 | 10 | – |
| Denmark | 16 | 24 | 31 | 6 | 21 |
| Finland | 19 | 38 | 37 | na | na |
| France | na | na | na | na | na |
| Germany | 5 | 18 | 56 | 6 | 10 |
| Greece | –[a] | 3 | 82[b] | 10 | 3 |
| Ireland | 1 | 2 | 72 | 23 | 3 |
| Italy | 4 | 27 | 44 | 10 | 10 |
| Luxembourg | – | 10 | 65 | 5 | – |
| Netherlands | 31 | 18 | 34 | 4 | 9 |
| Norway | 10 | 20 | 50 | 10 | 5 |
| Portugal | 12 | 9 | 65 | 7 | 3 |
| Spain | 3 | 16 | 63 | 13 | 3 |
| Sweden | 23 | 39 | 23 | 4 | 5 |
| Switzerland | 8 | 27 | 46 | na | na |
| Turkey | 6 | 4 | 60 | 15 | 5 |

Note: [a] Less than 0.5 per cent; [b] including panel turnover.
Source: *Report of ESOMAR Working Party on 1991 Market Statistics* (1992).

another reason is the unwillingness of people to respond. Research agencies and managers also have preferred methods, so they will also exert some personal influence on the choice of method.

*Sampling plans*    Marketing researchers usually draw conclusions about large groups of consumers by studying a small sample of the total consumer population. A **sample** is a segment of the population selected to represent the population as a whole. Ideally, the sample should be representative so that the researcher can make accurate estimates of the thoughts and behaviours of the larger population.

Designing the sample calls for three decisions. First, *who* is to be surveyed (what *sampling unit*)? The answer to this question is not always obvious. For example, to study the decision-making process for a family car purchase, should the researcher interview the husband, wife, other family members or all of these? The responses obtained from different family members varies so the researcher must determine the information needed and from whom.[23]

Second, *how many* people are to be surveyed (what *sample size*)? Large samples give more reliable results than small samples. However, it is not necessary to sample the entire target market or even a large portion to get reliable results. If well chosen, samples of less than 1 per cent of a population can often give good reliability.

Third, *how* are the people in the sample *to be chosen* (what *sampling procedure*)? Table 6.5 describes different kinds of samples. Using *probability samples*, each population member has a known chance of being included in the sample and researchers can calculate confidence limits for sampling error. But when probability sampling costs too much or takes too much time, marketing researchers often take *nonprobability samples*, even though their sampling error is not measurable. These varied ways of drawing samples have different costs and time limitations, as well as different accuracy and statistical properties. Which method is best depends on the needs of the research project.

*Research instruments*    In collecting primary data, marketing researchers have a choice of two main research instruments: the *questionnaire* and *mechanical devices*.

The *questionnaire* is by far the most common instrument. Broadly speaking, a questionnaire consists of a set of questions presented to a respondent for his or her

| **TABLE 6.5**    *Types of sampling* | |
|---|---|
| **Probability sample** | |
| Simple random sample | Every member of the population has a known and equal chance of selection. |
| Stratified random sample | The population is divided into mutually exclusive groups (such as age groups), and random samples are drawn from each group. |
| Cluster (area) sample | The population is divided into mutually exclusive groups (such as blocks), and the researcher draws a sample of the groups to interview. |
| **Nonprobability sample** | |
| Convenience sample | The researcher selects the easiest population members from which to obtain information. |
| Judgement sample | The researcher uses his or her judgement to select population members who are good prospects for accurate information. |
| Quota sample | The researcher finds and interviews a prescribed number of people in each of several categories. |

---

**TABLE 6.6**   *A 'questionable questionnaire'*

Suppose that a summer camp director had prepared the following questionnaire to use in interviewing the parents of prospective campers. How would you assess each question?

1. What is your income to the nearest hundred dollars?
   *People don't usually know their income to the nearest hundred dollars nor do they want to reveal their income that closely. Moreover, a researcher should never open a questionnaire with such a personal question.*
2. Are you a strong or a weak supporter of overnight summer camping for your children?
   *What do 'strong' and 'weak' mean?*
3. Do your children behave themselves well at a summer camp?
   Yes ( ) No ( )
   *'Behave' is a relative term. Furthermore, are 'yes' and 'no' the best response options for this question? Besides, will people want to answer this? Why ask the question in the first place?*
4. How many camps mailed literature to you last April? This April?
   *Who can remember this?*
5. What are the most salient and determinant attributes in your evaluation of summer camps?
   *What are 'salient' and 'determinant' attributes? Don't use big words on me!*
6. Do you think it is right to deprive your child of the opportunity to grow into a mature person through the experience of summer camping?
   *A loaded question. Given the bias, how can any parent answer 'yes'?*

---

answers. The questionnaire is very flexible – there are many ways to ask questions. Questionnaires need to be developed carefully and tested before their large-scale use. A carelessly prepared questionnaire usually contains several errors (see Table 6.6).

In preparing a questionnaire, the marketing researcher must decide what questions to ask, the form of the questions, the wording of the questions and the ordering of the questions. Questionnaires frequently leave out questions that need answering, but include questions that cannot be answered, will not be answered, or need not be answered. Each question should be checked to see that it contributes to the research objectives.

The *form* of the question can influence the response. Marketing researchers distinguish between closed-end and open-end questions. **Closed-end questions** include all the possible answers, and subjects make choices among them. Part A of Table 6.7 shows the most common forms of closed-end questions as they might appear in an SAS survey of airline users. **Open-end questions** allow respondents to answer in their own words. The most common forms are shown in part B of Table 6.7. Open-end questions often reveal more than closed-end questions because respondents are not limited in their answers. Open-end questions are especially useful in exploratory research in which the researcher is trying to find out *what* people think but not measuring *how many* people think in a certain way. Closed-end questions, on the other hand, provide answers that are easier to interpret and tabulate.

Researchers should also use care in the *wording* of questions. They should use simple, direct, unbiased wording. The questions should be pretested before use. The *ordering* of questions is also important. The first question should create interest if possible. Ask difficult or personal questions last so that respondents do not become defensive. The questions should be in a logical order.

Although questionnaires are the most common research instrument, *mechanical instruments* are also used. We discussed two mechanical instruments – people meters and supermarket scanners – earlier in the chapter. Another group of mechanical devices measures subjects' physical responses. For example, a galvanometer (lie

| TABLE 6.7 | *Types of questions* |
|---|---|

**A. Closed-end questions**

| Name | Description |
|---|---|
| Dichotomous | A question offering two answer choices. |
| Multiple choice | A question offering three or more choices. |
| Likert scale | A statement with which the respondent shows the amount of agreement or disagreement |
| Semantic differential | A scale is inscribed between two bipolar words, and the respondent selects the point th represents the direction and intensity of his or her feelings. |
| Importance scale | A scale that rates the importance of some attribute from 'not at all important' to 'extremely important'. |
| Rating scale | A scale that rates some attribute from 'poor' to 'excellent'. |
| Intention-to-buy scale | A scale that describes the respondent's intentions to buy. |

**B. Open-end questions**

| Name | Description |
|---|---|
| Completely unstructured | A question that respondents can answer in an almost unlimited number of ways. |
| Word association | Words are presented, one at a time, and respondents mention the first word that come to mind. |
| Sentence completion | Incomplete sentences are presented, one at a time, and respondents complete the sente |
| Story completion | An incomplete story is presented, and respondents are asked to complete it. |
| Picture completion | A picture of two characters is presented, with one making a statement. Respondents are asked to identify with the other and fill in the empty balloon. |
| Thematic Apperception Tests (TAT) | A picture is presented, and respondents are asked to make up a story about what they think is happening or may happen in the picture. |

## Example

'In arranging this trip, did you personally phone Delta?'   Yes ☐   No ☐

'With whom are you travelling on this flight?'

| | | | |
|---|---|---|---|
| No one | ☐ | Children only | ☐ |
| Spouse | ☐ | Business associates/friends/relatives | ☐ |
| Spouse and children | ☐ | An organized tour group | ☐ |

'Small airlines generally give better service than large ones.'

| Strongly disagree | Disagree | Neither agree nor disagree | Agree | Strongly agree |
|---|---|---|---|---|
| 1 ☐ | 2 ☐ | 3 ☐ | 4 ☐ | 5 ☐ |

*Delta Airlines*

Large    __X__ : ____ : ____ : ____ : ____ :   Small

Experienced    ____ : ____ : ____ : ____ : __X__ : ____ :   Inexperienced

Modern    ____ : ____ : ____ : __X__ : ____ : ____ :   Old-fashioned

'Airline food service to me is'

| Extremely important | Very important | Somewhat important | Not very important | Not at all important |
|---|---|---|---|---|
| 1 ____ | 2 ____ | 3 ____ | 4 ____ | 5 ____ |

'Delta's food service is'

| Excellent | Very good | Good | Fair | Poor |
|---|---|---|---|---|
| 1 ____ | 2 ____ | 3 ____ | 4 ____ | 5 ____ |

'If in-flight telephone service were available on a long flight, I would'

| Definitely buy | Probably buy | Not certain | Probably not buy | Definitely not buy |
|---|---|---|---|---|
| 1 ____ | 2 ____ | 3 ____ | 4 ____ | 5 ____ |

## Example

'What is your opinion of Delta Airlines?' _____

'What is the first word that comes to your mind when you hear the following?'

Airline _____

Delta    _____

Travel    _____

'When I choose an airline, the most important consideration in my decision is _____

'I flew Delta a few days ago. I noticed that the exterior and interior of the plane had very bright colours. This aroused in me the following thoughts and feelings.' *Now complete the story.*

WELL HERE'S THE FOOD.

Fill in the empty balloon.

Make up a story about what you see.

detector) measures the strength of interest or emotions aroused by a subject's exposure to different stimuli: for instance, an ad or picture. The galvanometer detects the minute degree of sweating that accompanies emotional arousal. The tachistoscope flashes an ad to a subject at an exposure range from less than one-hundredth of a second to several seconds. After each exposure, the respondents describe everything they recall. Eye cameras study respondents' eye movements to determine at what points their eyes focus first and how long they linger on a given item.[24]

### Presenting the research plan

At this stage, the marketing researcher should summarize the plan in a *written proposal*. A written proposal is especially important when the research project is large and complex or when an outside firm carries it out. The proposal should cover the management problems addressed and the research objectives, the information obtained, the sources of secondary information or methods for collecting primary data, and the way the results will help management decision making. The proposal should also include research costs. A written research plan or proposal makes sure that the marketing manager and researchers have considered all the important aspects of the research and that they agree on why and how to do the research.

### Implementing the research plan

The researcher next puts the marketing research plan into action. This involves collecting, processing and analysing the information. Data collection can be by the company's marketing research staff or, more usually, by outside firms. The company keeps more control over the collection process and data quality by using its staff. However, outside firms that specialize in data collection can often do the job more quickly and at lower cost.

The data collection phase of the marketing research process is generally the most expensive and the most subject to error. The researcher should watch fieldwork closely to make sure that the plan is implemented correctly and to guard against problems with contacting respondents, with respondents who refuse to cooperate or who give biased or dishonest answers, and with interviewers who make mistakes or take short cuts.

Researchers must process and analyse the collected data to isolate important information and findings. They need to check data from questionnaires for accuracy and completeness and code it for computer analysis. The researchers than tabulate the results and compute averages and other statistical measures.

### Interpreting and reporting the findings

The researcher must now interpret the findings, draw conclusions and report them to management. The researcher should not try to overwhelm managers with numbers and fancy statistical techniques. Rather, the researcher should present important findings that are useful in the important decisions faced by management.

However, interpretation should not be by the researchers alone. They are often experts in research design and statistics, but the marketing manager knows more about the problem and the decisions needed. In many cases, findings can be interpreted in different ways and discussions between researchers and managers will help point to the best interpretations. The manager will also want to check that the research project was conducted properly and that all the necessary analysis was completed. Or, after seeing the findings, the manager may have additional questions that can be answered from the data. Finally, the manager is the one who must ultimately decide what action the research suggests. The researchers may even make the data directly available to marketing managers so that they can perform new analyses and test new relationships on their own.

Interpretation is an important phase of the marketing process. The best research is meaningless if the manager blindly accepts wrong interpretations from the researcher. Similarly, managers may have biased interpretations – they tend to accept research results that show what they expected and to reject those that they did not expect or hope for. Thus managers and researchers must work together closely when interpreting research results and both share responsibility for the research process and resulting decisions.[25]

## Demand estimation

When a company finds an attractive market, it must estimate that market's current size and future potential carefully. The company can lose much profit by overestimating or underestimating the market.

Demand is measured and forecasted on many levels. Figure 6.3 shows *ninety* types of demand measurement! Demand might be measured for six different *product levels* (product item, product form, product line, company sales, industry sales and total sales); five different *space levels* (customer, territory, country, region, world); and three different *time levels* (short range, medium range and long range).

Each demand measure serves a specific purpose. A company might forecast short-run total demand for a product as a basis for ordering raw materials, planning production and borrowing cash. Or it might forecast long-run regional demand for a big product line as a basis for designing a market expansion strategy.

### DEFINING THE MARKET

Market demand measurement calls for a clear understanding of the market involved. The term *market* has acquired many meanings over the years. In its original

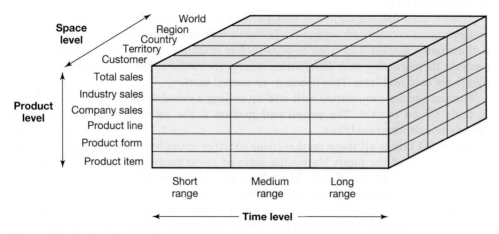

**Figure 6.3**    Ninety types of demand measurement (6 × 5 × 3).

meaning, a market is a physical place where buyers and sellers gather to exchange goods and services. Medieval towns had market squares where sellers brought their goods and buyers shopped for goods. Markets still dominate retailing in the Third World and remain in many towns, but most of today's buying and selling occurs in shopping areas.

To an economist, a market describes all the buyers and sellers who transact over some good or service. Thus the soft-drink market consists of sellers such as Coca-Cola, Pepsi-Cola, Tango and Lilt and all the consumers who buy soft drinks. The economist's interest is the structure, conduct and performance of each market.

To a marketer, a **market** is the set of all actual and potential buyers of a product or service. A market is the set of buyers and an **industry** is the set of sellers. The size of a market hinges on the number of buyers who might exist for a particular market offer. Potential buyers for something have three characteristics: *interest, income* and *access*.

Consider the consumer market for Finnish Tunturi exercise cycles. To assess its market, Tunturi must first estimate the number of consumers who have a potential interest in owning an exercise bike. To do this, the company could contact a random sample of consumers and ask the following question: 'Do you have an interest in buying and owning an exercise bike?' If one person out of ten says yes, Tunturi can assume that 10 per cent of the total number of consumers would constitute the potential market for exercise bikes. The **potential market** is the set of consumers who profess some level of interest in a particular product or service.

Consumer interest alone is not enough to define the exercise bike market. Potential consumers must have enough income to afford the product. They must be able to answer yes to the following question: 'Would you pay Fmk 1,000 for an exercise bike?' The higher the price, the fewer the number of people who can answer yes to this question. Thus market size depends on both interest and income.

1 ecu = US$1.26
= Fmk 5.53
(Finnish markka)

Access barriers further reduce exercise bike market size. If Tunturi has no distributors for its products in some areas, potential consumers in those areas are not available as customers. The **available market** is the set of consumers who have interest, income and access to a particular product or service.

Tunturi might restrict sales to certain groups. Excessive repetitive exercise can damage young children, so sale of exercise bikes to anyone under 12 years of age may be discouraged. The remaining adults make up the **qualified available market** – the set of consumers who have interest, income, access and qualifications for the product or service.

Tunturi now has the choice of going after the whole qualified available market or concentrating on selected segments. Tunturi's **served market** is the part of the qualified available market it decides to pursue. For example, Tunturi may decide to concentrate its marketing and distribution efforts in northern Europe where the winter nights are cold and long. This becomes its served market.

Tunturi and its competitors will end up selling a certain number of exercise bikes in their served market. The **penetrated market** is the set of consumers who have already bought exercise bikes.

Figure 6.4 brings all these market ideas together using hypothetical numbers. The bar on the left of the figure shows the ratio of the potential market – all interested persons – to the total population. Here the potential market is 10 per cent. The bar on the right shows several possible breakdowns of the potential market. The available market – those who have interest, income and access – is 40 per cent of the potential market. The qualified available market – those who can meet the legal requirements – is 50 per cent of the available market (or 20 per cent of the potential market).

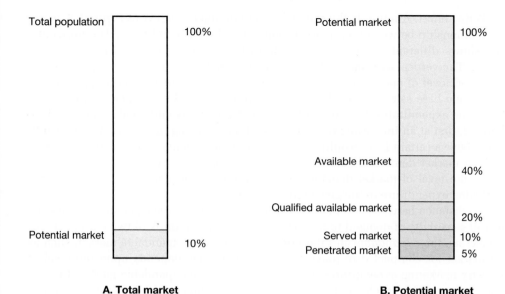

**Figure 6.4** Levels of market definition.

Tunturi concentrates its efforts on 50 per cent of the qualified available market – the served market, which is 10 per cent of the potential market. Finally, Tunturi and its competitors have already penetrated 50 per cent of the served market (or 5 per cent of the potential market).

These market definitions are a useful tool for marketing planning. If Tunturi is unsatisfied with current sales, it can take a number of actions. It can expand to other available markets in Europe or elsewhere. It can lower its price to expand the size of the potential market. It can try to attract a larger percentage of buyers from its served market through stronger promotion or distribution efforts to current target consumers. Or it can try to expand the potential market by increasing its advertising to convert noninterested consumers into interested consumers. Concern over heart diseases means that many middle-aged people who have avoided exercise for years are being encouraged to do more. Perhaps Tunturi can work through the health industry to attract these.

## MEASURING CURRENT MARKET DEMAND

Marketers need to estimate three aspects of current market demand: total market demand, area market demand and actual sales and market shares.

### Estimating total market demand

The **total market demand** for a product or service is the total volume that would be bought by a defined consumer group in a defined geographic area in a defined time period in a defined marketing environment under a defined level and mix of industry marketing effort.

Total market demand is not a fixed number, but a function of the stated conditions. One of these conditions, for example, is the level and mix of industry marketing effort. Another is the state of the environment. Part A of Figure 6.5 shows the relationship between total market demand and these conditions. The horizontal axis shows different possible levels of industry marketing expenditure in a given period. The vertical axis shows the resulting demand level. The curve represents the estimated level of market demand for varying levels of industry marketing expenditure. Some base sales (called the *market minimum*) would take place without any marketing expenditures. Greater marketing expenditures would yield higher levels of demand, first at an increasing rate and then at a decreasing rate. Marketing expenditures above a certain level would not cause much more demand, suggesting an upper limit to market demand called the *market potential*. The industry market forecast shows the level of market demand corresponding to the planned level of industry marketing expenditure in the given environment.[26]

The distance between the market minimum and the market potential shows the overall sensitivity of demand to marketing efforts. We can think of two extreme types of markets, the *expandable* and the *nonexpandable*. An expandable market, such as the market for compact disc players, is one whose size depends upon the level of industry marketing expenditures. For Figure 6.5A, in an expandable market, the distance between $Q_0$ and $Q_1$ would be fairly large. In a nonexpandable market, such as that for opera, marketing expenditures generate little demand; the distance between $Q_0$ and $Q_1$ would be fairly small. Organizations selling in a nonexpandable market can take **primary demand** – total demand for all brands of a given product or service – as given. They concentrate their marketing resources on building **selective demand** – demand for *their* brand of the product or service.

Given a different marketing environment, we must estimate a new market demand curve. For example, the market for exercise bikes is stronger during prosperity than during recession. Figure 6.5B shows the relationship of market demand to the environment. A given level of marketing expenditure will always result in more demand during prosperity than it would during a recession. The main point is that marketers should carefully define the situation for which they are estimating market demand.

Companies have developed various practical methods for estimating total market demand. We will illustrate two here. Suppose Dutch-owned Polygram wants to estimate the total annual sales of recorded compact discs. A common way to estimate total market demand is as follows:

$$Q = n \times q \times p$$

Market demand in the specified period

$Q_1$: Market potential

Market forecast

$Q_2$: Market minimum

Planned expenditure

Industry marketing expenditure

**A. Market demand as a function of industry marketing expenditure (assumes a marketing environment of prosperity)**

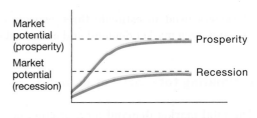

Market demand in the specified period

Market potential (prosperity)

Market potential (recession)

Prosperity

Recession

Industry marketing expenditure

**B. Market demand as a function of industry marketing expenditure (under prosperity vs. recession)**

**Figure 6.5**   Market demand.

where

   $Q$ = total market demand;
   $n$ = number of buyers in the market;
   $q$ = quantity purchased by an average buyer per year; and
   $p$ = price of an average unit.

Thus, if there are 10 million buyers of CDs each year and the average buyer buys six discs a year and the average price is DFl 40, then the total market demand for cassette tapes is DFl 8,400 million (= 10,000,000 × 6 × DFl 40).

A variation on the preceding equation is the *chain ratio method*. Using this method, the analyst multiplies a base number by a chain of adjusting percentages. For example, Britain has no national service, so the British Army needs to attract 20,000 new male recruits each year. There is a problem here, since the Army is already under strength and the population of 16 to 19 year olds is declining. The marketing question is whether this is a reasonable target in relation to the market potential. The Army estimates market potential using the following method:

1 ecu = US$1.26
= DFl 2.12
(Dutch guilders)

| | |
|---|---|
| Total number of male high-school graduating students | 1,200,000 |
| Percentage who are militarily qualified (no physical, emotional, or mental handicaps) | × 0.50 |
| Percentage of those qualified who are potentially interested in military service | × 0.05 |
| Percentage of those qualified and interested in military service who consider the Army the preferred service | × 0.60 |

This chain of numbers shows a market potential of 18,000 recruits, fewer than needed. Since this is less than the target number of recruits sought, the Army needs to do a better job of marketing itself. They responded by doing motivational research that showed existing advertising did not attract the target age group, although a military career did give them what they wanted. A new campaign therefore aimed to increase the attractiveness of a military career.[27]

## Estimating area and market demand

Companies face the problem of selecting the best sales territories and allocating their marketing budget optimally among these territories. Therefore they need to estimate the market potential of different cities, states, and even nations (see Marketing Highlight 6.3). Two main methods are available: the market-build-up method, used primarily by business-goods firms, and the market-factor index method, used primarily by consumer-goods firms.

The **market-build-up method** identifies all the potential buyers in each market and estimates their potential purchases. Suppose a manufacturer of mining instruments developed an instrument for assessing the actual proportion of gold content in gold-bearing ores. The portable instrument tests gold ore in the field. By using it, miners would not waste their time digging deposits of ore containing too little gold to be commercially profitable. It sees each mine as buying one or more instruments, depending on the mine's size. The company wants to determine the market potential for this instrument in each gold-mining country and whether to hire a salesperson to cover it.

## KFC gets Japan finger lickin'

Everyone is familiar with complaints about the bilateral trade deficits of the European Union (EU) and United States with Japan. There are many reasons why the Japanese market is 'impenetrable': because it is a closed market, the nontariff barriers, the stranglehold of the *keiretsu kigyō* (banking groups), the archaic tied distribution system of mama and papa stores, or just because the Japanese are 'workaholics' who live in 'little more than rabbit hutches'. If these claims are true, the fast-food market must be particularly hard to crack in a country that cooks creatures alive in Cruel Grill and Hell Tufo cuisine.

But not so – KFC (previously known as Kentucky Fried Chicken) is now the second largest fast-food chain in Japan. It is also the market leader in China, South Korea, Malaysia, Thailand, and Indonesia, and it is second to only McDonald's in Singapore. KFC's 1,470 Asian outlets average US$1.2 million[*] per store, about 60 per cent more than its US average. In Tiananmen Square, KFC operates its busiest outlet, a 701-seat restaurant serving 2.5 million customers a year. No wonder KFC plans to double its number of Asian outlets during the next five years.

Why is KFC so successful in Asia? First, many of the large Asian cities have a growing concentration of young middle-class urban workers with rising incomes. Fast-food outlets represent a step up from buying food at hawkers' stalls, and Asians are willing to pay more for sitting in an American-style restaurant. Second, Asian women have been entering the labour force in large numbers, leaving them with less time for cooking meals at home. Third, chicken is more familiar to the Asian palate than pizza, and more available than beef. Further, chicken faces none of the religious strictures that beef faces in India or that pork faces in Muslim countries. KFC serves its standard chicken, mashed potatoes, and coleslaw throughout Asia but has offered a few adaptations, such as Hot Wings, a spicier chicken, in Thailand, and fried fish and chicken curry in Japan.

As *Le Monde* recognized years ago: 'To continue to complain about the bilateral deficit with Japan as the result of Japanese protectionism only serves to obscure the problem, not resolve it'. All markets have entry barriers and Japan's are more discouragement to enter than real costs. Japan is the largest market that America and Europe have never been close to. It has a strong culture that is so different from our own that we have to try very hard to grasp it. The trade barriers are often an excuse for European and US failures to penetrate the Japanese market. Often those who complain most loudly about the barriers are business people who have never tried or who have tried once and failed. The Japanese rarely give up after only one attempt.

KFC have tried and won. So have Nestlé, and KitKat is now Japan's second top-selling confectionery. Clearly companies can succeed if they view the world as their market and take the time to learn. They must find those areas that promise the greatest potential sales and profit growth, whether in their neighbourhood, state or nation or even in Japan.

[*]1 ecu = US$1.26.

Source:   Andrew Tanzer, 'Hot wings take off', *Forbes* (18 January 1993), 74; George Staunton, 'Tokyo: aller au fond des choses', *Le Monde* (12 December 1977), 7; Endymion Wilkinson, *Japan Versus the West: Image and Reality* (London: Penguin, 1990); Leonard Koren, *283 Useful Ideas from Japan* (San Francisco: Chronicle, 1988); Sheridan M. Tatsumo, *Created in Japan: From Imitation to World-Class Innovators* (London: Harper & Row, 1990).

To estimate the market potential in each country the manufacturer first finds out the number of gold-mining operations in each country, their locations, the number of employees, annual sales and net worth. This will be harder in some countries than others since some have poor records and others, like China, are secretive about gold mining. Using this data, the company can estimate the market potential of each country based on the number of mines that are big enough and wealthy enough to buy the instrument.

The **market-factor index method** estimates the market potential for consumer goods. Consider the following example. An American manufacturer of men's dress shirts wishes to evaluate its sales performance with market potential in the Indianapolis region. It estimates total national potential for dress shirts at $2 billion per year. The company's current nationwide sales are $140 million – about a 7 per cent share of the total potential market. Its sales in the Indianapolis metropolitan area are $1,100,000. It wants to know whether its share of the Indianapolis market is higher or lower than its national 7 per cent market share. To find this out, the company first needs to calculate market potential in the Indianapolis area.

One way of calculating this is to multiply together population and the area's income per capita by the average share of income spent on shirts. The product then compares with that for the whole country. Using this calculation, the shirt manufacturer finds that Indianapolis accounts for 0.51 per cent of the nation's total potential demand for dress shirts. Since the total national potential is $2 billion each year, total potential in Indianapolis equals $10,200,000 (= $2 billion × 0.0051). Thus the company's sales in Indianapolis of $1,100,000 amount to a 10.8 per cent share (= $1,100,000/ $10,200,000) of area market potential. Comparing this with the 7 per cent national share, the company appears to be doing better in Indianapolis than in other parts of the country.

## Estimating actual sales and market shares

Besides estimating total and area demand, a company will want to know the actual industry sales in its market. Thus it must identify its competitors and estimate their sales.

The industry's trade association will often collect and publish total industry sales, although not listing individual company sales separately. In this way, each company can evaluate its performance against the industry as a whole. Suppose the company's sales are increasing at a rate of 5 per cent a year and industry sales are increasing at 10 per cent. This company is losing its relative standing in the industry.

Another way to estimate sales is to buy reports from marketing research firms that audit total sales and brand sales. For example, Nielsen, AGB and other marketing research firms use scanner data to audit the retail sales of various product categories in supermarkets and drugstores and sell this information to interested companies. A company can obtain data on total product category sales as well as brand sales. It can compare its performance with that of the total industry or any particular competitor to see whether it is gaining or losing in its relative standing.[28]

## FORECASTING FUTURE DEMAND

Having looked at ways to estimate current demand, we now examine ways to forecast future market demand. **Forecasting** is the art of estimating future demand by anticipating what buyers are likely to do under a given set of conditions. Very few products or services lend themselves to easy forecasting. Those that do generally involve a product with steady sales, or sales growth in a stable competitive situation. But most markets do not have stable total and company demand, so good forecasting

| TABLE 6.8 | *Common sales forecasting techniques* |
|---|---|
| **Based on:** | **Methods** |
| What people say | Surveys of buyers' intentions<br>Composite salesforce opinions<br>Expert opinion |
| What people do | Test markets |
| What people have done | Time-series analysis<br>Leading indicators<br>Statistical demand analysis |

becomes a key factor in company success. Poor forecasting can lead to excessively large inventories, costly price markdowns, or lost sales due to being out of stock. The more unstable the demand, the more the company needs accurate forecasts and elaborate forecasting procedures.

Companies commonly use a three-stage procedure to arrive at a sales forecast. First they make an *environmental forecast*, followed by an *industry forecast*, followed by a *company sales forecast*. The environmental forecast calls for projecting inflation, unemployment, interest rates, consumer spending and saving, business investment, government expenditures, net exports and other environmental events important to the company. The result is a forecast of gross national product used along with other indicators to forecast industry sales. Then the company prepares its sales forecast assuming a certain share of industry sales.

Companies use several specific techniques to forecast their sales. Table 6.8 lists some of these techniques.[29] All forecasts build on one of three information bases: what people say, what people do, or what people have done. The first basis – *what people say* – involves surveying the opinions of buyers or those close to them, such as salespeople or outside experts. It includes three methods: surveys of buyer intentions, composites of salesforce opinions and expert opinion. Building a forecast on *what people do* involves another method, that of putting the product into a test market to assess buyer response. The final basis – *what people have done* – involves analysing records of past buying behaviour or using time-series analysis or statistical demand analysis.

## Survey of buyers' intentions

One way to forecast what buyers will do is to ask them directly. This suggests that the forecaster should survey buyers. Surveys are especially valuable if the buyers have clearly formed intentions, will carry them out and can describe them to interviewers.

Several research organizations conduct periodic surveys of consumer buying intentions. These organizations ask questions like the following:

**Do you intend to buy a car within the next six months?**

| 0.0 | 0.1 | 0.2 | 0.3 | 0.4 | 0.5 | 0.6 | 0.7 | 0.8 | 0.9 | 1.0 |
|---|---|---|---|---|---|---|---|---|---|---|
| No chance | | Slight chance | | Fair chance | | Good chance | | Strong chance | | For certain |

This is a *purchase probability scale*. In addition, the various surveys ask about the consumer's present and future personal finances and their expectations about the economy. Consumer durable goods companies subscribe to these indexes to help them anticipate significant shifts in consumer buying intentions, so that they can adjust their production and marketing plans accordingly. For *business buying*, various agencies carry out intention surveys about plant, equipment and materials purchases. These measures need adjusting when conducted across nations and cultures. Overestimation of intention to buy is higher in southern Europe than it is in northern Europe and the United States. In Asia, the Japanese tend to make fewer overstatements than the Chinese.[30]

## Composite of salesforce opinions

When buyer interviewing is impractical, the company may base its sales forecasts on information provided by the salesforce. The company typically asks its salespeople to estimate sales by product for their individual territories. It then adds up the individual estimates to arrive at an overall sales forecast.

Few companies use their salesforce's estimates without some adjustments. Salespeople are biased observers. They may be naturally pessimistic or optimistic, or they may go to one extreme or another because of recent sales setbacks or successes. Furthermore they are often unaware of larger economic developments and do not always know how their company's marketing plans will affect future sales in their territories. They may understate demand so that the company will set a low sales quota. They may not have the time to prepare careful estimates or may not consider it worthwhile.

Accepting these biases, a number of benefits can be gained by involving the salesforce in forecasting. Salespeople may have better insights into developing trends than any other group. After participating in the forecasting process, the salespeople may have greater confidence in their quotas and more incentive to achieve them. Also, such 'grassroots' forecasting provides estimates broken down by product, territory, customer and salesperson.[31]

## Expert opinion

Companies can also obtain forecasts by turning to experts. Experts include dealers, distributors, suppliers, marketing consultants and trade associations. Thus motor vehicle companies survey their dealers periodically for their forecasts of short-term demand. Dealer estimates, however, are subject to the same strengths and weaknesses as salesforce estimates.

Many companies buy economic and industry forecasts. These forecasting specialists are in a better position than the company to prepare economic forecasts because they have more data available and more forecasting expertise.

Occasionally companies will invite a special group of experts to prepare a forecast. They exchange views and come up with a group estimate (group discussion method). Or they may supply their estimates individually, with the company analyst combining them into a single estimate (pooling of individual estimates). Or they may supply individual estimates and assumptions reviewed by a company analyst, revised and followed by further rounds of estimation (Delphi method).[32]

Experts can provide good insights upon which to base forecasts, but they can also be wrong (see Marketing Highlight 6.4). Where possible, the company should back up experts' opinions with estimates obtained using other methods.

## Sometimes 'expert opinion' isn't all it should be

Before you rely too heavily on expert opinion, you might be interested in learning how some past 'experts' came out with their predictions:

- 'Rail travel at high speed is not possible, because passengers, unable to breathe would die of asphyxia.' Dr Dioysy Larder (1828) in the year Stephenson's *Rocket* commenced service.
- 'No large steamship will ever cross the Atlantic, since it would require more coal than it could carry.' Dr Larder (1859) again. Two years later the *Great Eastern* crossed the Atlantic.
- 'Flight by machines heavier than air is unpractical and insignificant, if not impossible.' Simon Newcombe (1901). Eighteen months later the Wright brothers flew.
- 'My imagination refuses to see any sort of submarine doing anything but suffocating its crew and foundering at sea.' H. G. Wells (1902).
- 'Airplanes are interesting toys, but of no military value.' France's Marshal Foch (1911).
- 'The energy produced by the breaking down of the atom is a very poor kind of thing. Anyone who expects a source of power from the transformation is talking moonshine.' Ernest Rutherford (1919), after he had split the first atom.
- 'I think there's a world market for about five computers.' Thomas J. Watson, IBM Chairman (1943).
- 'TV won't be able to hold on to any market it captures after the first six months. People will soon get tired of staring at a plywood box every night.' Daryl F. Zanuck, head of 20th Century Fox (1946).
- 'By 1980, all power (electric, atomic, solar) is likely to be virtually costless.' Henry Luce, founder and publisher of *Time, Life*, and *Fortune* (1956).
- '[He] is an unspeakably untalented and vulgar young entertainer. Where do you go from Elvis Presley, short of obscenity – which is

“Everything that can be invented has *been* invented.”

1899 Director of the US Patent Office urging the office's abolition.

It's easy to make a wrong decision without the right research. At NOP Consumer Market Research we have over 50 researchers to help you cut through stale judgements and come up with fresh ideas daily. For the best attention, design and execution, call us and we'll deliver the best thing since...

**NOP** Make the right decision

NOP CONSUMER MARKET RESEARCH. CONTACT ROCKEY MORRISON OR ALAN WOOD, TOWER HOUSE, SOUTHAMPTON STREET, LONDON WC2 7HN TELEPHONE: 0171 813 6190

against the law.' John Crosby, syndicated TV critic (1954).
- 'With over 50 foreign cars already on sale here, the Japanese auto industry isn't likely to carve out a big slice of the US market for itself.' *Business Week* (1958).
- 'We don't like their sound. Groups of guitars are on the way out.' Decca Recording Company (1962), when turning down the Beatles. They were also rejected by Pye, Columbia and HMV before signing with EMI.

Source: 'Sometimes expert opinion isn't all it should be', *Go* (Sept.–Oct. 1985), 2; Terry Coleman, *The Liners* (Harmondsworth: Penguin, 1976); Stephen Pile, *The Book of Heroic Failures* (London: Futura, 1980); Charles Gillett, *The Sound of the City: The rise of rock and roll* (London: Souvenir, 1983); *Encarta: Multimedia Encyclopaedia* (Microsoft, 1993).

## Test-market method

Where buyers do not plan their purchases carefully or where experts are not available or reliable, the company may want to conduct a direct test market. This is especially useful in forecasting new-product sales or established-product sales in a new distribution channel or territory. Test marketing appears in Chapter 13.

## Time-series analysis

Many firms base their forecasts on past sales. They assume that statistical analysis can uncover the causes of past sales. Then analysts can use the causal relations to predict future sales. **Time-series analysis** consists of breaking down the original sales into four components – trend, cycle, season and erratic components – then recombining these components to produce the sales forecast.

**Trend** is the long-term, underlying pattern of growth or decline in sales resulting from basic changes in population, capital formation and technology. It is found by fitting a straight or curved line through past sales. **Cycle** captures the medium-term, wavelike movement of sales resulting from changes in general economic and competitive activity. The cyclical component can be useful for medium-range forecasting. Cyclical swings, however, are difficult to predict because they do not occur on a regular basis. **Seasonality** refers to a consistent pattern of sales movements within the year. The term *season* describes any recurrent hourly, weekly, monthly, or quarterly sales pattern. The seasonal component may relate to weather factors, holidays and trade customs. The seasonal pattern provides a norm for forecasting short-range sales. Finally, *erratic events* include fads, strikes, snow storms, earthquakes, riots, fires and other disturbances. These components, by definition, are unpredictable and should be removed from past data to see the more normal behaviour of sales.

Suppose an insurance company sold 12,000 new life insurance policies this year and wants to predict next year's December sales. The long-term trend shows a 5 per cent sales growth rate per year. This information alone suggests sales next year of 12,600 (= 12,000 × 1.05). However, a business recession is expected next year, which will probably result in total sales achieving only 90 per cent of the expected trend-adjusted sales. Sales next year are therefore more likely to be 11,340 (= 12,600 × 0.90). If sales were the same each month, monthly sales would be 945 (= 11,340/12). However, December is an above-average month for insurance policy sales, with a seasonal index standing at 1.30. Therefore December sales may be as high as 1,228.5 (= 945 × 1.3). The company expects no erratic events, such as strikes or new insurance regulations. Thus it estimates new policy sales next December at 1,228.5 policies.

## Leading indicators

Many companies try to forecast their sales by finding one or more **leading indicators**: that is, other time series that change in the same direction but ahead of company sales. For example, a plumbing supply company might find that its sales lag behind the housing starts index by about four months. An index of housing starts would then be a useful leading indicator.

## Statistical demand analysis

Time-series analysis treats past and future sales as a function of time, rather than as a function of any real demand factors. But many real factors affect the sales of any product. **Statistical demand analysis** is a set of statistical procedures used to discover the most important real factors affecting sales and their relative influence. The factors most commonly analysed are prices, income, population and promotion.

Statistical demand analysis consists of expressing sales ($Q$) as a dependent variable and trying to explain sales as a function of a number of independent demand variables $X_1, X_2, ..., X_n$. That is:

$$Q = f(X_1, X_2, ..., X_n)$$

Using multiple-regression analysis, various equations can be fitted to the data to find the best predicting factors and equation.

For example, the South of Scotland Electricity Board developed an equation that predicted the annual sales of washing machines (Q) to be:[33]

$$Q = 210,739 - 703P + 69H + 20Y$$

where

    P  = average installed price;
    H = new single-family homes connected to utilities; and
    Y  = per capita income.

Thus in a year when an average installed price is £387, there are 5,000 new connected homes, and the average per capita income is £4,800, from the equation we would predict the actual sales of washing machines to be 379,678 units:

$$Q = 210,739 - 703(387) + 69(5,000) + 20(4,800)$$

The equation was found to be 95 per cent accurate. If the equation predicted as well as this for other regions, it would serve as a useful forecasting tool. Marketing management would predict next year's per capita income, new homes and prices and use them to make forecasts.

Statistical demand analysis can be very complex and the marketer must take care in designing, conducting and interpreting such analysis. Yet constantly improving computer technology has made statistical demand analysis an increasingly popular approach to forecasting.

## Information analysis

Information gathered by the company's marketing information systems often requires more analysis and sometimes managers may need more help in applying it to marketing problems and decisions. This help may include advanced statistical analysis to learn more about both the relationships within a set of data and their statistical reliability (Chapters 9 and 10 show these factors used in segmentation and positioning research). Such analysis allows managers to go beyond means and standard deviations in the data. In an examination of consumer nondurable goods in the Netherlands, regression analysis gave a model that forecast a brand's market share ($B_t$) based upon predicted marketing activity:[34]

$$B_t = -7.85 - 1.45P_t + 0.08A_{t-1} + 1.23D_t$$

where

$P_t$   = relative price of brand;
$A_{t-1}$ = advertising share in the previous period; and
$D_t$   = effective store distribution.

This, and models like it, can help answer marketing questions such as:

- What are the chief variables affecting my sales and how important is each one?
- If I raised my price 10 per cent and increased my advertising expenditures 20 per cent, what would happen to sales?
- How much should I spend on advertising?
- What are the best predictors of which consumers are likely to buy my brand versus my competitor's brand?
- What are the best variables for segmenting my market and how many segments exist?

Information analysis might also involve a collection of mathematical models that will help marketers make better decisions. Each model represents some real system, process or outcome. These models can help answer the questions of *what if* and *which is best*. During the past twenty years, marketing scientists have developed numerous models to help marketing managers make better marketing-mix decisions, design sales territories and sales-call plans, select sites for retail outlets, develop optimal advertising mixes and forecast new-product sales.[35]

## DISTRIBUTING INFORMATION

Information has no value until managers use it to make better marketing decisions. The information gathered needs distributing to the right marketing managers at the right time. Most companies have centralized marketing information systems that provide managers with regular performance reports, intelligence updates and reports on the results of studies. Managers need these routine reports for making regular planning, implementation and control decisions. But marketing managers may also need nonroutine information for special situations and on-the-spot decisions. For example, a sales manager having trouble with a large customer may want a summary of the account's sales and profitability over the past year. Or a retail store manager who has run out of a best-selling product may want to know the current inventory levels in the chain's other stores. In companies with only centralized information systems, these managers must request the information from the MIS staff and wait. Often, the information arrives too late to be useful.

The globalization of business is extending the task facing managers. Now managers have to manage campaigns across countries and with different countries. Even gathering basic secondary information in many countries is difficult and primary information can present even more problems (see Marketing Highlight 6.5). Increasingly the marketing information systems have to support people working in different countries or even in different continents. Developments in information handling are now making that task easier. With recent advances in computers, software and telecommunications, many companies are decentralizing their marketing information systems. They are giving managers direct access to information stored in the system. In some companies, marketing managers can use a personal computer to tie into the company's information network. From any location, they can obtain information from internal records or outside information services, analyse the informa-

## International studies

International marketing researchers follow the same steps as domestic researchers, from defining the research problem and developing a research plan to interpreting and reporting the results. However, these researchers often face more and different problems. Whereas domestic researchers deal with fairly homogeneous markets within a single country, international researchers deal with markets in many different countries. These different markets often vary dramatically in their levels of economic development, cultures and customs and buying patterns.

In many foreign markets, the international researcher has a difficult time finding good *secondary data*. Whereas many marketing researchers can obtain reliable secondary data on their domestic market, many countries have almost no research services at all. Some international market research firms operate in several large economies, but most countries are not covered by any. Thus, even when secondary information is available, it must usually be obtained from many different sources on a country-by-country basis, making the information difficult to combine or compare.

Because of the scarcity of good secondary data, international researchers must often collect their own primary data. Here again, researchers face problems not encountered domestically. For example, they may find it difficult simply to develop appropriate samples. Whereas researchers in developed countries can use current telephone directories, census data and any of several sources of socioeconomic data to construct samples, such information is lacking or unreliable in many countries. Reaching respondents is often not so easy in other parts of the world. In some countries, few people have phones – there are only four phones per thousand people in Egypt, six in Turkey and thirty-two in Argentina. In other countries, the postal system is notoriously unreliable. In Brazil, for instance, an estimated 30 per cent of the mail is never delivered. In many developing countries, poor roads and transportation systems make certain areas hard to reach, making personal interviews difficult and expensive.[1]

Differences in cultures from country to country cause additional problems for international researchers.

Language is the most obvious culprit. For example, questionnaires must be prepared in one language and then translated into the languages of each country researched. Responses must then be translated back into the original language for analysis and interpretation. This adds to research costs and increases the risks of error:

> Translating a questionnaire from one language to another is far from easy. ... Many points are [lost], because many idioms, phrases and statements mean different things in different cultures. A Danish executive observed: 'Check this out by having a different translator put back into English what you've translated from the English. You'll get the shock of your life. I remember [an example in which] "out of sight, out of mind" had become "invisible things are insane"'.[2]

Buying roles and consumer decision processes vary greatly from country to country, further complicating international marketing research. Consumers in different countries also vary in their attitudes toward marketing research. People in one country may be very willing to respond; in other countries, nonresponse can be a difficult problem. For example, custom in some Islamic countries prohibits people from talking with strangers – a researcher simply may not be allowed to speak by phone with women about brand attitudes or buying behaviour. In certain cultures, research questions are often considered too personal. For example, in many Latin American countries, people may feel too embarrassed to talk with researchers about their choice of shampoo, deodorant, or other personal care products. Even when respondents are *willing* to respond, they may not be *able* to because of high functional illiteracy rates. And middle-class people in developing countries often make false claims in order to appear well-off. For example, in a study of tea consumption in India, over 70 per cent of middle-income respondents claimed that they used one of several national brands. However, the researchers had good reason to doubt these results – more than 60 per cent of the tea sold in India is unbranded generic tea.

Despite these problems, the recent growth of international marketing has resulted in a rapid increase in the use of international marketing research. Global companies have little choice but to conduct such research. Although the costs and problems associated with international research may be high, the costs of not doing it – in terms of missed opportunities and mistakes – might be even higher. Once recognized, many of the problems associated with international marketing research can be overcome or avoided.

## European research

Neither Europe, nor even the European Union, can be researched as one market. The market is getting closer to fulfilment, but some difficulties remain. The market research industry structure is fairly standard across the EU and most services are available everywhere. However, many large agencies including Control Data Corporation, IRI, GfK and Video Research cover only a few countries.[3] Frequently, if conducting international studies, agencies have to use the facilities provided by local research companies. To serve multinational clients better, many large and small firms are now forming alliances in order to ease cross-border research. Cooperative ventures have allowed medium-sized companies to build a reputation for international research. For example, Research Services and its associates conduct both the European Businessman's Readership Survey and the Asian Businessman's Readership Survey. Euroline is a one-stop-shop telephone interviewing consortium set up by agencies in France, Germany, Italy, Spain and the United Kingdom. This will allow one questionnaire to be written, transmitted to other countries, translated, then hopefully checked carefully.

There is a huge disparity of incomes and consumption within the European Union (EU): Denmark, Germany and Luxembourg have a gross domestic product per capita more than four times that of Portugal and three times that of Greece. Differences in wealth only account for a small part of the variation in consumption and consumer behaviour. Some differences, like eating habits, are clearly rooted in the different languages, cultural traditions and cuisine of the EU, but there are also big differences in the consumption of modern industrial goods. In Spain,

the penetration of consumer durables shows they are in the early stages of a slowly unwinding product life cycle, whereas the same products are maturing elsewhere. For example, in Spain penetration of home computers (11 per cent), CD players (9) and microwave ovens (9) contrasts with the penetration of home computers in Belgium (29 per cent), CD players in the Netherlands (60 per cent) and microwave ovens in the United Kingdom (60 per cent).

Competition and distribution also vary. Many European markets have locally dominant companies and competitive structures that are unique to them. The big multinationals now operate in most markets, but their strength in each market varies. The structure of retailing within the EU varies massively. The greatest contrast is between the United Kingdom dominated by a few large retailers and Italy where mama and papa stores dominate. Europe has many large chains, such as Germany's Tengelmann, France's Leclerc, Britain's J. Sainsbury and Dutch Ahold, but most of these are little known outside their home country.[4]

European primary and secondary data sources have yet to harmonize. Differences exist in the most basic of issues: variations in life-cycle groupings make comparisons awkward. In Germany, adulthood ranges from 18 onwards, but in other countries it is as low as 12 years, thus eliminating the teenage market. In Japan, adulthood does not depend on age: all persons living at home with their parents are defined as children. Social class scales also differ. The British scale – A, B, C1, C2, D and E – which is built up from ten components (e.g. age, income, occupation, and so on), is widely used, but in Germany the definition of social scale uses a point scale roughly depending upon three components: income, profession and education. In France, the scale depends upon where as well as what is done: for example, working in public or private sectors.[5]

The European Society for Opinion and Marketing Research (ESOMAR) set up working parties in 1982 to find a set of demographic questions that could be asked in any European country. The questions cover basic issues like sex, age, economic status, and so on. These questions

## MARKETING HIGHLIGHT 6.5 (cont)

Table I    The European Union 1995: in the club, in the queue and in the distance

| Status Population | Country |
| --- | --- |
| EU countries 287.8 m. | Belgium, Denmark, France, Germany, Greece, Holland, Ireland, Italy, Luxembourg, Portugal, Spain and United Kingdom. |
| Membership agreed 25.7 m. | Austria, Finland, Norway* and Sweden. |
| Already applied 65.6 m. | Cyprus, Malta, Switzerland* and Turkey. |
| Applications expected soon 64.2 m. | Czech Republic, Hungary, Poland and Slovakia. |
| Intend to apply 44.9 m. | Albania, Bulgaria, Estonia, Latvia, Lithuania, Romania and Slovenia. |
| Anyone's guess | Belarus, Bosnia and Herzegovina, Croatia, Macedonia, Moldova, Russia, Serbia and Ukraine. |

Note:    *Referendum against membership.

have been adopted by the European Barometer Service. Soon ESOMAR will be publishing a standardized format in a book that includes a sample questionnaire and information on how to code the answers.

While ESOMAR move slowly towards a single research market, the growth of the EU will make it less of a standardized market. The list is always changing, but Table I shows the present position. Expect the EU to be an ever-expanding and diverging marketplace.[6]

### References

1. Many of the examples in this section, along with others, are found in Subhash C. Jain, *International Marketing Management*, 3rd edn (Boston: PWS-Kent Publishing, 1990), 334–9; see also Vern Terpstra and Ravi Sarathy, *International Marketing* (Chicago: Dryden Press, 1991), 208–13.
2. Jain, *International Marketing Management*, 338.
3. Philip Klienman, 'A rise in cross border activity', *Financial Times* (30 March 1994), 15.
4. Figures taken from the following excellent annual guide to the European market: *European Market Pocket Book: 1994* (Henley-on-Thames, UK: NTC Publications, 1994); see also a series of journal articles reviewing consumers in different European countries starting with Peter S. H. Leeflang and W. Fred van Raaij, 'The changing consumer in the Netherlands: recent changes in environmental variables and their consequences for future consumption and marketing', *International Journal of Research in Marketing*, 12, 5 (1995), 345–63.
5. See Marieke de Mooij, 'Research for worldwide advertising', in *id., Advertising Worldwide* (Hemel Hempstead: Prentice Hall, 1994), 365–430; and Louella Miles, 'Single market research', *Marketing Business* (July–Aug. 1994), 40–1.
6. 'A touch of Eastern promise', *The Economist* (26 March 1994), 40; 'A rude awakening: a survey of the European Community', *The Economist* (3 July 1994).

tion using statistical packages and models, prepare reports on a word processor, and communicate with others in the network.

Such systems offer exciting prospects. They allow the managers to get the information they need directly and quickly and to tailor it to their needs. As managers develop the skills needed and as the systems become cheaper, companies will increasingly use decentralized marketing information systems.

## SUMMARY

In carrying out their marketing responsibilities, marketing managers need a great deal of information. Despite the growing supply of information, managers often lack enough information of the right kind or have too much of the wrong kind. To overcome these problems, many companies are taking steps to improve their marketing information systems.

A well-designed *marketing information system* (MIS) begins and ends with the user. The MIS first *assesses information needs* by interviewing marketing managers and surveying their decision environment to determine what information is desired, needed and feasible to offer. The MIS next *develops information* and helps managers to use it more effectively. *Internal records* provide information on sales, costs, inventories, cash flows and accounts receivable and payable. Such data are quick and cheap, but must often be adapted for marketing decisions. The *marketing intelligence system* supplies marketing executives with everyday information about developments in the external marketing environment. Intelligence can be from company employees, customers, suppliers and resellers; or by monitoring published reports, conferences, advertisements, competitor actions and other activities in the environment.

*Marketing research* involves collecting information relevant to a specific marketing problem facing the company. All marketers need marketing research and most large companies have their own marketing research departments. Marketing research involves a four-step process. The first step consists of the manager and researcher carefully *defining the problem and setting the research objectives*. The objectives may be *exploratory*, *descriptive*, or *causal*. The second step consists of developing the *research plan* for collecting data from primary and secondary sources. *Primary data collection* calls for choosing *a research approach* (observation, survey, experiment); choosing a *contact method* (mail, telephone, personal); designing a *sampling plan* (whom to survey, how many to survey and how to choose them); and developing *research instruments* (questionnaire, mechanical). The third step consists of *implementing the marketing research plan* by collecting, processing and analysing the information. The fourth step consists of *interpreting and reporting the findings*. Further information analysis helps marketing managers to apply the information and provides advanced statistical procedures and models to develop more rigorous findings from the information.

Finally, the marketing information system distributes information gathered from internal sources, marketing intelligence and marketing research to the right managers at the right times. More and more companies are decentralizing their information systems through networks that allow managers to have direct access to information. To carry out their responsibilities, marketing managers need measures of current and future market size. We define a *market* as the set of actual and potential consumers of a market offer. Consumers in the market have *interest*, *income* and *access* to the market offer. The marketer has to distinguish various levels of the market, such as the *potential market*, *available market*, *qualified available market*, *served market* and *penetrated market*.

One task is to *estimate current demand*. Marketers can estimate total demand through the chain ratio method, which involves multiplying a base number by successive percentages. Estimating actual industry sales requires identifying competitors and using some method of estimating the sales of each. Companies then estimate the market shares of competitors to judge their relative performance. For *estimating future demand*, the company can use one or a combination of seven possible forecasting methods, based on what consumers say (*buyers' intentions surveys*, *composite of salesforce opinions*, *expert opinion*); what consumers do (*market tests*); or what consumers have done (*time-series analysis*, *leading indicators* and *statistical demand analysis*). The best method to use depends on the purpose of the forecast, the type of product and the availability and reliability of data.

# ■ DISCUSSING THE ISSUES

1. You are a marketing research supplier, designing and conducting studies for a variety of companies. What is the most important thing you may do to ensure your clients will get their money's worth from your services?

2. Companies often face rapidly changing environments. Can market research information go stale? What issues does a manager face in using these research results?

3. What type of research would be appropriate in the following situations and why?

   - Nestlé wants to investigate the impact of children on their parents' decisions to buy breakfast foods.
   - A college or university bookstore wants to get some insights into how students feel about the store's merchandise, prices and service.
   - Gillette wants to determine whether a new line of deodorants for teenagers will be profitable.

- Virgin is considering where to locate a new music store in a fast-growing suburb.
- Nintendo intends to develop a new range of multimedia products for older children and adults and wants to test the feasibility of the idea.

4. In market measurement and forecasting, what is the more serious problem: to overestimate demand or to underestimate it? Give your reasons.

5. As marketing manager for Pedigree Chum cat food, you have seen sales jump 50 per cent in the last year after years of relatively stable sales. How will you forecast sales for the coming year?

6. What leading indicators might help you predict sales of cars? mobile phones? baby foods? Describe a general procedure for finding leading indicators of product sales?

# ■ APPLYING THE CONCEPTS

1. People often make their own judgements about the potential for new products. You may hear someone say a new product will 'never sell' or that it will 'sell like hot cakes'. Recall some recent new products or services that you saw or heard about and made an informal prediction. What attracted your attention enough to get you to comment on the future of the products or service? What was your forecast? Were you correct?

2. Run a small focus group to learn about the pros and cons of this technique.

- Pick one member in the group as a moderator and select six to eight other volunteers. Try to include at least one strong personality and one shy member. Set the group up in a circle in front of the class.
- Discuss a moderately controversial issue that is of interest to the class, but avoid issues that are very controversial or emotional. Run the group for 10 to 15 minutes.
- Discuss the focus group 'results' with the class. Were the conclusions fair or biased?
- What did the class find useful about the technique and what problems did they see?

# ■ REFERENCES

1. Hamish McDonald, 'Caught on the hop', *Far Eastern Economic Review* (18 February 1988), 72–3; 'Qantas embarks on major fleet expansion plan', *Aviation Week & Space Technology* (20 June 1988), 39, 42–3; Michael Westlake, 'Stand-by room only', *Far Eastern Economic Review* (2 June 1988), 72–5; and Paul Proctor, 'Pacific Rim carriers struggle to cope with impending traffic boom', *Aviation Week & Space Technology* (20 November 1989), 110–11; 'Asia's profitable skies', *The Economist* (7 July 1990), 73–4; 'Asia's airlines: learning how to fly economy', *The Economist* (21 May 1994); 'Airlines going global', *The Economist* (19 December 1992); Ivan Verchère, 'The fatal flaws in aviation economics', *The European* (26 Aug.–1 Sept. 1994), 17; Simon Holberton and Liam Strong, 'How BA tries to make friends and keep them', *Financial Times* (4 September 1990), 16; Tony Patey, 'Lufthansa lends an ear to passenger', *The European*, (29 Apr.–5 May 1994), 22; additional information supplied by Qantas Airways Ltd. (April 1993).

2. Marion Harper, Jr., 'A new profession to aid management', *Journal of Marketing* (January 1961), 1.

3. Rashi Glazer, 'Marketing in an information-intensive environment: strategic implications of knowledge as an asset', *Journal of Marketing* (October 1991), 1–19; Paul Turner, 'Using information to enhance competitive advantage – the marketing option', *European Journal of Marketing*, **25**, 6 (1991), 55–64.

4. John Neisbitt, *Megatrends: Ten new directions transforming our lives* (New York: Warner Books, 1984).

5. 'Harnessing the data explosion', *Sales & Marketing Management* (January 1987), 31; and Joseph M. Winski, 'Gentle rain turns into torrent', *Advertising Age* (3 June 1991), 34.

6. Neisbitt, *Megatrends, op. cit.*, 16.

7. See 'Business is turning data into a potent strategic weapon', *Business Week* (22 August 1983), 92; and 'Decision systems for marketers', *Marketing Communications* (March 1986), 163–90; and Jeffrey Rotfeder and Jim Bartimo, 'How software is making food sales a piece of cake', *Business Week* (2 July 1990), 54–5; Victoria Griffith, 'Smart selling to big spenders', *Financial Times* (1 July 1994), 16.

8. Louella Miles, 'Leader of the pack', *Marketing Business* (Dec.–Jan. 1992/3), 31–7; Louella Miles, 'Single market research', *Marketing Business* (July–Aug. 1994), 40–1; Philip Klienman, 'A rise in cross border activity', *Financial Times* (30 March 1990), 15.

9. See Christel Beard and Betsy Wiesendanger, 'The marketer's guide to online databases', *Sales & Marketing Management* (January 1993), 36–41.

10. *Ibid.*, 46; and Leonard M. Fuld, 'Competitor intelligence: can you plug the leaks?', *Security Management* (August 1989), 85–7; Kate Button, 'Spies like us', *Marketing Business* (March 1994), 7–9.

11. See Howard Schlossberg, 'Competitive intelligence pros seek formal role in marketing', *Marketing News* (5 March 1990), 2, 28; Gary B. Roush, 'A program for sharing corporate intelligence', *Journal of Business Strategy* (Jan.–Feb. 1991), 4–7; and Michele Galen, 'These guys aren't spooks: they're "competitive analysts"', *Business Week* (14 October 1991), 97.

12. Isabel Conway, 'Now there's a slimming pill for podgy pooches', *The European – élan* (30 Sept.–6 Oct. 1994), 5.

13. The American Marketing Association officially adopted this definition in 1987.

14. Peggy Hollinger, 'Europe reaches for the cereals', *Financial Times* (4 October 1994), 21.

15. For more information on secondary sources of business and marketing data, see Gilbert A. Churchill, Jr., *Marketing Research: Methodological foundations*, 5th edn (Chicago: Dryden Press, 1991), 287–303; *The Best 100 Sources of Marketing Information*, a supplement to *American Demographics*, 1989; 'Research business report', *Advertising Age* (3 June 1991), 31–5; 'The Honomichl 50: The 1992 Honomichl Business Report on the Marketing Research Industry', a special section in *Marketing News* (2 June 1992); and '1993 Directory of International Marketing Research Firms', *Marketing News* (1 March 1993).

16. See Rebecca Pirate, 'Do not adjust your set', *American Demographics* (March 1993), 6; Zachary Schiller, 'Thanks to the checkout scanner, marketing is losing some of its mystery', *Business Week* (28 August 1989), 57; and Lynn G. Coleman, 'IRI, Nielsen slug it out in the scanning wars', *Marketing News* (2 September 1991), 1, 47; Philip Kleinman, 'Electronics the tool in interviewer's armoury', *Financial Times* (30 March 1990), 16.

17. Mikael Hernant and Per-Göran Persson, 'A study of consumers' usage of sales promotions introducing a new type of single source data', in Josée Bloemer, Jos Lemmink and Hans Kasper, *European Marketing Academy Proceedings*, Maastricht (1994), 335–53.

18. Jacob Hornik and Tamar Zaig, 'Increasing compliance in costly telephone interviews: a test of four inducement techniques', *International Journal of Research in Marketing*, **8**, 2 (1991), 147–53.

19. Considerable research has been conducted on how best to increase the response rate of mail interviews. For a review see David Jobber, 'An examination of the effects of questionnaire factors on response to an industrial mail survey', *International Journal of Research in Marketing*, **6**, 2 (1989), 129–40; David Jobber and John Saunders, (1993), 'A note on the applicability of the Bruvold–Comer model of mail survey response rates to commercial populations', *Journal of Business Research*, 26(3), 223–36.

20. See Thomas L. Greenbaum, 'Focus group spurt predicted for the '90s', *Marketing News* (8 January 1990), 21, 22; and *Marketing News*, special issue on focus groups (27 May 1991).

21. Selwyn Feinstein, 'Computers replacing interviewers for personnel and marketing tasks', *Wall Street Journal* (9 October 1986), 35; and Diane Crispell, 'People talk, computers listen', *American Demographics* (October 1989), 8; Helen Slingsby, 'A high street revolution', *Financial Times* (30 March 1990), 17.

22. Cath Mersh, 'Danes develop a mobile phone to try to cut health risk concerns', *The European* (7–13 October 1993), 24.

23. For an international review of response differences see Robert A. Peterson, Dana L. Alden, Mustafa O. Attir and Alain J. P. Jolibert, 'Husband–wife report disagree-

ment: a cross-national investigation', *International Journal of Research in Marketing*, **5**, 2 (1988), 125–36.

24. For more on mechanical measures, see Michael J. McCarthy, 'Mind probe', *Wall Street Journal* (22 March 1991), B3.

25. For an interesting discussion of the importance of the relationship between market researchers and research users, see Christine Moorman, Gerald Zaltman, and Rohit Deshpande, 'Relationships between providers and users of market research: the dynamics of trust within and between organizations', *Journal of Marketing Research* (August 1992), 314–28; and Christine Moorman, Rohit Deshpande, and Gerald Zaltman, 'Factors affecting trust in market research relationships', *Journal of Marketing* (January 1993), 81–101.

26. For further discussion, see Gary L. Lilien, Philip Kotler, and K. Sridhar Moorthy, *Marketing Models* (Englewood Cliffs, NJ: Prentice Hall, 1992).

27. For more on forecasting total market demand, see F. William Barnett, 'Four steps to forecast total market demand', *Harvard Business Review* (July–Aug. 1988), 28–34; David Churchill, 'Marilyn's bait for the boys', *Financial Times* (30 March 1994), 17.

28. For a more comprehensive discussion of measuring market demand, see Philip Kotler, *Marketing Management: Analysis, planning, implementation and control*, 8th edn (Englewood Cliffs, NJ: Prentice Hall, 1994), ch. 10.

29. For a listing and analysis of these and other forecasting

techniques, see David M. Georgoff and Robert G. Murdick, 'Manager's guide to forecasting', *Harvard Business Review* (Jan.–Feb. 1986), 110–20; and Donald S. Tull and Del I. Hawkins, *Marketing Research: Measurement and method*, 6th edn (New York: Macmillan, 1990), ch. 21.

30. Lynn Y. S. Lin, 'Comparison of survey responses among Asian, European and American consumers and their interpretations', ESOMAR Conference, Venice (18–20 June 1990), 120–32.

31. For more on the salesforce composite method, see Tull and Hawkins, *Marketing Research*, op. cit., 705–6.

32. See Kip D. Cassino, 'Delphi method: a practical "crystal ball" for researchers', *Marketing News* (6 January 1984), sect. 2, pp. 10–11.

33. From Luiz Moutinho, *Problems in Marketing* (London: Chapman, 1991).

34. Karel Jan Alsem, Peter S. H. Leeflang and Jan C. Reuyl, 'The forecasting accuracy of market share models using predicted values of competitive marketing behaviour', *International Journal of Research in Marketing*, **6**, 3 (1989), 183–98.

35. For more on statistical analysis, consult a standard text, such as Donald S. Tull and Del I. Hawkins, *Marketing Research* (New York: Macmillan, 1993). For a review of marketing models, see Gary L. Lilien and Philip Kotler, and Sridhar Moorthy, *Marketing Models* (Englewood Cliffs, NJ: Prentice Hall, 1992).

## CASE 6

## Ballygowan springs into new age Kisqua    *Brenda Cullen**

In January 1991 Geoff Read, managing director of Ballygowan Spring Water Company, had to make a decision that could alter the whole direction of the company. Since August 1988 the management team had shaped a strategy to launch a drink to develop upon the success of Ballygowan Spring Water. The objective was to provide Ballygowan with a product to enter the soft-drinks market and so remove the weakness of being a one-product company. After identifying the market for 'new age' products, and carrying out research at each stage in the product development process, the results of a final test market were disappointing. Ballygowan had to consider whether to with-

draw the product, to redesign and reposition the new range or to go ahead and launch as originally planned.

### Ballygowan

Geoff Read founded Ballygowan in 1981. Initially the idea of selling bottled water to the Irish consumer met with scepticism from the banks. However, by 1991 Ballygowan exported to 15 countries and held 77 per cent of the 12.5 million litre water market in Ireland and had developed an extensive range of bottled spring water products.

Between 1987 and 1989 the company grew to be a medium-sized enterprise geared for expansion and growth. A joint investment with Anheuser Busch

* University College Dublin, Ireland.

provided a very modern production facility covering 270,000 square feet with a capacity of 600 bottles per minute. Ballygowan's success came from being an innovator in the market for water-based products, and also from astute management of the Ballygowan brand franchise. Management now saw the need to exploit the assets of the company more profitably. In particular the plant was not at full capacity and the company's strong distribution network and experienced management were not being fully utilized.

### Bottled water market

By the end of 1985 the bottled water market in Ireland was I£1.2 million* (2.8 million litres) with about 10 per cent of adults drinking mineral water regularly. By 1990 it had grown to I£12.5 million (12.5 million litres), about 5.5 per cent of the Irish soft drinks market (see Exhibit 6.1). The bottled water market was 'one of the fastest growing sectors in the food trade in both Ireland and the UK'. Reasons for this were reduction in the quality of tap water, and changing attitudes towards health and fitness, which led to an increase in the demand for drinks perceived as natural, alcohol free and with fewer calories. Furthermore, *increasingly* stringent drink-driving legislation was leading to an increase in the consumption of bottled water. A Euromonitor survey in 1989 showed that the Irish consumed far less bottled water per person than other countries (Ireland: 3 litres; United Kingdom: 5.5; Italy: 80; Germany: 76; France: 68; and the United States: 30).

The market potential for spring water in Ireland was small considering the number of competitor brands on the market (see Exhibit 6.2). While some niche brands had high prices, low prices were becoming common because of aggressive high-street pricing, own-label products, and cheap imports. With a proliferation of products and the threat of commoditization it was becoming difficult to develop new niches in the market.

### Ballygowan Spring Water

Ballygowan's success came from the sparkling and non-sparkling waters – Ballygowan Sparkling Irish

*1 ecu = US$1.26 = I£0.81 (Irish Punt) = 81p

**Exhibit 6.1** Irish bottled water market: segment growth

| Year | Still lit./m. | Sparkling lit./m. | Petillant lit./m. |
|------|------|------|------|
| 1988 | 28% | 72% | – |
| 1989 | 34% | 66% | – |
| 1990 | 33% | 65% | 2% |

**Exhibit 6.2** Dominant brands in the Irish bottled water market (% volume)

| Year | Ballygowan | Tipperary | Perrier | Other |
|------|------|------|------|------|
| 1987 | 75.0 | 9.5 | 13.0 | 2.5 |
| 1988 | 76.0 | 11.0 | 8.0 | 5.0 |
| 1989 | 77.0 | 12.8 | 7.0 | 3.2 |
| 1990 | 78.0 | 13.5 | 4.0 | 4.5 |

Source: A.C. Nielsen.

Spring Water and Ballygowan Natural Irish Spring Water. A later addition to the range was Ballygowan Light, and in 1988 Ballygowan successfully launched a range of flavoured spring waters. By 1990 the company's turnover was I£10 million, a figure they hoped to double within the next two years. An important part of this strategy was the launch of soft drinks, a market where the company saw significant volume potential.

The management wanted to launch a new drink to bring Ballygowan further into the mainstream soft-drinks market. It would enhance the company's reputation for innovation, market leadership, excellence and product quality. The product would be purer, juicier, fruitier and healthier than any other soft drink on the market. The brand should be consistent with developing consumer behaviour, particularly attitudes and behaviours towards healthy diets and lifestyles.

The Irish carbonated soft-drinks market in 1990 was about 235 million litres including approximately 40 million litres of adult soft drinks (see Exhibit 6.3). Soft-drink consumers were the target market for the proposed new product. They were likely to be more adult than young and would prefer to drink 7Up or Club Orange to Coke or Pepsi. The profile of this consumer was 'a sophisticated, self-righteous and reasonably health-conscious adult', 18–30 years old, who wants and will pay for drinks which look good, taste good and portray a certain image.

## CASE 6 (cont)

**Exhibit 6.3**    Irish carbonated drinks market

| Year | Litres (m.) | Increase on previous year (%) |
|---|---|---|
| 1987 | 179 | 7 |
| 1988 | 195 | 9 |
| 1989 | 224 | 15 |
| 1990 (estimated) | 285 | 27 |
| 1991 (projected) | 320 | 12 |

| Packaging 1990 | Share of total market (%) | Litres (m.) |
|---|---|---|
| Glass returnable | 16 | 46.0 |
| Glass nonreturnable | 8 | 23.0 |
| Pet | 55 | 157.0 |
| Cans | 19 | 54.0 |
| Disposable | 3 | 7.0 |
| Total | 100 | 287.0 |

| Flavour analysis 1990 | Share of total market (%) |
|---|---|
| Lemonade (inc. 7-Up) | 38 |
| Cola | 24 |
| Orange | 25 |
| Tonic/mixer | 8 |
| Other | 5 |

Source:   SDDB & A.

A product development process identified product development, brand development and business planning stages. The Ballygowan company employed a marketing consultancy firm to help in the first two stages.

### Product development process

In December 1988 Ballygowan instructed Dimension, a marketing consultancy. The consultancy's brief was:

- Identify and brief three companies to develop prototype products based on pure juices and Ballygowan Spring Water with natural flavours and sweeteners, carbonated, containing preservatives, but not pasteurized.
- Develop formulations for up to six flavours.
- Develop name, branding, positioning, communication and marketing strategies.
- Target the branded soft-drink sector – Coke, 7-Up, Club, Lilt, and so on.

- Develop a brand with a premium but accessible imagery, and superior product quality but priced competitively with major brands.
- The brand should have no overt Ballygowan endorsement.
- Packed in 1.5 litre plastic bottles, 330 ml. cans, 250 ml. glasses.
- Primary focus to be the Irish market, but with export potential.

### Product sourcing

The first task was to find a company that could manufacture the pure fruit juice to mix with Ballygowan Spring Water. Criteria for the selection of a company were degree of technological sophistication, ability to produce a range of flavours, expertise in producing fruit juices and flavours, product quality, hygiene standards and speed of response. Three short-listed companies were briefed. Visits to each company appraised their production processes and capabilities.

The three companies each made laboratory-scale products, which were tested using a structured questionnaire assessing aroma, appearance, taste and overall opinion on each of the test products. All tests were 'blind', and the products were compared with successful brands already on the market as 'controls'. The range of flavours screened included orange, lemon, apple, passion fruit, grapefruit, peach, pineapple, blackberry and blackcurrant. The aim was to achieve product ratings competitive with the 'controls' (see Exhibit 6.4).

After the analysis of each batch, the three companies were rebriefed, shown the taste test results and told the changes required. After repeating the process six times a German company, which responded particularly well to the product brief and to the taste tests, was appointed as the supplier. Both companies then agreed plant and equipment specifications.

### Product formulations

Six products were produced for a quantitative market research survey conducted in May 1989 by Behaviour & Attitudes, a market research agency in Dublin. A questionnaire, developed from Dimension's earlier

**Exhibit 6.4** Taste test

| Product | Aroma[*] | Appearance[*] | Taste[*] | Overall score | Likelihood of purchase[**] |
|---|---|---|---|---|---|
| Club Orange | 6.9 | 7.5 | 7.3 | 7.4 | 3.5 |
| Dohler Orange | 5.9 | 5.6 | 6.1 | 6.1 | 2.6 |
| Dohler Orange and Peach | 7.4 | 7.2 | 7.1 | 7.5 | 3.3 |
| Dohler Orange and Passion Fruit | 6.6 | 6.3 | 7.0 | 7.0 | 3.2 |
| Dohler Orange and Lemon | 6.4 | 6.4 | 6.9 | 7.2 | 3.2 |
| Club Lemon | 6.7 | 6.5 | 7.2 | 7.4 | 3.5 |
| Dohler Lemon | 6.5 | 6.9 | 6.9 | 7.4 | 3.2 |
| Dohler Grapefruit and Pineapple | 5.8 | 6.2 | 5.5 | 6.1 | 2.5 |

Note: [*]Average scores on nine-point scale, in which 9 = most favourable and 1 = least favourable; [**] on a scale of 1 to 5.
Source: Dimension, March 1989.

one, focused on aroma, appearance and flavour. The flavours tested were 10 per cent orange juice, 15 per cent orange peach juice, 15 per cent orange passion fruit juice, 10 per cent orange lemon juice, 10 per cent lemon juice, and 15 per cent grapefruit and pineapple juice, with Club Orange and Club Lemon as 'controls'. Each of 200 respondents taste-tested two Ballygowan samples and one of the 'controls', to give 75 assessments of each Ballygowan product.

The results convinced the Ballygowan team to focus on orange, orange and peach, orange and passion fruit, and orange and lemon. Lemon, and grapefruit and pineapple, could extend the range later (see Exhibit 6.5). Since the results of the orange formulation were not satisfactory a second round of quantitative market research would take place with performance isolated from packaging and advertising effects.

Some questions remained. Should the products be pasteurized, and should essence or preservatives be used? Each of these options had complications. Pasteurization meant that it would not be possible to use plastic bottles and there were also shelf-life implications. However, with pasteurization, the product ingredients are '100 per cent natural'. Using essence would overcome shelf-life difficulties but their use would not be consistent with the brand propositions. Finally, preservatives were in most soft drinks on the market but the management felt that they could compromise Ballygowan's image of purity and naturalness.

### Product concept and brand name development

The development of the product concept and branding began with brainstorming sessions by Dimension. Ballygowan's specification for the name was that it should be relevant, attractive, distinctive, memorable, registerable and have the attributes of a global brand name. Out of the hundreds of names generated Juisca, Juzze, Artesia, Kisqua, Prima, and Viva became prototype brand names. Five positioning options also helped explore the attitudes and motivations of soft-drink consumers:

1. *Health drink.* A pure, natural and healthy drink for mainstream soft-drink consumers who care about what they consume.
2. *Sophisticated.* A high-status drink of superior quality for discerning consumers.
3. *Healthy lifestyle.* For those who unselfconsciously lead and aspire to a healthy but full lifestyle in terms of diet, exercise and a relaxed but full life.
4. *Youthful peer groupies.* The Pepsi/Club generation.
5. *Generic.* Refreshment, cooling, youthful and Coke sociability values.

A market research agency, Behaviour & Attitudes, designed and conducted four focus groups representing market segments with different relationship to soft drinks (see Exhibit 6.6). The focus groups aimed to:

## CASE 6 (cont)

**Exhibit 6.5**   Summary ratings

| | Orange peach (15% juice) | Orange lemon (10% juice) | Club orange | Orange (10% juice) | Orange passion fruit (15% juice) | Lemon (10% juice) | Club lemon | Grapefruit and pineapple (15% juice) |
|---|---|---|---|---|---|---|---|---|
| *Aroma* | | | | | | | | |
| Attractiveness | 5 | 3 | 4 | 2 | 3 | 4 | 4 | 2 |
| Naturalness | 5 | 2 | 2 | 2 | 4 | 3 | 3 | 2 |
| Overall | 5 | 3 | 3 | 2 | 3 | 4 | 4 | 2 |
| *Appearance* | | | | | | | | |
| Attractiveness | 4 | 2 | 5 | 1 | 3 | 5 | 2 | 3 |
| Naturalness | 5 | 3 | 4 | 1 | 3 | 5 | 3 | 3 |
| Overall | 5 | 3 | 5 | 2 | 3 | 5 | 4 | 2 |
| *Flavour* | | | | | | | | |
| Good taste | 4 | 3 | 5 | 1 | 3 | 4 | 5 | 1 |
| Real fruit flavour | 5 | 3 | 3 | 1 | 4 | 5 | 3 | 1 |
| Sweetness (right) | 5 | 3 | 3 | 3 | 3 | 5 | 5 | 3 |
| Refreshment | 5 | 3 | 5 | 1 | 3 | 5 | 5 | 1 |
| Overall taste | 5 | 3 | 4 | 1 | 4 | 4 | 4 | 1 |
| Overall rating | 5 | 4 | 4 | 1 | 3 | 4 | 5 | 1 |

Key:   5   Well above average
       4   Above average
       3   Average
       2   Below average
       1   Well below average

Source:   Behaviour & Attitudes, Market Research Survey, May 1989.

- Investigate the response to five prototype brand names.
- Explore reaction to seven prototype pack designs.
- Consider pack designs and bottling formats.
- Give direction to brand positioning.

Discussions with each group followed a similar pattern. Initially respondents freely discussed their use and purchase of soft drinks. This naturally led to conversations about different brands. Next, the groups were told about the new idea for a soft drink and shown a board illustrating the new product concept. Following their responses to the concept the groups were told that there were alternative prototype brand names and packaging designs. These were presented one by one, with the order of presentation being rotated between different groups. Proposed brand names and pack designs were presented separately.

Later, discussion group members were asked to help market the new brand; 'mood boards' were presented and associated with the different brand names and pack designs. Finally, copy statements, presented on boards representing different positioning options, were discussed.

In September 1989, Behaviour & Attitudes debriefed Ballygowan about the research. First, they presented consumer attitudes to soft drinks generally (see Exhibit 6.7). The research indicated that teenage men, teenage girls and young married women had different attitudes and motivations to soft drinks. Secondly, they examined consumer attitudes to soft-drink brands (see Exhibit 6.8) and consumer reaction to the five prototype brands (see Exhibit 6.9). Behaviour & Attitudes made the following points about reactions to the product concepts:

1. The ingredients make it more sophisticated than mainstream soft drinks.

**Exhibit 6.6**   Focus groups

The four groups were:

1. Young teenage girls   Middle class
2. Young men          18–24   $C_1 C_2$
3. Women             22–32   $C_2$ with children
4. Women             22–32   $B_1 B_2$ with children

Target   markets

| Primary | Secondary |
|---|---|
| Health/body conscious ABCI | Soft-drink consumers |
| Late teens/twenties | |
| Young and early teens | |
| Teenage adults | |

Source:   Behaviour & Attitudes, Market Research, August 1989.

2. It was not seen as a totally novel idea. Consumers were aware of Nashs, Citrus Spring and Britvic.
3. The pleasant product and the endorsement of Ballygowan aroused a high predisposition to try it.
4. Price parity with Coke and 7-Up raised consumers' disposition to try the product.

A series of meetings between Dimension and the Ballygowan management team considered brand positioning and target market strategies. They chose Kisqua as the brand name. It was stylish, novel, distinctive, memorable, appropriate, warm and had the attributes of a world brand name. Ballygowan Spring Water's name would endorse Kisqua. Ballygowan also applied for registration of Artesia in case the company should wish to launch an up-market spring water.

*Marketing mix*

The Ballygowan company next needed to know the impact of the brand name, label design, price, positioning and advertising options on Kisqua's branding strategy. A further question was the reason for people's preference for Kisqua or Club Orange. In October 1989 Behaviour & Attitudes researched these key areas. They used a central location to approach a quota sample of 200 respondents. The respondents were in two equal subgroups: one group to taste-test Club Orange and Kisqua blind, and the other group with both products branded. The results in percentages were:

| | Blind | Branded |
|---|---|---|
| Prefer Club a lot | 59 | 39 |
| Prefer Club a little | 16 | 19 |
| Prefer Kisqua a lot | 19 | 0 |
| Prefer Kisqua a little | 6 | 6 |
| No preferences | 6 | 3 |

**Exhibit 6.7**   General consumer attitudes to soft drinks

| Young men | Young girls | Young married women |
|---|---|---|
| • Perceived as the province of children and teenagers<br>• Believe they are not emotionally involved in the market<br>• Yet they are regular consumers – for thirst/refreshment<br>• Therefore taste and refreshment are their criteria for judging soft drinks<br>• Coca-Cola is the preferred brand<br>• They associate 7-Up with contemporary youth, and refreshment<br>• Will be difficult to impress – little emotional interest in soft drinks | • Very involved with brands as badges of both individuality and groups<br>• Very conscious of style and fashion<br>• Very high level of health consciousness<br>• Brands reflect social valuations and status – Ballygowan, Perrier and 7-Up are stylish, sophisticated and healthy<br>• Are high-volume users of soft drinks | • Regular purchasers for themselves and their families<br>• Soft drinks are an essential household purchase item<br>• Oriented towards health and exercise, and reflected in their attitude to food and drink brands<br>• Disposed towards natural products, and low-calorie products<br>• 'Natural' products identified as contemporary and fashionable<br>• Working class want brands to be accessible – middle class focus on style |

**CASE 6 (cont)**

**Exhibit 6.8**   Consumer attitudes to soft-drink brands

*Coke*
- Perceived as the archetypal soft drink.
- Strong consistent branding, massive advertising support.
- Two problems: perceived by some as harsh, causing tooth decay, overly masculine personality.

*Club Orange*
- The archetypal orange soft drink.
- Its appeal is primarily based on its product characteristics – real orange taste with lots of orange in it.
- Advertising not consistent with the brand.

*Lilt*
- Has no clear product focus – a mix of different things.
- Dissonance between advertising and product knowledge.

*7-Up*
- Very coherent brand, with well-rounded persona.
- Very popular and the most contemporary soft drink.
- 'The soft drink for the 1990s.'
- Healthy perception – clean and clear.
- Appeals to male and female.
- Not limited to teenagers: helped by its mixer usage; helped by its healthy image.
- Strong perception of being refreshed.

*Club Lemon*
- Valued for its product characteristics of taste and refreshment.
- Very loyal consumers – almost a cult.

*Lucozade*
- Strong healthy drink imagery.
- Regarded as a soft drink by young men.
- Well out of its old hospital/sick bed positioning.
- Reparative quality for handling hangovers.

**Exhibit 6.9**   Consumer reactions to five prototype brands

| Prototype brand | Reaction to name | Reaction to design |
| --- | --- | --- |
| Artesia | • Distinctive but difficult to come to terms with.<br>• Far too up-market/exclusive.<br>• Not appropriate to the product concept.<br>• Will not appeal to a mass market.<br>• More relevant to wine. | • Very up-market, albeit very beautiful.<br>• Very designery, 'yuppie' and exclusive.<br>• Very aspirational.<br>• Very distinctive, but so sophisticated as to exclude the large majority. |
| Prima | • Very favourably received by working class – very easy to empathize with.<br>• Straightforward, direct and impactful for the working class.<br>• Targeted at mass market – no pretensions.<br>• But, rejected by middle class.<br>• Just another name, pedestrian.<br>• Little depth of imagery.<br>• Association with Pennys gives it a downmarket image.<br>• No distinctiveness. | • Appealed only to a small minority, and contemporary.<br>• Otherwise perceived as oriented to very young children.<br>• Very dissonant with product concept. |
| Viva | • Strong appeal to teenage girls – they associated it with beauty, fashion and style.<br>• International – but cliché and pedestrian.<br>• Strong negative Spanish association: cheap Spanish orange drink; 'Viva España'; Costa del Sol.<br>• Lively, bright, extrovert and exuberant.<br>• Dynamic and modern brand. | • Lacked novelty, not stylish, not sophisticated.<br>• Cheap.<br>• Dissonant with the Ballygowan heritage.<br>• Looked Spanish – negative imagery.<br>• Blue colour not liked. |

### Exhibit 6.9   *(cont)*

| Prototype brand | Reaction to name | Reaction to design |
|---|---|---|
| Juzze | • Significant pronunciation difficulties.<br>• Superficial and artificial.<br>• Yet youthful, contemporary and up to date.<br>• International.<br>• Correlated with the product concept, except for a phoniness in its spelling.<br>• Associated with zest, zing and vitality.<br>• Suggested pure fruit juice. | • In mainstream of soft-drinks market.<br>• Very OK, but no surprise, or aspirational qualities.<br>• Lacks excitement or fun, too logical.<br>• Consistently compared with Squeez and Britvic – but concentrated – is not pure orange juice.<br>• Might position it against Britvic rather than Club. |
| Kisqua | • Pronunciation initially difficult, but quickly overcome.<br>• Very definite and individualistic name.<br>• Novel and unique brand name.<br>• Drew favourable emotional relationships.<br>• International and cosmopolitan – potential to be a 'world brand'.<br>• Elegant and sophisticated.<br>• High quality and accessible. | • The best representative of the new product.<br>• Much more depth than other concept alternatives.<br>• Good impact, will generate trial easily.<br>• Stylish yet solidly in the mainstream of soft drinks – but a bit too straightforward?<br>• Very good typography. |

Ballogowan believed that by working on Kisqua's colour and sweetness they could significantly improve its appeal to the market, and also develop much higher ratings by fine-tuning Kisqua's advertising strategy. Response to Kisqua's name was positive: 71 per cent liked the name Kisqua compared to 20 per cent who did not. When assessing Kisqua's label, 36 per cent of respondents considered it above average, 36 per cent average and 26 per cent below average.

Two advertising concepts were presented. 'Kisqua – what could be more natural' received better than average scores from 38 per cent of respondents, while 45 per cent rated it average. Projective tests associated Kisqua with sports-minded and health-conscious people and with people who really care about quality and who may be described as trendsetters. The target market was confirmed as soft-drink consumers in social classes ABC1C2, 15–30 years, and of either sex. Following the research, Dimension made the appropriate adjustment to the advertising concept.

Pack design was a very important aspect of this project. Ballygowan had proprietorial rights to their distinctive bottle designs used for their spring water range. However, they believed that Kisqua should be differentiated from their other products and that the branding and bottle design of Kisqua should help distinguish it within the soft-drinks market. The pack design assumed that Kisqua would compete directly with Club Orange.

### Business plan

Initially the business plan had Kisqua available in three pack sizes: 1.5 litre plastic, 250 ml. glass and 330 ml. cans. Distribution would be through the existing Ballygowan network of grocery, wholesalers (grocery and bottlers), cash-and-carry and independent outlets.

Three pricing options were considered: a low pricing strategy which would put Kisqua into the market with prices comparable to Coke and 7-Up, a medium pricing strategy, and a high pricing strategy positioning Kisqua as a premium brand. Early projections gave strategies yielding the following percentage market shares in 1990:

| | Plastic | Cans | Overall[1] |
|---|---|---|---|
| Low-price strategy | 4.2 | 3.1 | 3.0 |
| Medium-price strategy | 3.3 | 2.2 | 2.1 |
| High-price strategy | 2.1 | 1.5 | 1.6 |

## CASE 6 (cont)

**Exhibit 6.10** Profit projections before tax for Kisqua (I£'000)

|  | Year 1 | Year 2 | Year 3 |
|---|---|---|---|
| *Low price strategy* |  |  |  |
| Low volume | (311) | (129) | (36) |
| Likely volume | (33) | 241 | 382 |
| High volume | 262 | 634 | 825 |
| *Medium price strategy* |  |  |  |
| Low volume | (371) | (211) | (128) |
| Likely volume | (63) | 200 | 336 |
| High volume | 341 | 702 | 902 |
| *High price strategy* |  |  |  |
| Low volume | (346) | (177) | 90 |
| Likely volume | (84) | 172 | 304 |
| High volume | 297 | 690 | 876 |

The Marketing Department projected that these volumes would increase by 33 per cent during the second year and by 16 per cent during the third year. After three years and assuming a medium pricing strategy, Kisqua's market share would be approximately 3 per cent of Ireland's soft-drinks market. This compared with Club Orange's 10 per cent market share in 1990.

With a capital investment of I£1.5 million and I£120,000 for additional technical staff, generous trade margins and all other relevant costs, the profits projections before tax for Kisqua were as set out in Exhibit 6.10.

The medium pricing strategy aimed at a retail selling price of I£1.19 per 1.5 litre bottle and 40p per can in supermarkets. This gave a reasonable return on investment and room to discount to supermarkets to compete with Coke and 7-Up if necessary (see Exhibit 6.11).

### Test market

From August to October 1990 Ballygowan test marketed Kisqua as a pasteurized drink in 250 ml. glass bottles. The test was conducted in the Dublin area using Ballygowan's main independent distributor serving 250 CTNs (combined confectioner, tobacconist and newsagent's), delicatessens and petrol stations. The results were discouraging. Most of the negative reaction centred around the pack and retailers not knowing where to position the range in their store. Ballygowan now faced a difficult decision. Should they withdraw Kisqua altogether, redesign and reposition it, or go ahead as originally planned? They knew that if they were to delay and relaunch, the payback of the expensive research and development would be put back considerably.

**Exhibit 6.11** Kisqua: business plan for Year 1

|  | 1.5L Pet | 250 ml. bottles | 330 ml. cans |
|---|---|---|---|
| *Retail selling price (I£)* | 1.05 | – | 0.33 |
| Net revenue per case wholesale (I£) | 8.44 | 7.00 | 5.30 |
| Volume (cases) |  |  |  |
| low | 200,000 | 30,000 | 125,000 |
| likely | 300,000 | 50,000 | 175,000 |
| high | 400,000 | 75,000 | 225,000 |
| *Retail selling price (I£)* | 1.19 | – | 0.40 |
| Net revenue per case wholesale (I£) | 8.93 | 7.00 | 6.00 |
| Volume (cases) |  |  |  |
| low | 125,000 | 30,000 | 75,000 |
| likely | 200,000 | 50,000 | 125,000 |
| high | 300,000 | 75,000 | 175,000 |
| *Retail selling price (I£)* | 1.29 | – | 0.45 |
| Net revenue per case wholesale (I£) | 9.68 | 7.00 | 6.50 |
| Volume (cases) |  |  |  |
| low | 100,000 | 30,000 | 60,000 |
| likely | 150,000 | 50,000 | 85,000 |
| high | 225,000 | 75,000 | 125,000 |

## CASE 6 (cont)

### Questions

1. Examine the types of market research used by Ballygowan in the development of Kisqua. What sort of information were they hoping to get from the different methods they used? Is quantitative marketing research intrinsically more reliable than qualitative research?

2. Relate the market research to the stages in the product development process and explain their use. Were the methods appropriately used? What alternatives would you suggest? How did they contribute to Ballygowan's understanding of the strategy for launching Kisqua?

3. Why could in-depth marketing research lead to wrong strategic choices? Do marketing research errors explain Kisqua's poor test market showing? What does explain the poor showing? Was too much, or too little, market research done by Ballygowan?

4. Where should Ballygowan go from here? What extra research should they do, if any? Should they go ahead with the existing marketing strategy, reposition the product, start again or give in?

### Note

1. Includes plastic bottles, cans and glass bottles.

# Mitsui & Company

## Colin Egan and Peter McKiernan*

Mitsui & Co. is one of Japan's leading and oldest general trading corporations (GTC, or *sogo shosha*). Its activities include import–export, commercial development, technology transfer and offshore trade. Mitsui is also a core company of the Mitsui Group, which comprises over 70 large Japanese firms. By the late 1980s, Mitsui itself had 219 overseas subsidiaries, and about 165 overseas offices. Total trading transactions for fiscal year 1988–9 (ending 31 March) were ¥16,800bn, of which 14.2 per cent were from its European operations. European trade transactions amounted to ¥2,390bn, up 33.6 per cent on the year.

1 ecu = US$1.26 = ¥122 (Japanese yen)

Only four years after Mitsui's formation in 1876, it opened its first European trading office in London. Following World War II, Mitsui returned to Europe and had developed substantial trading subsidiaries in London, Stockholm, Oslo, Helsinki, Dusseldorf, Hamburg, Munich, Brussels, Amsterdam, Paris, Milan, Lisbon, Madrid and Barcelona, with offices also in Dublin, Athens and Vienna. In 1974, it established a regional headquarters (RHQ) in London under the name of Mitsui Europe Ltd to manage operations in Western and Eastern Europe as well as in Africa. The new RHQ coordinated the local offices, which operated principally in their own countries. By 1989, Mitsui had 26 offices and 32 affiliated companies in nineteen European countries.

## RESPONDING TO A SINGLE EUROPE

Mitsui responded positively to the prospect for West European economic integration. The company's president, Koichiro Ejiri, was also head of the Keidanren (Japan's most influential business group) EC committee and had been trying to calm Japanese corporate worries about 'Fortress Europe'. The company advocated an 'insiderization' strategy. Regarding post-1992 Europe, the company's 1989 annual report said: 'Mitsui will not be on the outside looking in. Mitsui will be an insider at the grassroots level ... Mitsui is at home everywhere in the world.' Moreover, unification of the European market would allow Mitsui to realize significant economies of scale in administration and trading activity.

---

* Of Leicester Business School and Warwick Business School, with permission based on 'Mitsui' in Colin Egan and Peter McKiernan, *Inside Fortress Europe: Strategies for the single market* (Wokingham, Berks.: Addison-Wesley, 1994).

## THE FIRST STEP

After the Single European Act, Japanese interest in how to cope with the prospect of European integration soared. To fortify Mitsui's already strong position in Europe, the company established an EC '92 task force to monitor the progress of the Single Market. The task force was set up simultaneously in the Tokyo head office and in the London RHQ. The Tokyo group had seven or eight representatives from key corporate divisions, including finance, accounting, tax, legal, credit, corporate planning and information and research.

After its establishment in mid-1988, the task force focused initially on internal corporate education. They set up a centralized location in Tokyo to collect all documents, press articles or other material from banks or private companies on the EC. Mitsui also held educational seminars for company executives and managers and began publishing an EC newsletter on the progress of EC integration.

By 1989, the task of internal education had largely been accomplished and the overall strategy determined. Mitsui ceased general educational activities in favour of assisting the various operating groups – from motor vehicles to food – to solve their individual problems and determine their strategies. The task force acted as an information clearing house and a consultant for Mitsui operating groups and clients as well as for companies not associated with the Mitsui group.

The Information and Research Division (I&RD) gathered information on the progress of EC integration. I&RD sometimes drafted reports on significant events and distributed them among Mitsui and other business people. Requests for assistance soon focused on concrete business questions since general information was no longer so important. However, very specialized information, strictly connected with business activity, was needed by Mitsui's affiliates and clients.

The combination of the discussions coordinated by the EC '92 task force and Mitsui's long-term direction towards globalization resulted in a strategy for EC '92. It stressed the reorganization of Mitsui's European operations on a pan-European basis and a campaign to establish Mitsui and its associates as European 'insiders' through a massive increase in European investment.

## INSIDERIZATION

The number of Mitsui affiliated manufacturing and service companies with investments in the Community doubled from thirty-three in August 1987 to sixty-seven by August 1988, when even more projects were pending. Among the investments was the establishment by Mitsui's Iron & Steel Group of Mi-King Ltd, a service centre joint venture, with William King Ltd (the largest independent steel service centre in the United Kingdom) to handle steel processing and storage for automotive and other manufacturers. Mitsui also entered into a joint venture with Italy's Olivetti and Japan's Sanyo Electric Co. Ltd to manufacture facsimile machines in Italy and market them in Europe and the United States.

In keeping with its functions as a *sogo shosha*, Mitsui also helped smaller firms to set up in the EC under the slogan 'Let's Go With Mitsui!'. Mitsui found that medium-sized companies usually lacked the staff and organizational resources to effectively enter the EC on their own. They believed that by using this approach, the opportunities for a general trading company in the EC were enormous.

Most of those smaller companies were parts and component makers associated with big Japanese automotive, electronics or electrical machinery firms. However,

Mitsui had also made a variety of investments in the retail field to enhance its sales network. These included a high-class boutique in London's stylish Bond Street together with large Japanese retailers Isetan, Japan Travel Bureau and Nitto Kogyo.

## INTERNAL REORGANIZATION

EC '92 would give Mitsui an opportunity to reorganize its operations on a pan-European basis. This could significantly enhance the role of the RHQ in London relative to local Mitsui offices and affiliates and the head office in Tokyo. The vehicle for this revamping of European operations could be the passage of a European Company Statute (ECS). Until the late 1980s, the subsidiaries or offices in the United Kingdom, West Germany, France, Benelux, Italy, Spain and Portugal had been 100 per cent owned by Mitsui in Tokyo. This state of affairs should change with the ECS.

One of the main concerns of Mitsui and other Japanese companies with the proposed ECS was labour management. Firms that decided to operate under the ECS would have to choose one of three worker-participation models: the German system of codetermination; the Belgian, French and Italian system of independent internal workers' councils; or a Scandinavian-type approach where the form of worker representation was determined through companywide collective bargaining.

The move could create separate and independent 'inside' owners not controlled from Tokyo. Mitsui state that their European operation will face towards the EU, not Japan. In preparation for this development, Mitsui strengthened the RHQ. The ceiling for new investments (including manufacturing investments, acquisitions or other forms of participation) the RHQ could launch without approval from Tokyo was substantially raised. Moreover additional staff bolstered the RHQ.

Although Mitsui acknowledged that the primary responsibility for strategy would still rest in Tokyo, EC matters were to be resolved by the RHQ. Thus the company would need more staff, especially in the field of corporate planning, to advise the decision makers in the European headquarters.

It would also affect Mitsui's marketing and distribution management. In 1989, each country subsidiary carried out its own distribution, focusing mainly on bulk raw materials or industrial machinery along with consumer goods. Although the activities were common, the merchandise was not necessarily the same; for example, France and Germany sold different brands of industrial machinery. Mitsui encouraged its country offices to assume pan-European sectoral or product specializations. For example, Mitsui UK took the initiative in fertilizers, while the Brussels office specialized in dairy products throughout the EC. This effort paved the way for a more unified marketing and distribution agreement post-1992.

## QUESTIONS

1. Describe each of the steps taken by Mitsui in reaction to the Single Market. Explain the reason for each step. Why is it necessary for Mitsui to react in the way it did?
2. How does Mitsui handle information about European integration? What sort of information do you think should be in Mitsui's information system for Europe? How much importance do Mitsui attach to information and education? Is their interest in education and training typical of other Japanese or European companies?

3. Why do you think American and Japanese companies have been faster in taking a pan-European approach than many European companies? Given the diversity of economies and consumers, is Mitsui too early in adopting a pan-European strategy?

4. What does Mitsui gain from having a strengthened RHQ? What advantages are gained from the pan-European and sector responsibilities of the country offices? Why do you think they were only 'encouraged' to take on these roles? Do you think the new structure will slow down Mitsui's decision making and make their European operation slower and more difficult to control than it was before?

# Buyer behaviour

## CHAPTER SEVEN

# Consumer markets

## CHAPTER OBJECTIVES

After reading this chapter, you should be able to:

- Define the consumer market and construct a simple model of consumer buying behaviour.

- Tell how culture, subculture and social class influence consumer buying behaviour.

- Describe how consumers' personal characteristics and primary psychological factors affect their buying decisions.

- Discuss how consumer decision making varies with the type of buying decision.

- Explain the stages of the buyer decision and adoption processes.

## CHAPTER PREVIEW

### Porsche: a special car for the special few

Top managers at Porsche spend a great deal of time thinking about customers. They want to know who their customers are, what they think and how they feel and why they buy a Porsche rather than a Jaguar, a Ferrari or a Mercedes coupé. These are difficult questions – even Porsche owners themselves don't know exactly what motivates their buying. But management needs to put top priority on understanding customers and what makes them tick.

Porsche appeals to a very narrow segment of financially successful people – achievers who set very high goals for themselves and then work doggedly to meet them. They expect no less from 'their hobbies or the clothes they wear or the restaurants they go to or the cars they drive'. These achievers see themselves not as a regular part of the larger world, but as exceptions. They buy Porsches because the car mirrors their self-image – it stands for the things owners like to see in themselves and in their lives.

Most people buy what Porsche executives call utility vehicles – 'cars to be used: to go to work, to deliver the kids, to go shopping'. We base buying decisions on facts like price, size, function, fuel economy and other practical considerations. But a Porsche is more than a utility car – it is to be enjoyed, not just used. Most Porsche buyers are moved not by facts, but by feelings – they are trying to match their dreams. A Porsche is like a piece of clothing, 'something the owner actually wears and is seen in. … It's a very personal relationship, one that has to do with the way the car sounds, the way it vibrates, the way it feels.' People buy Porsches because they enjoy driving the car, just being in it. 'Just to get there, they could do it a lot less expensively. The car is an expression of themselves.' Surprisingly, many Porsche owners are not car enthusiasts – they are not interested in racing or learning how to drive a high-performance car. They simply like the way a Porsche makes them feel or what the car tells others about their achievements, lifestyles and stations in life.

A Porsche costs a lot of money, but price isn't much of an issue with such car buyers. The company deals often with people who can buy anything they want. To many Porsche owners, the car is a hobby. In fact, Porsche's competition comes not just from other cars, but from such things as yachts, country cottages and light aircraft. But 'most of those objects require a lot of one thing these people don't have – time. If you have a Porsche and make *it* your hobby, you can enjoy it every day on your way to work and on your way to the airport, something you can't do with a yacht or country cottage'.

Porsche has traditionally worked hard to meet its buyers' expectations, but in the mid-1980s, the company made a serious marketing blunder. It increased its sales goal by nearly 50 per cent, to 60,000 cars a year. To meet this volume goal, Porsche emphasized lower-priced models that sold for as little as DM 30,000. The chance to buy a Porsche at close to regular car prices attracted many new customers and in 1986 the company sold 49,976 – more than 60 per cent of them in the United States. Porsche had shifted from *class* to *mass* marketing. Also, after decades of priding itself on progressive engineering, high performance and tasteful and timeless styling, the company allowed its models to date. The first 911 Ferdinand Porsche appeared at the 1963 Frankfurt motor show. These moves tarnished Porsche's exclusive image and confused its loyal but demanding customers. At the same time, Porsche was battered by a falling US dollar and increasingly fierce competition from the Nissan 300ZX, Mazda RX-7, Honda NXS and other rivals pushing new luxury sports cars. As a result, Porsche's sales fell by 51 per cent in 1988.

1 ecu = US$1.26 = DM 1.89 (Deutschmarks)

Porsche fought to rebuild its damaged image and to regain rapport with its customers. It revamped its model lines, once again targeting the high end of the market. Production of the cheap, four-cylinder Porsche 924 ended; the 1989 range started at DM 60,000 and went up to DM 115,000. It revised its sales goal to 40,000 cars a year but by 1992 sales dropped to 23,060 with the United States accounting for only 4,133. Costly production added to Porsche's problems. Even after taking drastic action in cutting the workforce and using lean production, by 1994 it still took Porsche 85 hours to make a 911 compared with Honda's 50 hours for their NXS.

The company now looks for only moderate but profitable growth; it wants to make one less Porsche than the demand. 'We need to reach competitive prices worldwide,' says Kurt Wald, Porsche's production director. Hopes are pinned on the launch of the new Boxster model in 1996. This DM 75,000 car aimed at 'the low-price market' was designed in a new way for Porsche. 'In the past, we would have developed the car, then worked out how much it would cost to build,' admits Horst Marchart, their engineering chief. The Boxster will take 60 hours to build compared with the 85 hours for the 911.

According to one executive: 'we aren't looking for volume … we're searching for exclusivity.' Porsche does all it can to make Porsche ownership very special. It has even hired a representative to sell its cars to celebrities, executives of large companies, top athletes and other notables. Having high-profile individuals driving Porsches and talking to their friends about them is the best advertising the company could get.

Thus understanding Porsche buyers is an essential but difficult task – the company must carefully craft the car and its image to match buyer needs and desires. But buyers are moved by a complex set of deep and subtle motivations. Buyer behaviour springs from deeply held values and attitudes, from their views of the world and their place in it, from what they think of themselves and what they want others to think of them, from rationality and common sense and from whimsy and impulse. The chief executive at Porsche summed it up this way: 'If you really want to understand our customers, you have to understand the phrase, "If I were going to be a car, I'd be a Porsche".'[1]

---

The Porsche example shows that many different factors affect consumer buying behaviour. Buying behaviour is never simple, yet understanding it is the essential task of marketing management.

This chapter and the next explore the dynamics of consumer behaviour and the consumer market. **Consumer buying behaviour** refers to the buying behaviour of final consumers – individuals and households who buy goods and services for personal consumption. All of these final consumers combined make up the **consumer market**. The world consumer market consists of about 5.5 billion people, but the billion people living in North America, Western Europe and Japan make up 70 per cent of the world's spending power.[2] Even within these wealthy consumer markets, consumers vary tremendously in age, income, education level and tastes. They also buy an incredible variety of goods and services. How these diverse consumers make their choices among various products embraces a fascinating array of factors.

## MODELS OF CONSUMER BEHAVIOUR

In earlier times, marketers could understand consumers well through the daily experience of selling to them. But as firms and markets have grown in size, many marketing decision makers have lost direct contact with their customers and must now turn to consumer research. They now spend more money than ever to study consumers, trying to learn more about consumer behaviour. Who buys? How do they buy? When do they buy? Where do they buy? Why do they buy?

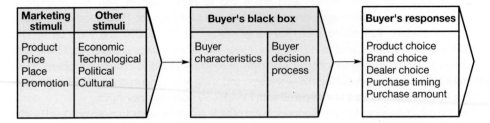

**Figure 7.1**    Model of buyer behaviour.

The central question for marketers is: How do consumers respond to various marketing stimuli the company might use? The company that really understands how consumers will respond to different product features, prices and advertising appeals has a great advantage over its competitors. Therefore, companies and academics have researched heavily the relationship between marketing stimuli and consumer response. Their starting point is the stimulus–response model of buyer behaviour shown in Figure 7.1. This figure shows that marketing and other stimuli enter the consumer's 'black box' and produce certain responses. Marketers must figure out what is in the buyer's black box.[3]

Marketing stimuli consist of the four Ps: product, price, place and promotion. Other stimuli include significant forces and events in the buyer's environment: economic, technological, political and cultural. All these stimuli enter the buyer's black box, where they are turned into a set of observable buyer responses (shown on the right side of Figure 7.1): product choice, brand choice, dealer choice, purchase timing and purchase amount.

The marketer wants to understand how the stimuli are changed into responses inside the consumer's black box, which has two parts. First, the buyer's characteristics influence how he or she perceives and reacts to the stimuli. Second, the buyer's decision process itself affects the buyer's behaviour. This chapter looks first at buyer characteristics as they affect buying behaviour, and then examines the buyer decision process. We will never know what exactly is in the black box or be able perfectly to predict consumer behaviour, but the models can help us understand consumers, help us to ask the right questions, and teach us how to influence them.[4]

## CHARACTERISTICS AFFECTING CONSUMER BEHAVIOUR

Consumer purchases are influenced strongly by cultural, social, personal and psychological characteristics, as shown in Figure 7.2. For the most part, marketers cannot control such factors, but they must take them into account. We illustrate these characteristics for the case of a hypothetical customer, Elena Klein. Elena is a married graduate who works as a brand manager in a leading consumer packaged-goods company. She wants to buy a camera to take on holiday. Many characteristics in her background will affect the way she evaluates cameras and chooses a brand.

### Cultural factors

Cultural factors exert the broadest and deepest influence on consumer behaviour. The marketer needs to understand the role played by the buyer's culture, subculture and social class.

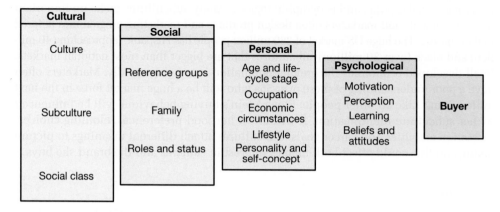

**Figure 7.2** Factors influencing behaviour.

## Culture

**Culture** is the most basic cause of a person's wants and behaviour. Human behaviour is largely learned. Growing up in a society, a child learns basic values, perceptions, wants and behaviours from the family and other important institutions. Like most Western people, in her childhood Elena observed and learned values about achievement and success, activity and involvement, efficiency and practicality, progress, material comfort, individualism, freedom, humanitarianism, youthfulness, and fitness and health. Sometimes we take these values for granted, but they are not cultural universals. Germany's Free Democratic Party found this when they ran a standard campaign across the whole of Germany. Its slogans and posters that concentrated on Leistungsfähigkeit (efficiency) meant nothing to the easterners, explained Wulf Oehme, FDP's party manager:

> There is, as yet, no strong entrepreneurial middle-class elite in eastern Germany. Also, if we used slogans extolling liberation values, which is also the basis of our support in the west, we found that these values had little relevance for the easterners.[5]

Elena Klein's wanting a camera is a result of being raised in a modern society which has developed camera technology and a whole set of consumer learning and values. Elena knows what cameras are. She can read instructions and her society has accepted the idea of photography.

Marketers are always trying to spot *cultural shifts* in order to imagine new products that might be wanted. For example, the cultural shift towards greater concern about health and fitness has created a huge industry for exercise equipment and clothing, lower-calorie and more natural foods, and health and fitness services. This allowed Snapple to change the face of the US soft-drinks market with its 'new age' iced teas and fruit-flavoured drinks. The shift towards informality has resulted in more demand for casual clothing, simpler home furnishings and lighter entertainment. And the increased desire for leisure time has resulted in more demand for convenience products and services, such as microwave ovens, fast food and direct line financial services such as First Direct and Direct Line.[6]

## Subculture

Each culture contains smaller **subcultures** or groups of people with shared value systems based on common life experiences and situations. Subcultures include nationalities, religions, racial groups, and geographic regions. Many subcultures make up important market segments and marketers often design products and marketing programmes tailored to their needs.[7] The huge US market of 260 million people has Hispanic (approaching 40 million) and black (over 30 million) subcultures that are bigger than most national markets. In all developed economies the greying population is growing rapidly. Marketers often have a poor understanding of these over-55s who will be a huge market force in the next millennium.[8] Like all other people, Elena Klein's buying behaviour will be influenced by her subculture identification. It will affect her food preferences, clothing choices, recreation activities and career goals. Subcultures attach different meanings to picture taking and this could affect both Elena's interest in cameras and the brand she buys.

### Social class

Almost every society has some form of social class structure. **Social classes** are society's relatively permanent and ordered divisions whose members share similar values, interests and behaviours. The British scale with six social classes is widely used, although all big countries have their own system (see Table 7.1). In these social class is not determined by a single factor, such as income, but is measured as a combination of occupation, income, education, wealth and other variables.

Not only do class systems differ in various parts of the world: the relative sizes of the classes vary with the relative prosperity of countries. The 'diamond'-shaped classification (few people at the top and bottom with most in the middle) in Table 7.1 is typical of developed countries, although the Japanese and Scandinavian scales are flatter. In less developed countries, as in Latin America and Africa, the structure is 'pyramid' shaped with a concentration of poor people at the base. As countries develop, their class structure moves towards the diamond shape, although there is now evidence that the gap between the richest and poorest in the English-speaking countries is now widening.

Some class systems have a greater influence on buying behaviour than others. In most Western countries 'lower' classes may exhibit upward mobility, showing buying behaviour similar to that of the 'upper' classes. But in other cultures, where a caste system gives people a distinctive role, buying behaviour is more firmly linked to social class. Upper classes in almost all societies are often more similar to each other than they are to the rest of their own society. They make choices which are less culture-bound when selecting products and services, including food, clothing, household items and personal-care products, than the lower classes. Generally, the lower social classes are more culture-bound, although young people of all classes less so.[9]

| TABLE 7.1 | *UK socioeconomic classification scheme* | | |
|-----------|------------------|--------------------------------|---|
| Class name | Social status | Occupation of head of household | % of population |
| A | Upper middle | Higher managerial, administrative or professional | 3 |
| B | Middle | Intermediate managerial, administrative or professional | 14 |
| C1 | Lower middle | Supervisors or clerical, junior managerial, administrative or professional | 27 |
| C2 | Skilled working | Skilled manual workers | 25 |
| D | Working | Semiskilled and unskilled manual workers | 19 |
| E | Those at lowest levels of subsistence | State pensioners or widows, casual or lower-grade workers | 12 |

Source:   Office of Population Censuses and Surveys.

Elena Klein's social class may affect her camera decision. If she comes from a higher social class background, her family probably owned an expensive camera and she may have dabbled in photography.

## Social factors

A consumer's behaviour is also influenced by social factors, such as the consumer's small groups, family, and social roles and status. Because these social factors can strongly affect consumer responses, companies must take them into account when designing their marketing strategies.

### Groups

A person's behaviour is influenced by many small groups. Groups which have a direct influence and to which a person belongs are called **membership groups**. Some are *primary groups* with whom there is regular but informal interaction − such as family, friends, neighbours and fellow workers. Some are *secondary groups*, which are more formal and have less regular interaction. These include organizations like religious groups, professional associations and trade unions.

**Reference groups** are groups that serve as direct (face-to-face) or indirect points of comparison or reference in forming a person's attitudes or behaviour. People are often influenced by reference groups to which they do not belong. For example, an **aspirational group** is one to which the individual wishes to belong, as when a teenage soccer player hopes to play some day for Manchester United. He identifies with them, although there is no face-to-face contact between him and the team.

Marketers try to identify the reference groups of their target markets. Reference groups influence a person in at least three ways. They expose the person to new behaviours and lifestyles. They influence the person's attitudes and self-concept because he or she wants to 'fit in'. They also create pressures to conform that may affect the person's product and brand choices. (See Marketing Highlight 7.1.)

The importance of group influence varies across products and brands, but it tends to be strongest for conspicuous purchases.[10] A product or brand can be conspicuous for one of two reasons. First, it may be noticeable because the buyer is one of few people who owns it − luxuries, such as a vintage Wurlitzer juke box or a Rolex, are more conspicuous than necessities because fewer people own the luxuries. Second, a product such as Carlsberg ICE beer or Perrier can be conspicuous because the buyer consumes it in public where others can see it. Figure 7.3 shows how group influence might affect product and brand choices for four types of products − public luxuries, private luxuries, public necessities and private necessities.

A person considering the purchase of a public luxury, such as a yacht, will gener-ally be influenced strongly by others. Many people will notice the yacht because few people own one. If interested, they will notice the brand because the boat is used in public. Thus both the product and the brand will be conspicuous and the opinions of others can strongly influence decisions about whether to own a boat and what brand to buy. At the other extreme, group influences do not much affect decisions for pri-vate necessities because other people will notice neither the product nor the brand.

Manufacturers of products and brands subject to strong group influence must fig-ure out how to reach the opinion leaders in the relevant reference groups. **Opinion leaders** are people within a reference group who, because of special skills, knowl-edge, personality or other characteristics, exert influence on others. Opinion leaders

## Using reference groups to sell: home-party and office-party selling

Many companies capitalize on reference-group influence to sell their products. Home-party and office-party selling involves throwing sales parties in homes or workplaces and inviting friends and neighbours or co-workers to see products demonstrated. Companies such as Mary Kay Cosmetics, Avon and Tupperware are masters at this form of selling.

Mary Kay Cosmetics provides a good example of home-party selling. A Mary Kay beauty consultant (of which there are 170,000) asks different women to host small beauty shows in their homes. Each hostess invites her friends and neighbours for a few hours of refreshments and informal socializing. Within this congenial atmosphere, the Mary Kay representative gives a two-hour beauty plan and free make-up lessons to the guests, hoping that many of them will buy some of the demonstrated cosmetics. The hostess receives a commission on sales plus a discount on personal purchases. Usually, about 60 per cent of the guests buy something, partly because of the influence of the hostess and the other women attending the party.

In recent years, changing demographics have adversely affected home-party selling. Increasingly, women are working, which leaves fewer women with the time for shopping and fewer women at home to host or attend home sales parties. To overcome this problem, most party-plan sellers have followed their customers into the workplace with office-party selling. For example, Avon now trains its 400,000 salespeople to sell through office parties during coffee and lunch breaks and after hours. The company once sold only door to door, but currently picks up a quarter of its sales from buyers at businesses. The well-known home Tupperware party has also invaded the office, as Tupperware 'rush-hour parties' held at the end of the workday in offices. At these parties, office workers meet in comfortable, familiar surroundings, look through Tupperware catalogues, watch product demonstrations and discuss Tupperware products with their friends and associates. Tupperware's 85,000 sales representatives now make about 20 per cent of their sales outside the home.

Home-party and office-party selling are now being used to market everything from cosmetics, kitchenware and lingerie to exercise instruction and handmade suits. Such selling requires a sharp understanding of reference groups and how people influence each other in the buying process.

Sources: See Shannon Thurman, 'Mary Kay still in the pink', *Advertising Age* (4 January 1988), 32; Len Strazewski, 'Tupperware locks in a new strategy', *Advertising Age* (8 February 1988), 30; Kate Ballen, 'Get ready for shopping at work', *Fortune* (15 February 1988), 95–8; and Vic Sussman, 'I was the only virgin at the party', *Sales & Marketing Management* (September 1989), 64–72.

are found in all strata of society and one person may be an opinion leader in certain product areas and an opinion follower in others. Marketers try to identify the personal characteristics of opinion leaders for the products, determine what media they use and direct messages at them.

If Elena Klein buys a camera, both the product and the brand will be visible to others she respects. Her decision to buy the camera and her brand choice may therefore be influenced strongly by some of her groups, such as friends who belong to a photography club.

### Family

Family members can strongly influence buyer behaviour. We can distinguish between two families in the buyer's life. The buyer's parents make up the *family of orientation*. Parents provide a person with an orientation towards religion, politics and economics and a sense of personal ambition, self-worth and love. Even if the buyer no longer interacts very much with parents, they can still significantly influence the

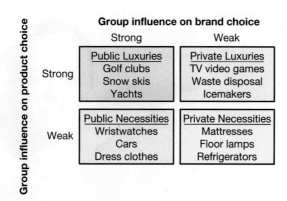

**Figure 7.3** Extent of group influence on product and brand choice. (Source: Adapted from William O. Bearden and Michael J. Etzel, 'Reference group influence on product and brand purchase decisions', *The Journal of Consumer Research* (September 1982), 185. © Journal of Consumer Research Inc., 1982. All rights reserved.)

buyer's behaviour. In countries where parents continue to live with their children, their influence can be crucial.

The *family of procreation* – the buyer's spouse and children – have a more direct influence on everyday buying behaviour. This family is the most important consumer buying organization in society and it has been researched extensively. Marketers are interested in the roles and relative influence of the husband, wife and children on the purchase of a large variety of products and services.

Husband–wife involvement varies widely by product category and by stage in the buying process. Buying roles change with evolving consumer lifestyles. Almost everywhere in the world, the wife is traditionally the main purchasing agent for the family, especially in the areas of food, household products and clothing. But with over 60 per cent or more women holding jobs outside the home in developed countries and the willingness of some husbands to do more of the family's purchasing, all this is changing. For example, in the United States women now buy about 45 per cent of all cars and men account for about 40 per cent of expenditure on food-shopping.[11] Such roles vary widely in different countries and social classes. As always, marketers must research specific patterns in their target markets.

In the case of expensive products and services, husbands and wives more often make joint decisions. Elena Klein's husband may play an *influencer role* in her camera-buying decision. He may have an opinion about her buying a camera and about the kind of camera to buy. At the same time, she will be the primary decider, purchaser and user.[12]

*Consumers' buying roles* Group members can influence purchases in many ways. For example, men normally choose their own newspaper and women choose their own pantyhose. For other products, however, the **decision-making unit** is more complicated with people playing one or more roles:

■ **Initiator** The person who first suggests or thinks of the idea of buying a particular product or service. This could be a parent of friends who would like to see a visual record of Elena's holiday.

■ **Influencer** A person whose view or advice influences the buying decision, perhaps a friend who is a camera enthusiast or a salesperson.

Flora is bought by women (*buyer*) who care about their men (*user*).

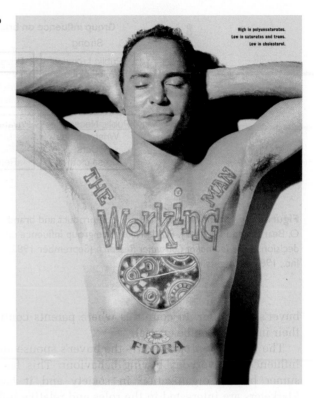

■ **Decider** The person who ultimately makes a buying decision or any part of it – whether to buy, what to buy, how to buy or where to buy.

■ **Buyer** The person who makes an actual purchase. Once the buying decision is made, someone else could make the purchase for the decider.

■ **User** The person who consumes or uses a product or service. Once bought, Elena's camera could be used by other members of her family.

### Roles and status

A person belongs to many groups – family, clubs, organizations. The person's position in each group can be defined in terms of both *role* and *status*. With her parents, Elena Klein plays the role of daughter; in her family, she plays the role of wife; in her company, she plays the role of brand manager. A **role** consists of the activities people are expected to perform according to the persons around them. Each of Elena's roles will influence some of her buying behaviour.

Each role carries a **status** reflecting the general esteem given to it by society. People often choose products that show their status in society. For example, the role of brand manager has more status in our society than the role of daughter. As a brand manager, Elena will buy the kind of clothing that reflects her role and status.

## Personal factors

A buyer's decisions also are influenced by personal characteristics such as the buyer's age and life-cycle stage, occupation, economic situation, lifestyle, and personality and self-concept.

## Age and life-cycle stage

People change the goods and services they buy over their lifetimes. Tastes in food, clothes, furniture and recreation are often age related. Buying is also shaped by the stage of the **family life cycle** – the stages through which families might pass as they mature over time. Table 7.2 lists the stages of the family life cycle. Marketers often define their target markets in terms of life-cycle stage and develop appropriate products and marketing plans for each stage.

Psychological life-cycle stages have also been identified.[13] Adults experience certain passages or transformations as they go through life. Thus Elena Klein may move from being a satisfied brand manager and wife to being an unsatisfied person searching for a new way to fulfil herself. In fact, such a change may have stimulated her strong interest in photography. The main stimuli to people taking photographs are holidays, ceremonies marking the progression through the life cycle (weddings, graduations, and so on), and having children to take photographs of. Marketers must pay attention to the changing buying interests that might be associated with these adult passages.

## Occupation

A person's occupation affects the goods and services bought. Blue-collar workers tend to buy more work clothes, whereas white-collar workers buy more suits and ties. Marketers try to identify the occupational groups that have an above-average interest in their products and services. A company can even specialize in making products needed by a given occupational group. Thus computer software companies will design different products for brand managers, accountants, engineers, lawyers and doctors.

| TABLE 7.2 *Family life-cycle stages* | | |
|---|---|---|
| **Young** | **Middle-aged** | **Older** |
| Single | Single | Older married |
| Married without children | Married without children | Older unmarried |
| Married with children | Married with children | |
|   Infant children |   Young children | |
|   Young children |   Adolescent children | |
|   Adolescent children | Married without dependent children | |
| Divorced with children | Divorced without children | |
| | Divorced with children | |
| |   Young children | |
| |   Adolescent children | |
| | Divorced without dependent children | |

Sources: Adapted from Patrick E. Murphy and William A. Staples, 'A modernized family life cycle', *Journal of Consumer Research* (June 1979), 16; © Journal of Consumer Research, Inc., 1979. Also see Janet Wagner and Sherman Hanna, 'The effectiveness of family life cycle variables in consumer expenditure research', *Journal of Consumer Research* (December 1983), 281–91.

*Economic circumstances*

A person's economic situation will affect product choice. Elena Klein can consider buying an expensive Olympus autofocus superzoom camera if she has enough spendable income, savings or borrowing power. Marketers of income-sensitive goods closely watch trends in personal income, savings and interest rates. If economic indicators point to a recession, marketers can take steps to redesign, reposition and reprice their products.

*Lifestyle*

People coming from the same subculture, social class and occupation may have quite different lifestyles. **Lifestyle** is a person's pattern of living as expressed in his or her activities, interests and opinions. Lifestyle captures something more than the person's social class or personality. It profiles a person's whole pattern of acting and interacting in the world.

The technique of measuring lifestyles is known as *psychographics*. It involves measuring the primary dimensions shown in Table 7.3. The first three are known as the *AIO dimensions* (activities, interests, opinions). Several research firms have developed lifestyle classifications. The most widely used is the SRI *Values and Lifestyles (VALS)* typology. The original VALS typology classifies consumers into nine lifestyle groups according to whether they were inner directed (for example, 'experientials'); outer directed ('achievers', 'belongers'); or need driven ('survivors'). Using this VALS classification, a bank found that the businessmen they were targeting consisted mainly of 'achievers' who were strongly competitive individualists. The bank designed highly successful ads showing men taking part in solo sports such as sailing, jogging and water skiing.[14]

The more recent version, VALS 2, classifies people according to their consumption tendencies – by how they spend their time and money. It divides consumers into eight groups based on two principal dimensions: self-orientation and resources (see Table 7.4). The *self-orientation* dimension captures three different buying approaches: *principle-oriented* consumers buy based upon their views of how the world is or should be; *status-oriented* buyers base their purchases on the actions and opinions of others; and *action-oriented* buyers are driven by their desire for activity, variety and risk-taking. Consumers within each orientation are further classified into

**TABLE 7.3**   *Lifestyle dimensions*

| Activities | Interests | Opinions | Demographics |
|---|---|---|---|
| Work | Family | Themselves | Age |
| Hobbies | Home | Social issues | Education |
| Social events | Job | Politics | Income |
| Vacation | Community | Business | Occupation |
| Entertainment | Recreation | Economics | Family size |
| Club membership | Fashion | Education | Dwelling |
| Community | Food | Products | Geography |
| Shopping | Media | Future | City size |
| Sports | Achievements | Culture | Stage in life cycle |

Source:   Joseph T. Plummer, 'The concept and application of lifestyle segmentation', *Journal of Marketing* (January 1974), 34.

**TABLE 7.4**   *VALS 2: lifestyles*

**Self-orientation**

Principle oriented

Fulfilleds
Mature, responsible, well-educated professionals. Their leisure activities centre on their homes, but they are well informed about what goes on in the world, and they are open to new ideas and social change. They have high incomes, but they are practical, value-oriented consumers.

Believers
Principle-oriented consumers with more modest incomes. They are conservative and predictable consumers who favour domestic products and established brands. Their lives are centred on family, church, community, and nation.

Status oriented

Achievers
Successful, work-oriented people who get ther satisfaction from their jobs and their families. They are politically conservative and respect authority and the status quo. They favour established products and services that show off their success.

Strivers
People with values similar to those of achievers, but fewer economic, social, and psychological resources. Style is extremely important to them as they strive to emulate consumers in other, more resourceful groups.

Action oriented

Experiencers
People who like to affect their environment in tangible ways. They are the youngest of all groups. They have a lot of energy, which they pour into physical exercise and social activities. They are avid consumers, spending heavily on clothing, fast food, music, and other youthful favourites. They especially like new things.

Makers
People who like to affect their environment, but in more practical ways. They value self-sufficiency. They are focused on the familiar – family, work, and physical recreation – and have little interest in the broader world. As consumers, they are unimpressed by material possessions other than those with a practical or functional purpose.

**Resources**

Actualizers
People with the highest incomes and so many resources that they can indulge in any or all self-orientations. Image is important to them, not as evidence of status or power, but as an expression of their taste, independence, and character. Because of their wide range of interests and openness to change, they tend to buy 'the finer things in life'.

Strugglers
People with the lowest incomes and too few resources to be included in any consumer orientation. With their limited means, they tend to be brand-loyal consumers.

Source:   See Martha Farnsworth Riche, 'Psychographics for the 1990s', *American Demographics* (July 1989), 25–31.

one of two *resource* segments, depending on whether they have high or low levels of income, education, health, self-confidence, energy and other factors. Consumers with either very high or very low levels of resources are classified into separate groups without regard to their self-orientations (actualizers, strugglers). The eight VALS 2 lifestyle groups are described in Table 7.4. A person may progress through several of these lifestyles over the course of a lifetime. People's lifestyles affect their buying behaviour. Like all psychographic schemes, VALS 2 segments are most effective for products that engage a consumer's ego. In clothes, fragrances and cars it works, but is less effective for private necessities, such as pencils, baked beans and toilet paper.[15]

## European lifestyle research

Does the 'European Consumer' exist and do lifestyles transcend European borders? These questions have troubled politicians and global companies alike. Several marketing research agencies have conducted pan-European research to find the answer.

Everyday-Life Research by SINUS GmbH, a German company, has identified 'social milieus' covering France, Germany, Italy and the United Kingdom. This study describes the structure of society with five social classes and value orientations:

- Basic orientation: traditional – *to preserve*.
- Basic orientation: materialist – *to have*.
- Changing values: hedonism – *to indulge*.
- Changing values: postmaterialism – *to be*.
- Changing values: postmodernism – *to have, to be and to indulge*.

It distinguishes two types of values: traditional values, emphasizing hard work, thrift, religion, honesty, good manners and obedience; and material values concerned with possession and a need for security. From these, SINUS developed a typology of social milieus (see Table 1): groups of people who share a common set of values and beliefs about work, private relationships, leisure activities and aesthetics, and a common perception of future plans, wishes and dreams. The size and exact nature of these milieus vary between the countries studied but there are broad international comparisons.

Knowing the social milieu of a person can provide information about their everyday life, such as work likes and dislikes, which helps in product development and advertising. The study has found that the up-market segments share a similar structure in all four countries; and it has identified trendsetting milieus in each country, containing heavy consumers with comparable attitudinal and sociodemographic characteristics. Important values shared by all these

### Table 1 Typology of social milieus

| Milieu | Germany | France | Italy | UK | Description |
|---|---|---|---|---|---|
| Upper conservative | Konservatives-gehobenes | Les Héritiers | Neoconservatori | Upper class | Traditional upper-middle class conservatives |
| Traditional mainstream | Kleinbürgerliches | Les conservateurs installés | Piccola borghesia | Traditional middle class | *Petit bourgeois* group mainly oriented to preserving the status quo |
| Traditional working class | Traditionsloses Arbeitermilieu | Les laborieux traditionnels | Cultura operaia | Traditional working class | Traditional blue-collar worker |
| Modern mainstream | Aufstiegsorien-tiertes | Les nouveaux ambitieux | Rampanti, plus crisaldi | Social climbers, plus progressive working class | Social climber and achievement-oriented white- and blue-collar workers |
| Trendsetter | Technokratisch-liberales | Les managers moderns | Borghesia illuminata | Progressive middle class | Technocratic-liberals with a postmaterial orientation |
| Avant-garde | Hedonistisches | Les post-modernistes | Edonisti | 'Thatcher's children' | Mainly young pleasure seekers |
| Sociocritical | Alternatives | Les néo-moralistes | Critica sociale | Socially centred | Pursuing an alternative lifestyle |
| Under-privileged | Traditionsloses Arbeitermilieu | Les oubliés, plus les rebelles hédonistes | Sotto-proletariato urbano | Poor | Uprooted blue-collar workers and destitute |

consumers include: tolerance, open-mindedness, an outward-looking approach; career and success; education and culture; high standard of living; hedonistic luxury consumption; individualism; and Europe.

The Anticipating Change in Europe (ACE) study, by the RISC research agency of Paris, investigated social changes in twelve European countries, the United States, Canada and Japan. The objective was to try to understand how social changes influence market trends. RISC describes people using sociodemographic characteristics, sociocultural profile, activities (sports, leisure, culture), behaviour towards the media (press, radio, television), political inclinations and mood. Using these dimensions, RISC developed six Eurotypes:

1. *The traditionalist* (18 per cent of the European population) is influenced by the culture, socioeconomic history and unique situation of his or her country, with a profile reflecting deep-rooted attitudes specific to that country. Consequently, this is the least homogeneous group across countries.
2. *The homebody* (14 per cent) is driven by a strong attachment to his or her roots and childhood environment. Less preoccupied with economic security than the traditionalist, the homebody needs to feel in touch with the social environment. The homebody seeks warm relationships, and has difficulty coping with violence in society.
3. *The rationalist* (23 per cent) has an ability to cope with unforeseeable and complex situations, and a readiness to take risks and start new endeavours. Personal fulfilment is more about self-expression than financial reward. The rationalist believes science and technology will help resolve the challenges facing humanity.
4. *The pleasurist* (17 per cent) emphasizes sensual and emotional experiences, preferring nonhierarchically structured groups built around self-reliance and self-regulation and not around leaders or formal decision-making processes.
5. *The striver* (15 per cent) holds the attitudes, beliefs and values that underlie the dynamics of social change.

The striver believes in autonomous behaviour and wants to shape his or her life and to exploit mental, physical, sensual and emotional possibilities to the full.

6. *The trend-setter* (13 per cent) favours nonhierarchical social structures and enjoys spontaneity rather than formal procedures. Trendsetters see no need to prove their abilities. Even more individualistic than strivers, they exemplify the flexibile response to a rapidly changing environment.

There are clear similarities between the ACE Eurotypology and the SINUS milieu. The division between *trendsetters* and *traditionalists* occurs in both, as do variations on the *pleasurist* and *strivers*. The French Centre de Communication Avancée (CCA) base their Euro'styles on three dimensions also discernible within the other two studies:

1. Progressive–conservative.
2. Material–spiritual.
3. Rational–emotional.

Many of the sixteen sociostyles found come close to the ACE and SINUS types, although their names are more original. CCA found the first dimension the most powerful. This distinguished between the progressive Euro'dandies, Euro'business, Euro'protests and Euro'pioneers and the conservative Euro'prudents, Euro'vigilantes, Euro'gentry and Euro'stricts. Another group, the Euro'rockies, is highly emotional and materialistic but is neither progressive nor conservative.

These studies do suggest that there are European lifestyles although, as with social class, there is greater similarity between wealthy Europeans than between poor ones. For this reason, luxury brands and their advertising are often more standardized internationally than other products.

The lifestyles give some insight into how Europeans live, work and play, but, like national lifestyles, they do not show how consumers relate to brands or markets. To understand this factor requires more detailed information on attitudes and behaviours towards the product class.

Source: RISC SA, *ACE* (Lyon: RISC SA, 1989); CCA, *CCA Euro'styles* (Paris: CCA, 1989); Norbert Homma and Jorg Uelzhoffer, 'The internationalisation of everyday-life and milieus', ESOMAR Conference on America, Japan and EC'92: The Prospects for Marketing, Advertising and Research, Venice, 18–20 June 1990; Marieke de Mooij, *Advertising Worldwide: Concepts, theories and practice of international and global advertising* (Hemel Hempstead: Prentice Hall, 1994).

Lifestyle classifications are not universal – they can vary significantly from country to country. McCann-Erickson London, for example, found the following British lifestyles: *Avant Guardians* (interested in change); *Pontificators* (traditionalists, very British); *Chameleons* (follow the crowd); and *Sleepwalkers* (contented underachievers). Contrast this with Survey Research Malaysia's seven categories from their developing country: *Upper Echelons* (driven by status and desire to stand out in society); *Not Quite Theres* (ambition for self and family); *Rebel Hangouts* (want to look off mainstream); *Sleepwalkers* (want to get through the day); *Inconspicuous* (want to blend in); *Kampung Trendsetters* (ambitious, city influenced, village dwellers) and *Rural Traditionalists* (abide by traditional rules).[16] Marketing Highlight 7.2 tells of cross-cultural lifestyle systems.

The lifestyle concept, when used carefully, can help the marketer understand changing consumer values and how they affect buying behaviour. Elena Klein, for example, can choose to live the role of a capable homemaker, a career woman or a free spirit – or all three. She plays several roles, and the way she blends them expresses her lifestyle. If she ever became a professional photographer, this would change her lifestyle, in turn changing what and how she buys.

### Personality and self-concept

Each person's distinct personality influences his or her buying behaviour. **Personality** refers to the unique psychological characteristics that lead to relatively consistent and lasting responses to one's own environment. Personality is usually described in terms of traits such as self-confidence, dominance, sociability, autonomy, defensiveness, adaptability and aggressiveness.[17] Personality can be useful in analysing consumer behaviour for certain product or brand choices. For example, coffee makers have discovered that heavy coffee drinkers tend to be high on sociability. Thus Nescafé ads show people coming together over a cup of coffee.

Many marketers use a concept related to personality – a person's **self-concept** (also called *self-image*). The basic self-concept premise is that people's possessions contribute to and reflect their identities: that is, 'we are what we have'. Thus, in order to understand consumer behaviour, the marketer must first understand the relationship between consumer self-concept and possessions. For example, Elena Klein may see herself as outgoing, fun and active. Therefore, she will favour a camera that projects the same qualities. In that case the Polaroid Vision autofocus SLR could attract her. 'The fun develops instantly'.[18]

The concept, admittedly, is not that simple. What if Elena's *actual self-concept* (how she views herself) differs from her *ideal self-concept* (how she would like to view herself) and from her *others self-concept* (how she thinks others ses her)? Which self will she try to satisfy when she buys a camera? Because this is unclear, self-concept theory has met with mixed success in predicting consumer responses to brand images.

## Psychological factors

A person's buying choices are further influenced by four important psychological factors: motivation, perception, learning, and beliefs and attitudes.

### Motivation

We know that Elena Klein became interested in buying a camera. Why? What is she *really* seeking? What *needs* is she trying to satisfy?

A person has many needs at any given time. Some are *biological*, arising from states of tension such as hunger, thirst or discomfort. Others are *psychological*, arising from the need for recognition, esteem or belonging. Most of these needs will not be strong enough to motivate the person to act at a given point in time. A need becomes a *motive* when it is aroused to a sufficient level of intensity. A **motive** (or *drive*) is a need that is sufficiently pressing to direct the person to seek satisfaction. Psychologists have developed theories of human motivation. Two of the most popular – the theories of Sigmund Freud and Abraham Maslow – have quite different meanings for consumer analysis and marketing.

*Freud's theory of motivation*  Freud assumes that people are largely unconscious about the real psychological forces shaping their behaviour. He sees the person as growing up and repressing many urges. These urges are never eliminated or under perfect control; they emerge in dreams, in slips of the tongue, in neurotic and obsessive behaviour or ultimately in psychoses.

Thus Freud suggests that a person does not fully understand his or her motivation. If Elena Klein wants to purchase an expensive camera, she may describe her motive as wanting a hobby or career. At a deeper level, she may be purchasing the camera to impress others with her creative talent. At a still deeper level, she may be buying the camera to feel young and independent again.

Motivation researchers collect in-depth information from small samples of consumers to uncover the deeper motives for their product choices. They use nondirective depth interviews and various 'projective techniques' to throw the ego off guard – techniques such as word association, sentence completion, picture interpretation and role playing.

Motivation researchers have reached some interesting and sometimes odd conclusions about what may be in the buyer's mind regarding certain purchases. For example, one classic study concluded that consumers resist prunes because they are wrinkled looking and remind people of sickness and old age. Despite its sometimes unusual conclusions, motivation research remains a useful tool for marketers seeking a deeper understanding of consumer behaviour (see Marketing Highlight 7.3).[19]

*Maslow's theory of motivation*  Abraham Maslow sought to explain why people are driven by particular needs at particular times.[20] Why does one person spend much time and energy on personal safety and another on gaining the esteem of others? Maslow's answer is that human needs are arranged in a hierarchy, from the most pressing to the least pressing. Maslow's hierarchy of needs is shown in Figure 7.4. In order of importance, they are (1) *physiological* needs, (2) *safety* needs, (3) *social* needs, (4) *esteem* needs, and (5) *self-actualization* needs. A person tries to satisfy the most important need first. When that important need is satisfied, it will stop being a motivator and the person will then try to satisfy the next most important need. For example, a starving man (need 1) will not take an interest in the latest happenings in the art world (need 5), nor in how he is seen or esteemed by others (need 3 or 4), nor even in whether he is breathing clean air (need 2). But as each important need is satisfied, the next most important need will come into play:

> The wine market shows how the different levels of the need hierarchy can be at play at the same time. Buyers of premium wines are seeking self-esteem and self-actualisation. They may achieve this by showing their knowledge by buying 1986 Chateaux Ausone from a specialist wine merchant. Wine buying makes many other people anxious, particularly if it is a gift. They buy the product to fill a social need but are unable to gauge quality. To be safe

## 'Touchy-feely' research into consumer motivations

The term *motivation research* refers to qualitative research designed to probe consumers' hidden, subconscious motivations. Because consumers often don't know or can't describe just why they act as they do, motivation researchers use a wide variety of nondirective and projective techniques to uncover underlying emotions and attitudes towards brands and buying situations. The techniques range from sentence completion, word association and inkblot or cartoon interpretation tests, to having consumers describe typical brand users or form daydreams and fantasies about brands or buying situations. Some of these techniques verge on the bizarre. One writer offers the following tongue-in-cheek summary of a motivation research session:

> Good morning, ladies and gentlemen. We've called you here today for a little consumer research. Now, lie down on the couch, toss your inhibitions out the window and let's try a little free association. First, think about brands as if they were your *friends* ... think of your shampoo as an animal. Go on, don't be shy. Would it be a panda or a lion? A snake or a woolly worm? For our final exercise, let's all sit up and pull out our magic markers. Draw a picture of a typical cake-mix user. Would she wear an apron or a negligee? A business suit or a can-can dress?

Other researchers use *transaction analysis* (TA), based originally on psychoanalytic theory, to study the relationship between the consumer and the brand. In this the consumer and the brand role player assume the 'ego states' of a parent, adult (equal) or child. Data are obtained from recording a dialogue between the consumer and a brand:

> Smoker to ideal cigarette: 'I can taste you; your tobacco is good ... I like you. Smart box ... You taste nice ... not harsh.'

> Ideal cigarette to smoker: 'If I can make you relaxed and happy, that's what I am here for. I always try to please my customers.'

Such projective techniques seem dotty, but more and more marketers are turning to these touchy-feely, motivation research approaches to help them probe consumer psyches and develop better marketing strategies.

Many advertising agencies employ teams of psychologists, anthropologists and other social scientists to carry out their motivation research. Says the research director of one large agency: 'We believe people make choices on a basic primitive level ... we use the probe to get down to the unconscious.' This agency routinely conducts one-on-one, therapy-like interviews to delve into the inner workings of consumers. Another agency asks consumers to describe their favourite brands as animals or cars (say, Saab versus BMW) in order to assess the prestige associated with various brands. Still another agency has consumers draw figures or make clay models of typical brands or brand users:

they buy from a reputable store (Marks and Spencer) or a brand legitimised by advertising (Le Piat d'Or).[21]

Maslow's hierarchy is not universal for all cultures. As the heroes of Hollywood movies amply show, Anglo-Saxon culture values self-actualization and individuality above all else, but that is not universally so. In Japan and German-speaking countries people are most highly motivated by a need for personal security and conformity, while in France, Spain, Portugal and other Latin and Asian countries, people are most motivated by the need for security and belonging.[22]

What light does Maslow's theory throw on Elena Klein's interest in buying a camera? We can guess that Elena has satisfied her physiological, safety and social needs; they do not motivate her interest in cameras. Her camera interest might come from a strong need for more esteem from others. Or it might come from a need for self-actualization – she might want to be a creative person and express herself through photography.

In one instance, the agency asked 50 interviewees to sketch likely buyers of two different brands of cake mixes. Consistently, the group portrayed Pillsbury customers as apron-clad, grandmotherly types, while they pictured Duncan Hines purchasers as svelte, contemporary women.

In a similar study, American Express had people sketch likely users of its gold card versus its green card. Respondents depicted gold card holders as active, broad-shouldered men; green card holders were perceived as 'couch potatoes' lounging in front of television sets. Based on these results, the company positioned its gold card as a symbol of responsibility for people capable of controlling their lives and finances.

Some motivation research studies employ more basic techniques, such as simply mingling with consumers to find out what makes them tick:

> Saatchi & Saatchi, the London based ad agency, recently hired anthropologist Joe Lowe to spend a week in Texas sidling up to wearers of Wranglers blue jeans at rodeos and barbecues. His findings reinforced what the jeans company suspected:

buyers associated Wranglers with cowboys. The company responded by running ads with plenty of Western touches. For a consumer-goods manufacturer, Lowe went to health clubs where he observed patrons applying deodorant. And for shampoo maker Helene Curtis, he spent three days in salons before coming to a somewhat predictable conclusion – going to the beauty shop makes women feel good.

Some marketers dismiss such motivation research as mumbo-jumbo. And these approaches do present some problems: they use small samples and researcher interpretations of results are often highly subjective, sometimes leading to rather exotic explanations of otherwise ordinary buying behaviour. However, others believe strongly that these approaches can provide interesting nuggets of insight into the relationships between consumers and the brands they buy. To marketers who use them, motivation research techniques provide a flexible and varied means of gaining insights into deeply held and often mysterious motivations behind consumer buying behaviour.

Sources: Excerpts from M. Blackthorn and M. Holmes, 'The use of transactional analysis in the development of a new brand's personality', ESOMAR Seminar on New Product Development, 1983; G. De Groot, 'Deep, dangerous or just plain dotty?', ESOMAR Seminar on Qualitative Methods of Research, Amsterdam, 1986; Annetta Miller and Dody Tsiantar, 'Psyching out consumers', Newsweek (27 February 1989), 46–7; see also Sidney J. Levy, 'Dreams, fairy tales, animals and cars', Psychology and Marketing (summer 1985), 67–81; Peter Sampson, 'Qualitative research and motivational research', in Robert Worcester (ed.), Consumer Marketing Research Handbook (London: McGraw-Hill 1986), 29–55; Ronald Alsop, 'Advertisers put consumers on the couch', Wall Street Journal (13 May 1988), 21; Rebecca Piirto, 'Measuring minds in the 1990s', American Demographics (December 1990), 31–5, and 'Words that sell', American Demographics (January 1992), 6.

## Perception

A motivated person is ready to act. How the person acts is influenced by his or her perception of the situation. Two people with the same motivation and in the same situation may act quite differently because they perceive the situation differently. Elena Klein might consider a fast-talking camera salesperson loud and phoney. Another camera buyer might consider the same salesperson intelligent and helpful.

Why do people perceive the same situation differently? All of us learn by the flow of information through our five senses: sight, hearing, smell, touch and taste. However, each of us receives, organizes and interprets this sensory information in an individual way. Thus **perception** is the process by which people select, organize and interpret information to form a meaningful picture of the world.

People can form different perceptions of the same stimulus because of three perceptual processes: selective attention, selective distortion and selective retention.

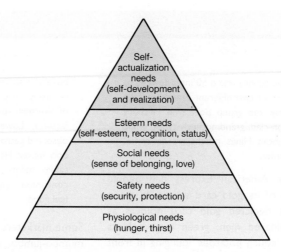

**Figure 7.4**   Maslow's hierarchy of needs. (Source: Adapted from Abraham H. Maslow, *Motivation and Personality*, 2nd edn (1970). © Abraham H. Maslow, 1970. Reprinted by permission of Harper & Row Inc.)

*Selective attention*   People are exposed to a great amount of stimuli every day. For example, the average person may be exposed to more than 1,500 ads a day. It is impossible for a person to pay attention to all these stimuli and some studies show people remembering only three or four.[23] **Selective attention** – the tendency for people to screen out most of the information to which they are exposed – means that marketers have to work especially hard to attract the consumer's attention. Their message will be lost on most people who are not in the market for the product. Moreover even people who are in the market may not notice the message unless it stands out from the surrounding sea of other ads.

*Selective distortion*   Even noted stimuli do not always come across in the intended way. Each person fits incoming information into an existing mind-set. **Selective distortion** describes the tendency of people to adapt information to personal meanings. Elena Klein may hear the salesperson mention some good and bad points about a competing camera brand. Because she already has a strong leaning towards Nikon, Olympus or Polaroid, she is likely to distort those points in order to conclude that one camera is better than the others. People tend to interpret information in a way that will support what they already believe. Selective distortion means that marketers must try to understand the mind-sets of consumers and how these will affect interpretaions of advertising and sales information:

> Cathay Pacific, the Hong Kong based airline, found out that although Caucasians saw Cathay as an Asian airline, Asians perceived the airline as being well managed and safe, but not Asian. Seeing their future in Asia where 80 per cent of their passengers came from, Cathay wants to change their view. Peter Sutch, Cathay's chairman, explains their new livery: 'We wanted something Asian in appearance: we wanted a quality look with an Asian flavour.' The airline now offers a wide range of Asian meals and communicates in many Asian languages. In-flight information is now in Japanese, Korean, Mandarin and Cantonese as well as English.[24]

*Selective retention*   People will also forget much of what they learn. They tend to retain information that supports their attitudes and beliefs. Because of **selective retention**, Elena is likely to remember good points made about the Nikon and forget

Selected perception: the average person is exposed to more than 1500 ads per day – in magazines and newspapers, on radio and TV, and all around them.

good points made about competing cameras. She may remember Nikon's good points because she 'rehearses' them more whenever she thinks about choosing a camera.

Because of selective exposure, distortion and retention, marketers have to work hard to get their messages through. This fact explains why marketers use so much drama and repetition in sending messages to their market. Although some consumers are worried that they will be affected by marketing messages without even knowing it, most marketers worry about whether their offers will be perceived at all.[25]

## Learning

When people act, they learn. **Learning** describes changes in an individual's behaviour arising from experience. Learning theorists say that most human behaviour is learned. Learning occurs through the interplay of *drives, stimuli, cues, responses* and *reinforcement*.

We saw that Elena Klein has a drive for self-actualization. A *drive* is a strong internal stimulus that calls for action. Her drive becomes a motive when it is directed towards a particular *stimulus object*, in this case a camera. Elena's response to the idea of buying a camera is conditioned by the surrounding cues. *Cues* are minor stimuli that determine when, where and how the person responds. Seeing cameras in a shop window, hearing a special sale price, and her husband's support are all cues that can influence Elena's *response* to her interest in buying a camera.

Suppose Elena buys the Nikon. If the experience is rewarding, she will probably use the camera more and more. Her response to cameras will be *reinforced*. Then the next time she shops for a camera, binoculars or some similar product, the probability is greater that she will buy a Nikon product. We say that she *generalizes* her response to similar stimuli.

The reverse of generalization is *discrimination*. When Elena examines binoculars made by Olympus, she sees that they are lighter and more compact than Nikon's binoculars. Discrimination means that she has learned to recognize differences in sets of products and can adjust her response accordingly.

The practical significance of learning theory for marketers is that they can build up demand for a product by associating it with strong drives, using motivating cues and providing positive reinforcement. A new company can enter the market by appealing to the same drives that competitors appeal to and by providing similar cues, because buyers are more likely to transfer loyalty to similar brands than to dissimilar ones (generalization). Or a new company may design its brand to appeal to a different set of drives and offer strong cue inducements to switch brands (discrimination).

### Beliefs and attitudes

Through doing and learning, people acquire their beliefs and attitudes. These, in turn, influence their buying behaviour. A **belief** is a descriptive thought that a person has about something. Elena Klein may believe that a Nikon camera takes great pictures, stands up well under hard use and is good value. These beliefs may be based on real knowledge, opinion or faith and may or may not carry an emotional charge. For example, Elena Klein's belief that a Nikon camera is heavy may or may not matter to her decision.

Marketers are interested in the beliefs that people formulate about specific products and services, because these beliefs make up product and brand images that affect buying behaviour. If some of the beliefs are wrong and prevent purchase, the marketer will want to launch a campaign to correct them.

People have attitudes regarding religion, politics, clothes, music, food and almost everything else. An **attitude** describes a person's relatively consistent evaluations, feelings and tendencies towards an object or idea. Attitudes put people into a frame of mind of liking or disliking things, of moving towards or away from them. Thus Elena Klein may hold such attitudes as 'Buy the best', 'The Japanese make the best products in the world', and 'Creativity and self-expression are among the most important things in life'. If so, the Nikon camera would fit well into Elena's existing attitudes.

Attitudes are difficult to change. A person's attitudes fit into a pattern and to change one attitude may require difficult adjustments in many others. Thus a company should usually try to fit its products into existing attitudes rather than try to change attitudes. Of course, there are exceptions in which the great cost of trying to change attitudes may pay off. For example:

> In the late 1950s, Honda entered the US motorcycle market facing a major decision. It could either sell its motorcycles to the small but already established motorcycle market or try to increase the size of this market by attracting new types of consumers. Increasing the size of the market would be more difficult and expensive because many people had negative attitudes toward motorcycles. They associated motorcycles with black leather jackets, switchblades and outlaws. Despite these adverse attitudes, Honda took the second course of action. It launched a major campaign to position motorcycles as good clean fun. Its theme 'You meet the nicest people on a Honda' worked well and many people adopted a new attitude toward motorcycles. In the 1990s, however, Honda faces a similar problem. With the ageing of the baby boomers, the market has once again shifted toward only hard-core motorcycling enthusiasts. So Honda has again set out to change consumer attitudes. Its 'Come Ride With Us' campaign aims to re-establish the wholesomeness of motorcycling and to position it as fun and exciting for everyone.[26]

## CONSUMER DECISION PROCESS

The consumer's choice results from the complex interplay of cultural, social, personal and psychological factors. Although many of these factors cannot be influenced by the marketer, they can be useful in identifying interested buyers and in shaping products and appeals to better serve their needs. Marketers have to be extremely careful in analysing consumer behaviour. Consumers often turn down what appears to be a winning offer. Polaroid found this out when it lost millions on its Polarvision instant home movie system; Ford when it launched the Edsel; RCA on its Selecta-Vision and Philips on its LaserVision video-disc player; Sony with DAT tapes and Bristol with their trio of the Brabazon, Britannia and Concorde airliners. So far we have looked at the cultural, social, personal and psychological influences that affect buyers. Now we look at how consumers make buying decisions. First, the types of decisions consumers face. Then the main steps in the buyer decision process. Finally, the process by which consumers learn about and buy new products.

## TYPES OF BUYING DECISION BEHAVIOUR

Consumer decision making varies with the type of buying decision. Consumer buying behaviour differs greatly for a tube of toothpaste, a tennis racket, an expensive camera and a new car. More complex decisions usually involve more buying participants and more buyer deliberation. Figure 7.5 shows types of consumer buying behaviour based on the degree of buyer involvement and the degree of differences among brands.[27]

### Complex buying behaviour

Consumers undertake **complex buying behaviour** when they are highly involved in a purchase and perceive significant differences among brands or when the product is expensive, risky, purchased infrequently and highly self-expressive. Typically, the consumer has much to learn about the product category. For example, a personal computer buyer may not know what attributes to consider. Many product features carry no real meaning: an 'Intel 90MHz Pentium Processor', 'SVGA display', '8Mb RAM, 256 Kb Cache' or even a 'PCI#9 GXE PRO 64-Bit Graphics card'.

This buyer will pass through a learning process, first developing beliefs about the product, then attitudes, and then making a thoughtful purchase choice. Marketers of high-involvement products must understand the information-gathering and evaluation behaviour of high-involvement consumers. They need to help buyers learn about product-class attributes and their relative importance and about what the company's brand offers on the important attributes. Marketers need to differentiate their

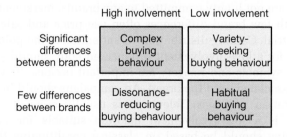

**Figure 7.5**    Four types of buying behaviour. (Source: Adapted from Henry Assael, *Consumer Behavior and Marketing Action* (Boston: Kent Publishing Company, 1987), 87. © Wadsworth Inc. 1987. Reprinted by permission of Kent Publishing Company, a division of Wadsworth Inc.)

brand's features, perhaps by describing the brand's benefits using print media with long copy. They must motivate store salespeople and the buyer's acquaintances to influence the final brand choice. Recognizing this problem, Dixons, the electrical retailers, are setting up the Link chain of stores dedicated to helping baffled buyers on to the information superhighway and multimedia.[28]

## Dissonance-reducing buying behaviour

**Dissonance-reducing buying behaviour** occurs when consumers are highly involved with an expensive, infrequent or risky purchase, but see little difference among brands. For example, consumers buying carpeting may face a high-involvement decision because carpeting is expensive and self-expressive. Yet buyers may consider most carpet brands in a given price range to be the same. In this case, because perceived brand differences are not large, buyers may shop around to learn what is available, but buy relatively quickly. They may respond primarily to a good price or to purchase convenience. After the purchase, consumers might experience postpurchase dissonance (after-sales discomfort) when they notice certain disadvantages of the purchased carpet brand or hear favourable things about brands not purchased. To counter such dissonance, the marketer's after-sale communications should provide evidence and support to help consumers feel good both before and after their brand choices.[29]

## Habitual buying behaviour

**Habitual buying behaviour** occurs under conditions of low consumer involvement and little significant brand difference. For example, take salt. Consumers have little involvement in this product category – they simply go to the store and reach for a brand. If they keep reaching for the same brand, it is out of habit rather than strong brand loyalty. Consumers appear to have low involvement with most low-cost, frequently purchased products.

Consumers do not search extensively for information about the brands, evaluate brand characteristics and make weighty decisions about which brands to buy. Instead, they passively receive information as they watch television or read magazines. Ad repetition creates *brand familiarity* rather than *brand conviction*. Consumers do not form strong attitudes towards a brand; they select the brand because it is familiar and consumers may not evaluate the choice even after purchase.

Because buyers are not highly committed to any brands, marketers of low-involvement products with few brand differences often use price and sales promotions to stimulate product trial. Gaining distribution and attention at the point of sale is critical. In advertising for a low-involvement product, ad copy should stress only a few key points. Visual symbols and imagery are important because they can be remembered easily and associated with the brand. Ad campaigns should include high repetition of short-duration messages. Television is usually more effective than print media because it is a low-involvement medium suitable for passive learning. Advertising planning should be based on classical conditioning theory, in which buyers learn to identify a certain product by a symbol repeatedly attached to it.

Products can be linked to some involving personal situation. Nestlé did this in a recent series of ads for Gold Blend/Tasters Choice coffee, each consisting of a new soap-opera-like episode featuring the evolving romantic relationship between neighbours, Sharon and Tony. Nestlé's success in doing this contrasts with the tea market in the United Kingdom where, although it is the national drink, sales promotions dominate sales.

### Variety-seeking buying behaviour

Consumers undertake **variety-seeking buying behaviour** in situations characterized by low consumer involvement, but significant perceived brand differences. In such cases, consumers often do a lot of brand switching. For example, when purchasing biscuits, a consumer may hold some beliefs, choose a biscuit without much evaluation, then evaluate that brand during consumption. But the next time, the consumer might pick another brand out of boredom or simply to try something different. Brand switching occurs for the sake of variety rather than because of dissatisfaction.

In such product categories, the marketing strategy may differ for the market leader and minor brands. The market leader will try to encourage habitual buying behaviour by dominating shelf space, avoiding out-of-stock conditions and running frequent reminder advertising. Challenger firms will encourage variety seeking by offering lower prices, deals, coupons, free samples and advertising that presents reasons for trying something new.

## THE BUYER DECISION PROCESS

Most large companies research consumer buying decisions in great detail to answer questions about what consumers buy, where they buy, how and how much they buy, when they buy and why they buy. Marketers can study consumer purchases to find answers to questions about what they buy, where and how much. But learning about the *whys* of consumer buying behaviour and the buying decision process is not so easy – the answers are often locked within the consumer's head.

We will examine the stages buyers pass through to reach a buying decision. We will use the model in Figure 7.6, which shows the consumer as passing through five stages: *need recognition, information search, evaluation of alternatives, purchase decision* and *post purchase behaviour*. Clearly the buying process starts long before actual purchase and continues long after. This encourages the marketer to focus on the entire buying process rather than just the purchase decision.

This model implies that consumers pass through all five stages with every purchase. But in more routine purchases, consumers often skip or reverse some of these stages. A woman buying her regular brand of toothpaste would recognize the need and go right to the purchase decision, skipping information search and evaluation. However, we use the model in Figure 7.6 because it shows all the considerations that arise when a consumer faces a new and complex purchase situation.

To illustrate this model, we return to Elena Klein and try to understand how she became interested in buying a camera and the stages she went through to make the final choice.

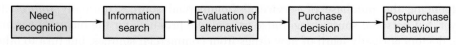

**Figure 7.6**   Buyer decision process.

## Need recognition

The buying process starts with **need recognition** – the buyer recognizing a problem or need. The buyer senses a difference between his or her *actual* state and some *desired* state. The need can be triggered by *internal stimuli* when one of the person's normal needs – hunger, thirst, sex – rises to a level high enough to become a drive. From previous experience, the person has learned how to cope with this drive and is motivated towards objects that he or she knows will satisfy it.

A need can also be triggered by *external stimuli*. Elena passes a bakery and the smell of freshly baked bread stimulates her hunger; she admires a neighbour's new car; or she watches a television commercial for a Caribbean vacation. At this stage, the marketer needs to determine the factors and situations that usually trigger consumer need recognition. The marketer should research consumers to find out what kinds of needs or problems arise, what brought them about and how they led the consumer to this particular product. Elena might answer that she felt she needed a camera after friends showed her the photographs they took on holiday. By gathering such information, the marketer can identify the stimuli that most often trigger interest in the product and can develop marketing programmes that involve these stimuli.

## Information search

An aroused consumer may or may not search for more information. If the consumer's drive is strong and a satisfying product is near at hand, the consumer is likely to buy it then. If not, the consumer may simply store the need in memory or undertake an **information search** related to the need.

At one level, the consumer may simply enter *heightened attention*. Here Elena becomes more receptive to information about cameras. She pays attention to camera ads, cameras used by friends and camera conversations. Or Elena may go into *active information search*, in which she looks for reading material, phones friends and gathers information in other ways. The amount of searching she does will depend upon the strength of her drive, the amount of information she starts with, the ease of obtaining more information, the value she places on additional information and the satisfaction she gets from searching. Normally the amount of consumer search activity increases as the consumer moves from decisions that involve limited problem solving to those that involve extensive problem solving.

The consumer can obtain information from any of several sources:

- *Personal sources*: family, friends, neighbours, acquaintances.
- *Commercial sources*: advertising, salespeople, dealers, packaging, displays.
- *Public sources*: mass media, consumer-rating organizations.
- *Experiential sources*: handling, examining, using the product.

The relative influence of these information sources varies with the product and the buyer. Generally, the consumer receives the most information about a product from commercial sources – those controlled by the marketer. The most effective sources, however, tend to be personal. Personal sources appear to be even more important in influencing the purchase of services.[30] Commercial sources normally *inform* the buyer, but personal sources *legitimize* or *evaluate* products for the buyer. For example, doctors normally learn of new drugs from commercial sources, but turn to other doctors for evaluative information.

As more information is obtained, the consumer's awareness and knowledge of the available brands and features increases. In her information search, Elena learned about the many camera brands available. The information also helped her drop certain brands from consideration. A company must design its marketing mix to make prospects aware of and knowledgeable about its brand. If it fails to do this, the company has lost its opportunity to sell to the customer. The company must also learn which other brands customers consider so that it knows its competition and can plan its own appeals.

The marketer should identify consumers' sources of information and the importance of each source. Consumers should be asked how they first heard about the brand, what information they received and the importance they place on different information sources.

## Evaluation of alternatives

We have seen how the consumer uses information to arrive at a set of final brand choices. How does the consumer choose among the alternative brands? The marketer needs to know about **alternative evaluation** – that is, how the consumer processes information to arrive at brand choices. Unfortunately, consumers do not use a simple and single evaluation process in all buying situations. Instead, several evaluation processes are at work.

Certain basic concepts help explain consumer evaluation processes. First, we assume that each consumer is trying to satisfy some need and is looking for certain *benefits* that can be acquired by buying a product or service. Further, each consumer sees a product as a bundle of *product attributes* with varying capacities for delivering these benefits and satisfying the need. For cameras, product attributes might include picture quality, ease of use, camera size, price and other features. Consumers will vary as to which of these attributes they consider relevant and will pay the most attention to those attributes connected with their needs.

Second, the consumer will attach different *degrees of importance* to each attribute. A distinction can be drawn between the importance of an attribute and its salience. *Salient attributes* are those that come to a consumer's mind when he or she is asked to think of a product's characteristics. But these are not necessarily the most important attributes to the consumer. Some of them may be salient because the consumer has just seen an advertisement mentioning them or has had a problem with them, making these attributes 'top-of-the-mind'. There may also be other attributes that the consumer forgot, but whose importance would be recognized if they were mentioned. Marketers should be more concerned with attribute importance than attribute salience.

Third, the consumer is likely to develop a set of *brand beliefs* about where each brand stands on each attribute. The set of beliefs held about a particular brand is known as the **brand image**. The consumer's beliefs may vary from true attributes based on his or her experience and the effect of selective perception, selective distortion and selective retention.

Fourth, the consumer is assumed to have a *utility function* for each attribute. The utility function shows how the consumer expects total product satisfaction to vary with different levels of different attributes. For example, Elena may expect her satisfaction from a camera to increase with better picture quality; to peak with a medium-weight camera as opposed to a very light or very heavy one; to be a compact 35-mm camera rather than a single lens reflex camera with interchangeable lenses. If we combine the attribute levels at which her utilities are highest, they make up Elena's ideal camera. The camera would also be her preferred camera if it were available and affordable.

Fifth, the consumer arrives at attitudes towards the different brands through some *evaluation procedure*. Consumers have been found to use one or more of several evaluation procedures, depending on the consumer and the buying decision.

In Elena's camera-buying situation, suppose she has narrowed her choice set to four cameras: Nikon AF400, Olympus Superzoom 110, Pentax Espio Jr. and Ricoh RW1. In addition, let us say she is interested primarily in four attributes – picture quality, ease of use, camera size and price. Table 7.5 shows how she believes each brand rates on each attribute.[31] Elena believes the Nikon will give her picture quality of 8 on a 10-point scale; is easy to use, 8; is of medium size, 9; and is very inexpensive, 10. Similarly, she has beliefs about how the other cameras rate on these attributes. The marketer would like to be able to predict which camera Elena will buy.

Clearly, if one camera rated best on all the attributes, we could predict that Elena would choose it. But the brands vary in appeal. Some buyers will base their buying decision on only one attribute and their choices are easy to predict. If Elena wants low price above everything, she should buy the Nikon, whereas if she wants the camera that is easiest to use, she could buy either the Olympus or the Pentax.

Most buyers consider several attributes, but assign different importance to each. If we knew the importance weights that Elena assigns to the four attributes, we could predict her camera choice more reliably. Suppose Elena assigns 40 per cent of the importance to the camera's picture quality, 30 per cent to ease of use, 20 per cent to its size and 10 per cent to its price. To find Elena's perceived value for each camera, we can multiply her importance weights by her beliefs about each camera. This gives us the following perceived values:

Nikon   = 0.4(8) + 0.3(8)  + 0.2(9) + 0.1(10) = 8.4
Olympus = 0.4(8) + 0.3(10) + 0.2(7) + 0.1(4)  = 8.0
Pentax   = 0.4(8) + 0.3(10) + 0.2(9) + 0.1(6)  = 8.8
Ricoh   = 0.4(6) + 0.3(8)  + 0.2(9) + 0.1(8)  = 7.4

We would predict that Elena will favour the Pentax.

This model is called the *expectancy value model* of consumer choice.[32] This is one of several possible models describing how consumers go about evaluating alternatives. Consumers might evaluate a set of alternatives in other ways. For example, Elena might decide that she should consider only cameras that satisfy a set of minimum attribute levels. She might decide a camera must have a superzoom lens. In this case, we would predict that she would choose Olympus because it is the only one

**TABLE 7.5**   *A consumer's brand beliefs about cameras*

| Camera | Attribute | | | |
| | Picture quality | Ease of use | Camera size | Price |
|---|---|---|---|---|
| Nikon | 8 | 8 | 9 | 10 |
| Olympus | 8 | 10 | 7 | 4 |
| Pentax | 8 | 10 | 9 | 6 |
| Ricoh | 6 | 8 | 9 | 8 |

that satisfies that requirement. This is called the *conjunctive model* of consumer choice. Or she might decide that she would settle for a camera that had a picture quality greater than 7 *or* ease of use greater than 9. In this case, the Nikon, Olympus or the Pentax would do since they all meet at least one of the requirements. This is called the *disjunctive model* of consumer choice.

How consumers go about evaluating purchase alternatives depends on the individual consumer and the specific buying situation. In some cases, consumers use careful calculations and logical thinking. At other times, the same consumers do little or no evaluating; instead they buy on impulse and rely on intuition. Sometimes consumers make buying decisions on their own; sometimes they turn to friends, consumer guides or salespeople for buying advice.

Marketers should study buyers to find out how they actually evaluate brand alternatives. If they know what evaluative processes go on, marketers can take steps to influence the buyer's decision. Suppose Elena is now inclined to buy a Pentax camera because of its ease of use and lightness. What strategies might another camera maker, say Olympus, use to influence people like Elena? There are several. Olympus could modify its camera to produce a version that has fewer features but is lighter and cheaper. It could try to change buyers' beliefs about how its camera rates on key attributes, especially if consumers currently underestimate the camera's qualities. It could try to change buyers' beliefs about Pentax and other competitors. Finally, it could try to change the list of attributes that buyers consider or the importance attached to these attributes. For example, it might advertise that all good cameras need a superzoom lens to get the picture quality that active people like Elena want.

## Purchase decision

In the evaluation stage, the consumer ranks brands and forms purchase intentions. Generally, the consumer's **purchase decision** will be to buy the most preferred brand, but two factors, shown in Figure 7.7, can come between the purchase *intention* and the purchase *decision*. The first factor is the *attitudes of others*. For example, if Elena Klein's husband feels strongly that Elena should buy the lowest-priced camera, then the chance of Elena buying a more expensive camera is reduced. He may like the specification of the Pentax but be offended by its name being Espio Jr (junior). How much another person's attitudes will affect Elena's choices depends both on the strength of the other person's attitudes towards her buying decision and on Elena's motivation to comply with that person's wishes.

Purchase intention is also influenced by *unexpected situational factors*. The consumer may form a purchase intention based on factors such as expected family income, expected price and expected benefits from the product. When the consumer is about to act, unexpected situational factors may arise to change the purchase

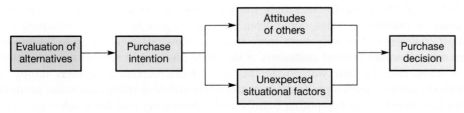

**Figure 7.7**  Steps between evaluation of alternatives and a purchase decision.

intention. Elena may lose her job, some other purchase may become more urgent or a friend may report being disappointed in her preferred camera. Thus preferences and even purchase intentions do not always result in actual purchase choice. They may direct purchase behaviour, but may not fully determine the outcome.

A consumer's decision to change, postpone or avoid a purchase decision is influenced heavily by *perceived risk*. Many purchases involve some risk taking.[33] Anxiety results when consumers cannot be certain about the purchase outcome. The amount of perceived risk varies with the amount of money at stake, the amount of purchase uncertainty and the amount of consumer self-confidence. A consumer takes certain actions to reduce risk, such as avoiding purchase decisions, gathering more information and looking for national brand names and products with warranties. The marketer must understand the factors that provoke feelings of risk in consumers and must provide information and support that will reduce the perceived risk.

## Postpurchase behaviour

The marketer's job does not end when the product is bought. After purchasing the product, the consumer will be satisfied or dissatisfied and will engage in **postpurchase behaviour** of interest to the marketer. What determines whether the buyer is satisfied or dissatisfied with a purchase? The answer lies in the relationship between the *consumer's expectations* and the product's *perceived performance*. If the product falls short of expectations, the consumer is disappointed; if it meets expectations, the consumer is satisfied; if it exceeds expectations, the consumer is delighted.

Consumers base their expectations on messages they receive from sellers, friends and other information sources. If the seller exaggerates the product's performance, consumer expectations will not be met – a situation that leads to dissatisfaction. The larger the gap between expectations and performance, the greater the consumer's dissatisfaction. This fact suggests that the seller should make product claims that represent faithfully the product's performance so that buyers are satisfied.

Motoring organizations regularly give pessimistic quotes about how long they will take to reach a customer whose car breaks down. If they say they will be 30 minutes and get there in 20 the customer is impressed. If, however, they get there in 20 minutes after promising 10, the customer is not so happy.

Almost all large purchases result in **cognitive dissonance** or discomfort caused by postpurchase conflict. Consumers are satisfied with the benefits of the chosen brand and glad to avoid the drawbacks of the brands not purchased. On the other hand, every purchase involves compromise. Consumers feel uneasy about acquiring the drawbacks of the chosen brand and about losing the benefits of the brands not purchased. Thus consumers feel at least some postpurchase dissonance for every purchase.[34]

Why is it so important to satisfy the customer? Such satisfaction is important because a company's sales come from two basic groups – *new customers* and *repeat customers*. It usually costs more to attract new customers than to retain current ones. Keeping current customers is therefore often more critical than attracting new ones, and the best way to do this is to make current customers happy. A satisfied customer buys a product again, talks favourably to others about the product, pays less attention to competing brands and advertising, and buys other products from the company. Many marketers go beyond merely *meeting* the expectations of customers – they aim to *delight* the customer. A delighted customer is even more likely to purchase again and to talk favourably about the product and company.

A dissatisfied consumer responds differently. Whereas, on average, a satisfied customer tells three people about a good product experience, a dissatisfied customer gripes to eleven people. In fact, one study showed that 13 per cent of the people who had a problem with an organization complained about that company to more than twenty people.[35] Clearly, bad word of mouth travels farther and faster than good word of mouth and can quickly damage consumer attitudes about a company and its products.

Therefore, a company would be wise to measure customer satisfaction regularly. It cannot simply rely on dissatisfied customers to volunteer their complaints when they are dissatisfied. In fact, 96 per cent of unhappy customers never tell the company about their problem. Companies should set up suggestion systems to *encourage* customers to complain. In this way, the company can learn how well it is doing and how it can improve. The 3M Company claims that over two-thirds of its new-product ideas come from listening to customer complaints. But listening is not enough – the company must also respond constructively to the complaints it receives.

Thus, in general, dissatisfied consumers may try to reduce their dissonance by taking any of several actions. In the case of Elena – a Pentax purchaser – she may return the camera, or look at Pentax ads that tell of the camera's benefits, or talk with friends who will tell her how much they like her new camera. She may even avoid reading about cameras in case she finds a better deal than she got.

Beyond seeking out and responding to complaints, marketers can take additional steps to reduce consumer postpurchase dissatisfaction and to help customers feel good about their purchases. For example, car dealers can write to or phone new car owners with congratulations on having selected a fine car. They can place ads showing satisfied owners driving their new cars.

Understanding the consumer's needs and buying process is the foundation of successful marketing. By understanding how buyers go through need recognition, information search, evaluation of alternatives, the purchase decision and postpurchase behaviour, the marketer can pick up many clues as to how to meet the buyer's needs. By understanding the various participants in the buying process and the strongest influences on their buying behaviour, the marketer can develop an effective programme to support an attractive offer to the target market.

## THE BUYER DECISION PROCESS FOR NEW PRODUCTS

We have looked at the stages buyers go through in trying to satisfy a need. Buyers may pass quickly or slowly through these stages and some of the stages may even be reversed. Much depends on the nature of the buyer, the product and the buying situation.

We now look at how buyers approach the purchase of new products. A **new product** is a good, service or idea that is perceived by some potential customers as new. It may have been around for a while, but our interest is in how consumers learn about products for the first time and make decisions on whether to adopt them. We define **adoption process** as 'the mental process through which an individual passes from first learning about an innovation to final adoption',[36] and **adoption** as the decision by an individual to become a regular user of the product.

## Stages in the adoption process

Consumers go through five stages in the process of adopting a new product:

1. *Awareness.* The consumer becomes aware of the new product, but lacks information about it.
2. *Interest.* The consumer seeks information about the new product.
3. *Evaluation.* The consumer considers whether trying the new product makes sense.
4. *Trial.* The consumer tries the new product on a small scale to improve his or her estimate of its value.
5. *Adoption.* The consumer decides to make full and regular use of the new product.

This model suggests that the new-product marketer should think about how to help consumers move through these stages. A manufacturer of large-screen televisions may discover that many consumers in the interest stage do not move to the trial stage because of uncertainty and the large investment. If these same consumers would be willing to use a large-screen television on a trial basis for a small fee, the manufacturer should consider offering a trial-use plan with an option to buy.

## Individual differences in innovativeness

People differ greatly in their readiness to try new products. In each product area, there are 'consumption pioneers' and early adopters. Other individuals adopt new products much later. This has led to a classification of people into the adopter categories shown in Figure 7.8.

After a slow start, an increasing number of people adopt the new product. The number of adopters reaches a peak and then drops off as fewer nonadopters remain. Innovators are defined as the first 2.5 per cent of the buyers to adopt a new idea (those beyond two standard deviations from mean adoption time); the early adopters are the next 13.5 per cent (between one and two standard deviations); and so forth.

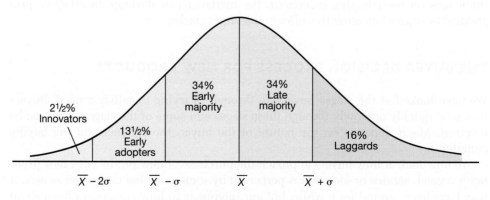

**Time of adoption of innovations**

**Figure 7.8** Adopter categorization on the basis of relative time of adoption of innovations. (Source: Redrawn from Everett M. Rogers, *Diffusion of Innovations*, 3rd edn (New York: Macmillan, 1983), 247. Adapted with permission of Macmillan Publishing Company Inc. © 1962, 1971, 1983 by the Free Press.)

The five adopter groups have differing values. *Innovators* are venturesome: they try new ideas at some risk. *Early adopters* are guided by respect: they are opinion leaders in their community and adopt new ideas early but carefully. The *early majority* are deliberate: although they rarely are leaders, they adopt new ideas before the average person. The *late majority* are sceptical: they adopt an innovation only after most people have tried it. Finally, *laggards* are tradition bound: they are suspicious of changes and adopt the innovation only when it has become something of a tradition itself.

This adopter classification suggests that an innovating firm should research the characteristics of innovators and early adopters and should direct marketing efforts to them. For example, home computer innovators have been found to be middle-aged and higher in income and education than noninnovators and they tend to be opinion leaders. They also tend to be more rational, more introverted and less social. In general, innovators tend to be relatively younger, better educated and higher in income than later adopters and nonadopters. They are more receptive to unfamiliar things, rely more on their own values and judgement and are more willing to take risks. They are less brand loyal and more likely to take advantage of special promotions such as discounts, coupons and samples.[37]

## Role of personal influence

Personal influence plays a distinctive role in the adoption of new products. **Personal influence** describes the effect of statements made by one person on another's attitude or probability of purchase. Consumers consult each other for opinions about new products and brands and the advice of others can strongly influence buying behaviour.

Personal influence is more important in some situations and for some individuals than for others. Personal influence is more important in the evaluation stage of the adoption process than in the other stages. It has more influence on later adopters than on early adopters and it is more important in risky buying situations than in safe situations.

## Influence of product characteristics on rate of adoption

The characteristics of the new product affect its rate of adoption. Some products catch on almost overnight (frisbees), whereas others take a long time to gain acceptance (Sony MiniDisc). Five characteristics are especially important in influencing an innovation's rate of adoption. For example, consider the characteristics of the MiniDisc in relation to the rate of adoption:

- *Relative advantage.* The degree to which the innovation appears superior to existing products. The greater the perceived relative advantage of using a MiniDisc over a cassette – say, does not tangle or lose quality – the sooner MiniDiscs will be adopted.
- *Compatibility.* The degree to which the innovation fits the values and experiences of potential consumers. MiniDiscs, for example, are highly compatible with an active lifestyle.
- *Complexity.* The degree to which the innovation is difficult to understand or use. CDs have already introduced customers to the benefits of digital recordings so the idea no longer seems complex.

- *Divisibility*. The degree to which the innovation may be tried on a limited basis. MiniDisc have a problem here. MiniDiscs require a big investment if people are to replace their in-home, in-car and on-street music systems. And what if the technology changes again?
- *Communicability*. The degree to which the results of using the innovation can be observed or described to others. The benefits of MiniDiscs are easy to demonstrate on a hi-fi system, but is the difference big enough to show in a car or Walkman?

Other characteristics influence the rate of adoption, such as initial and ongoing costs, risk and uncertainty, social approval and the efforts of opinion leaders. The new-product marketer has to research all these factors when developing the new product and its marketing programme.

## SUMMARY

Markets have to be understood before marketing strategies can be developed. The consumer market buys goods and services for personal consumption. Consumers vary tremendously in age, income, education, tastes and other factors. Marketers must understand how consumers transform marketing and other inputs into buying responses. *Consumer behaviour* is influenced by the buyer's characteristics and by the buyer's decision process. *Buyer characteristics* include four main factors: cultural, social, personal and psychological.

*Culture* is the most basic determinant of a person's wants and behaviour. It includes the basic values, perceptions, preferences and behaviours that a person learns from family and other key institutions. Marketers try to track cultural shifts that might suggest new ways to serve customers. *Social classes* are subcultures whose members have similar social prestige based on occupation, income, education, wealth and other variables. People with different cultural, subculture and social class characteristics have different product and brand preferences.

*Social factors* also influence a buyer's behaviour. A person's *reference groups* – family, friends, social organizations, professional associations – strongly affect product and brand choices. The person's position within each group can be defined in terms of *role and status*. A buyer chooses products and brands that reflect his or her role and status.

The buyer's age, life-cycle stage, occupation, economic circumstances, lifestyle, personality and other *personal characteristics* and *psychological factors* influence his or her buying decisions. Young consumers have different needs and wants from older consumers; the needs of young married couples differ from those of retired people; consumers with higher incomes buy differently from those who have less to spend.

Before planning its marketing strategy, a company needs to understand its consumers and the decision processes they go through. The number of buying participants and the amount of buying effort increase with the complexity of the buying situation. There are three types of *buying decision behaviour*: *routine response behaviour*, *limited problem solving* and *extensive problem solving*.

In buying something, the buyer goes through a decision process consisting of *need recognition*, *information search*, *evaluation of alternatives*, *purchase decision* and *post-purchase behaviour*. The marketer's job is to understand the buyers' behaviour at each stage and the influences that are operating. This allows the marketer to develop a significant and effective marketing programme for the target market. With regard to new products, consumers respond at different rates, depending on the consumer's characteristics and the product's characteristics. Manufacturers try to bring their new products to the attention of potential early adopters, particularly those with opinion leader characteristics.

A person's buying behaviour is the result of the complex interplay of all these cultural, social, personal and psychological factors. Although many of these factors cannot be controlled by marketers, they are useful in identifying and understanding the consumers that marketers are trying to influence.

# ■ DISCUSSING THE ISSUES

1. Thinking about the purchase of an audio hi-fi system, indicate the extent to which cultural, social, personal and psychological factors affect how a buyer evaluates hi-fi products and chooses a brand.

2. Describe and contrast any differences in the buying behaviour of consumers for the following products: Bruce Springsteen's new album; a notebook computer; a pair of jogging shoes; and a breakfast cereal.

3. Why might a detailed understanding of the model of the consumer buying decision process help marketers develop more effective marketing strategies to capture and retain customers? How universal is the model? How useful is it?

4. In designing the advertising for a soft drink, which would you find more helpful: information about consumer demographics or about consumer lifestyles? Give examples of how you would use each type of information.

5. Take, for example, a new method of contraception, which is being 'sold' to young males. It is a controversial, albeit innovative concept. Your firm is the pioneer in launching this device. What are the main factors your firm must research when developing a marketing programme for this product?

6. It has been said that consumers' buying behaviour is shaped more by perception than by reality. Do you agree with this comment? Why or why not?

# ■ APPLYING THE CONCEPTS

1. Different types of products can fulfil different functional and psychological needs.

   ■ List five luxury products or services that are very interesting or important to you. Some possibilities are cars, clothing, sports equipment, cosmetics, golf club membership. List five other necessities that you use which have little interest to you, such as pens, laundry detergent or petrol.

   ■ Make a list of words that describe how you feel about each of the products/services listed. Are there differences between the types of word you used for luxuries and necessities? What does this tell you about the different psychological needs these products fulfil?

2. Different groups may have different types of effects on consumers.

   ■ Consider an item you bought which is typical of what your peers (a key reference group) buy, such as a compact disc, a mountain bike or a brand of athletic shoes. Were you conscious that your friends owned something similar when you made the purchase? Did this make you want the item more or less? Why or why not?

   ■ Now, think of brands that you currently use which your parents also use. Examples may include soap, shaving cream or margarine. Did you think through these purchases as carefully as those influenced by your peers or were these purchases simply the result of following old habits?

# ■ REFERENCES

1. Quotes are from Peter Schutz and Jack Cook, 'Porsche on Nichemanship', *Harvard Business Review* (Mar.–Apr. 1986), 98–106. Copyright © 1986 by the President and Fellows of Harvard College; all rights reserved. See also Cleveland Horton, 'Porsche's ads get racy in '88 with tie to Indy', *Advertising Age* (2 November 1987), 34; Mark Maremont, 'Europe's long, smooth ride in luxury cars is over', *Business Week* (17 March 1988), 57; Stuart Cramer, 'Porsche: the myth and the marketing', *Marketing Business* (June 1990), 12–13; David Waller, 'By-word for glamour that few people can afford', *Financial Times* (6 November 1992), 31; 'Life in the fast lane again', *The Economist* (6 November 1993), 100; John Eisenhammer, 'Porsche hopes to squeak into the black', *Independent* (19 January 1994), 27, and 'Porsche plans ahead to reduce $67m loss', *The European* (25–31 March 1994), 25.

2. World Bank Atlas, 1994 and Microsoft Bookshelf, 1994.

3. Several models of the consumer buying process have been developed by marketing scholars. The most prominent models are those of John A. Howard and Jagdish N. Sheth, *The Theory of Buyer Behavior* (New York: Wiley, 1969); Francesco M. Nicosia, *Consumer Decision Processes* (Englewood Cliffs, NJ: Prentice Hall, 1966); James F. Engel, Roger D. Blackwell and Paul W. Miniard, *Consumer Behavior*, 5th edn (New York: Holt, Rinehart & Winston, 1986); and James R. Bettman, *An Information Processing Theory of Consumer Choice* (Reading, MA: Addison-Wesley, 1979). For a summary, see Leon G. Schiffman and Leslie Lazar Kanuk, *Consumer Behavior*, 4th edn (Englewood Cliffs, NJ: Prentice Hall, 1991), Ch. 20.

4. For an insight into this problem see Rik Pieters, 'A control view on the behaviour of consumers: turning the triangle', *European Journal of Marketing*, **27**, 8 (1993), 17–27.

5. The quote is from Judy Dempsey, 'Polls apart', *Financial Times* (3 November 1994), 19; for more on the European east/west divide see Graham J. Hooley (ed.), 'Marketing in Central and Eastern Europe', special edition of the *European Journal of Marketing*, **27**, 11/12 (1993), 1–120; and for a general review see Schiffman and Kanuk, *Consumer Behavior*, op. cit., Ch. 14.

6. Richard Tomkin, 'Quaker buys "new age" drinks', *Financial Times* (3 November 1994), 25; Sara McConnell, 'Banks put their future on the line', *The Times* (9 October 1994), 29; and Ralph Atkins, 'Families choose direct insurers', *Financial Times* (8/9 October 1994), 5.

7. For more on marketing to Hispanics, blacks, mature consumers and Asians, see Gary L. Berman, 'The Hispanic market: getting down to cases', *Sales &*

*Marketing Management* (October 1991), 65–74; Christy Fisher, 'Poll: Hispanics stick to brands', *Advertising Age* (15 February 1993), 6; Melissa Campanelli, 'The African-American market: community, growth and change', *Sales & Marketing Management* (May 1991), 75–81; Eugene Morris, 'The difference in black and white', *American Demographics* (January 1993), 44–9; Melissa Campanelli, 'The senior market: rewriting the demographics and definitions', *Sales & Marketing Management* (February 1991), 63–70; Joseph M. Winski, 'The mature market: marketers mature in depicting seniors', *Advertising Age* (16 November 1992), S1; Tibbett L. Speer, 'Older consumers follow different rules', *American Demographics* (February 1993), 21–2; Maria Shao, 'Suddenly, Asian-Americans are a marketer's dream', *Business Week* (17 June 1991), 54–5; and Carol J. Fouke, 'Asian-American market more important than ever', *Marketing News* (14 October 1991), 10.

8. Richard P. Coleman, 'The continuing significance of social class to marketing', *Journal of Consumer Research* (December 1983), 265–80; Laura Mazur, 'Golden oldies', *Marketing Business* (February 1993), 10–13; David Nicholson-Lord, 'Mass leisure class is on the way, say forecasters', *Independent* (18 April 1994), 4.

9. For a broad discussion of international social class see Edward W. Cundiff and Marye Tharp Higler, *Marketing in the International Environment* (Hemel Hempstead: Prentice Hall, 1988); Ernest Dichter, 'The world customer', *Harvard Business Review* (July–Aug. 1962), 113–23 and 'Rich man, poor man', *The Economist* (24 July 1993), 73; 'Slicing the cake' and 'For richer, for poorer', *The Economist* (5 November 1994), 13–14 and 19–21 respectively.

10. William O. Bearden and Michael J. Etzel, 'Reference group influence on product and brand purchase decisions', *Journal of Consumer Research* (September 1982), 185.

11. Debra Goldman, 'Spotlight men', *Adweek* (13 August 1990), M1–M6; Dennis Rodkin, 'A manly sport: building loyalty', *Advertising Age* (15 April 1991), S1, S12; Nancy Ten Kate, 'Who buys the pants in the family?', *American Demographics* (January 1992), 12; Laura Zinn, 'Real men buy paper towels, too', *Business Week* (9 November 1992), 75–6 and 'The war between the sexes', *The Economist* (5 March 1994), 96–7.

12. For more on family decision making, see Schiffman and Kanuk, *Consumer Behavior*, op. cit., Ch. 12; Rosann L. Spiro, 'Persuasion in family decision making', *Journal of Consumer Research* (March 1983), 393–402; Michael B. Menasco and David J. Curry, 'Utility and choice: an empirical study of husband/wife decision making', *Journal of Consumer Research* (June 1989), 87–97; and

Eileen Fisher and Stephen J. Arnold, 'More than a labor of love: gender roles and Christmas gift shopping', *Journal of Consumer Research* (December 1990), 333–45.

13. See Lawrence Lepisto, 'A life span perspective of consumer behavior', in Elizabeth Hirshman and Morris Holbrook, *Advances in Consumer Research*, vol. 12 (Provo, UT: Association for Consumer Research, 1985), 47.

14. Kim Foltz, 'Wizards of Marketing', *Newsweek* (22 July 1985), 44.

15. For more on VALS and on psychographics in general, see William D. Wells, 'Psychographics: a critical review', *Journal of Marketing Research* (May 1975), 196–213; Arnold Mitchell, *The Nine American Lifestyles* (New York: Macmillan, 1983); Rebecca Piirto, 'Measuring minds in the 1990s', *American Demographics* (December 1990), 35–9, and 'VALS the second time', *American Demographics* (July 1991), 6. For more reading on the pros and cons of using VALS and other lifestyle approaches, see Lynn R. Kahle, Sharon E. Beatty and Pamela Homer, 'Alternative measurement approaches to consumer values: the list of values (LOV) and values and life styles (VALS)', *Journal of Consumer Research* (December 1986), 405–9; and Mark Landler, 'The bloodbath in market research', *Business Week* (11 February 1991), 72–4.

16. Based on details in Marieke de Mooij, *Advertising Worldwide* (Hemel Hempstead: Prentice Hall, 1994), who obtained his information from Eugine Wong of Survey Research Malaysia.

17. See Harold H. Kassarjian and Mary Jane Sheffet, 'Personality in consumer behavior: an update', in Harold H. Kassarjian and Thomas S. Robertson (eds), *Perspectives in Consumer Behavior* (Glenview, IL: Scott Foresman, 1981), 160–80; and Joseph T. Plummer, 'How personality can make a difference', *Marketing News* (Mar.–Apr. 1984), 17–20.

18. See M. Joseph Sirgy, 'Self-concept in consumer behavior: a critical review', *Journal of Consumer Research* (December 1982), 287–300; and Russel W. Belk, 'Possessions and the extended self', *Journal of Consumer Research* (September 1988), 139–59.

19. See Annetta Miller and Dody Tsiantar, 'Psyching out consumers', *Newsweek* (27 February 1989), 46–7; and Rebecca Piirto, 'Words that sell', *American Demographics* (January 1992), 6.

20. Abraham H. Maslow, *Motivation and Personality*, 2nd edn (New York: Harper & Row, 1970), 80–106.

21. Robert L. Gluckman, 'A consumer approach to branded wines', *European Journal of Marketing*, **24**, 4 (1990), 27–46.

22. Geert Hofstede, *Cultural Consequences* (London: Sage, 1984).

23. John Fiske, *Understanding Popular Culture* (London: Routledge, 1989).

24. Simon Holberton, 'Cathay Pacific puts its future in Hong Kong', *Financial Times* (3 November 1994), 32.

25. For a discussion of subliminal perception see Timothy Moore, 'What you see is what you get', *Journal of Marketing* (spring 1982); Walter Weir, 'Another look at subliminal "facts"', *Advertising Age* (15 October 1984), 46.

26. See 'Honda hopes to win new riders by emphasizing "fun" of cycles', *Marketing News* (28 August 1989), 6.

27. Henry Assael, *Consumer Behavior and Marketing Action* (Boston: Kent Publishing, 1987), ch. 4. An earlier classification of three types of consumer buying behaviour – routine response behaviour, limited problem solving, and extensive problem solving – can be found in John A. Howard and Jagdish Sheth, *The Theory of Consumer Behavior* (New York: Wiley, 1969), 27–8. Gordon R. Foxall proposes a more sophisticated Behavioural Perspective Model (BPM) in 'A behavioural perspective on purchasing and consumption', and 'Consumer behaviour as an evolutionary process', *European Journal of Marketing*, **27**, 8 (1993), 7–16 and 46–57 respectively; see also John A. Howard, *Consumer Behavior in Marketing Strategy* (Englewood Cliffs, NJ: Prentice Hall, 1989).

28. Tom Stevenson, 'Dixons opens shops for baffled buyers', *Independent* (17 October 1994), 28.

29. V. W. Mitchell and Pari Boustani, 'A preliminary investigation into pre- and post-purchase risk perception and reduction', *European Journal of Marketing*, **28**, 1 (1990), 56–71.

30. Keith B. Murray, 'A test of services marketing theory: consumer information acquisition theory', *Journal of Marketing* (January 1991), 10–25.

31. The ratings are based on those given in 'Product test: compact cameras', *Which?* (November 1994), 21–6.

32. This was developed by Martin Fishbein. See Martin Fishbein and Icek Ajzen, *Belief, Attitude, Intention, and Behavior* (Reading, MA: Addison-Wesley, 1975). For a critical review of this model, see Paul W. Miniard and Joel B. Cohen, 'An examination of the Fishbein–Ajzen behavioral intentions model's concepts and measures', *Journal of Experimental Social Psychology* (May 1981), 309–99.

33. Raymond A. Bauer, 'Consumer behavior as risk taking', in Donald F. Cox (ed.), *Risk Taking and Information Handling in Consumer Behavior* (Boston: Division of Research, Harvard Business School, 1967); John W. Vann, 'A multi-distributional conceptual framework for the study of perceived risk', in Thomas C. Kinnear

(ed.), *Advances in Consumer Research*, vol. 11 (Provo, UT: Association for Consumer Research, 1983), 442–6; and Robert B. Settle and Pamela L. Alreck, 'Reducing buyers' sense of risk', *Marketing Communications* (January 1989), 19–24.

34. See Leon Festinger, *A Theory of Cognitive Dissonance* (Stanford, CA: Stanford University Press, 1957); and Schiffman and Kanuk, *Consumer Behavior*, op. cit., 304–5.

35. See Karl Albrect and Ron Zemke, *Service America!* (Homewood, IL: Dow-Jones Irwin, 1985), 6–7; and

Frank Rose, 'Now quality means service too', *Fortune* (22 April 1991), 97–108.

36. The following discussion draws heavily from Everett M. Rogers, *Diffusion of Innovations*, 3rd edn (New York: Free Press, 1983); see also Hubert Gatignon and Thomas S. Robertson, 'A propositional inventory for new diffusion research', *Journal of Consumer Research* (March 1985), 849–67.

37. See Schiffman and Kanuk, *Consumer Behavior*, op. cit., ch. 18.

## CASE 7

# Bic versus Gillette: the disposable wars

About half of all Western men get up each morning, confront their stubble in the bathroom mirror and reach for a 30 cent disposable plastic razor. Schick, Bic, Gillette, Wilkinson or whatever, most men think that one brand does as well as the next. Also, the razor makers seem always to have them on sale, so you can scoop up a dozen of them for next to nothing.

The Gillette Company does not like this sort of thinking. Of course, women also use Gillette's razors, but Gillette worries about the growing number of men who use disposables. The company makes about three times more money per unit on cartridge refills for its Atra and Trac II razor systems than it does on its Good News! disposables. However, since the first disposables appeared in 1975, their sales have grown faster than those of system razors. By 1988, disposables accounted for 40 per cent of shaving-product dollar sales and more than 50 per cent of unit sales.

### Gillette: the defender

Gillette dominates the world wet-shave industry with a 61 per cent share. Schick is second with a 16.2 per cent share, Bic has 9.3 per cent and others, including Wilkinson, account for most of the rest of the market. In 1988 Gillette's blades and razors produced 32 per cent of its $3.5bn[*] sales and 61 per cent of its $268 million net income.

[*] 1 ecu = US$1.26.

Gillette earned its dominant position in the market through large investments in research and development and through careful consumer research. Every day, about 10,000 men carefully record the results of their shaves for Gillette. Five hundred of these men shave in special in-plant cubicles under carefully controlled and monitored conditions, including observation through two-way mirrors and video cameras. Shavers record the precise number of nicks and cuts. In certain cases, researchers even collect sheared whiskers to weigh and measure. As a result, Gillette scientists know that an average man's beard grows 0.04 cm a day (14 cm per year) and contains 15,500 hairs. During an average lifetime, a man will spend 140 days scraping 8.4 metres of whiskers from his face. Gillette even uses electron microscopes to study blade surfaces and miniature cameras to analyse the actual shaving process.

Armed with its knowledge of shavers and shaving, Gillette prides itself in staying ahead of the competition. As soon as competitors adjust to one shaving system, Gillette introduces another advance. In 1971 Gillette introduced the Trac II, the first razor system featuring two parallel blades mounted in a cartridge. In 1977, following $8 million in R&D expenditure the company introduced Atra, a twin-blade cartridge that swivels during shaving to follow the face's contours. In 1985, Gillette launched the Atra Plus, which added a lubricating strip to the Atra cartridge to make shaving even smoother.

Although the company's founder, King Gillette, considered developing a disposable product, Gillette's marketing strategy has focused on developing products that use refill blades on a permanent handle. Gillette works to give its blades, and especially its handles, an aura of class and superior performance. By promoting new captive systems, in which blade cartridges fit only a certain razor handle, Gillette raise price and profit margins with each new technological leap. Atra cartridges do not fit the Trac II handle, so men had to buy a new handle to allow them to use the Atra blades when Gillette introduced that system.

Gillette has never bothered with the low end of the market – cheap, private-label blades. Status-seeking men, it believes, will always buy a classy product. Most men see shaving as a serious business and their appearance as a matter of some importance. Therefore, most men will not skimp and settle for an ordinary shave when, for a little more money, they can feel confident that Gillette's products give them the best shave.

### Bic: the challenge

The rapid rise of the disposable razor has challenged Gillette's view of men's shaving philosophy. Bic first introduced the disposable shaver in 1975 in Europe and then a year later in Canada. Realizing that the United States would be next, Gillette introduced the first disposable razor to the US market in 1976 – the blue plastic Good News! that used a Trac II blade. Despite its defensive reaction, Gillette predicted that men would use the disposable only for trips and in the locker room when they had forgotten their real razor. Disposables would never capture more than 7 per cent of the market, Gillette asserted.

Marcel Bich, Bic's French founder, is devoted to disposability. Bich made his money by developing the familiar ballpoint pen. He pursues a strategy of turning status products into commodities. Often a product has status because it is difficult to make and must sell at a high price. However, if a manufacturer develops ways to mass produce the product at low cost with little loss of functional quality, its status and allure disappear. Consumers will then not feel embarrassed to buy and be seen using the new, cheaper version of the product. Bich brands his products, strips them of their glamour, distributes them widely and sells them

cheaply. His marketing strategy is simple: maximum service; minimum price.

Bic attacks the shaving business in a very different manner from Gillette. It does not have anyone exploring the fringe of shaving technology; it does not even own an electron microscope; and it does not know or care how many hairs the average man's beard contains. The company maintains only a small shave-testing panel consisting of about 100 people. The Bic shaver (which sells for 25 cents or less) has only one blade mounted on a short, hollow handle. Nevertheless, the Bic disposable razor presents Gillette with its most serious challenge since the company's early days. In 1988, Bic's shaving products achieved $52 million in sales with a net income of $9.4 million and held a 22.4 per cent share of the disposable market.

### Early battles

In their pursuits of disposability, Gillette and Bic have clashed before on other product fronts. First, in the 1950s, they fought for market share in the writing pen market. Gillette's Paper Mate products, however, were no match for Bic's mass market advertising and promotion skills. The two firms met again in the 1970s in the disposable cigarette lighter arena, where they again made commodities of what had once been prestigious and sometimes expensive items. Although Gillette did better in disposable lighters than it had in pens, Bic's lighter captured the dominant market share.

In the most recent skirmish, however, Gillette's Good News! brand is winning with a 58 per cent market share in the disposable razor market. For Gillette, the victory is bittersweet. Good News! sells for a lot less than any of Gillette's older products. The key to commodity competition is price. To stay competitive with the 25 cent Bic razor and with other disposables, Gillette has to sell Good News! for much less than the retail price of an Atra or Trac II cartridge. As many Trac II and Atra users have concluded, why pay 56 cents for a twin-blade refill cartridge from Gillette when the same blade mounted on a plastic handle costs 25 cents? Good News! not only produces less revenue per blade sold, it also costs more because Gillette has to supply the handle as well as the cartridge. Each time Good News! gains a market share point, Gillette loses millions of dollars in sales and profits from its Atra and Trac II products.

## The psychology of shaving

The battle between Bic and Gillette represents more than a simple contest over what kinds of razors people want to use. It symbolizes a clash over one of the most enduring daily rituals. Before King Gillette invented the safety razor, men found shaving a tedious, difficult, time-consuming and often bloody task that they endured at most twice a week. Only the rich could afford to have a barber shave them daily.

Gillette patented the safety razor in 1904, but it was not until World War I that the product gained wide consumer acceptance. Gillette had the brilliant idea of having the military give a free Gillette razor to every soldier. In this manner, millions of men just entering the shaving age were introduced to the daily, self-shaving habit.

The morning shaving ritual continues to occupy a very special place in most men's lives – it affirms their masculinity. The first shave remains a rite of passage into manhood. A survey by New York psychologists reported that, although men complain about the bother of shaving, 97 per cent would not want to use a cream that would permanently rid them of all facial hair. Gillette once introduced a new razor that came in versions for heavy, medium, and light beards. Almost no one bought the light version, because few men wanted to publicly acknowledge their modest beard production. Although shaving may require less skill and involve less danger than it once did, many men still want the razors they use to reflect their belief that shaving is a serious business. A typical man regards his razor as an important personal tool, a kind of extension of self, like an expensive pen, cigarette lighter, attaché case or set of golf clubs.

## Gillette's fight back

For more than 80 years Gillette's perception of the men's shaving market and the psychology of shaving has been perfect. Its products hold a substantial 61 per cent share and its technology and marketing philosophy have held sway over the entire industry. Gillette has worked successfully to maintain the razor's masculine look, weight and feel as well as its status as an item of personal identification. Now, however, millions of men are scraping their faces each day with small, nondescript, passionless pieces of plastic costing 25 cents – an act that seems to be the ultimate denial of the shaving ritual. Good News! is bad news for Gillette. Gillette must find a way to dispose of the disposables.

## Questions

1. Who is involved in a man's decision to buy a disposable razor and what roles do various participants play? Do these participants and roles differ for the decision to buy a system razor?

2. What types of buying-decision behaviour do men exhibit when purchasing razors?

3. Examine a man's decision process for buying a wet-shave razor. How have Gillette and Bic pursued different strategies concerning this process?

4. What marketing strategy should Gillette adopt to encourage men to switch from disposables to system razors? How would buyer decision processes toward new products affect your recommendations?

5. What explains Bic's differing success in competing against Gillette in the disposable pen, lighter and shaver market? Why do you think Bic perfume failed?

Source:   Portions adapted from 'The Gillette Company', in Subhash C. Jain, *Marketing Strategy & Policy*, 3rd edn (Cincinnati, OH: Southwestern, 1990). Used with permission.

## CHAPTER EIGHT

# Business markets and business buyer behaviour

## CHAPTER OBJECTIVES

After reading this chapter, you should be able to:

- Explain how business markets differ from consumer markets.

- Identify the main factors that influence business buyer behaviour.

- List and define the steps in the business buying decision process.

- Explain how institutional and government buyers make their buying decisions.

## CHAPTER PREVIEW

### Selling business jets: the ultimate executive toy

On 3 November 1994 Tiny Rowland agreed to retire from the board of Lonrho after a long and bitter struggle against German property owner, Dieter Bock. On that day he lost more than the job he had held for thirty-three years, he also lost access to Lonrho's Gulfstream executive jet. Tiny Rowland often used the jet to visit Lonrho's 500 companies or many international contacts, especially in Africa, but it was a £2m. a year item that many of Lonrho's shareholders resented.

1 ecu =
UK£0.83

The shareholders' views on Lonrho's business jet were akin to those held by many people. As Brian Barents, president of Learjet explained: 'The business jet has gone from being the sign of a dynamic, fast-moving, entrepreneurial corporation to one of corporate privilege and excess.' The business jet market was hitting hard times. Businesses were looking at their costs and there seemed to be fewer and fewer charismatic and powerful people like Tiny Rowland or King Fahd of Saudi Arabia who were willing and able to buy a jet. Shareholders had reason to be sceptical about the cost-effectiveness of the jets. Unlike commercial airlines that spend most of their time flying, business jets spend most of their time on the ground. In Europe they fly on average for only about six hours a week.

'There is simply not enough viable business for seven or eight competing manufacturers,' complained one business jet marketing executive. 'There is bound to be more consolidation, since there is probably room for only three or four manufacturers.' Business jets' low utilization means that they last a long time and ownership is limited. The United States is by far the biggest market with 4,000 business jets operating, France has 490, Germany 360 and the United Kingdom 260. Japan is a very wealthy market but government restrictions have kept private ownership down to 90.

Recognizing potential buyers is simple – the organizations that can afford to own and operate a business jet are easily identified. The difficult problem is reaching key decision makers for jet purchases, understanding their complex motivations and decision processes, analysing what factors will be important in their decisions, and designing marketing approaches.

There are *rational* motives and *subjective* factors in buyers' decisions. A company buying a business jet will evaluate the aircraft on quality and performance, prices, operating costs and service. At times, these may appear to be the only things that drive the buying decision. But having a superior product isn't enough to land the sale: marketers must also consider the more subtle *human factors* that affect the choice of a jet. According to Gulfstream, a leading American supplier of business jets:

> The purchase process may be initiated by the chief executive officer (CEO), a board member wishing to increase efficiency or security, the company's chief pilot, or through vendor efforts like advertising or a sales visit. The CEO will be central in deciding whether to buy the jet, but he or she will be heavily influenced by the company's pilot, financial officer and perhaps by the board itself.
>
> Each party in the buying process has subtle roles and needs. The salesperson who, for example, tries to impress both the CEO with depreciation schedules and the chief pilot with minimum runway statistics will almost certainly not sell a plane if he or she overlooks the psychological and emotional components of the buying decision. 'For the chief executive', observes one salesperson, 'you need all the numbers for support, but if you can't find the kid inside the CEO and excite him or her with the raw beauty of the new plane, you'll never sell the equipment. If you sell the excitement, you sell the jet.'
>
> The chief pilot, as an equipment expert, often has veto power over purchase decisions and may be able to stop the purchase of a certain brand of jet by simply expressing a negative opinion about, say, the plane's bad weather capabilities. In this sense, the pilot not only influences the decision but also serves as an information 'gatekeeper' by advising management on the equipment to select. Though the corporate legal staff will handle the purchase agreement and the purchasing department will acquire the jet, these parties may have little to say about whether or how the plane will be obtained and which type will be selected. The users of the jet – middle and upper management of the buying company, important customers and others – may have at least an indirect role in choosing the equipment.
>
> The involvement of many people in the purchase decision creates a group dynamic that the selling company must factor into its sales planning. Who makes up the buying group? How will the parties interact? Who will dominate and who submit? What priorities do the individuals have?

Two European companies think they have an answer to competing in this competitive and increasingly cost-conscious business aircraft market. France's Aérospatiale's Socata subsidiary, with Mooney of the United States, have spent FFr500 million developing the TBM700, a single-engined turboprop aircraft. It is smaller and slower than conventional twin-engined business jets but much less expensive to buy and run. Aérospatiale, who claims the TBM700 has some of the capabilities and comfort of the larger executive jets, hopes to sell 600 of them.

The other market entrant is JetCo. They do not make aircraft but offer a 'fractional ownership' scheme that claims to offer all the benefits of private ownership at a fraction of the cost. 'As little as $7,000' per month buys a share in one of JetCo's fleet of Hawker 800 or Beechjet 400A 860-plus kilometres per hour jets, or Beechcraft Super King Air B200 twin-turboprop aircraft. Michael Riegal, managing director of JetCo, explains the financial advantages of JetShare: 'A corporate jet is an extremely expensive asset with annual

1 ecu = US$1.26
= FFr 6.47
(French francs)

operating cost of between $800,000 and $1m if you include fixed and variable cost as well as depreciation.' As an alternative JetShare offers one-quarter ownership of a corporate jet, with an entitlement to
150 flying hours, for $287,500 per year. When in use, JetCo puts a temporary company logo on the front
of the jet and will even personalize 'cushion covers and things – items that are easily changeable'.

Not all business jet makers are taking the frugal route. Canada's Bombardier is developing the
Global Express (Gex) BD-700 business jet capable of carrying eight passengers and four crew non-
stop on sectors such as San Francisco–Tokyo, London–Tokyo and Paris–Buenos Aires. Gex is faster
than other business jets: cruising at Mach 0.88 (that is, 88 per cent of the speed of sound) it will
knock an hour off their times on shorter routes like Johannesburg–Moscow or Berlin–Los Angeles.
Launched at the end of 1993 with a development cost of C$1.4bn, within a year the company had
orders and options for forty aircraft worth C$1.5bn. Wow, some toy![1]

1 ecu = US$1.26
= C$1.72
(Canadian dollars)

In some ways, selling corporate jets to business buyers is like selling cars and
kitchen appliances to families. Business jet makers ask the same questions as consumer marketers: Who are the buyers and what are their needs? How do buyers make
their buying decisions and what factors influence these decisions? What marketing
programme will be most effective? But the answers to these questions are usually different in the case of the business buyer. Thus the jet makers face many of the same
challenges as consumer marketers – and some additional ones.

In one way or another, most large companies sell to other organizations. Many
companies, such as Asea Brown Boveri, Norsk Hydro, Du Pont and countless other
firms, sell *most* of their products to other businesses. Even large consumer-products
companies, which make products used by final consumers, must first sell their products to other businesses. For example, Allied Domecq makes many consumer products – La Ina sherry, Presidente brandy, Tetley tea and others. To sell these products
to consumers, Allied Domecq must first sell them to wholesalers and retailers that
serve the consumer market. Allied Domecq also sells food ingredients directly to
other businesses through its Margetts Food and DCA Food Industries subsidiaries.

The **business market** consists of all the organizations that buy goods and services
to use in the production of other products and services that are sold, rented or supplied to others. It also includes retailing and wholesaling firms that acquire goods for
the purpose of reselling or renting them to others at a profit. The **business buying
process** is the decision-making process by which business buyers establish the need
for purchased products and services, and identify, evaluate and choose among alternative brands and suppliers.[2] Companies that sell to other business organizations
must do their best to understand business markets and business buyer behaviour.

## BUSINESS MARKETS

The business market is *huge*: most businesses just sell to other businesses and sales
to businesses far outstrip those to consumers. The reason for this is the number of
times parts of a consumer product is bought, processes and resold before reaching
the final consumer. For example, Figure 8.1 shows the large number of business
transactions needed to produce and sell a simple pair of shoes. Hide dealers sell to
tanners, who sell leather to shoe manufacturers, who sell shoes to wholesalers, who
in turn sell shoes to retailers, who finally sell the shoes to consumers. Each party in
the chain also buys many other related goods and services. This example shows why
there is more business buying than consumer buying – many sets of *business* purchases were made for only one set of *consumer* purchases.

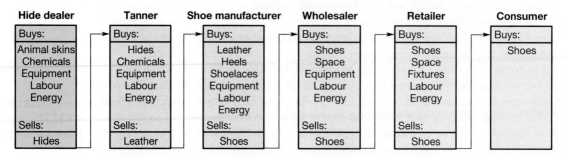

| Hide dealer | Tanner | Shoe manufacturer | Wholesaler | Retailer | Consumer |
|---|---|---|---|---|---|
| **Buys:** | **Buys:** | **Buys:** | **Buys:** | **Buys:** | **Buys:** |
| Animal skins<br>Chemicals<br>Equipment<br>Labour<br>Energy | Hides<br>Chemicals<br>Equipment<br>Labour<br>Energy | Leather<br>Heels<br>Shoelaces<br>Equipment<br>Labour<br>Energy | Shoes<br>Space<br>Equipment<br>Labour<br>Energy | Shoes<br>Space<br>Fixtures<br>Labour<br>Energy | Shoes |
| **Sells:** | **Sells:** | **Sells:** | **Sells:** | **Sells:** | |
| Hides | Leather | Shoes | Shoes | Shoes | |

**Figure 8.1**    Business transactions involved in producing and distributing a pair of shoes.

## Characteristics of business markets

In some ways, business markets are similar to consumer markets. Both involve people who assume buying roles and make purchase decisions to satisfy needs. However, business markets differ in many ways from consumer markets.[3] The main differences are in market structure and demand, the nature of the buying unit, and the types of decisions and the decision process involved.

### Market structure and demand

The business marketer normally deals with *far fewer but far larger buyers* than the consumer marketer does. For example, when Michelin sells replacement tyres to final consumers, its potential market includes the owners of cars currently in use. But Michelin's fate in the business market depends on getting orders from a few large

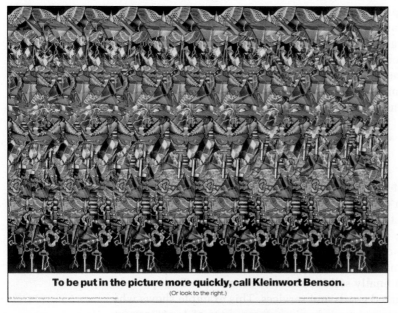

**To be put in the picture more quickly, call Kleinwort Benson.**
(Or look to the right.)

**Kleinwort Benson.
The power house.**

**Kleinwort Benson**

**We're focused.**

Merchant Banks, like Kleinwort Benson, have few large buyers who are concentrated in the world's financial market. Their 3D image campaign promotes their strength in sector expertise.

Courtaulds Fibres sells Tencel to the people who sell fabrics, to the people who sell garments, to the retailers who sell them to consumers. Advertising Tencel to consumers pulls the fibre through the chain.

car makers. These sales of original equipment are doubly important since many people replace their tyres with the brand already on the car. Even in large business markets, a few buyers normally account for most of the purchasing.

Business markets are also more *geographically concentrated*: international financial services in London, petrochemicals and synthetic fibres around Rotterdam and Amsterdam, and the movie industry in Hollywood. Further, business demand is **derived demand** – it ultimately derives from the demand for consumer goods. Mercedes buys steel because consumers buy cars. If consumer demand for cars drops, so will the demand for steel and all the other products used to make cars. Therefore, business marketers sometimes promote their products directly to final consumers to increase business demand (see Marketing Highlight 8.1).[4]

Many business markets have **inelastic demand**; that is, total demand for many business products is not affected much by price changes, especially in the short run. A drop in the price of leather will not cause shoe manufacturers to buy much more leather unless it results in lower shoe prices that, in turn, will increase consumer demand for shoes.

Finally, business markets have more *fluctuating demand*. The demand for many business goods and services tends to change more – and more quickly – than the demand for consumer goods and services does. A small percentage increase in consumer demand can cause large increases in business demand. Sometimes a rise of only 10 per cent in consumer demand can cause as much as a 200 per cent rise in business demand during the next period.

## Intel (not) inside

In mid-1991, Intel launched its two-year, $100-million 'Intel Inside' advertising campaign to sell personal computer buyers on the virtues of its 386 and 486 microprocessors, the tiny chips that serve as the brains of microcomputers. In 1994 that was followed by an $80-million campaign to persuade consumers and businesses to buy PCs based on its latest Pentium microprocessor. So what, you say? Lots of companies run big consumer ad campaigns. However, although such a campaign might be business as usual for companies like Nestlé, Shell or Unilever that market products directly to final consumers, it is anything but usual for Intel.

Computer buyers can't purchase a microprocessor chip directly – in fact, most will never even see one. Demand for microprocessors is *derived demand* – it ultimately comes from demand for products that *contain* microprocessors. Consumers simply buy the computer and take whatever brand of chip the computer manufacturer chose to include as a component. Traditionally, chip companies like Intel market only to the manufacturers who buy chips directly. In contrast, the innovative 'Intel Inside' campaign appeals directly to computer buyers – its customers' customers. If Intel can create brand preference among buyers for *its* chips, this in turn will make Intel chips more attractive to computer manufacturers. According to industry observers: 'Intel is treating the (PC) industry merely as a distribution arm, seeing the PC user as its ultimate consumer.'

Intel invented the first microprocessor in 1971 and for 20 years has held a near-monopoly, dominating the chip market for desktop computers. Its sales and profits have soared accordingly. In the decade since IBM introduced its first PCs based on Intel's 8088 microprocessor, Intel sales have jumped fivefold to more than $5 billion and its earnings have grown even faster. Its popular 286, 386, 486 and Pentium

chips power most of the microcomputers in use today.

Recently, however, a rush of imitators – Advanced Micro Devices (AMD), Chips & Technologies, Cyrix and others – have begun to crack Intel's monopoly, marketing new and improved clones of Intel chips. AMD claims more than a third of the 386 chip market although Intel retains roughly 90 per cent share of the world microprocessor market. So far the onslaught of 386 and 486 clones has not dented Intel's 63 per cent gross margin. Intel has the next-generation Pentium market to itself for now, but AMD, Nexgen and Cyrix cloners will soon offer 'Pentium class' chips as well.

Intel has responded fiercely to the cloners, slashing prices, spending heavily to develop new products, and advertising to differentiate its products. It has cut prices on its 486s faster than for any new chip in its history. Moreover, in 1993, Intel invested a whopping $2.5 billion in R&D to get new products to the market more quickly. The new Pentium microprocessor is a veritable one-chip mainframe. The Pentium contains 3 million transistors and will process 100 million instructions per second (MIPS), as compared to only one-half million transistors and five MIPS for the 386 chip. Intel's in-store demonstrations have a Pentium PC whizzing through tasks while older 486SX machines crank away behind. Pentium is not the end; Intel plans to create a new chip family every two years. The next generation, codenamed the P6, is not far off, and by the year 2000, it will offer a chip with 100 million transistors and 2 *billion* instructions per second – that's roughly equal to today's supercomputers.

Still, the clone makers are likely to continue nipping at Intel's heels, and advertising provides another means by which Intel can differentiate its 'originals' from competitors' imitations. The 'Intel Inside' campaign advances on two fronts. First, in its brand-

### Nature of the buying unit

Compared with consumer purchases, a business purchase usually involves *more buyers* and a *more professional purchasing effort*. Often, business buying is done by trained purchasing agents who spend their working lives learning how to buy better. The more complex the purchase, the more likely that several people will participate in the decision-making process. Buying committees made up of technical experts

awareness ads, Intel attempts to convince microcomputer buyers that Intel microprocessors really are better. The ads carry the message 'It's amazing what you can do with a Pentium processor'.

As a second important element of the 'Intel Inside' campaign, Intel also subsidizes ads by PC manufacturers that include the 'Intel Inside' logo. So far, more than 100 companies have featured the logo in their ads, including dan, NCR, Dell, Zenith and AST. Participating manufacturers claim that the campaign has increased their advertising effectiveness. 'The "Intel Inside" programme has been a good programme for us,' says the advertising manager of a large computer manufacturing firm. 'It has helped add some credibility and enhancements to our messages.' In the first six months of the campaign, more than 1,500 pages of 'Intel Inside' ads were run.

It remains to be seen whether the 'Intel Inside' campaign can convince buyers to care about what chip comes in their computers. But as long as microprocessors remain anonymous little lumps hidden inside a user's computer, Intel remains at the mercy of the clone makers. In contrast, if Intel can convince buyers that its chips are superior, it will achieve even more power in the market.

The reaction of IBM and Compaq, the leading PC supplier in the United States and Europe, suggests that Intel may be being too successful. For years Intel and Compaq collaborated in bringing Intel microprocessor-based PCs to markets, but the two firms are hardly on speaking terms now. Eckhard Pfeffer, Compaq president and chief executive, has accused

Intel of undermining Compaq's marketing effort. 'What upsets us generally is that a component supplier should try to influence the end user. The end user market is not their business. They are interfering' says Andreas Barth, head of Compaq's European operations. Not surprisingly, Compaq's latest PCs for the consumer market will have an AMD microprocessor inside.

Compaq are also annoyed by Intel forcing the pace of change in the industry. Intel's Pentium campaign started after Compaq had built up stocks of $2.2bn as backing for its campaign to increase its world market share. Most of the stocks are sophisticated machines but with the old Intel 486 chip inside. Intel is not sympathetic. 'The 486-based PC is not the machine you should be buying,' according to Hans Geyer, Intel's European operations head. 'Any company that has an inventory of one kind of product when the market prefers another is in a dangerous position.'

IBM are also annoyed about the rapid obsolescence of the Intel products they buy. 'Customers are telling us to slow down the pace of technology,' says IBM's Chairman, Lou Gerstner. 'How powerful a computer do you really need on a desk?' To challenge Intel's dominance, IBM are linking with Nexgen and Cyrix to give credibility to their clones.

Have Intel successfully assured their dominance of the microprocessor market or have they forgotten the golden rule: the customer is always right? To Compaq, it seems as though Intel is saying to them loud and clear, 'You, our biggest customer, are wrong'.

Sources: Quotes from Kate Bertrand, 'Advertising a chip you'll never see', *Business Marketing* (February 1992), 19; and Richard Brandt, 'Intel: way out in front, but the footsteps are getting larger', *Business Week* (29 April 1991), 88–9; see also Robert D. Hof, 'Inside Intel', *Business Week* (1 June 1992), 86–94; Bertrand, 'Chip wars', *Business Marketing* (February 1992), 16–18; Alan Deutschman, 'If they're gaining on you, innovate', *Fortune* (2 November 1992), 56–61; Richard Brandt, 'Intel: what a tease – and what a strategy', *Business Week* (22 February 1993), 40; Louise Kehoe and Alan Cane, 'Chips down for PC partner', *Financial Times* (20 September 1994), 21; and Louise Kehoe and Geoff Wheelwright, 'Breaking windows', *Financial Times* (4 October 1994), 16.

and top management are common in the buying of primary goods. Therefore, business marketers must have well-trained salespeople to deal with well-trained buyers.

## Types of decisions and the decision process

Business buyers usually face *more complex* buying decisions than do consumer buyers. Purchases often involve large sums of money, complex technical and economic considerations, and interactions among many people at many levels of the buyer's organization. Because the purchases are more complex, business buyers may take longer to make their decisions. For example, the purchase of a large computer system might take many months or more than a year to complete and could involve millions of dollars, thousands of technical details and dozens of people ranging from top management to lower-level users.

The business buying process tends to be *more formalized* than the consumer buying process. Large business purchases usually call for detailed product specifications, written purchase orders, careful supplier searches and formal approval. The buying firm might even prepare policy manuals that detail the purchase process.

Finally, in the business buying process, buyer and seller are often much *more dependent* on each other. Consumer marketers are usually at a distance from their customers. In contrast, business marketers may roll up their sleeves and work closely with their customers during all stages of the buying process – from helping customers define problems, to finding solutions, to supporting after-sale operation. For instance, 60 per cent of the money needed to develop Bombardier's Gax business jet came from suppliers, and risk-sharing partners including engine suppliers BMW/Rolls-Royce. They customize their offerings to meet individual customer needs. In the short run, orders go to suppliers who meet buyers' immediate product and service needs. However, business marketers must also build close *long-run* relationships with customers. In the long run, business marketers keep a customer's orders by meeting current needs *and* thinking ahead to meet the customer's future needs.

> Volkswagen is breaking new ground at its Skoda factory by having suppliers' operations directly inside the car plant. Lucas, Johnson Controls and Pelzer are producing rear axles, seats and carpets in the Czech factory. This is one step ahead of Japanese manufacturers who often have suppliers near by.[5]

### Other characteristics of business markets

*Direct purchasing*  Business buyers often buy directly from producers rather than through middlemen, especially for items that are technically complex or expensive. For example, in the United States, Ryder buys thousands of trucks each year in all shapes and sizes. It rents some of these trucks to move-it-yourself customers (yellow Ryder trucks), leases some to other companies for their truck fleets and uses the rest in its own freight-hauling business. When Ryder buys GMC trucks, it purchases them directly from General Motors rather than from independent GM truck dealers. Similarly, airlines buy aircraft directly from Boeing, European Airbus or McDonnell Douglas, Kroger buys packaged goods directly from Procter & Gamble, and universities buy mainframe computers directly from IBM, Bull, and so on.

*Reciprocity*  Business buyers often practise *reciprocity*, selecting suppliers who also buy from them. For example, a paper company might buy needed chemicals from a chemical company that in turn buys the company's paper.

> Shaken by European Airbus's success in the airliner market, market leader Boeing has started a worldwide review of its purchasing policies. They intend to match aircraft parts contracts to countries who buy Boeings. With an apparent eye on the Canadian government's purchase of search-and-rescue helicopters and Canadian Airlines International's 737 replacements, Boeing warned: 'Our Canadian business placement must understandably be market based, as it is elsewhere.'[6]

*Leasing*  Business buyers increasingly are leasing equipment instead of buying it outright. Everything from printing presses to power plants, business jets to hay balers, and office copiers to off-shore drilling rigs. The biggest buyer of airliners in the world is not a large airline but GPA, a company based in Ireland who buys airliners to resell or lease. The lessee can gain a number of advantages, such as having more available capital, getting the seller's latest products, receiving better servicing and gaining some tax advantages. The lessor often ends up with a larger net income and the chance to sell to customers who might not have been able to afford outright purchase.

## A model of business buyer behaviour

At the most basic level, marketers want to know how business buyers will respond to various marketing stimuli. Figure 8.2 shows a model of business buyer behaviour. In this model, marketing and other stimuli affect the buying organization and produce certain buyer responses. As with consumer buying, the marketing stimuli for business buying consist of the four *P*s: product, price, place and promotion. Other stimuli include influential forces in the environment: economic, technological, political, cultural and competitive. These stimuli enter the organization and are turned into buyer responses: product or service choice; supplier choice; order quantities; and delivery, service and payment terms. In order to design good marketing-mix strategies, the marketer must understand what happens within the organization to turn stimuli into purchase responses.

Within the organization, buying activity consists of two main parts: the buying centre, made up of all the people involved in the buying decision, and the buying decision process. Figure 8.2 shows that the buying centre and the buying decision process are influenced by internal organizational, interpersonal and individual factors as well as by external environmental factors.

## BUSINESS BUYER BEHAVIOUR

The model in Figure 8.2 suggests four questions about business buyer behaviour: What buying decisions do business buyers make? Who participates in the buying process? What are the strongest influences on buyers? How do business buyers make their buying decisions?

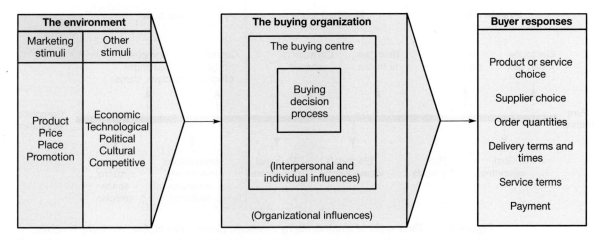

**Figure 8.2**   A model of business buyer behaviour.

## What buying decisions do business buyers make?

The business buyer faces a whole set of decisions in making a purchase. The number of decisions depends on the type of buying situation.

### Main types of buying situations

There are three main types of buying situations.[7] At one extreme is the *straight rebuy*, which is a fairly routine decision. At the other extreme is the *new task*, which may call for thorough research. In the middle is the *modified rebuy*, which requires some research. (For examples, see Figure 8.3.)

*Straight rebuy*    In a **straight rebuy**, the buyer reorders something without any modifications. It is usually handled on a routine basis by the purchasing department. Based on past buying satisfaction, the buyer simply chooses from the various suppliers on its list. 'In' suppliers try to maintain product and service quality. They often propose automatic reordering systems so that the purchase agent will save reordering time. The 'out' suppliers try to offer something new or exploit dissatisfaction so that the buyer will consider them. 'Out' suppliers try to get their foot in the door with a small order and then enlarge their purchase share over time.

*Modified rebuy*    In a **modified rebuy**, the buyer wants to modify product specifications, prices, terms, or suppliers. The modified rebuy usually involves more decision participants than the straight rebuy. The 'in' suppliers may become nervous and feel pressured to put their best foot forward to protect an account. 'Out' suppliers may see the modified rebuy situation as an opportunity to make a better offer and gain new business.

*New task*    A company buying a product or service for the first time faces a **new task** situation. In such cases, the greater the cost or risk, the larger will be the number of decision participants and the greater their efforts to collect information. The new-task situation is the marketer's greatest opportunity and challenge. The marketer not only tries to reach as many key buying influences as possible, but also provides help and information.

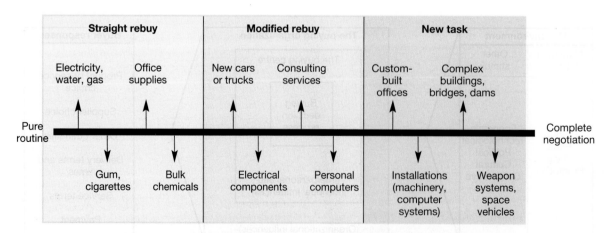

**Figure 8.3**    Three types of business buying situations. (Source: Ben M. Enis, *Marketing Principles*, 3rd edn (1980) © 1980 Scott, Foresman and Co. Reprinted by permission.)

## Specific buying decisions

The buyer makes the fewest decisions in the straight rebuy and the most in the new-task decision. In the new-task situation, the buyer must decide on product specifications, suppliers, price limits, payment terms, order quantities, delivery times and service terms. The order of these decisions varies with each situation and different decision participants influence each choice.

## Systems buying and selling

Many business buyers prefer to buy a packaged solution to a problem from a single seller. Called **systems buying**, this practice began with government buying of powerful weapons and communication systems. Instead of buying and putting all the components together, the government asked for bids from suppliers who would supply the components *and* assemble the package or system.

Sellers increasingly have recognized that buyers like this method and have adopted systems selling as a marketing tool.[8] Systems selling is a two-step process. First, the supplier sells a group of interlocking products: for example, the supplier sells not only glue, but also applicators and dryers. Second, the supplier sells a system of production, inventory control, distribution and other services to meet the buyer's need for a smooth-running operation.

Systems selling is a key business marketing strategy for winning and holding accounts. The contract often goes to the firm that provides the most complete system meeting the customer's needs. Consider the following:

> The Indonesian government requested bids to build a cement factory near Jakarta. An American firm's proposal included choosing the site, designing the cement factory, hiring the construction crews, assembling the materials and equipment and turning the finished factory over to the Indonesian government. A Japanese firm's proposal included all of these services, plus hiring and training workers to run the factory, exporting the cement through their trading companies and using the cement to build some needed roads and new office buildings in Jakarta. Although the Japanese firm's proposal cost more, it won the contract. Clearly the Japanese viewed the problem not as one of just building a cement factory (the narrow view of systems selling) but of running it in a way that would contribute to the country's economy. They took the broadest view of the customers' needs. This is true systems selling.

## Who participates in the business buying process?

Who buys the goods and services needed by business oganizations? The decision-making unit of a buying organization is called its **buying centre**, defined as all the individuals and units that participate in the business decision-making process.[9]

The buying centre includes all members of the organization who play any of five roles in the purchase decision process.[10]

1. **Users**. Members of the organization who will use the product or service. In many cases, users initiate the buying proposal and help define product specifications.
2. **Influencers**. People who affect the buying decision. They often help define specifications and also provide information for evaluating alternatives. Technical personnel are particularly important influencers.
3. **Buyers**. People with formal authority to select the supplier and arrange terms of purchase. Buyers may help shape product specifications, but they play their most important role in selecting vendors and in negotiating. In more complex purchases, buyers might include high-level officers participating in the negotiations.

JetCo's jet sharing service offers convenience to the *user* and economics to the *buyer*.

EVERY BUSINESSMAN'S DREAM...
...AT A FRACTION OF THE COST.

If you have travelled using a corporate jet you know how productive, convenient and flexible this type of travel is. Unfortunately, few corporate aircraft owners fly enough to make a dedicated aircraft cost-effective.

The answer is jet sharing, a revolutionary new way of owning a corporate jet that cuts the cost of ownership whilst giving you more of the benefits you would expect from corporate aviation. Jet sharing also eliminates the hassle often associated with corporate aircraft ownership.

Jet sharing allows you to buy only the time you need on an aircraft by offering for sale as little as a one eighth fraction; and we can offer you a choice of brand new jet aircraft from the market leading manufacturer, Cessna Aircraft Company.

You can purchase a share from as little as US$500,000, giving you a guaranteed number of flight hours per annum on our fleet of identical aircraft. Thereafter you pay modest fixed monthly and hourly charges. You do not pay for empty positioning flights nor are there any other nasty financial surprises. JetCo guarantees aircraft availability, fixed depreciation and the highest standards of operation, all at a fraction of the cost of traditional aircraft ownership.

JetCo is backed by Air London International PLC in co-operation with Avcon Ltd. With US$ 60 million of combined turnover, over 10,000 flights per annum and 50 aircraft under management, JetCo offers you cost-effective European corporate aviation from two of Europe's largest, and most experienced, companies.

JETCO

*Jet sharing from JetCo - Cutting the cost of corporate aviation.*

Air London
INTERNATIONAL

4. **Deciders**. People who have formal or informal power to select or approve the final suppliers. In routine buying, the buyers are often the deciders or at least the approvers.
5. **Gatekeepers**. People who control the flow of information to others. For example, purchasing agents often have authority to prevent salespersons from seeing users or deciders. Other gatekeepers include technical personnel and even personal secretaries.

The buying centre is not a fixed and formally identified unit within the buying organization. It is a set of buying roles assumed by different people for different purchases. Within the organization, the size and make-up of the buying centre will vary for different products and for different buying situations. For some routine purchases, one person – say, a purchasing agent – may assume all the buying centre roles and serve as the only person involved in the buying decision. For more complex purchases, the buying centre may include twenty or thirty people from different levels and departments in the organization. One study of business buying showed that the typical business equipment purchase involved seven people from three management levels representing four different departments.

The buying-centre concept presents a significant marketing challenge. The business marketer must learn who participates in the decision, each participant's relative influence and what evaluation criteria each decision participant uses. Consider the following example:

Baxter sells disposable surgical gowns to hospitals. It tries to identify the hospital personnel involved in this buying decision. They turn out to be the purchasing manager, the operating room administrator and the surgeons. Each participant plays a different role. The vice-president of purchasing analyses whether the hospital should buy disposable gowns or reusable gowns. If analysis favours disposable gowns, then the operating room administrator compares competing products and prices and makes a choice. This administrator considers the gown's absorbency, antiseptic quality, design and cost and normally buys the brand that meets requirements at the lowest cost. Finally, surgeons affect the decision later by reporting their satisfaction or dissatisfaction with the brand.

The buying centre usually includes some obvious participants who are involved formally in the buying decision. For example, the decision to buy a corporate jet will probably involve the company's chief pilot, a purchasing agent, some legal staff, a member of top management and others formally charged with the buying decision. It may also involve less obvious, informal participants, some of whom may actually make or strongly affect the buying decision. Sometimes, even the people in the buying centre are not aware of all the buying participants. For example, the decision about which corporate jet to buy may actually be made by a corporate board member who has an interest in flying and knows a lot about aircraft. This board member may work behind the scenes to sway the decision. Many business buying decisions result from the complex interactions of ever-changing buying-centre participants.

## What are the main influences on business buyers?

Business buyers are subject to many influences when they make their buying decisions. Some marketers assume that the strongest influences are economic. They think buyers will favour the supplier who offers the lowest price or the best product or the most service. They concentrate on offering strong economic benefits to buyers. However, business buyers actually respond to both economic and personal factors:

> It has not been fashionable lately to talk about relationships in business. We're told that it has to be devoid of emotion. We must be cold, calculating and impersonal. Don't you believe it. Relationships make the world go round. Business people are human and social as well as interested in economics and investments and salespeople need to appeal to both sides. Purchasers may claim to be motivated by intellect alone, but the professional salesperson knows that they run on both reason and emotion.[11]

When suppliers' offers are very similar, business buyers have little basis for strictly rational choice. Because they can meet organizational goals with any supplier, buyers can allow personal factors to play a larger role in their decisions. However, when competing products differ greatly, business buyers are more accountable for their choice and tend to pay more attention to economic factors.

Figure 8.4 lists various groups of influences on business buyers – environmental, organization, interpersonal and individual.[12]

### *Environmental factors*

Business buyers are influenced heavily by factors in the current and expected *economic environment*, such as the level of primary demand, the economic outlook and the cost of money. As economic uncertainty rises, business buyers cut back on new investments and attempt to reduce their inventories.

An increasingly important environmental factor is shortages in key materials. Many companies are now more willing to buy and hold larger inventories of scarce materials to ensure adequate supply. Business buyers are also affected by technological, political and competitive developments in the environment. Culture and customs can strongly influence business buyer reactions to the marketer's behaviour and strategies, especially in the international marketing environment (see Marketing

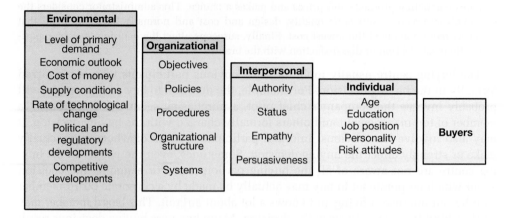

**Figure 8.4**    Main influences on business buying behaviour.

Highlight 8.2). The business marketer must watch these factors, determine how they will affect the buyer, and try to turn these challenges into opportunities.

## Organizational factors

Each buying organization has its own objectives, policies, procedures, structure and systems, which must be understood by the business marketer. Questions such as these arise: How many people are involved in the buying decision? Who are they? What are their evaluative criteria? What are the company's policies and limits on its buyers? In addition, the business marketer should be aware of the following organizational trends in the purchasing area.

*Upgraded purchasing*    Buying departments have often occupied a low position in the management hierarchy, even though they often manage more than half of the company's costs. In some industries, such as telecommunications, manufacturers buy in items approaching 80 per cent of total cost. With good reason many companies are upgrading their purchasing activities. Some companies have combined several functions – such as purchasing, inventory control, production scheduling and traffic – into a high-level function called *strategic materials management*. Buying departments in many multinational companies have responsibility for buying materials and services around the world. Many companies are offering higher compensation in order to attract top talent in the buying area. This means that business marketers must also upgrade their salespeople to match the quality of today's business buyers.[13]

*Centralized purchasing*    In companies consisting of many divisions with differing needs, much of the purchasing is carried out at the division level. Recently, however, some large companies have tried to centralize purchasing. Headquarters identifies materials purchased by several divisions and buys them centrally. Centralized purchasing gives the company more purchasing clout, which can produce substantial savings.

> PepsiCo aims to save $100m. a year, out of total costs of $2bn, by combining the buying power of their separate businesses. Paul Steele, their European vice-president of sales and marketing: 'When we went through the list it was surprising. For example, Pizza Hut buys an enormous quantity of cardboard for the boxes; Pepsi-Cola buys cardboard for soft drink trays. We're looking at whether we can leverage the sale.' They will try the same with buy-

ing flour, salt, spices, cooking oil and TV advertising air-time. 'The businesses developed very separately. We didn't have the scale to do this before, but it has suddenly become a very exciting proposition.'[14]

For the business marketer, this development means dealing with fewer, higher-level buyers. Instead of using regional salesforces to sell a large buyer's separate plants, the seller may use a *national account salesforce* to service the buyer. For example, at Xerox, over 250 national account managers each handle one to five large national accounts with many scattered locations. The national account managers coordinate the efforts of an entire Xerox team – specialists, analysts, salespeople for individual products – to sell and service important national customers.[15] National account selling is challenging and demands both a high-level salesforce and sophisticated marketing effort.

*Long-term contracts*   Business buyers are increasingly seeking long-term contracts with suppliers. For example, GM wants to buy from fewer suppliers who are willing to locate close to their plants and produce high-quality components. Business marketers also are beginning to offer *electronic order interchange* systems to their customers. When using such systems, the seller places terminals hooked to its own computers in customers' offices. Then the customer can order needed items instantly by entering orders directly into the computer. The orders are transmitted automatically to the supplier. Many hospitals order directly from Baxter using order-taking terminals in their stockrooms. And many bookstores order from Follett's in this way.

*Purchasing performance evaluation*   Some companies are setting up incentive systems to reward purchasing managers for especially good purchasing performance, in much the same way that salespeople receive bonuses for especially good selling performance. These systems should lead purchasing managers to increase their pressure on sellers for the best terms.

*Just-in-time production systems*   The emergence of *just-in-time production systems* has had a considerable impact on business purchasing policies. Marketing Highlight 8.3 describes the effects of just-in-time on business marketing.

### Interpersonal factors

The buying centre usually includes many participants who influence each other. The business marketer often finds it difficult to determine what kinds of *interpersonal factors* and group dynamics enter into the buying process. As one writer notes: 'Managers do not wear tags that say "decision maker" or "unimportant person". The powerful are often invisible, at least to vendor representatives.'[16] Nor does the buying-centre participant with the highest rank always have the most influence. Participants may have influence in the buying decision because they control rewards and punishments, are well liked, have special expertise, or have a special relationship with other important participants. Interpersonal factors are often very subtle. Whenever possible, business marketers must try to understand these factors and design strategies that take them into account.

### Individual factors

Each participant in the business buying-decision process brings in personal motives, perceptions and preferences. These individual factors are affected by personal

## International marketing manners: when in Rome ...

Consolidated Amalgamation, Inc., thinks it's time that the rest of the world enjoyed the same fine products it has offered American consumers for two generations. It dispatches vice-president Harry E. Slicksmile to Europe to explore the territory. Mr Slicksmile stops first in London, where he makes short work of some bankers – he rings them up on the phone. He handles Parisians with similar ease: after securing a table at La Tour d'Argent, he greets his luncheon guest, the director of an industrial engineering firm, with the words, 'Just call me Harry, Jacques'.

In Germany, Mr Slicksmile is a powerhouse. Whisking through a lavish, state-of-the-art marketing presentation, complete with the flip charts and audio-visuals, he shows 'em that this Georgia boy *knows* how to make a buck. Heading on to Milan, Harry strikes up a conversation with the Japanese businessman sitting next to him on the plane. He flips his card onto the guy's tray and, when the two say good-bye, shakes hands warmly and clasps the man's right arm. Later, for his appointment with the owner of an Italian packaging-design firm, our hero wears his comfy corduroy sport coat, khaki pants and Topsiders. Everybody knows Italians are zany and laid back, right?

Wrong. Six months later, Consolidated Amalgamation has nothing to show for the trip but a pile of bills. There was nothing wrong with Consolidated Amalgamation's products but the orders probably went to firms whose representative had not antagonized and insulted people as much as Harry did. In Europe, they weren't wild about Harry.

This case has been exaggerated for emphasis. People are seldom such dolts as Harry E. Slicksmile, but success in international business has a lot to do with knowing the territory and its people. Poor Harry tried, all right, but in all the wrong ways. The British do not, as a rule, make deals over the phone as much as Americans do. It's not so much a 'cultural' difference as a difference in approach. A proper Frenchman neither likes instant familiarity – questions about family, church or alma mater – nor refers to strangers by their first names. 'That poor fellow, Jacques, probably wouldn't show anything, but he'd recoil. He'd *not* be pleased,' explains an expert on

French business practices. 'It's considered poor taste,' he continues. 'Even after months of business dealings, I'd wait for him or her to make the invitation [to use first names] ... You are always right, in Europe, to say "Mister".'

Harry's flashy presentation was probably also a flop with the Germans, who dislike overstatement and ostentatiousness. According to one German expert, however, German businessmen have become accustomed to dealing with Americans. Although differences in body language and customs remain, the past 20 years have softened them. 'I hugged an American woman at a business meeting last night,' he said. 'That would be normal in France, but [older] Germans still have difficulty [with the custom].' He says that calling secretaries by their first names would still be considered rude: 'They have a right to be called by the surname. You'd certainly ask – and get – permission first.' In Germany people address each other formally and correctly: for example, someone with two doctorates (which is quite common) must be referred to as 'Herr Doktor Doktor'.

When Harry Slicksmile grabbed his new Japanese acquaintance by the arm, the executive probably considered him disrespectful and presumptuous. The Japanese, like many others in Asia, have a 'no contact culture' in which even shaking hands is a strange experience. Harry made matters worse by tossing his business card. Japanese people revere the business card as an extension of self and as an indicator of rank. They do not *hand* it to people, they *present* it – with both hands. In addition, the Japanese are sticklers about rank. Unlike Americans, they don't heap praise on subordinates in a room; they will praise only the highest-ranking official present.

Hapless Harry's last gaffe was assuming that Italians are like Hollywood's stereotypes of them. The flair for design and style that has characterized Italian culture for centuries is embodied in the business people of Milan and Rome. They dress beautifully and admire flair, but they blanch at garishness or impropriety in others' attire.

In order to compete successfully in global markets, or even to deal effectively with international firms in their home markets, companies must help their managers to understand the needs, customs and cultures of international business buyers. Here are additional examples of a few rules of social and business etiquette that managers should understand when doing business in another country.

| | |
|---|---|
| France | Dress conservatively, except in the south where more casual clothes are worn. Do not refer to people by their first names – the French are formal with strangers. |
| Germany | Be especially punctual. A businessman invited to someone's home should present flowers, preferably unwrapped, to the hostess. During introductions, greet women first and wait until, or if, they extend their hands before extending yours. |
| Indonesia | Learn how to sing at least one song. At the end of formal gatherings people often take turns in singing unaccompanied. |
| Italy | Whether you dress conservatively or go native in a Giorgio Armani suit, keep in mind that Italian business people are style conscious. Make appointments well in advance. Prepare for and be patient with Italian bureaucracies. |
| Japan | Don't imitate Japanese bowing customs unless you understand them thoroughly – who bows to whom, how many times and when. It's a complicated ritual. Presenting business cards is another ritual. Carry many cards, present them with both hands so your name can be easily read and hand them to others in order of descending rank. Expect Japanese business executives to take time making decisions and to work through all of the details before making a commitment. |
| Saudi Arabia | Although men will kiss each other in greeting, they will never kiss a woman in public. An American woman should wait for a man to extend his hand before offering hers. If a Saudi offers refreshment, accept – it is an insult to decline it. |
| United Kingdom | Toasts are often given at formal dinners. If the host honours you with a toast, be prepared to reciprocate. Business entertaining is done more often at lunch than at dinner. |
| United States | Expect to be asked to meet and work at any time, over breakfast, lunch and dinner. Do not be taken in by street attire; American managers' dress code at work is very formal and conservative. |

Do not panic. Most business people you are likely to meet are used to dealing with overseas guests and are used to forgiving their failings. There is, however, a big gap between being forgiven for social transgressions and getting the best deal.

Sources: Adapted from Susan Harte, 'When in Rome, you should learn to do what the Romans do', *The Atlanta Journal-Constitution* (22 January 1990), D1, D6; see also Lufthansa's *Business Travel Guide/Europe*; Sergey Frank, 'Global negotiating', *Sales & Marketing Management* (May 1992), 64–9; and Malcolm Wheatley, 'Going, going, gone', *Business Life* (October 1994), 65–8.

## Just-in-time production changes organizational selling

Over the past several years, as Western businesses have studied the reasons for Japanese success in world markets, they have learned about and adopted several new manufacturing concepts such as just-in-time (JIT), early supplier involvement, value analysis, total quality management and lean manufacturing. Some, like Leyland Trucks, practice JIT across the whole value chain, and consequently only need to start production after they have orders. These practices greatly affect how business marketers sell to and service their customers.

JIT, in particular, has produced notable changes in business marketing. Just-in-time means that production materials arrive fit for use at the customer's factory exactly when needed for production, rather than being stored in the customer's inventory until used. The goal of JIT is zero inventory with 100 per cent quality. It calls for coordination between the production schedules of supplier and customer, so that neither has to carry much inventory. Effective use of JIT reduces inventory and lead times and increases quality, productivity and adaptability to change.

Business marketers need to be aware of the changes that JIT has caused in business purchasing practices and they must exploit the opportunities that JIT creates. Just-in-time has several important features and effects.

- *Strict quality control.* Buyers can achieve maximum cost savings from JIT only if they receive consistently high-quality goods. In fact, many analysts link JIT with the recent 'total quality management' movement.

> Most of the gains made in quality by American firms over the past decade can be credited to the JIT movement. JIT raised everyone's 'quality consciousness'; indeed, it has made quality 'job 1'. ... JIT brought the quality issue out in the open. You can't operate in a JIT mode without good quality.

Thus, JIT buyers expect suppliers to maintain strict quality. The business marketer needs to work closely with customers and meet their high quality standards.

- *Frequent and reliable delivery.* Daily delivery is often the only way to avoid inventory build-up. Increasingly, customers are setting delivery dates with penalties for not meeting them. Apple even penalizes for early delivery. Thus JIT means that business marketers must develop reliable transportation arrangements.
- *Closer location.* Since JIT involves frequent delivery, many business marketers have set up locations closer to their large JIT customers. Closer locations enable them to deliver smaller shipments more efficiently and reliably. Many firms have set up plants close to Nissan's car plant in the north of England and VW now has suppliers producing inside their Czech Skoda plant. Thus JIT means that a business marketer may have to make large commitments to important customers.

---

characteristics such as age, income, education, professional identification, personality and attitudes towards risk. Also, buyers have different buying styles. Some may be technical types who make in-depth analyses of competitive proposals before choosing a supplier. Other buyers may be intuitive negotiators who are adept at pitting the sellers against one another for the best deal.

> Secretaries and personal assistants are an important target for DHL, the express courier; they may be told by their boss to send a package but have the discretion to choose the courier. To contact them they advertise in *Executive PA* and other secretarial type publications and 'always attend the Secretaries Show'. In contrast UPS, who has a bias towards small business-to-business parcels, finds that most decisions are made by traffic, distribution and logistics managers. To contact them it schedules its TV advertising around sports events, prime time films and documentaries.[17]

- *Telecommunication.* New communication technologies let suppliers set up computerized purchasing systems that are hooked up to their customers. One large customer even requires that suppliers put their inventory figures and prices in the system. This allows for on-line JIT ordering as the computer looks for the lowest prices for available inventory. Such systems reduce transaction costs, but put pressure on business marketers to keep prices very competitive.

- *Single sourcing.* JIT requires that the buyer and seller work closely together to reduce costs. Often the business customer awards a long-term contract to only one trusted supplier. Single sourcing is increasing rapidly under JIT. Thus, whereas General Motors still uses more than 3,500 suppliers, Toyota, which has totally adopted JIT, uses fewer than 250 suppliers.

- *Value analysis.* The chief objectives of JIT are to reduce costs and improve quality, and value analysis is critical to that. To reduce costs of its product, a customer must not only reduce its own costs but also get its suppliers to reduce their costs. Suppliers with strong value analysis programmes have a competitive edge because they can contribute to their customers' value analysis.

- *Early supplier involvement.* Business buyers are increasingly bringing business marketers into the design process. Philips have involved suppliers in the development of their CDI compact disc-based entertainment system since it was in the concept stage. At Eindhoven Philips and Motorola, one of the main suppliers, has a joint design team working on the project. Thus business marketers must employ quality people who can work with customers' design teams.

- *Close relationship.* To make JIT successful, the business marketer and customer must work closely together to satisfy the customer's needs. If the company can customize offerings for the particular business customer, it will win the contract for a specific term. Both parties may invest lots of time and money to set up the JIT relationship. Because the costs of changing suppliers are high, business customers are very selective in choosing suppliers. Thus business marketers must improve their skill in *relationship marketing* as compared to *transaction marketing*. The marketer must try to achieve maximum profits over the entire relationship rather than over each transaction.

Sources: The quotation is from Ernest Raia, 'Just-in-time USA', *Purchasing* (13 February 1986), 48–62; see also G.H. Manoochehri, 'Suppliers and the just-in-time concept', *Journal of Purchasing and Materials Management* (winter 1984), 16–21; Eric K. Clemons and F. Warren McFarlan, 'Telecom: hook up or lose out', *Harvard Business Review* (July–Aug. 1986), 91–7; Gary L. Frazier, Robert E. Spekman and Charles R. O'Neal, 'Just-in-time exchange relationships in industrial markets', *Journal of Marketing* (October 1988), 52–7; Quote from Ernest Raia, 'JIT in the '90s: Zeroing in on leadtimes', *Purchasing* (26 September 1991), 54–7; Michiyo Nakamoto, 'Building networks', *Financial Times*, (13 November 1992), 8; Richard Gourlay, 'From fat to lean enterprises', *Financial Times* (8 November 1994), 11; and Carlos Cordon, 'Doing justice to just in time', *Financial Times* (9 November 1994), 14.

## How do business buyers make their buying decisions?

Table 8.1 lists the eight stages of the business buying process.[18] Buyers who face a new-task buying situation usually go through all stages of the buying process. Buyers making modified or straight rebuys may skip some of the stages. We will examine these steps for the typical new-task buying situation.

### Problem recognition

The buying process begins when someone in the company recognizes a problem or need that can be met by acquiring a specific good or a service. **Problem recognition** can result from internal or external stimuli. Internally, the company may decide to

| | Buying situations | | |
|---|---|---|---|
| | **New** | **Modified** | **Straight** |
| Stages of the buying process | Task | Rebuy | Rebuy |
| 1. Problem recognition | Yes | Maybe | No |
| 2. General need description | Yes | Maybe | No |
| 3. Product specification | Yes | Yes | Yes |
| 4. Supplier search | Yes | Maybe | No |
| 5. Proposal solicitation | Yes | Maybe | No |
| 6. Supplier selection | Yes | Maybe | No |
| 7. Order-routine specification | Yes | Maybe | No |
| 8. Performance review | Yes | Yes | Yes |

**TABLE 8.1** *Key stages of the business buying process in relation to important buying situations*

Source: Adapted from Patrick J. Robinson, Charles W. Faris, and Yoram Wind, *Industrial Buying and Creative Marketing* (Boston: Allyn & Bacon, 1967), 14.

launch a new product that requires new production equipment and materials. Or a machine may break down and need new parts. Perhaps a purchasing manager is unhappy with a current supplier's product quality, service or prices. Externally, the buyer may get some new ideas at a trade show, see an ad or receive a call from a salesperson who offers a better product or a lower price.

### General need description

Having recognized a need, the buyer next prepares a **general need description** that describes the characteristics and quantity of the needed item. For standard items, this process presents few problems. For complex items, however, the buyer may have to work with others – engineers, users, consultants – to define the item. The team may want to rank the importance of reliability, durability, price and other attributes desired in the item. In this phase, the alert business marketer can help the buyers define their needs and provide information about the value of different product characteristics.

### Product specification

The buying organization next develops the item's technical **product specifications**, often with the help of a value analysis engineering team. **Value analysis** is an approach to cost reduction in which components are studied carefully to determine if they can be redesigned, standardized, or made by less costly methods of production. The team decides on the best characteristics and specifies them accordingly. Sellers, too, can use value analysis as a tool to help secure a new account. By showing buyers a better way to make an object, outside sellers can turn straight rebuy situations into new-task situations which give them a chance to obtain new business.

### Supplier search

The buyer now conducts a **supplier search** to find the best vendors. The buyer can compile a small list of qualified suppliers by reviewing trade directories, doing a computer search or phoning other companies for recommendations. The newer the buying task and the more complex and costly the item, the greater the amount of time the buyer will spend searching for suppliers. The supplier's task is to get listed in the big directories and build a good reputation in the marketplace. Salespeople should watch for companies in the process of searching for suppliers and make certain that their firm is considered.

## Proposal solicitation

In the **proposal solicitation** stage of the business buying process, the buyer invites qualified suppliers to submit proposals. In response, some suppliers will send only a catalogue or a salesperson. However, when the item is complex or expensive, the buyer will usually require detailed written proposals or formal presentations from each potential supplier.

Business marketers must be skilled in researching, writing and presenting proposals in response to buyer proposal solicitations. Proposals should be marketing documents, not just technical documents. Presentations should inspire confidence and should make the marketer's company stand out from the competition.

## Supplier selection

The members of the buying centre now review the proposals and select a supplier or suppliers. During **supplier selection**, the buying centre will often draw up a list of the desired supplier attributes and their relative importance. In one survey, purchasing executives listed the following attributes as most important in influencing the relationship between supplier and customer: quality products and services, on-time delivery, ethical corporate behaviour, honest communication and competitive prices.[19] Other important factors include repair and servicing capabilities, technical aid and advice, geographic location, performance history and reputation. The members of the buying centre will rate suppliers against these attributes and identify the best suppliers. They often use a supplier evaluation method similar to the one shown in Table 8.2.

The importance of various supplier attributes depends on the type of purchase situation the buyer faces.[20] One study of 220 purchasing managers showed that economic criteria were most important in situations involving routine purchases of standard products. Performance criteria became more important in purchases of non-standard, more complex products. The supplier's ability to adapt to the buyer's changing needs was important for almost all types of purchases.

Buyers may attempt to negotiate with preferred suppliers for better prices and terms before making the final selections. In the end, they may select a single supplier or a few suppliers. Many buyers prefer multiple sources of supplies to avoid being totally dependent on one supplier and to allow comparisons of prices and performance of several suppliers over time.

## Order-routine specification

The buyer now prepares an **order-routine specification**. It includes the final order with the chosen supplier or suppliers and lists items such as technical specifications, quantity needed, expected time of delivery, return policies and warranties. In the case of maintenance, repair and operating items, buyers are increasingly using *blanket contracts* rather than periodic purchase orders. A blanket contract creates a long-

**TABLE 8.2**   *An example of vendor analysis*

| Attributes | Rating scale | | | | |
| --- | --- | --- | --- | --- | --- |
| | Unacceptable (0) | Poor (1) | Fair (2) | Good (3) | Excellent (4) |
| Technical and production capabilities | | | | | x |
| Price competitiveness | | | x | | |
| Product quality | | | | | x |
| Delivery reliability | | | x | | |
| Service capability | | | | | x |

4 + 2 + 4 + 2 + 4 = 16
Average score: 16/5 = 3.2

Note: This vendor shows up as strong except on two attributes. The purchasing agent has to decide how important the two weaknesses are. The analysis could be redone using importance weights for the five attributes.
Source: Adapted from Richard Hill, Ralph Alexander, and James Cross. *Industrial Marketing*, 4th edn (Homewood, IL: Irwin, 1975), 101–4.

term relationship in which the supplier promises to resupply the buyer as needed at agreed prices for a set time period. The seller holds the stock and the buyer's computer automatically prints out an order to the seller when stock is needed. A blanket order eliminates the expensive process of renegotiating a purchase each time stock is required. It also allows buyers to write more, but smaller purchase orders, resulting in lower inventory levels and carrying costs.

Blanket contracting leads to more single-source buying and to buying more items from that source. This practice locks the supplier in tighter with the buyer and makes it difficult for other suppliers to break in unless the buyer becomes dissatisfied with prices or service.

### Performance review

In this stage, the buyer reviews supplier performance. The buyer may contact users and ask them to rate their satisfaction. The **performance review** may lead the buyer to continue, modify or drop the arrangement. The seller's job is to monitor the same factors used by the buyer to make sure that the seller is giving the expected satisfaction.

We have described the stages that typically would occur in a new-task buying situation. The eight-stage model provides a simple view of the actual business buying-decision process. The actual process is usually much more complex. In the modified rebuy or straight rebuy situation, some of these stages would be compressed or bypassed. Each organization buys in its own way and each buying situation has unique requirements. Different buying-centre participants may be involved at different stages of the process. Although certain buying-process steps usually do occur, buyers do not always follow them in the same order and they may add other steps. Often, buyers will repeat certain stages of the process.

## INSTITUTIONAL AND GOVERNMENT MARKETS

So far, our discussion of organizational buying has focused largely on the buying behaviour of business buyers. Much of this discussion also applies to the buying practices of institutional and government organizations. However, these two nonbusiness markets have additional characteristics and needs. Thus, in this final section, we will address the special features of institutional and government markets.

### Institutional markets

The **institutional market** consists of schools, hospitals, nursing homes, prisons and other institutions that provide goods and services to people in their care. Institutions differ from one another in their sponsors and in their objectives. For example, in the United Kingdom, BUPA hospitals are operated for profit and are predominantly used by people with private medical insurance, National Health Service trust hospitals provide health care as part of the welfare state, while charities, such as the Terrence Higgins trust and many small hospices, run centres for the terminally ill.

Many institutional markets are characterized by low budgets and captive patrons. For example, many campus-based students have little choice but to eat whatever food the university supplies. A catering organization decides on the quality of food to buy for students. The buying objective is not profit because the food is provided as a part of a total service package. Nor is strict cost minimization the goal – students receiving poor-quality food will complain to others and damage the college's reputation. Thus the university purchasing agent must search for institutional food vendors whose quality meets or exceeds a certain minimum standard and whose prices are low.

Many marketers set up separate divisions to meet the special characteristics and needs of institutional buyers. For example, Heinz produces, packages and prices its ketchup and other products differently to better serve the requirements of hospitals, colleges and other institutional markets.

### Government markets

The **government market** offers large opportunities for many companies. Government buying and business buying are similar in many ways. But there are also differences that must be understood by companies wishing to sell products and services to governments. To succeed in the government market, sellers must locate key decision makers, identify the factors that affect buyer behaviour and understand the buying decision process.

Government buying organizations are found at national and local levels. The national level is the largest and its buying units operate in both the civilian and military sectors. Various government departments, administrations, agencies, boards, commissions, executive offices and other units carry out buying. Sometimes, the *central buying operation* helps to centralize the buying of commonly used items in the civilian section (for example, office furniture and equipment, vehicles, fuels) and in standardizing buying procedures for the other agencies. Federal military buying is usually carried out by Defence Ministries for the Forces.

## Political graft: wheeze or sleaze?

On 26 May 1994 at the White House, President Bill Clinton's chef de cabinet was forced to resign. He had used a government helicopter to take him to a game of golf. He was ordered to reimburse the Treasury for the cost of his jaunt, $13,129.66.[*] Other continents, other morals.

On 20 June 1994 in Paris, the new MEPs [Members of the European Parliament] were invited to a briefing on the many perks attached to their new status. The subject excited Jean-François Hory, president of Bernard Tapie's socialist MRG party. From his place in the front row he turned in his seat, fixed a knowing eye on his new colleagues and addressed them in the manner of an old hand talking down to university freshmen: 'One thing you need to know about travel allowances – they'll want to know your address. If you have one or more second homes, make sure you list the one furthest from Brussels.' Obviously, a

return flight from Marseilles to Brussels is worth more than the tram fare from Loos-lès-Lille to Brussels. Do you detect a whiff of moral purity?

Political corruption used to be a thing other countries did, but no more. In the United States, United Kingdom, France, Spain, Italy, Japan and elsewhere, accusations of political corruption involving businesses have shaken the countries' leaders. Eurofraud is estimated to cost EU taxpayers over ecu 10 billion per year. Sometimes the fiddles are minor, like exaggerating expenses claims on Eurojaunts, but often they are not. In 1991 Antonio Quatraro leapt to his death from a Brussels window. He was a European Commission official responsible for authorizing subsidies. In 1990 a fraud was discovered where he allegedly received backhanders for rigging the auc-

### Table 1   Government codes of practice in various countries

| Country | Compulsory register of interests? | Register open to the public? | Register of income/shares details? | MPs declare interest in debate? | Must declare free Ritz weekend? |
|---|---|---|---|---|---|
| France | Assets | No | No | No | No |
| Germany | Yes | Yes | No | No | No |
| Italy | Income | Yes | Yes | No | No |
| Spain | Yes | No | No | No | No |
| United Kingdom | Yes | Yes | No | Yes | Yes |
| United States | Yes | Yes | Yes | No | Yes[a] |

Note: [a] Gifts over $250 not acceptable.

### Strong influences on government buyers

Like consumer and business buyers, government buyers are affected by environmental, organizational, interpersonal and individual factors. One unique thing about government buying is that it is carefully watched by outside publics, ranging from elected representatives to a variety of private groups interested in how the government spends taxpayers' money. Because their spending decisions are subject to public review, government organizations are buried in paperwork. Elaborate forms must be filled and signed before purchases are approved. The level of bureaucracy and political sensitivities are high and marketers must cut through this red tape. Ways of dealing with governments vary greatly from country to country and a knowledge of local practices is critical to achieving sales successes (see Marketing Highlight 8.4).

tion of Greek-grown tobacco to benefit Italian traders.

The auction rigging would be illegal anywhere but often what is common practice in one country will bring a senior politician down in another. All governments have codes of practice, but as Table 1 shows, they are not consistent. There are also different cultural traditions about obeying rules. In Britain a Treasury minister had to fight for his political life following accusations that a controversial Arab businessman had paid for a weekend the minister had had at the Paris Ritz Hotel. The bill was less than Ffr4,000* and in no other European country would he have had to declare such a gift. German political representatives have to sign a register but the Bundestag's guidelines suggest only declaring gifts over DM10,000.*

In Japan the attitude towards political corruption is changing slowly. In 1988 Kiichi Miyazawa resigned as finance minister after being caught up in the Recruit scandal. Recruit, an employment agency, had secretly given large tranches of its own shares to politicians, including cabinet ministers, in exchange for political favours. But, by 1991, Mr Miyazawa was sufficiently rehabilitated to become prime minister. This follows the 'traditional' pattern for Japanese

politicians caught taking bribes or *o-shoku*, 'defiling one's job'. *O-shoku* carries no moral overtones about wrong doing, it just means that through carelessness the publicity has dishonoured the politician's honoured position. The usual line of defence in the Diet is that the politicians knew nothing since their aides took the money. In that way the politician does not lose face, junior aides are not worth prosecuting, and everyone is happy.

The mood changed after the 1992 Sagawa scandal. Shin Kanemaru needed money to split the ruling LDP and start one of his own. He needed a lot of cash and most of it came from Sagawa Kyubin, a trucking company who wanted political favour in order to expand its business. Gold bars and bonds were found in Mr Kanemaru's home and office. He was found guilty of not reporting ¥250m.* in 'political donations' but fined less than ¥100,000. After this, a new term entered the Japanese political vocabulary, *seiji fuhai* or 'politics rotten to the point of disintegration'.

When selling to government, especially foreign ones, marketers face a great dilemma. Should they follow St Ambrose's advice to St Augustine: 'When you are at Rome live in the Roman style; when you are elsewhere live as they live elsewhere.'? Or should they behave like a saint?

* 1 ecu = US$1.26 = FFr 6.47 (French francs) = DM 1.89 (Deutschmarks) = ¥122 (Japanese yen).

Sources: The leading quotation is from 'An open letter to those unnerved by the little judges', by MEP Thierry Jean-Pierre Terry; other sources are Terry McCarthy, 'It's not graft, just duty and obligation', *Independent* (27 October 1994), 16; 'Hands up all those hit by sleaze', *The Economist* (29 October 1994), 49–51; 'The sour taste of gravy', *The Economist* (5 November 1994), 50; Alix Christie and Julie Read, 'Fraud crusader gears up for a fight', *The European* (11–17 November 1994), 11.

Noneconomic criteria also play a growing role in government buying. Government buyers are asked to favour: depressed business firms and areas; small business firms; and business firms that avoid race, sex or age discrimination. Politicians will fight to have large contracts awarded to firms in their area or for their constituency to be the site of big construction projects. EuroDisney is an extreme case, the Humber Bridge and the Nimrod AWAC aircraft are others. Sellers need to keep these factors in mind when deciding to seek government business.

Government organizations typically require suppliers to submit bids and they normally award contracts to the lowest bidders. In some cases, however, government buyers make allowances for superior quality or for a firm's reputation for completing contracts on time. Governments will also buy on a negotiated contract basis for complex projects that involve substantial R&D costs and risks or when there is little effective competition. Governments tends to favour domestic suppliers over foreign suppliers, which is a repeated complaint of multinational businesses. Each country tends to favour its own nationals, even when nondomestic firms make superior offers. The European Economic Commission is trying to reduce such biases.

### How do government buyers make their buying decisions?

Government buying practices often seem complex and frustrating to suppliers, who have voiced many complaints about government purchasing procedures. These include too much paperwork and bureaucracy, needless regulations, emphasis on low bid prices, decision-making delays, frequent shifts in buying personnel and too many policy changes. Yet, despite such obstacles, selling to the government can often be mastered in a short time. The government is generally helpful in providing information about its buying needs and procedures, and is often as eager to attract new suppliers as the suppliers are to find customers.

> When the mighty US Fleet edged its way up The Gulf during Desert Storm it was led by five little plastic boats. The little Royal Navy Hunt Class MCMVs (Mine Counter-Measure Vessels) were in a league of their own at the dangerous job of clearing a path for the main fleet. They were made by Vosper Thornycroft, a small British company who are master at selling to governments around the world. While the world's leading defence contractors seek alliances and mergers to meet the 'peace dividend's' reduced demand, Vosper have an order book worth £600m and 14 vessels under construction, 95 per cent of them for export. Part of their strength is Vosper's dominance in the niche for glass-reinforced plastic (GRP) mine hunters, corvettes and patrol craft. Just the sort of ships that small navies want.
>
> Vosper's strength extends beyond the vessels. With their vessels they offer a maritime training and support service where they have pioneered computer-based learning. Many clients come from the Middle East and travel with their families, so Vosper have built an Arabic school for 70 pupils next to the maritime training centre. They now do training for other firms selling to the Middle East, so strengthening their position in the region. Others of Vosper's activities get them closely involved in their customer operations. The company has a three-year contract for the Ministry of Defence's Record Data Centre and has a five-year contract to operate maritime services craft for the Royal Air Force. Not bad for a company sold by British Shipbuilders to a management team in 1985 for £18.5m – in 1994 the company's value was £236m.[21]

Many companies that sell to the government are not so marketing oriented as Vosper Thornycroft for a number of reasons. Total government spending is determined by elected officials rather than by any marketing effort to develop this market. Government buying has emphasized price, making suppliers invest their effort in technology to bring costs down. When the product's characteristics are specified carefully, product differentiation is not a marketing factor. Nor do advertising or personal selling matter much in winning bids on an open-bid basis.

More companies now have separate marketing departments for government marketing efforts. British Aerospace, Eastman Kodak and Goodyear are examples. These companies want to coordinate bids and prepare them more scientifically, to propose projects to meet government needs rather than just respond to government requests, to gather competitive intelligence, and to prepare stronger communications to describe the company's competence.

## SUMMARY

The business market is vast. In many ways, business markets are like consumer markets, but business markets usually have fewer, larger buyers who are more geographically concentrated. Business demand is *derived*, largely *inelastic* and more *fluctuating*. More buyers usually are involved in the business buying decision and business buyers are better trained and more professional than are consumer buyers. In general, business purchasing decisions are more complex and the buying process is more formal than consumer buying.

The *business market* includes firms that buy goods and services in order to produce products and services to sell to others. It also includes retailing and wholesaling firms that buy goods in order to resell them at a profit. Business buyers make decisions that vary with the three types of buying situations: *straight rebuys, modified rebuys* and *new tasks*. The decision-making unit of a buying organization – the *buying centre* – may consist of many persons playing many roles. The business marketer needs to know the following: Who are the main participants? In what decisions do they exercise influence? What is their relative degree of influence? And what evaluation criteria does each decision participant use? The business marketer also needs to understand the primary environmental, interpersonal and individual influences on the buying process. The business buying-decision process itself consists of eight stages: *problem recognition, general need description, product specification, supplier search, proposal solicitation, supplier selection, order-routine specification* and *performance review*. As business buyers become more sophisticated, business marketers must keep in step by upgrading their marketing accordingly.

The *institutional market* consists of schools, hospitals, prisons and other institutions that provide goods and services to people in their care. These markets are characterized by low budgets and captive patrons. The *government market* is also vast. Government buyers purchase products and services for defence, education, public welfare and other public needs. Government buying practices are highly specialized and specified, with open bidding or negotiated contracts characterizing most of the buying. Government buyers operate under the watchful eye of politicans and many private watchdog groups. Hence, they tend to require more forms and signatures and to respond more slowly in placing orders.

## ■ DISCUSSING THE ISSUES

1. Identify the ways in which the fashion clothing market differs from the military uniform market.

2. Which of the main types of buying situations are represented by the following individual circumstances?

   ■ BMW's purchase of computers that go in cars and adjust engine performance to changing driving conditions.

   ■ Volkswagen's purchase of spark plugs for its line of Jettas.

   ■ Honda's purchase of light bulbs for a new Legend model.

3. How would a marketer of office equipment identify the buying centre for a law firm's purchase of dictation equipment for each of its partners?

4. Discuss the principal environmental factors that would affect the purchase of radar speed detectors by national and local police forces.

5. Industrial products companies have advertised products to the general public that consumers are not able to buy. How does this strategy help a company sell products to resellers?

6. Assume you are selling a fleet of fork-lift trucks to be used by a large distribution and warehousing firm. The drivers of the fork-lift trucks need the latest technology that provides comfort, makes driving easy and improves manoeuvrability. This means more expensive trucks that are more prof-

itable for you. The fleet buyer, however, wants to buy established (not necessarily latest) technology that gives the highest productivity. Who might be in the buying centre? How might you meet the varying needs of these participants?

## ■ APPLYING THE CONCEPTS

1. Take your college/university as an example of a business customer for books and other educational materials. Imagine that you are a representative from a publisher who intends to establish sales to the college/university. How might you use the model of business buyer behaviour to help you develop a strategy for marketing effectively to this customer? How useful is the model? What (if any) are the limitations? Are there different levels of customers in this situation (e.g. the library as a buying centre; course team members who agree on the textbooks to recommend for student adoption and library stocks; the individual tutor

who chooses recommended textbooks and requests the library to stock; or the college/university bookshop)? How might you deal with these different levels of customer?

2. Thinking about a local government institution or agency, make a list of the key factors it might consider when deciding to purchase new coffee-making machines for users in its offices. Remembering how government buyers make their buying decisions, suggest a scenario that you, as a potential supplier, would use to sell to this institutional buyer.

## ■ REFERENCES

1. Excerpts from 'Major sales: who really does the buying', by Thomas V. Bonoma (May–June 1982). Copyright © 1982 by the President and Fellows of Harvard College; all rights reserved. See also Scott Ticer, 'Why Gulfstream's rivals are gazing up in envy', *Business Week* (16 February 1987), 66–7; David Boggis, 'Consolidation is the key to economy and progress', *Financial Times* (2 September 1992), XIII; Chuck Hawkins, 'Can a new bird get Gulfstream flying?', *Business Week* (15 February 1993), 114–16; Roland Rudd and Robert Peston, 'Tiny Rowland faces his day of reckoning', *Financial Times* (31 August 1994), 17; Paul Betts, 'Weighed down by high-flying image', *Financial Times* (28 September 1994), 24; Robert Peston, 'Rowland to quit Lonrho board', *Financial Times* (4 November 1994), 1; Penny Hughes, 'The $600 million gamble', *BusinessAge* (November 1994), 30B; Ian Verchère, 'Long-haul luxury from bombardier', *The European* (4–10 November 1994), 30.

2. This definition is adapted from Frederick E. Webster, Jr. and Yoram Wind, *Organizational Buying Behavior* (Englewood Cliffs, NJ: Prentice Hall, 1972), 2.

3. For discussions of similarities and differences in consumer and business marketing, see Edward F. Fern and James R. Brown, 'The industrial/consumer marketing

dichotomy: a case of insufficient justification', *Journal of Marketing* (Fall 1984), 68–77; and Ron J. Kornakovich, 'Consumer methods work for business marketing: yes; no', *Marketing News* (21 November 1988), 4, 13–14.

4. See William S. Bishop, John L. Graham and Michael H. Jones, 'Volatility of derived demand in industrial markets and its management implications', *Journal of Marketing* (spring 1984), 68–77.

5. See James C. Anderson and James A. Narus, 'Value-based segmentation, targeting and relationship-building in business markets', ISBM Report No.12 – 1989, The Institute for the Study of Business Markets, Pennsylvania State University, University Park, PA, 1989; Lawrence A. Crosby, Kenneth R. Evans and Deborah Cowles, 'Relationship quality and services selling: an interpersonal influence perspective', *Journal of Marketing* (July 1990), 68–81; Barry J Farber and Joyce Wycoff, 'Relationships: six steps to success', *Sales & Marketing Management* (April 1992), 50–8; and Kevin Done, 'Harmony under the bonnet', *Financial Times* (8 November 1994), 17.

6. Bernard Simon and Paul Betts, 'Boeing may tie component deals to aircraft sales', *Financial Times* (8 November 1994), 1.

7. Patrick J. Robinson, Charles W. Faris and Yoram Wind, *Industrial Buying Behavior and Creative Marketing* (Boston: Allyn & Bacon, 1967). Also see Erin Anderson, Weyien Chu and Barton Weitz, 'Industrial purchasing: an empirical exploration of the buyclass framework', *Journal of Marketing* (July 1987), 71–86.

8. For more on systems selling, see Robert R. Reeder, Edward G. Brierty and Betty H. Reeder, *Industrial Marketing: Analysis, planning and control* (Englewood Cliffs, NJ: Prentice Hall, 1991), 264–7.

9. Webster and Wind, *Organizational Buying Behavior*, op.cit., 6. For more reading on buying centres, see Bonoma, 'Major sales', op. cit.; and Donald W. Jackson, Jr., Janet E. Keith and Richard K. Burdick, 'Purchasing agents' perceptions of industrial buying center influence: a situational approach', *Journal of Marketing* (Fall 1984), 75–83.

10. Webster and Wind, *Organizational Buying Behavior*, op.cit., 78–80.

11. Clifton J. Reichard, 'Industrial selling: beyond price and persistence', *Harvard Business Review* (Mar.–Apr. 1985), 128.

12. Webster and Wind, *Organizational Buying Behavior*, op.cit., 33–7.

13. Peter W. Turnbull, 'Organisational buying behaviour', in Michael J. Baker (ed.), *The Marketing Book* (London: Heinemann, 1994), 147–64.

14. Diane Summers, 'Living life to the max', *Financial Times* (29 September 1994), 15.

15. Thayer C. Taylor, 'Xerox's sales force learns a new game', *Sales & Marketing Management* (1 July 1985), 48–51.

16. Bonoma, 'Major sales', op.cit., 114. Also see Ajay Kohli, 'Determinants of influence in organizational buying: a contingency approach', *Journal of Marketing* (July 1989), 50–65.

17. Malcom Brown, 'Signed, sealed, delivered', *Marketing Business* (June 1992), 30–2.

18. Robinson, Faris and Wind, *Industrial Buying Behavior*, op.cit., 14.

19. See 'What buyers really want', *Sales & Marketing Management* (October 1989), 30.

20. Donald R. Lehmann and John O'Shaughnessy, 'Decision criteria used in buying different categories of products', *Journal of Purchasing and Materials Management* (spring 1982), 9–14.

21. General H. Norman Schwartzkopf, *It Doesn't Take a Hero* (London: Bantam, 1992); General Sir Peter de la Billiere, *Storm Command* (London: HarperCollins, 1992); and Andrew Bolgar, 'Diversifying out of lumpiness', *Financial Times* (2 November 1994), 26.

CASE 8

## Troll-AEG *Javier Sarda, Franscesc Parés and Lluís G. Renart\**

J. Feliu de la Peña, SA (JFP) is a Spanish manufacturer of electric lamps[1] known for their modern Troll products. In the late afternoon of 21 January 1992 Miguel Tey Feliu de la Peña, JFP's managing director, was reflecting on the reciprocal commercial distribution contracts to be signed the next day with the managers of AEG's Technical Lighting Business Area (AEG Aktiengesellschaft Fachbereich Lichttechnik or AEG-LT) from Germany.

The first JFP 'mirror' contract granted AEG a non-exclusive right to distribute its products in Germany. The second granted JFP and its subsidiary Troll-France a nonexclusive right to distribute AEG products in Spain and France. Miguel Tey did not doubt

*IESE, University of Navarra, Barcelona-Madrid.
This is a revised version of the case TROLL-AEG that won the 'Joint Ventures and Alliances' category in the European Foundation of Management Development 1995 European Case Writing Competition. The full original version is available from IESE.

that the contracts needed signing but reflected on several questions:

> First, when I review the decisions that have been taken up to this point in time, I wonder if we are doing the right thing in entering into this type of agreement or whether it would have been better to continue following our own fully autonomous growth path, as we have done until now. At the same time, I wonder whether AEG is the best partner for us. Also, when I reread the two contracts, I wonder if something is missing or should not be there, or whether any of the sections should be reworded.
>
> Second, if we accept everything done until now and do sign the contracts, then there are two major questions with regard to our immediate future that must be answered: What must we decide and do to ensure that this new reciprocal relationship between Troll and AEG works, and works well? And finally, how will all this end up? In other words, where will

our company be three, five or ten years from now? Will these agreements still be in full force?

No doubt because of the obvious difference in size between JFP and AEG, someone had recently said, only half joking: 'In no time at all, we'll all be wearing AEG T-shirts ...'.

### J. Feliu de le Peña, SA (JFP)

Mr Julio Feliu de la Peña, grandfather of the brothers Xavier and Miguel Tey Feliu de la Peña, started manufacturing 'classic' design lamps in 1929, in Barcelona. Miguel joined the company as a 15-year-old apprentice in 1960. One year later, he was managing the business. Meanwhile, his elder brother, Xavier, continued his university studies to obtain a doctorate in industrial engineering.

In 1974, Miguel and Xavier became owners of the business, which then operated from a ground floor premises very close to the centre of Barcelona. Miguel describes the situation:

> The company was completely outmoded. It had 15 very old employees, who basically carried out assembly tasks. We were not experts in anything and sold classic design lamps through salesmen who were paid a fixed salary plus commission. Although it was small, the company had a reputation for being reliable and serious. In addition to making its own lamps, the company also had exclusive distribution agreements with other lamp manufacturers. It had one sales outlet for both wholesale and retail sales.

In the same year, 1974, Nordart Industria, SA offered them the possibility of selling its products marketed under the Troll brand. It was a new lighting system made up by spot projectors, power tracks and adapters (the adapter being the part linking the spot projector to the power-carrying track). Miguel saw that the product had a well-presented, modern design and offered to buy their entire output if given exclusive sales rights for Spain. Nordart Industria, SA was a small factory without any salesforce who were badly stung when a distributor had copied their product and left them in the lurch. Joaquim Masó, the company's owner, accepted the appointment of JFP as its sole agent after establishing that JFP would oper-

*1 ecu = US$1.26 = Pta 161 (Spanish pesetas).

ate with a gross margin of 30 per cent. In the remaining six months of 1974, they sold about Pta 16 million* worth of Troll products. By 1977, their Troll sales had increased to Pta 130 million. Miguel realized that 'the future was Troll'.

In 1978, Joaquim Masó and the Tey brothers agreed to merge both companies. Each partner owned one-third of the resulting company, which continued as J. Feliu de la Peña, SA. During the next decade, the company's sales grew at slightly more than 50 per cent per annum. The workforce increased from 25 to 100 employees and the company became market leader in Spain in this type of accent lighting elements. JFP's success is attributable to the changes in the distribution channel and the continuous improvement and redesign of its products. JFP ceased selling through traditional (normally classic design) lamp retailers and pioneered the sale of spotlights and down-lights through electrical goods wholesalers-stockists.

Miguel Tey considered that this change of distribution policy had only been partly successful. He soon realized his limited negotiating power with these wholesalers:

> I was the 'fellow selling spots', in other words, a rather unwelcome visitor who was attempting to sell them a very limited range of products, which was relatively new or unusual in their stores and which accounted for only a minute fraction of their total sales. No doubt that was the reason why most often I only got to speak with one of the electrical goods store's sales assistants.

To counteract this, Miguel sought an alliance with non-competing companies whose products sold through the same electrical goods stores. He managed to persuade the general managers of a wire company, a transformer company and a cable fastener company to join in an alliance. A network of self-employed representatives sold the products of all four manufacturers. All four manufacturers placed their products on consignment in the representative's warehouse. The representative would then sell and deliver the goods, sending the delivery note to each manufacturer. In Spain, this kind of wholesaler-stockist sells mostly to contractors specializing in electrical installations, either in new buildings or in building refurbishing jobs. Most of their sales were 'counter' sales, made on the spot to contractors who came to their outlet with a list of their immediate needs and would take the goods with them. In exchange for these functions, the representative received a commission agreed upon separately with each one of the four manufacturing companies. Thirteen joint 'branches' covered practically the entire Spanish market.

> And all that with just paying a commission, that is, a variable cost, and with a minimum investment in stock in all thirteen warehouses. An important point to remember is that thanks to our pioneering role in selling accent lighting elements in Spain, JFP's margins were very high. Our sale price to the electrical goods store was between 2.5 and 3 times our manufacturing cost!

In time JFP became the unofficial leader of the network as the representatives mainly followed Miguel Fey's lead. JFP's young general manager had managed to win them over through a combination of an extremely cordial personal relationship, an excellent service from his company, a product range with skyrocketing sales and a 10 per cent commission. The other three companies paid them 5 per cent commission or less.

### Range changes

Design changes helped JFP's success. Originally each lamp model and variants, of which there were about fifty, came in sixteen colours and consisted of several parts that were specific to each model. In total, there were about 3,200 different stock-keeping units (skus). Miguel reduced the colour range from sixteen to four (white, black, gold and stainless steel). The most important change was in the design of the lamp parts. A new system of universal connector secured all parts by simple pressure plus a security screw. This innovation made the four basic parts of the lighting systems manufactured fully interchangeable, which allowed the number of skus to be cut down to less than 200. This produced a dramatic increase in turnover for warehouses in the logistics chain for JFP and their immediate customers.

Miguel also implemented significant changes in the design process of its lighting elements. By 1985, Miguel decided that he needed to create an aesthetic consistency and identifying style in his lighting ele-

ment designs and started to commission original designs from two freelance industrial designers. He wanted his lighting elements to be immediately recognizable.

> I wanted people to say, when they saw one of our lamps: 'That's Troll', without having to read the brand name. 'Braun' was my guiding light in design. I wanted to be 'the Braun of lighting' ... two designers were recruited to the company as full-time, salaried employees.

The combination of pioneering accent lighting in Spain (with down-lights, spots and tracks), the network of 'branches' made up of the thirteen independent representatives, a well-designed product range and ample margins turned the company into one of the most profitable in Spain in this industry. Forecast sales for 1989 were about Pta 1.5 billion, net income of about Pta 400 million and a market share between 25 and 30 per cent of indoor accent lighting elements.

### Recruitment of Javier Rocasalbas

Faced with a strong increase in demand, the company no longer had sufficient capacity to supply all the orders. Furthermore Miguel was in serious danger of being overwhelmed by the increasing complexity of the company's management. Consequently in 1988, he decided to recruit Javier Rocasalbas as general manager. Miguel became managing director and his brother Xavier became president. Javier Rocasalbas was 40 years old. He had graduated as an industrial engineer but his early work experience was in engineering production. Before joining JFP, he had worked in a plastics factory where, for the first time, his duties went beyond the technical.

Javier describes what he found when he joined the company:

> J. Feliu de la Peña, SA was the typical family business where the management style was heavily influenced by the owner's personality. The chief problem was purely industrial. On the one hand, on occasion the lead-times quoted to the customers were very long. Furthermore, there was a clear lack of internal organisation in production, even though JFP was (and still is in 1992) basically a design and assembly company. My first actions were therefore eminently

industrial in nature, and included computerising the production process.

Rocasalbas realized that though the products were aesthetically excellent their technical quality was poor. The electromechanical aspects had been neglected to a considerable extent, which led to difficulties when attempting to assemble the lamps on an industrial scale. In 1989, he increased the design team by recruiting Carlos Galán, an industrial engineer and electromechanical designer, as its manager. A designer specialized in mechanical functions and a draughtsman were also recruited to the team.

By the end of 1991, the design and quality department had between twelve and fourteen people responsible for product performance, compliance with electrical safety standards, and aesthetic quality of the products as individual items and as parts of the entire collection. The company changed from a design process in which the cost price was only known at the end, to one where a cost price was set before starting the design work.

The 'star' products in 1988 were the fixed, low-voltage built-in down-light in black or white and the swivelling ball-spot. They were relatively simple products to design, manufacture, assemble and install at the point of use. They were standard products of average quality, usually bought by electricians or electrical contractors for easy installation in private homes, shops, offices and so forth. The 'branches' — the thirteen sales representatives with their own warehouse — sold indiscriminately and massively, without distinguishing between different types of customer. JFP published a single price list, which carried a 45 per cent discount for all customers.

### Tensions in the range

From 1988, competition in Spain became much fiercer. A large number of lamp manufacturers appeared, flooding the market with lighting elements that had designs very similar to Troll's. Some even used Troll products to take the photographs for some competitor's catalogue. By the end of 1991, between twenty-five and thirty Spanish lamp manufacturers offered virtually identical, standard accent lighting elements. The resulting price war severely eroded sales margins from about 30 per cent in 1988 to about 15 per cent in 1991.

Miguel's response was to decide that if Troll products sold well in Spain, they should also be successful in France, which had accounted for almost Pta 4 million of the company's exports. Always impulsive and quick off the mark, Miguel went to Lyon and bought an old building near the high-speed train (TGV) station and recruited Josep Sitjà as general manager of Troll-France. A Catalan by birth, he had worked until that time as an electrical contractor in Marseilles.

By 1988, JFP was exporting Pta 46 million worth of products to France, but part of this export figure included the start-up stock of finished product shipped to Lyon. The standard products also had serious difficulties in the French market. The quality was not right, the price was not right and it was not certified as conforming with the French standards. However, aesthetically they were very well accepted and that could become the decisive factor differentiating Troll lamps.

It was very difficult to achieve a significant level of sales in France without offering an integral, complete and coherent product range. The Troll range was solely interior accent lighting elements, that is, tracks and spots, down-lights and suspended fluorescent lights self-connected by jacks. They had no built-in fluorescent panels (used mainly in offices), industrial lights (for lighing factories) or any type of lighting elements for installation and use outdoors, to light public highways, parks and gardens, tunnels, sports facilities and so on.

Miguel and Javier's reaction to this setback was a firm resolve to gain a presence on the European market, and to do this by changing their product range, slowly phasing out their standard products and starting to design, manufacture and sell technical architectural lighting elements. Rocasalbas explains:

> We considered that the more sophisticated features of the new generation of lighting elements we wanted to design and launch onto the market would be more difficult for our direct competitors to imitate, most of which were small companies. We were up against companies who were not only limited by their technical skills but also by their financial possibilities, as an 'architectural' lighting element of this type may mean investing about Pta 20 million in design, tooling, moulds, etc.
>
> It was rather an intuitive change; I don't think we really knew what we were letting ourselves in for.

Or, at least, at that time, we were not aware that the change in focus of the product range would also necessarily involve a drastic change in the type of final customer, in distribution channels, and in the marketing resources to be used to promote our products.

When they launched the first new-generation lighting elements on the market, the electrical goods wholesaler-stockholders neither bought nor distributed technical architectural lighting products. These were too sophisticated, designed for specific applications, slow-selling and their installation required a prior analysis to ensure their match with specific lighting needs, circumstances or environments.

## The prescribers

Technical architectural lighting was promoted by persuading the prescribers to use them. Within the field of technical lighting, a prescriber could be an architect, an interior decorator, a shop window designer, an engineer or technician specializing in lighting, an engineering firm, and so on. When faced with a lighting requirement (a hotel, a stadium, a modern shop, a hospital, etc.), the prescriber studied the lighting needs (light intensity, colorimetry, possible combinations within the surroundings, etc.) and decided the type, quantity, characteristics and location of each lighting point to be installed in order to obtain the desired decorative and lighting results. In the case of new buildings, it was vital to incline the prescriber in favour of a certain light brand and model while the architectural design was still on the drawing-board. Rocasalbas explains:

> The prescriber was a new factor to be reckoned with during the sales process carried out by JFP ... Until then, we had not taken any steps to influence their decisions because, given the relative simplicity of our products, it was simply not necessary ... We realized that the image they had of us – if they had any at all – would be something like that of SEAT, when it was manufacturing the '600', while now we had decided to make Mercedes Benz! ... Perhaps at that time we might have given other strategic responses to our competitors, such as trying to cut them short by lowering prices or creating a second 'fighting' brand name but the fact is we consciously didn't. This does not mean, however, that we did not fight hard to

defend our position in the standard product market, as we were fully aware that the bulk of our sales were precisely composed – and, at the close of 1991, they still are – of these standard products.

Meanwhile the Madrid and Barcelona representatives had secretly come to an agreement in 1988 to propose a change in their role. They wanted to be fully independent and exclusive distributors in their geographical area, buying set quantities and reselling the product on their own account, thus earning a margin instead of a commission. The proposal had a mixed reception from the four manufacturers in the alliance. The transformer manufacturer accepted the proposed change but the cable manufacturer not only rejected the proposal but cancelled the agency agreement with them.

Rocasalbas turned down the proposal but continued to work with them, trying to get them to start promoting to prescribers while continuing to sell the standard lighting elements. To help them they took on four middle-aged, well-groomed women (two in Madrid and two in Barcelona). These ladies would start to contact prescribers, introducing them to the company and telling them that JFP was entering the technical architectural lighting market. Said Rocasalbas:

> We were not yet out 'project hunting'. But we soon realised that 'good grooming' was not enough. We had to be able to solve the prescriber's problem or at least to be able to provide them with all the necessary means for them to solve it themselves. This included providing prescribers with all the necessary technical data, free product samples and to have a showroom where they could handle the lights and test lighting effects.
>
> The selling process was very complex because the final decision on the light brand and model to be installed not only depends on the prescriber but also on the contractor installing the entire electrical and lighting system and, in the final analysis, on the building's owner, as the person footing the bill.
>
> Later on, we began to notice certain strange behaviours. In some cases, a certain lighting installation was literally 'auctioned off' to see which manufacturer finally offered the best price. Sometimes, we have suspected that some manufacturers, particularly foreign manufacturers eager to get a foothold in the Spanish market, seemed to be prepared to quote at

cost price or even below cost price in order to be able to install its lighting elements in a particularly unique or emblematic building and thus be able to use it as an example and show it. In other cases, a customer's association with a certain corporation tips the balance in favour of a manufacturer of lighting elements who happens to be linked with the same corporation … In short, the sale of lighting projects is neither as easy nor as clear-cut nor as technically aseptic as we originally, and perhaps rather naively, thought.

JFP managed slowly to penetrate the technical architectural lighting market, selling by promoting and carrying out projects for the prescriber. However, in 1990, this market only accounted for about 5 per cent of JFP's total sales, and marketing and sales costs had increased substantially.

To speed up the change process, in 1991 they decided to terminate their relationship with the Barcelona and Madrid representatives and open a sales office with showroom. Their Barcelona branch – responsible for promotion and sales through Catalonia – had two sales teams. One team of three full-time employed salesmen covered the electrical goods wholesaler-stockists while the other focused on speciality retailers, mainly selling them the more 'standard' product range. By the end of 1991, the other Barcelona-Catalonia sales team targeted the prescription market. It had three salaried salesmen who visited prospective customers and another person who drew up the design projects. The first team was much more profitable than the second as, at the end of 1991, sales of standard products continued to account for about 80 per cent of the company's total sales.

There was a possibility that, in the future, JFP would open similar fully owned branches in other large Spanish cities. The decision would depend on two factors: first, the degree of sales and financial success achieved by the two JFP branches already operating (Barcelona and Madrid); and second, the current 'old' representatives' attitude and behaviour. They had to show their willingness and effectiveness in promoting the new generation of architectural technical lighting products.

At the end of 1991, Javier Rocasalbas commented:

Perhaps I'm wrong, but I think that even the minimally observant person had realized that lighting in houses

and apartments, offices, shops, public areas, etc., had become increasingly sophisticated. Indeed, lighting was becoming an increasingly important part of the building's or premises' aesthetics. The challenge for us, then, is to *give* Troll lamps the technical capacity to contribute lighting solutions, on the one hand, and to be able to integrate themselves aesthetically with their surroundings, on the other hand. But we also have to explain this to prescribers, without forgetting to 'lose the loop', that is, acting actively and positively on the contractor and on the building's owner or his purchasing manager. Any one of these people, at any particular time, can act for or against a type, brand or model of lamp. It is crucial to identify new projects at an early stage, in order to mature the final decision in our favour. This selling and 'maturing' process can take several months, with a significant investment in time. And even with all that, we only manage to get one out of every ten projects we bid for! To put it another way, when we 'mature' a project, we are not selling 'lighting elements'. We are selling 'a particular lighting solution'.

In 1991 the company had spent a total of about Pta 100 million in advertising expenses, brochures and product catalogues, and attending trade fairs. This amount includes the cost of similar expenses by Troll-France, SA.

## Internationalization

### The French connection

In mid-1990 Philippe Martinez became Troll-France, SA's new general manager. He was of Spanish descent but was very knowledgeable about the French lighting market. He quickly established a team of six salaried sales reps selling only Troll products. They had two tasks: to 'sell in' to the wholesaler-stockists and to promote to prescribers. As in Spain, they never sold directly to contractors or to end customers.

By the end of 1991, JFP re-evaluated their French venture. Troll-France had used Pta 250 million start-up funds and between 1988 and 1991 had had Pta 120 million. 'From a strictly economic point of view, the economic effort undertaken in France was highly questionable,' commented Miguel Tey. But, he continued, 'If we had not taken the good (even if expensive) decision to go out of Spain at the time the Spanish economy was buoyant, we would find ourselves in a difficult position today, when the Spanish market is stagnant.'

JFP's activities soon came to the notice of other multinationals interested in buying an interest in the Catalan company.

### The Austrian connection

A large Austrian company wanted to buy 30 per cent of JFP to turn Troll into its technical indoor decorative lighting division. The company impressed JFP's managers but they rejected the deal. They would only sell for a high premium and did not want to lose their independence for a minority holding.

### The Dutch connection

The first contact with a Dutch company was at the 1990 Hanover trade fair. The multinational wanted to turn JFP into its workshop; a supplier of accent lighting elements sold by the Dutch company's marketing organization under its own brand. The Dutch already had a limited range of indoor accent lighting elements and wanted to expand it. Although an agreement of this type could generate significant sales for JFP, the managers of the Catalan company did not feel very happy about the loss of identity this could involve. Also, they feared that they might become too dependent on this kind of sale. In a final agreement JFP would manufacture a JFP-designed adapter and a transformer for the Dutch.

This relationship was still in force in early 1992, although it only accounted for a relatively small part of JFP's sales. The managers of the Catalan company did not plan to increase its scope or sales volume:

> Our priority objective is to build and strengthen the Troll brand. This does not mean that we won't accept manufacturing for another company under their brand but, obviously, it is not our greatest priority. For the same reason, we are not actively looking for other customers like the Dutch.

### The Belgian connection

JFP approached a Belgian company, one of the largest classic lamp manufacturers in Europe. Their proposal was to form an alliance to sell Troll lamps in the Benelux countries, subsequently expanding the distribution area in gradual stages. In the end, the conversations with the Belgians were dropped. JFP's

managers observed that there were fundamental differences in 'lighting culture' between them. The Belgians had a classic lamp manufacturer mentality. Furthermore contacts with AEG were already in an advanced stage and JFP's managers felt more in tune with them than with the Belgian managers. Although the agreement with AEG would only cover the German market, neither Miguel Tey nor Javier Rocasalbas wanted two agreements with two partners to cover different countries.

### The contacts and negotiations with AEG

AEG belongs to the Daimler-Benz Group. AEG-LT specialized in manufacturing lighting elements, particularly fluorescent strip lighting. Its product range included almost all categories of technical lighting for indoors or outdoors, the only exception being accent lighting. Its sales were Pta 23 billion in 1990, two-thirds indoor-lighting elements and the remainder outdoor lighting.

Dr Kappler of AEG started contacts with JFP in April 1990. From the start, his proposal was crystal-clear in that he was offering JFP a double contract for reciprocal distribution. It was not his intention to buy JFP but only to reach a commercial agreement. AEG-LT did not have a range of technical decorative indoor accent lighting elements. Its present customers in Germany were asking for this type of lighting elements, but they did not want to develop this new line themselves as the investment required would be too large. They preferred an agreement with a company like JFP that had already developed such a product line. The German company's managers had been watching the development of JFP since 1987, mainly at the international trade fairs, and considered that the company was following a line that could be interesting for them.

Initially, JFP's management, especially Miguel, was very wary of starting discussions. The early contacts were fairly informal: visits to each other's factory, lunches together, and so on. However, they picked up pace and consolidated significantly when Dr Kappler transferred to another area and Dr Herbert Willmy became the business area's new president. Until then, Dr Willmy had been the area's marketing and sales director. 'Willmy is overwhelmingly straightforward and clear. He is a person who immediately wins you over with his humanity and honesty,' reports Rocasalbas.

The negotiator for AEG was Willmy in person. The negotiators for JFP were Miguel Tey and Javier Rocasalbas, who explains: 'The negotiation was very much based on the human relationship between both parties and was by no means plain sailing because Miguel had difficulties in following the English.'

Apparently AEG-LT's managers were attracted by JFP's advanced and original design, good in-house and subcontract industrial production capacity, and good range of indoor accent lighting elements – all in an effectively managed and economically sound company. Rocasalbas commented:

> I think that they were aware that there was only 'an embryo' AEG distributor in Spain and France. However, even so, we were perhaps the best distributor available to them.
>
> Sometimes, the negotiations were even fun. For example, sometimes we were wary and even expressed fears that, should we sign an agreement with AEG-LT, somehow we would be putting ourselves in their power and that 'if they sneezed, we could catch a double pneumonia'. On these occasions, in order to get the negotiations out of the rut, Willmy suggested that we do a kind of role-playing, challenging us to put ourselves in his place, as if Miguel and I were the managers of the AEG-LT business area, and try to identify decisions or actions that could harm JFP. As soon as we said something, each time Willmy would come up with the defensive or protective countermeasure that JFP could take, thus effectively knocking down all our objections. Willmy caught on very quickly to JFP's way of operating and doing business.

The possibility of obtaining a high-volume and almost instantaneous distribution of Troll lighting elements in Germany, through AEG-LT's sales network of about seventy sales engineers attracted JFP. Also, the link with the Daimler-Benz Group, and through them Deutsche Bank, could lead to 'captive' or induced sales. Purchasing priority was presumably given to AEG-LT by the other companies in the Group. They also hoped that their association with AEG-LT would be a decisive factor in helping them rapidly to obtain the 'VDE' certifications in Germany for their lighting elements. In addition, wherever AEG had a subsidiary in Europe, JFP could sell through them their accent lighting elements. However, if JFP managers considered that some or any of AEG's subsidiaries were not adequate for this task, they could freely choose any other distributor or marketing channel.

JFP also saw big advantages in distributing AEG-LT's products in Spain and France:

> Obviously, the AEG brand, and its German origin, count for a lot. We realised that AEG-LT's products would be positioned in the high-quality, high-price segment in Spain, so perhaps we might not achieve high sales volumes or high margins for JFP as importers-distributors. However, it was clear to us that the 'partnership' with AEG-LT would give prestige to JFP in Spain and would help us consolidate the image of the Troll products and our image as a company. This would help us to gain easier access to prescribers.
>
> Also, it would obviously help us complete the product range we could offer in France and Spain. Now, we would be able to quote virtually all the lighting elements needed for an entire new building or for a complete architectural project. In other words, we would have a complete product range, and we could suggest a solution for any technical lighting need, in the broadest sense.

Rocasalbas expected that distributing AEG-LT lighting elements in Spain and France would not require any more salesmen but would need higher stocks and more warehouse space. Negotiating the agreement had not been without its problems and there had even been moments when it seemed that negotiations would break down. One of them concerned setting each company's sales targets and purchase commitments for the other company's products. Another difficulty appeared when Miguel Tey said that he would not stop supplying Troll lamps to Ulrich Settler, an electrical contractor with a retail store in Stuttgart. He had been JFP's importer-distributor since 1989 and had bought about one million Deutschmarks' worth in 1991. Miguel did not want to lose this sales volume and thought it would be wise to keep Settler on, just in case the agreement with AEG did not happen or did not work out properly.

### Reflections before the signing

Everything seemed taken care of, but there were still a number of points that worried Miguel. On one

**CASE 8 (cont)**

hand, there was the 'big guy will eat the little guy' complex. He felt that if AEG's purchases were to attain very high volumes, the Germans would have too much power over the Catalans and would end up taking them over. Was this a real danger? How could he prevent it? Another point was that he did not know to what extent he should commit himself to this alliance. Should it be a purely commercial alliance or should it include other aspects? How could they get maximum benefit from the alliance? What other synergies were there that might be yet untapped? He also wondered what he should do with Settler, the German distributor, and whether AEG had any kind of 'hidden agenda'.

It was late afternoon on 21 January 1991, when Miguel got up, went to his desk and started to read, once again, the contracts that had to be signed the next day. It seemed to him that for both companies, the 'Spain sells to Germany' flow or relationship was much more important than the 'Germany sells to Spain and France' relationship. Miguel estimated the weighting of the former as 90 and that of the latter at perhaps only 10 ...

## Questions

1. What are the chief strengths and weaknesses of the Catalan company? How and why did they change over time? What were the vital strategic shifts of JFP and what stimulated them?
2. What are the roles in the buying centre for lamps towards the end of the case? How does the market vary across Europe?
3. How does JFP seek to influence people in the buying process? What mistakes were made in Spain and France?
4. Was JFP internationalization wise and successful? What are they looking for in their joint ventures? Would you recommend them to sign the deal with AEG-LT?

## Note

1. In the trade 'lamp' and 'lighting elements' refer to lamp holders that hold the light bulb or other light source. 'Spot' lights or 'accent' lighting elements create a specific field of light while leaving the surrounding areas comparatively dark.

# Jacobs Kaffee Wien

## Spreading a golden light

*Verena M. Priemer*[*]

Klaus Jacobs founded Jacobs Kaffee Wien in 1961 as the first foreign subsidary of Jacobs Kaffee Bremen. It has four business areas: coffees for private households are the dominant part in the Jacobs product range, coffee for the catering trade, the coffees of the Hag Company (Café Hag and Columbia), and finally, the food sector with brands including Suchard Express (cocoa), Mirácoli (ready-to-serve meals), Reisfit (rice) or Philadelphia (cream cheese).

In the household coffee sector, Jacobs' most important brands in 1991 were Monarch, Night & Day, Mild & Fine, Carte Noire, Edelmocca, Meisterröstung, and Merido. By offering these brands, Jacobs makes allowances for different buyer segments in the coffee market: the premium or quality segment, the decaffeinated segment, the mild segment (a mild coffee contains caffeine, but fewer irritants), and the price segment. The brands' positions fit the segments: Monarch is 'Austria's best coffee with *the* highest flavour-enjoyment', Night & Day as a decaffeinated coffee, Mild & Fine as a coffee that does not irritate the stomach, and finally Meisterröstung, Edelmocca and Merido for price-sensitive buyers.

Jacobs sells its coffees in Germany, Austria, Switzerland, France, Canada and in the United States. However, because of the coffee drinkers' varying likes, the products are not the same in these countries. German coffee drinkers, for instance, like fine sour flavours, whereas the Austrians prefer a stronger coffee. Jacobs' local brand managers take these variations into account. In some cases strong local brands in the markets, such as Monarch in Austria or Krönung in Germany, are both positioned the same (highest quality, perfect flavour), but have different brand names and different recipes. Even with the same brand name, such as Night & Day, country specific product modifications meet local coffee preferences.

In 1992, the Austrian coffee market was 46,500 metric tons, the average per capita consumption being about 6.3 kilograms. Exhibit 3.1 shows the strengths and main strategic areas of Jacobs/Hag and their main competitors Eduscho, Hofer, and Alvorada. Monarch is the market leader with 10.6 per cent market share of the Austrian coffee market.

Coffee has high penetration: 96 per cent of the Austrian households buy coffee. The Austrians drink coffee at various occasions and times of the day, but mostly in the early morning and afternoon. There is little brand loyalty. According to market research, only about 15 per cent of the coffee purchasers are loyal to a single brand. Coffee drinkers usually switch depending on the consumption occasion. The brand

[*]University of Vienna, Austria.

**Exhibit 3.1**    Leading coffees in the Austrian market.

| Competitor | Share (%) | Strengths | Main strategic area | | | |
|---|---|---|---|---|---|---|
| | | | Premium | Decaf' | Mild | Price |
| Jacobs | 21.5 | Leader in the traditional grocery trade, and Monarch is the market leader with a 10.6% share. | ■ | | | |
| Hag | 6.2 | Café Hag is synonymous with decaffeinated coffee. | | ■ | | |
| Eduscho | 22.1 | Chain of coffee stores | ■ | ■ | ■ | |
| Hofer (Aldi) | 13.5 | Chain stores | | | | ■ |
| Alvorada | 6.4 | Low-priced supplier | | | | ■ |

Source: GfK 1991 cum.

used depends upon whether it is a weekday or holiday, daytime or night-time, or for own consumption or a gift. The evoked set of the average consumer consists of two or three brands belonging to the same segment; the consumer seldom makes his or her choice between a premium and a low-priced brand. Buyers usually decide the brand at the point of sale; they do not know which brand to buy before entering the shop. There are some exceptions to this: for example, the main competitor, Eduscho, has coffee shops selling only Eduscho coffee, and some retailers, such as Hofer, sell only private brands. In these cases, store choice determines the brand decision. As a result, Eduscho buyers show a higher brand loyalty. The same applies for the purchasers in the decaffeinated segment. Decaffeinated coffee drinkers are seeking security. The health hazard of caffeine leads consumers to need to rely on the product they buy. However, the share of users who exclusively drink decaffeinated coffee is rather small. Many consumers switch between decaffeinated coffee and caffeinated coffee depending on the time of day and the amount of coffee they have already consumed.

People's coffee drinking habits and their preferences for special brands form when they are young and living with their parents. In Austria, the love of coffee is also part of the traditional coffee-house culture. Here, coffee is not just a drink, it is part of the social ritual, and for many consumers it is a natural part of everyday life. The motive for having a cup of coffee is 'to spoil oneself'. This is a big difference between the Austrian and most other European coffee drinkers. Ads show the different roles that coffee plays in people's lives. German coffee ads and TV spots, for example, often show problem situations – providing for the family, having company or a celebration – where social recognition of the buyer depends on the choice of the correct or the wrong coffee. In contrast, Austrian coffee ads suggest harmony, atmosphere, enjoyment and self-actualization.

The European coffee market has two important trends. First, the market is polarizing into premium and price-conscious segments. Customers want either high quality or a very low price. The potential for brands between these two positions is decreasing. Secondly, lifestyle issues are growing in importance. People care more about their health, and prefer environmentally friendly products and socially responsible producers. Consumers, especially the young ones, are cutting their coffee consumption. Tea, mineral water or soft drinks are replacing coffee. But, here again, Austria's coffee-house culture makes it an exception.

These developments stimulated Jacobs' plan to launch a new product. They started with consumer segmentation that showed a market niche for products that contain less caffeine and irritants than the regular coffee but, at the same time, offer complete enjoyment and flavour. The idea of a 'light-coffee' was born.

A concept test of this new light-coffee showed that 'light' conveyed unambiguously the impression of a reduced content of caffeine and irritants. To counter the association of 'light' with 'empty of flavour' Jacobs decided also to use it in conjunction with the brand name Monarch, a brand name that stood for 'the highest flavour'. Monarch's image would be transferred to a new coffee named Monarch Light. Monarch Light should attract consumers who like the taste of Monarch and wanted a coffee with reduced caffeine and irritants. A new recipe gave the taste of Monarch but with different physiological effects.

Several more name tests found 'Monarch Golden Light' suggested the best combination of perceived quality and favourable emotional impressions. Alternative package designs were tested. The final pack chosen gave the highest similarity between Monarch and Monarch Golden Light on quality, flavour and taste while scoring Monarch Golden Light high on mild, light, modern, and gentle.

## QUESTIONS

1. Describe an extensive, a limited, and a routine coffee purchase. Which of them occurs most often and why?
2. What are possible stimuli that may start the buyer decision process? How can the process be influenced in Jacobs' favour?
3. How does the buyer decision process for Jacobs coffee compare with that of Eduscho coffee? What factors affect the behaviour of coffee consumers? Would you recommend the introduction of Monarch Golden Light into the German market also?
4. Why should consumers judge Monarch Golden Light differently from a neutral light-coffee? What dangers are inherent within the proposed brand extension?

Source: P. Kefer, 'Effiziente Markteinführung und Line Extension von Monarch light' in: *Werbeforschung und Praxis*, **38** (April 1993), 150–1; we thank Dr Peter Kefer, Marketing Director of Jacobs Kaffee GmbH Wien, for his cooperation.

# Core strategy

## CHAPTER NINE

# *Market segmentation and targeting*

## CHAPTER OBJECTIVES

After reading this chapter, you should be able to:

■ Define market segmentation and market targeting.

■ List and discuss the primary bases for segmenting consumer and business markets.

■ Explain how companies identify attractive market segments and choose a market-coverage strategy.

## CHAPTER PREVIEW

### Procter & Gamble: how many is too many?

Procter & Gamble is the market leader in the United States and the European detergent markets. In the United States it markets nine brands of laundry detergent (Tide, Cheer, Gain, Dash, Bold 3, Dreft, Ivory Snow, Oxydol and Era). The cultural and competitive diversity in Europe mean that even more brands, such as Ariel, are used to serve that market. Why so many?

Besides its many detergents Procter & Gamble sells eight brands of hand soap (Zest, Coast, Ivory, Safeguard, Camay, Oil of Ulay, Kirk's and Lava); six shampoos (Prell, Head & Shoulders, Ivory, Pert, Pantene and Vidal Sassoon); four brands each of liquid dish-washing detergents (Joy, Ivory, Dawn and Liquid Cascade), toothpaste (Crest, Gleam, Complete and Denquel), coffee (Folger's, High Point, Butternut and Maryland Club) and toilet tissue (Charmin, White Cloud, Banner and Summit); three brands of floor cleaner (Spic & Span, Top Job and Mr Clean); and two brands each of deodorant (Secret and Sure), cooking oil (Crisco and Puritan), fabric softener (Downy and Bounce) and disposable nappies (Pampers and Luvs). Moreover many of the brands are offered in several sizes and formulations (for example, you can buy large or small packages of powdered or liquid Tide in any of three forms – regular, unscented or with bleach).

These P&G brands compete with one another on the same supermarket shelves. Why would P&G introduce several brands in one category instead of concentrating its resources on a single leading brand? The answer lies in different people wanting different *mixes of benefits* from the products they buy. Take laundry detergents as an example. People use laundry detergents to get their clothes clean. They also want other things from their detergents – such as economy, bleaching powder, fabric softening, fresh smell, strength or mildness and suds. We all want *some* of every one of these benefits from our detergent, but we may have different *priorities* for each benefit. To some people, cleaning and bleaching power are most important; to others, fabric softening matters most; still others want a mild, fresh-scented detergent. Thus there are groups – or segments – of laundry detergent buyers and each segment seeks a special combination of benefits.

Procter & Gamble has identified at least nine important laundry detergent segments, along with numerous subsegments, and has developed a different brand designed to meet the special needs of each. The nine P&G brands aim at different segments:

1. *Tide* is 'so powerful, it cleans down to the fibre'. It's the all-purpose family detergent for extra-tough laundry jobs. 'Tide's in, dirt's out'. *Tide with Bleach* is 'so powerful, it whitens down to the fibre'.
2. *Cheer* with Colour Guard gives 'outstanding cleaning *and* colour protection. So your family's clothes look clean, bright and more like new'. Cheer is also formulated for use in hot, warm, or cold water – it's 'all tempera-Cheer'. *Cheer Free* is 'dermatologist tested … contains no irritating perfume or dye'.

3. *Oxydol* contains bleach. It 'makes your white clothes really white and your coloured clothes really bright. So don't reach for the bleach – grab a box of Ox!'
4. *Gain*, originally P&G's 'enzyme' detergent, was repositioned as the detergent that gives you clean, fresh-smelling clothes – it 'freshens like sunshine'.
5. *Bold* is the detergent with fabric softener. It 'cleans, softens and controls static'. Bold liquid adds 'the fresh fabric softener scent'.
6. *Ivory Snow* is 'Ninety-nine and forty-four one hundredths percentages pure'. It's the 'mild, gentle soap for diapers and baby clothes'.
7. *Dreft* is also formulated for baby's nappies and clothes. It contains borax, 'nature's natural sweetener' for 'a clean you can trust'.
8. *Dash* is P&G's value entry. It 'attacks tough dirt', but 'Dash does it for a great low price'.
9. *Era Plus* has 'built-in stain removers'. It 'gets tough stains out and does a great job on your whole wash too'.

By segmenting the market and having several detergent brands, P&G has an attractive offering for customers in all important preference groups. All its brands combined hold a market share much greater than any single brand could obtain.

## MARKETS

Organizations that sell to consumer and business markets recognize that they cannot appeal to all buyers in those markets, or at least not to all buyers in the same way. Buyers are too numerous, too widely scattered and too varied in their needs and buying practices. Companies vary widely in their abilities to serve different segments of the market. Rather than trying to compete in an entire market, sometimes against superior competitors, each company must identify the parts of the market that it can serve best. Segmentation is thus a compromise between the rash assumption that all people are the same and the uneconomic assumption that each person needs a dedicated marketing effort. Sellers have not always practised this philosophy. Their thinking has passed through three stages:

1. *Mass marketing.* In mass marketing, the seller mass produces, mass distributes and mass promotes one product to all buyers. At one time, Coca-Cola produced only one drink for the whole market, hoping it would appeal to everyone. The argument for mass marketing is that it should lead to the lowest costs and prices and create the largest potential market.
2. *Product-variety marketing.* Here, the seller produces two or more products that have different features, styles, quality, sizes, and so on. Later, Coca-Cola produced several soft drinks packaged in different sizes and containers. Each was designed to offer variety to buyers rather than to appeal to different market segments. The argument for product-variety marketing is that consumers have different tastes that change over time. Consumers seek variety and change.
3. *Target marketing.* Here, the seller identifies market segments, selects one or more of them and develops products and marketing mixes tailored to each. For example, Coca-Cola now produces soft drinks for the sugared-cola segment (Coca-Cola Classic and Cherry Coke), the diet segment (Diet Coke and Tab), the no-caffeine segment (Caffeine Free Coke) and the noncola segment (Minute Maid sodas).

Today's companies are moving away from mass marketing and product-variety marketing and towards target marketing. Target marketing can better help sellers find their marketing opportunities. Sellers can develop the right product for each target market and adjust their prices, distribution channels and advertising to reach the target market efficiently. Instead of scattering their marketing efforts (the 'shotgun' approach), they can focus on the buyers who have greater purchase interest (the 'rifle' approach).

As a result of the fragmentation of mass markets into hundreds of micromarkets with different needs and lifestyles, target marketing is increasingly taking the form of **micromarketing**. Using micromarketing, companies tailor their marketing programmes to the needs and wants of narrowly defined geographic, demographic, psychographic or behaviour segments. *Customized marketing* is the ultimate form of target marketing where the company adapts its product and marketing programme to the needs of a specific customer or buying organization.

Figure 9.1 shows the three main steps in target marketing. The first is **market segmentation**: dividing a market into distinct groups of buyers with different needs, characteristics, or behaviour who might require separate products or marketing mixes. The company identifies ways to segment the market and develops profiles of the resulting market segments. The second step is **market targeting**: evaluating each market segment's attractiveness and selecting one or more of the market segments to enter. The third step is **market positioning**: setting the competitive positioning for the product and creating a detailed marketing mix.

## MARKET SEGMENTATION

Markets consist of buyers, and buyers differ in one or more ways. They may differ in their wants, resources, locations, buying attitudes and buying practices. Any of these variables can segment a market.

## Segmenting a market

Because buyers have unique needs and wants, each buyer is potentially a separate market. Ideally, then, a seller might design a separate marketing programme for each buyer. For example, Airbus Industries manufacturers aeroplanes for only a few buyers and customizes its products and marketing programme to satisfy each specific customer.

However, most sellers face larger numbers of small buyers and do not find complete segmentation worthwhile. Instead, they look for broad *classes* of buyers who

**Figure 9.1**   Three steps in market segmentation, targeting, and positioning.

Occasion segmentation: Kodak has developed special versions of its single-use camera for any picture-taking occasion, from underwater photography to taking baby pictures.

differ in their product needs or buying responses. For example, high- and low-income groups differ in their car-buying needs and wants. It also knows that young consumers' needs and wants differ from those of older consumers. Thus Renault has designed specific models for different income and age groups. It also sells models for segments with varied *combinations* of age and income. For instance, Renault's stylish Clio Be Bop is aimed at young singles, while their seven-seater Espace RXE V6 is for affluent families.

## Bases for segmenting consumer markets

There is no single way to segment a market. A marketer has to try different segmentation variables, alone and in combination, to find the best way to view the market structure. Table 9.1 outlines the major variables used in segmenting consumer markets. Here we look at the major *geographic*, *demographic*, *psychographic* and *behavioural variables*.

### Geographic segmentation

**Geographic segmentation** calls for dividing the market into different geographical units such as nations, states, regions, counties, cities or neighbourhoods. A company may decide to operate in one or a few geographical areas, or to operate in all areas but pay attention to geographical differences in needs and wants.

International lifestyles are emerging but there are counterforces that continue to shape markets. Cross-cultural research has defined five 'mentality fields' for cars in Europe.[1] These show how much language demarcates common cultures and ways of life:

1. The north (Scandinavia)
2. Northwest (Britain, Iceland and parts of Norway, Belgium and Holland)
3. The centre (German mentality field extending to Switzerland and parts of Eastern Europe)

| TABLE 9.1 | *Market segmentation variables for consumer markets* |
|---|---|
| Variable | Typical breakdowns |
| *Geographic* | |
| Region | In the US these are Pacific, Mountain, West North Central, West South Central, East North Central, East South Central, South Atlantic, Middle Atlantic, New England. Each country has its own variation on this. |
| County size | A, B, C, D. |
| City size | Under 5,000; 5,000–20,000; 20,000–50,000; 50,000–100,000; 100,000–250,000; 250,000–500,000; 500,000–1,000,000; 1,000,000–4,000,000; 4,000,000 and over. |
| Density | Urban, suburban, rural. |
| Climate | Northern, Southern. |
| *Demographic* | |
| Age | Under 6, 6–11, 12–19, 20–34, 35–49, 50–64, 65+. |
| Gender | Male, female. |
| Family size | 1–2, 3–4, 5+. |
| Family life cycle | Young, single; young, married, no children; young, married, youngest child under 6; young, married, youngest child 6 or over; older, married with children; older, married, no children under 18; older, single; other. |
| Income | Under $10,000; $10,000–$15,000; $15,000–$20,000; $20,000–$30,000; $30,000–$50,000; $50,000–$75,000; $75,000 and over. |
| Occupation | Professional and technical; managers, officials, and proprietors; clerical, sales; craftsmen, foremen; operatives; farmers; retired; students; homemakers; unemployed. |
| Education | Grade school or less; some high school; high school graduate; some college; college graduate. |
| Religion | Catholic, Protestant, Jewish, other. |
| Race | White, Black, Asian, Hispanic, other. |
| Nationality | American, British, French, German, Scandinavian, Italian, Latin American, Middle Eastern, Japanese, other. |
| *Psychographic* | |
| Social class | Lower lowers, upper lowers, working class, middle class, upper middles, lower uppers, upper uppers. |
| Lifestyle | Achievers, believers, strivers. |
| Personality | Compulsive, gregarious, authoritarian, ambitious. |
| *Behavioural* | |
| Purchase occasion | Regular occasion, special occasion. |
| Benefits sought | Quality, service, economy. |
| User status | Nonuser, ex-user, potential user, first-time user, regular user. |
| Usage rate | Light user, medium user, heavy user. |
| Loyalty status | None, medium, strong, absolute. |
| Readiness state | Unaware, aware, informed, interested, desirous, intending to buy. |
| Attitude towards product | Enthusiastic, positive, indifferent, negative, hostile. |

4. West (the French-speaking area, including parts of Switzerland and Belgium)
5. South (the Mediterranean, covering Spanish, Portuguese, Italian and Greek languages)

Self-expression is important to car buyers in all the geographical regions but the similarity ends there. The western group seek quality and practicality, the south want value for money, while the northwestern group see their car in very personal terms.

The differences influence the cars they buy and how they are equipped. Although all developed nations worry about the environment, they do so in different ways. In Italy, Britain and France, motorists do not see their car as a source of pollution, while in Germany, demand for environmentally friendly cars is growing fast.

> Pargasa, the large Swiss investment group, concentrates on francophone Europe. It has ten core holdings including French Paribas, Swiss Orior and Belgium's Petrofina, but these and other holdings are all concentrated in France and the French-speaking parts of Belgium and Switzerland. According to Aimery Langois-Meurinne, the group's chief executive, they would like to extend their core holdings to much more than ten. Geographically they are pulling in their wings from the United Kingdom and the United States but they want to expand closer to home. 'We are trying to understand Germany and German-speaking Switzerland', he says, 'but we are starting from a low base'.[2]

Climatic differences lead to different lifestyles and eating habits. In countries with warm climates social life takes place outdoors and furniture is less important than in Nordic countries. Not noticing the different sizes of kitchens has caused many marketing mistakes. Philips only started making profits in the Japanese market after it made small coffee-makers to fit the cramped conditions there. In Spain, Coca-Cola withdrew its two-litre bottle after finding it did not fit local refrigerators.[3]

Many companies today have regional marketing programmes within national boundaries – localizing their products, advertising, promotion and sales efforts to fit the needs of individual regions, cities and even neighbourhoods. Others are seeking to cultivate yet untapped territory. For example, IKEA expanded globally using its large blue-and-yellow stores and dedicated out-of-town sites. IKEA were part of a marked 1980s trend towards out-of-town shopping. Its stores attracted customers from great distances so that countries were served by a handful of stores. IKEA changed their strategy when acquiring the Habitat furniture chain from Storehouse in the early 1990s. The small stores gave them access to passing trade and new customer segments who are less willing to travel. The Habitat chain also serves small towns. In making this significant shift IKEA is also following the European trend towards town-centre malls. Having seen American urban decay, European politicians are resisting out-of-town developments.[4]

## Demographic segmentation

**Demographic segmentation** consists of dividing the market into groups based on variables such as age, gender, family size, family life cycle, income, occupation, education, religion, race and nationality. Demographic factors are the most popular bases

Demographic segmentation: Johnson & Johnson targets children with Band Aid Sesame Street bandages; Big Bird and Cookie Monster 'help turn little people's tears into great big smiles'. Toyota seeks a 'beautiful new relationship' with women.

for segmenting customer groups. One reason is that consumer needs, wants and usage rates often vary closely with demographic variables. Another is that demographic variables are easier to measure than most other types of variables. Even when market segments are first defined using other bases – such as personality or behaviour – their demographics need knowing to assess the size of the target market and to reach it efficiently.

*Age*    Consumer needs and wants change with age. Some companies use **age and life-cycle segmentation**, offering different products or using different marketing approaches for different age and life-cycle groups. For example, Life Stage vitamins come in four versions, each designed for the special needs of specific age segments: chewable Children's Formula for children from 4 to 12 years old; Teen's Formula for teenagers; and two adult versions (Men's Formula and Women's Formula). Johnson & Johnson developed Affinity Shampoo to help women over 40 overcome age-related hair changes. McDonald's targets children, teens, adults and seniors with different ads and media. Its ads to teens feature dance-beat music, adventure and fast-paced cutting from scene to scene; ads to seniors are softer and more sentimental.

Lego's range shows the limits of age-based segmentation. For babies there are Duplo rattles (0 to 3 months), then there are round-edged activity toys made of two or three pieces (3 to 18 months). All these have the familiar Lego lugs so that they will fit onto Lego products. Next comes Duplo construction kits or toys (2 to 5 years). Duplo bricks look like Lego bricks but are twice the size so that young children can manipulate but not swallow them. Duplo kits start simple but there are more com-

By segmenting by age Lego products grow with the children.

plex ones – like train sets or zoo sets – that are suitable for children with increasing sophistication. By the age of 3, children have developed the manipulative skills that allow them to progress to Lego Basic. These are targeted at 3 to 12 year olds. The progression is made easy by the small Lego bricks fitting to Duplo ones.

Age-based segmentation works until children are 5 years old when fewer and fewer girls buy Lego and boys' interests diversify. In comes Lego pirates (6–12 years), Space Police (6–12), Railways (6–12), Technic (7–12), Model Team (9–12), and so on. To counter girls' decline in interest, Lego launched Fabuland, a heavily merchandised product backed by Ladybird books and videos. It failed, leaving Legoland with an incongruous Fabuland monorail and play area. Pastel coloured Fantia is their current attempt to attract older girls.

*Life-cycle stage*     Life-cycle stage is important in recreation markets. In the holiday market, for instance, Club 18–30 aims at young singles seeking the four Ss: sun, sand, sea and sex. This boisterous segment does not mix well with the families that the Club Mediterranean caters for. Children's activities and all-day child care are an important part of their provision. Saga Holidays cater for older people. Their prices are kept low by travelling off-peak. Saga also provides insurance for older people and aims to set up and run radio stations for them. Given the ageing population in Europe and other developed economies, Saga looks set to grow.[5]

In the United Kingdom housing market, Barratts was the first to identify two life-cycle stage segments. They provided Solo apartments as starter homes for young people. These had full furnishing and household equipment included in the basic price. These extras would not have appealed to Barratts' other target market, older people with 'empty nests' trading down to a small, single-floor home.

*Gender*     **Gender segmentation** is usual in clothing, hairdressing, cosmetics and magazines. Recently, marketers have noticed other opportunities for gender segmentation. For example, both men and women use most deodorant brands. Procter & Gamble, however, developed Secret as the brand specially formulated for a woman's chemistry and then packaged and advertised the product to reinforce the female image. In contrast, Gillette's association with shaving makes its deodorant male oriented.

The car industry has also begun to use gender segmentation extensively. Women are a growing part of the car market. 'Selling to women should be no different than selling to men', notes one analyst. 'But there are subtleties that make a difference'.[6] Women have different frames, less upper-body strength and greater safety concerns.

To address these issues, car makers are redesigning their cars with bonnets and boots that are easier to open, seats that are easier to adjust and seat belts that fit women better. They have also increased their emphasis on safety, highlighting features such as air bags and remote door locks. In their advertising, some manufacturers target women directly. Indeed, much TV advertising of small cars is now aimed at women, pioneered by Volkswagen: an angry, smartly dressed woman leaves a town house – she throws away a ring, discards a fur coat but, after hesitating, keeps the keys to the Volkswagen Golf. Volkswagen now devotes 30 per cent of its television advertising budget to advertisements for women.

Large advertising spreads are designed especially for women consumers in such magazines as *Cosmopolitan* and *Vogue*. Other companies avoid direct appeals, fearing that it will offend women. It sometimes comes across as condescending. Some companies, such as Toyota and GM, try to include a realistic balance of men and women in their ads without specific reference to gender. Sometimes the medium changes but the message does not. Alongside the traditionally feminine ads for fragrances and fashion in one issue of *Vogue* are product ads for the BMW 850Csi, Audi S2, Toyota MR2, etc., showing no people. Rover's ad for their Metro Manhattan differentiates: 'For the woman who has everything'. Ford's ad for their Maverick 4 × 4 is interesting: it shows two pictures with a man driving and a woman by his side.

*Income*    **Income segmentation** is often used for products and services such as cars, boats, clothing, cosmetics and travel. Many companies target affluent consumers with luxury goods and convenience services. The brands behind the French LVMH group's initials betray its focus on affluent consumers: Louis Vuitton luggage, Moet & Chandon champagne and Hennessy cognac. The group's links with Britain's Guinness, who own Johnnie Walker Red and Black Labels as well as Guinness, mean it has an interest in five out of Europe's top ten brands. Not surprisingly LVMH is growing fast and appears recessionproof. The company's brands are growing and they are seeking other luxury brands. Besides its *haute couture* activities, LVMH own Parfums Christian Dior, have taken control of Guerain, the French fragrance house, and are stalking Van Clef & Aprels, the Paris-based jeweller.[7]

However, not all companies grow by retaining their focus on the top-income segment. Foreign and long-haul travel was once for the wealthy, but the travel market is now a mass industry. P&O aim to do the same with cruises. Once the preserve of the rich and retired, P&O Cruises are entering the mass market. With the help of their German-built Oriana they intend to bring prices down. For example, in 1995 a 12-day Mediterranean cruise on their *Canberra* for two adults and two children will cost

1 ecu = UK£0.83     £2,877, cheaper by £640 than the 1994 price. The mass-market tour operator, Airtours, is also entering the cruise market and aiming even further down market. They will sail the Mediterranean and the Canary Islands with a ship bought from Closter Cruise of Norway. P&O's marketing director welcomes Airtours' market entry: 'What Airtours are good at is talking to a slightly younger, more down-market group of customers. They will put cruising in people's minds'. Airtours' managing director pledged to: 'revolutionize the market ... You've seen nothing yet. This is a different end of the market to where cruising has been before'.[8]

Established retailers, following the wheel of retailing and developing more sophisticated stores with added values, have allowed new entrants to succeed by targeting less affluent market segments. In the United Kingdom grocery market, Kwik Save did this with a lean organization, economically located stores, and a no-frills operation that kept prices to the minimum. The more up-market positioning of other United Kingdom grocers has also allowed Germany's cost-cutting Aldi into the market.

## Geodemographics

**Geodemographics** is a relatively new and increasingly used segmentation method. Originally developed by the CACI Market Analysis Group as ACORN (A Classification Of Residential Neighbourhoods) it uses forty variables from population census data to group residential areas (Table 9.2). In the United Kingdom, for example, ACORN identifies 54 types within 17 groups in 6 main categories (see Marketing Highlight 9.1). To compensate for the lack of detail in the census data, each neighbourhood type is also surveyed to give information on their demographics and consumer behaviour. Its strength is in micromarketing and direct mail promotions, since geodemographic databases hold the names and addresses of everyone in each of the neighbourhood types. For example, in the autumn Harrods, the exclusive London store, could mail ACORN categories A (thriving) and B (expanding) with a catalogue for their Christmas hampers. Alternatively, in winter a local travel agent could promote details of off-peak holidays to groups 2 (affluent, grey, rural communities), 3 (prosperous pensioners, retirement areas) and 13 (older people, less prosperous areas) within a 12 km radius.

Geodemographics is developing fast. Databases are now available in all the large economies. ACORN has been joined by PIN (Pinpoint Identified Neighbourhoods), Mosaic and Super Profile. In the Netherlands, the Post Office and Dutch *Readers Digest* have produced Omnidata based on telephone subscribers, and, in Sweden,

---

**TABLE 9.2**   *A classification of residential neighbourhoods (ACORN)*

*UK ACORN categories*

| Category | Name | % |
|---|---|---|
| A | Thriving | 19.8 |
| B | Expanding | 11.6 |
| C | Rising | 7.5 |
| D | Settling | 24.1 |
| E | Aspiring | 13.7 |
| F | Striving | 22.8 |

*UK ACORN category A groups*

| Group | Name | % |
|---|---|---|
| 1 | Wealthy achievers, suburban areas | 15.1 |
| 2 | Affluent greys, rural communities | 2.3 |
| 3 | Prosperous pensioners, retirement areas | 2.3 |

*UK ACORN group 1 types*

| Type | Name | % |
|---|---|---|
| 1.1 | Wealthy suburbs, large detached houses | 2.6 |
| 1.2 | Villages with wealthy commuters | 3.2 |
| 1.3 | Mature affluent home-owning areas | 2.7 |
| 1.4 | Affluent suburbs, older families | 3.7 |
| 1.5 | Mature, well-off suburbs | 3.0 |

Source:   CACI Market Analysis Group.

## ACORN and related classificatory systems

As a direct challenge to the socioeconomic classification system, the ACORN (A Classification Of Residential Neighbourhoods) system was developed by the CACI Market Analysis Group.[1] The system is based on population census data and classifies residential neighbourhoods into 54 types within 17 groups and 6 main categories. The groupings were derived through a clustering of responses to census data required by law on a regular basis. The groupings reflect neighbourhoods with similar characteristics.

Early uses of ACORN were by local authorities to isolate areas of inner-city deprivation (the idea came from a sociologist working for local authorities), but it was soon seen to have direct marketing relevance, particularly because the database enabled post codes to be ascribed to each ACORN type. Hence its use particularly in direct mail marketing.

The introduction of CACI's ACORN geodemographic database represented one of the biggest steps forward in segmentation and targeting techniques. Although the measure is crude, the great strength of the service depends on CACI's own research linking the neighbourhood groups to demographics and buyer behaviour, together with the ability to target households. The system, therefore, provides a direct link between off-the-peg segmentation and individuals, unlike earlier methods which only provided indirect means of contacting the demographic or personality segments identified.

Like the other a priori techniques, the limitations of CACI's approach are the variability within neighbourhoods and the similarity between their buying behaviour for many product classes. English[2] provides an example of this where five enumeration districts (individual neighbourhood groups of 150 households) are ranked according to geodemographic techniques. Of the five, two were identified as being prime mailing prospects. However, when individual characteristics were investigated, the five groups were found to contain 31, 14, 10, 10 and 7 prospects respectively: the enumeration districts had been ranked according to the correct number of prospects, but neighbourhood classifications alone appeared to be a poor method of targeting. With only 31 prime target customers being in the most favoured enumeration district, 119 out of 150 households would have been mistargeted.

### IKEA's catalogue targeting[3]

Many companies now use geodemographic segmentation to help their decision making. IKEA, the Swedish furniture retailer, used it to analyse their customer base. The store provides a vast range of stylish and original furniture, fittings and fabrics at affordable prices. The IKEA concept is a simple and effective one that has worked throughout the world. They retail from large out-of-town stores and sell furniture in easy-to-assemble kit format, passing on the cost savings they gain from this to the customer.

A key element in IKEA's success is their catalogue: produced once a year, it features a broad selection of products, showing the depth and breadth of the range available in the stores. Their local catalogue distribution around each of their stores represents a large promotional investment. Geodemographic analysis of their store catchment areas helps IKEA define their local distribution plans for the catalogue and to evaluate how effective the previous distribution had been. To do this, IKEA analysed their customer data to see where customers were coming from, and also their level of expenditure before and after the distribution. This helped IKEA predict likely return on their investment in the next catalogue distribution. The analysis also looked at the size of purchase, frequency of purchase and the distance their customers live from each store. Using this information combined with their ACORN classification types

Postaid is run by a subsidiary of the Post Office. Both these systems are voluntary, and are sold to consumers as a way of avoiding junk mail. The power of basic geodemographic databases is being increased by linking them to consumer panel databases. This allows trends to be tracked: for example, over a four-year period, 28 per cent more people living in 'less well-off public housing' took package holidays.[9]

has allowed IKEA to improve understanding of the relationship between each of these elements. In addition to determining the postcode sectors which offer best potential for catalogue distribution, this information will help IKEA across their marketing mix to assess other promotional opportunities.

### Targeting Sottini's customers[4]

Ideal Standard is a leading manufacturer of bathrooms. Their range covers a wide selection of prices and styles, from cost-effective suites for first-time buyers through to the top of the range for those who want the very best that money can buy. The company used geodemographics to understand more about customers' perception of the luxury Sottini range. The company knew that the Sottini range was bought by a very distinctive type of customer: they wanted more detailed information about these customer types so that they could target dealerships more accurately and provide local dealer support for the Sottini product.

Sottini is sold through a network of independent retail outlets. As such, they had only limited information on their end customers, collected from responses to advertisements. CACI was able to take this information and substantiate it with data from the Target Group Index survey of people with high levels of spend on bathroom suites and home enhancement. CACI profiled this data using the ACORN consumer classification. This analysis generated a strong profile which showed that the Sottini range was bought primarily by wealthy achievers in suburbs and better-off retirement areas. A typical Sottini customer would have a large disposable income – with their mortgage paid off and cash to spend – and would live in an affluent area.

The information helped find large concentrations of Sottini's target market and define the optimum catchment area for the Sottini dealers. Comparing the customer profiles with the catchment areas of dealers showed where to concentrate marketing support.

As a second phase to this project Ideal Standard is looking at individual dealers. Within each dealer's catchment, specific postal areas of highest customer potential can be identified. The dealers can then use this information for direct marketing campaigns or door-to-door leaflet distributions to raise awareness of the Sottini product and inform people about their local Sottini dealership.

Kelvin Baldwin, Commercial Executive at Ideal Standard, states: the 'analysis helped us to evaluate potential for the Sottini brand across the country. We are now assessing how we can use this information at individual dealership level to aid us in dealer-support activities for our Sottini products, such as identifying new customers and locating new areas for the introduction of the Sottini product'.

To be fair, like other means of off-the-peg segmentation discussed, geodemographics are powerful when related to products linked directly to characteristics of the neighbourhood districts: for instance, the demand for double glazing or gardening equipment. Even in the case described above, targeting the best enumeration districts increases the probability of hitting a target customer from less than 10 per cent to over 20 per cent, but misses are still more common than hits.

### References

1. *ACORN User Guide*, CACI Information Services, London, 1993.
2. J. English, 'Selecting and analysing your customer/market through efficient profile modelling and prospecting', Institute of International Research Conference on Customer Segmentation and Lifestyle Marketing, London, 11–12 December 1989.
3. Mark Mulcahey, 'CACI's customer analysis helping IKEA define their target markets', *Marketing Systems*, **9**, 1 (1994), 11.
4. Julie Randall, 'CACI working with Ideal Standard to identify their optimum dealership areas', *Marketing Systems*, **9**, 1 (1994), 12.

*Psychographic segmentation*

**Psychographic segmentation** divides buyers into different groups based on social class, lifestyle or personality characteristics. People in the same demographic group can have very different psychographic make-ups.

*Social class*    In Chapter 7, we described social classes and showed how they affect preferences in cars, clothes, home furnishings, leisure activities, reading habits and retailers. Many companies design products or services for specific social classes, building in features that appeal to them. In Britain, Butlin's holiday camps cater for working-class families. They cater for the whole family, but prominent attractions are variety shows, bingo, slot machines, discos, dancing and organized entertainment. The camps are very busy and the emphasis is upon fun. Much of the accommodation is basic, regimented, crowded and self-catering. The almost industrial atmosphere contrasts with Center Parc's woodlands, where in these middle-class establishments, the layout and attractions are unregimented, and the emphasis is on sporting activities and relaxation.

*Lifestyle*    As discussed in Chapter 7, people's interest in goods is affected by their lifestyles. Reciprocally, the goods they buy express their lifestyles. Marketers are increasingly segmenting their markets by consumer lifestyles. For example, General Foods used lifestyle analysis in its successful repositioning of Sanka decaffeinated coffee. For years Sanka's staid, older image limited the product's market. To turn this situation around, General Foods launched an advertising campaign that positioned Sanka as an ideal drink for today's healthy, active lifestyles. The campaign targeted achievers of all ages, using a classic achiever appeal that Sanka 'Lets you be your best'. Advertising showed people in adventurous lifestyles, such as kayaking through rapids.[10]

Lifestyle segments are either off-the-shelf methods from agencies or customized methods for individual companies. Many companies opt for off-the-shelf methods because of their familiarity and the high cost and complexity of developing their own. The ad agency Young and Rubican's Cross-Cultural Consumer Characterisation (4Cs) is a typical off-the-shelf method. It has three main segments:

1. *The Constrained.* People whose expenditure is limited by income. It includes the *resigned poor* who have accepted their poverty and the more ambitious *struggling poor.*
2. *The Middle Majority.* This segment contains *mainstreams* – the largest group of all – *aspirers* and *succeeders.*
3. *The Innovators.* A segment consisting of *transitionals* and *reformers.*

The *succeeders* are a successful group of people who like to feel in control. By showing travellers – having lost their travellers cheques and had them quickly returned – in complete control of the situation American Express advertising would appeal to this segment. They would be equally attracted to the ability to customize their Mercedes-Benz car. In contrast *mainstreams* need security. They will buy well-known, safe major brands and avoid risk. Britain's Tory party under Margaret Thatcher is believed to have won elections by appealing to this segment's fear of change. Highly educated *reformers* would have none of that. They would trust their own judgement and try new ideas. These people are at the forefront of many new trends such as ecologically friendly products and new tourist destinations.

Lifestyle segments can be superimposed on other segmentation methods. For instance, Third Age Research recognizes the different lifestyles of older people. They identify *explorers* who like to take up new activities, the *organizers*, the *apathetic*, the *comfortable*, the *fearful*, the *poor me*, the *social lion* and the *status quo.*

Based on a study of over 2,000 respondents and 30,000 'snacking occasions' Nestlé developed their own lifestyle segments of the snacking market. Two major segments they identified were the very different *depressive chocolate lovers* and *energetic males*. The *depressive chocolate lovers* are predominantly young women who buy fast food and eat chocolate. They eat chocolate at anytime but particularly when depressed, to unwind or when bored in the evening at home. For these people taste is important, so they buy expensive products, like boxed chocolates, for themselves. Terry's Chocolate Orange, All Gold, Cadbury's Milk Flake or Black Magic appeal to them. In contrast *energetic males* are young and disproportionately C2 in social class. They live at a fast pace, work hard, eat fast food and are reckless shoppers. Work tires them but they exercise regularly and like lively places. They also eat chocolate in a hurry in the evening, at lunch or at mid-morning or afternoon breaks. Boxed chocolates are not for them but they get their energy fix from countlines like KitKat, Lion, Snickers, and so on.

Being multi-dimensional, lifestyle segments provide a rich picture of consumers. The *depressive chocolate lovers* and *energetic males* may be the same age and social class but the lifestyle segments start to tell us about the people and what appeals to them. An ad for the *energetic males* needs to be lively, social and fast – the product grabbed firmly and eaten. Hofmeister used such a campaign showing George the Bear on a night out with the lads to revitalise the sales and image of their lager. In contrast, Cadbury's adverts show a quiet, solitary woman anticipating and indulging herself with a Milk Flake.[11]

*Personality*    Marketers also have used personality variables to segment markets, giving their products personalities that correspond to consumer personalities. Successful market segmentation strategies based on personality work for products such as cosmetics, cigarettes, insurance and alcohol.[12] Honda's marketing campaign for its motor scooters provides another good example of personality segmentation:

> Honda *appears* to target its Spree, Elite and Aero motor scooters at the hip and trendy 16- to 22-year-old age group but the company's ads aim at a much broader personality group. One ad, for example, shows a delighted child bouncing up and down on his bed while the announcer says, 'You've been trying to get there all your life'. The ad reminds viewers of the euphoric feelings they got when they broke away from authority and did things their parents told them not to do. And it suggests that they can feel that way again by riding a Honda scooter. So even though Honda seems to be targeting young consumers, the ads appeal to trend setters and independent personalities in all age groups. In fact, over half of Honda's scooter sales are to young professionals and older buyers – 15 per cent are purchased by the over-50 group. Thus, Honda is appealing to the rebellious, independent kid in all of us.[13]

### Behavioural segmentation

**Behavioural segmentation** divides buyers into groups based on their knowledge, attitudes, uses, or responses to a product. Many marketers believe that behaviour variables are the best starting point for building market segments.

*Occasions*    Buyers can be grouped according to occasions when they get the idea to buy, make their purchase or use the purchased item. **Occasion segmentation** can help firms build up product usage. For example, most people drink orange juice at breakfast, but orange growers have promoted drinking orange juice as a cool and refreshing drink at other times of the day. Mother's Day and Father's Day are promoted to increase the sale of confectionery, flowers, cards and other gifts. The turkey farmer, Bernard Matthews, fought the seasonality in the turkey market. In some European countries the American bird was as synonymous with Christmas as Santa Claus. He had a problem. In most families, Christmas dinner was the only meal big enough to justify buying such a big bird. His answer was to repackage the meat as turkey steaks, sausages and burgers and promote them for year-round use. His reformulated turkey is so successful that he is now reformulating New Zealand lamb.

Kodak uses occasion segmentation in designing and marketing its single-use cameras, consisting of a roll of film with an inexpensive case and lens sold in a single, sealed unit. The customer simply snaps off the roll of pictures and returns the film, camera and all, to be processed. By mixing lenses, film speeds and accessories, Kodak has developed special versions of the camera for about any picture-taking occasion, from underwater photography to taking baby pictures:

> Standing on the edge of the Grand Canyon? [Single-use cameras] can take panoramic, wide-angle shots. Snorkelling? Focus on that flounder with a [different single-use camera]. Sports fans are another target: Kodak now markets a telephoto version with ultra fast … film for the stadium set. … Planners are looking at a model equipped with a short focal-length lens and fast film requiring less light … they figure parents would like … to take snapshots of their babies without the disturbing flash. … In one Japanese catalogue aimed at young women, Kodak sells a package of five pastel-coloured cameras … including a version with a fish-eye lens to create a rosy, romantic glow.[14]

Polaroid show different uses for their instant camera. Originally promoted as capturing happy family events, the product is now shown in other uses – to photograph a damaged car, an antique seen in a shop or a possible house purchase.

*Benefits sought*   A powerful form of segmentation is to group buyers according to the different *benefits* that they seek from the product. **Benefit segmentation** requires finding the main benefits people look for in the product class, the kinds of people who look for each benefit and the major brands that deliver each benefit. One of the best examples of benefit segmentation was for the toothpaste market (see Table 9.3). Research found four benefit segments: economic, medicinal, cosmetic and taste. Each benefit group had special demographic behavioural and psychographic characteristics. For example, the people seeking to prevent decay tended to have large families, were heavy toothpaste users and were conservative. Each segment also favoured certain brands. Most current brands appeal to one of these segments. For example, Crest tartar control toothpaste stresses protection and appeals to the family segment; Aim looks and tastes good and appeals to children.

Colgate-Palmolive used benefit segmentation to reposition its Irish Spring soap. Research showed three deodorant soap benefit segments: men who prefer lightly scented deodorant

**TABLE 9.3**   *Benefit segmentation of the toothpaste market*

| Benefit segments | Demographics | Behaviour | Psychographics | Favoured brands |
|---|---|---|---|---|
| Economy (low price) | Men | Heavy users | High autonomy, value oriented | Brands on sale |
| Medicinal (decay prevention) | Large families | Heavy users | Hypochondriacal, conservative | Crest |
| Cosmetic (bright teeth) | Teens, young adults | Smokers | High sociability, active | Aqua-Fresh, Ultra Brite |
| Taste (good tasting) | Children | Spearmint lovers | High self-involvement, hedonistic | Colgate, Aim |

Source: Adapted from Russell J. Haley, 'Benefit segmentation: a decision-oriented research tool', *Journal of Marketing* (July 1968), 30–5; see also Haley, 'Benefit segmentation: backwards and forwards', *Journal of Advertising Research* (Feb.–Mar. 1984), 19–25; and Haley, 'Benefit segmentation – 20 years later', *Journal of Consumer Marketing*, 1 (1984), 5–14.

soap; women who want a mildly scented, gentle soap; and a mixed, mostly male segment that wanted a strongly scented, refreshing soap. The original Irish Spring did well with the last segment, but Colgate wanted to target the larger middle segment. Thus it reformulated the soap and changed its advertising to give the product more of a family appeal.[15]

In short, companies can use benefit segmentation to clarify why people should buy their product, define the brand's chief attributes and clarify how it contrasts with competing brands. They can also search for new benefits and launch brands that deliver them.

*User status*   Some markets segment into nonusers, ex-users, potential users, first-time users and regular users of a product. Potential users and regular users may require different kinds of marketing appeals. For example, one study found that blood donors are low in self-esteem, low risk takers and more highly concerned about their health; nondonors tend to be the opposite on all three dimensions. This suggests that social agencies should use different marketing approaches for keeping current donors and attracting new ones.

A company's market position will also influence its focus. Market share leaders will aim to attract potential users, whereas smaller firms will focus on attracting current users away from the market leader. Golden Wonder concentrated on regular users to give them a dominant market share with their Pot Noodle and Pot Rice. They were first on the market with their dehydrated snack meals in pots but new entrants took sales from them. They gained 80 per cent market share by making their brand more appealing to existing users. Kellogg's took a different approach with their Bran Flakes breakfast cereal. Rather than keeping to the original health conscious users, they aimed at nonusers promoting the superior flavour of the product.[16]

*Usage rate*   Some markets also segment into light, medium and heavy-user groups. Heavy users are often a small percentage of the market, but account for a high percentage of total buying. Figure 9.2 shows usage rates for some popular consumer products. Product users were divided into two halves, a light-user and a heavy-user half, according to their buying rates for the specific products. Using beer as an example, the figure shows that 41 per cent of the households studied buy beer. However, the heavy-users accounted for 87 per cent of the beer consumed – almost seven times as much as the light-users. Clearly, a beer company would prefer to attract one heavy user to its brand rather than several light users.

Airlines' frequent flyer programmes are aimed at heavy users who, because they are business travellers, also buy expensive tickets. British Airways Executive Club blue card members get free AirMiles each time they travel and other priority benefits when booking and checking in. As usage mounts Club members are upgraded to Silver and Gold cards, each giving extra benefits and services. Almost all airlines offer similar incentives, but since benefits mount with usage, it pays the frequent flyer to be loyal. Some operators share their schemes to provide wider benefits to the regular traveller. American Express's Membership Miles scheme integrates Air France's Frequence Plus, Austrian Swissair's Qualiflyer, Virgin's Freeway and Continental Airline's OnePass together with a string of hotel chains and car rental firms. Continental's scheme is already bundled with others, so with it comes Air Canada, BWIA International Airways, Malaysian Airlines and Cathay Pacific.

*Loyalty status*   Many firms are now trying to segment their markets by loyalty and using loyalty schemes to do it. They assume that some consumers are completely loyal – they buy one brand all the time. Others are somewhat loyal – they are loyal to

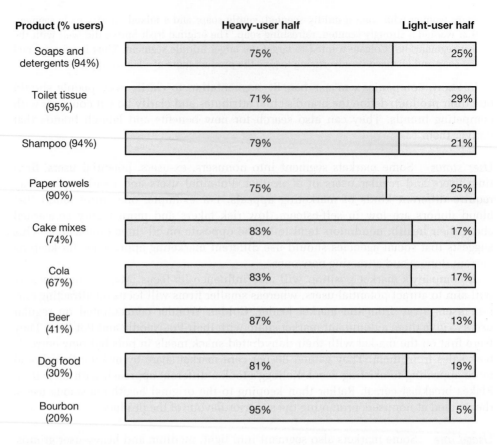

| Product (% users) | Heavy-user half | Light-user half |
|---|---|---|
| Soaps and detergents (94%) | 75% | 25% |
| Toilet tissue (95%) | 71% | 29% |
| Shampoo (94%) | 79% | 21% |
| Paper towels (90%) | 75% | 25% |
| Cake mixes (74%) | 83% | 17% |
| Cola (67%) | 83% | 17% |
| Beer (41%) | 87% | 13% |
| Dog food (30%) | 81% | 19% |
| Bourbon (20%) | 95% | 5% |

**Figure 9.2** Heavy and light users of common consumer products. (Sources: Victor J. Cook and William A. Mindak, 'A search for constants: the "heavy user" revisited!', *Journal of Consumer Marketing*, 1, 4 (spring 1984), 80.)

two or three brands of a given product or favour one brand while sometimes buying others. Still other buyers show no loyalty to any brand. They either want something different each time they buy or always buy a brand on sale. In most cases marketers split buyers into groups according to their loyalty to their product or service, then focus on the profitable loyal customers.

Loyalty schemes go beyond the continuity programmes, like Esso Tiger Cards, that have been used for decades. They seek to build a relationship between the buyer and the brand. In Australia members of Unilever's Omomatic Club – for people with front-loading washing machines – get newsletters, brochures, samples and gift catalogues. 'Front loaders' are rare in Australia so the club keeps Unilever in touch with a micromarket that their Omomatic detergent is made for. Nestlé's Casa Buitoni Club is for people interested in an Italian lifestyle and cooking. The pasta market is fragmented and penetrated by retailers' own brands so the club aims to build loyalty and Buitoni's brand heritage of focusing on enthusiasts. The Swatch's Club was formed after Swatch studied the market for cult objects. Members are helped to build up their Swatch collection and offered special editions.

The effectiveness of loyalty schemes and segmentation by loyalty is limited by how people buy. Loyal customers are few and very hard to find in most markets. Most customers are promiscuous and polygamous in their relationship with brands. Those with favoured brands will promiscuously try alternatives occasionally and most customers choose from a repertoire of favourites. But even the polygamous brand users change their repertoires and make opportunistic purchases. There is also a limit to the attention customers devote to some brands, plus the low cost of switching from one brand to another. In many markets, attempts to build brand loyalty will, like most sales promotions, only last as long as the campaign. There is also a danger of loyalty being displaced from the brand to the loyalty scheme – the air miles acquired becoming more important than the airline flown.[17]

*Buyer-readiness stage*    A market consists of people in different stages of readiness to buy a product. Some people are unaware of the product; some are aware; some are informed; some are interested; some want the product; and some intend to buy. The relative numbers at each stage make a big difference in designing the marketing programme. Car dealers use their databases to increase customer care and to estimate when customers are ready to buy. Guarantees lock customers into having the first few services from a dealer but, after that, the dealer can estimate when services are needed. Close to the due date the customer is sent a reminder or rung to arrange for a service. Some time later the dealer can estimate that the customer is getting ready to buy a new car and can then send out details of new models or deals. Indiscriminate mailing that does not take into account the buyer-readiness stage can damage relationships. By sending unwanted brochures the dealer becomes a source of junk mail. Even worse, a recent customer's satisfaction reduces if they are told about a better deal or replacement model soon after their purchase.

*Attitude towards product*    People in a market can be enthusiastic, positive, indifferent, negative or hostile about a product. Door-to-door workers in a political campaign use a given voter's attitude to determine how much time to spend with that voter. They thank enthusiastic voters and remind them to vote; they spend little or no time trying to change the attitudes of negative and hostile voters. They reinforce those who are positive and try to win the votes of those who are indifferent. In such marketing situations, attitudes can be effective segmentation variables.

The world charity Oxfam needs to keep donations up and costs down. Segmentation helps them do this. They value all donors but treat segments differently. A lot of their income is from *committed givers* who donate regularly but want low involvement with the charity. They get *Oxfam News*, special appeals and gift catalogues. *Oxfam Project Partners* want and get much more contact with Oxfam. These are further segmented by their choice of project on which they get regular feedback. Through this scheme, Oxfam, like Action Aid, develop a relationship between the giver and the final recipient. *Leading donors* receive special customer care and information about how their money was spent. Many donors can give little time to Oxfam, but other groups enjoy working in the charities shops or are enthusiastic *lottery ticket vendors*.[18]

## Segmenting business markets

Consumer and business marketers use many of the same variables to segment their markets. Business buyers segment geographically or by benefits sought, user status, usage rate, loyalty status, readiness state and attitudes. Yet business marketers also use some additional variables which, as Table 9.4 shows, include business customer *demographics* (industry, company size); *operating characteristics*; *buying approaches*; *situational factors*; and *personal characteristics*.[19]

**TABLE 9.4    *Primary segmentation variables for business markets***

**Demographics**
*Industry.* Which industries that buy this product should we focus on?
*Company size.* What size companies should we focus on?
*Location.* What geographical areas should we focus on?

**Operating variables**
*Technology.* What customer technologies should we focus on?
*User/nonuser status.* Should we focus on heavy, medium, or light users or nonusers?
*Customer capabilities.* Should we focus on customers needing many services or few services?

**Purchasing approaches**
*Purchasing function organizations.* Should we focus on companies with highly centralized or decentralized purchasing organizations?
*Power structure.* Should we focus on companies that are engineering dominated, financially dominated, or marketing dominated?
*Nature of existing relationships.* Should we focus on companies with which we already have strong relationships or simply go after the most desirable companies?
*General purchase policies.* Should we focus on companies that prefer leasing? Service contracts? Systems purchases? Sealed bidding?
*Purchasing criteria.* Should we focus on companies that are seeking quality? Service? Price?

**Situational factors**
*Urgency.* Should we focus on companies that need quick delivery or service?
*Specific application.* Should we focus on certain applications of our product rather than all applications?
*Size of order.* Should we focus on large or small orders?

**Personal characteristics**
*Buyer–seller similarity.* Should we focus on companies whose people and values are similar to ours?
*Attitudes towards risk.* Should we focus on risk-taking or risk-avoiding customers?
*Loyalty.* Should we focus on companies that show high loyalty to their suppliers?

Source:    Adapted from Thomas V. Bonoma and Benson P. Shapiro, *Segmenting the Industrial Market* (Lexington, MA: Lexington Books, 1983); see also John Berrigan and Carl Finkbeiner, *Segmentation Marketing: New methods for capturing business* (New York: Harper Business, 1992).

The table lists important questions that business marketers should ask in determining which customers they want to serve. By going after segments instead of the whole market, companies have a much better chance to deliver value to consumers and to receive maximum rewards for close attention to consumer needs. Thus Pirelli and other tyre companies should decide which *industries* they want to serve. Manufacturers buying tyres vary in their needs. Makers of luxury and high-performance cars want higher-grade tyres than makers of economy models. In addition, the tyres needed by aircraft manufacturers must meet much higher safety standards than tyres needed by farm tractor manufacturers.

Within the chosen industry, a company can further segment by *customer size* or *geographic location*. The company might set up separate systems for dealing with larger or multiple-location customers. For example, Steelcase, a big producer of office furniture, first segments customers into ten industries, including banking, insurance and electronics. Next, company salespeople work with independent Steelcase dealers to handle smaller, local, or regional Steelcase customers in each segment. Many national, multiple-location customers, such as Shell or Philips, have special needs that may reach beyond the scope of individual dealers. So Steelcase uses national accounts managers to help its dealer networks handle its national accounts.

Within a given target industry and customer size, the company can segment by *purchase approaches and criteria.* For example, government, university and industrial laboratories typically differ in their purchase criteria for scientific instruments. Government labs need low prices (because they have difficulty in getting funds to buy instruments) and service contracts (because they can easily get money to maintain instruments). University labs want equipment that needs little regular service because they do not have service people on their payrolls. Industrial labs need highly reliable equipment because they cannot afford downtime.

Table 9.4 focuses on business buyer *characteristics.* However, as in consumer segmentation, many marketers believe that *buying behaviour* and *benefits* provide the best basis for segmenting business markets. For example, a recent study of the customers of Signode Corporation's industrial packaging division revealed four segments, each seeking a different mix of price and service benefits:

1. *Programmed buyers.* These buyers view Signode's products as not very important to their operations. They buy the products as a routine purchase, usually pay full price and accept below-average service. Clearly this is a highly profitable segment for Signode.
2. *Relationship buyers.* These buyers regard Signode's packaging products as moderately important and are knowledgeable about competitors' offerings. They prefer to buy from Signode as long as its price is reasonably competitive. They receive a small discount and a modest amount of service. This segment is Signode's second most profitable.
3. *Transaction buyers.* These buyers see Signode's products as very important to their operations. They are price and service sensitive. They receive about a 10 per cent discount and above-average service. They are knowledgeable about competitors' offerings and are ready to switch for a better price, even if it means losing some service.
4. *Bargain hunters.* These buyers see Signode's products as very important and demand the deepest discount and the highest service. They know the alternative suppliers, bargain hard and are ready to switch at the slightest dissatisfaction. Signode needs these buyers for volume purposes, but they are not very profitable.[20]

This segmentation scheme has helped Signode to do a better job of designing marketing strategies that take into account each segment's unique reactions to varying levels of price and service.[21]

## Segmenting international markets

Few companies have either the resources or the will to operate in all, or even most, of the more than 170 countries that dot the globe. Although some large companies, such as Unilever or Sony, sell products in more than 100 countries, most international firms focus on a smaller set. Operating in many countries presents new challenges. The different countries of the world, even those that are close together, can vary dramatically in their economic, cultural and political make-up. Thus, just as they do within their domestic markets, international firms need to group their world markets into segments with distinct buying needs and behaviours.

Companies can segment international markets using one or a combination of several variables. They can segment by *geographic location*, grouping countries by regions such as Western Europe, the Pacific Rim, the Middle East, or Africa. Countries in many regions already have organized geographically into market groups or 'free trade zones', such as the European Union, the Association of Southeast Asian Nations and the North American Free Trade Association. These associations reduce trade barriers between member countries, creating larger and more homogeneous markets.

Geographic segmentation assumes that nations close to one another will have many common traits and behaviours. Although this is often the case, there are many exceptions. For example, although the United States and Canada have much in common, both differ culturally and economically from neighbouring Mexico. Even within a region, consumers can differ widely:

> Many marketers think everything between the Rio Grande and Tierra del Fuego at the southern tip of South America is the same, including the 400 million inhabitants. They are wrong. The Dominican Republic is no more like Argentina than Sicily is like Sweden. Many Latin Americans do not speak Spanish, including 140 million Portuguese-speaking Brazilians and the millions in other countries who speak a variety of Indian dialects.[22]

Some world markets segment on *economic factors*. For example, countries might group by population income levels or by their overall level of economic development. Some countries, such as the so-called Group of Seven – the United States, Britain, France, Germany, Japan, Canada and Italy – have established highly industrialized economies. Other countries have newly industrialized or developing economies (Singapore, Malaysia, Taiwan, South Korea, Brazil, Mexico and now China). Still others are less developed (India, sub-Saharan Africa). A company's economic structure shapes its population's product and service needs and, therefore, the marketing opportunities it offers.

*Political and legal factors* such as the type and stability of government, receptivity toward foreign firms, monetary regulations and the amount of bureaucracy can segment countries. Such factors can play a crucial role in a company's choice of which countries to enter and how. *Cultural factors* can also segment markets. International markets can group according to common languages, religions, values and attitudes, customs and behavioural patterns.

Segmenting international markets by geographic, economic, political, cultural and other factors assumes that segments should consist of clusters and countries. However, many companies use a different approach, called *intermarket segmentation*. Using this approach, they form segments of consumers who have similar needs and buying behaviour even though they are from different countries.[23] For example, BMW, Mercedes-Benz, Saab and Volvo target the world's well-to-do, regardless of their country. Similarly, an agricultural chemicals manufacturer might focus on small farmers in a variety of developing countries:

> These [small farmers], whether from Pakistan or Indonesia or Kenya or Mexico, appear to represent common needs and behaviour. Most of them till the land using bullock carts and have little cash to buy agricultural inputs. They lack the education ... to appreciate fully the value of using fertiliser and depend on government help for such things as seeds, pesticides and fertiliser. They acquire farming needs from local suppliers and count on word-of-mouth to learn and accept new things and ideas. Thus, even though these farmers are continents apart and even though they speak different languages and have different cultural backgrounds, they may represent a homogeneous market segment.[24]

## Multivariate segmentation

Most of the time companies integrate ways of segmenting markets. We have already mentioned how Lego segment by age until children develop different interests or how Third Age Research first focus on older people, then form lifestyle segments. There are several ways of combining segments.

### Simple multivariate segmentation

Many companies segment markets by combining two or more demographic variables. Consider the market for deodorant soaps. Many different kinds of consumers use the top-selling deodorant soap brands, but gender and age are the most useful in distinguishing the users of one brand from those of another. In the United States men and women differ in their deodorant soap preferences. Top men's brands include Dial, Safeguard and Irish Spring – these brands account for over 30 per cent of the men's soap market. Women, in contrast, prefer Dial, Zest and Coast, which account for 23 per cent of the women's soap market. The leading deodorant soaps also appeal differently to different age segments. For example, Dial appeals more to men aged 45 to 68 than to younger men; women aged 35 to 44, however, are more likely than the average woman to use Dial. Coast appeals much more to younger men and women than to older people – men and women aged 18 to 24 are about a third more likely than the average to use Coast.[25]

Demographic variables can also be combined with segmentation variables – social class, for instance. In Figure 9.3 social class and age are used to describe the UK media scene. This shows how the media is segmented, together with some successful, and some less successful attempts at segmentation. It is noticeable how most media appeal to older people in social classes C2, D and E. In the United Kingdom, only cinema hits younger ABC1s. Newspaper readership is clearly segmented by social class. The *Sun* and *Mirror* are popular tabloid newspapers that focus on personal interest stories, TV, pop and sport to appeal to social classes C2, D and E. The

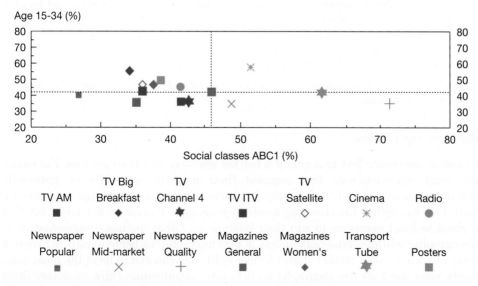

**Figure 9.3** The UK media scene.

*Daily Mail* and *Daily Express* are mid-market newspapers. They are tabloid in size but focus on national and international news. *The Times*, *Telegraph* and *Guardian* are broadsheet quality newspapers that appeal to A, B and C1 social groups. These segments are very strongly divided. When a price war had *The Times* and *Telegraph* slashing their prices, *The Times* reduction from 45p to 20p had no influence on the demand for popular tabloids.

1 ecu = UK£0.83
= 83 p

The similarity in the appeal of the two independent television stations, ITV and Channel 4, shows little segmentation of their overall appeal. In contrast Big Breakfast appeals to a segment quite different from the BBC's and ITV's serious morning programmes. Its zany humour and regular features, such as 'the Crunch with Zig and Zag', 'Snap, Crackle and Pop' and 'Paula's Boudoir' interviews – conducted in her bed with famous people – appeals most to young C2DEs.

### Advance multivariate segmentation

In multivariate segmentation segments are formed using a number of variables simultaneously. We have already introduced some of these, for example, geodemographic segmentation based on census data and lifestyle segments based on psychographic variables – Marketing Highlight 9.2 tells how this is done. Since multivariate segments are composed of several dimensions they provide a much fuller picture of the consumer.

A multinational drug company used to segment their market geographically until they found that their sales budgets were limited by legislation. That meant that they had to use their detailers (ethical drug salespeople) more carefully. They developed their multivariate segments using the prescribing habits of doctors for numerous drugs. They identified nine segments of doctors with clear marketing implications. Among them were:

■ *Initiators* who prescribed a wide range of drugs in large volumes but were also eager to try new ones. They were opinion leaders and researchers but did not have time to see detailers. This group are hard for detailers to see but critical to the success of new products. They were recognized as 'thought leaders' and had special, research-based promotions and programmes designed for them.

■ *Kinderschrecks* have quite high prescription rates and were willing to see detailers but had few children patients. They are an accessible and attractive target but not for children or postnatal products.

■ *Thrifty housewives* were often married women with children who did not run their medical practice full time. They had few patients, prescribed very few drugs and were usually unavailable to detailers. This segment was not attractive.

This allowed the drug company to select target markets for campaigns and help detailers when selling to them.[26]

### Multistage segmentation

It is often necessary first to segment a market one way and then another. For example, most multinationals first segment their markets regionally or nationally (macrosegmentation) and then by another means inside each area (microsegmentation). This can reflect the changing needs of geographical areas or the autonomy that is given to local managers to run their businesses. Often the macrosegmentation is demographic while microsegmentation is psychographic or behavioural. A Swedish study of an industrial market shows a clear split.[27] At the macro level the most commonly used methods are geographical, firm size, organization (how customer firms are structured), age of firm and age of the chief executive. At the micro level there is more variety: firms goals, market niches, competition, competitive advantage, expansion plans, personal needs, type of work done, customer type and size of customers.

At times segmentation may reach to three or more levels. In industrial markets, for instance, a third level could be the individuals within a buying centre – the likely user of a machine tool being approached in a different way to the financial director who would have to pay for it.

## Developing market segments

Segmenting markets is a research-based exercise with several stages. These apply irrespective of whether the method used is simple demographics or complex and multivariate.

1. *Qualitative research.* Exploratory research techniques find the motivations, attitude and behaviour of customers. Typical methods are focus group interviewing, elicitation interviews or repertory grid techniques. At the same time the researcher can find out the customers' view of competitive products. It is easy for a maker to define the competition in terms of those making similar products, whereas the customers take a broader view. Once brewers realized that people sometimes drank mineral water or soft drinks instead of beer, they knew the structure of their market was changing.
2. *Quantitative research.* Quantitative research identifies the important dimensions describing the market. Data are gathered by mail or personal interviews from enough customers to allow analysis. The sample size will depend upon the level of accuracy needed, the limits of the statistical techniques to be used and the need for sufficient information on each segment. The usual minimum is one hundred interviews per segment; if, therefore, there are three or four unequal segments, several hundred completed questionnaires will do. These are used to produce a structured questionnaire measuring:
   (a) attributes and their importance ratings;
   (b) brand awareness and brand ratings;
   (c) product-usage patterns;
   (d) attitude towards the product category; and
   (e) demographics, psychology and media habits.
3. *Analysis.* The data collected depend on the sort of analysis to be used. The most common process is the use of *factor analysis* to remove highly correlated variables, then *cluster analysis* to find the segments. Other techniques are available. Practitioners often use *Automatic Interaction Detection* (AID), and *conjoint analysis* is growing in popularity. These techniques are discussed in more depth in Marketing Highlight 9.2.
4. *Validation.* It is important to check if the segments are real or have occurred by chance. *Cluster analysis* has an ability to extract interesting looking clusters from random data, so this stage is critical. Validation can be by analysing the statistics from the analysis, replicating the results using new data, or experimenting with the segments.
5. *Profiling.* Each cluster is profiled to show its distinguishing attitudes, behaviour, demographics, and so forth. Usually they get a name that describes the clusters. We have seen some of those earlier: *thrifty housewives* and *initiators* among doctors, *organizers* and *explorers* among older people, or the *energetic male* and *depressive chocolate eater*.

## Ways of segmenting markets

The aim in segmentation is to find groups of people who are sufficiently alike in some way to make them a target market. There are broadly two ways of doing this. The first way is the a priori approach that splits a market by some predetermined criteria like age, sex or social class. This method works when products closely align with the a priori segments but often they do not. A priori segmentation sometimes works in new markets but becomes inadequate as the market becomes more sophisticated. For example, when the paper-nappy market started it had one design aimed at one a priori segment – people with babies. The market became more complicated as products were made to fit different sized bottoms – P&G Pampers Phases have six sizes for babies as they grow from infant to walker. P&G also discovered that the different plumbing of babies mattered and developed special versions – it seems that baby girls squirt downward, while baby boys squirt upwards and have bits sticking out. Then came products of different quality, compact versions and environmentally friendly ones. P&G market up-market Luvs and Kimberly-Clark has Huggies with elasticated waist and Pull-Up trainer pants.[1] The market was once segmented by a single a priori criterion but became complicated.

### Automatic interaction detection

Automatic Interaction Detection (AID) breaks a market down according to a series of a priori criteria, taking one after another. The First Direct telephone banking service used AID to identify twelve segments. They started with the knowledge of the revenue from customers and discriminating variables including residential status (owning or renting a home), occupational status, age, income and frequency of income payments (weekly, monthly, etc.).

AID analyses the discriminating variables one at a time (see Table 1) in order to find out which has most impact on the dependent variable – in this case, customer revenue:

1. It starts with all customers and then searches to find the discriminating variable with the most impact on revenue. If it finds out whether a customer is part of a family or not, the first division AID performs is to split customers into families and nonfamilies.
2. In the second stage AID first looks at families to see what factor most discriminates between them in terms of revenue. In this case it is the distinction between low- and high-income families. In the same way it splits nonfamilies into young and grey.
3. In the third stage it determines what discriminates between high-income families (social class) and so on.

Division after division occurs until there are too few people in each segment or no further discrimination. Looking at the twelve segments (see Table 2), First Direct could see that they were very 'skewed towards young, upscale and high-salaried segments compared with the bank population as a whole'.[2]

AID is useful because it can quickly form segments that differ in important ways. It is also good at handling variables like gender, occupation and home ownership. In First Direct's case it is revenue, but it could be usage rate, brand loyalty or profitability. The segments are also unique and distinct. AID does, however, have drawbacks. It only looks at one dimension at

Table 1     The AID process

| Start | First division | Second division | Third division |
|-------|----------------|-----------------|----------------|
| All customers | Family | High income | Social classes AB |
| | | | Social classes C1C2 |
| | | Low income | Social classes BC1 |
| | | | Social classes C2D |
| | Nonfamily | Young | Student |
| | | | Nonstudent |
| | | Grey | Couple |
| | | | Widow |

Table 2 First Direct's twelve segments from AID

| Segment | 1 | 2 | 3 | 4 | 5 | 6 | 7 | 8 | 9 | 10 | 11 | 12 |
|---|---|---|---|---|---|---|---|---|---|---|---|---|
| Married | Widow | Single | Single | Widow | Single | Single | Single | Couple | Family | Family | Family | Family |
| Age | Grey | Young | Young | Grey | Young | Young | Young | Grey | Middle | Middle | Middle | Middle |
| Home | Rent | Rent | Rent | Rent | Buy | Rent | Own | Own | Buy | Buy | Buy | Buy |
| Income | – | – | – | – | – | – | – | Med | Low | Low | High | High |
| Class | E | AB | E | C2D | C2D | C2D | BC1 | AB | C2D | BC1 | BC1 | AB |
| Employment | – | Student | – | – | – | Self | Self | – | – | – | – | – |

a time and it can miss segments where the discriminating variables interact. Also, since it keeps splitting the data, it quickly cuts the sample into groups that are too small for further analysis.[3]

Chi-square Interaction Detection (CHAID) is a development of AID that overcomes some of its limitations without sacrificing the benefits. Its principal applications so far are in direct marketing, but its applications are expected to widen.[4]

### Cluster analysis

1. Whereas AID starts with a population and splits it thin, cluster analysis usually starts with individuals and builds them into groups. Cluster analysis starts with details of more than 200 individuals. The measures can be demographic (as used in the geodemographic segmentation), psychographic (as in lifestyle segmentation), or both. Cluster analysis is also different to AID in the way it examines all the discriminating variables at once. Usually all the data gathered are on a set of uniform scales (say 1 to 7), used to represent demographic attitude, or other dimensions. Cluster analysis first looks at all the individuals and determines which two are most alike. Measures describe how alike the individuals are.
2. It then joins the most alike pair into a cluster that thus becomes a composite individual.
3. Cluster analysis then looks for the next most alike pair and joins them. This could involve the composite cluster joining with one other individual.
4. The process continues until measurements show that the individuals or clusters to be joined are *not* alike.

A dendrogram shows the individual clusters and how easy it is to join them. In Figure 1 the cluster containing 1, 2, 3 and 10 forms early and so do the clusters containing 4, 7 and 9, and 5, 6 and 8. These three clusters could become segments since they each include objects that look alike. If we try to force the three clusters to make two, there is a jump in 'error' as clusters 4, 7 and 9 and 5, 6 and 8 combine. The big jump suggests there are three natural segments. The individuals in the cluster are not exactly alike but they may be close enough to be treated as segments.[5]

Cluster analysis identified three benefit segments from 199 meat eaters in the Netherlands.[6] Table 3 gives some of the details and names the segments. Cluster analysis of the discriminating variables gave the segments. The descriptive variables were not used to find the clusters but they show cluster differences and help target them.

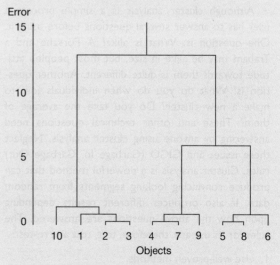

**Figure 1** Dendrogram showing cluster formation.

Table 3   The use of cluster analysis: three benefit segments identified among meat eaters

|  | Segment | | |
|---|---|---|---|
|  | Rural fat man | Urban quality seeker | Rounded meat eater |
| Cluster size (%) | 35 | 41 | 24 |
| *Discriminating variables* | | | |
| Quality | 1.88 | 2.20 | 1.42 |
| Fatness | 0.03 | −0.88 | −0.63 |
| Exclusiveness | −0.92 | 0.53 | 0.23 |
| Convenience | 0.55 | 0.59 | 0.45 |
| *Descriptive variables* | | | |
| Preferences | | | |
| Sirloin steak | 2.70 | 6.94 | 7.52 |
| Pork belly steaks | 7.81 | 4.17 | 5.56 |
| Brisket beef steaks | 6.16 | 4.93 | 5.69 |
| *Demographics* | | | |
| Region | East | North | West |
| Residence | Rural | Urban | − |
| Gender | Male | Female | − |

The segments can help market meat products in the Netherlands. None of the segments like fatty meats but the 'rural fat man' is not worried about fat, likes cheap cuts and is not looking for exclusivity. The 'urban quality seeker' is different. She wants quality, exclusiveness and no fat. She tends to live in northern towns and prefers steak to other cuts of meat.

Although cluster analysis is a simple process a user has to answer several questions before using it. One question is: What is alike? A Porsche and a Trabant may be alike in size, but most people's attitude towards them is quite different. Another question is: What do you do when individuals join to make a new cluster? Do you take the average of them? These and other technical questions need answering by anyone using cluster analysis. Neglect these issues and GIGO (Garbage In, Garbage Out) rules. Cluster analysis is a powerful method that can produce convincing looking segments from random data. It also produces different results depending upon how the above questions are answered. The rules for its use are, therefore, test, test and re-test:

1. Use well-proven methods.

2. See if the clusters are 'natural' by recreating them using different measures of alikeness.
3. Use some other data to see if the same clusters emerge from them.
4. Test the clusters practically to see if they do behave differently. This can sometimes be done using old data. Recently a bank was able to validate its segments by showing how they had responded differently to past sales promotions.

### Factor analysis

Factor analysis is often used in conjunction with cluster analysis. It identifies correlated variables and can reduce their combined effect. Researchers often collect much psychographic and other data in segmentation studies and usually much of it is intercorrelated. For example, age, income, family size, size of house and debt are all interrelated for middle-class people. Factor analysis could combine them into a single factor called 'maturity'. This reduces the computational effort in clustering and prevents the results being biased towards groups of correlated variables.

**MARKETING HIGHLIGHT 9.2 (cont)**

### Conjoint analysis

Conjoint analysis is a powerful tool that can measure the weight individuals put on the elements of a product or service. It often helps form customer segments. For example, Novotel could examine how much extra customers are willing to pay for a larger room, more expensive furnishings, a better TV in the room and so on. Sometimes it is called trade-off analysis because customers trade-off one desirable feature against another: a king-sized bed versus a Teletext TV maybe. Conjoint analysis examines the desires of individual customers. Often researchers use cluster analysis to combine these into segments.[7]

### References

1. 'High and dry', *The Economist* (28 September 1991), 108.
2. Patrick Moynagh, 'Exploiting the potential of your database to improve customer service and relationship building', Institute for International Research Conference on Advanced Customer Profiling, Segmentation and Analysis, London, 10 February, 1994.
3. Peter Doyle and Ian Fenwick, 'The pitfalls of AID analysis', *Journal of Marketing*, **12**, 4 (1975), 408–13.
4. Steve Baron and Dianne Phillips, 'Attitude survey data reduction using CHAID: an example in shopping centre market research', *Journal of Marketing Management*, **10**, 1–3 (1994), 75–88.
5. John Saunders, 'Cluster analysis', *Journal of Marketing Management*, **10**, 1–3 (1994), 13–28.
6. Michel Wedel and Cor Kistemaker, 'Consumer benefit segmentation using clusterwise linear regression', *International Journal of Research in Marketing*, **6**, 1 (1989), 45–59.
7. Dick R. Wittink, Marco Vriens and Wim Burhenne, 'Commercial use of conjoint analysis in Europe: results and critical reflection', *International Journal of Research in Marketing*, **11**, 1 (1994), 73–84.

## Requirements for effective segmentation

Clearly there are many ways to segment a market, but not all segmentations are effective. For example, buyers of table salt may divide into blond and brunette customers but hair colour obviously does not affect the purchase of salt. Furthermore, if all salt buyers bought the same amount each month, believed all salt is the same and wanted to pay the same price, the company would not benefit from segmenting this market.

To be useful, market segments must have the following characteristics:

- **Measurability**. The size, buying power and profiles of the segments need measuring. Certain segmentation variables are difficult to measure. For example, there are 30 million left-handed people in Europe – almost equalling the entire population of Canada – yet few firms target them. The crucial problem may be that the segment is hard to identify and measure. There are no data on the demographics of left-handed people and governments do not keep track of left-handedness in their surveys. Private data companies keep reams of statistics on other demographic segments, but not on left-handers.[28]
- **Accessibility**. Can market segments be effectively reached and served? There are many heavy drinkers but their imbibing is all they have in common. Except for a few Islamic states, heavy drinkers come from all countries, covering all ages, income groups, psychologies and both genders. Unless this group lives or shops at certain places or sees certain media, its members will be difficult to target.
- **Substantiality**. The market segments are large or profitable enough to serve. A segment should be the largest possible homogeneous group worth pursuing with a tailored marketing programme. It would not pay, for example, for a car manufacturer to develop cars for persons whose height is less than four feet.
- **Actionability**. Effective programmes need to attract and serve the segments. For example, although the Midland Bank identified seven market segments and developed Vector and Orchard accounts for them, its resources were too small to develop special marketing programmes for each segment. It had a limited advertising budget and had to serve all the segments using the same people in the branches.

## MARKET TARGETING

Marketing segmentation reveals the firm's market-segment opportunities. The firm now has to evaluate the various segments and decide how many and which ones to target. At this point we will look at how companies evaluate and select target segments.

### Evaluating market segments

In evaluating different market segments, a firm must look at two dimensions: segment attractiveness and company fit.

#### Segment attractiveness

The company must first collect and analyse data on current sales value, projected sales-growth rates and expected profit margins for the various segments. Segments with the right size and growth characteristics are interesting. But 'right size and growth' are relative matters. Some companies will want to target segments with large current sales, a high growth rate and a high profit margin. However, the largest, fastest-growing segments are not always the most attractive ones for every company. Smaller companies may find that they lack the skills and resources needed to serve the larger segments or that these segments are too competitive. Such companies may select segments that are smaller and less attractive, in an absolute sense, but that are potentially more profitable for them.

A segment might have desirable size and growth and still not be attractive from a profitability point of view. The company must examine several significant structural factors that affect long-run segment attractiveness.[29] For example, the company should assess current and potential *competitors*. A segment is less attractive if it already contains many strong and aggressive competitors. Marketers also should consider the threat of *substitute products*. A segment is less attractive if actual or potential substitutes for the product already exist. Substitutes limit the potential prices and profits from segments. The relative *power of buyers* also affects segment attractiveness. If the buyers in a segment possess strong or increasing bargaining power relative to sellers, they will try to force prices down, demand more quality or services, and set competitors against one another. All these actions will reduce the sellers' profitability. Finally, segment attractiveness depends on the relative *power of suppliers*. A segment is less attractive if the suppliers of raw materials, equipment, labour and services in the segment are powerful enough to raise prices or reduce the quality or quantity of ordered goods and services. Suppliers tend to be powerful when they are large and concentrated, when few substitutes exist, or when the supplied product is an important input.

#### Business strengths

Even if a segment has the right size and growth and is structurally attractive, the company must consider its objectives and resources for that segment. It is best to discard some attractive segments quickly because they do not mesh with the company's *long-run objectives*. Although such segments might be tempting in themselves, they might divert the company's attention and energies away from its main goals. They might be a poor choice from an environmental, political, or social-responsibility viewpoint. For example, in recent years, several companies and industries have been criticized for unfairly targeting vulnerable segments – children, the aged, low-income minorities and others – with questionable products or tactics.

Even powerful companies find it hard making headway in markets where they start weak. RTZ is the world's largest mineral extraction company, but when it moved into bulk chemicals and petroleum it found it could not compete. Before moving into a segment, a firm should consider its current position in that market. A low *market share* indicates weakness. Has the firm the energy, will or resources to build it up to economical levels? A firm's *growing market share* suggests strength, while, conversely, a declining market share suggests a weakness that entering new segments may not help. If a segment uses a firm's *marketing assets*, then it fits the company's strengths. If not, the segment could be costly to develop. Mars' excursion into the iced confectionery market has proved difficult for them. The European iced confectionery market is growing, Mars have the technology and brands that stretched well into ice-cream but they did not have freezers in shops. Freezers are usually owned by Unilever's Walls or Nestlé's Lyons Maid, both experts in frozen food, who had no reason to let Mars in. However, Mars' *unique products* and *valued reputation* allowed them to gain market share against established competitors.

Nonmarketing dimensions influence the ability of a company to succeed in a segment. Has it *low costs*, or has it *underutilised capacity* to use? Also, does the segment fit the firm's *technology strengths* – Daimler-Benz has bought high-technology businesses because it believes it will gain from them information and skills it could use in its core car and truck activities. Final considerations are the resources the firm can bring to the market. These include appropriate *marketing skills*, *general management strengths* and the chance for *forward or backwards integration* into the firm's other activities. IBM and Philips have huge resources, and great technology and marketing skills, but not of the type that will allow them to compete effectively in the dynamic PC market.

### Selecting market segments

Royal Dutch Shell's directional policy matrix plots market attractiveness of segments against business strengths. We introduced the method, along with GE's matrix, in Chapter 3. Originally developed as a way of balancing business portfolios, it is also well suited to decision making about which markets to target.[30] Figure 9.4 shows an application by an Austrian industrial engineering and construction company.[31]

When a segment fits the company's strengths, the company must then decide whether it has the skills and resources needed to succeed in that segment. Each segment has certain success requirements. If the company lacks and cannot readily obtain the strengths needed to compete successfully in a segment, it should not enter the segment. Even if the company possesses the *required* strengths, it needs to employ skills and resources *superior* to those of the competition to really win in a market segment. The company should enter segments only where it can offer superior value and gain advantages over competitors. The company in Figure 9.4 is not very strong in any of the most attractive segments. Segments 13 and 17 look most appealing because they are moderately attractive and fit the firm's strengths. Segment 3 is similar but the firm needs to build its strengths if it is to compete there. Segments 1, 6 and 9 are attractive but do not fit the firm's strengths. The firm has to develop new strengths if it is to compete in them. Without the investment the segments are not worth entering so the firm has to consider the investment needed to enter more than one. Although the firm's strengths are suitable for segments 2 and 12, they are not attractive.

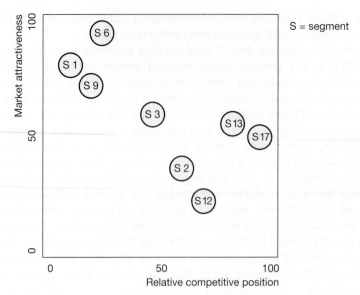

**Figure 9.4**  Portfolio of customer segments. (Source: Angelika Dreher, Angelika Ritter and Hans Mühlbacher, 'Systematic positioning: a new approach and its application', in European Marketing Academy Proceedings, Aarhus, Denmark, 26–29 May 1992, p. 324.)

## Segment strategy

After evaluating different segments, the company must now decide which and how many segments to serve. This is the problem of *target-market selection*. A **target market** consists of a set of buyers who share common needs or characteristics that the company decides to serve. Figure 9.5 shows that the firm can adopt one of three market-coverage strategies: undifferentiated marketing, differentiated marketing, and concentrated marketing.

### Undifferentiated marketing

Using an **undifferentiated marketing** strategy, a firm might decide to ignore market segment differences and go after the whole market with one offer. This can be because there are weak segment differences or through the belief that the product's appeal transcends segments. The offer will focus on what is *common* in the needs of consumers rather than on what is *different*. The company designs a product and a marketing programme that appeal to the largest number of buyers. It relies on quality, mass distribution and mass advertising to give the product a superior image in people's minds. Advertising and promotions have to avoid alienating segments, and so are often based on product features, like 'Polo, the mint with the hole', or associated with a personality of broad appeal, like Esso's tiger.

Undifferentiated marketing provides cost economies. The narrow product line keeps down production, inventory and transportation costs. The undifferentiated advertising programme keeps down advertising costs. The absence of segment marketing research and planning lowers the costs of market research and product management.

Most modern marketers, however, have strong doubts about this strategy. Difficulties arise in developing a product or brand that will satisfy all consumers. Firms using undifferentiated marketing typically develop an offer aimed at the

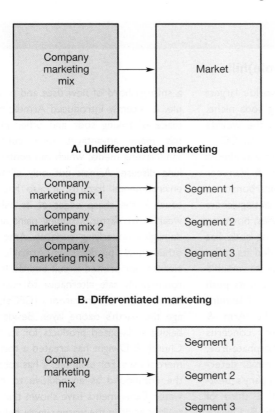

**A. Undifferentiated marketing**

**B. Differentiated marketing**

**C. Concentrated marketing**

**Figure 9.5** Three alternative market-coverage strategies.

largest segments in the market. When several firms do this, there is heavy competition in the largest segments and neglected customers in the smaller ones. The result is that the larger segments may be less profitable because they attract heavy competition. Recognition of this problem has led to firms addressing smaller market segments. Another problem is erosion of the mass market as competitors develop new appeals or segments. For example, Polo mints have faced attacks from competitors aiming at different benefit segments: Extra Strong mints for people who want a strong taste and Clorets as breath fresheners. At the same time, Polo faces direct competition from similarly packaged Trebor Mints in Europe and Duplex in Southeast Asia.

*Differentiated marketing*

Using a **differentiated marketing** strategy, a firm decides to target several market segments and designs separate offers for each. General Motors tries to produce a car for every 'purse, purpose and personality'. By offering product and marketing variations, it hopes for higher sales and a stronger position within each market segment. GM hopes that a stronger position in several segments will strengthen consumers' overall identification of the company with the product category. It also hopes for greater repeat buying because the firm's offer better matches the customer's desire.

Originally Martini products were not marketed separately. Advertising concentrated on the Martini brand and its exciting international lifestyle: 'anytime, anyplace,

## MARKETING HIGHLIGHT 9.3

# Market niching: king of the (mole)hill

Church & Dwight is not one of the world's largest businesses but it is a giant in its baking soda niche. Founded in 1846, Church & Dwight is the world's leading producer of sodium bicarbonate – $NaHCO_3$.

Until the late 1960s, Church & Dwight was almost a one-product company marketing Arm & Hammer baking soda to consumers or sodium bicarbonate to companies for use in cake mixes, fire extinguishers and so forth. During the past two decades, however, as the consumer market for pure baking soda has matured, Church & Dwight has expanded its niche dramatically by finding ever more uses for its versatile white powder. In 1970, the company began its push into new consumer markets with a line of laundry products that capitalized both on the Arm & Hammer brand name and on consumer concerns about the environment. It introduced phosphate-free, but sodium-bicarbonate-rich, Arm & Hammer detergent, which has since become the company's best-selling product, accounting for about a third of total sales. During the 1980s, Church & Dwight followed with a number of well-known consumer products ranging from carpet deodorizers to air fresheners.

Although baking soda-based consumer products make up the bulk of Church & Dwight's current sales, the usefulness of sodium bicarbonate extends well beyond household cooking and cleaning. Church & Dwight also does a brisk and growing industrial business, which now contributes about 25 per cent of annual sales. Business applications range from baking soda as a leavening agent in bakery products to use in oil well drilling mud. It's even used in animal nutrition products. For example, Church & Dwight markets an Arm & Hammer product called Megalac, a high-energy feed supplement that helps dairy cows neutralize digestive acids and supplements the sodium bicarbonate produced naturally. It results in better feed efficiency and increased milk production for farmers.

Business markets may provide some of Church & Dwight's best opportunities for growth. As the world looks for new, more environmentally friendly solutions to nagging problems, the company has responded with a smorgasbord of new uses and products. For example, it recently introduced Armex, a blasting material made of baking soda and other ingredients. Armex has many advantages over current silicon-based sandblasting media, which can contribute to silicosis, a lung disease. Armex not only eliminates health and environmental hazards, it also has a more delicate touch – the sharp edges of its baking soda crystals wear down faster, stripping paint and grime without damaging underlying surfaces. Among the company's other new products is Armakleen, an industrial cleanser for printed circuit boards. It provides an environmentally safe alternative to current cleaners that contain chlorofluorocarbons (CFCs), thought to damage the earth's ozone layer. Besides developing new baking soda-based products for its business markets, Church & Dwight has created a torrent of new commercial uses. For example, it has recently begun selling the compound as an additive to municipal drinking water. Experiments have shown that baking soda neutralizes acids in the water supply, helping to inhibit corrosion and preventing lead and other toxic metals from leaching out of the plumbing. The company is even rumoured to be experimenting with baking soda as a safe and effective fungicide for plants.

Church & Dwight battles daily with much larger competitors – consumer companies like Procter & Gamble, Unilever and Colgate, and such international heavyweights as Rhône Poulenc and Solvay. At first glance, the company may appear to be fighting a losing battle. For example, in the $3.6 billion[*] United States detergent market, Arm & Hammer commands only a 4 per cent market share, compared with P&G's 55 per cent and Colgate's 24 per cent. However, Arm & Hammer dominates the baking soda segment of the detergent market.

Another success is Arm & Hammer Dental Care – 'The Baking Soda Toothpaste'. Arm & Hammer was surprisingly slow to recognize the opportunity inherent in the old recommendation by dentists that 'brushing teeth with baking soda helps promote clean

[*]1 ecu = US$1.26

Well-focused Church & Dwight has built a commanding position by concentrating on small, highly specialized niches.

and healthy teeth and gums'. Established toothpaste manufacturers were slow to see it, too. The product took the United States market by storm and quickly became a main brand. Their familiar brand name helped the company's cause and their baking soda fame made it difficult for competitors to fight back with me-toos. Now Arm & Hammer is launching Dental Care in Europe. What next with baking soda?

Church & Dwight is 'king of the hill' for anything to do with baking soda – capturing 60 per cent of the world market for sodium bicarbonate. Even if the hill is more of a molehill than a mountain, Church & Dwight outperforms many of its much larger competitors. The well-focused company has built a commanding position by concentrating on small, highly specialized market niches. During the past ten years, its annual sales have more than tripled, to $492 million, and profits have increased fourfold. Thus Church & Dwight has proved again what many concentrated marketers have learned – small can be beautiful.

Sources: James P. Meagher, 'Church & Dwight: it scores big with the brand-name pull of Arm & Hammer', *Barron's* (10 December 1990), 49–50; Peter Coombes, 'Church & Dwight: on the rise', *Chemical Week* (20 September 1989), 16–18; Peter Nulty, 'Church & Dwight: no product is too dull to shine', *Fortune* (27 July 1992), 95–6; Riccardo A. Davis, 'Arm & Hammer seeks growth abroad', *Advertising Age* (17 August 1992), 3, 42.

anywhere'. That changed to having the main Martini brands aimed at clearly defined target markets:

- Martini Rosso, the most popular variety, is aimed at a broad sector of the market. Its ads show it being enjoyed by an attractive young couple with 'Our martini is Rosso' or by a small chic group relaxing in elegant surroundings: 'The bitter sweet sensation'.
- Martini Bianco is targeted at people in their twenties who like light alcoholic drinks. It is shown being casually drunk with ice by a sporty, boisterous set, out of doors: 'The sunny side of life'.
- Martini Extra Dry is for the sophisticated drinker. The advertising focuses on the bottle and the product in an atmosphere of quiet sophistication.[32]

Differentiated marketing typically creates more total sales than does undifferentiated marketing. KLM could fill all the seats on its New York flights charging APEX fares, but its own income, and the number of flyers, is increased by segmenting the market. In the main cabin or on the upper deck of each Boeing 747-400 taking off from Schiphol Airport there will be about 300 economy passengers. Some of these, holding restricted APEX tickets costing about DFl1,000, will be sat next to people who have paid over DFl2,000 for the same flight. They may have booked late or have an open ticket. Forward of them will be about eighty Flying Dutchmen, KLM business-class passengers whose companies paid DFl6,000 for each seat. In the extreme nose could be about twenty first-class passengers at over DFl10,000 each. The flight could not operate if everyone paid APEX fares because the Boeing would be full before the airline had covered the operating cost. If only full economy fares were charged, many passengers could not afford to fly, so an economy-class 747-400 could not be justified. Also some first-class passengers would be deterred from travelling with the crowd. First-class passengers demand big seats, and their catering alone costs over DFl250 each, but they help maximize the revenue of the airline and the number of people flying.

1 ecu = US$1.26
= DFl 2.12
(Dutch guilders)

### Concentrated marketing

A third market-coverage strategy, **concentrated marketing**, is especially appealing when company resources are limited. Instead of going after a small share of a large market, the firm goes after a large share of one or a few submarkets. For example, Oshkosh Truck is the world's largest producer of airport rescue trucks and front-loading concrete mixers. Recycled Paper Products concentrates on the market for alternative greeting cards and Ecover concentrates on a narrow segment of environmentally friendly detergents. Concentrated marketing is an excellent way for small new businesses to get a foothold against larger competitors.

Through concentrated marketing, a firm can achieve a strong market position in the segments (or niches) it serves because of its greater knowledge of the segments and its special reputation (see Marketing Highlight 9.3). It also enjoys many operating economies because of specialization in production, distribution and promotion. A firm can earn a high rate of return on its investment from well-chosen segments.

At the same time, concentrated marketing involves higher than normal risks. A particular market segment can turn sour. For example, when the 1980s boom ended, people stopped buying expensive sports cars and Porsche's earnings went deeply into the red. Another risk is larger competitors entering the segment. High margins, the glamour and lack of competition in the sports car market has attracted Mazda, Toyota and Honda as powerful competitors in that market. Fashion changes can also damage the niche's credibility. The yuppies who made Porsche's fortunes in the

1980s are over the recession but have grown up, have kids and a different lifestyle. Big, chunky, luxuriously appointed 4 × 4 land cruisers are what they want now.

## Choosing a market-coverage strategy

Many factors need considering when choosing a market-coverage strategy. The best strategy depends on *company resources*. Concentrated marketing makes sense for a firm with limited resources. The best strategy also depends on the degree of *product variability*. Undifferentiated marketing is suitable for uniform products such as grapefruit or steel. Products that can vary in design, such as cameras and cars, require differentiation or concentration. Consider the *product's stage in the life cycle*. When a firm introduces a new product, it is practical to launch only one version, and undifferentiated marketing or concentrated marketing therefore makes the most sense. In the mature stage of the product life cycle, however, differentiated marketing begins to make more sense. Another factor is *market variability*. Undifferentiated marketing is appropriate when buyers have the same tastes, buy the same amounts and react the same way to marketing efforts. Finally, *competitors' marketing strategies* are important. When competitors use segmentation, undifferentiated marketing can be suicidal. Conversely, when competitors use undifferentiated marketing, a firm can gain by using differentiated or concentrated marketing.

## SUMMARY

Sellers can take three approaches to a market. *Mass marketing* is the decision to mass-produce and mass-distribute one product and attempt to attract all kinds of buyers. *Product-variety marketing* is the decision to produce two or more market offers differentiated in style, features, quality, or size, designed to offer variety to the market and to set the seller's products apart from competitors' products. *Target marketing* is the decision to identify the different groups that make up a market and to develop products and marketing mixes for selected target markets. Sellers today are moving away from mass marketing and product differentiation towards target marketing because this approach is more helpful in spotting market opportunities and developing more effective products and marketing mixes.

The key steps in target marketing are market segmentation, market targeting and market positioning. *Market segmentation* is the act of dividing a market into distinct groups of buyers who might merit separate products or marketing mixes. The marketer tries different variables to see which give the best segmentation opportunities. For consumer marketing, the chief segmentation variables are geographic, demographic, psychographic and behavioural. Business markets segment by business consumer demographics, operating characteristics, buying approaches and personal characteristics. The effectiveness of segmentation analysis depends on finding segments that are *measurable*, *accessible*, *substantial* and *actionable*.

Next, the seller has to target the best market segments. The company first evaluates each segment's size and growth characteristics, structural attractiveness and compatibility with company resources and objectives. It then chooses one of three market-coverage strategies. The seller can ignore segment differences (*undifferentiated marketing*), develop different market offers for several segments (*differentiated marketing*), or go after one or a few market segments (*concentrated marketing*). Much depends on company resources, product variability, product life-cycle stage and competitive marketing strategies.

# ■ DISCUSSING THE ISSUES

1. What are the benefits of mass marketing versus market segmentation for a business? Discuss in relation to examples of product and service providers.

2. What variables are used for segmenting the market for: (a) casual clothing; (b) beer; and (c) holidays?

3. The European Union, with its fifteen member states, is now viewed as an attractive and distinctive geographic market segment. Do you agree with this view? To what extent can businesses market in the same way to different consumers in member states? What does this imply about market segmentation?

4. Some industrial suppliers make above-average profits by offering service, selection and reliability – at a premium price. How might these suppliers segment the market to locate customers who are willing to pay more for these benefits?

5. What are the merits and limitations of differentiated, undifferentiated and concentrated marketing? Give examples of product or service providers that have pursued these market coverage strategies. How successful were these strategies?

6. Financial services providers are looking to segment their markets in the face of greater competition and ever more demanding customers. Would segmentation work for financial services? Show how financial services providers might go about segmenting their markets and implementing selected targeting strategies.

# ■ APPLYING THE CONCEPTS

1. Thinking about the participants in this course, segment them into different groups (allocate a mnemonic to each group if you wish). What is your chief segmentation variable? Select several products or services and assess if you could effectively market them to these segments. How effective was your segmentation effort in the first instance?

2. By looking at advertising and at the products themselves, we can often see what target segments marketers hope to reach. Find advertisements of several products. Can you gauge what target markets the ads are aimed at? Do you think the products have distinctive target markets? Are some more clearly defined than others?

# ■ REFERENCES

1. Jocken Pläcking, *Marketing-Kommunikation im Autobilmarkt Europa* (Stuttgart: Motor-Presse, 1990).

2. Ian Rogers, 'Pergesa emerges from the gloom under a new guise', *Financial Times* (3 August 1994), 21.

3. Marieke De Mooij, *Advertising Worldwide Concepts, Theories, and Practical Multinational and Global Advertising*, 2nd edn (London: Prentice Hall, 1994).

4. 'High street renaissance', *The Economist* (16 October 1993), 35–6.

5. 'Can Europe compete? Aging Europe', *Financial Times* (8 March 1994), 14.

6. See Frieda Curtindale, 'Marketing cars to women', *American Demographics* (November 1988), 29–31; and Betsy Sharkey, 'The many faces of Eve', *Adweek* (25 June 1990), 44–9. The quote is from 'Automakers learn better roads to women's market', *Marketing News* (12 October 1992), 2.

7. Alice Rawsthorn, 'LVMH see strong profits growth', *Financial Times* (18/19 June 1994), 11; 'LVMH and Guinness: rearranging their affairs', *EuroBusiness* (February 1994), 6; David Short, 'Nescafé still strongest brew on top shelf', *The European* (22–28 July 1994), 22; Ian Harding,

'Take-overs fail to slake Arnault's thirst for a fight', *The European* (5–11 August 1994), 32.

8. Michael Skapinker, 'Cruise industry charts mass-market course', *Financial Times* (10 June 1994), 11.

9. Graham J. Hooley and John Saunders, *Competitive Positioning* (London: Prentice Hall, 1993); David Tonks, 'Market segmentation', in Michael J. Thomas (ed.), *Marketing Handbook* (Aldershot: Gower, 1989), 573–87.

10. Bickley Townsend, 'Psychographic glitter and gold', *American Demographics* (November 1985), 22.

11. Peter Field and Adam Morgan, 'Hofmeister: a study of advertising and brand imagery in the lager market', in Charles Channon (ed.), *20 Advertising Histories* (London: Cassell, 1989), 16–29.

12. For a detailed discussion of personality and buyer behaviour, see Leon G. Schiffman and Leslie Lazar Kanuk, *Consumer Behavior*, 4th edn (Englewood Cliffs, NJ: Prentice Hall, 1991), ch. 4.

13. See Laurie Freeman and Cleveland Horton, 'Spree: Honda's scooters ride the cutting edge', *Advertising Age* (5 September 1985), 3, 35.

14. Mark Maremont, 'The hottest thing since the flashbulb', *Business Week* (7 September 1992).

15. See Schiffman and Kanuk, *Consumer Behavior*, op. cit., 48.

16. Jeremy Elliott, 'Breaking the bran barrier – Kellogg's Bran Flakes', in Charles Channon (ed.), *20 Advertising Histories* (London: Cassell, 1989), 1–15; Terry Bullen, 'Golden Wonder: a potted success', in Channon (ed.), *20 Advertising Histories*, op. cit., 178–98.

17. For a comprehensive discussion of loyalty schemes see Mark Uncles, 'Do you or your customers need a loyalty scheme', *Journal of Targeting, Measurement and Analysis for Marketing*, **2**, 4 (1994), 335–50; see also F. F. Reichheld, 'Loyalty-based management', *Harvard Business Review* (Mar.–Apr. 1993), 64–73; Andrew S. C. Ehrenberg, 'Locking them in forever', *Admap*, **28**, 11 (1992), 14.

18. Martin Howard, 'The practicalities of developing better analysis and segmentation techniques for fine focusing and improving targeting', Institute for International Research, Conference on Advanced Customer Profiling, Segmentation and Analysis, London, 10 February 1994.

19. See Thomas V. Bonoma and Benson P. Shapiro, *Segmenting the Industrial Market* (Lexington, MA: Lexington Books, 1983). For examples of segmenting business markets, see Kate Bertrand, 'Market segmentation: divide and conquer', *Business Marketing* (October 1989), 48–54.

20. V. Kasturi Rangan, Rowland T. Moriarty and Gordon S. Swartz, 'Segmenting customers in mature industrial markets', *Journal of Marketing* (October 1992), 72–82.

21. For another interesting approach to segmenting the business market, see John Berrigan and Carl Finkbeiner, *Segmentation Marketing: new methods for capturing business* (New York: Harper Business, 1992).

22. Marlene L. Rossman, 'Understanding five nations of Latin America', *Marketing News* (11 October 1985), 10; as quoted in Subhash C. Jain, *International Marketing*

*Management*, 3rd edn (Boston: PWS–Kent Publishing, 1990), 366.

23. For more on intermarket segmentation, see Jain, *International Marketing Management*, op. cit., 369-70.

24. Ibid., 370–1.

25. Thomas Exter, 'Deodorant demographics', *American Demographics* (December 1987), 39.

26. Taken from Jens Maier and John Saunders, 'The implementation of segmentation in sales management', *Journal of Personal Selling and Sales Management*, **10**, 1 (1990), 39–48.

27. Gert-Olof Boström and Timothy L. Wilson, 'Market segmentation in professional services – case of CAD adoption amongst architectural firms', European Marketing Academy Proceedings, Barcelona, Spain, 25–28 May 1993, pp. 249–60.

28. See Joe Schwartz, 'Southpaw strategy', *American Demographics* (June 1988), 61; and 'Few companies tailor products for lefties', *Wall Street Journal* (2 August 1989), 2.

29. See Michael Porter, *Competitive Advantage* (New York: Free Press, 1985), 4–8, 234–6.

30. The methods are introduced in S. J. Q. Robinson, R. E. Hitchins and D. P. Wade, 'The directional policy matrix: tool for strategic planning', *Long Range Planning*, **11**, 3 (1978), 8–15; Yoram Wind and Vejay Mahajan, 'Designing product and business portfolios', *Harvard Business Review* (Jan.–Feb. 1981), 155–65. They are reviewed in Robin Wensley, 'Strategic marketing: boxes, betas or basics', *Journal of Marketing*, **45**, 3 (Summer 1981), 173–82.

31. Angelika Dreher, Angelika Ritter and Hans Mühlbacher, 'Systematic positioning: a new approach and its application', European Marketing Academy Proceedings, Aarhus, Denmark, 26–29 May 1992, pp. 313–29.

32. Rein Rijkens, *European Advertising Strategies* (London: Cassell, 1992), 121–32.

## CASE 9

## Coffee-Mate

The coffee creamer market grew consistently following its introduction in the United Kingdom in the early 1970s to approximately £25m.* in 1992. In volume terms, however, the creamer market is small, with a household penetration of 18 per cent (see Exhibit 9.1). Coffee-Mate has dominated the market since its launch as a result of strong brand and consis-

tent advertising. Despite the growth of private labels in the late 1980s Coffee-Mate's increased advertising spending (from £428,000 to £1,482,000 in 1990) has enabled it to squeeze both private label and other brands (see Exhibit 9.2). Coffee-Mate has maintained its leadership position and in 1992 enjoys volume and sterling brand shares of 55.5 per cent and 62.9 per cent respectively (see Exhibits 9.3 and 9.4).

*1 ecu = UK£0.83.

**CASE 9** (*cont*)

**Exhibit 9.1**   Coffee creamers market (% of total market)

|                          | 1987 | 1988 | 1989 | 1990 | 1991 | 1992 |
|--------------------------|------|------|------|------|------|------|
| Coffee creamers          | 13   | 13   | 11   | 11   | 18   | 18   |
| Coffee-Mate (regular)    | 6    | 6    | 5    | 6    | 12   | 9    |
| Coffee-Mate Lite         | –    | –    | –    | –    | –    | 6    |
| Total Coffee-Mate        | 6    | 6    | 5    | 6    | 12   | 13   |
| Total creamer sales (£m.)| 17.5 | 18.5 | 19.4 | 21.1 | 22.9 | 24.9 |

Source: Nielson and AGB TCA panel (1987-90) and Superpanel (91-2)

**Exhibit 9.2**   Media advertising on milk (£'000s)

|                         | 1986   | 1987   | 1988  | 1989   | 1990   |
|-------------------------|--------|--------|-------|--------|--------|
| Breakfast Milk          | 70     |        |       |        |        |
| Cadbury Marvel          | 125    | 87     | 63    |        |        |
| Cadbury Choc            |        |        | 739   | 1,036  | 616    |
| Carnation Coffee-Mate   | 893    | 755    | 428   | 1,154  | 1,482  |
| Carnation Evaporated    | 864    | 679    | 846   | 978    | 398    |
| Carnation Light Skimmed |        | 87     | 95    | 157    | 166    |
| Cereal Mate Soya        | 75     |        |       |        |        |
| DCNI                    | 152    | 180    | 287   | 307    | 173    |
| Express Vital           |        | 232    |       |        |        |
| Fresh 'n' Low           |        |        |       | 104    | 157    |
| Fit 'N' Lite Skimmed    | 112    |        |       |        |        |
| Kerrygold Light Skimmed |        |        |       | 226    | 211    |
| MMB Cans                |        |        |       | 279    | 286    |
| NDC                     | 10,078 | 12,154 | 9,830 | 9,217  | 10,427 |
| NDC Cans                | 135    |        |       |        |        |
| NDC Milk Race           |        | 116    | 171   | 80     | 1,664  |
| Nestlé Condensed        | 252    | 362    | 241   | 241    |        |
| Nestlé TipTop           | 960    | 955    | 973   | 820    | 1,443  |
| SMCP                    | 1,142  | 1,540  | 874   | 793    | 703    |
| St Ivel Shape           | 130    |        |       |        |        |
| Others                  | 250    | 209    | 109   | 149    | 211    |

Source: MEAL

**Exhibit 9.3**   Volume brand shares (%)

| Brand               | Share |
|---------------------|-------|
| Coffee-Mate – total:| 55.5  |
|    standard | 41.0 |
|    Lite     | 14.5 |
| Compliment          | 2.6   |
| Kenco               | 3.0   |
| Compleat            | 1.4   |
| Own label           | 37.3  |
| All others          | 0.3   |

**Exhibit 9.4**   Coffee creamer market shares (%)

|                | 1987 | 1988 | 1989 | 1990 | 1991 | 1992 |
|----------------|------|------|------|------|------|------|
| Coffee-Mate    | 52   | 55   | 56   | 56   | 61   | 63   |
| Private brands | 34   | 35   | 34   | 34   | 31   | 31   |
| Others         | 14   | 10   | 10   | 10   | 8    | 6    |

## Instant milk

The coffee creamer market is distinct from the instant dry milk market, which includes brands such as Marvel, St Ivel Five Pints and Pint Size which, although worth £43m., has seen a 25 per cent decline since 1988. Dried or powdered milk had been associated with slimming (e.g. Marvel adopted this positioning). The availability of low-fat, skimmed and semi-skimmed milks has had a substantial impact upon sales in this sector. Dried/instant milk, used for its convenience and low cost, has shown a 6 per cent decline in value sales in real terms consequent upon the increased availability of skimmed milk. Dried or powdered milk is not a direct substitute for coffee creamers because of its poor mixing qualities. It is used as a whitener in tea or coffee only in emergency situations in which the household has run out or run low on supplies of milk.

## Competition in the coffee creamer market

The dynamics of the coffee creamer market appear to be undergoing a change in parallel with consumers' developing tastes for skimmed and semiskimmed milk within their coffee. Milk is the most popular whitener for coffee. Although cream is thought to be the best whitener, it represents an aspirational flavour goal only for some. Most consumers perceive cream as a reserved, ritualistic practice, whose taste, while appropriate for an occasion, is not to be replicated on a daily basis.

Powdered or dried milk is a distress product, only used in emergency situations. As such, the brands are bought, but the product is only tolerated. Creamers are regarded more as an indulgence and treat by users, although nonusers did not see creamers as anything like a substitute for cream and were generally highly negative and suspicious of the product (consumers' and nonusers' perceptions of the product category will be described in a later section).

## Coffee-Mate

Coffee-Mate is a blend of dried glucose and vegetable fat, but cannot be legally defined as nondairy, since it also contains milk derivatives. Recent improvements to the product include the relaunch of Coffee-Mate 100 gm and 200 gm in straight-sided glass jars with paper labels, and a 'Nidoll-contoured' jar with shrink-wrapped label. Packs of 500 gm and 1 kg are available in cartons with an inner bag. At the end of 1990, Coffee-Mate Lite, a low-fat alternative to Coffee-Mate, was introduced. Cannibalization of volume has been minimal. The volume generated by Lite has been a key feature in the development of the brand, which has experienced a 10 per cent growth in sales volume over the three years since Lite's launch (see Exhibit 9.5).

**Exhibit 9.5**  Coffee-Mate and Coffee-Mate Lite (000s standard cases)

|  | 1987 | 1988 | 1989 | 1990 | 1991 | 1992 |
|---|---|---|---|---|---|---|
| Coffee-Mate | 1,310 | 1,370 | 1,450 | 1,490 | 1,400 | 1,400 |
| Lite | 0 | 0 | 0 | 0 | 300 | 450 |

## Coffee-Mate consumer

The demographic profile of Coffee-Mate and Lite buyers is summarized in Exhibit 9.6. The average Coffee-Mate consumer buys 1.5 kg annually. AGB Superpanel data suggest that buyers of Coffee-Mate tend to use all brands and types of coffee. The market is characterized by its low interest level, since most buyers do not see it as a weekly shopping item. The main reason given by respondents for not purchasing Coffee-Mate is preference for milk in their coffee: as many as one-third of nonusers gave this as their reason for rejecting the product. An equally high proportion of the nonusers simply have no reason to purchase, because they don't drink coffee, drink it black, or simply have no need to use the creamer. Reasons given spontaneously for lapsed usage were very similar to the main ones articulated by nonusers: 50 per cent of respondents stated they preferred milk in coffee, while around 21 per cent said that they don't drink coffee, drink it black or don't think to buy creamers (Exhibit 9.7).

Because Coffee-Mate and Coffee-Mate Lite are 'consumed' with coffee, popularity and demand will also be affected by the annual coffee consumption in the United Kingdom, which has been static at under 3 kg per head since 1985, compared with over 5 kg in Italy, France and Germany, and well below countries like Finland and the Netherlands with 11–13 kg. Exhibit 9.8 shows the coffee consumption in the UK between 1950–90.

**Exhibit 9.6** Coffee creamer buyers: demographic profile

| Product | Profile |
|---|---|
| Coffee creamers | No *strong* demographic bias. Slightly skewed towards 45–64 year olds, 2-person households, and households without children. |
| Coffee-Mate – std | Slight bias towards C2, DE and 45+ households as heavier buyers; 2–3 person households and households with children. |
| Coffee-Mate Lite | Slightly biased towards 45–64 year olds, full-time working housewives, and households without children. |

**Exhibit 9.7** Reasons for lapsing and rejection (number of respondents)

| Spontaneous response | Lapsing | Rejection |
|---|---|---|
| Don't drink coffee | 11 | 22 |
| Drink black coffee | 5 | 6 |
| Prefer milk | 50 | 33 |
| Prefer skimmed milk | 5 | 3 |
| Don't like them | 10 | 18 |
| Leaves coffee too hot | 2 | 1 |
| No need to use them | 5 | 5 |
| Don't think to buy them | 1 | 4 |
| Doesn't mix | 4 | 1 |
| Prefer pure things | 4 | 3 |
| Fattening | 2 | 2 |
| Too rich/creamy | 1 | 2 |
| Other | 5 | 3 |
| Don't know | 4 | 9 |
| Total sample | 409 | 664 |

The National Food Survey (EIU Retail Business 1992) suggests that the higher a household's income, the more it spends on coffee (Exhibit 9.9). Childless households are the most intense coffee drinkers (Exhibit 9.10).

### Consumers' perceptions of dried powdered milks and whiteners

For both users and nonusers, consumers' perceptions, attitudes towards, and motivations behind usage of whiteners and creamers vary.

Overall, consumers display a relatively clear understanding of the whitener market, which they tend to define under two headings: *dried* or *powdered milks*, and *whiteners*.

### Dried or powdered milk

Perceptually, the dried- or powdered-milk product is more prominent. The product's great versatility and its heritage ('milk') are responsible for this. Consumers regard dried milk as a substitute product, the alternative to turn to in an emergency when the real thing, milk, has run out or is running low. There was also an association with slimming, with brands such as Marvel adopting precisely this positioning. The advent of skimmed milk has, however, made the role in this respect redundant. A few older respondents who used powdered milk in cooking and baking nonetheless reported beneficial results, such as lighter cakes.

The prevailing image of powdered milk as a distress or convenience product means that the *brand* is *bought*, but the *product* is *tolerated*: 'You tend to buy powdered milk thinking that you will need it when you run out, and occasionally you do.' 'Powdered milk is useful if you run out of real milk. You can make it up and use it just like the real thing, but it doesn't taste too good. You have to be a bit desperate to want to use it.'

Other negatives are attached to dry milk. Respondents considered it to be an inconvenient product to prepare. Frequently the product's performance is perceived as disappointing. Consumers here spoke of the product's poor mixing qualities: it is 'lumpy', resulting in 'bits' floating on the top of their coffee. The product also tended to 'congeal' when spooned into tea or coffee. When made up and poured the product's poor taste qualities were also apparent: 'We have had it in our cornflakes when we've run out, but quite honestly, it tastes so disgusting that in the future I don't think I'd bother.' 'It's all right for baking but if you want to use it like real milk, it's not really advisable.'

A stigma is attached to dried milk because of its poor performance and taste delivery. The image of dried milk was consistent across both users and nonusers. Negative perceptions of the product do, however, impact on consumers' perceptions of coffee creamers or whiteners, acting to constrain or to taint perceptions, especially among nonusers.

**Exhibit 9.8**   Coffee consumption (gm/person/week)

| Year | 1950 | 1960 | 1970 | 1980 | 1986 | 1987 | 1988 | 1989 | 1990 |
|---|---|---|---|---|---|---|---|---|---|
| Amount | 0.69 | 1.09 | 1.60 | 1.88 | 2.02 | 1.88 | 1.96 | 1.82 | 1.76 |

Source: National Food Survey

**Exhibit 9.9**   Consumption by income group (per person/week)

| Weekly income (£) | Consumption (gm) | Expenditure (p) |
|---|---|---|
| 645+ | 2.60 | 25.20 |
| 475–644 | 1.79 | 19.30 |
| 250–474 | 1.76 | 20.03 |
| 125–249 | 1.54 | 18.20 |
| 0–124 | 1.62 | 17.24 |
| 125+ (no earners) | 3.08 | 32.19 |
| 0–124 | 1.65 | 19.41 |
| OAPs | 1.76 | 18.64 |

Source: National Food Survey

**Exhibit 9.10**   Consumption by household size (per person/week)

| Number of Adults | Children | Consumption (gm) | Expenditure (p) |
|---|---|---|---|
| 1 | 0 | 2.32 | 27.24 |
| 1 | 1+ | 1.18 | 14.82 |
| 2 | 0 | 2.32 | 25.34 |
| 2 | 1 | 1.68 | 17.97 |
| 2 | 2 | 1.34 | 14.55 |
| 2 | 3 | 1.26 | 14.63 |
| 2 | 4+ | 1.12 | 11.38 |
| 3 | 0 | 1.93 | 22.95 |
| 3+ | 1-2 | 1.43 | 15.51 |
| 3+ | 3+ | 0.92 | 12.22 |
| 4+ | 0 | 2.07 | 25.42 |

Source: National Food Survey

### Whiteners/coffee creamers

Coffee creamers have a more polarized image across users and nonusers. First, *loyal or confirmed creamer users* regard creamers as almost a treat. It is looked upon as an indulgence, solely for their pleasure. These hedonistic and indulgent properties are sometimes enhanced by the brand (e.g. Coffee-Mate) being perceived as having relaxing or comforting benefits: 'Creamers are a little bit of an indulgence. They make coffee taste so much better. They add something to it which improves the taste.' 'First thing in the morning I tend to have coffee with semiskimmed milk, but towards 11 o'clock I want something which is more relaxing, more substantial, so I have coffee with Coffee-Mate. It seems to be comforting.'

Creamers' taste benefits are undoubtedly a motivating force behind usage. Loyal users enjoy and appreciate the thicker, creamier taste. Creamers are considered to supplement the taste of coffee, to complement and improve its flavour. Where Coffee-Mate is concerned, the perceptions are extremely positive. Users enjoy its sweet delivery, stating that they need not add sugar to it. Coffee-Mate fans feel that it does produce a creamy cup of coffee whether or not it is added to instant or freshly brewed 'real' coffee: 'Coffee without Coffee-Mate, just made with milk, tastes like it's got something missing.' 'Coffee-Mate kind of lifts the flavour. It makes a richer, better tasting cup of coffee, whether it be an instant or a real one.'

Secondly, amongst *non-users* their perceptions of coffee creamers are tainted by their generally negative attitudes towards dried milk. Creamers are something you have by for an emergency. You don't really want to use them – they're only there if there's no other choice: 'If someone gave me a cup of coffee with creamer in it, I would think they were doing it because they had run out of milk. I wouldn't have thought it was because they like the taste of it. Surely nobody could like the taste'.

Thus, in marked contrast to the users, where the creamy taste of Coffee-Mate is a totally apposite adjective, nonusers criticized its sweetness. Nonusers describe creamers as changing the taste of coffee, masking its pure taste rather than enhancing it. They also criticized its high sugar content, given that it is a glucose-based product. These consumers feel that Coffee-Mate delivers a flavour that is unacceptably sweet. They are not impressed with the product and perceived it to be a poor synthetic alternative to cream: 'You can always tell when someone's used creamers, it just tastes powdery. It doesn't taste like cream, it has a taste all of its own'. 'Whiteners taste nothing like cream. They taste powdery. You always know when they're there'.

The polarized perceptions of users and nonusers are therefore summarized as follows:

| Taste reactions of users | Taste reactions of nonusers |
|---|---|
| Creamy, rich, comforting, sweet and relaxing. | Creamy, powdery, sickly, clawy, heavy and sweet. |
| 'Coffee without Coffee-Mate tastes as if it's lacking something'. | 'You lose the flavour of the coffee'. |

Thirdly, *lapsed users* still see creamers as a bit of an indulgence and a treat. However, they feel an element of guilt in using the product, and often it has been this anxiety that has caused them to drift away from it: 'I like coffee creamers – I like the taste. But I stopped using them because I felt I was putting on too much weight and I needed to cut down. I just think there is too much in there, it's just glucose syrup and vegetable fat'. 'My husband had to go on a low cholesterol diet and I figured that there was just too much fat in the coffee creamers. We've become accustomed now to drinking it black, or with very little skimmed milk'.

### Changing tastes in coffee consumption

Looking ahead, health concerns are having an impact upon milk consumption, particularly the use of skimmed milk and other low fat varieties. This change has been prompted by consumers' concern over health in general, and their level of fat intake in particular. Some consumers found it difficult to wean themselves and their families off milk, initially, and then semiskimmed milk, in favour of the fully skimmed variety. However, many are persistent in adopting an overall preventative health maintenance regime as well as controlling their weight. So, while a few respondents retained the notion that a cup of real coffee made with cream was still the ideal coffee,

many others considered their ideal to be coffee drunk with just a dash of milk or black. Unfortunately, Coffee-Mate is perceived to be too close to cream in its taste and textural delivery and is in danger of being rendered redundant since its creamy association is increasingly deemed undesirable. Coffee-Mate Lite may, however, redeem the situation by offering the same benefits of creamy and rich taste without causing injury to health and weight.

### Consumer analyses

TGI User Surveys covering instant/ground coffee and powdered milk/coffee creamer markets yielded five potential consumer groups for Coffee-Mate, some of which are potentially more attractive than others. These clusters warrant further evaluation.

### Cluster 1: 'Sharon and Tracy' – experimentalists (sample proportion: 15.4 per cent)

Like to enjoy themselves and try new things. Spend money happily and seem to be very materialistic and status conscious. Holiday abroad, go out frequently and are uninterested in political or environmental issues. Product of the Thatcher years.

Heavy users of instant coffee but low-level use of ground coffee. Claim to use Nescafé granules and Maxwell House powder most often. Are below-average users of the category and average users of Coffee-Mate, but heavy users of cream.

Younger (15–44 years) and mid- to down-market bias (C2D), with children. Middle income (£15,000 up to £30,000) but in council property, in fading industrial areas and underprivileged areas. Tend to be found in the north of the country (e.g. Scotland, Yorkshire, North-East).

Read many of the tabloids (e.g. *The Sun*, *Daily Star*, *Today*, *News of the World*) and the 'mums' magazines such as *Bella*, *Chat*, *Woman* and so on. Heavy users of ITV (not Channel 4), TVAM and satellite, and heavy listeners to independent radio. They cannot resist buying magazines, and read papers for entertainment rather than for news.

Spend average to high amounts on the main grocery shop, and shop at Asda and M&S (all those exciting new foods). They love shopping for anything, be it food, clothes, kitchen gadgets, and so forth.

They like to keep up with fashion and believe they are stylish, and feel it is important to try to keep looking young. They will try anything new. They will respond to seeing new things in advertising or in the store.

They are very gregarious and socialize often (heavy users of pubs, wine bars and restaurants). They like to enjoy life and not worry about the future. They holiday abroad (eat, lie and drink in the sun) and like to treat themselves. A fairly hedonistic bunch, they tend to spend money without thinking, spend more with their credit card, and are no good at saving their money. They feel that it is important for people to think they are doing well. They buy cars for their looks and believe that brands are better than own labels.

At present they are not really using Coffee-Mate as much as one would have expected.

### Cluster 2: 'Eileen and Mary' – cost constrained, older, conservative (sample proportion: 23.6 per cent)

Very price aware, budget when shopping and look for lowest prices. Very traditional in their habits (don't like foreign food or foreign holidays) but worry about whether food is safe to eat or not. Health conscious and worry about what goes into food, but don't do much about it, perhaps because they can't afford to. Seem to be looking back.

They are light users of instant coffee compared with the population as a whole, but when they do use instant coffee they claim to use Maxwell House granules and powder most often. They are average users of the category and buy Marvel and St Ivel. They are not really users of Coffee-Mate and never use cream. Older (55+) and down-market (C2DE). Are not working or are retired in 1 or 2-person households and hence fewer of these types have children at home. Live in multiethnic areas, council areas, and underprivileged areas on a low household income (£5,000–£11,000).

They read the tabloid press and *Bella* and *Chat*. They are also heavy users of ITV, Channel 4 and TVAM, and listen to independent radio.

Not surprisingly, their expenditure on the main grocery shop is low and they tend to shop daily at places such as Kwik Save and the Co-op. They enjoy shopping but always look for the lowest prices,

decide what they want before they go shopping and budget for every penny. They frequently enter competitions, find saving difficult, save for items they want, and like to pay cash.

They are by nature very conservative. They like routine, dislike untidiness, would buy British if they could, have a roast on Sundays and prefer brands to own label. They believe job security is more important than money, would rather have a boring job than no job, and prefer to do rather than take responsibility. Due to both their age and financial constraints they socialize rarely. Most of this group never entertain friends to a meal, and never go to a pub, a wine bar or a restaurant.

They seem to worry about food (food is not safe nowadays, feel safe using products recommended by experts, think fast food is junk, and think it is worth paying more for organic fruit and vegetables and environmentally friendly products), but it is doubtful that they can do much about it.

### Cluster 3: 'Sarah and Anna' – affluent, young foodies (sample proportion: 24.4 per cent)

Unencumbered by children and well off, they love both travelling and food (many claim to be vegetarian). They do not have to budget and can afford to treat themselves to perfume and foreign holidays, preferably more than once a year. They are not interested in additional channels on satellite TV and tend to be light users of all media.

Heavy users of coffee and ground coffee. They buy decaffeinated, Gold Blend, Alta Rica, Cap Colombie, Sainsbury, M&S and Tesco. They are above average users of the category, claim to buy Coffee-Mate and Marvel most often, and they also use cream.

Aged 35–54, predominantly ABC1, they earn above-average incomes and tend to be working full time. They live in areas of affluent minorities, young married suburbs and metro singles 1 or 2-person households. They are more likely to be found in London, the south and the south-west.

They read the quality press including the *Guardian*, the *Independent*, *The Times*, the *Financial Times* and the *Daily Telegraph*. They also read the *Mail* and the *Express* and all the equivalent Sunday papers including the *Observer*. They are light users of independent radio but they do listen to the radio in the car.

They have a high expenditure on their main grocery shop (£71+) but shop infrequently at, of course, Sainsbury, Tesco and Safeway. They really enjoy cooking and food, read recipes in magazines and like to try out new foods. Their tastes will be varied as they also enjoy travelling abroad on holiday where they avoid the package trips and like to do as much as possible.

They entertain frequently and invite friends for meals. They also use pubs and wine bars, though not as much as 'Sharon and Tracy,' and they are heavy users of restaurants.

They are health conscious (well, they can afford to be) and claim to include fibre in their diet, eat wholemeal bread, eat less fat in their diet and fewer sweets and cakes. They are prepared to pay more for food without additives and for environmentally friendly products. They also claim to exercise.

They can afford to treat themselves and prefer to buy one good thing rather than many cheap ones. They also like to keep up with technology and want to stand out from the crowd. In their fortunate position they enjoy life and don't worry about the future.

They also claim never to buy any product tested on animals, buy unleaded petrol, use recycling banks and disapprove of aerosols more than the population at large. They make use of credit cards, especially for business, like to be well insured, and consult professional advisors.

### Cluster 4: 'Dawn and Lisa' – cost constrained, young families (sample proportion: 13.9 per cent)

Rather like 'Eileen and Mary', this group is severely constrained by their low incomes. But unlike the previous group, they are often younger and often working part time or are unemployed or students, although they may have children. They are also not remotely concerned about health or the environment. Many left school before the age of 16.

They are heavy users of instant coffee but do not use ground coffee. They buy Nescafé granules and Maxwell House powder. They are below average users of the category and never use cream.

This group is biased towards the 15–34 age group and is down-market (C2DE) with low incomes (£5,000–£11,000). They are to be found in council estates, fading industrial areas and underprivileged areas in the east, north-east and London. They have

young families and there is a slight bias to larger families than in other groups.

They read the tabloid press, *Bella* and *Chat*, and they are heavy viewers of ITV, TVAM and satellite, and heavy listeners to independent radio.

Their expenditure on the main grocery shop is low and they shop daily or once a week at Kwik Save. They always look for the lowest price, watch what they spend, budget for every penny and look out for special offers. They want to save but find it difficult.

As a result of their difficult financial circumstances, they rarely use wine bars, pubs or restaurants. They claim to enjoy going to the pub but cannot afford to these days. Similarly, when they can afford a holiday, they prefer to holiday in the United Kingdom.

They have little time or money to worry about the environment or health issues and claim that health food is bought by fanatics. They believe that frozen food is as nutritious as fresh foods. They tend to buy own label, presumably because it is cheaper rather than because they believe own-label goods are better than branded goods.

### Cluster 5: 'Dorothy and Amy' – affluent (sample proportion: 22.7 per cent)

This group does not have to be price conscious. They are older, sometimes retired or working part time, and are well off. Often they own their house outright. They are, however, fairly traditional. They are not interested in holidaying abroad, they are not health conscious and they are not media aware.

They are the people most likely to be buying Coffee-Mate. They buy instant coffee to the same degree as the rest of the population and are light users of ground coffee. But they use the category as well as cream.

Dorothy and Amy are older (55+) and are upmarket (AB and C1). They still have a reasonable household income despite being retired (£25,000+) and their children have left home. They are clearly a group who have disposable income as many own their homes, and are not worried about budgeting. They are to be found in affluent minorities, older suburbs and young married suburbs in the northeast, Scotland, Wales and the west.

**CASE 9 (cont)**

*Proposed TV ad*

A TV campaign aims to boost sales. The following ad is proposed.

| Vision | Sound |
|---|---|
| Jane and John, an affluent thirty something couple, are entertaining two other similar couples. | Soft soul music playing throughout. |
| They are ending their meal by drinking coffee out of fine china cups and eating After Eights. | John (to one of the other guests): 'Do you want another cup?'<br>Guest 1: 'Yes, please'.<br>Guest 2: 'Me, too! With cream!' |
| Jane looks alarmed at John.<br>John glances at the empty cream jug. | Jane (thinking quickly): 'I'll make it!' |
| Jane rushes into kitchen and frantically looks for cream (there is none) and milk (all gone). | |
| Jane pauses, smiles, then gets out the Coffee-Mate. | |
| Jane pours the coffee and adds the Coffee-Mate. | |
| Jane returns with coffee. | |
| Guest sips the coffee containing Coffee-Mate. | Guest 1: 'Lovely, even better than the last one!'<br>Guest 2: 'Yes, how do you do it?' |
| John smiles quizzically (and admiringly) at Jane.<br>Jane leans back in her chair, smiling knowingly. | Voice: 'Coffee-Mate, never be without it!' |

They are readers of quality press and light viewers of ITV. They rarely watch Channel 4 and never listen to independent radio. They are not media aware, claiming to watch little TV and not to notice posters, and do not expect ads to entertain. They are not interested in satellite TV or more channels.

Expenditure on the main grocery shop is above average, although they shop infrequently at places such as Safeway, Budgens and the Co-op. They do not enjoy shopping as much as other groups and they are not price conscious at all but are prudent with money (consider themselves good at saving). They do not want to try new things, are not keen to keep up with the latest fashion, and are not concerned with their appearance. They prefer to buy British if possible, and will pay extra for quality goods, but are not really indulgent.

This is a group whose attitudes tend to lag the other groups. They get a great deal of pleasure from gardening and others often ask their advice on the matter. As a group they are happy with their standard of living. They do not often go to pubs, wine bars or restaurants but they do have people in for meals.

*Questions*

1. What are the main benefits of Coffee-Mate and what is limiting its sales? How would the promotion of Coffee-Mate change with the benefits promoted and the competition targeted?
2. Should Coffee-Mate be mass marketed, aimed at one segment or multiple segments? How would the different alternatives alter the marketing mix used to market Coffee-Mate? Why launch Coffee-Mate Lite?
3. Evaluate the alternative ways of segmenting the Coffee-Mate market. Make your choice and defend your choice of segmentation method, segmentation strategy and target segment.
4. Evaluate the segments from TGI's user survey for target attractiveness and their fit to Coffee-Mate's strengths. Which of the segments would you target and why? Evaluate the proposed ad for target market and benefits promoted. Will the ad help propel Coffee-Mate's further growth? Create an alternative ad for your chosen target market.

Sources: Economist Intelligence Unit, *Retail Business*, No. 418 (December 1992); British Market Research Bureaux, *Instant Powdered Milk and Coffee Creamers* (1992); company sources.

## CHAPTER TEN

# Positioning

## CHAPTER OBJECTIVES

After reading this chapter, you should be able to:

- Define differentiation and market positioning.

- Explain why companies seek to differentiate their markets and use positioning strategies.

- List and discuss the principal ways in which companies can differentiate their products.

- Explain how companies can position their products for maximum competitive advantage in the marketplace.

## CHAPTER PREVIEW

### Castrol: liquid engineering

#### The enthusiast

Antoni carefully measured four litres of Syntec into his greatest love, his new Van Dieman Formula Ford single-seater racing car. Tomorrow he was racing her for the first time at Silverstone and wanted to do well. Racing the Formula Fords was exciting but his real dream was to race for Ferrari. That is why he had left his home in Barcelona to work for a specialist engineering firm in rural England.

Leaving Spain was hard, but he was now near where he needed to be: at the heart of the world's motor sports industry. It still seemed odd to him that a sport as international as motor racing was so localized but the evidence was all around. More than three-quarters of the world's purpose-built single-seater cars – including 10,000 Formula Fords – came from small firms like Reynard, Ralt and Van Dieman. Many of the Grand Prix teams were also close by – McLaren, Williams, Lotus, Tyrell, Lola, March, Arrow and, best of all, Benetton. Much of the design work on the new

Castrol's positioning varies from market to market. In this case they aim a specialist oil at motor sports enthusiasts.

Ferraris was also done by local engineers. Local firms even dominated the United States 'Indy' car championships. Few of the 450,000 people watching the Indianapolis 500 race knew that almost all the cars and engines originated in rural England.

Antoni got his Syntec oil from an American friend, and fellow motor enthusiast, living nearby. He was glad of the gift since the synthetic motor oil cost four times that of regular lubricants. In motor racing every little helps and the oil could make the difference between winning and losing. Even if he had not been given the oil, he would have bought some.

## Syntec

Syntec is Burmah Castrol's 'flagship' product. Targeted at enthusiasts and technically advanced users of motor oil, the product appeared on the United States market with a $20m. budget. Despite its high price Syntec sells well and should break even in 1994. It will never have a high market share but the 'flagship' product allows Castrol to create gradations in the market at intermediate prices.

I ecu = US$1.26

Syntec fits Castrol's strategy of having a high price and high marketing expenditure. Sponsorship of rallying, Grand Prix racing and the Indy car series in the United States positions Castrol as a quality, high-performance product used by the experts. Their TV advertising shows Castrol GTX as 'liquid engineering' and so encourages motorists to cosset their engines by using premium-priced product. In the United States the campaign has helped Castrol increase its share of the DIY market from 5 to 15 per cent in ten years. Sales are now just behind Pennzoil, the market leader.

### The 'have somes' and 'near haves'

Castrol has operations in fifty countries and sells to another hundred. Some of its greatest successes are in developing countries where economic development fuels growth. The company's positioning in the developing world is not the same as in developed countries. According to Ian Pringle, Castrol's Asia director, 'have somes' are the key to their marketing in Asia. They are the real middle class of Asia who want to buy cars, houses and consumer durables. They treasure and care for their possessions and look after them. The segment is growing fast. For instance, in India the domestically produced Maruti-Suzuki 800 cc car is *the* status symbol of the rapidly growing middle class. By a combination of political patronage and Japanese technology the company has 71 per cent of the Indian car market that grew by 30 per cent in 1993. Castrol estimates that in 1994 Asia had 55m. to 60m. of these 'have somes', but that there would be 300m. by the end of the century.

Castrol's marketing also covers the Asian 'near haves' who are likely to buy a motor cycle as their first vehicle. According to Mr Pringle, these groups are important because of the way that rapid economic development leads to consumers 'leapfrogging' intermediate technologies: for example, people progressing from having no telephone direct to a cellular phone, or from no radio to hi-fi system with a compact disc player. These changes happen quickly and, Mr Pringle believes, some brand loyalty persists when 'near haves' become 'have somes'. That is why Castrol has made the motor-cycle market central to their marketing strategy in Vietnam and Thailand. In Thailand, Castrol concentrated on building distribution and its image among motorcyclists despite government controls restricting profits in the 1970s. Then, when the motorcycle population leapt from 1m. to 5m. in the late 1980s they were able to hold on to their leading position.

### World coverage

Appropriate targeting and positioning of Castrol lubricants ensures that the company makes profits in markets as different as Vietnam's 'near haves' and the US enthusiasts. By positioning product to fit the market's stage of development, Castrol is profitable in both mature and developing markets. In 1993 the United States and Germany were the two most profitable markets, but India was the third and Thailand the sixth.

**Burmah Castrol: Lubricants Division, 1993**

1 ecu = UK£0.83

| Region | Turnover (£m.) | Operating profits (£m.) |
| --- | --- | --- |
| Europe | 679.4 | 95.9 |
| North America | 502.5 | 50.7 |
| Asia | 242.2 | 40.0 |
| Southern hemisphere | 201.3 | 15.8 |

Mr Tim Stevenson, Castrol's chief executive, says that they have 'proved wrong the sceptics who for years have been arguing that Castrol is a mature business, liable to be snuffed out by the major oil dinosaurs'. He has good reason to boast. Excluding the 1990 Gulf crisis year, Castrol's profits have maintained a 14 per cent compound annual growth rate since 1985. While the world lubricant market has been almost flat over the last ten years, Castrol has increased its sales by 6 per cent per year on average – some maturity; some snuffing out.[1]

## CORE STRATEGY

**Core strategy** is at the hub of marketing strategy, where the strengths of a company meet market opportunities. It has two parts. First, the identification of a group of customers for whom the firm has a differential advantage, and second, positioning itself in that market. Castrol did that. While the big oil companies saw the lubricant market as mature, Castrol identified target markets and built strengths in them. Their motor racing experience, knowledge of high-performance oils, and brand name were competitive advantages in the motor enthusiast market. In the United States, their support of Grand Prix and Indy car racing helped position Castrol Syntec as a high-performance product. In developing countries, their early investments in distribution gave them a differential advantage in the emergent markets. There too, Castrol's association with Grand Prix racing gives the products an exotic international appeal.

## DIFFERENTIATION

Consumers typically choose products and services that give them the greatest value. Thus the key to winning and keeping customers is to understand their needs and buying processes better than competitors do and to deliver more value. To the extent that a company can position itself as providing superior value to selected target markets, either by offering lower prices than competitors do or by providing more benefits to justify higher prices, it gains **competitive advantage**.[2] Solid positions are not built upon empty promises. If a company positions its product as *offering* the best quality and service, it must then *deliver* the promised quality and service. Positioning therefore begins with *differentiating* the company's marketing offer so that it will give consumers more value than competitors' offers do (see Marketing Highlight 10.1). It is not just a matter of being different; success comes from being different in a way that customers want. Arby's, the fast food chain, explain how they compete by being different: 'Being different makes you more interesting. Of course it's not always good to be different (you don't want to be the only one standing up in an electrical storm). But in most cases being different is good. Great tasting, lean Roast Beef and 3 fantastic ways. And *no* dull, boring burger!'

Not every company can find many opportunities for differentiating its offer and gaining competitive advantage. In some industries it is harder than others. The Boston Consulting Group explains four types of industry based on the number of competitive advantages and the size of those advantages (see Figure 10.1). The four industry types are:

1. **Volume industry** where there are a few large advantages to be had. The airline industry is one of these. A company can strive for low costs or differentiate by service quality but can win 'big' on both bases. In these industries profitability is correlated with company size and market share. As a result most minor airlines lose money while the main players try to form global alliances to build share. In this case almost all the industry leaders, like United Airlines, Singapore International Airlines and British Airways, are large, low-cost operators providing a high-quality service.

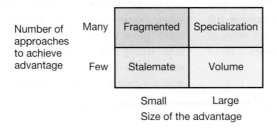

**Figure 10.1**   The new BCG matrix.

# Nintendo: more than just fun and games

In the early 1980s, no home could be without a video game console and a dozen or so cartridges. By 1983, Atari, Coleco, Mattel, and a dozen other companies offered some version of a video game system and industry sales topped $3.2 billion.* Then, by 1985, home video game sales had plummeted to a meagre $100 million. Game consoles gathered dust in closets, and cartridges, originally priced as high as $35 each, sold for $5. Industry leader Atari, a subsidiary of Warner Communications, was hardest hit when the bottom fell out of the market. Amid soaring losses, Warner fired Atari's president, sacked 4,500 employees, and sold the subsidiary at a fraction of its 1983 worth. Most industry experts simply shrugged their shoulders and blamed the death of the video game industry on fickle consumer tastes. Video games, they asserted, were just another fad.

However, one company, Nintendo, a 100-year-old toy company from Kyoto, Japan, did not agree. In late 1985, on top of the still smouldering ruins of the video game business, the company introduced its Nintendo Entertainment System (NES). By the end of 1986, just one year later, Nintendo had sold over 1 million NES units. By 1991, Nintendo and its licensees were reaping annual sales of $4 billion in a now revitalized $5 billion video game industry. Nintendo had captured an astounding 80 per cent share of the market, and more than one out of every five United States households, slightly fewer in the EU, and 40 per cent of Japanese households had a Nintendo system hooked up to one of its television sets.

How did Nintendo manage to single-handedly revive a dying industry? First, it recognized that video game customers were not so much fickle as bored. The company sent researchers to visit popular video arcades to find out why alienated home video game fans still spent hours happily pumping quarters into arcade machines. The researchers found that Nintendo's Donkey Kong and similar games were still mainstays of the arcades even though home versions were failing. The reason? The arcade games offered

better quality, full animation, and challenging plots. Home video games, on the other hand, offered only crude quality and simple plots. Despite their exotic names and introductory hype, each new home game was boringly identical to all the others, featuring slow characters who moved through ugly animated scenes to the beat of monotonous, synthesized tones. The video kids of the early 1980s had quickly outgrown the elementary challenges of these first-generation home video games.

Nintendo saw the fall of the video game industry not as a catastrophe, but as a golden opportunity. It set out to differentiate itself from the ailing competition by offering superior quality - by giving home video game customers a full measure of quality entertainment value for their money. Nintendo designed a basic game system that sold for under $100 yet boasted near arcade-quality graphics. Equally important, it also developed innovative and high-quality software, or 'Game Paks' as Nintendo calls them, to accompany the system. The company's Game Pak library features 150 titles. New games constantly appear and mature titles are weeded out to keep the selection fresh and interesting. The games contain consistently high-quality graphics, and game plots vary and challenge the user. Colourful, cartoon-like characters move fluidly about cleverly animated screens. Amidst a chorus of bongs, whistles, and bleeps, players can punch out the current heavyweight boxing champ or wrestle Hulk Hogan, play ice hockey or golf, or solve word and board games. The most popular games, however, involve complex sword-and-sorcery conflicts, or the series of Super Mario Brothers fantasy worlds, where young heroes battle to save endangered princesses or fight the evil ruler, Wart, for peace in the World of Dreams.

Nintendo's quest to deliver superior quality and value, however, goes far beyond selling its home video game system. The company also worked to build lasting relationships with its ever-growing customer base. For example, to help young customers who are having trouble navigating a passage in one of

*1 ecu = US$1.26.

its games, Nintendo set up one of the most extensive telephone hotline systems in the country. Some 100,000 game players telephone each week, seeking tips on game strategy from one of 250 Nintendo games counsellors. The calls not only help create happy customers, they also provide Nintendo with valuable game-development and marketing information – the company learns at first hand what is hot and what is not. Nintendo has also introduced *Nintendo Power*, a bimonthly magazine that discusses the latest developments in home video entertainment systems. The magazine became the fastest-growing paid-subscription magazine ever – in a little over one year, the magazine's circulation rocketed to more than 1.8 million subscribers. Nintendo further cements its customer relationships by licensing its most popular characters for a variety of uses, not just T-shirts and posters, but also movies, a syndicated TV show, cartoons, and magazines.

Thus, by differentiating itself through superior products and service, and by building strong relationships with its customers, Nintendo has built a seemingly invincible quality position in the video game market. Still, the company knows that it cannot simply rest on past success. The Euromonitor forecasts that the world market for video games will fall by 30 per cent by the year 2000. New competitors such as Sega and NEC have already exploited opportunities created as Nintendo junkies became bored and sought the next new video thrill. Sega beat Nintendo at its own game – product superiority – when it hit the market first with its Genesis machine, an advanced new system that offered even richer graphics, more lifelike sound, and more complex plots. Nintendo countered with the Nintendo Super NES and a fresh blast of promotion, but the competition has intensified. Nintendo must continue to find new ways to differentiate itself from aggressive competitors.

Meanwhile the world of Nintendo has been attacked for being 'violent, destructive, xenophobic, racist and sexist'. Sega Europe has also been attacked for marketing gruesome games such as Mortal Kombat and Night Trap. In Japan, where many of the games come from, consumers are more broad-minded than in most Western countries. Nintendo needs to extend its customer range beyond the easily bored and terminally fickle teenage males. Girls and young women are put off by the sexism of much of the software: from computerized knights rescuing busty damsels to neopornographic exploitation and sadistic violence. In the past there has been little overt attempt to market to girls although they account for 30 per cent of purchases. Sega took the lead by sponsoring roadshows with teen magazines. It is now thinking seriously of putting girls in its TV ads after complaints from schoolchildren on its 'advisory board' about sexism in advertising. In addition to adjusting the marketing of its regular product, Sega Europe has created a new toy division to target 'housewives with kids, instead of 14-year-old boys'. The first product will be Pico, an electronic learning aid for kids that has taken a 'significant' share of the Japanese hi-tech toys market. The US$8m. European launch will include TV, press and posters with full below-the-line campaign. Next will be an 'electronic learning aid that thinks it's a toy' for the three- to seven-year-olds. Will Sega be as successful with these customers as they have been with young boys? Several leading toy makers are already firmly established in the electronic toy market and, as any parent will confirm, toy buyers are fickle too. The company's future success in the home video game market will involve more than the old fun and games. It means keeping abreast of social changes and keeping the fun *in* the games.

Sources: See Rebecca Fannin, 'Zap?', *Marketing and Media Decisions* (November 1989), 35-40; Raymond Roel, 'The power of Nintendo', *Direct Marketing* (September 1989), 24-9; Stewart Wolpin, 'How Nintendo revived a dying industry,' *Marketing Communications* (May 1989), 36-40; Kate Fitzgerald, 'Nintendo, Sega slash price of videogames', *Advertising Age* (8 June 1992), 44; and Richard Brandt, 'Clash of the Titans', *Business Week* (7 September 1992), 34; Mark Jones and Margaret Bennett, 'Game Over?', *Marketing Business* (Dec.-Jan. 1993/4), 8-11; Ros Snowden, 'New Sega arm targets mothers', *Marketing Week* (7 October 1994), 9.

2. **Stalemate industries** produce commodities where there are few potential advantages and each is small. Many old industries like steel and bulk chemicals fall into this category. In these industries it is hard to differentiate products or have significantly lower costs. European firms in these sectors often lose money since they are unable to compete with products from low-cost labour economies. Even size and modern plant cannot counter high labour costs.

3. **Fragmented industries** offer many opportunities to differentiate, but each opportunity is small. Many service industries are fragmented. Restaurants are an extreme example: Hard Rock Café has a global reputation and long queues, but its overall share of the market is small. Even market leaders, like McDonald's and KFC, have a small share of the market relative to leaders in other industries. In fragmented industries profitability is not closely related to size. For many years global Pizza Hut was not profitable, while every large town has restaurateur millionaires who own few eating places. At the same time, many small restaurants fail each year.

4. **Specialized industries** offer companies many opportunities to differentiate in a way that gives a high pay-off. Pharmaceuticals is a specialized industry. A disproportionately large proportion of the world's most successful companies come from the sector where firms like Merck, Glaxo, and Ciba-Geigy are market leaders for particular treatment. Less conspicuous specialized industries are those for scientific instruments and publishing.

Figure 10.2 shows the returns to be had from differentiation. It shows results taken from the Profit Implications of Marketing Strategy (PIMS) study of American and European firms.[3] This study shows that firms with the lowest return on investment (ROI) operate in commodity markets where there is no differentiation on quality or anything else, the coal industry for example. Where there is room for differentiation losers have inferior quality (Aeroflot) and more returns than winners (KLM). The most highly performing group of companies are 'power companies' who have superior quality in differentiable markets (BMW, Mercedes, Toyota and General Motors). These are ahead of nichers (local airlines) who score lower on quality and ROI than the 'power companies'. According to PIMS, often the 'power companies' have a high market share since quality, share and ROI are interrelated.

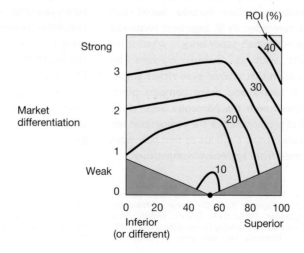

**Figure 10.2** How differentiation and quality drive profitability (Source: SPI's Quality/Differentiation Data Base).

Differentiation may be harder in some industries than others but creative firms have shown that any market can be differentiated.[4] Few people see the brick market as exciting but one brick company found a way of getting a competitive advantage. Bricks used to be delivered to building sites in a truck that tipped them onto the ground. In the process many bricks got broken or lost. Workers on the site also had to spend time stacking the bricks. The brick company's idea was to put the bricks on pallets that were lifted off the truck by a small integral crane. The idea was so successful that soon all bricks came that way. The firm's next idea was to carry a small off-the-road fork-lift truck with the bricks so that they could deliver them to the exact spot where the site manager wanted them.

Oil is a *stalemate industry* but Shell remains the leading petroleum retailer by understanding that fuel is a distress purchase that people do not enjoy. They succeed by making their petrol stations easy to use and paying attention to all the other reasons people stop on a journey: to find their way, get a snack, make a phone call or go to a clean toilet.

Differential advantages can be transient. Some companies find many major advantages that are easily copied by competitors and are, therefore, highly perishable. This is particularly true in financial services where successful ideas are quickly followed by competitors. The Bank of Scotland's Direct Line insurance company succeeded by offering an economic and high-quality personal insurance service through television advertising and telephone selling. It was so successful that established insurers had to follow. Zurich Insurance intends to attack the conservative German and Italian insurance markets in the same way.[5]

The solution for companies facing the erosion of their advantage is to keep identifying new potential advantages and to introduce them one by one to keep competitors off balance. These companies do not expect to gain a single substantial permanent advantage. Instead, they hope to manage a series of advantages that will increase their share over time. This is how market leaders like Canon, Hewlett-Packard, Sony and Gillette have held their position for so long. The true competitive advantage of these firms is their market knowledge, technological expertise, creativity and entrepreneurship that gives them the ability to develop products quickly.

## Differentiating markets

In what specific ways can a company differentiate its offer from those of competitors? A company or market offer can be differentiated along the lines of product, services, personnel, or image.

### *Product differentiation*

A company can differentiate its physical product. At one extreme, some companies offer highly standardized products that allow little variation: chicken, steel, aspirin. Yet even here, some meaningful differentiation is possible. For example, Perdue claims that its branded chickens are better – fresher and more tender – and gets a 10 per cent price premium based on this differentiation.

Other companies offer products that can be highly differentiated, such as cars, commercial buildings, and furniture. Here the company faces an abundance of design parameters.[6] It can offer a variety of standard or optional *features* not provided by competitors. Thus Volvo provides new and better safety features, while Lufthansa offers wider seats to business-class flyers. In Britain, Whitbread has targeted its chain of

In the vastly competitive fashion market Damart differentiates itself on comfort and thermal performance.

Brewers Fayre pubs at families. Besides the usual food and drink, most Brewers Fayres have a toddlers' area, a play zone for bigger children and a 'Charlie Chalk Fun Factory – a large self-contained area full of games, toys and adventure equipment'.

Companies can also differentiate their products on *performance*. Whirlpool designs its dishwasher to run more quietly; Unilever formulates Radion to remove odours as well as dirt from washing. *Style* and *design* can also be important differentiating factors. Thus many car buyers pay a premium for Jaguar cars because of their extraordinary look, even though Jaguar has sometimes had a poor reliability record. Similarly, companies can differentiate their products on such attributes as *consistency*, *durability*, *reliability* or *repairability*.

### Services differentiation

In addition to differentiating its physical product, the firm can also differentiate the services that accompany the product. Some companies gain competitive advantage through speedy, reliable, or careful *delivery*. Harrods, the luxury retailer, delivers to its customers using replica vintage vans – a service particularly popular at Christmas. At the other end of the scale Domino's Pizza promises delivery in less than 30 minutes or takes $3 off the price.

*Installation* can also differentiate one company from another. IBM, for example, is known for its quality installation service. It delivers all pieces of purchased equipment to the site at one time rather than sending individual components to sit and wait for others to arrive. And when asked to move IBM equipment and install it in another location, IBM often moves competitors' equipment as well. Companies can further distinguish themselves through their *repair* services. Many a car buyer would gladly pay a little more and travel a little farther to buy a car from a dealer that provides topnotch repair service.

Some companies differentiate their offers by providing a *customer training* service. For instance, General Electric not only sells and installs expensive X-ray equipment in hospitals, but also trains the hospital employees who will use the equipment. Other companies offer free or paid *consulting services* – data, information systems and advising services that buyers need. For example, M&G, a big reinsurance company, provides information and advice to its customers. It also provides specialist help in developing new products.

Companies can find many other ways to add value through differentiated services. In fact, they can choose from a virtually unlimited number of specific services and benefits through which to differentiate themselves from the competition. Milliken & Company provides one of the best examples of a company that has gained competitive advantage through superior service:

> Milliken sells shop towels to industrial launderers who rent them to factories. These towels are physically similar to competitors' towels. Yet Milliken charges a higher price for its towels and enjoys the leading market share. How can it charge more for essentially a commodity? The answer is that Milliken continuously 'decommoditizes' this product through continuous service enhancement for its launderer customers. Milliken trains its customers' salespeople; supplies prospect leads and sales promotional material to them; supplies on-line computer order entry and freight optimization systems; carries on marketing research for customers; sponsors quality improvement workshops; and lends its salespeople to work with customers on Customer Action Teams. Launderers are more than willing to buy Milliken shop towels and pay a price premium because the extra services improve their profitability.[7]

*Speed* of service is a competitive advantage used by many firms. Fast food is now common on the world's high streets and malls, along with services like one-hour photo-processing and Vision Express's one-hour service for spectacles. These services provide a direct benefit to customers by giving rapid gratification and allowing services to be completed within one shopping trip. Speed also helps sell more expensive goods. Abbey National found that their success in providing large mortgages depended upon how fast they could confirm that they would give a person a home loan. They responded by allowing local managers to make loan decisions rather than processing applications centrally. In the car market Toyota's two-day policy means that they can supply a well-equipped Lexus within two days, while many other luxury car makers expect prospects to wait several weeks for custom-built cars.

The success of courier services like TNT and DHL show that many people are willing to pay extra for a quick, secure service. A study of the importance of service responsiveness to users of small business-computer-based systems shows how speed is valued:

- Eighty-five per cent of users were willing to pay a 10 per cent premium price for same-day service; 60 per cent would pay 20 per cent more; and 40 per cent would pay a 30 per cent premium.
- On average, same-day service was worth twice as much as brand name and distributor reputation and worth four times more than technical features.[8]

## Personnel differentiation

Companies can gain a strong competitive advantage through hiring and training better people than their competitors do. Singapore Airlines enjoys an excellent reputation largely because of the grace of its flight attendants. McDonald's people are courteous, IBM people are professional and knowledgeable, and Mark Warner's resort staff are friendly and upbeat. Marks & Spencer helps differentiate its stores by careful selection, training and looking after its staff.

| | Local community pub | Broad-based local | Young persons' circuit pub | Quality traditional dry |
|---|---|---|---|---|
| **TABLE 10.1** | *Allied Breweries pub segments* | | | |
| Segment | | | | |
| Location | Public housing estates or old terraced housing | Housing estates | Town centre or suburban high street | Prosperous villages or remote country sites |
| Customer demographics | Generally males of all ages | Men and women aged 18 to 44 | Aged 18 to 24. Single sex groups at lunch time | Aged 35 plus as couples or with family. Managerial and professional |
| Customer geography | Local | Work within a mile of the pub | From 5-mile radius | Five miles or over |
| Pub journey | Walk | Walk or car | Public transport | Car |
| Consumer behaviour | Price conscious, shop locally but do not drink at home | Price conscious, like pub games | Fashion-conscious and like background noise | Dislike pub games and background noise |
| Readership | Popular newspapers | Popular newspapers | Music press | Quality newspapers |
| Drinks | Thirty per cent standard lager and white spirits | Beer, wine and whisky | Standard lagers plus some premium lagers and spirits | Drinks only 60 per cent of sales |
| Food | Basic lunch-time sandwiches | A little more than the local community pubs | Little | Appreciate good food |

Personnel differentiation requires that a company should select its customer-contact people carefully and train them well. These personnel must be competent – they must possess the required skills and knowledge. They need to be courteous, friendly, and respectful. They must serve customers with consistency and accuracy. And they must make an effort to understand customers, to communicate clearly with them, and to respond quickly to customer requests and problems.

The Allied Breweries subsidiary of Allied Lyons linked staff needs to the market segments they served. A segmentation study identified four pub segments in the United Kingdom (see Table 10.1) and the managers needed to run them. *Local community pubs* needed a good controller who was mature and experienced. He or she had to be 'one of the crowd', be involved in the local community and be an organizer of pub teams and other events. The personality of the manager is the key to success of *broad-based locals*. They need to maintain a high profile and set the mood of the pub and other staff. *Young persons' circuit pubs* need good organizers who are tolerant but firm. These places are very busy at peak times, so service standards have to be high and efficient. Users of *quality traditional dry pubs* expect attention to detail and high professional standards. Good food is important, so the manager's job is more complicated than for other pubs. The manager may not have a strong personality but organizational and financial skills are important.

## Image differentiation

Even when competing offers look the same, buyers may perceive a difference based on company or brand images. Thus companies work to establish *images* that differentiate them from competitors. A company or brand image should convey a singular and distinctive message that communicates the product's main benefits and positioning. Developing a strong and distinctive image calls for creativity and hard work. A company cannot implant an image in the public's mind overnight using only a few advertisements. If 'IBM means service', this image must be supported by everything the company says and does.

*Symbols* can provide strong company or brand recognition and image differentiation. Companies design signs and logos that provide instant recognition. They associate themselves with objects or characters that symbolize quality or other attributes, such as the Mercedes star, the Johnnie Walker character, the Michelin man or the Lecoste crocodile. The company might build a brand around some famous person, as with perfumes such as Passion (Elizabeth Taylor) and Uninhibited (Cher). Some companies even become associated with colours, such as Kodak (yellow) or Benson & Hedges (gold).

The chosen symbols must be communicated through advertising that conveys the company or brand's personality. The ads attempt to establish a story-line, a mood, a performance level – something distinctive about the company or brand. The atmosphere of the physical space in which the organization produces or delivers its products and services can be another powerful image generator. Hyatt hotels have become known for their atrium lobbies and TGI Friday's restaurants for American memorabilia. Thus a bank that wants to distinguish itself as the 'friendly bank' must choose the right building and interior design – layout, colours, materials and furnishings – to reflect these qualities.

A company also can create an image through the types of events it sponsors. Perrier, the bottled water company, became known by laying out exercise tracks and sponsoring health sports events. Other organizations have identified themselves closely with cultural events, such as orchestral performances and art exhibits. Still other organizations support popular causes. For example, Heinz gives money to hospitals and Quaker gives food to the homeless.

## WHAT IS MARKET POSITIONING?

A **product's position** is the way the product is *defined by consumers* on important attributes – the place the product occupies in consumers' minds relative to competing products. Thus Tide is positioned as a powerful, all-purpose family detergent, Radion removes odours, and Fairy is gentle. Skoda and Subaru are positioned on economy, Mercedes and Jaguar on luxury, and Porsche, Saab and BMW on performance.

A firm's *competitive advantage* and its *product's position* can be quite different. A competitive advantage is the strength of a company while a product's position is a prospect's perception of a product. A competitive advantage, like low costs or high quality, could influence a product's position but in many cases they are not central to it. For instance, low costs and access to Heathrow are two of British Airways' competitive advantages, but its position is based on popularity and its global network, 'The world's favourite airline'. Similarly, Toyota's low costs are a significant competitive advantage but its products are sold on quality and technical excellence, not price.

Consumers are overloaded with information about products and services. They cannot re-evaluate products every time they make a buying decision. To simplify buying decision making, consumers organize products into categories – that is they 'position' products, services and companies in their minds. A product's position is the complex set of perceptions, impressions and feelings that consumers hold for the product compared with competing products. Consumers position products with or without the help of marketers. But marketers do not want to leave their products' positions to chance. They *plan* positions that will give their products the greatest advantage in selected target markets, and they *design* marketing mixes to create these planned positions.

The word *positioning* was popularized by advertising executives Al Ries and Jack Trout.[9] They saw positioning as a creative exercise done with an existing product:

> Positioning starts with a product, a piece of merchandise, a service, a company, an institution or even a person…But positioning is not about what you do to a product. Positioning is what you do to the mind of the prospect. That is, you position products in the mind of the prospect.

They argue that current products generally have a position in the minds of consumers. Thus Rolex is thought of as the world's top watch, Coca-Cola as the world's largest soft drink company, Porsche as one of the world's best sports cars, and so on. These brands own those positions and it would be hard for a competitor to steal them.

Ries and Trout show how familiar brands can acquire some distinctiveness in an 'overcommunicated society' where there is so much advertising that consumers screen out most of the messages. A consumer can only know about seven soft drinks even though there are many more on the market. Even then, the mind often knows them in the form of a *product ladder*, such as Coke>Pepsi>Fanta or Hertz>Avis>Budget. In such a ladder, the second firm usually has half the business of the first firm, and the third firm enjoys half the business of the second firm. Furthermore, the top firm is remembered best.

People tend to remember *number one*. For example, when asked, 'Who was the first person to successfully fly the Atlantic Ocean?' people usually answer, 'Charles Lindbergh'. When asked, 'Who was the second person to do it?' we draw a blank. That is why companies fight for the number-one position. In reality, the first people to fly the Atlantic were Alcock and Brown, but Charles Lindbergh won the publicity battle.

Ries and Trout point out that the 'size' position can be held by only one brand. What counts is to achieve a number-one position along some valued attribute, not necessarily 'size'. Thus 7-Up is the number-one 'Uncola', Porsche is the number-one small sports car and Foster's is Australia's top-selling lager. In the United States Heineken is 'the' imported beer because it was the first heavily promoted imported beer. The marketer should identify an important attribute or benefit that can convincingly be won by the brand. In that way brands hook the mind in spite of the incessant advertising bombardment reaching consumers.

According to Ries and Trout, there are three positioning alternatives:

1. The first strategy they suggest is to strengthen a brand's *current position* in the mind of consumers. Thus Avis took its second position in the car rental business and made a strong point about it: 'We're number two. We try harder'. This was believable to the consumer. 7-Up capitalized on *not* being a cola soft drink by advertising itself as the Uncola.

2. Their second strategy is to search for a new *unoccupied position* that is valued by enough consumers and grab it: 'Cherchez le creneau', 'Look for the hole'. Find a hole in the market and fill it, they say. Vidal Sassoon's Wash & Go was based on recognizing that the fashion for exercise meant that people washed their hair frequently, quickly and away from home. By combining a shampoo and hair conditioner in one they were able to fill a latent market need. Similarly, after recognizing that many housewives wanted a strong washing powder to treat smelly clothes, Unilever successfully launched Radion.

Across Europe new 'newspapers' have filled a down-market gap left by the traditional press. In Britain the *Sunday Sport* started as a weekly paper reporting on sensationalist stories – 'Double decker bus found in iceberg' – sport and sex, but has now grown into a daily paper. In France the new *Infos du Monde* reached sales of 240,000 a week after just two months. 'Our readers don't want "dirty" news', say *Infos*. They instead seek the bizarre in ordinary life; fairground freaks are popular – 'Four-legged woman from Cannes looks for love'. Another sensationalist publication is the German-owned *Voici*, a glossy scandal sheet full of show-biz personalities. *Infos* has sent some of its staff to the United States to learn from their *Weekly World News*, a magazine specialising in blood, sex and gore. Some newspaper vendors are embarrassed about the newspapers and the established press see the new publications as distasteful. They also worry about the disturbing misinformation they monger. But, as a Gare du Nord news kiosk seller says: 'If people lead such dull and boring lives that their day is brightened by reading about a man with an axe stuck in his head, what's wrong with that?'[10]

3. Their third strategy is to *deposition* or *reposition* the competition. Most US buyers of dinnerware thought that Lenox china and Royal Doulton both came from England. Royal Doulton countered with ads showing that Lenox china is from New Jersey, but theirs came from England. In a similar vein, Stolichnaya vodka attacked Smirnoff and Wolfschmidt vodka by pointing out that these brands were made locally but 'Stolichnaya is different. Similarly, it is Russian.' Guinness, the world's leading brown ale, has strong Irish associations. However, the focus on individuality in its Rutger Hauer 'Pure Genius' campaign has allowed Murphy's and Beamish to attack Guinness's Irish heritage. A final example is Kaliber no-alcohol beer drunk by people who want a good time or, as Billy Connolly says in their ads posted next to those for Wonderbra, 'Hello girls!'

Ries and Trout essentially deal with the psychology of positioning – or repositioning – a current brand in the consumer's mind. They acknowledge that the positioning strategy might call for changes in the product's name, price and packaging, but these are 'cosmetic changes done for the purpose of securing a worthwhile position – in the prospect's mind'.

## PERCEPTUAL MAPPING

**Perceptual maps** are a valuable aid to product positioning. These maps use *multidimensional scaling* of perceptions and preferences that portray psychological distance between products and segments, using many dimensions. They contrast with conventional maps that use two dimensions to show the physical distance between objects. Physical and psychological maps of the same items can be quite different. Disneyland in California and Disney's Magic Kingdom in Florida are thousands of kilometres apart physically but psychologically close together.

In their simplest form perceptual maps use two dimensions. For example, Figure 10.3 shows the average *value for money* and *accessibility* rating of European holiday destinations.[11] The perceptual map shows that France, Germany and the Netherlands, which are physically close together, are also psychologically close holiday destinations using these two criteria. In contrast, Spain and the United Kingdom are psychologically close together but are physically distant. France is Europe's most popular holiday destination and this map partly shows why: it offers the best value for money amongst the accessible nations. The lack of destinations in the high *value for money* and easy *access* quadrant suggests a *cherchez le creneau* positioning opportunity for new destinations. Hungary and Czechoslovakia could fill the hole in the market.

This award-winning campaign attracted immense attention without offending women. Sales of Wonderbra were reported to have more than doubled as a result.

This poster ad promotes a distinct advantage of no-alcohol beer when meeting the girl in the Wonderbra.

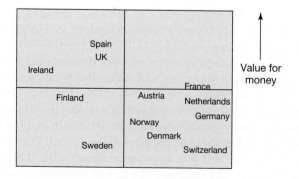

**Figure 10.3**   Two-dimensional perceptual maps of European tourist destinations.

Of course, holiday-makers have a more complicated view of destinations than the two-dimensional map suggests. And if the map had other dimensions it would change: for instance, adding weather would certainly separate Spain and the United Kingdom. Multidimensional scaling produces maps that show many dimensions at the same time (Figure 10.4). To read these maps, trace back the individual

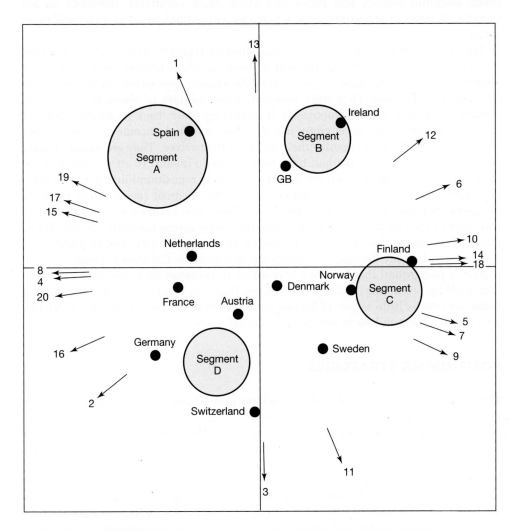

**Attribute key:**

| | | | |
|---|---|---|---|
| 1 | Good value for money | 11 | Poor value for money |
| 2 | Accessible | 12 | Inaccessible |
| 3 | Good facilities | 13 | Poor facilities |
| 4 | Good entertainments | 14 | Poor entertainments |
| 5 | Peaceful and quiet | 15 | Not quiet |
| 6 | Friendly and hospitable | 16 | Unfriendly |
| 7 | Wild areas | 17 | No wild areas |
| 8 | Good cultural experience | 18 | Poor cultural experience |
| 9 | Beautiful scenery | 19 | Not scenic |
| 10 | Unique and different | 20 | Similar to others |

**Figure 10.4** Internal property-fitting analysis using PREFMAP. (Source: G. Hooley, 'The Finnish Tourist Board', in Peter Doyle and Norman Hart (eds), *Case Studies in International Marketing* (London: Heinemann, 1982), 68.)

dimensions one at a time. For example, the perception is that Switzerland has *good facilities*; Germany and Sweden quite good ones; Denmark, the Netherlands and Norway average ones; and the United Kingdom, Spain and Ireland *poor facilities*. Finland has an extreme position on the map. Prospective travellers see its people as *friendly and hospitable* while the country is a *unique and different* place with *wild areas*, *beautiful scenery* and *peace and quiet*. More negatively, travellers do not perceive Finland as *accessible*, or as a place for *entertainment*, or as a *cultural experience*.

The perceptual map shows how holiday-makers segment, as well as the possible destinations. A, the largest segment, wants cheap, sunshine holidays and liked Spain. Segment C, who represented 15 per cent of the sample population, are a natural target market for Finland. They want peaceful, quiet holidays in places with beautiful scenery. Norway is already successful at marketing these 'back to nature' ideals as 'natural tourism'.[12] The target group mainly consists of high-income couples or families with one child who organize their holidays themselves. They are mainly Dutch, German or Scandinavian, but half have never visited Finland. To attract this segment the Finnish Tourist Board does not need to massively reposition Finland as a holiday destination. It needs to promote the country as the segment sees it while reducing the perception that it is an *inaccessible* place. Promoting luxury car ferries that allow travellers to start their holiday with a relaxing cruise across the Baltic Sea would be one way of doing this. Strangely Barbados has a similar positioning problem to Finland as a holiday destination. Europeans perceive the Caribbean island as a millionaire's playground that is a long way away. In response Barbados tries to reposition itself by promoting 'Barbados. It's closer than you think … A sunshine holiday there can cost as little as one of Europe's premier resorts.' (Marketing Highlight 10.2 gives more advice on how to develop perceptual maps.)

## POSITIONING STRATEGIES

Marketers can follow several positioning strategies. These strategies use associations to change consumers' perception of products.

*Product attributes* position many technical products. The positioning of Ericsson's EH237 mobile phone is its *low weight* and number of *features* while much of BMW's advertising promotes individual *technical items* like fresh air filters. In the exclusive watch market Breitling, Baume & Mercier and Audemars Piguet's positioning are on their mechanical movements. Some of their designs leave the mechanisms exposed and one ad argues 'Since 1735 there has never been a quartz Blancpain. And there never will be.'

The *benefits* they offer or the needs they fill position many products – Crest toothpaste reduces cavities. Aim tastes good and Macleans Sensitive relieves the pain of sensitive teeth. In the confectionery industry Italian Baci and Ferrero Rocher are gifts while Mars and Snickers bars satisfy hunger.

*Usage occasions* positions many products. Mentadent Night Action toothpaste, for instance, is for evening use. In the summer, Gatorade is positioned as a drink for replacing athletes' body fluids; in the winter, it can be positioned as the drink to use when the doctor recommends plenty of liquids. KitKat and After Eight mints sell alongside Snickers and Ferrero Rocher but the positioning is on usage occasion. Internationally KitKat means 'Have a break' while After Eight is an after-dinner mint to share.

Red Bull, a soft drink made by a small Austrian company, is a huge success in Germany and is rolling out across Europe. According to their sales director: 'We don't want to be compared with the soft drink market. Of course, Red Bull has quite a key position in the market

Carlsberg positions ICE using strong personalities.

but it is mainly a sports drink.' Red Bull's origin is in the huge Japanese market for energy drinks. Each can has 80 milligrammes of caffeine, a third more than the equivalent amount of Coca-Cola. This had made the drink popular with teetotaller young ravers who can consume several cans a night.[13]

*Users* help position products. Johnson & Johnson improved the market share for its baby shampoo from 3 per cent to 14 per cent by repositioning the product towards a new *user category* of adults who wash their hair frequently and need a gentle shampoo. Often products are positioned by associating them with their *user class*. Nescafé Gold Blend increased sales dramatically after showing a series of ads romancing thirty somethings as did Tango soft drinks as a result of the youthful 'You've been Tangoed' campaign. Woolworths give their products credibility among teenagers by using and promoting successful young people as models – Sega champion Karl Roberts, rapper and dance champion Jermaine Emmanuel; mountain bike champion Zoe Read.

*Activities* are often used to sell expensive products. The Geneva-based SMH group position their watches using sports. Thus Rado has come to specialize in tennis, Omega in sailing and aerospace, 'the first and only watch on the moon', and Longines in skiing and aviation.[14] This positioning activity goes beyond advertising and promotions. Rolex position their watches using adventurers and back this with their SFr450,000 Awards for Enterprise. Over thirty people are Rolex Laureate for their original and creative schemes.[15]

*Personalities* often help positioning. Nike started 1990 as the third-place sports shoe after Reebok and Adidas but grew to number one by associating their products with the basketball star Michael Jordan and other famous sports personalities.

1 ecu = US$1.26 = SFr 1.56 (Swiss francs)

# Building perceptual maps of markets

The most important part of perceptual mapping is collecting the right data in the right way. This marketing highlight takes you through the data stages of data collection and introduces ways of making perceptual maps.[1]

## *Defining the competitors*

Defining the competition is not a trivial task since perceptual mapping is about how consumers see markets and that may differ from the map maker's view.[2] For instance, the Range Rover is a four-wheel-drive cross-country vehicle, yet research shows that customers do not see it as an alternative to other four-wheel-drive recreational vehicles. From the customer's perspective, it is one of the automotive nobility and is an alternative to a Jaguar, a large BMW or Mercedes-Benz, or even a Porsche or Rolls-Royce.[3]

One way of defining competitors is to look at panel data to see what customers have done in the past. By tracking the past purchasers of customers, it may be possible to identify product alternatives when switching takes place. The danger in this approach is the dissociation of the purchasers from the user's situation and the user. For instance, a buying pattern that shows the purchase of low-alcohol lagers, lemonade, beer and coke could represent products consumed by different people at different times, rather than switching between alternatives. Another approach is to determine which brands buyers consider. For consumer nondurables, customers are asked what other brands they considered in their buying process. This could show the present tendency for customers to buy soda water and tonic water – traditionally mixers – as an alternative to mineral water or other soft drinks. For low-involvement products, it may be inappropriate to ask buyers about a particular purchase decision, so instead they ask what brands they would consider if their favourite brand was not available.

A more exhaustive process and cost-effective way of mapping product markets uses a structured series of interviews. Start by asking twenty or so respondents the use context of a product, say, a low-alcohol lager. For each use context so identified – such as the lunch-time snack, with an evening meal, or at a bar – respondents identify all alternative drinks. For each drink identified, the respondent has to identify an appropriate use context. The process continues until there is a full list of contexts and drinks. A second group of respondents is asked to make a judgement on how appropriate each drink would be for each usage situation. Then cluster the drinks by the similarity of their use. For instance, if both low-alcohol lager and coke were appropriate for a company lunch-time snack but inappropriate for an evening meal, they are direct competitors.[4]

## *The competitive dimensions*

There are three ways of seeking competitive dimensions that we do not recommend. The first is to use experts' judgements, which, like their judgements of competitors, are likely to be different from those of customers. The second is to look too closely at the perceptual map in an attempt to work out what the dimensions represent. Such maps are often ambiguous and there is a particular danger of researchers superimposing their own views on it. Thirdly, a better, but still imperfect, technique is to ask customers directly how they differentiate the market. The problem here is that customers may give a relatively simplistic answer which may not represent all the dimensions they may use to differentiate product offerings.

Kelly grids are a popular market research technique that identifies the dimensions underlying a market.[5]

1. Give respondents three stimuli (say, Pepsi Max, Schweppes Soda Water and Perrier) and ask them to state which two are alike but unlike the third. 'Tonic water and Perrier are alike but different from Pepsi Max', could be the answer.
2. Next, ask how tonic water and Perrier are alike. The answer could be, 'low calorie and natural'. These factors are labelled 'the emergent pole'. 'Youthful' could be the answer to the question why Pepsi Max is different from the other two. That answer is 'the implicit pole'.
3. Sort the stimuli (Pepsi Max, Schweppes Soda Water, Perrier and other drinks) equally between the two poles.

4. Another three stimuli are selected and the process is repeated until the respondents can think of no new reasons why the triad are alike or dissimilar.

## Determine the competitors' positions

It is an odd feature of many of the techniques used in positioning research that the competitors' positions appear before understanding how customers differentiate between them. For example, in *similarities-based multidimensional scaling*, respondents sort a stack of cards that contain pairs of competing products: for instance, card one could read 'Pepsi Max and Coca-Cola', card two, 'Perrier and 7-Up', card three 'Pepsi Max and Dr Pepper', and so on. Then ask the respondents to rank the pairs according to their similarity, the pair most alike on the top and the pair most unalike on the bottom. Since this can be a rather cumbersome process, it is best first to ask respondents to stack the cards into three piles representing those pairs that are very similar, those pairs that are very unalike and a middling group. The respondents then rank the pairs within each group.

The objective is now to develop a plot of the stimuli (drinks) that shows those that people saw as

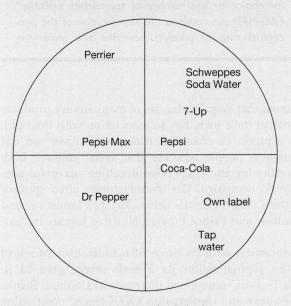

**Figure 1**  Perceptual maps of soft drinks

similar close together and those that respondents said were dissimilar far apart. Although this is a difficult task to conduct manually, computers are particularly adept at finding solutions and there are many computer packages that can be used.[6] A computer package called KYST produces perceptual maps from the similarities matrix provided and many sorts of data.[7] The map in Figure 1 shows Pepsi Max and Coca-Cola positioned well away from the economic drink, tap water. Noticeably, Perrier has also distanced itself from tap water, hence its premium price.

The map is not a perfect fit to reality. It is in two dimensions whereas the customers' perception of the market is rather more complex than that. The map is also an aggregate of a number of customers' views, so it is an average picture. KYST can produce a perceptual map of a single customer, but it is more common to produce a map which either aggregates all customers or aggregates all the people in a segment.

## Adding competitive dimensions

To find out how the dimensions fit the perceptual map, respondents rate each drink on the basis of the attributes identified. The result is another series of matrices that are difficult to analyse manually, and again, computers must come to our aid: in this case, a package called PREFMAP takes the perceptual map of product positions and fits the dimensions as they best describe the respondents' perceptions (see Figure 2).[8]

Again, it is likely that the map does not show respondents' individual or aggregated scores perfectly. This is inevitable, given that the picture is trying to represent ever more information in the same two dimensions. This problem can be reduced by using three or more dimensions, but usually the situation then becomes less rather than more comprehensible as the map goes beyond our normal experience. It may also be that segments of the market have distinctly different views and therefore it is more appropriate to produce maps that represent their different perceptions, rather than aggregate the market as has been done so far.

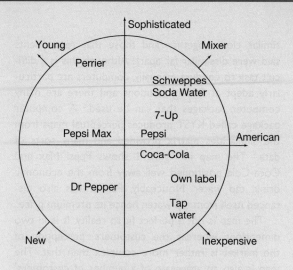

**Figure 2** Perceptual map of soft drinks showing competition dimensions

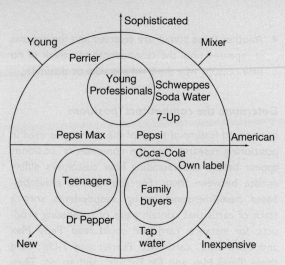

**Figure 3** Perceptual map of soft drinks showing customer positions

### Adding customers

A two-stage process adds customer positions to the drinks map. First, respondents rate the drinks on their preference. Cluster analysis then segments those respondents with similar preferences (see Marketing Highlight 9.2 to find out about this), which indicates the presence of three main clusters. Analysis of their demographic characteristics shows these clusters to be: young professionals, who found Perrier and Schweppes most attractive; family buyers,

who preferred own brands; and teenagers, attracted by Pepsi Max and Coke. Again, PREFMAP can locate these segments on the product map (see Figure 3).

### Alternative ways of mapping

In developing positioning maps, researchers are spoilt for choice by the number of approaches available.[9] PREFMAP can combine the identification of the perceptual map of product positions and underlying

Prestigious brands are often positioned that way. For buyers of many luxury products it is hard to show situations better than their own, but an association with the right, successful personality can add to a product's character. American Express run ads showing caricatures of famous business people who are also users; Jameson Irish Whiskey use sportsmen in their positioning and Hugo Boss identifies successful people as models in their 'Men at Work' campaign. Car manufacturers often sponsor favourable personalities. The sprinter Linford Christie drives Toyota's fastest car and the Queen and her sons Prince Andrew and Prince Edward all drive Jaguars by 'private arrangement'.[16]

*Origin* positions product by association with its place of manufacture. Much of Perrier's success depended on the sophistication its French origin gave to it. Similarly Audi's 'Vorsprung Durch Technik' positioned their cars as German. Drinks are often positioned using origin. Foster's and Castlemaine XXXX lagers' positioning uses their Australian heritage, plus masculine humour to reinforce their character. The strategy also works at a local level. Boddington's was a local Manchester beer

dimensions.[10] This program would require respondents to rate drinks along each of the dimensions, such as 'exciting' or 'natural', and would then involve aggregating the results to arrive directly at a map. Correspondence Analysis is another method that is now widely acclaimed by practitioners. It is popular because it makes maps using cross-tabulated data that often already exist. However, this convenience is achieved at the cost of not mapping meaningful interpoint distances. As a result, when correspondence analysis shows Pepsi Max and 7-Up closer together on a map than are Perrier and Schweppes, this does not mean that Pepsi Max and 7-Up are particularly close together.[11]

Anyone who starts to use this diversity of approaches will find that the map produced depends upon the approach used. This is because of the differences in the data-gathering techniques and the methods used to optimize the results. In that way, the use of multidimensional scaling is similar to cluster analysis, where the results depend on the method used. But as in cluster analysis, this should not be regarded as a defect but as an indication that there are numerous ways of looking at a market. Life would be convenient if there were just one map that represented a market, but any attempt to compress the richness of a market into so simple a perspective is likely to result in opportunities being missed.

A few years ago, access to these software packages was difficult and the programs hard to use. Now

the situation has changed completely. These programs, along with other reasonably user-friendly data analysis packages, are available in PC form[12] and are used routinely by many market researchers.

## References

1. This highlight draws mainly from Graham Hooley and John Saunders, *Competitive Positioning: The key to market success* (Hemel Hempstead, Herts: Prentice Hall, 1993).
2. John Saunders and Ann Watt, 'Do brand names differentiate identical industrial products?', *Industrial Marketing Management*, **8**, 2 (1979), 114-33.
3. Tony Lewin, 'Rebirth of the Range Rover', *The European* (30 Sept.-6 Oct. 1994), 23.
4. G. S. Day, A. D. Shocker and R. K. Srivastava, 'Customer oriented approach to identifying product markets,' *Journal of Marketing*, **43**, 4 (1979), 8-19.
5. Peter Sampson, 'Qualitative research and motivational research', in Robert M. Worcester and John Downham (eds), *Consumer Marketing Research Handbook* (London: McGraw-Hill, 1986), 29-55.
6. P. E. Green, F. J. Carmone and S. M. Smith, *Multidimensional Scaling: Concepts and applications* (London: Allyn and Bacon, 1989).
7. J. B. Kruskal, F. W. Young and J. B. Seery, 'How to use KYST: a flexible programme to do multidimensional scaling' (Multidimensional Scaling Package of Bell Labs: Murry Hill, NJ, 1973).
8. J. J. Chang and J. D. Carol, 'How to use PREFMAP and PREFMAP 2: programs which relate preference data to multidimensional scaling solutions' (Multidimensional Scaling Package of Bell Labs: Murry Hill, NJ, 1972).
9. Graham Hooley and Michael K. Hussey, 'Quantitative methods in marketing: the multivariate jungle revisited – introduction and overview to special edition', *Journal of Marketing Management*, **10**, 1-3 (1994), 3-12.
10. J. J. Chang and J. D. Carol, 'How to use MDPREF: a computer program for multidimensional analysis of preference data', (Multidimensional Scaling Package of Bell Labs: Murry Hill, NJ, 1969).
11. Donna Hoffman and George F. Franke, 'Correspondence analysis: graphical presentation of categorical information in marketing research', *Journal of Marketing Research*, **23** (August 1986), 213-27.
12. S. M. Smith, *PC-MDS Version 5.1: Multidimensional statistics package* (Prova, UT: Brigham Young University, 1990).

that was not in Britain's top ten sellers. Then, in 1992 it was relaunched with a campaign using Manchester people and a setting that played upon the creamy froth on the product. Plays on ice-cream, face cream, smooth, rich cream helped to make the product the top take-home beer.

*Other brands* can help position products. Clinique's advertising for their 'skin supplies for men' prominently features a Rolex watch. Where firms have traditionally crafted products, such as Wilkinson's Sword or Holland & Holland shotguns, these lend glamour to more recent products – in these instances, shaving products and men's clothing respectively. After Volkswagen bought the Czech Skoda company they used the VW name to transfer some of their strong reputation to Skoda. 'Volkswagen were so impressed, they bought the company' ran one press ad. The responsible ad agency, GGK, explains: 'The Volkswagen connection hit the spot. People immediately latched on to it. It allowed susceptible people [who might be persuaded to buy a Skoda] a route into the brand.' Dealers reported 50 per cent sales increases.[17]

*Competitors* provide two positioning alternatives. A product can also be positioned directly *against a competitor*. For example, in ads for their personal computers, Compaq and Tandy have directly compared their products with IBM personal computers. The direct-selling computer company dan compare their performance with all other suppliers: '1st in repurchase intention, 1st in repair satisfaction', and so on. In its famous 'We're number two, so we try harder' campaign, Avis successfully positioned itself against the larger Hertz. A product may also be positioned *away from competitors* – 7-Up became the number-three soft drink when it was positioned as the 'Uncola', the fresh and thirst-quenching alternative to Coke and Pepsi. River Island Expeditions position their holidays, their adventures for travellers, away from package holidays and the tourists who go on them. They quote: 'The traveller is active; he goes strenuously in search of people, of adventure, of experience. The tourist is passive; expects interesting things to happen to him. He goes "sight-seeing"' (Daniel J. Boorstin, 1962).

*Product class* membership is the final means of positioning. For example, Van Den Bergh's I Can't Believe It's Not Butter is clearly positioned against butter while other yellow fats are promoted as cooking oils. Camay hand soap is positioned with bath oils rather with soap. Marketers often use a *combination* of these positioning strategies. Johnson & Johnson's Affinity shampoo is positioned as a hair conditioner for women over 40 (product class *and* user). And in their Christmas campaigns Martell cognac and Glenlivet malt whisky both neglect the lucrative 18- to 35-year olds to concentrate on the over-35s (*usage situation* and *user).*

The Ruhr's advertising positions it *against the competition* at the heart of Europe.

I Can't Believe It's Not Butter uses dual positioning: it is 'light' but it tastes like 'butter'.

## CHOOSING AND IMPLEMENTING A POSITIONING STRATEGY

Some firms find it easy to choose their positioning strategy. For example, a firm well known for quality in certain segments will go for this position in a new segment if there are enough buyers seeking quality. In many cases two or more firms will go after the same position: for instance, British Airways and Lufthansa in the European business market. Then, each will have to find other ways to set itself apart, such as Lufthansa's promise of reliability and wider seats, and BA's spacious cabins and executive lounges. Each firm must differentiate its offer by building a unique bundle of competitive advantages that appeal to a substantial group within the segment.

Having identified a set of possible competitive advantages upon which to build a position, the next stages are to select the right competitive advantages and effectively communicate the chosen position to the market (see Marketing Highlight 10.3).

### Selecting the right competitive advantages

Suppose a company is fortunate enough to have several potential competitive advantages. It must now choose the ones upon which it will build its positioning strategy. It must decide *how many* differences to promote and *which ones*.

#### How many differences to promote?

Many marketers think that companies should aggressively promote only one benefit to the target market. Ad man Rosser Reeves, for example, said a company should

## Battling for position in the fast lane

In the late 1980s, Europe dominated the world luxury car market. Germany reigned with Mercedes, BMW and Audi followed by Sweden's Saab and Volvo. Britain's newly independent Jaguar trailed well behind but was making up ground. Even Rover was again aiming at the luxury market after finding the going too tough against European and Japanese economy cars. They had drastically reduced their range and completely pulled out of the sports car market that they had once dominated. Austin Healey, MG and Triumph were no more.

Rover's re-entry into the luxury car market contained a clue about the future. Realizing they did not have the scale to design and build a range of cars by themselves they made a deal with Honda, Japan's third largest car manufacturer. For Rover it was to be the 800, a replacement for their SD1; for Honda, the Legend. Both firms intended to sell them in the North American market. Rover got there first in 1986. The car was good value and fitted well with Britain's reputation for traditional luxury products. The Rover 800 sold in the United States as the Stirling, with no Rover badge, to avoid association with the SD1's unsuccessful career in the United States. Although voted *International Car of the Year* when it was launched in 1977, the SD1 had quickly acquired a reputation for poor quality and unreliability. In 1987 initial sales of the Stirling were good, reaching 14,000. Then, by 1988, they had dropped to less than 9,000. Again unreliability killed Rover in the United States market. Quality problems plagued the Stirling. It was not ready for any market, let alone the American market.

Honda's aims for the Legend were higher than Rover's. The Honda Accord was already America's top-selling car. It had an excellent reputation for economy, reliability and comfort, and was number one in the United States compact car market. Honda, however, had its sights on the United States luxury market dominated by the Europeans. The market was growing fast, and margins were high and were expected to remain so for several years. To attack the luxury end Honda had to straddle the United States car market. Being a compact car, the Accord was smaller and less expensive than regular American cars. In contrast, the European luxury cars now targeted were exclusive and priced above regular autos. Honda realized that to succeed they had to position the Accord and Legend differently, and that is what they did. The Legend was already bigger and more expensive than the Accord but that was not enough. Honda decided not to extend the Honda brand name but to launch the Legend as an Acura, a new luxury brand. They also established a new Acura distribution chain and set up a special hot-line service for Acura suppliers and users. However, unlike Mercedes and BMW, they intended to sell their cars fully equipped to luxury standards - cruise control, air conditioning, the lot. With the cars being made in Japan it would have taken too long to have them 'made to measure' and shipped.

Honda had decided to take on Europe's leading car manufacturers in the world's largest car market — and with a new product, in a segment they did not know, using a new brand name and new dealerships, and pricing higher than they had ever done before. Honda's declared aim was to give the discerning Acura driver 'total customer satisfaction'. Honda's Legend did much better than Rover's Stirling in the United States market. In 1988 70,770 Acuras were sold, 80 per cent more than Mercedes who had been the class leader up to that point. The Acura also had one of the best reliability records in the United States market and one of the highest residual values. However, Acura supremacy in the United States did not last long: Toyota soon followed with their luxury Lexus range.

America's economic recession and their loss of market share to the Japanese hit European luxury car makers. Some responded with violent repositioning to help attract new customers. In 1992, Mercedes tried to adjust their staid, reliable, quality reputation and so address customer's views that 'I can't afford one at the moment' and 'I'm not old enough yet'. One Mercedes ad asked: 'Has our reputation for the highest quality also given us a reputation for the highest price?' and then explains how inexpensive they are. They wanted to be sporty too. One ad headlined 'What do 27 of the 34 Grand Prix drivers drive on their day off?'

Mercedes' concern about perceived expense continues. They advertise their S-class using quotes from *Autocar & Motor* who say it is the best car in the world: 'Sit in an S-class, regardless of engine size, and you know you've arrived'. But, the ad continues: '"A genuine bargain": as *What Car?* so neatly puts it.' The ad's headlines betrays their positioning dilemma: 'It wouldn't be the best car in the world if nobody could afford it.'

Volvo are also repositioning their products. In 1990 their position was clear when they ran an ad with five pictures of toddlers with the headline: 'Are they as safe around town as they are around the house?' It goes on: 'If you'd like your children to be as safe as houses on the road...' Shortly after, Volvo's TV ads were showing a horse galloping through a dark wood, the car had become so exciting to drive it was almost alive – a position close to BMW's 'The Ultimate Driving Machine'.

Saab's repositioning is no less dramatic. In the late 1980s Saab's Carlsson series ads had the car juxtaposed with the (somewhat ageing) Saab Viggen jet fighters: 'For Saab Viggen, getting behind the controls is proof of incredible mental and physical stamina, years of intensive training and an ally or two at the Royal Swedish Air Force'. Their strapline was 'Saab: The Aircraft Manufacturer'. The aggressive masculinity of the product is now gone. The strapline has gone and the Saab is a thoughtfully designed car. Designers appear in the ads and one of them is a woman, 'Aina Nilsson, chief interior designer of the Saab 900'.

The 1990 European launch positioned Lexus as one of the great marques. Names like Rolls-Royce, Mercedes, BMW and Jaguar littered the copy. They ignored Japanese cars such as the Acura Legend and Nissan Infiniti. The car impressed the press, so later ads incorporated their favourable comments: 'Imagine a big saloon that is faster than a BMW 735i, quieter than a Jaguar Sovereign and as meticulously engineered as a Mercedes. The Lexus LS400 is all of these and more.' By 1994 Toyota were using a different endorsement: '100% of owners are completely satisfied with the Lexus LS400. Where do we go from here?'

The launches of other Japanese models have used positioning strategies similar to that used by Toyota for Lexus. Nissan's new coupé used a quotation from *Autocar & Motor* as a headline: 'Brilliant new 200SX, Ferrari looks, Porsche pace'. Underneath the Nissan logo they also promote: 'Nissan UK Ltd, Worthing, Sussex'. Mazda's attack with their MX-3 coupé is more direct: 'Does your GTi still look modern?'

The positioning of some new Japanese cars addresses the past – designs for people who yearn for cars of character. Nissan's 1988 nostalgia cars evoke the spirit of Citroën 2CV. Their austere Pio is close to the 1950s basic 2CV AZL. It has a single dashboard dial, old-fashioned flick switches, simple seats, corrugated body panels, but with a 985 cc engine. The S-Cargo (Escargot) is like a more modern and exotic 2CV with a 1487 cc engine. The cars are odd but the Pio price is twice that of the similarly sized Nissan Micra.

Mazda's MX-5 Miata is in the mood of more exotic antiques and must have Rover sobbing. It was designed in Britain but, when being road tested in California, the drivers were plagued by people demanding to know where they could get one. The car's launch used 1960s imagery and profuse references to Austin Healey, MG and Triumph. Like Nissan's nostalgia cars, the MX-5 is a 'back to basics' car whose performance is not outstanding but, as *What Car?* says, it has 'Sixties looks with Nineties fun and finesses...Over to you MG'.

References: Timothy Jacobs, *The World's Worst Cars* (London: Bison, 1991); Nick Georgano, *Cars of the Seventies and Eighties* (Gothenburg: Crescent, 1990); Peter Nunn, 'Class barriers fall', *Financial Times* (18 September 1994), XI; Neil Weinberg, 'Domestic luxury car sales accelerate', *Financial Times* (25 June 1994), VI; Michiyo Nakamoto, 'A taste of their own medicine', *Financial Times* (30 June 1994), 11.

develop a **unique selling proposition (USP)** for each brand and stick to it. Each brand should pick an attribute and tout itself as 'number one' on that attribute. Buyers tend to remember 'number one' better, especially in an overcommunicated society. Thus Crest toothpaste consistently promotes its anticavity protection, and Mercedes promotes its great automotive engineering. What are some of the 'number one' positions to promote? The most significant ones are 'best quality', 'best service', 'lowest price', 'best value', and 'most advanced technology'. A company that hammers away at one of these positions and consistently achieves it will probably become best known and remembered for it.

The difficulty of keeping functional superiority has made firms focus on having a unique **emotional selling proposition (ESP)** instead of a USP. The product may be similar to competitors but it has unique associations for consumers. Leading names like Rolls-Royce, Ferrari and Rolex have done this. Other cars outperform Ferrari on the road and track but 'the red car with the prancing horse' is the world's number-one sports car. Many Formula One racing drivers still dream of racing a Ferrari, even when the team is not winning.

Other marketers think that companies should position themselves on more than one differentiating factor. This may be necessary if two or more firms are claiming to be best on the same attribute. Steelcase, an office furniture systems company, differentiates itself from competitors on two benefits: best on-time delivery and best installation support. Volvo positions its automobiles as 'safest' and 'most durable'. Fortunately, these two benefits are compatible – a very safe car would also be very durable.

Today, in a time when the mass market is fragmenting into many small segments, companies are trying to broaden their positioning strategies to appeal to more segments. For example, Beecham promotes its Aquafresh toothpaste as offering three benefits: 'anti-cavity protection', 'better breath', and 'whiter teeth'. Clearly, many people want all three benefits, and the challenge is to convince them that the brand delivers all three. Beecham's solution was to create a toothpaste that squeezed out of the tube in three colours, thus visually confirming the three benefits. In doing this, Beecham attracted three segments instead of one.

However, as companies increase the number of claims for their brands, they risk disbelief and a loss of clear positioning. Usually, a company needs to avoid three serious positioning errors. The first is **underpositioning** – that is, failing to position the company at all. Some companies discover that buyers have only a vague idea of the brand or that they do not really know anything special about it. This has occurred with dark spirits – whisky and brandy – where young drinkers have drifted away from them. United Distillers and Hiram Walker aim to reverse this trend with their Bells and Teacher's brands by targeting 25- to 35-year-old men. There is much focus on extending the use of both brands as a mixer. This is an anathema to many whisky drinkers but United Distillers have successfully promoted it as a mixer in both Spain and Greece.[18] The second positioning error is **overpositioning** – that is giving buyers too narrow a picture of the company. Thus a consumer might think that the Steuben glass company makes only fine art glass costing $1,000 and up, when it also makes affordable fine glass starting at around $50.

Finally, companies must avoid **confused positioning** – that is, leaving buyers with a confused image of the company. For example, Burger King has struggled without success for years to establish a profitable and consistent position. Since 1986, it has undertaken five separate advertising campaigns, with themes ranging from 'Herb the nerd doesn't eat here', and 'This is a Burger King town', to 'The right food for the right times', and 'Sometimes you've got to break the rules'. This barrage of positioning statements has left consumers confused and Burger King with poor sales and profits.[19]

## Which differences to promote?

Not all brand differences are meaningful or worthwhile. Not every difference makes a good differentiator. Each difference has the potential to create company costs as well as customer benefits. Therefore, the company must carefully select the ways in which it will distinguish itself from competitors. A difference is worth establishing insofar as it satisfies the following criteria:

- *Important.* The difference delivers a highly valued benefit to target buyers.
- *Distinctive.* Competitors do not offer the difference, or the company can offer it in a more distinctive way.
- *Superior.* The difference is superior to other ways that customers might obtain the same benefit.
- *Communicable.* The difference is communicable and visible to buyers.
- *Pre-emptive.* Competitors cannot easily copy the difference.
- *Affordable.* Buyers can afford to pay for the difference.
- *Profitable.* The company can introduce the difference profitably.

Many companies have introduced differentiations that failed one or more of these tests. The Westin Stamford hotel in Singapore advertises that it is the world's tallest hotel, a distinction that is not important to many tourists – the fact scared many. AT&T's original picturevision phones failed, partly because the public did not think that seeing the other person was worth the phone's high cost. Philips Laservision failed too. Although the laser disks gave excellent picture quality there were few disks available and the machines could not record. These drawbacks meant that consumers saw Laservision as offering no advantage over video tape machines.

Some competitive advantages are too slight, too costly to develop, or too inconsistent with the company's profile. Suppose that a company is designing its positioning strategy and has narrowed its list of possible competitive advantages to four. The company needs a framework for selecting the one advantage that makes the most sense to develop. Table 10.2 shows a systematic way of evaluating several potential competitive advantages and choosing the right one.

In the table, the company compares its standing on four attributes – technology, cost, quality and service – to the standing of its chief competitor. Let's assume that both companies stand at 8 on technology (1 = low score, 10 = high score), which means that they both have good technology. The company questions whether it can gain much by improving its technology further, especially given the high cost of new

**TABLE 10.2** *Finding competitive advantage*

| Competitive advantage | Company standing (1-10) | Competitor standing (1-10) | Importance of improving standing (H-M-L) | Affordability and speed (H-M-L) | Competitor's ability to improve standing (H-M-L) | Recommended action |
|---|---|---|---|---|---|---|
| Technology | 8 | 8 | L | L | M | Hold |
| Cost | 6 | 8 | H | M | M | Watch |
| Quality | 8 | 6 | L | L | H | Watch |
| Service | 4 | 3 | H | H | L | Invest |

technology. The competitor has a better standing on cost (8 instead of 6), and this can hurt the company if the market gets more price sensitive. The company offers higher quality than its competitor (8 instead of 6). Finally, both companies offer below-average service (4 and 3).

At first glance, it appears that the company should go after cost or service to improve its market appeal over the competitor. However, it must consider other factors. First, how important are improvements in each of these attributes to the target customers? The fourth column shows that both cost and service improvements would be highly important to customers. Next, can the company afford to make the improvements? If so, how fast can it complete them? The fifth column shows that the company could improve service quickly and affordably. But if the firm decided to do this, would the competitor be able to improve its service also? The sixth column shows that the competitor's ability to improve service is low, perhaps because the competitor does not believe in service or has limited funds. The final column then shows the appropriate actions to take on each attribute. It makes the most sense for the company to invest in improving its service. Service is important to customers; the company can afford to improve its service and can do it fast, and the competitor probably will not be able to catch up.

## Communicating and delivering the chosen position

Once it has chosen a position, the company must take strong steps to deliver and communicate the desired position to target consumers. All the company's marketing-mix efforts must support the positioning strategy. Positioning the company calls for concrete action – it is not just talk. If the company decides to build a position on better quality and service, it must first *deliver* that position. Designing the marketing mix – product, price, place and promotion – involves working out the tactical details of the positioning strategy. Thus a firm that seizes upon a 'high-quality position' knows that it must produce high-quality products, charge a high price, distribute through high-quality dealers, and advertise in high-quality media. It must hire and train more service people, find retailers who have a good reputation for service, and develop sales and advertising messages that broadcast its superior service. This is the only way to build a consistent and believable high-quality, high-service position.

Calvin Klein Cosmetics have noticed a shift in the fragrance market. Shiseido launched a classic fragrance by Jean-Paul Gaultier, *enfant terrible* of French fashion, that broke industry rules with its punky advertising and packaging – a bottle in the shape of a woman's torso encased in an aluminium can. L'Oréal responded with Eden, a new Cacharel fragrance for ecologically concerned consumers.

Calvin Klein's response is *cK one,* a 'shared fragrance for young consumers who, he believes, are ready to buy a scent created for both sexes'. The designer's other fragrances, Obsession, Eternity and Escape, are for women only. The positioning of *cK one* is radical and covers the whole marketing mix. The range will include youth-oriented products, such as massage oil. The bottles and display material are by Fabien Baron, designer of advertising campaigns for other Calvin Klein products as well as Valentino, Burberry's and Giorgio Armani. He also collaborated with Madonna in the production of her Sex book. He says Calvin's response to the bottle was 'Boom! Yeah! Right on.' It is a frosted glass flask with aluminium top and recycled paper packaging.

The rest of the marketing mix backs *cK one*'s radical positioning. Prices are low – about 70 per cent of Obsession's – and it will sell in novel distribution outlets, notably Tower Records. To ensure that the multi-million dollar launch is a success, Calvin Klein's corporation will send 12,000 gorgeous members of both sexes to stores to splash it on shoppers.[20]

Companies often find it easier to come up with a good positioning strategy than to implement it. Establishing a position or changing one usually takes a long time. In contrast, positions that have taken years to build can quickly disappear. Once a company has built the desired position, it must take care to maintain the position through consistent performance and communication. It must closely monitor and adapt the position over time to match changes in consumer needs and competitors' strategies. This is how world leading brands Coca-Cola, Nescafé, Snickers, BMW, Rolex, Estée Lauder, Johnnie Walker and Chanel have remained pre-eminent so long. The company should avoid abrupt changes that might confuse consumers. Coca-Cola forgot this when they introduced their disastrous new Coke, Marlboro's price cuts made the brand fall from being the most highly valued brand to out of the top ten, and Unilever's hasty introduction of the Persil/Omo Power benefited Procter & Gamble. Violent changes rarely succeed – a product's position should evolve as it adapts to the changing market environment.

## SUMMARY

The *core strategy* of a company shows how it will address the markets it has targeted. By *differentiation* it develops the strengths of the company so that they meet the target markets' needs then, by market positioning, it manages the way consumers view the company and its products.

*Differentiation* helps a firm compete profitably. It gives it a *competitive advantage*. If a firm does not differentiate, it will be like 'all the rest' and be forced to compete on price. Differentiation is harder in some industries than others, but it is rare that a creative marketer cannot differentiate a market in some way. There are four main ways to differentiate: *product differentiation*, *service differentiation*, *personnel differentiation* and *image differentiation*. The ease of following new technological innovations means that the product is becoming an increasingly difficult way to differentiate. Now service and image are the main ways people distinguish between products. As systems and methods become more common, personnel differentiation becomes more important. The firm is its people and they are usually what the customer is most sensitive to.

A firm's functional strengths give it its competitive advantage. Market positioning is about managing customers' view of the company and its products. It is about perception. *Perceptual maps* are a way of revealing how customers see markets. They show which products customers see as alike and those that are not. They can also show segments and the dimensions customers use to split up the market.

There are several positioning strategies for shifting and holding customers' perceptions. Positioning works by associating products with product attributes or other stimuli. Successful firms usually maintain a clear differential advantage and do not make violent changes to their market positions.

# ■ DISCUSSING THE ISSUES

1. In marketing products and services, 'being different is good', so the pros say. Why should firms differentiate their product or service offerings? What are the specific ways in which a producer of goods or services differentiates its offer from those of competitors? Discuss, using specific examples.

2. What roles do product attributes and perceptions of attributes play in positioning a product? Can an attribute held by several competing brands be used in a successful positioning strategy?

3. A company is looking to deposition or reposition the competition. What does this mean? How might the company go about depositioning its rivals in the marketplace?

4. Think of well-known beer or lager brands. How well are these positioned in relation to one another? Are the positioning themes used by manufacturers clear or confusing? Are the differences they promote meaningful or worthwhile?

5. Perceptual mapping is a valuable aid to product positioning. What are its benefits and limitations?

6. Is positioning helpful to not-for-profit organizations? If so, how should a charity select and implement a positioning strategy? If not, why?

# ■ APPLYING THE CONCEPTS

1. By looking at advertising and at products themselves, we can often see how marketers are attempting to position their products and what target market they hope to reach.

   ■ Define the positionings of and target markets for Coca-Cola, Pepsi Cola, Red Bull, Tango and 7-Up.

   ■ Define the positionings of and target markets for KitKat, Lion Bar, Snickers, Aero, Mars Bars and Twix.

   ■ Do you think that the soft drinks and confectionery industries achieve distinctive positionings and target markets? Are some more clearly defined than others?

2. It is possible to market people as well as products or services. When marketing a person, we can *position* that individual for a particular target market. Describe briefly how you could position yourself for the following target markets: (a) for a potential employer; (b) for a potential boyfriend or girlfriend; (c) for your boyfriend or girlfriend's mother and father. How could you position yourself differently for the different target markets? Do you position yourself differently for them? How do the positionings differ? Why do the positionings differ?

# ■ REFERENCES

1. Based on John Griffiths, 'The pace hots up', *Financial Times* (26 January 1990), I; Andrew Bolger, 'Growth by successful targeting', *Financial Times* (21 June 1994), 12; Shiraz Sidhva, 'Carmakers drive deep into India', *Financial Times* (20 July 1994), 28; David Done, 'Benetton Grand Prix team changes gear', *Financial Times* (24 August 1994), 2; Meg Carter, 'Wheels of fortune', *Marketing Week* (26 August 1994), 28–30; Anil Bhoyrul, 'Devil take the hindmost', *Business Age*, **4**, 49 (1994), 20–3.

2. For a discussion of the concepts of differentiation and competitive advantage and methods for assessing them, see Michael Porter, *Competitive Advantage* (New York: Free Press, 1985), ch. 2; George S. Day and Robin Wensley, 'Assessing advantage: a framework for diagnosing competitive superiority', *Journal of Marketing* (April 1988), 1–20; Philip Kotler, *Marketing Management*, 7th edn (Englewood Cliffs, NJ: Prentice Hall, 1991), ch. 11; and Grahan Hooley and John Saunders, *Competitive Positioning: The key to market success* (Hemel Hempstead, Herts: Prentice Hall, 1993).

3. For a review of this and other results see Robert D. Buzzell and Bradley T. Gale, *The PIMS Principle: Linking strategy to performance* (New York: Free Press, 1987).

4. Theodore Levitt, 'Making success through differentiation – of anything', *Harvard Business Review* (Jan.–Feb. 1980).

5. 'Western Europe's insurance tangle', *The Economist* (18 June 1994), 115–6.

6. See David A. Garvin, 'Competing on the eight dimensions of quality', *Harvard Business Review* (Nov.–Dec. 1987), 101–9.

7. See Tom Peters, *Thriving on Chaos* (New York: Knopf, 1987), 56–7.

8.  For details of this and other examples see George Stalker and Thomas M. Hout, *Competing Against Time* (London: Collier Macmillan, 1990).

9.  Positioning was introduced in the seminal work by Al Ries and Jack Trout, *Positioning: The battle for your mind* (New York: McGraw-Hill, 1981); see also Al Ries and Jack Trout, *Marketing Warfare* (New York: McGraw-Hill, 1986). Al Ries develops his ideas in 'The mind is the ultimate battlefield', *The Journal of Business Strategy* (July–Aug. 1988), 4–7.

10. Julie Street, 'Success crowns crash course in sensationalism', *The European – élan* (10-16 June 1994), 5.

11. These figures and others relating to European tourist destinations are based on a study by A. Haahti, Helsinki School of Economics, R. R. van den Heuvel, Groningen University and G. J. Hooley of Aston University. The results are disguised for the purpose of confidentiality. A case study called 'Finnish Tourist Board' by Graham Hooley appears in Peter Doyle and Norman Hart (eds), *Case Studies in International Marketing* (London: Heinemann, 1982), 61–86.

12. Leiv Gunner Lie, 'Norway cashes in on the magic of the mountains, *The European* (10–16 June 1994), 20.

13. David Short, 'Red Bull set to lock horns with multinationals', *The European* (19–25 August 1994).

14. Susan Jacquet, 'Ethics and responsibility', *Swiss Quality Timing*, **6** (spring 1994), 40–1.

15. Birna Helgadottir, 'Time has come to realise your dreams', *The European – élan* (16–22 September 1994), 6.

16. Mike Baldwin, 'Nice car, shame about the driver', *Today* (20 September 1994), 7.

17. Diane Summers, 'Skoda's sales drive is no joke', *Financial Times* (12 May 1994), 11.

18. Ros Snowden, 'Spirit of adventure', *Marketing Week* (15 August 1994), 32–5.

19. Mark Landler and Gail DeGeorge, 'Tempers are sizzling over Burger King's new ads', *Business Week* (12 February 1990), 33; and Philip Stelly, Jr., 'Burger King rule breaker', *Adweek* (9 November 1990), 24, 26.

20. Alice Rawsthorn, 'A nose for innovation', *Financial Times* (4 August 1994), 11; Bronwyn Cosgrove, 'Fabulous Fabien's pure object of desire', *The European – élan* (23–29 September 1994), 14–15.

## CASE 10

# Cadbury's TimeOut: choc around the clock   *Damien McLoughlin\* and Benoit Heilbrunn\*\**

### Introduction

Cadbury's TimeOut is the most successful product ever developed and launched by Cadbury in Ireland. The development was by the management of Cadbury Ireland, at their plant in Coolock, Dublin. The product's success came from a combination of technological advance, strong domestic and international market orientation and original positioning strategy at the time of launch.

Cadbury started manufacturing in Ireland in the 1930s, at a time when the protectionist policies of the Irish government effectively forbade the importation of chocolate to Ireland. Ireland and the United Kingdom's entry to the EEC in 1973 made them an open market for confectionery. The effect on the industry in Ireland was that several indigenous firms such as Lemons (hard-boiled sweets) and Urnies

(chocolates) disappeared from the marketplace. The implication for Cadbury Ireland was the need to reshape its manufacturing so that it was positioned to benefit from economies of scale internationally rather than simply domestically.

### Cadbury Ireland as a partner in Cadbury Schweppes International

Within the Cadbury-Schweppes group, Cadbury Ireland identified its particular strengths and competencies and set out to develop in these areas. The company identified three technologies in which it felt that it had, or could develop global expertise. These three areas were:

1.  *Extrusion.* This involves putting one form of confectionery inside another: for example, Cadbury's Eclairs wrapped chocolate in caramel; or the Moro bar, which is a centre of chocolate paste with biscuit encased in caramel and covered in chocolate.

\* Marketing Group, DCUBS, Dublin City University, Dublin, Ireland.
\*\* Department of Marketing, Graduate School of Business, UCD, Blackrock, Co. Dublin, Ireland.

2. *Flake chocolate manufacture.* Cadbury's Flake is a light, crumbly, melt-in-the-mouth product positioned in the indulgence section of the confectionery market. The Flake brand is very well established and its advertising is legendary. The brand has been leveraged to include confectionery, catering and ice-cream usage. However, the Flake recipe and process provide unique product properties, which were the key for future development.

3. *Wafer making and baking.* Wafer is an important part of a number of strong-selling products in Ireland, in particular the 'pink Snack brand'. Cadbury Ireland is the only Cadbury-Schweppes affiliate in the northern hemisphere to manufacture the wafer product.

### Building on core competencies at Cadbury Ireland

Since the mid 1970s Cadbury Ireland had developed centres of excellence around these core competencies. The strong product development process in Cadbury Ireland had produced products such as Cadbury's Chomp, Moro, TimeOut and Twirl. Twirl is a two-finger casual chocolate snack based on flake technology. These developments have led to a doubling of Cadbury Ireland's throughput and allowed it to develop its brand successfully on both the domestic and international markets.

### The perspective of Cadbury Ireland on the marketplace

Cadbury sees itself as a 'range house'. This describes a company which provides the consumer with a complete range of options in every segment of the market. In addition, all Cadbury products bear the distinctive Cadbury logo. The core product of the Cadbury group is Dairy Milk chocolate, which is used in its products and which is also marketed under the Dairy Milk brand name. This chocolate, which uses fresh Irish milk, has been the basis of success in a great number of segments. Cadbury defines segments on the basis of how customers buy rather than on how a product is made. For example, they identify products as serving impulse markets, take-home markets or gift usage. This has allowed Cadbury Ireland management to identify a significant consumption pattern whereby the take-home segment is increasing its share of the confectionery market. This trend is driven by supermarket purchases of chocolate. In addition, they had noticed a certain overlap in the marketplace where brands which were traditionally seen as bars - for example, Twix and KitKat - were extending their franchise into the biscuit market. The main snack brands in Ireland (see Exhibit 10.1) are as follows:

■ **KitKat.** KitKat was first sold in Ireland in 1937. It has become one of the most popular brands on the market with in the region of I£11m.[*] sales in 1992. KitKat had initiated the move into the biscuit market with the memorable advert debating '...it's a biscuit...it's a bar'. This ad showed the product being used in different ways and suggested that it had multiple uses. Nestlé-Rowntree, the owners of the brand, maintained this position by heavy advertising and maintaining the price of the product at a below market par level. Usually 2 to 4p below its main competitors, KitKat is also available in bar and snack size formats.

■ **Twix.** Owned by the Mars corporation, Twix was launched in Ireland in 1968. The effort was made to develop a position for the product in the snack market with the advertising slogan 'Whenever there is a snack gap, Twix fits'. Its packaging format, in a flow wrapper, however, also allowed it to fit in to the bar/impulse market segment. The success of Twix has been attributed to its good value-for-money position and the heavy advertising support that it has traditionally received. Total brand sales in 1992 were estimated to be in the region of I£6–7m. Twix was among the first products to be sold in the snack and fun-size formats.

**Exhibit 10.1** The main snack brands in Ireland, 1992

|  | Manufacturer | Launched | Sales (I£m.) |
|---|---|---|---|
| KitKat | Nestlé-Rowntree | 1937 | 11.0 |
| Twix | Mars | 1968 | 6.5 |
| Jacobs Club Milk | Jacobs | 1900s | 5.0 |
| Cadbury's Snack | Cadbury | 1960s | 11.0 |

[*]1 ecu = US$1.26 = I£0.81 (Irish punt) = 81p.

- **Jacob's Club Milk**. The oldest brand on the market, Jacob's Club Milk has been sold in Ireland since the 1900s. It is sold singly and in family six-pack formats. The Club Milk acts as a flagship for a range of different flavoured, chocolate-covered Club biscuits. For example, the Club bar is available in Club Orange and Club Mint formats. The position of Club Milk in the snack market is firmly achieved with the advertising message 'If you're going to have a cuppa have a Club'.
- **Cadbury's Snack**. Since its launch in the 1960s, the Cadbury's Snack brand has grown to lead the chocolate snack market. This domination is achieved through grocery sales but also includes the important catering market. The Snack comes in three formats, differentiated by the colour of the packaging. The 'yellow' snack comprises a chocolate-covered shortcake biscuit. The 'purple' snack is a sandwich-filled biscuit heavily covered with thick milk chocolate. The third option is the 'pink' snack, which comprises three fingers of chocolate-covered wafer. Cadbury's Snack is sold in a variety of formats incorporating single bar, multipacks and treat size. Its combined sales from grocery, newsagent and catering outlets were in excess of I£11m. in 1992.

### The snack market

The snack is a particularly prominent product market in Great Britain and Ireland. It is essentially a lifestyle market linked to a destructured approach to food. Snack products are most successful in those countries in which eating habits are not centred around two or three main meals. In these countries the consumption of food may be scattered around various occasions during the day. Thus the 11 a.m. and 4 p.m. snack breaks are usual practice in Irish and English lifestyles. These breaks generally consist of a cup of tea/coffee together with fruit, a chocolate bar or a scone. Internationally, this snack habit is linked to the grazing phenomenon, which is representative of the slow but steady change in cultural habits concerning eating (destruction of family meals and less time devoted to meals) and accounts for the growth of the snack market in other European countries. That the Irish are accomplished 'snackers' is evidenced by their large confectionery market with annual sales in 1992 of over I£240m. (see Exhibit 10.2).

**Exhibit 10.2** The confectionery market in Ireland

|  | 1988 | 1989 | 1990 | 1991 | 1992 |
|---|---|---|---|---|---|
| Estimated market value at RSP (I£m.) | 210 | 216 | 228 | 245 | 242 |
| Annual growth rate (%) | — | 3.0 | 5.0 | 3.0 | 2.9 |

Source: Nestlé-Rowntree.

### Break time in Ireland

Ireland is also a great tea-drinking nation. A survey carried out by Nielsen in 1993 in Ireland showed that twenty of the top 100 grocery brands are liquid consumables. However, leading tea brands in Ireland are positioned on value for money rather than taste. This means that tea might be viewed as a depersonalized drink. Therefore there is considerable need for a beverage complement with strong personality in order to personalize break times.

In trying to meet this need Cadbury were faced with what was a mature marketplace. Irish consumption of confectionery is the highest in Europe (see Exhibit 10.3). Chocolate consumption alone is 8.3 kilos per annum per capita. This figure is matched only by their British neighbours.

### The concept of TimeOut

Based on these trends in the marketplace and Cadbury's core technological competencies, the management of Cadbury Ireland saw the opportunity to bring confectionery values to the biscuit market and biscuit values to the confectionery market. In this sense TimeOut set out specifically to target the bridge-brand position and satisfy all uses from mainstream confectionery luxury to straight beverage accompaniment, but with values firmly rooted in the break market.

It also had to compete with existing competitors in this market, particularly KitKat and Twix, both brands which had also targeted the bridge-brand position for the future. TimeOut therefore 'institutionalized' the coexistence of three elements: the need for a break during the day, tea or coffee as a liquid consumable, and the need for a snack to accompany that

**Exhibit 10.3**   EU consumption of confectionery (kg per capita)

|  | Ireland | UK | Greece | Belgium | Denmark | West Germany | France | Nether-lands | Italy | Spain | Portugal | EU average |
|---|---|---|---|---|---|---|---|---|---|---|---|---|
| Chocolate | 8.3 | 8.3 | 2.4 | 7.0 | 7.2 | 5.9 | 5.2 | 6.0 | 1.3 | 2.3 | 0.5 | 4.8 |
| Biscuits | 17.9 | 13.0 | 17.9 | 5.2 | 5.5 | 3.1 | 6.5 | 2.8 | 5.9 | 5.2 | 4.6 | 6.6 |
| Ice cream | 8.0 | 7.1 | 5.3 | 9.8 | 9.1 | 7.8 | 4.7 | 4.5 | 6.1 | 3.8 | 1.8 | 6.0 |
| Total | 34.2 | 28.4 | 25.6 | 22.0 | 21.8 | 16.8 | 16.4 | 13.3 | 13.3 | 11.3 | 6.9 | 17.4 |

Source: In *Irish Consumer Market Handbook: A guidebook for marketing managers*, ed. M. V. Lambkin (Dublin: Marketing Society of Ireland, 1993), adapted from *European Marketing Data and Statistics*, 27th edn (London: Euromonitor, 1992).

drink. This can be paraphrased as 'Wherever you are, whatever you are doing, when it's that time (i.e. your time for a break) it's TimeOut time'.

### The positioning mix for the launch of TimeOut

#### Product

TimeOut stems from a technological advance at Cadbury Ireland which allowed them to layer flake on to wafer. The competitive advantage of this product lies in the unique blend of flake sandwiched between two wafers and covered in dairy milk chocolate. In product terms, TimeOut bridges both the snack and bar markets as the Flake ingredient was sufficiently biscuity to be a suitable accompaniment to a beverage break. On the one hand its biscuit constituency made it an ideal snack, while its Flake content made it a suitable bar of chocolate in its own right.

#### The branding ingredients: brand name, logo and identity colours

Many names were proposed for the new product including 'Switch' and 'Ultra'. However, it was discovered that using a name indicating the timing and situation in which the bar should be consumed greatly enhanced the consumer's understanding of what the product was designed for. The TimeOut name was proposed and accepted as it more clearly communicated the desired position as *the snack* accompaniment. These brand-name objectives were supported by the use of a clock (suggesting that any time is suitable for TimeOut) and a mug (which reinforced the beverage break accompaniment role).

The new brand needed a strong visual identity system to reinforce the other positioning elements.

Hence the use of bold primary colours on the packaging to attract attention and create competitive distinction. The two main colours used were blue, considered the main identity colour, and red, which is used to write the brand name. The brand name is surrounded by yellow; this blue/red/yellow association is the colour scheme most easily associated with light biscuity bars. Blue also has a symbolic connotation and is considered as a peaceful and resting colour. The choice of colour is interesting because the market is dominated by darker brand colours such as black/brown (Mars) and gold (Twix).

#### Pricing

Consumer knowledge of price in the snack market, given its habitual nature, is high. However, the standard-size chocolate bars are only slightly differentiated in terms of price. Given the power of retailers, the producer often has little discretion in the determination of price. TimeOut was launched at a price of 28p, while a standard bar was priced at 30p.

#### Packaging configuration

Packaging was particularly important in positioning TimeOut as a bridge brand. Most brands establish themselves in standard format initially and then expand to different formats. TimeOut, however, was required to meet the needs of a number of groups and so came in a variety of formats from the start:

- **Standard**. The standard product to be sold in newsagents, workplace restaurants and coffee shops. The format is two full-size fingers in a flow wrapper. In newsagents or supermarkets TimeOut is placed with other Cadbury brands.

- **5-pack**. The five-pack format was five TimeOut fingers in a convenience pack to allow the product to be bought in bulk from supermarkets. It is positioned with the multipacks for other confectionery products.
- **Breakpack**. The breakpack consisted of six shorter twin-finger packs individually wrapped. This is also sold in supermarkets and is intended for the home snack market. In supermarkets the breakpack would be put on shelf space with the biscuit range.
- **Treat-size**. The treat-size format is intended to meet the demands of the children's treat/party market. The treat-size format was 14 full-size individually wrapped TimeOut fingers. These are mainly distributed through supermarkets. The shelf position for the treat size is with the treat and fun-size formats of other confectionery products.

### Advertising and promotion

At its initial launch in early 1992 TimeOut was supported by a complete range of advertising and promotion. Heavy TV and radio advertising emphasized the 'TimeOut at any time' theme. Promotions included balloon releases at several centres around the country, a variety of street activities involving a national radio station and using branded characters, and participation at the annual St Patrick's Day parade in Dublin. Free samples were generously distributed at street activities and during in-store promotions. TimeOut has also made effective and large-scale use of poster advertising.

TimeOut used both family brand promotions and brand alliance promotions in its initial positioning. An example of the family brand promotions was one with Lyons tea, the largest selling brand of tea in Ireland. The promotion gave customers a free bar of TimeOut with every standard box of tea. This achieved two goals. First, given the market share of Lyons, it facilitated trial of the product. Secondly, it was an opportunity to nail down the position of TimeOut as a beverage accompaniment. The overall promotional message was one of a new, friendly, modern, fun and young, beverage-break accompaniment that was suitable for use at any time.

### The success of TimeOut

Six to eight months after its launch a national trade magazine completed a brand evaluation of TimeOut (*Checkout*, July/August 1993). Primary research completed by an independent research company highlighted some extraordinary results.

### User profile

The user profile of the brand demonstrated a widespread acceptance. The vast majority of adults and all children had used the brand at some stage since its introduction (see Exhibit 10.4). Women, a prime market for chocolate consumption, represented over 60 per cent of TimeOut consumers. Users were drawn from all areas of Ireland but were particularly strong in urban areas. This user profile was assisted by a high conversion ratio for both adults and children (see Exhibit 10.5).

### Attitudes towards the brand

As might be expected given the high levels of trial achieved for the brand, consumer attitudes towards the brand were very positive (see Exhibit 10.6). This is particularly evidenced by the positive appeal which

**Exhibit 10.4** Brand acceptance among adults and children (%)

|  | Adults (15 years +) | Children (11–14 years) |
|---|---|---|
| Aware | 86 | 100 |
| Ever used | 68 | 97 |
| Used once/twice | 23 | 13 |
| Occasional user | 22 | 41 |
| Regular user | 14 | 43 |

Source: Lansdowne Market Research.

**Exhibit 10.5** Cadbury's TimeOut conversion ratio (%)

|  | Adults (15 years +) | Children (11–14 years) |
|---|---|---|
| Awareness to trial | 69 | 97 |
| Trial to repeat user | 61 | 87 |
| Won over consumers | 66 | 86 |
| Lost consumers | 7 | 1 |

Source: Lansdowne Market Research.

**CASE 10** (*cont*)

**Exhibit 10.6**  Cadbury's TimeOut brand appeal (%)

|  | Adults (15 years +) | Children (11–14 years) |
| --- | --- | --- |
| Positive | 66 | 86 |
| Neutral | 27 | 14 |
| Negative | 7 | 1 |

the brand had for both adults and children. Among the target group of 11-25 year olds there was virtually no criticism of the brand. This sort of consumer support should allow TimeOut to build on its initial success even after its large-scale media support is reduced.

**Questions**

1. What criteria did Cadbury Ireland use in developing TimeOut? What role did they play in the positioning strategy of TimeOut?

2. TimeOut has adopted what it describes as a 'bridge-brand' position. What are the risks of the 'bridge-brand' position? Which marketing mix variables were most important in positioning TimeOut?

3. How did the positioning and marketing strategies of its main competitors influence TimeOut's positioning?

4. Discuss the promotional strategy used to launch TimeOut. What are the cultural factors that account for the success of TimeOut? Could TimeOut be successful in other European countries?

## CHAPTER ELEVEN

# Building customer satisfaction through quality, value and service

## CHAPTER OBJECTIVES

After reading this chapter, you should be able to:

- Define *customer value* and discuss its importance in creating customer satisfaction and company profitability.

- Discuss the concepts of *value chains* and *value delivery* systems and explain how companies go about producing and delivering customer value.

- Explain the importance of retaining current customers as well as attracting new ones.

- Discuss customer relationship marketing and the main steps in establishing a customer relationship programme.

- Define quality and explain the importance of total quality marketing in building value-laden, profitable relationships with customers.

## CHAPTER PREVIEW

### Rubbermaid: Want to buy an expensive rubber dustpan?

The best selling car in the world is not a VW, Toyota or Chevy but the Little Tikes Cozy Coupé – a leg-powered, Flintstones-like car for toddlers. It is one of the thousands of products made by one of the world's most successful companies, Rubbermaid. The company's rise started in 1934 when the then Wooster Rubber Company made a little-noticed addition to its line of balloons: a rubber dustpan. It sold the new dustpan door to door for twice what competitors were charging for their metal versions. But this dustpan was special – it was well-designed, long-lasting and very high in quality – it was good value. The Wooster Rubber Company became Rubbermaid and that lowly dustpan turned out to be a real winner. Since then, the same concepts that led to the development

I ecu = US$1.26

of the rubber dustpan have transformed Rubbermaid from a sleepy, small-town rubber-products company into a dynamic market leader.

Today, Rubbermaid thoroughly dominates its fragmented industry, without serious competition. It produces a dazzling array of more than 5000 products, ranging from food containers, pedal bins and home organizers to toy cars, mailboxes and plastic bird feeders. It sells $2.2 billion worth of rubber and plastic household goods, toys, outdoor furniture and office products each year. Rubbermaid's rise has been spectacular. In the past decade or so, its sales have quadrupled and profits have grown sixfold. It has achieved fifty-four consecutive years of profits, fifty-seven consecutive quarters of sales and earnings growth and 15 per cent average earnings per share since 1985. *Fortune* magazine has rated Rubbermaid among the top seven most admired US corporations for ten years running.

Rubbermaid's success results from a simple but effective competitive marketing strategy: to consistently offer the best value to customers. First, the company carefully studies and listens to consumers. It uses demographic and lifestyle analysis to spot consumer trends and conducts focus groups, interviews and in-home product tests to learn about consumer problems and needs, likes and dislikes. Then it gives consumers what they want — a continuous flow of useful, innovative and high-quality products.

Rubbermaid has forged a strong market position. To most consumers, the Rubbermaid name has become the gold standard of good value and quality. Customers know that Rubbermaid products are well designed and well made and they willingly pay premium prices to own them. Rubbermaid management jealously protects this reputation. The company has an obsession with quality. Under its strict quality-control programme, no product with so much as a scratch ever leaves the factory floor. It's said that former Rubbermaid CEO Stanley Gault, who guided the company through its spectacular growth during the 1980s, used to visit retail stores several times a week to see how the company's products were displayed and to check on quality and workmanship. If he found a problem, he bought up the merchandise on the spot, brought it back to headquarters and severely lectured responsible company executives. Throughout the company, he was known to get livid about product defects.

Rubbermaid thrives on finding new ways to serve customers. Innovation and new-product development have become a kind of religion in the company. Rubbermaid introduced a staggering 365 new products in 1992 and over 400 in 1994. Its goal is to generate at least 33 per cent of its total sales from products less than five years old, a goal that it usually meets or exceeds. The company even bases part of its executive compensation on new products' share of sales. Despite the hectic pace of new introductions, Rubbermaid has met with astonishing success. In a fiercely competitive industry where 90 per cent of all new products typically fail, Rubbermaid boasts an amazing 90 per cent *success* rate for its new products.

To speed up the flow of new products, Rubbermaid assigns small teams – made up of experts from marketing, design, manufacturing and finance – to each of its fifty or so product categories. These teams identify new product ideas and usher them through design, development and introduction. The teams tackle the new-product development challenge with enthusiasm. For example, the manager of Rubbermaid's bath accessories, decorative coverings and home organizational products notes that her 'bath team' lives and breathes soap dishes, vanity wastebaskets and shower caddies. Team members go to trade shows, scour magazines, scan supermarket shelves and travel the globe searching for new product ideas. 'We are like sponges,' she says.

Rubbermaid's versions of ordinary products usually offer simple but elegant improvements. For example, its simple yet stylish new Sidekick 'litter-free' lunch box features plastic containers that hold a sandwich, a drink and another item, eliminating the need for plastic wrapping, milk cartons, cans and other potential litter. The Sidekick is priced 20 per cent higher than competing products. Still, the colourful new lunch box has become all the rage among parents worried about America's garbage glut and among school children who have had environmental messages pounded into them at school. Rubbermaid's share of the lunch box market is expected to continue to exhibit strong growth and the company plans to introduce new Sidekick versions.

In addition to developing new products from scratch, Rubbermaid has been very successful at buying up and building small, undervalued companies. For example, in 1984 it added Little Tikes, a small producer of plastic toys, to its portfolio of businesses. In 1991, with the acquisition of Eldon Industries, it established its Office Products Group, which makes desktop accessories, office containers and organizers, modular furniture and other products for home and commercial offices. Such smart strategic planning moves have paid off. Little Tikes is now the company's second largest unit – it introduced over 50 new toys last year and currently contributes about 25 per cent of total sales. Rubbermaid is also gearing up to expand its dominance into global markets. By the year 2000, it plans to generate 30 per cent of sales from outside the United States, compared to the current 15 per cent.

Rubbermaid has also built strong relationships with its 'other customers' – retailers who operate the more than 120,000 outlets in the United States alone that sell Rubbermaid products. Retailers appreciate the company's consistent high quality, larger margins, outstanding service and strong consumer appeal. In fact, Rubbermaid recently received 'Vendor of the Year' honours from the mass-merchandising industry. It has built alliances aggressively with fast-growing discount stores which account for the bulk of household goods sales. It created 'Rubbermaid boutiques', which are whole sections within stores that stock only Rubbermaid products. For example, Twin Valu stores set up ten 24-foot-long shelves with Rubbermaid products, displacing between 20 and 490 feet of competing products. As a result, most of Rubbermaid's competitors have trouble simply getting shelf space.

Thus Rubbermaid has done all of the things that an outstanding marketing company must do to establish and retain its leadership. As one industry analyst notes: '[Rubbermaid has] the ability to execute strategy flawlessly. There's something about Rubbermaid that's magical, that is so difficult for competitors to replicate.' Rubbermaid has positioned itself strongly and gained competitive advantage by providing the best value to consumers. It has set the pace for its industry and kept competitors at bay through continuous innovation. Finally, it has developed a constant stream of useful, high-quality products in a constant quest to deliver ever more value to consumers. In fact, some observers wonder if Rubbermaid can maintain its current torrid pace. How many more new products and approaches, they ask, can the company find? 'It's a little like in 1900, when there was legislation to close the patent office,' answers a Rubbermaid executive. 'The country was convinced that everything that could be invented already was. [But when it comes to fresh and saleable new ways to serve our customers], we're never going to run out of ideas.'[1]

## SATISFYING CUSTOMER NEEDS

Today's companies face tough competition and things will only get harder. In previous chapters, we argued that to succeed in today's fiercely competitive markets, companies have to move from a *product and selling philosophy* to a *customer and marketing philosophy*. This chapter tells in more detail how companies can win customers and outperform competitors. The answer lies in the marketing concept – in doing a better job of *meeting and satisfying customer needs*.

In sellers' markets – those characterized by shortages and near-monopolies – companies do not make special efforts to please customers. In Eastern Europe, for example, millions of would-be consumers used to stand sullenly in line for hours only to receive poorly made clothes, toiletries, appliances and other products at high prices. Producers and retailers showed little concern for customer satisfaction with goods and services. Sellers pay relatively little heed to marketing theory and practice.

In buyers' markets, in contrast, customers can choose from a wide array of goods and services. In these markets, if sellers fail to deliver acceptable product and service quality, they will quickly lose customers to competitors. Also, what is acceptable today may not be acceptable to tomorrow's ever-more-demanding consumers. Consumers are becoming more educated and demanding and their quality expectations have been raised by the practices of superior manufacturers and retailers. The decline of many traditional Western industries in recent years – cars, cameras, machine tools, consumer electronics – offers dramatic evidence that firms offering only average quality lose their consumer franchises when attacked by superior competitors.

To succeed or simply to survive, companies need a new philosophy. To win in today's marketplace, companies must be **customer-centred** – they must deliver superior value to their target customers. They must become adept in *building customers*, not just *building products*. They must be skilful in *market engineering*, not just *product engineering*. New chief executive of Lucas Industries, George Simpson's views were honed at Rover where the corporate culture had to shift to the notion that customers need to like the cars they buy. There was, he says, 'a bit of a tendency at Lucas to have technology for technology's sake'.[2]

Too many companies think that obtaining customers is the job of the marketing or sales department. But winning companies have come to realize that marketing cannot do this job alone. Although marketing plays a leading role, it is only a partner in attracting and keeping customers. The world's best marketing department cannot successfully sell poorly made products that fail to meet consumer needs. The marketing department can be effective only in companies in which all departments and employees have teamed up to form a competitively superior *customer value-delivery system*.

Consider McDonald's. People do not swarm to the world's 11,000 McDonald's restaurants only because they love the chain's hamburgers. Many other restaurants make better-tasting hamburgers. Consumers flock to the McDonald's *system*, not just to its food products. Throughout the world, McDonald's finely tuned system delivers a high standard of what the company calls QSCV – Quality, Service, Cleanliness and Value. The system consists of many components, both internal and external. McDonald's is only effective to the extent that it successfully partners its employees, franchisees, suppliers and others in jointly delivering exceptionally high customer value.

This chapter discusses the philosophy of customer-value-creating marketing and the customer-focused firm. It addresses several important questions: What are customer value and customer satisfaction? How do leading companies organize to create and deliver high value and satisfaction? How can companies keep current customers as well as get new ones? How can companies practice total quality marketing?

## DEFINING CUSTOMER VALUE AND SATISFACTION

More than thirty-five years ago, Peter Drucker observed that a company's first task is 'to create customers'. However, creating customers can be a difficult task. Today's customers face a vast array of product and brand choices, prices and suppliers. The company must answer a key question: How do customers make their choices?

The answer is that customers choose the marketing offer that gives them the most value. Customers are value-maximizers, within the bounds of search costs and limited knowledge, mobility and income. They form expectations of value and act upon them. Then they compare the actual value they receive in consuming the product to the value expected and this affects their satisfaction and repurchase behaviour. We will now examine the concepts of customer value and customer satisfaction more carefully.

### Customer value

Consumers buy from the firm that they believe offers the highest **customer delivered value** – the difference between *total customer value* and *total customer cost* (see Figure 11.1). For example, suppose that an Irish farmer wants to buy a tractor. He can buy the equipment from either his usual supplier Massey-Ferguson or a cheaper East European product. The salespeople for the two companies carefully describe their respective offers to the farmer.

The farmer evaluates the two competing tractors and judges that Massey-Ferguson's tractor provides higher reliability, durability and performance. The customer also decides that Massey-Ferguson has better accompanying services – delivery, training and maintenance – and views Massey-Ferguson personnel as more knowledgeable and responsive. Finally, the customer places higher value on Massey-Ferguson's reputation. The farmer adds all the values from these four sources – *product, services, personnel* and *image* – and decides that Massey-Ferguson offers more **total customer value** than does the East European tractor.

Does the farmer buy the Massey-Ferguson tractor? Not necessarily. The firm will also examine the **total customer cost** of buying the Massey-Ferguson tractor versus the East European tractor product. First, the buying firm will compare the prices it must pay for each of the competitors' products. The Massey-Ferguson's tractor costs a lot more than the East European tractor does, so the higher price might offset the

| | Total customer value | (Product, services, personnel, and image values) |
|---|---|---|
| *minus* | Total customer cost | (Monetary, time, energy, and psychic costs) |
| *equals* | Customer delivered value | ('Profit' to the consumer) |

**Figure 11.1**    Customer delivered value.

higher total customer value. Moreover, total customer cost consists of more than just monetary costs. As Adam Smith observed more than two centuries ago: 'The real price of anything is the toil and trouble of acquiring it.' Total customer cost also includes the buyer's anticipated time, energy and psychic costs. The farmer will evaluate these costs along with monetary costs to form a complete estimate of his costs.

The farmer compares total customer value to total customer cost and determines the total delivered value associated with Massey-Ferguson's tractor. In the same way, he assesses the total delivered value for the East European tractor. The farmer then will buy from the competitor that offers the highest delivered value.

How can Massey-Ferguson use this concept of buyer decision making to help it succeed in selling its tractor to this buyer? Massey-Ferguson can improve its offer in three ways. First, it can increase total customer value by improving product, services, personnel or image benefits. Second, it can reduce the buyer's nonmonetary costs by lessening the buyer's time, energy and psychic costs. Third, it can reduce the buyer's monetary costs by lowering its price, providing easier terms of sale or, in the longer term, lowering its tractor's operating or maintenance costs.

1 ecu = US$1.26
= I£0.81
(Irish punt)

Suppose Massey-Ferguson carries out a *customer value assessment* and concludes that buyers see Massey-Ferguson's offer as worth I£20,000. Further suppose that it costs Massey-Ferguson I£14,000 to produce the tractor. This means that Massey-Ferguson's offer potentially generates I£6,000 (I£20,000 − I£14,000) of *total added value*. Massey-Ferguson needs to price its tractor between I£14,000 and I£20,000. If it charges less than I£14,000 it won't cover its costs. If it charges more than I£20,000, the price will exceed the total customer value. The price Massey-Ferguson charges will determine how much of the total added value will be delivered to the buyer and how much will flow to Massey-Ferguson. For example, if Massey-Ferguson charges I£16,000, it will grant I£4,000 of total added value to the customer and keep I£2,000 for itself as profit. If Massey-Ferguson charges I£19,000, it will grant only I£1,000 of total added value to the customer and keep I£5,000 for itself as profit. Naturally, the lower Massey-Ferguson's price, the higher the delivered value of its offer will be and, therefore, the higher the customer's incentive to purchase from Massey-Ferguson. Delivered value should be viewed as 'profit to the customer'. Given that Massey-Ferguson wants to win the sale, it must offer more delivered value than the East European tractor does.[3]

Some marketers might rightly argue that this concept of how buyers choose among product alternatives is too rational. They might cite examples in which buyers did not choose the offer with an objectively measured highest delivered value. Consider the following situation:

> The Massey-Ferguson salesperson convinces the farmer that, considering the benefits relative to the purchase price, Massey-Ferguson's tractor offers a higher delivered value. The salesperson also points out that the East European tractor uses more fuel and requires more frequent repairs. Still, the farmer decides to buy the East European tractor.

How can we explain this appearance of non-value-maximizing behaviour? There are many possible explanations. For example, perhaps the farmer has a long-term friendship with the East European tractor salesperson. Or the farmer might have a policy of buying at the lowest price. Or perhaps the farmer is short of cash, and therefore chooses the cheaper East European tractor, even though the Massey-Ferguson machine will perform better and be less expensive to operate in the long run.

Clearly, buyers operate under various constraints and sometimes make choices that give more weight to their personal benefit than to company benefit. However, the customer delivered value framework applies to many situations and yields rich insights. The framework suggests that sellers must first assess the total customer value and total customer cost associated with their own and competing marketing offers to determine how their own offers measure up in terms of customer delivered value. If a seller finds that competitors deliver greater value, it has two alternatives. It can try to increase customer value by strengthening or augmenting the product, services, personnel or image benefits of the offer. Or it can decrease total customer cost by reducing its price, simplifying the ordering and delivery process, or absorbing some buyer risk by offering a warranty.[4]

## Customer satisfaction

Consumers form judgements about the value of marketing offers and make their buying decisions based upon these judgements. *Customer satisfaction* with a purchase depends upon the product's performance relative to a buyer's expectations. A customer might experience various degrees of satisfaction. If the product's performance falls short of expectations, the customer is dissatisfied. If performance matches expectations, the customer is satisfied. If performance exceeds expectations, the customer is highly satisfied or delighted.

But how do buyers form their expectations? Expectations are based on the customer's past buying experiences, the opinions of friends and associates, and marketer and competitor information and promises. Marketers must be careful to set the right level of expectations. If they set expectations too low, they may satisfy those who buy but fail to attract enough buyers. In contrast, if they raise expectations too high, buyers are likely to be disappointed. For example, Holiday Inn ran a campaign a few years ago called 'No Surprises', which promised consistently trouble-free accommodation and service. However, Holiday Inn guests still encountered a host of problems and the expectations created by the campaign only made customers more dissatisfied. Holiday Inn had to withdraw the campaign.

Still, some of today's most successful companies are raising expectations – and delivering performance to match. These companies embrace *total customer satisfaction*. For example, Honda claims, 'One reason our customers are so satisfied is that we aren't' or, as dan Technology puts it, 'We value your business. We want you to buy from us again.' These companies aim high because they know that customers who are *only* satisfied will still find it easy to switch suppliers when a better offer comes along. In one consumer packaged-goods category, 44 per cent of consumers reporting satisfaction later switched brands. In contrast, customers who are *highly satisfied* are much less ready to switch. One study showed that 75 per cent of Toyota buyers were highly satisfied and about 75 per cent said they intended to buy a Toyota again. Thus *customer delight* creates an emotional affinity for a product or service, not just a rational preference, and this creates high customer loyalty.

Today's winning companies track their customers' expectations, perceived company performance and customer satisfaction. They track this for their competitors as well. Consider the following:

> A company was pleased to find that 80 per cent of its customers said they were satisfied with its new product. However, the product seemed to sell poorly on store shelves next to the leading competitor's product. Company researchers soon learned that the competitor's product attained a 90 per cent customer satisfaction score. Company management was further dismayed when it learned that this competitor was aiming for a 95 per cent satisfaction score.

Marketing Highlight 11.1 describes the way in which companies can track customer satisfaction.

# Tracking customer satisfaction

The tools used to track and measure customer satisfaction range from the primitive to the sophisticated. Companies use many methods to measure how much customer satisfaction they are creating.

## Complaint and suggestion systems

A customer-centred organization makes it easy for customers to make suggestions or complaints. Restaurants and hotels provide forms upon which guests can check off their likes and dislikes. Hospitals place suggestion boxes in the corridors, supply comment cards to existing patients and employ patient advocates to solicit grievances. Some customer-centred companies, such as P&G, General Electric and Whirlpool, set up customer hot lines with 800 numbers to make it easy for customers to enquire, suggest or complain. It is important to measure how difficult it is for customers to complain and get their problems solved.

Successful companies try very hard. Among leaflets selling mortgages, loans and other services, the Hong Kong and Shanghai Bank's branches has one informing customers how to complain. All visitors to Richer Sounds shops get a card showing the shop's team and saying: 'We're listening.' It's a Freepost letter addressed to Julian Richer, the owner of the chain. Inside it reads:

'*Thank you* for your support and making us the UK's most successful hi-fi retailer. In order to maintain No. 1 position, we need to know where we've gone wrong. Suggestions or comments regarding customer service, however small, are gratefully received. Every one has Mr Richer's personal attention ... Please, please, please let us know, as we really do care!'

Such systems not only help companies to act more quickly to resolve problems, but they also provide companies with many good ideas for improved products and service.

## Customer satisfaction surveys

Simply running complaint and suggestion systems may not give the company a full picture of customer satisfaction and dissatisfaction. Studies show that one out of every four purchases results in consumer dissatisfaction but that less than 5 per cent of dissatisfied customers complain. Customers may feel that their complaints are minor or that they will be treated harshly if they complain or that the company will do little to remedy the problem anyway. Rather than complain, most customers simply switch suppliers. As a result, the company needlessly loses customers.

Responsive companies take direct measures of customer satisfaction by conducting regular surveys. They send questionnaires or make telephone calls to a sample of recent customers to find out how they feel about various aspects of the company's performance. They also survey buyers' views on competitor performance. Whirlpool surveys customer satisfaction on a massive scale, then acts on the results:

When customers talk, Whirlpool listens. Each year the company mails its Standardised Appliance Measurement Satisfaction (SAMS) survey to 180,000 households, asking people to rate all their appliances on dozens of attributes. When a competitor's product ranks higher, Whirlpool engineers rip it apart to see why. The company [also] pays hundreds of consumers to fiddle with computer-simulated products at the company's Usability Lab while engineers record the users' reactions on videotape.

Belgacom is the new name for Belgium's revitalised Régie des Télégraphes et des Téléphones, the state-owned telecommunications monopoly. They placed a questionnaire about their service in newspapers and got 65,000 replies. These highlighted the firm's weaknesses and reputation for 'customer unfriendliness'. Not surprising when a law exists that allows Belgacom employees to slam the phone down on irate customers. Belgacom has changed its ways so as not to be crushed in the European telecom market by BT, Deutsche Telekom and American telecom giants. To start, the word 'subscriber' was banned and employees were taught to think of 'the customer'.

A company can measure customer satisfaction in a number of ways. It can measure satisfaction directly by asking: 'How satisfied are you with this product? Are you highly dissatisfied, somewhat dissatisfied, neither satisfied nor dissatisfied, somewhat satisfied or highly satisfied?' Or it can ask respondents to rate how much they expected of certain attributes and how much they actually experienced. Finally, the company can ask respondents to list any problems they have had with the offer and to suggest improvements.

While collecting customer satisfaction data, companies often ask additional useful questions. They often measure the customer's *repurchase intention*; this will usually be high if customer satisfaction is high. According to CEO John Young at Hewlett-Packard, nine out of ten customers in HP surveys who rank themselves as highly satisfied say that they would definitely or probably buy from HP again. The company might also ask about the customer's likelihood or willingness to recommend the company and brand to other people. A strongly positive word-of-mouth rating suggests high customer satisfaction.

## Ghost shopping

Another useful way of assessing customer satisfaction is to hire people to pose as buyers and then to report their experiences in buying the company's and competitors' products. These 'ghost shoppers' can even present specific problems in order to test whether the company's personnel handle difficult situations well. For example, ghost shoppers can complain about a restaurant's food to see how the restaurant handles this complaint. Research International's Mystery Shopper surveys can measure many dimensions of customer performance. By telephoning it can measure a firm's telephone technique: how many rings it takes to answer, the sort of voice and tone and, if transferred, how many leaps it took before being correctly connected? Not only should companies hire ghost shoppers, but managers themselves should leave their offices from time to time and experience first-hand the treatment they receive as 'customers'. As an alternative, managers can phone their companies with different questions and complaints to see how the call is handled.

## Lost customer analysis

Companies should contact customers who have stopped buying or those who have switched to a competitor, to learn why this happened. When IBM loses a customer, it mounts a thorough effort to learn how it failed: was IBM's price too high, its service poor or its products substandard? Not only should the company conduct such *exit interviews*, it should also monitor the *customer loss rate*. A rising loss rate indicates that the company is failing to satisfy its customers.

## Independent surveys

Magazines and consumers' associations often conduct independent surveys. Honda, Dell and dan Technologies strive to come out on top in these measures. They find them good publicity and a useful way of overcoming biased self-assessments. Companies can easily be deluded by their own results. For instance, a conference centre may be happy that 85 per cent of its customers say its service is good, but what if 95 per cent of the customers also rate a competitor as excellent? The ad agency Bozell Worldwide's Quality Poll gives a league table and shows how biased local perceptions can be. Gallup conducted a study that asked 20,000 people in twenty countries to rate the quality of manufactured goods from 12 countries. The results show countries in four distinct bands (see Table 1).

All countries rated themselves higher than other people did. The French put French goods on top while the Japanese gave themselves twice the rating (76 per cent) that the full sample did (38.5). All other countries were optimistic too: Germans gave themselves 49 per cent against the full sample's 36 per cent and the United Kingdom 39 per cent against 22 per cent.

## Some cautions in measuring customer satisfaction

Customer satisfaction ratings are sometimes difficult to interpret. When customers rate their satisfaction with some element of the company's performance, say, delivery, they can vary greatly in how they define good delivery. It might mean early delivery, on-time delivery, order completeness or something else. Yet,

**MARKETING HIGHLIGHT 11.1 (cont)**

Table 1    Quality rating of manufactured goods

| Band | Scores (respondents rating goods very good or excellent) | Members (ranked in order of their score) |
| --- | --- | --- |
| One | About 30 to 40 per cent | Japan, Germany and US |
| Two | About 15 to 20 per cent | UK, France, Canada and Italy |
| Three | About 10 per cent | Spain, China and Taiwan |
| Four | About 5 per cent | Mexico and Russia |

if the company tried to define every element in detail, customers would face a huge questionnaire.

Companies must also recognize that two customers can report being 'highly satisfied' for different reasons. One might be easily satisfied most of the time, whereas the other might be hard to please but was pleased on this occasion. Further, managers and salespeople can manipulate their ratings on customer satisfaction. They can be especially nice to customers just before the survey or try to exclude unhappy customers from being included in the survey. Finally, if customers know that the company will go out of its way to please customers, even if they are satisfied some customers may express high dissatisfaction in order to receive yet more concessions.

Source:  Quote from Sally Solo, 'Whirlpool: how to listen to consumers', *Fortune* (11 January 1993), 77-9; see also *Measure* (July-Aug. 1990), 28. 'A new line for Belgacom', *The Economist* (8 January 1994), 6; Peter Barley, 'Looking for trouble', *Marketing Business* (September 1994),

21-4, Richard Tomkins, 'Japan tops consumer list for best quality goods', *Financial Times* (11 February 1994), 6; Bozell Worldwide, *Bozell-Gallup Worldwide Quality Poll* (New York: Bozell Worldwide, 1994); David Reed, 'Setting a new benchmark', *Marketing Week* (4 November 1994), 55-8.

For customer-centred companies, customer satisfaction is both a goal and an essential factor in company success. Companies that achieve high customer satisfaction ratings make sure that their target market knows it. In the car industry, the Honda Accord received the number-one rating in customer satisfaction by J. D. Powers for several years running and Honda advertising touting helped sell more Accords. Similarly dan Technology's success in the personal computer industry was partly because it achieves and advertises its number-one ranking.[5]

These and other companies realize that highly satisfied customers produce several benefits for the company. They are less price sensitive and they remain customers for a longer period. They buy additional products over time as the company introduces related products or improvements. And they talk favourably to others about the company and its products.

Although the customer-centred firm seeks to deliver high customer satisfaction relative to competitors, it does not attempt to *maximize* customer satisfaction. A company can always increase customer satisfaction by lowering its price or increasing its services, but this may result in lower profits. In addition to customers, the company has many stakeholders, including employees, dealers, suppliers and stockholders. Spending more to increase customer satisfaction might divert funds from increasing the satisfaction of these other 'partners'. Thus the purpose of marketing is to generate customer value profitably. Ultimately, the company must deliver a high level of customer satisfaction while at the same time delivering at least acceptable levels of satisfaction to the firm's other stakeholders. This requires a very delicate balance: the marketer must continue to generate more customer value and satisfaction but not 'give away the house'.[6] Many of the world's most successful companies

KLM satisfy their high-paying and frequent-flying business user by giving them more room.

build their strategies on customer satisfaction but, as Marketing Highlight 11.2 shows, you do not have to be big to succeed.[7]

## DELIVERING CUSTOMER VALUE AND SATISFACTION

Customer value and satisfaction are important ingredients in the marketer's formula for success. But what does it take to produce and deliver customer value? To answer this, we will examine the concepts of a *value chain* and *value delivery system*.

### Value chain

Michael Porter proposed the **value chain** as the main tool for identifying ways to create more customer value (see Figure 11.2).[8] Every firm consists of a collection of activities performed to design, produce, market, deliver and support the firm's products. The value chain breaks the firm into nine value-creating activities in an effort to understand the behaviour of costs in the specific business and the potential sources

**MARKETING HIGHLIGHT 11.2**

## Cold turkey has got me on the run

'Oh dear! Am I in trouble now'. It was a week before Christmas as the recalcitrant academic trudged up and down Castle Street trying to buy a goose for Christmas dinner. Long before Charles Dickens' time, when Scrooge sent 'the prize Turkey ... the big one' to Bob Cratchit's house, goose was the traditional English Christmas fayre. Introduced to Europe from America in the sixteenth century, turkey had displaced goose in all of Castle Street's butchers. Sick of having cold turkey salad, turkey sandwiches and that dreadful turkey curry for days after Christmas, the academic's family had decided to have goose 'for a change'. His job was to get one, but he had left it too late.

Butcher after butcher came out with the worn-out lines, 'You should have ordered one weeks ago', 'We can't get them anywhere', or 'There's no call for them these days'. Even, 'A goose? They're so greasy. How about a nice fat turkey. It'll last you for days.' SCREAM!

Defeated, he slumped in his car to drive home. It was dark and on the way through a village he saw the lights of a small shop he had not noticed before. A small independent butcher, well stocked, brightly lit and full of customers. 'Funny', he thought, 'there are not many of those these days. Still, let's have one last try'.

On joining the festive throng inside, he noticed a sign on the wall. It read:

*The ten commandments of good business*

1.   The customer is the most important person in my business.
2.   The customer is not dependent on us; we are dependent on him.
3.   A customer is not an interruption of our work; he is the purpose of it.
4.   A customer does us a favour when he calls; we are not doing him a favour by serving him.
5.   The customer is part of our business, not an outsider.
6.   The customer is not a cold statistic; he is a flesh and blood human being with feelings and emotions like ours.
7.   The customer is not someone to argue or match wits with.
8.   The customer brings us his wants; it is our job to fill those wants.
9.   The customer is deserving of the most courteous and attentive treatment we can give him.
10.  The customer is the lifeblood of this, and every other, business.

'Merry Christmas, what can I do for you?' asked the butcher.
'Have you a goose?' the academic asked timidly.
'I haven't got any in but I'll get one for you. What size do you want?'

Later on, at The Pheasant Inn, the talk turned to food. 'Have you come across that great butcher in the next village?'
'Great butcher? Come off it. A butcher's a butcher's a butcher!'
'Not this one, he will do anything for you. Nice guy, too.'

Lesson: You do not have to be big to be great.

Sources:   Charles Dickens, *A Christmas Carol* (London: Hazell, Watson & Viney, 1843); John Lennon, *Cold Turkey* (London: Apple, 1969); Microsoft, *Encarta, electronic multimedia encyclopedia* (Microsoft Corporation, 1993).

of competitive differentiation. The nine value-creating activities include five primary activities and four support activities.

The primary activities involve the sequence of bringing materials into the business (inbound logistics), operating on them (operations), sending them out (outbound logistics), marketing them (marketing and sales) and servicing them (service). For a long time firms have focused on the product as the primary means of adding value but customer satisfaction also depends upon the other stages of the value chain.[9] The support activities occur within each of these primary activities. For example, procurement involves obtaining the various inputs for each primary activity – only a fraction of procurement is done by the purchasing department. Technology development and human-resource management also occur in all departments. The

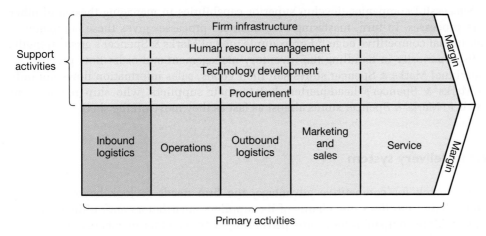

**Figure 11.2** The generic value chain. (Source: Michael E. Porter, *Competitive Advantage* (New York: Free Press, 1985), 37.)

firm's infrastructure covers the overhead of general management, planning, finance, accounting and legal and government affairs borne by all the primary and support activities.

Under the value-chain concept, the firm should examine its costs and performance in each value-creating activity to look for improvements. It should also estimate its competitor's costs and performances as benchmarks. To the extent that the firm can perform certain activities better than its competitors, it can achieve a competitive advantage.

The firm's success depends not only on how well each department performs its work, but also on how well the activities of various departments are coordinated. Too often, individual departments maximize their own interests rather than those of the total company and the customer. For example, a credit department might attempt to reduce bad debts by taking a long time to check the credit of prospective customers: meanwhile, salespeople get frustrated and customers wait. A distribution department might decide to save money by shipping goods by rail; again the customer waits. In each case, individual departments have erected walls that impede the delivery of quality customer service.

To overcome this problem, companies should place more emphasis on the smooth management of *core business processes*, most of which involve inputs and cooperation from many functional departments. Among others, these core business processes include the following:

- *Product development process.* All the activities involved in identifying, researching and developing new products with speed, high quality and reasonable cost.
- *Inventory management process.* All the activities involved in developing and managing the right inventory levels of raw materials, semi-finished materials and finished goods so that adequate supplies are available while avoiding the costs of high overstocks.
- *Order-to-payment process.* All the activities involved in receiving orders, approving them, shipping the goods on time and collecting payment.
- *Customer service process.* All the activities involved in making it easy for customers to reach the right parties within the company to obtain service, answers and resolutions of problems.

Successful companies develop superior capabilities in managing these and other core processes. In turn, mastering core business processes gives these companies a substantial competitive edge.[10] For example, one of Marks & Spencer's great strengths is its superiority in handling the inventory management and order flow process. As individual Marks & Spencer stores sell their goods, sales information flows not only to Marks & Spencer's headquarters but to their suppliers, who ship replacement goods to Marks & Spencer stores almost as fast as they move off the shelf.

## Value delivery system

In its search for competitive advantage, the firm needs to look beyond its own value chain, into the value chains of its suppliers, distributors and, ultimately, customers. More companies today are 'partnering' with the other members of the supply chain to improve the performance of the **customer value delivery system**. For example:

> Campbell Soup operates a qualified supplier programme in which it sets high standards for suppliers and chooses only the few suppliers who are willing to meet its demanding requirements for quality, on-time delivery and continuous improvement. Campbell then assigns its own experts to work with suppliers to constantly improve their joint performance.

> Marks & Spencer places its staff at its suppliers' sites to maintain quality standards and improve the speed and reduce the costs of supplying to Marks & Spencer stores.

An excellent value delivery system connects jeans maker Levi Strauss with its suppliers and distributors. One of Levi's biggest retailers is Sears. Every night, Levi's learns the sizes and styles of its blue jeans that sold through Sears and other large outlets. Levi's then electronically orders more fabric from the Milliken Company, its fabric supplier. In turn, Milliken relays an order for more fibre to DuPont, the fibre supplier. In this way, the partners in the supply chain use the most current sales information to manufacture what is selling, rather than to manufacture based on potentially inaccurate sales forecasts. This is known as a *quick response* system, in which goods are pulled by demand, rather than pushed by supply.

As companies struggle to become more competitive, they are turning, ironically, to greater cooperation. Companies used to view their suppliers and distributors as cost centres and in some cases, as adversaries. Today, however, they are selecting partners carefully and working out mutually profitable strategies. Increasingly in today's marketplace, competition no longer takes place between individual competitors. Rather, it takes place between the entire value delivery systems created by these competitors. Thus, if Levi Strauss has built a more potent value delivery system than Wrangler or another competitor, it will win more market share and profit.

Therefore, marketing can no longer be thought of as only a selling department. That view of marketing would give it responsibility only for formulating a promotion-oriented marketing mix, without much to say about product features, costs and other important elements. Under the new view, marketing is responsible for *designing and managing a superior value delivery system to reach target customer segments*. Today's marketing managers must think not only about selling today's products but also about how to stimulate the development of improved products, how to work actively with other departments in managing core business processes and how to build better external partnerships.[11]

## RETAINING CUSTOMERS

Beyond building stronger relations with their partners in the supply chain, companies today must work to develop stronger bonds and loyalty with their ultimate customers. In the past, many companies took their customers for granted. Customers often did not have many alternative suppliers, or the other suppliers were just as poor in quality and service, or the market was growing so fast that the company did not worry about fully satisfying its customers. A company could lose 100 customers a week but gain another 100 customers and consider its sales to be satisfactory. Such a company, operating on a 'leaky bucket' theory of business, believes that there will always be enough customers to replace the defecting ones. However, this high *customer churn* involves higher costs than if a company retained all 100 customers and acquired no new ones.

### The cost of lost customers

Companies must pay close attention to their customer defection rate and undertake steps to reduce it. First, the company must define and measure its retention rate. For a magazine, it would be the renewal rate; for a consumer packaged-good firm, it would be the repurchase rate.

Next, the company must identify the causes of customer defection and determine which of these can be reduced or eliminated. Not much can be done about customers who leave the region or about business customers who go out of business. But much can be done about customers who leave because of shoddy products, poor service or prices that are too high. The company needs to prepare a frequency distribution showing the percentage of customers who defect for different reasons.

Companies can estimate how much profit they lose when customers defect unnecessarily. For an individual customer, this is the same as the *customer's lifetime value*. Rob Walker, quality director of Rank Xerox, quantifies the problem:

> Last year, customers discontinued using 5,500 machines out of 140,000 installed. If Rank Xerox had retained them all, the impact on its bottom line would have been over £5m. in the first year and over £19m. in three years. 'If you then add on the opportunity cost the effect on the bottom line is large,' he says. 'Not all of this is, however, controllable and recoverable. But we reckon that 30 per cent of it is. So the financial impact of dissatisfied customers is large.'[12]

1 ecu = UK£0.83

The company needs to work out how much it would cost to reduce the defection rate. If the cost is less than the lost profits, the company should spend that amount to reduce customer defections. In this example, if the company could spend up to £1.5m. (0.3 × £5m.) to retain the lost accounts, it would be wise to do so.

### The need for customer retention

Today, outstanding companies go all out to retain their customers. Many markets have settled into maturity and there are not many new customers entering most categories. Competition is increasing and the costs of attracting new customers are rising. In these markets, it might cost five times as much to attract a new customer as to keep a current customer happy. Offensive marketing typically costs more than defensive marketing, because it takes a great deal of effort and spending to coax satisfied customers away from competitors.

Unfortunately, classic marketing theory and practice centres on the art of attracting new customers rather than retaining existing ones. The emphasis has been on creating *transactions* rather than *relationships*. Discussion has focused on *pre-sale activity* and *sale activity* rather than on *post-sale activity*. Today, however, more companies recognize the importance of retaining current customers. According to one report, by reducing customer defections by only 5 per cent, companies can improve profits anywhere from 25 per cent to 85 per cent.[13] Unfortunately, however, most company accounting systems fail to show the value of loyal customers.

Thus, although much current marketing focuses on formulating marketing mixes that will create sales and new customers, the firm's first line of defence lies in customer retention. And the best approach to customer retention is to deliver high customer satisfaction that results in strong customer loyalty.

## The key: customer relationship marketing

**Relationship marketing** involves creating, maintaining and enhancing strong relationships with customers and other stakeholders. Increasingly, marketing is moving away from a focus on individual transactions and towards a focus on building value-laden relationships and marketing networks. Relationship marketing is oriented more towards the long term. The goal is to deliver long-term value to customers and the measure of success is long-term customer satisfaction. Relationship marketing requires that all of the company's departments work together with marketing as a team to serve the customer. It involves building relationships at many levels – economic, social, technical and legal – resulting in high customer loyalty.

We can distinguish five different levels or relationships that can be formed with customers who have purchased a company's product, such as a car or a piece of equipment:

- *Basic.* The company salesperson sells the product but does not follow up in any way.
- *Reactive.* The salesperson sells the product and encourages the customer to call whenever he or she has any questions or problems.
- *Accountable.* The salesperson phones the customer a short time after the sale to check whether the product is meeting the customer's expectations. The salesperson also solicits from the customer any product improvement suggestions and any specific disappointments. This information helps the company to continuously improve its offering.
- *Proactive.* The salesperson or others in the company phone the customer from time to time with suggestions about improved product use or helpful new products.
- *Partnership.* The company works continuously with the customer and with other customers to discover ways to deliver better value.

Figure 11.3 shows that a company's relationship marketing strategy will depend on how many customers it has and their profitability. For example, companies with many low-margin customers will practice *basic* marketing. Thus Heineken will not phone all of its drinkers to express its appreciation for their business. At best, Heineken will be reactive by setting up a customer information service. At the other extreme, in markets with few customers and high margins, most sellers will move towards partnership marketing. In developing the Airbus A3XX, a very large commercial transport, Airbus Industries will work closely with the aero-engine manufacturers as well as with British Airways and Singapore Airlines, the first two operators interested in buying the super jumbo.

**Profit margins**

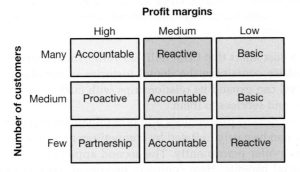

Figure 11.3 shows a 3×3 matrix:

|  | High | Medium | Low |
|---|---|---|---|
| Many | Accountable | Reactive | Basic |
| Medium | Proactive | Accountable | Basic |
| Few | Partnership | Accountable | Reactive |

(Rows labelled "Number of customers": Many, Medium, Few)

**Figure 11.3** Relationship levels as a function of profit margin and number of customers.

What specific marketing tools can a company use to develop stronger customer bonding and satisfaction? It can adopt any of three customer value-building approaches.[14] The first relies primarily on adding *financial benefits* to the customer relationship. For example, airlines offer frequent-flyer programmes, hotels give room upgrades to their frequent guests and supermarkets give patronage refunds. Procter & Gamble recently offered a unique money-back guarantee on its Crest toothpaste in an effort to build a long-term bond with customers:

> [P&G advertises] a toll-free number customers can call to join a money-back guarantee programme for Crest toothpaste. P&G supplies dental patients with evaluation forms that they

**Together we lead the world in aviation technology.**

The combination of European skills and resources from our partners in France, Germany, the UK and Spain has put Airbus Industrie in a leading position in civil aviation. Our constantly evolving Airbus family of aircraft, with its 30% market share worldwide, shows how European co-operation can make a significant impact on a highly competitive international business.

AIRBUS INDUSTRIE
TAKING THE WORLD VIEW

Airbus Industrie's programme shows relationships in many directions: with customers, with suppliers, across airframe makers in foreign countries and with governments.

take to their local dentists. Dentists check for cavities and tartar build-up. After six months of Crest use and a return trip to the dentist, patients who haven't improved are refunded the money they spent on Crest.[15]

Beyond assuring customers that Crest delivers value, this promotion helps P&G build a customer database containing the dental histories of families that sign up. Using this database, P&G can expand its relationships with customers by offering additional related products and services to them.

Although these reward programmes and other financial incentives build customer preference, they can be easily imitated by competitors and thus may fail to differentiate the company's offer permanently. The second approach is to add *social benefits* as well as financial benefits. Here company personnel work to increase their social bonds with customers by learning individual customers' needs and wants and then individualizing and personalizing their products and services. Heinz Weightwatchers Clubs have very effectively done that for people who are worried about their weight. They turn their *customers* into *clients*:

> Customers may be nameless to the institution; clients cannot be nameless. Customers are served as part of the mass or as part of larger segments; clients are served on an individual basis. ... Customers are served by anyone who happens to be available; clients are served ... by the professional ... assigned to them.[16]

The third approach to building strong customer relationships is to add *structural ties* as well as financial and social benefits. For example, a business marketer might supply customers with special equipment or computer linkages that help them manage their orders, payroll or inventory. Investment bankers J. P. Morgan provides its RiskMetrics financial risk measurement system free of charge to its customers. It has two reasons for doing so. First, say the company, it will promote greater transparency to risk and so help identify problems. Second, J. P. Morgan must also be hoping that the association of its name with a widely accepted benchmarking system will yield long-term commercial advantages, partly through strengthening ties with existing customers. There are clear customer needs here. In the twelve months prior to RiskMetrics' release, estimated derivatives losses, by firms including Metallgesellschaft and Kashima Oil, approached DM10bn.[17]

1 ecu = US$1.26
= DM1.89
(Deutschmarks)

The main steps in establishing a relationship marketing programme in a company are:

- *Identify the key customers meriting relationship management.* Choose the largest or best customers and designate them for relationship management. Other customers can be added who show exceptional growth or who pioneer new industry developments.
- *Assign a skilled relationship manager to each key customer.* The salesperson currently servicing the customer should receive training in relationship management or be replaced by someone more skilled in relationship management. The relationship manager should have characteristics that match or appeal to the customer.
- *Develop a clear job description for relationship managers.* Describe their reporting relationships, objectives, responsibilities and evaluation criteria. Make the relationship manager the focal point for all dealings with and about the client. Give each relationship manager only one or a few relationships to manage.
- *Have each relationship manager develop annual and long-range customer relationship plans.* These plans should state objectives, strategies, specific actions and required resources.

■ *Appoint an overall manager to supervise the relationship managers.* This person will develop job descriptions, evaluation criteria and resource support to increase relationship manager effectiveness.

When it has properly implemented relationship management, the organization begins to focus on managing its customers as well as its products. At the same time, although many companies are moving strongly towards relationship marketing, it is not effective in all situations:

> When it comes to relationship marketing ... you don't want a relationship with every customer. ... In fact, there are some bad customers. [The objective is to] figure out which customers are worth cultivating because you can meet their needs more effectively than anyone else.[18]

In the end, companies must judge which segments and which specific customers will be profitable. Marketing Highlight 11.3 discusses the importance of relationships in business marketing and the types of situations in which relationship marketing proves most effective.

## The ultimate test: customer profitability

Ultimately, marketing is the art of attracting and keeping *profitable customers*. Yet, companies often discover that between 20 per cent and 40 per cent of their customers are unprofitable. Further, many companies report that their most profitable customers are not their largest customers but their mid-size customers. The largest customers demand greater service and receive the deepest discounts, thereby reducing the company's profit level. The smallest customers pay full price and receive less service, but the costs of transacting with small customers reduce their profitability. In many cases, mid-size customers who pay close to full price and receive good service are the most profitable. This helps to explain why many large firms that once targeted only large customers are now invading the middle market.

A company should not try to pursue and satisfy every customer. For example, if business customers of Courtyard (Marriott's less expensive motel) start asking for Marriott-level business services, Courtyard should say 'no'. Providing such service would only confuse the respective positionings of the Marriott and Courtyard systems. Similarly, airlines differentiate between tourist- and business-class flyers and Visa offer more service to gold-card users.

> Some organizations ... try to do anything and everything customers suggest. ... Yet, while customers often make many good suggestions, they also suggest many courses of action that are unactionable or unprofitable. Randomly following these suggestions is fundamentally different from market-focus – making a disciplined choice of which customers to serve and which specific combination of benefits and price to deliver to them (and which to deny them).[19]

What makes a customer profitable? We define a *profitable customer* as a person, household or company whose revenues over time exceed, by an acceptable amount, the company costs of attracting, selling and servicing that customer. Note that the definition emphasizes lifetime revenues and costs, not profit from a single transaction. Here are some dramatic illustrations of **customer lifetime value**:

> Stew Leonard, who operates a highly profitable single-store supermarket, says that he sees $50,000 flying out of his store every time he sees a sulking customer. Why? Because his average customer spends about $100 a week, shops 50 weeks a year and remains in the area

# When – and how – to use relationship marketing

Although relationship marketing may not be effective in all situations, it works extremely well in the right situations. Transaction marketing, which focuses on one sales transaction at a time, is more appropriate than relationship marketing for customers who have short time horizons and who can switch from one supplier to another with little effort or investment. This situation often occurs in 'commodity' markets, such as steel, where various suppliers offer largely undifferentiated products. A customer buying steel can buy from any of several steel suppliers and choose the one offering the best terms on a purchase-by-purchase basis. The fact that one steel supplier works at developing a longer-term relationship with a buyer does not automatically earn it the next sale; its price and other terms still have to be competitive.

In contrast, relationship marketing can pay off handsomely with customers who have long time horizons and high switching costs, such as buyers of office automation systems. Such major system buyers usually

research competing suppliers carefully and choose one from whom they can expect state-of-the-art technology and good long-term service. Both the customer and the supplier invest a lot of money and time in building the relationship. The customer would find it costly and risky to switch to another supplier and the seller would find that losing this customer would be a considerable loss. Thus each seeks to develop a solid long-term working relationship with the other. It is with such customers that relationship marketing has the greatest pay-off.

In these situations, the 'in-supplier' and 'out-supplier' face very different challenges. The in-supplier tries to make switching difficult for the customer. It develops product systems that are incompatible with those of competing suppliers and installs its own ordering systems that simplify inventory management and delivery. It works to become the customer's indispensable partner. Out-suppliers, in contrast, try to make it easy and less costly to switch suppliers. They design product systems that are compatible

---

for about 10 years. If this customer has an unhappy experience and switches to another supermarket, Stew Leonard has lost $50,000 in revenue. The loss can be much greater if the disappointed customer shares the bad experience with other customers and causes them to defect.

Tom Peters, noted author of several books on managerial excellence, runs a business that spends $1,500 a month on Federal Express service. His company spends this amount 12 months a year and expects to remain in business for at least another 10 years. Therefore, he expects to spend more than $180,000 on future Federal Express service. If Federal Express makes a 10 per cent profit margin, Peters' lifetime business will contribute $18,000 to Federal Express's profits. Federal Express risks all of this profit if Peters receives poor service from a Federal Express driver or if a competitor offers better service.

Few companies actively measure individual customer value and profitability. For example, banks claim that this is hard to do because customers use different banking services and transactions are logged in different departments. However, banks that have managed to link customer transactions and measure customer profitability have been appalled by how many unprofitable customers they find. Some banks report losing money on over 45 per cent of their retail customers. It is not surprising that many banks now charge fees for services that they once supplied free.

A useful type of profitability analysis is shown in Figure 11.4.[20] Customers make up the columns of the figure and products or services make up the rows. Each cell contains a symbol for the profitability of selling a given product or service to a given customer. Customer 1 is very profitable – he or she buys two profit-making products, product A and product B. Customer 2 yields mixed profitability, buying one profitable product and one unprofitable product. Customer 3 generates losses by purchas-

with the customer's system, that are easy to install and learn, that save the customer a lot of money, and that promise to improve through time.

Some marketers believe that the issue of transaction versus relationship marketing depends not so much on the type of industry as on the wishes of the particular customer. Some customers value a high-service supplier and will stay with that supplier for a long time. Other customers want to cut their costs and will switch suppliers readily to obtain lower costs. In the latter case, the company can still try to keep the customer by agreeing to reduce the price, providing that the customer is willing to accept fewer services. For example, the customer may forgo free delivery, design assistance, training or some other extra. However,

the seller should probably treat this type of customer on a transaction basis rather than on a relationship-building basis. As long as the company cuts its own costs by as much as or more than its price reduction, the transaction-oriented customer will still be profitable.

Thus relationship marketing is not the best approach in all situations. For some types of customers, heavy relationship investments simply don't pay off. But relationship marketing can be extremely effective with the right types of customers – those who make hefty commitments to a specific system and then expect high-quality, consistent service over the long term. To win and keep such accounts, the marketer will have to invest heavily in relationship marketing. But the returns will be well worth the investment.

Sources: See Barbara Bund Jackson, *Winning and Keeping Industrial Customers: The dynamics of customer relationships* (Lexington, MA: Heath, 1985); James C. Anderson and James A. Narus, 'Value-based segmentation, targeting and relationship-building in business markets', ISBM Report No. 12, The Institute for the Study of Business Markets, Pennsylvania State University, University Park, PA (1989); Lawrence A. Crosby, Kenneth R. Evans and Deborah Cowles, 'Relationship quality and services selling: an interpersonal influence perspective', *Journal of Marketing* (July 1990), 68–81; and Barry J. Farber and Joyce Wycoff, 'Relationships: six steps to success', *Sales & Marketing Management* (April 1992), 50–8.

ing the company's two unprofitable products ('loss leaders'). What can the company do about consumers like customer 3? First, the company should consider raising the prices of its less profitable products or eliminating them. The company can also try to cross-sell its profit-making products to its unprofitable customers. If these actions cause unprofitable customers to defect, it may be for the good. In fact, the company might benefit by *encouraging* its unprofitable customers to switch to competitors.

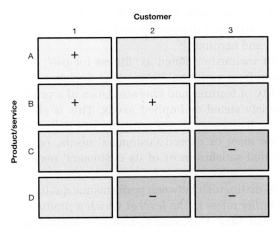

**Figure 11.4**  Customer/product profitability analysis.

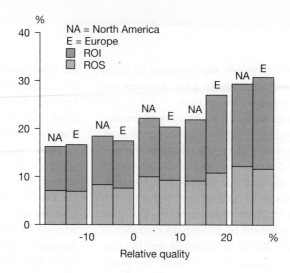

**Figure 11.5**  Relative quality boosts rate of return. (Source: Bob Luchs, 'Quality as a strategic weapon: measuring relative quality, value and market differentiation', *European Business Journal*, 2, 4 (1990), 39.)

## IMPLEMENTING TOTAL QUALITY MARKETING

Customer satisfaction and company profitability are linked closely to product and service quality. Higher levels of quality result in greater customer satisfaction, while at the same time supporting higher prices and often lower costs. Therefore, *quality improvement programmes* normally increase profitability. The Profit Impact of Marketing Strategies studies show similarly high correlations between relative product quality and profitability for Europe and the United States (see Figure 11.5).[21]

The task of improving product and service quality should be a company's top priority. Much of the striking global successes of Japanese companies has resulted from their building exceptional quality into their products. Most customers will no longer tolerate poor or average quality. Companies today have no choice but to adopt *total quality management* (TQM) if they want to stay in the race, let alone be profitable. According to GE's chairman, John F. Welch, Jr.: 'Quality is our best assurance of customer allegiance, our strongest defence against foreign competition and the only path to sustained growth and earnings.'[22]

Quality has been variously defined as 'fitness for use', 'conformance to requirements', and 'freedom from variation'.[23] American Society for Quality Control defines **quality** as the totality of features and characteristics of a product or service that bear on its ability to satisfy stated or implied needs. This is clearly a customer-centred definition of quality. It suggests that a company has delivered quality whenever its product and service meet or exceed customers' needs, requirements and expectations. A company that satisfies most of its customers' needs most of the time is a quality company.

It is important to distinguish between performance quality and conformance quality. *Performance quality* refers to the *level* at which a product performs its functions. Compare two German cars: Volkswagen, Europe's leading volume car maker, and Mercedes, Europe's leading luxury car maker. A Mercedes provides higher performance quality than a VW: it has a smoother ride, handles better and lasts longer. It is more expensive and sells to a market with higher means and requirements. *Conformance quality* refers to freedom from defects and the *consistency* with which a product delivers a specified level of performance. Both a Mercedes and a VW could offer equivalent conformance quality to their respective markets since each consistently delivers what its market expects. A DM 50,000 car that meets all of its requirements is a quality car; so is a DM 15,000 car that meets all of its requirements. However, if the Mercedes handles badly or if the VW gives poor fuel efficiency, then both cars have failed to deliver quality, and customer satisfaction suffers accordingly.

Total quality is the key to creating customer value and satisfaction. Total quality is everyone's job, just as marketing is everyone's job:

> Marketers who don't learn the language of quality improvement, manufacturing and operations will become as obsolete as buggy whips. The days of functional marketing are gone. We can no longer afford to think of ourselves as market researchers, advertising people, direct marketers, marketing strategists – we have to think of ourselves as customer satisfiers – customer advocates focused on whole processes.[24]

Marketing management has two responsibilities in a quality-centred company. First, marketing management must participate in formulating strategies and policies designed to help the company win through total quality excellence. Second, marketing must deliver marketing quality as well as production quality. It must perform each marketing activity – marketing research, sales training, advertising, customer service and others – to high standards.

Marketers play several important roles in helping their companies to define and deliver high-quality goods and services to target customers. First, marketers bear the main responsibility for correctly identifying the customers' needs and requirements and for communicating customer expectations correctly to product designers. Second, marketers must make sure that the customers' orders are filled correctly and on time, and must check to see that customers have received proper instructions, training and technical assistance in the use of the product. Third, marketers must stay in touch with customers after the sale to make sure that they remain satisfied. Finally, marketers must gather and convey customer ideas for product and service improvements to the appropriate company departments.

At the same time, ironically, one study found that marketing people were responsible for more customer complaints than any other department (35 per cent). Marketing mistakes included cases in which the salesforce ordered special product features for customers but failed to notify manufacturing of the changes; in which incorrect order processing resulted in the wrong product being made and shipped; and in which customer complaints were not properly handled.[25]

The implication here is that marketers must spend time and effort not only to improve external marketing, but also to improve internal marketing. Marketers must be the customer's watchdog or guardian, complaining loudly for the customer when the product or the service is not right. Marketers must constantly uphold the standard of 'giving the customer the best solution'. Marketing Highlight 11.4 presents some important conclusions about total marketing quality strategy.

## SUMMARY

Today's customers face a growing range of choices in the products and services they can buy. They base their choices on their perceptions of *quality*, *value* and *service*.

## Pursuing a total quality marketing strategy

Design to Distribution (D2D), winner of the 1994 European Quality Award, attributes its improved performance to total quality management (TQM). 'Quality management satisfies customers, reduces costs and motivates people', says Alistair Kelly, D2D's managing director. TQM helped D2D, a contract electronics manufacturer, increase labour productivity by 300 per cent and save £2m. a year by 'getting things right first time'.

Not long ago, many companies were complacent about product and service quality. Then they awoke to the realization that the Japanese were gaining market domination by offering products of superior design and quality. The first to be hurt were makers of overexpensive shabby goods, but even top manufacturers have now learned that what was the best is no longer good enough. Leica, now owned by the Swiss Anova company, invented the 35 mm camera and still makes cameras renowned for their beautifully engineered bodies with lenses giving razor-sharp pictures. At DM 4,000 their M6 is still a great status symbol, but now nearly all professional photographers use Japanese-made Canon, Nikon, Minolta or their like. Leica now have a technology cooperation agreement with Minolta that has helped them produce their Leica Mini that sells for about DM 400.

The Japanese took early to TQM. In 1947 General Douglas MacArthur invited W. Edwards Deming to Japan to help assess their postwar industrial needs. Deming was no ordinary management consultant; he was the man who invented quality. To the Japanese he was a prophet whom they invited back many times to lecture on quality and statistical theory. Meanwhile the United States and Europe ignored him. In 1951 the Japanese created the Deming Prize, an award that symbolized Japanese industry's commitment to Deming's quality ideals. Honda, Nissan, Toyota, Nippondenso, Tanabe Seiyaku and Matsushita all won that prize more than thirty years ago. Consumers around the world flocked to buy high-quality Japaese products, leaving many American and European firms trying to catch up.

TQM recognizes the following premises:

1. *Quality is in the eyes of the customer.* Quality must begin with customer needs and end with customer perceptions. As Motorola's vice-president of quality suggests: 'Quality has to do something for the cus-tomer ... Beauty is in the eye of the beholder. If [a product] does not work the way that the user needs it to work, the defect is as big to the user as if it doesn't work the way the designer planned it. Our definition of a defect is, "if the customer doesn't like it, it's a defect".' Thus the fundamental aim of today's quality movement has now become 'total customer satisfaction'. Quality improvements are meaningful only when perceived by customers. British Telecom's first quality programme launched in the late 1980s became bogged down in its quality processes and bureaucracy. It failed to focus its efforts on customers.

2. *Quality must reflect not just in the company's products, but in every company activity.* 'Quality is a way of life,' declares Jan Timmer, president of Philips Electronics. 'Total quality is not a passing business fad but embedded in the permanent principles of human philosophy', says Louis Schweitzer, président directeur général of Renault.

3. *Quality requires total employee commitment.* Quality comes only from companies whose employees commit to quality and who have the motivation and training to deliver it. Successful companies remove the barriers between departments. Their employees work as a team to carry out core business processes and to create desired outcomes. Employees work to satisfy their internal customers as well as external customers.

4. *Quality requires high-quality partners.* Quality comes only from companies whose value chain partners also deliver quality. Therefore, a quality-driven company must find and align itself with high-quality suppliers and distributors. 'Unless suppliers are in tune with quality demands of their customers they will not be able to meet their demands', says Clive Capp of Howard UK.

5. *A quality programme cannot save a poor product.* The Pontiac Fiero launched a quality programme but because the car didn't have a performance engine to support its performance image, the quality programme did not save the car. A quality drive cannot compensate for product deficiencies.

6. *Quality can always improve.* The best companies believe in the Japanese idea of *kaizen*: 'Continuous improvement of everything by everyone.' The best way to improve quality is to benchmark the compa-

ny's performance against the 'best-of-class' competitors or the best performers in other industries, striving to equal or even surpass them. For example, Alcoa measured the best-of-class competitors and then set a goal of closing the gap by 80 per cent within two years.

**7.** *Quality improvement sometimes requires quantum leaps.* Although the company should strive for continuous quality improvement, it must at times seek a quantum quality improvement. Companies can sometimes obtain small improvements by working harder. But large improvements call for fresh solutions and for working smarter. For example, John Young of Hewlett-Packard did not ask for a 10 per cent reduction in defects, he asked for a tenfold reduction and got it.

**8.** *Quality does not cost more.* Philip Crosby argues that 'quality is free'. Managers once argued that achieving more quality would cost more and slow down production. But improving quality involves learning ways to 'do things right the first time'. Quality is not *inspected* in – it is *designed* in. Doing things right the first time reduces the costs of salvage, repair and redesign, not to mention losses in customer goodwill. Motorola claims that its quality drive has saved $700 million in manufacturing costs during the last five years.

**9.** *Quality is necessary but may not be sufficient.* Improving a company's quality is necessary to meet the needs of more demanding buyers. At the same time, higher quality may not ensure a winning advantage, especially as all competitors increase their quality to approximately the same extent. For example, Singapore Airlines enjoyed a reputation as the world's best airline. However, competing airlines have attracted larger shares of passengers recently by narrowing the perceived gap between their service quality and Singapore's service quality.

**10.** *Quality needs long-term commitment.* It is not a quick fix. A 'blitz approach' can lead to disaster, says John Oakland of Bradford Management Centre. 'You raise employees' expectations but they are invariably not given the means of doing things differently ... People talk the language of quality but the capability of the organisation doesn't live up to the language; it's still using lousy systems and materials'.

In recent years, some European and US firms have struggled to close the quality gap between them and the Japanese. About ten years ago Motorola, Texas Instruments and Harley Davidson took up TQM. Rank Xerox, one of the earliest European adherents, started some years later. Many started their TQM programmes to compete on a global and domestic basis against the Japanese. Europe's acceptance of TQM remains well behind that of the United States and Japan. A survey by the Brussels-based European Foundation for Quality Management (EFQM) found that only 30 per cent of European companies claim to have adopted TQM compared with 55 per cent in the United States and 53 per cent in Asia.

The European Commission worries about this quality shortfall and its failure to reach some European countries, such as Germany, where it has made little impact. 'In Germany where quality has always been established, TQM is not as easily accepted as in many other countries,' says Geert de Raad, EFQM's general secretary. Such complacency is dangerous. An IBM–London Business School study shows that only one in fifty manufacturers in four European countries were world class, although three-quarters believed that they could compete with their best international rivals. Britain had the most 'punch-bags' – weak on both practice and performance – while Finland had no world-class manufacturers at all. Germany had most (2.9 per cent) world-class manufacturers, but also large numbers who wrongly thought they were. Many had not realized that total quality and customer service are no longer a source of sustainable advantage, but merely a qualification for competing.

Sources: Quotes from Lois Therrien, 'Motorola and NEC: going for glory', *Business Week*, special issue on quality (1991), 60–1; and Simon Holberton, 'An idea whose time has not only come but will prevail', *Financial Times* (20 March 1991), 10. See also David A. Garvin, 'Competing on eight dimensions of quality', *Harvard Business Review* (Nov.–Dec. 1987), 109; Robert Jacobson and David A. Aaker, 'The strategic role of product quality', *Journal of Marketing* (October 1987), 31–44; and Frank Rose, 'Now quality means service too', *Fortune* (22 April 1992), 97–108; Frederick Stüdemann, 'Leica develops a sharper focus', *The European* (30 Sep.–6 Oct. 1994), 32; Tom Lloyd, 'How Mr Quality made his mark', *The European* (11–17 February 1994), 20; 'The cracks in quality', *The Economist* (18 April 1992), 85–6; Vanessa Houlder, 'Satisfaction guaranteed' and 'Two steps forward, one step back', *Financial Times* (23 October 1994), 10; Jessica Berry, 'Scathing survey blames inertia for poor manufacturing performance', *The European* (25 Nov.–1 Dec. 1994), 28; Christopher Lorenz, '"World-class" delusion of multinationals', *Financial Times* (2 December 1994), 11; IBM, *Made in Europe* (London: IBM UK, 1994).

Companies need to understand the determinants of *customer value* and *satisfaction*. *Customer delivered value* is the difference between *total customer value* and *total customer cost*. Customers will normally choose the offer that maximizes their delivered value.

Customer satisfaction is the outcome felt by buyers who have experienced a company performance that has fulfilled expectations. Customers are satisfied when their expectations are met and delighted when their expectations are exceeded. Satisfied customers remain loyal longer, buy more, are less price sensitive and talk favourably about the company.

To create customer satisfaction, companies must manage their own *value chains* and the entire *value delivery system* in a customer-centred way. The company's goal is not only to get customers, but, even more importantly, to retain customers. *Customer relationship marketing* provides the key to retaining customers and involves building financial and social benefits as well as structural ties to customers. Companies must decide the level at which they want to build relationships with different market segments and individual customers, from such levels as basic, reactive, accountable and proactive to full partnership. Which is best depends on a customer's lifetime value relative to the costs required to attract and retain that customer.

*Total quality management* has become a leading approach to providing customer satisfaction and company profitability. Companies must understand how their customers perceive quality and how much quality they expect. Companies must then do a better job of meeting consumer quality expectations than their competitors do. Delivering quality requires total management and employee commitment as well as measurement and reward systems. Marketers play an especially critical role in their company's drive towards higher quality.

## ■ DISCUSSING THE ISSUES

1. Describe a situation in which you became a 'lost customer'. Did you drop the purchase because of poor product quality, poor service quality or both? What should the firm do to 'recapture' lost customers?

2. Recall a purchase experience in which the sales assistant or sales representative went beyond the normal effort and 'gave his all' to produce the utmost in quality. What impact did the noticeable effort have on purchase outcome? (Did you buy the product as a result? If it was a frequently purchased product, did you repeatedly buy the product from the same outlet or company?) Give reasons for your answer.

3. Total quality management is an important approach to providing customer satisfaction and company profits. How might total quality be managed for the following product and service offerings: (a) a packaged food product; (b) a restaurant meal; (c) a new car; (d) a family holiday; and (e) a university education?

4. Who should define quality standards: research and development, design, engineering, operations/production, or marketing? Give reasons for your choice.

5. Thinking of a service provided by a not-for-profit organization, propose some meaningful ways to measure quality that could be used in efforts to improve the service.

6. Just-in-time inventory management makes suppliers responsible for delivering parts in exact quantities at precisely the right time. Companies that succeed with JIT find that benefits often go beyond inventory cost savings and that quality improvements come from the process of working very closely with suppliers. Are the ideas of a value chain used in JIT management? Can JIT succeed without using the concepts in the value chain? Explain.

# APPLYING THE CONCEPTS

1. Write a letter of complaint to a firm about one of their products or services. What was the firm's response? Did you receive a refund or replacement product, a response letter or no reply at all? How does the type of response affect your attitude towards the company?

2. Identify a product, service or activist person that has clearly developed a strong relationship with its customers (e.g. BMW cars, a popular politician, Oxfam) . Talk to several customers that strongly identify with one such 'product'. How do they see their relationship to the product? What are the key 'values' they receive? What 'if anything' does the producer do to maintain this relationship?

# REFERENCES

1. Quotes from Valerie Reitman, 'Rubbermaid turns up plenty of profit in the mundane', *Wall Street Journal* (27 March 1992), B4; see also Erik Calonius, 'Smart moves by the quality champs', in *The New American Century*, special issue of *Fortune* (1991), 24–8; Cristy Marshall, 'Rubbermaid: yes, plastic', *Business Month* (December 1988), 38; Maria Mallory, 'Profits on everything but the kitchen sink', *Business Week*, special issue on innovation (1991), 122; William Band, 'Use Baldridge criteria as guide to improving quality', *Marketing News* (1 October 1991), 2, 18; Zachary Schiller, 'At Rubbermaid, little things mean a lot', *Business Week* (11 November 1991); and 'Rubbermaid: breaking all the molds', *Sales & Marketing Management* (August 1992), 42.

2. Paul Cheeseright, 'Simpson aims to accelerate Lucas', *Financial Times* (11 October 1994), 21.

3. For more on measuring customer delivered value, and on 'value/price ratios', see Irwin P. Levin and Richard D. Johnson, 'Estimating price–quality tradeoffs using comparative judgements', *Journal of Consumer Research* (11 June 1984), 593–600.

4. For an interesting discussion of value and value strategies, see Michael Treacy and Fred Wiersema, 'Customer intimacy and other value disciplines', *Harvard Business Review* (Jan.–Feb. 1993), 84–93.

5. For more on the measurement and effect of customer satisfaction see Chow-Hou Wee and Celine Cheong, 'Determinants of consumer satisfaction/dissatisfaction towards dispute settlements in Singapore', *European Journal of Marketing*, **25**, 1 (1991), 6–16; Harald Biong, 'Satisfaction and loyalty to suppliers within the grocery trade', *European Journal of Marketing*, **27**, 7 (1993), 21–38; Fred Selnes, 'An examination of the effect of product performance on brand reputation, satisfaction and loyalty', *European Journal of Marketing*, **27**, 9 (1993), 19–35.

6. Thomas E. Caruso, 'Got a marketing topic? Kotler has an opinion', *Marketing News* (8 June 1992), 21.

7. 'Europe's most respected companies', *Financial Times* (27 June 1994), 8–9.

8. Michael E. Porter, *Competitive Advantage: Creating and sustaining superior performance* (New York: Free Press, 1985).

9. For an analysis of the relative contribution of the product, sales service and after-sales service, see José M. M. Bloemer and Jos G. A. M. Lemmink, 'The importance of customer satisfaction in explaining brand and dealer loyalty', *Journal of Marketing Management*, **8**, 4 (1992), 351–64.

10. See George Stalk, Philip Evans, and Laurence E. Shulman, 'Competing capabilities: the new rules of corporate strategy', *Harvard Business Review* (Mar.–Apr. 1992), 57–69; and Benson P. Shapiro, V. Kasturi Rangan, and John J. Sviokla, 'Staple yourself to an order', *Harvard Business Review* (July–Aug. 1992), 113-22.

11. For more discussion, see Frederick E. Webster, Jr., 'The changing role of marketing in the corporation', *Journal of Marketing* (October 1992), 1–17.

12. Simon Holberton, 'In pursuit of repeat business', *Financial Times* (31 May 1991), 14.

13. Redrick F. Reicheld and W. Earl Sasser, Jr., 'Zero defections: quality comes to service', *Harvard Business Review* (Sept.–Oct. 1990), 301–7.

14. Leonard L. Berry and A. Parasuraman, *Marketing Services: Competing through quality* (New York: Free Press, 1991), 136–42.

15. Aimee L. Stern, 'Courting consumer loyalty with the feel-good bond', *New York Times* (17 January 1993), F10.

16. James H. Donnelly, Jr., Leonard L. Berry, and Thomas W. Thompson, *Marketing Financial Services: A strategic vision* (Homewood, IL: Dow Jones–Irwin, 1985), 113.

17. Richard Lapper, 'JP Morgan offers free use of its toolbox', *Financial Times* (11 October 1994), 27.

18. Thomas E. Caruso, 'Kotler: future marketers will focus on customer data base to compete globally', *Marketing News* (8 June 1992), 21.

19. Michael J. Lanning and Lynn W. Phillips, 'Strategy shifts up a gear', *Marketing* (October 1991), 9.

20. See Thomas M. Petro, 'Profitability: The fifth "P" of marketing', *Bank Marketing* (September 1990), 48–52.

21. Specifically Bob Luchs, 'Quality as a strategic weapon: measuring relative quality, value, and market differentiation', *European Business Journal*, **2**, 4 (1990), 34–47; and generally Robert D. Buzzell and Bradley T. Gale, *The PIMS Principles: Linking strategy to performance* (New York: Free Press, 1987), ch. 6.

22. 'Quality: the US drives to catch up', *Business Week* (November 1982), 66–80: 68. For a recent assessment of progress, see 'Quality programs show shoddy results', *Wall Street Journal* (14 May 1992), B1.

23. See 'The gurus of quality: American companies are heading the quality gospel preached by Deming, Juran, Crosby, and Taguchi', *Traffic Management* (July 1990), 35–9.

24. J. Daniel Beckham, 'Expect the unexpected in health care marketing future', *The Academy Bulletin* (July 1992), 3.

25. Kenneth Kivenko, *Quality Control for Management* (Englewood Cliffs, NJ: Prentice Hall, 1984); see also Kate Bertrand, 'Marketing discovers what "quality" really means', *Business Marketing* (April 1987), 58–72.

## CASE 11

# Feinschmecker Sauce: pricey n' spicy   *Verena M. Priemer*

Uncle Ben's Rice is the market leader in the Austrian market for parboiled rice. According to a survey, 75 per cent of the Austrian households knew the brand, a figure that increased to 95 per cent for the aided recall. Seventy-eight per cent of all households had used the brand at least once, 36 per cent bought it most of the time, and 50 per cent of them claimed that Uncle Ben's was their preferred brand.

Consumers saw Uncle Ben's Rice as having superior quality and taste, easy to prepare, modern, wholesome and nutritious. It was seen as a relatively expensive brand, but consumers thought the brand's outstanding quality made it worth the high price. Uncle Ben's many brand strengths made its owner, Master Foods Austria (MFA), think it was the ideal vehicle for brand extension. However, care was needed. The brand extension must meet the high quality of Uncle Ben's Rice to avoid damaging the reputation of the mother brand.

MFA's first task was to find out from customers the kinds of products that would sell with Uncle Ben's Rice. A survey of consumers' associations was carried out regarding Uncle Ben's, which revealed some potential product fields (see Exhibit 11.1). The general trend towards international eating encouraged MFA to extend Uncle Ben's umbrella to ready-to-serve sauces with exotic tastes. Both Uncle Ben's rice and sauce would be fast and easy to cook, and so could be used together. To enhance its image of high quality and naturalness, the product would contain whole pieces of vegetables. MFA produced Uncle Ben's sauces in 350 gram glass jars rather than in the usual can. Users needed to add about 200 grams of their own meat to the sauce to make a meal. The chosen name, Uncle Ben's Feinschmecker (gourmet) Sauce, focused on the quality and refinement of the product.

The 350 gram jars fitted the needs of two-person households, which were the main target market. These would be typically women between the ages of 20 and 40 years who were interested in food and variety. Being well educated, the target segment would be open-minded towards new and foreign ideas. The target group also had the necessary high income to match the pricey sauce. A selling price of nearly Sch 30* was needed to cover high production costs and import duties.

Feinschmecker Sauces had varieties to suit the tastes of different market segments. For example, adults, who wanted exotic and spicy dishes, were expected to buy flavours such as 'Karibisch', while children would prefer the mild 'Chinesisch', a taste that they already know from restaurant food. The latter variety was viewed as a 'gateway sauce' for consumers who are unused to more exotic dishes. Concept tests showed that people were attracted to the more exotic sauces: 55 per cent of the informants said that they were interested in 'Karibisch', 45 per cent in 'Mexikanisch', 45 per cent in 'Indisch', but only 5 per cent in 'Italienisch'. The range of Feinschmecker Sauces would satisfy a variety of consumers' needs, thus increasing the buying frequency.

* University of Vienna, Austria.

*1 ecu = US$1.26 = Sch13.2 (Austrian schillings).

## CASE 11 *(cont)*

**Exhibit 11.1**  Potential product fields for an expansion of the Uncle Ben's brand

| Associations with Uncle Ben's | → | Potential product fields |
|---|---|---|
| Rice – different kinds of rice | → | rice plus sauce, rice plus vegetables, rice meals, rice pudding |
| Rice – cereals, flour, grain | → | wholesome nutrition |
| Garnishing | → | different garnishings, noodles |
| American | → | fast food, prepared food |
| Helpful, prepared | → | ready-to-serve meals, mixed spices |
| Quality, cooking | → | ready-to-serve meals, frozen food |

The main reasons for purchasing Uncle Ben's Sauces would be quality, comfort, confidence in the product and the attraction of a foreign flavour that would be hard to find elsewhere. Meals would be easy to prepare with the sauces so that even nonexpert cooks could produce exotic food at home. The sauces also gave people the chance to try foreign meals without buying numerous unfamiliar ingredients.

Some opposition was expected from some consumers to using the sauces. Certain people disapproved of ready-to-eat meals or disliked exotic flavours, for instance, while the high price would deter others. The danger of spoiling the meat when adding the sauce would be seen by some as a further obstacle.

In September 1992 MFA launched six varieties of Uncle Ben's Feinschmecker Sauce in Austria and two more varieties were later added (see Exhibit 11.2). Uncle Ben's sauces were launched in other European countries too, but because of the divergent tastes within Europe, the varieties, recipes and the brand name varied from country to country. The advertis-ing concentrated on creating awareness and interest, a task simplified by the strength of the Uncle Ben's brand reputation. It emphasized the link between Uncle Ben's Feinschmecker Sauce and Uncle Ben's Rice, and aimed to transfer the quality image from the rice to the sauce while at the same time strengthening Uncle Ben's position in the saturated rice market. Point-of-sales promotions gave consumers a chance to try the product.

The launch of Uncle Ben's Feinschmecker Sauce was successful. By November 1993, 6 per cent of Austrian households had bought the product once and 7 per cent had bought it more often. The repurchase rate by the GfK panel of households after the first six months of 1993 was 32 per cent. Of the varieties 8 per cent of purchasers had tried 'Mexikanisch Chili', 7 per cent 'Chinesisch süß-sauer', 5 per cent 'Indisch Curry', 3 per cent 'Neapolitanisch raffiniert gewürzt', 2 per cent 'Provenzalisch mit feinen Kräutern', and 1 per cent 'Karibisch exotisch fruchtig'.

**Exhibit 11.2**  Varieties of Uncle Ben's Feinschmecker Sauce

| Variant name | Translation |
|---|---|
| Chinesisch süß-sauer | Chinese sweet and sour |
| Provenzalisch mit feinen Kräutern | Provençal with fine herbs |
| Indisch Curry | Indian curry |
| Karibisch exotisch fruchtig | Caribbean exotic fruity |
| Mexikanisch Chili | Mexican chilli |
| Neapolitanisch raffiniert gewürzt | Neapolitan sophisticated seasoned |
| Chinesisch Szechuan | Chinese Szechuan |
| Stroganoff | Stroganoff |

Sources:  Thanks to Dr Ingrid Kauper-Petschnikar of Master Foods Austria GmbH and research by the Institut für Motivforschung, A+U Gallup-Institut, and Telebus, INTEGRAL.

Purchase frequencies of Uncle Ben's Feinschmecker Sauce varied from group to group. Younger women (up to 34 years old) had bought Feinschmecker Sauce disproportionately often: a survey showed that their share of purchase (33 per cent) was higher than the sample average (20 per cent). Thirty per cent of the buyers came from the highest social class although they accounted for only 14 per cent of the sample. The survey also showed variations in the products consumed. Households with children bought mainly 'Neapolitanisch raffiniert gewürzt' (50 per cent), but seldom the spicy variety 'Mexikanisch Chili' (16 per cent). Higher-income consumers bought spicy 'Karibisch exotisch fruchtig' more often than the more familiar 'Chinesisch süß-sauer' (19 per cent).

The popularity of the sauces contrasted sharply with what the concept test had suggested. The mild 'Chinesisch süß-sauer' was the most popular variety (40 per cent of purchases), 'Mexikanisch Chili' and 'Provenzalisch mit feinen Kräutern' each had only 10 per cent of purchases, while 'Karibisch' – the most popular flavour during the concept tests – was the least popular of the range!

Consumer research showed people mainly bought Feinschmecker Sauce in order to prepare meals quickly and easily, particularly when coming home late in the evening or when short of time. In contrast to ready-to-serve meals, consumers still added their own seasoning to create a meal to their liking – they wanted to remove the trouble of preparing a meal but still wanted the dish served to be essentially their own. Although preprepared, Feinschmecker Sauce appeared wholesome, so consumers had no qualms about enjoying it.

The sauce was convenient to transport and store, and was also easy to open and reclose for later use. Uncle Ben's Feinschmecker Sauce gained the same reputation for high quality, security and modernity as Uncle Ben's Rice. Consumers prepared the sauces in various ways: with or without meat, and with rice or noodles. They perceived the product as special and quite different from other dried and frozen sauces.

## Questions

1. What internal or external stimuli may start the buyer decision process for Uncle Ben's Feinschmecker Sauce? Compare the buyer decision process of an initial purchase and a repeat purchase. What is the type of buying decision behaviour in each case? How does the brand name Uncle Ben's influence the decision?

2. Show the importance of the post-purchase behaviour for Uncle Ben's Feinschmecker Sauce. What figures in the case study indicate consumers' satisfaction with the product? How can MFA influence the level of customer satisfaction achieved? How does MFA's targeting help achieve customer satisfaction?

3. Several stores sell the product below the price of Sch 30. Why should they do that and could it harm Uncle Ben's reputation?

4. What explains the big difference between the concept test results and eventual buyer behaviour? Does the difference in the results matter?

5. How does this brand extension endanger the standing of Uncle Ben's Rice? Was the brand extension worth the risk? Do you agree that Feinschmecker Sauce is a success?

## CHAPTER TWELVE

# Creating competitive advantage

## Competitor analysis and competitive marketing strategies

### CHAPTER OBJECTIVES

After reading this chapter, you should be able to:

■ Explain the importance of developing competitive marketing strategies that position the company against competitors and give it the strongest possible competitive advantage.

■ Identify the steps companies go through in analysing competitors.

■ Discuss the competitive strategies that market leaders use to expand the market and to protect and expand their market shares.

■ Describe the strategies market challengers and followers use to increase their market shares and profits.

■ Discuss how market nichers find and develop profitable corners of the market.

### CHAPTER PREVIEW

#### Federal Express: losing a packet in Europe

Federal Express (FedEx), pioneer of the express-delivery industry as we now know it, has pulled out of the European market with a red face and an even redder balance sheet. Left to fight for Europe's express package deliveries market are Brussels-based DHL, Australian TNT and, new entrant from Connecticut, UPS (United Parcel Service).

Founded in 1973, FedEx got off to a slow start – educating the American public about the value of overnight delivery took time. However, building doggedly on the advertising promise, 'When it absolutely, positively *has* to be there on time', FedEx went on to become one of the fastest start-ups in American history. Central to its success was the company's innovative and now much-copied

'hub-and-spoke' distribution system. This capital-intensive system had vans picking up parcels and delivering them to local airports. That night FedEx's aircraft then flew to the national hub for sorting onto a same-night flight out to their destination and final delivery by van.

1 ecu = US$1.26

By the early 1990s the US express-delivery market was for 3 million packages shipped daily, generating more than $20 million in annual revenues. Despite strong challenges from a glut of imitators in the United States, FedEx remains the undisputed market leader. It has 45 per cent US market share, comfortably ahead of the main challengers UPS at 25 per cent, Airborne at 14 per cent, and the US Postal Service at about 8 per cent.

FedEx did not succeed by being the lowest-priced express-delivery service. Even in the face of cutthroat pricing by competitors, the company has been careful not to let cost cutting undermine its main source of competitive advantage – superior quality. FedEx traditionally has differentiated itself not by luring customers with low prices, but by giving them unbeatable reliability and service. Over the years, it has sunk money and effort into improving service quality. In 1987, it established a formal Quality Improvement Process, which set simple yet lofty quality goals: 100 per cent on-time deliveries, 100 per cent accurate information on every shipment to every location in the world, and 100 per cent customer satisfaction.

At Federal Express, quality goes beyond slogans. In 1980 FedEx became the first service organization to receive the Malcolm Baldridge National Quality Award for outstanding quality leadership. It developed a Service Quality Index (SQI – pronounced 'sky'), made up of twelve things that it knows disappoint customers – how many packages were delivered on the wrong day, how many were late, how many were damaged, how many billing corrections the company had to make, and other such mistakes. It computes the SQI daily and takes it very seriously. 'Quality action teams' study SQI results, looking for trouble spots and ways to eliminate them. Even management bonuses are keyed to achieving SQI goals. Each year, the company invests more than $200 on each of its 86,000 employees for quality initiatives. FedEx believes that top-flight quality is well worth the heavy investment, even if it results in higher prices. In an industry where late delivery can spell disaster, even a 98 per cent success rate isn't good enough. Most customers will gladly pay a little more for the added peace of mind that comes with superior service and unwavering reliability.

In the early 1980s, flush with domestic success, FedEx decided that the time had come to go global. To recreate its phenomenal performance overseas, it began to buy into Europe through a series of small acquisitions including Lex Wilkinson and Littlewoods' Home Delivery Service. It invested heavily to set up a European hub-and-spoke system, and prepared to launch a full frontal assault on Europe. In 1989, to cap its global network it bought the legendary Flying Tigers, the world's largest carrier of heavyweight cargo. With this acquisition, it could move freight of any size. By the early 1990s FedEx had poured $2.5bn into international expansion to become the world's largest express transportation company, with 441 aircraft and 30,000 pick-up and delivery vans serving 173 countries. Its new global goal: to be able to deliver freight anywhere in a global network within just two days.

Despite its high hopes and heavy investment, however, the global effort turned out to be a disaster. FedEx's American success had been followed by others and some of these already competed globally. Whereas FedEx is the clear market leader in the United States, in Europe it was a challenge. To win in Europe, it had to take on a well-entrenched competitor, DHL, the world leader in international express delivery. FedEx's aggressive attack on international markets provoked an equally aggressive defence, not just from DHL, but also from UPS, TNT and other large international rivals. For example, DHL strengthened its international base by forging new relationships with Lufthansa and Japan Airlines. TNT had a joint venture with GD Net, an express delivery network set up by the post offices of Canada, France, Germany, the Netherlands and Sweden. UPS invested heavily to strengthen its global delivery network, expanding coverage to 175 countries. Once all these competitors had set up their expensive networks with high fixed costs, the marketing departments had to compete intensively to get business.

The basis of the courier business is people's willingness to pay more for a fast and reliable service, a basic quality the European competitors found hard to achieve. In July 1991 the business journal, *Management Today*, experimented by sending their magazines by five carriers (DHL, FedEx, Securicor, TNT and UPS) from London to Dusseldorf, Paris and Milan. The times ranged from 16 hours to 49 hours for Paris; from 18 to 46 hours for Dusseldorf and from 19 hours to 10 days for Milan. Also, in each case the slowest delivery was by the most expensive courier. Customs and border controls were part of the problem, a barrier FedEx did not have in the United States. A 1994 experiment by the *Business Age* magazine found that the situation had not improved. Eighteen parcels were sent by different couriers from London to Hong Kong expecting a two-day service. Three parcels arrived in 19 hours but half were late. Once again the cheapest service, DPE, was the fastest and the worst cost almost four times DPE's price. Surprisingly the five couriers with the lowest prices were also the best on booking, collection and delivery.

It is not surprising that Europeans were not enthusiastic users of expensive overnight delivery services. As Martin White, of Coopers & Lybrand explains: 'they realized that they get the same level of reliability as they get on an overnight contract, but at a price 30 to 40 per cent lower.' Experienced users quickly started trading on domestic services but the habit quickly spread to the international market also. The diminished interest in speed took away the aircraft operators' big advantages. FedEx appears to have overestimated the European market for overnight delivery, which reached a maximum of only 100,000 packages daily. Europe's rail network also worked against aircraft: DHL already has a Paris-Brussels train link and plans to increase the triangle to include London. The six-wagon train carries 60 tonnes and costs $11,000 to run, the same as a 12-tonne capacity aircraft.

While the attention of FedEx was on its losing international operations, competitors were busy stealing customers at home. In 1989 US competitor Airborne had its best year in company history, achieving an astounding 171 per cent increase in sales. TNT caused a tumult in the industry when in a surprise move they bought up the world's supply of British Aerospace Quiet Trader 146 aircraft, now known in the industry as the quiet profit-makers. This aircraft could fly at night from any airport denied to the noisier old jets used by FedEx and others. This facility proved to be a boon in environmentally conscious California and Germany, where TNT has its European hub.

Flying Tigers also became an albatross: although international sales doubled in the year after purchase, earnings plummeted – FedEx lost $1.2 billion in four years. FedEx could carry bigger loads than rivals, but they were losing the edge to competitors like UPS who focus on small business-to-business parcels.

In May 1992, FedEx began a decisive retreat from its disastrous European campaign. It closed down operations in more than 100 countries, fired 6,600 employees, and contracted with other companies to handle its deliveries to all but sixteen large European cities – such as London, Paris, and Milan – that it still serves directly. FedEx executives insist that the retreat doesn't mean surrender. The company still leads in the US market, and it has retained a strong base for building more solid international operations. 'Fear of failure must never be a reason not to try something,' said FedEx's chairman and chief executive, Fred Smith. It is an attitude that has cost him dearly.[1]

## GAINING A COMPETITIVE ADVANTAGE

Today, understanding customers is not enough. The 1990s is a decade of intense competition, both foreign and domestic. Many economies are deregulating and encouraging market forces to operate. The EU is removing trade barriers among Western European nations and deregulating many previously protected markets. Multinationals are moving aggressively into the rapidly growing Southeast Asian markets and competing globally. The result is that companies have no choice but to be 'competitive'. They must start paying as much attention to tracking their competitors as to understanding target customers.

Under the marketing concept, companies gain **competitive advantage** by designing offers that satisfy target-consumer needs *better than competitors' offers*. They might deliver more customer value by offering consumers lower prices than competitors for similar products and services or by providing more benefits that justify higher prices. Marketing strategies must consider the strategies of competitors as well as the needs of target consumers. The first step is **competitor analysis**, the process of identifying key competitors; assessing their objectives, strengths and weaknesses, strategies and reaction patterns; and selecting which competitors to attack or avoid. The second step is developing **competitive strategies** that strongly position the company against competitors and that give the company the strongest possible competitive advantage.

## COMPETITOR ANALYSIS

To plan effective competitive marketing strategies, the company needs to find out all it can about its competitors. It must constantly compare its products, prices, channels and promotion with those of close competitors. In this way the company can find areas of potential competitive advantage and disadvantage. It can launch more effective marketing campaigns against its competitors and prepare stronger defences against competitors' actions.

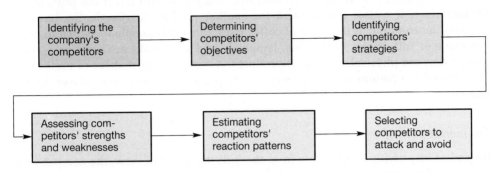

**Figure 12.1**   Steps in analysing competitors.

What do companies need to know about their competitors? They need to know: Who are our competitors? What are their objectives? What are their strategies? What are their strengths and weaknesses? What are their reaction patterns? Figure 12.1 shows the main steps in analysing competitors.

## Identifying the company's competitors

Normally, it would seem a simple task for a company to identify its competitors. Coca-Cola knows that Pepsi is its strongest competitor; and Caterpillar knows that it competes with Komatsu. At the most obvious level, a company can define its competitors as other companies offering a similar product and services to the same customers at similar prices. Thus Volvo might see Saab as a foremost competitor, but not Fiat or Ferrari.

In competing for people's money, however, companies actually face a much wider range of competitors. More broadly, the company can define competitors as all firms making the same product or class of products. Volvo could see itself as competing against all other car manufacturers. Even more broadly, competitors might include all companies making products that supply the same service. Here Volvo would see itself competing against not only other car manufacturers but also against the makers of trucks, motorcycles or even bicycles. Finally and still more broadly, competitors might include all companies that compete for the same consumer's money. Here Volvo would see itself competing with companies that sell major consumer durables, foreign holidays, new homes or extensive home repairs or alterations.

> Companies must avoid 'competitor myopia'. A company is more likely to be 'buried' by its latent competitors than its current ones. For example, Eastman Kodak worries about growing competition for its film business from Fuji, the Japanese film maker. However, Kodak faces a much greater threat from the recent advances in 'filmless camera' technology. These cameras, sold by Canon and Sony, take video still pictures transmitted on a TV set, turned into hard copy and later erased. What greater threat is there to a film business than a filmless camera?[2]

## The industry point of view

Many companies identify their competitors from the *industry* point of view. An **industry** is a group of firms that offer a product or class of products which are close substitutes for each other. We talk about the car industry, the oil industry, the pharmaceutical industry or the beverage industry. In a given industry, if the price of one product rises, it causes the demand for another product to rise. In the beverage industry, for example, if the price of coffee rises, this leads people to switch to tea or lemonade or soft drinks. Coffee, tea, lemonade and soft drinks are substitutes, even though they are physically different products. A company must strive to understand the competitive pattern in its industry if it hopes to be an effective 'player' in that industry.

### The market point of view

Instead of identifying competitors from the industry point of view, the company can take a *market* point of view. Here it defines competitors as companies that are trying to satisfy the same customer need or serve the same customer group. From an industry point of view, Heineken might see its competition as Beck's, Guinness, Carlsberg and other brewers. From a market point of view, however, the customer may really want 'thirst quenching' or 'social drinking'. Iced tea, fruit juice, 'designer' water or many other drinks could satisfy the needs. Similarly, Crayola might define its competitors as other makers of crayons and children's drawing supplies. Alternately, from a market point of view, it would include as competitors all firms making recreational products for the children's market. Generally, the market concept of competition opens the company's eyes to a broader set of actual and potential competitors. This leads to better long-run market planning.

The key to identifying competitors is to link industry and market analysis by mapping out product/market segments. Figure 12.2 shows the product/market segments in the toothpaste market by product types and customer age groups. We see that P&G (with several versions of Crest and Gleam) and Colgate-Palmolive (with Colgate) occupy six of the segments. Lever Brothers (Aim), Beecham (Aqua Fresh) and Topol each occupy two segments. If Topol wanted to enter other segments, it would need to estimate the market size of each segment, the market shares of the current competitors, and their current capabilities, objectives and strategies. Clearly each product/market segment would pose different competitive problems and opportunities.

**Customer segmentation**

|  | Children/teens | Age 19–35 | Age 36+ |
|---|---|---|---|
| Plain toothpaste | Colgate-Palmolive Procter & Gamble | Colgate-Palmolive Procter & Gamble | Colgate-Palmolive Procter & Gamble |
| Toothpaste with fluoride | Colgate-Palmolive Procter & Gamble | Colgate-Palmolive Procter & Gamble | Colgate-Palmolive Procter & Gamble |
| Gel | Colgate-Palmolive Procter & Gamble Lever Bros. | Colgate-Palmolive Procter & Gamble Lever Bros. | Colgate-Palmolive Procter & Gamble Lever Bros. |
| Striped | Beecham | Beecham |  |
| Smoker's toothpaste |  | Topol | Topol |

(Product segmentation)

**Figure 12.2**  Product/market segments for toothpaste. (Source: William A. Cohen, *Winning on the Marketing Front* (New York: Wiley, 1986), 63.)

## Determining competitors' objectives

Having identified the main competitors, marketing management now asks: What does each competitor seek in the marketplace? What drives each competitor's behaviour?

The marketer might at first assume that all competitors will want to maximize their profits and choose their actions accordingly. However, companies differ in the emphasis they put on short-term versus long-term profits and some competitors are oriented towards 'satisfying' rather than 'maximizing' profits. They have profit goals that satisfy them, even if the strategies could produce more profits.

Marketers must look beyond competitors' profit goals. Each competitor has a mix of objectives, each with differing importance. The company wants to know the relative importance that competitors place on current profitability, market share growth, cash flow, technological leadership, service leadership and other goals. Knowing a competitor's objectives reveals if it is satisfied with its current situation and how it might react to competitive actions. For example, a company that pursues low-cost leadership will react much more strongly to a competitor's cost-reducing manufacturing breakthrough than to the same competitor's advertising increase. A company must also monitor its competitors' objectives for attacking various product/market segments. If the company finds that a competitor has discovered a new segment, this might be an opportunity. If it finds that competitors plan new moves into segments now served by the company, it will be forewarned and, hopefully, forearmed.

## Identifying competitors' strategies

The more that one firm's strategy resembles another firm's strategy, the more the firms compete. In most industries, the competitors sort into groups that pursue different strategies. A **strategic group** is a group of firms in an industry following the same or a similar strategy in a given target market. For example, in the major appliance industry, Electrolux, Hotpoint and Zanussi all belong to the same strategic group. Each produces a full line of medium-price appliances supported by good service. Quality-oriented Bosch and stylish Alessi, on the other hand, belong to a different strategic group. They both produce a narrow line of appliances and charge a premium price.

Some important insights emerge from strategic group identification. For example, if a company enters one of the groups, the members of that group become its key competitors. Thus, if the company enters the first group against Electrolux, Hotpoint and Zanussi, it can succeed only if it develops some strategic advantages over these large competitors.

Although competition is most intense within a strategic group, there is also rivalry among groups. First, some of the strategic groups may appeal to overlapping customer segments. For example, no matter what their strategy, all major appliance manufacturers will go after the apartment and home builders segment. Second, the customers may not see much difference in the offers of different groups – they may see little difference in quality between Electrolux and Bosch. Finally, members of one strategic group might expand into new strategy segments as Hotpoint have done by extending their washing machine range to approach Bosch's prices.

The company needs to look at all the dimensions that identify strategic groups within the industry. It needs to know each competitor's product quality, features and mix; customer services; pricing policy; distribution coverage; salesforce strategy; and advertising and sales promotion programmes. It must study the details of each competitor's R&D, manufacturing, buying, financial and other strategies.

## Assessing competitors' strengths and weaknesses

Can a company's competitors carry out their strategies and reach their goals? This depends on each competitor's resources and capabilities. Marketers need to accurately identify each competitor's strengths and weaknesses.

As a first step, a company gathers key data on each competitor's business over the last few years. It wants to know about competitors' goals, strategies and performance. Admittedly, some of this information will be hard to collect. For example, industrial goods companies find it hard to estimate competitors' market shares because they do not have the same syndicated data services that are available to consumer packaged goods companies. Still, any information they can find will help them form a better estimate of each competitor's strengths and weaknesses.

Companies normally learn about their competitors' strengths and weaknesses through secondary data, personal experience and hearsay. They can also increase their knowledge by conducting primary marketing research with customers, suppliers and dealers. Recently, a growing number of companies have turned to **benchmarking**, comparing the company's products and processes to those of competitors or leading firms in other industries to find ways of improving quality and performance. Benchmarking has become a powerful tool for increasing a company's competitiveness (see Marketing Highlight 12.1).

In searching for competitors' weaknesses, the company should try to identify any assumptions they make about their business and the market that are no longer valid. Some companies believe they produce the best quality in the industry when this is no longer true. Many companies are victims of rules of thumb such as 'customers prefer full line companies', 'the salesforce is the only important marketing tool', or 'customers value service more than price'. If a competitor is operating on a significant wrong assumption, the company can take advantage of it.

## Estimating competitors' reaction patterns

A competitor's objectives, strategies and strengths and weaknesses explain its likely actions, and its reactions to moves such as a price cut, a promotion increase or a new product introduction. In addition, each competitor has a certain philosophy of doing business, a certain internal culture and guiding beliefs. Marketing managers need a deep understanding of a given competitor's mentality if they want to anticipate how that competitor will act or react.

Each competitor reacts differently. Some do not react quickly or strongly to a competitor's move: they may feel that their customers are loyal, they may be slow in noticing the move; they may lack the funds to react. Some competitors react only to certain types of assaults and not to others. They might always respond strongly to price cuts in order to signal that these will never succeed. But they might not respond at all to advertising increases, believing these to be less threatening. Other competitors react swiftly and strongly to any assault. As Unilever have found with their Persil/Omo Power, P&G does not let a new detergent come easily into the market. Many firms avoid direct competition with P&G and look for easier prey, knowing that P&G will fight fiercely if challenged. Finally, some competitors show no predictable reaction pattern. They might or might not react on a given occasion and there is no way to foresee what they will do based on their economics, history or anything else.

In some industries, competitors live in relative harmony; in others, they fight constantly. Knowing how key competitors react gives the company clues on how best to attack competitors or how best to defend the company's current positions.[3]

## Selecting competitors to attack and avoid

Management has already largely determined its main competitors through prior decisions on customer targets, distribution channels and marketing-mix strategy. These decisions define the strategic group to which the company belongs. Management must now decide which competitors to compete against most vigorously. The company can focus its attack on one of several classes of competitors.

### Strong or weak competitors

Most companies prefer to aim their shots at their weak competitors. This requires fewer resources and time. Conversely, the firm may gain little. Alternatively, the firm should also compete with strong competitors to sharpen its abilities. Furthermore, even strong competitors have some weaknesses and succeeding against them often provides greater returns.

A useful tool for assessing competitor strengths and weaknesses is **customer value analysis**, asking customers what benefits they value and how they rate the company versus competitors on important attributes (see Marketing Highlight 12.2). Customer value analysis also points out areas in which the company is vulnerable to competitors' actions.

### Close or distant competitors

Most companies will compete with those competitors who resemble them the most. Thus, Citroën/Peugeot competes more against Renault than against Porsche. At the same time, the company may want to avoid trying to 'destroy' a close competitor. Here is an example of a questionable 'victory':

> Bausch & Lomb in the late 1970s moved aggressively against other soft lens manufacturers with great success. However, this led one after another competitor to sell out to larger firms such as Revlon, Schering-Plough and Johnson & Johnson. The result was that Bausch & Lomb faced much larger competitors – and it suffered the consequences. For example, Johnson & Johnson acquired Vistakon, a small nicher that served the tiny portion of the contact-lens market for people with astigmatism. Backed by J&J's deep pockets, however, Vistakon proved a formidable opponent. When the small but nimble Vistakon unit introduced its innovative Acuvue disposable lenses, the much larger Bausch & Lomb had to take some of its own medicine. According to one analyst, 'The speed of the [Acuvue] roll-out and the novelty of [J&J's] big-budget ads left giant Bausch & Lomb ... seeing stars.' By 1992, J&J's Vistakon was No 1 in the fast-growing disposable contact-lens market.[4]

In this case, the company's success in hurting a close rival brought in tougher competitors.

### 'Well-behaved' or 'disruptive' competitors

A company really needs and benefits from competitors. The existence of competitors results in several strategic benefits. Competitors may help increase total demand.

## How benchmarking helps improve competitive performance

In most industries, one or more companies are known to outperform their competitors. According to McKinsey, the management consultants, industry leaders typically develop products two-and-a-half times faster than the industry average. Anderson Consulting consistently found 2:1 differences in productivity between world-class plants and the remainder. The quality gaps they found ranged from 9:1 to a staggering 170:1. Richard Buetow, Motorola's director of quality, sees even bigger differences: 'Best-in-class companies', he says, 'have error rates 500 to 1,000 times lower than average.' Benchmarking is the art of finding out how and why some companies perform tasks much better than others. 'If you're gonna succeed, you've gotta steal shamelessly,' says John Milliken, president of Milliken & Co., one of the most profitable US textile manufacturers.

A benchmarking company aims to imitate, or better still, to improve upon, the best practices of other companies. The Japanese used benchmarking persistently after World War II, copying many American products and practices. In 1979, Xerox undertook one of the first Western benchmarking projects. Xerox wanted to learn how Japanese competitors were able to produce more reliable copiers and charge prices below Xerox's production costs. They started with their Japanese subsidiary Fuji Xerox where they found that Canon could sell a photocopier for less than Xerox could make one in the United States. By buying Japanese copiers and analysing them through 'reverse engineering', Xerox learned how to greatly improve its own copiers' reliability and costs. However, Xerox did not stop there. It went on to ask additional questions: Are Xerox scientists and engineers among the best in their respective specialities? Are Xerox marketing and sales people and practices among the best in the world? To answer these questions, the company had to identify world-class, 'best practices' companies and learn from them. Although benchmarking initially focused on studying other companies' products and services, it later expanded to include benchmarking work processes, staff functions, organizational performance and the entire customer value delivery process.

Another early benchmarking pioneer was Ford. Ford was losing sales to Japanese and European car makers. Don Peterson, then chairman of Ford, instructed his engineers and designers to build a new car that combined the 400 features that Ford customers said were the most important. If Saab made the best seats, then Ford should copy Saab's seats. If Toyota had the best fuel gauge and BMW had the best tyre and jack storage system, then Ford should copy these features also. Peterson went further: he asked the engineers to 'better the best' where possible. When finished, Peterson claimed that the highly successful new car (the Taurus) had improved upon, not just copied, the best features found in competing cars.

In another benchmarking project, Ford discovered that it employed 500 people to manage its accounts payable operation, whereas its partly owned Japanese partner, Mazda, handled the same task with only 10 people. After studying Mazda's system, Ford installed an 'invoiceless system' and reduced its staff to 200.

Ind Coope Retail and Woolworth use statistical models to benchmark the performance of their outlets. This allows them to compare the performance of pubs and shops even though they operate in different environments. Benchmarking has also meant them finding other companies with similar systems in use. 'We've learnt an awful lot,' commented Nick Lighton, marketing and development director of Ind Coope Retail.

Today many companies, such as AT&T, Du Pont, Elida Gibbs, Ind Coope, Intel, InterCity, Lucas, Marriott and Motorola, use benchmarking as a standard tool. Some companies benchmark the best companies in their industry. For instance, ICL, a British computer company now owned by Japan's Fujitsu, benchmarks Sun Microsystems for manufacturing. However, when ICL wanted to benchmark distribution systems, it chose retailer Marks & Spencer as the best benchmark. In this sense, benchmarking goes beyond standard 'competitive analysis'. Benchmark against the 'best practices' in the world, not just against direct competitors. Motorola, for example, starts each benchmarking project with a search for 'best of breed' in the world. According to one of its executives, 'The further away from our industry we reach for comparisons, the happier we are. We are seeking competitive superiority, after all, not just competitive parity.'

Benchmarking involves seven steps: (1) determine which functions to benchmark; (2) identify the key performance variables to measure; (3) identify the best-in-class companies; (4) measure performance of best-in-class companies; (5) measure the company's performance; (6) specify programmes and actions to close the gap; and (7) implement and monitor results.

Once a company commits to benchmarking, it may try to benchmark every activity. It may set up a benchmarking department to promote the practice and to teach benchmarking techniques to departmental people. Yet benchmarking takes time and costs money. Companies should focus their benchmarking efforts only on critical tasks that deeply affect customer satisfaction and company costs and for which substantially better performance is known to exist.

How can a company identify 'best-practice' companies? As a good starting point, it can ask customers, suppliers and distributors who they rate as doing the best job. Alternatively, it can contact big consulting firms that have built large files of 'best practices'. An important point is that benchmarkers need to resort to industrial espionage. Japan's Canon and Britain's Lucas Industries encourage reciprocal visits from companies they use as benchmarks. Motorola and General Electric gain access to firms by sharing what they learn with firms they use as benchmarks. 'Industrial dating agencies', such as the Benchmarking Centre and the International Benchmarking Clearing House (IBC), now exist to help firms find partners.

After identifying the 'best practice' companies, the company needs to measure their performance regarding cost, time and quality. For example, a company studying its supply management process found that its buying cost was four times higher, its supplier selection time four times longer, and its delivery time sixteen times worse than world-class competitors.

Some critics suggest that companies must be careful not to rely *too* much on benchmarking. They warn that, because benchmarking takes other companies' performance as a starting point, it might hamper real creativity. It might lead to an only marginally better product or practice when other companies are leapfrogging ahead. Too often, benchmarking studies take many months, so by the time they are completed, better practices may have emerged elsewhere. Benchmarking might cause the company to focus too much on competitors while losing touch with consumers' changing needs. Finally, benchmarking might distract from making further improvements in the company's core competencies.

When Roberto Schisano left Texas Instruments to join Alitalia he found another way in which benchmarking can go wrong. Our previous benchmarks were the so-so bunch,' he said, 'the other European state airlines, not those seeking to be market leaders like British Airways or Southwest in the US. And when one mentioned losses, the reply was, "Oh, we're not as bad as Air France".'

Nevertheless, a company must do more than simply look inside when trying continuously to improve its performance. To gain competitive advantage, it must compare its products and processes to those of its competitors and leading companies in other industries. Thus benchmarking remains one of the most powerful tools for improving quality and competitive performance.

Sources: Robert C. Camp, *Benchmarking: The search for industry-best practices that lead to superior performance* (White Plains, NY: Quality Resources, 1989); A. Steven Walleck, David O'Halloran and Charles Leader, 'Benchmarking world class performance', *McKinsey Quarterly*, 1 (1990), 3–24; 'First find your bench', *The Economist* (11 May 1991), 102; Robert Osterhoff, William Locander and Gregory Bounds, *Competitive Benchmarking at Xerox* (London: Quorum Books, 1991); Michael J. Spendolini, *The Benchmarking Book* (New York: AMACOM, 1992); Jeremy Main, 'How to steal the best ideas around', *Fortune* (19 October 1992); Betsy Weisendanger, 'Benchmarking for beginners', *Sales & Marketing Management* (November 1992), 59–64; Robert Graham, 'Alitalia tries to fly higher', *Financial Times* (1 August 1994), 12; John Griffin, 'Streets ahead', *Financial Times* (4 November 1994), 11; David Reed, 'Setting a new benchmark', *Marketing Week* (4 November 1994), 55–8.

## Customer value analysis: the key to competitive advantage

In analysing competitors and searching for competitive advantage, one of the most important marketing tools is *customer value analysis*. The aim of a customer value analysis is to determine the benefits that target customers value and how they rate the relative value of various competitors' offers. The main steps in customer value analysis are as follows:

1. *Identify the chief attributes that customers value.* Various people in the company may have different ideas on what customers value. Thus the company's marketing researchers must ask customers themselves what features and performance levels they look for in choosing a product or seller. Different customers will mention different features and benefits. If the list gets too long, the researcher can remove overlapping attributes.

2. *Assess the importance of different attributes.* Ask customers to rate or rank the importance of the different factors. If the customers differ very much in their ratings, group them into different customer segments.

3. *Assess the company's and the competitors' performance on different customer values against the values' rated importance.* Next ask customers where they rate each competitor's performance on each attribute. Ideally, the company's performance will be high on the attributes the customers value most and low on the attributes which customers value least. Two pieces of bad news would be: (a) the company's performance ranks high on some

minor attributes – a case of 'overkill'; and (b) the company's performance ranks low on some important attributes – a case of 'under-kill'. The company must also look at how competitors rate on the important attributes.

4. *Examine how customers in a specific segment rate the company's performance against a specific large competitor on an attribute-by-attribute basis.* The key to gaining competitive advantage is to take each customer segment and examine how the company's offer compares with that of its main competitor. If the company's offer exceeds the competitor's offer on all important attributes, the company can charge a higher price and earn higher profits or it can charge the same price and gain more market share. If the company is performing at a lower level than its main competitor on some important attributes, it must invest in strengthening those attributes or finding other important attributes where it can build a lead on the competitor.

5. *Monitor customer values over time.* Although customer values are fairly stable in the short run, they will probably change as competing technologies and features appear and as customers face different economic climates. A company that assumes that customer values will remain stable flirts with danger. The company must review customer values and competitors' standing periodically if it wants to remain strategically effective.

---

They share the costs of market and product development and help to legitimize new technology. They may serve less attractive segments or lead to more product differentiation. Finally, they may improve bargaining power against labour or regulators.

However, a company may not view all of its competitors as beneficial. An industry often contains 'well-behaved' competitors and 'disruptive' competitors.[5] Well-behaved competitors play by the rules of the industry. They favour a stable and healthy industry, set prices in a reasonable relation to costs, motivate others to lower costs or improve differentiation, and accept a reasonable level of market share and profits. Disruptive competitors, on the other hand, break the rules. They try to buy share rather than earn it, take large risks, invest in overcapacity and generally shake up the industry. For example, British Airways finds KLM and United to be well-behaved competitors because they play by the rules and attempt to set their fares sensibly. Conversely, BA finds Air France and Olympic disruptive competitors because they destabilize the airline industry through their overextended networks and dependence on state handouts. A company might be smart to support well-behaved competitors, aiming its attacks at disruptive competitors, as, for instance, in the attempt by several airlines, spearheaded by BA, KLM and SAS, to block the European Commission's approval of a FFr20 billion package of state aid for Air France.[6]

1 ecu = US$1.26
= FFr 6.47
(French francs)

The implication is that 'well-behaved' companies should try to shape an industry that consists only of well-behaved competitors. Through careful licensing, selective retaliation and coalitions, they can shape the industry, making competitors behave rationally and harmoniously, follow the rules, try to earn share rather than buy it, and differentiate somewhat to compete less directly.

## Designing the competitive intelligence system

We have described the main types of information that company decision makers need to know about their competitors. This information needs collecting, interpreting, distributing and using. Although the cost in money and time of gathering competitive intelligence is high, the cost of not gathering it is higher. Yet the company must design its competitive intelligence system in a cost-effective way.

The competitive intelligence system first identifies the vital types of competitive information and the best sources of this information. Then the system continuously collects information from the field (salesforce, channels, suppliers, market research firms, trade associations) and from published data (government publications, speeches, articles). Next the system checks the information for validity and reliability, interprets it and organizes it in an appropriate way. Finally, it sends key information to relevant decision makers and responds to enquiries from managers about competitors.

With this system, company managers will receive timely information about competitors in the form of phone calls, bulletins, newsletters and reports. In addition, managers can contact the system when they need an interpretation of a competitor's sudden move, or when they require to know a competitor's weaknesses and strengths or how a competitor will respond to a planned company move.

Smaller companies that cannot afford to set up a formal competitive intelligence office can assign specific executives to watch specific competitors. Thus a manager who used to work for a competitor might follow closely all developments connected with that competitor; he or she would be the 'in-house' expert on that competitor. Any manager needing to know the thinking of a given competitor could contact the assigned in-house expert.[7]

## COMPETITIVE STRATEGIES

Having identified and evaluated the main competitors, the company must now design competitive marketing strategies that best position its offer against competitors' offerings.[8] What broad marketing strategies can the company use? Which ones are best for a particular company or for the company's different divisions and products?

No one strategy is best for all companies. Each company must determine what makes the most sense, given its position in the industry and its objectives, opportunities and resources. Even within a company, different businesses or products need different strategies. Johnson & Johnson uses one marketing strategy for its leading brands in stable consumer markets and a different marketing strategy for its new high-tech healthcare businesses and products. Recognizing the difference in the way its business had to be treated, the ICI chemicals company spun off its biosciences activities as a separately quoted company, Zeneca.[9] We now look at broad competitive marketing strategies companies can use.

## Competitive positions

Firms competing in a given target market will, at any moment, differ in their objectives and resources. Some firms will be large, others small. Some will have great resources; others will be strapped for funds. Some will be old and established, others new and fresh. Some will strive for rapid market share growth, others for long-term profits. And the firms will occupy different competitive positions in the target market.

Michael Porter suggests four basic competitive positioning strategies that companies can follow – three winning strategies and one losing one.[10] The three winning strategies are:

1. *Overall cost leadership.* Here the company works hard to achieve the lowest costs of production and distribution so that it can price lower than its competitors and win a large market share. Texas Instruments and Amstrad are leading practitioners of this strategy. In the steel industry big is not beautiful any more; small mini-

Boddington's single-mindedly focus on the product's attribute, smoothness – as evidenced by the creamy head – to differentiate itself.

BODDINGTONS. THE CREAM OF MANCHESTER.
Boddingtons Draught Bitter. Brewed at the Strangeways Brewery since 1778.

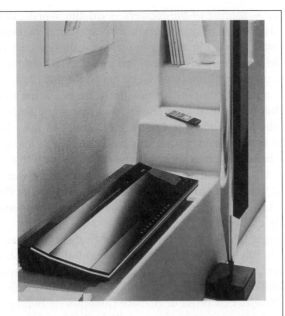

The magic of
Bang & Olufsen
is not magic.
It's logic.

The design is, of course, what sets Bang & Olufsen apart from other manufacturers. But the significant difference is the quality of what is inside; intelligent technology and well thought-out concepts.

Take Beocenter 9300 for example. It has a built-in CD player, cassette recorder, radio and amplifier. Furthermore it is filled with electronic intelligence that allows it to run a BeoLink system. This means you can connect other Bang & Olufsen equipment to the system and deliver the music wherever you want it. To the TV in your bedroom, to your extra speakers in the kitchen, or in the bathroom.

Beocenter 9300 is based on the idea that you want to have the sound where you are, not where the equipment is placed. Sounds logical, doesn't it.

BEOCENTER 9300 FROM **Bang & Olufsen**

Bang & Olufsen consumer products' distinctive design make them instantly recognizable and differentiate them from other makes.

mills, including Nucor and Chaparral Steel, who use electric furnaces to convert scrap metal, are undercutting the large integrated suppliers.

2. *Differentiation.* Here the company concentrates on creating a highly differentiated product line and marketing programme so that it comes across as the class leader in the industry. Most customers would prefer to own this brand if its price is not too high. Bose and Glaxo follow this strategy in ultrasmall speakers and ethical drugs, respectively.

3. *Focus.* Here the company focuses its effort on serving a few market segments well rather than going after the whole market. Many firms in northern Italy excel at this. Among them are Luxottica, the world's leading maker of spectacle frames, pasta makers Barilla and many dynamic small firms in the Prato textile industry. In 1993 Novo Nordisk was Denmark's twelfth largest company by turnover but made more profits than any other by focusing on Insulin and industrial enzymes. It is a research-led company that 'continues to take market share away from its competitors on the back of sophisticated delivery systems.'[11]

Companies that pursue a clear strategy – one of the above – are likely to perform well. The firm that carries out that strategy best will make the most profits. Firms that do not pursue ·a clear strategy – *middle-of-the-roaders* – do the worst. VW, Olivetti, Philips and International Harvester all came upon difficult times because they did not stand out as the lowest in cost, highest in perceived value or best in serving some market segment. Middle-of-the-roaders try to be good on all strategic counts, but end up being not very good at anything (see Marketing Highlight 12.3).

We will adopt a different classification of competitive positions, based on the role firms play in the target market – that of leading, challenging, following or niching. Suppose that an industry contains the firms shown in Figure 12.3. Some 40 per cent of the market is in the hands of the **market leader**, the firm with the largest market share. Another 30 per cent is in the hands of a **market challenger**, a runner-up that is fighting hard to increase its market share. Another 20 per cent is in the hands of a **market follower**, another runner-up that wants to hold its share without rocking the boat. The remaining 10 per cent is in the hands of **market nichers**, firms that serve small segments not being pursued by other firms.

We now look at specific marketing strategies that are available to market leaders, challengers, followers and nichers. In the sections that follow, you should remember that the classifications of competitive positions often do not apply to a whole company, but only to its position in a specific industry. For example, large and diversified companies such as P&G, Unilever, Nestlé, Procordia or Société Générale de Belgique – or their individual businesses, divisions or products – might be leaders in some markets and nichers in others. For example, Procter & Gamble leads in dishwashing and laundry detergents, disposable nappies and shampoo, but it is a challenger to Unilever in hand soaps. Companies' competitive strengths also vary geographically. Buying Alpo from Grand Metropolitan in 1994 made Nestlé the challenger in the US petfoods market behind Ralston Purina's 18 per cent share. However, in the submarket for US canned cat food Nestlé has a commanding 39 per cent share. By contrast, in the fragmented European petfoods market Nestlé Friskies languishes in fourth place behind Mars' Pedigree (47 per cent), Dalgety and Quaker. However, even with that low base, Nestlé's Go Cat is Europe's top-selling dry cat food.[12]

## Market-leader strategies

Most industries contain an acknowledged market leader. The leader has the largest market share and usually leads the other firms in price changes, new product introductions, distribution coverage and promotion spending. The leader may or may not be admired, but other firms concede its dominance. The leader is a focal point for competitors, a company to challenge, imitate or avoid. Some of the best-known market leaders are Boeing (airliners), Nestlé (food), Microsoft (software), L'Oréal (cosmetics), Royal Dutch/Shell (oil), McDonald's (fast food) and De Beer (diamonds).

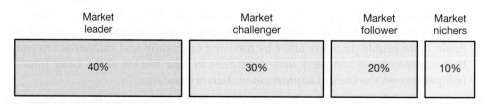

| Market leader | Market challenger | Market follower | Market nichers |
|---|---|---|---|
| 40% | 30% | 20% | 10% |

**Figure 12.3**  Hypothetical market structure.

The London International Group defend their leading position focusing on the growth markets they dominate.

A leading firm's life is not easy. It must maintain a constant watch. Other firms keep challenging its strengths or trying to take advantage of its weaknesses. The market leader can easily miss a turn in the market and plunge into second or third place. A product innovation may come along and hurt the leader – as when Tylenol's nonaspirin painkiller took the lead from Bayer Aspirin or when P&G's Tide, the first synthetic laundry detergent, beat Unilever's leading brands. Sometimes leading firms grow fat and slow, losing out against new and more energetic rivals – Xerox's share of the world copier market fell from over 80 per cent to less than 35 per cent in just five years when Fuji and Canon challenged them with cheaper and more reliable copiers.

Leading firms want to remain number one. This calls for action on three fronts. First, the firm must find ways to expand total demand. Second, the firm must protect its current market share through good defensive and offensive actions. Third, the firm can try to expand its market share further, even if market size remains constant.

## Expanding the total market

The leading firm normally gains the most when the total market expands. If people take more pictures, then as the market leader, Kodak stands to gain the most. If Kodak can persuade more people to take pictures or to take pictures on more occasions or to take more pictures on each occasion, it will benefit greatly. Generally, the market leader should look for new users, new uses and more usage of its products.

*New users* Every product class can attract buyers who are still unaware of the product or who are resisting it because of its price or its lack of certain features. A

## Competitive strategy: don't play in the middle of the road

Being mainstream used to be a blessing for products. Now it is becoming a curse. Today, companies in most industries face slow-growing and fiercely competitive markets. Solid middle-of-the-road names like Olivetti, VW or Holiday Inn are struggling against a lot of new competitors that strike from both above and below. Encircled by rivals offering either more luxurious goods or plain cheaper ones, companies with products in the middle are finding their market shares dwindling. They are striving to break away from the image of being 'just average'. 'Getting stuck in the middle is a terrible fate,' notes one advertising agency executive. '[You remain] a mass brand as the market splinters.'

Examples abound of products and services caught in the middle – adequate but not exciting – losing ground to more clearly positioned competitors at both the high and low ends. For example, swanky stores such as Timberland and budget outlets such as Aldi are prospering, while bread-and-butter Argyll stores flounder. Häagen-Dazs, Ben & Jerry's and other 'super-premium' ice creams are thriving – as are grocers' own bargain labels – while middle brands

such as Crosse & Blackwell are struggling. Travellers want either economy lodging at chains such as Travel Lodge or to sleep in the lap of luxury, leaving adequate but neither inexpensive nor plush hoteliers such as Novotel or Holiday Inn in the lurch. Thus brands in the 'murky middle' are facing increasing pressure from competitors at both ends of the spectrum. Notes the advertising executive: 'There's no future for products everyone likes a little.'

If a brand in the middle cannot sell on prestige, it has to compete on value. To make Sealtest stand out against own-brand ice creams, Kraft borrowed tactics from fancier brands. It recently added a layer of cellophane inside the carton. It also made the package's graphics cleaner and more modern. The idea is to keep the price about in the middle but to come across as better value. Still, the product remains in that not-cheap, not-expensive limbo – a very tough sell.

An average image also haunts Sears in the United States, which has seen its middle-income customer defect either to discount outlets or to trendier speciality stores. It is scrambling to revitalize sales by

seller can usually find new users in many places. For example, L'Oréal might find new fragrance users in its current markets by convincing women who do not use expensive fragrance to try it. Or it might find users in new demographic segments: for instance, men's fragrances are currently a small but fast growing market. Or it might expand into new geographic segments, perhaps by selling its fragrances to the new wealthy in Eastern Europe or Southeast Asia.

Johnson's Baby Shampoo provides a classic example of developing new users. When the baby boom had passed and the birth rate slowed down, the company grew concerned about future sales growth. J&J's marketers noticed that other family members sometimes used the baby shampoo for their own hair. Management developed an advertising campaign aimed at adults. In a short time, Johnson's Baby Shampoo became a leading brand in the total shampoo market.

*New uses*    The marketer can expand markets by discovering and promoting new uses for the product. DuPont's nylon is an example of new-use expansion. Every time nylon became a mature product, some new use appeared. Nylon was first used as a fibre for parachutes; then for women's stockings; later as a leading material in shirts and blouses; and still later in vehicle tyres, upholstery and carpeting. Another example of new-use expansion is Arm & Hammer baking soda. Its sales had flattened after 125 years. Then the company discovered that consumers were using baking soda as a

stocking more national brands and running slicker, more stylish ads to project an image that's a step up from plain vanilla. Sears claims that this image-building programme has been successful, but consumer perceptions die hard. Sears has yet to establish a clear and distinctive position. As one image consultant suggests: 'Sears doesn't stand for anything consumers aspire to.'

For some, it finally gets to the point where the middle market just is not worth it. Marriott tried to string its Bob's Big Boy, Allie's and Wag's coffee shops into a single chain of casual restaurants. It was a vague niche that few consumers wanted. The restaurants were not as cheap or as appealing to children as fast food nor could they please adults with an attractive dining-out atmosphere. Marriott ended up quitting the restaurant business. 'We were sandwiched in the middle,' a Marriott spokesman says.

In the hotel industry, where chains have spread rapidly, companies are trying to escape the middle by extending their reach to cover people needing smaller units or wanting higher-priced ones. Holiday Inn, which no longer has the casual family traveller all to itself, has added a more up-market Holiday Inns Crown Plaza.

Thus, to win in the marketplace, a company must gain competitive advantage by offering something that competitors do not. It might offer consumers the best price for a given level of quality or offer a differentiated product – one with unique features or higher quality for which consumers are willing to pay a higher price. It might focus on serving the special needs of a specific market segment. Sadly, companies in the middle usually end up not being very good at anything. Some big losers finally have to seek protection from creditors in the bankruptcy courts. That happened to Germany's Klöckner-Werke, a high-cost, undersized steel and engineering group. The moral? Do not play in the murky middle of the road.

Sources: 'Is there room for Volkswagen?', *The Economist* (28 August 1993), 55; *The Financial Times – FT500* (10 February 1993), and portions adapted from Kathleen Deveny, 'Middle-price brands come under siege', *Wall Street Journal* (2 April 1990), B1, B7.

refrigerator deodorizer. It launched a heavy advertising and publicity campaign focusing on this use and persuaded consumers to place an open box of baking soda in their refrigerators and to replace it every few months.

*More usage*  A third market expansion strategy is to persuade people to use the product more often or to use more per occasion. Campbell encourages people to consume more of its soup by running ads using it as an ingredient in recipes in women's magazines. P&G advises users that its Head & Shoulders shampoo is more effective with two applications instead of one per hair wash.

The Michelin Tyre Company found a creative way to increase usage per occasion. It wanted French car owners to drive more miles per year, resulting in more tyre replacement. Michelin began rating French restaurants on a three-star system and publishing them in its Red Guides. It reported that many of the best restaurants were in the South of France, leading many Parisians to take weekend drives south. Michelin also publishes its Green Guide containing maps and graded sights to encourage additional travel.

### Protecting market share

While trying to expand total market size, the leading firm must also constantly protect its current business against competitor attacks. Shell must constantly guard against BP, Exxon and Elf Aquitane; Gillette against Bic; Kodak against Fuji; Boeing against Airbus; Nestlé against BSN.

What can the market leader do to protect its position? First, it must prevent or fix weaknesses that provide opportunities for competitors. It needs to keep its costs down and its prices in line with the value the customers see in the brand. The leader should 'plug holes' so that competitors do not jump in. The best defence is a good offence and the best response is *continuous innovation*. The leader refuses to be content with the way things are and leads the industry in new products, customer services, distribution effectiveness and cost cutting. It keeps increasing its competitive effectiveness and value to customers. It takes the offensive, sets the pace and exploits competitors' weaknesses.

Increased competition in recent years has sparked management's interest in models of military warfare. Leader companies can protect their market positions with competitive strategies patterned after successful military defence strategies. Figure 12.4 shows six defence strategies that a market leader can use.[13]

*Position defence*    The most basic defence is a position defence in which a company builds fortifications around its current position. Simply defending one's current position or products rarely works. Henry Ford tried it with his Model T and brought an enviably healthy Ford Motor Company to the brink of financial ruin. Even lasting brands such as Coca-Cola and Nescafé cannot supply all future growth and profitability for their companies. These brands must be improved and adapted to changing conditions and new brands developed. Coca-Cola today, in spite of being the world leader in soft drinks, is aggressively extending its beverage lines and has diversified into desalinization equipment and plastics.

*Flanking defence*    When guarding its overall position, the market leader should watch its weaker flanks closely. Smart competitors normally will attack the company's

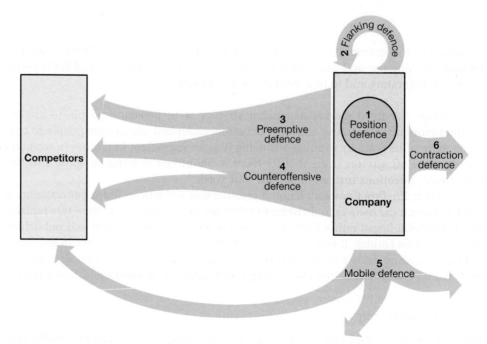

**Figure 12.4**    Defence strategies.

weaknesses. Thus the Japanese successfully entered the US small car market because local car makers left a gaping hole in that submarket. Using a flanking defence, the company carefully checks its flanks and protects the more vulnerable ones. In this way Nestlé's Nescafé and Gold Blend have the support of flanking brands Blend 37, Alta Rica and Cap Colombie. By acquiring Rover, BMW obtained access to small cars and cross-country vehicles and so defend their flanks in two growing sectors of the luxury car market where they were not active.

*Pre-emptive defence*     The leader can launch a more aggressive pre-emptive defence, striking competitors before they can move against the company. A pre-emptive defence assumes that an ounce of prevention is worth a pound of cure. Thus, when threatened in the mid-1980s by the impending entry of Japanese manufacturers into the US market, Cummins Engine slashed its prices by almost a third to save its number-one position in the $2 billion heavy-duty truck engine market. Today, Cummins claims a commanding 50 per cent market share in North America and not a single US-built tractor-trailer truck contains a Japanese engine.[14]

*Counteroffensive defence*     When attacked, despite its flanking or pre-emptive efforts, a market leader can launch a counteroffensive defence. When Fuji attacked Kodak in the film market, Kodak counterattacked by dramatically increasing its promotion and introducing several innovative new film products. Mars' attack on the ice-cream market using its brand extensions of Mars Bars, Snickers, Bounty, and so on, created a new product class of ice-confectionery. Unilever's Walls ice-cream division, which is market leader in parts of Europe, had difficulty countering this because it had no confectionery brands to use in that way. It overcame the problem by developing brand extensions of Cadbury's products, a competitor of Mars, which has no ice-cream interests. In other parts of Europe Nestlé is leader in the ice-cream market. With its strength in both confectionery and ice-cream it was able to launch brand extensions to match Mars.

Sometimes companies hold off for a while before countering. This may seem a dangerous game of 'wait and see', but there are often good reasons for not jumping in immediately. By waiting the company can understand more fully the competitor's offence and perhaps find a gap through which to launch a successful counteroffensive.

*Mobile defence*     A mobile defence involves more than aggressively defending a current market position. The leader stretches to new markets that can serve as future bases for defence and offence. Through *market broadening*, the company shifts its focus from the current product to the broader underlying consumer need. For example, Armstrong Cork redefined its focus from 'floor covering' to 'decorative room covering' (including walls and ceilings) and expanded into related businesses balanced for growth and defence. *Market diversification* into unrelated industries is the other alternative for generating 'strategic depth'. When the tobacco companies like British American Tobacco (BAT) and Philip Morris faced growing curbs on cigarette smoking, they moved quickly into new consumer products industries. Philip Morris bought up General Foods and Kraft to become the world's largest consumer packaged goods company and BAT Industries is now one of Europe's largest firms.

*Contraction defence*     Large companies sometimes find they can no longer defend all of their positions. Their resources are spread too thin and competitors are nibbling away on several fronts. The best action then appears to be a contraction defence (or strategic withdrawal). The company gives up weaker positions and concentrates its resources on stronger ones. During the 1970s, many companies diversified wildly and spread themselves too thin. In the slow-growth 1980s, ITT, Paribas, Suez, ENI, Gulf & Western, Quaker, Storehouse and dozens of other companies pruned their portfolios to concentrate resources on products and businesses in their core industries. These companies now serve fewer markets, but serve them much better.

The British motor cycle industry showed an extreme case of a contracting defence. Norton, Triumph, BSA and the like, once dominated the world motor-cycle market. First challenged by the small bikes made by Honda, Yamaha and others, they contracted into making medium-sized (250cc) to super-bikes. When the Japanese made 250cc machines, the British market retreated from entry-level machines to concentrate on larger ones. Eventually only Triumph and Norton super-bikes remained as small, out-of-date specialist manufacturers facing the Japanese giants, and they did not last long. A successful contracting defence must be a retreat into a position of strength.

### Expanding market share

Market leaders can also grow by increasing their market shares further. In many markets, small market-share increases mean very large sales increases. For example, in the coffee market, a 1 per cent increase in market share is worth $48 million; in soft drinks, $440 million! No wonder normal competition turns into marketing warfare in such markets.

Many studies have found that profitability rises with increasing market share.[15] Businesses with very large relative market shares averaged substantially higher returns on investment. Because of these findings, many companies have sought expanded market shares to improve profitability. General Electric, for example, declared that it wants to be at least number one or two in each of its markets or else get out. GE shed its computer, air-conditioning, small appliances and television businesses because it could not achieve a top-dog position in these industries. Nestlé intend to hold their position as the world's leading food company although France's Danone also have designs on that spot. Both have been acquiring businesses, Nestlé buying Perrier and Rowntree among others, while Danone own Jacobs, Kronenbourg, Amora, Lee & Perrins and HP sauce.[16]

Other studies have found that many industries contain one or a few highly profitable large firms, several profitable and more focused firms, and a large number of medium-sized firms with poorer profit performance:

> The large firms ... tend to address the entire market, achieving cost advantages and high market share by realizing economies of scale. The small competitors reap high profits by focusing on some narrower segment of the business and by developing specialized approaches to production, marketing and distribution for that segment. Ironically, the medium-sized competitors ... often show the poorest profit performance. Trapped in a strategic 'No Man's Land', they are too large to reap the benefits of more focused competition, yet too small to benefit from the economies of scale that their larger competitors enjoy.[17]

Thus it appears that profitability increases as a business gains share relative to competitors in its *served market*. For example, BMW holds only a small share of the total car market, but it earns high profit because it is a high-share company in its luxury car segment. It achieved this high share in its served market because it does other things right, such as producing high quality, giving good service and holding down its costs.

Companies must not think, however, that gaining increased market share will improve profitability automatically. Much depends on their strategy for gaining increased market share. We see many high-share companies with low profitability and many low-share companies with high profitability. The cost of buying higher market share may far exceed the returns. Higher shares tend to produce higher profits only when unit costs fall with increased market share or when the company's premium price covers the cost of supplying higher-quality goods.

## Market-challenger strategies

Firms that are second, third or lower in an industry are sometimes quite large, such as Colgate, Fiat, Toyota, Roche, Sandoz, HSBC (Hong Kong and Shanghai Banking Corp,), Carlsberg and PepsiCo. These runner-up firms can adopt one of two competitive strategies: they can attack the leader and other competitors in an aggressive bid for more market share (market challengers); or they can play along with competitors and not rock the boat (market followers). We now look at competitive strategies for market challengers.

### Defining the strategic objective and the competitor

A market challenger must first define its strategic objective. Most market challengers seek to increase their profitability by increasing their market shares. The strategic objective chosen depends on who the competitor is. In most cases, the company can choose which competitors it will challenge.

The challenger can attack the market leader, a high-risk but potentially high-gain strategy that makes good sense if the leader is not serving the market well. To succeed with such an attack, a company must have some sustainable competitive advantage over the leader – a cost advantage leading to lower prices or the ability to provide better value at a premium price. In the construction equipment industry, Komatsu successfully challenged Caterpillar by offering the same quality at much lower prices. Glaxo became Europe's leading drug company by aggressively marketing Zantac, its anti-ulcer drug.[18]

The challenger can avoid the leader and instead attack firms its size or smaller local and regional firms. Many of these firms are underfinanced and will not be serving their customers well. Several of the large beer companies grew to their present size not by attacking large competitors, but by gobbling up small local or regional competitors.

Thus the challenger's strategic objective depends on which competitor it chooses to attack. If the company goes after the market leader, its objective may be to wrest a certain market share. Bic knows that it cannot topple Gillette in the razor market – it simply wants a larger share. Or the challenger's goal might be to take over market leadership. Compaq entered the personal computer market late, as a challenger, but quickly became the market leader. If the company goes after a small local company its objective may be to put that company out of business. The important point remains: the company must choose its opponents carefully and have a clearly defined and attainable objective.

### Choosing an attack strategy

How can the market challenger best attack the chosen competitor and achieve its strategic objectives? Figure 12.5 shows five possible attack strategies.

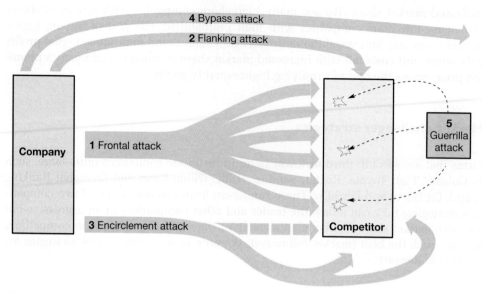

**Figure 12.5**   Attack strategies.

*Frontal attack*    In a full frontal attack, the challenger matches the competitor's product, advertising, price and distribution efforts. It attacks the competitor's strengths rather than its weaknesses. The outcome depends on who has the greater strength and endurance. Even great size and strength may not be enough to challenge a firmly entrenched and resourceful competitor successfully.

> Unilever has twice the worldwide sales of P&G and five times the sales of Colgate-Palmolive but its American subsidiary trails P&G by a wide margin in the US. Unilever launched a full frontal assault against P&G in the detergent market while Unilever's Wisk was already the leading liquid detergent. In quick succession, it added a barrage of new products – Sunlight dishwashing detergent, Snuggle fabric softener, Surf laundry powder – and backed them with aggressive promotion and distribution efforts. P&G spent heavily to defend its brands and held on to most of its business. It counterattacked with Liquid Tide, which came from nowhere in just 17 months to run neck-and-neck with Wisk. Unilever did gain market share, but most of it came from smaller competitors.[19]

If the market challenger has fewer resources than the competitor, a frontal attack makes little sense.

*Flanking attack*    Rather than attacking head on, the challenger can launch a flanking attack. The competitor often concentrates its resources to protect its strongest positions, but it usually has some weaker flanks. By attacking these weak spots, the challenger can concentrate its strength against the competitor's weakness. Flank attacks make good sense when the company has fewer resources than the competitor.

When Airbus Industries started making airliners they were up against Boeing, a company that dominates the industry. Lockheed and McDonnell Douglas had once challenged Boeing as plane makers but Lockheed had withdrawn from the industry and McDonnell Douglas was reduced to making derivatives of their old aircraft. Airbus's first move was to develop the A300 with range and payload performance different from Boeing's established 727, 737 and 747 range.

**If you think Airbus Industrie makes only one aircraft, maybe this will change your view.**

Airbus Industrie has achieved a 30% share of the international civil aviation market because its long-term business strategy, based on a clear vision of the world's air transport needs, has created not just one aircraft but a family of seven: including the world's largest twin-aisle twin and the longest range jetliner in aviation history. Sales of all seven members of the Airbus family now total nearly 2000 aircraft worldwide.

© *AIRBUS INDUSTRIE TAKING THE WORLD VIEW*

Airbus challenges the market leader, Boeing, by providing an ever-increasing range of airliners.

Another flanking strategy is to find gaps that are not being filled by the industry's products, fill them and develop them into strong segments. European and Japanese car makers do not try to compete with American car makers by producing large, flashy, gas-guzzling contraptions. Instead they recognized an unserved consumer segment that wanted small, fuel-efficient cars and moved to fill this hole. To their satisfaction and Detroit's surprise, the segment grew to be a large part of the market.

*Encirclement attack*    An encirclement attack involves attacking from all directions, so that the competitor must protect its front, sides and rear at the same time. The encirclement strategy makes sense when the challenger has superior resources and believes that it can break the competitor's hold on the market quickly. An example is Seiko's attack on the watch market. For several years, Seiko has been gaining distribution in every big watch outlet and overwhelming competitors with its variety of constantly changing models. In most markets Seiko offers about four hundred models, but its marketing strength is backed by the 2,300 models it makes and sells worldwide.

*Bypass attack*    A bypass attack is an indirect strategy. The challenger bypasses the competitor and targets easier markets. The bypass can involve diversifying into unrelated products, moving into new geographic markets or leapfrogging into new technologies to replace existing products. Technological leapfrogging is a bypass strategy used often in high-technology industries. Instead of copying the competitor's product and mounting a costly frontal attack, the challenger patiently develops the next technology. When satisfied with its superiority, it launches an attack where it has an advantage. Thus Minolta toppled Canon from the lead in the 35 mm SLR camera market when it introduced its technologically advanced auto-focusing Maxxum camera. Canon's market share dropped towards 20 per cent while Minolta's zoomed passed 30 per cent. It took Canon three years to introduce a matching technology.[20]

*Guerrilla attack*   A guerrilla attack is another option available to market challengers, especially smaller or poorly financed ones:

> When entrepreneur Freddie Laker frontally attacked the established airlines (then BOAC and TWA) by offering cheap transatlantic flights, they fought back and bankrupted him. Now TWA has all but disappeared and British Airways is facing Virgin Atlantic run by a much more wily entrepreneur, Richard Branson. He makes guerrilla attacks on his much larger competitors. In these attacks the agile challenger typically makes small, periodic attacks to harass and demoralise the competitor, hoping eventually to establish permanent footholds. It might use selective price cuts, novel products, executive raids, intense promotional outbursts or assorted legal actions. Virgin has been successful so far and taken 22 per cent of the London to New York market. He is also expanding quickly using franchising, an approach new to the airline industry.[21]

Normally, guerrilla actions are by smaller firms against larger ones. The smaller firms need to be aware, however, that continuous guerrilla campaigns can be expensive and must eventually be followed by a stronger attack if the challenger wishes to 'beat' the competitor. Thus guerrilla campaigns are not necessarily cheap.

## Market-follower strategies

Not all runner-up companies will challenge the market leader. The effort to draw away the leader's customers is never taken lightly by the leader. If the challenger's lure is lower prices, improved service or additional product features, the leader can quickly match these to diffuse the attack. The leader probably has more staying power in an all-out battle. A hard fight might leave both firms worse off and this means the challenger must think twice before attacking. Many firms therefore prefer to follow rather than attack the leader.

A follower can gain many advantages. The market leader often bears the huge expenses involved with developing new products and markets, expanding distribution channels and informing and educating the market. The reward for all this work and risk is normally market leadership. The market follower, on the other hand, can learn from the leader's experience and copy or improve on the leader's products and marketing programmes, usually at a much lower investment. Although the follower will probably not overtake the leader, it can often be as profitable.[22]

In some industries – such as steel, fertilizers and chemicals – opportunities for differentiation are low, service quality is often comparable and price sensitivity runs high. Price wars can erupt at any time. Companies in these industries avoid short-run grabs for market share because the strategy only provokes retaliation. Most firms decide against stealing each other's customers. Instead they present similar offers to buyers, usually by copying the leader. Market shares show a high stability.

This is not to say that market followers are without strategies. A market follower must know how to hold current customers and win a fair share of new ones. Each follower tries to bring distinctive advantages to its target market – location, services, financing. The follower is a primary target of attack by challengers. Therefore, the market follower must keep its manufacturing costs low and its product quality and services high. It must also enter new markets as they appear. Following is not the same as being passive or a carbon copy of the leader. The follower has to define a growth path, but one that does not create competitive retaliation.

The market-follower firms fall into one of three broad types. The *cloner* closely copies the leader's products, distribution, advertising and other marketing moves. It originates nothing – it simply attempts to live off the market leader's investments. IBM's demise started after outsourcing (286 chips from Intel and the MS-DOS operating system from Microsoft) and open architecture allowed low-cost market entrants to copy their PCs.

> Dutch flower growers, who dominate the international flower trade, are facing intense competition from growers in Israel, Kenya and Zimbabwe. They can grow exactly what the Dutch do but, unlike the North Europeans, have no big heating bills, cheap labour and unregulated use of fertilisers. The flood of foreign stems has knocked 40 per cent off rose prices and Dutch growers are increasingly resigned to losing the rose and carnation trade.[23]

The *imitator* copies some things from the leader but maintains some differentiation with packaging, advertising, pricing and other factors. The leader does not mind the imitator as long as the imitator does not attack aggressively. The imitator may even help the leader avoid the charges of monopoly.

> Today's imitators are often retailers making look-alike own brands. The British Producers and Brand Owners Group (BPOG) was formed in response to own brands aping the market leaders too closely. Sainsbury's highly publicised launch of Classic Cola precipitated BPOG's formation and resulted in the retailer backing off. Other confrontations include Sainsbury's Full Roast (based on Nescafé) and Tesco's Unbelievable low-fat spread (close to Van den Bergh's I Can't Believe It's Not Butter).[24]

Finally, the *adapter* builds on the leader's products and marketing programmes, often improving them. The adapter may choose to sell to different markets to avoid direct confrontation with the leader. Many IBM PC clones did this – Amstrad was one of the earliest selling its ready and running machines through conventional electrical goods retailers. Now Dell and dan Technologies combine direct selling with excellent customer support. Often the adapter grows into a future challenger, as many Japanese firms have done after adapting and improving products developed elsewhere.

## Market-nicher strategies

Almost every industry includes firms that specialize in serving market niches. Instead of pursuing the whole market or even large segments of the market, these firms target segments within segments or niches. This is particularly true of smaller firms because of their limited resources. Smaller divisions of larger firms also pursue niching strategies. EG&G is an example of a large company that profitably employs a niching strategy:

> EG&G is a $1.4 billion industrial equipment and components company consisting of over 175 distinct and independent business units, many with less than $10 million in sales in markets worth $25 million. Many EG&G business units have their own R&D, manufacturing and salesforce operations. The company is currently the market or technical leader in 80 per cent of its niche markets. More astonishing, EG&G ranked second in earnings per share and first in profitability in the *Fortune 1000*. EG&G illustrates how niche marketing may pay larger dividends than mass marketing.

## Concentrated marketing: two nice niches

Jo Brand is a size-challenged new comedienne whose act often includes two themes, her size and her love for cakes. The following two niche companies are for her. One is old and one is new. They are Betty's Café Tea Rooms and 1647, the clothes shops owned by comedienne Dawn French.

### Betty's Café Tea Room

There are only four Betty's Café Tea Rooms and one Taylor's Tea Room, all in Yorkshire, but they serve 2m. cups of tea a year – it is *the* British tea room. They do not advertise, yet year round people queue for a chance to taste their exquisitely expensive tea, coffee and cakes. Once inside, the guests find themselves in a quiet room where a pianist plays light classical music. The rooms are simple but rich with atmosphere of times past. Serving are waiters, formally dressed, or waitresses wearing black skirt, starched white blouse and apron – the embodiment of Victorian servants. Betty's is proud of its heritage and quietly boasts of the York Betty's being built by 'the same team of craftsmen who were responsible for the ornate decor of the luxury liner, the Queen Mary ... During the last war it was the favourite haunt of the thousands of airmen and servicemen stationed around York. Many left there a permanent reminder of their visit by inscribing their names onto the mirror which now hangs in the Oak Room.'

The first Betty's was opened in Harrogate in 1919 by Fredrick Belmont, a Swiss confectioner who trav-

elled to London to make his fortune. He visited the Yorkshire Dales, liked it, stayed and started Betty's. His timing was as good as his patisserie. Harrogate was booming and Betty's was just about the only place an unchaperoned woman could go. Then and now Betty's succeeds because of the quality of what it serves and its employees. The range and quality of cakes are such that customers need a description of what each is. The pastries range from exotic Amadeus tort and Venetian festival cake to local Yorkshire curd tarts and fat rascals. Here Betty's keeps close to its Swiss roots; the bakers and confectioners train at Richemont College, Lucerne.

Like many smart companies, Betty's is a multiple nicher. It has diversified into other businesses close to its original business. At each of its Café Tea Rooms it also has a retail outlet selling expensive gift-oriented confectionery, which suits their location in tourist towns. They also have a mail-order business selling cakes, chocolates, and speciality teas and coffees by post. Finally, they market Yorkshire Tea, a brand sold and positioned nationally as a traditional Yorkshire cuppa. As part of the promotion for this brand the tea is supplied, free of charge, to all northern branches of the Women's Institute, a long-established organization of middle-aged, middle-class gentlewomen.

### Dawn French Fashions

A study of the contours of 5,000 women just after World War II links Betty's golden age to Dawn

---

The main point is that firms with low shares of the total market can be highly profitable through smart niching (see Marketing Highlight 12.4).

One study of highly successful mid-size companies found that, in almost all cases, these companies niched within a larger market rather than going after the whole market.[25] Two of 'Europe's most respected companies',[26] De La Rue and Reuters, both fall into this category. De La Rue's niche is banknote printing and payment handling systems while Reuters provides news and financial information, usually screen-based.

Why is niching profitable? The main reason is that the market nicher ends up knowing the target customer group so well that it meets their needs better than other firms which casually sell to this niche. As a result, the nicher can charge a substantial mark-up over costs because of the added value. Whereas the mass marketer achieves *high volume*, the nicher achieves *high margins*.

French's fashions. The study's results gave the British Standard Sizes – 12, 14, 16 and so on – that have pained many people ever since. The sizes worked well in the 1950s when food rationing had just ended and people walked a lot, but not now. A recent study of women's contours by JD Williams shows things have changed. For years the company has been selling mail-order clothes to women with a fuller figure who were unable to get suitable clothes from high-street stores. Nigel Green, marketing director of JD Williams' Classic Combinations catalogue business, explains:

Today's woman enjoys a far more self-indulgent lifestyle and is not only taller, but has a noticeably bigger and lower bust, an appreciably larger waist and rib cage, a more rounded tummy, a larger and flatter bottom and far fuller upper arms. And while her hip size may still be 36 inches [1 in = 2.54 cm], the standard British figure [the original size 12] is now more likely to be 38-28-36 than 36-24-36 … The old-fashioned dress sizes meant that women in this country have learned to live with ill-fitting clothes: blouses that gape, waistbands that cut and skirts that ride up.

Nigel Green believes these new sizes will give his niche company an extra USP (unique selling proposition).

Other moves are afoot in the high street. 'Women are no longer prepared to put their lives on hold until they can starve themselves down to size 14', says Christina Bounce, group marketing and merchandising director for Country Casuals Holdings. She goes on: 'They are generally feeling happier about their own size, even when it doesn't conform to fashion stereotypes.' C&A and DH Evans, the Outsize Shop, have long served the outsize market but the emerging market shows that women no longer feel the need to don masks before entering the premises.

Dawn French's shops, 1647, sell high fashions designed – not just upsized 12s, cover-all T-shirts and leggings – for the amply proportioned. Few in the trade believe the claim implicit in the shop name that 47 per cent of women are over size 16, but the huge success of niche retailers aiming at the market shows where the future lies. Within a year of start-up Ann Harvey shops, for sizes 16 to 26, grew from the initial twenty stand-alone stores to thirty-eight, and two concessions and a further twelve are scheduled.

'There is correlation between age and increased size and obesity,' says Verdict's Clive Vaughan. So, as the middle-aged market grows in number, affluence and girth, the outsize market is a good niche to target. But as Joan Miller, training coordinator of Betty's Café Tea Rooms, says: 'If everyone round here decides to get health conscious we're in real trouble.'

Sources: Nicholas Lander, 'British tea and torte', *Financial Times* (4–5 June 1994), XI; Virginia Matthews, 'Oversized and over here', *Marketing Week* (23 September 1994), 25.

Nichers try to find one or more market niches that are safe and profitable. An ideal market niche is big enough to be profitable and has growth potential. It is one that the firm can serve effectively. Perhaps most importantly, the niche is of little interest to large competitors. The firm can build the skills and customer goodwill to defend itself against an attacking big competitor as the niche grows and becomes more attractive.

The key idea in nichemanship is specialization. The firm has to specialize along market, customer, product or marketing mix lines. Here are several specialist roles open to a market nicher:

- *End-use specialist.* The firm specializes in serving one type of end-use customer. For example, Reuters provides financial information and news to professionals and Moss Bros's strength is in clothes hire.

- *Vertical-level specialist.* The firm specializes at some level of the production–distribution cycle. For example, the Dutch based Anglo-Italian company, EVC, is Europe's leading manufacturer of polyvinylchloride (PVC), while Country Homes' niche is as a middleman between owners of country cottages and people who want to hire them for holidays.
- *Customer-size specialist.* The firm concentrates on selling to either small, medium or large customers. Many nichers specialize in serving small customers neglected by the large companies. Fuji gained its initial success in the photocopying market by specializing on small firms neglected by Xerox. Many regional advertising agencies also specialize in serving medium-sized clients.
- *Specific-customer specialist.* The firm limits its selling to one or a few large customers. There are many firms like this in the motor industry: for example, Unipart who devote most of their time to BMW/Rover.
- *Geographical specialist.* The firm sells only in a certain locality, region or area of the world. Most retail banks stay within their national boundaries. Two odd exceptions to this rule are the European HSBC and Standard & Charter whose main interest is Southeast Asia.
- *Product or feature specialist.* The firm specializes in producing a certain product, product line or product feature – Rolls-Royce is the only supplier of tilt-thrust jet engines.
- *Quality–price specialist.* The firm operates at the low or high end of the market. For example, Hewlett-Packard specializes in the high-quality, high-price end of the hand-calculator market, while Tring International sells very cheap CDs.
- *Service specialist.* The firm offers one or more services not available from other firms: for example, NASA's ability to recover and repair satellites.

Niching carries a very significant risk in that the market niche may dry up or be attacked. Porsche was hit by both of these threats when the demand for luxury cars declined in the early 1990s and Honda, Toyota and Mazda attacked the sports car market. On a different scale, innovation and intense competition between multinationals and social trends eventually killed off Pollards Cornish Ice Cream.[27] Their niche was selling high-fat dairy ice cream – estimated 100 calories per cone – to the declining number of tourists in the south-west of England.

The danger of the disappearing niche is why many companies use *multiple niching*. By developing two or more niches, the company increases its chances of survival. Most of the wealth of successful healthcare companies comes from their each having products in a few niches that they dominate. For instance, Sweden's Gambio concentrates on renal care, cardiovascular surgery, intensive care and anaesthesia, blood compound technology and preventative health services. The need for multiple niching is shown by SmithKline Beecham's Tagamet sales dropping 76 per cent in the quarter that it lost patent cover in the United States.[28]

## BALANCING CUSTOMER AND COMPETITOR ORIENTATIONS

We have stressed the importance of a company watching its competitors closely. Whether a company is a market leader, challenger, follower or nicher, it must find the competitive marketing strategy that positions it most effectively against its competitors. It must continually adapt its strategies to the fast-changing competitive environment.

This question now arises: Can the company spend too much time and energy tracking competitors, damaging its customer orientation? The answer is yes! A

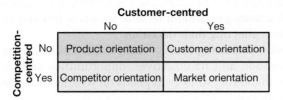

**Figure 12.6**   Evolving company orientations.

company can become so competitor-centred that it loses its even more important customer focus. A **competitor-centred company** is one whose moves are based mainly on competitors' actions and reactions. The company spends most of its time tracking competitors' moves and market shares and trying to find strategies to counter them.

This mode of strategy planning has some pluses and minuses. On the positive side, the company develops a fighter orientation. It trains its marketers to be on a constant alert, watching for weaknesses in their position and watching for competitors' weaknesses. On the negative side, the company becomes too reactive. Rather than carrying out its own consistent customer-oriented strategy, it bases its moves on competitors' moves. As a result, it does not move in a planned direction towards a goal. It does not know where it will end up, since so much depends on what the competitors do.

A **customer-centred company**, in contrast, focuses more on customer developments in designing its strategies. Clearly, the customer-centred company is in a better position to identify new opportunities and set a strategy that makes long-run sense. By watching customer needs evolve, it can decide what customer groups and what emerging needs are the most important to serve, given its resources and objectives.

In practice, today's companies must be **market-centred companies**, watching both their customers and their competitors. They must not let competitor watching blind them to customer focusing. Figure 12.6 shows that companies have moved through four orientations over the years. In the first stage, they were product-oriented, paying little attention to either customers or competitors. In the second stage, they became customer-oriented and started to pay attention to customers. In the third stage, when they started to pay attention to competitors, they became competitor-oriented. Today, companies need to be market-oriented, paying balanced attention to both customer and competitors. A market orientation pays big dividends – one recent study found a substantial positive relationship between a company's marketing orientation and its profitability, a relationship that held regardless of type of business or market environment.[29]

## SUMMARY

To prepare an effective marketing strategy, a company must consider its competitors as well as its actual and potential customers. It must continuously analyse its competitors and develop competitive marketing strategies that effectively position it against competitors and give it the strongest possible *competitive advantage*.

*Competitor analysis* first involves identifying the company's main competitors, using both an industry and a market-based analysis. The company then gathers information on competitors' objectives, strategies, strengths and weaknesses, and reaction patterns. With this information to hand, it can select competitors to attack or avoid.

Competitive intelligence must be collected, interpreted and distributed continuously. Company marketing managers should be able to obtain full and reliable information about any competitor affecting their decisions.

Which *competitive marketing strategy* makes the most sense depends on the company's industry position and its objectives, opportunities and resources. The company's competitive marketing strategy depends on whether it is a market leader, challenger, follower or nicher.

A *market leader* faces three challenges: expanding the total market, protecting market share and expanding market share. The market leader wants to find ways to expand the total market because it will benefit most from any increased sales. To *expand market size*, the leader looks for *new users* of the product, *new uses* and *more usage*. To protect its existing market share, the *market leader* has several defences: *position defence, flanking defence, pre-emptive defence, counteroffensive defence, mobile defence* and *contraction defence*. The most sophisticated leaders cover themselves by doing everything right, leaving no openings for competitive attack. Leaders can also try to increase their market shares. This makes sense if profitability increases at higher market-share levels.

A *market challenger* is a firm that aggressively tries to expand its market share by attacking the leader, other runner-up firms or smaller firms in the industry. The challenger can choose from a variety of *attack strategies*, including a *frontal attack, flanking attack, encirclement attack, bypass attack* and *guerrilla attack*.

A *market follower* is a runner-up firm that chooses not to rock the boat, usually out of fear that it stands to lose more than it might gain. The follower is not without a strategy, however, and seeks to use its particular skills to gain market growth. Some followers enjoy a higher rate of return than the leaders in their industry.

A *market nicher* is a smaller firm that serves some part of the market that is not likely to attract the larger firms. Market nichers often become specialists in some end use, vertical level, customer size, specific customer, geographic area, product or product feature, or service.

A competitive orientation is important in today's markets, but companies should not overdo their focus on competitors. Companies are more likely to be hurt by emerging consumer needs and new competitors than by existing competitors. Companies that balance consumer and competitor considerations are practising a true market orientation.

## ■ DISCUSSING THE ISSUES

1. 'Well-behaved' companies prefer well-behaved competition. Should it make any difference to consumers whether competition is 'well-behaved' or 'disruptive'? Why or why not?

2. Consider Richard Branson's attempts at taking on market leaders in the airlines (e.g. British Airways on transatlantic routes), soft drinks (e.g. Coca-Cola) and, more recently, financial services (as seen in the launch of Virgin Direct which would challenge current providers of traditional and direct insurance products). What market-leader strategies would you recommend for the number-one competitor in each of these sectors? Why?

3. Thinking about the market for athletic shoes (as exemplified by brands such as Adidas, Nike or Puma), how might the total market be expanded? Are there some routes to total market expansion that might be more effective than others? What are they? Explain why they are successful.

4. Many medium-sized firms occupy an unprofitable middle ground between large firms and smaller,

more focused competitors. Discuss how medium-sized competitors could use market-nicher strategies to strengthen their competitive position and improve profitability.

5. The goal of the marketing concept is to satisfy customer wants and needs. What is the goal of a competitor-centred strategy? Discuss whether the marketing concept and competitor-centred strategy are in conflict.

6. Assume you are the product manager for the number-two brand in the antiseptic mouthwash market. The number-one brand enjoys a 60 per cent share of the domestic market and has been known to aggressively defend its market leadership position. Few of the smaller competitors further down the league have been successful. You are, however, determined to increase your business in this market. What would your strategy be for achieving this objective?

## APPLYING THE CONCEPTS

1. Select one of these industries: cars, cameras or personal computers. Study a purchasing guide (normally sold at newsstands, newsagents or bookstores). Examine different aspects of the products, including features, style, image and price.

   ■ Identify competitors that you think are competing based upon the market point of view.
   ■ What sort of competitive strategies do you see being used by market leaders, followers, challengers and nichers?
   ■ What different strategic groups might be identified in the industry you have selected? Which groups compete with which other groups?

2. Market leaders often try to expand the total market, especially in slower-growing, mature markets.

   ■ Look at the ads in several issues of women's magazines. Find examples in which manufacturers or service providers are attempting to expand the total market demand for their goods or services.
   ■ Look for similar examples in your local grocery and other retail stores.
   ■ What specific strategies are reflected by these expansion attempts: new users, new uses or more usage?
   ■ Rate the probability of success for each example you have found. Explain why you think the chances of success are high or low.

## REFERENCES

1. Chuck Hawkins, 'FedEx: Europe nearly killed the messenger', *Business Week* (25 May 1992), 124–6; Erik Calonius, 'Federal Express's battle overseas', *Fortune* (3 December 1990), 137–40; Joseph Maglitta, 'Being the best in the business', *Computer World* (25 February 1991), 61–4; Shlomo Maital, 'When you absolutely, positively have to give the better service', *Across the Board* (March 1991), 8–12; 'Pass the parcel', *The Economist* (21 March 1992), 73–4; Nikki Tait, 'FedEx wraps up its European dream', *Financial Times* (23 March 1992), 1; Phillip Hastings, 'On track for a faster service', *Financial Times* (20 May 1992); III; Janina Walker, 'Fleets take on a greener shade', *Financial Times* (20 May 1992), V; Malcolm Brown, 'Signed, sealed, delivered', *Marketing Business* (June 1992), 30–2; and Phillip Hastings, 'Today or tomorrow please', *Financial Times* (21 September 1994), III; Dan Keeler, 'A litany of broken promises', *BusinessAge*, **4**, 50 (1994), 40B–47B; 'Unafraid to fail', *BusinessAge*, **4**, 50 (1994), 2C–4C.

2. For an insight perception of competitors see Leslie de Chertony, Kevin Daniels and Gerry Johnson, 'A cognitive perspective on managers' perceptions of competition', *Journal of Marketing Management*, **9**, 4 (1992), 373–81.

3. For a good discussion of the underlying rules of competitive interaction and reaction, see Gloria P. Thomas and Gary F. Soldow, 'A rules-based approach to competitive interaction', *Journal of Marketing* (April 1988), 63–74.

4. See Joseph Weber, 'How J&J's foresight made contact lenses pay', *Business Week* (4 May 1992), 132.

5. See Michael E. Porter, *Competitive Advantage* (New York: Free Press, 1985), 226–7.

6. Ian Verchère, 'Sabina seeks divorce from Air France', *The European* (7–13 October 1994), 1; John Ridding, 'Air France reduces loss to Ffr 2.61bn', *Financial Times* (3 October 1994), 22.

7. For more discussion, see William L. Sammon, Mark A. Kurland, and Robert Spitalnic, *Business Competitor*

*Intelligence* (New York: Ronald Press, 1984); Leonard M. Fuld, *Monitoring the Competition* (New York: Wiley, 1988); Howard Schlossberg, 'Competitive intelligence pros seek formal role in marketing', *Marketing News* (5 March 1990), 2, 28; Michele Galen, 'These guys aren't spooks, they're "competitive analysts"', *Business Week* (14 October 1991), 97; James W. Taylor, 'Competitive intelligence: a status report on US business practices', *Journal of Marketing Management*, **8**, 2 (1992), 117–26; Peter Marsh, 'Is there a spy in your boardroom?', *Financial Times* (18 October 1994), 35.

8.  See Porter, *Competitive Advantage*, op. cit.; Pankaj Ghemawat, 'Sustainable advantage', *Harvard Business Review* (Sept.–Oct. 1986), 53–8; Michael E. Porter, 'From competitive advantage to corporate strategy', *Harvard Business Review* (May–June 1987), 43–59; and George S. Day and Robin Wensley, 'Assessing competitive advantage: a framework for diagnosing competitive superiority', *Journal of Marketing* (April 1988), 1–20; Graham Hooley and John Saunders, *Competitive Positioning: The key to marketing success* (Hemel Hempstead: Prentice Hall, 1993).

9.  Clive Cookson and Tony Jackson, 'An institution under threat', *Financial Times* (18 May 1991), 6; Richard Gourlay, 'Shaping up for a split decision', *Financial Times: FT 500* (10 February 1993), 19.

10.  Michael E. Porter, *Competitive Strategy: Techniques for Analyzing Industries and Competitors* (New York: Free Press, 1980), ch. 2. Other strategy types have been suggested. See Richard Speed, 'An approach to operationalising and validating strategic typologies in marketing strategy research', European Marketing Academy Proceedings, Aarhus, 26–29 May 1992, pp. 1093–108; Dale Littler and Fiona Leverick, 'Strategic archetypes in nascent technology sectors', European Marketing Academy Proceedings, Aarhus, 26–29 May 1992, pp. 801–17; Eivor Huldén, 'Strategy types in the European children's wear industry', European Marketing Academy Proceedings, Maastricht, 17–20 May 1994, pp. 429–49.

11.  Martin Dickens, 'Small is powerful', *Financial Times* (28 March 1991), 12; Marcus Gibson, 'Bose leaps out of the sound coffin', *The European* (7–13 October 1994), 32; Marcus Gibson, 'Firm focus on research pays leading dividends', *The European* (28 January–3 February 1994), 28; Ruth Sullivan, 'Barilla's Italian recipe for success', *The European* (24–30 June 1994), 32; Ruth Sullivan, 'One man's vision which put Luxottica in the frame', *The European* (14–20 October 1994), 32; Robert Graham, 'Prato textile industry: remarkable resilience', *Financial Times* (25 October 1994), 34.

12.  David Blackwell, 'Making a meal of a dog's dinner', *Financial Times* (25 October 1994), 21.

13.  For more discussion on defence and attack strategies, see Philip Kotler, *Marketing Management: Analysis, planning, implementation, and control* (Englewood Cliffs, NJ: Prentice Hall, 1994), ch. 14.

14.  See Lois Therrien, 'Mr. Rust Belt', *Business Week* (17 October 1988), 72–80.

15.  See Robert D. Buzzell, Bradley T. Gale, and Ralph G.M. Sultan, 'Market share – the key to profitability', *Harvard Business Review* (Jan.–Feb. 1975), 97–106; and Ben Branch, 'The laws of the marketplace and ROI dynamics', *Financial Management* (summer 1980), 58–65. Others suggest that the relationship between market share and profits has been exaggerated. See Carolyn Y. Woo and Arnold C. Cooper, 'Market-share leadership – not always so good', *Harvard Business Review* (Jan.–Feb. 1984), 2–4; and Robert Jacobson and David A. Aaker, 'Is market share all it's cracked up to be?', *Journal of Marketing* (Fall 1985), 11–22.

16.  Ian Harding, 'BSN provide food for thought', *The European* (25–31 March 1994), 28.

17.  See John D.C. Roach, 'From strategic planning to strategic performance: closing the achievement gap', *Outlook*, quarterly house magazine of Booz, Allen & Hamilton, New York (spring 1981), 21. Michael Porter makes the same point in his *Competitive Strategy*, op.cit.

18.  See Michael E. Porter, 'How to attack the industry leader', *Fortune* (19 April 1985), 153–66; 'Life after Zantac', *The Economist* (3 July 1993), 65.

19.  See Andrew C. Brown, 'Unilever fights back in the US', *Fortune* (26 May 1986), 32–8.

20.  See Otis Port, 'Canon finally challenges Minolta's mighty Maxxum', *Fortune* (2 March 1987), 89–90.

21.  'Virgin Atlantic: still on course', *The Economist* (22 January 1994), 63–4.

22.  See Daniel W. Haines, Rajan Chandran, and Arvind Parkhe, 'Winning by being first to market … or last?', *Journal of Consumer Marketing* (winter 1989), 63–9.

23.  Michael Griffin, 'Imports cut into Dutch flower power', *Financial Times* (5 August 1994), 22.

24.  Claire Murphy, 'Brand owners plot fresh assault', *Marketing Week* (3 June 1994), 7.

25.  Donald K. Clifford and Richard E. Cavanagh, *The Winning Performance: How America's high- and midsize growth companies succeed* (New York: Bantam Books, 1985).

26.  'Europe's most respected companies', *Financial Times* (27 June 1994), 8–9.

27.  Tim Burt, 'Tourists lose their taste for Pollards Cornish Ice Cream', *Financial Times* (25 October 1994), 24.

28.  Robert Taylor, 'Gambio: looking forward to a healthy future', *Financial Times: FT500* (10 February 1993), 17; Daniel Green, 'Tagamet's US sales fall 76% in quarter', *Financial Times* (19 October 1994), 25.

29.  See John C. Narver and Stanley F. Slater, 'The effect of a market orientation on business profitability', *Journal of Marketing* (October 1990), 20–35.

# BMW: putting the 'brrrrum' back in Brum

The 63-year-old widow scorns expensive jewellery, drinks mineral water and tea, gives no parties and rarely attends them. Outside her family she has few friends and, like many other middle-class German women, she takes her car when she goes shopping. However, unlike most shoppers', her car is a BMW 525. She also has a Mercedes 500 and a chauffeur-driven 12-cylinder 7 series BMW. She is Mrs Joanna Brauhn, one of Europe's richest people, whose DM 7 billion[*] business interests stretch from baby food to batteries. She also owns Bayerische Motorenwerke (Bavarian Motor Works), better known as BMW.

After a decade of success BMW faced problems in the early 1990s. Between 1992 and 1993 European car sales dropped 16 per cent and BMW did worse than average. Their arch rival, Mercedes, and the Japanese car makers had also lost, but not as badly as BMW. Only one of the world's car makers had gained over that period – Rover's sales grew 9 per cent in 1993.

## Under attack

BMW was squeezed on several fronts. Recessions in Europe, Japan and the United States brought car sales down in all the world's major markets. Like Audi, Mercedes and Porsche, BMW's sales were also hit by Japan's aggressive and successful attack on the US luxury car market. In less than a year after launch Honda's Acura range became America's top-selling luxury car, knocking Mercedes off the top spot. Toyota soon followed with their Lexus, a car that quickly became the benchmark for luxury and quality. As Japan's luxury car sales grew in the United States, German sales declined: BMW's US sales fell from 97,000 in 1986 to 57,000 in 1991. BMW could not follow two leading trends in the car market – the shift towards smaller cars, and to large off-the-road vehicles. In Europe, the number of wealthy working women was increasing rapidly and these were opting to buy fashionable super-minis or small sporty cars, not BMW's executive saloons. In addition, senior executives who had once bought 5 or 7 series BMWs

increasingly opted for Range Rovers, Toyota Land Cruisers or other bulky giants. Volvo was similarly hit as wealthy parents opted for an off-the-road vehicle rather than a Volvo estate to transport their children.

## Honda

Honda caused BMW particular problems. Japan's third largest car maker, behind Toyota and Nissan, Honda positioned itself close to BMW. Even before the launch of Acura, Honda had an excellent reputation for quality, reliability and being sporty. Honda cars also came well equipped and had many advanced features. BMW, like Mercedes, could have sophisticated accessories, such as microscopic air filters and parking aids, but these were rarely fitted to cars unless customers paid extra for them. Even radios are optional extras on most BMWs. Unlike BMW, Honda also made small sports cars and the Civic, an attractive small family car. One motoring correspondent said: 'If Mercedes ever made a small car, it would be like the Civic.'

In the early 1990s, Europe's 13 million cars a year industry had 2 million cars a year excess capacity, and too many manufacturers making too many models. This did not stop Toyota, Nissan and Honda building further new factories, mostly in England. By doing this the Japanese avoided their own country's high labour costs, gained access to Britain's flexible and inexpensive workforce, and avoided the European Union's Japanese car import quotas. The strategy proved successful. The workers quickly learned to produce cars of Japanese quality. Japanese management practices (just-in-time, total quality, continuous improvement, and so forth) blended easily with the British tradition of improvisation. In their Sunderland plant, well away from the traditional car-making area round Coventry and Birmingham (Brum), Nissan achieved production rates equal to those in Japan – 80 cars per worker per year. This compares with a European average of 45 cars per worker per year achieved only after productivity gains in the early 1990s.

Being smaller than Toyota and Nissan, Honda initially chose a joint venture with Britain's Rover as an

[*] 1 ecu = US$1.26 = DM 1.89 (Deutschmarks).

**CASE 12** *(cont)*

**Exhibit 12.1**    The Honda–Rover deal

| Agreement | Content |
| --- | --- |
| Equity holding | Honda owns 20 per cent of Rover Cars. |
|  | Rover owns 20 per cent of Honda (UK). |
| Licensing | Honda car designs for Rover 200, 400, 600 and 800. |
|  | Honda component designs, such as gearbox for 2-litre Rover engine. |
|  | Honda supplies production equipment and technology to Rover for its 200, 400 and 600 series cars. |
| Component supplies | Each sells the other about £400m. worth of car parts and components a year: for example, Honda sells 1.6, 2.0, 2.3 and 2.7 litre engines to Rover; Honda sells Rover fascias for 600 series; and Rover sells body panels for UK-made Honda Accords. |
| Vehicle sales | Rover makes Honda Concertos in Birmingham and supplies Land Rover Discoveries for sales as Honda Crossroads in Japan. |

inexpensive way of entering the European market. Honda took a 20 per cent stake in Rover, the other 80 per cent being owned by British Aerospace (BAe). In exchange BAe took a 20 per cent share of Honda (UK). Exhibit 12.1 shows the extent of the deal.

### Rover, by any other name

The Rover group in 1990 was the product of governments, not enterprise. The company has its origins in the early days of the motor industry, the first Rover being a bicycle made by the Starley company in 1884. In 1938 Lord Nuffield combined the Riley, Wolseley, Morris and MG companies. Austin and Vanden Plas joined them in 1952 to form the British Motor Corporation (BMC). Then, with the addition of Jaguar and Daimler in 1966, the group became British Motor Holdings (BMH).

Successive Labour governments encouraged these and further mergers. Prime Minister Harold Wilson explained that the policy was 'to encourage the UK's chief strategic industry to become more internationally competitive'. The idea was to merge companies, and then to select the best managers to run them. The clear failure of the earlier mergers did not deter the government who, in 1968, encouraged the formation of British Leyland (BL) by combining BMH with Rover, Triumph and Leyland. Leyland's Donald Stokes took over the group, which made over 1 million cars a year, had 40 per cent of the UK car market, thirty factories, thirteen brands and dozens of models.

Donald Stokes, whose reputation came from selling buses and trucks worldwide, was out of his depth

running this hugely complex and underinvested company. Under his directorship BL deteriorated. It faced increasing competition from European rivals and started losing its traditional overseas markets. The company became synonymous with low quality, strikes and trade unions resistant to the reform of working practices. In 1973 the oil supply crisis sent the company reeling. Even the successful truck and bus division struggled after being starved of cash to subsidize the loss-making car business. Finally, in 1975, the Labour government nationalized BL and brought in Michael Edwards, a South African, as chief executive. He persuaded first the Labour government, and then the Conservative government that succeeded it, to give BL money to revamp its range. To help do this, he established the company's first links with Honda. BL continued losing money, but Michael Edwards succeeded – where Donald Stokes had failed – in breaking the power of the trade unions. Under the premiership of Margaret Thatcher he threatened the unions with the ultimate sanction – to close the company!

While state-owned, BL absorbed £2 billion[*] in government aid and accumulated a further £2.6 billion losses – £200 worth of aid for each person in the United Kingdom. Margaret Thatcher refused to give BL any more. The sale of Jaguar provided some funds, but by 1986 Margaret Thatcher had lost patience and called in Graham Day, a Canadian, to sort out BL. He had earlier 'rationalized' British Shipbuilding. Taking

[*]1 ecu = UK£0.83.

BMW as a model, Graham Day shifted the product range up-market and, with the help of Honda, rationalized products and introduced new work practices. In cut after cut, some of the great names of the car industry disappeared: Vanden Plas, Riley, Austin-Healey, Wolseley, Triumph, Morris and Austin. BL was sliced and sold off: trucks to Daf of the Netherlands; buses went eventually to Sweden's Volvo; the spares operation, Unipart, to a group of financial institutions; and finally Rover, the renamed rump of the company, to BAe. Both Ford and GM tried to buy parts of Rover, particularly the famous Land Rover division. However, fearing the political backlash, the sales fell through. Now Thatcher's government could boast that the deal kept Rover 'British' by putting it safely in the hands of Britain's biggest engineering group – an aeroplane maker.

### Rover: going Japanese

The link with Honda saved Rover from extinction. It provided product and manufacturing knowledge that Rover lacked. They gained first-hand experience of Japan's world-beating manufacturing ways and drank deeply from the pool of experience. Licensing Honda's car designs allowed Rover's 2,000 engineering and development staff to concentrate upon their own new K-series engine and off-the-road vehicle design.

One of the most valuable lessons Rover learned from Honda was how to break down barriers between departments to ease production and product development. They were taught how to bring product to market more quickly and with fewer mistakes in product development. Product development was done at production plants rather than at a centralized location. For the new Rover 600, the project leader was based at Cowley where the car would be made. He chose a team from around the company who worked out of one room while shaping the car. In this way Rover developed their small capacity multi-valve K-series engine from scratch. Its 4- and 6-cylinder developments could power almost any of Rover's future cars.

Land Rover had made civilian and military off-road vehicles for years, but changed direction in 1970 with their Range Rover – a luxury vehicle with polished wood trim and the capability to cross fields, streams, deserts and jungles. Designed for Britain's wealthy country-living classes, the 'Hollywood Jeep' appeared wherever there was money. The Range Rover defined a new product class. It became a fashion statement – the only vehicle to have been exhibited in the Louvre in Paris as a work of art. People who never got their shoes nor car dirty liked the Range Rover classic design and the way it allowed its drivers to stare over and look down on other road users. Other car makers followed Rover's lead and helped Europe's off-the-road sports/utility vehicle market grow from 50,000 in 1980 to 300,000 in 1990. Rover's newfound product development skills allowed it to defend Land Rover's strong position at the top of the market. Their all-new Rover Discovery model went into production in a record breaking twenty-one months. Launched in 1989, it helped Land Rover's sales to grow from 46,700 in 1988 to 73,527 in 1993, during a period in which other car makers suffered declining sales. Priced between £17,500 and £26,800 the Discovery is not cheap, but it has allowed Land Rover to move its new generation, 200 kph, £31,950 to £43,950 Range Rover up-market to compete with top-of-the-range BMW, Mercedes, Jaguar and Lexus.

Honda saved Rover – but at a price. The sumo held the recovering Rover in a constricting embrace. Honda protected Rover but stopped the car business making profits. Rover had to pay Honda handsomely for the floor-plans and engines it needed for its larger models. They also paid a royalty to Honda for each jointly developed car Rover sold. The technology agreement barred Rover from selling Honda-based models in markets Honda wanted for themselves, such as the United States. Rover needed a better deal with Honda but their weak position and Honda's intractability left BAe in a jam. 'We were involved in some kind of Japanese poker game,' said Richard Evans, chief executive of BAe.

### Enter BMW

The play of Richard Evans's last poker card sent Honda reeling. On 29 January 1994, BAe sold their 80 per cent stake in Rover to BMW. With one bold move BMW's share of the European car market doubled to 6.4 per cent, they became market leader in

## CASE 12 (cont)

**Exhibit 12.2**   Ranges

| Type | Honda | Rover | BMW | Rolls-Royce |
|------|-------|-------|-----|-------------|
| Basic | | Mini | | |
| Super Mini | | Metro | | |
| Small family | Civic | 200* | | |
| Saloon | Concerto | 400* | | |
| | | Maestro | | |
| Large family | | Montego | 300 | |
| Saloon | | | | |
| Executive | Accord | 600* | 500 | |
| Luxury | Legend | 800* | 700 | |
| Exotic | | | 800 | All |
| Off-the-road | | Defender | | |
| | | Discovery | | |
| | | Range Rover | | |

Note: * Based on Honda.

the off-the-road market, and they gained a range of small cars, a low-cost manufacturing base, and access to Honda's production know-how. Simultaneously, they wrecked Honda's European strategy.

The speed of Honda's undoing left their managers in Tokyo bewildered and resentful. 'Now our partner has been acquired by our competitor we must start to reassess our entire operation in Europe', said Kiyoshi Ikemi, councillor to Honda's president, Nobuhiko Kawamoto. 'Mr. Kawamoto has made it quite clear that he has no intention of collaborating with BMW in the UK. We did not want to collaborate with Rover through BMW. Such a collaboration was not called for – we had nothing to gain from it.' According to industry observers, the collapse of Honda's European alliance could not have happened at a worse time for the company. Management attention was on the very depressed Japanese market and the United States where Honda were losing share to the revitalized American car makers. Honda had offered to buy a 47.5 per cent share in Rover, but, explained Mr. Kawamoto, 'We did not want to make Rover Japanese. We wanted to increase Rover's Roverness. We wanted it to be more British – that was the way the collaboration would work best.'

BMW's campaign on Honda's seemingly impregnable position had started in September 1993. It had identified Rover as a target that would extend its car range and achieve economies of scale in distribution, component sourcing and R&D. BMW's initial offer to

BAe was repulsed because of Rover's relationship with Honda. Despite the rebuff, BMW continued scrutinizing Rover. Wolfgang Reitzle, BMW's R&D director, quietly visited Rover's plants and, back in Germany, test drove the entire fleet (see Exhibit 12.2). Hagan Lüderitz, BMW's director of corporate planning, says BMW delivered a letter to Honda's Mr Kawamoto, stating their interest in Rover. He got no response. Mr Kawamoto's councillor, Mr Ikemi, denies any direct approach, saying Honda only had indirect hints of BMW's interest. 'We weren't informed properly until Friday last week [the day before the BMW deal],' he protested.

After the deal, the mood amongst BMW's management was different to Honda's. Mr Volker Doppelfeld, BMW's finance director, explained that they had taken the shortest and cheapest route to fulfil their long-term aim of expanding BMW's core car business into new market segments. The long route would have meant a step-by-step move from BMW's up-market saloon base. In the event, the DM2,000 million paid for Rover is what BMW would normally spend on developing a single new model. Included in the price, he explained, were seventeen brands, including Land Rover and Range Rover, which came equipped with 'the most interesting, the best, and the longest heritage in off-the-road vehicles'. There was talk of how the Mini could become an up-market small car, the rebirth of the MG, and licensing Rover technology to Malaysia and Korea. However, within a few days BMW's euphoria declined. Honda threatened not to honour their deals with BAe and questioned their own future in Europe.

In December 1994 BMW signed another deal with another British company, Rolls-Royce. After beating off competition from Mercedes, BMW will supply V8 and V12 engines for Rolls-Royce and Bentley cars. Soon Mrs Joanna BraUhn will have an even bigger choice of cars when she goes for a spin.

## Questions

1. Why did the combining of a large number of car makers to form British Leyland not help the country's 'chief strategic industry?' Why did British Leyland's broad range of vehicles not allow it to defend its position in the world's markets?

2. Attacking the US luxury car market forced Honda, Toyota and Nissan to move from making cars equivalent to American inexpensive 'compacts' to large expensive luxury Acura, Infiniti and Lexus models. Why do you think they attacked these segments rather than the mass market for 'regular' sized cars in the United States? Why did the Japanese attack the luxury car market in the United States rather than taking the battle to Europe?

3. What enabled Land Rover to hold its position in the market even though the Rover group could not? Why did Rover manage to increase sales when the rest of the world's car industry was in decline? Given Rover's much wider range, why were they not as successful as BMW who had a much smaller range of vehicles to sell?

4. If BAe wanted to get rid of Rover, and Honda did not want it, what good is it to BMW? What do you think explains Honda's reaction to the supposed contact with BMW? Would you recommend Honda to pull-the-plug on their deal with Rover?

Sources: Simon Davies, 'BAe flies away from Rover with a sack full of cash', *Financial Times* (1 February 1994), 1; Christopher Parkes, 'A quick route into new market segments', *Financial Times* (1 February 1994), 22; Paul Abrahams and John Griffiths, 'Honda's European strategy wrecked', *Financial Times* (1 February 1994), 22; Kenneth Gooding, 'Rich British ancestry fails to provide independent future', *Financial Times* (1 February 1994), 23; 'Europe's car makers: then there were seven', *The Economist* (5 February 1994), 19–24; Andrew Lorenz and Matthew Lynn, 'BMW drives in', *Sunday Times: Business Focus* (6 February 1994), 2–3; Peter Miller, 'One careful lady owner', *Sunday Times: News Review* (6 February 1994), 1; B. John Griffiths, 'Capable of producing from the ground up', *Financial Times* (22 February 1994), 24; Tony Lewin, 'Rebirth of the Range Rover', *The European* (30 Sept.–6 Oct. 1994), 23; 'Ecstasy meets Mercedes', *The Economist* (17 December 1994), 72; John Griffiths, 'Rolls-Royce keep hold of the steering wheel', *Financial Times* (20 December 1994), 8.

# A cola challenge

## Cola with breakfast

Ron Watson wrestled his 18-wheeler on to an exit ramp on Interstate 85 south of the Virginia–North Carolina border. Although it was only 7.00 a.m., Ron had already been driving almost four hours since leaving his trucking company's main terminal in Charlotte, North Carolina. The 26-year-old driver's stomach felt empty. Ron pulled in to a truck stop and parked. He picked up the morning paper as he entered the restaurant, then sauntered over to the counter. A half-asleep waitress handed Ron a menu and asked if he was ready to order.

'Sure,' he nodded, 'I'd like two eggs, sunny-side up, a side order of pancakes and a Pepsi.' The waitress, who had been busy scribbling his order, stopped writing and eyed Ron suspiciously. Another customer seated nearby looked up from his paper.

'Did you say Pepsi?' the waitress asked as if her sleepiness had affected her hearing.

'That's right,' Ron replied, a smile brightening his face. 'Been drinking Pepsi with breakfast for years. You ought to give it a try.'

'No thanks!', the waitress replied as she wrote 'Pepsi' on the order pad and turned towards the kitchen. As she walked away, she mumbled, 'Takes all kinds.'

Ron Watson was used to funny looks when he orders breakfast, but he's not alone. Thousands of other customers have joined the ranks of those who like a cold cola drink with breakfast instead of the traditional hot coffee. In fact, the Coffee Development Group, an industry trade association, estimates that per capita daily coffee consumption peaked in 1962 at 3.12 cups. Since then, coffee consumption has steadily declined to the present level of 1.76 cups. At the same time, the soft-drink industry calculates that morning soft-drink consumption accounts for 12 per cent of total soft-drink sales, up from 9 per cent ten years ago.

Soft-drink manufacturers have paid close attention to this gain of three percentage points in a market where 1 per cent of market share represents more than $400 million in retail sales. Although the change has been gradual, industry analysts argue that the trend testifies to the power of sophisticated advertising. In recent decades, they note, soft-drink manufacturers have outspent almost all other producers of non-alcoholic drinks. They poured money into advertising designed to persuade young people to drink more soda. These young people have grown up with soft drinks and are now a very significant buying force. Further, the rapid growth in fast-food merchandising, the explosive growth of the vending industry and the proliferation of convenience stores have made soft drinks available almost everywhere at almost any time. As a result, the *Beverage Industry Digest* reports that people between the ages of 24 and 44 represent the largest group of soft-drink consumers, accounting for 27 per cent of total market sales.

Citing what it calls a 'watershed movement', Coca-Cola became the first company to take direct action in order to capitalize on the growth in morning consumption of soft drinks. In 1987, the company tested a promotional campaign dubbed 'Coke in the Morning' in cities across the United States. Early in 1988, Coca-Cola made the programme available to its bottlers across the country. The campaign does not directly attack coffee, which accounts for 47 per cent of morning beverages sold. The consumption of all other drinks is much lower: 21 per cent for juices, 17 per cent for milk, 7 per cent for tea and only 4 per cent for soft drinks. Rather, the campaign, designed by Coca-Cola's advertising agency McCann-Erickson, focuses on the time after the consumer leaves home in the morning and on the mid-morning coffee break.

At first, Pepsi-Cola Company, like the rest of the industry, stood by to see what would result from Coca-Cola's efforts. Now, however, Pepsi-Cola appears to be charging in with an even more aggressive strategy than Coca-Cola's. In late 1989, Pepsi-Cola announced that it was launching its new strategy in test markets in the Midwest. Those test markets revealed just how aggressive the new strategy will be. First, rather than just positioning its regular product for morning consumption, Pepsi-Cola has developed a new brand, Pepsi A.M. – available in both diet and regular forms – designed specifically for the morning segment. Whereas regular Pepsi contains 3.2 milligrams of caffeine per fluid ounce and Coca-Cola Classic contains 3.8 milligrams, Pepsi A.M. has 4 milligrams. Still, Pepsi A.M.'s caffeine level contains only one-quarter the level of caffeine found in a cup of regular coffee. Pepsi-Cola have also lowered the level of carbonation in the new drink to help with digestion.

Pepsi-Cola's promotional strategy for Pepsi A.M. is as important to the marketing effort as the product change. The ads attack coffee head on. For example, one print ad shows a series of cups of coffee and one Pepsi A.M. can. Printed under the Pepsi A.M. can is the message, 'A refreshing break from the daily grind'.

Both Coca-Cola, with its subtle approach, and Pepsi-Cola, with its aggressive campaign, face a challenge in attempting to pry open the morning drink market. Coffee drinkers are loyal. Furthermore, both companies must overcome the 'Yuck factor'. Like Ron Watson's waitress, many consumers find drinking cola in the morning disgusting. Finally, the coffee industry is not likely to sit quietly by and watch Pepsi and Coke steal its market.

Pepsi and Cola may one day challenge one another for shares of a growing morning-cola market. But before they can do battle against each other for that segment, they must first win the battle with tradition to obtain a place for colas at the breakfast table and in the coffee break.

## QUESTIONS

1. What is the target audience for Coca-Cola's 'Coke in the Morning' campaign? What is the target for Pepsi A.M.? Are these audiences the same?
2. What buyer responses are Coca-Cola and Pepsi-Cola trying to generate from their target customers?
3. What general message content and message structure decisions should the two companies make in setting their message strategies?
4. What promotion mixes should the companies use? Should the two companies use the same or different mixes? Why?
5. Given the promotion mixes you recommend, what specific ads and other promotion ideas would you recommend to Pepsi-Cola and Coca-Cola to help them win over the morning-cola market?
6. Should Pepsi-Cola be concerned about the ethical issue raised by encouraging consumers to have colas with breakfast, especially if its efforts encourage young children to drink colas with breakfast?

# Product

Product

## CHAPTER THIRTEEN

# Designing products

## New-product development and product life-cycle strategies

## CHAPTER OBJECTIVES

After reading this chapter, you should be able to:

- Describe the new-product development process.

- Explain how companies find and develop new-product ideas.

- Describe the stages of the product life cycle.

- Explain how marketing strategy changes during a product's life cycle.

## CHAPTER PREVIEW

### Aerostructures Hamble

Markets do not stand still. When customer needs and technology change, companies, big or small, must create new products and invest in new technology to keep abreast of such changes in the marketplace.

Aerostructures Hamble, a Hampshire (UK)-based aircraft components manufacturer, is a good example of a company that has survived many changes in its industry. Through its emphasis upon customer-oriented innovation and lean management techniques to speed up product development, it has maintained outstanding performance in a highly competitive aircraft components industry.

The company started in 1936 making the Midge and Gnat aircraft. Hawker Siddeley took it over in 1963. The aircraft manufacturing side of Hawker Siddeley was nationalized as part of the British Aircraft Corporation, which was privatized in 1979. It became Aerostructures Hamble in 1989 when British Aerospace decided to make it more accountable as a profit centre. In 1990, Andy Barr, chief executive, joined from Rover Group and led a £46.7 million management buyout.

1 ecu = UK£0.83

With a small team of ten senior managers, including Mr Barr and an operations director, Mr Wyman, who had also come from Rover, new management techniques were introduced – notably Japanese techniques devised by car manufacturers.

In the 1930s, the slipway of Aerostructures Hamble was used to launch seaplanes. In the 1990s it is being used to dispatch cargo doors of transport planes. Its transformation from aircraft to aircraft component manufacturer is not the surprising element in Aerostructure's strategy, which reflects the many changes undergone by the British aerospace industry. What is noteworthy is the speed of execution of the order and its on-time delivery, something, Mr Wyman claims is totally alien to the aircraft industry.

The company stresses the need to introduce the 'right product' first time, like the Japanese car makers do. It is hard work but all functions in the firm must be involved in innovation.

The company has invested heavily in new plant equipment, including riveting machinery, a large press, machine tools and a world-class aluminium finishing plant. It also sets tight parameters for component manufacture using computer technology and techniques such as statistical process control, which ensure that a part will fit and comes out right first time.

In order to get things right first time, the firm approaches each new project through a multidisciplinary team with a manager who becomes the main contact with the customer. People are seconded from other parts of the firm. The manager sticks with the team from the initial bid through to completion of the project. While some of the team members might change, there is a consistent thread running right through the project, from initial conception to final delivery. The goal is to achieve a 'seamless' process as Mr Wyman suggests, which is in marked contrast with the old method of passing a project from one department to another.

Quality is given heavy emphasis, and quality control techniques, including suggestion schemes in which over 50 per cent of the staff have taken part, have borne fruitful results.

Other parts of its operations have been reworked or reorganized to allow the company to utilize just-in-time delivery of components to specific parts of its factory. It has introduced 'kitting', through which parts are dispatched to a customer in a carefully laid out package. This simple innovation enables any part missing to be immediately visible and has revolutionized the traceability of orders and saved hours of dispute.

The company's reliance on its former owner, British Aerospace, which accounted for 93 per cent of its business in 1990, fell to 78 per cent in 1993 and is expected to fall further in the late 1990s. It has successfully secured new orders and acquired an impressive blue chip customer base, including Boeing, McDonnell Douglas, Vought and Raytheon.

The company claims its methods are new in the aircraft components industry. While the new techniques ensure that it creates new products which are a perfect fit with customer requirements, management are well aware that it gets tougher as they go on – customers and market needs are continually evolving and products and methods must follow suit.[1]

## INTRODUCTION

In the face of changing customer needs, technologies and competition, product innovation or the development of new products, has become vital to a company's survival. Introducing new products, however, is not sufficient. The firm must also know how to manage the new product as it goes through its life cycle: that is, from its birth, through growth and maturity, to eventual demise as newer products come along that better serve consumer needs.

This product life cycle present two principal challenges. First, because all products eventually decline, the firm must find new products to replace ageing ones (the problem of *new-product development*). Second, the firm must understand how its products age and adapt its marketing strategies as products pass through life-cycle stages (the problem of *product life-cycle strategies*). We therefore look initially at the problem of finding and developing new products, and then at the challenge of managing them successfully over their life cycles.

## INNOVATION AND NEW-PRODUCT DEVELOPMENT

Given the rapid changes in taste, technology and competition, a company cannot rely solely on its existing products to sustain growth or to maintain profitability. The firm can hope to maintain market and profit performance only by continuous product innovation. Product innovation encompasses a variety of product development activities – product improvement, development of entirely new ones, and extensions that increase the range or number of lines of product the firm can offer. Product innovations are not to be confused with **inventions**. The latter are a new technology or product which may or may not deliver benefits to customers. An **innovation** is defined as *an idea, product or piece of technology that has been developed and marketed to customers who perceive it as novel or new*. We may call it a process of identifying, creating and delivering new product values that did not exist before in the marketplace. In this chapter we look specifically at new products as opposed to value creation through marketing actions (such as product/brand repositioning, segmentation of current markets).

We also need to distinguish between obtaining new products through **acquisition** – by buying a whole company, a patent, or a licence to produce someone else's product – and through **new-product development** in the company's own research and development department. As the costs of developing and introducing major new products have climbed, many large companies have decided to acquire existing brands rather than to create new ones. Other firms have saved money by copying competitors' brands or by reviving old brands. These routes can contribute to a firm's growth and have both advantages and limitations. In this chapter, we are mainly concerned with how businesses create and market new products. By new products we mean original products, product improvements, product modifications and new brands that the firm develops through its own research and development efforts.

### Risks and returns in innovation

Innovation can be very risky for a number of reasons:

1. New product development is an expensive affair – it cost Tate & Lyle around £150 million to develop a new sugar substitute; pharmaceutical firms spend an average of £100–150 million to develop a new drug, whilst developing a super-jumbo project could cost billions of pounds.
2. New-product development takes time. Although companies can dramatically shorten their development time (see 'Speeding up new product development' later in this chapter), in many industries, such as pharmaceuticals, biotechnology, aerospace and food, new-product development cycles can be as long as ten to fifteen years. The uncertainty and unpredictability of market environments further raise the risks of commercialization.[2] Boots had to withdraw Manoplex, a heart drug, less than a year after its launch in the United Kingdom in September 1992,

after a trial on 3,000 patients in the United States and Scandinavia suggested an adverse effect on patient survival. The pharmaceuticals division lost about £200 million on the drug, which cost nearly £100 million to develop over a period of 12 years, and about £20 million was spent on promoting and marketing it.

3. Unexpected delays in development are also a problem. History is littered with grand pioneering engineering projects which have failed to satisfy the original expectations of bankers, investors and politicians. The Seikan rail tunnel, connecting the island of Hokkaido to mainland Japan was completed fourteen years late and billions of pounds over budget; the £10 billion cost of the Channel tunnel, which opened on 6 May 1994, a year later than originally planned, is more than double the £4.8 billion forecast in 1987.

4. The new product success record is not encouraging either. New products continue to fail at a disturbing rate. One recent study estimated that new consumer packaged goods (consisting mostly of line extensions) fail at a rate of 80 per cent. The same high failure rate appears to afflict new financial products and services, such as credit cards, insurance plans and brokerage services. Another study found that about 33 per cent of new industrial products fail at launch.[3]

Despite the risks, firms that learn to innovate well become less vulnerable to attacks by new entrants who discover new ways of delivering added values, benefits and solutions to customers' problems.

## Why do new products fail?

Concorde aircraft (an Anglo-French project), PCjr personal computer (IBM), Betamax video cassette recorder (Sony), EuroDisneyland (Walt Disney/EuroDisney Group), the C5 (Clive Sinclair's electric car) all have one thing in common – they all failed to meet target returns on investment, and therefore join the ranks of new-product failure.

Why do so many new products fail? There are several reasons. Although an idea may be good, the market size may have been overestimated. Perhaps the actual product was not designed as well as it should have been. It may be a 'me too' product that is no better than products which are already established in the marketplace. Or maybe it was incorrectly positioned in the market, priced too high or advertised and promoted poorly. A high-level executive might push a favourite idea despite poor marketing research findings. Sometimes the costs of product development are higher than budgeted and sometimes competitors fight back harder than expected.

## What governs new product success?

Because so many new products fail, companies are anxious to learn how to improve their chances of new-product success. One way is to identify successful new products and find out what they have in common. A recent study of 200 moderate- to high-technology new-product launches, which looked for factors shared by successful products but not by product failures, found that the number one success factor is a *unique superior product*, one with higher quality, new features, higher value in use and other such attributes. Specifically, products with a high product advantage succeed 98 per cent of the time, compared to products with a moderate advantage (58 per cent success) or minimal advantage (18 per cent success). Another key success factor is a *well-defined product concept* prior to development, in which the company

Amstrad attempts to create value that has never existed before.

carefully defines and assesses the target market, the product requirements, and the benefits before proceeding. New products that *meet market needs* more closely than existing products invariably do well. Other success factors included *technological and marketing synergy, quality of execution in all stages* and *market attractiveness.*[4] Thus to create successful new products, a company must understand its consumers, markets and competitors and develop products that deliver superior value to customers.

Successful new-product development may be even more difficult in the future. Keen competition has led to increasing market fragmentation – companies must now aim at smaller market segment rather than the mass market, and this means smaller sales and profits for each product. New products must meet growing social and government constraints such as consumer safety and environmental standards. The costs of finding, developing and launching new products will increase steadily due to rising manufacturing, media and distribution costs. Many companies cannot afford or cannot raise the funds needed for new-product development. Instead, they emphasize product modification and imitation rather than true innovation. Even when a new product is successful, rivals are so quick to follow suit that the new product typically is fated to have only a short happy life.

So, companies face a problem – they must develop new products, but the odds weigh heavily against success. The solution lies in careful *new product planning*. Top management is ultimately accountable for the new-product success record. It must take the lead, rather than simply ask lower-level staff or the new-product manager to come up with great ideas. It must define the business domains and product categories that the company wants to focus on. Many or most new product ideas are likely to be unsuitable for development. Management must encourage the search for a large pool of ideas from which potential winners emerge. To facilitate the selection process, it must establish specific criteria for new-product idea acceptance, especially in large multidivisional companies where all kinds of projects bubble up as favourites of various managers. These criteria will vary with the specific *strategic role* the product is expected to play. The product's role might be to help the company maintain its industry position as an innovator, to defend a market-share position, or to get a foothold in a future new market. Or the new product might help the company to take advantage of its special strengths or exploit technology in a new way. For example, an electronics firm set the following screening criteria for new products aimed at exploiting a technology in a new way: (1) the product can be introduced within five years; (2) the product has a market potential of at least £50 million and a 15 per cent growth rate; (3) the product will provide at least 30 per cent return on sales and 40 per cent on investment; and (4) the product will achieve technical or market leadership.

Another crucial decision facing top management is how much to budget for new-product development New-product outcomes are so uncertain that it is difficult to use normal investment criteria for budgeting. Some companies solve this problem by encouraging and financing as many projects as possible, hoping to achieve a few winners. Other companies set their R&D budgets by applying a conventional percentage-to-sales figure or by spending what the competition spends. Still other companies decide how many successful new products they need and work backwards to estimate the required R&D investment.

Another important factor in new-product development work is to set up effective organizational structures for nurturing innovation and handling new products. Successful new-product development requires a total-company effort. Successful innovative companies make a consistent commitment of resources to new-product development, design and new-product strategy that is linked to their strategic planning process, and set up formal and sophisticated organizational arrangements for managing the new-product development process (see Marketing Highlight 13.1).

## NEW-PRODUCT DEVELOPMENT PROCESS

The new-product development process for finding and growing new products consists of nine main steps (see Figure 13.1).

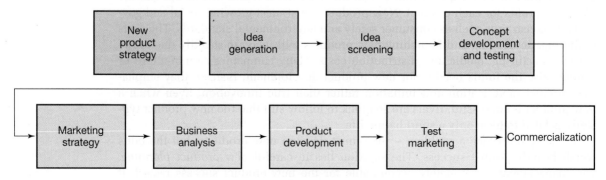

**Figure 13.1**    Steps in new-product development.

## New-products strategy

Effective product innovation is guided by a definite *corporate strategy* for new products. Without a clear strategy, the new-product programme lacks direction; without good direction the new-product team members are unlikely to operate effectively and achieve new product objectives. The new-products strategy achieves four main goals: first, it *focuses team effort*; second, it brings about *integration* of functional or departmental efforts; third, it acts as a *delegation* tool by letting team members operate independently, effectively and efficiently while remaining integrated with the rest of the project team; and fourth, the very act of producing and getting management agreement on strategy requires *proactive*, not reactive, management, which increases the likelihood of a more thorough search for innovation opportunities. For example, Bausch & Lomb, the contact lens and lens-care products maker, was on the verge of losing its market position in the late 1980s because its managers had concentrated for too long on product improvement. It almost missed new product opportunities like extended-wear contact lenses. Fortunately, managers reviewed their new-product strategy and spotted many more opportunities for innovation, which they eventually capitalized on.[5]

Successful innovative companies that think strategically are placing more emphasis upon the use of definitive strategy statements or a **product innovation charter** (PIC). The PIC draw managers' attention to the reasons or *rationale* behind the firm's search for innovation opportunities, the *product/market* and *technology* to focus on, the miscellaneous *goals* or *objectives* (e.g., market share, cash flow, profitability, etc.) to be achieved, and *guidelines* on the nature or level of innovativeness that will sell the new product.[6] The charter should therefore state the effort to be allocated to developing breakthrough products, changing existing ones, and imitating competitors' products.

## Idea generation

The PIC should then direct the search for new-product ideas. **Idea generation** should be systematic rather than haphazard. Otherwise, although the company will find many ideas, most will not be good ones for its type of business. A company typically has to generate many ideas in order to find a few good ones.

To obtain a flow of new-product ideas, the company can tap many sources. Chief sources of new-product ideas include internal sources, customers, competitors, distributors and suppliers and others.

### Internal sources

Studies have found that nearly half or more of all new-product ideas come from within the company.[7] The company can find new ideas through formal research and development. It can pick the brains of its scientists, engineers, designers and manufacturing people. Or company executives can brainstorm new-product ideas. The company's salespeople are another good source of ideas because they are in daily contact with customers. Formal or informal suggestion schemes also can be used to tap staff's ideas. Toyota claims that employees submit two million ideas annually – about 35 suggestions per employee – and that more than 85 per cent of these ideas are implemented.

## 3M: championing innovation

The 3M Company markets more than 60,000 products. These products range from sandpaper, adhesives, and floppy disks to contact lenses, laser optical disks, aerosol inhalers, heart-lung machines, translucent braces, and futuristic synthetic ligaments; from coatings that sleeken boat hulls to hundreds of sticky tapes – Scotch Tape, masking tape, superbonding tape and even refastening disposable nappy tape. 3M views innovation as its path to growth, and new products as its lifeblood. Up till 1992, the company's longstanding goal was to derive 25 per cent of annual sales from products which had been on the market for less than five years. In 1992, in the light of increasing competition, it decided to raise its sights. An astonishing 30 per cent of each year's sales should come from products introduced within the previous four years. More astonishing, it has succeeded in achieving the new target. Its legendary emphasis on innovation has consistently made 3M one of America's, and possibly the world's, most admired companies.

New products don't just happen. 3M's impressive record is due to several factors. The company works hard to create an environment that supports innovation. It invests nearly 7 per cent of annual group sales in research and development – twice as much as the average company. Its Innovation Task Force seeks out and destroys corporate bureaucracy that might interfere with new-product progress. Hired consultants help 3M find ways to make employees more inventive.

3M's culture is innovative. Its management encourages everyone to look for new products. The company's renowned '15 per cent rule' allows all employees to spend up to 15 per cent of their time 'bootlegging' – that is, working on projects of personal interest whether or not those projects directly benefit the company. When a promising idea comes along, 3M forms a venture team made up of the researcher who developed the idea and volunteers from manufacturing, sales, marketing, and legal. Developing cross-functional teams is the touchstone of 3M's efforts to facilitate the flow of technology around the company. The team nurtures the product and protects it from company bureaucracy. Team members stay with the product until it succeeds or fails and then return to their previous jobs. Some teams have tried three or four times before finally making a success of an idea. Each year, 3M hands out Golden Step Awards to venture teams whose new products earned more than US$2 million* in US sales, or US$4 million in worldwide sales, within three years of introduction.

3M's management culture encourages the cross-fertilization of ideas between its forty or more business units. Much of this is done through informal networking such as employee-run technical forums or getting technicians to go out and meet customers. Cross-fertilization is also reinforced by official bodies, such as audit teams, whose main function is to go round laboratory groups and assess the commercial potential of their new-product programmes. Often they come across developments in one lab which can be helpful to another.

The company knows that it must try thousands of new-product ideas to hit one big jackpot. One well-worn slogan at 3M is, 'You have to kiss a lot of frogs to find a prince'. 'Kissing frogs' often means making mistakes, but 3M accepts blunders and dead ends as a normal part of creativity and innovation. In fact, its philosophy seems to be, 'if you aren't making mistakes, you probably aren't doing anything'. Dating back to 1941, a paper spelling out 3M's management philosophy declared that employees must be allowed to perform their work in their own way and be allowed to make mistakes – what we call worker 'empower-

*1 ecu = US$1.26.

### Customers

Almost 28 per cent of all new-product ideas come from watching and listening to customers. The company can conduct surveys to learn about consumer needs and wants. It can analyse customer questions and complaints to find new products that better solve consumer problems. Company engineers or salespeople can meet with customers to get suggestions. General Electric's Video Products Division, Sony, Toyota and many other

Championing innovation: 3M's innovation track record is hard to beat.

chemical eventually became Scotchgard fabric protector.

And then there's the one about 3M scientist Spencer Silver. Silver started out to develop a super-strong adhesive; instead he came up with one that didn't stick very well at all. He sent the apparently useless substance on to other 3M researchers to see whether they could find something to do with it. Nothing happened for several years. Then Arthur Fry, another 3M scientist, had a problem ... and an idea. As a choir member in a local church, Mr Fry was having trouble marking places in his hymnal – the little scraps of paper he used kept falling out. He tried dabbing some of Mr Silver's weak glue on one of the scraps. It stuck nicely and later peeled off without damaging the hymnal. Thus were born 3M's ubiqui-tous Post-it notes, a product that now has sales of almost $100 million a year!

3M recognizes that to maintain its formidable rep-utation for innovation, management must keep alive its traditional innovative culture. It must be willing to engage in self-criticism and benchmarking against other companies to ensure that it continues to create products that become winners in the marketplace. Staff must keep close to customers, be given the freedom to 'bootleg', and communication channels around the company must remain open, with cross-functional teamwork upheld to ensure inventiveness is maximized, not stifled. Reward systems must recognize group efforts, given that get-ting inventions and new ideas to market invariably require extremely complex corporate teamwork. 3M stays on its toes. There is no room for complacency if you want to remain a corporate superstar.

ment' today. As it turns out, 'blunders' have turned into some of 3M's most successful products. Old-timers at 3M love to tell the story about the chemist who accidentally spilled a new chemical on her tennis shoes. Some days later, she noticed that the spots hit by the chemical had not become dirty. Eureka! The

Sources: Martin Dickson, 'Back to the future', *Financial Times* (30 May 1994), 7; '3M, 60,000 and counting', *The Economist* (30 November 1991), 86–89; Russel Mitchell, 'Master of innovation: how 3M keeps its new products coming', *Business Week* (10 April 1989), 58–64; Joyce Anne Oliver, '3M vet enjoys taking risks, knocking down barriers', *Marketing News* (15 April 1991), 13; and Kevin Kelly, '3M running scared? Forget about it', *Business Week* (16 September 1991), 59–62.

effective innovators are known to have their design engineers talk with final consumers to get ideas for new products. Many new ideas come from simply observing consumers.[8]

Honda's highly acclaimed City model was conceived in this manner. Honda sent designers and engineers from the City project team to Europe to 'look around' for the best product concept for the City. Based on the British Mini-Cooper, developed decades earlier, the Honda team designed a 'short and tall' car which countered the prevailing wisdom that cars should be long and low.

Observing the growing market potential in Third World countries, Boeing sent a team of engineers to those countries to study the idiosyncrasies of Third World aviation. The engineers found that many runways were too short for jet planes. Boeing redesigned the wings on its 737, added lower pressure tyres to prevent bouncing on short landings, and redesigned the engines for quicker takeoff. As a result, the Boeing 737 became the best-selling commercial jet in history.

Finally, consumers often create new products on their own, and companies can benefit by finding these products and putting them on the market. Pillsbury gets promising new recipes through its annual Bake-Off. One of Pillsbury's four cake-mix lines and several variations of another came directly from Bake-Off winners' recipes. About one-third of all the software IBM leases for its computers is developed by outside users.[9]

### Competitors

About 30 per cent of new-product ideas come from analysing competitors' products. The company can watch competitors' ads and other communications to get clues about their new products. Companies buy competing products, take them apart to see how they work, analyse their sales, and decide whether the company should bring out a new product of its own. For example, when designing its highly successful Taurus, Ford tore down more than 50 competing models, layer by layer, looking for things to copy or improve upon. It copied the Audi's accelerator-pedal 'feel', the Toyota Supra fuel gauge, the BMW 528e tyre and jack storage system and 400 other such outstanding features. Ford did this again when it redesigned the Taurus in 1992.[10]

### Distributors, suppliers and others

Resellers are close to the market and can pass along information about consumer problems and new-product possibilities. Suppliers can tell the company about new concepts, techniques and materials that can be used to develop new products. Other idea sources include: trade magazines, shows, and seminars; government agencies; new-product consultants; advertising agencies; marketing research firms; university, commercial laboratories and science parks; and inventors.

## Idea screening

The purpose of idea generation is to create a large number of ideas. The purpose of the succeeding stages is to *reduce* that number to a manageable few which deserve further attention. The first idea-reducing stage is **idea screening**. The purpose of screening is to spot good ideas and drop poor ones as soon as possible. As product-development costs rise greatly in later stages, it is important for the company to go ahead only with those product ideas that will turn into profitable products.

Most companies require their executives to write up new-product ideas on a standard form that can be reviewed by a new-product committee. The write-up describes the product, the target market, and the competition, and makes some rough estimates of market size, product price, development time and costs, manufacturing costs, and rate of return. The committee then evaluates the idea against a set of general criteria. At Kao Company of Japan, for example, the committee asks questions such as these: Is the product truly useful to consumers and society? Is this product good for our particular company? Does it mesh well with the company's objectives and strategies? Do we have the people, skills, and resources to make it succeed? Is its cost performance superior to competitive products? Is it easy to advertise and distribute?

Surviving ideas can be screened further using a simple rating process such as the one shown in Table 13.1. The first column lists factors required for the successful launching of the product in the marketplace. In the next column, management rates these factors on their relative importance. Thus management believes that marketing skills and experience are very important (0.20) and purchasing and supplies competence is of minor importance (0.05).

Next, on a scale of 0.0 to 1.0, management rates how well the new product idea fits the company's profile on each factor. Here management feels that the product idea fits very well with the company's marketing skills and experience (0.9), but not too well with its purchasing and supplies capabilities (0.5). Finally, management multiplies the importance of each success factor by the rating of fit to obtain an overall rating of the company's ability to launch the product successfully. Thus, if marketing is an important success factor and if this product fits the company's marketing skills, this will increase the overall rating of the product idea. In the example, the product idea scored 0.74, which places it at the high end of the 'fair idea' level.

The checklist promotes a more systematic product idea evaluation and basis for discussion. However, it is *not* designed to make the decision for management.

## Concept development and testing

Attractive ideas must now be developed into product concepts. It is important to distinguish between a *product idea*, a *product concept* and a *product image*. A **product idea** is an idea for a possible product that the company can see itself offering to the market. A **product concept** is a detailed version of the idea stated in meaningful consumer terms. A **product image** is the way consumers perceive an actual or potential product.

**TABLE 13.1**    *Product idea rating process*

| New-product success factors | (A) Relative importance | (B) Fit between product idea and company capabilities | | | | | | | | | | | Idea rating (A × B) |
|---|---|---|---|---|---|---|---|---|---|---|---|---|---|
| | | 0.0 | 0.1 | 0.2 | 0.3 | 0.4 | 0.5 | 0.6 | 0.7 | 0.8 | 0.9 | 1.0 | |
| Company strategy and objectives | 0.20 | | | | | | | | | x | | | 0.160 |
| Marketing skills and experience | 0.20 | | | | | | | | | | x | | 0.180 |
| Financial resources | 0.15 | | | | | | | | x | | | | 0.105 |
| Channels of distribution | 0.15 | | | | | | | | | x | | | 0.120 |
| Production capabilities | 0.10 | | | | | | | | | x | | | 0.080 |
| Research and development | 0.10 | | | | | | | | x | | | | 0.070 |
| Purchasing and supplies | 0.05 | | | | | | x | | | | | | 0.025 |
| Total | 1.00 | | | | | | | | | | | | 0.740* |

Note: *Rating scale: 0.00–0.40, poor; 0.50–0.75, fair; 0.76–1.00, good. Minimum acceptance level: 0.70.

### Concept development

Suppose a car manufacturer figures out how to design an electric car that can go as fast as 90 km per hour and as far as 170 km before needing to be recharged. The manufacturer estimates that the electric car's operating costs will be about half those of a regular car.

This is a product idea. Customers, however, do not buy a product idea; they buy a product *concept*. The marketer's task is to develop this idea into some alternative product concepts, find out how attractive each concept is to customers, and choose the best one.

The marketer might create the following product concepts for the electric car.

- *Concept 1* — An inexpensive subcompact designed as a second family car to be used around town. The car is ideal for loading groceries and hauling children and it is easy to enter.
- *Concept 2* — A medium-cost, medium-size car designed as an all-purpose family car.
- *Concept 3* — A medium-cost sporty compact appealing to young people.
- *Concept 4* — An inexpensive subcompact appealing to conscientious people who want basic transportation, low fuel cost, and low pollution.

To increase the likelihood of concept acceptance, some firms involve the customer (or potential customer) in concept development – as in the case of Aerostructures Hamble, the aircraft components manufacturer, who invites customers to its design reviews in the early stages of the new product process.

### Concept testing

**Concept testing** calls for testing new-product concepts with a group of target consumers. The concepts may be presented to consumers symbolically or physically. Here in, words, is *Concept 1:*

> An efficient, fun-to-drive, electric-powered subcompact car that seats four. Great for shopping trips and visits to friends. Costs half as much to operate as similar gasoline-driven cars. Goes up to 90 km per hour and does not need to be recharged for 170 km. Priced at £6,000.

In this case, a word or picture description might be sufficient. However, a more concrete and physical presentation of the concept will increase the reliability of the concept test. Today, marketers are finding innovative ways to make product concepts more real to concept-test subjects (see Marketing Highlight 13.2).

After being exposed to the concept, consumers then may be asked to react to it by answering the questions in Table 13.2. The answers will help the company decide which concept has the strongest appeal. For example, the last question asks about the consumer's intention to buy. Suppose 10 per cent of the consumers said they 'definitely' would buy and another 5 per cent said 'probably'. The company could project these figures to the population size of this target group to estimate sales volume. Concept testing offers a rough estimate of potential sales, but, managers must view this with caution. They must recognize that the estimate is only a broad pointer and is uncertain largely because consumers do not always carry out stated intentions.[11] Drivers, for example, might like the idea of the electric car that is kind to the environment, but might not want to pay for one! It is, nonetheless, important to carry out such tests with product concepts so as to gauge customers' response as well as identify aspects of the concept that are particularly liked or disliked by potential buyers. Feedback might suggest ways to refine the concept, thereby increasing its appeal to customers.

## The new world of concept testing: stereolithography and virtual reality

Product concept testing can be reliable only to the extent that the concept can be made real to consumers. The more the presentation of the concept resembles the final product or experience, the more dependable the concept testing. Today, many firms are developing interesting new methods for product concept testing.

For example, 3D Systems, Inc., uses a technique known as 3-D printing – or 'stereolithography' – to create three-dimensional models of physical products, such as small appliances and toys. The process begins with a computer-generated, three-dimensional image of the prototype:

> A three-dimensional design is first simulated on a computer, which then electronically 'slices' the image into wafer-thin segments. The digital information that designs each of these segments is then used to guide a robotically controlled laser beam, which focuses on a soup of liquid plastic formulated to turn solid when exposed to light. The laser builds the object as it creates layer upon microthin layer of hardened plastic.

Within a few hours, the process turns out plastic prototypes that would otherwise take weeks to create. Researchers can show these models to consumers to gather their comments and reactions.

Stereolithography has produced some amazing success stories. Logitech, a company that produces computer mice and other peripherals, used stereolithography to win a highly sought contract from a big computer maker. Logitech was delighted when the computer maker requested a bid to manufacturer a specific mouse. The only hitch was that the bid had to be submitted within just two weeks. Using stereolithography, Logitech was able to design, build, and assemble a full functional, superior-quality prototype within the allotted time. The disbelieving customer awarded the contract to Logitech on the spot.

Beyond making prototypes, 3-D printing (also called 'desktop manufacturing') offers exciting prospects for manufacturing custom-made products at the push of a button:

> In the future lie 3-D 'factories' churning out custom-designed parts, companies storing their entire inventory electronically in a computer's memory banks, and possibly even the ability to 'fax' a solid object to distant locations.

When a large physical product such as an automobile is involved, it can be tested using a radically new approach called 'virtual reality'. Researchers use a software package to design a car on a computer. Subjects can then manipulate the simulated car as if it were a real object. By operating certain controls, a respondent can approach the simulated car, open the door, sit in the car, start the engine, hear the sound, drive away, and experience the ride. The entire experience can be enriched by placing the simulated car in a simulated showroom and having a simulated salesperson approach the customer with a certain manner and words. After completing this experience, the respondent is asked a series of questions about what he or she liked and disliked, as well as the likelihood of buying such a car. Researchers can vary car features and salesroom encounters to see which have the greatest appeal. Although this approach may be expensive, researchers learn a great deal about designing the right car before investing millions of dollars to build the real product.

Sources: Benjamin Wooley, *Virtual Worlds* (London: Blackwell, 1992); and 'The world leader in senseware orchestrates a sales tour de force using solid imaging', *The Edge*, 3D Systems, Inc., (spring 1993), 4–5; see also quotations taken from 'The ultimate widget: 3-D "printing" may revolutionize product design and manufacturing', *US News & World Report* (20 July 1992), 55.

## Marketing strategy development

Suppose *Concept 1* for the electric car tests best. The next step is to develop a **marketing strategy** for introducing this car to the market.

The **marketing strategy statement** consists of three parts. The first part describes the target market, the planned product position, and the sales, market share and profit goals for the first few years. Thus:

| **TABLE 13.2**    *Questions for electric car concept test* |
| :--- |

1.   Do you understand the concept of an electric car?
2.   Do you believe the claims about the electric car's performance?
3.   What are the main benefits of the electric car compared with a conventional car?
4.   What improvements in the car's features would you suggest?
5.   For what uses would you prefer an electric car to a conventional car?
6.   What would be a reasonable price to charge for the electric car?
7.   Who would be involved in your decision to buy such a car? Who would drive it?
8.  Would you buy such a car? (Definitely, probably, probably not, definitely not)

> The target market is households that need a second car for going shopping, running errands, and visiting friends. The car will be positioned as more economical to buy and operate, and more fun to drive than cars now available to this market. The company will aim to sell 200,000 cars in the first year, at a loss of not more than £2 million. In the second year, the company will aim for sales of 200,000 cars and a profit of £3 million.

The second part of the marketing strategy statement outlines the product's planned price, distribution and marketing budget for the first year.

> The electric car will be offered in three colours and will have optional air-conditioning and power-drive features. It will sell at a retail price of £8,000 – with 15 per cent off the list price to dealers. Dealers who sell more than ten cars per month will get an additional discount of 5 per cent on each car sold that month. An advertising budget of £10 million will be split fifty-fifty between national and local advertising. Advertising will emphasize the car's economy and fun. During the first year, £60,000 will be spent on marketing research to find out who is buying the car and to determine their satisfaction levels.

The third part of the marketing strategy statement describes the planned long-run sales, profit goals, and marketing mix strategy:

> The company intends to capture a 3 per cent long-run share of the total auto market and realize an after-tax return on investment of 15 per cent. To achieve this, product quality will start high and be improved over time. Price will be raised in the second and third years if competition permits. The total advertising budget will be raised each year by about 10 per cent. Marketing research will be reduced to £40,000 per year after the first year.

## Business analysis

Once management has decided on its product concept and marketing strategy, it can evaluate the business attractiveness of the proposal. **Business analysis** involves a review of the sales, costs, and profit projections for a new product to find out whether they satisfy the company's objectives. If they do, the product can move to the product-development stage.

To estimate sales, the company should look at the sales history of similar products and should survey market opinion. The firm should estimate minimum and maximum sales to learn the range of risk. After preparing the sales forecast, management can estimate the expected costs and profits for the product, including marketing, R&D, manufacturing, accounting and finance costs. The company then uses the sales and costs figures to analyse the new product's financial attractiveness.

## Product development

If the product concept passes the business test, it moves into **product development**. Here, R&D or engineering develop the product concept into a physical product. So far, the product has existed only as a word description, a drawing, or perhaps a crude mock-up. The product-development step, however, now calls for a large jump in investment. It will show whether the product idea can be turned into a workable product.

The R&D department will develop one or more physical versions of the product concept. R&D hopes to design a prototype that will satisfy and excite consumers and that can be produced quickly and at budgeted costs.

Developing a successful prototype can take days, weeks, months, or even years. The prototype must have the required functional features and also convey the intended psychological characteristics. The electric car, for example, should strike consumers as being well built and safe. Management must learn what makes consumers decide that a car is well built. Some consumers slam the door to hear its 'sound'. If the car does not have 'solid-sounding' doors, consumers may think it is poorly built.

When the prototypes are ready, they must be tested. Functional tests are then conducted under laboratory and field conditions to make sure that the product performs safely and effectively. The new car must start easily; it must be comfortable; it must be able to go around corners without overturning. Consumer tests are conducted, in which consumers test-drive the car and rate its attributes. Consider the following example:

> In the 1980s, Philips Consumer Electronics, Sony and Matsushita joined forces to develop a common format for consumer-based multimedia systems using compact discs. CD-interactive or CD-i was the result.
>
> The CD-i player plugs into a TV set and the user interface is a remote control device. The initial use of CD-i is for playing games and watching movies, but other applications such as home shopping are potentially very probable.
>
> Philips, however, recognises that, as with any new technology, the potential for home shopping must be demonstrated. First, home shopping companies are unlikely to replace their current paper-based shopping catalogues with CDs without knowing if the multimedia home shopping system works.
>
> Philips launched the HOMESTEAD (Home Shopping by Television and Discs) ESPRIT project in June 1992 which involved several user organisations – Freemans, one of the largest home shopping catalogue companies in the UK, Page & Moy, a major holiday provider, Barclays Bank and Little Big One, a Belgian audio-visual company.
>
> Barclays and Little Big One each received a 'multimedia toolkit' developed earlier by Philips. The toolkit was designed to be versatile and to allow the user company to assemble CD-based multimedia catalogues for itself and its partners. The customer test results were exceedingly encouraging: for example, Freeman's clothes catalogue showed their clothes and accessories in full-motion video and allowed consumers to either browse through the catalogue or go straight to the section that interested them. The Page & Moy catalogue helped users plan their cruise holidays, which were brought to life on the TV screen. The package takes the user on a tour of the ships from five different cruise companies, while also providing all the itinerary and booking details.
>
> Philips then started an extensive consumer trial in the middle of 1994, the largest of its type ever undertaken – 5,500 homes were issued the Freeman, Page & Moy and Barclays catalogues and a questionnaire designed to obtain consumers' response. Some 300 homes had never used CD-i and were vital for providing information on how the new product might be promoted to non-users of CD-i.[12] Tests such as these can be expensive, but the feedback from potential customers is invaluable in helping the firm to prepare for next steps in the new product programme.

When designing products, the company should look beyond simply creating products that satisfy consumer needs and wants. Too often, companies design their new products without enough concern for how the designs will be produced – their main goal is to create customer-satisfying products. The designs are then passed along to manufacturing, where engineers must try to find the best ways to produce the product.

Recently, many companies have adopted a new approach toward product development called *design for manufacturability and assembly* (DFMA). Using this approach, companies work to fashion products that are *both* satisfying *and* easy to manufacture. This often results not only in lower costs but also in higher quality and more reliable products. For example, using DFMA analysis, Texas Instruments redesigned an infrared gun-sighting mechanism that it supplies to the Pentagon. The redesigned product required seventy-five fewer parts, 78 per cent fewer assembly steps, and 85 per cent less assembly time. The new design did more than reduce production time and costs, it also worked better than the previous, more complex version. Thus DFMA can be a potent weapon in helping companies to get products to market sooner and to offer higher quality at lower prices.[13]

## Test marketing

If the product passes functional and consumer tests, the next step is **test marketing**, the stage at which the product and marketing programme are introduced into more realistic market settings.

Test marketing lets the marketer get experience with marketing the product. It allows the marketer to find potential problems and learn where more information is needed before going to the great expense of full introduction. The basic purpose of test marketing is to test the product itself in real market situations. But test marketing also allows the company to test its entire marketing programme for the product – its positioning strategy, advertising, distribution, pricing, branding and packaging, and budget levels. The company uses test marketing to learn how consumers and dealers will react to handling, using and repurchasing the product. The results can be used to make better sales and profit forecasts. Thus a good test market can provide a wealth of information about the potential success of the product and marketing programme.

The amount of test marketing needed varies with each new product. Test marketing costs can be enormous and test marketing takes time that may allow competitors to gain advantages. When the costs of developing and introducing the product are low or when management is already confident that the new product will succeed, the company may do little or no test marketing. Minor modifications of current products or copies of successful competitors' products might not need standard testing. But when the new-product introduction requires a large investment, or when management is not sure of the product or marketing programme, the company should do a lot of test marketing. In fact, some products and marketing programmes are tested, withdrawn, changed and retested many times during a period of several years before they are finally introduced. The costs of such test markets are high, but they are often small compared with the costs of making a serious mistake.

Thus whether or not a company test markets, and the amount of testing it does, depends on the cost and risk of introducing the product on the one hand, and on the testing costs and time pressures on the other. Test-marketing methods vary with the type of product and market situation, and each method has advantages and disadvantages.

When using test marketing, consumer-products companies usually choose one of three approaches – standard test markets, controlled test markets, or simulated test markets.

## Standard test markets

Standard test markets test the new consumer product in situations similar to those it would face in a full-scale launch. The company finds a small number of representative test cities where the company's salesforce tries to persuade resellers to carry the product and give it good shelf space and promotion support. The company puts on a full advertising and promotion campaign in these markets and uses store audits, consumer and distributor surveys, and other measures to gauge product performance. It then uses the results to forecast national sales and profits, to discover potential product problems and to fine-tune the marketing programme.

Standard market tests have some drawbacks. First, they take a long time to complete – sometimes from one to three years. If the testing proves to be unnecessary, the company will have lost many months of sales and profits. Second, extensive standard test markets may be very costly. Finally, standard test markets give competitors a look at the company's new product well before it is introduced nationally. Many competitors will analyse the product and monitor the company's test market results. If the testing goes on too long, competitors will have time to develop defensive strategies and may even beat the company's product to the market. For example, prior to its launch in the United Kingdom, Carnation Coffee-Mate, a coffee-whitener, was test marketed over a period of six years. This gave rival firm Cadbury ample warning and the opportunity to develop and introduce its own product – Marvel – to compete head on with Coffee-Mate.

Furthermore competitors often try to distort test-market results by cutting their prices in test cities, increasing their promotion or even buying up the product being tested. Despite these disadvantages, standard test markets are still the most widely used approach for significant market testing. But many companies today are shifting toward quicker and cheaper controlled and simulated test-marketing methods.

## Controlled test markets

Several research firms keep controlled panels of stores which have agreed to carry new products for a fee. The company with the new product specifies the number of stores and geographical locations it wants. The research firm delivers the product to the participating stores and controls shelf location, amount of shelf space, displays and point-of-purchase promotions, and pricing according to specified plans. Sales results are tracked to determine the impact of these factors on demand.

Controlled test-marketing systems are particularly well developed in the United States. Systems like Nielsen's Scantrack and Information Resources Inc.'s (IRI) BehaviorScan track individual behaviour from the television set to the checkout counter. IRI, for example, keeps panels of shoppers in carefully selected cities. It uses microcomputers to measure TV viewing in each panel household and can send special commercials to panel member television sets. Panel consumers buy from cooperating stores and show identification cards when making purchases. Detailed electronic-scanner information on each consumer's purchases is fed into a central computer, where it is combined with the consumer's demographic and TV viewing information and reported daily. Thus BehaviorScan can provide store-by-store, week-by-week reports on the sales of new products being tested. And because the scanners record the specific purchases of individual consumers, the system also can provide information on repeat purchases and the ways that different types of consumers are reacting to the new product, its advertising, and various other elements of the marketing programme.[14]

Controlled test markets take less time than standard test markets (six months to a year) and usually cost less (a year-long BehaviorScan test in the United States might cost from $200,000 to $2,000,000). However, some companies are concerned that the limited number of small cities and panel consumers used by the research services may not be representative of their products' markets or target consumers. And, as in standard test markets, controlled test markets allow competitors to get a look at the company's new product.

### Simulated test markets

Companies also can test new products in a simulated shopping environment. The company or research firm shows, to a sample of consumers, ads and promotions for a variety of products, including the new product being tested. It gives consumers a small amount of money and invites them to a real or laboratory store where they may keep the money or use it to buy items. The researchers note how many consumers buy the new product and competing brands. This simulation provides a measure of trial and the commercial's effectiveness against competing commercials. The researchers then ask consumers the reasons for their purchase or nonpurchase. Some weeks later, they interview the consumer by phone to determine product attitudes, usage, satisfaction, and repurchase intentions. Using sophisticated computer models, the researchers then project national sales from results of the simulated test market.

Simulated test markets overcome some of the disadvantages of standard and controlled test markets. They usually cost much less ($35,000 to $75,000), can be run in eight weeks, and keep the new product out of competitors' view. Yet, because of their small samples and simulated shopping environments, many marketers do not think that simulated test markets are as accurate or reliable as larger, real-world tests. Still, simulated test markets are used widely, often as 'pretest' markets. Because they are fast and inexpensive, one or more simulated tests can be run to quickly assess a new product or its marketing programme. If the pretest results are strongly positive, the product might be introduced without further testing. If the results are very poor, the product might be dropped or substantially redesigned and retested. If the results are promising but indefinite, the product and marketing programme can be tested further in controlled or standard test markets.[15]

### Test marketing industrial goods

Business marketers use different methods for test marketing their new products, such as: product-use tests; trade shows; distributor/dealer display rooms; and standard or controlled test markets.

*Product-use tests*   Here the business marketer selects a small group of potential customers who agree to use the new product for a limited time. The manufacturer's technical people watch how these customers use the product. From this test the manufacturer learns about customer training and servicing requirements. After the test, the marketer asks the customer about purchase intent and other reactions.

*Trade shows*   These shows draw a large number of buyers who view new products in a few concentrated days. The manufacturer sees how buyers react to various product features and terms, and can assess buyer interest and purchase intentions.

*Distributor and dealer display rooms*    Here the new industrial product may stand next to other company products and possibly competitors' products. This method yields preference and pricing information in the normal selling atmosphere of the product.

*Standard or controlled test markets*    These are used to measure the potential of new industrial products. The business marketer produces a limited supply of the product and gives it to the salesforce to sell in a limited number of geographical areas. The company gives the product full advertising, sales promotion, and other marketing support. Such test markets let the company test the product and its marketing programme in real market situations.

## Commercialization

Test marketing gives management the information needed to make a final decision about whether to launch the new product. If the company goes ahead with **commercialization** – that is, introducing the new product into the market – it will face high costs. The company will have to build or rent a manufacturing facility. It must have sufficient funds to gear up production. And it may have to spend millions of pounds for advertising and sales promotion in the first year. For example, Spillers spent £3 million for its launch of GoodLife Breakfast dog meal in October 1993. Gillette spent £8 million in the UK launch of its new shaving system – the Sensor Excel – in July 1994. Unilever spent nearly £200 million to promote Omo and Persil Power across Europe, in addition to the £100 million already invested in three new factories to produce its revolutionary laundry powder.

The company launching a new product must make four decisions.

### When?

The first decision is whether the time is right to introduce the new product. If it will eat into the sales of the company's other products, its introduction may be delayed. If it can be improved further, or if the economy is down, the company may wait until the following year to launch it.[16]

### Where?

The company must decide whether to launch the new product in a single location, or region, several regions, the national market, or the international market. Few companies have the confidence, capital, and capacity to launch new products into full national or international distribution. They will develop a planned market roll-out over time. In particular, small companies may select an attractive city and conduct a blitz campaign to enter the market. They may then enter other cities one at a time. Larger companies can introduce their products into a whole region and then expand into the next region. Companies with national distribution networks, such as auto companies, often launch their new models in the national market.

Companies with international distribution systems are increasingly introducing their new products in swift global assaults. Procter & Gamble did this with the Pampers Phases line of disposable nappies. In the past, P&G typically introduced a new product in the US market. If it was successful, overseas competitors would copy the product in their home markets before P&G could expand distribution globally.

With Pampers Phases, however, the company introduced the new product into global markets within one month of introducing it in the United States. It planned to have the product on the shelf in ninety countries within just twelve months of introduction. Such rapid worldwide expansion solidified the brand's market position before foreign competitors could react. P&G has since mounted worldwide introductions of several other new products.[17]

### To whom?

Within the roll-out markets, the company must target its distribution and promotion to customer groups who represent the best prospects. These prime prospects should have been profiled by the firm in earlier research and test marketing. The firm must now fine-tune its targeting efforts, looking especially for early adopters, heavy users and opinion leaders. Opinion leaders are particularly important as their endorsement of the new product has a powerful impact upon adoption by other buyers in the marketplace.

### How?

The company also must develop an *action plan* for introducing the new product into the selected markets. It must spend the marketing budget on the marketing mix and various other activities. Thus when Spillers Foods launched GoodLife Breakfast dog meal, which was a particularly innovative product, being the first of its type on the UK market, Spillers had to do a lot of educating and convincing. The main thrust was to get sampling. Trial boxes were banded to magazines and samples were given away at point-of-sale. The national, hobby and trade press were each invited to breakfast launches. Vets were also mailed nutritional briefings. A TV news video featuring dog owners admitting what their dog ate for breakfast (human breakfast cereals were not uncommon!) was run by two regional stations. A radio interview with an animal nutritionist was recorded and mailed as a news item to radio stations. Trade advertisements were also placed. In the spring of 1994, a TV ad campaign was launched. As you can see, the GoodLife Breakfast launch was incredibly thorough, with sales promotions sustained over an eight- to twelve-week period. The communications strategy was not just about shouting loudly but doing so in focused ways with media specifically chosen to reach different target audiences.[18]

## Speeding up new-product development

Many companies organize their new-product development process into an orderly sequence of steps, starting with idea generation and ending with commercialization. Under this **sequential product-development** approach, one company department works individually to complete its stage of the process before passing the new product along to the next department and stage. This orderly, step-by-step process can help bring control to complex and risky projects. But it also can be dangerously slow. In fast-changing, highly competitive markets, such slow-but-sure product development can cost the company potential sales and profits at the hands of more nimble competitors.

Today, in order to get their new products to market more quickly, many companies are dropping the sequential product development method in favour of the faster, more flexible **simultaneous product-development** approach. Under the new approach, various company departments work closely together, overlapping the steps in the product-development process to save time and increase effectiveness (see Marketing Highlight 13.3).

## Organization for innovation

Table 13.3 illustrates the most common form of organization for new-product development: product managers, new-product managers, new-product committees/departments and venture teams.

The organizational format used in a new-product development project can influence the time taken to complete the new-product project. As suggested in Marketing Highlight 13.3, multidisciplinary teams and a concurrent approach to handling new-product process activities have been the main driving force behind fast-paced innovation.

But successful new-product development is not just about having a special organizational *structure* for new-product development. An innovative organization must have, at its helm, *top management* that gives priority to new products. Their *vision* for innovation is also clearly communicated to, and its *value shared by staff* at all levels of the organization. Top management not only believes wholeheartedly in, but also commits adequate resources to new product development, which is seen as a means of creating customer value that guarantees company survival and longevity. A successful innovative organization is also strongly committed to its people (*staff*) and continually invests in their *skills* to maintain innovation prowess. Lines of communication are kept open to ensure information gets to those that need it most to make critical new-product development decisions. Knowledge is used to facilitate learning, a key characteristic of innovation-oriented firms. Because innovation is a risky activity, the firm must foster an *entrepreneurial climate* with planning, control and

---

**TABLE 13.3**   *Ways companies organize for new-product development*

*Product managers*
Many companies assign responsibility for new-product ideas to their product managers. Because these managers are close to the market and competition, they are ideally situated to find and develop new-product opportunities. In practice, however, this system has several faults. Product managers are usually so busy managing their product lines that they give little thought to new products other than brand modifications or extensions. They also lack the specific skills and knowledge needed to evaluate and develop new products.

*New-product managers*
Some companies have new-product managers who report to group product managers. This position 'professionalizes' the new-product function. On the other hand, new-product managers tend to think in terms of product modifications and line extensions limited to their current product and markets.

*New-product committees*
Most companies have a high-level management committee charged with reviewing and approving new-product proposals. It usually consists of representatives from marketing, manufacturing, finance, engineering, and other departments. Its function is not developing or coordinating new products so much as reviewing and approcing new-product plans.

*New-product departments*
Large companies often establish a new-product department headed by a manager who has substantial authority and access to top management. The department's chief responsibilities include generating and screening new ideas, working with the R&D department, and carrying out field testing and commercialization.

*New-product venture teams*
A more free-standing approach involves assigning major new-product development work to venture teams. A venture team is a group brought together from various operating departments and charged with developing a specific product or business. Team members are relieved of their other duties, and given a budget and a time frame. In some cases, this team stays with the product long after it is successfully introduced.

## Simultaneous product development: speeding new products to market

Philips, the giant Dutch consumer electronics company, marketed the first practical video cassette recorder in 1972, gaining a three-year lead on its Japanese competitors. But in the seven years that it took Philips to develop its second generation of VCR models, Japanese manufacturers had launched at least three generations of new products. A victim of its own creaky product-development process, Philips never recovered from the Japanese onslaught. Today, the company is an also-ran with only 2 per cent market share; it still loses money on VCRs. The Philips story is typical – during the past few decades, dozens of large companies have fallen victim to competitors with faster, more flexible new-product development programmes. In today's fast-changing, fiercely competitive world, turning out new products too slowly can result in product failures, lost sales and profits, and crumbling market positions. 'Speed to market' has become a pressing concern to companies in all industries.

Large companies traditionally have used a sequential product-development approach in which new products are developed in an orderly series of steps. In a kind of relay race, each company department completes its phase of the development process before passing the new product on. The sequential process has its merits – it helps bring order to risky and complex new-product development projects. But the approach also can be fatally slow.

To speed up their product-development cycles, many companies are now adopting a faster, more agile, team-oriented approach called 'simultaneous product development'. Instead of passing the new product from department to department, the company assembles a team of people from various departments that stays with the new product from start to finish. Such teams usually include representatives from the marketing, finance, design, manufacturing, and legal departments, and even supplier companies. Simultaneous development is more like a rugby match than a relay race – team members pass the new product back and forth as they move down field toward the common goal of a speedy and successful new-product launch.

Top management gives the product development team general strategic direction, but on a clear-cut product idea or work plan. It challenges the team with stiff and seemingly contradictory goals – 'turn out carefully planned and superior new products, but do it quickly' – and then gives the team whatever freedom and resources it needs to meet the challenge. The team becomes a driving force that pushes the product forward. In the sequential process, a bottleneck at one phase can seriously slow or even halt the entire project. In the simultaneous approach, if one functional area hits snags, it works to resolve them while the team moves on.

The Allen-Bradley Company, a maker of industrial controls, provides an example of the tremendous benefits gained by using simultaneous development. Under the old sequential approach, the company's marketing department handed over a new product

reward systems geared towards risk-taking as opposed to risk avoidance. Last, but not least, new-product teams almost invariably perform better if guided by a clear *strategy* that is strongly supported at the top. The organization also needs *product champions* who strive to take the project to completion against all the odds. The product champion, in turn, needs the backing of an executive champion whose authority becomes invaluable in fighting off the political battles that interfere with new-product progress. In summary, to innovate effectively, firms must build customer-focused, functionally integrated and entrepreneurial, yet strategically directed, organizations. In successful innovative firms, new-product development is seldom left to chance. There may be an element of luck underpinning successful commercialization of innovations. Luck, however, is not easy to replicate. The lessons of strategic new product planning and implementation are.

idea to designers. The designers, working in isolation, prepared concepts and passed them along to product engineers. The engineers, also working by themselves, developed expensive prototypes and handed them on to manufacturing, which tried to find a way to build the new product. Finally, after many years and dozens of costly design compromises and delays, marketing was asked to sell the new product – which it often found to be too highly priced or sadly out of date. Now, Allen-Bradley has adopted the simultaneous product-development approach. All of the company's departments work together – from beginning to end – to design and develop new products that meet customer needs and company capabilities. The results have been astonishing. For example, the company recently developed a new electrical control in just two years; under the old system, it would have taken six years.

The auto industry also has discovered the benefits of simultaneous product development. The approach is called 'simultaneous engineering' at GM, the 'team concept' at Ford, and 'process-driven design' at Chrysler. The first American cars built using this process, the Ford Taurus and Mercury Sable, have been great marketing successes. Using simultaneous product development, Ford slashed development time from sixty months to less than forty. It squeezed

fourteen weeks from its cycle by simply getting the engineering and finance departments to review designs at the same time instead of sequentially. It claims that such actions have helped cut average engineering costs for a project by 35 per cent. In an industry that has typically taken five or six years to turn out a new model, Mazda now brags about two-to-three-year product-development cycles – a feat that would be impossible without simultaneous development.

However, the simultaneous approach has some limitations. Superfast product development can be riskier and more costly than the slower, more orderly sequential approach. And it often creates increased organization tension and confusion. But in rapidly changing industries facing increasingly shorter product life cycles, the rewards of fast and flexible product development far exceed the risks. Companies that get new and improved products to the market faster than competitors gain a dramatic competitive edge. They can respond more quickly to emerging consumer tastes and charge higher prices for more advanced designs. As one motor industry executive states, 'What we want to do is get the new car approached, built, and in the consumer's hands in the shortest time possible .... Whoever gets there first gets all the marbles.'

Sources: Hirotake Takeuchi and Ikujiro Nonaka, 'The new product development game', *Harvard Business Review* (Jan.–Feb. 1986), 137–46; Bro Uttal, 'Speeding new ideas to market', *Fortune* (2 March 1987), 62–5; John Bussey and Douglas R. Sease, 'Speeding up: manufacturers strive to slice time needed to develop new products', *Wall Street Journal* (23 February 1988), 1, 24; Paul Kunkel, 'Competing by design', *Business Week* (25 March 1991), 51–63; and Homer F. Hagedorn, 'High performance in product development: an agenda for senior management', in Arthur D. Little Company, *PRISM* (1st Quarter 1992), 47–58.

## PRODUCT LIFE-CYCLE STRATEGIES

After launching the new product, management wants the product to enjoy a long and healthy life. Although it does not expect the product to sell forever, managment wants to earn a decent profit to cover all the effort and risk that went into launching it. Management is aware that each product will have a life cycle, although the exact shape and length is not known in advance.

Figure 13.2 shows a typical **product life cycle (PLC)**, the course that a product's sales and profits take over its lifetime. The product life cycle has five distinct stages:

1. *Product development* begins when the company finds and develops a new-product idea. During product development, sales are zero and the company's investment costs mount.

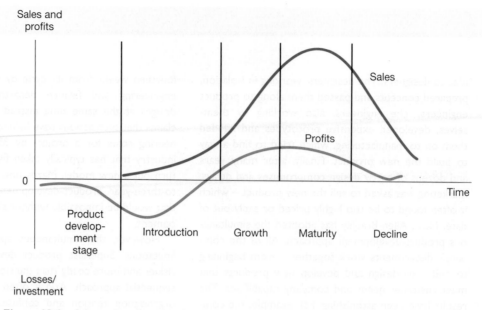

**Figure 13.2** Sales and profits over the product's life from inception to demise.

2. *Introduction* is a period of slow sales growth as the product is being introduced in the market. Profits are nonexistent in this stage because of the heavy expenses of product introduction.
3. *Growth* is a period of rapid market acceptance and increasing profits.
4. *Maturity* is a period of slowdown in sales growth because the product has achieved acceptance by most potential buyers. Profits level off or decline because of increased marketing outlays to defend the product against competition.
5. *Decline* is the period when sales fall off and profits drop.

Not all products follow this S-shaped product life cycle. Some products are introduced and die quickly; others stay in the mature stage for a long, long time. Some enter the decline stage and are then cycled back into the growth stage through strong promotion or repositioning.

The PLC concept can describe a product class (petrol-engined cars), a product form (coupé), or a brand (the BMW 325is). The PLC concept applies differently in each case. Product classes have the longest life cycles. The sales of many product classes stay in the mature stage for a long time. Product forms, in contrast, tend to have the standard PLC shape. Product forms such as 'cream deodorants', the 'dial telephone' and 'phonograph records' passed through a regular history of introductions, rapid growth, maturity, and decline. A specific brand's life cycle can change quickly because of changing competitive attacks and responses. For example, although teeth-cleaning products (product class) and toothpaste (product form) have enjoyed fairly long life cycles, the life cycles of specific brands have tended to be much shorter.

The PLC concept can also be applied to what are known as styles, fashions and fads. Their special life cycles are shown in Figure 13.3. A **style** is a basic and distinctive mode of expression. For example, styles appear in British homes (Edwardian, Victorian, Georgian); clothing (formal, casual); and art (realistic, surrealistic, abstract). Once a style is invented, it may last for generations, coming in and out of vogue. A style has a cycle showing several periods of renewed interest.

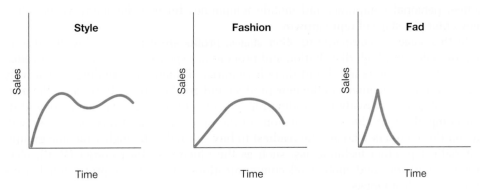

**Figure 13.3**   Marketers need to understand and predict style, fashion, and fad.

A **fashion** is a currently accepted or popular style in a given field. For example, the 'preppie look' in the clothing of the late 1970s gave way to the 'loose and layered' look of the 1980s, which in turn yielded to the less conservative but more tailored look of the 1990s. Fashions pass through many stages. First, a small number of consumers typically take an interest in something new that sets them apart. Then other consumers take an interest out of a desire to copy the fashion leaders. Next, the fashion becomes popular and is adopted by the mass market. Finally, the fashion fades away as consumers start moving toward other fashions that are beginning to catch their eye. Thus fashions tend to grow slowly, remain popular for a while, then decline slowly.

**Fads** are fashions that enter quickly, are adopted with great zeal, peak early, and decline very fast. They last only a short time and tend to attract only a limited following. Fads often have a novel or quirky nature, as when people start buying Rubik's cubes, 'pet rocks', or yo-yos. Fads appeal to people who are looking for excitement, a way to set themselves apart or something to talk about to others. Fads do not survive for long because they normally do not satisfy a strong or lasting need or satisfy it well.

The PLC concept can be applied by marketers as a useful framework for describing how products and markets work. But using the PLC concept for forecasting product performance or for developing marketing strategies presents some practical problems.[19] For example, managers may have trouble identifying which stage of the PLC the product is in, pinpointing when the product moves into the next stage, and determining the factors that affect the product's movement through the stages. In practice, it is difficult to forecast the sales level at each PLC stage, the length of each stage and the shape of the PLC curve.

Using the PLC concept to develop marketing strategy can also be difficult because strategy is both a cause and a result of the product's life cycle. The product's current PLC position suggests the best marketing strategies and the resulting marketing strategies affect product performance in later life-cycle stages. Yet when used carefully, the PLC concept can help in developing good marketing strategies for different stages in the product life cycle.

We looked at the product-development stage of the product life cycle in the first part of the chapter. Now let us look at strategies for each of the other life-cycle stages.

## Introduction stage

The **introduction stage** starts when the new product is first launched. Introduction takes time, and sales growth is apt to be slow. Well-known products such as instant coffee, personal computers and mobile telephones lingered for many years before they entered a stage of rapid growth.

In this stage, as compared to other stages, profits are negative or low because of the low sales and high distribution and promotion expenses. Much money is needed to attract distributors and build their inventories. Promotion spending is relatively high to inform consumers of the new product and get them to try it. Because the market is not generally ready for product refinements at this stage, the company and its few competitors produce basic versions of the product. These firms focus their selling on those buyers who are the readiest to buy – usually the higher-income groups. For radical product technologies, such as the video cassette recorder (VCR), electronic calculators and mobile telecommunications, business or professional users were the earliest targets.

A company might adopt one of several marketing strategies for introducing a new product. It can set a high or low level for each marketing variable, such as price, promotion, distribution, and product quality. Considering only price and promotion, for example, management might *skim* the market *slowly* by launching the new product with a high price and low promotion spending. The high price helps recover as much gross profit per unit as possible while the low promotion spending keeps marketing spending down. Such a strategy makes sense when the market is limited in size, when most consumers in the market know about the product and are willing to pay a high price (these consumers are typically called the 'innovators'), and when there is little immediate potential competition. If, however, most consumers in the limited market are unaware and know little about the innovation, and require education and convincing, a high promotion spending is required. A high price–high promotion strategy also helps the firm to *rapidly skim* the price-insensitive end of the market in the early stages of the new product's launch.

On the other hand, a company might introduce its new product with a low price and heavy promotion spending (a *rapid penetration* strategy). This strategy promises to bring the fastest market penetration and the largest market share, and it makes sense when the market is large, potential buyers are price sensitive and unaware of the product, there is strong potential competition, and the company's unit manufacturing costs fall with the scale of production and accumulated manufacturing experience. A low price, but low promotion spend (or *slow penetration* strategy) may be chosen instead if buyers are price conscious, but the firm wants to keep its launch costs down because of resource constraints.

A company, especially the *market pioneer*, must choose its launch strategy consistent with its intended product positioning. It should realize that the initial strategy is just the first step in a grander marketing plan for the product's entire life cycle. If the pioneer chooses its launch strategy to make a 'killing', it will be sacrificing long-run revenue for the sake of short-run gain. As the pioneer moves through later stages of the life cycle, it will have continuously to formulate new pricing, promotion and other marketing strategies. It has the best chance of building and retaining market leadership if it plays its cards correctly from the start.

### Growth stage

If the new product meets market needs or stimulates previously untapped needs, it will enter a **growth stage**, in which sales will start climbing quickly. The early adopters will continue to buy, and later buyers will start following their lead, especially if they hear favourable word of mouth. Attracted by the opportunities for profit, new competitors will enter the market. They will introduce new product features, improve on the pioneer's product and expand the market for the product. The increase in competitors leads to an increase in the number of distribution outlets, and sales jump just to build reseller inventories. Prices remain where they are or fall only slightly. Companies keep their promotion spending at the same or a slightly higher level. Educating the market remains a goal, but now the company must also meet the competition.

Profits increase during the growth stage, as promotion costs are spread over a large volume and as unit-manufacturing costs fall. The firm uses several strategies to sustain rapid market growth as long as possible. It improves product quality and adds new product features and models. It enters new market segments and tries to grow sales further by selling through new distribution channels. It shifts some advertising from building product awareness to building product conviction and purchase, and it lowers prices at the right time to attract more buyers.

In the growth stage, the firm faces a trade-off between high market share and high current profit. By spending a lot of money on product improvement, promotion, and distribution, the company can capture a dominant position. In doing so, however, it gives up maximum current profit, which it hopes to make up in the next stage.

## Maturity stage

At some point, a product's sales growth will slow down, and the product will enter a **maturity stage**. This maturity stage normally lasts longer than the previous stages, and it poses strong challenges to marketing management. Most products are in the maturity stage of the life cycle, and, therefore, most of marketing management deals with the mature product.

The slowdown in sales growth results in many producers with many products to sell. In turn, this overcapacity leads to greater competition. Competitors begin to cut prices, increase their advertising and sale promotions and increase their R&D budgets to find better versions of the product. These steps lead to a drop in profit. Often some of the weaker competitors start to lag behind and soon drop out of the industry, which eventually contains only well-established competitors.

Although many products in the mature stage appear to remain unchanged for long periods, most successful ones stay alive through continually evolving to meet changing consumer needs (see Marketing Highlight 13.4). Product managers should do more than simply ride along with or defend their mature products – a good offensive is the best defence. They should stretch their imagination and look for new ways to innovate in the market (market development), or to modify the product (product development) and the marketing mix (marketing innovation).

### Market development

Here, the company tries to increase the consumption of the current product. It looks either for new users or to enter a market new to the company, as when Johnson & Johnson targeted the adult market with its baby powder and shampoo. The company may want to reposition the brand to appeal to a larger or faster-growing segment, as Lucozade did when it introduced its new line of drinks that were aimed at younger users, not convalescents, the original target segment for the brand.

## Crayola crayons: a long and colourful life cycle

Binney & Smith Company began making crayons in Bushkill Creek near Peekskill, New York, in 1903. Partner Edwin Binney's wife, Alice, named them Crayola crayons – after the French *craie*, meaning 'stick of colour', and the Spanish *ola*, meaning 'oil'. In the 90-odd years since, Crayola crayons have become a household staple, not just in the United States, but in more than sixty countries around the world, in boxes printed in eleven languages. If you placed all the Crayola crayons made in a single year end to end, they would circle the earth four-and-a-half times.

Few people can forget their first pack of '64s' – sixty-four beauties neatly arranged in the familiar green and yellow flip-top box with a sharpener on the back. The aroma of a freshly opened Crayola box still drives kids into a frenzy and takes members of the older generation back to some of their fondest childhood memories. Binney & Smith, now a subsidiary of Hallmark, dominates the crayon market. Sixty-five per cent of all American children between the ages of 2 and 7 pick up a crayon at least once a day and colour for an average of twenty-eight minutes – 80 per cent of the time, they pick up Crayolas.

In some ways, Crayola crayons haven't changed much since 1903, when they were sold in an eight-pack for a nickel. Crayola has always been the num-ber one brand, and the crayons are still made by hand in much the same way as then. But a closer look reveals that Binney & Smith has made many adjust-ments in order to keep the Crayola brand in the mature stage and out of decline. Over the years, the company has added a steady stream of new colours, shapes, sizes and packages. It increased the number of colours from the original eight in 1903 (red, yel-low, blue, green, orange, black, brown and white) to forty-eight in 1949, to sixty-four in 1958. In 1972, it added eight fluorescent colours – with hot names like Laser Lemon, Screamin' Green, and Atomic Tangerine; and in 1990, an additional seven fluores-cents, including Electric Lime and Razzle-Dazzle Rose. Most recently, it created a new line of Silver Swirls colours – Cerulean Frost, Cosmic Cobalt, Misty Moss, Rose Dust, and twenty others. In all, Crayola crayons now come in 103 colours and a variety of packages, including a 72-crayon attaché-like case.

Over the years, the Crayola line has grown to include many new sizes and shapes. In addition to the standard $3^5/_8$-inch crayon, it now includes flat, jumbo, and 'So Big' crayons. Crayola Washable Crayons were added in 1991. Binney & Smith also extended the Crayola brand to new markets when it developed Crayola Markers and related products. Finally, the

### Product development

The product manager can also change product characteristics, such as quality, features or style, to attract new users and to inspire more usage.

A strategy of *quality improvement* aims at increasing product performance – its durability, reliability, speed, taste. This strategy is effective when the quality can be improved, when buyers believe the claim of improved quality, and when enough buyers want higher quality.

A strategy of feature improvement adds new features that expand the product's usefulness, safety, or convenience. Feature improvement has been used successfully by Japanese makers of watches, calculators, and copying machines. For example, Seiko keeps adding new styles and features to its line of watches.

A strategy of *style improvement* aims to increase the attactiveness of the product. Thus car manufacturers restyle their cars to attract buyers who want a new look. The makers of consumer food and household products introduce new flavours, colours, ingredients or packages to revitalize consumer buying.

company has added several programmes and services to help strengthen its relationships with Crayola customers. For example, in 1984 it began its Dream Makers art education programme, a national elementary-school art programme designed to help students capture their dreams on paper and to use the artistic process to make the dreams more tangible. In 1986, it set up a toll-free 1-800-CRAYOLA hotline to provide better customer service. And it recently implemented a national recycling effort. Each store now has a crayon collection bin – the collected bits and pieces of crayon are melted down and used to make the most-used hue – black.

Not all of Binney & Smith's life-cycle adjustments have been greeted with open arms by consumers. For example, facing flat sales throughout the 1980s, the company conducted market research which showed that children were ready to break with tradition in favour of some exciting new colours. They were seeing and wearing brighter colours and wanted to be able to colour with them as well. So, in 1990, Binney & Smith retired eight colours from the time-hon-

oured box of sixty-four – raw umber, lemon yellow, maize, blue grey, orange yellow, orange red, green blue and violet blue – in to the Crayola Hall of Fame. In their place, it introduced eight more modern shades – Cerulean, Vivid Tangerine, Jungle Green, Fuchsia, Dandelion, Teal Blue, Royal Purple and Wild Strawberry. The move unleashed a ground swell of protest from loyal Crayola users, who formed such organizations as the Raw Umber and Maize Preservation Society and the National Committee to Save Lemon Yellow. Binney & Smith receive an average of 334 calls a month from concerned customers. Company executives were flabbergasted: 'We were aware of the loyalty and nostalgia surrounding Crayola crayons,' a spokeperson says, 'but we didn't know we [would] hit such a nerve.' Still, fans of the new colours outnumbered the protestors, and the new colours are here to stay. However, the company did revive the old standards for one last hurrah in a special collector's tin – it sold all of the 2.5 million tins made. Thus the Crayola brand continues through its long and colourful life cycle.

Sources: Quote from 'Hue and cry over Crayola may revive old colors', *Wall Street Journal* (14 June 1991), B1; see also Margaret O. Kirk, 'Coloring our children's world since '03', *Chicago Tribune* (29 October 1986), sect. 5, p. 1: Catherine Foster, 'Drawing dreams', *Christian Science Monitor* (5 June 1989), 13; Mike Christiansen, 'Waxing nostalgic: Crayola retires a colorful octet', *Atlanta Constitution* (8 August 1990), B1, B4; and Ellen Neuborne, 'Expansion goes outside crayon lines', *USA Today* (2 October 1992), B1, B2.

*Marketing innovation*

Marketers can also try to improve sales by changing one or more marketing-mix elements. Price cuts attract new users and competitors' customers. They can launch a better advertising campaign or use aggressive sales promotions – trade deals, discounts, premiums, and contests. The company can also move into larger market channels as Dell Computers did with mail-order selling of personal computers, or use mass merchandisers, if these channels are growing. Finally, the company can deliver even better value by offering new or improved services to buyers.

## Decline stage

The sales of most product forms and brands eventually dip. The decline may be slow, as in the case of oatmeal cereal, or rapid, as in the case of gramophone records.

Sales may plunge to zero, or they may drop to a low level where they continue for many years. This is the **decline stage**.

Sales decline for many reasons, including technological advances, shifts in consumer tastes, and increased competition. As sales and profits decline, some firms withdraw from the market. Those remaining may reduce the number of their product offerings. They may drop smaller market segments and marginal trade channels, or they may cut the promotion budget and reduce their prices further.

Carrying a weak product can be very costly to a firm, and not just in profit terms. There are many hidden costs. A weak product may take up too much of management's time. If often requires frequent price and inventory adjustments. It requires advertising and sales force attention that might be better used to make 'healthy' products more profitable or to create new ones. A product's failing reputation can cause customer concerns about the company and its other products. The biggest cost may well lie in the future. Keeping weak products delays the search for replacements, creates a lopsided product mix, hurts current profits and weakens the company's foothold on the future.

For these reasons, companies need to pay more attention to their ageing products. The firm's first task is to identify those products in the decline stage by regularly reviewing sales, market shares, costs, and profit trends. Then management must decide whether to maintain, harvest for cash or drop each of these declining products.

Management may decide to *maintain* its brand without change in the hope that competitors will leave the industry. For example, Procter & Gamble made good profits by remaining in the declining liquid soap business as others withdrew. Or management may decide to reposition the brand in hopes of moving it back into the growth stage of the product life cycle.

Management may decide to harvest the product, which means reducing various costs (plant and equipment, maintenance, R&D, advertising, salesforce) and hoping that sales hold up. If successful, harvesting will release cash and increase the company's profits in the short run. Or management may decide to drop the product from the line. It can sell it to another firm or simply liquidate it at salvage value. If the company plans to find a buyer, it will not want to run down the product through harvesting.[20]

Table 13.4 summarizes the key characteristics of each stage of the product life cycle. The table also lists the marketing objectives and strategies for each stage.[21]

## SUMMARY

Organizations must develop new products and services. Their current products face limited life spans and must be replaced by newer products. But new products can fail – the risks of innovation are as great as the rewards. The key to successful innovation lies in a total-company effort, strong planning, a marketing focus and a *systematic new-product development process*.

The new-product development process consists of nine stages: *new product strategy determination, idea generation, idea screening, concept development and testing, marketing strategy development, business analysis, product development, test marketing*, and *commercialization*. The purpose of each stage is to decide whether the idea should be further developed or dropped. The company wants to minimize the chances of poor ideas moving forward and good ideas being rejected.

| TABLE 13.4 | Summary of product life-cycle characteristics, objectives, and strategies | | | |
|---|---|---|---|---|
| | Introduction | Growth | Maturity | Decline |
| *Characteristics* | | | | |
| Sales | Low sales | Rapidly rising sales | Peak sales | Decling sales |
| Costs | High cost per customer | Average cost per customer | Low cost per customer | Low cost per customer |
| Profits | Negative | Rising profits | High profits | Declining profits |
| Customers | Innovators | Early adopters | Middle majority | Laggards |
| Competitors | Few | Growing number | Stable number beginning to decline | Declining number |
| *Marketing objectives* | Create product awareness and trial | Maximize market share | Maximize profit while defending market share | Reduce expenditure and milk the brand |
| *Strategies* | | | | |
| Product | Offer a basic product | Offer product extensions, service, warranty | Diversify brand and models | Phase out weak items |
| Price | Use cost-plus | Price to penetrate market | Price to match or beat competitors | Cut price |
| Distribution | Build selective distribution | Build intensive distribution | Build more intensive distribution | Go selective: phase out unprofitable outlets |
| Advertising | Build product awareness among early adopters and dealers | Build awareness and interest in the mass market | Stress brand differences and benefits | Reduce to level needed to retain hard-core loyals |
| Sales promotion | Use heavy sales promotion to entice trial | Reduce to take advantage of heavy consumer demand | Increase to encourage brand switching | Reduce to minimal level |

*Source:* Philip Kotler, *Marketing Management: Analysis, planning, implementation, and control*, 8th edn (Englewood Cliffs, NJ: Prentice Hall, 1994), 365.

Each product has a *life cycle* marked by a changing set of problems and opportunities. The sales of the typical product follow an S-shaped curve made up of five stages. The cycle begins with the *product-development* stage when the company finds and develops a new-product idea. The *introduction stage* is marked by slow growth and low profits as the product is being pushed into distribution. If successful, the product enters a *growth stage* marked by rapid sales growth and increasing profits. During this stage, the company tries to improve the product, enter new market segments and distribution channels, and reduce its prices slightly. Then comes a *maturity stage* in which sales growth slows down and profits stabilize. The company seeks strategies to revitalize sales growth, including market, product and marketing-mix modification. Finally, the product enters a *decline stage* in which sales and profits dwindle. The company's task during this stage is to identify the declining product and decide whether it should be maintained, harvested, or dropped. If dropped, the product can be sold to another firm or liquidated for salvage value.

# ◾ DISCUSSING THE ISSUES

1. Ericsson, the Swedish telecommunications group increased its spending on new product development in the early 1990s. Its chief executive, Lars Ramqvist, extols the power of innovation: invest to the utmost in new products or services, forget about short-term profits and be willing to take risks. As it turned out, in the tough, fast-moving global telecommunications market, Ericsson now enjoys a 40 per cent share of the world market for mobile phone systems and one of over 50 per cent in digital cellular equipment. Why do you think a willingness to take risks is so important when making heavy investments in developing new products and services? Is technology alone sufficient for success? What other factors do you think facilitate the successful commercialization of new products and technologies?

2. Less than a third of new-product ideas come from the customer. Does this low percentage conflict with the marketing concept's philosophy of 'find a need and fill it'? Why or why not?

3. Many businesses have formal new-product development systems. Yet recent studies suggest that most successful new products were those that had kept away from the formal system. Why might this be true?

4. What factors must be considered when deciding whether to test-market a new product or not? Give examples of types of new product or service that should be test-marketed prior to commercialization.

5. Do you think that the product life-cycle concept is a useful marketing-planning tool? Why or why not?

6. Recent evidence suggests that consuming a high-fibre diet may be helpful in reducing cholesterol levels. What impact might this health benefit have on the life cycle of high-fibre (e.g. oatmeal and oat-based) food products?

# ◾ APPLYING THE CONCEPTS

1. List ten new-product ideas for your favourite chocolate or candy bar. Out of all these ideas, which (if any) do you think would have a good chance of success? What percentage of your ideas were rated as having a good chance of success? Is this a high or low percentage? If the answer is high, can you explain why the potentially successful ideas seem stronger?

2. Go to a grocery store you normally shop at. Make a list of ten items that appear to be new products. Rate each product for its level of innovation: give a '10' score for extremely novel and highly innovative products and '1' for a very minor change such as an improved package or fragrance. How truly new or innovative are these products overall? Do you think companies are being too risk averse because 'pioneers are the ones who get shot'?

# ◾ REFERENCES

1. David Blackwell, 'Taking a leaf from the car industry's book', *Financial Times* (21 July 1994), 26.
2. Liz Hunt, 'Boots withdraws heart drug less than a year after launch', *Independent* (20 July 1993), 1.
3. Kevin J. Clancy and Robert S. Shulman, *The Marketing Revolution: A radical manifesto for dominating the marketplace* (New York: Harper Business, 1991), 6; and Robert G Cooper, 'New product success in industrial firms', *Industrial Marketing Management*, **21** (1992), 215–23; see also Brian Dumane, 'Closing the innovation gap', *Fortune* (2 December 1991), 56–62; and Gary Strauss, 'Building on brand names: companies freshen old product lines', *USA Today* (20 March 1992), B1, B2.
4. Robert G. Cooper and Elko J. Kleinschmidt, *New Product: The key factors in success* (Chicago: American Marketing Association, 1990); see also Axel Johne and Patrician Snelson, *Successful Product Development: Lessons from American and British firms* (Oxford: Basil Blackwell, 1990).
5. 'Bausche and Lomb is correcting its vision of research', *Business Week* (30 March 1987), 91.
6. C. Merle Crawford, *New Products Management*, 4th edn. (Boston, MA: Irwin, 1994), ch.3.
7. See Leigh Lawton and A. Parasuraman, 'So you want your new product planning to be productive', *Business Horizons* (December 1980), 29–34. The percentages in this section add to more than 100 because more than one source was named for some products in the study. 'Why innovation can become a risky business', *Financial Times* (12 May 1992), 13.

8. For these and other examples see Michael Czinkota and Masaaki Kotabe, 'Product development the Japanese way', *The Journal of Business Strategy* (Nov.–Dec. 1990), 31–6; and Jennifer Reese, 'Getting hot ideas from customers', *Fortune* (18 May 1992), 86–7.

9. See 'Listening to the voice of the marketplace', *Business Week* (21 February 1983), 90; and Eric von Hipple, 'Get new products from consumers', *Harvard Business Review* (Mar.–Apr. 1982), 117–22.

10. Russel Mitchel, 'How Ford hit the bullseye with Taurus', *Business Week* (30 June 1986), 69–70; 'Copycat Stuff? Hardly!', *Business Week* (14 September 1987), 112; and Jeremy Main, 'How to steal the best ideas around', *Fortune* (19 October 1992), 102–6.

11. For more on product concept testing, see William L. Moore, 'Concept testing', *Journal of Business Research*, **10** (1982), 279–94; and David A. Schwartz, 'Concept testing can be improved – and here's how', *Marketing News* (6 January 1984), 22–3.

12. Tony Scott, 'Demonstrating the future', *Innovation & Technology Transfer*, **4/94** (July 1994), 18.

13. See Otis Port, 'Pssst! Want a secret for making super-products?' *Business Week* (2 October 1989), 106–10.

14. See Howard Schlossberg, 'IRI, Nielsen slug it out in "Scanning Wars"', *Marketing News* (2 September 1991), 1, 47.

15. For more on simulated test markets, see Kevin Higgins, 'Simulated test marketing winning acceptance', *Marketing News* (1 March 1985), 15, 19; and Howard Schlossberg, 'Simulated vs. traditional test marketing', *Marketing News* (23 October 1989), 1–2.

16. See Robert J. Thomas, 'Timing – the key to market entry', *The Journal of Consumer Marketing* (Summer 1985), 77–87.

17. Jennifer Lawrence, 'P&G rushes on global diaper roll-out', *Advertising Age* (14 October 1991), 6; and Zachary Schiller, 'No more Mr Nice Guy at P&G – not by a long shot', *Business Week* (3 February 1992), 54–6.

18. Hester Thomas, 'Launching pad', *Marketing Business* (April 1994), 41–2.

19. See George S. Day, 'The product life cycle: analysis and applications issues', *Journal of Marketing* (Fall 1981), 60–7; John E. Swan and David R. Rink, 'Fitting marketing strategy to varying life cycles', *Business Horizons* (Jan.–Feb. 1982), 72–6; and Sak Onkvist and John J. Shaw, 'Competition and product management: can the product life cycle help?' *Business Horizons* (July–Aug. 1986), 51–62.

20. See Laurence P. Feldman and Albert L. Page, 'Harvesting: the misunderstood market exit strategy', *Journal of Business Strategy*, (spring 1985), 79–85.

21. For a more comprehensive discussion of marketing strategies over the course of the product life cycle, see Philip Kotler, *Marketing Management*, 8th edn (Englewood Cliffs, NJ: Prentice Hall, 1994), ch.14.

## CASE 13

# The Swatchmobile: any colour combination, including black

In February 1994 Jacques Chirac went to meet his old friend Nicolas Hayek in Geneva. The media clamour made it like he was running his campaign for the French presidency from the capital of the Swiss watch industry. It was a meeting between giants. Hayek, a Beirut-born Palestinian is fond of saying he is 'better known than the Swiss president'. He has reason to boast. Since emigrating to Switzerland in 1955 his Swatch range had increased the country's share of the world watch market from 15 to 50 per cent. By the turn of the century Swatch was set to overtake Seiko to become the world leader. While the Swatch was going from success to success in the 1990s, the leading Japanese were losing sales, market share and profits. They blamed the recession and the overvalued yen for making them unprofitable.

### SMH and Swatch

Following the lead taken by Clive Sinclair's Black Watch, the Japanese had used electric movements and digital technology to dominate the industry. The mechanically based Swiss watch industry had been damaged badly by the technological change. The market was left split between the luxury market dominated by Swiss brands like Blancpain, Audemas Piguet and Rolex and cheaper reliable products by the Japanese Casio, Seiko, Pulsar and others. Hayek's company, Ste Suisse Microélectronique et d'Horlogerie (SMH), rushed into the gap between them with the beautifully engineered, fashion-led Swatch range. The plastic-bodied ever-changing range of watches with quartz movements combined Swiss reliability and quality with fun and economy.

In its short life Swatch had become a fashion-oriented youth product and a collectable cult object. Enthusiasts will pay SFr 500 for originals that cost SFr 50 in 1983 and only SFr 60 today. Some members of the 100,000 plus Swatch Club had paid over SFr 100,000 for limited edition 'art' Swatches. In 1993, when Harrods had 500 limited editions to sell 'it stopped just short of fisticuffs' as 1,500 buffs fought over them.

### The Swatchmobile

In 1992 SMH's profit grew 64 per cent to SFr 413m. and was set to grow 23 per cent in 1993. But after years of steady growth its share price was levelling out. Swatch sales were saturating and Hayek had his eyes on the car market. He was being criticized for spending too much time working on his Swatchmobile and not enough on his core business.

His idea was to market a tiny car only 2.41 m long and 1.4 m wide – a Fiat 500 is 3.18 m by 1.32 m. Its light-weight plastic body was designed to carry two people and their shopping through dense city traffic. There would be a range of alternative underfloor power plants from electric to petrol. The most discussed option was an energy efficient electro-petrol hybrid. The performance of that version would be equal to a basic Ford Escort but would have a range of 550 km on a tank of petrol. According to Hayek, to be successful on a global scale today, a wrist watch – and by extension, a microcar – 'must also be a *provocation*'.

Although he was an engineer, he does not design Swatches nor will he design Swatchmobiles. He saw marketing energy and style as his strength. Swatches were designed by an in-house team of Swiss engineers led by Jacques Müller. He aimed to employ dozens of designers and artists as well as engineers to work on the Swatchmobile. 'Expect it to be offered in any colour – and any combination of colours you want, *including* black', says Hayek.

### Please, not another European car maker

Some saw Hayek's ideas as foolhardy. There was already overcapacity in the world car market. The European industry was in deep recession and had high labour

costs – Japan's were SFr 26 per hour compared with Germany's SFr 40. In addition, further traffic growth was seen by some as an impossibility on the world's over-crowded roads. Bankers and other potential backers were openly critical of the venture. It was one step too far at the wrong time and in the wrong market.

MORI's survey for the 1994 *Lex Report on Marketing* sheds another light on the changing market. Their study showed that 85 per cent of drivers still saw their car as an essential part of their lives. The younger generation agreed: 80 per cent of 13- to 16-year-olds said that cars were indispensable. People still wanted cars but the report showed a sea change in attitudes. Security and environmental friendliness were top of the new car-buyer's agenda, especially for women and the young. Top speed had dropped to tenth place in the priority. Few drivers were happy about their car's safety standards. Most wanted air bags, antilocking brakes and catalytic converters in their next car and wanted to trade up to get them. A similar survey in Japan showed similar attitude shifts. The report heralded the 'light green' consumers who rely on their car but care about its environmental impact.

SMH wanted a partner for their new venture. They tried with Volkswagen, with the idea of making a SFr 10,000 Swatch-VW in China. Then, in 1993, VW pulled out. They were short of money and doubted the Swatchmobile's economic viability. They opted instead for the Chico, a more conventional car than Hayek envisaged. They will also bring back the Beetle. In 1999 production of the 'back to the future' design based on VW's Concept 1 prototype will start in Mexico.

The meeting between Chirac and Hayek stimulated speculation about a French suitor for SMH. There was the prospect of an exciting alliance combining French style, Swiss engineering excellence and Hayek's marketing hype. Was there to be a deal with Matra-Hachette, Renault or Peugeot-Citroën? Chirac left the meeting smiling but saying nothing. Hayek told reporters that the partner would certainly not be GM but they would have to wait until the Geneva Motor Show to find out more.

### A Swatchmomerc?

The news finally broke at the Stuttgart Motor Show where the prototype Swatch Eco-Sprinter coupé and

*1 ecu = US$1.26 = SFr1.56 (Swiss francs).

**CASE 13 (cont)**

Eco-Speedster convertible were revealed. They were expected to cost between SFr 15,000 and SFr 21,000. Now the partner was Mercedes-Benz, the German executive and luxury car maker. The board of their parent company, Daimler-Benz, had given their permission for the car division to set up a development company with SMH. They said that the joint venture, called Micro-Compact-Car had 'promising possibilities for the development, manufacture and marketing of automobiles geared particularly to city use'. Hayek aimed to launch the car at the 1996 Olympic Games in Atlanta, United States, for sale in Europe in 1997/98 with an initial production of 100,000 to 150,000 cars a year.

The deal fitted Mercedes' growth plans and 'Made in Germany' policy. To lower their high labour costs and counter the recession, the company had cut their workforce for the first time. They were radically transforming their new model development programme. Cars were now being designed to a cost target, rather than designing the best cars possible and then pricing them. They also intended to broaden their product range to cover four-wheel-drive sports/recreational vehicles, people carriers and small cars. The plan to build 200,000 small family cars a year in Germany had recently been announced. Their Vision A-93 concept car had been shown at several motor shows. It was smaller than the VW Golf or Ford Escort but much larger than the Swatchmobile.

Some industry observers were not impressed by the joint venture. Was it one diversification too far for both Mercedes and Swatch? How could the flamboyant Hayek work with Mercedes' technocrats? Would the Swatch and Mercedes brand names fit together?

## Questions

1. How was Hayek able to make such a great success of Swatch, and can those ideas be transferred to other products in other markets? Would the ideas transfer to hi-fi, pens, kitchen goods, and so forth? How were Swatch able to beat the huge and established Japanese competitors?

2. What is Hayek's role in the new product development process? Why does he need the help of a partner?

3. Is the Swatchmobile a market-driven idea? Is there now any justification for not basing new products on marketing research?

4. What market research would you conduct to test the market for the Swatchmobile and when would you do it?

5. How should the Swatchmobile be branded? Should it be a Swatchmobile Eco-Speedster, Mercedes Eco-Speedster, Mercedes Swatch Eco-Speedster, Swatch Eco-Speedster, Micro-Compact-Car Eco-Speedster, MCC Eco-speedstern, or some other combination? What are the pros and cons of the various names? Does the name really matter if the product is right?

Sources: 'Japan's carmakers: the car as a fashion statement', *The Economist* (21 October 1989); Tony Lewis, 'What's safe, green and doesn't go too fast?', *The European* (4–10 February 1994), 12; John Parry, 'Clock turns slowly as Hayek dreams about his green car', *The European* (4–10 February 1994), 17; Kevin Done, 'Mercedes and Swatch in minicar venture', *Financial Times* (23 February 1994), 1; Jonathan Glancey, 'Watch this car', *Independent* (10 March 1994), 23; *Financial Times*, 'Volkswagen to produce new beetle', (28 November 1994), 3; 'Decision on "Swatchmobile" site', *Financial Times* (29 November 1994), 3; and John Parry, 'Swatchmobile set for Germany', *The European* (2–8 December 1994), 16.

## CHAPTER FOURTEEN

# Designing products

## Products, brands, packaging and services

## CHAPTER OBJECTIVES

After reading this chapter, you should be able to:

- Define *product* and the main classifications of consumer and industrial products.

- Explain why companies use brands and identify the chief branding decisions.

- Describe the roles of product packaging and labelling.

- Explain the decisions companies make when developing product lines and mixes.

## CHAPTER PREVIEW

### Revlon

Revlon sells cosmetics, toiletries, and fragrances to consumers around the world. Revlon is the number-one firm in the popular-price segment of the fragrance market. Revlon's perfumes are no more than careful mixtures of oils and chemicals that have nice scents. But Revlon knows that when it sells perfume, it sells much more than fragrant fluids – it sells what the fragrances can do for the women who use them.

Perfume is actually shipped from the fragrance houses in big, ugly drums. Although a £100-an-ounce perfume may cost no more than £7 to produce, to perfume consumers the product is much more than a few pounds' worth of ingredients and a pleasing smell.

Many things beyond the ingredients and scent add to a perfume's allure. In fact, the scent may be the *last* element developed. Revlon first researches women's feelings about themselves and their relationships with others. It then develops and tests new perfume concepts that match women's changing values, desires and lifestyles. When Revlon finds a promising new concept, it creates and names a scent to fit the idea. Revlon's research in the early 1970s showed that women were feeling

I ecu = UK£0.83

more competitive with men and that they were striving to find individual identities. For this woman of the 1970s, Revlon created Charlie, the first of the 'lifestyle' perfumes. Thousands of women adopted Charlie as a bold statement of independence, and it quickly became the world's best-selling perfume.

In the late 1970s, Revlon research showed a shift in women's attitudes: 'women had made the equality point, which Charlie addressed. Now women were hungering for an expression of femininity.' They now wanted perfumes that were subtle rather than shocking. Thus Revlon subtly shifted Charlie's position. The perfume still made its 'independent lifestyle' statement, but with an added tinge of 'femininity and romance'. Revlon also launched a perfume for the woman of the 1980s, Jontue, which was positioned on a theme of romance.

Revlon continues to refine Charlie's position, now targeting the woman of the 1990s who is 'able to do it all, but smart enough to know what she wants to do'. After almost twenty years, aided by continuous but subtle repositioning, Charlie remains the best-selling mass-market perfume.

A perfume's *name* is an important product attribute. Revlon uses such brand names as Charlie, Fleurs de Jontue, Ciara, Scoundrel, Guess and Unforgettable to create images that support each perfume's positioning. Competitors offer perfumes with such names as Obsession, Passion, Uninhibited, Opium, Joy, White Linen and Eternity. These names suggest that the perfumes will do something more than just make you smell better.

Revlon must also carefully *package* its perfumes. To consumers, the bottle and package are the most tangible symbol of the perfume and its image. Bottles must feel comfortable, be easy to handle and look impressive when displayed in stores. Most important, they must support the perfume's concept and image.

So when a woman buys perfume, she buys much, much more than simply fragrant fluids. The perfume's image, its promises, its scent, its name and package, the company that makes it and the stores that sell it all become a part of the *total* perfume *product*. When Revlon sells perfume, it sells more than the tangible product. It sells lifestyle, self-expression and exclusivity; achievement, success, and status; femininity, romance, passion and fantasy; memories, hopes and dreams.[1]

---

## INTRODUCTION

Clearly, perfume is more than just perfume when Revlon sells it. Revlon's great success in the rough-and-tumble fragrance world comes from developing an innovative product concept. An effective product concept is the first step in marketing-mix planning.

This chapter begins with a deceptively simple question: *What is a product?* After answering this question, we look at ways to classify products in consumer and business markets and look for links between types of products and types of marketing strategies. Next, we see that each product requires several decisions that go beyond product design. These decisions involve *branding, packaging* and *labelling*, and *product-support services*. Finally, we move from decisions about individual products to decisions about building *product lines* and *product mixes*.

## WHAT IS A PRODUCT?

A pair of Adidas trainers, a Vidal Sassoon haircut, a Bruce Springsteen concert, a EuroDisney vacation, advice from a solicitor, a Volvo truck and tax preparation services are all products. We define *product* as follows: A **product** is anything that is offered to a market for attention, acquisition, use or consumption and that might satisfy a want or need; it includes physical objects, services, persons, places, organizations and ideas.

Product planners need to think about the product on three levels. The most basic level is the **core product**, which addresses the question: *What is the buyer really buying?* As Figure 14.1 illustrates, the core product stands at the centre of the total product. It consists of the problem-solving services or core benefits that consumers seek when they buy a product. A woman buying lipstick buys more than lip colour. Charles Revson of Revlon saw this early: 'In the factory, we make cosmetics; in the store, we sell hope.' Theodore Levitt has pointed out that buyers 'do not buy quarter-inch drills; they buy quarter-inch holes'. Thus when designing products, marketers must first define the core of *benefits* the product will provide to consumers.

The product planner must next build an **actual product** around the core product. Actual products may have as many as five characteristics: a *quality level, features, design*, a *brand name* and *packaging*. For example, Sony's Handycam camcorder is an actual product. Its name, parts, styling, features, packaging, and other attributes have all been combined carefully to delivery the core benefit – a convenient, high-quality way to capture important moments.

Finally, the product planner must build an **augmented product** around the core and actual products by offering additional consumer services and benefits. Sony must offer more than a camcorder. It must provide consumers with a complete solution to their picture-taking problems. Thus when consumers buy a Sony Handycam, they receive more than just the camcorder itself. Sony and its dealers also might give buyers a warranty on parts and workmanship, free lessons on how to use the camcorder, quick repair services when needed, and a freephone number to call if they have problems or questions. To the consumer, all of these augmentations become an important part of the total product.

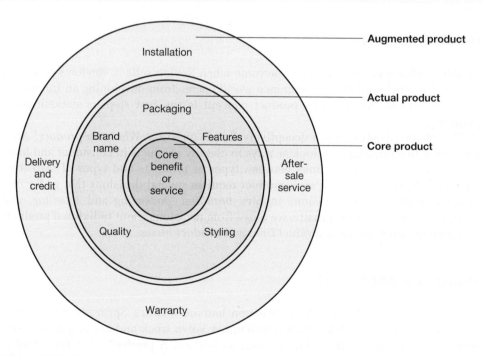

**Figure 14.1**   Three levels of product.

Therefore, a product is more than a simple set of tangible features. In fact, some products, such as a haircut or a doctor's examination, have no tangible features at all. Consumers tend to see products as complex *bundles of benefits* that satisfy their needs. When developing products, marketers first must identify the *core* consumer needs the product will satisfy, then design the *actual* product and finally find ways to *augment* it in order to create the bundle of benefits that will best satisfy consumers.

Today, most competition takes place at the product augmentation level. Successful companies add benefits to their offers that will not only *satisfy*, but will also *delight* the customer. For instance, hotel guests find chocolates on the pillow or a bowl of fruit or a VCR with optional videotapes. The company is saying 'we want to treat you in a special way'. However, each augmentation costs the company money, and the marketer has to ask whether customers will pay enough to cover the extra cost. Moreover augmented benefits soon become *expected* benefits: hotel guests now expect cable television sets, small trays of toiletries and other amenities in their rooms. This means that competitors must search for still more features and benefits to distinguish their offers.

## PRODUCT CLASSIFICATIONS

In seeking marketing strategies for individual products and services, marketers have developed several product-classification schemes based on product characteristics. We now examine these schemes and characteristics.

### Durable goods, nondurable goods, and services

Products can be classified into three groups according to their *durability* or *tangibility*.[2] **Nondurable goods** are consumer goods that are normally consumed in one or a few uses, such as beer, soap and salt. **Durable goods** are consumer goods that are used over an extended period of time and that normally survive many uses. Examples include refrigerators, cars and furniture. **Services** are activities, benefits or satisfactions that are offered for sale, such as haircuts and home repairs. Services are essentially intangible and do not result in the ownership of anything. (Because of the growing importance of services, we will look at them more closely in Chapter 15.)

### Consumer goods

**Consumer goods** are those bought by final consumers for personal consumption. Marketers usually classify these goods based on *consumer shopping habits*. Consumer goods include *convenience goods, shopping goods, speciality goods* and *unsought goods* (see Figure 14.2).[3]

**Convenience goods** are consumer goods and services that the consumer usually buys frequently, immediately and with a minimum of comparison and buying effort. They are usually low priced and widely available. Examples include tobacco products, soap, and newspapers. Convenience goods can be divided further into *staples, impulse goods* and *emergency goods*.

*Staples* are goods that consumers buy on a regular basis, such as ketchup, toothpaste, or bread. *Impulse goods* are purchased with little planning or search effort. These goods are normally available in many places because consumers seldom seek

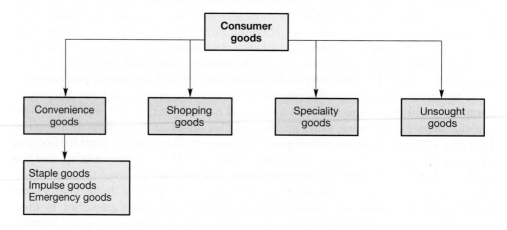

**Figure 14.2** Classification of consumer goods.

them out. Thus chocolate bars and magazines are placed next to checkout counters because shoppers may not otherwise think of buying them. *Emergency goods* are purchased when a need is urgent – umbrellas during a rainstorm, or boots and shovels during the year's first snowstorm. Manufacturers of emergency goods will place them in many outlets to make them readily available when the customer needs them.

**Shopping goods** are consumer goods that the customer, in the process of selection and purchase, usually compares as alternative brands on such bases as suitability, quality, price and style. When purchasing shopping goods, consumers spend considerable time and effort in gathering information and making comparisons. Examples include furniture, clothing, used cars and large appliances. Shopping goods can be divided into *uniform* and *nonuniform* goods. The buyer sees uniform shopping goods, such as big appliances, as similar in quality but different enough in price to justify shopping comparisons. The seller has to 'talk price' to the buyer. However, when a consumer is shopping for clothing, furniture and other nonuniform goods, product features are often more important than price. If the buyer wants a new suit, the cut, fit and look are likely to be more important than small price differences. The seller of nonuniform shopping goods therefore must carry a wide assortment to satisfy individual tastes and must have well-trained salespeople to give information and advice to customers.

**Speciality goods** are consumer goods with unique characteristics or brand identification for which a significant group of buyers is willing to make a special purchase effort. Examples include specific brands and types of cars, high-priced home entertainment systems, photographic equipment and custom-made men's suits. A jukebox, for example, is a speciality good because buyers are usually willing to travel great distances to buy one. Buyers normally do not compare speciality goods. They invest only the time needed to reach dealers carrying the wanted products. Although these dealers do not need convenient locations, they must still let buyers know where to find them.

**Unsought goods** are consumer goods that the consumer either does not know about or knows about but does not normally think of buying. A new product like the digital audio tape player is unsought until the consumer becomes aware of it through advertising. Classic examples of known but unsought goods are life insurance, home security systems and encyclopaedias. By their very nature, unsought goods require a lot of advertising, personal selling and other marketing efforts. Some of the most advanced personal selling methods have developed out of the challenge of selling such goods.

## Industrial goods

**Industrial goods** are those bought by individuals and organizations for further processing or for use in conducting a business. Thus the distinction between a consumer good and an industrial good is based on the *purpose* for which the product is purchased. If a consumer buys a lawn mower for use around the home, the lawn mower is a consumer good. If the same consumer buys the same lawn mower for use in a landscaping business, the lawn mower is an industrial good.

Industrial goods can be classified according to how they enter the production process and according to what they cost. There are three groups: *materials and parts, capital items*, and *supplies and services* (see Figure 14.3).

**Materials and parts** are industrial goods that enter the manufacturer's product completely, either through further processing or as components. They fall into two class: raw materials and manufactured materials and parts.

*Raw materials* include farm products (wheat, cotton, livestock, fruits, vegetables) and natural products (fish, timber, crude petroleum, iron ore). Farm products are supplied by many small producers who turn them over to marketing intermediaries that

Raw materials: this ad positions NutraSweet's sweetener as the important ingredient in the success of other brands, the sweetener that creates added value for its customers.

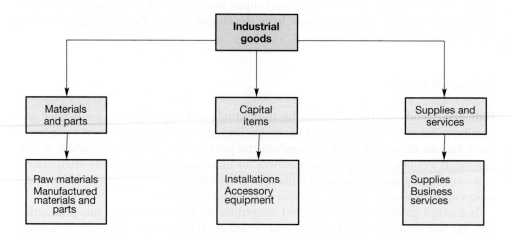

**Figure 14.3**   Classification of industrial goods.

process and sell them. Natural products usually have great bulk and low unit value and require a lot of transportation to move them from producer to user. They are supplied by fewer and larger producers, who tend to market them directly to industrial users.

*Manufactured materials and parts* include component materials (iron, yarn, cement, wires) and component parts (small motors, tyres, castings). Component materials are usually processed further – for example, pig iron is made into steel and yarn is woven into cloth. Component parts enter the finished product complete with no further change in form, as when small motors are put into vacuum cleaners and tyres are added to automotives. Most manufactured materials and parts are sold directly to industrial users. Price and service are the most significant marketing factors, and branding and advertising tend to be less important.

**Capital items** are industrial goods that partly enter the finished product. They include two groups: installations and accessory equipment. *Installations* consist of buildings (factories, offices) and fixed equipment (generators, drill presses, large components, elevators). Because installations are substantial purchases, they are usually bought directly from the producer after a long decision period. **Accessory equipment** includes portable factory equipment and tools (hand tools, lift trucks) and office equipment (fax machines, desks). These products do not become part of the finished product. They have a shorter life than installations and simply aid in the production process. Most sellers of accessory equipment use middlemen because the market is spread out geographically, the buyers are numerous and the orders are small.

**Supplies and services** are industrial goods that do not enter the finished product at all. *Supplies* include operating supplies (lubricants, coal, computer paper, pencils) and repair and maintenance items (paint, nails, brooms). Supplies are the convenience goods of the industrial field because they are usually purchased with a minimum of effort or comparison. *Business services* include maintenance and repair services (window cleaning, computer repair) and business advisory services (legal, management consulting, advertising). These services are usually supplied under contract. Maintenance services are often provided by small producers, and repair services are often available from the manufacturers of the original equipment.

Thus we see that a product's characteristics have a marked effect on marketing strategy. At the same time, marketing strategy also depends on factors such as the product's stage in its life cycle, the number of competitors, the degree of market segmentation, and the condition of the economy.

## INDIVIDUAL PRODUCT DECISIONS

Let us now look at decisions relating to the development and marketing of individual products. We will focus on decisions about *product attributes, branding, packaging, labelling,* and *product-support services.*

### Product attribute decisions

Developing a product involves defining the benefits that the product will offer. These benefits are communicated and delivered by tangible product attributes, such as *quality, features* and *design.* Decisions about these attributes are particularly important as they greatly affect consumer reactions to a product. We will now discuss the issue involved in each decision.

#### Product quality

Quality has two dimensions: level and consistency. In developing a product, the marketer must first choose a *quality level* that will support the product's position in the target market. Quality is one of the marketer's main positioning tools. Here, **product quality** stands for the ability of a product to perform its functions. It includes the product's overall durability, reliability, precision, ease of operation and repair, and other valued attributes. Although some of these attributes can be measured objectively, from a marketing point of view, quality should be measured in terms of buyers' perceptions. Companies rarely try to offer the highest possible quality level – few customers want or can afford the high levels of quality offered in products such as a Rolls-Royce, a Sub Zero refrigerator or a Rolex watch. Instead, companies choose a quality level that matches target market needs and the quality levels of competing products.

No matter what the targeted quality level, all companies shoulds strive for high levels of *quality consistency.* That is, beyond quality level, high quality can also mean consistently delivering the targeted level of quality to consumers. In this sense, quality means 'absence of defects or variation'.

During the past decade, a renewed emphasis on quality has spawned a global quality movement. Japanese firms have long practised 'total quality management' (TQM), an effort to constantly improve product and process quality in every phase of their operations. For more than forty years, the Japanese have awarded the Demming prize (named after quality pioneer W. Edwards Demming) to companies that have achieved outstanding quality. In these forty years, a focus on quality has turned Japan from a maker of knick-knacks into an economic powerhouse – and European and US companies are now being forced to respond. The result has been a global revolution affecting every facet of business.[4]

To some companies, improving quality means using better quality control to reduce defects that annoy consumers. To others, it means making lofty speeches about the importance of quality and passing out lapel pins with quality slogans on them. But total quality management means much more than this. It requires a total-company dedication to continuous quality improvement. Quality starts with a strong commitment by top management – many companies have now created 'total quality

## Motorola's customer-defined, 'six-sigma' quality

Founded in 1928, Motorola introduced the first car radio – hence the name Motorola, suggesting 'sound in motion'. During World War II, it developed the first two-way radios ('walkie-talkies'), and by the 1950s, Motorola had become a household name in consumer electronics products. In the 1970s, however, facing intense competition, much of it from Japanese firms, Motorola abandoned the radios and televisions that had made it famous. Instead, it focused on advanced telecommunications and electronics products – semiconductors, two-way radios, pagers, cellular telephones, and related gear. But by the early 1980s, Motorola still faced a challenge. Japanese competitors were threatening Motorola with higher-quality products at lower prices.

Then things changed. During the past decade, Motorola has come roaring back. It is now one of the leaders not only in its own home (US) market for semiconductors, but also ranks number one worldwide in the fast-growing cellular telephone industry. It dominates the world's two-way mobile radio market and leads all competitors in pagers. Rather than suffering at the hands of Japanese competitors, Motorola now has them on the run, even on their home turf. It ranks third in the fiercely competitive Asian chip market and is threatening to overtake Toshiba at number two. Once in danger of being forced out of the pager market altogether, Motorola now holds the top position in the world. And the company has become Asia's leading supplier of two-way radios and digital cordless phones.

How has Motorola achieved such remarkable leadership? The answer is deceptively simple: an obsessive dedication to *quality*. In the early 1980s, Motorola launched an aggressive crusade to improve product quality, first by tenfold, then by a hundredfold. Ultimately, it set the unheard-of goal of 'six-sigma' quality by 1992. Six sigma is a statistical term that means 'six standard deviations from a statistical performance average'. In plain English, the six-sigma standard mean that Motorola set out to slash product defects to fewer than 3.4 per million components manufactured – that is, 99.9997 per cent defect free. 'Six sigma' became Motorola's rallying cry, and the company is now an acknowledged pioneer in quality, achieving constant quality improvement by applying quality principles to every phase of company operations. In 1988, Motorola received one of the first annual Malcolm Baldrige National Quality Awards recognizing 'pre-eminent quality leadership'.

Motorola's initial efforts were focused on improving product quality through manufacturing improvements. This involved much more than simply increasing the number of quality control inspectors. The goal was to prevent defects from occurring in the first place. This mean *designing* products from the onset for quality and making things right *first* time and *every* time. For example, Motorola's highly successful MicroTAC foldable, hand-held cellular phone has only one-eighth the number of parts contained in its original 1978 portable telephone; components snap together instead of being joined by screws or fasteners. This simpler design results in fewer component defects and production errors.

Meeting the six-sigma standard means that everyone in the organization must be dedicated to quality. Motorola spends $120 million* annually to educate employees about quality – to teach them to inspect their own work and improve their own performance. Then it rewards people when they make things right. Finally, because Motorola's products can be only as good as the components that go into them, the company forces its suppliers to meet the same exacting quality standards. Some suppliers grumble, but those that survive benefit greatly from their own quality improvements. As an executive from one of Motorola's suppliers puts it, 'if we can supply Motorola, we can supply God'. Thus total quality has

*1 ecu = US$1.26.

programmes' headed by vice-presidents or directors of quality. Employees at all levels of the organization must then be educated and motivated to put quality first.

Rather than catching and correcting defects after the fact, total quality management involves preventing defects before they occur, through better product design and improved manufacturing processes. Beyond simply reducing product defects,

become an important part of Motorola's basic corporate culture, and everyone associated with Motorola strives for quality improvement.

More recently, as Motorola has developed a broader and deeper understanding of the meaning of quality, its initial focus on preventing manufacturing defects has evolved into an emphasis on improving customer value. 'Quality', notes Motorola's vice-president of quality, 'has to do something for the customer.' Thus, the fundamental aim of the company's quality movement is 'total customer satisfaction'.

> [The focus of the first quality-improvement efforts] was very internal, looking at things like defects on printed circuit boards manufacturered in the factory. ... Now we're taking the customer's values and establishing quality criteria directly [from those] ... Beauty is in the eye of the user. If [a product] does not work the way that the user needs it to work, the defect is as big to the user as if it doesn't work the way the designer planned it. Our definition of a defect is 'if the customer doesn't like it, it's a defect'.

This concept of *customer-defined quality* has put more pressure on the company to understand the customer better. Instead of concentrating solely on manufacturing defects, Motorola now surveys customers about their quality needs, analyses customer complaints, and studies service records, in a constant quest to improve value to the customer. Motorola's executives routinely visit customers' offices to gain more detailed, deeper insights into customer needs. As a result, Motorola's total quality management programme has done more than reduce product defects: it has helped the company to shift from an inwardly focused engineering orientation to a market-driven, customer-focused one.

Although Motorola missed its target of 3.4 defects per million in 1992, it did improve manufacturing quality 170-fold, to a current 30 defects per million compared to 6,000 per million just five years ago. Building on this success, Motorola has set a new quality goal: to cut defects by 90 per cent every two years throughout the 1990s. And it has now expanded the quality goal to all of its departments and processes, from manufacturing and product development to market research, finance, and even advertising. Each department now has its own six-sigma quality goal.

Some sceptics are concerned that Motorola's obsession with quality might result in problems. For example, the company's products have sometimes been late to the market. Others worry that building so much quality into a product might be too expensive. Not so, claims Motorola. In fact, the reverse is true – superior quality is the lowest-cost way to do things. The costs of monitoring and fixing mistakes can far exceed the costs of getting things right in the first place. Motorola estimates that its quality efforts have resulted in savings of more than $3 billion during the past six years. Finally, the sceptics fear that the quality crusade might stifle innovation by forcing research, design and production staff to stick with safe, proven methods and technologies. But the results suggest otherwise. 'We're doing a lot more now than we've every done,' says Motorola's chairman, 'and doing most of it better.'

And so Motorola's quest for quality continues. By the year 2001, Motorola is shooting for near perfection – a mind-boggling rate of just *one* defect per billion.

Sources: Quotes from 'Future perfect', *The Economist* (4 January 1992), 61; Lois Therrien, 'Motorola and NEC: going for glory', *Business Week*, special issue on quality (1991), 60–1; and B. G. Yovovich, 'Motorola's quest for quality', *Business Marketing* (19 September 1991), 14–16; see also William Wiggenhorn, 'Motorola U: when training becomes an education', *Harvard Business Review* (July–Aug. 1990), 71–83; and Ernest Raia, '1991 Medal of Professional Excellence', *Purchasing* (26 September 1991), 38–57.

the ultimate goal of total quality is to improve *customer value*. Some argue that total quality is not merely a manufacturing issue but a powerful weapon for achieving 'total customer satisfaction'. This is possible if quality is defined from the customers' perspective and if product defects are interpreted in terms of customer need and expectations (see Marketing Highlight 14.1).

Many companies have turned quality into a potent strategic weapon. *Strategic quality* involves gaining an edge over competitors by consistently offering products and services that better serve customers' needs and preferences for quality. As one expert proclaims: 'Quality is not simply a problem to be solved; it is a competitive opportunity.'[5] Others suggest, however, that quality has now become a competitive *necessity* – that in the 1990s and beyond, only companies with the best quality will thrive.

## Product features

A product can be offered with varying features. A 'stripped-down' model, one without any extras, is the starting point. The company can add more features and create higher-level models. Features are a competitive tool for differentiating the company's product from competitors' products. Being the first producer to introduce a needed and valued new feature is one of the most effective ways to compete. Some companies are very innovative in adding new features.

To identify new features and decide which ones to add to its product the company should periodically survey buyers who have used the product and ask these questions: How do you like the product? Which specific features of the product do you like most? Which features could we add to improve the product? How much would you pay for each feature? The answers provide the company with a rich list of feature ideas, each of which should be assessed on the basis of its *customer value* versus its *company cost*. The analysis should give insight into features that customers value highly in relation to costs, and which would truly improve the current product's competitive position.

## Product design

Another way to add product distinctiveness is through **product design**. Some companies have reputations for outstanding design, such as Black & Decker in cordless appliances and tools, Olivetti in office equipment and Braun in shavers and small

Honda's unbeatable 'extras': the new Honda Civic 5-door is the only car in the class that includes a passenger airbag as standard.

household appliances. Many companies, however, lack a 'design touch'. Their product designs function poorly or are dull or common looking. Yet design can be one of the most powerful competitive weapons in a company's marketing arsenal.

Design is a broader concept than style. *Style* simply describes the appearance of a product. A sensational style may grab attention, but it does not necessarily make the product *perform* better. In some cases, it might even result in worse performance. For example, a chair may look great yet be extremely uncomfortable. Unlike style, *design* is more than skin deep – it goes to the very heart of a product. Good design contributes to a product's usefulness as well as to its looks. A good designer considers appearance but also creates products that are easy, safe, inexpensive to use and service, and simple and economical to produce and distribute.

As competition intensifies, design will offer one of the most potent tools for creating competitive distinctiveness for products of all kinds. That investment in design pays off has certainly been recognized by global companies which have embraced design – Minolta (cameras), Sony (hi-fis), Philips (compact disc players and shavers), Ford (cars) and Swatch (watches) are just a few examples of such firms that have profited from their commitment to product design. Differentiating through design is also a familiar strategy in premium products such as Rolex watches, Porsche cars and Herman Miller office furniture. These products stand out from the crowd. Good design can attract attention, improve product performance, cut production costs, and give the product a strong competitive advantage in the target market.[6]

## Brand decisions

Consumers view a brand as an important part of a product, and branding can help to differentiate a firm's product from that of its competitors product. A successful brand, besides meeting the basic functional requirements of consumers, also has added values that fulfil customers' psychological needs. These added values are not usually specific, tangible product features, but intangible benefits best interpreted as inspiring consumers' confidence in the brand as they perceive it to be of superior quality and more desirable than competitive brands in the market.

Branding has become a central issue in product strategy. On the one hand, developing a branded product requires a great deal of long-term marketing investment, especially for advertising, promotion, and packaging. Manufacturers often find it easier and less expensive simply to make the product and let others do the brand building. Taiwanese manufacturers, for example, have taken this course. They make a large amount of the world's clothing, consumer electronics and computers, but these products are sold under non-Taiwanese brand names.

On the other hand, most manufacturers eventually learn that the power lies with the companies that control the brand names. For example, brand-name clothing, electronics, and computer companies can replace their Taiwanese manufacturing sources with cheaper sources in Malaysia and elsewhere. The Taiwanese producers can do little to prevent the loss of sales to less expensive suppliers – consumers are loyal to the brands, not to the producers. Japanese and South Korean companies, however, have not made this mistake. They have spent heavily to build up brand names such as Sony, Panasonic, JVC, Hyundai, Goldstar and Samsung for their products. Even when these companies can no longer afford to manufacture their products in their homelands, their brand names continue to command customer loyalty.[7]

Powerful brand names have *consumer franchise* – that is, they command strong consumer loyalty. This means that a sufficient number of customers demand these brands and refuse substitutes, even if the substitutes are offered at somewhat lower prices. Companies that develop brands with a strong consumer franchise are insulated from competitors' promotional strategies. Thus it makes sense for a supplier to invest heavily to create strong national or even global recognition and preference for its brand name. If customers perceive its brand as superior, then they will prefer it and pay more for it.

## What is a brand?

Perhaps the most distinctive skill of professional marketers is their ability to create, maintain, protect, reinforce and enchance brands. A **brand** is a name, term, sign, symbol, design or a combination of these, which is used to identify the goods or services of one seller or group of sellers and to differentiate them from those of competitors.[8] Thus a brand identifies the maker or supplier of a product. Take a product such as a cola drink – any manufacturer can produce a cola drink but only the Coca-Cola Company can produce Coke.

Branding is not a new phenomenon. In the last hundred years, however, its use has developed considerably. Legal systems recognize that brands are also property in a very real sense. Currently, over 160 countries have trademark laws allowing owners of brands to claim title in their brand names and logos through trademark registration. But brands, unlike other forms of intellectual property, such as patents and copyrights, do not have expiration dates and their owners have exclusive rights to use their brand name for an unlimitd period of time.

A brand conveys a specific set of features, benefits and services to buyers. The best brands, for example, often stand for quality, value and product satisfaction. According to one marketing executive, a brand can deliver up to four levels of meaning:

1. *Attributes.* A brand first brings to mind certain product attributes. For example, Mercedes suggests such attributes as 'well engineered', 'well built', 'durable', 'high prestige', 'fast', 'expensive' and 'high resale value'. The company may use one or more of these attributes in its advertising for the car. For years, Mercedes advertised 'Engineered like no other car in the world'. This provided a positioning platform for other attributes of the car.
2. *Benefits.* Customers do not buy attributes, they buy benefits. Therefore, attributes must be translated into functional and emotional benefits. For example, the attribute 'durable' could translate into the functional benefit, 'I won't have to buy a new car every few years'. The attribute 'expensive' might translate into the emotional benefit, 'The car makes me feel important and admired'. The attribute 'well-built' might translate into the functional and emotional benefit, 'I am safe in the event of an accident'.
3. *Values.* A brand also says something about the buyers' values. Thus Mercedes buyers value high performance, safety, and prestige. A brand marketer must identify the specific groups of car buyers whose values coincide with the delivered benefit package.
4. *Personality.* A brand also projects a personality. Motivation researchers sometimes ask, 'If this brand were a person, what kind of person would it be?' Consumers might visualize a Mercedes automobile as being a wealthy, middle-aged business executive. The brand will attract people whose actual or desired self-images match the brand's image.[9]

All this suggests that a brand is a complex symbol. If a company treats a brand only as a name, it misses the point of branding. The challenge of branding is to develop a deep set of meanings for the brand.

Given the four levels of a brand's meaning, marketers must decide the levels at which they will build the brand's identity. It would be a mistake to promote only the brand's attributes. Buyers are not so much interested in brand attributes as in brand benefits. Moreover competitors can easily copy attributes. Or the current attributes may later become less valuable to consumers, hurting a brand that is tied too strongly to specific attributes.

Even promoting the brand on one or more of its benefits can be risky. Suppose Mercedes touts its main benefit as 'high performance'. If several competing brands emerge with as high or higher performance, or if car buyers begin placing less importance on performance as compared to other benefits, Mercedes will need the freedom to move into a new benefit positioning.

The most lasting and sustainable meanings of a brand are its values and personality. They define the brand's essence. Thus Mercedes stands for 'high achievers and success'. The company must build its brand strategy around creating and protecting this brand personality. Although Mercedes has recently yielded to market pressures by introducing lower-price models, this might prove risky. Marketing less expensive models might dilute the value and erode the personality that the Mercedes brand has built up over the decades.

## Brand equity

Brands vary in the amount of power and value they have in the marketplace. At one extreme are brands that are largely unknown to most buyers in the marketplace. Next are brands with a fairly high degree of consumer *brand awareness*. Still other brands enjoy *brand preference* – buyers select them over the others. Finally, some brands command a high degree of *brand loyalty*. A top executive at H. J. Heinz proposes this test of brand loyalty: 'My acid test ... is whether a [consumer], intending to buy Heinz Ketchup in a store but finding it out of stock, will walk out of the store to buy it elsewhere or switch to an alternative product.'

A powerful brand has high **brand equity**. Brands have higher brand equity to the extent that they have higher brand loyalty, name awareness, perceived quality, strong brand associations, and other assets such as patents, trademarks, and channel relationships.[10] A brand with strong brand equity is a valuable asset. In fact, it can even be bought or sold for a price. Many companies base their growth strategies on acquiring and building rich *brand portfolios*. For example, Grand Metropolitan acquired various Pillsbury brands, including Green Giant vegetables, Häagen-Dazs ice cream and Burger King restaurants. Switzerland's Nestlé bought Rowntree (UK), Carnation (US), Stouffer (US), Buitoni-Perugina (Italy) and Perrier (France), making it the world's largest food company controlling many desirable 'brands'.

Measuring the actual equity of a brand name is difficult.[11] Because it is so hard to measure, companies usually do not list brand equity on their balance sheets. Still, they pay handsomely for it. For example, Nestlé paid £2.5 billion to buy Rowntree, six times its reported asset value. And when Grand Metropolitan bought Heublein, it added $800 million to its assets to reflect the value of Smirnoff and other names. According to one estimate, the brand equity of Marlboro is $31 billion, Coca-Cola $24 billion, and Kodak $13 billion.

The world's top brands include such superpowers as Coca-Cola, Campbell, Disney, Kodak, Sony, Mercedes-Benz and McDonald's (see Marketing Highlight 14.2). High brand equity provides a company with many competitive advantages. Because a powerful brand enjoys a high level of consumer brand awareness and loyalty, the company will incur lower marketing costs relative to revenues. Because consumers

# The world's most powerful brand names

Companies around the world invest billions each year to create awareness and preference for their top brands. Powerful brand names command strong consumer loyalty and provide competitive advantage in the marketplace.

What are the world's most powerful brands? In a recent study, Landor Associates, an image consulting firm, surveyed 9,000 consumers in the United States, Western Europe, and Japan about their familiarity with and esteem for more than 6,000 brands. It then combined the familiarity and esteem scores to develop brand 'image-power' rankings. Listed in Table 1 are the top ten brands for each part of the world.

Table 1    The world's most powerful brand names

| United States | Europe | Japan |
|---|---|---|
| Coca-Cola | Coca-Cola | Sony |
| Campbell | Sony | National |
| Disney | Mercedes-Benz | Mercedes-Benz |
| Pepsi-Cola | BMW | Toyota |
| Kodak | Philips | Takashimaya (store) |
| NBC | Volkswagen | Rolls-Royce |
| Black & Decker | Adidas | Seiko |
| Kellogg | Kodak | Matsushita |
| McDonald's | Nivea | Hitachi |
| Hershey | Porsche | Suntory |

The Landor study suggests some interesting conclusions. Perhaps most notably, the top brands varied greatly across regions. In recent years, many companies have worked to build global brands that are recognized and preferred not only in their home countries, but by consumers around the world. However, the Landor study suggests that few brands have yet achieved true global status. Although some twenty brands were internationally known, and another forty-five were poised for global prominence, only two brands – Coca-Cola and Sony – appeared in the top-40 image-power rankings in all three markets. And only six other brands made the top 100 in each market: Disney, Nestlé, Toyota, McDonald's, Panasonic, and Kleenex. No product made it into the top 10 lists of all three countries.

Further, the study appears to counter the recent contention, summarized by Chrysler chairman Lee Iacocca, that US consumers believe 'Everything from Japan is perfect. Everything from America is lousy.' The study reveals that Americans do like American products. According to Don Casey, Landor's president, 'What's playing in America today is warm and fuzzy and family and traditional.' The list of top-10 American brands bears this out – it reads like a page out of the corporate American history book. And of

expect stores to carry the brand, the company has more leverage in bargaining with retailers. And because the brand name carries high credibility, the company can more easily launch brand extensions. Above all, a powerful brand offers the company some defence against fierce price competition.

Marketers need to manage their brands carefully in order to preserve brand equity. They must develop strategies that effectively maintain or improve brand awareness, perceived brand quality and usefulness, and positive brand associations over time. This requires, in the first instance, continuous R&D investment to provide a constant flow of improved and innovative products to satisfy customers' changing needs, in addition to skilful advertising, and excellent trade and consumer service. Some companies even appoint 'brand equity managers' to guard their brands' images, associations, and quality. They work to prevent brand managers from overpromoting brands in order to produce short-term profits at the expense of long-term brand equity.

Some analysts see brands as *the* most enduring asset of a company, outlasting the company's specific products and facilities. Yet, behind every powerful brand stands a set of loyal customers. Therefore, the basic asset underlying brand equity is *cus-*

the top-100 ranked brands in the United States, ninety-seven claim American roots. Brand consultants see the high recognition of American brands as proof that it takes decades to construct an image power-house such as Coca-Cola or Kodak. For instance, 'The Great American Chocolate Bar' Hershey, which ranks highest among candidates in America, was also the nation's top-ranked candy in 1925.

The rankings also suggest strong cultural differences among consumers in Europe, the United States and Japan. For example, European and Japanese consumers seem to have more expensive tastes, at least as reflected by the brands they hold in high regard. Casey believes that these differences are tied not just to differing appetites, but to varying aspirations. 'I think that there is a sense of realism in this country of what you can expect from your life,' he says. 'The mindset of Americans is more practical than it is aspirational.' Americans appear food oriented – six of the top ten brands are food related. In the other regions, cars and high-tech brands are more revered. Based on the top-10 list, American consumers appear satis-fied with simple pleasures like a Big Mac, chocolates, and – as a real self-indulgent treat – luxury ice creams. Thus the Landor study suggests that a global marketer may face many cultural hurdles in its attempts to create worldwide brands.

The power of a brand is very difficult to measure. Some critics question the value of asking consumers to rate brands on such subjective factors as 'esteem'. People will probably hold a Mercedes in higher esteem than a brand of laundry detergent. Thus noticeably absent from the list are top brands from some of the world's most powerful marketers, including such giant consumer goods companies as Procter & Gamble, Unilever, and Philip Morris. Further, people often don't buy the brands they regard most highly – many people who hold a Mercedes in high esteem can't afford one. But no matter how you measure brand power, few marketers doubt the value of a powerful brand, as both a verbal and visual entity. Almost any-where in the world, as one brand consultant states, 'When you mention Kodak, I'm pretty sure everyone sees that yellow box.'

Sources: Portions adapted from Cathy Taylor, 'Consumers know native brands best', *Adweek* (17 September 1990), 31; see also Kathleen Deveny, 'More brand names gain recognition around the world', *Wall Street Journal* (13 September 1990), B7; 'Hard sellers: the leading adver-tisers', *Wall Street Journal* (21 March 1991), B4; R. Craig Endicott, 'The top 200 brands', *Advertising Age* (9 November 1992), 16; and Interbrand, *World's Greatest Brands* (New York: Wiley, 1992).

*tomer equity*. This suggests that marketing strategy should focus on extending *loyal customer lifetime value*, with brand management serving as an essential marketing tool.

Branding poses challenging decisions to the marketer. Figure 14.4 shows the key branding decisions.

### To brand or not to brand

The company must first decide whether it should put a brand name on its product. Branding has become so strong that today hardly anything goes unbranded. Salt is packaged in branded containers, common nuts and bolts are packaged with a distrib-utor's label, and automotive parts – spark plugs, tyres, filters – bear brand names that differ from those of the auto makers. Even fruits and vegetables are branded – Sunkist oranges, Dole pineapples and Chiquita bananas.

Recently, however, there has also been a return to 'nonbranding' certain consumer goods. In the late 1970s, 'generic' products took brand name manufacturers by sur-prise. Generics are unbranded, plainly packaged, less expensive versions of common

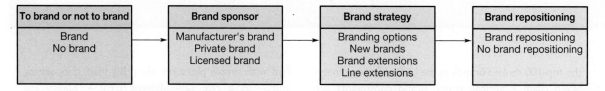

| To brand or not to brand | Brand sponsor | Brand strategy | Brand repositioning |
|---|---|---|---|
| Brand<br>No brand | Manufacturer's brand<br>Private brand<br>Licensed brand | Branding options<br>New brands<br>Brand extensions<br>Line extensions | Brand repositioning<br>No brand repositioning |

**Figure 14.4** Major branding decisions.

products such as spaghetti, paper towels, and canned peaches. They often bear only black-stencilled labels – TOWELS, SUGAR, CAT FOOD – and offer prices as much as 40 per cent lower than those of main brands. The lower price is made possible by lower-quality ingredients, lower-cost packaging, and lower advertising costs.

Although generics are probably here to stay, it appears that their popularity peaked in the early 1980s. Since then, the market share for generics has dropped, largely as a result of better marketing strategies by brand-name manufacturers. These marketers responded by emphasizing brand image and quality.

Despite the decline in the popularity of generics, the issue of whether or not to brand is very much alive today. This situation highlights some key questions: Why have branding in the first place? Who benefits? How do they benefit? At what cost?

Branding helps buyers in a number of ways:

■ Brand names tell the buyer something about product quality. Buyers who always buy the same brand know that they will get the same quality each time they buy.
■ Brand names also increase the shopper's efficiency. Imagine a buyer going into a supermarket and finding thousands of generic products.
■ Brand names help call consumers' attention to new products that might benefit them. The brand name becomes the basis upon which a whole story can be built about the new product's special qualities.

Branding also gives the supplier several advantages:

■ The brand name makes it easier for the supplier to process orders and track down problems.
■ The supplier's brand name and trademark provide legal protection for unique production features that otherwise might be copied by competitors.
■ Branding helps the supplier attract a loyal and profitable set of customers.
■ Branding helps the supplier to segment markets. For example, Cadbury can offer Dairy Milk, Milk Tray, Roses, Flake, Fruit and Nut and many other brands, not just one general confectionery product for all consumers.

Branding also adds value to consumers and society:

Those who favour branding suggest that it leads to higher and more consistent product quality.

■ Branding also increases innovation by giving producers an incentive to look for new features that can be protected against imitating competitors. Thus, branding results in more product variety and choice for consumers.
■ Branding increases shopper efficiency because it provides much more information about products and where to find them.

*Brand sponsor*

A manufacturer has three sponsorship options. The product may be launched as a **manufacturer's brand** as when Lever Brothers, Nestlé and IBM sell their output under their own manufacturer's brand names. Or the manufacturer may sell to resellers who give it a **private brand** (also called *retailer brand, distributor brand,* or *store brand*). For example, Jaka Foods, a Danish company, manufactures tinned food products (notably ham) for sale to own-label retailers like Marks & Spencer. Cott, a Canadian company, makes store-branded foods and drinks, and supplies to retailers worldwide – in the United Kingdom, it sells cola to J. Sainsbury. Fruit juice manufacturers like Del Monté and Gerber makes own-label products for the big supermarket groups. Finally, although most manufacturers create their own brand names, others market *licensed brands*. They choose this route because it takes years to create their own brand names. They can acquire a name quickly by *licensing*, for example, names or symbols previously created by other manufacturers, names of well-known celebrities, characters from popular movies and books – for a fee, any of these can provide an instant and proven brand name. Some apparel and accessories sellers pay large royalties to adorn their products with the names or initials of fashion innovators such as Calvin Klein, Pierre Cardin, and Gucci. Sellers of children's products attach an almost endless list of character names to clothing, toys, school supplies, linens, dolls, lunch boxes, cereals and other items. The character names include such classics as Mickey and Minnie Mouse, Peanuts, Barbie, the Flintstones, Muppets, Garfield, Batman and the Simpsons. The newest form of licensing is **corporate licensing** – renting a corporate trademark or logo made famous in one category and using it in a related category. Some examples include Old Spice shaving mugs and razors, Fabergé costume jewellery, Porsche sunglasses and accessories, and Coppertone swimwear.

In recent times, many large retailers and wholesalers have developed their own private brands. Despite the fact that private brands are often hard to establish and costly to stock and promote, middlemen develop private brands because they can be profitable. Middlemen can often locate manufacturers with excess capacity who will produce the private label at a low cost, resulting in a higher profit margin for the middleman. Private brands also give middlemen exclusive products that cannot be bought from competitors, resulting in greater store traffic and loyalty. A good example of a retailer that has created and sustained a successful private brand is Marks & Spencer with their St Michael label. Another example is the British supermarket chain, Sainsbury, that has recently taken on consumer packaged goods manufacturers like P&G and Lever Brothers by marketing its own Novon brand of detergents.

The competition between manufacturers' and middlemen's brands is called the *battle of the brands*. In this battle, middlemen have many advantages. Retailers control scarce shelf space. Many supermarkets in the United States, for example even charge **slotting fees** – payments demanded by retailers from producers before they will accept new products and find 'slots' for them on the shelves. For example, Safeway required a payment of $25,000 from a small pizza roll manufacturer to stock its new product. Middlemen give their own brands better display space and make certain they are better stocked. They price their store brands lower than comparable manufacturers' brands, thereby appealing to budget-conscious shoppers, especially in difficult economic times. And most shoppers know that store brands are often made by one of the larger manufacturers anyway.

As a result, the dominance of manufacturers' brands is weakening. Today's more financially squeezed consumers, hard pressed to spend wisely, are increasingly sensitive to quality, price, and value. The barrage of coupons and price specials has trained a generation of consumers to buy on price. Product proliferation and the seemingly endless stream of brand extensions and line extensions have blurred brand identity. Consumers see ever-greater similarities across brands, as competing manufacturers and retailers copy the qualities of the best brands. As store brands improve in quality, and as consumers gain confidence in their store chains, store brands are posing a strong challenge to manufacturer's brands (see Marketing Highlight 14.3).

Not surprisingly manufacturers of national brands are very frustrated by the growing power of retailers. As one executive remarks:

> A decade ago, the retailer was a Chihuahua nipping at the manufacturer's heels – a nuisance, yes, but only a minor irritant. You fed it and it went away. Today it's a pit bull and it wants to rip your arms and legs off. You'd like to see it roll over, but you're too busy defending yourself to even try.[12]

Some marketing analysts predict that middlemen's brands eventually will knock out all but the strongest manufacturers' brands.

To retain their power relative to the trade, leading brand marketers must, therefore, invest in R&D to create new brands, new features and continuous quality improvements. They must design strong advertising programmes to differentiate their brands, and maintain high brand awareness and preference. But most importantly, they must find ways to 'partner' with large distributors in a search for distribution economies and competitive strategies that improve their joint performance. It is only through such efforts at creating a 'win-win' situation that manufacturers will sustain their position in an increasingly competitive marketplace.

## Brand strategy

A company must define its overall branding strategy which affects all of its products. This strategy will also guide the branding of new products. Four key areas where decisions must be taken are: *branding options, new brands, brand extensions* and *line extensions.*

*Branding options*    Companies have adopted a number of brand strategy options:

1. **Corporate brand.** At one extreme, the firm makes its company name the dominant brand identity across all of its products, as in the case of Mercedes-Benz, Philips and Heinz. The main advantages are economies of scale in marketing investments and wider recognition of the brand name. It also facilitates introduction of new products especially when the corporate name is well established.

2. **Multibrand.** At the other extreme, companies exemplified by Unilever, Mars and Procter & Gamble, have used individual brand identities for each of their products. Unilever's line of laundry detergents – Persil, Wisk, Surf, Radion, etc. – have distinct labels, with the corporate name hardly featured. Like Unilever, Procter & Gamble produces at least nine brands of laundry products. These manufacturers argue that managing a stable of brand names within the some product category permits finer segmentation of the market, with each brand name suggesting different functions or benefits for different customer segments. Another advantage is that the firm can differentiate its new products more effectively with individual brand names, whilst also reducing the risk of individual brand failures harming the company's overall reputation.

3. **Company and individual brand.** This is a middle approach which focuses both on the corporate and individual brand names. Kelloggs (e.g. Cornflakes, Raisin

Bran, Rice Krispies, Coco Pops, etc.) and Cadbury's (e.g Wispa, Flake, Roses, Fruit and Nut, Milk Tray, Wholenut, Dairy Milk) are supporters of this branding strategy.

4. **Range branding.** Some companies have developed separate range names for different families of product, as in the case of Japan's Matsushita which own Technics, National, Panasonic and Quasar.

*New brands*    Firms that favour a multibrand approach are likely to create a new brand to differentiate a new product whether it is introduced into an existing or a new-product category. However, for some companies, a new brand may be created because it is entering a new-product category for which none of the company's current brands seem appropriate. For example, Toyota established a separate family name – the Lexus – for its new luxury executive cars in order to create a distinctive identity for the latter and to position these well away from the traditional mass-market image of the 'Toyota' brand name. Alternatively, a company may be compelled to differentiate its new product, and a new brand is the best route to signal its identity. Seiko introduced a line of lower-priced watches under the Pulsar brand name, which is used as a *flanker* or *fighter brand* aimed at customers who want a less expensive watch.

Introducing new brands within a product category can be risky as each brand might obtain only a small market share and none may be very profitable. The company will have spread its resources over several brands instead of building one or a few brands to a highly profitable level. Companies should weed out weaker brands and set high standards for choosing new brands. Ideally, the firm's brands should take sales away from competitors' brands, not from each other.

*Brand extensions*    A **brand-extension** (or brand-stretching) strategy is any effort to use a successful brand name to launch new or modified products in a new category. Procter & Gamble put its Fairy name on laundry powder and dishwashing detergent with effective results. Swatch spread from watches into telephones. Dunhill, long ago, successfully extended its range of smokers' requisites to include pens and watches. And Honda stretched its company name to cover such different products as its automobiles, motorcyles, snowblowers, lawn mowers, marine engines, and snow-mobiles. This allows Honda to advertise that it can fit 'six Hondas in a two-car garage'.

A brand extension strategy offers many advantages. A recent study found that brand extensions capture greater market share and realize greater advertising efficiency than individual brands.[13] Launching a new brand is risky and the odds on failure are high. By contrast, a well-regarded brand name gives a new product an implicit quality guarantee. It helps the company enter new product categories more easily as it increases initial reaction, interest and willingness to try the product. Sony puts its name on most of its new electronic products, creating an instant perception of high quality and faster acceptance for each new product. Brand extensions also save the high advertising cost usually required to familiarize consumers with a new brand name.

At the same time, a brand extension strategy involves some risk. Badly thought-out brand extensions such as Bic pantyhose, Heinz pet food and Cadbury soup met early deaths. In each of these cases the brand name was not appropriate to the new product, even though it was well made and satisfying. This problem occurs when the established brand name is launched into a very different market from the original brand and target customers in the new market do not value the brand's associations. Imagine a Pepsi single malt whiskey or Chanel galoshes?

# The battle for the brands

'Consumers still prefer to buy a branded product. They don't want to walk around with Brand X in their hand,' says PepsiCola.

'Consumers are smarter now than they were 20 years ago. ... They are no longer prepared to pay a "brand tax" – the extra costs of hiring rock stars and the like to promote and sustain a brand's image. You can only pay so long for an icon,' argues Cott, the Canadian private label foods and drinks maker who supplies leading food retailers and supermarkets like J. Sainsbury in the United Kingdom.

This exchange of words represents the battle for customer loyalty that is hotting up between large international food/drinks manufacturers who own established brands and retailers. In recent times, big supermarket chains have stepped up their efforts to boost sales by introducing more and more of their own private label goods. A recent study by McKinsey, the management consultant, shows the extent of own-label penetration in food as well as nonfood sectors (see Table 1). The report shows that Britain leads the Western world in penetration of own-label groceries. The reason is that the market share of its large supermarket chains, like Tesco, Asda and Sainsbury, is far higher than in any other country. The

growth of private label is not unique to the United Kingdom. In Germany and Switzerland, high private-label penetration has occurred and this is largely due to own-label clothing dominance of the Aldi and Migros chains. The McKinsey study reports that private label's market share in other European countries would eventually reach the levels of Britain and Germany and that further growth is predicted even for these two countries.

Business observers sometimes call the 1980s the 'decade of the brand'. Big brands (and their owners) were performing spectacularly well throughout the 1980s. They were seen as perpetual treasures. Companies (or predators) keen to lay their hands on these jewels paid hefty premiums for them, as witnessed in some of the most memorable mega-takeover deals that occurred in the late 1980s – Kohlberg Kravis Roberts paid $25 billion for RJR Nabisco (more than double its book value); Philip Morris bought Kraft for $12.9 billion (four times its book value) and Nestlé bought Rowntree for $4.5 billion/£2.6 billion (five times book value). Companies such as Kelloggs and Heinz were also on a roll – by exploiting consumers' loyalty to their brand name, they were able to charge a premium and, with price hikes of well above inflation, these companies' profits soared in the order of 15 per cent a year.

By the early 1990s, however, things were beginning to change. Brand owners were finding that consumers had become more price sensitive and their loyalty to famous brands was waning – many were no longer prepared to pay more for the name. There are several explanations for this. In part, the economic downturn of the 1990s was to be blamed for the fading popularity of famous brand names. Consumers were becoming more concerned with getting good quality at a low price than about the name on the product. In the food and drinks market, this gave way to the rising popularity of retailers' own-label goods. However, recession was not the only culprit. Manufacturers themselves were partly to be blamed – they had been encouraging consumers to buy on price by bombarding them with special offers. Still others argue that the damage that brand owners are currently suffering is a consequence of their own

Table 1   Own-label grocery penetration

| Country | Percentage own-label* |
|---|---|
| United Kingdom | 30 |
| Germany | 23 |
| Switzerland | 23 |
| France | 20 |
| Sweden | 20 |
| United States | 18 |
| Belgium | 18 |
| Denmark | 18 |
| Netherlands | 18 |
| Austria | 11 |
| Spain | 7 |
| Italy | 7 |
| Norway | 3 |
| Portugal | 1 |

Note: *1991 value.
Source: Nielsen; McKinsey analysis.

short-sightedness, greed and bad marketing decisions.

Many food and drinks manufacturers neither saw nor appreciated the long-term shift in the balance of power from manufacturer to multiple retailer. The writing has been on the wall for some time. Big brand names do not have a perpetual value and their owners must continually find ways to keep strong brands strong. A salutary lesson for owners of big brands comes from an event that will live in infamy – 2 April 1993 or 'Marlboro Friday'.

On that day, Philip Morris, the world's largest consumer products group, slashed the price in America of its top-selling cigarette, Marlboro, by 20 per cent – 40 cents a pack – in a desperate attempt to shore up the brand's collapsing sales and to stop the erosion of its market share by lower-priced cigarettes most people have never heard of. What happened next? In just one day, investors not only wiped $13.4 billion off Philip Morris's stockmarket value, but also dumped shares in scores of other consumer goods firms, causing a worldwide slump in the shares of branded goods companies. RJR Nabisco (Philip Morris's main rival who also subsequently cut its prices), P&G, Coca-Cola, PepsiCo, Gillette and Quaker Oats were all hit by traders who were convinced that the explosive profit growth previously enjoyed by branded standard-bearers had come to an end. Something like $24 billion was shed off the combined market value of America's top five consumer product groups. A year on, Philip Morris's share price remained more than 20 per cent below their level of 2 April. As for the industry, the cuts engulfed competitors as the group extended the discounts to its other premium brands – Benson & Hedges, Virginia Slims, Merit and Parliament. Rivals like American Brands and Ligget have been driven into loss and RJR, in 1994, considered quitting the tobacco business altogether. So much for the invincibility of brands!

Marlboro Friday cannot be dismissed as a one-off event. Across the Atlantic, Britain's equivalent of Marlboro Friday arrived on Wednesday, 3 November 1993. On this day, J. Sainsbury, the leading supermarket group, slashed prices of 300 best-selling own-label items, an activity that would force branded-product prices to come down significantly to compete.

Let us look at Britain's own-label threat and the pioneering efforts of Sainsbury and followers such as Tesco, Asda and Safeway, as a prime example of how supermarkets have utilized basic marketing principles to create and sustain a competitive advantage in their continuing battle with traditional branded-product manufacturers.

Sainsbury in the United Kingdom has a long-established reputation for supplying good-quality own-label grocery products that match branded equivalents. In its continuous drive to protect sales, and with the advent of discount retailers like Food Giant and Kwik Save threatening margins, the supermarket chain has stepped up efforts, over the late 1980s and early 1990s, to push more new private-label food and non-food products onto its shelves. For example, it launched 1,300 new private-label products in 1990. At the same time, it has launched a drive to expand sales of these goods by capitalizing on 'lookalike' packaging. Sainsbury's launch of 'Classic Cola', 'Creme' and 'Johara' (see 'lookalike' pictures overleaf), are just a few powerful examples of the growing trend sweeping the United Kingdom and Europe. By playing on consumers' perceived product parity, together with its high product-quality image and lower prices, its own labels are seen to offer much better value for money. Sainsbury is not alone in getting to the number-one brands. Tesco, Britain's number-two food retailer, has also been testing the strength of brand owners' resolve. Its Unbelievable brand of a low-fat spread closely resembles Van den Bergh Foods' I Can't Believe It's Not Butter brand (see picture overleaf). These bold forays of retailers mark a new era of brand competition that is expected to gather pace throughout the 1990s. Not surprisingly, developments like these are a big worry for suppliers like P&G, Nestlé, Unilever and Coca-Cola, who still rely very much on their name to shift products often costing twice as much as the private label.

Brand owners, and especially the giants, are however, not easily defeated. They are stoutly defending their market shares. P&G, for example, acknowledges that many housewives prefer own-label pasta to a branded product, but, where detergents are concerned, its washing powders are markedly superior

Own brands versus manufacturers' brands: witness here the essence of the 'product lookalike' threat confronting brand owners in the UK grocery and packages goods market.

to own-label alternatives. It would vigorously defend its hard-won market position. For many brand owners, that means having to cut prices to remain competitive.

The tough private-label competition in the United Kingdom had precipitated the formation, in 1994, of an informal alliance – the British Producers and Brand Owners (BPBOG) – comprising top international corporations, including Unilever, P&G, Nestlé and Mars (see photo above), whose main focus then was to lobby Parliament to amend its trademarks bill to restrict the use of lookalikes. They, were, however, unsuccessful. In the medium term, the issue of whether future new legislation is needed to curb lookalikes remains an open question. There seems to be some respite. In June 1994, Sainsbury decided to redesign its Full Roast Coffee, after pressure from Nestlé. The climbdown followed another earlier concession to Coca-Cola in May 1994, when it changed the design of its Classic Cola. Meanwhile, fair or

unfair competition, it seems likely that supermarkets in Britain are set to continue their advance in the private-label war. Brand owners can do little to block this assault. Their best chance of an effective defence is to step up investment in marketing and innovation. They also have to learn to deliver far better value to the more demanding consumers of today.

Critics say that the main reason behind brand owners' plight against own-labels is that their brands have lost the direct power of communication with the consumer – once the manufacturer's strength – because of its failure to invest in its brand through advertisement and promotions over the 1980s. Going back to the 1960s and early 1970s, brands were launched by manufacturers and 'pulled through' the outlets by the power of the advertising communication that the manufacturer and brand owner enjoyed with the consumer. The retail outlet or supermarket, in the case of food and drink products, was merely a conduit for the passage of brands from the factory to the household.

But, in the last two decades, manufacturers have slowly lost that link with the customer by failing to maintain the desired level of communications. Meanwhile, supermarkets have increased their commitment to marketing. Many manufacturers reduced advertising spent over the recession whilst retailers increased this expenditure in attempts to increase their profile and to communicate their company 'brand' values to the consumer. Retailers like Tesco, Asda and Sainsbury have, over the years, stepped up their dialogue with consumers using innovative forms of communications, such as direct marketing. They were deploying sales promotions methods that enabled them to collect customers' names and build databases. The use of direct marketing to build direct links with customers was not taken seriously by manufacturers in the United Kingdom, despite retailers'

In 1979, Levi Strauss introduced a line of trousers and blazers under the name David Hunter. They were marketed as 'classically tailored clothes from Levi'. A contradiction in terms? The men who bought classically tailored clothes thought so too. The range sank without trace. Levi learnt that the 'Levi' name, although having an outstanding reputation in denim jeans and casual wear, was not as 'elastic' as management thought it to be. It snapped.[14]

growing strength, or in Europe, where the multiple retailers' grip is less strong. Recently, more emphasis has been placed upon product packaging and, rightly or wrongly, retailers' lookalikes signal a new era of aggression from competition which traditional brand owners can no longer be complacent about. The war has not stopped with packaging alone either. Sainsbury took the lead in putting its redesigned Classic Cola on British TV in June 1994, and spending £750,000 on the ad campaign that used the catchline, 'A Classic taste from America at a Sainsbury price'.

In the past, the willingness of brand owners to make own-label lookalikes and tastealikes for the big retail outlets also contributed to the current problem. They did own-label supplies for a number of reasons. First, it keeps production lines busy and running at full capacity. Second, by increasing the volume of units coming from a production line or factory, it improves line/plant profitability. Besides, own-label production was profitable because there was no additional promotional spend or marketing overheads to bear. Smarter brand owners like Heinz, Nestlé and Kellogg avoid supplying private labels, but the existence of own-label suppliers like the Canadian Cott company inevitably fuels the growth of this sector.

Big brand owners, having learnt the lessons of their previous complacency, are nonetheless fighting back. Unilever, for instance, firmly believes that to combat the increasing competition from own-label (and branded rivals), the firm must continuously invest in innovations, relentlessly keep costs down and maintain capital efficiency, but never, never stop striving to develop superior understanding of the consumer and to satisfy consumer needs. Such views have been echoed by other leading brand owners. Brand strength, whether measured by customers' preference/perceptions, or by the brand's overall market share and superior performance in direct competition with private-label goods, will depend more and more on the intrinsic quality and features of the products themselves. But as customers' needs and wants are changing all the time, manufacturers will have to accelerate their innovation efforts, both in developing and manufacturing new products, and to focus on marketing campaigns that clearly differentiate their products from other branded rivals' and private labels. Furthermore, just as the retailers' close involvement with suppliers of own-label goods has given them first-hand experience of production methods, branded-product owners must learn to deepen their knowledge of modern sales and distribution techniques. All these help to build and sustain a brand's value over time.

Interestingly, in instances where manufacturers' brands continue to dominate the market in spite of retailers' efforts to expand private-label sales, as in coffee and breakfast cereals, it is because the traditional market leaders have successfully defended their position by commitment to staying ahead through innovation, advanced production and delivery technologies, and single-minded marketing. For them, the secret of success lies, not in the product's name, but in the benefits it delivers to target customers. Ultimately, that is the name of the game!

Sources:   Richard Tomkins, 'Cola warriors identify new enemy', *Financial Times* (11–12 June 1994), 11; Claire Murphy, 'Sainsbury's angers IDV with Archer's lookalike', *Marketing Week* (10 June 1994), 7; Helen Slingsby, 'Sainsbury's put classic on TV', *Marketing Week* (10 June 1994), 8; Claire Murphy, 'Brand owners plot fresh assault', *Marketing Week* (3 June 1994), 7; Haari Laaksonen, 'Own brands in food retailing across Europe', (Oxford: *Oxford Institute of Retail Management*, 1994); Claire Murphy,

'Tesco joins lookalike war with low-fat spread brand', *Marketing Week* (27 May 1994), 7; Tim O'Sullivan, 'Minister says no to brand owners', *Marketing Week* (20 May 1994), 36–8; Andrew Lorenz, 'Brands fight back', *Sunday Times*, (3 April 1994), 3; Guy de Jonquieres, 'Brands left on the shelf', *Financial Times* (31 October 1991), 11; 'Shoot out at the check out', *The Economist* (5 June 1993), 81–2.

A brand name may also lose its special positioning in the consumer's mind through overuse. *Brand dilution* occurs when consumers no longer associate a brand with a specific product or even highly similar products. Consider the contrast between how Hyatt and Marriott hotels are named:

Hyatt practices a brand extension strategy. Its name appears in every hotel variation – Hyatt Resorts, Hyatt Regency, Hyatt Suites and Park Hyatt. Marriott, in contrast, practises multibranding. Its various types of hotels are called Marriott Marquis, Marriott, Residence Inn, Courtyard and Fairfield Inns. It is harder for Hyatt guests to know the differences between Hyatt hotel types, whereas Marriott more clearly aims its hotels at different segments and builds distinct brand names and images for each.

Finally, brand extensions can hurt the core values of the original product when managers get it wrong. The American Milwaukee Miller Brewing Company stuck the Miller name, synonymous with a hefty 'good-ol'-boys' brew, on its new 'Lite' beer. Miller Lite became a highly successful beer, but by muddying the sharp associations of the Miller name, the company hurt Miller High Life, the original beer, whose sales subsequently plummeted. Miller's original beer was advertised to older drinkers on the basis of traditional American values, while Miller Lite targeted the under-24s using tongue-in-cheek endorsements from sportsmen and comics.

Transferring an existing brand name to a new customer segment or product group requires great care. The best result is one when the extension enhances the core brand and builds the sales of both current and new products. An acceptable outcome is when the new product sells well without damaging existing product sales. The worst is when the new product fails and sales of the existing products are hurt.

*Line extensions*    **Line extensions** occur when a company introduces additional items in a given product category under the same brand name, such as new flavours, forms, colours, ingredients or package sizes.

By far the most new-product activity consists of line extensions. For example, according to one study, of the 6,125 new products accepted by grocery stores in the first five months of 1991, only 5 per cent bore new brand names, 6 per cent were brand extensions, and 89 per cent were line extensions. A company might introduce line extensions for any of several reasons. It might want to meet the consumer desires for variety or it might recognize a latent consumer want and try to capitalize on it. Excess manufacturing capacity might drive the company to introduce additional items, or the company might want to match a competitor's successful line extension. Some companies introduce line extensions simply to command more shelf space from resellers.

Line extensions, like brand extensions, involve some risks. The brand name might lose its specific meaning – some marketing strategies call this the 'line-extension trap'.[15] In the past, when consumers asked for a Coke, they received a 6-ounce bottle of the classic beverage. Today the vendor has to ask: New, Classic, or Cherry Coke? Regular or diet? Caffeine or caffeine free? Bottle or can? Another risk is that many line extensions will not sell enough to cover their development and promotion costs. Or even when they sell enough, the sales may come at the expense of other items in the line. A line extension works best when it takes sales away from competing brands, not when it 'cannibalizes' the company's other items.

### Brand repositioning

However well a brand is initially positioned in a market, the company may have to reposition it later. A competitor may launch a brand position next to the company's brand and cut into its market share. Or customer wants may shift, leaving the company's brand with less demand. Marketers should consider repositioning existing brands before introducing new ones. In this way, they can build on existing brand recognition and consumer loyalty.

Repositioning may require changing both the product and its image. For example, Arrow added a new line of casual shirts before trying to change its image. Kentucky Fried Chicken changed its menu, adding lower-fat skinless chicken, and nonfried items such as broiled chicken and chicken salad sandwiches to reposition itself toward more health-conscious fast-food consumers. It is also changing its name – to KFC. A brand can also be repositioned by changing only the product's image. Johnson & Johnson's baby shampoo was repositioned with a physical change from a 'baby shampoo' to a 'mild shampoo' for adults who wash their hair frequently and want a gentle alternative. Similarly, Bulmer the United Kingdom's leading cider maker, successfully repositioned its mainstream brands, Strongbow and Woodpecker, by giving them a more contemporary lifestyle image, a marked contrast to cider's traditional rustic image. Bulmer spend around £10 million in 1988 in a series of advertising campaigns to revitalize these two brands.

### Brand name selection

The brand name should be carefully chosen. A good name can add greatly to a product's success. Most large marketing companies have developed a formal, brand name selection process. Finding the best brand name is a difficult task. It begins with a careful review of the product and its benefits, the target market, and proposed marketing strategies.

Desirable qualities for a brand name include the following:

1. It should suggest something about the product's benefits and qualities. Examples: Bounty, Kleenex, Frisp (a light savoury snack).
2. It should be easy to pronounce, recognize and remember. Short names help. Examples: Dove (soap), Yale (security products), Hula Hoops (potato crisps shaped like the name). But longer ones are sometimes effective. Examples: 'Love My Carpet' carpet cleaner, 'I Can't Believe It's Not Butter' margarine, Better Business Bureau.
3. The brand name should be distinctive. Examples: Shell, Kodak, Virgin.
4. The name should translate easily into foreign languages. Before spending $100 million to change its name to Exxon, Standard Oil of New Jersey tested the name in fifty-four languages in more than 150 foreign markets. It found that the name Enco referred to a stalled engine when pronounced in Japanese.
5. It should be capable of registration and legal protection. A brand name cannot be registered if it infringes on existing brand names. Also, brand names that are merely descriptive or suggestive may be unprotectable. For example, the Miller Brewing Company registered the name Lite for its low-calorie beer and invested millions in establishing the name with customers. But the courts later ruled that the terms *lite* and *light* are generic or common descriptive terms applied to beer and that Miller could not use the Lite name exclusively.[16]

Once chosen, the brand name must be protected. Many firms try to build a brand name that will eventually become identified with the product category. Brand names such as Hoover, Frigidaire, Kleenex, Levi's, Scotch Tape, Formica and Fiberglas have succeeded in this way. However, their very success may threaten the company's rights to the name. Many originally protected brand names, such as cellophane, aspirin, nylon, kerosene, linoleum, yo-yo, trampoline, escalator, thermos and shredded wheat, are now names that any seller can use.[17]

## Packaging decisions

Many products offered to the market have to be packaged. Some marketers have called packaging a fifth *P*, along with price, product, place and promotion. Most marketers, however, treat packaging as an element of product strategy.

**Packaging** includes the activities of designing and producing the container or wrapper for a product. Packaging performs a vital function for most products. It protects goods from being damaged before you buy them, helps keep, for example, foodstuffs hygienic and fresh, and is often necessary for labelling and information reasons.

Although the primary function of the package was to contain and protect the product, in recent times, however, many factors have made packaging an important marketing tool. An increase in self-service means that packages must now perform many sales tasks – from attracting attention, to describing the product, to making the sale. Rising consumer affluence means that consumers are willing to pay a little more for the convenience, appearance, dependability, and prestige of better packages.

Good packaging creates instant consumer recognition of the company or brand. For example, in an average supermarket, which stocks 15,000 to 17,000 items, the typical shopper passes by some 300 items per minute, and 53 per cent of all purchases are made on impulse. In this highly competitive environment, the package may be the seller's last chance to influence buyers. Manufacturers must use pack graphics to reinforce and communicate brand values.

Innovative packaging can give a company an advantage over competitors. Take creative packages such as those for Perrier, Jiff Lemon, Grolsch. These enjoy excellent recall – try thinking about Jiff without picturing a lemon – and good market results. Coke and Jack Daniels whisky bottles are so distinctive and have such strong identity with their brands that the packaging of each product not only says it all, but has also become a classic. Equally, the first companies to put their fruit drinks in airtight foil and paper cartons (aseptic packages) and toothpastes in pump dispensers also attracted many new customers. In contrast, poorly designed packages can cause headaches for consumers and lost sales for the company.

In recent years, product safety has also become a major packaging concern. We have all learned to deal with hard-to-open 'childproof' packages. And after the rash of product tampering scares during the 1980s, most drug producers and food makers are now putting their products in tamper-resistant packages.[18]

Developing a good package for a new product requires making many decisions. The first task is to establish the packaging concept. The **packaging concept** states what the package should *be* or *do* for the product. Should the main functions of the package be to offer product protection, introduce a new dispensing method, communicate certain qualities about the product or the company, or something else? Decisions, then, must be made on package design that cover specific elements of the package, such as size, shape, materials, colour, text and brand mark. These various elements must work together to support the product's position and marketing strategy. The package must be consistent with the product's advertising, pricing, and distribution.

Companies usually consider several different package designs for a new product. To select the best package, they usually test the various designs to find the one that stands up best under normal use, is easiest for dealers to handle, and receives the most favourable consumer response. Consider the following 'birth of a package':

A lot of thought goes into packaging design. Take, for example, the package for one of a range of Marks & Spencer Chinese-styled chilled meals. In this particular case, M & S employed design consultants, Fisher, Ling & Bennion (FLB) to develop the packaging. M & S wanted the pack to have an oriental look, but not a stereotyped Chinese image, and still be recognisable as an M & S product. FLB produced several sketches, some of which were developed. M & S liked a white background which was different from the usual Chinese image as well as from the packaging used for Indian dishes they will be displayed next to. FLB then made a mock-up of the approved design and a colour coding was worked out – blue in this case. A red seal highlighted the Chinese theme. The chicken dish was photographed for the final version. Finally, a conventional typeface, not Chinese-style lettering, was chosen.[19]

After selecting and introducing the package, the company should check it regularly in the face of changing consumer preferences and advances in technology. In the past, a package design might last for 15 years before it needed changes. However, in today's rapidly changing environment, most companies must recheck their packaging every two or three years.[20]

Keeping a package up to date usually requires only minor but regular changes – changes so subtle that they may go unnoticed by most consumers. But some packaging changes involve complex decisions, drastic action, high cost and risk. Marketers must, nonetheless, weigh packaging costs against the risks on the one hand, and on the other, against consumer perceptions of the value added by the packaging and the role of packaging in helping to attain marketing objectives. In making packaging decisions, the company also must heed growing environmental concerns about packaging and make decisions that serve society's interests as well as immediate customer and company objectives. However, determining just what serves the best interests of consumers and society can sometimes be tricky (see Marketing Highlight 14.4).

## Labelling decisions

Labels may range from simple tags attached to products to complex graphics that are part of the package. They perform several functions. At the very least, the label *identifies* the product or brand, such as the name 'Sunkist' stamped on oranges. The label might also *grade* the product, or *describe* several things about the product – who made it, where it was made, when it was made, its contents, how it is to be used and how to use it safely. Finally, the label might *promote* the product through attactive graphics.

There has been a long history of legal concerns about labels. Labels can mislead customers, fail to describe important ingredients or fail to include needed safety warnings. As a result, many countries have laws to regulate labelling. Sellers must ensure that their labels contain all the required information and comply with national or international (e.g. US, EU), requirements.

## Product-support services decisions

Customer service is another element of product strategy. A company's offer to the marketplace usually includes some services, which can be a minor or a major part of the total offer. In fact, the offer can range from a pure good on the one hand to a pure service on the other. In the next chapter, we will discuss services as products in themselves. Here, we address **product-support services** – services that augment actual products. More and more companies are using product-support services as a vital tool in gaining competitive advantage.

Good customer service makes sound business sense. It costs less to keep the goodwill of existing customers than it does to attract new customers or woo back lost customers. Firms that provide high-quality service usually outperform their less service-oriented competitors. A study by the Strategic Planning Institute compared the performance of businesses that had high customer ratings of service quality with

## Eyeful power: packaging toys is not kids' stuff

Designing effective packaging for toys is getting increasingly difficult as this is an area that manufacturers claim is strewn with clichés and restrictions. Why is this so?

Take a typical toy store. In it, often hundreds to thousands (in the case of Toys 'R' Us) of items are stacked from floor to ceiling and all rely upon eye-catching packaging to attract little consumers', and their parents', attention. Being noticed among all this is akin to trying to whistle a jingle while a Nirvana record plays.

In the battle to gain attention, toy manufacturers have literally to 'turn up the visual volume' to the extent that packaging in the norm becomes violently loud. This loud visual display is exemplified by banks of pink, pale blue and frills (reminiscent of an evening with Dame Edna) with Barbie, Sindy, My Little Pony and their 'me-toos' and accessories reaching out to small girls. These are counter-matched by the fluorescent yellows, oranges, blacks and blues of ever larger, uglier and more deadly looking toy weapons, vehicles, Crash Dummies and Biker Mice from Mars – all seeking to attract the boys. Political correctness has no place here! Toy packaging aimed at children aged five years and older is apparently violently garish (and unashamedly sexist).

Interestingly, only in the pre-school and more educational categories does some tranquillity (in terms of colours) reign, maybe because these are targeted at parents who are doing the choosing.

Old-timers like Matchbox are abandoning its old, dated blue-grid packs and introducing the 'obligatory' fluorescents. Bright orange and yellow are found across its full product mix of 340 different lines. Matchbox has had to jettison its familiar old blue look and move in pace with everything else on the shelves.

Packaging design, however, seems to look different and dull when it comes to educational toys for 8 year olds and older children. Here manufacturers avoid sledgehammer colours and brash presentation on packaging because these toys are generally aimed at both sexes.

Manufacturers seem to face a general problem in finding a balance between worthiness and aspiration. For example, the 'Fun With ...' range is, by most parents' standards, a worthy toy because of the educational benefits offered to kids. But it comes in exceptionally dull packaging that seems to contradict the aspirational value of the toy (the pack features two children using the product, but even they do not seem to be having much fun).

Manufacturers can get it right sometimes. Hornby's The Eliminator (a big-gun toy) and Duplo's new 1994 range are presented in packaging that effectively communicates the benefits of their individual products.

Hornby's packaging for The Eliminator, sporting sci-fi style with lots of exaggerated perspective, is

---

those that had lower ratings. It found that the high-service businesses managed to charge more, grow faster, and make more profits.[21] Clearly, marketers need to think about their service strategies.

### Deciding on the service mix

A company should design its product and support services to meet the needs of target customers. Thus the first step in deciding which product-support services to offer is to determine both the services that target consumer value and the relative importance of these services. Customers vary in the value they assign to different services. Some consumers want credit and financing services, fast and reliable delivery, or quick installation. Others put more weight on technical information and advice, training in product use, or after-sale service and repair.

Determining customers' service needs involves more than simply monitoring complaints that come in over free telephone hot lines or on comment cards. The compa-

Toy packaging: loud and violent colours reign when it comes to packaging toys for boys.

dramatic and exciting. It clearly conveys the toy's fantasy value. The box size – almost as big as the child – is also important. The colours are loud but still manage to stand out from the general clutter of colour on-shelf. Uses and benefits are also clearly explained on the front of the box, just as an adult would expect these to be displayed on a drill's packaging.

Duplo's new packaging has been designed to appeal to under-5s, although parents are the main buyers for this age group. Duplo has strong brand identification, which helps, given that this is a very important element for mums and dads. The packaging's visual character is supposed to amplify the product inside. The happy, smiling child showing off the end result of play reinforces the worthiness of the

toy (and fulfils mum's and dad's aspirations for the child!). The pack's exciting physical presence also has an edge – you can tell it is Duplo from a mile off.

Packaging design for toys is not just getting 'eyeful power'. Manufacturers say that it is easy to get it wrong, difficult to strike a balance between aspirations and worthiness, and difficult to be really innovative. Manufacturers must, nonetheless, pay attention to target consumers (who uses the toy, who does the choosing, etc.) and design appropriate packaging that will effectively do the job of attracting and communicating with its target audience. Only then will it stand out from the crowd – on-shelf and in sales!

Source   Rod Springett, 'Eyeful power', *Marketing Week*, (29 April 1994), 48–9.

ny should periodically survey its customers to get ratings of current services as well as ideas for new ones.

Products can often be designed to reduce the amount of required servicing. Thus companies need to coordinate their product-design and service-mix decisions. For example, the Canon home copier uses a disposable toner cartridge that greatly reduces the need for service calls. Kodak and 3M design products that can be 'plugged in' to a central diagnostic facility that perform tests, locates troubles, and fixes equipment over telephone lines. A key to successful service strategy therefore, is to design products that rarely break down and are easily fixable with little service expense.

### Delivering product-support services

Finally, companies must decide how they want to deliver product-support services to customers. For example, consider the many ways an electrical appliance manufacturer might offer repair services on its main appliances. It could hire and train its own service people and locate them across the country. It could arrange with distributors and dealers to provide the repair services, or it could leave it to independent companies to provide these services.

Most equipment companies start out with providing their own service. This allows them to stay close to the equipment and know its problems. They can also make good money running the 'parts and service business' or even charge a premium price, if they are the only supplier of the needed parts. Indeed, some equipment manufacturers like Rank-Xerox make more than half of their profits in after-sale service.

Over time, producers may shift more of the maintenance and repair service to authorized distributors and dealers who are closer to customers, have more locations and can offer quicker if not better service. The producer still makes a profit on selling the parts but leaves the servicing cost to middlemen.

Still later, independent service firms emerge. They typically offer lower cost or faster service than the manufacturer or authorized middlemen do.

Ultimately, some large customer start to handle their own maintenance and repair services. Thus, a company with several hundred personal computers, printers and related equipment might find it cheaper to have its own service people on site.

### The customer service department

Given the importance of customer service as a marketing tool, many companies have set up strong customer service departments to handle complaints and adjustments, credit service, maintenance service, technical service and consumer information. Many others have set up hot lines to handle consumer complaints and requests for information. By keeping records on the types of requests and complaints, the custmer service department can press for needed changes in product design, quality control, high-pressure selling, and so on. An active customer service department coordinates all the company's services, creates consumer satisfaction and loyalty, and helps the company to further set itself apart from competitors.

## PRODUCT LINE DECISIONS

We have looked at product strategy decisions such as branding, packaging, labelling and services for individual products. But product strategy also calls for building a product line. A **product line** is a group of products that are closely related because they function in a similar manner, are sold to the same customer groups, are marketed through the same types of outlets, or fall within given price ranges. For example, Volvo produces several lines of cars, Philips produces several lines of hi-fi systems and IBM produces several lines of computers. In formulating product line strategies, marketers have to consider the length of the line and distinctive features that differentiate items within the line.

### Product line-length decisions

How long should a firm's product line be? Product line length is influenced by company objectives. Companies that want to be positioned as full-line companies or that are seeking high market share and market growth, usually carry longer lines. They are less concerned when some items do not add to profits. Companies that are keen on high short-term profitability generally carry shorter lines consisting of selected items.

Over time, product line managers tend to add new products either to use up excess manufacturing capacity, or because the salesforce and distributors are calling for a more complete product line to satisfy their customers, or because the firm needs to add items to the product line to increase sales and profits.

However, as the manager adds items, several costs rise: design and engineering costs, inventory carrying costs, manufacturing changeover costs, order processing costs, transportation costs, and promotional costs to introduce new items. As such, the company must plan product line growth carefully. It can systematically increase the length of its product line in two ways: by *stretching* its line and by *filling* its line.

## Product line-stretching decisions

Every company's product line covers a certain range of the products offered by the industry as a whole. For example, BMW automobiles are located in the medium-high price range of the automobile market. Nissa focuses on the low-to-medium price range. **Product line stretching** occurs when a company lengthens its product line beyond its current range. Figure 14.5 shows that the company can stretch its line downward, upward, or both ways.

### Downward stretch

Downward stretching occurs when a company that is located at the upper end of the market later stretches its lines downward. The firm may have first entered the upper end to establish a quality image and intended to roll downward later. It may be responding to an attack on the upper end by invading the low end. Or a company may add a low-end product to plug a market hole that otherwise would attract a new competitor. It may find faster growth taking place at the the low end. Thus Compaq and IBM both added inexpensive personal computer lines to fend off competition

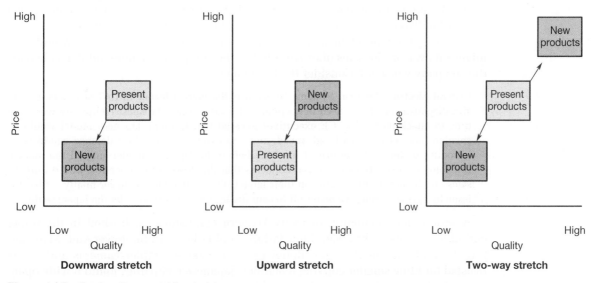

**Figure 14.5**  Product line-stretching decision.

BMW has recently 'downward stretched' its product line, with the Compact set to attack the 'small-size high-volume' car sector.

from low-priced 'clones' and to take advantage of faster market growth at the lower end of the market.

In stretching downwards, the company faces some risks. The low-end item might provoke competitors to counteract by moving into the higher end. The company's dealers may not be willing or able to handle the lower-end products. Or the move may confuse the customer. Parker Pen introduced a cheap disposable ball point, called Itala, in 1976, in an attempt to take on the Japanese in the low end of the market. Parker had always been positioned at the top end of the market as a high-quality high-price product (it cost more but delivered more). The foray into the disposable pen sector was a classic brand-confusing error. According to Mr Jacques Margry, Parker's chairman: 'By going down-market we confused the customer; the consumer no longer knew what Parker stood for. We were all over the place, dissipating the advertising'.[22]

A more serious problem with downward stretching is that the new low-end item might eat away at the sales of or *cannibalize* the company's higher-end items, leaving the company worse off. Consider the following:

> General Electric's Medical Systems Division is the market leader in CAT scanners, expensive diagnostic machines used in hospitals. GE learned that a Japanese competitor was planning to attack its market. GE executives guessed that the new Japanese model would be smaller, more electronically advanced, and less expensive. GE's best defence would be to introduce a similar lower-priced machine before the Japanese model entered the market. But some GE executives expressed concerns that this lower-priced version would hurt the sales and higher profit margins on their large CAT scanner. One manager finally settled the issue by saying: 'Aren't we better off to cannibalize ourselves than to let the Japanese do it?'

A serious miscalculation of many Western companies established in the upper end of their markets has been their failure to plug holes in the lower end. Mercedes resisted building smaller cars, Rollei resisted making simpler cameras and Xerox resisted building smaller copying machines. Japanese companies found a wide opening at the lower end and moved in quickly and successfully.

*Upward stretch*

Companies at the lower end of the market may want to enter the higher end. They may be attracted by a faster growth rate or higher margins at the higher end, or they may simply want to position themselves as full-line manufacturers. Sometimes, companies move up market in order to add prestige to their current products, as when America's Chrysler purchased Lamborghini, the maker of exotic, hand-crafted sports cars.

An upward stretch decision can be risky. The higher-end competitors are not only well entrenched, but may also strike back by entering the lower end of the market. Prospective customers may not believe that the newcomer can produce quality products. Finally, the company's salespeople and distributors may lack the talent and training to serve the higher end of the market.

*Two-way stretch*

Companies in the middle range of the market may decide to stretch their lines in both directions. Sony did this to hold off copycat competitors of its Walkman line of personal tape players. Sony introduced its first Walkman in the middle of the market. As imitative competitors moved in with lower-priced models, Sony stretched downward. At the same time, in order to add lustre to its lower-priced models and to attract more affluent consumers keen to trade up to a better model, Sony stretched the Walkman line upward. It now sells more than 100 models ranging from a plain playback-only version for £20 to a high-tech, high-quality £350 version that both plays and records. Using this two-way stretch strategy, Sony now dominates the global personal tape player market.

## Product line-filling decisions

Rather than stretching into lower- or higher-end segments, the firm can lengthen its product line by adding more items within the present range of the line. There are several reasons for **product line filling**: reaching for extra profits, trying to satisfy dealers, trying to use excess capacity, trying to be the leading full-line company, and trying to plug holes to keep out competitors. Thus Sony filled its line by adding solar-powered and waterproof Walkmans and an ultralight model that attaches to a sweatband for joggers, cyclists, tennis players, and other exercisers.

However, marketers must avoid overdoing this as it results in cannibalization and customer confusion. The company should, therefore, ensure that new items are *noticeably different* from existing ones.

## Product line-modernization decisions

In some cases, product line performance may be improved, not so much by extending the number of items, but by modernizing or revamping them. For example, a company's machine tools may have a 1950s look and lose out to better-styled competitors' lines.

The firm can overhaul the line piecemeal or all at once. A piecemeal approach allows the company to test customers' and dealers' response to the new styles before changing the whole line. It also causes less drain on the company's cash flow. A big disadvantage, however, is that it forewarns competitors and allows them to retaliate quickly by redesigning their own lines.

## PRODUCT MIX DECISIONS

Some companies may offer, not one, but several lines of products which form a **product mix** or *product assortment*. For example, a cosmetics firm may have four main product lines in its product mix: cosmetics, jewellery, fashions and household items. Each product line may consist of a range of items or sublines. Take cosmetics. This could be broken down into several sublines – lipstick, powder, nail varnish, eye-shadows, and so on. Each subline may have many individual items. For example, eye-shadows contain a string of items ranging from different colours to alternative application modes (e.g. pencil, roll-on, powder, etc.).

A company's product mix has four important dimensions: width, length, depth and consistency. Table 14.1 illustrates these concepts with selected Procter & Gamble consumer products.

The *width* of the product mix refers to the number of different product lines the company carries – six in the case of Procter & Gamble. (In fact, P&G produces many more lines, including mouthwashes, paper towels, disposable nappies, pain relievers and cosmetics.)

The *length* of P&G's product mix refers to the total number of items the company carries, which is forty-two. We can also compute the average length of a line at P&G by dividing the total length (here forty-two) by the number of lines (here six). So, the average P&G product line consists of seven brands.

The *depth* or number of versions offered of each brand or product in the line can also be counted. Thus, if Crest comes in three sizes and two formulations (paste and gel), Crest has a depth of six.

**TABLE 14.1**  *Product mix width and product line length shown for selected Procter & Gamble products*

Product mix width

| | Detergents | Toothpaste | Bar soap | Deodorants | Fruit juices | Lotions |
|---|---|---|---|---|---|---|
| | Ivory Snow | Gleem | Ivory | Secret | Citrus Hill | Wondra |
| | Dreft | Crest | Camay | Sure | Sunny Delight | Noxema |
| | Tide | Complete | Lava | | Winter Hill | Oil of Ulay |
| | Joy | Denquel | Kirk's | | Texsun | Camay |
| | Cheer | | Zest | | Lincoln | Raintree |
| | Oxydol | | Safeguard | | Speas Farm | Tropic Tan |
| Product line length | Dash | | Coast | | | Bain de Soleil |
| | Cascade | | Oil of Ulay | | | |
| | Ivory Liquid | | | | | |
| | Gain | | | | | |
| | Dawn | | | | | |
| | Era | | | | | |
| | Bold 3 | | | | | |
| | Liquid Tide | | | | | |
| | Solo | | | | | |

The *consistency* of the product mix refers to how closely related the various product lines are in end use, production requirements, distribution channels, or in some other way. P&G's product lines are consistent insofar as they are consumer goods that go through the same distribution channels. The lines are less consistent insofar as they perform different functions for buyers.

These product mix dimensions provide the handles for defining the company's product strategy. The company can increase its business in four ways:

1. It can add new product lines, thus widening its product mix. In this way, its new lines build on the company's reputation in its other lines.
2. The company can lengthen its existing product lines to become a more full-line company.
3. It can add more product versions of each product and thus deepen its product mix.
4. The company can pursue more product line consistency, or less, depending on whether it wants to have a strong reputation in a single field or in several fields.

## INTERNATIONAL PRODUCT DECISIONS

International marketers face special product and packaging challenges. As discussed in Chapter 5, they must decide what products to introduce in which countries, and how much of the product to standardize or adapt for world markets. Companies usually must respond to national differences by adapting their product offerings. Something as simple as an electrical outlet can create big product problems:

> Those who have travelled to Europe know the frustration of electrical plugs, different voltages, and other annoyances of international travel. ... Philips, the electrical appliance manufacturer, has to produce 12 kinds of irons to serve just its European market. The problem is that Europe still lacks a universal [electrical] standard. The ends of irons bristle with different plugs for different countries. Some have three prongs, others two; prongs protrude straight or angled, round or rectangular, fat, thin, and sometimes sheathed. There are circular plug faces, squares, pentagons, and hexagons. Some are perforated and some are notched. One French plug has a niche like a keyhole; British plugs carry fuses.[23]

Packaging also presents new challenges for international marketers. Penn Racquet Sports, the American sports equipment company, found this out when it attempted to launch its line of tennis balls in Japan in a 'traditional' three-ball can. After netting an initial 8 per cent market share, Penn's Japanese sales quickly plummeted to less than 1 per cent. The problem: poor packaging. Whereas Americans play with three balls, the Japanese use only two. Explains one Penn manager: 'The Japanese thought a three-ball can was a discount, and they passed us over. Our big mistake was that we didn't know the market.' Penn redesigned its package and sales recovered. It now designs its containers to fit the needs of each market: Japan gets a two-ball can, whereas Australia and Europe receive four-ball plastic tubes.[24]

Packaging issues can be subtle. For example, names, labels and colours may not translate easily from one country to another. Consumers in different countries also vary in their packaging preferences. Europeans like efficient, functional, recyclable boxes with understated designs. In contrast, the Japanese often use packages as gifts. Thus in Japan, Lever Brothers packages its Lux soap in stylish gift boxes. Packaging may even have to be tailored to meet the physical characteristics of consumers in various parts of the world. For instance, soft drinks are sold in smaller cans in Japan to better fit the smaller Japanese hand.

Companies may have to adapt their packaging to meet specific regulations regarding package design or label contents. For instance, some countries ban the use of any foreign language on labels; other countries require that labels be printed in two or more languages. Labelling laws vary greatly from country to country. The international firm would do well to study these and modify their product packaging and labels to conform with local requirements.

In summary, whether domestic or international, product strategy calls for complex decisions on product mix, product line, branding, packaging, and service strategy. These decisions must be made not only with a full understanding of consumer wants and competitors' strategies, but also with considerable sensitivity to the regulatory environment affecing both product and packaging.

## SUMMARY

*Product* is not merely a physical item but a complex concept that must be defined carefully. Marketers must develop a product strategy that calls for coordinated decisions on product items, product lines and the product mix.

Each product item offered to customers can be viewed on three levels. The *core product* is the essential benefit the customer is really buying. The *actual product* includes the features, styling, quality, brand name, and packaging of the product offered for sale. The *augmented product* is the actual product plus the various services offered with it, such as warranty, installation, maintenance and free delivery.

All products can be classified into three groups according to their durability or tangibility: nondurable goods, durable goods, and services. *Consumer goods* are usually distinguished according to consumer shopping habits: convenience goods, shopping goods, speciality goods and unsought goods. *Industrial goods* are grouped according to their cost and the way they enter the production process: materials and parts, capital items and supplies and services.

Companies have to develop strategies for the items in their product lines. Key decisions have regard to product attributes, branding, packaging, labelling, and product-support services. *Product attribute decisions* involve the product quality, features, and design the company will offer. For *brands*; the company must decide on whether to brand or not, its brand sponsorship policy, brand strategy and repositioning opportunities.

Marketers have to make *packaging decisions* to create benefits such as protection, preservation, economy, convenience, and promotion. A firm must develop and test its packaging concept to be sure that it both achieves desired objectives and is compatible with public policy.

Products also require *labelling* for identification and possible grading, description, and promotion of the product. The firm must check that its product labels comply with national or individual country labelling regulations.

*Product-support services* add value for customers and are effective weapons against competitors. The company must determine the most importance services to offer and the best ways to deliver these services. The *service mix* should be coordinated by a customer service department that handles complaints and adjustments, credit, maintenance, technical service, and customer information. *Customer service* should be used as a marketing tool to create customer satisfaction and competitive advantage.

Most companies produce a group of products or a *product line* instead of a single product. Each product line requires a product strategy. Managers have to decide on:

*line stretching* options – whether a line should be extended downward, upward, or in both directions; *line filling* opportunities – whether additional items should be added within the present range of the line; and *line modernization* prospects – when and how to revamp older-styled products.

Many firms may offer several product lines to form a *product mix* or *product assortment*. Marketing people face the additional task of determining dimensions, such as the *width, length, depth* and *consistency* of the firm's *product mix*.

The astute market-oriented firm uses the product as a means of creating a differential advantage. A sound product strategy always takes customers' needs and wants into consideration, with marketing decision makers then exploiting the many dimensions of the product concept as tools for creating competitive advantage.

## ■ DISCUSSING THE ISSUES

1. What are the core, tangible and augmented products of the educational experience that universities offer?

2. How would you classify the product offered by restaurants: as durable goods or as services? Why?

3. In recent years, many European and US auto makers have tried to reposition many of their brands. Thinking about examples of such repositioning efforts, describe whether a brand has moved to a high-quality end of the market or moved down-market. How easy is it for car makers to reposition their brands? What else could they do to change consumers' perceptions of their cars?

4. Why are many people willing to pay more for branded products than for unbranded products? What does this say about the value of branding?

5. Coca-Cola started with one type of cola drink. Now we find Coke in nearly a dozen varieties. Why do consumer-goods manufacturers extend their brands? What issues do these brand extensions raise for manufacturers, retailers and consumers?

6. Compare brand extension by the brand owner with licensing a brand name for use by another company. What are the opportunities and risks of each approach?

## ■ APPLYING THE CONCEPTS

1. Different areas of a town may attract different sorts of businesses. (a) Go to a town shopping centre and note the variety of shops in the centre. Count the number of outlets for each type of consumer good: convenience, shopping, speciality or unsought goods. (b) Take a trip to a local or neighbourhood shopping street and do a similar count. (c) Calculate what percentage of businesses fall into each category for the two areas. Are there any differences? If so, why do you think these differences exist?

2. Go to a number of grocery stores which you think are direct competitors. Compare the product mix. Are there differences in width or depth? Suggest ways in which the retailers could stretch their lines upwards or downwards.

# ■ REFERENCES

1. See 'What lies behind the sweet smell of success', *Business Week* (27 February 1984), 139–43; S.J. Diamond, 'Perfume equals part mystery, part marketing', *Los Angeles Times* (22 April 1988), sect. 4, p. 1; Pat Sloan, 'Revlon leads new fragrance charge', *Advertising Age* (16 July 1990), 14; and Joanne Lipman, 'Big "outsert" really puts Revlon in vogue', *Wall Street Journal* (17 September 1992), B6.

2. See Peter D. Bennett, *Dictionary of Marketing Terms* (Chicago: American Marketing Association, 1988).

3. Ibid. For more information on product classifications, see Patrick E. Murphy and Ben M. Enis, 'Classifying products strategically', *Journal of Marketing* (July 1986), 24–42.

4. Otis Port, 'The quality imperative: questing for the best', *Business Week*, special issue on quality (1991), 7.

5. David A. Garvin, 'Competing on eight dimensions of quality', *Harvard Business Review* (Nov.–Dec. 1987), 109. Also see Robert Jacobson and David A. Aaker, 'The strategic role of product quality', *Journal of Marketing* (October 1987), 31–44; and Frank Rose, 'Now quality means service too', *Fortune* (22 April 1992), 97–108.

6. For more on design, see Christopher Lorenz, *The Design Dimension* (Oxford: Blackwell, 1990); see also Philip Kotler, 'Design: a powerful but neglected strategic tool', *Journal of Business Strategy* (Fall 1984), 16–21; and Stephen Potter, Robin Roy, Claire H. Capon, Margaret Bruce, Vivien Walsh, and Janny Lewis, *The Benefits and Costs of Investment in Design: Using professional design expertise in product, engineering and graphics projects*, (Manchester: Open University/UMIST, September 1991).

7. Pete Engardio, 'Quick, name five Taiwanese PC makers', *Business Week* (18 May 1992), 128–9.

8. See Bennett, *Dictionary of Marketing Terms*, op. cit.

9. Jean-Noel Kapferer, *Strategic Brand Management: New approaches to creating and evaluating brand equity* (London: Kogan Page, 1992), 38 ff.

10. David A. Aaker, *Managing Brand Equity* (New York: Free Press, 1991).

11. See T.P. Barwise, C.J. Higson, J.A. Likierman and P.R. Marsh, *Accounting for Brands* (London: Institute of Chartered Accountants in England and Wales, 1990); Peter H. Farquhar, Julia Y. Han, and Yuji Ijiri, 'Brands on the balance sheet', *Marketing Management* (winter 1992), 16–22; and Kevin Lane Keller, 'Conceptualising, measuring, and managing customer-based brand equity', *Journal of Marketing* (January 1993), 1–22.

12. Kevin Price, quoted in 'Trade promotion: much ado about nothing', *Promo* (October 1991), 37.

13. Daniel C. Smith and C. Whan Park, 'The effects of brand extensions on market share and advertising efficiency', *Journal of Marketing Research* (August 1992), 296–313; for more on the use of brand extensions and consumer attitudes toward them, see David A. Aaker and Kevin L. Keller, 'Consumer evaluations of brand extensions', *Journal of Marketing* (January 1990), 27–41; and Julie Liesse, 'Brand extensions take centre stage,' *Advertising Age* (8 March 1993), 12.

14. 'Brand stretching can be fun and dangerous', *The Economist* (5 May 1990), 105–6, 110; and Hugh Aldersey-Williams, 'Elastic band', *Marketing Week* (29 April 1994), 43–5, 47.

15. Al Ries and Jack Trout, *Positioning: The battle for your mind* (New York: McGraw-Hill, 1981).

16. Thomas M.S. Hemnes, 'How can you find a safe trademark?', *Harvard Business Review* (Mar.–Apr. 1995), 44.

17. For a discussion of legal issues surrounding the use of brand names, see Dorothy Cohen, 'Trademark strategy', *Journal of Marketing* (January 1986), 61–74; 'Trademark woes: help is coming', *Sales & Marketing Management* (January 1988), 84; and Jack Alexander, 'What's in a name? Too much, said the FCC', *Sales & Marketing Management* (January 1989), 75–8.

18. See Fred W. Morgan, 'Tampered goods: legal developments and marketing guidelines', *Journal of Marketing* (April 1988), 86–96.

19. 'Packaging unwrapped', *Which?* (August 1990), 427.

20. See Alicia Swasy, 'Sales lost their vim? Try repackaging', *Wall Street Journal* (11 October 1989), B1.

21. Bro Uttal, 'Companies that serve you best', *Fortune* (7 December 1987), 98–116; see also William H. Davidow, 'Customer service: the ultimate marketing weapon', *Business Marketing* (October 1989), 56–64; and Barry Farber and Joyce Wycoff, 'Customer service: evolution and revolution', *Sales & Marketing Management* (May 1991), 44–51.

22. Gary Mead, 'Parker prepares to write a new chapter;', *Financial Times* (10 February 1992), 13.

23. Philip Cateora, *International Marketing*, 7th edn (Homewood, IL: Irwin, 1990), 260.

24. David J. Morrow, 'Sitting pretty: how to make your package stand out in a crowd', *International Business* (November 1991), 30–2.

## Colgate: one squeeze too many?

You probably know about Colgate toothpaste – perhaps you have even used it. But what would you think of Colgate aspirin or Colgate antacid? Would you buy Colgate laxatives or Colgate dandruff shampoo?

That is exactly what Colgate-Palmolive would like to know. Colgate wants to investigate the possibility of entering the over-the-counter (OTC) drug market. Can it use its Colgate brand name, developed in the oral-care products market, in the OTC healthcare market?

Why does the OTC market interest them? The first reason is market size. The worldwide OTC market annually accounts for about $30 bn sales.* The US OTC marekt is $12 bn and Europe's is $8 bn. It is the largest nonfood consumer products industry, and it is growing at over 6 per cent annually.

Several trends are fuelling this rapid growth. Consumers are more sophisticated than they were and they increasingly seek self-medication rather than seeing a doctor. Companies are also switching many previously prescription-only drugs to OTC drugs. The companies can do this when they can show, based on extensive clinical tests, that the drug is safe for consumers to use without monitoring by a doctor. Moreover OTC drugs tend to have very long product life cycles. Medical researchers are also discovering new drugs or new use or benefits of existing drugs. For example, researchers have found that the psyllium fibre used in some OTC natural laxatives is effective in controlling cholesterol.

Beyond the size and growth of the market, Colgate also knows that the OTC market can be extremely profitable. Analysts estimate that the average cost of goods sold for an OTC drug is only 29 per cent, leaving a gross margin of 71 per cent. Advertising and sales promotions are the largest expenditure categories for these products, accounting for an average of 42 per cent of sales. OTC drugs produce on average 11 per cent after-tax profit.

Because of the OTC market's attractiveness, Colgate conducted studies to learn the strength of its brand name with consumers. Colgate believes in the

*1 ecu = US$1.26

following equation: brand awareness + brand image = brand equity. Its studies found that Colgate was number one in brand awareness, number two in brand image, and number two in brand equity among OTC consumers, even though it did not sell OTC products. The Tylenol brand name earned the number-one spot in both brand image and brand equity.

Thus Colgate's research shows that the OTC market is very large, is growing rapidly and is very profitable, and that Colgate has a strong brand equity position with OTC consumers. Most companies would find such a situation very attractive.

Colgate realizes that entering the OTC market will not be easy. First, its research suggests that the typical OTC product does not reach the breakeven point for four years and does not recover development costs until the seventh year. OTC firms must therefore be correct in their product development decisions or they risk losing a great deal of money.

Second, OTC drugs require a high level of advertising and promotion expenditures: 25 per cent of sales on year-round media alone. A firm must have substantial financial resources to enter this market.

Third, because of the market's attractiveness, entering firms face stiff competition. The market has many competitors and is the least concentrated of any large consumer market. In Europe, no company has more than 3.5 per cent of the market and the top fifteen companies only account for 25 per cent market share. Established companies like Bayer, Rhône-Poulenc Rorer, Sanofi, Boots, Boehringer Ingelheim and Warner-Lambert have strong salesforces and marketing organizations. They are strong financially and are willing to take competitors to court if they perceive any violations of laws or regulations. These firms also have strong research and development organizations that spin out new products. As governments squeeze state drug budgets, ethical drug companies have been aggressively working their way into the OTC market. Amongst notable acquisitions are Hoffmann-La Roche's of Nicholas Laboratories and SmithKline Beecham's purchase of Stirling Winthrop from Kodak, while Merck, America's leading drug company has teamed up with Johnson & Johnson in the OTC market. Market leaders have also bought interests in drug distribution, such as SmithKline Beecham's acquisition of Diversified Pharmaceuticals Services, US pharmacy benefits managers.

Fourth, because of the high and rising level of fixed costs, such as the costs of advertising and R&D, many smaller firms are leaving the industry or being acquired by larger firms. Many of the world's leading ethical drug companies' industry observers estimate that an OTC firm must have at least several hundred million dollars in sales. They need this to cover fixed costs and to have the power to match big retailers. So the OTC firms are growing larger and larger, and they are willing to fight aggressively for market share.

Given all these barriers to entry, you might wonder why Colgate would want to pursue OTC products, even if the industry is growing and profitable. Colgate has adopted a strategy that aims to make it the best global consumer products company. It believes that oral-care and OTC products are very similar. Both rely on their ingredients for effectiveness, are highly regulated and use similar marketing channels.

Colgate set up its Colgate Health Care Laboratories to explore product and market development opportunities in the OTC market. In 1987 and 1988 Colgate carried out a test market for a line of OTC products developed by its Health Care Laboratories. It test marketed a wide line of OTC products, from a nasal decongestant to a natural fibre laxative, under the brand name Ektra. The predominantly white packages featured the Ektra name with the Colgate name in smaller letters below it.

Following the test market results, Colgate quietly established another test market to test a line of ten OTC healthcare products, all using the Colgate name as the brand name. The line includes Colgate aspirin-free pain reliever to compete against Tylenol, Colgate ibuprofen (versus Advil), Colgate cold tablets (v. Contact), Colgate night-time cold medicine (v. Nyquil), Colgate antacid (v. Rolaids), Colgate natural laxative (v. Metamucil) and Colgate dandruff shampoo (v. Head and Shoulders).

Industry observers realize that the new line represents a significant departure from Colgate's traditional, high-visibility household goods and oral-care products. Responding to enquiries, Colgate chairman Reuben Marks suggests that: 'The Colgate name is already strong in oral hygiene, now we want to learn whether it can represent health care across the board. We need to expand into more profitable categories.'

Colgate will not talk specifically about its new line. Drugstore operators say, however, that Colgate has blitzed the town with coupons and ads. Representatives have given away free tubes of toothpaste with purchases of the new Colgate products and have handed out coupons worth virtually the full price of the new products. One store owner noted: 'They're spending major money out there.'

If all that promotion was not enough, the manager of one store points out that Colgate has priced its line well below competing brands – as much as 20 per cent below in some cases. The same manager reports that the new products' sales are strong but also adds: 'With all the promotion they've done, they should be. They're cheaper, and they've got Colgate's name on them.'

Yet even if Colgate's test proves a resounding success, marketing consultants say expanding the new line could prove dangerous and, ultimately, more expensive than Colgate can imagine. 'If you put the Colgate brand name on a bunch of different products, if you do it willy-nilly at the lowest end, you're going to dilute what it stands for – and if you stand for nothing, you're worthless,' observes Clive Chajet, chairman of Lipincott and Margolies, a firm that handles corporate identity projects.

Mr Chajet suggests that Colgate also might end up alienating customers by slapping its name on so many products. If consumers are 'dissatisfied with one product, they might be dissatisfied with everything across the board. I wouldn't risk it,' he says. What would have happened to Johnson & Johnson during the Tylenol poison scare, he asks, if the Tylenol name appeared on everything from baby shampoo to birth control pills?

Colgate's test is one of the bolder forays into line extensions by consumer products companies. Companies saddled with 'mature' brands – brands that cannot grow much more – often try to use those brands' solid gold name to make a new fortune, generally with a related product. Thus Procter & Gamble's Ivory soap came up with a shampoo and conditioner. Mars bars were turned into ice-confectionery. Persil extended into washing-up liquids.

**CASE 14** *(cont)*

Unlike those products, however, Colgate's new line moves far afield from its familiar turf. Although its new line is selling well, sales might not stay so strong without budget prices and a barrage of advertising and promotion. 'People are looking at it right now as a generic-style product,' observes one store manager. 'People are really price conscious, and as long as the price is cheaper, along with a name that you can trust, people are going to buy that over others.'

Al Ries, chairman of Trout & Ries marketing consultants, questions whether any line extensions make sense – not only for Colgate, but other strong brand names. He says the reason Colgate has been able to break into the OTC drug market is that other drugs have expanded and lost their niches. Tylenol and Alka-Seltzer both now make cold medicines, for example, and 'that allows an opportunity for the outsiders, the Colgates, to come in and say there's no perception that anybody is any different. The consumer will look for any acceptable brand name.'

Mr Ries argues that Colgate and the traditional OTC medicine companies are turning their products into generic drugs instead of brands. They are losing 'the power of a narrow focus', he says, adding, 'It reflects stupidity on the part of the tradional over-the-counter marketers. ... If the traditional medicines maintained their narrow focus, they wouldn't leave room for an outsider such as Colgate.'

If Colgate is too successful, meanwhile, it also risks cannibalizing its flagship product. Consultants note that almost all successul line extensions and many not-so-successful ones, hurt the product from which they took their name. They cite Miller High Life, whose share of the US beer market has dwindled since the introduction of Miller Lite. 'If Colgate made themselves to mean over-the-counter medicine, nobody would want to buy Colgate toothpaste,' contends Mr Ries.

Mr Chajet agrees. Colgate could 'save tens of millions of dollars by not having to introduce a new brand name' for its new products, he says. But in doing so, it might also 'kill the goose that laid the golden egg'. Other marketing consultants believe that Colgate may be able to break into the market but that it will take much time and money. 'They just don't bring a lot to the OTC party', one consultant indicates.

Although chairman Marks admits that Colgate will continue to try to build share in its traditional cleanser and detergent markets, the company seems to consider personal care a stronger area. Leveraging a name into new categories can be tricky, requiring patience from sceptical retailers and fickle consumers. 'It isn't so much a question of where you can put the brand name,' says one marketing consultant. 'It's what products the consumer will let you put the brand name on.'

### Questions

1. What core product is Colgate selling when it sells toothpaste or the other products in its new line?
2. How would you classify these new products? What implications does this classification have for marketing the new line?
3. What brand decisions has Colgate made? What kinds of product line decisions? Are these decisions consistent?
4. If you were the marketing manager for the extended Colgate line, how would you package the new products? What risks do you see in these packaging decisions?

Source   Adapted from Joanne Lipman, 'Colgate tests putting its name on over-the-counter drug line', *Wall Street Journal* (19 July 1989). Used with permission. See also Dan Koeppel. 'Now playing in Peoria: Colgate generics', *Adweek's Marketing Week* (18 September 1989), 5; Sean Brierley, 'Drug Dependence', *Marketing Week* (14 November 1994), 32–5; Clive Cookson, 'Roche deal puts fizz in the drug races', *Financial Times* (4 June 1991), 19; Paul Abrahams, 'A dose of OTC medicine for growth strategy', *Financial Times* (30 August 1994), 19; 'Hoffmann-La Roche: staying calm', *The Economist* (28 September 1991), 120; Colgate Health Care Laboratories also cooperated in the development of this case.

## CHAPTER FIFTEEN

# *Marketing services*

## CHAPTER OBJECTIVES

After reading this chapter, you should be able to:

- Define a *service*.

- Describe the distinctive characteristics that affect the marketing of services.

- Explain how service business can improve their differentiation, quality and productivity.

## CHAPTER PREVIEW

### Lufthansa: listening to customers

> When an airline has a young fleet, experienced pilots, attentive cabin crew, and the pickiest ground technicians in the world, it is free to concentrate on what is really important: you.

So runs a recent Lufthansa Airline ad.

A decade ago, this German airline company could never make such claims to offering the customer its undivided attention and care. Today, it is taking great pride in its newly earned reputation – not just for quality, but also for being a 'good listener'. It has learnt that superior quality service pays off, and, most importantly, that doing what the customer wants is the key to customer retention.

As one of the world's largest route network operations, Lufthansa conducted in the early 1990s one of the most comprehensive passenger surveys ever carried out. Airline researchers tend to ask only a few thousand travellers for their views and comments. The German airline surveyed some 300,000 European business travellers who fly with them or other airlines. It is not so much the survey results that are noteworthy, but Lufthansa's response to what business customers want.

If your copy of the Business Class Survey results has already been taken from this issue, please call 0800 300 747.

**86,000 British business travellers responded:**
## Europe's largest Business Class Survey was a great success.

Well over 200,000 business travellers throughout Europe participated in the Lufthansa Business Class Survey — giving us their opinions, views and expectations The results were not only overwhelmingly positive, but highly constructive too. They confirmed that by setting our sights on quality improvements throughout the Lufthansa service both on the ground and in the air, we are right on target. They also helped us to highlight the areas that you felt we should improve upon. Our sincere thanks go out to all of you who helped us by responding to the survey.

⊖ **Lufthansa**

Lufthansa takes the pursuit of customer satisfaction seriously: this Business Class Survey ad thanks the 200,000 business travellers who responded to their survey for their role in helping the airlines further improve its service.

Top of the list of wants for a better flight for business customers was more leg-room and elbow-room, followed in third and fourth places by designated lounges and non-smoking aircraft. Separate check-ins and passport control were the top two most important convenience factors stressed by the business customers surveyed.

Lufthansa has taken note and tests were carried out on wider seating arrangements for business-class passengers on selected German domestic and European routes. Responses were very positive. It has redesigned – a unique response where the airline world is concerned – business-class seats to make them wider. Previously a heavy demand on business class meant an overspill into economy class. Redesign means, however, that any overspill into economy class is now met by telescoping seats on one side of the aisle and extending them on the other to make the seats wider. The new seats are 48 cm wide on the left of the aisle. In economy class, the centre seat of the three can be removed by telescoping it into two. On the right of the aisle, the usual three seats can be extended into wider ones. The centre seat is 50 cm wide. The new seats are installed in Lufthansa's Boeing 737, Airbus A320 and A321 jets. Wide-body Airbus A300 and 310 aircraft are also equipped with modified versions.

To ensure that they got things right first time, the design of the new seat was carefully thought out. Airline seat manufacturer, Recaro, who was commissioned to do the redesign, was brought in to work with Lufthansa's marketing and technical staff. Other conveniences were also incorporated into the new seats. For example, they are equipped with modern communication systems, and a credit-card-operated telephone is installed in each armrest![1]

Finding out what target customers require or desire is one thing. Responding to these demands and to the satisfaction of customers is another. Lufthansa ran an ad campaign to thank respondents. But, as the story above shows, a customer focus can benefit service businesses. To improve service quality, the firm must listen to what customers want and then commit resources to deliver precisely that. The application of marketing in service organizations is the focus of this chapter.

Marketing developed initially for selling physical products, such as toothpaste, cars, steel and equipment. But this traditional focus may cause people to overlook the fact that other types of things are marketed. In this chapter, we look at the special marketing requirements for *services*.

## SERVICES MARKETING

One of the chief trends in our modern economy in the past two decades has been the dramatic growth of services. In the big European countries, America and Japan, more people are employed in services than in all other sectors of the economy put together. Both public and private sector services in these countries account for between 60 and 70 per cent of national output. In international trade, services make up 20 per cent of total world exports.[2] Service jobs include not only those in service industries – hotels, airlines, banks, and others – but also service jobs in product-based industries, such as design, advertising, public relations and financial services, corporate lawyers, medical staff and sales trainers. Consumer services are marketed to individuals and households while industrial services are those offered to business and other organizations. The increase in demand for consumer and industrial services has been attributed to a number of factors. First, rising affluence has increased consumers' desire to contract out mundane tasks such as cleaning, cooking and other domestic activities, giving rise to a burgeoning convenience industry. Second, rising incomes and more leisure time have created greater demand for a whole array of leisure services and sporting activities. Third, higher consumption of sophisticated technologies in the home (e.g. home computers, multimedia entertainment equipment, security systems) has triggered the need for specialist services to install and maintain them. In the case of business clients, more complex markets and technologies mean that companies are in greater need of the expertise and knowledge of service organizations, such as market research agencies, marketing and technical consultants. Furthermore businesses are under increasing pressure to reduce fixed costs, so that many are buying in services rather than incur the overheads involved in performing specialized tasks in-house. Finally, as an increasing number of firms are keen to focus on their core competencies, they begin to contract out noncore activities, such as warehousing and transportation, thus stimulating the growth of specialist business service organizations. All these developments have, in turn, led to a growing interest in the special problems of marketing services.

Service industries vary greatly. In most countries, the *government sector* offers services: for example, legal, employment, health care, military, police, fire and postal services, education and regulatory agencies. The *private nonprofit* sector offers services such as museums, charities, churches, colleges, foundations and hospitals. A large part of the *business sector* includes profit-oriented service suppliers like airlines, banks, hotels, insurance companies, consulting firms, medical and law practices, entertainment companies, advertising and research agencies and retailers.

Some service businesses are very large, as in the case of international airlines, finance and retailing. There are also many smaller service providers. As a whole, selling services presents some special problems calling for special marketing solutions.[3]

Let us now examine the nature and special characteristics of service organizations.

### Nature and characteristics of a service

A **service** is any activity or benefit that one party can offer to another which is essentially intangible and does not result in the ownership of anything. Its production may or may not be tied to a physical product. Activities such as renting a hotel room, depositing money in a bank, travelling on an airplane, visiting a doctor, getting a haircut, having a car repaired, watching a professional sport, seeing a movie, having clothes cleaned at a dry cleaner, getting advice from a lawyer – all involve buying a service.

A company must consider five main service characteristics when designing marketing programmes: *intangibility, inseparability, variability, perishability* and *lack of ownership*. We will look at each of these characteristics in the following sections.[4]

### Intangibility

**Service intangibility** means that services cannot be readily displayed, so cannot be seen, tasted, felt, heard or smelled before they are bought. A buyer can examine in detail before purchase the colour, features and performance of an audio hi-fi system he or she wishes to buy. In contrast, a person getting a hair-cut cannot see the result before purchase, just as an airline passenger has nothing but a ticket and the promise of delivery to a chosen destination.

Because service offerings lack tangible characteristics that the buyer can evaluate before purchase, uncertainty is increased. To reduce uncertainty, buyers look for signs of service quality. They draw conclusions about quality from the place, people, equipment, communication material, and price that they can see. Therefore, the service provider's task is to make the service tangible in one or more ways. Whereas product marketers try to add intangibles (e.g. fast delivery, extended warranty, after-sales service) to their tangible offers, service marketers try to add tangible cues suggesting high quality to their intangible offers.[5]

Consider a bank that wants to convey the idea that its service is quick and efficient. It must make this positioning strategy tangible in every aspect of customer contact. The bank's physical setting must suggest quick and efficient service: its exterior and interior should have clean lines; internal traffic flow should be planned carefully; waiting lines should seem short; and background music should be light and upbeat. The bank's staff should be busy and properly dressed. The equipment – computers, copying machines, desks – should look modern. The bank's ads and other communications should suggest efficiency, with clean and simple designs and carefully chosen words and photos that communicate the bank's positioning. The bank should choose a name and symbol for its service that suggest speed and efficiency. Because service intangibility increases purchase risk, buyers tend to be more influenced by word of mouth, which gives credibility to the service, than by advertising messages paid for by the service provider. As such, the service marketer (the bank in this case) should stimulate word of mouth communication by targeting opinion leaders who could be motivated to try its services, and satisfied customers who could be encouraged to recommend its service(s) to peers and friends. Its pricing for various services should be kept simple and clear.

### Inseparability

Physical goods are produced, then stored, later sold, and still later consumed. In contrast, services are first sold, then produced and consumed at the same time and in the same place. **Service inseparability** means that services cannot be separated from their providers, whether the providers are people or machines. If a person provides the service, then the person is a part of the service. A rock concert is an example. The pop group or band is the service. It cannot deliver the service without consumers (the audience) being present. A teacher cannot deliver a service if there are no students attending class. Because the customer is also present as the service is produced, *provider–client interaction* is a special feature of services marketing. Both the provider and the client affect the service outcome. If the audience comprises ardent fans of the pop group, they are likely to be ecstatic with the service. The teacher, who has taught well and is liked by her students, will have effectively satisfied her clients. It is important for service staff to be trained to interact well with clients.

A second feature of the inseparability of services is that other customers are also present or involved. The concert audience, students in the class, other passengers in a train, customers in a restaurant, all are present while an individual consumer is consuming the service. Their behaviour can determine the satisfaction that the service delivers to the individual customers. For example, an unruly crowd in the restaurant would disenchant other customers dining there and reduce satisfaction. The implication for management would be to ensure at all times that customers involved in the service do not interfere with each other's satisfaction.

Because of the simultaneity of service production and consumption, service providers face particular difficulty when demand rises. A goods manufacturer can make more, or mass produce and stock up in anticipation of growth in demand. This is not possible for service operators like restaurants. Service organizations have therefore to pay careful attention to managing growth, given the constraints. A high price is used to ration the limited supply of the provider's service. Several other strategies exist for handling the problem of demand growth. First, the service provider can learn to work with larger groups so that more customers are serviced simultaneously. Bigger sites or premises are used by retailers to accommodate larger numbers of customers. For example, a pop concert will cater for a larger audience if held in an open air sports arena than in an enclosed concert hall. Second, the service provider can learn to work faster. Productivity can be improved by training staff to do tasks and utilize time more efficiently. Finally, a service organization can train more service providers.

### Variability

As services involve people in production and consumption, there is considerable potential for variability. **Service variability** means that the quality of services depends on who provides them, as well as when, where and how they are provided. For example, some hotels have reputations for providing better service than others. Within a given hotel, one registration-desk employee may be cheerful and efficient, whereas another, standing just a few feet away, may be unpleasant and slow. Even the consistency in quality of a single employee's service varies according to his or her energy and frame of mind at the time of each customer contact. For example, two services offered by the same solicitor may not be identical in performance.

Service firms can take several steps towards quality control.[6] First, they can select and train their personnel carefully. Airlines, banks, and hotels invest large sums of money in training their employees to give good service. Business-class customers flying SIA should find friendly and helpful personnel servicing them whatever the time, duration and destination of their travel. Second, they can motivate staff by providing employee incentives that emphasize quality, such as employee-of-the-month awards or bonuses based on customer feedback. Third, they can make service employees more visible and accountable to consumers – auto dealerships can let customers talk directly with the mechanics working on their cars. A firm can check customer satisfaction regularly through suggestion and complaint systems, customer surveys and comparison shopping. When poor service is found, it is corrected.

Fourth, service firms can increase the consistency of employee performance by substituting equipment for staff (e.g. vending machines, automatic cash dispensers), and through heavy enforcement of standardized as well as detailed job procedures (e.g. Walt Disney's theme parks, McDonald's, Mark Warner, the British equivalent of Club Med).

### Perishability

**Service perishability** means that services cannot be stored for later sale or use. In some countries dentists and general practitioners charge patients for missed appointments because the service value existed only at that point and disappeared when the patient did not show up. The perishability of services is not a problem when demand is steady. When demand fluctuates, however, service firms often have difficult problems. For example, public transportation companies have to own much more equipment because of rush-hour demand than they would if demand were even throughout the day.

Service firms can use several strategies for producing a better match between demand and supply. On the demand side, differential pricing – that is, charging differnt prices at different times – will shift some demand from peak periods to off-peak periods. Examples include cheaper low-season holidays and air fares. Or nonpeak demand can be increased, as in the case of business hotels developing minivacation weekends for tourists. Complementary services can be offered during peak times to provide alternatives to waiting customers, such as cocktail lounges to sit in while waiting for a restaurant table and automatic tellers in banks. Reservation systems can also help manage the demand level – airlines, hotels and doctors use them regularly.

On the supply side, firms can hire part-time employees to serve peak demand. Schools add part-time teachers when enrolment goes up, and restaurants call in part-time waiters and waitresses to handle busy shifts. Peak-time demand can be handled more efficiently by rescheduling work so that employees do only essential tasks during peak periods. Some straightforward tasks can be shifted to consumers (e.g. pack-

Services are perishable: empty seats at slack times cannot be stored for later use during peak periods.

ing their own groceries). Or providers can share services, as when several hospitals share an expensive piece of medical equipment. Finally, a firm can plan ahead for expansion, as when an airline company buys more wide-bodied jumbo jets in anticipation of future growth in international air travel.

### Lack of ownership

When customers buy physical goods, such as cars and computers, they have personal access to the product for an unlimited time. They actually own the product. They can even sell it when they no longer wish to own it. In contrast, service products lack that quality of ownership. The service consumer often has access to the service for a limited time. An insurance policy is yours only when you have paid the premium and continue to renew it. A holiday is experienced and, hopefully, enjoyed, but after the event, it remains ephemeral, unlike a product in the hand. Because of the lack of ownership, service providers must make a special effort to reinforce their brand identity and affinity with the consumer by one or more of the following methods:

1. They could offer incentives to consumers to use their service again, as in the case of frequent-flyer schemes promoted by British Airways and other big airlines.
2. They could create membership clubs or associations to give an impression of ownership (e.g. British Airways' executive clubs for air travellers, Toshiba's cookery clubs for microwave oven users).
3. Where appropriate, service providers might turn the disadvantage of nonownership into a benefit: for example, an industrial design consultant might argue that

British Airways Executive Club reinforces British Airways brand identity and consumer belonging. *Executive Club News* informs members of British Airways services and promotions that are specifically targeted at them.

by employing his or her expertise, the customer would actually be reducing costs, given that the alternative would be for that customer to employ a full-time designer with equally specialized knowledge. Paying for access to services rather than perfoming the activities in-house (e.g. warehousing) reduces capital cost while also giving greater flexibility to a business.

## Marketing strategies for service firms

Until recently, service firms lagged behind manufacturing firms in their use of marketing. Many service businesses are small (shoe repair shops, barbershops) and often consider marketing unnecessary or too costly. Some service businesses (e.g. schools, churches) were at one time so much in demand that they did not need marketing until recently. Others (e.g. legal, medical and accounting practices) believed that it was unprofessional to use marketing. Still others who sell sensitive services did not contemplate using marketing techniques because it was not discreet to do so (see Marketing Highlight 15.1).

Furthermore service businesses are more difficult to manage when using only traditional marketing approaches. In a product business, products are fairly standardized and sit on shelves waiting for customers. In a service business, however, the customer interacts with a service provider whose service quality is less certain and more variable. The service outcome is affected not just by the service provider but by the whole supporting production process. Thus service marketing requires more than just traditional external marketing using the four *P*s. Figure 15.1 shows that service marketing also requires both *internal marketing* and *interactive marketing*.

**Internal marketing** means that the service firm must invest heavily in employee quality and performance. It must effectively train and motivate its customer-contact employees and all the supporting service *people* to work as a *team* to provide customer satisfaction. For the firm to deliver consistently high service quality, everyone must practise a customer orientation. It is not enough to have a marketing

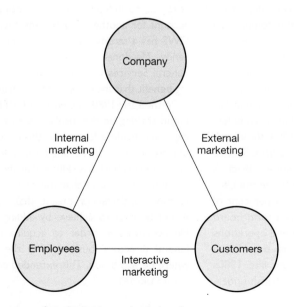

**Figure 15.1**    Three types of marketing in service industries.

# The death business: marketing funeral services

People rarely like to be reminded of their mortality. If you were in the funeral industry – the business of dealing with death (and, indeed, one which depends on death for its survival) – how would traditional marketing practices be of use in selling such a sensitive service? In recent years, funeral companies in Britain have not only increasingly adopted a more commercially minded approach to selling funeral services, but have also introduced relatively *innovative marketing* practices to maintain and increase market share.

Since the Independent Television Commission changed its rules in 1993 – governing the broadcast of 'sensitive' advertising – undertakers are using TV advertising to persuade viewers to arrange and pay for their own funerals years before they could actually expect to die. Funeral directors Great Southern (now owned by America's Service Corporation International (SCI), the world's largest funeral services company) did just that with 'Chosen Heritage', its prepayment scheme first advertised in the London TV area in early 1994. It had amassed over £40 million* in sales from 67,000 people, by September 1994.

Funeral directors must develop greater marketing sense because of a number of changes in their environment. First, the demographics of death mean that the number of funerals per year until the end of the century will remain constant at about 650,000 a year, although the numbers are set to rise after that. Second, within such a static market the competition is intensifying, with many funeral directors seeking to safeguard future market share. Larger operations have bought smaller chains of undertakers in order to boost market share in the 1980s. Family-run firms, in particular, have been hit. Furthermore the trend has been towards greater invasion of the European funeral market by foreign operators. In 1994, America's (and the world's) largest funeral services firm, Service Corporation International (SCI), acquired Britain's Great Southern and Plantsbrook, to become the UK's number-one operator having secured 15 per cent of the market. SCI, which sees Britain as a springboard into Europe, is set to buy up other funeral operations in Europe. The onset of recession in the United Kingdom and high interest rates in the late 1980s have also made it more difficult for big British under-

takers to raise the funds to maintain their acquisition trail. The large groups have been forced to look for other ways to increase market share (e.g. advertising on TV to attract new business).

The funeral directors who have adopted marketing thinking do not see themselves as merely directing funerals, but are sensitive to their role as a business that, while performing a very sensitive service, must remain profitable to survive in the long term.

The UK funeral market is worth about £650 million a year, with the average cost of a funeral being just under £1,000. Funeral directors range from small independent directors to chains such as the Co-operative Wholesale Society (CWS) Funeral Services Group. There are some 3,500 funeral directors in Britain. Small independent firms, probably looking after only a few hundred funerals each year, make up 60 per cent of this total. This figure contrasts with ten years ago when independents accounted for about 87 per cent of the market. At that time, working practices were reminiscent of a cottage industry. When funeral directors bothered to think about marketing, it was probably only a small, discreet advertisement in the local paper or an entry in the *Yellow Pages*. The only strong brand name most people associate with funerals is Co-op. The CWS now accounts for about 10 per cent of all funerals in Britain, while the twenty-seven or so independent retail cooperative societies account for another 15 per cent between them. The CWS has a strong identity in the public mind, which Sandy Macdonald, operations manager for CWS Funeral Services Group, claims is an obvious marketing benefit that they work hard to maintain.

In the early 1980s, however, a Mr Howard Hodgson began shaking up the insular world of funeral directing – and made a fortune in the process. He bought out his father's undertaking busines for £14,000, having honed his business skills selling life insurance.

Hodgson realized that the operating inefficiencies in most undertakers meant that scale economies would be easy to achieve by adding extra business. He borrowed in order to acquire small, moribund funeral directors' businesses in the West Midlands where he was based. This extended *distribution* cover-

*1 ecu = UK£0.83.

age. More importantly, by a shrewd and hands-on management approach, he managed to improve the *productivity* of the acquired businesses. Hodgson joined the unlisted securities market (USM) in 1986 and continued to buy market share and improve operations and profitability. The strategy was followed by Hodgson's main rivals – CWS, Great Southern and Kenyon Securities. In 1986 Hodgson merged with Kenyon to form PFG Hodgson Kenyon International, later renamed Plantsbrook Group. Kenyon was 29 per cent owned by France's largest funeral group, Pompes Funèbres Générales, who liked Hodgson's management style. Plantsbrook came to enjoy a market share of 11 per cent compared with about 25 per cent for the Co-op Group as a whole and 5 per cent for Great Southern.

With growth by acquisition put aside for the time being after the heady pace of change in the 1980s, the funeral business has turned to marketing. A greater understanding of what the *target customer wants* is important. Some people may want to delay their purchase of a headstone, others want a proper funeral for the deceased. Some are cutting back on flowers.

*Pricing* issues have also risen in importance. A recent survey conducted by the Old Fellows Friendly Society, which sells insurance plans to cover funeral costs, found that the average cost of a funeral had risen by 14 per cent over 1993–4 for burials and by 19 per cent for cremations. The average cost of a burial was £1,022 and a cremation, £806. The survey showed that Britain is one of the cheapest places to die in Europe: a burial in France, for example, costs £1,102, in Germany, £1,127 and in Belgium, £1,159. A *Which?* (magazine for the Consumers' Association) survey highlighted that prices quoted varied between funeral directors, and pointed out that: 'People visiting funeral directors tend to be under a lot of emotional stress, and so it is particularly important that they're given clear information about how much a funeral is going to cost.'

Funeral directors are under increasing pressure to abide by the voluntary codes of practice and enforcement procedures operated by the industry's main body, the National Assocation of Funeral Directors. So excessive pricing is often inappropriate as a means of propping up margins. Pricing uncertainty, however, has favoured funeral directors: it has helped encourage people to take advantage of the prepayment funeral schemes – a US idea – thus allowing undertakers to price their service in advance.

Funeral directors use a variety of methods to *promote* their service. As noted earlier, TV advertising and other media advertising are used to create awareness of prepayment schemes. Some organizations like the Co-op extend this awareness by holding 'open days' at its funeral homes, where visitors are greeted with a video, say, and literature about the work carried out in preparing for a funeral. Personal or word-of-mouth recommendation is, however, still the most effective marketing tool used by independent undertakers.

Funeral businesses are well aware of the changing attitudes of people regarding death. All the marketing efforts in the 1990s are based on the assumption that the taboo about funerals has gone, and that people are becoming more conscious of the cost of dying and are therefore more willing to think and plan ahead than ever before.

Educating the public to consider funerals in advance is hard going. But there are signs that people are prepared to be more imaginative about funerals – one man recently arranged to have a jazz band play at his – although most customers still opt for a tradiational funeral.

Some countries are less inhibited. In Japan, for example, death can be celebrated with a gusto few in the West embrace. It has been reported that the Gyokuzenin funeral busines charges £3,000 for a 60-minute 'music and light' funeral in which synthesized Buddhist chants, together with an elaborate laser show, take the deceased to a new hi-tech world.

The case of funeral businesses highlights the applicability of marketing in even the most insular of service organizations. Those that are aware of marketplace sensitivities and able to respond to customer needs will survive in the tougher conditions of the 1990s.

Sources: Drawn extensively from David Churchill, 'Grave undertakings', *Marketing Business* (October 1992), 43–5; Stephen Nathan, 'Invasion of the body snatchers', *The European* (9–15 September 1994), 29; Caroline Southey, 'Plantsbrook advances 8 per cent despite fall in death rate', *Financial Times* (9 September 1994), 20.

department doing traditional marketing while the rest of the company goes its own way. Marketers must also encourage everyone else in the organization to practise marketing. In fact, internal marketing must *precede* external marketing. It makes little sense to advertise excellent service before the company's staff is ready, willing and able to provide it.

**Interactive marketing** means that perceived service quality depends heavily on the quality of the buyer–seller interaction. In product marketing, product quality often depends little on how the product is obtained. But in services marketing, service quality depends on both the service deliverer and the quality of the delivery, especially in professional services. The customer judges service quality not just on *technical quality* (e.g. the success of the surgery) but also on its *functional quality* (e.g. whether the doctor showed concern and inspired confidence). Thus professionals cannot assume that they will satisfy the client simply by providing good technical service. They have to master interactive marketing skills or functions as well.[7]

Today, as competition and costs increase, and as productivity and quality decrease, more marketing sophistication is needed. Service companies face three major marketing tasks: they want to increase their *competitive differentiation, service quality* and *productivity*.

## Managing differentiation

Service differentiation poses particular problems. First, service intangibility and inseparability mean that consumers rarely compare alternative service offerings in advance of purchase in the way that potential buyers of products do. Differences in the attractiveness or value of competing services are not readily obvious to the potential buyer. Service providers often use pricing to differentiate their offering. However, pricing strategies (e.g. price cuts) are quickly emulated by competitors. Furthermore intense price competition erodes margins and does not create a sustainable differential advantage over the long term.

Service differentiation: Virgin Atlantic uses in-flight entertainment to provide a very different service in a very competitive market.

The solution to price competition is to develop a differentiated *offer, delivery*, and *image*. The offer can include *innovative features* that set one company's offer apart from its competitors' offers. For example, airlines have introduced such innovations as in-flight movies, advance seating, air-to-ground telephone service, and frequent-flyer awareness programmes to differentiate their offers.

Unfortunately, this exposes a second problem – service innovations cannot be patented and are easily copied. Still, the service company that regularly finds desired service innovations will usually gain a succession of temporary advantages, and, by earning an innovative reputation, may keep customers who want to go with the best.

Third, the variability of services suggests that standardization and quality are difficult to control. Consistency in quality is generally hard to obtain, but firms that persistently cultivate a customer orientation and execute sound internal marketing schemes will increase their ability to differentiate their brand by offering superior quality service *delivery*.

The service company can differentiate its service *delivery* in three ways: through *people, physical environment*, and *process*. These means are often referred to as the additional three *P*s in service marketing. The company can distinguish itself by having more able and reliable customer-contact people than its competitors have. The smart appearance of front-line customer-contact staff also helps. Or it can develop a superior physical environment in which the service product is delivered. Finally, it can design a superior delivery process. For example, a bank might offer its customers home banking as a better way to use banking services than by having to drive, park, and wait in line.

Finally, service intangibility and variability mean that a consistent service brand image is not easily built. Brand image also takes time to develop and cannot be copied by competitors. Service companies that work on distinguishing their service by creating unique and powerful images, either through symbols or branding, will gain a lasting advantage over competitors with lack-lustre images. For example, the Ritz, Sheraton, Hard Rock Café, British Airways, Citibank, Swissair, Benetton all enjoy superior brand positioning which has taken years of effort to develop. Organizations such as Lloyd's Bank (who adopted the black horse as its symbol of strength), McDonald's (personified by its Ronald McDonald clown), and the International Red Cross, have all differentiated their images through symbols.

Service firms are under increasing pressure to adopt a marketing-oriented approach to thrive. Management must develop effective strategies for the seven *P*s of service marketing: product (the service), price, place, promotion, people, physical environment and process.

### Managing service quality

One of the principle ways in which a service firm can differentiate itself is by delivering consistently higher quality than its competitors. Like manufacturers before them, many service industries have now joined the total quality management revolution. Studies have shown that service quality affects customer satisfaction, which in turn affects buying intentions.[8] Many companies are finding that outstanding service quality can give them a potent competitive advantage which leads to superior sales and profit performance.

Quality in service industries is harder to define, judge or quantify than product quality. It is hard to quantify service quality because intangibility means that there are seldom physical dimensions, like performance, functional features or maintenance cost, which can be used as benchmarks and measured. It is harder to get agreement on the quality of a haircut than on that of a hair dryer, for instance. The inseparability of production and consumption means that service quality must be defined on the basis of both the process in which the service is delivered and the actual outcome experienced by the customer. Again, it is difficult to quantify standards or reference points against which service delivery process and performance outcome are measured.

Studies suggest that they key to measuring service quality is to determine how customers of the service assess quality, and that customer assessments of service quality are the result of a comparison of service expectations with actual performance.[9] To create a differential advantage, the firm should exceed the customers' service = quality *expectations*. As the chief executive at American Express puts it, 'Promise only what you can deliver and deliver more than you promise!' True, offering greater service quality results in higher costs. However, investments usually pay off because greater customer satisfaction leads to increased customer retention and sales.

To improve quality, service marketers have to identify: the key determinants of service quality (i.e. what criteria customers use to judge quality); what target customers' expectations are; and how customers rate the firm's service in relation to these criteria against what they expected.

### Determining service quality

An important study highlights ten key determinants of perceived service quality – criteria used by consumers to judge quality.[10] Figure 15.2 shows these dimensions: *access* (is the service easy to get access to and delivered on time?); *credibility* (is the company credible and trustworthy?); *knowledge* (does the service provider really understand customers' needs?); *reliability* (how dependable and consistent is the service?); *security* (is the service low-risk and free from danger?); *competence* (are

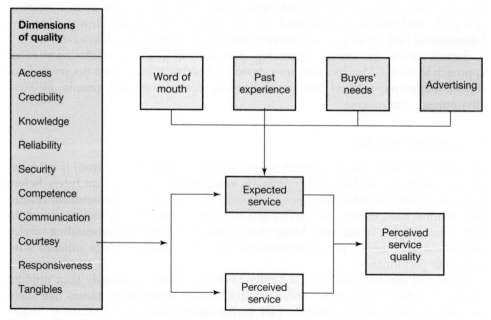

**Figure 15.2**  Key determinants of perceived service quality.

staff knowledgeable and in possession of the skills required to delivery good service?); *communication* (how well has the company explained its service?); *courtesy* (are staff polite, considerate and sensitive to customers?); *responsiveness* (are stafff willing and quick to deliver the service?) and *tangibles* (does the appearance of staff, the physical environment and other tangible representations of the service reflect high quality?). The first five are concerned with the quality of the *outcome* of service provided, while the last five are related to the quality of the delivery *process*.

To achieve high-quality service, the firm has to focus on the key determinants of service outcome and delivery process quality.

To a large extent, aspects such as good understanding of customers' needs and the ability to provide consistent and dependable service are achieved through internal marketing and continual investment in employee quality and performance. The reputation and credibility of the service provider and customers' perceived risk are interrelated. If the consumer trusts the service provider, he or she expects that the service is free from danger or perceives little risk in using the service. Credibility can be improved through effective communication of service quality through advertising and/or satisfied customers. Access can be improved by having multisite locations (e.g. Pizza Hut, McDonald's, Benetton), and waiting times can be reduced through synchronizing supply and demand and/or tackling staff productivity problems.

During the past decade, many service companies have invested heavily to develop streamlined and efficient service-delivery systems. They have attempted to ensure that customers will receive consistently high-quality service in every service encounter. Unlike product manufacturers who can adjust their machinery and inputs until everything is perfect, service quality will always vary, depending on the interactions between employees and customers. Problems inevitably will occur:

> Mistakes are a critical part of every service. Hard as they try, even the best service companies can't prevent the occasional late flight, burned steak, or missed delivery. The fact is, in services, often performed in the customer's presence, errors are inevitable. But dissatisfied customers are not. While companies may not be able to prevent all problems, they can learn to recover from them. A good recovery can turn angry, frustrated customers into loyal ones. It can, in fact, create more good will than if things had not gone badly in the first place.[11]

Thus although a company may not be able to prevent service problems, it must learn to recover when they occur. Good *service recovery* can win customer purchasing and loyalty.

The first step is to *empower* front-line service employees – that is, to give them the authority, responsibility and incentives to recognize, care about and tend to customer needs. Such empowered employees can act quickly and effectively to keep service problems from resulting in lost customers.

Studies in well-managed service companies show that they share a number of common virtues regarding service quality:

1. Top service companies are '*customer obsessed*'. They have developed a distinctive strategy for satisfying these customer needs that wins enduring customer loyalty. At British Telecom, liaison panels are set up which demonstrate management commitment to listen to customers and ensure that the ethos of customer care is embedded in the whole company.
2. They have a history of *top management commitment to quality*. Management at companies such as Marks & Spencer, American Express, Swissair and McDonald's look not only at financial performance but also at service performance.

3. The best service providers *set high service quality standards*. Swissair, for example, aims to have 96 per cent or more of its passengers rate its service as good or superior; otherwise, it takes action. The standards must be set *appropriately* high. A 98 per cent accuracy standard may sound good but, using this standard, 64,000 Federal Express packages would be lost each day, ten words would be misspelled on each page, 400,000 prescriptions would be misfilled daily, and drinking water would be unsafe eight days a year. Top service companies do not settle merely for 'good' service, they aim for 100 per cent defect-free service.[12]

4. Top service firms *watch service performance closely* – both their own and that of competitors. Good service companies also communicate their concerns about service quality to employees and provide performance feedback. They use methods such as comparison shopping, customer surveys, suggestion schemes and customer complaint programmes. Customer complaints are an opportunity for companies to remedy poor service, and, when they are dealt with promptly and effectively, customer care in service-recovery situations can be a source of unrivalled competitive advantage (see Marketing Highlight 15.2).

5. Well-managed service companies *satisfy employees as well as customers*. They believe that good employee relations will result in good customer relations. Whatever the level of service they intend to deliver, it is important that management should clearly define and communicate that level so that, first, its employees know what service targets they must achieve, and secondly, its customers know what to expect to receive from their interaction with the service provider.

Management must also create an environment of employee support, reward good service and monitor employee job satisfaction. For example, the Danish-based international cleaning services giant ISS (International Service System) stresses good working relations and utilization of human resources. Staff are encouraged to join trade unions. Total quality management is firmly upheld – staff are trained so that they can do their jobs well and derive satisfaction from them – happy satisfied customers yield happy employees. It has also gone to the extreme of moving into palatial new headquarters in a wooded country estate in northern Copenhagen – an absence of air-conditioning or dust-hugging carpets, together with soothing colours, reflect management's belief that scientific cleaning can help reduce staff illness.

6. Quality-oriented service firms also learn to *manage customers' service expectations*. They are careful not to oversell their firm's service levels. Overpromising and underdelivering invariably reduces perceived service quality and leads to dissatisfied consumers. Expectations are based on past experiences, word of mouth, buyers' needs and service firms' advertising. If *perceived service* exceeds *expected service*, perceived service quality will be high, resulting in delighted customers who are likely to use the service again.

Arguably, managers should measure customer retention to gauge service quality. The service firm's ability to retain customers depends on how consistently it delivers value to them. The service provider's goal is therefore 'zero customer defections' as opposed to 'zero defects', the product manufacturer's quality goal.

### Managing productivity

Rising costs put service firms under great pressure to increase service productivity. The problem is particularly acute where the service is labour intensive. Productivity can be improved in several ways:

1. The service providers can better train current employees, or they can hire new ones who will work harder or more skilfully for the same pay.
2. The service providers can increase the quantity of their service by giving up some quality (e.g. doctors having to handle more patients by giving less time to each).
3. The provider can 'industrialize the service' by adding equipment and standardizing production (McDonald's production-line approach to fast-food retailing is a good example). Commercial dishwashing, jumbo jets, and multiple-unit movie theatres all represent the use of technological advances to increase service output.
4. Service providers can also increase productivity by designing more effective services. How-to-quit-smoking clinics and exercise recommendations may reduce the need for expensive medical services later on.
5. Providers can also give customers incentives to substitute company labour with their own labour – that is, increase customer participation. For example, business firms that sort their own mail before delivering it to the post office pay lower postal rates. Self-service restaurants are another case in point. Pay-and-display facilities in car parks alleviate the need to employ attendants (as well as reducing waiting time).
6. Service providers who have to deal with fluctuating demand can increase productivity by increasing flexibility and reshaping demand. Supplier flexibility – the ability to improve supply capacity – is increased by using part-time workers, shared facilities and rescheduling peak-time facilities and work. Demand movements are reshaped by differential pricing, reservation systems and stimulating nonpeak usage.

However, companies must avoid pushing productivity so hard that doing so reduces perceived quality. Some productivity steps help standardize quality, increasing customer satisfaction. But other productivity steps lead to too much standardization and can rob consumers of a customerized service. Attempts to industrialize a service or to cut costs can make a service company more efficient in the short run but reduce its longer-run ability to innovate, maintain service quality and flexibility, or respond to consumer needs and desires. In some cases, service providers accept reduced productivity in order to create more service differentiation or quality.[13]

## International services marketing

An Italian sportswear manufacturer calls her advertising agency in London to confirm plans for new billboards in Venezuela. A German businessman checks into his hotel room in Atlanta – the hotel is owned by a British company and managed by an American firm. The Zurich branch of a Japanese bank participates in a debt offering for an aircraft-leasing company in Ireland. These are just a few examples of the thousands of service transactions that take place each day around the globe. More and more, the global economy is dominated by services. In fact, a variety of service industries – from banking, insurance, and communications to transportation, travel, and entertainment – now account for well over 60 per cent of the economy in developed countries around the world. The worldwide growth rate for services (16 per cent in the past decade) is almost double the growth rate of manufacturing.[14]

Some industries have a long history of international operations. For example, the commercial banking industry was one of the first to grow internationally. Banks had to provide global services in order to meet the foreign exchange and credit needs of their home-country clients wanting to sell overseas. In recent years, however, as the

## Turning customer complaints into opportunities

Customers are becoming more demanding. They like to see things right first time. But if things go wrong, companies must be responsive and remedy poor service to recover customer confidence and loyalty.

Leading service companies show customer service and care characteristics that make them stand out in the crowd. Not only do they believe strongly in giving the customer good service, they have systems and procedures installed to offer a high level of customer service and care in service-recovery situations, especially in handling complaints. Firms that view complaints as a valuable source of opportunities establish effective complaint procedures to capture these opportunities. Customer complaint programmes pay off because:

- The complaint itself points to possible improvement areas.
- They offer another chance to give service and satisfaction to the dissatisfied customer.
- Complaints that are put right to the full satisfaction of the customer prevent customer loss and are an excellent opportunity to strengthen loyalty.
- They can enhance the firm's standing and may generate further businesses as a result of recommendations made by satisfied customers.

To build effective complaint procedures, management must first be aware of the factors that impede them: managers see complaints as personal attacks; complaints are viewed as problems; someone is to be blamed; and dissatisfied customers are discouraged from, or do not know the most effective way of, complaining.

The firms must therefore develop strategies to ensure that complaints are attracted, listened to and resolved to the satisfaction of the customer. The latter is crucial because the customer may still be dissatisfied if the complaint was badly handled. Worse, the level of the complaint may be raised if the firm's response was not satisfactory.

Because only a small minority of dissatisfied customers ever complain, the firm should proactively seek to attract complaints from disenchanted customers. The firm should keep channels of communication open to permit customers access and to make it easy for them to give feedback. Free telephones, regular follow-up of customer surveys, and staff training are required, which may increase costs, but in the long run satisfied customers are more valuable and are an inexpensive way of developing the firm's business. Customers themselves may use different channels of complaint: telephone, fax, letter or personal call. Complaints about the time a product or service is delivered are often made by phone, whilst broader policy issues and billing disputes are usually written. The tone of a complaint must be heeded. Whatever tone the customer adopts, it is important for the firm to respond with the urgency and seriousness that is expected by the customer – an abusive customer is as valuable over a lifetime as any other and is more damaging if not satisfied.

Organizations must develop a nonthreatening culture which does not penalize the 'mistake', in order to encourage staff to analyse and resolve complaints and realize beneifts for the organization. A no-blame orientation is a prerequisite for a culture that wishes to attract and learn from complaints. Staff must be rewarded for creating service-recovery opportunities.

Avis, the car rental company, found that the cost of handling complaints was out of all proportion to the transactions involved. There was also the hidden cost of the delay between the complaint being made and finally resolved, which resulted in Avis losing the customer despite its generous recompense. Avis decided to give its counter staff the authority to satisfy customers, based on their own judgements: that is, to empower its employees. The scheme saved money and increased the number of loyal customers.

Another company, British Gas, has also benefited from having a customer complaint scheme. British Gas, which is now privatized, faces mounting competition in the marketplace for the first time. It therefore has to develop a policy that will retain customers in a competitive environment. In the current tight economic situation, a profitable company like British Gas can be seen as a natural target for complaint and indeed a service provider of this stature has a moral and ethical duty to be a good corporate citizen.

Research among managers in the British Gas South Eastern area shows some of the issues which affect the resolution of customer complaint-handling. Interviews were carried out among the customer managers in the ten districts of the region. There was an overwhelming consensus amongst the managers that complaints deserved to be dealt with individually and that remedies to customer complaints should be rapid and adequate. However, the managers were also found to be protective towards their staff and systems. There was even a sense of resentment or hurt about some of the ways in which customers chose to complain.

The tone of complaint affected the way it was received. Managers responded adversely to sarcastic, carping letters and also to complaints that were directed through more than one channel. All managers claimed not only to have investigated and resolved complaints, but to have learned from them and applied the lessons. However, there is no follow-up of complaints and 'learning' is sometimes only feedback to the management team.

A series of standards of service has been agreed with Ofgas, the industry watchdog. In some cases, breach of these standards will give rise to a fixed compensation payment. The company will not wait for payments to be claimed, but adopt a proactive stance. Publication of these standards and of the complaints and compensation scheme is consistent with the ideals of the Citizen's Charter. (In Britain, the Competition and Services Utilities Act 1992 requires the utility monopolies to relate to the principles set out in the Citizen's Charter – legislation that enshrines the ethos of customer care and service satisfaction.)

Another quality-conscious service organization is Marks & Spencer. The following are excerpts taken from a set of correspondence made by the company and its supplier to a customer who returned a can of Danish Lean Ham to the local store after he discovered a piece of paper in the product. They show how Marks & Spencer resolved the complaint promptly, for the letters arrived within days of the complaint being made:

> I very much regret that despite this care [numerous quality checks], you were unfortunate enough to experience a problem of this nature. Please accept our apologies for this lapse in our quality.

> Thank you for having taken the trouble to bring this matter to our attention. I would like to assure you that the problem will be reported to our Buying Department and Supplier as a matter of urgency. The investigations as a result of this complaint will help to ensure the elimination of problems of this kind in the future. ... We always wish our customers to enjoy the food products they purchase from us without experiencing any problems. Therefore I have pleasure in enclosing Marks & Spencer gift vouchers to the value of £3.00 as a sincere gesture of our customer good will.

(Customer Advisor, Food Division, Marks & Spencer plc)

(Note: The customer paid only £1.45 for the product that was returned. He was also given another can of Danish Lean Ham plus a refund at the time of making the complaint.)

The same day, the customer also received a letter from the company who supplied Marks & Spencer Danish Lean Ham:

> We are sorry to learn about your complaint. ... Our Parent Company will be informed of this immediately and you can expect to hear from them in the very near future. ... In the meantime, we thank you for bringing the matter to the attention of Marks & Spencer, and for our part, we apologise for any inconvenience which you may have been caused.

(Technical Manager, Jaka Foods Group Limited)

A week later, the response from Jaka Foods (the parent company in Denmark) arrived.

> We were most concerned to learn that you had reason to complain about the product.... In producing for Marks & Spencer, no effort is spared to ensure the highest quality of the products.... We have passed on your complaint to our quality control department for examination.
>
> However, they are unfortunately at a loss to explain the origin of this piece of paper. The production lines where this product is made are subject to very high hygienic standards which include an hourly wash-down of all machinery. In view of this, and as we have received no other complaints, we believe this to be an isolated, but not less regrettable incident.... We apologise for any inconvenience this matter may have caused you and thank you for bringing it to our attention.... We hope you will continue to shop at Marks & Spencer and to purchase St

Michael's products with the same confidence as ... you have always done prior to this incident.

(Export Manager)

It is evident from the Danish Lean Ham incident that Marks & Spencer and its supplier take customer complaints very seriously. The customer who complained was treated with reverence – he received apologies, explanations and more than sufficient compensation.

Resolving customer complaints quickly, efficiently, effectively and incisively requires the firm to set a clear policy on solutions and compensation. The company should adapt resources to fit customer requirements. Resources must be planned before-

hand to ensure that when complaints occur, departments handling these complaints are able to resolve them. Staff must be both aware and knowledgeable, and have sufficient network contacts within the firm and with outside suppliers to exercise chosen solutions as and when necessary. It is also vital that, in order to reduce argument and paperwork, recovery action and compensation are agreed quickly with the customer, particularly where there has been substantial inconvenience or economic loss.

In conclusion, unless the firm is open and honest with its customers, agrees solutions, and keeps its promises of customer care and service recovery, its complaint programme will not achieve the goal of retaining customers through increasing their satisfaction.

Sources: Peter Barbey, 'Looking for trouble', *Marketing Business* (September 1994), 21–4; 'Effective complaint systems', leaflet (London: HMSO, 1993); see also David Clutterbuck, Graham Clark and Colin Armistead, *Inspired Customer Service* (London: Kogan Page, 1993).

scope of international financing has broadened, many banks have become truly global operations. Germany's Deutsche Bank, for example, has branches in forty-one countries. Thus, for its clients around the world who wish to take advantage of growth opportunities created by German reunification, Deutsche Bank can raise money not just in Frankfurt, but also in Zurich, London, Paris and Tokyo.

The travel industry also moved naturally into international operations. American hotel and airline companies grew quickly in Europe and the Far East during the economic expansion that followed World War II. Credit card companies soon followed – the early worldwide presence of American Express has recently been matched by Visa and MasterCard. Business travellers and holiday-makers like the convenience and they have now come to expect that their credit cards will be honoured wherever they go.

Professional and business services industries such as accounting, management consulting, and advertising have only recently started operating on a worldwide scale. The international growth of these firms followed the globalization of the manufacturing companies they serve. For example, increasingly globalized manufacturing firms have found it much easier to have their accounts prepared by a single accounting firm, even when they operate in two dozen countries. This set the stage for rapid international consolidation in the accounting industry. During the late 1980s, established accounting companies around the world quickly merged with America's 'Big Eight' to become the international 'Big Six' almost overnight. Similarly, as their client companies began to employ global marketing and advertising strategies, advertising agencies and other marketing services firms responded by globalizing their own operations.[15]

The rapidly expanding international marketplace provides many attractive opportunities for service firms. It also creates some special challenges, however. Service companies wanting to operate in other countries are not always welcomed with open arms. Whereas manufacturers usually face straightforward tariff, quota or currency restrictions when attempting to sell their products in another country, service providers are likely to face more subtle barriers. In some cases, rules and regulations affecting international services firms reflect the host country's traditions. In others, they appear to protect the country's own fledgling service industries from large global competitors with greater resources. In still other cases, however, the restrictions seem to have little purpose other than to make entry difficult for foreign service firms.

> Most of the industrialized nations want their banks, insurance companies, construction firms and other service providers to be allowed to move people, capital and technology around the globe unimpeded. Instead they face a bewildering complex of national regulations, most of them designed to guarantee jobs for local competitors. A new Turkish law, for example, forbids international accounting firms to bring capital into the country to set up offices and requires them to use the names of local partners, rather than prestigious international ones, in their marketing. To audit the books of a multinational company's branch in Buenos Aires, an accountant must have the equivalent of a high school education in Argentinian geography and history. ... India is perhaps the most [difficult] big economy in the world [to enter] these days. ... New Delhi prevents international insurance companies from selling property and casualty policies to the country's swelling business community or life insurance to its huge middle class.[16]

Despite such difficulties, the trend toward growth of global service companies will continue, especially in banking, telecommunications, and professional services. Today service firms are no longer simply following their manufacturing customers. Instead, many are taking the lead in international expansion.

## SUMMARY

Marketing has been broadened in recent years to cover services.

As developed countries move increasingly toward a *service economy*, marketers need to know more about marketing services. *Services* are activities or benefits that one party can offer to another which are essentially intangible and *do not result in* the *ownership* of anything. Services are *intangible, inseparable, variable*, and *perishable*. Each characteristic poses problems and requires strategies. Marketers have to find ways to make the service more tangible; to increase the productivity of providers who are inseparable from their products; to standardize the quality in the face of variability; and to improve demand movements and supply capacities in the face of service perishability.

Service industries have typically lagged behind manufacturing firms in adopting and using marketing concepts, but this situation is now changing. Services marketing strategy calls not only for external marketing, but also for *internal marketing* to motivate employees and *interactive marketing* to create service delivery skills among service providers. To succeed, service marketers must create *competitive differentiation*, offer high service quality and find ways to increase *service productivity*.

# ■ DISCUSSING THE ISSUES

1. Why is demand for services growing? How would marketers gain a competitive advantage by satisfying the growing demand for increased services?

2. How can a theatre deal with the intangibility, inseparability, variability and perishability of the service it provides? Give examples.

3. A fast-food restaurant serves its hamburgers 'fresh off the grill'. This ensures high quality but creates leftover hamburgers if the staff overestimates demand. The restaurant solves this perishability problem by using the leftover meat in other dishes such as meat pies and sphaghetti sauce. How do airlines solve the perishability of unsold seats? Give additional examples of perishability and how service firms address it.

4. Services marketing calls for external, internal and interactive marketing. Select examples of firms that provide services to other business organizations (e.g. an advertising agency, a transportation firm or a management consultancy). Explain how these other types of marketing can help such service firms create and maintain a competitive advantage.

5. Marketing is defined as satisfying needs and wants through exchange processes. What exchanges occur in marketing nonprofit organizations, such as a museum, the Red Cross or other charities?

6. Referring to examples of nonprofit (both public and private) service organizations, discuss how their effectiveness and efficiency might be increased by applying marketing principles.

# ■ APPLYING THE CONCEPTS

1. Select an educational institution you are familiar with (it could be the one at which you are currently studying for a qualification). Take the concept of the marketing mix as a framework to guide your evaluation of the organization. Start with the product (i.e. the service offering), then work through pricing, promotion, place and the other three Ps – people, physical environment and process. Show how attention to all seven Ps can affect the effectiveness and efficiency of the institution you have selected.

2. Perishability is very important in the airlfine industry: unsold seats are gone forever, and too many unsold seats mean large losses. With computer-

ized ticketing, airlines can easily use pricing to deal with perishability and variations in demand.

■ Call a travel agent or use an on-line service that is accessible to check airline fares. Get prices on the same route for 60 days in advance, two weeks, one week, and today. Is there a clear pattern to the fares?

■ When a store is overstocked on ripe fruit, it may lower the price to sell out quickly. What are airlines doing to their prices as the seats get close to 'perishing'? Why? What would you recommend as a pricing strategy to increase total revenues?

# ■ REFERENCES

1. Tony Patey, 'Lufthansa lends an ear to passengers', *The European* (29 April–5 May 1994), 22.
2. 'The manufacturing myth', *The Economist* (19 March 1994), 98–9.
3. See Leonard L. Berry, 'Services marketing is different', *Business* (May–June 1980), 24–30; Eric Langeard, John E. G. Bateson, Christopher H. Lovelock, and Pierre Eiglier, *Services Marketing: New insights from consumers and managers* (Cambridge, MA: Marketing Science Institute, 1981); Karl Albrecht and Ron Zemke, *Service America! Doing Busines in the New Economy* (Homewood, IL: Dow-Jones-Irwin, 1985); Karl Albrecht, *At America's Service* (Homewood, IL: Dow-Jones-Irwin, 1988); and William H. Davidow and Bro Uttal, *Total Customer Service: The ultimate weapon* (New York: Harper & Row, 1989).
4. For more on definitions and classifications of services, see John E. Bateson, *Managing Services Marketing: Text and readings* (Hinsdale, IL: Dryden Press, 1989); and Christopher H. Lovelock, *Services Marketing* (Englewood Cliffs, NJ: Prentice Hall, 1991).
5. See Theodore Levitt, 'Marketing intangible products and product intangibles', *Harvard Business Review*, (May–June, 1981), 94–102.

6.  For more discussion, see James L. Heskett, 'Lessons in the service sector', *Harvard Business Review* (Mar.–Apr. 1987), 122–4.

7.  For more reading on internal and interactive marketing, see Christian Gronroos, 'A service quality model and its marketing implications', *European Journal of Marketing*, **18**, 4 (1984), 36–44; and Leonard Berry, Edwin F. Lefkowith, and Terry Clark, 'In services, what's in a name?', *Harvard Business Review* (Sept.–Oct. 1988), 28–30.

8.  See Joseph Cronin, Jr. and Steven A. Taylore, 'Measuring service quality: a re-examination and extension', *Journal of Marketing* (July 1992), 55–68.

9.  A. Parasuraman, Valarie Zeithaml and Leonard Berry, 'Servqual: a multi-item scale for measuing consumer perceptions of service quality', *Journal of Retailing*, **63** (spring 1988), 12–40; A. Parasuraman, Valarie A. Zeithaml and Leonard L. Berry, 'A conceptual model of service quality and its implications for future research', *Journal of Marketing*, **49** (fall 1985), 41–50; Valarie Zeithaml, Leonard L. Berry and A. Parasuraman, 'Communication and control processes in the delivery of service quality', *Journal of Marketing*, **52** (April 1988), 35–48.

10.  Parasuraman *et al.*, 'A conceptual model', op. cit.

11.  Christopher W. L. Hart, James L. Heskett, and W. Earl Sasser, Jr., 'The profitable art of service recovery', *Harvard Business Review* (July–Aug. 1990), 148–56.

12.  See James L. Heskett, W. Earl Sasser, Jr., and Christopher W. L. Hart, *Service Breakthroughs* (New York: Free Press, 1990).

13.  See Stephen S. Roach, 'Services under siege – the restructuring imperative', *Harvard Business Review* (Sept.–Oct. 1991), 83; and Leonard A Schlesinger and James L. Heskett, 'The service-driven service company', *Harvard Business Review* (Sept.–Oct. 1991), 72–81.

14.  Nora E. Field and Ricardo Sookdeo, 'The global service 500', *Fortune* (26 August 1991), 166–70.

15.  Michael R. Czinkota and Ilkka A. Ronkainen, *International Marketing*, 2nd edn (Chicago: Dryden, 1990), 679.

16.  Lee Smith, 'What's at stake in the trade talks', *Fortune* (27 August 1990), 76–7.

## CASE 15

## Tibigarden: is there life after EuroDisney?

While EuroDisney was facing desperate meetings with their creditors in February 1994, Grand Peninsula was finalizing a deal to build the second biggest theme park in Europe. Their Tibigarden theme park outside Salou, near Tarragona on Spain's Mediterranean coast, needed Pta 41bn* of finance. Grand Peninsula, who owned the theme park, was created by Busch Entertainment. They already operated several theme parks in America as the leisure area of Annheuser Busch, the US beer and food giant.

Given EuroDisney's much publicized problems, it was not surprising that the original investors wanted to spread the risk of the new venture. The final agreement diluted Busch Entertainment's holdings to 20 per cent and would make the British Tussaud's group the largest shareholders (30 per cent) and park's manager. The Tussaud's group is part of Pearson, a communication conglomerate, that owns the *Financial Times* and *The Economist*, as well as big

attractions like Madame Tussaud's, Alton Towers and Warwick Castle. Other shareholders in the venture are: Fesca, a Barcelona-based electricity utility (10 per cent); Grand Tibidaba (20 per cent), a Barcelona holding group; and one other Spanish investor. With the finances in place, the theme park was to open in April 1995, but would this one fail too? EuroDisney omens were not good.

The gift from Michael Eisner (the chairman of Walt Disney) to Jacques Chirac (the then French premier) to mark the signing in 1987 of the agreement to open EuroDisney in France, now seems prophetic. It was an original Disney cartoon of the witch handing the poisoned apple to Snow White. Walt Disney have a 49 per cent stake in the park and it was the strength of their marketing and management reputation that convinced institutional and private investors that the park could not fail. Their past success in opening duplicates of the original Californian Disneyland led them to the idea of European expansion. Walt Disney World in Florida was the world's greatest attraction, and Tokyo

*1 ecu = US$1.26 = Pta161 (Spanish pesetas).

Disneyland, opened in 1984, had 10 million visitors in the first year. Even better, the guests had spent US$355m.* rather than the US$200m. estimated.

Disney had opted for the Marne-La-Vallée site 32 km east of Paris, rather than the south of Spain or London's Docklands, after a massive cross-party effort by the French government. Besides the conservative Jacques Chirac, the planning and building of EuroDisney spanned three socialist prime ministers – Laurent Fabian, Michel Rocard and Edith Cresson. Incentives to Disney included 1,943 hectares of land at a bargain price, an extension of the Paris rail network to the park's location, a promise of a TGV rail link and a soft loan covering 22 per cent (FFr20.8 bn*) of the park's development.

EuroDisney was to be Europe's leading tourist attraction and provide over 10,000 jobs. Hopes ran high and many investors in France, Britain and elsewhere bought shares at FFr72 when floated in 1989. Disney originally bought its shares for FFr10. 'The moment EuroDisney's gates opened', its promoters said, 'visitors would be overwhelmed by the professionalism and artistry of it all. Europeans would flock to the park.' Share prices soared to FFr164 in April 1992 just before the gates opened. 'I wonder what they were all on. I'd like to smoke some', said one financial analyst. Disney planned to make huge profits from reselling land close to the site and intended to open a second theme park in 1996. Predictions showed EuroDisney breaking even in its first year.

By February 1994 Europe's Magic Kingdom was a cultural Chernobyl. The 10.5m. visitors in the first year were only 500,000 short of target, but in the second year the number of visitors did not rise as predicted, but was down to 9.5m. Losses were FFr188m. in 1992 and FFr5.3bn in 1993, the first full year of trading. Worse still, the visitors stayed less than the three days forecast and spent about half the sum expected. The French stayed away and many northern Europeans made EuroDisney a day trip. The huge hotel complex serving EuroDisney had only 55 per cent occupancy and the park was getting adverse publicity. The Parisian weather was cold and damp, food, drinks and goods were expensive, and the hotels were extortionate.

EuroDisney frequently pointed out how unlucky they had been since the park opened. Europe was in a recession and the strong French franc had deterred visitors from Italy and the United Kingdom. Financial

troubles were now causing even more bad publicity. 'Why promise the kids a trip to Disney in summer if you can't be sure it will survive till then,' asked one German newspaper. Before the opening, managers estimated that the resort's labour costs would be 13 per cent of revenues. Rebecca Winnington-Ingram of London's Morgan Stanley merchant bank reckoned that the true figure for 1993 was close to 24 per cent. Disney's hoped-for profits from property development were also thin; little of the forecast Ffr2bn by 1996 has so far arrived.

Lack of magic and the financial structure were killing EuroDisney. The park's operations are self-financing, but it cannot service the FFr20.3bn debt resulting from construction overruns and trading difficulties. Disney agreed to keep the park going, but unless financially restructured it would be out of money 'by spring 1994'. The banks braced themselves for playing high-stakes poker against Mike Eisner – 'Ice Man Mike' as he is known in Hollywood. The costs of failure were awful to both sides. The French government had sunk a lot of money and prestige into the project. Besides the global embarrassment the 10,000 jobs in the park would be hard to replace while unemployment was already high and rising. They could encourage the banks to bail them out. The state-controlled Caisse des Depôts could reduce the 7.8 per cent interest rate on their FFr4.8bn loan.

EuroDisney was an 'albatross' for its US parent, dragging with losses. Disney's main negotiating weapon against the banks was to threaten to close the park. It could afford to do so and the losses made it an economic option. But the banks could gamble that Disney would be unwilling to damage their reputation as one of America's most successful businesses. Disney had already waived its 3 per cent management fee and the banks might ask them to cut their 10 per cent royalty fee on admissions and 5 per cent on food and merchandise sales. With share prices down to FFr30 no one was now expecting to get rich from EuroDisney.

The EuroDisney experience was sobering for Grand Peninsula. Only foolish managers would not have learnt from the debacle. Some had argued that

1 ecu = US$1.26 = FFr 6.47 (French francs).

EuroDisney was a mistake before it opened. It was in the wrong place. Why build fake castles in a continent full of castles, real and fake? French intellectuals' objections to the US culture led them to avoid EuroDisney, but other Europeans do not share their views. They have a more basic question: 'Why go to Paris rather than the real thing in Florida?' The Orlando alternative is no more expensive per night, has better hotels, has sunshine and is simply more fun. Maybe EuroDisney could have succeeded if it had been done differently. According to Rebecca Winnington-Ingram, 'Just because EuroDisney has got problems, it does not mean major theme parks in Europe are bound to fail.' Grand Peninsula aims to succeed by learning from the Paris venture and doing it differently. 'We have put together the profitable end of EuroDisney,' says Ole Bredbery, managing partner of Axel, a Madrid investment bank advising Grand Peninsula.

EuroDisney expected 11m. guests in the first year, where Tibigarden expects to be profitable with only 2.7m. In the next year attendance will rise to 3.5m. and eventually only reach 5m. after expansion. That will still make it the tenth largest non-Disney theme park in the first year and Europe's third largest. Denmark's Tivoli Gardens attract 4.5m. visitors and Sweden's Liseberg 2.8m. Tibigarden is just a theme park. To avoid high fixed costs, plans to build a large beachside hotel and 2,000 'living units' were shelved. Unlike EuroDisney, Tibigarden will not open all year round but for 156 days between April and October. During that time the climate is warm and sunny. More than 15m. already visit the coast within striking distance of the park. Within 200 km of the site there are already 800,000 hotel beds including Benidorm.

Tibigarden's financial structure is slimmer than EuroDisney. The Axel group estimate that EuroDisney's royalties and management fees were over 30 per cent of operating income when the park opened and would rise. In contrast, the combined fee for Busch Entertainment's design and Tussaud's man-

agement was little over 12.4 per cent and scheduled to decline. Finally, France was generally a poor place for theme parks. All but one of France's other theme parks were struggling. The exception was Futurescope, a small park near Poitiers, 330 km south-west of Paris. In 1992 its visitors increased by almost a third to 1.2m. and they made over FFr10m profit on FFr175 sales.

What accounts for Futurescope's success? It was cheap to build, has admission prices (FFr120 a day) almost half that of EuroDisney and provides accommodation for as little as FFr60 a night. Its educational high tech appeals to parents and kids and promotes itself through direct mailing to societies and schools. Futurescope is a successful operation but it is quite different from the conventional theme parks like EuroDisney and Tibigarden.

## Questions

1. What accounts for EuroDisney's failure to date? Would EuroDisney have worked if located elsewhere in Europe?
2. Were EuroDisney problems foreseeable? If so, why were they not seen? Are they solvable now? Will changing the name to Disneyland, Paris help?
3. Contrast the Tibigarden proposal with EuroDisney. What are the differences and does any give Tibigarden an advantage over EuroDisney?
4. Is the European theme park market already oversubscribed? Will Tibigarden succeed despite the failure of EuroDisney and the other theme parks in France?

Sources: Toni Burns, 'Riding the theme park roller coaster', *Financial Times* (14 February 1994), 15; Alice Rawsthorn, 'Only a month to make the refinancing fly', *Financial Times* (1 March 1994), 23; 'EuroDisney: waiting for Dumbo', *The Economist* (1 May 1993), 86; 'EuroDisney's plight worsens', *The European* (4–10 February 1994), 1; John Ridding, 'EuroDisney suffers huge loss', *Financial Times* (11 November 1993), 1; Mickael Skapinher and John Ridding, 'Unlucky or unwise', *Financial Times* (13–14 November 1993), 4; Alice Rawsthorn, 'Poisoned apple within the magic kingdom', *Financial Times* (25 November 1993), 6; 'Meltdown at the cultural Chernobyl', *The Economist* (5 February 1994) 69–70; 'A profitable theme', *The Economist* (1 May 1993), 86.

# Mapanza Breweries

*Hapenga M. Kabeta*[*]

The marketing and public relations manager of Mapanza Breweries Ltd lamented the pressure of foreign competition on his 'Kafue lager beer', a drink very popular in Zambia for over thirty years. He wondered how he could effectively counteract competition from the foreign, high-quality lager beers. He commissioned research to give him some insight into this and other marketing-mix questions, including the issues of beer consumption and preference patterns.

## ZAMBIA

The Republic of Zambia is a land-locked country lying close to the heart of Africa. It is mostly high-plateau country covered with thick forest drained by several important rivers. The Zambezi River includes the Victoria Falls and the huge artificial Lake Kariba, both bordering on Zimbabwe. In 1994 Zambia had an estimated population of 8.4 million inhabitants of which 98 per cent are members of Bantu-speaking ethnic groups. However, the official language is English and 70 per cent of the population is Christian; the rest follow traditional beliefs. With 53 per cent of this population living in urban areas it is the most urbanized country in sub-Saharan Africa. The economic growth rate of 3.6 per cent per annum is very high by African standards, and counterbalances the natural population increase of 3.7 per cent. Zambia's economy depends almost entirely on mineral extraction, notably copper. The urban population concentrates along the railway lines that serve the mines.

Zambia has a mixed economy. Between 1975 and 1991 the public sector controlled about 80 per cent of economic activity. The chairperson of the board of directors of the holding company of this state conglomerate is the President of the Republic of Zambia. Mapanza Breweries is a monopoly and a subsidiary of this holding company. In October 1991 a new government came into office after democractic presidential and general elections. The new government introduced market-based policies of liberalization and privatization, and adopted International Monetary Fund (IMF) and World Bank policies that encourage competition and the freeing of controls on foreign exchange. All policies that protected local industries disappeared in favour of freer trade. Zambia is also a member of both the Common Market for Eastern and Southern Africa (COMESA), aimed at regional economic integration and more free trade among COMESA members, and the General Agreement

*The Copperbelt University, Kitwe, Zambia.

on Tariffs and Trade (GATT), aimed at eliminating trade barriers and unfair trade practices.

## IMPORTED BEERS

Until recently Mapanza Breweries had a monopoly on the local brewing industry of clear beer. Now, following deregulation of the market, it is no longer protected from foreign competition by high tariff barriers. New policies have created a highly competitive market in beer. There is an influx of competing brands of lager beer from Zimbabwe and South Africa, brewed under licence and including such world brands as Carling Black Label and Heineken. Imported African brands, again coming mainly from Zimbabwe and South Africa, include Castle Lager, Lion Lager, Zambezi Lager, Olhssons and Castle Milk Stout. A new Zambian brand, Opaque, with hygienic disposable packaging has also appeared. This new competition and changing environment means Mapanza Breweries have to monitor the changes and respond.

## MAPANZA BREWERIES' POSITION

Mapanza Breweries had two plants, in Lusaka and Ndola, supplying their Kafue lager to all parts of Zambia. Kafue lager remains Zambia's most popular alcoholic drink and gives Mapanza Breweries about 60 per cent of the market. Local brews like Shake Shake, Chibuku and other traditional brews represent 30 per cent of consumption, with the remaining 10 per cent being shared evenly between brands from Zimbabwe and South Africa. However, imports are increasing their share of the market.

In 1993, Mapanza Breweries produced 88.5 million litres of Kafue lager, up from about 8 million litres ten years ago. However, the plants at both Ndola and Lusaka are very old and preventive maintenance is largely absent. As a result, production capacity is about 40 per cent of the installed capacity. Following deregulation of the market, a leading South African brewery bought the Lusaka plant and has promised to invest about ZK700 million in it. The new owners want to make Mapanza Breweries compete effectively against foreign brewers. The Lusaka plant has retained the Mapanza Breweries name while the Ndola plant is being advertised for privatization as Mukuba Breweries.

1 ecu = US$1.26 = ZK125 (Zambian kwacha) although annual inflation has approached 100 per cent in recent years.

## DISTRIBUTION

The distribution network in Zambia's brewing industry is mainly a direct route from manufacturer to bars, restaurants, hotels, motels, bottle stores, and so forth. Some produce goes through distributors, some of whom are wholesalers. Since Mapanza Breweries has depots in all provincial centres and rural districts, it uses few wholesalers. In the past Mapanza Breweries has found dealers and wholesalers to be very costly. Normally distributors and wholesalers handle imported beers, although some retailers procure goods directly from Zimbabwe and South Africa.

Bars are the predominant outlet in Zambia; in 1992, they sold on average fifty crates of Kafue lager to one case of imported lager. The ratio is different in hotels, which sell more imported lagers.

## PRODUCTS

Mapanza Breweries brews and bottles the Kafue brand of lager beer in 375 and 300 ml bottles. The dumpy bottle was launched in late 1992 to counteract imported lager. The packaging of Kafue is a plain brown bottle with a label and cap. The alcohol content is about 4.5 per cent, but it has a very short shelf life, a fact not disclosed on the label. In contrast, imported lagers are attractively packaged and usually have an alcohol content of 5 per cent. Nevertheless, a survey of 3,770 people showed that 'Kafue' retains a good image amongst some high- and middle-income groups of the population (see Exhibit 5.1), although this figure is lower than the brand's historic market share. When asked how they thought Kafue lager should be improved, the responses given varied with age (see Exhibit 5.2). Overall 38 per cent wanted an improved taste, but this figure rose to 69 per cent among younger people. Similarly, 60 per cent of the respondents wanted the alcohol content to be increased, a desire particularly strong amongst the under 35-year olds. Forty-two per cent would prefer Kafue canned while only 22 per cent preferred the dumpy bottle (see Exhibit 5.3). The packaging of all imported lager is either canned or in dumpy bottles with labels that consumers thought were very attractive and informative.

Mapanza Breweries' management thought that imported lagers reflected status position in society. Exhibit 5.4 shows consumers' perceptions of Kafue lager's packaging, price and availability relative to imported lagers. Kafue lager does relatively poorly on packaging and quality but well on availability. Although it is reasonably cheap, customers still feel that Kafue is too costly for a locally produced product.

**Exhibit 5.1**  Product preference amongst high and low income earners (% of respondents)

| Product | High income over ZK50,000* | Low income below ZK50,000* |
|---|---|---|
| Kafue lager | 40 | 48 |
| Imported lager | 25 | 11 |
| Spirits | 3 | 1 |
| Opaque/traditional brews | 32 | 40 |

Note: *Income per month.
Source: Research conducted by Samson Sakala and the author.

**Exhibit 5.2**  Desired improvements in Kafue

| Attribute | Respondents Age | % |
|---|---|---|
| Taste | Overall | 38 |
| | 18–35 years | 69 |
| | Over 36 | 31 |
| Alcohol content | Overall | 60 |
| | 19–35 years | 70 |
| | Over 36 | 31 |
| Colour | Overall | 5 |
| Flavour | Overall | 21 |

Source: Research conducted by Samson Sakala and the author.

**Exhibit 5.3**   Preferred packaging for Kafue

| Type of packaging | % |
|---|---|
| Current bottle (375 ml) | 17 |
| Plastic pack | 2 |
| Draught | 3 |
| Can | 42 |
| Dumpy | 22 |
| Others | 14 |

Source: Research conducted by Samson Sakala and the author.

**Exhibit 5.4**   Overall perception of Kafue (% of respondents)

| Level | Packaging | Quality | Price | Availability |
|---|---|---|---|---|
| Very Good | 13 | 21 | 8 | 46 |
| Good | 3 | 40 | 17 | 37 |
| Fair | 31 | 21 | 34 | 10 |
| Poor | 8 | 2 | 18 | 2 |
| Very Poor | 1 | 1 | 8 | 1 |

Source: Research conducted by Samson Sakala and the author.

## PRICE

In 1992 the price of Kafue (ZK350) was lower than imported lagers (ZK550). Up to that time the imported lagers had kept their prices down by evading customs duty and receiving a 20 per cent subsidy from their producers in Zimbabwe and South Africa. To counter this the Zambian government established the Zambia Revenue Authority (ZRA) to ensure full collection of all taxes and duties. Now, all lager importers pay tax. Mapanza Breweries also proved a 'dumping' case against the imported lagers and, in response, the government introduced an extra 20 per cent duty on them. As a result, by 1994 imported lagers were retailing at ZK750 compared with Kafue at ZK350. However, since the high income groups perceive imported lagers as of higher quality than Kafue, the demand for imported lager has not changed much.

## PROMOTION

Between 1975 and 1990 an unwritten law restricted advertising of alcohol, and so the only forms of publicity used by Mapanza Breweries were billboard and sports sponsorship. Since deregulation Mapanza Breweries has advertised on radio, television and newspapers. So far, sales promotions are rare.

Being used to having a monopoly, Mapanza Breweries has had difficulties in adjusting to the new competition. The marketing and public relations manager knows that he needs an effective marketing strategy to counteract competitive manoeuvres in the industry. He also knows that at least one new multinational company is entering the industry. Thus he needs to develop a marketing strategy soon to strengthen Mapanza Breweries' position in the market before yet another competitor arrives.

## QUESTIONS

1. What are the problems facing Mapanza Breweries in the marketplace? What are the brewery's main weaknesses and main strengths?
2. How should Mapanza Breweries respond to the threat from imported lagers? Should it change Kafue lager so that it competes with them more directly, or seek to avoid competition?
3. Mapanza Breweries have many ways they could develop Kafue but it is unlikely that they could do them all at once. What changes would you advise and how would you prioritize them? Which changes are likely to increase Kafue's sales most, and which are likely to cost most to implement?
4. Should Mapanza Breweries increase their product range? If so, what products should they introduce and how should they be positioned? What is the most important dimension in the beer market: the product, its taste, its strength, its packaging, its distribution or its image?

# Price

Price

## CHAPTER SIXTEEN

# Pricing products

## Pricing considerations and approaches

## CHAPTER OBJECTIVES

After reading this chapter, you should be able to:

- Understand the internal and external factors affecting price.

- Explain the impact of cost on price.

- See how market structures influence price setting.

- Compare and evaluate the general approaches to price setting.

## CHAPTER PREVIEW

### *The Times:* for a change

1 ecu = UK£0.83
= 83p

*The Times*' price cut from 45p to 30p in July 1993 shook Britain's quality newspaper industry. Rupert Murdoch's News International, whose *Times* newspaper had a circulation of 360,000, had declared war on the other quality daily newspapers: the *Daily Telegraph* (circulation 1,017,000), the *Guardian* (403,000), the *Independent* (336,000) and the *Financial Times* (288,000). It was not the first time News International (NI) had started a price war. NI, who own five of Britain's national papers as well as many others around the world, had already cut the price of their *Sun* tabloid newspaper from 25 to 20p. The move had consolidated the *Sun*'s position as market leader pushing up circulation from 3.43m. to 4.10m. within a year. Sales of the *Sun*'s chief competitor, the *Daily Mirror* dropped from 2.67m. to 2.50m. over the same period. People have very strong relationships to their daily newspapers and, given the papers' different political leanings, many in the industry thought the quality papers were not price sensitive. NI clearly thought otherwise. 'Obviously we would like to push it [*The Times*] to the same [circulation] level as the *Telegraph* and beyond,' said Gus Fischer, chief executive of NI.

Very soon NI were proved right. By April 1994 the *Times'* circulation had grown to 478,000 while most of the others had gone down: *Telegraph*, 999,000; *Guardian*, 397,000; and *Independent* 271,000. The specialist and expensive (65p) *Financial Times* was not affected at all; the left of centre *Guardian* and right of centre *Telegraph* saw sales drop a little, while the *Independent*, who had increased their price to 50p in response to *The Times'* price cut, had a 20 per cent sales drop. After an initial short-term sales decline, the mid-market dailies, *Today*, *Daily Express* and *Daily Mail*, were unaffected by the low prices of the *Sun* and *The Times*.

Before the price cut the quality newspapers had competed in other ways. Throughout the 1980s their strategy was to improve the product by adding sections. According to one senior executive, 'The daily market has been contracting every year. We have been almost excessively focused on sales promotion to encourage trial from rival papers. We hoped that the added value products would keep our readers more loyal.' But to the consumers, more did not mean better. Most of the brand extensions (supplements) were created to attract advertising revenue; not to keep readers' loyalty. By offering the advertisers 'high definition, high quality' targets, publishers had taken their eyes off the circulation figures. Wooing new advertisers did not keep customers happy. Increased pagination meant paper bills went up and consumers were frustrated at not being able to 'get through the paper' at one sitting. Loyalty was declining before *The Times'* price cut but its true magnitude only became known later. Analysis of Taylor Nelson AGB's Mediaspan panel showed that newspapers lose and gain at least 20 per cent of their 'loyal readers' each year. This switching excludes casual readers since loyal readers are defined as those 'almost always reading' a paper. Following the price cut, *The Times'* users showed much lower loyalty than usual. The paper boosted its regular readership by two-thirds, but one-third of the regular 1993 readership was lost by 1994. Further analysis in May 1994 using RSGB's Conversion Model showed that about half the readers of all quality newspapers were 'safe' (entrenched or average loyalty) while the rest of the readers were 'vulnerable' (shallow or convertible). The study also showed that *The Times* had fewer entrenched readers than the other quality newspapers.

After *The Times'* price cut the quality newspapers had fought hard to keep their customers. The *Telegraph* offered free books to people who collected tokens printed in the paper and the cash-strapped *Independent* ran a promotion competition with the prize equal to the winner's income tax bill. But the *Independent's* lost circulation hurt and cash was running out. When newspapers lose circulation two forms of income drop: income from the cover price, and advertising revenue. The fewer the readers, the lower the advertising rates. *The Independent* was the newest of the quality newspapers and also financially the weakest. Founded by the brilliant entrepreneur and editor, Whittam Smith, the *Independent's* biggest shareholders were Italy's *La Repubblica* and Spain's *El Pais* newspapers, neither very rich. After initially taking the market by storm the paper overextended itself on an overexpensive launch of the *Independent on Sunday* and a failed attempt to take over the *Observer*, another Sunday paper.

If it was to survive the circulation war, the *Independent* needed more money. Surprisingly for a newspaper facing a price war, there were three prospective new partners. One was Tony O'Reilly, Irish chairman of Heinz and owner of Independent Newspapers; another was Conrad Black, Canadian proprietor of the *Telegraph*; the third was Newspaper Publishing, publishers of the *Daily Mirror*. After reassuring the *Independent* about editorial independence, Newspaper Publishing bought the *Independent* and the battle continued.

After holding their prices up for eight months after *The Times'* first price cut, on 22 June 1994 Conrad Black cut the *Telegraph's* price from 48p to match *The Times* at 30p. *The Times* quickly responded with a cut to 20p two days later, determined to hang on to the 150,000 extra buyers from its first price cut. On that day the *Independent's* Whittam Smith moved his editorial to the front page accusing *The Times* of predatory pricing. 'Two right-wing ideologues, Rupert Murdoch and Conrad Black, have set about to destroy the quality newspaper market,' he thundered. NI were thought to be losing £45m. from their earlier price cutting of *The Times* and the *Sun*. Lost profits at *The Times* were thought to be about £17m. The extra cut to 20p would cost £12m. more a year if retailers were to maintain their current 17p a copy, and with printing costs running at 13p a copy. Shareholders were also unimpressed by the *Telegraph*'s action: £800m was wiped off the share value of the newspaper as a whole and it lost £200m. in value. The City were particularly angered since Conrad Black's Hollinger Group had sold 12.5m. shares, raising £73m., barely a month before the price cut.

In August 1994 the *Independent* caved in and reduced their price. Sales by then were as follows: *Telegraph*, 1,010,000; *The Times*, 510,000; *Guardian*, 400,000; and *Independent* 280,000. After market testing prices of 45p and 40p the *Independent* exceeded City expectations and cut their price to 30p. Newspaper International stressed the newspaper would not remain at 30p indefinitely – a move that would cost the newspaper £14m. per year in lost revenue. 'It is felt that the premium quality that the *Independent* achieves will, in the longer term, warrant a premium cover price,' said its editorial.[1]

## NAMING THE PRICE

All profit organizations and many non-profit organizations must set prices on their products or services. *Price* goes by many names:

> Price is all around us. You pay *rent* for your apartment, *tuition* for your education and a *fee* to your physician or dentist. The airline, railway, taxi and bus companies charge you a *fare*; the local utilities call their price a *rate*; and the local bank charges you *interest* for the money you borrow … The guest lecturer charges an *honorarium* to tell you about a government official who took a *bribe* to help a shady character steal *dues* collected by a trade association. Clubs or societies to which you belong may make a special *assessment* to pay unusual expenses. Your regular lawyer may ask for a *retainer* to cover her services. The 'price' of an executive is a *salary*, the price of a salesperson may be a *commission* and the price of a worker is a *wage*. Finally, although economists would disagree, many of us feel that *income taxes* are the price we pay for the privilege of making money.[2]

In the narrowest sense, **price** is the amount of money charged for a product or service. More broadly, price is the sum of all the values that consumers exchange for the benefits of having or using the product or service.

How are prices set? Historically, prices usually were set by buyers and sellers bargaining with each other. Sellers would ask for a higher price than they expected to get and buyers would offer less than they expected to pay. Through bargaining, they would arrive at an acceptable price. Individual buyers paid different prices for the same products, depending on their needs and bargaining skills.

Today, most sellers set *one* price for *all* buyers. Large-scale retailing led to the idea at the end of the nineteenth century. F. W. Woolworth and other retailers advertised a 'strictly one-price policy' because they carried so many items and had so many employees.

Historically, price has been the most significant factor affecting buyer choice. This is still true in poorer nations, among poorer groups and with commodity products. However, nonprice factors have become more important in buyer-choice behaviour in recent decades.

Price is the only element in the marketing mix that produces revenue; all other elements represent costs. Price is also one of the most flexible elements of the marketing mix. Unlike product features and channel commitments, price can be changed quickly. At the same time, pricing and price competition is the number-one problem facing many marketing executives. Yet many companies do not handle pricing well. The most common mistakes are: pricing that is too cost-oriented; prices that are not revised often enough to reflect market changes; pricing that does not take the rest of the marketing mix into account; and prices that are not varied enough for different products, market segments and purchase occasions.

In this and the next chapter, we focus on the problem of setting prices. This chapter looks at the factors marketers must consider when setting prices and at general pricing approaches. In the next chapter, we examine pricing strategies for new-product pricing, product mix pricing, price changes and price adjustments for buyer and situational factors.

## FACTORS TO CONSIDER WHEN SETTING PRICES

A company's pricing decisions are affected both by internal company factors and external environmental factors (see Figure 16.1).[3]

### Internal factors affecting pricing decisions

Internal factors affecting pricing include the company's marketing objectives, marketing-mix strategy, costs and organization.

#### Marketing objectives

Before setting price, the company must decide on its strategy for the product. If the company has selected its target market and positioning carefully, then its marketing-mix strategy, including price, will be fairly straightforward. For example, if Toyota decides to produce its Lexus cars to compete with European luxury cars in the high-income segment, this suggests charging a high price. Travel Lodge positions itself as motels that provide economical rooms for budget-minded travellers; this position requires charging a low price. Thus pricing strategy is largely determined by past decisions on market positioning.

At the same time, the company may seek additional objectives. The clearer a firm is about its objectives, the easier it is to set price. Examples of common objectives are *survival*, *current profit maximization*, *market-share maximization* and *product-quality leadership*.

Companies set *survival* as their fundamental objective if they are troubled by too much capacity, heavy competition or changing consumer wants. In Europe and Japan steel-makers sell steel at a loss as demand declines. To keep a plant going, a company may set a low price, hoping to increase demand. In this case, profits are less important than survival. As long as their prices cover variable costs and some fixed

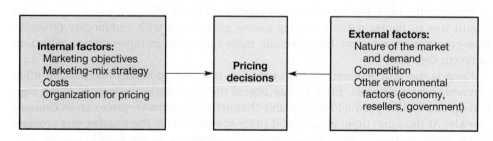

**Figure 16.1**  Factors affecting price decisions.

costs, they can stay in business. However, survival is only a short-term objective. In the long run, the firm must learn how to add value or face extinction.[4]

Many companies use *current profit maximization* as their pricing goal. They estimate what demand and costs will be at different prices and choose the price that will produce the maximum current profit, cash flow or return on investment. In all cases, the company wants current financial results rather than long-run performance. Other companies want to obtain *market-share leadership*. They believe that the company with the largest market share will enjoy the lowest costs and highest long-run profit. To become the market-share leader, these firms set prices as low as possible. A variation of this objective is to pursue a specific market-share gain. Say the company wants to increase its market share from 10 per cent to 15 per cent in one year. It will search for the price and marketing programme that will achieve this goal.

A company might decide that it wants to achieve product-quality leadership. This normally calls for charging a high price to cover such quality and the high cost of R&D:

> For example, Jaguar's limited edition XJ220 sold for £400,000 each but had wealthy customers queuing to buy one. Less exotically, Pitney Bowes pursues a product-quality leadership strategy for its fax equipment. While Sharp, Canon and other competitors fight over the low-price fax machine market with machines selling at around $500, Pitney Bowes targets large corporations with machines selling at about $5,000. As a result, it captures some 45 per cent of the large-corporation fax niche.[5]

1 ecu = US$1.26 = UK£0.83

A company might also use price to attain other more specific objectives. It can set prices low to prevent competition from entering the market or set prices at competitors' levels to stabilize the market:

> In 1994 grocery market leaders Sainsbury and Tesco used 'Essentials' and 'Everyday super value range' campaigns to counter the attack of discounters Aldi and Netto on the UK market. Originally projected to take 20 per cent of the grocery market by the year 2000, forecasters later predicted the discounters would take only 12 per cent.[6]

Prices can be set to keep the loyalty and support of resellers or to avoid government intervention. Prices can be reduced temporarily to create excitement for a product or to draw more customers into a retail store. One product may be priced to help the sales of other products in the company's line. Thus pricing may play an important role in helping to accomplish the company's objectives at many levels.

Non-profit and public organizations may adopt a number of other pricing objectives. A university aims for *partial cost recovery*, knowing that it must rely on private gifts and public grants to cover the remaining costs. A non-profit hospital may aim for *full cost recovery* in its pricing. A non-profit theatre company may price its productions to fill the maximum number of theatre seats. A social service agency may set a *social price* geared to the varying income situations of different clients.

## Marketing-mix strategy

Price is only one of the marketing-mix tools that a company uses to achieve its marketing objectives. Price decisions must be coordinated with product design, distribution and promotion decisions to form a consistent and effective marketing programme. Decisions made for other marketing-mix variables may affect pricing decisions. For example, producers using many resellers who are expected to support and promote their products may have to build larger reseller margins into their prices. The decision to position the product on high performance quality will mean that the seller must charge a higher price to cover higher costs. The perfume houses argue that their high margins, expensive advertising and exclusive distribution are essential to the brands and in the public interest.[7]

Companies often make their pricing decisions first and then base other marketing-mix decisions on the prices they want to charge. Here, price is a crucial product-positioning factor that defines the product's market, competition and design. The intended price determines what product features can be offered and what production costs can be incurred.

Many firms support such price-positioning strategies with a technique called **target costing**, a potent strategic weapon. Target costing reverses the usual process of first designing a new product, determining its cost and then asking 'Can we sell it for that?' Instead, it starts with a target cost and works back:

> Compaq Computer Corporation calls this process 'design to price'. After being battered for years by lower-priced rivals, Compaq used this approach to create its highly successful, lower-priced Prolinea personal computer line. Starting with a price target set by marketing and with profit-margin goals from management, the Prolinea design team determined what costs *had* to be in order to charge the target price. From this crucial calculation all else followed. To achieve target costs, the design team negotiated doggedly with all the company departments responsible for different aspects of the new product and with outside suppliers of needed parts and materials. Compaq engineers designed a machine with fewer and simpler parts, manufacturing overhauled its factories to reduce production costs and suppliers found ways to provide quality components at needed prices. By meeting its target *costs*, Compaq was able to set its target *price* and establish the desired price position. As a result, Prolinea sales and profits soared.[8]

Other companies deemphasize price and use other marketing-mix tools to create *nonprice* positions. Often, the best strategy is not to charge the lowest price, but rather to differentiate the marketing offer to make it worth a higher price (see Marketing Highlight 16.1).

> For example, in the US Johnson Controls, a producer of climate control systems for office buildings, used initial price as its primary competitive tool. However, research showed that customers were more concerned about the total cost of installing and maintaining a system than about its initial price. Repairing broken systems was expensive, time-consuming and risky. Customers had to shut down the heat or air conditioning in the whole building, disconnect a lot of wires and face the dangers of electrocution. Johnson decided to change its strategy. It designed an entirely new system called Metasys. To repair the new system, customers need only pull out an old plastic module and slip in a new one – no tools required. Metasys costs more to make than the old system and customers pay a higher initial price, but it costs less to install and maintain. Despite its higher asking price, the new Metasys system brought in $500 million in revenues in its first year.[9]

Thus the marketer must consider the total marketing mix when setting prices. If the product is positioned on nonprice factors, then decisions about quality, promotion and distribution will strongly affect price. If price is a crucial positioning factor, then price will strongly affect decisions made about the other marketing-mix elements. In most cases, the company will consider all the marketing-mix decisions together when developing the marketing programme.

## Costs

Costs set the floor for the price that the company can charge for its product. The company wants to charge a price that both covers all its costs for producing, distributing and selling the product and delivers a fair rate of return for its effort and risk. A company's costs may be an important element in its pricing strategy. Many companies work to become the 'low-cost producers' in their industries. Companies with lower costs can set lower prices that result in greater sales and profits (see Marketing Highlight 16.1).

*Types of Costs*    A company's costs take two forms, fixed and variable. **Fixed costs** (also known as overhead) are costs that do not vary with production or sales level. For example, a company must pay each month's bills for rent, heat, interest and executive salaries, whatever the company's output.

**Variable costs** vary directly with the level of production. Each personal computer produced by Compaq involves a cost of computer chips, wires, plastic, packaging and other inputs. These costs tend to be the same for each unit produced. They are called variable because their total varies with the number of units produced.

**Total costs** are the sum of the fixed and variable costs for any given level of production. Management wants to charge a price that will at least cover the total production costs at a given level of production. The company must watch its costs carefully. If it costs the company more than competitors to produce and sell its product, the company will have to charge a higher price or make less profit, putting it at a competitive disadvantage.

*Costs at different levels of production*    To price wisely, management needs to know how its costs vary with different levels of production. Glen Dimplex, the Irish domestic appliance company who own Murphy Richards, Dimplex and Belling, have taken over Roberts, Britain's maker of high-quality radios. As part of their plan to add new and innovative products to the Roberts range they could build a plant to produce 1,000 Roberts luxury travel clocks per day. Figure 16.2A shows the typical short-run average cost curve (SRAC). It shows that the cost per clock is high if Roberts' factory produces only a few per day. But as production moves up to 1,000 clocks per day, average cost falls. This is because fixed costs are spread over more units, with each one bearing a smaller fixed cost. Roberts can try to produce more than 1,000 clocks per day, but average costs will increase because the plant becomes inefficient. Workers have to wait for machines, the machines break down more often and workers get in each other's way.

If Roberts believed it could sell 2,000 clocks a day, it should consider building a larger plant. The plant would use more efficient machinery and work arrangements. Also, the unit cost of producing 2,000 units per day would be lower than the unit cost of producing 1,000 units per day, as shown in the long-run average cost (LRAC) curve (Figure 16.2B). In fact, a 3,000-capacity plant would be even more efficient, according to Figure 16.2B. But a 4,000 daily production plant would be less efficient because

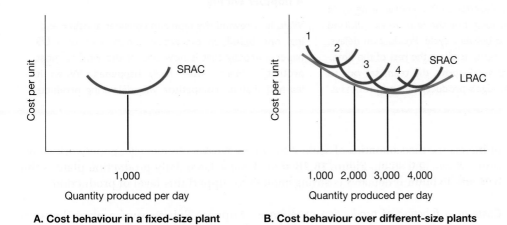

A. Cost behaviour in a fixed-size plant    B. Cost behaviour over different-size plants

**Figure 16.2**    Cost per unit at different levels of production.

# A pricing fable

Once upon a time there was a successful manufacturer of speciality papers called the Woodbridge Company. Woodbridge made coloured papers used by the food industry for packaging soup, ketchup, and food products. For years, it dominated its market. Woodbridge kept its customers happy, from the printers who bought paper directly, to the food companies who bought labels from the printers.

One day, however, a loyal customer – a local printer – informed Woodbridge that it was thinking of switching its business to a competitor, Mountain View Papers. According to the customer, Mountain View charged lower prices. Moreover the competitor could deliver on orders in only one week, compared with Woodbridge's four-week lead time. A few weeks later, another key customer, a soup manufacturer, lodged a similar complaint: 'We find that Mountain View can resupply us more quickly and cheaply when we run out of packages during promotions. We plan to switch about 40 per cent of our business to them.'

Woodbridge immediately set up a management team to investigate. The team learned that much of the problem resulted from Woodbridge's large product line. Woodbridge carried some 440 items, compared with only 140 for Mountain View and 240 for its other main competitor, Hyde Park Paper. Neither competitor offered special papers such as shiny vermilion and shamrock green, which Woodbridge ran in very small quantities, causing its setup time and costs to skyrocket. The team eventually discovered that 35 per cent of Woodbridge's products were unprofitable, low-volume items. Woodbridge's manufacturing cycle was only two days long; not the four weeks allotted for the full order-to-delivery cycle. Production delays, paper shuffling, and setup took up the rest of the time.

After identifying weak spots, the team set out to streamline Woodbridge's product line and processes.

It dropped shiny vermilion, shamrock green, and other low-volume papers. After just three months, Woodbridge had reduced its order-to-delivery cycle to only one and a half weeks, and had dropped prices to competitors' levels. Encouraged by this success, Woodbridge continued its quest to match competitors' processes, efficiency, and prices. Soon, the angry phone calls from customers had stopped. Market share, which had fallen at the rate of about 1 per cent per month for six months, stabilized. Everyone celebrated.

## An unhappy ending

End of the story? Well, not quite. Within a year, a frightening new marketplace pattern had emerged. Lead time was now the same for all competitors: about one week. After waves of product-line pruning by Woodbridge, the competitors' product lines looked alike and customers now ranked the three suppliers about equally on quality and customer service. The term *commodity* raised its ugly head. The three companies took turns initiating price cuts, and each met the others' prices as a matter of policy. Narrowing the Woodbridge product line had taken a heavy toll. 'All we've got to compete on now is price,' complained Woodbridge's marketers. Industry wide prices and margins declined steadily. Seven years later, all competitors were struggling to make even meagre profits.

## A happier ending

Wait, let's rewind the tape and consider another ending, one based on the actual experiences of a US paper company that is now one of the world's most profitable. Here's what *really* happened. When it learned that its competitor was delivering products

of increasing diseconomies of scale – too many workers to manage, paperwork slows things down and so on. Figure 16.2B shows that a 3,000 daily production plant is the best size to build if demand is strong enough to support this level of production.

*Costs as a function of production experience*    Suppose Roberts runs a plant that produces 3,000 clocks per day. As Roberts gains experience in producing hand-held clocks, it learns how to do it better. Workers learn short cuts and become more famil-

faster and at lower prices, Woodbridge invited the unhappy soup manufacturer and the local printer to a meeting to discuss their concerns. They learned that the soup manufacturer faced problems in handling promotions. 'We never know how successful we'll be until the promotion hits the stores,' commented one soup executive. 'When the promotion is successful, we run out of stock, costing us big money in lost sales and profits. The problem is that the printer can't print packages fast enough to avoid stock outs.'

'That's true,' the printer conceded, 'but we aren't the problem. We have old printing presses we could use if we could get paper faster. But Woodbridge takes four weeks to deliver.' Woodbridge's manufacturing vice president offered a solution. 'You know,' he said, 'we have an old paper machine we don't use anymore. It's not the fastest or cheapest machine. But it could help us in these situations.' The three managers quickly sketched out a system for handling stock-out emergencies.

The Woodbridge managers also learned that the manufacturer faced an increasingly competitive and fragmented market. 'The trick is to make our products stand out on the shelf,' noted the soup executive. 'In addition, we need to tailor our packages to the preferences of different markets. For example, consumers in Holland love red cans. In France, they prefer dark green. Dealing with this fragmentation is a nightmare.' Woodbridge's manufacturing vice president nodded. 'We have a similar problem,' he said. 'Our shiny vermilion, which must be for your Dutch market, is very hard to make. So is shamrock green. Actually, we're losing our shirt on those papers and are thinking about dropping them.'

'If you do that' the soup maker warned, 'you'll be like every other supplier. We might as well buy from whichever supplier charges the lowest price.' After a few moments of reflection, he added, 'But maybe we and the printer can agree on a higher price that makes these low-volume items more profitable for you.'

Within the next few months, Woodbridge redesigned its manufacturing system around the newly discovered customer needs. First, it set up the old paper machine for rush jobs. Next, it dedicated one of its smaller machines to making special, small-volume papers. Everyone involved agreed that Woodbridge would charge a premium price for these rush orders and special papers. Finally, Woodbridge devoted the rest of its machines to large-volume items, allowing it to dramatically reduce lead times and prices on these items.

Three years later, Mountain View announced that it was selling its coloured-packaging-paper business. Woodbridge had successfully stripped Mountain View of its only weapons – lower prices and shorter delivery times on high-volume products. At the same time, Woodbridge had bettered Mountain View by offering a fuller product line – now numbering 520 items – that closely matched the needs of soup manufacturers facing highly fragmented markets. Woodbridge succeeded not by *matching* Mountain View's prices and products, but by *differentiating* its offer to create greater value, even though many of its prices were higher. Woodbridge had beaten the competition by understanding its customers and they all lived happily ever after.

Lesson: if you do not know your customers, you will end up giving them something for nothing.

Sources: Based on portions of Francis J. Gouillart and Frederick D. Sturdivant, 'Spend a day in the life of your customers', *Harvard Business Review* (Jan.–Feb. 1994), 116–25; see also Minda Zetlin, 'Kicking the discount habit', *Sales & Marketing Management* (May 1994), 102–5.

iar with their equipment. With practice, the work becomes better organized and Roberts finds better equipment and production processes. With higher volume, Roberts becomes more efficient and gains economies of scale. As a result, average cost tends to fall with accumulated production experience. This is shown in Figure 16.3.[10] Thus the average cost of producing the first 100,000 clocks is I£10 per clock. When the company has produced the first 200,000 clocks, the average cost has fallen to I£9. After its accumulated production experience doubles again to 400,000,

1 ecu = US$1.26 = I£0.81 (Irish punt)

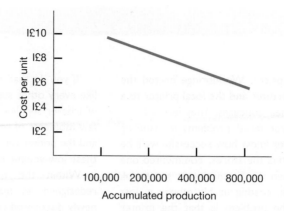

**Figure 16.3**  Cost per unit as a function of accumulated production: the experience curve.

the average cost is I£7. This drop in the average cost with accumulated production experience is called the **experience curve** (or the **learning curve**).

If a downward-sloping experience curve exists, this is highly significant for the company. Not only will the company's unit production cost fall, it will fall faster if the company makes and sells more during a given time period. But the market has to stand ready to buy the higher output. And to take advantage of the experience curve, Roberts must get a large market share early in the product's life cycle. This suggests the following pricing strategy. Roberts should price its clocks low; its sales will then increase and its costs will decrease through gaining more experience, and then it can lower its prices further.

Some companies have built successful strategies around the experience curve. For example, during the 1980s, Bausch & Lomb consolidated its position in the soft contact lens market by using computerized lens design and steadily expanding its one Soflens plant. As a result, its market share climbed steadily to 65 per cent. Yet a single-minded focus on reducing costs and exploiting the experience curve will not always work. Experience curves became somewhat of a fad during the 1970s and like many fads, the strategy was sometimes misused. Experience-curve pricing carries some serious risks. The aggressive pricing might give the product a cheap image. The strategy also assumes that competitors are weak and not willing to fight it out by meeting the company's price cuts.

> 1 ecu = US$1.26 = ¥122 (Japanese yen)
>
> An 'experience curve war' broke out between the Japanese makers of DRAM (dynamic random-access memory) chips, the semiconductor memory devices used in computers. Hitachi, Toshiba, NEC and Mitsubishi reduced the price of their 4-megabyte DRAMs from ¥12,000 to ¥2,500 within a year of its launch at the same time spending heavily to develop the next generation's 16-megabyte DRAM. Within two years 1-megabyte DRAM sold for ¥1,600, probably too low to recoup the cost of the production lines needed to make them.[11]

Finally, while the company is building volume under one technology, a competitor may find a lower-cost technology that lets it start at lower prices than the market leader, who still operates on the old experience curve.

### Organizational considerations

Management must decide who within the organization should set prices. Companies handle pricing in a variety of ways. In small companies, prices are often set by top management rather than by the marketing or sales departments. In large companies, pricing typically is handled by divisional or product line managers. In industrial markets, salespeople may be allowed to negotiate with customers within certain price ranges. Even so, top management sets the pricing objectives and policies and it often approves the prices proposed by lower-level management or salespeople. In industries in which pricing is a key factor (aerospace, railroads, oil companies), companies often will have a pricing department to set the best prices or help others in setting them. This department reports to the marketing department or top management. Others who have an influence on pricing include sales managers, production managers, finance managers and accountants.

## External factors affecting pricing decisions

External factors that affect pricing decisions include the nature of the market and demand, competition and other environmental elements.

### The market and demand

Whereas costs set the lower limit of prices, the market and demand set the upper limit. Both consumer and industrial buyers balance the price of a product or service against the benefits of owning it. Thus, before setting prices, the marketer must understand the relationship between price and demand for its product.

In this section, we explain how the price–demand relationship varies for different types of markets and how buyer perceptions of price affect the pricing decision. We then discuss methods for measuring the price–demand relationship.

*Pricing in different types of markets*   The seller's pricing freedom varies with different types of markets. Economists recognize four types of markets, each presenting a different pricing challenge.

Under **pure competition**, the market consists of many buyers and sellers trading in a uniform commodity such as wheat, copper or financial securities. No single buyer or seller has much effect on the going market price. A seller cannot charge more than the going price because buyers can obtain as much as they need at the going price. Nor would sellers charge less than the market price because they can sell all they want at this price. If price and profits rise, new sellers can easily enter the market. In a purely competitive market, marketing research, product development, pricing, advertising and sales promotion play little or no role. Thus sellers in these markets do not spend much time on marketing strategy.

Under **monopolistic competition**, the market consists of many buyers and sellers who trade over a range of prices rather than a single market price. A range of prices occurs because sellers can differentiate their offers to buyers. Either the physical product can be varied in quality, features or style or the accompanying services can be varied. Buyers see differences in sellers' products and will pay different prices for them. Sellers try to develop differentiated offers for different customer segments and, in addition to price, freely use branding, advertising and personal selling to set their offers apart. For example, Danone's Lea and Perrins and several other bottled sauces compete with dozens of national and international varieties differentiated by price and nonprice factors. Because there are many competitors, each firm is less affected by competitors' marketing strategies than in oligopolistic markets.

Under **oligopolistic competition**, the market consists of a few sellers who are highly sensitive to each other's pricing and marketing strategies. The product can be uniform

Monopolistic competition: in the
industrial market, Stanley sets its
hinges apart from dozens of other
brands using both price and nonprice
factors.

(steel, aluminium) or nonuniform (cars, computers). There are few sellers because it is difficult for new sellers to enter the market. Each seller is alert to competitors' strategies and moves. If a steel company slashes its price by 10 per cent, buyers will quickly switch to this supplier. The other steel makers must respond by lowering their prices or increasing their services. An oligopolist is never sure that it will gain anything permanent through a price cut. In contrast, if an oligopolist raises its price, its competitors might not follow this lead. The oligopolist would then have to retract its price increase or risk losing customers to competitors.[12]

In a **pure monopoly**, the market consists of one seller. The seller may be a government monopoly (a Postal Service), a private regulated monopoly (a power company) or a private nonregulated monopoly (Microsoft with DOS and Windows). Pricing is handled differently in each case. A government monopoly can pursue a variety of pricing objectives. It might set a price below cost because the product is important to buyers who cannot afford to pay full cost. Or the price might be set either to cover costs or to produce good revenue. It can even be set quite high to slow down consumption. In a regulated monopoly, the government permits the company to set rates that will yield a 'fair return', one that will let the company maintain and expand its operations as needed. Nonregulated monopolies are free to price at what the market will bear. However, they do not always charge the full price for a number of reasons: for example, a desire not to attract competition, a desire to penetrate the market faster with a low price, or a fear of government regulation.

*Consumer perceptions of price and value*   In the end, the consumer will decide whether a product's price is right. When setting prices, the company must consider consumer perceptions of price and how these perceptions affect consumers' buying decisions. Pricing decisions, like other marketing-mix decisions, must be buyer-oriented.

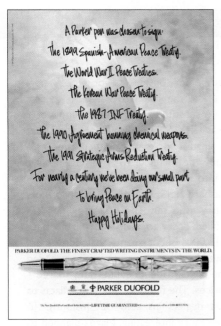

Perceived value: a less expensive pen might write as well, but some consumers will pay much more for the intangibles. This Parker model costs $185. Others are priced as high as $3500.

When consumers buy a product, they exchange something of value (the price) to get something of value (the benefits of having or using the product). Effective, buyer-oriented pricing involves understanding how much value consumers place on the benefits they receive from the product and setting a price that fits this value. These benefits can be actual or perceived. For example, calculating the cost of ingredients in a meal at a fancy restaurant is relatively easy. But assigning a value to other satis-factions such as taste, environment, relaxation, conversation and status is very hard. And these values will vary both for different consumers and different situations.

Thus the company will often find it hard to measure the values customers will attach to its product. But consumers do use these values to evaluate a product's price. If customers perceive that the price is greater than the product's value, they will not buy the product. If consumers perceive that the price is below the product's value, they will buy it, but the seller loses profit opportunities (see Marketing Highlight 16.2).

Marketers therefore must try to understand the consumer's reasons for buying the product and set the price according to consumer perceptions of the product's value. Because consumers vary in the values they assign to different product features, mar-keters often vary their pricing strategies for different segments. They offer different sets of product features at different prices. For example, Philips offers DFl 550 small 41 cm portable TV models for consumers who want basic sets and DFl 2,500 68 cm 100 Hz Nicam stereo models loaded with features for consumers who want the extras.

1 ecu = US$1.26
= DFl 2.12
(Dutch guilders)

*Analysing the price-demand relationship*    Each price the company might charge will lead to a different level of demand. The relation between the price charged and the resulting demand level is shown in the **demand curve** in Figure 16.4A. The demand curve shows the number of units the market will buy in a given time period at differ-ent prices that might be charged. In the normal case, demand and price are inversely related: that is, the higher the price, the lower the demand. Thus the company would sell less if it raised its price from $P_1$ to $P_2$. In short, consumers with limited budgets probably will buy less of something if its price is too high.

## Miata's popularity drives its prices

How much would you pay for a curvaceous new two-seat convertible that has the reliability of modern engineering yet the look, feel and sound of such classic roadsters as the 1959 Triumph TR3, the 1958 MGA, the 1962 Lotus Elan, or the Austin-Healey 3000? The car was the Mazda MX-5 Miata, *the* hot new car of 1990. It is a Japanese car designed in Europe for the US market. When being road tested in California the car was such an instant hit that passing drivers kept making it pull over to ask where they could buy one. Not only did consumers rave about its looks, car critics passionately praised its performance. According to *Car and Driver*, if the Miata 'were any more talented or tempting, driving one would be illegal'. Judging on design, performance, durability and reliability, entertainment, and value, *Road & Track* named it one of the five best cars in the world. Others included in the rankings along with the Miata included the Porsche 911 Carrera, the Corvette ZR-1, the Mercedes-Benz 300E and the $140,000 Ferrari Testarossa. Not bad company for a car with a base sticker price of only $13,800 and

designed 'just to be fun'. Besides its good looks, performance and price, the Miata rocketed to success because it had no substitutes. Its closest competitors were the Honda CRX Si and the Toyota MR2, but they lacked its singular looks and neither came as a convertible. Thus the Miata drove rivals to despair and customers into a covetous swoon.

Mazda had a hard time with the question of how to price its classy little car. The Japanese importer carefully controlled costs to keep the Miata's base price below $15,000. But it seems that consumers cared little about Mazda's costs, or about its intended price. When the Miata made its debut, sales soared – and so did its prices. The first few thousand Miatas to arrive at Mazda dealerships sold out instantly. To make things even more interesting, Mazda planned to ship only 20,000 Miatas (in three colours – red, white, and blue) to its 844 dealers in 1989, and only 40,000 more in 1990. Thus demand exceeded the limited supply by a reported ratio of ten to one.

The Miata was in such demand that dealers increased the price way beyond that advertised on

In the case of prestige goods, the demand curve sometimes slopes upwards. For example, one perfume company found that to be the case by raising its price on a more desirable perfume. However, if the company charges too high a price, the level of demand will be lower. The demand curve for theatre tickets can show similarly strange patterns. For mid-range tickets demand goes up as prices go down, but below a critical point demand declines with price as people assume the seats are no good. Also, demand for 'the best seats in the house' sometimes increases with price.[13]

Most companies try to measure their demand curves by estimating demand at different prices. The type of market makes a difference. In a monopoly, the demand curve shows the total market demand resulting from different prices. If the company faces competition, its demand at different prices will depend on whether competitors' prices stay constant or change with the company's own prices. Here, we will assume that competitors' prices remain constant. Later in this chapter, we will discuss what happens when competitors' prices change.

In measure the price–demand relationship, the market researcher must not allow other factors affecting demand to vary. For example, if Philips increased its advertising at the same time that it lowered its television prices, we would not know how much of the increased demand was due to the lower prices and how much was due to the increased advertising. The same problem arises if a holiday weekend occurs when the lower price is set – more gift-giving over some holidays causes people to buy more portable televisions. Economists show the impact of nonprice factors on demand through shifts in the demand curve rather than movements along it.

the sticker and still had barely enough cars to sell. Because of the car's popularity, customers were more than willing to pay the higher price. As one dealer noted: 'People are offering more than what we're asking just to get [the car].' On average, dealers across the US marked up prices $4,000; in California, they added as much as $8,000. Some enterprising owners even offered to sell their Miatas for prices ranging up to $45,000. Ads appeared daily in the *Los Angeles Times* from owners in Kansas, Nebraska, or Michigan proffering their Miatas for $32,000 plus delivery fees.

Thus although many companies focus on costs as a key to setting prices, consumers rarely know of or care about the seller's costs. What really counts is what consumers are willing to pay for the benefits of owning the product. To some consumers, the sharp little Miata added up to much more than the sum of its mechanical parts. To them, it delivered the same pleasures and prestige as cars selling at much higher prices. Therefore, even at above-sticker prices, most buyers got a good deal. Mazda on the other hand, may have left some money on the table.

Aside from its good looks, performance and price, the Mazda MX-5 rocketed to success because it had no substitutes.

Sources: Rebecca Fannin, 'Mazda's sporting chance', *Marketing & Media Decisions* (October 1989), 24–30; S. C. Gwynne, 'Romancing the roadster', *Time* (24 July 1989), 39; 'The roadster returns', *Consumer Reports* (April 1990), 232–4; and Larry Armstrong, 'After the Miata, Mazda isn't just idling', *Business Week* (2 September 1991), 35.

*Price elasticity of demand*   Marketers also need to know **price elasticity** – how responsive demand will be to a change in price. Consider the two demand curves in Figure 16.4. In Figure 16.4A, a price increase from $P_1$ to $P_2$ leads to a relatively small drop in demand from $Q_1$ to $Q_2$. In Figure 16.4B, however, a similar price increase leads to a large drop in demand from $Q_1$ to $Q_2$. If demand hardly changes with a small change in price, we say the demand is *inelastic*. If demand changes greatly, we say the demand is *elastic*. The price elasticity of demand is given by the following formula:

$$\text{Price elasticity of demand} = \frac{\%\ \text{change in quantity demanded}}{\%\ \text{change in price}}$$

Suppose demand falls by 10 per cent when a seller raises its price by 2 per cent. Price elasticity of demand is therefore −5 (the minus sign confirms the inverse relation between price and demand) and demand is elastic. If demand falls by 2 per cent with a 2 per cent increase in price, then elasticity is −1. In this case, the seller's total revenue stays the same: that is, the seller sells fewer items but at a higher price that preserves the same total revenue. If demand falls by 1 per cent when the price is increased by 2 per cent, then elasticity is $-\frac{1}{2}$ and demand is inelastic. The less elastic the demand, the more it pays for the seller to raise the price.

What determines the price elasticity of demand? Buyers are less price sensitive when the product they are buying is unique or when it is high in quality, prestige or exclusiveness. They are also less price sensitive when substitute products are hard to find or when they cannot easily compare the quality of substitutes. Finally, buyers

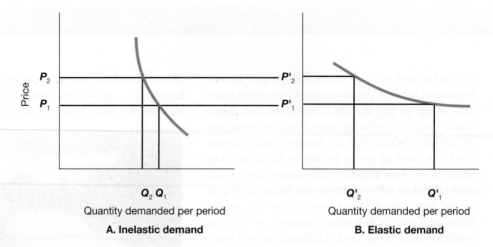

**Figure 16.4**   Inelastic and elastic demand.

are less price sensitive when the total expenditure for a product is low relative to their income or when the cost is shared by another party.[14]

If demand is elastic rather than inelastic, sellers will consider lowering their price. A lower price will produce more total revenue. This practice makes sense as long as the extra costs of producing and selling more do not exceed the extra revenue.

> Yorkshire Chemicals, a dyes and specialist chemicals manufacturer, shrugged off the effects of a depressed European market by 'producing and selling more at lower price levels'. Investments in extra efficient capacity allowed the dyestuffs division to keep profits constant after cutting prices 5 per cent and increasing sales 8 per cent.[15]

## Competitors' costs, prices and offers

Another external factor affecting the company's pricing decisions is competitors' costs and prices and possible competitor reactions to the company's own pricing moves. A consumer who is considering the purchase of a Canon camera will evaluate Canon's price and value against the prices and values of comparable products made by Nikon, Minolta, Pentax and others. In addition, the company's pricing strategy may affect the nature of the competition it faces. If Canon follows a high-price, high-margin strategy, it may attract competition. A low-price, low-margin strategy, however, may stop competitors or drive them out of the market.

Canon needs to benchmark its costs against its competitors' costs to learn whether it is operating at a cost advantage or disadvantage. It also needs to learn the price and quality of each competitor's offer. Canon might do this in several ways. It can send out comparison shoppers to price and compare the products of Nikon, Minolta and other competitors. It can get competitors' price lists and buy competitors' equipment and take it apart. It can ask buyers how they view the price and quality of each competitor's camera.

Once Canon is aware of competitors' prices and offers, it can use them as a starting point for its own pricing. If Canon's cameras are similar to Nikon's, it will have to price close to Nikon or lose sales. If Canon's cameras are not as good as Nikon's, the firm will not be able to charge as much. If Canon's products are better than Nikon's, it can charge more. Basically, Canon will use price to position its offer relative to the competition.

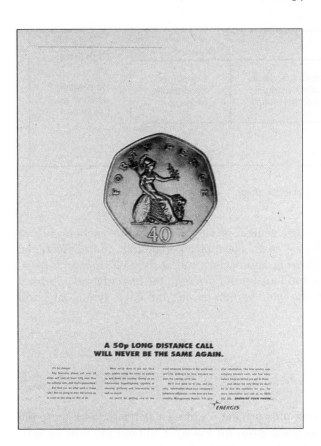

Low price is one of the strategies that Energis use against BT, the dominant competitor.

## Other external factors

When setting prices, the company must also consider other factors in its external environment. *Economic conditions* can have a strong impact on the firm's pricing strategies.[16] Economic factors such as boom or recession, inflation and interest rates affect pricing decisions because they affect both the costs of producing a product and consumer perceptions of the product's price and value. The company must also consider what impact its prices will have on other parties in its environment. How will *resellers* react to various prices? The company should set prices that give resellers a fair profit, encourage their support and help them to sell the product effectively. The *government* is another important external influence on pricing decisions. Finally, *social concerns* may have to be taken into account. In setting prices, a company's short-term sales, market share and profit goals may have to be tempered by broader societal considerations.

## GENERAL PRICING APPROACHES

The price the company charges will be somewhere between one that is too low to produce a profit and one that is too high to produce any demand. Figure 16.5 summarizes the primary considerations in setting price. Product costs set a floor to the price; consumer perceptions of the product's value set the ceiling. The company must consider competitors' prices and other external and internal factors to find the best price between these two extremes.

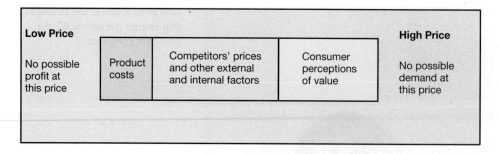

**Figure 16.5**  Primary considerations in price settings.

Companies set prices by selecting a general pricing approach that includes one or more of these three sets of factors – costs, consumer perception, and competitors' prices. We will examine the following approaches: the *cost-based approach* (cost-plus pricing, break-even analysis and target profit pricing); the *buyer-based approach* (perceived-value pricing); and the *competition-based approach* (going-rate and sealed-bid pricing).

## Cost-based pricing

### Cost-plus pricing

The simplest pricing method is **cost-plus pricing** – adding a standard mark-up to the cost of the product. Construction companies, for example, submit job bids by estimating the total project cost and adding a standard mark-up for profit. Lawyers, accountants and other professionals typically price by adding a standard mark-up to their costs. Some sellers tell their customers they will charge cost plus a specified mark-up; for example, aerospace companies price this way to the government. (For a detailed discussion of **mark-ups** and **markdowns** see Marketing Highlight 16.3.)

To illustrate mark-up pricing, suppose a toaster manufacturer had the following costs and expected sales:

| | |
|---|---|
| Variable cost | $10 |
| Fixed cost | $300,000 |
| Expected unit sales | 50,000 |

Then the manufacturer's cost per toaster is given by:

$$\text{Unit cost} = \text{Variable cost} + \frac{\text{fixed costs}}{\text{unit sales}} = \$10 + \frac{\$300,000}{50,000} = \$16$$

Now suppose the manufacturer wants to earn a 20 per cent mark-up on sales. The manufacturer's mark-up price is given by:

$$\text{Markup-price} = \frac{\text{unit cost}}{(1.0 - \text{desired return on sales})} = \frac{\$16}{(1.0 - 0.2)} = \$20$$

The manufacturer would charge dealers $20 a toaster and make a profit of $4 per unit. The dealers, in turn, will mark up the toaster. If dealers want to earn 50 per cent on sales price, they will mark up the toaster to $40 ($20 + 50 per cent of $40). This number is equivalent to a *mark-up on cost* of 100 per cent ($20/$20).

Does using standard mark-ups to set prices make logical sense? Generally, no. Any pricing method that ignores demand and competitors' prices is not likely to lead to the best price. Suppose the toaster manufacturer charged $20 but only sold 30,000 toasters instead of 50,000. Then the unit cost would have been higher since the fixed costs are spread over fewer units and the realized percentage mark-up on sales would have been lower. Mark-up pricing only works if that price actually brings in the expected level of sales.

Still, mark-up pricing remains popular for a number of reasons. First, sellers are more certain about costs than about demand. By tying the price to cost, sellers simplify pricing – they do not have to make frequent adjustments as demand changes. Second, when all firms in the industry use this pricing method, prices tend to be similar and price competition is thus minimized. Third, many people feel that cost-plus pricing is fairer to both buyers and sellers. Sellers earn a fair return on their investment but do not take advantage of buyers when buyers' demand becomes great.

## Breakeven analysis and target profit pricing

Another cost-oriented pricing approach is **breakeven pricing** or a variation called **target profit pricing**. The firm tries to determine the price at which it will break even or make the target profit it is seeking. Target pricing is used by General Motors, which prices its automobiles to achieve a 15 to 20 per cent profit on its investment. This pricing method is also used by public utilities, which are constrained to make a fair return on their investment. Businesses are increasingly basing their investment decisions on their Economic Value Added (EVA); this compares the revenue from a venture with the cost of capital to fund it (Marketing Highlight 16.4 shows how EVA works).

Target pricing uses the concept of a *breakeven chart*. A breakeven chart shows the total cost and total revenue expected at different sales volume levels. Figure 16.6

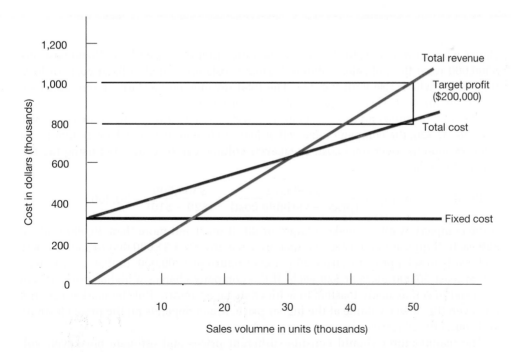

**Figure 16.6** Breakeven chart for determining target price.

## MARKETING HIGHLIGHT 16.3

### Mark-ups and markdowns

Retailers and wholesalers must understand **mark-ups** and **markdowns**. They need to make profit to stay in business and mark-ups affect profits.

Mark-ups and markdowns appear as percentages. There are two ways to compute mark-ups – on *cost* or on selling *price*:

Mark-up percentage on cost $= \dfrac{\text{dollar mark-up}}{\text{cost}}$

Mark-up percentage on selling price $= \dfrac{\text{dollar mark-up}}{\text{selling price}}$

Dale Parsons must decide which formula to use. If Parsons bought shirts for $15 and wanted to mark them up $10, his mark-up percentage on cost would be $10/$15 = 67.7 per cent. If Parsons based mark-up on selling price, the percentage would be $10/$25 = 40 per cent. In figuring mark-up percentage, most retailers use the selling price rather than the cost. Suppose Parsons knew his cost ($12) and desired mark-up on price (25 per cent) for a man's tie, and wanted to compute the selling price. The formula is:

Selling price $=$ cost $\times$ (100 per cent + mark-up)
Selling price $=$ $16

As a product moves through the channels of distribution, each channel member adds a mark-up before selling the product to the next member. This 'mark-up chain' for a suit bought by a Parsons customer for $200 is shown in Table 1.

Table 1   The mark-up chain for a product

|  |  | $ amount | % of selling price |
|---|---|---|---|
| Manufacturer | Cost | 108 | 90 |
|  | Mark-up | 12 | 10 |
|  | Selling price | 120 | 100 |
| Wholesaler | Cost | 120 | 80 |
|  | Mark-up | 30 | 20 |
|  | Selling price | 150 | 100 |
| Retailer | Cost | 150 | 75 |
|  | Mark-up | 50 | 25 |
|  | Selling price | 200 | 100 |

The retailer whose mark-up is 25 per cent does not necessarily enjoy more profit than a manufacturer whose mark-up is 10 per cent. Profit also

shows a breakeven chart for the toaster manufacturer discussed here. Fixed costs are $300,000 regardless of sales volume. Variable costs are added to fixed costs to form total costs, which rise with volume. The total revenue curve starts at zero and rises with each unit sold. The slope of the total revenue curve reflects the price of $20 per unit.

The total revenue and total cost curves cross at 30,000 units. This is the *breakeven volume*. At $20, the company must sell at least 30,000 units to break even: that is, for total revenue to cover total cost. Breakeven volume can be calculated using the following formula:

$$\text{Breakeven volume} = \frac{\text{fixed cost}}{(\text{price} - \text{variable cost})} = \frac{\$300,000}{(\$20 - \$10)} = 30,000$$

If the company wants to make a target profit, it must sell more than 30,000 units at $20 each. Suppose the toaster manufacturer has invested $1,000,000 in the business and wants to set a price to earn a 20 per cent return or $200,000. In that case, it must sell at least 50,000 units at $20 each. If the company charges a higher price, it will not need to sell as many toasters to achieve its target return. But the market may not buy even this lower volume at the higher price. Much depends on the price elasticity and competitors' prices.

The manufacturer should consider different prices and estimate breakeven volumes, probable demand and profits for each. This is done in Table 16.1. The table

depends on the number of items with that profit margin sold (stock turnover rate), and on operating efficiency (expenses). Sometimes a retailer wants to convert mark-ups based on selling price to mark-ups based on cost and vice versa. The formulas are:

Mark-up percentage on selling price =

$$\frac{\text{mark-up percentage on cost}}{(100 \text{ per cent} + \text{mark-up percentage on selling cost})}$$

Mark-up percentage on cost =

$$\frac{\text{mark-up percentage on selling price}}{(100 \text{ per cent} - \text{mark-up percentage on selling price})}$$

Suppose Parsons found that his competitor was using a mark-up of 30 per cent based on cost and wanted to know what this would be as a percentage of selling price. The calculation would be:

$$\frac{30 \text{ per cent}}{100 \text{ per cent} + 30 \text{ per cent}} = \frac{30 \text{ per cent}}{130 \text{ per cent}} = 23 \text{ per cent}$$

Because Parsons was using a 25 per cent mark-up on the selling price for suits, he felt that his mark-up was suitable compared with that of the competitor.

Near the end of the summer Parsons still had an inventory of summer slacks in stock. Therefore, he decided to use a markdown, a reduction from the original selling price. Before the summer he had bought 20 pairs at $10 each, and he had since sold 10 pairs at $20 each. He marked down the other pairs to $15 and sold five pairs. We compute his *markdown ratio* as follows:

$$\text{Markdown percentage} = \frac{\text{dollar markdown}}{\text{total net sales in dollars}}$$

The dollar markdown is $25 (five pairs at $5 each) and total net sales are $275 (ten pairs at $20 + five pairs at $15). The ratio, then, is $25/$275 = 9 per cent.

Larger retailers usually compute markdown ratios for each department rather than for individual items. The ratios provide a measure of relative marketing performance for each department and for departments over time. Markdown ratios can also compare the performance of different buyers and salespeople in a store's various departments.

shows that as price increases, breakeven volume drops (column 2). But as price increases, demand for the toasters also falls off (column 3). At the $14 price, because the manufacturer clears only $4 per toaster ($14 less $10 in variable costs), it must sell a very high volume to break even. Even though the low price attracts many buyers,

| TABLE 16.1 | Breakeven volume and profits at different prices | | | | |
|---|---|---|---|---|---|
| (1) | (2) | (3) | (4) | (5) | (6) |
| | Unit demand needed to | Expected unit demand at | Total revenues ($) | Total | Profit |
| Price ($) | break even | given price | (1) × (3) | costs ($)* | (4) − (5) |
| 14 | 75,000 | 71,000 | 994,000 | 1,100,000 | −32,000 |
| 16 | 50,000 | 67,000 | 1,072,000 | 970,000 | 102,000 |
| 18 | 37,500 | 60,000 | 1,080,000 | 900,000 | 180,000 |
| 20 | 30,000 | 42,000 | 840,000 | 720,000 | 120,000 |
| 22 | 25,000 | 23,000 | 506,000 | 530,000 | −24,000 |

Note:* Assumes fixed costs of $300,000 and constant unit variable costs of $10.

## Economic value added

### Sales volume (SV)

Increasing the quantity sold (sales volume) is the driving force behind marketing activity. There are good reasons for this:

- Increased sales show success and a growing company.
- Increased market share shows competitive success.
- If sales do not match production, capacity will be underused or customers disappointed.

### Net proceeds from sales (S)

An increased sales volume may show competitive success but net proceeds from sales show the cash flowing into the company. It is the value of sales made less returns. The popular idea of 'every-day low prices' can increase sales but not always by enough to cover lost margins. Sales value and sales volume sometimes do not move hand in hand. A company that increases sales by 5 per cent by cutting prices by 10 per cent increases sales volume but reduces sales value:

| Action | Regular price | 10% discount | Percentage change |
|---|---|---|---|
| Price ($) | 1.00 | 0.90 | (10.0) |
| Sales (units) | 100 | 105 | 5.0 |
| Sales ($) | 100.00 | 94.50 | (5.5) |

### Gross profit (GP)

Gross profit is the difference between net proceeds from sales (S) and the cost of goods sold (COGS). The costs are the variable costs incurred each time a product is made. It typically includes raw materials, labour, energy, and so on.

The interplay between gross profit and price is

dramatic. The 10 per cent price cut has much more impact on gross profits than sales:

| Action | Regular price | 10% discount | Percentage change |
|---|---|---|---|
| *Sales* | | | |
| Price ($) | 1.00 | 0.90 | |
| Sales (units) | 100 | 105 | |
| Sales ($) | 100.00 | 94.50 | (5.5) |
| *Cost of goods sold* | | | |
| Unit cost ($) | 0.50 | 0.50 | |
| Sales (units) | 100 | 105 | |
| Cost ($) | 50.00 | 52.50 | 5.0 |
| Gross profit | 50.00 | 42.00 | (8.0) |

### Net profit (NP)

Gross profit shows the contribution made to the company by each unit sold but neglects many other trading expenses incurred by a company. These included fixed costs like rates, staff, and so forth, and strategic expenditure like research and development. Interest paid on debts is sometimes not included because this depends upon the capital structure of the company.

The fixed cost means that net profit is more volatile than gross profit. This sensitivity encourages companies to convert some of their fixed costs into variable ones, for example, hiring trucks rather than buying them:

| Action | Regular price | 10% discount | Percentage change |
|---|---|---|---|
| Sales ($) | 100 | 94.5 | (5.5) |
| Cost of goods sold ($) | 50 | 52.5 | (5.0) |
| Gross profit ($) | 50 | 42.0 | (8.0) |
| Other trading expenses | 40 | 40.0 | 0.0 |
| Net profit | 10 | 2.0 | (80.0) |

## Return on sales (ROS)

ROS = NP/Sales

Return on sales (or margin) measures the ratio of profit to sales. This can be useful in comparing businesses over time. During a four-year period a company may find both sales and net profit increasing but are profits keeping pace with sales? The 10 per cent price promotion gives an increase in sales volume but a big reduction in return on sales:

| Action | Regular price | 10% discount | Percentage change |
|---|---|---|---|
| Sales ($) | 100 | 94.5 | (5.5) |
| Net profit ($) | 10 | 2.0 | (80.0) |
| Return on sales (%) | 10.0 | 2.1 | |

## Return on capital employed (ROCE)

Some companies, like grocery chains, can have low returns on sales but are very profitable. They achieve this because the critical measure is return on capital employed. This is the product of return on sales and the speed that assets are turned over (the activity ratio):

$$ROCE = ROS \times ACTIVITY$$
$$= \frac{NP}{Sales} \times \frac{Sales}{Assets}$$

By turning over its assets four times each year a supermarket can achieve a 20 per cent return on capital employed although its return on sales is only 5 per cent:

$$\text{Supermarket ROCE} = \frac{5}{100} \times \frac{100}{25} = 20 \text{ per cent}$$

In contrast, an exclusive clothes shop has very high margins but only turns its assets over slowly.

$$\text{Clothes shop ROCE} = \frac{40}{100} \times \frac{100}{300} = 13.3 \text{ per cent}$$

These are powerful ratios that can define how a company can do business. Aldi, the German discount grocery chain, succeeds with margins half those of many grocers. Its margins are very low (2–3 per cent) but it keeps its return on capital employed high by high stock turnover and keeping its other assets low – it has a small range of products, buys in great bulk and trades in less costly stores than traditional grocers.

There are two benefits from increasing asset turnover: improved return on capital employed, and reduced fixed costs. The firm that hires trucks rather than buying them reduces its fixed costs and, therefore, its sensitivity to volume changes. Also, by reducing its assets it increases its activity ratio and return on capital employed. Increased assets turnover is one of the direct benefits of JIT, lean manufacturing and re-engineering. JIT cuts down the assets tied up in stock, and improves quality. Lean manufacturing reduces investment in plant while re-engineering can reduce capital investments, costs and working capital.

## Capital cost covered (C³)

Assets cost money and return on capital costs takes that into account. It is a powerful tool because it combines three critical business ratios:

$$C^3 = ROS \times ACTIVITY \times CAPITAL\ EFFICIENCY$$
$$C^3 = \frac{NP}{Sales} \times \frac{Sales}{Assets} \times \frac{Assets}{Cost\ of\ capital}$$

The cost of capital is the weighted average cost of debt and shareholder equity. For a supermarket the figure could be:

| | Debt (after tax) | Equity | Weighted average cost of capital (%) |
|---|---|---|---|
| Debt/equity split | 0.50 | 0.50 | |
| Cost of capital (%) | 4.00 | 16.00 | |
| Partial cost of capital (%) | 2.00 | 8.00 | 10.00 |

At 4 per cent, debt cost less than equity (16 per cent), so by having both, the firm reduces the average weighted capital cost to 10.00 per cent. A firm can reduce its average cost of capital by taking out more debt but the amount used is limited by the risks involved.

Debt is relatively cheap because it bears no risk; equity is relatively expensive because it bears the whole risk of the business. If a firm tries to increase its lending too much, a bank, or other lending body, will refuse to give more money or demand a higher interest rate.

For the supermarket the asset of $25m. would cost $25m. $\times$ 010 = $2.5m. to finance. Therefore:

$$C^3 = \frac{5}{100} \times \frac{100}{25} \times \frac{25}{2.5} = \frac{NP}{CC} = 2.0$$

In other words, the net profit is double the capital cost – the company is healthy. This ratio is more discriminating than the familiar distinction between profit and loss. If the capital cost covered is below zero a firm is making a loss. A capital cost covered above zero indicates a profit. However, capital cost covered between zero and one shows a firm is in profit but not adding value – its profit does not cover its cost of capital.

### Economic value added (EVA)

Economic value added makes a direct comparison between the cost of capital and net profits. It is a simple idea that has hugely increased the value of companies using it. Christened EVA by Stern Stewart & Company of New York city, many leading companies see it as a way of examining the value of their investments and strategy. Amongst early users are Coca-Cola, AT&T, Quaker Oats and Briggs & Stratton. William Smithburg, Quaker's chief executive officer, explains that, 'EVA makes managers act like shareholders. It is the true corporate faith for the 1990s.'

EVA = Net profit – Cost of capital

For the supermarket:

Supermarket EVA = 5 – 2.5 = $2.5m.

Profit, economic value added and capital cost covered are related concepts: profit shows how a company's trading is going, economic value added shows a company's wealth creation in monetary terms, while capital cost covered gives the rate of wealth creation.

| Category | $C^3$ | EVA | NP | Economic state |
|---|---|---|---|---|
| I | >1 | >0 | >0 | A profitable company which is adding economic value |
| II | 1>0 | <0 | >0 | A company whose profits do not cover the cost of capital. No economic value is being added. |
| III | <0 | <0 | <0 | A loss-making company |

The supermarket is a clear category I company; this contrasts with the clothes store whose capital is more expensive because the clothes market is cyclical and fashion-dependent:

| Clothes store | Debt | Equity | Weighted average cost of capital (%) |
|---|---|---|---|
| Debt/equity split | 0.25 | 0.75 | |
| Cost of capital (%) | 5.0 | 20.0 | |
| Partial cost of capital (%) | 1.25 | 15.0 | 16.25 |

Assets of $300m. give a capital cost of $48.75m.

| | $C^3$ | EVA ($m.) | NP ($m.) | Category |
|---|---|---|---|---|
| Supermarket | 2.0 | 2.5 | 5 | I |
| Clothes store | 0.8 | (9.5) | 40 | II |

Sources: Alan Wolfe, 'Price Wars', *Marketing Business* (November 1991), 37–9; Shawn Tully, 'The real key to creating wealth', *Fortune* (20 September 1993), 24–30; Neil Buckley, 'Potential cost of selling it cheap every day', *Financial Times* (24 March 1994), 17; and Neil Buckley, 'Waging war over bread and baked beans', *Financial Times* (20 October 1994), 11.

demand still falls below the high breakeven point and the manufacturer loses money. At the other extreme, with a $22 price the manufacturer clears $12 per toaster and must sell only 25,000 units to break even. But at this high price, consumers buy too few toasters and profits are negative. The table shows that a price of $18 yields the highest profits. Note that none of the prices produce the manufacturer's target profit of $200,000. To achieve this target return, the manufacturer will have to search for ways to lower fixed or variable costs, thus lowering the breakeven volume.

## Value-based pricing

An increasing number of companies are basing their prices on the product's perceived value. **Value-based pricing** uses buyers' perceptions of value, not the seller's cost, as the key to pricing. Value-based pricing means that the marketer cannot design a product and marketing programme and then set the price. Price is considered along with the other marketing-mix variables *before* the marketing programme is set.

Figure 16.7 compares cost-based pricing with value-based pricing. Cost-based pricing is product driven. The company designs what it considers to be a good product, totals the costs of making the product and sets a price that covers costs plus a target profit. Marketing must then convince buyers that the product's value at that price justifies its purchase. If the price turns out to be too high, the company must settle for lower mark-ups or lower sales, both resulting in disappointing profits.

Value-based pricing reverses this process. The company sets its target price based on customer perceptions of the product value. The targeted value and price then drive decisions about product design and what costs can be incurred. As a result, pricing begins with analysing consumer needs and value perceptions and a price is set to match consumers' perceived value:

> Consider Thorn selling its 10W 2D energy saving electric light bulbs to a hotel manager. The SL18 costs far more to make than a conventional 60-watt tungsten light bulb so a higher price has to be justified. Value pricing helps by looking at the hotel manager's total cost of ownership rather than the price of electric light bulbs. The life cycle costs of the manager using a tungsten bulb for the 1000 hours that they last includes the price of the bulb (60p), the labour cost of replacing it (50p) and electricity (£4.80). The life cycle cost of the tungsten bulb is therefore £5.90. The Thorn 10W 2D bulb uses a sixth of the electricity of a conventional bulb and lasts eight times longer. Its life cycle cost must therefore be compared with the cost of owning eight tungsten bulbs: 8 x £5.90 = £47.20. To work out the value of the Thorn bulb its cost of ownership is also considered: changing the bulb 50p and electricity £6.40 (one sixth the electricity costs of eight tungsten bulbs). The maximum value-based price of the Thorn bulb to the hotel manager is therefore:

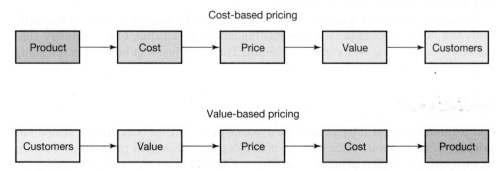

**Figure 16.7**   Cost-based versus value-based pricing. (Source: Thomas T. Nagle and Reed K. Holden, *The Strategy and Tactics of Pricing*, 2nd edn (Englewood Cliffs, NJ: Prentice Hall, 1995), 5.)

Maximum value based price = competitor's cost of ownership – own operating costs

$$= £47.20 – (£6.40 + 50p)$$
$$= £40.30$$

Using this evidence Thorn can argue that it is worth the hotel manager paying a lot more than 60p to buy the energy-saving bulb. It is unrealistic to think the manager would pay the full £40.30 but, based on these figures, the actual price of £10.00 for the Thorn energy saving bulb looks very reasonable. At first sight it seems hard to justify replacing a 60p tungsten bulb with a £10.00 energy saving one but value-based pricing shows the hotel manager is saving £30.00 by doing so. The value-based pricing using life-cycle costs can be used to justify paying a premium price on products: from low energy-condensation boilers as domestic boilers to low maintenance jet fighters.[17]

A company using perceived-value pricing must find out what value buyers assign to different competitive offers. However, measuring perceived value can be difficult. Sometimes consumers are asked how much they would pay for a basic product and for each benefit added to the offer. Or a company might conduct experiments to test the perceived value of different product offers. If the seller charges more than the buyers' perceived value, the company's sales will suffer. Many companies overprice their products and their products sell poorly. Other companies underprice. Underpriced products sell very well, but they produce less revenue than they would if prices were raised to the perceived-value levels.

## Competition-based pricing

Consumers will base their judgements of a product's value on the prices that competitors charge for similar products. Here, we discuss two forms of competition-based pricing: *going-rate pricing* and *sealed-bid pricing*.

### Going-rate pricing

In **going-rate pricing**, the firm bases its price largely on *competitors'* prices, with less attention paid to its *own* costs or to demand. The firm might charge the same, more or less than its chief competitors. In oligopolistic industries that sell a commodity such as steel, paper or fertilizer, firms normally charge the same price. The smaller firms follow the leader: they change their prices when the market leader's prices change, rather than when their own demand or costs change. Some firms may charge a bit more or less, but they hold the amount of difference constant. Thus, minor gasoline retailers usually charge a few cents less than the big oil companies, without letting the difference increase or decrease.

Going-rate pricing is quite popular. When demand elasticity is hard to measure, firms feel that the going price represents the collective wisdom of the industry concerning the price that will yield a fair return. They also feel that holding to the going price will prevent harmful price wars.

### Sealed-bid pricing

Competition-based pricing is also used when firms *bid* for jobs. Using **sealed-bid pricing**, a firm bases its price on how it thinks competitors will price rather than on its own costs or on the demand. The firm wants to win a contract and winning the contract requires pricing less than other firms.

Yet the firm cannot set its price below a certain level. It cannot price below cost

| **TABLE 16.2** | *Effect of different bids on expected profit* | | |
|---|---|---|---|
| Company's bid ($) | (1) Company's profit ($) | (2) Probability of winning with this bid (assumed) | (3) Expected profit (1) × (2) |
| 9,500 | 100 | 0.81 | 81 |
| 10,000 | 600 | 0.36 | 216 |
| 10,500 | 1,100 | 0.09 | 99 |
| 11,000 | 1,600 | 0.01 | 16 |

without harming its position. In contrast, the higher the company sets its price above its costs, the lower its chance of getting the contract.

The net effect of the two opposite pulls can be described in terms of the *expected profit* of the particular bid (see Table 16.2). Suppose a bid of $9,500 would yield a high chance (say, 0.81) of getting the contract, but only a low profit (say, $100). The expected profit with this bid is therefore $81. If the firm bid $11,000, its profit would be $1,600, but its chance of getting the contract might be reduced to 0.01. The expected profit would be only $16. Thus the company might bid the price that would maximize the expected profit. According to Table 16.2, the best bid would be $10,000, for which the expected profit is $216.

Using expected profit as a basis for setting price makes sense for the large firm that makes many bids. In playing the odds, the firm will make maximum profits in the long run. But a firm that bids only occasionally or needs a particular contract badly will not find the expected-profit approach useful. The approach, for example, does not distinguish between a $100,000 profit with a 0.10 probability and a $12,500 profit with an 0.80 probability. Yet the firm that wants to keep production going would prefer the second contract to the first.

## SUMMARY

Despite the increased role of nonprice factors in the modern marketing process, *price* remains an important element in the marketing mix. Many internal and external factors influence the company's pricing decisions. *Internal factors* include the firm's *marketing objectives*, *marketing-mix strategy*, *costs* and *organization for pricing*.

The pricing strategy is largely determined by the company's *target market and positioning objectives*. Common pricing objectives include survival, current profit maximization, market-share leadership and product-quality leadership.

Price is only one of the marketing-mix tools the company uses to accomplish its objectives, and pricing decisions affect and are affected by product design, distribution and promotion decisions. Price decisions must be carefully coordinated with the other marketing-mix decisions when designing the marketing programme.

*Costs* set the floor for the company's price – the price must cover all the costs of making and selling the product, plus a fair rate of return. Management must decide who within the organization is responsible for setting price. In large companies, some pricing authority may be delegated to lower-level managers and salespeople, but top management usually sets pricing policies and approves proposed prices. Production, finance and accounting managers also influence pricing.

*External factors* that influence pricing decisions include the nature of the market and demand; competitors' prices and offers; and factors such as the economy, reseller needs and government actions. The seller's pricing freedom varies with different types of markets. Pricing is especially challenging in markets characterized by monopolistic competition oligopoly.

In the end, the consumer decides whether the company has set the right price. The consumer weighs the price against the perceived values of using the product – if the price exceeds the sum of the values, consumers will not buy the product. Consumers differ in the values they assign to different product features and marketers often vary their pricing strategies for different price segments. When assessing the market and demand, the company estimates the demand curve, which shows the probable quantity purchased per period at alternative price levels. The more *inelastic* the demand, the higher the company can set its price. *Demand* and *consumer value perceptions* set the ceiling for prices.

Consumers compare a product's price to the prices of *competitors'* products. A company must learn the price and quality of competitors' offers and use them as a starting point for its own pricing.

The company can select one or a combination of three general pricing approaches: the *cost-based approach* (cost-plus pricing, break-even analysis and target profit pricing); the *value-based approach* (value-based pricing); and the *competition-based approach* (going-rate or sealed-bid pricing).

## ■ DISCUSSING THE ISSUES

1. Certain 'inexpensive products that waste energy, provide few savings per package or require frequent maintenance may *cost* much more to own and use than do products selling for a higher *price*. How would marketers use this information on 'true cost' to gain a competitive edge in pricing and promoting their products?

2. Companies must consider both the internal company factors and external environmental influences that impact on their pricing decisions. Consider a relatively new entrant in the world car industry – Malaysia's Proton Saga – which has sought a low-cost, value-for-money positioning in the volume sector. Its low price supports this positioning. What type of pricing approach is the manufacturer pursuing? How appropriate is this pricing approach, taking into consideration the key factors the company should evaluate when pricing its products? Explain your answer.

3. Sales of a brand of malt whisky increased when prices were raised 20 per cent over a two-year period. What does this tell you about the demand curve and the elasticity of demand for this whisky? What does this suggest about using perceived-value pricing in marketing alcoholic drinks?

4. Genentech, a high-technology pharmaceutical company, developed a clot-dissolving drug called TPA that would halt a heart attack in progress. TPA saves lives, minimizes hospital stays and reduces damage to the heart itself. It was initially priced at $2,200 per dose. What pricing approach does Genentech appear to have been using? Is demand for this drug likely to be elastic with price? Why or why not?

5. In the early years of global market expansion, Japanese car and camera makers took advantage of the experience or learning curve when pricing their products to penetrate overseas markets. What does this suggest about their pricing approach? How successful do you think this approach has been for the Japanese companies which have taken advantage of the learning curve?

6. Select a personal care product or cosmetic item that you regularly use. Notice the price of the item. What are the main benefits you are looking for in using this product? Does the price communicate the total benefits sought? Does the product's price suggest good value? Do you think the manufacturer or retailer is overcharging or undercharging consumers for this product. Why or why not? What pricing approach do you think is most appropriate for setting the price for this product?

# ■ APPLYING THE CONCEPTS

1. Do a pricing survey of several petrol stations in your town in different locations. If possible, check prices at the following: stations at a service area on a main highway/motorway, stations on a local street in or near the town, a station not near any other stations, and (where appropriate) a station that is tied to a supermarket. Write down the brand of petrol, prices of regular and premium grades, type of location, distance to the nearest competitor and the competitor's prices.

   ■ Is there a pattern to the pricing of petrol at various forecourts?

   ■ Are these stations using cost-based, buyer-based or going-rate pricing?

2. You are faced with setting the price for an automatic car-wash. Your annual fixed costs are £50,000 and variable costs are £0.50 per vehicle washed. You think customers would be wiling to pay £2.50 to have their car washed. What would be the breakeven volume at that price? What opportunities are there for pricing high? What might be the most significant constraints on your pricing decision?

# ■ REFERENCES

1. Allan Ruddock and Ivan Fallon, 'Blood begins to flow in the battle for the *Independent*', *Sunday Times* (6 February 1994), 3, 6; 'Newspapers: indirubber', *The Economist* (29 January 1994), 33–4; 'Cheaper *Times* here to stay', *The European* (10–16 June 1994), 22; Andreas Whittam Smith, 'An ugly struggle for dominance of the newspaper market', *Independent* (24 June 1994), 1; Roger Cowe, Tony May and Andrew Culf, '*Telegraph* in Shares Inquiry', *Guardian* (24 June 1994), 1; Tony Jackson, 'Ruthless killers or paper tigers', *Financial Times* (2–3 July 1994), 9; 'Scale of indies cut surprises ad industry', *Marketing Week* (5 August 1994), 14; and Raymond Snoddy, 'Undaunted by hit to newspaper profits', *Financial Times* (26 August 1994), 15.

2. See David J. Schwartz, *Marketing Today: A basic approach,* 3rd edn (New York: Harcourt Brace Jovanovich, 1981), 270–3.

3. For an excellent discussion of factors affecting pricing decisions, see Thomas T. Nagle and Reed K. Holden, *The Strategy and Tactics of Pricing*, 2nd edn (Englewood Cliffs, NJ: Prentice Hall, 1995), ch. 1.

4. Michiyo Makamoto, 'Weak Japanese recovery hits results at steelmakers', *Financial Times* (14 November 1994), 21; and Andrew Baxter, 'Sweet and sour flow from British Steel', *Financial Times* (14 November 1994), 19.

5. Norton Paley, 'Fancy footwork', *Sales & Marketing Management* (July 1994), 41–2.

6. Helen Slingsby, 'Discounters lose at their own game', *Marketing Week* (23 September 1994), 21–2; and Neil Buckley, 'Sainsbury launch price war campaign', *Financial Times* (10 October 1994), 8.

7. 'A funny smell from the scent counter', *Independent* (12 November 1993), 17.

8. Christopher Farrell, 'Stuck! How companies cope when they can't raise prices', *Business Week* (15 November 1993), 146–55; see also John Y. Lee, 'Use target costing to improve your bottom line', *The CPA Journal* (January 1994), 68–71; 'The Texas computer massacre', *The Economist* (2 July 1994), 65–6.

9. Brian Dumaine, 'Closing the innovation gap', *Fortune* (2 December 1991), 56–62.

10. Here accumulated production is drawn on a semi-log scale so that equal distances represent the same percentage increase in output.

11. 'Japan's chip makers: falling off the learning curve', *The Economist* (23 February 1991), 84–5.

12. For a view of how managers perceive these price response curves see A. Diamantopoulos and Brian P. Mathews, 'Managerial perceptions of the demand curve: evidence from multiproduct firms', *European Journal of Marketing*, **27**, 9 (1993), 5–18.

13. Paul A. Huntington, 'Perception of product quality in a static state utility model', *European Journal of Marketing*, **24**, 3 (1990), 57–71.

14. Nagle and Holden, *Strategy and Tactics of Pricing*, op. cit., ch. 4.

15. Tim Burt, 'Yorkshire Chemicals ahead 19%' *Financial Times* (3 August 1994), 20.

16. For an operable example of this see Kai Kristenson and Hans Jorn Juhl, 'Pricing and correspondence to market conditions: some Danish evidence', *European Journal of Marketing*, **24**, 5 (1989), 50–5.

17. Values taken from 'Energy-saving light bulbs', *Which?* (May 1993), 8–10.

## Proton MPi: Malaysian styling, Japanese engineering, and European pricing    *Richard Lynch**

Doreen and Shem felt criminal as they sidled into the second-hand car dealer's showroom. For years they bought a new Rover every four years, but this time, after carefully reading the *Which? Guide to New and Used Cars*, they were thinking of buying a second-hand car for the first time. Shem loved the smell and feel of a new car, and he could afford one, but the numbers just did not add up. As Doreen and he looked round the dealers he caught himself humming an old Bruce Springsteen song: 'Now mister, the day the lottery I win, I ain't ever gonna ride in no used car again.' 'Well,' thought Shem, 'I have not won the lottery. So here we are.'

Just then he felt a glow. He noticed Doreen looking at the new cars also sold by the dealer. Quite a nice looking car but with an unfamiliar name. A Proton MPi and from a far-away place too, Malaysia! Still the price looked reasonable and the label said Japanese engineering. 'Maybe we needn't buy a used car after all,' suggested Doreen. 'Maybe not,' replied Shem. 'We could also look at a Skoda,' he said, swallowing hard. 'They're not expensive and now made by VW or something.' The Proton salesperson overheard them. 'Lovely cars aren't they,' he said. 'We can give you a good deal too.'

It was late 1994 and Proton, the Malaysian maker of economical small cars had an opportunity. Proton cars were manufactured in Malaysia using Japanese car engineering and some car parts. They were then shipped to the United Kingdom for sale. They had a chance to seize an increased share of the market in the United Kingdom, their biggest export market. Sales of new cars to private buyers were plunging. Not because of lack of money or lack of consumer confidence, but because of discontent with high prices, fast depreciation and the knowledge that the price of cars in Britain was higher than in the United States and some neighbouring European countries. Evidence suggested that private buyers, like Doreen and Shem, who once bought new cars, were now buying two- or three-year-old, second-hand ones

instead. The buyers found the second-hand cars were problem-free and a bargain after two or three years of depreciation. Statistics from the Society of Motor Manufacturers and Traders showed that sales of all new cars rose 8.5 per cent in the first ten months of 1994 compared with the same period in 1993, but private sales were only up 2.2 per cent.

The private car buyers were, at last, getting their own back on the fleet buyers whom they had subsidized for years. Car makers' fleet-first policy in the United Kingdom meant that the average price of a medium-sized family car was £2,000* higher than it would otherwise be. In the United Kingdom, fleet buyers include car hire companies and cars bought as additional remuneration for professional employees. As a result the fleet buyers, accounting for 60 per cent of the market, were very influential and powerful buyers. The National Franchised Dealers Association director, Alan Pulham, explained why the private buyer had to pay so much:

- Dealers need to fund the discounts, free servicing and other inducements that are usually given to fleet buyers who have bargaining power. Private buyers, with little bargaining power, rarely get these perks but subsidize the fleet buyer by paying close to the list price.
- Cars in the United Kingdom are usually equipped to a high specification because that is what the fleet buyers want. The equipment was more than the private buyer often wanted or could afford, but that is what there was.

This price discrimination gave Proton a market opportunity. Although Britain had few British-owned car companies, fleet buyers followed a made-in-Britain policy (Ford, Rover or GM) or, increasingly, made in the EU. They also bought from the big dealers representing the market leaders. Proton was neither, so its price to private buyers did not have to subsidize fleet sales. Proton had a choice. It could cut prices to gain market share or charge moderate prices but keep the comfortable margins that the current prices gave them.

* Richard Lynch is managing director of Aldersgate Consultancy Ltd. This case is largely based, with permission, on 'European Car Pricing' from his book *Cases in European Marketing* (London: Kogan Page, 1993).

*1 ecu = UK£0.83.

## Background

According to the UK Monopolies and Mergers Commission's 1992 study of small cars in Europe, there are considerable variations in price between European Union (EU) countries. These cannot be explained by currency differences, tax variations or extra equipment supplied on some models. They originate with the manufacturers themselves and their ability to maintain higher prices in some EU countries, principally the United Kingdom.

On larger cars in Europe and taking into account the same factors, the study found that there was no significant difference in price levels between the countries. With the coming of the Single Market, should Proton and the other car manufacturers set the same prices across the EU? Should there be a pan-European pricing policy?

In 1990 the EU car market was larger than that in the United States. Sales in the EU were 12.4 million cars in 1990, with the United Kingdom entering a period of decline, but Germany, and to a lesser degree other EU countries, still showing significant growth. Exhibit 16.1 estimates annual registrations for countries. Then, in late 1992, the EU market produced its first real drop in volume.

For many years, some European car companies, such as American-owned Ford, have manufactured cars on a pan-European basis. For example, its small car, named the 'Fiesta', combined parts produced in the United Kingdom, Germany and Spain in the finished model. Other companies essentially produced one model in one location. For example, Germany's Volkswagen always produced its medium-sized Polo at Wolfsburg, Germany. The cars were then shipped across the EU.

The EU car market is not truly pan-European in the sense that any model can be readily sold in any other country. There are detailed car and legal regulations in each EU country – yellow headlights in France and car emission standards in Germany, for instance – that effectively stopped this happening. However, it was for precisely this reason that the Single Market Act 1986 was enacted: over time, it was envisaged that, apart from some obvious differences such as the British and Irish driving on the left, car market standards would become the same. At this time, if not before, prices also could surely become the same across Europe.

## Car prices across Europe

As champions of the European car customer, the Bureau Européenne des Unions des Consommateurs

**Exhibit 16.1**    Car ownership across the European Union

|  | Typical annual car registrations (millions) | GDP per head in 1992 (US$000)* | Cars per 1,000 of population in 1992 | % of senior managers with company cars 1991 |
|---|---|---|---|---|
| Germany | 2.9 | 15 | 469 | 80 |
| Italy | 2.3 | 9 | 457 | 75 |
| France | 2.4 | 11 | 420 | 53 |
| United Kingdom | 2.0 | 9 | 387 | 95 |
| Belgium/Luxemburg | 0.5 | 10 | 401 | n/a |
| Netherlands | 0.4 | 10 | 374 | 85 |
| Denmark | 0.1 | 12 | 309 | n/a |
| Spain | 1.1 | 5 | 419 | 50 |
| Ireland | 0.1 | 7 | 242 | n/a |
| Portugal | 0.3 | 3 | 163 | n/a |
| Greece | 0.2 | 3 | 178 | n/a |

Sources:   *Panorama of EU Industry* (New York: World Bank, 1991/2), 13–21; various OECD Statistics, Paris; and Aldersgate Consultancy estimates.

*1 ecu = US$1.26.

(BEUC) has been campaigning for many years to bring down car prices in the expensive countries in Europe. BEUC is made up of the national consumer associations of most EU member countries. It produces surveys of car prices such as that shown in Exhibit 16.2. From that survey there would appear to be large differences between prices in different countries. BEUC reported that average new car prices varied by 70 per cent between the lowest and highest countries net of tax. The difference including taxes was as much as 128 per cent. Since EU rules lay down that the maximum difference should only be 18 per cent, there was some concern expressed. It should be noted that the EU rules specifically exclude those countries with exceptionally high national taxes, such as Denmark and Greece. The price differences stimulated parallel imports, despite the process being complicated and risky. Two hundred thousand cars had been bought by UK residents between 1980 and 1985 from outside the United Kingdom, mainly from Belgium. The car manufacturers complained that this undermined their profitability.

According to BEUC, the main reason for these price differences was that the manufacturers were taking advantage of a system of exclusive dealerships in EU countries. These meant that manufacturers could stop shipping cars to any dealer who sold the cars to anyone resident in a country different from the dealer's own. The manufacturers argued a number of other essential reasons for the differences in price between EU countries: different tax systems, exchange rate variations, different car specifications,

different dealer discounts. They said it was not a question of 'what the market would bear'.

In 1984, the European Commission agreed a Block Exemption Regulation to exempt the passenger car industry from the Treaty of Rome rules on competition. It allowed the motor trade to operate a system of exclusive distributor franchises so that the market supply in an area was controlled by the manufacturer. The reason the Commission gave for allowing the exemption was that motor vehicles are complex products and require a high level of after-sales service, which would be best served by allowing dealers to have exclusive rights in a geographical area.

With the exemption coming up for review in 1994 and the Single European Market becoming more established, the manufacturers had to decide whether to seek a continuation of this policy. They said they would like to keep the special arrangement and, to the chagrin of many consumer movements, the European Commission agreed.

### Reasons for differing car prices across Europe

The real question is whether the reasons for the differences across Europe were sufficient to justify the absence of a pan-European pricing policy. The evidence comes under four headings: customers, tax variations, dealer arrangements and other areas.

***Customers*** As Exhibit 1 shows, car ownership across the EU follows wealth to a limited extent. It is distorted by the availability of public service trans-

**Exhibit 16.2**   New car prices across Europe

| Car | Prices in ecu | | | |
| --- | --- | --- | --- | --- |
| | Denmark | Germany | France | United Kingdom |
| BMW 316i | 8,926 | 10,919 | 11,071 | 13,218 |
| Citroen CX 22TRS | 8,982 | 13,012 | 12,361 | 14,282 |
| Fiat Tipo 1400 | 5,416 | 7,359 | 7,081 | 9,143 |
| Ford Orion 1400 | – | 8,197 | 7,837 | 10,799 |
| Renault 19 | 6,390 | 9,543* | 9,493 | 11,310 |

Notes:* With catalytic converter.
All prices per model, per country, net of taxes at June 1989.
Source:   BEUC.

**Exhibit 16.3**   VAT and additional sales taxes on new cars in 1992

| Country | VAT | Car tax |
|---|---|---|
| Belgium | 25% up to 3,000 cc | |
| | 33% above | None |
| Denmark | 22% | 105% up to DKr 19,750 |
| | | 180% on the rest |
| France | 22% | None |
| Germany | 14% | None |
| Greece | 6% | Between 45% and 400%, depending upon engine size |
| Italy | 19% up to 2,000 cc, 38% above | None |
| Luxembourg | 12% | None |
| Portugal | 17% | Esc 95–1,700 per cc on an increasing scale |
| Ireland | 21% | 21.7% up to 2,016 cc |
| | | 24.7% above |
| Spain | 33% | None |
| United Kingdom | 17.5% | 10% |

Source:   Monopolies and Mergers Study UK, 1992.

1 ecu = US$1.26 = DKr 7.33 (Danish kroner) = Esc 195 (Portuguese escudos).

port, the level of car sales taxes and the likelihood of obtaining a car as part of a work pay and remuneration package. The provision of company cars has distorted car prices. Company fleet buyers purchase in large quantities, and they are therefore able to get price discounts not available to private buyers. To maintain their profits, car companies charge private buyers high prices.

***Tax variations***   Exhibit 16.3 shows substantial variations across the EU in the tax on cars. When car manufacturers complained about price comparisons made by the consumer groups, their responses often concerned this area.

***Dealer arrangements***   Across Europe, car manufacturers have agreements with dealers in a geographical area for the sale of their product ranges. There are a number of restrictions placed on the dealers, which:

- Limit the dealer's ability to advertise outside its franchise area.
- Stop the dealer from acquiring or holding dealerships outside the existing area from other suppliers.
- Prevent the dealer acquiring or holding other dealerships except on a distinct and separate site.

- Restrict the ability of the dealer to sell other products, such as second-hand cars or car parts from other manufacturers.
- Limit the dealer to selling a maximum quantity of cars in a given period and to a maximum percentage of the total cars from the manufacturer in one year.

While these restrictions limit dealer freedom, the car manufacturers say that they do make it more likely that car service levels are of the highest quality. Moreover European car companies are engaged in a fiercely competitive battle in each EU country, so that the EU has accepted that these dealer restrictions are acceptable in terms of the EU Block Exemption Regulation.

Data have been published on the number of dealers that each of the main EU car manufacturers has in each country. In general terms in 1991, manufacturers tended to have rather more dealers in the main country of manufacture, e.g. Renault in France, Rover in the United Kingdom. The Japanese car companies had rather fewer dealers, but this would be consistent with their overall share of the European car market at around 9 per cent in 1989. The US multinationals, Ford and General Motors (trading as Opel in Germany and Vauxhall in the United Kingdom), were well represented in numbers of dealerships across Europe, reflecting their market share of 21 per cent. However, the *number* of dealers provides no indication of their *quality* in terms of location, size, trained staff, workshop facilities, and so forth. Proton dealers were almost exclusively confined to the United Kingdom.

**Other areas**   As will be generally true in all pricing decisions, the costs of car production need to be reflected in the prices: there would be no point in pricing below marginal costs. In fact, such a pricing policy is illegal in some EU countries. While European car manufacturers do not publish detailed comparative cost data for competitive reasons, outline data on wage costs by country are summarized in Exhibit 16.4.

Other areas that would need to be considered include the extra items added to some cars as standard, such as electric windows, in-car stereo systems, fuel injection. European car manufacturers have commented that this is the area which has made UK cars more expensive.

**Reasons for national price differences**   To assist understanding of how prices are constructed and explain why some national prices are higher than others, the European car manufacturer General Motors commissioned a study of comparative prices in 1991 (see Exhibit 16.5). The detailed study shows that significant price differences exist for what is basically the same car.

### Proton's pricing

Given a system which meant that the price of Doreen and Shem's car would subsidize fleet purchases, it seemed sensible for them to think about buying a 'second-hand new car'. In that way the private buyer benefits from fleet buyers absorbing the

**Exhibit 16.5**   Comparative car prices, 1991 ($)

|  | UK Astra GL 1.4 5-door noncatalytic | German Kadett GL 1.4 5-door catalytic | France Kadett GL 1.4 5-door noncatalytic |
|---|---|---|---|
| List price inc. tax | 8,749 | 7,407 | 7,764 |
| List excluding tax | 7,023 | 6,497 | 7,764 |
| Equipment adjustments (EA) | – | 482 | 257 |
| E.A. list price excluding tax | 7,023 | 6,979 | 6,468 |
| Discounts dealer (%) | 13.7 | 7.1 | 2.8 |
| On-road costs | 350 | 152 | 314 |
| On-road price ex tax | 5,411 | 6,636 | 6,601 |
| Financing support | 672 | 160 | – |
| On-the-road with finance | 5,739 | 6,578 | 6,601 |

Source: GM Vauxhall 1991 Survey.

**Exhibit 16.4**   Wage costs in some car-producing countries

|  | Deutschmarks per hour 1991 | Typical producers |
|---|---|---|
| Germany | 45 | Volkswagen and BMW |
| United States | 35 | GM and Ford |
| Japan | 34 | Toyota and Nissan |
| Italy | 32 | Fiat |
| Spain | 29 | SEAT (Volkswagen/Audi group) |
| France | 29 | Renault |
| United Kingdom | 29 | Rover |
| Malaysia | 15 | Proton |

Source:   German Auto Industry Association and Aldersgate Consultancy Ltd estimates.

1 ecu = US$1.26 = DM 1.89 (Deutschmarks).

## CASE 16 (cont)

heavy depreciation in the first few years of a car's life. Will the car manufacturers ever recapture the private-buyer market again? Car industry expert, Garel Rhys thinks not until 'prices of new cars in Europe ... come down in real terms to American levels'. He continues, 'That's when the fur will fly. There are simply too many car makers in Europe and they can't all survive.'

As a low-cost supplier of cars to the EU without a vested interest in fleet buyers and expensive dealerships, Proton could start the 'fur flying'. Should they or should they not cut prices to gain market share? What would happen if they did? Would the European manufacturers fight back or would the European Commission step in to limit Proton's access to the market? Charging a lower price would help Doreen and Shem, and many other private customers, but would it, in the long run, help Proton? Maybe they would do better to accept the high margins that the European car industry forces upon them.

### Questions

1. Clearly there is currently no pan-European pricing policy, but should that *ever* exist across the EU? Should the car companies continue with what are essentially national policies? Who is benefiting from the European Commission's intervention?

2. Is Shem justified in his concern about being charged too much for new cars in the UK? What explains the big difference between EU and US car prices? Does the price demand function vary from country to country in Europe and is that in the United States completely different?

3. How should Proton price their cars? Should they keep their list prices high, reduce them or give big discounts to buyer? Why might giving discounts be better than lowering the list price?

4. What is likely to happen if Proton cuts its prices to gain market share? Is the differential pricing policy across Europe and between private and fleet buyers a way for car makers to maximize profits or is it forced upon them by differences in EU governments and customers?

Sources: Song extract from Bruce Springsteen, 'Used Cars', on *Nebraska* (CBS 25100, 1982); other sources are Monopolies and Mergers Commission, *New Motor Cars* (HMSO, 1992); Y. Doz, *Strategic Management in Multinational Companies* (Oxford: Pergamon, 1986); John Griffith, 'Bad dreams return to the motor trade', *Financial Times* (10 May 1992), ii; John Griffith, 'Market distorted by use of company cars as perks,' *Financial Times* (6 February 1992), 6; European Commission, *Panorama of EC Industry 1991/92* (Luxemburg: OPECE, 1991), 30–8; D. Fisher, 'Time to become lean and mean', *Financial Times* (23 June 1992), 18; John Griffiths, 'Price is wrong for some motorists', *Financial Times* (26–27 November 1994), 9.

## CHAPTER SEVENTEEN

# Pricing products

## Pricing strategies

## CHAPTER OBJECTIVES

After reading this chapter, you should be able to:

- Understand new-product pricing strategies and know when to use them.

- Explain how pricing decisions are influenced by the product mix.

- Appreciate price adjustment strategies and how to make price changes.

- Differentiate between geographical pricing strategies and know their implications.

## CHAPTER PREVIEW

### Mobile phones: even more mobile customers

1 ecu = UK£0.83
= 83p

Vodafone and Cellnet, Britain's leading mobile phone suppliers are losing market share to new digital competitors, One-2-One and Orange. Between July and September 1994, 227,000 subscribers joined Vodafone but, more significantly, 104,000 left. The pricing policy explains why Vodafone and Cellnet gain and lose so many customers. Vodafone pump in about £300 subsidy into the sale of each phone and connection, and then make a huge profit on the phone's use. Often the mobile phone and its connection charge come free with a large purchase, such as a car or photocopier. Then, depending on the deal, subscribers pay between 15p and 50p per minute for what the cellular company pay 1.5p per minute off-peak and 0.5p for local calls. The margins helped Vodafone post pretax profits of £363m. on a turnover of £850m. Gerry Whent, Vodafone's chief executive describes the market, 'Every month people are leaving us for a variety of reasons. They've died, changed jobs, just decided to hand the phone back, or whatever. A lot of people we take on are attracted to the idea of using a mobile phone, until they see the bill. If they only use it once a day it's only a matter of time before they give it back.' He continues, 'This problem is not exclusive to us. I'd argue that Cellnet is losing just as many subscribers over the year. The important thing is that we are both taking in new ones.'

Li Ka-shing, Asian billionaire boss of Orange's parent company Hutchinson Whampoa, sees things differently. As Vodafone subscribers scrutinize their bills at renewal time they are tempted to switch to the cheaper and technically more advanced Orange or One-2-One services. As Hans Snook, Orange's UK manager says, 'Vodafone has rested on its laurels far too long. Now it's paying the price.' About 70 per cent of Orange's subscribers are switchers, not first-time buyers.

Hans Snook had better be right. By the end of 1995 Hutchinson will have spent £1bn on developing the UK market, 'the price for four brand new skyscrapers' in Li Ka-shing's Hong Kong home town. The investment is in the latest DCS 1800 digital technology that gives the same voice quality as conventional telephones. Digital is also intrinsically cheaper than Vodafone and Cellnet's older analogue systems and gives access to more features. The investment so far has bought the mobile phone system Orange 980 £75,000 Nokia base stations and aerials across the United Kingdom covering 50 per cent of the population. To get to their target 90 per cent coverage Orange will need 2,000 stations. The fruity brand name is already a success. Launched using a huge teaser campaign, customers are already asking people to 'Call me back on Orange' or saying 'Can I give you my Orange phone number?' One month after launch they already had 65 per cent unprompted name recognition.

Orange's pricing strategy is different to the analogue suppliers. Their phones are not cheap, costing between £150 and £300 each, and they don't give them away to get new customers. Instead they have introduced package calls to the market. Orange customers buy between £15 and £100 worth of calls a month. The cost per call is about half that of the traditional networks.

Mercury's One-2-One has taken a less aggressive approach to the cellular market. They did not strive to go national but concentrated on giving a cheap service to Londoners living within the M25 orbital motorway. That means that they can offer a package to users in their catchment area for much less than Orange. They give unlimited free local calls, too. Will their good value for the 'not very mobile' phone user work? So far it has, and it has also tempted about 10,000 new subscribers a month, about half of them coming from Vodafone. As a second careful step they have just extended One-2-One to the West Midland's, Britain's second largest conurbation, covering Birmingham and Coventry.

Orange and One-2-One are a hit with consumers and 25 December 1994 was the Christmas of the mobile phone, with many being given as gifts. The new growth markets switched from executives to travellers worried about being out alone at night. By 1999 forecasters expect Orange to outsell Vodafone to domestic consumers and One-2-One to be close to Cellnet in the same market. One-2-One have placed themselves firmly in the gift market by offering unlimited free phone calls on Christmas Day. Will anyone get through? Whatever happens, the signs are that the days of the 43 per cent profit margin for the cellular operators are coming to an end.[1]

## PRICING STRATEGIES

In this chapter, we will look at the complex dynamics of pricing. A company does not set a single price, but rather a *pricing structure* that covers different items in its line. This pricing structure changes over time as products move through their life cycles. The company adjusts product prices to reflect changes in costs and demand and to account for variations in buyers and situations. As the competitive environment changes, the company considers when to initiate price changes and when to respond to them. And as the cellular phone example demonstrates forcefully, pricing decisions are subject to an incredibly complex array of environmental and competitive forces.

This chapter examines the dynamic pricing strategies available to management. In turn, we look at *new-product pricing strategies* for products in the introductory stage of the product life cycle, *product-mix pricing strategies* for related products in the product mix, *price-adjustment strategies* that account for customer differences and changing situations and *strategies for initiating and responding to price changes*.[2]

## NEW-PRODUCT PRICING STRATEGIES

Pricing strategies usually change as the product passes through its life cycle. The introductory stage is especially challenging. We can distinguish between pricing a product that imitates existing products and pricing an innovative product that is patent protected.

A company that plans to develop an imitative new product faces a product-positioning problem. It must decide where to position the product versus competing products in terms of quality and price. Figure 17.1 shows four possible positioning strategies. First, the company might decide to use a *premium pricing* strategy – producing a high-quality product and charging the highest price. At the other extreme, it might decide on an *economy pricing* strategy – producing a lower quality product but charging a low price. These strategies can coexist in the same market as long as the market consists of at least two groups of buyers, those who seek quality and those who seek price. Thus, Tag-Heuer offers very high-quality sports watches at high prices, whereas Casio offers digital watches at almost throwaway prices.[3]

The *good-value* strategy represents a way to attack the premium pricer. Britain's leading grocery chain always uses the **strapline**: 'Good food costs less at Sainsbury's'. If this really is true and quality-sensitive buyers believe the good-value pricer, they will sensibly shop at Sainsbury's and save money – unless the premium product offers more status or snob appeal. Using an *overcharging* strategy, the company over-prices the product in relation to its quality. In the long-run, however, customers are likely to feel 'taken'. They will stop buying the product and will complain to others about it. Thus this strategy should be avoided.[4]

Companies bringing out an innovative, patent-protected product face the challenge of setting prices for the first time. They can choose between two strategies: *market-skimming pricing* and *market-penetration pricing*.

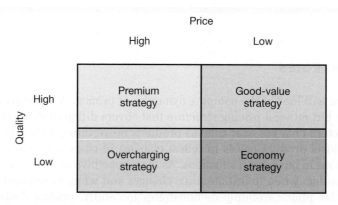

**Figure 17.1** Four price-positioning strategies.

## Market-skimming pricing

Many companies that invent new products initially set high prices to 'skim' revenues layer by layer from the market. Intel is a prime user of this strategy, called **market-skimming pricing**. When Intel first introduces a new computer chip, it charges the highest price it can, given the benefits of the new chip over competing chips. It sets a price that makes it *just* worthwhile for some segments of the market to adopt computers containing the chip. As initial sales slow down and as competitors threaten to introduce similar chips, Intel lowers the price to draw in the next price-sensitive layer of customers.

For example, when Intel first brought out its Pentium chips, it priced them at about $1,000 each. As a result, computer producers priced their first Pentium PCs at £3,500 or more, attracting as customers only serious computer users and business buyers. However, after introduction, Intel cut Pentium prices by 30 per cent per year, allowing the price of Pentium PCs to drop eventually into the typical price range of home buyers. In this way, Intel skimmed a maximum amount of revenue from the various segments of the market.[5]

1 ecu = US$1.26

Market skimming makes sense only under certain conditions. First, the product's quality and image must support its higher price and enough buyers must want the product at that price. Second, the costs of producing a smaller volume cannot be so high that they cancel the advantage of charging more. Finally, competitors should not be able to enter the market easily and undercut the high price.

## Market-penetration pricing

Rather than setting a high initial price to skim off small but profitable market segments, some companies use **market-penetration pricing**. They set a low initial price

France Telecom use market-penetration pricing to attract new corporate clients.

in order to *penetrate* the market quickly and deeply – to attract a large number of buyers quickly and win a large market share. The high sales volume results in falling costs, allowing the company to cut its price even further. For example, Dell and dan used penetration pricing to sell high-quality computer products through lower-cost mail-order channels. Their sales soared when IBM, Compaq, Apple and other competitors selling through retail stores could not match their prices. The Bank of Scotland and Winterthur of Switzerland both used their Direct Line, Privilege and Churchill subsidiaries to grab profits and share in the motor insurance market by selling direct to consumers at market-penetrating prices. The high volume results in lower costs which, in turn, allow the discounters to keep prices low.[6]

Several conditions favour setting a low price. First, the market must be highly price sensitive so that a low price produces more market growth. Second, production and distribution costs must fall as sales volume increases. Finally, the low price must help keep out the competition – otherwise the price advantage may only be temporary. For example, Dell faced difficult times when IBM and Compaq established their own direct distribution channels.

## PRODUCT-MIX PRICING STRATEGIES

The strategy for setting a product's price often has to be changed when the product is part of a product mix. In this case, the firm looks for a set of prices that maximizes the profits on the total product mix. Pricing is difficult because the various products have related demand and costs and face different degrees of competition. We now take a closer look at five *product mix pricing* situations summarized in Table 17.1.

### Product line pricing

Companies usually develop product lines rather than single products. For example, Merloni's sells Indesit, Ariston and Scholte with price and status ascending in that order. There are full ranges of Indesit to Ariston appliances, from washing machines to freezers, covering the first two price bands while Scholte sell expensive built-in kitchen equipment. Kodak offers not just one type of film, but an assortment including regular Kodak film, higher-priced Kodak Royal Gold film for special occasions and a lower-priced, seasonal film called Funtime that competes with store brands.

| TABLE 17.1 | Product mix pricing strategies | | | |
|---|---|---|---|---|
| Product line pricing | Optional-product pricing | Captive-product pricing | By-product pricing | Product-bundle pricing |
| Setting price steps between product line items | Pricing optional or accessory products sold with the main product | Pricing products that must be used with the main product | Pricing low-value by-products to get rid of them | Pricing bundles of products sold together |

Each of these brands is available in a variety of sizes and film speeds. In **product line pricing**, management must decide on the price steps to set between the various products in a line.

The price steps should take into account cost differences between the products in the line, customer evaluations of their different features and competitors' prices. If the price difference between two successive products is small, buyers will usually buy the more advanced product. This will increase company profits if the cost difference is smaller than the price difference. If the price difference is large, however, customers will generally buy the less advanced products.

In many industries, sellers use well-established *price points* for the products in their line. Thus record stores might carry CDs at four price levels: budget, mid-line, full-line and superstar. The customer will probably associate low to high-quality recordings with the four price points. Even if the four prices are raised a little, people will normally buy CDs at their own preferred price points. The seller's task is to establish perceived quality differences that support the price differences.[7]

## Optional-product pricing

Many companies use **optional-product pricing** – offering to sell optional or accessory products along with their main product. For example, a car buyer may choose to order power windows, cruise control and a radio with a CD player. Pricing these options is a sticky problem. Car companies have to decide which items to include in the base price and which to offer as options. BMW's basic cars come famously under-equipped. Typically the 318i is about DM 40,000, but the customer then has to pay extra for a radio (prices vary), electric windows (DM 700), sun roof (DM 1,800) and security system (DM 1,100). The basic model is stripped of so many comforts and conveniences that most buyers reject it. They pay for extras or buy a better-equipped version. More recently, however, American and European car makers have been forced to follow the example of the Japanese auto makers and include in the basic price many useful items previously sold only as options. The advertised price now often represents a well-equipped car.

1 ecu = US$1.26
= DM 1.89
(Deutschmarks)

## Captive-product pricing

Companies that make products that must be used along with a main product are using **captive-product pricing**. Examples of captive products are razors, camera film and computer software. Producers of the main products (razors, cameras and computers) often price them low and set high mark-ups on the supplies. Thus Polaroid prices its cameras low because it makes its money on the film it sells. And Gillette sells low-priced razors but makes money on the replacement blades. Camera or razor makers who do not sell film have to price their main products higher in order to make the same overall profit.

The strategy used by the cellular operators is called **two-part pricing**. The price of the service is broken into a *fixed fee* plus a *variable usage rate*. Thus a telephone company charges a monthly rate – the fixed fee – plus charges for calls beyond some minimum number – the variable usage rate. Amusement parks charge admission plus fees for food, midway attractions and rides over a minimum. The service firm must decide how much to charge for the basic service and how much for the variable usage. The fixed amount should be low enough to induce usage of the service and profit can be made on the variable fees.

*Price*

## By-product pricing

In producing processed meats, petroleum products, chemicals and other products, there are often **by-products**. If the by-products have no value and if getting rid of them is costly, this will affect the pricing of the main product. Using **by-product pricing**, the manufacturer will seek a market for these by-products and should accept any price that covers more than the cost of storing and delivering them. This practice allows the seller to reduce the main product's price to make it more competitive. By-products can even turn out to be profitable. For example, many lumber mills have begun to sell bark chips and sawdust profitably as decorative mulch for home and commercial landscaping.

## Product-bundle pricing

Using **product-bundle pricing** sellers often combine several of their products and offer the bundle at a reduced price. Thus theatres and sports teams sell season tickets at less than the cost of single tickets; hotels sell specially priced packages that include room, meals and entertainment; computer makers include attractive software packages with their personal computers. Price bundling can promote the sales of products consumers might not otherwise buy, but the combined price must be low enough to get them to buy the bundle.[8]

## PRICE-ADJUSTMENT STRATEGIES

Companies usually adjust their basic prices to account for various customer differences and changing situations. Table 17.2 summarizes seven price-adjustment strategies: *discount and allowance pricing, segmented pricing, psychological pricing, promotional pricing, value pricing, geographical pricing* and *international pricing*.

| **TABLE 17.2** | *Price adjustment strategies* | | | | | |
|---|---|---|---|---|---|---|
| Discount and allowance pricing | Discriminatory pricing | Psychological pricing | Value pricing | Promotional pricing | Geographical pricing | International pricing |
| Reducing prices to reward customer responses such as paying early or promoting the product | Adjusting prices to allow for differences in customers products, and locations | Adjusting prices for psychological effect | Adjusting prices to offer the right combination of quality and service at a fair price | Temporarily reducing prices to increase short-run sales | Adjusting prices to account for the geographic location of customers | Adjusting prices in international markets |

## Discount and allowance pricing

Most companies adjust their basic price to reward customers for certain responses, such as early payment of bills, volume purchases and off-season buying. These price adjustments – called *discounts* and *allowances* – can take many forms.

A **cash discount** is a price reduction to buyers who pay their bills promptly. A typical example is '2/10, net 30', which means that although payment is due within 30 days, the buyer can deduct 2 per cent if the bill is paid within 10 days. The discount must be granted to all buyers meeting these terms. Such discounts are customary in many industries and help to improve the sellers' cash situation and reduce bad debts and credit-collection costs.

A **quantity discount** is a price reduction to buyers who buy large volumes. A typical example might be '$10 per unit for less than 100 units, $9 per unit for 100 or more units'. Wine merchants often give 'twelve for the price of eleven' and Makro, the trade warehouse, automatically gives discounts on any product bought in bulk. Discounts provide an incentive to the customer to buy more from one given seller, rather than from many different sources.

A **quantity premium** is sometimes charged to people buying higher volumes. In Japan it often costs more per item to buy a twelve-pack of beer or sushi than smaller quantities because the larger packs are more giftable and therefore less price sensitive. Quantity surcharges can also occur when the product being bought is in short supply or in sets, for example, several seats together at a 'sold-out' rock concert or sports event, and some small restaurants charge a premium to large groups. Similarly, in buying antiques, it costs more to buy six complete place settings of cutlery than a single item. In this case the price will continue to increase with volume, eight place settings costing more than six, and twelve place settings costing more than eight. Quantity premiums are more common than people imagine, and that is why they work. Consumers expect prices to decrease with volume and so do not check unit prices. This allows retailers to slip in high-margin items. Quantity surcharge increases with the variety of complexity of pack sizes and, in some markets, over 30 per cent of ranges include some quantity surcharging.[9]

A **functional discount** (also called a *trade discount*) is offered by the seller to trade channel members who perform certain functions, such as selling, storing and record keeping. Manufacturers may offer different functional discounts to different trade channels because of the varying services they perform, but manufacturers must offer the same functional discounts within each trade channel.

A **seasonal discount** is a price discount to buyers who buy merchandise or services out of season. For example, lawn and garden equipment manufacturers will

Grundig offers a 'cash back', an increasingly popular price-adjustment strategy for expensive goods.

Photograph: Mary Ann Page

offer seasonal discounts to retailers during the autumn and winter to encourage early ordering in anticipation of the heavy spring and summer selling seasons. Hotels, motels and airlines will offer seasonal discounts in their slower selling periods. Seasonal discounts allow the seller to keep production steady during the entire year.

Allowances are another type of reduction from the list price. For example, **trade-in allowances** are price reductions given for turning in an old item when buying a new one. Trade-in allowances are most common in the automobile industry, but are also given for other durable goods. **Promotional allowances** are payments or price reductions to reward dealers for participating in advertising and sales-support programmes.

## Segmented pricing

Companies will often adjust their basic prices to allow for differences in customers, products and locations. In **segmented pricing**, the company sells a product or service at two or more prices, even though the difference in prices is not based on differences in costs. Segmented pricing takes several forms:

- *Customer-segment pricing.* Different customers pay different prices for the same product or service. Museums, for example, will charge a lower admission for young people the wageless, students and senior citizens. In many parts of the world, tourists pay more to see museums, shows and national monuments than do locals.
- *Product-form pricing.* Different versions of the product are priced differently, but not according to differences in their costs. For instance the Dutch company Skil prices its 6434H electric drill at DFl 200, which is DFl 125 more than the price of its 6400H. The 6434H is more powerful and has more features, yet this extra power and features cost only a few more guilders to build in.
- *Location pricing.* Different locations are priced differently, even though the cost of offering each location is the same. For instance, theatres vary their seat prices because of audience preferences for certain locations and EU universities charge higher tuition for non-EU students.

1 ecu =US$1.26
= DFl 2.12
(Dutch guilders)

■ *Time pricing.* Prices vary by the season, the month, the day and even the hour. Public utilities vary their prices to commercial users by time of day and weekend versus weekday. The telephone company offers lower 'off-peak' charges and resorts give seasonal discounts.

For segmented pricing to be an effective strategy, certain conditions must exist. The market must be segmentable and the segments must show different degrees of demand. Members of the segment paying the lower price should not be able to turn around and resell the product to the segment paying the higher price. Competitors should not be able to undersell the firm in the segment being charged the higher price. Nor should the costs of segementing and watching the market exceed the extra revenue obtained from the price difference. The practice should not lead to customer resentment and ill will. Finally, the segmented pricing must be legal.

## Psychological pricing

Price says something about the product. For example, many consumers use price to judge quality. A $100 bottle of perfume may contain only $3 worth of scent, but some people are willing to pay the $100 because this price indicates something special.

In using **psychological pricing**, sellers consider the psychology of prices and not simply the economics. For example, one study of the relationship between price and quality perception of cars found that consumers perceive higher-priced cars as having higher quality.[10] By the same token, higher-quality cars are perceived to be even higher priced than they actually are. When consumers can judge the quality of a product by examining it or by calling on past experience with it, they use price less to judge quality. When consumers cannot judge quality because they lack the information or skill, price becomes an important quality signal (see Marketing Highlight 17.1)

Another aspect of psychological pricing is **reference prices** – prices that buyers carry in their minds and refer to when looking at a given product. The reference price might be formed by noting current prices, remembering past prices or assessing the buying situation. Sellers can influence or use these consumers' reference prices when setting price. For example, a company could display its product next to more expensive ones in order to imply that it belongs in the same class. Department stores often sell women's clothing in separate departments differentiated by price: clothing found in the more expensive department is assumed to be of better quality. Companies also can influence consumers' reference prices by stating high manufacturer's suggested prices, by indicating that the product was originally priced much higher or by pointing to a competitor's higher price.

Even small differences in price can suggest product differences. Consider a stereo priced at $300 compared to one priced at $299.95. The actual price difference is only 5 cents, but the psychological difference can be much greater. For example, some consumers will see the $299.95 as a price in the $200 range rather than the $300 range. Whereas the $299.95 is more likely to be seen as a bargain price, the $300 price suggests more quality. Complicated numbers, such as $247.41, also look less appealing than rounded ones, such as $250. Some psychologists argue that each digit has symbolic and visual qualities that should be considered in pricing. Thus, 8 is round and even and created a soothing effect, whereas 7 is angular and creates a jarring effect.[11]

## Promotional pricing

With **promotional pricing**, companies will temporarily price their products below list price and sometimes even below cost. Promotional pricing takes several forms.

## How price signals product quality

Heublein produces Smirnoff, America's leading brand of vodka. Some years ago another brand, Wolfschmidt, attacked Smirnoff. Wolfschmidt claimed to have the same quality as Smirnoff but priced at one US dollar less per bottle. Concerned that customers might switch to Wolfschmidt, Heublein considered several possible counterstrategies. It could lower Smirnoff's price by one dollar to hold on to market share; it could hold Smirnoff's price but increase advertising and promotion expenditures; or it could hold Smirnoff's price and let its market share fall. All three strategies would lead to lower profits, and it seemed that Heublein faced a no-win situation.

At this point, however, Heublein's marketers thought of a fourth strategy – and it was brilliant. Heublein *raised* the price of Smirnoff by one dollar! The company then introduced a new brand, Relska, to compete with Wolfschmidt. Moreover it introduced yet another brand, Popov, priced even *lower* than Wolfschmidt. This product line-pricing strategy positioned Smirnoff as the élite brand and Wolfschmidt as an ordinary brand. Heublein's clever strategy produced a large increase in its overall profits.

The irony is that Heublein's three brands are much the same in taste and manufacturing costs. Heublein knew that a product's price signals its quality. Using price as a signal, Heublein sells roughly the same product at three different quality positions.

Supermarkets and department stores will price a few products as *loss leaders* to attract customers to the store in the hope that they will buy other items at normal mark-ups. Sellers will also use *special-event pricing* in certain seasons to draw in more customers. Thus linens are promotional priced every January to attract weary Christmas shoppers back into the stores. Manufacturers will sometimes offer *cash rebates* to consumers who buy the product from dealers within a specified time; the manufacturer sends the rebate directly to the customer. Rebates have recently been popular with auto makers and producers of durable goods and small appliances. Some manufacturers offer *low-interest financing, longer warranties* or *free maintenance* to reduce the consumer's 'price'. This practice has recently become a favourite of the auto industry. Or, the seller may simply offer *discounts* from normal prices to increase sales and reduce inventories.

### Value pricing

During the recessionary, slow-growth 1990s, many companies have adjusted their prices to bring them into line with economic conditions and with the resulting fundamental shift in consumer attitudes toward quality and value. More and more, marketers have adopted **value-pricing** strategies – offering just the right combination of quality and good service at a fair price. In many cases, this has involved the introduction of less expensive versions of established, brand name products. Thus Campbell introduced its Great Starts Budget frozen-food line, Holiday Inn opened several Holiday Express budget hotels, Revlon's Charles of the Ritz offered the Express Bar collection of affordable cosmetics, and McDonald's offered 'value menus'. In other cases, value pricing has involved redesigning existing brands in order to offer more quality for a given price or the same quality for less (see Marketing Highlight 17.2).

## Geographical pricing

A company also must decide how to price its products to customers located in different parts of the country or the world. Should the company risk losing the business of more distant customers by charging them higher prices to cover the higher shipping costs? Or should the company charge all customers the same prices regardless of location? We will look at five **geographical pricing** strategies for the following hypothetical situation:

> The Tromsø a.s. is a Norwegian paper products company selling to customers all over Europe. The cost of freight is high and affects the companies from whom customers buy their paper. Tromsø wants to establish a geographical pricing policy. It is trying to determine how to price a NKr 1,000 order to three specific customers: Customer A (Oslo); Customer B (Amsterdam) and Customer C (Barcelona).

1 ecu = US$1.26 = NKr 8.20 (Norwegian kroner)

One option is for Tromsø to ask each customer to pay the shipping cost from the factory to the customer's location. All three customers would pay the same factory price of NKr 1,000, with Customer A paying, say NKr 100 for shipping; Customer B, NKr 150; and Customer C, NKr 250. Called **FOB-origin pricing**, this practice means that the goods are placed *free on board* (hence, *FOB*) a carrier. At that point the title and responsibility pass to the customer, who pays the freight from the factory to the destination.

Because each customer picks up his own cost, supporters of FOB pricing feel that this is the fairest way to assess freight charges. The disadvantage, however, is that Tromsø will be a high-cost firm to distant customers. If Tromsø's main competitor happens to be in Spain, this competitor will no doubt outsell Tromsø in Spain. In fact, the competitor would outsell Tromsø in most of southern Europe, whereas Tromsø would dominate the north.

**Uniform delivered pricing** is the exact opposite of FOB pricing. Here, the company charges the same price plus freight to all customers, regardless of their location. The freight charge is set at the average freight cost. Suppose this is NKr 150. Uniform delivered pricing therefore results in a higher charge to the Oslo customer (who pays NKr 150 freight instead of NKr 100) and a lower charge to the Barcelona customer (who pays NKr 150 instead of NKr 250). On the one hand, the Oslo customer would prefer to buy paper from another local paper company that uses FOB-origin pricing. On the other hand, Tromsø has a better chance of winning over the Spanish customer. Other advantages of uniform delivered pricing are that it is fairly easy to administer and it lets the firm advertise its price nationally.

**Zone pricing** falls between FOB-origin pricing and uniform delivered pricing. The company sets up two or more zones. All customers within a given zone pay a single total price; the more distant the zone, the higher the price. For example, Tromsø might set up a Scandinavian zone and charge NKr 100 freight to all customers in this zone, a northern Europe zone in which it charges NKr 150 and a southern Europe zone in which it charges NKr 250. In this way, the customers within a given price zone receive no price advantage from the company. For example, customers in Oslo and Copenhagen pay the same total price to Tromsø. The complaint, however, is that the Oslo customer is paying part of the Copenhagen customer's freight cost. In addition, even though they may be within a few miles of each other, a customer just barely on the south side of the line dividing north and south pays much more than one who is just barely on the north side of the line.

Using **basing-point pricing**, the seller selects a given city as a 'basing point' and charges all customers the freight cost from that city to the customer location, regardless of the city from which the goods actually are shipped. For example, Tromsø might set Oslo as the basing point and charge all customers NKr 100 plus the freight from Oslo to their locations. This means that a Copenhagen customer pays the freight cost from Oslo to Copenhagen, even though the goods may be shipped from Tromsø. Using a basing-point location other than the factory raises the total price for customers near the factory and lowers the total price for customers far from the factory.

If all sellers used the same basing-point city, delivered prices would be the same for all customers and price competition would be eliminated. Industries such as sugar, cement, steel and automobiles used basing-point pricing for years, but this method has

## Value pricing: offering more for less

Marketers have a new buzzword for the 1990s and it's spelt V-A-L-U-E. Throughout the 1980s, marketers pitched luxury, prestige, extravagance − even expensiveness − for everything from ice cream to autos. But after the recession began, they started redesigning, repackaging, repositioning and remarketing products to emphasize value. Now, value pricing − offering more for a lot less by underscoring a product's quality while at the same time featuring its price − has gone from a groundswell to a tidal wave.

Value pricing can mean many things to marketers. To some, it means price cutting. To others, it means special deals, such as providing more of a product at the same price. And to still others, it means a new image − one that convinces consumers they're receiving a good deal. No matter how it's defined, however, value pricing has become a prime strategy for wooing consumers. The up-market tactics that dominated the 1980s have virtually disappeared. Now, 1980s pretentiousness is used as the antithesis. Take the magazine ad for Nissan's Maxima GXE: 'Today the idea of spending thousands more on a luxury sedan for the cachet of having a hood ornament appears hopelessly unjustified. No, these are the 1990s, an era of renewed sensibility.'

Marketers are finding that the flat economy and changing consumer demographics have created a new class of sophisticated, bargain-hunting shoppers who are careful of where and how they shop. Whereas it used to be fashionable to flaunt affluence and spend conspicuously, now it's fashionable to say you got a good deal. To convince consumers they're getting more for their money, companies from fast-food chains to stock brokerages and car makers have revamped their marketing pitches:

- 'Every day low prices' is the central philosophy of 'category killers', such as Toys 'R' Us and IKEA.

These often sell from low-cost out-of-town 'sheds' offering a huge range and good value. Economies of scale and buying power help these traders keep costs down but they also get customers to do more. Buy a bike from Toys 'R' Us or furniture from IKEA and you will have to assemble it yourself. IKEA also does not deliver, so keeps costs down by having a simple operation where customers work as warehouse, distribution and assembly staff.

- Marks & Spencer uses a similar 'Outstanding value' campaign across its European stores. It froze prices on 75 per cent of its items, and reduced the price of the remainder. They then continued to pass on their own efficiency gains and suppliers' price cuts to the customer. The suppliers rose to the challenge, cut their prices and gained a significant increase in sales volume during a recession. Marks & Spencer's profits also rose.

- PepsiCo's Taco Bell chain introduced an incredibly successful 'value menu' offering 59-cent tacos and fifteen other items for either 59 cents, 79 cents or 99 cents. McDonald's followed suit with its Extra-Value meals, underscored by the ad theme, 'Good food. Good value'. Soon, Wendy's, Burger King and other competitors entered the fray with their own value-pricing schemes.

- Stock broker Shearson-Lehman Hutton is searching for a new ad campaign to help it counter the low-price claims of discount stockbrokers. 'People are asking, "Am I getting what I paid for and is there value in it?"' notes a Shearson marketing executive. 'Companies are being challenged to [define] the value they offer versus the price they charge'. The new campaign will focus on services such as investment advice and financial planning that make Shearson's full-service offering a better value, even at the higher prices it charges.

become less popular today. Some companies set up multiple basing points to create more flexibility: they quote freight charges from the basing-point city nearest to the customer.

Finally, the seller who is anxious to do business with a certain customer or geographical area might use **freight-absorption pricing**. Using this strategy, the seller absorbs all or part of the actual freight charges in order to get the desired business.

---

- In a recent world tour, General Electric Chairman Jack Welch noted that customers around the globe are now more interested in price than technology. 'The value decade is upon us', he states. 'If you can't sell a top-quality product at the world's lowest price, you're going to be out of the game.' As a result, in products ranging from refrigerators to CAT scanners and jet engines, GE is working to offer basic, dependable units at unbeatable prices.

- Most office supplies are now bought direct from warehouses such as Office World, 'The No. 1 Office Supplies Discount Superstore' or by direct mail from 'Price Busters' such as Viking Direct. Software Warehouse has a price pledge: 'If you can find it cheaper – CALL US! We will beat ANY advertised price.' The low-cost, high-service approach to selling pioneered by Dell is rapidly becoming the favoured way to buy PCs.

- Makers of luxury goods are losing control of their premium prices and exclusive distribution. Chanel, Yves Saint Laurent and Christian Dior fragrances are discounted along with other goods by discounters such as Superdrug and grocery stores. Littlewoods, a big high-street chain, has struck 25 per cent off dozens of famous brands. Specialist discounters, What Everyone Wants and Eau Zone are also entering the fray. Selfridges, the exclusive department store claims it 'would never do anything as down-market as discounting', but even the snootiest retailers may find that they have to respond to the discounters.

Value pricing involves more than just cutting prices. It means finding the delicate balance between quality and price that gives target consumers the value they seek. To consumers, 'value' is not the same as 'cheap'. Value pricing requires price cutting coupled with finding ways to maintain or even improve the quality while still making a profit. Consumers who enjoyed high-quality brand-name products during the 1980s now want the same high quality, but at much lower prices. Thus value pricing often involves redesigning products and production processes to lower costs and preserving profit margins at lower prices. For example, before launching its value menu, Taco Bell redesigned its restaurants to increase customer traffic and reduce costs. It shrank its kitchens, expanded seating space, and introduced new menu items specifically designed for easy preparation in the new, smaller kitchens.

Although the trend toward value pricing began with the recession, its roots run much deeper. The trend reflects marketers' reactions to a fundamental change in consumer attitudes, resulting from the ageing of the baby boomers and their increased financial pressures. Today's 'squeezed consumers' – saddled with debt acquired during the free-spending 1980s and facing increased expenses for child rearing, home buying and pending retirement – will continue to demand more value long after the economy improves. Even before the economy soured, buyers were beginning to rethink the price–quality equation. Thus value pricing is likely to remain a crucial strategy throughout the 1990s and beyond. Winning over tomorrow's increasingly shrewd consumers will require finding ever-new ways to offer them more for less.

Sources: Portions adapted from 'Scenting trouble', *The Economist* (2 November, 1991), 38; Gary Strauss, 'Marketers plea: let's make a deal', *USA Today* (29 September, 1992), B1-B2. The Jack Welch quote is from Stratford Sherman, 'How to prosper in the value decade', *Fortune* (30 November, 1992), 90-104. Also Joseph B. White, '"Value pricing" is hot as shrewd consumers seek low-cost quality', *Wall Street Journal* (12 March, 1991), A1, A9; Faye Rice, 'What intelligent consumers want', *Fortune* (28 December 1992), 56-60; Bill Kelley, 'The new consumer revealed', *Sales & Marketing Management* (May 1993), 46-52. Bradford W. Morgan, 'Its the myth of the "value consumer"', *Brandweek* (28 February 1994), 17; Neil Buckley, 'Potential cost of selling cheap every day', *Financial Times* (24 March 1994), 17; The Lex Column, 'Sinking into the trough: Kingfisher', *Financial Times* (24 March, 1994), 22; and David Blackwell, 'M&S sees sales in Europe rise 20%', *Financial Times* (9 November 1994), 25; and Alan Mitchell, 'Going a bundle on marketing', *Marketing Week* (2 December, 1994), 30-31.

The seller might reason that if it can get more business, its average costs will fall and more than compensate for its extra freight cost. Freight-absorption pricing is used for market penetration and to hold on to increasingly competitive markets.

## International pricing

Companies that market their products internationally must decide what prices to charge in the different countries in which they operate. In some cases, a company can set a uniform worldwide price. For example, Airbus sells its jetliners at about the same price everywhere, whether in the United States, Europe or a Third World country. However, most companies adjust their prices to reflect local market conditions and cost considerations.

The price that a company should charge in a specific country depends on many factors, including economic conditions, competitive situations, laws and regulations and development of the wholesaling and retailing system. Consumer perceptions and preferences may also vary from country to country, calling for different prices. Or the company may have different marketing objectives in various world markets, which require changes in pricing strategy. For example, Sony might introduce a new product into mature markets in highly developed countries with the goal of quickly gaining mass-market share – this would call for a penetration pricing strategy. In contrast, it might enter a less developed market by targeting smaller, less price-sensitive segments – in this case, market-skimming pricing makes sense.

Costs play an important role in setting international prices. Travellers abroad are often surprised to find that goods which are relatively inexpensive at home may carry outrageously higher price tags in other countries. A pair of Levi's selling for $30 in the United States goes for about $63 in Tokyo and $88 in Paris. A McDonald's Big Mac selling for a modest $2.25 in the United States, costs $5.75 in Moscow. Pink Floyd's 'Dark Side of the Moon' CD sells for $14.99 in the United States, but costs about $22 in the EU. Conversely, a Gucci handbag going for only $60 in Milan, Italy, fetches $240 in the United States. In some cases, such price escalation may result from differences in selling strategies or market conditions. In most instances, however, it is simply a result of the higher costs of selling in foreign markets – the additional costs of modifying the product, higher shipping and insurance costs, import tariffs and taxes, costs associated with exchange-rate fluctuations and higher channel and physical distribution costs.

For example, Campbell found that its distribution costs in the United Kingdom were 30 per cent higher than in the United States. US retailers typically purchase soup in large quantities – 48-can cases of a single soup by the dozens, hundred or carloads. In contrast English grocers purchase soup in small quantities – typically in 24-can cases of *assorted* soups. Each case must be hand-packed for shipment. To handle these small orders, Campbell had to add a costly extra wholesale level to its European channel. The smaller orders also mean that English retailers order two or three times as often as their US counterparts, bumping up billing and order costs. These and other factors caused Campbell to charge much higher prices for its soups in the UK.[12]

Thus international pricing presents some special problems and complexities. We discuss international pricing issues in more detail in Chapter 5.

## PRICE CHANGES

After developing their price structures and strategies, companies often face situations in which they must initiate price changes or respond to price changes by competitors.

## Initiating price changes

In some cases, the company may find it desirable to initiate either a price cut or a price increase. In both cases, it must anticipate possible buyer and competitor reactions.

### Initiating price cuts

Several situations may lead a firm to consider cutting its price. One such circumstance is excess capacity. In this case, the firm needs more business and cannot get it through increased sales effort, product improvement or other measures. It may drop its follow-the-leader pricing – charging about the same price as their leading competitor – and aggressively cut prices to boost sales. But as the airline, construction equipment and other industries have learned in recent years, cutting prices in an industry loaded with excess capacity may lead to price wars as competitors try to hold on to market share.

Another situation leading to price changes is falling market share in the face of strong price competition. Several American industries – automobiles, consumer electronics, cameras, watches and steel, for example – lost market share to Japanese competitors whose high-quality products carried lower prices than did their American counterparts. In response, American companies resorted to more aggressive pricing action. General Motors, for example, cut its subcompact car prices by 10 per cent on the West Coast, where Japanese competition was strongest.[13]

A company may also cut prices in a drive to dominate the market through lower costs. Either the company starts with lower costs than its competitors or it cuts prices in the hope of gaining market share that will further cut costs through larger volume. Bausch & Lomb used an aggressive low-cost, low-price strategy to become an early leader in the competitive soft contact-lens market.

### Initiating price increases

In contrast, many companies have had to *raise* prices in recent years. They do this knowing that the price increases may be resented by customers, dealers and even their own salesforce. Yet a successful price increase can greatly increase profits. For example, if the company's profit margin is 3 per cent of sales, a 1 per cent price increase will increase profits by 33 per cent if sales volume is unaffected.

A considerable factor in price increases is cost inflation. Rising costs squeeze profit margins and lead companies to regular rounds of price increases. Companies often raise their prices by more than the cost increase in anticipation of further inflation. Another factor leading to price increases is overdemand: when a company cannot supply all its customers' needs, it can raise its prices, ration products to customers or both.

Companies can increase their prices in a number of ways to keep up with rising costs. Prices can be raised almost invisibly by dropping discounts and adding higher-priced units to the line. Or prices can be pushed up openly. In passing price increases on to customers, the company should avoid the image of price gouging. The price increases should be supported with a company communication programme telling customers why prices are being increased. The company salesforce should help customers find ways to economize.

Where possible, the company should consider ways to meet higher costs or demand without raising prices. For example, it can shrink the product instead of raising the price, as candy bar manufacturers do. Or it can substitute less expensive ingredients or remove certain product features, packaging or services. Or it can 'unbundle' its products and services, removing and separately pricing elements that were formerly part of the offer. IBM, for example, now offers training and consulting as separately priced services.

### Buyer reactions to price changes

Whether the price is raised or lowered, the action will affect buyers, competitors, distributors and suppliers and may interest government as well. Customers do not always interpret prices in a straightforward way. They may view a price *cut* in several ways. For example, what would you think if Sony were suddenly to cut its VCR prices in half? You might think that these VCRs are about to be replaced by newer models or that they have some fault and are not selling well. You might think that Sony is in financial trouble and may not stay in the business long enough to supply future parts. You might believe that quality has been reduced. Or you might think that the price will come down even further and that it will pay to wait and see.

Similarly, a price *increase*, which would normally lower sales, may have some positive meanings for buyers. What would you think if Sony *raised* the price of its latest VCR model? On the one hand, you might think that the item is very 'hot' and may be unobtainable unless you buy it soon. Or you might think that the recorder is an unusually good value. On the other hand, you might think that Sony is greedy and charging what the traffic will bear.

### Competitor reactions to price changes

A firm considering a price change has to worry about the reactions of its competitors as well as its customers. Competitors are most likely to react when the number of firms involved is small, when the product is uniform and when the buyers are well informed.

How can the firm figure out the likely reactions of its competitors? If the firm faces one large competitor and if the competitor tends to react in a set way to price changes, that reaction can be easily anticipated. But if the competitor treats each price change as a fresh challenge and reacts according to its self-interest, the company will have to figure out just what makes up the competitor's self-interest at the time.

The problem is complex because, like the customer, the competitor can interpret a company price cut in many ways. It might think the company is trying to grab a larger market share, that the company is doing poorly and trying to boost its sales or that the company wants the whole industry to cut prices to increase total demand.

When there are several competitors, the company must guess each competitor's likely reaction. If all competitors behave alike, this amounts to analysing only a typical competitor. In contrast, if the competitors do not behave alike – perhaps because of differences in size, market shares or policies – then separate analyses are necessary. However, if some competitors will match the price change, there is good reason to expect that the rest will also match it.

## Responding to price changes

Here we reverse the question and ask how a firm should respond to a price change by a competitor. The firm needs to consider several questions: Why did the competitor change the price? Was it to make more market share, to use excess capacity, to meet changing costs conditions or to lead an industrywide price change? Is the price change temporary or permanent? What will happen to the company's market share and profits if it does not respond? Are other companies going to respond? What are the competitor's and other firms' responses to each possible reaction likely to be?

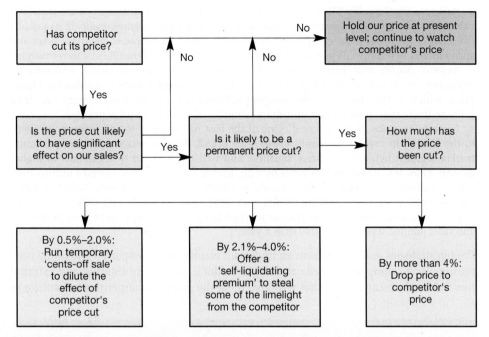

**Figure 17.2**   Price reaction programme for meeting a competitor's price cut. (Source: Redrawn with permission from a working paper by Raymond J. Trapp, Northwestern University, 1964)

Besides these issues, the company must make a broader analysis. It has to consider its own product's stage in the life cycle, its importance in the company's product mix, the intentions and resources of the competitor and the possible consumer reactions to price changes. The company cannot always make an extended analysis of its alternatives at the time of a price change, however. The competitor may have spent much time preparing this decision, but the company may have to react within hours or days. About the only way to cut down reaction time is to plan ahead for both possible price changes and possible responses by the competitor.

Figure 17.2 shows the ways a company might assess and respond to a competitor's price cut. Once the company has determined that the competitor has cut its price and that this price reduction is likely to harm company sales and profits, it might simply decide to hold its current price and profit margin. The company might believe that it will not lose too much market share or that it would lose too much profit if it reduced its own price. It might decide that it should wait and respond when it has more information on the effects of the competitor's price change. For now, it might be willing to hold on to good customers, while giving up the poorer ones to the competitor. The argument against this holding strategy, however, is that the competitor may get stronger and more confident as its sales increase and the company might wait too long to act.

If the company decides that effective action can and should be taken, it might make any of the four responses:

1. *Reduce price.* The leader might drop its price to the competitor's price. It may decide that the market is price sensitive and that it would lose too much market share to the lower-priced competitor. Or it might worry that recapturing lost market share later would be too hard. Cutting price will reduce the company's profits in the short run. Some companies might also reduce their product quality, services and marketing communications to retain profit margins, but this ultimately will hurt long-run market share. The company should try to maintain its quality as it cuts prices.

2. *Raise perceived quality.* The company might maintain its price but strengthen the perceived value of its offer. It could improve its communications, stressing the relative quality of its product over that of the lower-price competitor. The firm may find it cheaper to maintain price and spend money to improve its perceived quality than to cut price and operate at a lower margin.

3. *Improve quality and increase price.* The company might increase quality and raise its price, moving its brand into a higher price position. The higher quality justifies the higher price, which in turn preserves the company's higher margins. Or the company can hold price on the current product and introduce a new brand at a higher price position.

4. *Launch low-price 'fighting brand'.* One of the best responses is to add lower-price items to the line or to create a separate lower-price brand. This is necessary if the particular market segment being lost is price sensitive and will not respond to arguments of higher quality. Thus, when attacked on price by Fuji, Kodak introduced low-priced Funtime film. When challenged on price by store brands and other low-priced entrants, Nestlé turned a number of its brands into fighting brands, including Fussell's condensed milk. In response to price pressures, Miller cut the price of its High Life brand by 20 per cent in most markets and sales jumped 9 per cent in less than a year.[14]

Pricing strategies and tactics form an important element of a company's marketing mix. In setting prices, companies must carefully consider a great many internal and external factors before choosing a price that will give them the greatest competitive advantage in

## MARKETING HIGHLIGHT 17.3

### Excuse me but, do you accept money?

Cash is out of fashion. Increasingly people pay, for even small transactions, by credit card, debit card or, in many parts of Europe, by prepaid smart cards. People are as uninterested in seeing their money as they are the petrol they buy for their car, with a credit card, of course. Money, and the constraints it imposes, will disappear. Because of financial liberalization the spending of both households and companies is becoming less determined by immediate income or money in the bank, than by their expected wealth. Even the resistance of ultra conservative Germany and Marks & Spencer is crumbling; they will liberalize the use of credit and debit cards soon.

People and companies are increasingly turning to trading their skills and produce without using money. Want a plumbing job done? Fred will do it if you will mow his lawn for a week and baby sit one night. What if the plumber does not want anything you can provide? In that case, clubs exist to trade credits. The plumber does the job for you but he can use his credits to get goods or services from someone else and you have to work off your debt. These networks are growing so fast that governments are starting to worry about them. They exist outside the tax system so people pay no VAT or income tax. Maybe that is why people like them so much.

London's Capital Barter Corporation (CBC) orchestrates third-party deals for a pool of 150 companies that offer their services for trade credits rather than cash. CBC's deals range from a £15 restaurant meal to a £15,000 stock of computers. The most popular items are airline tickets, photocopiers and computers. Barter is not just for small deals between small firms – in the United States, Lufthansa, Playtex and US Networks have all had deals worth $2m. or more.

CBC and other barter companies, including The Bartering Company, Business Barter Exchange and Eurotrade, debit and credit its members' accounts in 'trade pounds'. Each member has a credit limit depending upon the size of the company and the tradability of its products. But why barter rather than get money instead? The marketing manager of Konica Business machines explains: 'A lot of companies, when they find out how much a fax machine is in trade pounds, say they can get a better deal by getting a discount in cash. But if they think how much it would cost to generate that cash, they would find it cheaper to do the deal in barter.' The value of bartering is best when the incremental cost of serving an extra client is low, explains the chief executive of the International Reciprocal Trade Association. Letting a

selected target markets. However, companies are not usually free to charge whatever prices they wish. Several laws restrict pricing practices and a number of ethical considerations affect pricing decisions. Pricing strategies and tactics also depend upon the way that we pay for things. Increasingly what we spend does not depend on how much money we have on us or how much we earned that week. These days our money is rarely something we see or feel, it is the electronic transmission of data between files. Also as currency is becoming an increasingly small part of our lives, barter is coming back in international and inter-personal dealing. Marketing Highlight 17.3 tells more about how money is changing.

## SUMMARY

Pricing is a dynamic process. Companies design a *pricing structure* that covers all their products. They change this structure over time and adjust it to account for different customers and situations.

Pricing strategies usually change as a product passes through its life cycle. The company can decide on one of several price–quality strategies for introducing an imitative product. In pricing innovative new products, it can follow a *skimming policy* by initially setting high prices to 'skim' the maximum amount of revenue from

room on barter, for example, only costs the hotel the price of laundry and cleaning since all the other costs are fixed. But the buying power it earns in trade pounds is equal to the full retail value of the room.

Internet, the information superhighway linking 30m. people and 20,000 firms now has its own money. Customers 'net-surfing' through on-line 'shops' in electronic 'shopping malls' usually buy information, but increasingly they buy music, books and clothes from 'e-catalogues'. How do they pay? Punching in credit card numbers is one way, but hackers make this method insecure. Lee Stern, a Californian entrepreneur thinks he has the answer with his First Virtual Holdings bank, 'The world's first truly electronic bank'. In this, both buyers and sellers must have accounts with the First Virtual. To buy through Internet the buyers give the sellers their account numbers and the goods are shipped. Periodically the seller reports sales to First Virtual who uses e-mail to ask the buyer for confirmation. That being done, the buyer's credit card is automatically debited.

The Dutch Firm, DigiCash is close to having a system that is simpler than the virtual banks. Its e-money

works like a prepaid smart card. The problem they have had to solve is, again, security. How to make sure the e-money is spent only once. DigiCash checks the card's electronic signature with the card's supplier for each transaction in order to make sure the transaction is valid. Governments worry about e-money. The 'virtual economy' is already the size of the Netherlands' and who can guess how big it will be within a decade? With digital cash zipping across the Internet's 'cyber-space' how can tax inspectors keep tabs on it? E-cash pushes the idea of money to the limit. It has no intrinsic value and hardly a trace of physical existence. Internet is pushing to the limits the question, what makes money worth what it is worth? Two Irish economists, Browne and Fell, see money disappearing altogether. They argue that e-money will replace cash, bonds will replace the money market, and a standard of value will be established in which prices are divorced from the means of payment. Values, they say, will ultimately be measured with a unit of account defined for a basket of goods. Maybe the Mars Bar will become the ultimate unit of currency because it contains a very representative balance of commodities and manufacture.

Sources: Neil Buckley, 'M&S close to accepting debit card payments', *Financial Times* (29 August 1994), 6; Motoka Rich, 'Abracadabra! It's the barter magicians', *Financial Times* (1–2 October 1994), 4; Michael Lindemann, 'Germany flexible at last on credit cards', *Financial Times* (11 November 1994), 3; Samuel Britten, 'Post-money world on our doorstep', *Financial Times* (17 November 1994), 20; and 'Electric money: so much for the cashless society', *The Economist* (26 November 1994), 25–30.

various segments of the market. Or it can use *penetration pricing* by setting a low initial price to win a large market share.

When the product is part of a product mix, the firm searches for a set of prices that will maximize the profits from the total mix. The company decides on *price steps* for items in its product line and on the pricing of *optional products*, *captive products*, *by-products* and *product bundles*.

Companies apply a variety of *price-adjustement strategies* to account for differences in consumer segments and situations. One is *discount and allowance pricing*, whereby the company establishes cash discounts, quantity discounts, functional discounts, seasonal discounts and allowances. A second is *segmented pricing*, whereby the company sets different prices for different customers, product forms, places or times. A third is *psychological pricing*, whereby the company adjusts the price to better communicate a product's intended position. A fourth is *promotional pricing*, whereby the company decides on loss-leader pricing, special-event pricing and psychological discounting. A fifth is *value-pricing*, whereby the company offers just the right combination of quality and good service at a fair price. A sixth is *geographical pricing*, whereby the company decides how to price to distant customers, choosing from such alternatives as FOB pricing, uniform delivered pricing, zone pricing, basing-point pricing and freight-absorption pricing. A seventh is *international pricing*, whereby the company adjusts its price to meet different conditions and expectations in different world markets.

When a firm considers initiating a *price change*, it must consider customers' and competitor's reactions. Customers' reactions are influenced by the meaning customers see in the price change. Competitors' reactions flow from a set reaction policy or a fresh analysis of each situation. The firm initiating the price change must also anticipate the probable reactions of suppliers, middlemen and government.

The firm that faces a price change initiated by a competitor must try to understand the competitor's intent as well as the likely duration and impact of the change. If a swift reaction is desirable, the firm should preplan its reactions to different possible price actions by competitors. When facing a competitor's price change, the company might sit tight, reduce its own price, raise perceived quality, improve quality and raise price, or launch a fighting brand.

## ■ DISCUSSING THE ISSUES

1. Describe which strategy – market skimming or market penetration – is appropriate for the following products: (a) Procter & Gamble's new Ariel Future laundry detergent; (b) Reebok's latest, 'new-tech' aerobics shoes; (c) an American Diner that has recently opened a restaurant right opposite McDonald's in the city's shopping centre. Why are these the right strategies for these companies?

2. American Express offers three tiers of 'product' to customers – a green card, a gold card and a platinum card. The membership fee (price) rises from £100 for the green card to £200 for the gold and £300 for the platinum. What pricing strategy is adopted by AmEx? Do you think this type of strategy is effective? Why or why not?

3. A leading brand of room spray is priced at £2.50 for a 150ml bottle. A close competitor launched a similar product priced at £1.99 for 300ml and quickly became the number-one brand. Discuss the psychological aspects of this pricing. What sort of company image do you think the competitor possesses to allow the use of this superb-value strategy. Would a similar strategy work for the number brand? Why or why not?

4. The formula for household chlorine bleaching agents is virtually identical for all brands. One brand, Clorox, charges a premium price for this same product, yet remains an unchallenged market leader in some national markets. What does this imply about the value of a brand name? Are there ethical issues involved in this type of pricing?

**5.** Manufacturers of clothing, confectionery, crockery and other consumer products are often faced with 'by-products' – such as reject goods that are not quite perfect and fail to meet the high standards of retailers and consumers. There is, however, a market for such 'rejects". What strategy should be used for pricing these products?

**6.** A Bodum coffee percolator sells for under £20 in a department store in London. The same device is priced at £80 in Tang's, a local department store in Singapore. What do you think accounts for the discrepancy in price? Can you list other products or services that would reflect a similar international pricing pattern?

## APPLYING THE CONCEPTS

**1.** Go to your local supermarket or a grocery store you regularly shop at. Take a few product categories. Observe the sizes and prices within product categories. Are the package sizes (weight or number of units contained) comparable across brands? Find instances where a manufacturer seems to have made a smaller package in order to charge (a) a lower price and (b) a higher price. Are there any instances where (a) a higher price is charged for larger packages and (b) a discount is given on larger packages? Why do you think manufacturers adopt these pricing strategies? Do they appear effective? Under what circumstances are they effective?

**2.** You probably are familiar with the seasonal sales that take place at certain times of the year. Examples are the 'summer sales', 'Christmas sales' and 'New Year sales'. Why do retailers run these sales each year? Would it be more effective for a retailer to differentiate from others by offering discounts outside, rather than during, the conventional seasonal sales periods? Why or why not? In general, how effective are discount and allowance pricing strategies?

## REFERENCES

1. Tom Rubython, 'A roll of the orange dice, *BusinessAge* (July 1994), 56–8; Anil Bhoyrul, 'Boom to gloom', *BusinessAge* (November 1994), 4B–6B; and Alan Cane, 'Santa receives a call for rapid growth', *Financial Times* (22 November 1994), 28.
2. For a comprehensive discussion of pricing strategies, see Thomas T. Nagle and Reed K. Holen, *The Strategy and Tactics of Pricing*, 2nd edn (Englewood Cliffs, NJ: Prentice Hall, 1995).
3. John Parry, 'Times are changing for Tag-Heuer', *The European* (11–17 November, 1994), 32; and Ian Fraser, 'Don't crack under the pressure, *European Business* (June 1994), 66–8.
4. Bridget Williams, *The Best Butter in the World: A history of Sainsbury's* (London: Ebury, 1994).
5. See David Kirkpatrick, 'Intel goes for broke', *Fortune* (16 May 1994), 62–8.
6. Ralph Atkins, 'A certain lack of drive', *Financial Times* (25 November 1994), 18.
7. Gregory Viscusi, 'Merloni makes a clean break for eastern markets', *The European* (25 November 1994), 21; 'Britain's music business: the sound barrier', *The Economist* (15 May 1993), 103.
8. Nagle and Holden *Strategy and Tactics of Pricing*, op cit., 225–8; and Manjit S. Yadav and Kent B. Monroe, 'How buyers perceive savings in a bundle price: an examination of a bundle's transaction value', *Journal of Marketing Research* (August 1993), 350-8.
9. S. M. Widrick, 'Measurement of incidence of quantity surcharge among selected grocery products', *Journal of Consumer Affairs* (summer 1979); and Yiorgos Zotos and Steven Lysonski 'An exploration of the quantity surcharge concept in Greece', *European Journal of Marketing*, **27**, 10 (1993), 5–18.
10. Gary M. Erickson and Johnny K. Johansson, 'The role of price in multi-attribute product evaluations', *Journal of Consumer Research* (September 1985), 195–9.
11. For more reading on reference prices and psychological pricing, see Nagle and Holden, *Strategy and Tactics of Pricing*, op cit., 12; and K. N. Rajendran and Gerard J. Tellis, 'Contextual and temporal components of reference price', *Journal of Marketing* (January 1994), 22–34.
12. Philip R. Cateora, *International Marketing*, 7th edn (Homewood, IL: Irwin, 1990), 540.
13. For more on price cutting and its consequences, see Kathleen Madigan, 'The latest mad plunge of the price slashers,' *Business Week* (11 May 1992), 36; and Bill Saporito, 'Why the price wars never end', *Fortune* (23 March 1992), 68–78.
14. Jonathon Berry and Zachary Schiller, 'Attack of the fighting brands', *Business Week* (2 May 1994), 125.

# Stena Sealink versus Le Shuttle, Eurostar and the rest

The Channel Tunnel: about as welcome to cross-channel ferry operators as Henry Ford was to carriage makers.

In July 1994 Stena Sealink, the Swedish ferry company, was waiting for the outcome of a battle caused by the opening of the Channel Tunnel between Folkestone and Calais. Although the tunnel only carried four Eurostar trains a day in each direction between London and Paris, cross-channel ferry prices had already dropped to 20 per cent of 1993 levels. On some routes the competition was particularly intensive and it had given rise to the court battle between France's Brittany Ferries and Britain's P&O. At the heart of the case was P&O's FFr 49* three-day return fare for passengers originating in France on the 'long route' between Cherbourg and Le Havre in France and Portsmouth in England.

To qualify for the reduced fare, passengers had to collect three coupons from *Ouest-France*, a regional newspaper covering the main catchment area for the Cherbourg–Portsmouth service. Brittany applied for an immediate injunction against P&O's 'loss-leading' prices at the Tribunal de Commerce in Rennes. Since Brittany Ferries' owners are 4,000 French farmers and regional councils, they have considerable influence in that part of France. Brittany Ferries' main accusation was: 'predatory pricing, which we believe breaks French law if it is proved to be intentionally aimed at eliminating rivals'. They complained that the massive price cut to 75 per cent of normal tariffs throughout the peak summer season made profits impossible. P&O asked the court to find itself unable to rule since it was impossible to stipulate fares when some sailings carried 1,600 passengers and others as few as 10. Industry experts say companies can gain by packing ferries with cheap-rate passengers who swell profits by spending on food, drink and souvenirs during the voyage.

Stena Sealink entered the fray at the end of the summer season when promotional fares in the United Kingdom dropped to £1.* The Central Committee of French Ship Owners (CCFSO) and their sailors' union demanded that the EU should impose minimum fares on cross-channel routes. They also wanted to bar all non-EU citizens from working on the ferries and claimed that, for safety reasons, all crew members must speak French. 'We believe it our duty to offer the keenest possible fare and that is what we do', argued P&O in defence of their low fares. 'We thrive on competition which benefits the consumer and we would oppose any move to disrupt that.' Stena Sealink added: 'It would be ridiculous to increase prices in such a competitive industry.' The CCFSO responded to these comments: 'It is not our intention to be protectionist. Protection is where you erect customs or other barriers to trade. It is not protectionist to seek to save the jobs of French seafarers.' Brittany Ferries has other problems, too. In 1993 they lost FFr 90 million on a turnover of FFr 500 million, and have borrowings of FFr 1,400 million.

## Competition by sea

Stena Sealink has 30 per cent of the cross-channel market of 30 million annual passengers. P&O is market leader with a 42 per cent share, and Brittany Ferries is number three with 9 per cent. Other contenders are Sally Line, owned by the Finnish Effjohn Oy group, and Britain's Hoverspeed, each with about 7 per cent of the market. Hoverspeed is unlike the other operators in that it uses fast car-carrying hovercraft and Seacats rather than boats. A further 40 million passengers cross the channel by air each year.

Short routes dominate the cross-channel market. Of the 24 million passengers travelling between Britain and France, 16 million take the intensively competitive Dover–Calais route. Of these, 9 million go by P&O, 6 million by Stena Sealink and 1 million by Hoverspeed. Although conspicuous for their consumer pricing and advertising, Sally Lines and Brittany Ferries are minor contenders on the short routes most threatened by the Channel Tunnel. Not only are fares down by an average of 20 per cent but the quality of the ships and the frequency of the service they offer is also up. Both P&O and Stena Sealink have five vessels on the route.

The short route is critical to both the big operators. In 1993 P&O made £77 million operating profits on sales of £615 million while Stena Sealink made

---

1 ecu = US$1.26 = FFr 6.47 (French francs) = UK£0.83

£24 million profits on £380 million sales. However, P&O depended upon duty and tax-free sales for one-third of their profits. The market will decline. Eurotunnel expects to have half of a 40 million sea-going cross-channel passenger market by 1996. In the opinion of London-based brokers, NatWest Markets: 'The route can work with six vessels between them operating a service every 45 minutes.' The competition has already claimed one victim. Olau Lines, subsidiary of the German TT Line, stopped trading in May 1994. As the Channel Tunnel's threat increases and competition on the short routes intensifies, Stena Sealink and P&O are looking to the less competitive long routes. Hence P&O's quick purchase of Olau's luxury ferries to compete against Brittany Ferries between Portsmouth and Le Havre.

The Channel Tunnel will not equally affect all ferry traffic. Travellers between England and western France and Spain can avoid London and the congested south-east of England by taking a ferry from the south coast to Brittany or Spain. Similarly, travellers to or from the Midlands or north of England have a choice of ferries from the east coast to north European destinations. A problem with these routes is time. Ferries are slow and the journeys take between several hours to over a day depending on the route. That means less regular services, provisions of cabins, bigger ships and, of course, higher costs. Nevertheless, Le Havre has spent £27 million building a new terminal to cope with increased demand and Dieppe has been given £6 million of regional funds to help pay for a new ferry terminal.

Ferry operators also hope to keep a high share of the commercial trade on the short routes. Along with the 4 million cars that cross the channel each year are 170,000 coaches and 1.3 million commercial vehicles. A survey amongst 102 senior transport executives found 62 per cent of transport companies believed that their drivers would prefer to stick with the ferries, while 84 percent thought that the ferries would offer better facilities than the tunnel. 'We've managed perfectly well without a tunnel; I don't see it making a big difference except for the novelty value', said one transport executive. Scania, the heavy-truck company who commissioned the survey commented: 'Eurotunnel has predicted it will carry more than 8 million tonnes of freight in its first full year of opera-

tion and it aims to take a significant share of the ferries' freight business. Our survey shows they may be in for a big surprise.'

The removal of customs between European countries has created a new business for the ferry companies. The British are pouring across the channel to buy alcoholic drinks in France, where excise duties are much lower than in the United Kingdom. France levies £1.57 less than Britain on a bottle of champagne; 99p less on a bottle of still wine; and 25p less on a pint[1] of beer. Since pretax prices are also low in France, total savings can be up to £60 on a case of champagne or £10 on six litres of some beers. The Wine and Spirits Federation reckon 9 per cent of domestic sales of wine and 15 per cent of beer drunk in British homes are personal imports that avoid UK taxes. Some of the imports are from holiday-makers 'stocking-up' on their way through France or from legitimate day-trippers whose main aim is to get the tax free booze. They can import up to a year's supply of booze for personal consumption. The ferry companies benefited from the doubling of the day-tripper market in 1994. However, Whitbread, the brewers, estimate that 30 per cent of the cross-channel booze trade, and the fastest growing part, was by organized bootleggers. They can profit £324 per journey and can make up to four trips a day. After each trip they unload their vans on to trucks at Dover for distribution in the north of England. The British government and the Brewers and Licensed Retailers Association are unhappy about this trade, but not the ferry companies.

## Competition under and over the sea

The Channel Tunnel poses two commercial challenges to Stena Sealink: Eurostar and Le Shuttle. Eurostar is a passenger rail service, initially operating on the main London–Brussels and London–Paris routes, and Le Shuttle transports cars, commercial vehicles, their drivers and passengers between Folkestone and Calais. Eurostar's pricing is targeting the business passenger between the European capitals, which are on Europe's busiest air routes. Eurostar's £195 first-class fare between London and Paris savagely undercuts British Airways' and Air France's £318 Business Class fare. However, both prices are well above the £79 first-class passenger rail fare for using British Rail, Stena Sealink and SNCF to get between the centres of London and Paris. In contrast, the cheapest Eurostar fare (£95) is more expensive than both the cheapest air fares (£85) and the lowest price for rail-sea-rail (£62).

Eurostar aims to capture 60 per cent of the London–Paris and London–Brussels traffic but British Airways see Eurostar as just another player in an already competitive market. The airline expects a dent in its business, but only in the London area. Many of its daily flights to Paris depart from elsewhere in the United Kingdom. Similarly, British Midland, a regional airline, is confident. They concede that Eurostar will have the benefit of novelty but do not think it will halt the airline's progress – they achieved a 27 per cent increase in year-on-year demand for their European services in the last quarter of 1994. British Midland believes that the inner-city location of the train terminals will count against Eurostar. Sabina, Belgium's national airline is similarly dismissive: 'The tunnel is not a major worry. Parking facilities are poor at both Waterloo and Gare du Midi in Brussels, which will be an off-putting factor for business people using the train. We're confident we can stay on top.' Nevertheless, Sabina has entered the fray by joining with Avis to give business people flying to Brussels from Gatwick or Manchester a free day's car hire. British Airways also admit that their £75 million relaunch of their Club Europe service for business travellers was in direct response to the tunnel. Eurostar has started small, but in 1995 services will run from Birmingham, Edinburgh, Glasgow and Manchester. By 1996 European Night Trains, whose sleeper will have *en suite* bathrooms, will run from London to Amsterdam, Dortmund and Frankfurt.

Stena Sealink's initial skirmish with Le Shuttle has given them confidence. The cross-channel freight and passenger businesses are very price sensitive. When Le Shuttle first started carrying trucks it did well, but then lost much of the business once initial price offers had finished. Le Shuttle's prices for the launch of their full service in June 1995 were also thought too high compared with those of ferries. Many in the industry believe that an attractive price would boost customers. Christopher Garnett, commercial director of Eurotunnel disagrees: 'Our research shows

that there is no requirement to undercut the ferries. People get worried when you talk about premium pricing but we have scope to add value and we will still be competitive.' Wendy Wong, Smith New Court analyst, explains the conflict: 'Eurotunnel has to be careful with any price-cutting – it has some anxious [and very long suffering] shareholders to consider.'

### Fast, luxurious or inexpensive

Consultants Healey & Baker think the days of ferries and short-hop air travel are numbered. They report that: 'it is now generally accepted that for distances over 300 km, rail is more economical than road.' Rail will compete with air for passengers' journeys within Europe and with road for freight. Realizing the importance of higher-speed travel, there has been wide-scale development of high-speed networks and rail terminals throughout Europe. Brave new ventures with high-speed trains have confounded critics. Spain's high-speed train, the AVE, almost broke even on its first full year of service. The train runs 471 km between Madrid and Seville using trains similar to France's Train à Grande Vitesse (TGV) and built by the same Anglo-French engineering group, GEC-Alsthom. The AVE slashed the rail time for the journey from 5 hours 55 minutes to 2 hours 40 and mirrors the TGV's results:

- The high-speed train captures most of the market. Before the AVE 51 per cent of travellers on the route went by car and only 20 per cent by rail. The figures are now 39 per cent by car and 44 per cent by AVE.
- Air travel is hard hit by high-speed trains. Iberia's share of the traffic on the route dropped from 18 to 7 per cent because of AVE.
- High-speed trains generate new customers. Twenty-four per cent of AVE users had never before travelled between Madrid and Seville. Originally the TGV between Paris and Lyon was projected to carry 6 million passengers a year; in 1993 21 million people travelled the route.

Eurostar achieves similar drastic cuts in travel time. Eurostar's journey time between London and Paris is 3 hours and between London and Brussels 3 hours and 15 minutes – times that will fall even further with the completion of Belgian and British high-speed links. Le Shuttle will take only 35 minutes and at peak times there will be four trains an hour. It will also be unaffected by weather and high seas. In competition P&O operate twenty-five sailings a day between Dover and Calais and a 'proven motorway-to-motorway time of 105 minutes.' They intend to speed up too, and have ordered a new high-speed Seacat for their Folkestone–Boulogne route.

The threat of the Channel Tunnel has stimulated other forms of competition besides price cutting and speed. Targeting the frequent traveller, Sally Line has extended its nautical miles-frequent-traveller programme. P&O's advertising promotes the pleasure of the sea crossing: 'Why sail across the channel when you can cruise across?' A substantial investment programme aims to give P&O 'the best appointed ships on the channel.' Borrowing a lesson from the airlines, sailings have a new Club Class. This provides comfortable lounges, guaranteed seating and free coffee and newspapers. Perhaps the ultimate attraction is peace and freedom from Euro-school children. The company also intend to give their passengers a lot more reason to spend money on board. P&O claim revenue from duty-free shops and other retail services already keeps fares down by an average of 25 per cent. Shipboard shoppers are a captive market with time on their hands. The whole 'cruise' experience contrasts with the service that Le Shuttle offers. 'People want style and comfort, not the commodity-like impersonal service of Le Shuttle,' says P&O's passenger marketing and sales director, Brian Langford. Le Shuttle's advantage is speed but 'the time advantage will be wiped out', says Langford, 'when people need to take a break after enduring the "spartan" 30-minutes tunnel journey'. Also, 'Le Shuttle will be charging a premium for speed', claims another P&O spokesman, 'so it's unlikely they can match our fares.' P&O's five-day return rates for a car and driver start at £57.

In many ways Eurotunnel's views concur with P&O's: 'You must remember', says Christopher Garnett, 'we're in the business of transport, not leisure.' Unlike truck drivers, who may leave their cabs for a quick meal in a separate carriage, car passengers must remain with their vehicles. There is nothing to see while in the tunnel and little for the passengers to do. 'Le Shuttle is a means to an end for most users and we will market it to those consumers simply as a way of reaching their chosen destination', says Garnett. 'But we can build our business by giving customers reasons to travel. We could, for example, use direct marketing to communicate with people we know enjoy practising sports in the north of France and persuade them to visit the area because of the ease of using the tunnel.' Wunderman Cato Johnson is handling the direct marketing and David Butter, their executive vice-president (Europe), predicts that Eurostar will be 'the leading brand in European travel'. He says Le Shuttle will 'change the way people relate to the Channel and remove it as an obstacle to travel.'

### Stena Sealink's dilemma

Stena Sealink had faced many sea squalls in the channel but nothing like the competitive squall it was facing now. Was the cross-channel ferry market going to collapse? If so, how could they justify the investment that was necessary for them to compete effectively? Should they cut prices to match P&O's bargain basement prices or invest in refurbishing ships to provide a luxury service? Could they cross-subsidize their price by getting passengers to spend more whilst on board or should they concentrate on running a basic efficient service like Le Shuttle? Should they invest in new terminals to help them serve the long channel crossings? One option was to invest in radically new ships. There was a chance to leapfrog the competition by buying huge high-speed high-tech catamarans costing £130 million each. Being the size of a football stadium the vessels would be the biggest ferries in the world and cruise at 40 knots. They could carry commercial vehicles, trailers, coaches and cars plus 1,500 passengers each. They would have much room for seating, bars, restaurants, cafeterias and duty-free shops, and, because of the unique hull construction, be stable in all weathers.

### Questions

1. Explain P&O's heavy discounting strategy. Explain Eurostar's pricing. Is Brittany Ferries right in saying the fares make profits impossible? Should prices

be fixed on cross-channel routes to prevent unprofitable price wars?

2. Should Stena Sealink follow P&O's price cutting? What else could they do? Can Stena Sealink get away with charging more than P&O at any time, any place, any way?

3. Is P&O discounting consistent with their luxury 'cruise' positioning? What prevents Le Shuttle driving the ferries out by cutting prices? Does Le Shuttle's speed advantage make its victory over the ferries inevitable?

4. Since the cross-channel ferry market will decline, explain their investment in gaining market share by

price cutting, operating new routes, refurbishing vessels and buying expensive fast Seacats. What strategy should Stena Sealink follow? Should they follow all P&O's moves, follow some, do something completely different or, like Olau Line, get out?

### Note

1. A pint is the standard serving of beer in a British pub and equals 0.568 litres; a US pint is 0.551 litres.

Sources: 'Rough waters for P&O' *Marketing Business* (June 1990, 4; Charles Batchelor, 'Freight companies to shun the tunnel', *Financial Times* (7 March 1994), 7; Tom Burns, 'Madrid–Seville fast rail link heads for profit', *Financial Times* (15 March 1994), 2; 'Cross-channel booze: glug glug', *The Economist* (23 April 1994), 30–1; Julie Read, 'Cut-price ferry fare sparks all-out war', *The European* (1–7 July 1994), 1; Chris Butler 'Ferries chart new course for survival', *The European* (1–7 July 1994), 19; Claire Murphy, 'A severe case of tun-nel vision', *Marketing Week* (2 September 1994), 21–2; Ian Fletcher, 'French sailors move to stop £1 ferry bargain', *Today* (20 September1994), 1–2; 'Tunnel Vision', *EuroBusiness* (October 1994), 18; Charles Batchelor, 'Watch out, the drive ahead could be rough', *Financial Times* (3 October, 1994), 14; Clive Branson, 'The impor-tance of being well connected', *The European* (21–27 October 1994), 25; Roderick Oram, 'A stiff one for drink lobby', *Financial Times* (22–23 October 1994), 6.

# Amaizer

## It tastes awful, but we're working on it

Amaizer is a new savoury snack made from maize. Its method of manufacture is similar to cornflakes breakfast cereal but it is to be sold as a savoury snack. Amaizers look like potato crisps but are more golden and regular in shape. Raw materials and manufacturing costs are higher than potato chips but they are healthier – in their basic form, they contain the same calories but are low in saturates and cholesterol.

Amaizer is sweeter than potato crisps but can be flavoured. Unfortunately, consumer trials showed that the Amaizer versions of popular crisp flavours – salt and vinegar, cheese and onion and so on – 'taste awful'. Research and development were still working on the taste of these flavours. Meanwhile, the aim was to launch the product with four flavours that consumers did like: regular, sweet and sour, honey roasted ham and '1,000 Islands' dressing.

Although originally designed to use spare breakfast cereal capacity, the developed product needed dedicated plant. This produces Amaizer for a direct cost of £1,500 per tonne, excluding the cost of capital. With potato snacks selling for £3,000 per tonne, the brand manager was confident about the product's profitability.

1 ecu = UK£0.83

The brand manager's confidence crashed, however, when sales, finance and market research each came up with recommended prices. The finance officer demanded that the price be set to cover the usual 100 per cent overhead charge plus a 20 per cent margin. His suggested price of £3,600 per tonne gave a very satisfactory £180,000 profit for the targeted 300 tonne annual sales.

Unfortunately, the finance officer's view conflicted with the sales manager's, who wanted the price to be £100 per tonne below potato crisps. The sales manager claimed that only with a price advantage could they achieve the target sales against the established competition. The sales manager added that a low initial price would also compensate traders for the extra shelf space Amaizer used. Amaizer was bulkier than potato crisps and therefore needed about 20 per cent extra shelf space.

The marketing researcher's contribution to the pricing debate confused the brand manager even more. Rather than giving a price, the researcher gave a string of prices and sales and, to the annoyance of the finance officer, some financial information:

| Price (£000) | 2.5 | 3.0 | 3.5 | 4.0 | 4.5 |
|---|---|---|---|---|---|
| Sales (tonnes) | 400 | 350 | 280 | 200 | 100 |

The researcher also estimated £300,000 annual fixed operating cost for the product and capital investment that depended upon the annual volumes produced.

| Annual sales (tonnes) | 400 | 350 | 280 | 200 | 100 |
|---|---|---|---|---|---|
| Capital investment (£000) | 2,250 | 2,000 | 1,650 | 1,200 | 600 |

'I assume you know that our average cost of capital is 15 per cent,' commented the finance officer.

'All very impressive,' said the brand manager, 'but what price should we charge?'

'That all depends on what you want to achieve,' replied the researcher.

## QUESTIONS

1. Evaluate the pricing suggestions of the sales, finance and market research officers. What criteria should be used to select the best price?

2. How could the price elasticities provided by the marketing researcher be estimated?

3. What prices give the highest gross margins, return on investment, capital cost covered ($C^3$) economic value added (EVA), net contribution, sales value and sales volume (Marketing Highlight 16.4 shows how to calculate these)? What price would you choose and why? What do you notice about the room to manoeuvre around the optimum prices?

4. Assuming a price of £3,500 per tonne, what would be the best advertising strategy, given the following advertising response?

| Advertising (£000) | 25 | 50 | 100 | 200 | 400 |
|---|---|---|---|---|---|
| Sales (tonnes) | 180 | 210 | 280 | 360 | 420 |
| Capital investment (£000) | 1,100 | 1,250 | 1,650 | 2,050 | 2,300 |

5. How does the optimum advertising agency strategy change with alternative manufacturing processes: one with a fixed cost of £300,000 and a variable cost of £1,500 per tonne and the other a fixed cost of £50,000 and a variable cost of £2,500 per tonne? What do these results tell you about the interaction between price (margin) and the other elements of the marketing mix?

Sources: Adapted from in-company information. Names and figures have been changed for commercial reasons.

# *Promotions*

# Promotions

## CHAPTER EIGHTEEN

# Promoting products

## Communication and promotion strategy

### CHAPTER OBJECTIVES

After reading this chapter, you should be able to:

- Name and define the four tools of the promotion mix.
- Discuss the elements of the marketing communications process.
- Explain the methods for setting the promotion budget.
- Discuss the factors that affect the design of the promotion mix.

### CHAPTER PREVIEW

#### British Home Stores

British Home Stores (BHS), the retailer which is part of Britain's Storehouse Group, recently embarked on a campaign to revamp its staid image. BHS has long been noted for its good quality and value-for-money range of clothing, household furnishings and appliances, and food. This long-established institution has been a big player in British high streets. The problem, however, is that in the face of increasing high-street competition and retailing innovations in the 1990s, the stores no longer came across as 'exciting' to consumers. Helen Packshaw, marketing director of BHS, put the problem this way: 'Not enough people get up in the morning and think "I must go to BHS". Shoppers just drift in to the store from the high street. Unlike Marks & Spencer, the BHS brand is "too neutral". There appeared to be a big gap between consumers' perception of what the BHS brand offered and the reality – good quality and well-priced products, besides the convenience of its high-street location. When you go in the store it is actually better than you expected!'

To remedy the situation, BHS has spent three to four years developing a new image and culture – a young, energetic organization – and defining the store's 'value propositions'. (These moves were all part of the restructuring and recovery of the Storehouse Group itself.) The BHS brand is promoted on three platforms: fashion-moderate products, which are up-to-date but mainstream, not at the cutting edge of fashion; consistent and appropriate quality, and low prices that are attractive to mothers on tight budgets, who are by far the largest group among BHS's customers.

The company undertook a vast brand-building exercise. The retailer's goal was to communicate its revamped positioning to its target market and to attract shoppers to the store.

BHS uses several promotion tools to communicate its new message to its customers. A chief component of its communication programme is TV advertising. The ads are adapted to show each season's clothes and can be extended to other BHS lines (e.g. lighting). In-store 'events', such as beach parties, are staged to display the season's fashions. These are organized in stores around the country to gain local publicity and as a general promotional tool.

The BHS logo is also being revamped. The new logo is a 'more feminine, more fluid' version of the one it replaces and seeks to communicate the feeling of 'excitement and energy' that is to be associated with the brand. To support the repositioning of the BHS brand, the company seeks to refurbish its stores and replace the old fasciae so as to reflect its new image. Not only do the inside of stores display the new logo, but carrier bags and labels also carry it. Moreover store interiors are revamped with a new look that is to communicate the brand's new and fresher image. In-store design aims to show off merchandise to greater effect and to 'allow it to breathe'.

BHS uses advertising to raise consumers' awareness of the BHS brand. The ad campaign is also about elevating the brand in the minds of people to whom it might be neutral. The public relations and sales promotions exercises, as in the case of in-store events, are used to draw consumers into the stores in order for them to see what the store really has to offer. The company also uses other elements in the marketing mix – product quality, the way merchandise is presented in the store, its logo and low price – to communicate its total offering to its target market. BHS has to coordinate all these aspects to get the most out of its promotional programme.[1]

Modern marketing calls for more than just developing a good product, pricing it attractively, and making it available to target customers. Companies must also *communicate* with their customers, and what they communicate should not be left to chance.

To communicate well, companies often hire advertising agencies to develop effective ads, sales-promotion specialists to design sales-incentive programmes, direct-marketing specialists to develop databases and interact with customers and prospects by mail and telephone, and public relations firms to develop corporate images. They train their salespeople to be friendly, helpful and persuasive. For most companies, the question is not *whether* to communicate, but *how much to spend* and *in what ways*.

A modern company manages a complex marketing communications system (see Figure 18.1). The company communicates with its middlemen, consumers and various publics. Its middlemen communicate with their consumers and publics. Consumers have word-of-mouth communication with each other and with other publics. Meanwhile, each group provides feedback to every other group.

A company's total marketing communications programme – called its **promotion mix** – consists of the specific blend of advertising, personal selling, sales promotion and public relations tools that the company uses to pursue its advertising and marketing objectives. Let us define the four main promotion tools:

- **Advertising.** Any paid form of nonpersonal presentation and promotion of ideas, goods or services by an identified sponsor.
- **Personal selling.** Oral presentation in a conversation with one or more prospective purchasers for the purpose of making sales.

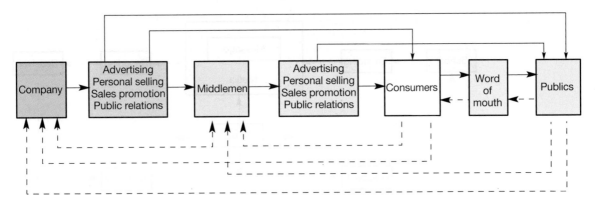

**Figure 18.1**  The marketing communications system.

- **Sales promotion.** Short-term incentives to encourage the purchase or sale of a product or service.
- **Public relations.** Building good relations with the company's various publics by obtaining favourable publicity, building up a good 'corporate image', and handling or heading off unfavourable rumours, stories and events.[2]

Within these categories are specific tools. For example, advertising includes print, broadcast, outdoor and other forms. Personal selling includes sales presentations, fairs and trade shows, and incentive programmes. Sales promotion includes activities such as point-of-purchase displays, premiums, discounts, coupons, competitions, speciality advertising and demonstrations. At the same time, communication goes beyond these specific promotion tools. The product's design, its price, the shape and colour of its package, and the stores that sell it – *all* communicate something to buyers. Thus although the promotion mix is the company's primary communication activity, the entire marketing mix – promotion *and* product, price and place – must be coordinated for greatest communication impact.

This chapter examines two questions. First, *what are the main steps in developing effective marketing communication?* Second, *how should the promotion budget and mix be determined?* In Chapter 20, we look at mass-communication tools, that is, advertising, sales promotion and public relations. Chapter 21 examines the salesforce as a communication and promotion tool.

## STEPS IN DEVELOPING EFFECTIVE COMMUNICATION

Marketers need to understand how communication works. Communication involves the nine elements shown in Figure 18.2. Two of these elements are the chief parties in a communication – the *sender* and the *receiver*. Another two are the essential communication tools – the *message* and the *media*. Four more are primary communication functions – *encoding, decoding, response* and *feedback*. The latest element is *noise* in the system. We will explain each of these elements using a McDonald's televisons ad:

- *Sender.* The *party sending the message* to another party – in this case, McDonald's.
- *Encoding.* The process of *putting the intended message or thought into symbolic form* – McDonald's advertising agency assembles words and illustrations into an advertisement that will convey the intended message.
- *Message.* The *set of word, pictures or symbols* that the sender transmits – the actual McDonald's advertisement.

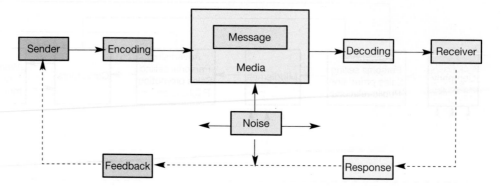

**Figure 18.2**  Elements in the communication process.

- *Media.* The *communication channels* through which the message moves from sender to receiver – in this case, television and the specific television programmes McDonald's selects.
- *Decoding.* The process by which the receiver *assigns meaning to the symbols* encoded by the sender – a consumer watches the McDonald's ad and interprets the words and illustrations it contains.
- *Receiver.* The *party receiving the message* sent by another party – the consumer who watches the McDonald's ad.
- *Response.* The *reactions of the receiver* after being exposed to the message – any of hundreds of possible responses, such as the consumer likes McDonald's better, is more likely to eat at McDonald's next time he or she eats fast food, or does nothing.
- *Feedback.* The part of the r*eceiver's response communicated back to the sender* – McDonald's research shows that consumers like and remember the ad, or consumers write or call McDonald's praising or criticizing the ad or McDonald's products.
- *Noise.* The *unplanned static or distortion* during the communication process, which results in the receiver getting a different message than the one the sender sent – for example, the consumer is distracted by family members while watching the ad.

This model points out the key factors in good communication. Senders need to know what audiences they want to reach and what responses they want. They must be good at encoding messages that take into account how the target audience decodes or interprets them. They must send the message through media that reach target audiences and they must develop feedback channels so that they can assess the audience's response to the message. Thus the marketing communicator must do the following: identify the target audience; determine the response sought; choose a message; choose the media through which to send the message; allocate the total promotion budget; choose the promotion mix; collect feedback to measure the promotion's results; and manage and coordinate the total marketing communications process. Let us now address each of these steps in turn.

### Identifying the target audience

A marketing communicator starts with a clear target audience in mind. The audience may be potential buyers or current users, those who make the buying decision or those who influence it. The audience may be individuals, groups, special publics or the general public. The target audience will heavily affect the communicator's decisions on *what* will be said, *how* it will be said, *when* it will be said, *where* it will be said and *who* will say it.

## Determining the response sought

Once the target audience has been defined, the marketing communicator must decide what response is sought. Of course, in most cases, the final response is *purchase*. But purchase is the result of a long process of consumer decision making. The marketing communicator needs to know where the target audience now stands and to what state it needs to be moved. To do this he or she must determine whether or not the customer is ready to buy.

The target audience may be in any of six **buyer-readiness states** – the states that consumers normally pass through on their way to making a purchase. These states include *awareness*, *knowledge*, *liking*, *preference*, *conviction*, or *purchase* (see Figure 18.3). The states can be described as a *hierarchy of consumer response stages*. The purpose of communication is to move the customer along these stages and ultimately to achieve final purchase.

### Awareness

The communicator must first know how aware the target audience is of the product or organization. The audience may be totally unaware of it, know only its name, or know one or a few things about it. If most of the target audience is unaware, the communicator tries to build awareness, perhaps starting with just name recognition. This process can begin with simple messages that repeat the company or product name. Even then, building awareness takes time. Suppose a new restaurant opens in town and wants to attract clientele. It has not established any reputation in the town. There are 100,000 residents in this town. Suppose some 20,000 may potentially be interested in dining at this restaurant. The restaurant may set the objective of making 50 per cent aware of its existence.

### Knowledge

The target audience might be aware of the existence of the company (there is a restaurant called Pinnochio's in town) or of the product (it is a wine bar that specializes in Italian food) but not know much more. Pinnochio's may want its target audience to know that it is a family-owned operation offering an exciting range of delicate Italian cuisine and served in a fun environment. Thus Pinnochio's needs to learn how many people in its target audience have little, some, or much knowledge about Pinnochio's and it may therefore decide to select product knowledge as its first communication objective.

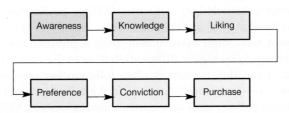

**Figure 18.3** Buyer readiness states.

### Liking

Assuming target audience members *know* the product, how do they *feel* about it? We can develop a scale covering degrees of liking – including dislike very much, dislike somewhat, indifferent, like somewhat and like very much. If the audience looks unfavourably on Pinnochio's, the communicator has to find out why, and then develop a communications campaign to generate favourable feelings. If the unfavourable view is based on real problems in the restaurant (its service is known to be slow; the food does not come across as good value for money; the wine list is not impressive), then communications alone cannot do the job. The owners must resolve those problems before they start to communicate on renewed quality. Good public relations call for 'good deeds followed by good works'.

### Preference

The target audience might *like* the product but not *prefer* it to others. In this case, the communicator must try to build consumer preference by promoting the restaurant's quality, value, friendly and efficient service, its ambience and other features. The communicator can check on the campaign's success by measuring the audience's preferences again after the campaign. If Pinnochio's finds that many potential customers like the restaurant, but choose to eat in other restaurants, it will have to identify those areas where its offerings are not as good as competing restaurants and where they are better. It must then promote its advantages to build preference among prospective clients, while redressing its weaknesses.

### Conviction

A target audience might *prefer* the product but not develop a *conviction* about buying it. Thus some customers may prefer Pinnochio's but may not be sure they want Italian food when they do eat out. The communicator's job is to build conviction that Italian food is fun and interesting.

### Purchase

Finally, some members of the target audience might have *conviction* but not quite get around to making the *purchase*. They may wait for opportunity, want more information or plan to act later. The communicator must lead these consumers to take the final step. Actions might include offering the product at a low price, offering a premium, or letting consumers try it on a limited basis. For instance, Pinnochio's might offer a discount on a meal for two while also inviting selected clientele to the restaurant to enjoy 'an Italian evening'. It may attract diners by distributing leaflets offering the chance to enter a competition with the first visit to the restaurant.

In discussing buyer readiness states, we have assumed that buyers pass through *cognitive* (awareness, knowledge); *affective* (liking, preference, conviction); and *behavioural* (purchase) stages, in that order. This '*learn–feel–do*' sequence is appropriate when buyers have high involvement with a product category and perceive brands in the category to be highly differentiated, as is the case when they purchase a product such as a car. But consumers often follow other sequences. For example, they might follow a '*do–feel–learn*' sequence for high-involvement products with little perceived differentiation, such as a central heating system. Still a third sequence is the '*learn–do–feel*' sequence, where consumers have low involvement and perceive little differentiation, as is the case when they buy a product such as salt. By understanding consumers' buying stages and their appropriate sequence, the marketer can do a better job of planning communications.

## Choosing a message

Having defined the desired audience response, the communicator turns to developing an effective message. Ideally, the message should get *Attention*, hold *Interest*, arouse *Desire* and obtain *Action* (a framework known as the AIDA model). In practice, few message take the consumer all the way from awareness to purchase, but the AIDA framework suggests the desirable qualities of a good message.

In putting the message together, the marketing communicator must solve three problems: what to say (*message content*), how to say it logically (*message structure*), and how to say it symbolically (*message format*).

### Message content

The communicator has to figure out an appeal or theme that will produce the desired response. There are three types of appeal: rational, emotional and moral. **Rational appeals** relate to the audience's self-interest. They show that the product will produce the desired benefits. Examples are messages showing a product's quality, economy, value, or performance. Thus, in its ads, Mercedes offers automobiles that are

### Before you invest in the latest technology, make sure it has a future.

Remember the furry radio? Back in the Fifties, no self-respecting Doris Day fan would have been without one. The very latest innovations are always the most exciting. But have you noticed that they're sometimes the least enduring? So, when it comes to investing in your business, you want to be certain that the communications technology you choose will be as relevant in 20 years' time as it is today. Which is why we developed the Alcatel 4000 Series, a range of advanced ATM compatible communications systems. Because they evolve with your business, they can be easily upgraded to incorporate new services, as and when you need them. If you'd like further information on business systems with a future, call (33.1) 47.69.48.82 or fax (33.1) 47.69.47.75. **Alcatel. Your reliable partner in communications systems.**

ALCATEL

This Alcatel ad is a good example of the use of 'fear appeal'. It stresses the upgradability of its innovations, arresting potential buyers' fear of technological obsolescence.

'engineered like no other car in the world', stressing engineering design, performance and safety. The Volvo 940 GL ad gives 'a whole stack of reasons' for buying the car – it has a rigid passenger safety cage, front and rear absorbing crumple zones, a catalytic converter that always works at peak efficiency, and many more reasons stressing design, safety and economy. When pitching computer systems to business users, IBM salespeople talk about quality, performance, reliability and improved productivity. Rational appeals emphasize the functional benefits – better performance, higher quality, outstanding value – of the product. This type of appeal is particularly appropriate in industrial buying situations and for the purchase of expensive consumer durable products.

**Emotional appeals** attempt to stir up either negative or positive emotions that can motivate purchase. These include fear, guilt and shame appeals that get people to do things they should (brush their teeth, buy new tyres) or to stop doing things they shouldn't (smoke, drink too much, overeat). For example, a recent Crest ad invoked mild fear when it claimed, 'There are some things you just can't afford to gamble with' (cavities). So did Michelin tyre ads that featured cute babies and suggested 'Because so much is riding on your tyres'.[3] Communicators of industrial goods can also use emotional appeals, as in the case of Alcatel who played on managers' fear of investing in technology that could become obsolete rapidly. Its ad says: 'Before you invest in the latest technology make sure it has a future.'

Advertisers also use positive emotional appeals such as love, humour, pride, promise of success and joy. Thus some ad themes, such as British Telecom's 'Make someone happy with a phone call' stir a bundle of strong emotions. An ad campaign for Häagen-Dazs in Britain equated ice cream with pleasure (foreplay, to be more

Moral and emotional appeals: not-for-profit organisations like the United Nations High Commission for Refugees (UNHCR) have successfully used moral and emotional appeals to market a good cause.

**WHAT'S WRONG HERE?**

Look at these nice happy people. Notice that each one has something: a tool or implement here, a bicycle or a briefcase there. All completely normal and unremarkable.

But wait. Something's amiss. That nice fellow near the bottom — third row down, second from the right. He doesn't seem to have anything.

Indeed. You see, he's a refugee. And as you can see, refugees are just like you and me except for one thing: everything they once had has been destroyed or taken away, probably at

gunpoint. Home, family, possessions, all gone.

They have nothing.

And nothing is all they'll ever have unless we help.

Of course, you can't give them back what's been destroyed, and we're not

asking for money (though every penny helps). But we are asking you to keep an open mind. And a smile of welcome.

It may not seem much. But to a refugee it can mean everything.

UNHCR is a strictly humanitarian organization funded only by voluntary contributions. Currently it is responsible for more than 23 million refugees around the world.

UNHCR Public Information
P.O. Box 2500
1211 Geneva 2, Switzerland

UNHCR
United Nations High Commissioner for Refugees

precise). 'It is the *intense* flavour of the finest ingredients combined with *fresh* cream that is essentially Häagen-Dazs', followed by the strapline. 'Now it's on everybody's lips'. The firm claimed that the ad was a success. During the three months it advertised in newspapers and their supplements, brand awareness doubled while sales in big outlets rose by a third. Over the year the campaign had boosted sales by 59 per cent.[4]

**Moral appeals** are directed to the audience's sense of what is 'right' and 'proper'. They are often used to urge people to support social causes such as a cleaner environment, better race relations, equal rights for women, and aid to the handicapped and needy. An example of a moral appeal is a recent *Financial Times* and Salomon Brothers ad drawing attention to a family festival and fun run in aid of Imperial Cancer Research Fund and the Queen Elizabeth's Foundation for Disabled People. The ad informs viewers of the date and time of a fun/entertainment event. Runners taking part in a three-mile competitive run and a one-mile fun run each donate £10    1 ecu = UK£0.83 to the charities. The ad stresses that the two charities count on the generosity of donors or sponsors to continue their vital work – in the United Kingdom alone, about 2.6 million people are severely disabled; cancer is a disease which affects one in three people and kills one in four. If readers want more information and an entry form, they are invited to complete the reply coupon at the end of the ad or to telephone the event hot line. Witness that the advertisement also uses an emotional appeal – concern and sympathy for sufferers – to convey its cause to the target audience.

### Message structure

The communicator also must decide on what is to be said and how to say it. To construct an effective message, the communicator must handle three message–structure issues. The first is whether to draw a conclusion or to leave it to the audience. Research shows that drawing a conclusion is usually more effective where the target audience is less likely to be motivated or may be incapable of arriving at the appropriate conclusion. Recent research suggests that in cases where the targets are likely to be interested in the product, the advertiser is better off asking questions to stimulate involvement and motivate customers to think about the brand, and then letting them come to their own conclusions.

The second message structure issue is whether to present a one-sided argument (mentioning only the product's strengths), or a two-sided argument (touting the product's strengths while also admitting its shortcomings). Usually, a one-sided argument is more effective in sales presentations – except when audiences are highly educated and negatively disposed. The third message-structure issue is whether to present the strongest arguments first or last. Presenting them first gets strong attention but may lead to an anticlimatic ending.[5]

### Message format

The communicator also needs a strong *format* for the message. The format depends upon the type of medium used. In a print ad, the communicator has to decide on the headline, copy, illustration and colour. To attract attention, advertisers can use: novelty and contrast: eye-catching pictures and headlines; distinctive formats; message size and position; and colour and shape. All these elements must be put together creatively to gain maximum impact with the effectiveness of the ad.

If the message is to be carried over the radio, the communicator has to choose words, sounds and voices. The 'sound' of an announcer promoting a used car should be different from one promoting quality furniture.

If the message is to be transmitted on television or conveyed in person, then all these elements plus body language have to be planned. Presenters plan their facial expressions, gestures, dress, posture and even their hairstyle. If the message is carried on the product or its package, the communicator has to watch texture, scent, colour, size and shape. For example, colour plays an important communication role in food preferences.

> When consumers sampled four cups of coffee that had been placed next to brown, blue, red and yellow containers (all the coffee was identical, but the consumers did not know this), 75 per cent felt that the coffee next to the brown container tasted too strong; nearly 85 per cent judged the coffee next to the red container to be the richest; nearly everyone felt that the coffee next to the blue container was mild; and the coffee next to the yellow container was seen as weak.

Thus, if a coffee company wants to communicate that its coffee is rich, it should probably use a red container along with label copy boasting the coffee's rich taste.

Even when an individual is exposed to a message, he or she may pay no attention to the message because it is either boring or irrelevant. The communicator increases the chances of the message attracting the attention of the target audience by taking into consideration the following factors:

- The message must be of practical value to the target audience because individuals are in the market for the product (for example, advertising pension schemes to undergraduates is a waste of time as they are likely to find such policies irrelevant to them for the time being).
- The message must interest the target group.
- The message must communicate new information about the product or brand. Consumers pay more attention to new messages.
- The message must reinforce or help to justify the buyer's recent purchase decisions – if you have recently bought a personal computer, it is likely that you will notice or your attention is quickly drawn to ads for the PC (the phenomenon is called cognitive dissonance reduction).
- The presentation of the message must be impactful. As explained above, this objective can be achieved by investing in message formats and enhancing the creativity with which the copy, artwork/illustrations and physical layout or presentation are delivered.

While advertisers' basic aim is to get their ads noticed, they must be sensitive to, and comply with, codes of practice operated by the industry watchdogs or country regulators alike. Messages should be designed to create maximum impact but, at the same time, not cause public offence and irritation (see Marketing Highlight 18.1).

### Selecting the message source

Studies show that the effectiveness of the **message source** – the company, the brand name, the spokesperson of the brand or the actor in the ad who endorses the product – depends upon its credibility and attractiveness.

Messages delivered by highly credible sources are more persuasive. Credibility is the extent to which the source is perceived by the audience as being an expert with regard to the product concerned and impartial in the claims that are made for it. Pharmaceutical firms want doctors to testify about their products' benefits because doctors rank high on expertise in their field, so have high credibility. Many food companies are now promoting to doctors, dentists and other healthcare experts to motivate these professionals to recommend their products to patients. For example, Sensodyne Toothpaste has, for years, promoted the product in dental surgeries, and ads use endorsements by dental practitioners to persuade target users to adopt the brand. However, the expert loses credibility if the audience believes the person is being paid to make product claims. To remain credible, the source must be seen by the target audience as being trustworthy: that is, objective and honest in their opinion of the benefits claimed for the product.

Advertisers often also use celebrities to be spokespeople for their products. For example, when the pan-European television station MTV launched its Britain-only music channel VH-1 in September 1994, it chose a cast of UK celebrities who would appeal to its target audience of 'older' viewers. Ads featured, among others, fashion designer Bruce Oldfield, England rugby captain Will Carling and Anglo-Norwegian television presenter Mariella Frostrup.[6]

Other notable examples are Michael Jackson who was the star in Pepsi-Cola's ad and O. J. Simpson for the car rental firm, Hertz. Celebrities are effective when they personify a key product attribute, but there can be a backlash, as in the case of both Jackson and Simpson, when they are caught up in unsavoury publicity and jeopardize their credibility and esteem with the audience.

Attractiveness is associated with the prestige of the source, his or her similarity with the receiver, and/or the physical or personal attractiveness of the source. It is also likely that the more attractive the source, the more he or she will be liked by the audience. It is therefore not surprising that many advertisers use well-known film stars, fashion models and top sports people to endorse their products.

## Choosing media

The communicator must now select *channels of communication*. There are two broad types of communication channels: personal and nonpersonal.

### Personal communication channels

In **personal communication channels**, two or more people communicate directly with each other. They might communicate face to face, person to audience, over the

Here, Anglo-Norwegian television presenter, Mariella Frostrup, takes part in VH-1's launch campaign to promote the new music channel in Britain.

## Communications: the fine line between attraction and irritation

Most marketers work hard to communicate honestly and openly with customers. Very few advertisers set out deliberately to trick, mislead, insult or offend the public. Those that do, face a backlash from consumers and other interested parties, or find themselves debarred at source from the means to further publicize their messages because the media reject the ads that conflict with a country's codes of advertising practices. Established brands supported by ill conceived promotions could backfire badly. Shock tactics can do as much damage, although observers argue that it is really a question of what is socially intolerable and a matter of taste.

### Teasers: good campaigns get the punters talking, a bad one attracts complaints

Advertisers acknowledge that getting viewers to solve a puzzle in an advertisement is fair game in advertising. However, one such campaign backfired. Britvic Soft Drinks' 'Still Tango' ad, aired in June 1994, teased its audience thus: the ad appealed to consumers to report any sightings of the apparently unlicensed product. Almost 30,000 consumers responded only to be told that it was all a joke. They'd been 'Tango'd'. Sixty-three of them were so annoyed, they complained to the Independent Television Commission (ITC). Britvic and its agency were accused of exploiting the credibility and authority of the medium – TV – to play a prank on viewers, all in pursuit of publicity. ITC added that it had to act because consumers were misled! People were irritated that the company had taken advantage of their 'public-spiritedness'. Britvic 'had gone too far'. People felt used. Britvic's teaser did grab customers' attention, but in quite the wrong way.

Observers agree that advertisers must be careful how far they keep consumers guessing. In the late 1980s, ad agency Young & Rubicam devised the 'Tell Sid' British Gas flotation campaign, arguably the first series of high-profile puzzle ads. The intrigue revolved around Sid – nobody knew who Sid was. The campaign had a huge media budget, so new material was churned out every fortnight. It also ran for weeks. However, it was very irritating for consumers to experience the build-up of the teaser ads only to find eventually that the product being launched was something trivial.

Yet another criticism has been levelled at the 'Que Signifie' campaign for Kronenbourg 1664 lager. The saga is conducted entirely in French. The puzzle – a mysterious woman. It was the subject of five episodes, with about a four-month gap between episodes. Throughout those months consumers remained none the wiser as to the significance of 1664, or the identity of the mystery woman. Despair!

A campaign of a different kind caused uproar in Spain. An agency in Madrid sent out love letters to 50,000 young mothers in a direct-marketing campaign for Fiat's Cinquento car. A second batch of letters was then sent revealing the Cinquento as the secret admirer. Rather than seeing this as an amusing piece of junk mail, it caused a storm of protest. The agency claimed the reaction was mainly positive. The Spanish Women's Institute denounced the campaign. Some women were so troubled they were scared to leave the house.

Experts are agreed that there is a fine dividing line between attracting and irritating consumers. For most of the time, people are prepared to enjoy a light-hearted puzzle. A little intrigue adds interest. But, as Britvic has discovered, the intrigue can only be stretched so far.

### Bad taste ads?

Bad taste ads also have their casualties.

For example, charities and pressure groups have inspired a considerable amount of criticism. The RSPCA (Royal Society for the Prevention of Cruelty to Animals) recently drew attention to the plight of horses exported for consumption by deploying a harrowing image of a dead pony hanging from a hook. The advertising watchdog, ASA, upheld complaints against the ad, not because it had any wish to frustrate the RSPCA's efforts to enlighten the public, but because the visual image used was deemed misleading and grossly offensive. The advertisement did not successfully reflect either the argument advanced in the text or the way live horses were actually herded for transportation.

A British Rail (BR) newspaper advertisement featuring twelve yellow condoms arranged in a circle against a blue background was severely criticized by the ASA for being 'grossly irresponsible in its encouragement of promiscuity', and for denigrating the flag of the European Union. The ad was intended to boost sales of BR's Young Person's European rail pass. It was headed 'Inter-Rail. You've got the rest of your life to be good' and it also referred to the European Commission's 'Europe Against Aids' initiative. The ASA received 164 complaints, which were upheld because the advertisement was irresponsible and caused widespread offence. BR argued that Inter-Rail did not encourage promiscuity but reflected their research which showed that a significant proportion of 18-25 year-olds had sexual encounters without a condom while on holiday. Moreover the ad supported the European Aids initiative. BR was urged to avoid further advertisements in that style!

Throughout the mid-1980s to early 1990s Benetton, the Italian clothing designer and manufacturer, used shock tactics to communicate the message about the company as a whole to the consumer. Increasingly, controversy dogged its series of United Colour ads. In 1989, public opinion in the United States forced it to withdraw those showing a black woman breast-feeding a white child. Another in 1991 – a blood-smeared newborn baby – received more than 800 complaints to the United Kingdom's Advertising Standards Authority (ASA), criticizing Benetton for provoking public distress and outrage: 'Benetton has displayed a conspicuous disregard for the sensitivities of the public.' On the advice of the ASA, Benetton agreed to withdraw the advertisement. The ASA was also supported in its ruling against Benetton by both magazine publishers and poster contractors who refused space to the advertiser. Other Benetton ads – a black child depicting a devil contrasting with a white cherub, a dying Aids patient, a baby's bottom stamped with 'HIV positive', the Queen of England as a black woman, the bloodied uniform of a dead Bosnian soldier – consistently created furore, with each being more criticized than praised. Benetton's spokespersons argue that the campaigns were not about sales building or pushing, nor were they intended to insult or hurt. Rather they were designed to capture people's interest and provoke reflection.

There is no question that Benetton's shocking ads have been successful in creating worldwide publicity and served to keep its name on everybody's lips. The question arises: Has it been good or bad publicity? In the short term, Benetton found that its worldwide sales and profits went up and remained buoyant (possibly thanks to the advertisements). But in early 1995, the company felt the backlash. Certain German franchised retailers withheld money from the parent firm because of mounting losses – in some cases more than 30 per cent of turnover – which they directly blamed on Benetton's 'misguided' and now notorious ad campaign. Benetton utterly refuted the accusation, blaming retailers' losses on poor local management, and sought legal action to recover the outstanding money. A flamboyant solicitor claimed to be representing at least 50 retailers with 150 stores – no small challenge. Whatever Benetton says, many believe that their 'bad taste' ads were indeed implicated in the company's plight, though not perhaps the only cause of it.

More recently Benetton changed style, dropping its shocking posters in favour of more subtle ways of reaching its audiences. To sell their message globally, the company is opening up shops all over the world – so what's the puzzle? These, apparently, are not ordinary shops. One in Milan for example is staffed by penniless North African immigrants. And there is a common thread – shops in the Bosnian capital of Sarajevo, in Siberia, Albania, Estonia, Ukraine, Libya, Cameroon and Croatia. 'Benetton's publicity is supposed to make consumers think', says the controversial Oliviero Toscani, Benetton's freelance photographer and advertising guru.

What, then can we make of Benetton's new-image shops? Well, the one opened in Milan was a response to European Union moves to restrict immigration to Europe. And the answer to the puzzle – Benetton's message remains the same as in its shocking posters, but now, these shops give Benetton another channel to make challenging gestures. The big question is, will this help to sell lots and lots of clothes?

Sources: 'Brands that backfired badly', *The European* (25–31 March, 1994), 22; Claire Murphy, 'When the teasers become unbearable', *Marketing Week* (15 July, 1994), 21; Diane Summers, 'BR's condom-flag advert is labelled "irresponsible"', *Financial Times* (5 October, 1994), 9; Louella Miles, 'Consumer speak', *Marketing Business* (November 1991), 29; Gary Mead and Haig Simonian, 'Shocking tone for United Colours', *Financial Times* (30 January, 1992), 12; Matti Alderson, 'Standard practice', *Marketing Business* (November (1992), 8–10; Sarah Cunningham, 'Benetton to drop its shock tactics', *The European* (8–14 July, 1994), 23; 'As you sow, so shall you reap' and 'Benetton cover story', *Marketing Week* (3 February 1995), 5 and 21 respectively.

telephone or even through the mail. Personal communication channels are effective because they allow for personal addressing and feedback.

Some personal communication channels are controlled directly by the communicator. For example, company salespeople contact buyers in the target market. But other personal communications about the product may reach buyers through channels not directly controlled by the company. These might include independent experts making statements to target buyers – consumer advocates, consumer buying guides and others. Or they might be neighbours, friends, family members and associates talking to target buyers. This last channel, known as **word-of-mouth influence**, has considerable effect in many product areas.

Personal influence carries great weight for products that are expensive, risky or highly visible. For example, buyers of automobiles and major appliances often go beyond mass-media sources to seek the opinions of knowledgeable people.

Companies can take several steps to put personal communication channels to work for them:

- They can devote extra effort to selling their products to well-known people or companies, who may, in turn, influence others to buy.
- They can create *opinion leaders* – people whose opinions are sought by others – by supplying certain people with the product on attractive terms. For example, companies can work through community members, such as leaders of local organizations.
- And they can use influential people in their advertisements or develop advertising that has high 'conversation value'.
- Finally, the firm can work to manage word-of-mouth communications by finding out what consumers are saying to others, by taking appropriate actions to satisfy consumers and correct problems, and by helping consumers seek information about the firm and its products.[7]

### Nonpersonal communication channels

**Nonpersonal communication channels** are media that carry messages without personal contact or feedback. They include important media, atmospheres, and events. Important **media** consist of print media (newspapers, magazines, direct mail); broadcast media (radio, television); and display media (billboards, signs, posters). **Atmospheres** are designed environments that create or reinforce the buyer's leanings towards buying a product. Thus lawyers' offices and banks are designed to communicate confidence and other factors that might be valued by their clients. **Events** are occurrences staged to communicate messages to target audiences. For example, public relations departments arrange press conferences, grand openings, public tours, and other events to communicate with specific audiences.

Nonpersonal communication affects buyers directly. In addition, using mass media often affects buyers indirectly by causing more personal communication. Mass communications affect attitudes and behaviour through a *two-step flow-of-communication process*. In this process, communications first flow from television, magazines and other mass media to opinion leaders and then from these opinion leaders to the less active sections of the population.[8] This two-step flow process means the effect of mass media is not as direct, powerful and automatic as once supposed. Rather, opinion leaders step between the mass media and their audiences. Opinion leaders are more exposed to mass media and carry messages to people who are less exposed to media.

The two-step flow concept challenges the notion that people's buying is affected by a 'trickle-down' of opinions and information from higher social classes. Because people mostly interact with others in their own social class, they pick up their fashion and other ideas from people *like themselves*, who are opinion leaders. The two-step flow concept also suggests that mass communicators should aim their messages directly at opinion leaders, letting them carry the message to others. Pharmaceutical firms direct their new drugs promotions at the most influential doctors and medical experts first – the 'thought leaders' in the profession; if they are persuaded, their opinions have an impact upon the new product's acceptance by others in the field. Thus opinion leaders extend the influence of the mass media. Or, they may alter the message or not carry the message, thus acting as gatekeepers.

We have looked at the steps involved in planning and sending communications to a target audience. But how does the company decide on the total *promotion budget* and its division among the major promotional tools to create the *promotion mix*? We now look at these questions.

## Setting the total promotion budget

One of the hardest marketing decisions facing a company is how much to spend on promotion. John Wanamaker, an American department store magnate, once said: 'I know that half of my advertising is wasted, but I don't know which half. I spent $2 million for advertising, and I don't know if that is half enough or twice too much.' It is not surprising, therefore, that industries and companies vary widely in how much they spend on promotion. Promotion spending may be 20 per cent to 30 per cent of sales in the cosmetics industry and only 5 per cent to 10 per cent in the industrial machinery industry. Within a given industry, both low- and high-spending companies can be found.

How does a company decide on its promotion budget? There are four common methods used to set the total budget for advertising: the affordable method, the percentage-of-sales method, the competitive-parity method and the objective-and-task method.[9]

### Affordable method

A common 'rule-of-thumb' used by many companies is the **affordable method**: they set the promotion budget at the level they think the company can afford. One executive explains this method as follows: 'Why it's simple. First, I go upstairs to the controller and ask how much they can afford to give us this year. He says a million and a half. Later, the boss comes to me and asks how much we should spend and I say "Oh, about a million and a half"'.[10]

Unfortunately, this method of setting budgets completely ignores the effect of promotion on sales volume. It leads to an uncertain annual promotion budget, which makes long-range planning difficult. Although the affordable method can result in overspending on advertising, it more often results in underspending.

### Percentage-sales method

Many companies use the **percentage-of-sales method**, setting their promotion budget at a certain percentage of current or forecasted sales. Or they budget a percentage of the sales price. Automotive companies usually budget a fixed percentage for promotion based on the planned car price. Fast-moving consumer goods companies usually set it at some percentage of current or anticipated sales.

The percentage-of-sales method has a number of advantages. First, using this method means that promotion spending is likely to vary with what the company can 'afford'. It also helps management think about the relationship between promoting spending, selling price and profit per unit. Finally, this method supposedly creates competitive stability because competing firms tend to spend about the same percentage of their sales on promotion.

Despite these claimed advantages, however, the percentage-of-sales method has little to justify it. It wrongly views sales as the *cause* of promotion rather than as the *result*. The budget is based on availability of funds rather than on opportunities. It may prevent the increased spending sometimes needed to turn around falling sales. It fails to consider whether a higher or lower level of spending would be more profitable. Because the budget varies with year-to-year sales, long-range planning is difficult. Finally, the method does not provide any basis for choosing a *specific* percentage, except what has been done in the past or what competitors are doing.

## Competitive-parity method

Other companies use the **competitive-parity method**, setting their promotion budgets to match competitors' outlays. They watch competitors' advertising or get industry promotion-spending estimates from publications or trade associations, and then set their budgets based on the industry average.

Two arguments support this method. First, competitors' budgets represent the collective wisdom of the industry. Second, spending what competitors spend helps prevent promotion wars. Unfortunately, neither argument is valid. There are no grounds for believing that the competition has a better idea of what a company should be spending on promotion than does the company itself. Companies differ greatly, in terms of market opportunities and profit margins, and each has its own special promotion needs. Finally, there is no evidence that budgets based on competitive parity prevent promotion wars.

## Objective-and-task method

The most logical budget setting method is the **objective-and-task method**, whereby the company sets its promotion budget based on what it wants to accomplish with promotion. Marketers develop their promotion budgets by (1) defining specific objectives: (2) determining the tasks that must be performed to achieve these objectives; and (3) estimating the costs of performing these tasks. The sum of these costs is the proposed promotion budget.

The objective-and-task method forces management to spell out its assumptions about the relationship between amount spent and promotion results. But it is also the most difficult method to use. They will have to set sales and profit targets and then work back to what tasks must be performed to achieve desired goals. Often it is hard to figure out which specific tasks will achieve specific objectives. For example, suppose Sony wants 95 per cent awareness for its latest camcorder model during the six-month introductory period. What specific advertising messages and media schedules would Sony need in order to attain this objective? How much would these messages and media schedules cost? Sony management must consider such questions, even though they are hard to answer. By comparing the campaign cost with unexpected profit gains, the financial viability of the promotions campaign can be determined.

The main advantage of this method is that it forces managers to define their communication objectives, to determine the extent to which each objective will be met using selected promotion tools and the financial implications of alternative communication programmes.

## Setting the promotion mix

The company must now divide the total promotion budget among the main promotion tools – advertising, personal selling, sales promotion and public relations. It must blend the promotion tools carefully into a coordinated *promotion mix* that will achieve its advertising and marketing objectives. Companies within the same industry differ greatly in how they design their promotion mixes. For example, Avon spends most of its promotion funds on personal selling and catalogue marketing (its advertising is only 1.5 per cent of sales), whereas Helene Curtis Industries spends heavily on consumer advertising (about 23 per cent of sales). Electrolux sells 75 per cent of its vacuum cleaners door to door, whereas Hoover relies more on advertising.

Companies are always looking for ways to improve promotion by replacing one promotion tool with another that will do the same job more economically. Many companies have replaced a portion of their field sales activities with telephone sales and direct mail. Other companies have increased their sales promotion spending in relation to advertising to gain quicker sales.

Designing the promotion mix is even more complex when one tool must be used to promote another. Thus when British Airways decides to offer air miles for flying with them (a sales promotion), it has to run ads to inform the public. When Lever Brothers uses a consumer advertising and sales promotion campaign to back a new washing powder, it has to set aside money to promote this campaign to the resellers to win their support.

Many factors influence the marketer's choice of promotion tools. We now look at these factors.

### The nature of each promotion tool

Each promotion tool – *advertising, personal selling, sales promotion* and *public relations* – has unique characteristics and costs. Marketers have to understand these characteristics in selecting their tools.

*Advertising*    Because of the many forms and uses of advertising, it is hard to generalize about its unique qualities as a part of the promotion mix. Yet several qualities can be noted:

■ Because many people see ads for the product, buyers know that purchasing the product will be understood and accepted publicly. Advertising's public nature suggests that the advertised product is standard and legitimate.
■ Advertising also lets the seller repeat a message many times, and it lets the buyer receive and compare the messages of various competitors.
■ Large-scale advertising by a seller says something positive about the seller's size, popularity and success.
■ Advertising is also very expensive, allowing the company to dramatize its products through the artful use of print, sound and colour.
■ On the one hand, advertising can be used to build up a long-term image for a product (such as Coca-Cola ads). On the other hand, advertising can trigger quick sales (as when a department store advertises a seasonal sale).
■ Advertising can reach masses of geographically spread-out buyers at a low cost per exposure.

Advertising also has some shortcomings:

■ Although it reaches many people quickly, advertising is impersonal and cannot be as persuasive as a company salesperson.

- Advertising is only able to carry on a one-way communication with the audience, and the audience does not feel that it has to pay attention or respond.
- In addition, advertising can be very costly. Although some advertising forms, such as newspaper and radio advertising, can be done on small budgets, other forms, such as network TV advertising, require very large budgets.

*Personal selling*    Personal selling is the most effective tool at certain stages of the buying process, particularly in building up buyers' preferences, convictions and actions. Compared to advertising, personal selling has several unique qualities:

- It involves personal interaction between two or more people, so each person can observe the other's needs and characteristics and make quick adjustments.
- Personal selling also allows all kinds of relationships to spring up, ranging from a matter-of-fact selling relationship to a deep personal friendship. The effective salesperson keeps the customer's interests at heart in order to build a long-term relationship.
- Finally, with personal selling the buyer usually feels a greater need to listen and respond, even if the response is a polite 'no thank you'.

These unique qualities come at a cost, however. A salesforce requires a longer-term commitment than does advertising – advertising can be turned on and off, but salesforce size is harder to change. Personal selling is also the company's most expensive promotion tool, costing industrial companies an average of almost £200 per sales call.

*Sales promotion*    Sales promotion includes a wide assortment of tools – coupons, contests, price reductions, premium offers, free goods and others – all of which have many unique qualities:

- They attract consumer attention and provide information that may lead to a purchase.
- They offer strong incentives to purchase by providing inducements or contributions that give additional value to consumers.
- Moreover sales promotions invite and reward quick response. Whereas advertising says 'buy our product', sales promotion offers incentives to consumers to 'buy it now'.

Companies use sales-promotion tools to create a stronger and quicker response. Sales promotion can be used to dramatize product offers and to boost sagging sales. Sales-promotion effects are usually short-lived, however, and are not effective in building long-run brand preference. To work, manufacturers agree that sales promotions must be carefully planned and offer target customers genuine value. Only then will they enhance perceived brand image, build sales and maintain customer loyalty (see Marketing Highlight 18.2).

*Public relations*    Public relations or PR offers several unique qualities. It is all those activities that the organization does to communicate with target audiences and which are not directly paid for.

- PR is very believable: news stories, features and events seem more real and convincing to readers than do ads.
- Public relations can also reach many prospects who avoid salespeople and advertisements since the message gets to the buyers as 'news' rather than as a sales-directed communication.
- And, like advertising, PR can dramatize a company or product. The Body Shop is amongst one of the few international companies that have used public relations as a more effective alternative to mass TV advertising.

Marketers tend to underuse public relations or to use it as an afterthought. Yet a well-thought-out public relations campaign used with other promotion mix elements can be very effective and economical.

### Factors in setting the promotion mix

Companies consider many factors when developing their promotion mixes, including type of product/market, the use of a push or pull strategy, the buyer-readiness stage and the product life-cycle stage.

*Type of product/market*    The importance of different promotion tools varies between consumer and business markets (see Figure 18.4). Consumer-goods companies usually put more of their funds into advertising, followed by sales promotion, personal selling and then public relations. Advertising is relatively more important in consumer markets because there are a larger number of buyers, purchases tend to be routines, and emotions play a more important role in the purchase-decision process. In contrast, industrial goods companies put most of their funds into personal selling, followed by sales promotion, advertising and public relations. In general, personal selling is used more heavily with expensive and risky goods and in markets with fewer and larger sellers.

Although advertising is less important than sales calls in business markets, it still plays an important role. Advertising can build product awareness and knowledge, develop sales leads and reassure buyers. Similarly, personal selling can add a lot to consumer goods marketing efforts. It is simply not the case that 'salespeople put products on shelves and advertising takes them off'. Well-trained consumer goods salespeople can sign up more dealers to carry a particular brand, convince them to give more shelf space and urge them to use special displays and promotions.

*Push versus pull strategy*    The promotional mix is affected by whether the company chooses a *push* or *pull* strategy. Figure 18.5 contrasts the two strategies. A *push strategy* involves 'pushing' the product through distribution channels to final consumers. The producer directs its marketing activities (primarily personal selling and trade

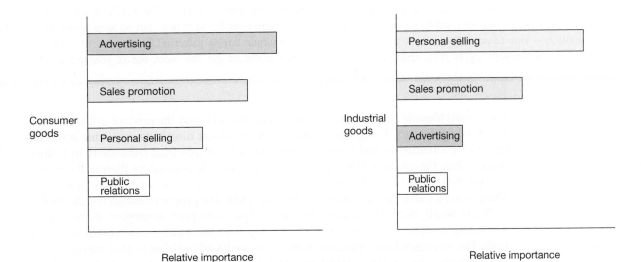

**Figure 18.4**    Relative importance of promotion tools in consumer versus industrial markets.

# Promotions for children: can childish things build sales and brand loyalty?

Sales promotions targeted at kids are successfully deployed by many consumer goods companies. Some argue that they are great for building sales and loyalty. Manufacturers also agree that children are not easy targets. They are fickle, so it is crucial for the firm to strike the right note. At the same time, the firm must be careful to avoid venturing too far into the delicate area of 'pester power'. The latter is a phenomenon many parents claim to be familiar with: the child demands a particular food or toy because it is the latest craze, often hyped on television. Observers argue that, in the long run, promotions which are not only fun but also educational, and offer real value to target consumers, will build loyalty – always assuming of course, that the product itself is right.

## Creating brand loyalty

One of the most successful kids' crazes in recent years has been dinosaurs – Dino stickers, Dino cups, Dino cards, Dino games, Dino chips, Dino biscuits – all stalk supermarket shelves. (Remember Ninja Turtles? Well, the story is very much the same, although parents were spared Ninja Turtle chips and cookies!) The Spielberg blockbuster, *Jurassic Park*, was partly responsible, but manufacturers and merchandisers have also deliberately focused upon kids' interest in the dinosaur itself – they learn about dinosaurs at school, how they lived and the mystery of their extinction. McDonald's, the restaurant chain, was one of the many big names who signed up for a themed promotion – kids could collect all six of its *Jurassic Park* cups. McDonald's argues that: 'children are very

finicky and anything that is of the moment will interest them, but this means you will have to be on top of the trends'. McDonald's, however, is a consistent investor in promotions, as reflected in its long standing concentration on its Happy Meals for children. They appear to be leading the way in terms of creating brand loyalty. The challenge lies in maintaining the appeal of the offers. Creativity in value creation is a must.

Sometimes, authorities can get in the way of booms. In Israel, consumers were urged to boycott food companies mounting such promotions because dinosaurs were ruled as not kosher. Moreover, they died 65 million years ago, so the rabbinical authorities decreed that they could never have existed as the world was only created 5,753 years ago.

There are, however, dangers inherent in blindly following fads. It is also difficult to decide whether the children themselves create the trends or simply follow them. Nevertheless, whatever the sequence, most people agree that promotions linked to current crazes have a superior chance of success. At the same time, the firm must follow trends discriminately and ensure that they do not conflict with the product.

Licensing has advantages, especially for an established brand. 'Thunderbirds' has been one of the most successful licences of recent years. Licensing also has inherent dangers. A small brand that buys the endorsement of a well-known character may be dwarfed by that character. The result is usually a short-term sales boost at best, but no long-term shift in consumer buying patterns. Sometimes, it takes a strong brand to get the most out of licensing (e.g.

promotion) towards channel members to induce them to carry the product and to promote it to final consumers. Using a *pull strategy*, the producer directs its marketing activities (primarily advertising and consumer promotion) towards final consumers to induce them to buy the product. If the pull strategy is effective, consumers then will demand the product from channel members, who will in turn demand it from producers. Thus under a pull strategy, consumer demand 'pulls' the product through the channels.

Some small industrial goods companies use only push strategies: some direct-marketing companies use only pull. Most large companies use some combinations of both. For example, Lever Brothers uses mass-media advertising to pull consumers to its products and, a large salesforce and trade promotions to push its products through the channels.

McDonald's and Walt Disney's 'Beauty and the Beast' cartoon characters).

### Backing up promotions

Jacob's, a biscuit manufacturer, joined the dinosaur boom and launched dinosaur biscuits, which have done very well on the Continent. The biscuits were promoted on television (breakfast time was popular) and in cinemas, and the company also sponsored a dinosaur exhibition at London's Alexandra Park. Extensive back-up is often required to build awareness for the promotion as well as to maintain the momentum over time.

For some products, such as milk drinks and food products, one difficulty lies in targeting the wide age range, from 3 to 12. In the United Kingdom, Crusha, a milk drink from Rayner Burgess, invested in a host of promotional tools – PR, sales promotions and competitions in women's magazines and youth press, and samplings at the Milk Marketing Board and National Dairy Council roadshows around the country. Crusha, with a limited promotions budget, focused on 'heavy users' who are primarily younger children. A recent outstanding promotion was T-shirts that changed design when worn. It had a redemption of 250 per cent higher than any previous offer. Parents like the product as it encourages kids to drink milk. The promotion also added genuine value to the product – kids do not just want instant appeal with no substance. Promotions therefore need to have real value. This requirement is borne out in another T-shirt offer. Walkers (crisps) offered Looney Tunes T-shirts as the incentive but made it more relevant and desirable by picking up one of the most popular characters within the Looney Tunes portfolio, the Tasmanian Devil, and positioning it as the Big Taz T. More importantly, it was imperative that the T-shirt itself was promoted on design, quality and positioning. Even the colour was carefully chosen – kids prefer coloured T-shirts to white.

### What appeals to children?

For promotional items, experts suggest that there are a number that retain popularity – particularly stickers, models and T-shirts. If these also leak into the current crazes, they have a good chance of success. Although kids still prefer traditional items, observers acknowledge that there are two main considerations when planning promotions for children. First, children are usually more comfortable with forms of modern technology than their parents are, so the promoter must avoid patronizing them. Secondly, children enjoy being required to make some effort (e.g. to patiently collect tokens, which they regard as a challenge, or competitions, which they are even more enthused with). Parents, on the other hand, may find it hard to summon the energy for such tasks. For children's promotions to work they must be in tune with children's current interests. But more importantly, they have to offer real value to their receivers (and parents must perceive this value factor too).

Source:    Louella Miles, 'Childish things', *Marketing Business* (Dec.–Jan. 1993), 36–8.

---

In recent years, consumer-goods companies have been decreasing the pull portions of their promotion mixes in favour of more push. There are a number of reasons behind this shift in promotion strategy. One is that mass-media campaigns have become more expensive and many companies in Europe, the United States and Japan have cut back due to recessionary pressures in the early 1990s. Many firms have also found advertising less effective in recent years. Companies are increasing their segmentation efforts and tailoring their marketing programmes more narrowly, making national advertising less suitable than localized retailer promotions. In these days of heavy brand extensions and me-too products, many companies are finding it difficult to feature meaningful product differentiations in advertising. Instead, they differentiate their brands through price reductions, premium offers, coupons and other promotions aimed at the trade. The growing strength of retailers is also a key factor speeding the shift from pull to push. Big retail chains in Europe and the United States have greater access to product sales and profit information. They have the power to demand and get what they want from suppliers. And what they want is margin improvements – that is, more push. Mass advertising bypasses them on its way to the consumers, push promotion benefits them directly. Consumer promotions give retailers an immediate sales boost and cash from trade allowances pads retailer profits. So, manufacturers are compelled to use push promotions just to obtain good shelf space and advertising support from their retailers.

However, reckless use of push promotion leads to fierce price competition and a continual spiral of price slashing and margin erosion, leaving less money to invest in the product R&D, packaging and advertising that is required to improve and maintain long-run consumer preference and loyalty. Robbing the advertising budget to pay for more sales promotion could mortgage a brand's long-term future for short-term gains. While push strategies will remain important, particularly in packaged goods marketing, companies that find the best mix between the two – consistent advertising to build long-run brand value and consumer preference and sales promotion to create short-run trade support and consumer excitement – are most likely to win the battle for loyal and satisfied customers.[11]

*Buyer-readiness state*    The effects of the promotional tools vary for the different buyer-readiness stages. Advertising, along with public relations. plays the leading

Advertising can play a dramatic role in industrial marketing, as shown in this classic McGraw-Hill ad.

"I don't know who you are.
I don't know your company.
I don't know your company's product.
I don't know what your company stands for.
I don't know your company's customers.
I don't know your company's record.
I don't know your company's reputation.
Now—what was it you wanted to sell me?"

MORAL: Sales start **before** your salesman calls—with business publication advertising.

McGRAW-HILL MAGAZINES
BUSINESS•PROFESSIONAL•TECHNICAL

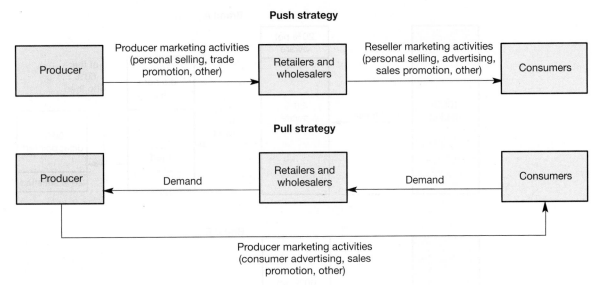

**Figure 18.5**   Push versus pull promotion strategy.

role in the awareness and knowledge stages, more important than that played by 'cold calls' from salespeople. Customer liking, preference and conviction are more affected by personal selling, which is closely followed by advertising. Finally, closing the sale is mostly done with sales calls and sales promotion. Clearly, advertising and public relations are the most cost effective at the early stages of the buyer decision process, while personal selling, given its high costs, should focus on the later stages of the customer buying process.

*Product life-cycle stage*   The effects of different promotion tools also vary with stages of the product life cycle. In the introduction stage, advertising and public relations are good for producing high awareness, and sales promotion is useful in promoting early trial. Personal selling must be used to get the trade to carry the product. In the growth stage, advertising and public relations continue to be powerful influences, whereas sales promotion can be reduced because fewer incentives are needed. In the mature stage, sales promotion again becomes important relative to advertising. Buyers know the brands and advertising is needed only to remind them of the product. In the decline stage, advertising is kept at a reminder level, public relations is dropped and salespeople give the product only a little attention. Sales promotion, however, might continue at a high level in order to stimulate trade and customers.

## Collecting feedback

After sending the message, the communicator must research its effect on the target audience. This involves asking the target audience members whether they remember the message, how many times they saw it, what points they recall, how they felt about the message and their past and present attitudes toward the product and company. The communicator also would like to measure behaviour resulting in the message – how many people bought a product, talked to others about it or visited the store.

Figure 18.6 shows an example of feedback measurement for two hypothetical brands. Looking at Brand A, we find that 80 per cent of the total market is aware of it,

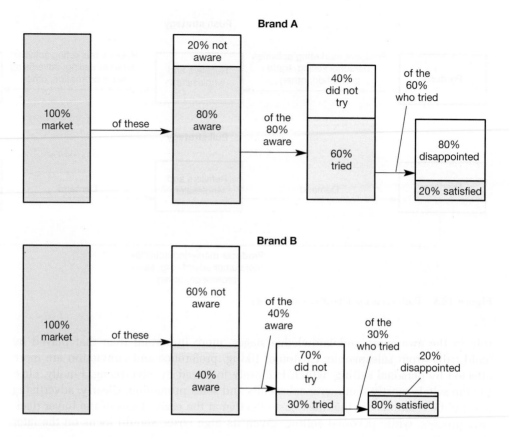

**Figure 18.6** Feedback measurements for two brands.

that 60 per cent of those aware of it have tried it, but that only 20 per cent of those who tried it were satisfied. These results suggest that although the communication programme is creating *awareness*, the product fails to give consumers the *satisfaction* they expect. Therefore, the company should try to improve the product while staying with the successful communication programme. In contrast, only 40 per cent of the total market is aware of Brand B, only 30 per cent of those aware of Brand B have tried it, but 80 per cent of those who have tried it are satisfied. In this case, the communication programme needs to be stronger to take advantage of the brand's power to obtain satisfaction.

## Managing and coordinating the marketing communications process

Members of the marketing department often have different views on how to split the promotion budget. The sales manager would rather hire a few more salespeople than spend £100,000 on a single television commercial. The public relations manager feels that he or she can do wonders with some money shifted from advertising to public relations. Little thought will be given to alternative forms of communication, like direct mail or telemarketing, unless someone in the organization champions it.

If companies leave promotional decisions to different people, and no one person is responsible for thinking through the roles of the various promotion tools and coordinating the promotion mix, they may lack consistency and may not be cost effective. The wide range of promotional tools and communication objectives make it imperative that they be coordinated. Increasingly, companies are adopting the concept of *integrated marketing communications.*

Under this concept, the company works out the roles that the various promotional tools will play and the extent to which each will be used. It carefully coordinates the promotional activities and their timing when big campaigns take place. It keeps track of its promotional expenditures by product, promotional tool, product life-cycle stage and observed effect in order to improve future use of the promotion mix tools. Finally, to help implement its integrated marketing strategy, the company appoints a marketing communications director who has overall responsibility for the company's persuasive communications efforts.

Integrated marketing communications produces better communications consistency and greater sales impact. It places the responsibility in someone's hands – where none existed before – to unify the company's image as it is shaped by thousands of company activities. It leads to a total marketing communication strategy aimed at showing how the company and its products can help customers solve their problems.

Whoever is in charge, people at all levels of the organization must be aware of the growing body of laws and regulations that governs marketing communications activities. Beyond understanding and abiding by these laws and regulations, companies should ensure that they communicate honestly and fairly with consumers and resellers.

## SUMMARY

*Promotion* is one of the four principal elements of the company's marketing mix. The main promotion tools – *advertising, sales promotion, public relations* and *personal selling* – work together to achieve the company's communication objectives.

In preparing marketing communications, the communicator has to understand the nine elements of any communication process: *sender, receiver, encoding, decoding, message, media, response, feedback* and *noise.* The communicator's first task is to identify the target audience and its characteristics. Next, the communicator has to define the response sought, whether it be *awareness, knowledge, liking, preference, conviction* or *purchase.* Then a message should be constructed with an effective *content, structure* and *format.* Media must be selected, both for *personal communication* and *non-personal communication.* The message must be delivered by a credible *source* – someone who is an expert and is trustworthy and likeable.

The company also has to decide how much to spend on promotion. The most popular approaches are to spend what the company can afford, to use a *percentage of sales,* to base promotion on *competitor's spending* or to base it on an analysis and costing of the communication *objectives* and *tasks.*

The company has to divide the *promotion budget* among the main tools to create the *promotion mix.* Companies are guided by the characteristics of each promotion tool, the type of product/market, the desirability of a *push* or *pull* strategy, the *buyer's readiness state* and the *product life-cycle stage.*

Finally, the communicator must *collect feedback* by watching how much of the market becomes aware, tries the product and is satisfied in the process. As with all marketing plans and programmes, all of the promotional activities must be managed and *coordinated* for maximum impact.

## ■ DISCUSSING THE ISSUES

1. Which forms of marketing communications does each of the following represent?

   - A Madonna T-shirt sold at a concert.
   - An interview with Eric Clapton on a late evening TV 'chat' programme arranged by his manager.
   - A record store selling Madonna albums at a 10 per cent discount during the week her latest music video debuts on national television.

2. Linda McCartney (wife of former Beatle, Paul McCartney) has been used to endorse a line of reduced calorie, health-food products. Her name is a key selling feature on the packaging of these products. Is she a credible source for the product? Is she chosen for her credibility as a spokesperson or for some other reason?

3. How does an organization get feedback on the effects of its communication efforts?

4. Companies spend a huge amount of money on advertising to build a quality image for their products. They spend even more on a discount-oriented sales promotions, offering lower price as the main reason to purchase. Discuss whether sales promotion enhances or reduces the effect of advertising. Where possible, offer examples where they enhance one another.

5. Consider a consumer goods company that has historically set the promotion budget as a percentage of anticipated sales. Make out a case for changing the method, indicating your preferred method, and explain why.

6. Charity Projects, the organization behind Comic Relief, most notable for the initiation of Red Nose Day, is planning a new fund-raising campaign to raise millions of pounds to support development and emergency projects in Asia and Eastern European economies. Outline a communication plan to achieve this objective.

## ■ APPLYING THE CONCEPTS

1. Think of a nationally advertised product or service that has been running an advertising message for a while. Go to a bookstore, newsagent and/or the library and seek out magazines and other relevant print media that may contain print advertising for the brand you have selected. Where possible, copy examples of the ads from current and back issues of the magazines and the printed material you have accessed. Now examine the ads closely.

   - How consistent are the message content, structure and format?
   - Which response(s) do you think the campaign is seeking: awareness, knowledge, liking, preference, conviction or purchase?

   - Do you think the ad campaign is successful in achieving the desired response? Why or why not?

2. Consider a car brand you are familiar with.

   - List examples of how this brand uses the range of promotional tools to communicate with its target audience. (Public relations examples may be difficult to spot, although you could consider how cars are used in films, television programmes or as celebrity vehicles for sports tournaments or public events.)
   - Does this car maker use the communication tools in a coordinated way that builds a consistent brand image, or are the efforts fragmented? Explain.

## ■ REFERENCES

1. Diane Summers, 'From neutral to high gear,' *Financial Times* (21 July 1994), 17.
2. For these and other definitions, see Peter D. Bennett, *Dictionary of Marketing Terms* (Chicago: American Marketing Association, 1988).
3. For more on fear appeals, see John F. Tanner, James B. Hunt, and David R. Eppright, 'The protection motivation model: a normative model of fear appeals', *Journal of Marketing* (July 1991), 36–45.
4. 'Repent, ye sinners, repent', *The Economist* (24 April 1993), 87–8; *Financial Times* (16 March 1992), 9.
5. For more on message content and structure, see Leon G. Schiffman and Leslie Lazar Kanuk, *Consumer Behavior*, 4th edn (Englewood Cliffs, NJ: Prentice Hall,

1991), ch. 10; Frank R. Kardes, 'Spontaneous inference processes in advertising: the effects of conclusion omission and involvement on persuasion', *Journal of Consumer Research* (September 1988), 225–53; Alan G. Sawyer and Daniel J. Howard, 'Effects of omitting conclusions in advertisements to involved and uninvolved audiences', *Journal of Marketing Research* (November 1991), 467–74; and Cornelia Pechmann, 'Predicting when two-sided ads will be more effective than one-sided ads: the role of correlational and correspondent inferences', *Journal of Marketing* (November 1992), 441–53.

6. David Short, 'Rival shows mean business,' *The European* (23–29 September, 1994), 25.

7. See K. Michael Haywood, 'Managing word of mouth communications', *Journal of Services Marketing* (spring 1989), 55–67).

8. See P. F. Lazarsfeld B. Berelson, and H. Gaudet, *The People's Choice*, 2nd edn (New York: Columbia University Press, 1948), 151; and Schiffman and Kanuk, *Consumer Behavior*, 571–2.

9. For a more comprehensive discussion on setting promotion budgets, see Michael L. Rothschild, *Advertising* (Lexington, MA: D. C. Heath, 1987), 20.

10. Quoted in Daniel Seligman, 'How much for advertising', *Fortune* (December 1956), 123.

11. Louis Therrien, 'Brands on the run,' *Business Week* (April 1993), 26–9; Karen Herther, 'Survey reveals implications of promotion trends for the 90's,' *Marketing News* (1 March 1993), 7; David Short, 'Advertisers come out to spend again,' *The European* (12–18 August, 1994), 21.

## CASE 18

## Absolut Vodka: absolutely successful
*Pontus Alenroth, Robert Björnström, Joakim Eriksson and Thomas Helgesson**

Little did Lars Olsson Smith know, when he introduced a new kind of vodka called 'Absolutely Pure Vodka' in 1879, that his unique concept would become the world's leading premium vodka a century later. Lars Olsson Smith, whose portrait embellishes every Absolut Vodka bottle, was a self-made spirits tycoon in nineteenth-century Sweden. He introduced a revolutionary new distillation method – the rectification method – which is still used today when producing Absolut Vodka. The result was a clear high-quality vodka free from dangerous and bad-tasting by-products. As its label shows, Absolut vodka trades on its heritage:

**ABSOLUT**
*Country of Sweden*
**VODKA**
*This superb vodka*
*was distilled from grain grown*
*in the rich fields of Sweden.*
*It has been produced by the famous*
*old distilleries of Åhus*
*in accordance with more than*
*400 years of Swedish tradition.*
*Vodka has been sold under the name*
*Absolut since 1879.*

Despite its long traditions, Absolut Vodka is a modern success. In 1979, when the 100th anniversary of Absolutely Pure Vodka was approaching, Vin & Sprit, the Swedish state-owned alcohol monopoly, decided to start exporting the vodka to the United States. After objections from American authorities the name Absolutely Pure Vodka was changed to Absolut Vodka. American consultants had surveyed the US spirits market and found 'a clearly discernible consumer trend towards "white spirits" [such as vodka, gin and white rum] as opposed to "brown spirits" [brandy, whiskey and dark rum]; white spirits are seen as being purer and healthier'. Vin & Sprit had no marketing or product design experience, and so they employed outside teams of marketing and management experts to create an adequate product for the newly discovered market.

The design of the bottle was recognized at an early stage as crucial to success. The final result is almost entirely the result of the persistence of one man, Gunnar Broman. Gunnar Broman got the idea when he saw some eighteenth-century medicine bottles in the window of an antique shop in the Old

* Halmstad University, Sweden.

Town in Stockholm. The bottles were elegant, different, simple and very Swedish. Actually vodka was sold as a medicine in not dissimilar bottles during the eighteenth and nineteenth centuries. Broman had to argue his case for more than a year until the bottle was finally approved and the manufacturing problems overcome: The resulting Absolut bottle was very different from competitors' bottles. The new version of an old medicine bottle was considered a masterpiece in glass design. The timeless shape, the fine lines and the exceptionally clear glass distinguish Absolut from other premium vodka brands.

Independently of each other, the marketing team in Sweden and Carillion, their US distributors, came up with marketing strategies that were almost identical. 'All advertising should centre around the bottle, the product should not be identified with any particular lifestyle, and the approach should have a timeless yet contemporary feel to it.' Every advertisement has two features in common: the depiction of an Absolut bottle and a two- or three-word caption beginning with the word 'Absolut'. It hit the US market in 1979 and became the biggest selling imported vodka brand. In 1993 Vin & Sprit shipped 4.5m. nine-litre cases to the United States alone.

The new innovative way of marketing Absolut contrasted directly with that of the established brands. As David Wachsman points out, the advertising of spirits in the United States used 'one of three formats: a roomful of exceedingly happy people, a celebrity holding a glass or old-fashioned settled family life.' Then came 'Absolut Perfection' and hundreds of different ads.

Absolut Vodka is a highly priced premium vodka and therefore has an aura of up-market exclusiveness. Considering the target market and the early magazine ads (Absolut Perfection, and so on), a tie-up with the arts world was inevitable. The first step in this direction was taken in 1985 when the New York cult pop artist Andy Warhol was commissioned to paint the Absolut Vodka bottle. Today Absolut cooperates with artists, chefs and designers in all the contemporary arts. 'The purity and clarity' of the product, says Vin & Sprits vice president Curt Nycander, is a 'timeless source of inspiration'. There are now over 3,000 works in the Absolut collection, all featuring some aspect of the bottle or label. Like other very successful campaigns, such as Benetton and Wonderbra, the marketing is so sensational that the product receives a huge amount of free media exposure. In Absolut's case this has even occurred in markets that did not allow alcohol advertising.

Due to the fame that Absolut's unconventional marketing has generated, the advertising agency receives thousands of requests for ad reprints of the product, which has become a modern icon. In 1993, besides having won the Effie and the Kelly awards, Absolut was honoured with an induction into the Marketing Hall of Fame. That seal of approval confirmed Absolut's success and impact on the American lifestyle, especially since the only other brands that have received such an honour are Coke and Nike. 'Absolut Art' is also achieving international recognition. Warhol and other key US works, together with others specially commissioned from French artists Bosser and Delprat, were shown at Paris's prestigious Lavignes-Bastille Gallery in late 1994. From there, the exhibition moved to London's Royal College of Art where new works by British artists, including Peter Blake, were added. The exhibition then travelled in turn to Berlin, Munich and Milan.

The modest sales during the first years contrast with the current situation where Absolut Vodka is recognized as the leading premium vodka and the second largest vodka brand overall. Absolut Vodka gave Vin & Sprit a lifeline amidst declining Swedish demand for spirits. Sales grew by more than 38 per cent in 1993 and accounted for a quarter of Vin & Sprit's Skr486 million* turnover.

An ingenious bottle and creative marketing played a crucial part in the Absolut saga, but Vin & Sprit's distribution partnership was also crucial to its success. Recently, however, Absolut bid farewell to Carillion, its international distributor. After a long and fruitful relationship Absolut has outgrown Carillion. The new choice is the US company Seagram, the world's leading alcohol distributor with an international distribution network spanning 150 countries. With Seagram's help Vin & Sprit intends to reinforce Absolut's presence in new markets, notably in Russia and the Far East. It also hopes to increase its penetration in the eighty-five countries where Absolut is already present.

*1 ecu = US$1.26 = Skr9.29 (Swedish kronor).

The Absolut Akademi aims to create 'a competitive edge through people'. 'The goal is to build a quality culture around a quality product.' Another tool in internal marketing is the *Absolut Reflexions* magazine which is distributed throughout Absolut Vodka's network. The magazine publishes instructions ranging from how Absolut should be introduced and presented to the customer to how public or professional audiences should be addressed.

Despite Absolut's success, Vin & Sprit's profits were less than one per cent of turnover in 1993. At the end of 1994 Vin & Sprit will also lose its monopoly status in Sweden. Other producers will be allowed and the company will no longer have exclusive rights regarding wholesale sales to the state retail company, System-Bolaget. Vin & Sprit are tackling the problem by economizing and expanding. Their Stockholm distillery will close in 1995 to concentrate production in three remaining plants. The total number of employees will also be reduced by a third.

While economizing at home Vin & Sprit aim to follow Absolut's success in America with an attack on the European, Asian and Pacific markets. Compared with the United States, the European market is slow growing, fragmented and conservative. Europe has many leisure drinking cultures, but these vary from region to region and there are well-established traditions everywhere. Except for countries where vodka is the national drink, the European vodka market is underdeveloped. Vodka is drunk by only 4 per cent of consumers in Europe, compared to 21 per cent of Americans. To repeat its American success, Absolut will need clever and innovative strategies tailored specifically for each of Europe's submarkets. Absolut are bullish about their chances in Europe. 'We have built up a wide experience of operating abroad and we are confident we can meet the competition,' says Vin & Sprit's Margareta Nyström. The company believe that wherever there is a demand for premium vodka, Absolut Vodka is the optimal choice. 'Absolut Vodka proves itself time and time again as more than just a fine vodka: it's an idea. And nothing can stop an idea whose time has come.'

## Questions

1. What is the foundation of Absolut Vodka's success? Is it the vodka, the bottle, the distribution or the promotion? Do Vin & Sprit's low profits suggest that Absolut is not a commercial success but one bought at the expense of losing their monopolistic powers elsewhere?

2. Absolut's successful advertising has benefited greatly from the publicity it generated. Can advertising campaigns be designed to create such media attention or is the success of Wonderbra, Benetton and their like, just good fortune? Compare the approaches of Absolut, Wonderbra, Nescafé Gold Blend, Boddingtons and others, in creating publicity-efficient campaigns. Is all such coverage good publicity? Does it involve the advertiser losing control of the brand?

3. How does Absolut's marketing build upon American trends in the late 1980s and early 1990s? Is Absolut a fashion product that will decline with the trends? Since Absolut Vodka is such a lifestyle product, would you recommend that Vin & Sprit should extend the brand into other markets in the same way as Virgin has extended into video games, PCs, cola and vodka?

4. Do you believe that Absolut Vodka 'is an idea whose time has come' and that nothing can stop its success? In what way are the conditions in the Russian, European and Far Eastern markets different from those in the United States? Vin & Sprit's European campaign uses ads in the same style that has been so successful in the United States. Do you think the US approach will work in other regions?

Sources: The leading article in *Marketing Business* (November 1992), 1; *Absolut Reflections* (July 1992), April and October 1993, February 1994); *Aftonbladet* (10 September, 1994); *Månadens Affärer* (August 1994); Gustavsson Tegnérlunden, Häggblom Tegnérlunden and Arne Lövgren, *The Storey* (Stockholm: Vin & Sprit, 1994); Greg McIvor 'Nordic drink groups shaken by changes', *The European* (16-22 September, 1994), 19; 'IPA Advertising Effectiveness Awards' (London: *Marketing*, 1994); and Henry Sutton, 'Absolutely in the spirit of art's sake', *The European* (23 Oct.–3 Nov. 1994), 21.

## CHAPTER NINETEEN

# Promoting products

## Advertising, sales promotion and public relations

## CHAPTER OBJECTIVES

After reading this chapter, you should be able to:

- Define the roles of advertising, sales promotion and public relations in the promotion mix.

- Describe the main decisions involved in developing an advertising programme.

- Explain how sales promotion campaigns are developed and implemented.

- Explain how companies use public relations to communicate with their publics.

## CHAPTER PREVIEW

### Promotions medley!

1 ecu = UK£0.83

'Scott backs the arrival of its softer, thicker toilet tissue brand with a £15 million TV, poster and press campaign featuring a family and their puppy.'

'Delta Airlines launches a new 96-sheet poster ad that would be seen on 250 sites throughout London ... which is part of the company's £24 million pan-European, image-building campaign.'

'The UK's third largest charity, the Royal National Lifeboat Institution (RNLI), is set to spend £1.5 million on direct marketing and will consider direct response television following a successful trial campaign ... in which more than £55 million in voluntary income was received ...'

'IBM will use generic advertising for its personal computers. To start off with, corporate advertising will emphasize IBM as a brand rather than a series of products. IBM also will run a £12 million pan-European advertising campaign for its new operating system ...'

'Spanish designer Paco Rabanne launches XS pour Elle, a women's version of its XS men's fragrance. TV advertisements break simultaneously in France, the UK and Belgium ...'

'Ready Brek, an instant hot oat cereal from Weetabix, teams up with Disney Home Video for an in-pack promotion. Children collect a set of eight moving picture cards based on original illustrations from the Disney film, *Snow White and the Seven Dwarfs*, The cards become available before the video of the film goes on sale. Children can also send away for a 12-page booklet in which to mount cards for £1.50 and one completed order form. Over the period of the in-pack promotion campaign, Ready Brek packs also offer "10 per cent extra free". A national TV ad campaign focuses on the *Snow White* promotion and a full publicity programme is implemented to raise awareness of the video release.'

'Richard Branson's everywhere – the beard, the smile, the stories about this irrepressibly optimistic businessman leaping out of every newspaper, television and radio station, the publication of the man's second biography in five years. Virgin is his brand and that is going places too – Virgin launches into vodka, Virgin takes on Coca-Cola, Virgin gets FM frequency in London … Radio 1 listeners vote Virgin's Branson the man they would most like to rewrite the ten commandments.' The moral of the story is that a well-lubricated PR (public relations) machine can work wonders for the company's leader and its brands.

These accounts are just a few examples reflecting the array of mass communication opportunities open to organizations seeking to create awareness for their products or services, to secure greater support for their brands or to generate sales.[1]

---

Companies must do more than offer good products or services. They must inform consumers about product or service benefits and carefully position these in consumers' minds. To do this, they must skilfully use the mass-promotion tools of *advertising*, *sales promotion* and *public relations*. We take a closer look at each of these tools in this chapter.

## ADVERTISING

We define *advertising* as any paid form of nonpersonal presentation and promotion of ideas, goods or services through mass media such as newspapers, magazines, television or radio by an identified sponsor. Advertising is used by many organizations to communicate specific messages about themselves, their products and services or their modes of behaviour to a predefined target audience, in order to stimulate a response from the audience. The response may be perceptual in nature: for example, the consumer develops specific views or opinions about the product or brand or these feelings are altered by the ad. The response could be behavioural: for instance, the consumer buys the product or increases the amount he or she buys. Advertisers who sponsor advertisements include not only business firms, but also non-profit and social institutions such as charities, museums and religious organizations that promote causes to various target publics. It is a good way to inform and persuade, whether the purpose is to build brand preference for Colgate toothpaste worldwide or to motivate a developing nation's consumers to drink milk or practise birth control.

European Union countries spend around ecu 45.4 billion on advertising a year. As recession in Europe lifts, and national economies revive, advertising spend in most EU countries has been forecast to rise in the late 1990s. Advertisers will, however, remain cautious in terms of how best to use their advertising budget in order to achieve desired communication goals[2].

Different organizations handle advertising in different ways. In small and medium-sized companies, advertising might be handled by someone in the sales or marketing department. Large companies might set up advertising departments whose job it is to set the advertising budget, work with the ad agency and handle direct-mail advertising, dealer displays and other advertising not done by the agency. Most companies, small or large, tend to use outside advertising agencies because they offer several advantages:

- Agencies have specialists who can perform specialist functions (e.g. research, creative work) better than a company's own staff.
- Agencies bring an outside point of view to solving a company's problems, together with years of experience from working with different clients and situations.
- Agencies have more buying power in media than the firm. They are also paid partly from media discount, which would cost the firm less.
- The client can drop its agency at any time. One could argue, on the other hand, that an agency would work hard to do a good job in order to get repeat business.

There are disadvantages in relinquishing the advertising function to an outside agency: loss of total control of the advertising process, a reduction in flexibility, conflicts arising when the agency dictates working practices, and the client is unable to exercise more control or coordination. Despite the potential problems, most firms find that they benefit from employing the specialized expertise of agencies.

## IMPORTANT DECISIONS IN ADVERTISING

Marketing management must make five important decisions when developing an advertising programme (see Figure 19.1).

### Setting objectives

The first step in developing an advertising programme is to set *advertising objectives.* These objectives should be in line with decisions about the target market, and the brand's positioning and marketing mix. Together these define the job that the advertising campaign must achieve in the total marketing programme.

An **advertising objective** is a specific communication *task* to be accomplished with a specific *target* audience during a specific period of *time.*[3] Advertising objectives can be classified by purpose: that is, whether their aim is to *inform, persuade* or *remind.* Table 19.1 lists examples of each of these objectives.

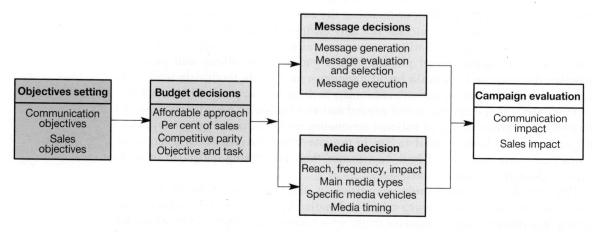

**Figure 19.1**   Main advertising decisions.

| **TABLE 19.1**  *Possible advertising objectives* | |
|---|---|

*To inform*

- Telling the market about a new product.
- Suggesting new uses for a product.
- Informing the market of a price change.
- Explaining how the product works.

- Describing available services.
- Correcting false impressions.
- Reducing buyers' fears.
- Building a company image.

*To persuade*

- Building brand preference.
- Encouraging switching to your brand.
- Changing buyer perceptions of product attributes.

- Persuading buyers to purchase now.
- Persuading buyers to receive a sales call.

*To remind*

- Reminding buyers that the product may be needed in the near future.
- Reminding buyers where to buy the product.

- Keeping the product in buyers' minds during off seasons.
- Maintaining top-of-mind product awareness.

**Informative advertising** is used heavily when introducing a new product category. In this case, the objective is to build primary demand. Thus producers of compact disc players first informed consumers of the sound and convenience benefits of CDs. **Persuasive advertising** becomes more important as competition increases. Here, the company's objective is to build selective demand. For example, when compact disc players became established and accepted, Sony began trying to persuade consumers that its brand offered the best quality for their money.

Some persuasive advertising has become **comparison advertising**, in which a company directly or indirectly compares its brand with one or more other brands:

Among the most frequent users of comparison advertising or *knocking copy* is the car industry. In the UK, Korean car maker, Hyundai, sought to raise awareness of its cars with a series of lighthearted efforts: 'Even a kettle has a longer guarantee than Rover'. Another example was the war of words between two yellow fat-manufacturers. Van den Berghs, part of Unilever, provoked a battle with a campaign for its low-fat spread, Delight, that made taste comparisons with St Ivel Gold, produced by Unigate, and parodied some of its ad lines. St Ivel retaliated with an ad for their Gold brand that targeted Flora, another Van Den Berghs product, and turned one of Flora's catchlines, 'For your blooming generation' into 'For your ballooning generation'. The argument was that Flora contained twice as much fat as Gold. This led to a telling-off from the UK's Advertising Standards Authority (ASA) on grounds that, as Flora was a different type of spread (a full-fat margarine), St Ivel was not comparing like with like. The ASA finally urged both advertisers to refrain from using the approach.[4]

There are potential dangers in using comparison advertising, especially when comparisons are unfair and escalate into denigration of a rival's brand. The approach is legal in both the United States and United Kingdom, but in some European countries it is banned. Belgium and Germany regard it as tantamount to unfair competition. Even the relatively innocuous Carlsberg commercial with the tagline, 'Probably the best lager in the world', could not be run in those countries. Similarly, the car-hire company Avis's 'We try harder' ad would not be allowed in Germany because, although nobody is named, Hertz, the number one, is presumed to be the only real competitor. Efforts to produce a European directive to harmonize rules on com-

Comparative advertising: this ad reflects the 'war of words' between St Ivel (Gold) and Van den Berghs (Flora).

parative advertising across the EU have been relatively unsuccessful to date. Until such a directive is issued, however, advertisers in the region must remain sensitive to individual nations' codes of practice and legislation. This style of communication will probably always exist in one form or another, as most advertising is essentially comparative – after all, the aim of the advertiser is to persuade the consumer to respond to one product offering rather than another.[5]

**Reminder advertising** is important for mature products as it keeps consumers thinking about the product. Expensive Coca-Cola ads on television are designed to remind people about Coca-Cola, not merely to inform or persuade them.

Advertisers might also seek to assure existing customers that they have made the right choice. For example, car firms might use reinforcement advertising that depicts satisfied owners enjoying some special feature of their new car.

The choice of advertising objective is based on a good understanding of the current marketing situation. If the product is new and the company is not the market leader, but the brand is superior to the leading brand, then the advertising objective is to inform and convince the market of the brand's superiority. On the other hand, if the market is mature and brand usage is declining, the advertising objective would probably be to stimulate sales by persuading customers to increase frequency of usage or by encouraging competitors' customers to switch.

## Setting the advertising budget

After determining its advertising objectives, the company next sets its *advertising budget* for each product. The role of advertising is to create demand for a product.

The company wants to spend the amount needed to achieve the sales goal. Four commonly used methods for setting the advertising budget were discussed in Chapter 18. Here we describe some specific factors which should be considered when setting that budget:

- *Stage in the product life cycle.* New products typically need large advertising budgets to build awareness and to gain consumer trial. Mature brands usually require lower budgets as a ratio to sales.
- *Market share.* High-market-share brands usually need more advertising spending as a percentage of sales than do low-share brands. Building the market or taking share from competitors requires larger advertising spending than does simply maintaining current share.
- *Competition and clutter.* In a market with many competitors and high advertising spending, a brand must advertise more heavily to be heard above the noise in the market.
- *Advertising frequency.* When many repetitions are needed to present the brand's message to consumers, the advertising budget must be larger.
- *Product differentiation.* A brand that closely resembles other brands in its product class (coffee powder, washing powder, chewing gum, beer, soft drinks) requires heavy advertising to set it apart. When the product differs greatly from competitors, advertising can be used to point out the differences to consumers.[6]

Setting the advertising budget is no easy task. How does a company know if it is spending the right amount? Some critics maintain that large consumer packaged-goods firms tend to overspend on advertising and industrial companies generally underspend on advertising. They claim also that the large consumer companies use image advertising extensively without really knowing its effects, overspending as a form of 'insurance' against not spending enough. Furthermore, what these companies decide to spend is based on traditional rules of thumb such as what can be afforded or normal industry advertising–sales ratios, which have little local validity.[7] On the other hand, industrial advertisers tend to rely too heavily on their salesforces to bring in orders, underestimating the power of the company and product image in preselling industrial customers. Thus they do not spend enough on advertising to build customer awareness and knowledge.

How much impact does advertising really have on consumer buying and brand loyalty? A research study analysing household purchases of frequently bought consumer products came up with the following surprising conclusion:

> Advertising appears effective in increasing the volume purchased by loyal buyers but less effective in winning new buyers. For loyal buyers, high levels of exposure per week may be unproductive because of a leveling off of ad effectiveness ... Advertising appears unlikely to have some cumulative effect that leads to loyalty ... Features, displays, and especially price have a stronger impact on response than does advertising.[8]

These findings did not sit well with the advertising community, and several people attacked the study's data and methodology. They claimed that the study measured mostly short-run sales effects. Thus it favoured pricing and sales-promotion activities, which tend to have more immediate impact. In contrast, most advertising takes many months, or even years, to build strong brand positions and consumer loyalty. These long-run effects are difficult to measure. However, recent research, which examined data over a ten-year period, found that advertising does produce long-term sales growth, even two years after a campaign ends.[9] This debate underscores the fact that measuring the results of advertising spending remains a poorly understood subject.

Companies can use advertising-expenditure models to help them decide how much to spend. An early model developed by Vidale and Wolfe called for a larger advertising budget – the higher the sales response rate, the higher the rate at which customers forget the advertising and brand, and the higher the untapped sales potential.[10] Such a model does not, however, consider competitors' advertising and whether or not the firm's ads are effective. An adaptive-control model has the firm experimenting with different rates of expenditure and measuring sales response to different levels of spending. Suppose the company has set an advertising expenditure rate based on its most recent information on sales response. It spends this rate in all of its markets except in a subset of $2n$ markets randomly chosen. In $n$ tests markets, the firm spends at a lower rate, and in the other $n$, a higher rate. This provides sales response to low, medium and high rates of advertising spend that is used to update the parameters of the sales-response function currently used. The updated sales-response function is used to determine the best advertising budget for the next period.[11]

## Creating the advertising message

A large advertising budget does not guarantee a successful advertising campaign. Two advertisers can spend the same amount on advertising, yet have very different results. Studies show that creative advertising messages can be more important to advertising success than the amount of money spent. No matter how big the budget, advertising can succeed only if commercials gain attention and communicate well. Therefore the budget must be invested in effective advertising messages.

Advertisers face an increasingly cluttered advertising environment. The average consumer has numerous television and radio stations to tune in to, and thousands of magazines to choose from. To these, add the countless catalogues, direct-mail ads and continuous barrage of other media. This clutter of media also causes big problems for advertisers – it is very costly. Advertisers could pay tens to hundreds of thousands of pounds for a 30-second slot on a prime-time TV programme. Also their ads are sandwiched in with a battery of other commercials and announcements in any viewing hour. With the growth in cable TV, video cassette recorders and remote-controlled technologies, today's audience can also tune out ads by either watching commercial-free channels or 'zapping' commercials by pushing the 'fast-forward' button during taped programmes. With remote-control, they can instantly turn off the sound during a commercial or 'zip' around channels to see what else is on. So, given the hundreds of other messages competing for attention and the brief attention scan a message is likely to receive, advertisers face a challenging task in designing messages that grab and hold viewers' attention as well as motivating them to respond, be it in a perceptual or behavioural manner. The advertising message must be better planned, more imaginative, more entertaining and more rewarding to consumers. The task requires imagination and innovation. Creative strategy, therefore, will play an increasingly important role in advertising success. Advertisers go through three steps to develop a creative strategy: message generation, message evaluation and selection, and message execution.

### Message generation

The message is the idea that underlies the communication. When deciding the advertising message, planners must have in mind the target audience (who the message must appeal to) and advertising objectives (the type of response that message would evoke in those that get the message). There are several creative message strategies that firms adopt:

- The message focuses on the brand's positioning (e.g. 'Stella Artois. Reassuringly expensive'; 'Simply years ahead', Philips; 'Have a break, have a Kit-Kat'; 'The world's most civilized spirit', Henessy cognac).
- The message taps one or other of the motivations that drive human consumption – for example, functional benefit ('Brain food – every Friday', *The Economist*), pleasure ('Never simply required reading – it is desired reading', *Wall Street Journal*, Europe), self-identity ('No *FT* Comment', *Financial Times*), image ('Many *Guardian* readers are just like their newspaper – eloquent, incisive and successful'), admiration ('Top people read *The Times*'), and altruism ('We don't cut down trees for our newsprint').[12]
- The idea could be spawned by addressing the ways in which product sales can be increased: current users must be encouraged to use more or new users are encouraged to start buying the product. For example, Reebok came up with a breakthrough idea of informing consumers that their running shoes are for everyday wear, thus creating a 'new use' for previously nonusers of the product category.
- The message homes in on the differences between the advertised product and competitors' offering: for example, Burger King's message to consumers is that their burger is 'Broiled, not fried'.
- The idea for the message could have developed from an in-depth knowledge of the consumer's own experience with the product, particularly the buying process, the process and effect of consumption, and the benefits sought. The advertiser must come very close to the consumer and follow his or her experience with the product, usually through lengthy, labour-intensive qualitative research, including point-of-purchase observations and analysis. Thus Contac 400 shows acute observation with its ad which assures cold sufferers that the drug 'dried up the symptoms of a cold'.

Creative ad people therefore have different ways of finding advertising-message ideas that will engage the attention of viewers. Many creative people start by talking to consumers, dealers, experts and competitors. Others try to imagine consumers using the product and then work out the benefits consumers seek when buying and using the product.

Generally advertisers create several possible messages. Logically, it makes sense to generate alternative themes, evaluate the appeal of each and select a preferred solution. We will address message evaluation next.

## Message evaluation and selection

How should we evaluate advertising messages? The appeals used in messages should have three characteristics:

1. They should be *meaningful*, pointing out benefits that make the product more desirable or interesting to target consumers.
2. They should be *distinctive* in terms of telling consumers how the product is better than the competing brands.
3. They should be *believable*. This last objective is difficult because many consumers doubt the truth of advertising in general. One study found that a full one-third of the public rates advertising messages as 'unbelievable.'[13]

Advertisers should therefore pre-test each ad to determine that it has the maximum impact, believability and appeal.

## Message execution

The impact of the message depends not only on *what* is said, but also on *how* it is said. This is the realm of message execution. Message execution is a difficult task for reasons mentioned earlier: the low level of attention consumers usually have in advertisements, media clutter, and saturation with competing messages. The advertiser has to present the message in a way that wins the target market's attention and interest – a message that 'grabs'.

The advertiser usually begins with a statement of the objective and approach of the desired ad:

> For example, in France, McClan's Whisky planned to use advertising to increase awareness and familiarity and to create an image as a real whisky with a distinct personality which was clearly within the values of the French whisky market. The target segment is regular whisky drinkers who are currently buying standard brands such as Johnny Walker and Ballantines, and who want good value but not the prestige of a premium or the money saving value of a cheap brand. The 'how' or advertising message proposed that McClan is the whisky that embodied the spirit of France today. It was the whisky for the 'new adventurers', who are dynamic and aspirational, but their ambition is directed to a full and varied experience of life, self-expression and appreciation of art and culture, not the desires for social standing or political power. The message was executed via an evocative visual campaign. It exploited the physical elements of the brand, which already evoke positive images among French whisky drinkers – the short, sharp, powerful name, the golden label, distinctive bottle shape and red typography. Since it is illegal to advertise spirits on French TV, luxury magazines which gave colour and a prestige environment were chosen.[14]

The creative people must find the best style, tone, words and format for executing the message. Any message can be presented in different *execution styles*, such as the following:

Message execution style: Singapore Airlines builds a mood around its services.

- *Slice of life.* This style shows one or more people using the product in a normal setting (the 'Oxo' gravy commercials which show the role of the mother who is tolerant of the domestic impositions of other members of her family).
- *Lifestyle.* This style shows how a product fits in with a particular lifestyle. For example, the 'After Eight' mints UK advertisement (elegant dinner party in a period house) appeals to aspirations more than anything else.
- *Fantasy.* This style creates a fantasy around the product or its use. For instance, 'Anything can happen after a Badedas bath' usually meant the arrival of a 'prince charming' with a romantic style of transport just after his mistress emerges from the bath.
- *Mood or image.* This style builds a mood or image around the product, such as beauty, love or serenity. No claim is made about the product except through suggestion. Timotei shampoo employs the mood for nature and simplicity, a strategy that has worked successfully in many countries across the globe.
- *Musical.* The ad is built around a song or some well-known music so that emotional responses to the music are associated with the product. Many soft-drink commercials (e.g. Coca-Cola, Pepsi-Cola) use this format.
- *Personality symbol.* This style creates a character that represents the product. The character might be *animated* (the Jolly Green Giant, Garfield the Cat) or *real* (Richard Branson and the American Express Card).
- *Technical expertise.* This style shows the company's expertise in making the product. Thus Maxwell House shows one of its buyers carefully selecting the coffee beans, and Audi cars implied superiority with 'Vorsprung durch Technik.'
- *Scientific evidence.* This style presents survey or scientific evidence that the brand is better or better liked than one or more other brands. For years, Crest toothpaste has used scientific evidence to convince buyers that Crest is better than other brands at fighting cavities. In Elida Gibbs' relaunch of the skin-care brand Pond's, the advertisement referred to the 'Pond's Institute' where women were

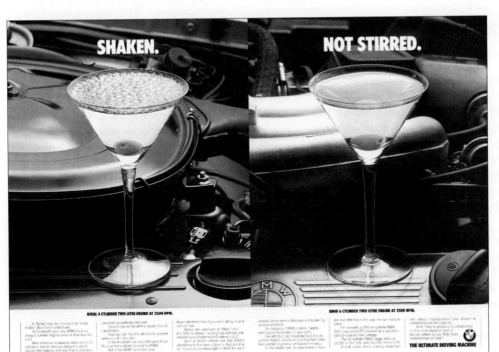

Here, BMW's highly acclaimed ad proudly presents BMWs as 'precise, cold, technical icons with jewel-like perfection.' The brand's functional excellence, consistently communicated by advertising over the last two decades, has helped to create and sustain the brand's superior value over time.

shown having their skin analysed, the ad emphasizing the brand's scientific problem-solving qualities.

- *Testimonial evidence.* This style features a highly believable or likable source endorsing the product. It could be a celebrity, like sports star Daley Thompson who was used to endorse SmithKline Beecham's energy drink Lucozade, which is targeted at young consumers, or ordinary people saying how much they like a given product.

The advertiser also must choose a *tone* for the ad. Positive appeals that evoke happiness, feelings of achievement, fun and so forth tend to be more effective than negative tones. Research has shown that negative appeals that evoke fear discourage viewers from looking at the advertisement, and so would be counterproductive (see Marketing Highlight 19.1).

The advertiser must also use memorable and attention-getting *words* in the ad. For example, the following themes on the left would have had much less impact without the *creative* phrasing on the right:

| *Theme* | *Creative copy* |
|---|---|
| Klm would like frequently flying business passengers to see it as the all-round, reliable specialist in air travel. | 'KLM – Royal Dutch Airlines – the Reliable Airline' |
| Nothing is too much trouble in the pursuit of creating the perfectly functioning mechanism. | 'Pure, Undiluted BMW' |

---

**MARKETING HIGHLIGHT 19.1**

### Hush little baby!

Here is an example of how 'tone' can break an ad.

Fisher-Price the international toy manufacturer, recently pre-tested a commercial called "Baby". The ad opens on an empty, sun-filled room with net curtains hanging from high windows and swaying above a polished wooden floor. A dramatic chord rings in the magical appearance of a perfect little boy on a white blanket. An enthusiastic, but gentle, voice-over suggests baby's thoughts: 'Where am I? How did I get here?'

Another chord and the baby is surrounded by Fisher-Price toys. Baby reveals his thoughts: 'What's the box? What if I push ... What if ... etc.' The ad closes with the thought: 'Fisher-Price, for the most enquiring minds in the world.'

The women in the focus group sessions related well to the ad. The agency were excited about it. They loved it. However, when the commercial was presented for the first time in general advertising, mothers admitted they were terrified by the opening sequence. The billowing curtains, the dramatic chord suggested Alfred Hitchcock, not creation. When the baby appeared, the mothers expected some harrowing warning (like ... 100 babies die each year through being left alone!), not plastic toys. The agency reviewed the mothers' reaction to the commercial. The ad was indeed impactful. It would, however, lead to a *negative* association for Fisher-Price toys.

The agency changed the beginning of the ad to remove the sinister overtones.

Source:   See Judith Corstjens, *Strategic Advertising* (Oxford: Heinemann, 1990), 145–6.

| | |
|---|---|
| Miele offers top-quality premium kitchen products that are miles ahead of the competition | 'Miele – there is no better one' (The German company's advertising for dishwashers and washing machines in Belgium, Holland, United States and Canada) |
| Philishave gives optimum shaving satisfaction due to its high quality and advanced technology, making it superior to competitors in every way. | 'For a better, closer shave – Philips' |
| 7-Up is not a cola. | 'The Uncola' |
| Stella Artois is a high-price high-quality beer. | 'Stella Artois – reassuringly expensive' |

Finally, *format* elements make a difference to an ad's impact as well as its cost. A small change in ad design can make a big difference on its effect. The *illustration* is the first thing the reader notices, so it must be strong enough to attract attention. Next, the *headline* must effectively entice the right people to read the copy. Finally, the *copy*, which is the main block of text in the ad, must be simple but strong and convincing. Moreover these three elements must effectively work *together*. Even then, less than 50 per cent of the exposed audience will notice even a truly outstanding ad: about 30 per cent will recall the main point of the headline; about 25 per cent will remember the advertiser's name; and less than 10 per cent will have read most of the copy. Less than outstanding ads, unfortunately, will not achieve even these results.

## Selecting advertising media

The advertiser must next decide upon the media to carry the message. The main steps in media selection are: (1) deciding on *reach*, *frequency*, and *impact*; (2) choosing among chief *media types*; (3) selecting specific *media vehicles*; and (4) deciding on *media timing*.

### Deciding on reach, frequency, and impact

To select media, the advertiser must decide what reach and frequency are needed to achieve advertising objectives. **Reach** is a measure of the *percentage* of people in the target market who are exposed to the ad campaign during a given period of time. For example, the advertiser might try to reach 70 per cent of the target market during the first three months of the campaign. **Frequency** is a measure of how many *times* the average person in the target market is exposed to the message. For example, the advertiser might want an average exposure frequency of three. The advertiser must also decide on the desired **media impact**, that is, the qualitative value of a message exposure through a given medium. For example, for products that need to be demonstrated, messages on television may have more impact than messages on radio because television uses sight and sound. The same message in a national newspaper may be more believable than in a local daily.

Suppose that the advertiser's product might appeal to a market of 1 million consumers. The goal is to reach 700,000 consumers (70 per cent of 1,000,000). Because the average consumer will receive three exposures, 2,100,000 exposures (700,000 × 3) must be bought. If the advertiser wants exposures of 1.5 impact (assuming 1.0 impact is the average), a rated number of exposures of 3,150,000 (2,100,000 × 1.5) must be bought. If a thousand exposures with this impact cost $10, the advertising　　1 ecu = US$1.26

budget will have to be $31,500,000 (3,150 × $10). In general, the more reach, frequency and impact the advertiser seeks, the higher the advertising budget will have to be.

### Choosing among chief media types

The media planner has to know the reach, frequency and impact of each of the major media types. Table 19.2 shows the available media in key western and Asian mar-

| TABLE 19.2 | Available media in major European, North American and Asian countries | | | | |
|---|---|---|---|---|---|
| | Daily newspapers, national/regional[1] | Executive media[1] | Consumer magazines, general interest[1] | Consumer magazines, special interest | Commercial TV stations[2] | TV households penetration (%)[2] |
| Austria | 20 | 20 | 29 | 55 | 2 | 97 |
| Belgium | 57 | 37 | 51 | 154 | 4 | 96 |
| Denmark | 47 | 12 | 19 | 84 | 4 | 95 |
| Finland | 55 | 12 | 20 | 44 | 6 | 98 |
| France | 86 | 26 | 68 | 153 | 5 | 94 |
| Germany | 232 | 33 | 99 | 327 | 5 | 96 |
| Greece | 110 | 16 | 54 | 30 | 30 | 93 |
| Ireland | 8 | 8 | 14 | 36 | 2 | 95 |
| Italy | 91 | 41 | 90 | 315 | 4 | 99 |
| Netherlands | 60 | 20 | 35 | 141 | 4 | 98 |
| Norway | 62 | 16 | 8 | 52 | 3 | 98 |
| Portugal | 18 | 6 | 17 | 33 | 2 | 95 |
| Spain | 106 | 22 | 58 | 147 | 13 | 99 |
| Sweden | 92 | 10 | 16 | 83 | 1 | 97 |
| Switzerland | 59 | 20 | 37 | 129 | 4 | 94 |
| Turkey | 47 | 10 | 10 | 16 | 7 | na |
| United Kingdom | 104 | 75 | 91 | 1,214[a] | 3 | 97 |
| Bulgaria | 14 | 2 | 5 | 11 | – | 95 |
| Czech Slov. Rep. | 27 | 8 | 25 | 44 | 2 | 96 |
| Hungary | 12 | 10 | 7 | 15 | 2 | 98 |
| Poland | 7 | 7 | 16 | 14 | na | 98 |
| Romania | 10 | 1 | 4 | 18 | na | 52 |
| United States | 1,159 | 85 | 112 | 561 | 1,426[†] | 97[†] |
| Canada | 97 | 43 | 41 | 160 | 132[†] | 69[†] |
| Australia | 47 | 19 | 44 | 217 | 52 | 99 |
| China | 27 | 9 | 9 | 51 | 292 | 57 |
| Hong Kong | 23 | 20 | 37 | 50 | 4 | 98 |
| India | 114 | 13 | 50 | 38 | na | 66 |
| Indonesia | 39 | 11 | 15 | 14 | 5 | 74 |
| Japan | 113 | 54 | 82 | 164 | 115 | 100 |
| Malaysia | 35 | 6 | 11 | 12 | 3 | 89 |
| New Zealand | 29 | 13 | 27 | 72 | 7 | 94 |
| Singapore | 9 | 11 | 20 | 40 | 5 | 100 |
| South Korea | 35 | 5 | 7 | 6 | 4 | 99 |
| Taiwan | 25 | 8 | 9 | 5 | 3 | 99 |

Notes:   Cable penetration * less than 0.5 per cent; DTH penetration: * less than 0.05 per cent; na – not available.
[a] *Benn's Media Directory* is a UK publication which gives information on the UK in far more detail than on other countries: this may explain the large number; [b] Jakarta only; [c] Tokyo & Osaka only; [†] *Euromonitor* 1992; [**] OAAA.
Sources:   [1] *Benn's Media Directory*, 1992; [2] *Zenith's Europe Market Media Facts*, 1992; [3] *BIB World Guide*, 1993.

kets. Table 19.3 displays the distribution of advertising spend by type of mass medium in these countries. The leading media have advantages and limitations, as shown in Table 19.4.

How do advertisers select appropriate media from the range of media available? Media planners consider many factors when making their media choices. The *media habits of target consumers* will affect media choice: for example, radio and television are the best media for reaching teenagers. So will the *nature of the product*: fashions,

| Cable penetration[3] (%) | DTH satellite penetration[3] (%) | VCR penetration (%)[3] | Commercial radio station[2] | Cinema screens number[2] | Outdoor poster panels[2] (000) |
|---|---|---|---|---|---|
| 23.0 | 3.4 | 42 | 2 | 395 | 106 |
| 87.0 | 0.3 | 39 | 610 | 393 | 100 |
| 47.0 | 3.0 | 53 | 80 | 276 | 18 |
| 37.0 | 0.7 | 55 | 52 | 340 | 100 |
| 4.0 | 0.2 | 41 | 1,397 | 3,058 | 575 |
| 33.0 | 7.6 | 26 | 157 | 3,170 | 358 |
| – | 0.2 | 46 | 245 | 323 | 13 |
| 38.0 | 2.4 | 44 | 22 | 183 | 7 |
| – | – | 40 | 4,000 | 3,000 | 100 |
| 86.0 | 3.6 | 55 | 200 | 422 | 75 |
| 44.0 | 5.4 | 60 | 404 | 292 | 13 |
| – | 0.7 | 36 | 294 | 400 | 16 |
| 5.0 | 1.5 | 45 | 840 | 2,160 | 45 |
| 46.0 | 4.5 | 61 | – | 550 | 11 |
| 77.0 | 1.1 | 63 | 35 | 330 | 150 |
| 1.0 | 0.8 | 40 | na | 355 | 3 |
| 1.0 | 11.0 | 64 | 109 | 1,791 | 101 |
| * | – | 7 | na | 558 | na |
| 2.0 | 2.0 | 16 | na | 2,778 | na |
| 27.0 | 1.7 | 28 | 6 | 1,603 | 7 |
| 2.0 | 1.7 | 20 | na | 1,600 | na |
| na | * | 12 | na | 630 | na |
| 60.0 | na | 72 | na | 23,132[†] | 399[**] |
| 74.0 | na | 68 | na | 790[†] | na |
| na | na | 73 | 151 | 744 | 53 |
| na | na | 3 | 568 | 8,090 | na |
| na | 7.5 | 70 | 3 | 154 | 7 |
| 7.7 | 5.0 | 17 | 85 | 10,000 | 6 |
| na | 1.0 | 13 | 694 | 1,654 | 32[b] |
| 16.5 | 8.2 | 67 | 88 | 1,600 | 72[c] |
| na | na | 33 | 1 | 237 | 2 |
| na | na | 69 | 66 | 87 | 2 |
| na | na | 78 | 11 | 71 | 15 |
| 1.0 | 1.0 | 44 | 7 | 671 | 3 |
| na | 10.0 | 62 | 33 | 600 | na |

**TABLE 19.3**    *Distribution of advertising expenditure by medium in major European, North American and Asian countries*

| | Total mass media (US$ m.) | Print (%) | TV (%) | Radio (%) | Cinema (% | Outdoor/ transit (%) |
|---|---|---|---|---|---|---|
| Austria | 1,012 | 56 | 26 | 12 | na | 6 |
| Belgium | 1,018 | 52 | 32 | 2 | 1 | 13 |
| Denmark | 1,081 | 83 | 12 | 2 | 1 | 2 |
| Finland | 7,993 | 45 | 32 | 8 | 1 | 14 |
| France | 1,482 | 79 | 14 | 4 | * | 3 |
| Germany (W) | 11,246 | 75 | 15 | 5 | 1 | 4 |
| Greece | 526 | 44 | 42 | 7 | * | 7 |
| Ireland | 311 | 55 | 27 | 11 | na | 7 |
| Italy | 5,710 | 43 | 51 | 2 | na | 4 |
| Netherlands | 2,712 | 83 | 12 | 2 | * | 3 |
| Norway | 786 | 93 | 3 | 1 | 1 | 2 |
| Portugal | 415 | 37 | 44 | 8 | na | 11 |
| Spain | 7,652 | 53 | 31 | 10 | 1 | 5 |
| Sweden | 1,837 | 93 | 2 | na | 1 | 4 |
| Switzerland | 2,421 | 78 | 7 | 2 | 1 | 12 |
| United Kingdom | 14,069 | 65 | 29 | 2 | * | 4 |
| United States | 80,389 | 53 | 35 | 11 | na | 1 |
| Canada (1988) | 4,781 | 54 | 22 | 12 | na | 12 |
| Australia | 3,848 | 48 | 35 | 9 | 2 | 6 |
| China | 297 | 54 | 40 | 6 | * | na |
| Hong Kong | 861 | 42 | 50 | 4 | 1 | 3 |
| India | 896 | 67 | 20 | 3 | * | 10 |
| Indonesia | 287 | 60 | 9 | 19 | 1 | 11 |
| Japan | 34,747 | 35 | 32 | 5 | na | 13 |
| Malaysia | 317 | 49 | 41 | 2 | * | 8 |
| New Zealand | 575 | 49 | 36 | 15 | na | na |
| Singapore | 313 | 65 | 30 | 2 | * | 3 |
| South Korea | 2,826 | 48 | 30 | 5 | na | 17 |
| Taiwan | 1,294 | 55 | 35 | 7 | * | 3 |

Notes:    * less than 0.5 per cent; na not available.

Source:    *World Advertising Expenditures*, 25th edn (New York: Starch Inra Hooper, Inc., in cooperation with the International Advertising Association, 1993).

for example, are best advertised in colour magazines and Nikon cameras are best demonstrated on television. Different *types of messages* may require different media: for instance, a message announcing a big sale tomorrow will require radio or newspapers; a message with a lot of technical data might require magazines or direct mailings. *Cost* is also an important consideration in media choice: thus whereas television is very expensive, newspaper advertising costs much less. The media planner looks at both the total cost of using a medium and at the cost per thousand exposures – that is, the cost of reaching 1,000 people using the medium.

Media impact and cost must be re-examined regularly. For a long time, television and magazines dominated in the media mixes of national advertisers, with other media often neglected. Recently, however, the costs and clutter of these media have

| TABLE 19.4 | *Advantages and limitations of media forms* | |
| --- | --- | --- |
| Medium | Advantages | Limitations |
| Newspapers | Flexibility; timeliness; local market coverage; broad acceptance; high believability. | Short life; poor reproduction quality; small pass-along audience. |
| Television | Combines sight, sound and motion; appealing to the senses; high attention; high reach. | High absolute cost; high clutter; fleeting exposure; less audience selectivity. |
| Radio | Mass use; high geographic and demographic slectivity; low cost. | Audio presentation only; lower attention than TV; fleeting exposure. |
| Magazines | High geographic and demographic selectivity; credibility and prestige; high-quality reproduction; long life; good pass-along readership. | Long ad purchase lead time; some waste circulation; no guarantee of position. |
| Outdoor | Flexibility; high repeat exposure; low cost; low competition. | No audience selectivity; creative limitations. |

gone up, audiences have dropped and marketers are adopting strategies aimed at narrower segments.[15] Advertisers are also turning increasingly to alternative media, ranging from cable TV and outdoor advertising to parking meters, taxis and even shopping trolleys.

Given these and other media characteristics, the media planner must decide how much of each media type to buy. For example, in launching a new health snack food, the company might decide to spend £1.75 million advertising in national television, £0.5 million in women's magazines and £0.2 million in radio advertising.

### Selecting specific media vehicles

The media planner now must choose the best **media vehicles**, that is, specific media within each general media type. In most cases, there is an incredible number of choices. For radio and television, and in any one country, there are numerous stations and channels to choose from, together with hundreds, even thousands, of programme vehicles – the particular programmes or shows where the commercial should be broadcast. Prime-time programmes are the favourites; the costs, however, tend to escalate with the popularity of the programme.

In the case of magazines, the media planner must look up circulation figures and the costs of different ad sizes, colour options, ad positions and frequencies for specific magazines. Each country has its own high- or general-circulation magazines (for example, TV guides) which reach general audience groups. There is also an array of special interest publications that enable advertisers to reach special groups of audience (for instance, business magazines to reach business executives). The planner selects the media that will do the best job in terms of reaching the target customer group – that is, their selectivity towards the target. Then he or she must evaluate each magazine on factors such as credibility, status, reproduction quality, editorial focus and advertising submission deadlines. The media planner ultimately decides which vehicles give the best reach, frequency and impact for the money. The selection of specific vehicles in other print media, such as newspapers, also follows the same logic.

Media planners have to compute the cost per thousand persons reached by a vehicle. For example, if a full-page, four-colour advertisement in *The Economist* costs £30,000 and its readership is 3 million people, the cost of reaching each group of 1,000 persons is about £10. The same advertisement in *Business Week* may cost only £20,000 but reach only 1 million persons, giving a cost per thousand of about £20. The media planner would rank each magazine by cost per thousand and favour those magazines with the lower cost per thousand for reaching target consumers.

Additionally, the media planner considers the cost of producing ads for different media. Whereas newspaper ads may costs very little to produce, flashy television ads may cost millions. Media costs vary across different countries, so care must be taken not to generalize the figures.

Thus the media planner must balance media cost measures against several media impact factors. First, the planner should balance costs against the media vehicle's *audience quality*. Second, the media planner should consider *audience attention*. Readers of *Vogue*, for example, typically pay more attention to ads than do *Business Week* readers. Third, the planner should assess the vehicle's *editorial quality*. For example, the *Financial Times* and *Wall Street Journal Europe* are more credible and prestigious than *News of the World*.

### Deciding on media timing

Another decision that must be made concerns timing: how to schedule the advertising over the course of a year. Suppose sales of a product peak in December and drop in March. The firm can vary its advertising to follow the seasonal pattern, to oppose the seasonal pattern, or to be the same all year. Most firms do some seasonal advertising. Some do *only* seasonal advertising: for example, many department stores advertise – usually their seasonal sales – in specific periods in the year, such as Christmas, Easter, summer. Finally, the advertiser has to choose the pattern of the ads. **Continuity** means scheduling ads evenly within a given period. **Pulsing** means scheduling ads unevenly over a given time period. Thus fifty-two ads could either be scheduled at one per week during the year or pulsed in several bursts. The idea is to advertise heavily for a short period to build awareness that carries over to the next advertising period. Those who favour pulsing feel that it can be used to achieve the same impact as a steady schedule, but at a much lower cost. However, some media planners believe that although pulsing achieves minimal awareness, it sacrifices depth of advertising communications.

## Advertising evaluation

The advertising programme should evaluate both the communication effects and the sales effects of advertising regularly.

### Measuring the communication and sales effects

Measuring the communication effect of an ad or **copy testing** tells whether the ad is communicating well. Copy testing can be done before or after an ad is printed or broadcast. There are three principal methods of *pretesting* in advertising. The first is through *direct rating*, where the advertiser exposes a consumer panel to alternative ads and asks them to rate the ads. These direct ratings indicate how well the ads gain attention and how they affect consumers. Although this is an imperfect measure of an ad's actual impact, a high rating indicates a potentially more effective ad. In *portfolio tests*, consumers view or listen to a portfolio of advertisements, taking as much time as they need. They are then asked to recall all the ads and their content, aided or unaided by the interviewer. Their recall level indicates the ability of an ad to stand out and for its message to be understood and remembered. *Laboratory tests* use equipment to measure consumers' physiological reactions to an ad, such as their heartbeat, blood pressure, pupil dilation and perspiration. These tests measure an ad's attention-getting power, but reveal very little about the overall impact on brand awareness, attitudes and brand preference of a completed advertising campaign.

There are two popular methods of *post-testing* ads. Using *recall tests*, the advertiser asks people who have been exposed to magazines or television programmes to recall everything they can about the advertisers and products they saw. Recall scores indicate the ad's power to be noticed and retained. In *recognition tests*, the researcher asks readers of a given issue of, say, a magazine to point out what they recognize as having seen before. Recognition scores can be used to assess the ad's impact in different market segments and to compare the company's ads with competitors' ads.

To identify the extent to which the campaign increased brand awareness, or affected brand comprehension, brand beliefs and preference or intentions to buy, the advertiser must, in the first instance, measure these levels before a campaign. It then draws a random sample of consumers after the campaign to assess the communication effects. If a company intended to increase brand awareness from 20 to 50 per cent, but only succeeded in increasing it to 30 per cent, then something is wrong: it is not spending enough, its ads are poor, its message is ill-targeted, or some other factor is missing.

Figure 19.2 shows the levels of communication effect which advertisers are likely to monitor and measure with respect to a campaign:

■ The change in brand awareness is determined by the number of customers who were previously *unaware* of the brand and the number who *notice* the advertisement and are now *aware* of the brand, or by the difference in the number of customers who are aware that the brand exists before and after the campaign. If there has been little increase or even a decline in brand awareness, the advertiser has to determine whether the reasons are due to the poor impact achieved by the communications campaign or if customers *forget* because of poor recall or inadequate advertising investment.

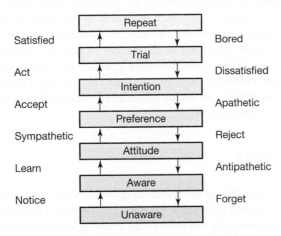

**Figure 19.2** Advertising: measuring communications and sales effectiveness.

- The nature of consumers' attitudes toward a brand can be ascertained before and after a campaign. An informative ad allows consumers to *learn* more about product/brand benefits. If the message is poorly targeted, conveys an undesirable or unbelievable message, consumers are *antipathetic* towards the brand. They do not develop any liking for the product. Advertisers may have to redesign the copy to generate greater interest among customers or improve message content in order to enhance the level of comprehension of brand benefits among target customers.

- Consumers who are *sympathetic* towards advertised brand benefits would manifest their favourable response in the form of stated brand performance. Similarly, before-and-after (the campaign) studies would enable changes in consumer brand preference to be determined. Reasons for brand *rejection* should be identified so that communication weaknesses can be redressed.

- An advertising campaign may be used to turn preference among customers into more definite *intention* to buy. Again, this response can be measured and changes in the level of buying intent may be determined.

- It is usually difficult to measure the sales effect of a campaign. Questions such as, 'What sales are caused by an ad that increases brand awareness by 20 per cent and brand preference by 10 per cent?', are not easy to answer. Sales or *trial* are affected by many factors besides advertising, such as product features, price and availability. One way to measure the sales effect of advertising is to compare past sales with past advertising expenditures. Another way is through experiments. For example, Du Pont, the world's largest chemical giant, was one of the first companies to use advertising experiments.[16] Du Pont's paint department divided fifty-six sales territories into high-, average- and low-market-share territories. In one-third of the group, Du Pont spent the normal amount for advertising; in another third, the company spent two-and-a-half times the normal amount; and in the remaining third, it allotted four times the normal amount. At the end of the experiment, Du Pont estimated how many extra sales resulted from higher levels of advertising expenditure. It found that higher advertising spending increased sales at a diminishing rate and that the sales increase was weaker in its high-market-share territories.

- If the customer is *satisfied* with the brand he or she has bought, this would lead to *repeat* purchase on another buying occasion. The extent to which advertising or a specific 'reminder' campaign affects repeat purchase is difficult to measure because of the difficulty of separating out the immediate and long-term effects of advertising. 'Before-and-after' type studies and controlled experiments can be used, nonetheless, to detect changes in purchase and usage frequency. Again, advertisers should obtain consumer feedback to increase their understanding of the impact of communications on repeat purchase. Advertising may not be blamed for nonrepeat sales due to the nature of product consumption: for example, consumers get *bored* with the same product and want variety. In this case, advertising is not powerful enough to arrest that desire. Few of us would relish the thought of surviving on an uninterrupted diet of Heinz beans, Heinz soup, Heinz sausages all year round!

### Advertising worldwide

We have discussed advertising decisions in general. Next we consider the key issues in planning the advertising effort that supports the firm's brand(s) in overseas markets. Although advertising remains the vehicle for creating brand awareness and maintaining brand value, the problems of international or worldwide advertising are more complex than those encountered by domestic advertisers. We define international or worldwide advertising as: *advertising that promotes a cause, or an organization and the sale of its goods or services in more than one country and in different parts of the world.*[17]

When developing advertising for international markets, two basic issues must be considered.

## Standardization or differentiation

The first issue concerns the degree to which advertising should be adapted to the unique characteristics of various country markets. Some large advertisers have attempted to support their global brands with highly standardized worldwide advertising. The chances of success for standardized advertising depend on how culture-bound a product or service is, the buying behaviour of consumers, the competition, and national laws and regulations. All these factors dictate how well the advertising concepts cross borders. Standardization produces many benefits, such as lower advertising costs, greater coordination of global advertising efforts and a more consistent worldwide company or product image. However, standardization also has drawbacks. Most importantly, it ignores the fact that country markets – not just across the continents, but also within the European Union – differ greatly in their cultures, demographics and economic conditions. Pan-European advertising, for example, is complicated because of the EU's cultural diversity as reflected in the differences in circumstances, language, traditions, music, beliefs, values and lifestyle amongst member nations. Ironically, the English have more in common with the Australians, who live on the opposite side of the globe, than they have with the Germans or the French, their closer neighbours. Although, like products, services and brands, advertising messages can be standardized, their executions cannot as culture invariably dominates communications.[18] Indeed, a recent survey in Europe among 210 pan-European brand managers showed that a majority (57 per cent) believe it is difficult to standardize advertising execution.[19] Most international advertisers must therefore think globally but act locally. They develop global advertising *strategies* that bring efficiency and consistency to their worldwide advertising efforts. Then they adapt their advertising *programmes* to make them more responsive to consumer needs and expectations within local markets. In many cases, even when a standard message is used, execution styles are adapted to reflect local moods and consumer expectations.

Companies also vary in the degree to which they adapt their advertising to local markets. For example, Kellogg's Frosted Flakes commercials are almost identical worldwide, with only minor adjustments for local cultural differences.[20] The advertising uses a tennis theme that has worldwide appeal and features teenage actors with generic good looks – neither too Northern European nor too Latin American. Of course, Kellogg translates the commercials into different languages. In the English version, for example, Tony growls 'They're Gr-r-reat!' whereas in the German version it's 'Gr-r-rossartig!' Other adaptations are more subtle. In the American ad, after winning the match, Tony leaps over the net in celebration. In other versions, he simply 'high fives' his young partner. The reason: Europeans do not jump over the net after winning at tennis.

In contrast, Parker Pen Company changes its advertising substantially from country to country:

> Print ads in Germany simply show the Parker Pen held in a hand that is writing a headline – 'This is how you write with precision.' In the UK, where it is the brand leader, [ads emphasize] the exotic processes used to make pens, such as gently polishing the gold nibs with walnut chips. ... In America, the ad campaign's theme is status and image. The head-

lines are ... 'Here's how you tell who's boss', and 'There are times when it has to be Parker.' The company considers the different themes necessary because of different product images and ... customer motives in each market.[21]

Successful standardized advertising is most likely to work for capital goods or business-to-business marketing, where targets are more homogeneous in their needs and buy the product for the same reasons. For example, whether it be a European, Asian or American construction company, the purchase of bulldozers is governed by similar economic rationality (for example, productivity, lifetime cost of running the equipment, parts delivery). Consumer goods advertising is less amenable to cross-cultural standardization, although considerable similarities are found in groups, such as the world's rich to whom brands like Cartier, Montblanc, Mercedes and Hugo Boss appeal.

Several basic conditions favour a standardized approach:

- Product or brand values offered to consumers and as conveyed by the advertisement are similar in every target country.
- Target customers in each country have similar expectations regarding the product and they do not differ in the way they evaluate the product. For example, business airline passengers' expectations of airline services are virtually the same in all countries.
- The target groups in each country are homogenous, so that similar media can be used to reach them.
- The advertised product is in the same stage of its life cycle in every country market. Different messages and executions are needed for the product that is newly launched into one market and one that is already in its growth stage in another.
- The brand is a true 'mega-brand' with a strong position in each market as well as the advertising budget necessary to support it in each market.
- The advertising idea must be transportable (universal, functional appeals, fantasies and symbols, fashions, movies/television, international celebrities and current events travel better than cultural values such as idiosyncratic lifestyles, habits and sports and leisure activities, local accents and language, and endorsements by local celebrities).
- The different countries can support the same advertising style of execution, or the company's preferred style can be accommodated in each country. Many European countries find the display of emotions in American ads ludicrous, and while lifestyle and glamour works well in the United States, innovative, modern and attention-getting styles are better received in France; humour, subtlety, understatement and irony are favoured in the United Kingdom; while in Germany, rational, descriptive and informative executions won't go wrong.
- If countries can be clustered on the basis of showing similar economic, cultural, legal and media characteristics, standardized advertising becomes more feasible.[22]

There is no simple solution for companies as to whether a standardized or differentiated approach would work best for their brand. They must therefore identify both the differences and similarities among target audiences in different national or regional markets, and determine opportunities for standardization or differentiation, as appropriate. It is unrealistic to expect that cultural differences will diminish in Europe because of the European Union. Cultural differences will also remain in Asian markets (the Japanese and Singaporean consumers are as alike as the Germans and Italians!). Where similarities in buying rationale occur, the astute advertiser should take the opportunity to design overlapping messages while taking into consideration the implications of cultural dissimilarities on delivery and execution.

## Centralization or decentralization

The second basic issue facing international advertisers is whether advertising decision making and implementation should be centralized or decentralized. This decision is directly linked to the decision about whether to follow a standardized or differentiated advertising approach, which, in turn, is affected by the similarities and differences in the marketing situations in different countries. Five key factors influence the choice between centralization and decentralization of the responsibility for international advertising decisions and implementation:

1. *Corporate and marketing objectives.* A company whose global marketing objectives dominate over domestic objectives is likely to centralize advertising and communications decisions. Where it emphasizes short-term profit and local objectives, decentralized decision making is favoured.
2. *Product uniformity.* The more similar the product or service marketed across different countries, the greater the feasibility of a uniform approach, which allows for centralized management of advertising.
3. *Product appeal.* Underpinning the product's appeal are the reasons why customers use the product. The reasons for consumption may differ amongst different cultures, whatever the demographic or psychographic characteristics of consumers. French women drink mineral water to stay slim, German women drink it to keep healthy. Golf club membership is a status purchase in Singapore, in Britain it is a moderate leisure activity, without the same label of exclusivity attached. Where underlying appeals vary significantly, decentralized decision making makes better sense.
4. *Cultural sensitivities.* Where a product's usage and appeal are culture-bound in terms of the local attitudes towards consumption, habits and preferences, as in the case of drinks and food products, more decentralization is necessary.
5. *Legal constraints.* Individual country rules and regulations affect advertising decisions and their implementation. Decentralization of responsibility, with the aim of tapping local wisdom and knowledge, is necessary where strict country regulations apply. In the European Union, until real 'harmonization' exists, cross-border advertisers must remain alert to subtle differences in nations' rules and codes of practice in order to avoid costly mistakes.

There has been a tendency for international organizations, especially in Europe, to centralize their marketing activities, resulting in more attempts to centralize the advertising function. Across many product categories, including cars, durable goods, electronics products, cosmetics and alcoholic beverages, European multinationals have adopted single-agency networks across Europe. Retailers, media companies and food and drinks manufacturers, however, remain less positive about centralization as they have to respond to cultural differences and legislation.[23]

The modes used by firms vary. Some organizations exert tight control from the centre and executional changes for local culture and conditions are closely monitored, as in the case of Unilever's Lever Europe. Some Corporations, like Nestlé, grant local management some degree of freedom to develop advertising within broad strategic guidelines, but with central directives on agencies and media buying groups. Yet others, such as Heinz, have tended to give local management total autonomy in both strategy determination and local implementation of product and advertising strategies.

*Worldwide advertising media*

The international media comprises an extensive mix:

- *Newspapers.* Faster and more efficient circulation is possible with new technologies, such as satellite printing, which allows advertising copy to be sent by satellite to the printers. Many international newspapers (e.g. *International Herald Tribune, Financial Times, Asahi Shimbun, Wall Street/Asian Wall Street Journal*) are printed simultaneously in more than one country. In general there have been enormous developments in local and global press and more newspapers have gone global to reach specific audiences.
- *Magazines.* There are some national and international journals which carry ads that target regional, international or global customers (e.g. *Newsweek, Time, The Economist*). Women's magazines, such as *Cosmopolitan, Elle, Vogue* and *Harper's Bazaar*, are printed in different editions for readers in different target countries/regions. And there are other international magazines such as *Reader's Digest* and men's magazines like *Playboy* and *Penthouse*.
- *Professional and technical magazines.* In Europe alone, there are more than 15,000 titles, and the number is rising yearly.
- *Cinema.* This is a relatively popular medium for reaching younger viewers, such as teenagers. In developing and less developed nations, cinema remains important.
- *Television.* There are few country markets where television is not available or where advertising is not carried via that medium. Satellite and cable opportunities have expanded enormously and accelerated the use of TV for international advertising.
- *Outdoor advertising and transport advertising.* This medium is used throughout the world. In the Western developed markets, advertisers are expanding their repertoire of outside media (e.g. park benches, trucks, taxis, bus stop shelters and so forth). This medium is used as an alternative in cases where the product category cannot be advertised on TV, as in the case of tobacco and alcoholic products. In some countries, like India and the People's Republic of China, outdoor advertising has become more important.
- *Interactive communication.* Interactive systems, such as videotext and pay-TV, are gaining importance as cable TV continues to develop. France's Minitel, for example, offers over 3,000 different services to subscribers.
- *Radio.* As a medium for international advertising, radio is constrained by availability in the sense that most commercial radio is regional. Radio Luxembourg, the international European station, transmits ads in several languages and reaches the whole of Europe.
- *Place-based media.* This is a worldwide development and advertisers are increasingly deploying the medium to reach audiences wherever they happen to be – at work, the fitness centre, the supermarket, airports and in the aeroplane. The programming and advertising can be produced internationally.
- *Trade fairs and exhibitions.* These can be costly, but are useful media for international communications.
- *Sponsorship.* Sponsorship of sports or art events, like the Olympic Games and the World Cup soccer match, offers vast audience reach. However, such global audiences are rare and the effectiveness of the initiatives is not easy to measure.
- *Other media.* Point-of-sale materials are not easy to reproduce internationally. Invariably, they have to be adapted to local conditions, specifically the language, regulations and distribution outlets. Direct mail is used in many countries, but it is primarily a local technique. As postal services vary from country to country, including within the EU, the medium has yet to be applied internationally. Nonetheless, credit card companies, that have an international customer database, can exploit this medium for worldwide communications.

There have been important trends in media development worldwide. Most notable are developments in TV and telecommunications. A second force is deregulation, which results in the proliferation of commercial TV and satellite broadcasting. In deregulated central Europe and in Asia, as state control over media relaxes, opportunities open for advertising. Another development in the 1990s is the emergence of megabrands as a result of merger activities. Such megabrands can concentrate media buying, which in turn influences media development. Furthermore, as more companies seek a pan-European or global approach to media buying, only large media groups with a broad European or international base, owning a network of media companies worldwide – such as Berlusconi, Bertelsmann, Time-Warner and Murdoch – are in a position to negotiate at this level and have their own grip on media developments.[24]

### Media buying and costs

International media planning is more complicated than local media planning as the media situation is not the same in all countries, due to cultural differences, history and economic development. In some countries, there is inadequate media research, or research techniques vary greatly across countries, making cross-country comparisons of media research data almost impossible. Research into international media is in its infancy and still relatively expensive. Unless reliable intercountry comparisons can be made, international advertisers will find it difficult to evaluate the effectiveness of different media.

Also, as noted earlier, media availability differs considerably from country to country. Some countries have too few media to handle all of the advertising offered to them. Other countries are peppered with so many media that an advertiser cannot gain national coverage at a reasonable cost.

International media buying is changing rapidly. Global advertisers have concentrated advertising budgets. They have the power of scale because of the revenues they generate for the media. They are in a position to require their agencies to negotiate the best prices for them. On the other hand, there are the few – large and powerful – international media barons who are in a position to influence prices and the outcome of negotiations given their cross-ownership across different media and countries. These media empires can offer multimedia advertising, one-stop media shopping, and even multimedia discount opportunities. So, for international advertising, prices must be negotiated. Prices may vary greatly per country. For example, one source shows that, for television, the cost per thousand to reach housewives in sixteen European countries ranged from ecu 8.37 in Ireland to ecu 35.5 in Sweden.[25] Nevertheless, firms that advertise their products in different country markets must decide on what media to use based on a consideration of their target groups, the budget available, and an understanding of the media scene and relative media costs efficiencies in these countries.

Countries also differ in the extent to which they regulate advertising practices. Many countries have extensive systems of laws restricting how much a company can spend on advertising, the media used, the nature of advertising claims, and other aspects of the advertising programme. Such restrictions often require that advertisers adapt their campaigns from country to country. Consider the following examples:

When 'G. I. Joe' war toys and soldiers were launched in Europe, two television commercials were developed – a general version for most European countries and another for countries that bar advertisements for products with military or violent themes. As a result, in the version running in Germany, Holland and Belgium, jeeps replaced the toy tanks and guns were removed from the hands of toy soldiers.[26]

A 30-second Kellogg cereal commercial produced for British TV would have to have [several] alterations to be acceptable [elsewhere] in Europe: Reference to iron and vitamins would have to be deleted in the Netherlands. A child wearing a Kellogg's T-shirt would be edited out in France where children are forbidden from endorsing products on TV. In Germany, the line 'Kellogg makes cornflakes the best they've ever been' would be cut because of rules against making competitive claims. After alterations, the 30-second commercial would be [only] about five seconds long.[27]

Thus although advertisers may develop global strategies to guide their overall advertising efforts, specific advertising programmes must usually be adapted to meet local cultures and customs, media characteristics and advertising regulations.

## SALES PROMOTION

An increasingly important communication tool is **sales promotion**. In Europe, this promotional vehicle has traditionally been labelled the 'poor relation' of advertising. Advertising assumed significance because there was greater scope for advertising agencies to differentiate brands through creative campaigns, which also helped to enhance their organization's profile. A number of pressures, which will be enumerated in this section, have fuelled the recent growth in emphasis on sales promotions. Sales promotion consists of short-term incentives, in addition to the basic benefits offered by the product or service, to encourage purchase or sales of that product or service. Whereas advertising offers reasons to buy a product or service, sales promotion offers reasons that would achieve immediate sales. It seeks to motivate the customer to buy *now*.

Sales promotion includes a wide variety of promotion tools designed to stimulate earlier or stronger market response. It can be targeted at three levels within the distribution chain – the consumer, the trade or retailer and the company's salesforce. **Consumer promotions** include prices-off, coupons, premiums, contests and others. **Trade promotions** range from special discounts, free goods and loyalty bonuses to training. **Salesforce promotions** include bonuses, commissions, free gifts and competitions. Table 19.5 lists the array of sales promotion vehicles that apply to each type of sales promotion target.

### Reasons for growth of sales promotion

There are several reasons for the recent rapid growth of sales promotion, especially in consumer markets:

- First, inside the company, promotion is now more readily accepted by top management as an effective sales tool, and more product managers are qualified to use sales promotion tools. There is increasing acceptance of the idea of creative sales promotions supporting the brand. Furthermore product managers face greater pressures to increase their current sales. In mature markets manufacturers are striving to maintain market share through a balance between longer-term 'share-of-voice' gained from advertising, and shorter-term incentives for the consumer.
- Second, externally, the company faces more competition, and competing brands are less differentiated. Competitors are using more and more promotions, and consumers have become more deal-prone.
- Third, advertising efficiency has declined because of rising costs, media clutter and legal restraints. Also, the minimum threshold cost for a national TV campaign

| TABLE 19.5 | *Sales promotion tools* | | |
|---|---|---|---|
| Targets | Vehicles | | |
| Salesforce | ■ Coupons <br> ■ Vouchers <br> ■ Commissions | ■ Competitions <br> ■ Free samples/gifts <br> ■ Bonus Scheme | ■ Points system with gift catalogue <br> ■ Club for high achievers |
| Consumer | ■ Demonstrations <br> ■ Competitions <br> ■ Sweepstake <br> ■ Premiums: <br>     Free with pack <br>     Free on-pack <br>     Free mail-in <br> ■ Self-liquidating | ■ Events <br> ■ Club for repeat buyers <br> ■ Money-back guarantees <br> ■ Joint promotion: <br>     Complimentary product <br>     with charity | ■ Reduced-price pack <br> ■ Extra-value pack <br> ■ Coupon <br> ■ Voucher with cash value <br> ■ Banded pack <br> ■ Collector series |
| Trade or retailer | ■ Credit/Extended credit <br> ■ Free services <br> ■ Training <br> ■ Club for special customers | ■ Competitions <br> ■ Free samples <br> ■ Discount on bulk purchases <br> ■ Discount for early payment | ■ Trade-in offers <br> ■ Sale or return <br> ■ Loyalty bonuses <br> ■ Range bonuses <br> ■ Reciprocal buying |

is prohibitive for many advertisers. Sales promotion used in conjunction with other communications, such as direct mail, can offer a more cost-effective route to reach target consumers.

- Retailers are demanding more deals from manufacturers.
- More agencies are aware of recent manufacturer pressure. They want to become involved in this fast-growing sector because sales promotion is an area creating opportunity for creativity and revenue.
- Developments in information technology, the reduction in data storage costs and retrieval, and increased sophistication of targeting techniques have facilitated implementation and enabled more effective measurement and control of sales promotion efforts.

The growing use of sales promotion has resulted in *promotion clutter*, similar to advertising clutter. Consumers who are continually bombarded with promotions are increasingly 'tuning out', so making the promotions less effective in triggering immediate purchase. Many sales promotions fail to create excitement among promotion-prone consumers. To capture the attention and interest of customers, manufacturers are now searching for ways to rise above the clutter, such as offering larger coupon values or creating more dramatic point-of-purchase displays or developing more creative campaigns that stand out from the crowd.

## Purpose of sales promotion

Sales-promotion tools vary in their specific objectives. For example, a free sample *stimulates consumer trial*; a free management advisory service *cements a long-term relationship* with a retailer. Sellers use sales promotions to *attract new triers*, to *reward loyal customers*, and to *increase the repurchase rates* of occasional users.

There are three types of new triers: consumers of the product category, loyal users of another brand, and users who frequently switch brands. Sales promotions often attract the last group – *brand switchers* – because nonusers and users of other brands do not always notice or act on a promotion. Brand switchers are looking mostly for low price or good value. Sales promotions are unlikely to turn them into loyal brand users. Thus sales promotions used in markets where brands are very similar usually produce high short-run sales response but little permanent market-share gain. In markets where brands differ greatly, however, sales promotions can alter market shares on a long-term basis.

Many sellers think of sales promotion as a tool for breaking down brand loyalty and advertising as a tool for building up brand loyalty. Thus an important issue for marketing managers is how to divide the budget between sales promotion and advertising. Ten years ago, marketing managers typically would first decide how much they needed to spend on advertising and then put the rest into sales promotion. Today, more and more marketing managers first decide how much they need to spend on trade promotion, then decide what they will spend on consumer promotion, and then budget whatever is left over for advertising.

There is a danger in letting advertising take a back seat to sales promotion, however. Reduced spending on advertising can result in lost consumer brand loyalty. One recent study of loyalty toward forty-five big packaged-goods brands showed that when share of advertising drops, so does brand loyalty. Since 1975, brand loyalty for brands with increased advertising spending fell 5 per cent. However, for brands with decreased ad spending, brand loyalty dropped 18 per cent.[28]

And there are other dangers. For instance, when a company uses price promotion for a brand too much of the time, consumers begin to think of it as a cheap brand. Soon, many consumers will buy the brand only when there is a special offer. No one knows when this will happen, but the risk increases greatly if a company puts a well-known, leading brand on promotion more than 30 per cent of the time. Marketers rarely use sales promotion for dominant brands because the promotions would do little more than subsidize current users.

Most analysts believe that sales promotion activities do not build long-term consumer preference and loyalty, as does advertising. Instead, promotion usually produces only short-term sales that cannot be maintained. Small-share competitors find it advantageous to use sales promotion because they cannot afford to match the large advertising budgets of the market leaders. Nor can they obtain shelf space without offering trade allowances or stimulate consumer trial without offering consumer incentives. Thus price competition is often used for small brands seeking to enlarge their shares, but it is usually less effective for a market leader whose growth lies in expanding the entire product category.[29]

The upshot is that many consumer packaged-goods companies feel that they are forced to use more sales promotion than they would like. Recently, traditional brand leaders like Kellogg, Kraft, Procter & Gamble and several other market leaders have announced that they will put more emphasis on pull promotion and increase their advertising budgets. They blame the heavy use of sales promotion for decreased brand loyalty, increased consumer price sensitivity, a focus on short-run marketing planning and an erosion of brand-quality image.

Some marketers dispute this criticism, however. They argue that the heavy use of sales promotion is a symptom of these problems, not a cause. They point to more basic causes, such as slower population growth, more educated consumers, industry overcapacity, the decreasing effectiveness of advertising, the growth of reseller power, and business's emphasis on short-run profits. These marketers assert that sales promotion provides many important benefits to manufacturers as well as to consumers. Sales promotions let manufacturers adjust to short-term changes in supply and demand and to differences in customer segments. They let manufacturers charge a higher list price to test 'how high is high' – that is, to ascertain the highest price the market will stand. Sales promotions encourage consumers to try new products instead of always staying with their current ones. They lead to more varied retail formats, such as the everyday-low-price store or the promotional-pricing store, which gives consumers more choice. Finally, sales promotions lead to greater consumer awareness of prices, and consumers themselves enjoy the satisfaction of feeling like smart shoppers when they take advantage of price specials.[30]

Sales promotions are usually used together with advertising or personal selling. Consumer promotions are normally advertised and can add excitement and pulling power to ads. Trade and salesforce promotions support the firm's personal selling process. In using sales promotion, a company must set objectives, select the right tools, develop the best programme, pretest and implement that programme, and evaluate the results. We will examine each of these issues in turn.

## Setting sales-promotion objectives

Sales-promotion objectives vary widely. Let us take *consumer promotions* first. Sellers may use consumer promotions to: (1) increase short-term sales; (2) help build long-term market share; (3) entice consumers to try a new product; (4) lure consumers away from competitors' products; (5) encourage consumers to 'load up' on a mature product; or (6) hold and reward loyal customers.

Objectives for *trade promotions* include: (1) motivating retailers to carry new items and more inventory; (2) inducing them to advertise the product and give it more shelf space; and (3) persuading them to buy ahead.

For the *salesforce*, objectives may be to: (1) prompt more salesforce support for current or new products; or (2) stimulate salespeople to sign up new accounts.

Objectives should focus on a realistic outcome and one which is measurable. Rather than saying that the aim of the promotion is to increase sales, the objective should be specific about the level of increase, who the main targets are, and whether increased sales are expected to come from new trialists or from current consumers who are loading up or bringing forward their purchase.

In general, sales promotions should be **consumer franchise building**. They should promote the product's positioning and include a selling message along with the deal. Ideally, the objective is to build long-run consumer demand rather than to prompt temporary brand switching. If properly designed, every sales-promotion tool has consumer franchise building potential.

## Selecting sales-promotion tools

Many tools can be used to accomplish sales promotion objectives. The promotion planner should consider the type of market, the sales-promotion objectives, the competition, and the costs and effectiveness of each tool. Descriptions of the main consumer- and trade-promotion tools follow.

### Consumer-promotion tools

The main consumer-promotion tools include samples, coupons, cash refunds, price packs, premiums, advertising specialities, patronage rewards, point-of-purchase displays and demonstrations, and contests, sweepstakes and games.

**Samples** are offers of a trial amount of a product. Some samples are free; for others, the company charges a small amount to offset its cost. The sample might be delivered door to door, sent by mail, handed out in a store, attached to another product or featured in an ad. Sampling is the most effective, but most expensive, way to introduce a new product. For example, Lever Brothers had so much confidence in its new Persil Power detergent that it spent millions of pounds to distribute free samples to British households.

**Coupons** are certificates that give buyers a saving when they purchase specified products. Coupons can be mailed, included with other products or placed in ads. They can stimulate sales of a mature brand or promote early trial of a new brand.

**Cash refund offers** (or **rebates**) are like coupons except that the price reduction occurs after the purchase rather than at the retail outlet. The consumer sends a 'proof of purchase' to the manufacturer, who then refunds part of the purchase price by mail.

**Price packs** or reduced prices offer consumers savings off the regular price of a product. The reduced prices are marked by the producer directly on the label or package. Price packs can be single packages sold at a reduced price (such as two for the price of one) or two related products banded together (such as a toothbrush and toothpaste). Price packs are very effective, even more so than coupons, in stimulating short-term sales.

**Premiums** are goods offered either free or at low cost as an incentive to buy a product. A premium may come inside the package (in-pack) or outside the package (on-pack). If reusable, the package itself may serve as a premium, such as a decorative tin. Premiums are sometimes mailed to consumers who have sent in a proof of purchase, such as a box top. A *self-liquidating premium* is a premium sold below its normal retail price to consumers who request it.

**Advertising specialities** are useful articles imprinted with an advertiser's name given as gifts to consumers. Typical items include pens, calendars, key rings, matches, shopping bags, T-shirts, caps and coffee mugs. Such items can be very effective. In a recent study, 63 per cent of all consumers surveyed were either carrying or wearing an ad speciality item. More than three-quarters of those who had an item could recall the advertiser's name or message before showing the item to the interviewer.[31]

**Patronage rewards** are cash or other awards offered for the regular use of a certain company's products or services. For example, airlines offer 'frequent flyer plans', awarding points for miles travelled that can be turned in for free airline trips. Some international hotels like Holiday Inn and Marriott Hotels have an 'honoured guest' plan that awards points to users of their hotels.

**Point-of-purchase (POP) promotions** include displays and demonstrations that take place at the point of purchase or sale. Unfortunately, many retailers do not like to handle the hundreds of displays, signs and posters they receive from manufacturers each year. Manufacturers have responded by offering better POP materials, tying them in with television or print messages, and offering to set them up.

Competitions, sweepstakes, lotteries and games give consumers the chance to win something, such as cash, trips or goods, by luck or through extra effort. A *competition* calls for consumers to submit an entry – a jingle, guess, suggestion – to be judged by a panel that will select the best entries. A *sweepstakes* calls for consumers to submit their names for a draw. For a *lottery*, consumers buy tickets which enter their names into a draw. A *game* presents consumers with something, such as bingo numbers or missing letters, every time they buy, which may or may not help them win a prize. A sales contest urges dealers or the salesforce to increase their efforts, with prizes going to the top performers.

The sales promotion industry is significantly more developed in the United States. In Europe, Britain leads other EU member states. In the United Kingdom, sales promotion activities are relatively free from legal constraints, with self-policing, in alignment with the industry's code of practice, being the norm. Supermarket retailing in the United Kingdom is dominated by a few key players and decisions regarding acceptance of manufacturers' sale promotion activities are centralized. Cost-effectiveness is increased as the sales promotion handling house is able to use the retailing groups' own administrative processes. Cultural differences also affect consumers' acceptance of different sales-promotion techniques. Furthermore, the legal position of sales-promotion techniques in different EU countries varies (see Table 19.6). In general, greater freedom is found in the United Kingdom, Ireland and Spain. Legal controls are stricter in the Benelux countries and, notably so, in Germany.

> For example, the use of sampling devices is banned in Germany if the product has been on the market for some time. Competitions are legal in Italy but are subject to tax. In Germany competitions are legal if used as 'attention getters', but illegal if authorities judge these to be used as 'inducements-to-buy'. In the Netherlands, games won by chance are not permitted, although those won by exercising skill are allowed if prizes are in cash or the service won has a monetary value not more than 2500 guilders. In Belgium, competitions are allowed if a reasonably high level of skill and judgement is needed to play the competition. With-purchase or in-pack premiums are illegal in Belgium, but permitted if the premium is an accessory to the main product or its value is low .... Free premiums are illegal in Germany. In the Netherlands, premiums must have a natural association with the product and be restricted to not more than 4 per cent of the value of the main product. In the UK, there are no restrictions on the use of premiums.[32]

*1 ecu = US$1.26 = DFl 2.12 (Dutch guilders).*

The European market for sales promotion remains fragmented for the time being and, until true harmonization is achieved, marketers must retain a sensitivity to national constraints and adapt strategies to fit individual country markets (see Marketing Highlight 19.2).

### Trade-promotion tools

Trade promotion can persuade retailers or wholesalers to carry a brand, give it shelf space, promote it in advertising and push it to consumers. Shelf space is so scarce these days that manufacturers often have to offer price-discounts, allowances, buy-back guarantees or free goods to retailers and wholesalers to get on the shelf and, once there, to stay on it.

Manufacturers use several trade-promotion tools. Many of the tools used for consumer promotions – contests, premiums, displays – can also be used as trade promotions. Alternatively, the manufacturer may offer a straight **discount** off the list price on each case purchased during a stated period of time (also called a *price-off, off-invoice* or *off-list*). The offer encourages dealers to buy in quantity or to carry a new item. Dealers can use the discount for immediate profit, for advertising or for price reductions to their customers.

Manufacturers also may offer an **allowance** (usually so much off per case) in return for the retailer's agreement to feature the manufacturer's products in some way. An *advertising allowance* compensates retailers for advertising the product. A *display allowance* compensates them for using special displays.

Manufacturers may offer *free goods*, which are extra cases of merchandise, to middlemen who buy a certain quantity or who feature a certain flavour or size. They may offer *push incentives* – cash or gifts to dealers or their salesforce to 'push' the manufacturer's goods. Manufacturers may give retailers free *speciality advertising items* that carry the company's name, such as pens, pencils, calendars, paperweights, matchbooks, memo pads, and ashtrays.

**TABLE 19.6** Sales promotions in the European Union: what is permitted, and what is not

| | Spain | Portugal | Greece | United Kingdom | Irish Republic | France | Italy | Netherlands | Belgium | Denmark | Luxembourg | Germany |
|---|---|---|---|---|---|---|---|---|---|---|---|---|
| On-pack price reductions | ✓ | ✓ | ✓ | ✓ | ✓ | ✓ | ✓ | ✓ | ✓ | ✓ | ✓ | ✓ |
| In-store demos | ✓ | ✓ | ✓ | ✓ | ✓ | ✓ | ✓ | ✓ | ✓ | ✓ | ✓ | ✓ |
| Free product | ✓ | ✓ | ✓ | ✓ | ✓ | ✓ | ✓ | ✓ | ✓ | ✓ | ✓ | ✓ |
| Reusable/alternative use pack | ✓ | ✓ | ✓ | ✓ | ✓ | ✓ | ✓ | ✓ | ✓ | ✓ | ✓ | ✓ |
| Extra product | ✓ | ✓ | ✓ | ✓ | ✓ | ✓ | ✓ | ✓ | ✓ | ✓ | ✓ | ? |
| Free mail-ins | ✓ | ✓ | ✓ | ✓ | ✓ | ✓ | ✓ | ✓ | ✓ | ✓ | ✓ | ? |
| Competitions | ✓ | ✓ | ✓ | ✓ | ✓ | ✓ | ✓ | ✓ | ✓ | ✓ | ✓ | ? |
| Self-liquidating premiums | ✓ | ✓ | ✓ | ✓ | ✓ | ✓ | * | ✓ | ? | ✓ | ✓ | ✓ |
| Cash backs | ✓ | ✓ | ✓ | ✓ | ✓ | ✓ | ✓ | ✓ | ? | ✓ | ✓ | ? |
| Multipurchase offers | ✓ | ✓ | ✓ | ✓ | ✓ | ✓ | ✓ | ✓ | ✓ | ✓ | ✓ | ? |
| Banded offers | ✓ | ✓ | ✓ | ✓ | ✓ | ✓ | ? | ? | ? | ✓ | ✓ | ? |
| Money-off vouchers | ✓ | ✓ | ✓ | ✓ | ✓ | ✓ | ? | ? | ? | ✓ | ✓ | * |
| Money-off next purchase | ✓ | ✓ | ✓ | ✓ | ✓ | ✓ | ✓ | ? | * | ✓ | ✓ | * |
| Collector devices | ✓ | ✓ | ✓ | ✓ | ✓ | ✓ | ✓ | ? | ? | ✓ | ✓ | * |
| Cross-product offers | ✓ | ✓ | ✓ | ✓ | ✓ | ✓ | ✓ | * | ? | ✓ | ✓ | * |
| With-purchase premiums | ✓ | ✓ | ✓ | ✓ | ✓ | ✓ | ✓ | ? | * | * | ✓ | * |
| Free draws | ✓ | ✓ | ✓ | ✓ | ✓ | ✓ | ✓ | ? | ? | ✓ | ✓ | * |
| In-pack premiums | ✓ | ✓ | ✓ | ✓ | ✓ | ✓ | ? | * | * | ? | ✓ | ? |
| Share-outs | ✓ | ✓ | ✓ | ✓ | ✓ | ✓ | ? | ? | ? | ? | ✓ | * |
| Sweepstake/lottery | ✓ | ✓ | ✓ | ? | ? | ✓ | ? | * | * | ? | ✓ | * |

Notes: ✓ Permitted; * not permitted; ? may be permitted.
Source: IMP London.

*Business-promotion tools*

Companies also promote to industrial customers. These business promotions are used to generate business leads, stimulate purchases, reward customers and motivate salespeople. Business promotion includes many of the same tools used for consumer or trade promotions. Here, we focus on two of the main business-promotion tools – conventions and trade shows, and sales contests.

*Conventions and trade shows*   Many companies and trade associations organize *conventions and trade shows* to promote their products. Firms selling to the industry show their products at the trade show. Vendors receive many benefits, such as opportunities to find new sales leads, contact customers, introduce new products, meet new customers, sell more to present customers and educate customers with publications and audiovisual materials.

Trade shows also help companies reach many prospects not reached through their salesforces. Business managers face several decisions, including which trade shows to participate in, how much to spend on each trade show, how to build dramatic exhibits that attract attention, and how to follow up on sales leads effectively.[33]

*Sales contests*   A *sales contest* is a contest for salespeople or dealers to motivate them to increase their sales performance over a given period. Most companies sponsor annual or more frequent sales contests for their salesforce. Called 'incentive programmes' these contests motivate and recognize good company performers, who may receive trips, cash prizes or other gifts. Some companies award points for performance, which the receiver can exchange for any of a variety of prizes. Sales contests work best when they are tied to measurable and achievable sales objectives (such as finding new accounts, reviving old accounts or increasing account profitability) and when employees believe they have an equal chance of winning. Otherwise, employees who do not think the contest's goals are reasonable or equitable will not take up the challenge.[34]

## Developing the sales promotion programme

The marketer must decide on the *creative idea* and the *mechanics* of the promotion. The creative idea concerns adding some kind of added value to the product. It is often difficult to generate an innovative idea which sets a sales promotion apart. Also, it is easy for competitors to copy as in the case of price reductions, free products or gifts, and in-store demonstrations. The marketer must take care to ensure the promotion does genuinely offer extra value and incentives to targets, and is not misleading, and that the firm will be able to honour redemptions. An example of a sales promotion campaign that backfired is the Hoover free-flights promotion in Britain and Ireland:

> Hoover offered consumers two free return flights to Europe or America if they bought any of its vacuum cleaners, washing machines or other household appliances worth more than £100. The campaign caused a great deal of damage and produced little benefit. What went wrong? The promotion was a ploy dreamed up to tempt people to buy a new appliance. At the time, it seemed to have the advantage of raising cash on extra sales now (and at a time when the UK market for household appliances was depressed), with costs that did not have to be incurred, until later, in the form of heavily discounted air tickets, when the appliance market would have improved. Hoover's mistake was to expect many consumers to be attracted by the promise of free flights, but to be deterred from redeeming their air tickets by

## Sales promotions: creating successful European-wide campaigns

Sales promotion tactics as marketing tools are difficult enough to gauge in domestic markets, let alone outside them. Like advertising, using a single theme, through one medium, to target a single audience across different countries is tempting, but rarely successful.

Some companies decide to take the risks in order to benefit from scale economies. IBM ran a pan-European campaign that featured the Pink Panther to revitalize the image of its personal computer division. Market research in five countries showed that people saw the character as smart, friendly and approachable. IBM also wanted to portray an image of quality, reliability and integrity. Customers anywhere in Europe could order by post, telephone or electronic-mail, and pay by credit card. The promotion was backed by a wide range of merchandise – pens, T-shirts, watches, ties, hats, balloons, badges, mouse mats and point-of-sale displays There was also a leaflet with twenty-eight products carrying the Pink Panther label. The promotion worked because IBM had homed in on cultural similarities in key segments – business executives, the metropolitan middle classes, and teenagers.

Iain Arthur, president of the European Federation of Sales Promotion, argues that the mechanics of promotional campaigns can translate well across national borders, on the basis that the most powerful word which is understood across cultures is 'free.' Giving away items free with a purchase tends to work well in most countries. Samples, where permitted, also work well, especially if they are attached to something bought or given away. Pan-European sampling campaigns were run for Procter & Gamble's new Wash & Go and Johnson & Johnson's pH 5.5 shampoo: the colours, on-card samples and branding were consistent in each market. Only the language on the packaging was changed. Minipack Sampling Solutions, the company that ran the campaigns, stressed that the principle behind pan-European sampling campaigns is to look for cross-country convergences, not differences, and to leverage these similarities.

Where there are cross-country segments that are looking for recognition and reward, then, according to

David Butter, Wunderman Cato Johnson Europe's vice president, promotions that give customers the chance to win competitions and draws are very powerful.

There are a number of barriers that marketers should understand. One is the differing *legislation* across individual countries. For example, it is very liberal in Italy, Spain and Portugal, where gifts-with-purchase, prizes-with-purchase and on-pack promotions are commonplace. In Germany, laws dating back to the 1930s mean that a free or very cheap premium is illegal, as is sampling if the product is not new. France is moderately liberal in allowing premiums so long as they do not exceed 7 per cent of the value of products up to and including FFr 500* or go above FFr 350. In the Netherlands, premiums must not exceed 4 per cent of the value of the main purchase, while in Belgium the ceiling is 5 per cent.

Another hurdle to overcome is *national safety standards*. In Germany, safety standards are particularly tight, requiring a higher testing procedure than in the United Kingdom. In France, the firm's logo must be incorporated into promotional products.

The concept of the Single Market is slowly making its impact on EC law. The latest ruling is that companies should not be disadvantaged due to individual national laws. Countries with restrictive legislation are compelled to open up to those which do not have the same restrictions. Thus German laws have been relaxed as a result. For example, the French cosmetics firm Yves Rocher produced catalogues full of special offers that were available in Germany but illegal. The European Court found in favour of Yves Rocher. Germany's *Rabattgesetz*, which forbids the offer of certain types of discounts has been amended. Discounting has since been permitted in Germany.

If it is becoming easier to get round national laws in Europe, it is not so easy to overcome *cultural differences*, *prejudices* and *suspicions*. If a German buyer is offered a discounted product he or she usually thinks that there is something wrong with it or it is deficient in some way. Any price reduction must therefore reassure the customer and offer a good rationalization for the discount. Cultural differences also affect the type

Pan-European sampling: Johnson & Johnson's pH5.5 sampling campaign worked on the basis of common packaging, with the language being changed for each different market.

of merchandise used in the promotion. Household items, especially electrical goods, are very popular in Germany. Beach towels, sunglasses and T-shirts are more popular in Spain and Portugal, while in France, it is pens, lighters and watches. In Italy, brand association is important – if the merchandise features a designer name, a recognized brand name or a football club, the chances are that it will be well received.

*Media costs* vary significantly and could affect the success of the campaign. Marketers must take care not to put money-off vouchers in publications that are worth less than the voucher, since dishonest shopkeepers will simply keep the newspaper or cut the coupons out. *Fraud* is a problem too. In poorer countries, if an incentive is worth cheating for, people will cheat. It is not problematic to offer a 50 pence* voucher in the United Kingdom, but 50p may be worth forging a voucher for in, say, Greece or southern Spain.

To achieve successful European promotional campaigns, managers have to carry out accurate research. Achieving economies of scale with global brands and consistent campaigns may be attractive, but insufficient. Successful Europeanwide promotions are invariably built around local and national criteria as opposed to being pan-European or global, says Iain Arthur. Other experts, however, argue that firms can

mix the two in the face of *mass customization* in many markets where the mass is the *core idea or strategy*, which is customized to suit different markets. For example, Schweppes tonic devised a core theme based on the game Trivial Pursuit, which they called *Schquiz*. In France, tonic is a soft drink, while in the United Kingdom it is a mixer, in Spain a refreshment, and, in Germany a 'sophisticated' drink. The main difference in image across the different countries was the relative strength of the brand. In Spain it is a much stronger brand, which is popular among older consumers. A TV phone-in was used for Schquiz because of this and the fact that TV is a stronger medium. In France, the smaller market for Schweppes tonic meant a smaller media spend for the brand and a radio phone-in was used instead.

Experts stress that it is a mistake to start with a single consumer group to target or a promotion vehicle like a contest or a premium, and then work out how the promotion will be executed on a pan-European level. Effective European promotional campaigns work best if marketers begin by clarifying and defining their objectives and then decide on the best means, within the limitations of budgets and resources, to meet these objectives on a country-by-country basis. It is also advisable to employ as much local knowledge as possible. By using experts on the ground, who understand the sales promotion business and their own consumers, marketers can avoid costly errors or embarrassments, like one such campaign run for a soap manufacturer in Thailand. Consumers had the chance to win a house if they pulled one of six gold coins out of a soap box. They queued at shops to buy the soap powder. They poured the powder in the street to look for the gold coins. Only five were found. People continued to buy the soap powder long after the campaign finished. The government had to intervene to put a stop to it in the end.

*1 ecu = US$1.26 = FFr 6.47 (French francs).
*1 ecu = 83 pence.

Source: Sean Brierley, 'Harmony in discount,' *Marketing Week* (14 October 1994), 61–2; David Waller, 'Charged up over competition law', *Financial Times* (23 June 1994), 16.

the offer's small print, which lays down conditions about when its flights can be and the choice of hotel accommodation. The company had, unfortunately, miscalculated, although, according to Mr Fallon, company lawyer for Hoover European Appliance Group, no fewer than three sales promotions agencies were involved in originating and costing the promotion. Each of them were sufficiently confident to accept the risk on take-up rates. As it happened, most consumers bought cheap vacuum cleaners that cost as little as £120. The cheapest pair of return air tickets to New York cost about £500. The firm was inundated with as many as 200,000 applications for free flights within the first ten months of the campaign. The company had only issued about 6,000 tickets within that same period. The travel agents hired by Hoover were also alleged to be unfairly dissuading consumers from taking up the offer. Angry customers were, nonetheless adamant and many were still waiting for their tickets. Although Hoover had put aside some money to cover the air fares, it was nothing like enough. The parent company, Maytag, had to come to the rescue by paying out $30 million. When the three agencies failed to fulfil their obligations, they left Hoover to honour their commitments. The debacle had cost the company £48 million. In Britain and Ireland, Hoover's name became a sick joke to millions of consumers. Which party is to be blamed? Hoover's management or the three expert promotions companies? Both parties displayed errors in judgement. While the experts have severely miscalculated, management at Hoover cannot put the blame entirely on them. It is up to the firm to question: How should they justify their spending on the sales promotion? What return on their promotional investment were they seeking? What would the take-up rates be and are they realistic? What would it cost the company given the size or attractiveness of the incentive?[35]

It follows that the marketer must cost the sales promotion and carefully evaluate take-up rates when deciding the *size of the incentive*. A certain minimum incentive is necessary if the promotion is to succeed; a larger incentive will produce more sales response. It is important to strike a balance between an incentive of sufficient substance to induce consumers to experiment and to tempt lapsed users to buy, and too huge an incentive that results in regular consumers heavily stocking up during the promotion, causing profitability to decline in the medium term as sales drop after the promotion period. Or, as in the Hoover example, the incentive is too generous, triggering an extreme rate of redemption that could financially cripple the firm.

Some of the large firms which sell consumer packaged goods have a sales-promotion manager who studies past promotions and uses past experience to decide on incentive levels to adopt. Many firms also use marketing companies and agencies to assist them in designing and implementing the sales-promotion campaign.

The marketer also must set *conditions for participation*. Incentives might be offered to everyone or only to select groups. For example, competitions may not be offered to families of company personnel or to people under a certain age. Conditions, such as the proof of purchase or closing date of the offer, must be clearly stated.

The marketer must then decide how to *promote and distribute the promotion* programme itself. A money-off coupon could be given out in a package, at the store, by mail or in an advertisement. Each distribution method involves a different level of reach and cost. Increasingly, marketers are blending several media into a total campaign concept. They also must decide on the choice of media used to announce the sales-promotion programme:

A food company plans to launch a campaign to promote a new health snack product. The peak purchasing period for health snacks is usually after the winter, particularly Christmas, indulgence period and before summer. It schedules TV and magazine advertising to coincide with this period. Some of the magazine advertising is used to announce a competition and free health booklet. It also plans a trade promotion to sustain retailer awareness and to ensure they stock up for demand. Salesforce incentives also are planned to bolster the effects of the trade promotion.

The *duration of the promotion* is also important. If the sales-promotion period is too short, many prospects (who may not be buying during that time) will miss it. If the promotion runs too long, the deal will lose some of its 'act now' force. Brand managers need to set calendar dates for the promotions. The dates will be used by production, sales and distribution. Some unplanned promotions may also be needed, requiring cooperation at short notice.

The marketer also must decide on the *response mechanism*: that is, the redemption vehicle to be used by the customer who takes part in the promotion. The easier it is for the customer to respond to an offer, the higher the response rate. Immediate gratification – for example, a price reduction, a free gift attached to the product on offer – often yields a higher response. If the incentive requires further action to be taken by the consumer – for instance, to make another purchase or to collect the required number of tokens in promotion packs and then post these off to claim a gift or free product – redemption rate can be reduced.

Finally, the marketer must determine *the sales promotion budget*, which can be developed in one of two ways. The marketer may choose the promotions and estimate their total cost. However, the more common way is to use a percentage of the total budget for sales promotion. One study found three serious problems in the way companies budget for sales promotion. First, they do not consider cost effectiveness. Second, instead of spending to achieve objectives, they simply extend the previous year's spending, take a percentage of expected sales or use the 'affordable approach.' Finally, advertising and sales promotion budgets are too often prepared separately.[36]

## Pretesting and implementing

Whenever possible, sales-promotion tools should be *pretested* to find out if they are appropriate and of the right incentive size. Consumer sales promotions can be pretested quickly and inexpensively. For example, consumers can be asked to rate or rank different possible promotions, or promotions can be tried on a limited basis in selected geographic areas.

Companies should prepare implementation plans for each promotion, covering lead time and sell-off time. *Lead time* is the time necessary to prepare the programme before launching it. *Sell-off time* begins with the launch and ends when the promotion ends.

## Evaluating the results

Evaluation is also very important. Many companies fail to evaluate their sales-promotion programmes while others evaluate them only superficially. Manufacturers can use one of many evaluation methods. The most common method is to compare sales before, during and after a promotion. Suppose a company has a 6 per cent market share before the promotion, which jumps to 10 per cent during the promotion, falls to 5 per cent right after and rises to 7 per cent later on. The promotion seems to have attracted new triers and more buying from current customers. After the promotion, sales fell as consumers used up their inventories. The long-run rise to 7 per cent means that the company gained some new users. If the brand's share had returned to the old level, then the promotion would have changed only the *timing* of demand rather than the *total* demand.

Consumer research would also show the kinds of people who responded to the promotion and what they did after it ended. *Surveys* can provide information on how many consumers recall the promotion, what they thought of it, how many took advantage of it and how it affected their buying. Sales promotions can also be evaluated through *experiments* that vary factors such as incentive value, timing, duration and distribution method.

Clearly, sales promotion plays an important role in the total promotion mix. To use it well, the marketer must define the sales promotion objectives, select the best tools, design the sales promotion programme, pretest and implement the programme, and evaluate the results.

## PUBLIC RELATIONS

Another important mass-promotion technique is **public relations**. This concerns building good relations with the company's various publics by obtaining favourable publicity, building up a good 'corporate image' and handling or heading off unfavourable rumours, stories and events. The old name for marketing public relations was **publicity**, which was seen simply as activities to promote a company or its products by planting news about it in media not paid for by the sponsor. Public relations is a much broader concept that includes publicity as well as many other activities. Public relations departments use many different tools:

- *Press relations.* Placing newsworthy information in the news media to attract attention to a person, product or service.
- *Product publicity.* Publicizing specific products.
- *Corporate communications.* Creating internal and external communications to promote understanding of the firm or institution.
- *Lobbying.* Dealing with legislators and government officials to promote or defeat legislation and regulation.
- *Counselling.* Advising management about public issues and company positions and image.[37]

Public relations is used to promote products, people, places, ideas, activities, organizations and even nations. Trade associations have used public relations to rebuild interest in declining commodities such as eggs, apples, milk and potatoes. Even nations have used public relations to attract more tourists, foreign investment and international support. Companies can use PR to manage their way out of crisis, as in the case of Johnson & Johnson's masterly use of public relations to limit the damage from its tainted Tylenol pain killers.

Public relations can have a strong impact on public awareness at a much lower cost than advertising. The company does not pay for the space or time in the media. Rather, it pays for a staff to develop and circulate information and to manage events. If the company develops an interesting story, it could be picked up by several different media, having the same effect as advertising that would cost a lot more money. And it would have more credibility than advertising.

Despite its potential strengths, public relations, like sales promotions, is often described as a marketing stepchild because of its limited and scattered use. The public relations department is usually located at corporate headquarters. Its staff is so busy dealing with various publics – stockholders, employees, legislators, regulators – that public relations programmes to support product marketing objectives may be ignored. Moreover marketing managers and public relations practitioners do not always talk the same language. On the one hand, many public relations practitioners see their job as simply communicating. On the other hand, marketing managers tend to be much more interested in how advertising and public relations affect sales and profits.

This situation is changing, however. Many companies now want their public relations departments to manage all their activities with a view toward marketing the company and improving the bottom line. Some companies are setting up special units to support corporate and product promotion and image making directly. Many companies hire marketing public relations firms to handle their PR programmes or to assist the company public relations team. In one survey of marketing managers, three-quarters reported that their companies use marketing public relations. They found it particularly effective in building brand awareness and knowledge for both new and established products. In several cases, it proved more cost effective than advertising.[38]

## Important public relations tools

There are a number of PR tools. One essential tool is *news*. PR professionals find or create favourable news about the company and its products or people. Sometimes news stories occur naturally. At other times, the PR person can suggest events or activities that would create news.

*Speeches* also create product and company publicity. Increasingly, company executives must field questions from the media or give talks at trade associations or sales meetings. These events can either build or hurt the company's image.

Another common PR tool is *special events*, ranging from news conferences, press tours, grand openings and fireworks displays to laser shows, hot-air balloon releases, multi-media presentations and star-studded spectaculars that will reach and interest target publics.

Public relations people also prepare *written materials* to reach and influence their target markets. These materials include annual reports, brochures, articles and company newsletters and magazines.

*Audiovisual materials*, such as films, slide-and-sound programmes and video and audio cassettes, are being used increasingly as communication tools.

*Corporate-identity materials* also help create a corporate identity that the public immediately recognizes. Logos, stationery, brochures, signs, business forms, business cards, buildings, uniforms and even company cars and trucks make effective marketing tools when they are attractive, distinctive, and memorable.

Companies might improve public goodwill by contributing to *public-service activities*: campaigns to raise funds for worthy causes – for example, to fight illiteracy, support the work of a charity, or assist the aged and handicapped – help to raise public recognition.

*Sponsorship* is any vehicle through which corporations gain public relations exposure. In Europe, the sponsorship industry is growing, with many firms committing huge sums of money around the world into the sponsorship of sport and the arts because it makes good sense as a marketing tool (see Marketing Highlight 19.3).

## Main public relations decisions

In considering when and how to use product public relations, management should set PR objectives; choose the PR messages and vehicles; implement the PR plan; and evaluate the results.

## Making sponsorship work for the company

Traditionally, sponsorship has been an underrated medium compared to its more glamorous cousin – advertising. Times are changing and, increasingly, marketers see this tool as an investment that makes good marketing sense. According to the market research company SRI, in 1992, businesses around the world spent $9.4 billion on sponsorship. For example, business sponsorship of the arts – investment in return for public relations exposure or corporate hospitality – has been one of the fastest and most sophisticated growth areas in the industry in recent years. In the United Kingdom particularly, companies have been establishing partnerships with the arts as a way of reaching specific target markets. Allied-Lyons, one of the world's largest drinks companies, boasted a £3.3 million sponsorship of the Royal Shakespeare Company. It uses the prestigious alliance to promote its corporate identity and, ultimately, to increase sales of individual brands. Marks & Spencer spent close to £50,000 a year on the London Philharmonic Orchestra's Concerts for Children, held three times a year at the London Festival Hall. M & S claims that it helps the company to gain access to inner city areas, to school children, their parents and their teachers. Ice cream manufacturer Häagen-Dazs sponsored an art exhibition called 'Some Went Mad, Some Ran Away' at London's Serpentine Gallery, as part of the company's 'Dedicated to Pleasure, Dedicated to the Arts' programme. The

German Beck's Bier was launched as a premium lager on the British market using arts sponsorship.

Common trends are emerging in almost all European countries, according to Anne Vanhaeverbeke of the Comité Européen pour le Rapprochement de l'Economie et de la Culture (Cerec). There are professional sponsorship associations in most countries in Europe and Cerec fosters closer ties between business and the arts and coordinates the network of sponsorship associations and its own business members. In Germany, however, due to high public subsidy for the arts and punishing levels of taxation, businesses play a lesser role. Those that do participate, however, like Daimler-Benz, BMW and Lufthansa, do seek public recognition and media coverage for their efforts.

Sponsorship can be cheaper than advertising. Sunkist's $3 million title sponsorship of a bowls championship generated $10.8 million worth of media impressions for the brand in the United States. Smaller sums can also result in spectacular returns from sponsorship investment. For example, for under £1,000, companies can get a match-day sponsorship at a small football club. The package includes a hospitality box, twelve seats in the main stand, a buffet and a free bar. The firm gets free advertising in the match programme, banners in the car-park area, the right to present the Man-of-the-Match award, and tickets to

### Setting public relations objectives

The first task is to set *objectives* for public relations. These are usually defined in relation to the types of news story to be communicated, the communication objectives to be achieved (for instance, awareness creation, knowledge dissemination, generation of specific publicity for target groups) and the specific target audiences.

### Choosing public relations messages and vehicles

The organization next finds interesting stories to tell about the product. Suppose a little-known company wants more public recognition. It will search for possible stories: Do any company staff have unusual backgrounds? Is the firm contributing to unusual community projects? Have any socially beneficial products been launched by the company? Usually, this search will uncover hundreds of stories that can be fed to the press. The chosen stories should reflect the image sought by the company.

If there are not enough stories, the company could sponsor newsworthy events. Here, the organization *creates* news rather than finds it. Ideas might include hosting

join players in the bar after the match. At under £100 per head, this is not bad for a day's entertainment for key customers – as long as the game is good! Furthermore it offers a sales opportunity and rewards the firm's best sales staff.

Sponsorship should not be used as a substitute for advertising, however. The two should go hand in hand. 'Integrated communications' yield more effective results. Sponsorship is a deed. Advertising tells the public about it. Sales promotion and direct marketing are integral, too. For example, a Diet Coke campaign used sponsorship of a London marathon as a vehicle for a sports T-shirt offer. Promotional vouchers that were returned had the name and address of the recipient filled in. This provided a useful basis for future communication between the company and customer.

A fast-growing area of sponsorship has been the one with an environmental focus. In the early 1990s, Volvo ran a £250,000 per annum two-year sponsorship programme in Britain to stress the fact that Volvo is Swedish and 'green.' The programme was run on two fronts. One, a research project into ground-level ozone, involving children growing and monitoring plants in their own gardens, was carried out in conjunction with the Society for Nature Conservancy Council (SNCC). The other concerned tie-ups among its dealer distribution points and the local

SNCC office, which involved building an owl sanctuary and protecting a bluebell wood. Such PR activities have served to reinforce the company's corporate identity.

To be a successful sponsor, the firm must meet certain requirements:

- There are clear marketing objectives.
- The objectives can be fulfilled by sponsorship.
- Legally, the contract is watertight, and has been vetted by a lawyer or a specialist in the field.
- The staff are prepared to work hard to make it a success – the launch of the campaign is the easy part, the hard grind comes later.
- Internally, staff have fully accepted the idea and various departments agree about its relevance.

The firm should decide its sponsorship target: for example, sports, the arts, a national event. It would do well to seek the advice of consultants or specialist bodies in order to decide the best sponsorship area that matches its objectives. Importantly, sponsorship can bring good results if used in conjunction with other elements of the communication mix.

Source: Louella Miles, 'Get noticed', *Marketing Business* (March 1992), 30-3; Terry Eccles, 'Why $9 billion is put on board the sponsorship bicycle', *The European* (6–12 May 1994), 20.

1 ecu = US$1.26 = UK£0.83

major conventions, inviting well-known celebrities and holding press conferences. Each event creates many stories for many different audiences.

Creating events is especially important in publicizing fund-raising drives for non-profit organizations. Fund-raisers have developed a large set of special events such as art exhibits, auctions, benefit evenings, book sales, contests, dances, dinners, fairs, fashion shows, marathons and walkathons.

## Implementing the public relations plan

Implementing public relations requires care. Take, for example, the placing of stories in the media. A *great* story is easy to place, but, unfortunately, most stories are not earth shattering and would not get past busy editors. Thus one of the main assets of public relations people is their personal relationships with media editors. In fact, PR professionals are often former journalists who know many media editors and know what they want. They view media editors as a market to be satisfied so that editors will continue to use their stories.

*Evaluating public relations results*

Public relations results are difficult to measure because PR is used with other promotion tools and its impact is often indirect. If PR is used before other tools come into play, its contribution is easier to evaluate.

The easiest measure of publicity effectiveness is the number of exposures in the media. Public relations people give the client a 'clippings book' showing all the media that carried news about the product and a summary such as the following:

> Media coverage included 3,500 column inches of news and photographs in 350 publications with a combined circulation of 79.4 million; 2,500 minutes of air time on 290 radio stations and an estimated audience of 65 million; and 660 minutes of air time on 160 television stations with an estimated audience of 91 million.

The summary would also give an indication of the cost of the time and space had they been purchased at current advertising rates.

This exposure measure is not very satisfying, however. It does not tell how many people actually read or heard the message, nor what they thought afterwards. In addition, because of the media overlap in readership and viewership, it does not give information on the *net* audience reached.

A better measure is the change in product awareness, knowledge and attitude resulting from the publicity campaign. Assessing the change requires measuring the before-and-after-the-campaign levels of these measures. Finally, sales and profit impact, if obtainable, is the best measure of public relations effort. If advertising and sales promotion had also been stepped up during the period of the PR campaign, their contribution has to be considered.

## SUMMARY

Three main tools of mass promotion are advertising, sales promotion and public relations. They are mass-marketing tools as opposed to personal selling, which targets specific buyers.

*Advertising* is the use of paid media by a seller to inform, persuade and remind target audiences about its products or organization. It is a powerful promotion tool. Advertisements take many forms and have many uses. *Advertising decision making* is a five-step process consisting of decisions about the objectives, the budget, the message, the media and, finally, the evaluation of results. Advertisers should set clear *objectives* as to whether the advertising is supposed to inform, persuade or remind buyers. The advertising *budget* can be based on what is affordable, on a percentage of sales, on competitors' spending, or on the objectives and tasks to be accomplished. Decisions about the *message* evolve around the designing of effective messages, evaluating them and executing them effectively. The *media decision* calls for a definition of reach, frequency and impact goals; choosing chief media types; selecting media vehicles; and scheduling the media. Finally, *evaluation* draws attention to the communication and sales effects of advertising before, during and after the advertising is placed. Companies that advertise their products in different country markets can apply the basic principles relating to domestic advertising, but must additionally take on board the differences in cultural, socioeconomic, political and regulatory environments across country markets. They should also take advantage of similarities across country markets when developing international advertising campaigns.

*Sales promotion* covers a wide variety of short-term incentives – coupons, premiums, contests, buying allowances – designed to stimulate consumers, the trade and the company's own salesforce. In many countries, sales promotion spending has been growing faster than advertising spending in recent years. Sales promotion calls for setting sales promotion objectives; selecting tools; developing, pretesting, and implementing the sales promotion programme; and evaluating the results.

*Public relations* is about gaining favourable publicity and creating a favourable company image. It is the least used of the main promotion tools, although it has great potential for building awareness and preference. Public relations involves setting PR objectives, choosing PR messages and vehicles, implementing the PR plan and evaluating PR results.

To maximize the results of the firm's investment in mass promotions, marketers must adopt a total promotion approach which coordinates resources, strategies, planning and implementation among the communications mix adopted.

## ■ DISCUSSING THE ISSUES

1. Comparison advertising is not permitted in some countries. What are some of the benefits and drawbacks of comparison advertising. Which has more to gain from using comparison advertising – the leading brand in a market or a lesser brand? Why?

2. Surveys show that many people are sceptical of advertising claims. Do you mistrust advertising? Why or why not? What should advertisers do to increase credibility?

3. What factors call for more *frequency* in an advertising media schedule? What factors call for more *reach*? How can you increase one without sacrificing the other or increasing the advertising budget?

4. An ad states that Brand Y's cookies are the 'moistest, chewiest, most perfectly baked cookies the world has ever tasted', aside from home-made cookies. You happen to prefer another brand of cookies that you think is moister or chewier than Brand Y. Is the Brand Y claim false? Should this type of claim be regulated? Why or why not?

5. Companies often run advertising, sales-promotion and public relations efforts at the same time. Can their efforts be separated? Discuss how a company might evaluate the effectiveness of each element in this mix.

6. Many companies are spending more on trade promotions and consumer promotions than on advertising. Why do you think this is so? Is heavy spending on sales promotions a good strategy for long-term profits? Why or why not?

## ■ APPLYING THE CONCEPTS

1. Buy a Sunday paper and sort through the colour advertising and coupon inserts. Find examples that combine advertising, sales promotion and/or public relations. For instance, a manufacturer may run a full page ad that also includes a coupon and information on its sponsorship of a charity event.

   ■ Do you think these approaches using multiple tools are more or less effective than a single approach? Why?

   ■ Try to find ads from two direct competitors. Are these brands using similar promotional tools in similar ways?

2. Look out for two current television ads that you think are particularly effective and two which you feel are ineffective.

   ■ Describe precisely why you feel the better ads are effective and explain why the ineffective ones fall short.

   ■ How would you improve the less effective ads? If you think they are too poor to be improved, write an alternative ad for each, describing why these would be more effective.

# ■ REFERENCES ■

1. Excerpts and accounts taken from: *Marketing Week* (21 October 1994), 9–12; *Marketing Week* (14 October 1994), 51; Nick Higham, 'Papers prove just the ticket', *Marketing Week* (21 October 1994), 19.

2. David Short, 'Advertisers come out to spend again', *The European* (12–18 August, 1994), 21.

3. See Russell H. Colley, *Defining Advertising Goals for Measured Advertising Results* (New York: Association for National Advertisers, 1961). In this well-known book, Colley lists fifty-two possible advertising objectives. He outlines a method called DAGMAR (after a book's title) for turning advertising objectives into specific measurable goals. For a more complete discussion of DAGMAR, see M. L. Rothschild, *Advertising* (Lexington, MA: D. C. Heath, 1987), 142–55.

4. Roger Trapp, 'Ads that hit raw nerves,' *Independent* (18 August 1994), 16.

5. Ibid.

6. See Donald E. Schultz, Dennis Martin, and William P. Brown, *Strategic Marketing Campaigns* (Chicago: Crain Books, 1984), 192–7.

7. See C. Gilligan, 'How British advertisers set budgets', *Journal of Advertising Research* (17 February 1977).

8. Gerard J. Tellis, 'Advertising exposure, loyalty, and brand purchase: a two-stage model of choice', *Journal of Marketing Research* (May 1988), 134–5. For counterpoints, see Magid M. Abraham and Leonard M. Lodish, 'Getting the most out of advertising and promotion,' *Harvard Business Review* (May–June 1990), 50–60.

9. Gary Levin, 'Tracing ads' impact', *Advertising Age* (4 November 1991), 49

10. M. L. Vidale and H. R. Wolfe, 'An operations research study of sales response to advertising', *Operations Research* (June 1957), 370–81.

11. John D. C. Little, 'A model of adaptive control of promotional spending', *Operations Research* (November 1966), 1075–97; see also Gary A. Lilien and Philip Kotler, *Marketing Decision Making: A model building approach* (New York: Harper & Row, 1983), 490–501; for an insight into the usefulness of a management-oriented model for determining the budget and profitability of alternative levels of advertising, see Peter Doyle and Marcel Corstjens, 'Budget determination for highly advertised brands', *Journal of Advertising*, 1 (1982), 39–48.

12. The examples are drawn from Judith Corstjens, *Strategic Advertising: A practitioner's handbook* (Oxford: Heinemann Professional Publishing, 1990).

13. See Faye Rice, 'How to deal with tougher customers', *Fortune* (3 December 1990), 38–48.

14. Corstjens, *Strategic Advertising*, op. cit., 58, 105.

15. See, for example, R. Dunn, 'Greater freedom of the airwaves and advertising cost-effectiveness', *Admap*, **25**, 6 (1989).

16. See Robert D. Buzzell, 'E. I. Du Pont de Nemours & Co.: measurements of effects of advertising', in *id.*, *Mathematical Models and Marketing Management* (Boston: Administration, Harvard University, 1964), 157–79.

17. This definition is adapted from Marieke De Mooij, *Advertising Worldwide*, 2nd edn (New York: Prentice Hall, 1994), 12; for other definitions see Rein Rijkens and Gordon Miracle, *European Regulations of Advertising* (Amsterdam: Elsevier, 1986); William Wells, John Burnett and Sandra Moriarty, *Advertising Principles and Practice* (New York: Prentice Hall, 1989): see also De Mooij, *Advertising Worldwide*, op. cit., 6–7, 198–230, for discussions of differences between international, multinational, global or transnational marketing and its relevance to advertising and worldwide advertising decisions respectively.

18. Phili Geier, 'Global products, localized messages', *Marketing Communications* (December 1986).

19. J. N. Kapferer and Eurocom, 'How global are global brands', ESOMAR Seminar on the Challenge of Branding Today and in the Future, Brussels, 28–30 October 1992.

20. Michael Lev, 'Advertisers seek global messages', *New York Times* (18 November 1991), D9.

21. Philip R. Cateora, *International Marketing*, 7th edn (Homewood, IL: Irwin, 1990), 462.

22. See Ullrich Applebaum and Chris Halliburton, 'International advertising campaigns: the example of the European food and beverage sector', *International Journal of Advertising*, **12**, 13 (September 1993); Robert T. Green, William Cunningham and Isabella Cunningham, 'The effectiveness of standardized global advertising', *Journal of Advertising*, **41**, (1975); Ven Sriram and Pradeep Gopalakrishna, 'Can advertising be standardized among similar countries? A cluster-based analysis', *International Journal of Advertising*, **10** (1991); Judie Lannon, 'Developing brand strategies across borders', ESOMAR Conference on International Marketing Research: New Tasks, New Methods, New Scenarios, Ljubljana, 14–16 February 1991.

23. Media and Marketing, Europe (February 1993); *The Campaign Report* (1990).

24. For excellent discussions of the media landscape worldwide and influences on development of pan-European advertising, see respectively De Mooij, *Advertising Worldwide*, op. cit., 262–346; and Susan Norgan, *Marketing Management: A European perspective* (Wokingham, Berks: Addison-Wesley, 1994), 342–9.

25. Initiative Media, *European Planning Guide, 1992–1993*, Media and Marketing, Europe.

26. Michael R. Czinkota and Ilkka A. Ronkainen, *International Marketing*, 2nd edn (Chicago: Dryden, 1990), 615.

27. Cateora, *International Marketing*, op. cit., 466–7.

28. Scott Hume, 'Brand loyalty steady', *Advertising Age* (2 March 1992), 19.

29. See F. Kent Mitchel, 'Advertising/promotion budgets: how did we get here, and what do we do now?' *Journal of Consumer Marketing* (Fall 1985), 405–47.

30. For more on the use of sales promotion versus advertising, see Paul W. Farris and John A. Quelch, 'In defense of price promotion', *Sloan Management Review* (Fall 1987); and John Philip Jones, 'The double jeopardy of sales promotions', *Harvard Business Review* (Sept.–Oct. 1990), 145–52.

31. See J. Thomas Russell and Ronald Lane, *Kleppner's Advertising Procedure*, 11th edn (Englewood Cliffs, NJ: Prentice Hall, 1990), 383–6; and 'Power to the key ring and T-shirt', *Sales and Marketing Management* (December 1989), 14.

32. For a more extensive discussion of the legal position of sales promotion methods across EU states and developments towards EU harmonization, consult: *European Promotional Legislation Guide*, 3rd edn (London: Institute of Sales Promotion, 1992); *European Code of Sales Promotion Practice* (London: Institute of Sales Promotion, March 1991); R. Lawson, 'Key problems in Europe: can you implement a pan-European promotion?', Incorporated Society of British Advertisers' Conference on 'Controlling Sales Promotion: Getting it Right is a Joint Responsibility', London, July 1991; J. Lyons, 'German suppliers are jealous of us in the UK', *Promotions and Incentives* (January 1989), 17–20.

33. See Thomas V. Bonoma, 'Get more out of your trade shows', *Harvard Business Review* (Jan.–Feb. 1983), 75–83; Jonathan M. Cox, Ian K. Sequeira and Alissa Eckstein, '1988 trade show trends: shows grow in size; audience quality remains high', *Business Marketing* (June 1989), 57–60; and Richard Szathmary, 'Trade shows', *Sales & Marketing Management* (May 1992), 83–4.

34. For more on sales contests, see C. Robert Patty and Robert Hite, *Managing Sales People*, 3rd edn. (Englewood Cliffs, NJ: Prentice Hall, 1988), 313–27.

35. Robert Janes, 'Earning by experience', *Marketing Week* (2 September 1994), 53; 'Hoover: it sucks', *The Economist* (3 April 1993), 88; 'Hoover fights offer: the facts', *Marketing Week* (21 October 1994), 36.

36. Roger A. Strang, 'Sales promotion, fast growth, faulty management', *Harvard Business Review* (July–Aug. 1976), 119.

37. Adapted from Scott M. Cutlip, Allen H. Center and Glen M. Brown, *Effective Public Reactions*, 6th edn (Englewood Cliffs, NJ: Prentice Hall, 1985), 7–17.

38. Tom Duncan, *A Study of How Manufacturers and Service Companies Perceive and Use Marketing Public Relations* (Muncie, IN: Ball State University, 1985).

## CASE 19

### Diesel Jeans & Workwear: 'We're all different, but aren't we all different in the same way?'[1]   *Malin Nilsson, Anki Sjöström, Anneli Zell and Thomas Helgesson**

During, the oil-crisis in 1978 the idea of a trademark called Diesel came to Renzo Rosso, the son of an Italian farmer. To him Diesel represented something that everybody needs and always will need. He kept this in mind until 1985, when the real Diesel story began. In that year he decided to produce and sell clothes that he himself liked to wear; clothes that represented his lifestyle. His wild and masculine 'Renzo Rosso style' is what Diesel Jeans & Workwear is all about. It is a way of living …

#### Get your blue jeans on

Blue jeans are the most successful clothes ever invented and the world's largest clothing companies

* Halmstad University, Sweden.

depend on them. Why has this 'all American' workwear become the global uniform? Sociologist John Fiske tries to explain. He once asked a class to write down what jeans meant to each of them. He got back a set of staggeringly uniform results. Jeans were American, informal, classless, unisex and appropriate in town or country. Wearing them was a sign of freedom from constraints on behaviour and of class membership. *Free* was the word most commonly used, usually expressing 'freedom to be oneself'. By wearing jeans Fiske's class were expressing their 'freedom to be themselves', yet 118 out of 125 students were 'being themselves' by wearing the same clothes, jeans. With everyone wearing the same clothes, people who are *really free* go one step further to express themselves. Rockers wore greasy ones, mods smart ones, hippies old ones, skinheads new ones, punks damaged ones, indies torn ones and grunge shabby ones – but all wore jeans.

## Fashion bubbles up

Jeans are no longer as uniform, or cheap, as they used to be. The generic jeans, foundation of the Levi Strauss and Wrangler empires, mean classless, country, communal, unisex, work, traditional, unchanging and American. But not so designer jeans. These reached their zenith when Pakistan-born Shami Ahmed exhibited his Manchester-made, diamond-studded, Joe Bloggs jeans costing £150,000* a pair. In contrast to generic jeans, designer jeans mean up-market, city, socially distinctive, (usually) feminine, leisure, contemporary, transient and not American. So transient and non-American are Joe Bloggs jeans that the range changes twelve times a year and West Indian cricketer, Brian Lara, promotes their 375 and 501 range. The ranges are named after Lara's record breaking batting scores although Levi are not happy about the Joe Bloggs 501 name.

Jeans are now not only high fashion but the foundation for many new fashions. Jeans are the uniform of the street culture, and leading designers, such as Versace, Westwood, Gaultier and Lagerfield, concede that there is now a very strong 'bubble up' effect where the streets lead fashion. Top jeans companies 'bubble up' in the same way as street fashions do. Shami Ahmed and Renzo Rosso are typical of the clothing entrepreneurs who are leading the way in Europe's dynamic and varied fashion market, and foremost among these businesses is Rosso's Diesel Jeans & Workwear, a European firm that aims to overtake Levi's and become the world's number-one jeans company.

## Diesel's concept

To work for Rosso, you have to understand the Diesel concept. You have to love Diesel and devote your life to the company. This company spirit imbues

1 ecu = US$1.26 = UK£0.83 = L2,066 (Italian lire).

the whole organization and is presumably the reason for Diesel's success. For example, Diesel is probably the only company where all employees, even the management team, wear Diesel clothes.

Rosso has managed to create a multinational concern out of Diesel. The turnover is approximately L 8,000,000 million* and rising. The profit margin of between 10 and 15 per cent is almost all reinvested in the company. This makes Diesel very strong financially. Today Diesel is number two in Europe after the American jeans-giant Levi's. Their goal is to become number one.

Diesel is today represented in sixty-nine countries worldwide. Of Diesel's 3,000 employees 150 work at their headquarters at Moldava, Italy. Small family-owned companies in Northern Italy carry out about 70 per cent of production, and the rest is spread around low-cost countries like Hong Kong, Thailand and Korea.

The Diesel collection contains jeans, jackets, sweaters, shoes, underwear and belts for both men and women. These account for 60 per cent of Diesel's products. The remainder includes sportswear, kidswear and perfume for men. Diesel's products are sold through hand-picked agents, licensees and subsidiaries. Franchising is not popular as there is a risk of losing control of the company profile. Education and training of the international network is intensive. The resellers have a lot to live up to. They have to understand the Diesel concept and sell clothes that go well with Diesel.

Diesel has only two shops of its own, one in Berlin and the other in Stockholm. New stores in Paris, Rome and New York will open soon. There were strategic reasons for opening the first two flagship stores in Stockholm and Berlin. Germany is Diesel's largest market: 25 per cent of production is sold there. Sweden is seen as receptive to new fashions and useful for test-marketing. Also, Diesel's vice-president and head of international marketing, Johan Lindeberg, is Swedish. Together with local advertising agency Paradiset, he directs all Diesel's marketing activities from his Swedish headquarters.

## Diesel's advertising

Lindeberg and Paradiset claim that much of their marketing success derives from their lack of respect for marketing strategies and their trend-setting advertising. Adverts are sent by courier-post from 'Paradiset' to distributors in other countries who decide the local marketing arrangements themselves. Local distributors spend 5 per cent of their turnover on national marketing, while Diesel spend 7 per cent of their total turnover on internationals such as MTV and Sky Sport.

'Paradiset' has two ideas in mind when creating an advert. The ad should be conspicuous and also contain an ironic message. Diesel's advertising is targeted at modern intelligent people. Diesel often makes fun of current myths, as, for example, in their 'How to ...' campaign. In this campaign, one advert showed the cranium of a girl sucking on a cigarette. The text read, 'How to smoke 145 a day' and 'Man, who needs two lungs anyway'? This message caused much controversy in the United States, where Diesel were criticized for encouraging young people to smoke.

Rosso has his own way of running a company. He follows his own path, ignoring conventional marketing approaches – and it certainly works! Diesel has great growth potential. Rosso believes that, in the long run, a good organization structure is much more important than good advertising. According to Rosso, a strong company is one 'with strong collaborators'. This requires work that employees enjoy, and above all, work that they find interesting. 'When you trust your own and your collaborators' intuitions, feelings and judgements, and not only text-book theories,' says Rosso, 'then you have reached the Diesel feeling.' Since Rosso owns 100 per cent of Diesel he has his hands free to do whatever he wants. To buy other companies or to be listed on the stock exchange is not 'the Renzo Rosso style' and neither would he leave Moldava. The company's vision is expressed in their slogan, you need Diesel 'for successful living'.

Note:   1. The quotation is copy from a 1970s Levi ad.

Sources: John Fiske, *Understanding Popular Culture* (Routledge: London, 1990); Hunter Davies, 'Not any old Joe Bloggs',

## Questions

1. Since jeans are street-led fashions, do jeans companies have to follow, not create, the demand for their products? Are sociologists correct in their perception of the cultural significance of jeans or are they merely inexpensive, practical clothes? How and why have European jeans producers been able to edge into the traditionally American jeans market?

2. How does the advertising for *generic* and *designer* jeans differ? Can one brand and advertising campaign straddle both markets? Explain Joe Bloggs' choice of Lara and the £150,000 jeans as a way of promoting the brand. Are twelve ranges a year really necessary?

3. What explains Rosso's choice of Sweden, rather than Italy, as the base for his international marketing activity? Why choose an agency and location outside the London and New York heartlands of modern global advertising? Can 'the Renzo Rosso style' be separated from the brand identity and the advertising used? Are such organizational issues separate from the marketing of the products? How well does 'the Renzo Rosso style' fit the needs of the jeans market and why?

4. What is the controversial style of Diesel's advertising trying to achieve? Do you think it is effective? Ethical? Appropriate for all markets? How does the centralized nature of Diesel's advertising fit the entrepreneurial style of the company? How can the advertising be linked in with the rest of the marketing mix in the many markets and distributors that Diesel serves?

*Independent* (15 November 1994), 23; and Stephanie Theobald, 'European street style', *The European-élan* (11–17 November, 1994), 13–16.

## CHAPTER TWENTY

# Promoting products

## Personal selling and sales management

## CHAPTER OBJECTIVES

After reading this chapter, you should be able to:

- Discuss the role of a company's salespeople.

- Identify the six main salesforce management steps.

- Explain how companies set salesforce objectives and strategy.

- Explain how companies recruit, select, and train salespeople.

- Describe how companies supervise salespeople and evaluate their effectiveness.

## CHAPTER PREVIEW

### Airbus

1 ecu = US$1.26

Airbus, the Toulouse-based aircraft manufacturer, announces sales of thirty A340-300e aircraft, worth $5.4 billion inclusive of spare parts, to Singapore Airlines. The airline has also placed an order for twenty-two Boeing 747-400 'Megatops' worth $4.9 billion. Deliveries are scheduled for the period 1996–2003. In late June 1994, British Airways was reported to be talking to Airbus about buying a range of jets from the company. Any orders from the 'Boeing-only' British carrier would be a significant boost for Airbus (and for European cooperation in aircraft manufacture).

The European Airbus has about 30 per cent of the world market for large aircraft and has set itself a target to increase this share to 50 per cent over the next decade, according to Jean Pierson, chief executive of Airbus. This target is particularly challenging given the tough competition in the commercial aircraft industry, which is currently dominated by Airbus's rival, Boeing, the US aerospace giant. Boeing is noted for its obsessive dedication to making a sale. In a field where big sales are seldom big news, Boeing held everyone's attention when, on one occasion, it received orders worth $18 billion in little more than a week. Despite difficult times for the aerospace industry in recent years, Boeing has managed to maintain its dominant share leadership. Airbus must learn to compete with and outsell its rival if it is successfully to fulfil its stated sales growth objectives for the decade ahead.

Most of the responsibility for marketing Airbus commercial aircraft falls on the shoulders of the company's salesforce. In some ways, selling airplanes differs from selling other industrial products. Worldwide, there are only about a hundred or so potential customers; there are only three big manufacturers (Boeing, McDonnell-Douglas and Airbus); and the high-tech product is especially complex and challenging. But in many other ways, selling commercial aircraft is like selling any other industrial product. The salespeople determine needs, demonstrate how their product meets these needs, try to close the sale, and then follow up after the sale.

To determine needs, Airbus salespeople become experts on the airlines for which they are responsible, much like stockmarket analysts would. They find out where each airline wants to grow, when it wants to replace planes, and details of its financial situation. They then find ways to fulfil customer needs. They run Airbus and competing planes through computer systems, stimulating the airline's routes, cost per seat and other factors, to show that their planes are better or more efficient. And it is probable that they will bring in financial, planning and technical people to answer any questions.

Then the negotiations begin. Deals are made, discounts agreed and training programmes offered. Sometimes top executives from both the airline and Airbus are brought in to close the deal. The selling process is nerve-wrackingly slow – it can take two or three years from the first sales presentation to the day the sale is announced. After receiving the order, salespeople must stay in almost constant touch with the customer in order to keep track of the account's equipment needs and to make certain the customer remains satisfied. Success depends on building solid, long-term relationships with customers, based on performance and trust. Airbus's salespeople are the vehicle by which information is collected and contacts are made so that the whole process can take place.

The Airbus salesforce consists of experienced salespeople who use a conservative, straightforward sales approach. They are knowledgeable, and trained to sell on facts and logic rather than hype and promises. They must effectively communicate, but not overestimate, product benefits. To secure customer satisfaction and long-term customer retention, Airbus must ensure that, after the sale, their product will live up to expectations.

'Mega' orders for Airbus are a boost to salespeople's morale. The company's sales team have to fight against tough Boeing salespeople who have a head start on the competition. Boeing has a relatively broad mix of excellent products to sell, and Boeing's size and reputation help them get orders. The company's salespeople are proud to be selling Boeing aircraft, and their pride creates an attitude of success that is perhaps best summed up by the company's director of marketing communications. 'The popular saying is that Boeing is the Mercedes of the airline industry. We think that's backward. We like to think that Mercedes is the Boeing of the auto industry'.

Airbus is making headway in this business. The future augers well for the European manufacturer. In fact, Airbus is collaborating with Boeing on a possible development of a super jumbo jet, demand for which is expected to emerge in the next decade – a long time from now. Nonetheless, the long order-to-development-to-delivery time in this business means that companies must think and plan well ahead, and in advance of sales, if they are to win.[1]

Robert Louis Stevenson once noted that 'everyone lives by selling something'. Salesforces are found in nonprofit as well as profit organizations. Churches use membership committees to attract new members. Hospitals and museums use fundraisers to contact donors and raise money.

The people who do the selling go by many names: *salespeople, sales representatives, account executives, sales consultants, sales engineers, field representatives, agents*, *district managers* and *marketing representatives*, to name a few. Selling is one of the oldest professions in the world.

There are many stereotypes of salespeople. 'Salesman' may bring to mind the image of Arthur Miller's pitiable Willy Loman in *Death of a Salesman* or Meredith Willson's cigar-smoking, back-slapping, joke-telling Harold Hill in *The Music Man*. Salespeople typically are portrayed as outgoing and sociable, although many salespeople actually dislike unnecessary socializing. They are blamed for forcing goods on people, although buyers themselves often seek out salespeople.

Actually the term **salesperson** covers a wide range of positions whose differences are often greater than their similarities. Here is one popular classification of sales positions:

- Positions in which the salesperson's job is largely to *deliver* the product, such as milk, bread, fuel or oil.
- Positions in which the salesperson is largely an inside *order taker*, such as the department store salesperson standing behind the counter or an outside order taker, such as the home improvement or insurance salespeople who call on households and persuade them to buy their products.
- Positions in which the salesperson is not expected or permitted to take an order but only *builds goodwill* or *educates buyers* (called 'missionary' selling), as in the case of the 'detailer' for a pharmaceutical company who calls on doctors to educate them about the company's drug products and to urge them to prescribe these products to their patients.
- Positions in which the basic emphasis is on *technical knowledge* – the engineering salesperson who is mostly a consultant to client companies.
- Positions that demand the *creative selling* of tangible products, such as appliances, houses, or industrial equipment, or of intangibles, such as insurance, advertising services, or education.[2]

This list ranges from the least to the most creative types of selling. For example, the jobs at the top of the list call for servicing accounts and taking orders, whereas the others call for simply hunting down buyers and getting them to buy.

In this chapter, we focus on the more creative types of selling and on the process of building and managing an effective salesforce. We define **salesforce management** as the analysis, planning, implementation and control of salesforce activities. It

The term 'salesperson' covers a wide range of jobs, from shop assistant to sales staff involved in consulting with client companies.

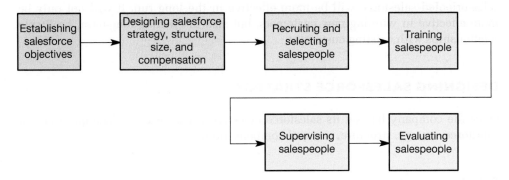

**Figure 20.1**    Primary steps in salesforce management

includes setting salesforce objectives, designing salesforce strategy and recruiting, selecting, training, supervising, and evaluating the firm's salespeople. The primary salesforce management decisions are shown in Figure 20.1. The salesforce serves as the company's personal link with customers. In many cases, the sales representative is the company to many of its customers. Also, sales personnel bring back to the company much-needed intelligence about the customer. Hence, the company must pay particular attention to these decisions.

## SETTING SALESFORCE OBJECTIVES

Companies set different objectives for their salesforces. Salespeople usually perform one or more of the following tasks:

- *Prospecting.* They find and develop new customers.
- *Communicating.* They communicate information about the company's products and services.
- *Selling.* They sell products by approaching customers, presenting their products, answering objections and closing sales.
- *Servicing.* In addition, salespeople provide services to customers (e.g. consulting on problems, providing technical assistance, arranging finance).
- *Information gathering.* Salespeople carry out market research and intelligence work and fill out sales call reports.

Some companies are very specific about their salesforce objectives and activities. One company advises its salespeople to spend 80 per cent of their time with current customers and 20 per cent with prospects and 85 per cent of their time on current products and 15 per cent on new products. This company believes that if such norms are not set, salespeople tend to spend almost of all of their time selling current products to current accounts and neglect new products and new prospects.

In market-led companies, the salesforce needs to be market focused and customer oriented. The old view was that salespeople should worry about sales and the company should worry about profit. However, the contemporary view holds that salespeople should be concerned with more than just producing *sales*. They must also know how to produce *customer satisfaction* and *company profit*. They should know how to look at sales data, measure market potential, gather market intelligence and develop marketing strategies and plans. Salespeople need marketing analysis skills, especially at higher levels of sales management. A market-oriented rather than a sales-oriented salesforce will be more effective in the long run. It will not only be more effective in winning new customers, but also in creating long-term, profitable relationships with existing customers.

## DESIGNING SALESFORCE STRATEGY

Once the company has set its salesforce objectives, it is ready to face questions of salesforce strategy, structure, size and compensation.

### Salesforce strategy

Every company competes with other firms to get orders from customers. Thus it must base its strategy on an understanding of the customer buying process. A company can use one or more of several sales approaches to contact customers. An individual salesperson can talk to a prospect or customer in person or over the phone, make a sales presentation to a buying group. Similarly, a sales *team* (such as a company executive, a salesperson and a sales engineer) can make a sales presentation to a buying group. In *conference selling* a salesperson brings resource people from the company to meet with one or more buyers to discuss problems and opportunities. In *seminar selling,* a company team conducts an educational seminar about state-of-the-art developments for a customer's technical people.

Thus the salesperson often acts as an 'account manager' who arranges contacts between people in the buying and selling companies. Because salespeople need help from others in the company, selling calls for teamwork. Others who might assist salespeople include top management, especially when big sales are at stake; technical people who provide technical information to customers; customer service representatives who provide installation, maintenance and other services to customers; and office staff, such as sales analysts, order processors and secretaries.

Once the company decides on a desirable selling approach, it can use either a direct or a contractual salesforce. A *direct (or company) salesforce* consists of full- or part-time employees who work exclusively for the company. This salesforce includes *inside salespeople*, who conduct business from their offices via telephone or visits from prospective buyers, and *field salespeople*, who travel to call on customers. A *contractual salesforce* consists of manufacturers' reps, sales agents or brokers who are paid a commission based on their sales.

### Salesforce structure

Salesforce strategy influences the structure of the salesforce. The salesforce structure decision is simple if the company sells one product line to one industry with customers in many locations. In that case the company would use a *territorial salesforce structure*. If the company sells many products to many types of customers, it might need either a *product salesforce structure* or *a customer salesforce structure*.

#### Territorial salesforce structure

In the **territorial salesforce structure**, each salesperson is assigned to an exclusive territory in which to sell the company's full line of products or services. This salesforce structure is the simplest sales organization and has many advantages. First, it clearly defines the salesperson's job, and because only one salesperson works the territory, he or she gets all the credit or the blame for territory sales. Second, the territorial structure increases the salesperson's desire to build local business ties that, in turn, improve the salesperson's selling effectiveness. Finally, because each salesperson travels within a small geographic area, travel expenses are relatively small.

## Product salesforce structure

Salespeople must know their products. The task is not easy if the company's products are numerous, unrelated and technically complex. To overcome this problem, many companies adopt a **product salesforce structure**, in which the salesforce sells along product lines. For example, Kodak uses different salesforces for its film products than for its industrial products. The film products salesforce deals with simple products that are distributed intensively, whereas the industrial products salesforce deals with complex products that require technical understanding.

The product structure can lead to problems, however, if a given customer buys many of the company's products. For example, a hospital supply company has several product divisions, each with a separate salesforce. Several salespeople might end up calling on the same hospital on the same day. This means that they travel over the same routes and wait to see the same customer's purchasing agents. These extra costs must be weighed against the benefits of better product knowledge and attention to individual products.

## Customer salesforce structure

Companies might use a **customer salesforce structure**, whereby they organize the salesforce along customer or industry lines. Separate salesforces may be set up for different industries, for serving current customers versus finding new ones, and for large accounts versus regular accounts. For example, a company selling photocopiers could divide its customers into four main groups, each served by a different salesforce. The top group consists of large national accounts with multiple and scattered locations, which would be handled by *national account managers*. Next are large accounts that, although not national in scope, may have several locations within a region and are handled by *senior account managers*. Customers with lower annual sales potential could be served by *account representatives* and all other customers could be handled by *marketing representatives*.

Organizing its salesforce around customers can help a company to become more customer focused. For example, giant ABB, the Swiss-based industrial equipment maker, recently changed from a product-based to a customer-based salesforce. The new structure resulted in a stronger customer orientation and improved service to clients:

> Until four months ago, David Donaldson sold boilers for ABB....After 30 years, Donaldson sure knew boilers, but he didn't know much about the broad range of other products offered by ABB's US Power Plant division. Customers were frustrated because as many as a dozen ABB salespeople called on them at different times to peddle their products. Sometimes representatives even passed each other in customers' lobbies without realizing that they were working for the same company. ABB's bosses decided that this was a poor way to run a salesforce. So, David Donaldson and 27 other power plant salespeople began new jobs. [Donaldson] now also sells turbines, generators, and three other product lines. He handles six major accounts...instead of a [mixed batch] of 35. His charge: Know the customer intimately and sell him the products that help him operate productively. Says Donaldson: 'My job is to make it easy for my customer to do business with us...I show him where to go in

ABB whenever he has a problem.' The president of ABB's power plant businesses [adds]: 'If you want to be a customer-driven company, you have to design the sales organization around individual buyers rather than around your products.'[3]

### Complex salesforce structures

When a company sells a wide variety of products to many types of customers over a broad geographical area, it often combines several types of salesforce structures. Salespeople can be specialized by territory and product, by territory and market, by product and market, or by territory, product and market. A salesperson might then report to one or more line and staff managers.

### Salesforce size

Once the company has set its strategy and structure, it is ready to consider *salesforce size*. Salespeople constitute one of the company's most productive, and most expensive, assets. Therefore, increasing their number will increase both sales and costs.

Many companies set salesforce size based on an evaluation of workload. Under this **workload approach**, a company groups accounts according to size and then determines the number of salespeople needed to call on them the desired number of times. The logic is as follows: Suppose we have 1,000 Type-A accounts and 2,000 Type-B accounts. Type-A accounts require 36 calls a year and Type-B accounts require 12 calls a year. In this case, the salesforce's *workload*, as defined by the number of calls it must make per year, is 60,000 calls [(1,000 × 36) + (2,000 × 12) = 36,000 + 24,000 = 60,000)]. Suppose our average salesperson can make 1,000 calls a year. The company thus needs 60 salespeople (60,000/1,000).

### Salesforce compensation

To attract salespeople, a company must have an attractive compensation plan. These plans vary greatly both by industry and by companies within the same industry. The level of compensation must be close to the 'going rate' for the type of sales job and needed skills. This varies from country to country. To pay less than the going rate would attract too few quality salespeople; to pay more would be unnecessary.

Compensation is made up of several elements – a fixed amount, a variable amount, expenses and fringe benefits. The fixed amount, usually a salary, gives the salesperson some stable income. The variable amount, which might be commissions or bonuses based on sales perfomance, rewards the salesperson for greater effort. Expense allowances, which repay salespeople for job-related expenses, let salespeople undertake needed and desirable selling efforts. Fringe benefits, such as paid vacations, sickness or accident benefits, pensions and life insurance, provide job security and satisfaction. Management must select the combination of compensation elements that makes the most sense for each sales job. There are four basic types of compensation plans based on whether these elements are fixed or variable: straight salary, straight commission, salary plus bonus and salary plus commission. The advantages and disadvantages are summarized in Table 20.1.

| TABLE 20.1 | *Advantages and disadvantages of sales compensation plans* | |
|---|---|---|
| Sales compensation plan | Advantages | Disadvantages |
| *Straight salary*<br>This pays a fixed salary and expenses. | Easy to explain and administer; can alter sales duties without strong objection; simplifies task of projecting sales payroll; a stable income helps to secure higher salesforce morale | Does not induce the sales rep to do a better than average job; does not discriminate between salespeople's ability; fails to attract or hold the more aggressive sales representatives |
| *Straight commission*<br>This pays some fixed or sliding rate related to sales or profits | Stimulates sales reps to work at maximum capacity; ties selling expenses to current revenue; different commissions can be set for different products and sales tasks, thus influencing how the salespeople spend their time. | Salespersons may resist doing tasks that do not generate immediate income; it encourages high-pressure tactics or price discounting; it is costly to administer; it provides little income security; it lowers morale if sales decline through no fault of the salesperson. |
| *Salary plus bonus*<br>This gives a fixed salary and payments for extra efforts and results | Advantages for fixed salary as indicated above; also stimulates salespeople to perform desirable tasks which are not normally rewardable through commissions (e.g. generating useful selling ideas, speed in furnishing reports). | Given that managerial judgement is involved in determining the bonus, salespersons whose expectations are not met could raise questions about fairness. |
| *Salary plus commission* | The sales plan combines the advantages of each approach; also the firm does not have to absorb inflexible selling costs during sales downswings, and salespeople do not lose all their income. | Disadvantages of straight salary and commission-only plans apply, although somewhat minimized. |

## RECRUITING AND SELECTING SALESPEOPLE

Having set the salesforce strategy, structure, size and compensation, the company now must set up systems for *recruiting and selecting, training, supervising,* and *evaluating salespeople.*

### Importance of careful selection

At the heart of any successful salesforce operation is the selection of good salespeople. There can be a big difference in the performance levels of an average and a top salesperson. In a typical salesforce, the top 30 per cent of the salespeople might bring 60 per cent of the sales. Thus careful salesperson selection can greatly increase overall salesforce performance.

Beyond the differences in sales performance, poor selection results in costly turnover. When a salesperson quits, the costs of finding and training a new salesperson, plus the costs of lost sales, could be considerable. Also, a salesforce with many new people is less productive than one with a stable membership.

## What makes a good salesperson?

Selecting salespeople would not be a problem if the company knew what traits to look for. If it knew that good salespeople were outgoing, aggressive and energetic, for example, it could simply check applicants for these characteristics. Many successful salespeople, however, are also bashful, mild-mannered and very relaxed. Successful salespeople include some individuals who are tall and others who are short, some who speak well and some poorly, some who dress well and some shabbily.

Still, the search continues for the magic list of traits that spells sure-fire sales ability. One survey suggests that good salespeople have a lot of enthusiasm, persistence, initiative, self-confidence and job commitment. They are committed to sales as a way of life and have a strong customer orientation. Another study suggests that good salespeople are independent and self-motivated and are excellent listeners. Still another study advises that salespeople should be a friend to the customer as well as persistent, enthusiastic, attentive, and above all, honest.[4] Charles Garfield found that good salespeople are goal-directed risk takers who identify strongly with their customers.

How can a company find out what traits salespeople in its industry should have? A good start is to look at the job *duties* involved, which would suggest some of the traits a company should look for. For instance, is a lot of paperwork required? Does the job call for much travel? Will the salesperson face a lot of rejections? The successful sales candidate should possess qualities ideally suited to these duties. The company should also look at the characteristics of its most successful salespeople for clues to needed traits.

## Recruiting procedures and selection

Having determined its selection criteria, management proceeds to *recruit* the desired candidate. The human resources department looks for applicants by getting names from current salespeople, using employment agencies and placing classified ads.

Recruiting will attract many applicants, from which the company must select the best. The selection procedure can vary from a single informal interview to lengthy testing and interviewing. Many companies give formal tests to sales applicants. Tests typically measure sales aptitude, analytical and organizational skills, personality traits and other characteristics.[5] Companies do take test results seriously. Gillette, for example, claims that tests have reduced turnover by 42 per cent and that test scores have correlated well with the later performance of new salespeople. But test scores provide only one piece of information in a set that includes personal characteristics, references, past employment history, and interviewer reactions.

## TRAINING SALESPEOPLE

Many companies used to send their new salespeople into the field almost immediately after hiring them. They would be given samples, order books and general instructions. Training programmes were luxuries. To many companies, a training programme translated into much expense for instructors, materials, space and salary for a person who was not yet selling, and a loss of sales opportunities because the person was not in the field.

Today's new salespeople, however, may spend anywhere from a few weeks to many months in training. The average training period is four months. IBM spends $1 billion

Companies spend hundreds of millions of dollars to train their salespeople in the art of selling.

a year educating its workforce and customers. Initial sales training lasts thirteen months, and new salespeople typically are not on their own for two years! IBM also expects its salespeople to spend 15 per cent of their time each year in additional training.[6]

Training programmes have several goals. Salespeople need to know and identify with the company, so most companies spend the first part of the training programme describing the company's history and objectives, its organizations, its financial structure and facilities, and its chief products and markets. Because salespeople also need to know the company's products, sales trainees are shown how products are produced and how they work. Salespeople also need to know customers' and competitors' characteristics, so the training programme teaches them about competitors' strategies and about different types of customers and their needs, buying motives and buying habits. Learning how to make effective presentations is another important component in the firm's sales training programmes. Training courses should therefore cover the principles of selling and outline the chief sales argument for each product. Finally, salespeople need to understand field procedures and responsibilities. They learn how to divide time between active and potential accounts and how to use an expense account, prepare reports and route communications effectively.

## SUPERVISING SALESPEOPLE

New salespeople need more than a territory, compensation and training – they need *supervision*. Through supervision, the company *directs* and *motivates* the salesforce to do a better job.

### Directing salespeople

To what extent should sales management be involved in helping salespeople manage their territories? It depends on everything from the company's size to the experience of its salesforce. Consequently, companies vary widely in how closely they supervise their salespeople. Furthermore, what works for one company may not work for another.[7]

#### Developing customer targets and call norms

Most companies classify customers based on sales volume, profit and growth potential, and set call norms accordingly. Thus salespeople may call weekly on accounts with large sales or potential but only infrequently on small accounts. Beyond account size and potential, call norms may also depend on other factors such as competitive call activity and account development status.

Companies often specify how much time their salesforce should spend prospecting for new accounts. For example, a company may want its salespeople to spend 25 per cent of their time prospecting and to stop calling on a prospect after three unsuccessful calls. Companies set up prospecting standards for several reasons. If left alone, many salespeople will spend most of their time with current customers, who are better-known quantities. Moreover, whereas a prospect may never deliver any business, salespeople can depend on current accounts for some business. Therefore, unless salespeople are rewarded for opening new accounts, they may avoid new-account development. Some companies even may rely on a special salesforce to open new accounts.

### Using sales time efficiently

Salespeople need to know how to use their time efficiently. One tool is the *annual call schedule* that shows which customers and prospects to call on in which months

---

**MARKETING HIGHLIGHT 20.1**

## So you want to be a professional salesperson?

Salespeople are often said to be unloved, foot-in-the-door creatures, whose superiors motivate them mainly in the form of alternate bouts of public humiliation and recognition. It is not surprising that many people commonly regard selling as a very low form of life. The frequent portrayal of salespeople as sweet-talking, hard-selling pedlars does not boost their self-perception either. Rather it only fuels the already uncertain public perception of a stereotypical salesrep. This is, of course, an unfair representation of company staff who are under constant pressure to create and keep a customer. Furthermore salespeople are expected to perform many other tasks, most of which are arguably related to creating and maintaining sales for the company.

What do salespeople in fact do with their time? Given the many tasks they are expected to perform, how many are truly professional in what they do? Do salespeople use their time well?

A recent international survey was carried out by Kinnaird Communications Group, a Glasgow-based consultancy, which covered about 1,000 salesmen and women operating in the United Kingdom, France, Italy and Germany. The investigation was based on looking at sales records, and, talking to chief executives, supervisors and customers. The consultancy's

findings were also supplemented by observations over many years among clients' salesforces.

The Kinnaird study reported that only 5 per cent of field sales staff surveyed 'possess the natural selling skills that make them stand out as a professionals'. The survey claimed that 35 per cent of salespeople 'just manage to pay their way', while 'an astounding 60 per cent (are) just there for the beer'. The study claimed that many of the salesreps 'drifted into the profession, attracted by the freedom, car and expense account'.

In terms of how salespeople spend their time, Kinnaird found that out of the average salesperson's day, 42 per cent of the time is spent in the car, while 26 per cent is spent at home, planning, having lunch, telephoning, writing reports and parking the car (see Table 1). Less than one-third of the time is spent on customers' premises, and all of that time – except for about 6 per cent – is spent on fruitless 'cold' calls, waiting in reception, interruptions and, in the case of the poorest salespeople, inadequate forward planning and an excess of 'small talk'. Although 20 per cent of time is spent in face-to-face contact (including 'small talk': 7.5 per cent; customer interruptions, phone, colleagues, and so forth: 7.5 per cent; and actual selling negotiation: 5 per cent), the survey found that much of this invaluable activity was spent talking

and which activities to carry out. Activities include taking part in trade shows, attending sales meetings, and carrying out marketing research. Another tool is *time-and-duty analysis.* In addition to time spent selling, the salesperson spends time travelling, waiting, eating, taking breaks and doing administrative chores (see Marketing Highlight 20.1). Because of the tiny portion of the day most sales staff actually spend selling or negotiating and talking face-to-face with potential customers, companies must look for ways to save time. This can be done by getting salespeople to use phones instead of travelling, simplifying record-keeping forms, finding better call and routing plans, and supplying more and better customer information.

Advances in information and computer technology, such as laptop computers, telecommunications, personal selling software, videodisc players, automatic dialers and others, have encouraged many firms to adopt *salesforce automation systems*, computerized sales operations for more efficient order-entry transactions, improved customer service, and better salesperson decision-making support. Many salesforces have truly gone 'electronic'. A recent study of 100 large companies found that 48 per cent are 'actively pursuing' salesforce automation; another 34 per cent are planning or considering it.[8] Salespeople use computers to profile customers and prospects, analyse and forecast sales, manage accounts, schedule sales calls, enter orders, check

Table 1: A day in the life of a typical salesperson

| Activity | % of total time |
| --- | --- |
| Selling or negotiation | 5.0 |
| Home-planning | 5.0 |
| 'Cold canvass' calls – leaving card, no interview | 6.0 |
| Waiting in reception | 6.0 |
| 'Small talk' | 7.5 |
| Customer interruptions, phone, colleagues, and so forth | 7.5 |
| Walking, parking, taking notes telephoning, and so on | 8.0 |
| Lunch | 13.0 |
| Car travel | 42.0 |

Note: * Based on a nine-hour day.
Source: Kinnaird 1994.

to individuals with no influence on the purchasing decision.

Kinnaird argues that what sets the upper 5 per cent sales élite apart from the rest is charisma in a sales situation. Arguably, charisma is elusive. However, there are other prime qualities to be found in a successful salesperson: a sense of humour; good planning and preparation skills; the ability to take initiatives (nearly all of the time, salesreps are on their own); a belief in their company and their products or services (if they don't, why should their customers?); a trust in their colleagues (that is, those in marketing, accounting, and distribution); and a belief in themselves. Other observers add to that list physical energy, tenacity and resilience in the face of rejection.

There are always going to be 'natural' salespeople, but for the rest, training is absolutely essential if their sales professionalism is to be developed. High-quality training in selling skills can overcome some of the deficiencies in personal skills. Another area that must be emphasized continually is management's commitment to providing marketing and advertising support for the salesforce. Yes, salespeople are frontline troops. They constitute a valuable bridge between the business and its customers, they act as information and intelligence satellites, and they can make or break the sale. Where selling is a key activity, businesses must learn to utilize this valuable marketing tool, the salesperson. The unloved ranks of salespeople must be loved again.

Source: Adapted from Diane Summers, 'Unloved and incompetent', *Financial Times* (25 August, 1994), 9.

inventories and order status, prepare sales and expense reports, process correspondence and carry out many other activities. Salesforce automation not only lowers salesforce calls and improves productivity, it also improves the quality of sales management decisions. Here are some examples of companies that have introduced computer and other sophisticated technologies successfully into their salesforce operations:

Shell Chemical Company developed a laptop computer package consisting of several applications. Although many salespeople initially resisted the computer – they couldn't type, or they didn't have time to learn the software, or whatever – some applications had great appeal. Salespeople responded first to the *automatic expense statement* programme, which made it easier for them to record expenses and get reimbursed quickly. Soon, they discovered the *sales inquiry function*, which gave them immediate access to the latest account information, including phone numbers, addresses, recent developments and prices. They no longer had to wait for the clerical staff to give them out-of-date information. Before long, salespeople were using the entire package. *Electronic mail* allowed them quickly to receive and send messages to others. Various *corporate forms*, such as territory work plans and sales call reports, could be filled out faster and sent electronically. Other useful applications included an *appointment calendar*, a '*to-do list*' *function*, a *spreadsheet programme*, and a *graphics package* that helped salespeople prepare charts and graphs for customer presentations. Today, even salespeople who initially resisted the computer package wonder how they ever got along without it.[9]

Construction machinery firm JCB has an internal database which covers over 35,000 records and details of all its franchised dealers and their salesforces. The database system provides each salesperson with a contact plan and diary, as well as giving JCB a direct mail facility, with every link in the distribution chain enjoying detailed management reporting through diary updates.[10]

Computers have also changed the way commercial insurance company, Sun Alliance International (SAI) uses information to support sales staff and to forge long-term relationships with customers and intermediaries. SAI deploys a PC-based sales system called ADAM – Agency Development and Management – among its 170-strong salesforce, including 26 home workers known as 'On the road sales staff' (OTRs). Much of SAI's business comes from overseas customers. Over 80 per cent of its business is generated by a network of agents, supported by a salesforce of 140 across the UK. Their job is to build relationships with brokers and other intermediaries (some 4000 agencies). According to Peter Burrows, sales and marketing manager at SAI, paper-based systems were sketchy: salespeople's natural instinct is not to complete records, frequently the paperwork is incomplete or their reports do not tell the whole story. ADAM is a sales system developed from the view of field-based sales staff who need to share data with office-based colleagues. Customer information is accessible by anyone – all view the same record which is synchronised in an overnight update. Burrows argue that 'the beauty of a distributed database is that you can share the information across a wide range of people. Gone are the days of relying on a dusty set of papers in someone's car 100 miles away'. Steve Ginn, an SAI sales development manager, stresses that 'One of the fundamentals of selling is an understanding of customers' needs. Once we know the customer sectors, we can work more closely in partnership with brokers and the customer sees a far more professional approach.' He has been using his Toshiba T1900 laptop for only seven months (he knew nothing about computers and never owned one before) but the benefits are already dawning on him. His menu shows a task organiser, in-tray, electronic mail and standard user reports and inquiries. The system would enable him to analyse work on current sales campaigns and see instantly how long it is since he contacted clients. He can also append notes to the agency records for his account 'caretakers'. The PC-based system offers a far more structured way to analyse and summarise information, something paper-based card systems could not do. The system facilitates home workers and results are promising. One salesperson whose performance once gave concern has become an OTR and an enthusiastic and highly effective ADAM user. According to Burrows, 'you have got to open people's eyes to what the technology can do for them', but 'you can't do it overnight'. The company trained total novices on the keyboard, and worked to put at rest the fears of those expelled from the cosy support of their office. For SAI, Burrows adds: 'the vast majority of staff, now they have seen it in action, see myriad advantages. ADAM converts task response into *customer care*, and that is what the technology can help us do.'[11]

To reduce time demands on their *outside salesforces*, many companies have increased the size of their *inside salesforces*. Inside salespeople included technical support people, sales assistants and telemarketers. *Technical support people* provide technical information and answers to customers' questions. *Sales assistants* provide clerical backup for outside salespeople. They call ahead and confirm appointments, conduct credit checks, follow up on deliveries and answer customers' questions when outside salespeople cannot be reached. *Telemarketers* use the phone to find new leads, qualify prospects, and sell to and service them.

The inside salesforce frees outside salespeople to spend more time selling to large accounts and finding good new prospects. Depending on the complexity of the product and customer, a telemarketer can make from twenty to thirty-three decision-maker contacts a day, compared to the average of four that an outside salesperson can see. And for many types of products and selling situations, telemarketing can be as effective as a personal call but at a much lower cost.

## Motivating salespeople

Some salespeople will do their best without any special urging from management. To them, selling may be the most fascinating job in the world. But selling can also be frustrating. Salespeople usually work alone, and they must sometimes travel away from home. They may face aggressive, competing salespeople and difficult customers. They sometimes lack the authority to do what is needed to win a sale and may thus lose large orders they have worked hard to obtain. Therefore, salespeople often need special encouragement to do their best. Management can boost salesforce morale and performance through its organizational climate, sales quota and positive incentives.

### Organizational climate

Organizational climate describes the feeling that salespeople have about their opportunities, value and rewards for a good performance within the company. Some companies treat salespeople as if they are not very important. Other companies treat their salespeople as their prime movers and allow virtually unlimited opportunity for income and promotion. Not surprisingly, a company's attitude toward its salespeople affects their behaviour. If they are held in low esteem, there is high turnover and poor performance. If they are held in high esteem, there is less turnover and higher performance.

Treatment from the salesperson's immediate superior is especially important. A good sales manager keeps close to their salesforce. They are in touch with salespeople through letters and phone calls, visits in the field and evaluation sessions in the home office. At different times, the sales manager acts as the salesperson's boss, companion, coach and confessor. Most importantly, sales management must be able to convince salespeople that they can sell more by working harder, by being trained to work smarter, and that the rewards – be they financial in nature or higher-order rewards for better performance, such as liking, peer recognition and respect and a sense of accomplishment – are worth the extra effort.

Many companies
award trips as
incentives for
outstanding sales
performance.

### Sales quotas

Many companies set **sales quotas** for their salespeople. Sales quotas are standards stating the amount they should sell and how sales should be divided among the company's products. Compensation is often related to how well salespeople meet their quotas.

Sales quotas are set at the time the annual marketing plan is developed. The company first decides on a sales forecast that is reasonably achievable. Based on this forecast, management plans production, workforce size and financial needs. It then sets sales quotas for its regions and territories. Generally, sales quotas are set higher than the sales forecast to encourage sales managers and salespeople to give their best effort. If they fail to make their quotas, the company may still make its sales forecast.

### Positive incentives

Companies also use several incentives to increase salesforce effort. *Sales meetings* provide social occasions, breaks from routine, chances to meet and talk with 'company brass', and opportunities to air feelings and to identify with a larger group. Companies also sponsor *sales contests* to spur the salesforce to make a selling effort above what would normally be expected. Other incentives include honours, merchandise and cash awards, trips, and profit-sharing plans.

## EVALUATING SALESPEOPLE

So far we have described how management communicates what salespeople should be doing and motivates them to do it. This process requires good feedback, which means getting regular information from salespeople to evaluate their performance.

## Sources of information

Management gets information about its salespeople in several ways. The most important source is the *sales report*. Additional information comes from personal observation, customers' letters and complaints, customer surveys and talks with other salespeople.

Sales reports are divided into plans for future activities and write-ups of completed activities. The best example of the first is the *work plan* that salespeople submit a week or month in advance. The plan describes intended calls and routing. From this report, the salesforce plans and schedules activities. It also informs management of the salespeople's whereabouts and provides a basis for comparing plans and performance. Salespeople can then be evaluated on their ability to 'plan their work and work their plan'. Sometimes, managers contact individual salespeople to suggest improvements in work plans.

Companies also require their salespeople to draft *annual territory marketing plans* in which they outline their plans for building new accounts and increasing sales from existing accounts. Formats vary greatly, in the sense that some ask for general ideas on territory development, while others ask for detailed sales and profit estimates. Sales managers study these territory plans, make suggestions and use the plans to develop sales quotas.

Salespeople write up their completed activities on *call reports*. Call reports keep sales managers informed of the salesperson's activities, show what is happening with each customer's account and provide information that might be useful in later calls. Salespeople also turn in *expense reports* for which they are partly or wholly repaid. Some companies also ask for reports on new business, lost business and local business and economic conditions.

These reports supply the raw data from which sales management can evaluate salesforce performance. For example, are salespeople making too few calls per day? Are they spending too much time per call? Are they spending too much money on entertainment? Are they closing enough orders per hundred calls? Are they finding enough new customers and holding on to enough old customers?

## Formal evaluation of performance

Using salesforce reports and other information, sales management formally evaluates members of the salesforce. Formal evaluation produces four benefits. First, management must develop and communicate clear standards for judging performance. Second, management must gather well-rounded information about each salesperson. Third, salespeople receive constructive feedback that helps them to improve future performance. Finally, salespeople are motivated to perform because they know that they will have to sit down one morning with the sales manager and explain their performance.

### Comparing salespeople's performance

One type of evaluation compares and ranks the sales performance of different salespeople. Such comparisons can be misleading, however. Salespeople may perform differently because of differences in territory potential, workload, level of competition, company promotion effort and other factors. Furthermore sales are not usually the best indicator of achievement. Management should be more interested in how much each salesperson contributes to net profits, a factor that requires analysis of each salesperson's sales mix and expenses.

### Comparing current sales with past sales

A second type of evaluation is to compare a salesperson's current performance with past performance. Such a comparison should directly indicate the person's progress. Table 20.2 provides an example.

The sales manager can learn many things about Chris Bennett from this table. Bennett's total sales increased every year (line 3). This does not necessarily mean that Bennett is doing a better job. The product breakdown shows that Bennett has been able to push the sales of product B further than those of product A (lines 1 and 2). According to the quotas for the two products (lines 4 and 5), the success in increasing product B sales may be at the expense of product A sales. According to gross profits (lines 6 and 7), the company earns twice as much gross profit (as a ratio to sales) on A as it does on B. Bennett may be pushing the higher-volume, lower-margin product at the expense of the more profitable product. Although Bennett increased total sales by £1,100 between 1993 and 1995 (line 3), the gross profits on these total sales actually decreased by £580 (line 8).

1 ecu = UK£0.83

Sales expense (line 9) shows a steady increase, although total expense as a percentage of total sales seems to be under control (line 10). The upward trend in Bennett's total expenses, in money terms, does not seem to be explained by any increase in the number of calls (line 11), although it may be related to his success in acquiring new customers (line 14). However, there is a possibility that in prospecting for new customers, Bennett is neglecting present customers, as indicated by an upward trend in the annual number of lost customers (line 15).

The last two lines on the table show the level and trend in Bennett's sales and gross profits per customer. These figures become more meaningful when they are compared with overall company averages. If Chris Bennett's average gross profit per customer is lower than the company's averages, Chris may be concentrating on the

**TABLE 20.2**     *Evaluating salespeople's performance*

| Territory: Midland | Salesperson: Chris Bennett 1992 | 1993 | 1994 | 1995 |
|---|---|---|---|---|
| 1. Net Sales product A (£) | £251,300 | £253,200 | £270,000 | £263,100 |
| 2. Net sales product B (£) | £423,200 | £439,200 | £553,900 | £561,900 |
| 3. Net sales total (£) | £674,500 | £692,400 | £823,900 | £825,000 |
| 4. Per cent of quota product A | 95.6 | 92.0 | 88.0 | 84.7 |
| 5. Per cent of quota product B | 120.4 | 122.3 | 134.9 | 130.8 |
| 6. Gross profits product A (£) | £50,260 | £50,640 | £54,000 | £52,620 |
| 7. Gross profits product B (£) | £42,320 | £43,920 | £53,390 | £56,190 |
| 8. Gross profits total (£) | £92,580 | £94,560 | £109,390 | £108,810 |
| 9. Sales expense (£) | £10,200 | £11,100 | £11,600 | £13,200 |
| 10. Sales expense to total sales (%) | 1.5 | 1.6 | 1.4 | 1.6 |
| 11. Number of calls | 1,675 | 1,700 | 1,680 | 1,660 |
| 12. Cost per call (£) | £6.09 | £6.53 | £6.90 | £7.95 |
| 13. Average number of customers | 320 | 324 | 328 | 334 |
| 14. Number of new customers | 13 | 14 | 15 | 20 |
| 15. Number of lost customers | 8 | 10 | 11 | 14 |
| 16. Average sales per customer (£) | £2,108 | £2,137 | £2,512 | £2,470 |
| 17. Average gross profit per customer (£) | £289 | £292 | £334 | £326 |

wrong customers or may not be spending enough time with each customer. Looking back at the annual number of calls (line 11), Bennett may be making fewer calls than the average salesperson. If distances in the territory are not much different, this may mean he is not putting in a full workday, he is poor at planning his routing or minimizing his waiting time, or he spend too much time with certain accounts.

### Qualitative evaluation of salespeople

A *qualitative evaluation* usually looks at a salesperson's knowledge of the company, products, customers, competitors, territory and tasks. Personal traits like manner, appearance, speech and temperament can be rated. The sales manager can also review any problems in motivation or compliance. Each company must decide what would be most useful to know. It should communicate these criteria to salespeople so that they understand how their performance is evaluated and can make an effort to improve it.

## PRINCIPLES OF PERSONAL SELLING

We now turn from designing and managing a salesforce to the actual personal selling process. Personal selling is an ancient art that has spawned a large literature and many principles. Effective salespeople operate on more than just instinct – they are highly trained in methods of territory analysis and customer management.

## The personal selling process

Companies spend a huge amount of money on seminars, books, cassettes and other materials to teach salespeople the 'art' of selling. Millions of books on selling are purchased every year, with tantalizing titles such as *How to Sell Anything to Anybody, How I Raised Myself from Failure to Success in Selling, The Four-Minute Sell, The Best Seller, The Power of Enthusiastic Selling, Where Do You Go from No. 1?*, and *Winning Through Intimidation*. One of the most enduring books on selling is Dale Carnegie's *How to Win Friends and Influence People*, which is marketed all over the world.

All of the training approaches try to convert a salesperson from a passive *order taker* to an active *order getter*. Order takers assume that customers know their own needs, that they would resent any attempt at influence, and that they prefer salespeople who are polite and reserved. An example of an order taker is a salesperson who calls on a dozen customers each day, simply asking if the customer needs anything.

There are two approaches to training salespeople to be *order getters* – a sales-oriented approach and a customer-oriented approach. The *sales-oriented approach* trains the salesperson in high-pressure selling techniques, such as those used in selling encyclopaedias or insurance policies. This form of selling assumes that the customers will not buy except under pressure, that they are influenced by a slick presentation and that they will not be sorry after signing the order (and that, even if they are, it no longer matters).

The *customer-oriented approach*, the one most often used in today's professional selling, trains salespeople in customer problem solving. The salesperson learns how to identify customer needs and to find solutions. This approach assumes that customer needs provide sales opportunities, that customers appreciate good suggestions and that customers will be loyal to salespeople who have their long-term interests at heart. One recent survey found that purchasing agents appreciate salespeople who understand their needs and meet them. As one purchasing agent states:

> My *expectation* of salespeople is that they've done their homework, uncovered some of our needs, probed to uncover other needs and presented convincing arguments of mutual benefits for both organisations...[The problem is that] I don't always see that.[12]

The qualities that purchasing agents *disliked most* in salespeople included being pushy, late and unprepared or disorganized. The qualities they *valued most* included honesty, dependability, thoroughness and follow-through. The problem-solver salesperson fits better with the marketing concept than does the hard seller or order taker.

## Steps in the selling process

Most training programmes view the **selling process** as consisting of several steps that the salesperson must master (see Figure 20.2)

### Prospecting and qualifying

The first step in the selling process is **prospecting** – identifying qualified potential customers. The salesperson must approach many prospects to get just a few sales. Although the company supplies some leads, salespeople need skill in finding their own. They can ask current customers for the names of prospects. They can build referral sources, such as suppliers, dealers, noncompeting salespeople and bankers. They can join organizations to which prospects belong or can engage in speaking and writing activities that will draw attention. They can search for names in newsletters or directories and use the telephone and mail to track down leads. Or they can drop in unannounced on various offices (a practice known as 'cold calling'). Cold calling, however, may not always be appropriate, as in the case of German or Japanese organizations, where third-party introduction is the norm.

Salespeople need to know how to *qualify* leads: that is, how to identify the good ones and screen out the poor ones. Prospects can be qualified by looking at their financial ability, volume of business, special needs, location and possibilities for sales growth.

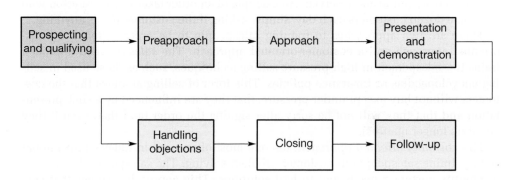

**Figure 20.2**  Primary steps in effective selling.

## Preapproach

Before calling on a prospect, the salesperson should learn as much as possible about the organization (what it needs, who is involved in the buying) and its buyers (their characteristics and buying styles). This step is known as the **preapproach**. The salesperson can consult standard business directories or information sources (e.g. *Moody's, Standard & Poor's, Dun & Bradstreet*), acquaintances and others to learn about the company. The salesperson should set *call objectives*, which may be to qualify the prospect, to gather information, or to make an immediate sale. Another task is to decide on the best approach, which might be a personal visit, a phone call or a letter. The best timing should be considered carefully because many prospects are busiest at certain times. Finally, the salesperson should give thought to an overall sales strategy for the account.

## Approach

During the **approach** step, the salesperson should know how to meet and greet the buyer, and get the relationship off to a good start. The salesperson's appearance, his or her opening lines and the follow-up remarks have a great deal of impact on relationship building at this early phase of the sales process. The opening lines should be positive: 'Mr Johnson, I am Chris Henderson from the Alltech Company. My company and I appreciate your willingness to see me. I will do my best to make this visit profitable and worthwhile for you and your company'. This opening might be followed by some key questions to learn more about the customer's needs, or the showing of a display or sample to attract the buyer's attention and curiosity.

## Presentation and demonstration

The **presentation** is that step in the selling process where the salesperson tells the product 'story' to the buyer, showing how the product will make or save money. The salesperson describes the product features but concentrates on presenting *customer benefits*.

Companies may use three styles of sales presentation: the canned approach; the formula approach; or the need-satisfaction approach. The *canned approach* is the

In the sales presentation, the salesperson tells the product story to the buyers.

Photograph: Mary Ann Page

oldest type and consists of a memorized or scripted talk covering the seller's main points. This approach has limited usefulness in industrial selling, but scripted presentations can be effective in some telephone-selling situations. A properly prepared and rehearsed script should sound natural and move the salesperson smoothly through the presentation. With electronic scripting, computers can lead the salesperson through a sequence of selling messages tailored on the spot to the prospect's responses.

Using the *formula approach*, the salesperson first identifies the buyer's needs, attitudes and buying style. The salesperson then moves into a formula presentation that shows how the product will satisfy that buyer's needs. Although not canned, the presentation follows a general plan.

The *need-satisfaction approach* starts with a search for the customer's needs by getting the customer to do most of the talking. This approach calls for good listening and problem-solving skills. One marketing director describes the approach this way:

> [High-performing salespeople] make it a point to understand customer needs and goals before they pull anything out of their product bag. ...Such salespeople spend the time needed to get an in-depth knowledge of the customer's business, asking questions that will lead to solutions our systems can address.[13]

Any style of sales presentation can be improved with demonstration aids, such as booklets, flip charts, slides, videotapes or videodiscs and product samples. If buyers can see or handle the product, they will better remember its features and benefits.

### Handling objections

Customers almost always have objections during the presentation or when asked to place an order. The problem can be either logical or psychological, and objections are often unspoken. In **handling objections**, the salesperson should use a positive approach, seek out hidden objections, ask the buyer to clarify any objections, take objections as opportunities to provide more information, and turn the objections into reasons for buying. Salespeople should learn to execute this task properly. As such, they need training in the skills of handling objections.

### Closing

After handling the prospect's objections, the salesperson now tries to close the sale. Some salespeople do not get around to **closing** or do not handle it well. They may lack confidence, feel guilty about asking for the order or fail to recognize the right moment to close the sale. Salespeople should know how to spot closing signals from the buyer, including physical actions, comments and questions. For example, the customer might sit forward and nod approvingly or ask about prices and credit terms. Salespeople can use one of several closing techniques. They can ask for the order, review points of agreement, offer to help write up the order, ask whether the buyer wants this model or that one, or point out to the buyer that he or she will lose out if the order is not placed now. The salesperson may offer the buyer special reasons to close, such as a lower price or an extra quantity at no charge.

### Follow-up

The last step in the selling process – **follow-up** – is necessary if the salesperson wants to ensure customer satisfaction and repeat business. Right after closing, the salesperson should complete any details on delivery time, purchase term and other matters. The salesperson should then schedule a follow-up call when the initial order is received to make sure there is proper installation, instruction and servicing. This visit would reveal any problems, assure the buyer of the salesperson's interest and reduce any buyer concerns that might have arisen since the sale.

### International selling

The typical sales process can be applied in international selling. However, intercultural trade always requires special efforts in tailoring sales and negotiation approaches. Marketing Highlight 20.2 illustrates the tortuous process of selling to Japan and how the Western approach should be adapted to reflect business customs and practices in that country.

## Relationship marketing

The principles of personal selling as described are *transaction oriented* in that their aim is to help salespeople close a specific sale with a customer. But in many cases, the company is not seeking simply a sale: it has targeted a significant customer account that it would like to win and serve. The company would like to demonstrate to the account that it has the capabilities to serve the account's needs in a superior way, especially if a *committed relationship* can be formed.

More companies today are moving their emphasis from transaction marketing to *relationship marketing*. The days of the lone salesperson working a territory and being guided only by a sales quota and a compensation plan are numbered. Today's customers are large and often global. They prefer suppliers who can sell and deliver a coordinated set of products and services to many locations. They want to do business with suppliers who can quickly solve problems that arise in their different parts of the nation or world, and who can work closely with customer teams to improve products and processes. Unfortunately, most companies are not set up to meet these requirements. They often sell their products through separate salesforces that do not work easily together. Their national account managers may be turned down when requesting help from a district salesperson. Their technical people may not be willing to lend time to educate a customer.

Companies recognize that *sales teamwork* will increasingly be the key to winning and maintaining accounts. Yet they recognize that just asking people for teamwork does not produce it. Companies must revise their compensation systems to give credit for work on shared accounts, while also setting up better goals and measures for their salesforce. They must stress the value of team-selling in their training programmes while also acknowledging the importance of individual initiative.[14]

Relationship marketing is based on the premise that important accounts need focused and continuous attention. Salespeople working with key customers must do more than call when they think a customer might be ready to place an order. They also should monitor each key account, know its problems and be ready to serve in a number of ways. They should call or visit frequently, make useful suggestions about how to improve the customer's business, take the customer to dinner and take an interest in the customer as a person. Taking care of customers by offering them gifts, free entertainment or corporate hospitality may be questioned by outsiders who equate such activities with bribery. Managers must therefore set guidelines on where to draw the line (see Marketing Highlight 20.3)

## Selling to the United States, Japan and China: some guidelines for European businesses

Selling to companies belonging to one's own culture and in one's home country is tough enough. Selling to foreign companies in overseas markets becomes even more exacting. Personal selling is the least easily controlled part of international marketing. Business people selling abroad must adapt selling styles and strategies even though, on the surface, international business executives reflect similar characteristics. In the Far East, for example, modern cities look disappointingly similar to Western ones, businessmen and women may wear Western clothes, drive Western cars, enjoy Western food, art and music or follow Western religions – but Eastern cultural traditions still dominate. Within a geographical region – for example, the Far East, the European Union – inter-country differences can be marked. European companies must help their managers not only to understand the needs, customs and cultures of international markets, but also to adjust their selling behaviour in accordance with the rules of social and business etiquette of the country in which they are doing business.

In this section we look at elements of selling, drawing particular attention to a few rules about selling to the United States, China and Japan. Close scrutiny reveals subtle differences between China and Japan, the two largest economies in that region, and the countries with which Western business people are still least familiar. Conversely, Eastern business people must also identify their approaches when sell-

In order to succeed in global markets, American companies must help their managers to understand the needs, customs and cultures of international business buyers.

ing to companies in the West. The US market presents huge opportunities for entrepreneurial and enterprising businesses in the East, but to sell successfully in the United States, foreign business people have also to acquire a sensitivity to US customs and business traditions. This rule applies equally to European companies seeking to do business with American customers. Let us now turn to elements in the sales process and examine the ways in which business behaviour varies across the three large economies – Japan, China and the United States.

| Sales process elements | United States | China | Japan |
|---|---|---|---|
| Preapproach – the entreé | Direct contact usually acceptable at junior level; cold-calling is common; salesperson telephones contact in the company. | Indirect, slow process; best to write to foreign trade corporations in Beijing or their branch offices, who act as intermediaries between their end-users and foreign firms; introductions via third parties/intermediaries (e.g. overseas offices, agents/ distributors in Hong Kong, Macau, Chinese embassies and liaison offices abroad); contact made at senior level. | Write to contact, but expect slow response; third-party introduction is preferable; develop contacts via Japanese companies' representatives in own country; use acquaintances, embassies to facilitate introduction; contact made at senior level; cold-calling is inadvisable. |

| Sales process elements | United States | China | Japan |
|---|---|---|---|
| Opening – the approach | Brisk; get down to business quickly; a confident, positive and business-like approach works well; breakfast meetings are common; business cards are exchanged with little ritual. | Assiduous preparation for talks; establish trust and friendship first; business cards are rarely distributed; contacts keep their status vague. | Assiduous preparation is the norm; introduction is a ritual, as is the exchange of business calling cards (*meishi*), which must be presented with both hands, and to contacts in order of descending status; bowing is common, but understand the ritual, which, again, is dictated by the seniority of individuals (handshakes will do when meeting Japanese business people who are used to dealing with Westerners); avoid using first names – the family name should be used to introduce oneself. |
| Presentation and demonstrations – the negotiations | Professional presentations are expected; tactical and straightforward styles are common; persuasion by logic is acceptable negotiating style; meetings involve a lot of talking, with details put down in writing later on. | Less formal; tends to be unstructured; can be exhaustive; expect lengthy decision-making; important to exercise patience, courtesy and self-control; they find being shamed intolerable, blame, even more so; a lot of technical information is expected; a discount on the final offer is expected, so always insert a cushion in one's quotation from the start. | Negotiations tend to be formal; ensure a high-ranking official in the company initially meets with an equal in the Japanese firm; expect the process to be lengthy because the Japanese negotiators must reach a consensus before making a commitment; expect long periods of silence (this means they are thinking and waiting for others to digest the information, but it could be that you have embarrassed them); probe (get details to help formulate a proposal that fits their needs); push (try all angles to get across issues that concern them); when desired results are not reached, they do not show emotions, but 'panic in silence', so try to salvage your position without causing embarrassment/shame or dishonour; beware, they try to 'save face' and avoid conceding by postponing the negotiation for further study. |

| Sales process elements | United States | China | Japan |
|---|---|---|---|
| Objections | Objections from audience are usually direct; the well-prepared salesperson is expected to openly counterdefend objections. | Objections are indirect (Confucian philosophy stresses need for harmony); difficult points have to be smoothed using compromise. | Objections are often indirect; open resistance is rare; beware, do not assume yes or *hai* in Japanese means agreement as it can also mean 'I see', 'I'll think about it' or 'I understand'; learn to read the objections – hesitancy in speech, facial expressions, unwillingness to be more specific, or silence are all signs of negative response. |
| Closing | Sales negotiator often asks for an order directly; deft footwork to persuade clients is acceptable. | The persuasive approach could cause great embarrassment, so avoid deft footwork; they emphasize good faith over legal safeguards in the business relationship; learn to read non-verbal signals and act as the situation arises. | Again, tactical close and hefty persuasion are alien to this group; like the Chinese, the Japanese emphasize friendship, loyalty and trust – a successful close occurs when the prospects feel the two parties have reached this state of mutual understanding. |
| Extra-business activities | Breakfast and lunch meetings are common; business entertaining is moderate (managers see it as time-wasting and, if lavish, a bit dubious); there is minimal celebration after the close. | Lavish entertainment is not the norm; the giving of gifts is not all that important, but, if offered, are not seen as a bribe. | Entertainment is the foundation of Japanese business; it never takes place in the executive's home and is done invariably in the evening rather than at lunch; present-giving is an established part of business etiquette – so, come prepared, and, when the Japanese counterpart offers gifts, it is rude to refuse them. |

Sources: Sergey Frank, 'Global negotiating', *Sales & Marketing Management* (May 1992), 64–9; John Saunders and Hon-Chung Ton, 'Selling to Japan', *Journal of Sales Management*, 1 (1984), 9–15; John Saunders and Hon-Chung Tong, 'Selling to the People's Republic of China', *Journal of Sales Management*, 1, 2 (1984), 16–20; J. C. Morgan and J. J. Morgan, *Cracking the Japanese Market* (New York: Free Press, 1991); F. Reinstein, 'Selling to Japan: we did it their way', *Export Today*, 3, 3 (1987), 19–24.

Recognition of the importance of relationship marketing has increased rapidly in the past few years. Companies are finding they earn a higher return from resources invested in retaining customers than from money spent to attract new ones. They are realizing the benefits of cross-selling opportunities with current customers. More and more, companies are forming strategic partnerships, making skilled relationship marketing essential. And for customers who buy large, complex products – such as robotics, large computer systems or aircraft equipment – the sale is only the beginning of the relationship. Thus although it is not appropriate in all marketing situations, relationship marketing continues to grow in importance. It is the key to establishing relationships and customer partnerships that last, and which in turn sustain, over the long term, company revenue and profits. For more discussion on relationship marketing refer back to Chapter 12.

## SUMMARY

Most companies use salespeople, and many companies assign them the key role in the marketing mix. The high cost of the salesforce calls for an effective *sales management process* consisting of six steps: setting *salesforce objectives*; designing *salesforce strategy*, *structure*, *size*, and *compensation*; *recruiting and selecting*; *training*; *supervising*; and *evaluating*.

As an element of the marketing mix, the salesforce is very effective in achieving certain marketing objectives and carrying out such activities as prospecting, communicating, selling and servicing and information gathering. A market-oriented salesforce needs skills in marketing analysis and planning in addition to the traditional selling skills.

Once the salesforce objectives have been set, strategy answers the questions of what type of selling would be most effective (solo selling, team selling); what type of salesforce structure will work best (territorial, product or customer structured); how large the salesforce should be; and how the salesforce should be compensated in terms of salary, commissions, bonuses, expenses and fringe benefits.

To hold down the high costs of hiring the wrong people, salespeople must be *recruited* and *selected* carefully. *Training* programmes familiarize new salespeople not only with the art of selling, but with the company's history, its products and policies, and the characteristics of its market and competitors. All salespeople need supervision, and many need continuous encouragement because they must make many decisions and face many frustrations. Periodically, the company must evaluate their performance to help them do a better job.

The art of selling involves a seven-step *selling process*: *prospecting and qualifying*, *preapproach*, *approach*, *presentation and demonstration*, *handling objections*, *closing*, and *follow-up*. These steps help marketers close a specific sale. However, a seller's dealings with customers should be guided by the larger concept of *relationship marketing* – the company's salesforce should work to develop long-term relationships with key accounts.

## ■ DISCUSSING THE ISSUES

1. The job of a salesperson can be exceedingly tough – it is challenging, varied, and the salesrep is under constant pressure to close and maintain sales. Describe the tasks performed by salespeople. Given the diversity of tasks and activities management expect of salespeople, are there ways of ensuring that the salesforce's time is spent more productively?

2. Who do so many salesforce compensation plans combine salary with bonus or commission? What are the advantages and disadvantages of using bonuses as incentives, as opposed to using commissions?

3. Salespeople are born, not made. Do you agree with this statement or not. Explain why or why not. What role does training play in helping someone develop selling skills?

## MARKETING HIGHLIGHT 20.3

### Corporate hospitality: drawing the line on freebies

Corporate entertaining or hospitality is an expected part of business life. But when does an all expenses-paid golfing trip, a free weekend in Paris or a case of finest Moet and Chandon stop being part of corporate life and begin to look like sleaze?

Freebies, such as a calendar or a fountain pen carrying the supplier's logo, are usually accepted by clients without a second thought. A nice dinner to keep in touch with a valued customer rarely raises an eyebrow, but is a free trip for a client and an accompanying partner to somewhere warm improper inducement, or merely a relaxing opportunity to build relations?

Even the most junior manager is likely to have been confronted with a freebie dilemma. What should business people do when faced with freeloading opportunities? In the absence of clear corporate or standard guidelines, how would managers decide if a gift, meal or trip is acceptable or sleazy?

Mr Mike Beard, head of public relations at international construction company, Taylor Woodrow, and president of the Institute of Public Relations, offers several useful guidelines:

1. The first test is what he calls the 'means test'. He draws the line at entertainment 'way beyond the level the person would normally be able to afford themselves'. It also depends on the level of superiority or importance of the individual. A steak in a wine bar at lunchtime is not beyond the means of most ordinary managers. However, if you want to talk business with the chief executive officer of a big company, you may have to meet him in more expensive surroundings.

2. The second test is the 'wow test'. When you open an envelope containing an invitation, you may say 'how nice' (or you may groan and say 'I suppose I had better be there!'). However, if you find yourself saying 'Wow!', then you had better think twice.

3. The third test is the *reciprocity test*. It is worthwhile occasionally to check that entertaining is reciprocal – suppliers buy you lunch, but you also buy them lunch back sometimes. That way, the relationship does not become too oppressive.

Corporate hospitality can be costly. At top sporting events – such as the football cup final at Wembley, or a day at Epsom for the horse racing, for example – the cost could reach Ritz-bill proportions. It costs something upwards of £1,500 per head to entertain at the Wimbledon men's tennis finals, but business people will pay that if they have big international customers coming into London to talk over deals that are worth millions of pounds. And don't ask what a meal for four in a Tokyo geisha club would amount to …

---

4. There has been an increasing trend towards the use of computers to help sales managers analyse, plan and coordinate salesforce activities. Discuss the effects of computer-based and related information technologies on the role of the salesforce.

5. In many companies, talented salespeople are frequently promoted to top marketing or management positions. What are the pros and cons of rewarding top salespeople in this way?

6. Salespeople doing business abroad must not only acquire an understanding of prospects' needs and requirements, but also develop a great deal of sensitivity to foreign customs, traditions and business etiquette. What are the key considerations the sales manager and his or her representatives must take on board when selling to business people in the Far East? You may discuss the question in relation to components of the selling process and how selling behaviour must be adapted to accommodate local business traditions.

Is corporate entertaining necessary? Even though hospitality events are felt to be part of work, very little work is actually discussed. Some managers argue that such events serve other purposes. The idea is to get the contact out for a good time. They feel good about you, and the next time you or your sales representatives call, they will receive you in front of the competition. Furthermore a night at the theatre or opera, with a ticket for an accompanying partner, is quite useful when overseas visitors need to be entertained in the evening. Weekend outings for clients and potential customers allow the company to buy a little of a contact's private time to talk about business. In some business cultures (e.g. Japan, Malaysia, Thailand and most countries in the Far East) offering and accepting hospitality is part of work. Contacts or customers often expect it. It is a way of cultivating friendship. Money sometimes counts as a 'gift', which may be offered to help a business contact or to express appreciation of friendship.

Some Western cultures frown upon others where special favours to family members or 'baksheesh' is a way of corporate life. Funnily enough, Americans and Japanese often frown on British standards. The Japanese are surprisingly quiet on the hospitality scene in Britain. They may visit clubs in their own time (after office hours), but are often horrified by the notion of taking a working day off to go to a sporting event. The Americans would think it 'barmy to spend thousands of pounds at Wimbledon. An MD of a big US corporation might entertain a senior partner at the ball game, but they would buy each other a hot dog and sit in public seats. How near you are to the Royal Enclosure at a race horse meeting and all those other layers of importance is very British,' according to Mr David Willis, a director of Britain's National Sporting Club.

Some companies actively discourage all employees from accepting hospitality. Some have no qualms about offering or receiving freebies. For those that have a problem on the morality or ethics side of all this, the experts have this to say: look at whether a mention of the hospitality arrangement – meal, trip or gift – in the press would cause embarrassment; try the 'means' test; do the *wow* test.

Source: Anil Bhoyrul, 'A man for all seasons', *BusinessAge Magazine*, **4**, 49 (1994), 104–6; Diane Summers, 'Hitching a ride on the corporate gravy train', *Financial Times* (24 October 1994), 7.

## ■ APPLYING THE CONCEPTS

1. Go to a retailer, such as a car dealership, a travel agency, a home appliance dealer or other outlets where salespeople are working on a commission basis.

   - Rate the salesperson who dealt with you. Was his or her approach, presentation and demonstration effective?
   - How did you respond to the sales pitch? Did you enjoy the experience or find it hard to endure? Why did you respond in this way?

2. Visit a retail outlet that specializes in complex products, such as audio and video equipment, computers and software or mobile telephones. Get a salesperson in the shop to explain the product to you and ask specific questions. Based on your experience of the sales situation:

   - Was the salesperson knowledgeable, helpful and able to answer your queries? Was he or she believable?
   - To what extent did the expertise of the salesperson help to 'add value' to the product in question?
   - If the product were available through mail order, would you rather buy it through that channel at a lower price, or from the salesperson you dealt with?

# REFERENCES

1. Portions adapted from Bill Kelley, 'How to sell air-planes, Boeing-style', *Sales & Marketing Management* (9 December 1985), 32–4; see also Dori Jones Yang and Andrea Rothman, 'Boeing cuts its altitude as the clouds roll in', *Business Week* (8 February 1993), 25; and Shawn Tully, 'Can Boeing reinvent itself?', *Fortune* (8 March, 1993), 10. '"Mega" orders for Airbus', *Eurobusiness* (July–Aug. 1994), 23; Paul Bells, 'Rolls-Royce seek bigger Airbus share', *Financial Times* (1 September 1994), 6.

2. For a comparison of several classifications, see William C. Moncrief III, 'Selling activity and sales position tax-onomies for industrial salesforces', *Journal of Marketing Research* (August 1986), 261–70.

3. Patricia Sellers, 'How to remake your salesforce', *Fortune* (4 May 1992), 96–103: at 96.

4. See Thayer C. Taylor, 'Anatomy of a star salesperson', *Sales & Marketing Management'* (May 1986), 49–51; Bill Kelley, 'How to manage a superstar', *Sales & Marketing Management* (November 1988), 32–4; and 'What is the best advice on selling you have ever been given?', *Sales & Marketing Management* (February 1990), 8–9.

5. See Richard Kern, 'IQ tests for salesmen make a come-back', *Sales & Marketing Management* (April 1988), 42–6; see also Robert G. Head, 'Systemizing salesper-son selection', *Sales & Marketing Management'* (February 1992), 65–8.

6. Patricia Sellers, 'How IBM teaches techies to sell', *Fortune* (6 June 1988), 141–6; see also *1991 Sales Manager's Budget Planner*, published by *Sales & Marketing Management* (17 June 1991), 77; and Matthew Goodfellow, 'Hiring and training: a call for action', *Sales & Marketing Management* (May 1992), 87–8.

7. See Bill Kelley, 'How much help does a salesperson need?', *Sales & Marketing Management* (May 1989), 32–5.

8. Thayer C. Taylor, 'SFA: the newest orthodoxy', *Sales & Marketing Management* (February 1993), 26–8; see also Rowland T. Moriarty and Gordon S. Swartz, 'Automation to boost sales and marketing', *Harvard Business Review* (Jan.–Feb. 1989), 100–8; Thayer C. Taylor, 'Back from the future', *Sales & Marketing Management* (May 1992), 47–60, and Taylor, 'Getting in step with the computer age', *Sales & Marketing Management* (March 1993), 52–60.

9. See 'Computer-Based Sales Support: Shell Chemical's System', (New York: The Conference Board, Management Briefing: Marketing, April/May 1989), 4–5.

10. 'The sweet SML of success', *Marketing Business* (December 1990), 2.

11. Claire Gooding, 'Salesforce put on the record', *Financial Times* (28 July 1994), 14.

12. Derrick C. Schnebelt, 'Turning the tables', *Sales & Marketing Management* (January 1993), 22–3.

13. Taylor, 'Anatomy of a Star Salesperson', op. cit., 50; see also Harvey B. Mackay, 'Humanize your selling strate-gy', *Harvard Business Review* (Mar.–Apr. 1988), 36–47; and Barry J. Farber and Joyce Wycoff, 'Relationships: six steps to success', *Sales & Marketing Management* (April 1992), 50–8.

14. See Frank V. Cespedes, Stephen X. Doyle, and Robert J. Freedman, 'Teamwork for today's selling', *Harvard Business Review* (Mar.–Apr. 1989), 44–54, 58.

## CASE 20

# Britcraft Jetprop: Whose sale is it anyhow?[1]

On 14 April 1992, Bob Lomas, sales administration manager at Britcraft Civil Aviation (BCA), received a telephone call from Wing Commander Weir, the air attaché for the United Kingdom in a European nation. The wing commander had found out that the national air force (NAF) of the European nation (hereafter Country) were looking for an aircraft to replace their ageing freight/transport aircraft for intra-European operations. They required equipment to fit between the large Lockheed Hercules that the air force had already decided to buy and lighter, utility/transport aircraft. The air attaché thought the Britcraft Jetprop was a suitable candidate.

## Britcraft aviation

Britcraft Aviation is the largest subsidiary owned by Britcraft Group Ltd, a British company with global engineering interests. Before being bought by Britcraft, the BCA was a differently named indepen-dent company founded by an aviation pioneer. They had designed and produced many famous military aircraft in the past. Military and executive aircraft were sold by the Britcraft Aviation (BMA) and Britcraft Executive Aviation (BEA) who were not based at the same site as the civil division. The Jetprop was BCA's top selling aircraft, but the company was also a big subcontractor to Airbus Industries and Boeing.

Production of the Jetprop started a few years after that of a similar aircraft made by Fokker, a Dutch company who was their main competitor. The Britcraft and Fokker aircraft were similar in many ways and used variants of the same engine. After intensive engineering and market research the Jetprop was designed as a regional airliner, particularly for developing countries. Unlike the Fokker, the Jetprop was a low-winged aircraft. Besides giving an unobstructed passenger area, Britcraft also claimed it gave their aircraft aerodynamic, structural and maintenance advantages. A primary design objective was for an aircraft that incurred low maintenance costs and that allowed high utilization by its operators. To achieve this, all components used on auxiliary services were selected for proven reliability, long overhaul life and ease of provisioning. Several important components were from aircraft already in service.

The aircraft was fully fail-safe. If there should be a failure of any part of the structure, sufficient members were available to allow redirection of loads. This gave a robust aircraft, where any failure due to fatigue developed sufficiently slowly for it to be detected during routine inspection before it became dangerous. To operate in the Third World the Jetprop needed short take-off and landing (STOL) performance from semi-prepared runways. Eventually the Jetprop became well known for its outstanding performance out of hot and high air strips. The company's sales literature explains:

> The Jetprop represents no great technological 'breakthrough'. It is instead a classical example of the application of 'state of the art' technology in achieving highly satisfactory performance, reliability and comfort.

The original design objectives remained the main selling features of the aircraft.

By 1992 the Jetprop was one of the United Kingdom's most successful commercial aircraft (see Exhibit 20.1), but several new products were now in the market, including a Japanese aircraft very similar

**Exhibit 20.1**   Commercial success of the Jetprop aircraft, 1992

| Continent | Number of Jetprops sold |
|---|---|
| Africa | 11 |
| America: North and South | 62 (4)* |
| Asia | 26 |
| Australasia | 11 |
| Europe | 25 (20)** |
| Oceania | 6 |

Notes:   * Figure in parentheses indicates total sales to US and Canada; ** Figures in parentheses indicates sales to UK operators.

to the Jetprop, although significantly larger. Britcraft worked closely with the Japanese during the project stage of this aircraft, hoping to be awarded a large share of the work associated with this venture, but this never occurred. Less competitive, and aimed at the military market, were Russian and Canadian turboprop aircraft and pure jet aircraft from the Netherlands and Germany.

### Sales organization

The BCA's sales organization was responsible for selling the Jetprop. It covered civil and military sales since several air forces had bought thirty Jetprops. A small number became VIP transports for heads of state. Each year markets were analysed and a list made of the most likely sales prospects for the coming twelve months. Area sales managers then received 'designated areas' comprising a number of prospective customers. These usually grouped geographically, although there were exceptions due to special relationships a salesperson had developed in the past. With time, new prospects were added to the designated areas, and the areas also had to be changed to balance the workload that developed.

Doug Watts was the area sales manager eventually responsible for the NAF prospect. Until then, his designated area included the air forces of Malaysia, Thailand, Zaire and Germany. Like several other area sales managers, he had joined Britcraft after a distinguished career in Britain's Royal Air Force (RAF). Immediately before joining the company in 1990 he was Group Captain, Air Plans RAF Germany. Three of the area sales managers had no RAF experience but had previously worked in one or more of the company's technical departments. One had been in the Sales Engineering Department for a number of years before being promoted to the Sales Department. In the company the Sales Department had a very high status, occupying a series of offices on the ground floor at the front of the Jetprop factory.

The sales engineers were all technically qualified, a number having postgraduate degrees. Most had become sales engineers directly after completing a technical apprenticeship with the company although some came from other technical departments. They were responsible for providing technical support to the Sales Department but also did much routine work associated with the sales effort. Although the sales engineers were not working directly for the area sales managers, the work of each sales engineer usually related to one part of the world, requiring frequent contact with one or two people in the Sales Department. The Sales Engineering Department was close to the Sales Department and could be reached by a corridor that led from the 'front corridor' to the Sales Department in a corner of the design office occupied by the sales engineers.

Ian Crawford, the marketing director of all Britcraft, worked at Britcraft's HQ in London. He was responsible for marketing for the whole of Britcraft Aviation in the United Kingdom and overseas. He also managed Britcraft Aviation's regional executives – senior executives strategically based to cover all the world's markets.

### The opening phase

After receiving the telephone call from Wing Commander Weir, Bob Lomas circulated news of the prospect while Doug Watts took overall responsibility for the prospect. Although BCA had agents in the Country, these had either not heard of the NAF requirement or failed to tell the company about it. Since the agents seemed dormant, BCA made direct contact with the national authorities in the Country. Following a visit to Herr Hans Schijlter, the defence secretary, Bob Lomas was asked to send copies of the standard Jetprop military brochure directly to the

Ministry of Defence for the minister. A few days later, Lieutenant Colonel Schemann, junior defence secretary, wrote thanking Bob Lomas. The next contact made was with Lieutenant General Baron von Forster, defence attaché to the Country's embassy in London, whom Bob Lomas had met at the Hanover Air Show. The general confirmed the NAF's interest in new equipment and asked for details of the Jetprop to pass on the authorities.

On 6 July, Air Commodore Netherton informed John Upton of Britcraft that the NAF probably had a requirement for a state VIP aircraft. The air commodore had lived in the capital of the Country for eight years since retiring from the RAF where he had been responsible for the Queen's Flight. After completing his military career he had become a founder member of Eilluft AG, a group that dominated civil aircraft maintenance and light aircraft operations in the Country. Britcraft had later used him as an *ad hoc* agent for the prospective sale of fighter aircraft. Having become an accredited agent for BMA, he was proposed as an agent in the Country for BCA.

Besides the Jetprop, Britcraft made another aircraft sold for VIP purposes. This was the Britcraft Executive Jet, a small, twin-jet aircraft manufactured and marketed by BEA. The sales organizations of both BEA and BCA were told of the sales opportunity.

In response, Geoff Lancaster, deputy sales manager of Britcraft Civil Aviation sent copies of the Jetprop brochure to Air Commodore Netherton requesting that they be passed on to the prospective customer. As the air commodore was not familiar with the Jetprop, a letter enclosed with the brochures outlined some of the selling points that he could use:

> Although the JETPROP does not have the glamour of a fast jet aircraft, it has many other advantages which make it perhaps the most suitable choice for a State Aircraft ... the size of the accommodation coupled with reasonably low purchase price. Most VIP layouts consist of a large rear state room with seats for four or five persons. These would be of the fully reclining and swivelling type. The forward part of the cabin would accommodate anything up to 20 attendants. The large size of the Jetprop also allows full galley and toilet facilities to be placed if need be both forward and aft in the aircraft, so that the VIP party could have complete privacy ... uses short airfields ... credit terms are available.

The letter also mentioned that the Country's minister of defence had recently flown in a Jetprop of the Queen's Flight and was favourably impressed.

On 10 July, Air Commodore Netherton met the officer in charge of the Operations Requirements Branch of the NAF. They confirmed that there was a study into the replacement of several types of transport aircraft. Simultaneously, Wing Commander Weir contacted Ron Hill, the executive director of marketing for BCA, saying that it was imperative that the company made direct contact with the Long Term Planning Department of the NAF about their requirement. Major Graff was the best contact, although Colonel Beauers and Lieutenant Colonel Horton were suitable alternatives if he was not available. Since Doug Watts was out of the country, Brian Cowley, the Jetprop sales manager arranged a meeting. An exploratory meeting on 26 July proceeded another on 7 August when Ron Hill would meet the senior personnel responsible for aircraft procurement.

Work in Iran prevented Ron Hill from attending the meeting so Steve Williams, his executive assistant, took his place. The discussions – between Steve Williams, Air Commodore Netherton, Major Graff and Lieutenant Colonel Horten – went well. Lieutenant Colonel Horten, the second in command of the Planning Department, outlined the need for NAF to completely re-equip their tactical and transport squadrons before 1996. Large Lockheed Hercules had already been ordered but they were still looking for a small, more flexible aircraft. Major Graff, the officer in command of re-equipment evaluations, explained that he had already completed preliminary analysis of suitable replacements, which had included the Jetprop. Fokker had already demonstrated their aircraft, which many in the NAF favoured because a large part of the airframe was constructed in the Country. The final requirement would be for two or three general transport aircraft plus possibly one for the paratroop training school at NAF-Graz. A Short Skyvan had already given a demonstration as a paradrop aircraft and the Canadians wanted to demonstrate their aircraft.

The Jetprop's demonstration to the NAF would be on 20 October. Major Graff asked for further evidence to support the Jetprop. The advantages of the Jetprop over the Fokker aircraft were highlighted, which were lack of bonding and spot welding, no pneumatics, fail-safe design, progressive maintenance and rough-airfield performance. Also, since Hercules were already ordered, it would be advantageous if there was commonality of avionics.

During the visit they met briefly with Colonel Beauers, the officer commanding the Long Range Planning Department. Air Commodore Netherton had known him well for a number of years but found that Colonel Beauers was soon to move to NATO HQ and would be replaced by an officer whom he did not know. After the meeting the air commodore expressed the hope that, provided the presentation in October went well and the NAF wanted the aircraft, the political people would agree to the purchase. He added that the sale of the paradrop aircraft seemed likely to depend upon support from Colonel Smit, the commanding officer of NAF-Graz, while the main issue, he thought, would be the aircraft's ability to operate safely, fully loaded for a parachute-training mission, from the NAF-Graz airstrip, which was grass and only 650 metres long.

Following the visit, Ernie Wise, a senior sales engineer, managed the technical selling effort. Through the Sales Department customer specifications engineer, the Production Planning Department were asked for a delivery schedule and the Estimating Department were requested to cost the aircraft. Other technical departments also became involved in supplying cost and performance evaluations. Eventually it would fall to the Contracts Department to negotiate a price for the package of aircraft, spares, guarantees, and after-sales services required.

Glynn Wills, a sales engineer who worked closely with Ernie Wise in the specification and requisitioning of artwork for the demonstration, became particularly involved with the avionics requirements. Several requests for detailed information were received from Major Graff, including details of the take-off and landing performance of the Jetprop at NAF-Graz. Since it was marginal, Air Commodore Netherton concluded that the only course was to convince the airfield's commanding officer to extend the runway.

Before the scheduled demonstration, the UK's biennial Farnborough Air Show took place. Invitations to attend went to a number of the NAF personnel, several of whom visited the show where they were entertained by Britcraft. The guests were: Lt. Col. Horten (chief of Plans and Studies), Lt. Col. Wabber (chief of Pilot Training), Major Bayer and Major Graff (Plans and Studies). The meeting progressed well, providing a useful prelude to the full demonstration. Then nine NAF officers visited BCA for the demonstration of the Jetprop in October, including officers from NAF Planning, Plans and Studies, Avionics, Technical Section, Supply/Spares and HQ Transport.

During the visit, technical specialists looked after most of the NAF officers while the Long Range Planning Department people discussed contractual details. Prices presented for the aircraft in three configurations were £900,000 for the basic version, £950,000 for the basic version with strengthened floor for cargo operations, and £1,125,000 for the basic version with strengthened floor and large freight door. The cost of avionics, spares and other equipment that allowed the aircraft to perform a wide variety of roles would be additional.

On the whole, the demonstration and presentation went very well, although Major von Betterei, 'from whom it was difficult even to wring a smile', was evidently 'Fokker oriented'. Air Commodore Netherton and he had been able to talk separately with the senior officer present with whom they had a 'long and useful discussion about compensation'.

### The second phase

Compensation or offset is an increasingly common part of large international sales. It usually involves a provision being made for the vendor or the vendor's country to buy goods from the customer's country. The size of the offset varies considerably, ranging from a fraction of the contracted price to, on rare occasions, more than the contracted price. The discussion with Colonel Zvinek, of NAF Planning, Plans and Studies, during the demonstration marked the first occasion when offset appeared accompanying the NAF's procurement of transport aircraft.

BCA conducted investigations to determine the importance of offset arrangements to the Country's national government. News from BEA suggested offset was critical. They had been attempting to sell two executive jet aircraft to the NAF: 'sales of the

Britcraft Executive Jet failed mainly due to offset being ignored.' Two French aircraft were bought instead by the NAF as VIP transports as part of a deal with very high offset. This had been easy for the French to arrange as the aircraft were partly built in the Country. While continuing internal studies into offset, BMA warned BCA not to use any of the compensation they had already earmarked for a possible sale of military trainer aircraft.

To clarify the offset situation Air Commodore Netherton visited Herr Maximilian, an under-secretary in the Ministry of Economic Affairs, who was responsible for advising the Country's ministerial committee on such matters. Herr Maximilian said offset had recently been between 60 and 70 per cent of the value of a contract and had been completed by the delivery date of the last aircraft. He felt that ideally the work should relate directly to the major project being considered but should not involve the manufacture of main subassemblies such as wings, air frames or engines. He concluded by saying that negotiations were the responsibility of the vendor alone who should not increase prices as a result of the required activities.

Soon after his visit to Herr Maximilian, the air commodore had obtained some encouraging information about the prospective sale. The NAF had given the replacement top priority with a schedule for action defined as follows:

| March 1993 | Finalized requirement. |
| Mid 1993 | Signing of letter of intent. |
| Late 1993 | Signing of contract and deposit payment. |
| 1994 | Delivery and full payment. |

Colonel Zvinek, who had originally been doubtful about the Jetprop, had been converted since the demonstration, together with all the other important NAF officers concerned. Also, since the government had already earmarked funds for the procurement of three aircraft, all that was necessary was to assemble an acceptable offset.

Some time passed with little further progress being made with the sale. It became evident that, although the NAF staff officers favoured the Jetprop, Fokker were offering a very substantial offset. One reason for Fokker's ability to do this was their shareholding in Baden GmbH who themselves owned Nationale Flugzeugwerke AG (NFW), the Country's largest airframe manufacturer. Since NFW already manufactured Fokker parts it was easy for them to show an advantageous offset capability.

Early in 1993, Kevin Murphy, the contracts manager for Britcraft Civil Aviation, sent a firm proposal to Colonel Zvinek. Simultaneously, members of the Sales Engineering Department were attempting to persuade the NAF to accept performance and weight information that showed Jetprop in a better light. The original figures requested by the NAF to allow direct comparison with the Fokker aircraft did not favour the Jetprop. The conditions for the 'paper comparison' were Fokker's and, not surprisingly, those conditions favoured their aircraft.

Some days later an urgent fax came from Roger Woods of Britcraft who had met Colonel Horten at a cocktail party in the capital. He said that Fokker's exceptional offset looked like losing Britcraft the deal. Panic abated, however, when Air Commodore Netherton talked to Colonel Horten and confirmed that the offset was 'not big business'. Further, Messrs Jones and Bedwell of BMA, who were in the Country at that time negotiating a large offset deal with the Ministry of Economic Affairs, found that 'offset would not really be involved on such a small order'.

Major Graff and Air Commodore Netherton visited BCA on 11 April 1993, to discuss the contract. Major Graff said there was a feeling that the Jetprop was inferior to the Fokker on several technical grounds. Also the price of £1,393,000, being asked for an aircraft with a large cargo door and the required equipment, compared unfavourably with the Fokker offer. In addition, when adding the price of spares to the aircraft cost, the total was more than the amount budgeted. Negotiations centred on reducing the number of roles the aircraft had to perform, so reducing the amount of optional equipment supplied. By eliminating paradropping, supply-dropping, and aero-medical capabilities the price reduced to a more acceptable £1,323,000. A new formal offer went to the Country before the end of April. This included details of an increased 'all up weight' for the aircraft, which would allow it to carry an extra 1,000 kg of fuel, thereby increasing performance over longer flights.

At the Paris Air Show on 13 June, Doug Watts again met Major Graff. They talked over two issues. First, the NAF desired to change the specifications of the aircraft to such an extent that a new quotation would be necessary. Secondly, Major Graff emphasized the importance of offset. Since by this time Steve Williams had left Britcraft, Geoff Lancaster took over negotiations. Wing Commander Weir, the air attaché in the capital, was contacted and questioned about the sale. He said he would probably be able to help in arranging some offset deal but added that diplomatic circles generally felt that it was 'Britain's turn' to obtain a contract.

On 16 July Geoff Lancaster, Major Graff and Air Commodore Netherton visited Herr Maximilian at the Ministry of Economic Affairs to discuss alternative offset arrangements that the company could provide. There were four suggestions:

1. Bought-out equipment for the Jetprop could be purchased from the Country's firms.
2. Basic aircraft could be flown to the Country to be finished and new avionics fitted by a NAF contractor.
3. Britcraft's vendors could subcontract work into the Country.
4. The Country's industry could build a future batch of Jetprops.

Herr Maximilian's response to the suggestion was not enthusiastic. His main point was that offset must not relate directly to the main contract in question, nor should it involve the NAF or the government. He explained how critical offset arrangements were to the Country's aerospace industry, which designed and marketed few aircraft and was almost totally dependent upon outside work. To underline his government's concern he quoted the offset associated with the recent sale of two Boeing aircraft to the Country's national airline. Boeing had agreed to place £3,000,000 of work with the Country's industry in the first year and £15,000,000 over the next ten years. The figures suggested that the offset was far more than the price of the two aircraft.

After leaving the ministry, Geoff Lancaster told Major Graff the consequence of further delay in placing a firm order. The three aircraft set aside for the NAF would go to other customers and eventually be supplied from a later batch of aircraft. Since each batch was costed separately the price per aircraft could increase to almost £1,000,000. The longer the delay, the less likely it would become that Britcraft could supply at the original price. Furthermore, as several customers were on the verge of signing contracts for Jetprops, there was even greater need for a quick decision. Major Graff worried about the delay but said there was little he could do. His recommendations for purchase would go on to General Petsch, at which stage they would constitute the official NAF requirements. They would then go to the air force advisor, and from him to the Defence Secretary, who would examine the report closely but would not consider offset. The defence secretary, General Keil, would then receive the documents and pass them to the minister of defence. He, together with the Prime Minister and the minister for economic affairs, would make the final decision. Before Geoff Lancaster left the Country it was agreed to arrange for a group of NAF officers to visit Schiller Aviation, an independent airline who had recently bought some Jetprops.

When the visit to Schiller took place, as the visitors' chief concern was the operation and maintenance of the aircraft, Chris Dyer helped. As an assistant customer liaison manager for Britcraft he had been working closely with Schiller Aviation during the early stages of their Jetprop operation. Air Commodore Netherton escorted the group on the visit and later reported that the airline was 'very complimentary' about the aircraft and Britcraft support.

### The offset

In an attempt to arrange the necessary offset, several channels were investigated. One of the main problems facing Britcraft was the large part of a completed Jetprop aircraft being accounted for by very specialized bought-out equipment. There was little chance of this equipment being bought from anyone other than the normal vendor. The largest bought-out items were the engines. One source for the offset was for the aero-engine supplier to place work with Baden GmbH, who had been undertaking subcontract work for a number of years. Although there was a chance that the aero-engine supplier would help, since they supplied the same engines to Fokker, the offset would not give Britcraft any advantage over the competing supplier.

A team of Britcraft design and production engineers investigated what work could be 'put out' to subcontractors in the Country. They identified three types:

1. Design work on the Britcraft Quiet Jet, a small jet transport aircraft still at the project stage.
2. Machining of components required in small quantities, but which were difficult and heavy.
3. Sheet-metal work construction.

Negotiations with Nationale Flugzeugworke (NFW), aimed at their doing about £1,000,000 of work, were started. However, although several exchanges of personnel, specifications and estimates took place, there was little progress towards a satisfactory agreement.

Meanwhile, Geoff Lancaster contacted Coles & Turf Ltd, a London-based company who had previously helped the company with offset. They offered to buy £4,500,000 worth of the Country's goods for a commission of 10 per cent. Within days the company again contacted Britcraft saying they had £1,500,000 worth of lard that was available for use as part of an offset. Meanwhile, Britcraft felt that the commission rate requested left no room for them to make a profit on the contract, so they wrote to Coles & Turf explaining this and stating that they needed £1,500,000 of offset rather than £4,500,000. Coles & Turf's response was to suggest that 10 per cent commission on £1,500,000 would leave plenty of room for Britcraft to make a profit and subsequently offered alternative products for offset. Finally Roden AG, a subsidiary of The Roden Company Ltd was contacted by Britcraft. After initial talks, packages of parts and drawings went to the company so that they could estimate prices for manufacture and assembly.

The situation became critical on 9 October when Air Commodore Netherton requested an urgent meeting with Geoff Lancaster at the NFA HQ. It seemed possible to sign 'a letter of intent' by 1 November, with the final contract signed by 1 April 1994. To achieve this, however, a global level for the total offset had to be presented, with details of it to be broken down. Negotiations with NFW, Coles & Turf, and Roden intensified as the deadline approached.

On 16 October there came a blow to the NAF deal. A Brazilian operator signed a contract for six aircraft. This meant that the NAF aircraft would be from the more expensive batch 15 rather than the original batch 14. The aircraft would be of slightly different configurations, and would cost more. The new price estimated for an aircraft, with strengthened floor and large freight door, was £1,470,000. The NAF reluctantly accepted the price increase and signed a letter of intent. Roden AG agreed to accept £450,000 worth of specified subcontract work. With this deal, it looked as though future activities would be mainly the responsibility of the Contracts Department. The pressure was off!

As April approached, a team at Britcraft was preparing to make a trip to the Country for final negotiations and contract signing. Then, a day before they were due to leave, Dick Drake, the commercial director, received a fax from the Country's authorities. It read:

> Department of Economic Affairs urgently expect more precision about your commitment and also a sensible increase of work for national industry. It is quite obvious that the 10 per cent offset is absolutely unsatisfactory. A reply is expected by 29 April.

A copy of the message went to Air Commodore Netherton, to which Dick Drake added:

> It is virtually certain that it will be necessary for me to reply on Friday that we regret we are unable to increase our commitment and the only other offset

is that which they already know about from the aero engine supplier. However, before replying, I would like to know whether Weir still believes it is Britain's turn.

## Questions

1. Trace the stages in the buying process and how the Country's interests changed from one stage to the next. Why were the Country's interests changing and was Britcraft keeping pace with the changes? How well did the strengths of the Jetprop match the needs of the NAF?
2. Identify the players in the buying centre and gauge their role and influence. How well did Britcraft manage the complexity of the buying centre and their diverse needs?
3. Discriminate between the sales roles of the people in Britcraft. Did Britcraft's structure help or hinder their sales campaign? How could it be changed for the better?
4. What characterizes the sale described in the case? What were Britcraft's main failings and strengths? Do you think they will win the sale or are they too out of touch with the needs of the NAF and the Country's government? What could they do at this late stage? Is it still 'Britain's turn'?

Note:
1. This case is based on in-company records and documents. For this reason the identity of the buyer and the seller and the names of the people in the case have been disguised.

# Bang & Olufsen

## Different by design

*Anton Hartmann-Olesen*[*]

In 1983 Bang & Olufsen, a small Danish manufacturer of stylish consumer electronics products, had to make a double-or-quits decision. Should it try to further penetrate the German market or get out altogether? If it was to stay in, how was it to gain the market share it needed?

The company's German operation based in Hamburg had so far been unable to make much impression on the huge German market. Over the last five years, sales had grown by less than 3 per cent and the financial results were poor. The only way to motivate the dealer base had been a series of expensive special offers: 'this week's special offer', 'buy 10 and pay for 8', or 'buy now and we will offer you terms of payment of 120 days, better than anyone else in the market'.

Relationships with Bang & Olufsen's 450 dealers were difficult. Bang & Olufsen's turnover in the individual shops was so small that it did not matter to the dealer. Also, since turnover on the German market accounted for only 3 per cent of Bang & Olufsen's turnover in the Danish parent company, the German market was not significant to them either. Several other markets looked more attractive than Germany. The United States, Canada and Japan showed high growth and, due to the high value of the dollar, they also looked very profitable. The question often came up: 'Should Bang & Olufsen concentrate on selling in the most profitable markets and close the German subsidiary? Alternatively, should they re-establish and re-position the brand following a new marketing strategy?'

Until 1983 the company had had little experience of selling outside Denmark. The sales organization looked very professional with sales subsidiaries in the United States, Japan and every country in Europe. However, there were problems beneath the surface. Almost all subsidiaries were acquired as bankrupt agents. These agents could no longer handle the changed distribution systems. Everywhere in Europe there was a shift from specialized, selective radio and TV dealer-network to the very competitive and hard-selling mass-distributors. Bang & Olufsen had traditionally used a push strategy that focused on getting retailers to stock Bang & Olufsen's products. Once displayed, the consumers would buy Bang & Olufsen's distinctively designed consumer electronics.

The international sales organization was large but ill-defined. There was no common communication strategy, no distribution development strategy, no common

[*] Herning, Denmark.

approach to training, and no corporate image strategy. As a result, each country developed their own strategy and became a series of independent 'kingdoms'.

## Under new management

In early 1984 a new management team started analysing the situation. The new managing director faced several problems, and one of the most serious problems was on Bang & Olufsen's doorstep. Germany is one of the world's largest markets for consumer electronics and, like Denmark, part of the EU. Bang & Olufsen Germany had to be healthy. But, first of all:

- *An overall target market* had to be defined. Until then each of the subsidiary 'kingdoms' had defined a target group that depended on local preferences and circumstances.
- *A new marketing strategy* needed formulating. The old push-orientation was failing and could not resolve Bang & Olufsen's poor position in the market.
- *A new dealer base* was needed to increase the quality and profitability of the operation.
- *A new organization* had to meet the demands from the new marketing strategy. A move from Hamburg to Munich would signal that Bang & Olufsen Germany was part of the most dynamic, business and growth-oriented section of the country.

## THE 7 CIC

The changes followed from Bang & Olufsen's 7 CIC (Corporate Identity Components) that defined the *corporate culture* and the *product strategy*:

1. *Authenticity.*   It is the company's aim to make products that guarantee faithful reproduction of programme material.
2. *Autovisuality.*   The company's products must provide immediate understanding of their capabilities and manner of operation.
3. *Credibility.*   We must constantly strive towards establishing confidence in the company, its actions, dealings and in its products.
4. *Domesticity.*   The products are for use by people in the home. They must be problem-free and easy to operate – even though technically advanced. Technology is for the benefit of people – not the reverse.
5. *Essentiality.*   The products must be concept bearing. Design must focus on the essentials of the concept.
6. *Individuality.*   Bang & Olufsen has elected to be an alternative to the mass-producing giants of the trade.
7. *Inventiveness.*   Product development and other tasks must be inventive. New approaches to solving practical tasks should characterize the company and its products.

## THE CONSUMER TARGET

So far, in the whole global Bang & Olufsen operation there was no single definition of the target group but where they did exist they used traditional demographic criteria: age, sex, income, education or geographic location. Experience had proved them to be no longer valid, if they ever had been. Bang & Olufsen saw the 1990s consumers turning away from indiscriminate consumption. They instead chose a lifestyle and arranged their possessions to fit it with great care. The pan-European sociocultural ACE research identifies different groups of these people. The research divides the European population into ten homogeneous groups. The groups are of equal size but differ sociologically and culturally.

A diamond-shaped model represents the ten segments (see Exhibit 7.1). This diagram indicates that:

- People close to the top of the diamond are vital and open-minded. They influence society and society influences them.
- People in the bottom groups focus on a secure and stable life. They are passive and will often resist change.
- The groups on the left have strong ethical anchors in life. They feel responsible for themselves and society.
- The groups on the right are constantly trying to bring pleasure and new experience into their lives.

Bang & Olufsen has selected the northern groups A, B1 and B2 as their primary target groups – 30 per cent of Europe's population. The were selected because:

> Their attitudes and interests are in harmony with Bang & Olufsen's philosophy. They influence public opinion compared to other groups, they are more frequent buyers of and more likely to pay high prices for audio and video products.

Characteristically the groups are curious, open-minded and have a strong desire to learn new things. They are always changing.

The targeted groups A, B1 and B2 account for 30 per cent of Europe's total population, but only some 17 per cent in West Germany (as it then was). In contrast A, B1

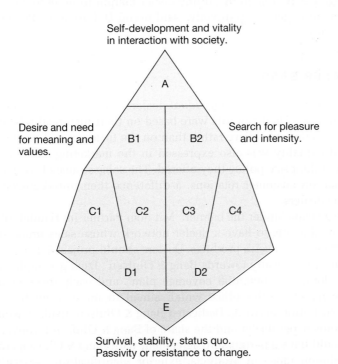

**Exhibit 7.1**   Pan-European consumer groups. (Source: ACE Research.)

and B2s make up 35 per cent of France's population and 37 per cent in Italy. This suggests that German consumers, on average, are more conservative than the French and Italians. For Germans, adjustment to change is the responsibility of institutions rather than individuals.

## A NEW PROMOTIONS STRATEGY

The limitations of the push strategy used by Bang & Olufsen Germany showed in the low consumer awareness (10 per cent) and preference (2 per cent) for Bang & Olufsen products by Germans in 1984. Comparable figures in Denmark were 98 per cent awareness and 48 per cent preference. The situation had to improve and could only improve. A switch from a push to a pull strategy was needed to redress the balance between consumer demand and the availability of the products. The advertising strategy was built upon four ideas:

1. *Quality of advertising medium* has great influence on the attention and the effect of the advertising message.
2. *Activation of the main target group* by the careful choice of media (exclusive special magazines concerning *living, design, lifestyle*, and so on) creates multiple purchase incentives without cannibalizing the Bang & Olufsen main target group.
3. *Target group analysis and purchase motives.* Main income and education levels decide the interest in the product and bear on the purchase decision.
4. *Increase in awareness of Bang & Olufsen.* Through advertising in high-profile *general-interest-magazines* the company would achieve a clear increase in the Bang & Olufsen awareness to an above-average level.

Marketing expenses increased from 3 to 10 per cent to support the new promotional effort – a change partly funded by cutting dealer margin from 38 to 33 per cent. 'We approach our main target group directly,' said Bernd D. Ehrengart, President of Bang & Olufsen Germany.

## A NEW DEALER BASE

In 1984 the dealer base was 450 *individual* dealers, each with a different agreement with Bang & Olufsen. Their rewards were based on their historical relationship with Bang & Olufsen's sales subsidiary rather than on the turnover and profits they generated. Their individuality was also expressed in the marketing strategy, the service performance and the price policy they offered. The sales strategy focused on transactions rather than on customer relations, a difference then unrecognized by Bang & Olufsen and the dealers.

A new strategy came under the banner: 'Mit dem Partner im Handel' (Relationship Marketing). The aim was to have a dealer network whose sales processes matched the quality of Bang & Olufsen's products. Dealers should project a 'perception of high quality' and 'heighten loyalty towards Bang & Olufsen'. Each geographical sales area would have a 'long-term potential coverage plan', and each area's plan would be tracked by the national sales office which aimed to increase quality and loyalty within their distribution network. Dedicated Bang & Olufsen displays would increase the average turnover per dealer and the share of Bang & Olufsen turnover per dealer. Each dealer would have a partnership agreement with Bang & Olufsen covering: presentation, minimum range of products, exterior identification, service/installation provision, promotional activity policies, training, and minimum turnover.

Bang & Olufsen's message to their chosen dealers was:

- Bang & Olufsen makes you an up-market store.
- Bang & Olufsen offers unique high technology on a full range of exclusive products.
- Bang & Olufsen caters for customers who want qualified guidance.
- Bang & Olufsen conducts its marketing in cooperation with its specialized dealers.

## A NEW ORGANIZATION

In 1984 Bang & Olufsen Germany had twenty-five staff. These worked mainly on the internal administration of stock keeping, servicing, book keeping and recording orders. The average sales per employee were DKr 452,000. The new marketing strategy required the staff to be more externally oriented, with a focus on communication, technical and sales training, distribution development, service and working in the field implementing the new marketing strategy. More staff were needed, but increased sales per employee would more than cover their cost.

1 ecu = US$1.26
= DKr 7.33
(Danish kroner)

## QUESTIONS

1. Distinguish between the old push and the new pull policies followed by Bang & Olufsen. Why do you think the push strategy was not working? Is it likely that the pull strategy will increase sales significantly without making Bang & Olufsen's products more attractive to German consumers?
2. How is the new pull strategy being funded? In what way is the new strategy attractive or not attractive to distributors? What compensates the retailers for having a lower margin and investing more in Bang & Olufsen's stock and display area?
3. How does the target market influence Bang & Olufsen's promotional strategy? Since there are so few of the target customers in Germany, would it pay Bang & Olufsen to target other groups in that market? Does it seem likely that the European market segments into ten equally sized groups that are similar across all European countries?
4. Would you 'double or quit' the German market? Why were Bang & Olufsen more attracted to the United States and other markets than to Germany, and were they right in being so? What is the rationale behind Bang & Olufsen's new marketing and distribution strategy for Europe? Do you think it will work in Germany?

# *Place*

Place

## CHAPTER TWENTY ONE

# *Placing products*

## Distribution channels and logistics management

## CHAPTER OBJECTIVES

After reading this chapter, you should be able to:

- Explain why companies use distribution channels and the functions these channels perform.

- Discuss how channel members interact and how they organize to carry out the work of the channel.

- Identify the main distribution channel options open to an organization.

- Explain how businesses select, motivate and evaluate channel members.

- Isolate the key issues managers face when setting up physical distribution systems.

## CHAPTER PREVIEW

### Economos

1 ecu = US$1.26

Economos is a small Austrian company that makes seals. These are rubber or plastic rings that are fitted at joints in fluid pipes to prevent leakage. It is difficult for anyone, even engineers, to get excited about seals. Economos, however, can. The company, founded by Helmùt Mayerhofer, has achieved tremendous success in this $4bn annual worldwide market through an impressive series of innovations in materials and production technologies and distribution methods. Economos has shaken up the world seal industry, and distribution advances have been a cornerstone of its market-ing strategy.

There are thousands of seal types and sizes. Customers expect their distributors to keep stocks available of most of them. Seal makers like Economos also expect their distributors to buy large stocks. In this business, it is also apparent that the firm's own production technologies and the injection moulding process it uses encourages it to manufacture large batches of the product. The traditional production methods, however, mitigated against fast response to customers who ordered a small quantity of an item not in stock. Economos was considering how to overcome the inflexibility which, in a way, confined the company to the use of third-party distributors who are put under pressure to keep large inventories.

In the mid-1980s, Helmut Mayerhofer and his associates started to examine the possibility of developing compounds that could be machined on a numerically controlled lathe. When a customer ordered a small quantity of an item that was not in stock, the firm could simply take a rough block of synthetic rubber or polyurethane and turn out the required number of pieces. At that time, few of the existing polyurethane substances could be machined. Those that could were not sufficiently flexible to make suitable seals. Economos approached the Department of Material Science and Material Testing of the Mining University of Leoben in Styria in 1988 whose assistance resulted in the development of a formula that produced machinable polyurethane suitable for seals. A plastics machine maker who Economos was working with developed a process for extruding the material into rough seal moulds, resembling lengths of pipe, in industrial quantities. The company also came up with a third innovation – a lathe, cutting tools and software for machining the rough stock into precisely dimensioned seals. This enabled the firm to produce a finished product that had highly consistent elastic properties and was free of bubbles. As a result of the speed and automation of the company's lathe, it could now machine a seal in about one minute, slice it off the rough stock and immediately machine another from the remaining stock. Economos could use its system to produce normal as well as occasional seals.

It is clear that once such a system is enforced, Economos could create a competitive advantage in fast, flexible, manufacturing which could be translated into higher service levels for its customers: that is any size of seal could be delivered to them in small or large quantities and, most importantly, quickly.

Since production could be done in immediate response to orders, Economos decided to set up as close to customers as possible. Its distributors would no longer need to carry large inventories, which meant lower prices and higher margins for their customers. Machinery makers could also contemplate abandoning the stocking and supplying of replacement seals. More recently, Economos has set up, together with local partners, seal service centres worldwide. It supplies the rough blocks of materials and the lathes to the local entrepreneur, who, under a franchise agreement, machines and supplies seals in response to manufacturers' orders. To date, there are 250 such service centres operating with the brand name Seal-Jet. The company's managing director, Ernst Stocker, estimates that their combined annual sales is about Sch 1,424m. Economos' own revenues of Sch 420m. in 1993 have come from selling not only seals, but also, increasingly, machines and materials.

1 ecu = US$1.26
= Sch 13.2
(Austrian schillings)

The Austrian group is set to adapt its strategy over the 1990s to obtain greater control over its seal service businesses in overseas markets. Through investment in technological innovation, the company has transformed the way it delivers value to its distributors and customers, while creating extra revenues for the firm. Through the transformation of its distribution method, Economos has been able to improve its delivery service in particular, thus lowering costs and improving margins for its customers. A seal is a seal is a seal – maybe for most people, but for Economos it is serious business in which the integration of production (in this case) and marketing channel strategies have created a significant source of competitive advantage, and a win-win situation for the company, its customers, and distributors alike.[1]

This story about Economos shows how a firm can use technological innovations to achieve greater distribution effectiveness (including international expansion) and efficiency and enhance customer service delivery. Increasingly, many firms, operating in all types of product sectors, are utilizing technical advances in areas such as information gathering and processing, communications and logistical processes, and methods to improve distribution channel performance. In this chapter, we will take a closer look at an important, albeit often neglected, component of the marketing mix – place – and focus on decisions and activities relating to distribution channels and logistics management.

## INTRODUCTION

Distribution channel decisions and processes are among the most important elements of the marketing mix. They determine how well target customers gain access to the firm's product or service and whether the distribution-channel system is cost-effective for the organization concerned. A company's channel decisions directly affect every other marketing decision. The company's pricing depends on whether it uses mass merchandisers or high-quality speciality stores. The firm's salesforce and advertising decisions depend on how much persuasion, training and motivation the dealers need. Whether a company develops or acquires certain new products may depend on how well those products fit the abilities of its channel members.

Companies often pay too little attention to their distribution channels. Managers who see channel functions merely as the physical transportation, storage and distribution of finished goods to the end-user fail to utilize the channel of distribution as a competitive weapon. As we saw in the case of Economos, like the rest of its competitors in the seal-making industry, the firm had relied on the use of a rigid distribution channel system. Constraints in materials and production technologies were generally accepted to rule out speed and flexibility in small-order delivery. However, by forceful investment in technological innovations. Economos overcame these barriers and found a means of creating superior channel advantage – closeness to customers, flexibility, no order-size restriction, faster customer-order response time, international reach, lower costs, higher margins and rewards for its distributors and entrepreneurial franchises. It had used a more imaginative distribution system to *gain* a competitive advantage.

Distribution channel decisions often involve long-term commitments to other firms. For example, companies can easily change their advertising, pricing or promotion programmes. They can scrap old products and introduce new ones as market tastes demand. But when they set up distribution channels through contacts with franchises, independent dealers or large retailers, they cannot readily replace these channels with company-owned stores if conditions change. Therefore, management must design its channels carefully, with an eye on tomorrow's likely selling environment as well as today's. In the case of Economos, the use of franchises has enabled it to expand its distribution network outside Austria, but, these intermediaries must be properly managed if they are to successfully maintain sales, the Seal-Jet brand name and market position. Economos has to revise its channel strategy to maintain cost-effective service delivery to customers. Companies like Safeway, BASF, Häagen-Dazs, Lucas Industries and Texaco Oils, in Britain also periodically review their channel arrangements with their existing distributor, Christian Salvesen, a distribution and specialist hire company, renewing the distribution contract only if agreed performance is maintained.

Single Market reforms in the European Union have forced many companies to review their entire distribution strategy. The use of third-party as opposed to in-house distribution in the grocery retailing sector, for example, is predicted to rise over the 1990s, and current operators in Europe must look for new ways to differentiate their services by taking advantage of the trend. In the EU as a whole, the distribution industry in 1992 was worth over £81bn, with the trend towards usage of third-party distributors, over the first half of the 1990s, forecast to grow by 5 to 10 per cent in the United Kingdom, and a similar trend likely to follow in the rest of the EU, as competitive pressures mount. Third-party distribution is also becoming more popular as companies seek to reduce fixed costs.[2]

1 ecu = UK£0.83

This chapter examines four main questions concerning distribution channels:

- What is the nature of distribution channels?
- How do channel firms interact and organize to do the work of the channel?
- What problems do companies face in designing and managing their channels?
- What role does physical distribution play in attracting and satisfying customers?

Then in Chapter 22, we will look at distribution channel issues from the viewpoint of retailers and wholesalers.

## THE NATURE OF DISTRIBUTION CHANNELS

Most producers use third parties or intermediaries to bring their products to market. They try to forge a **distribution channel** – a set of interdependent organizations involved in the process of making a product or service available for use or consumption by the consumer or business user.[3] The channel of distribution is therefore all those organizations through which a product must pass between its point of production and consumption.[4]

### Why are marketing intermediaries used?

Why do producers give some of the selling job to intermediaries? After all, doing so means giving up some control over how and to whom the products are sold. The use of intermediaries results from their greater efficiency in making goods available to target markets – in contracting out distribution is more cost-effective. Through their contacts, experience, specialization and scale of operation, intermediaries usually offer the firm more than it can achieve on its own. Moreover it allows the producer to concentrate on its core activities.

Figure 21.1 shows how using intermediaries can provide economies. Part A shows three manufacturers, each using direct marketing to reach three customers. This system requires nine different contacts. Part B shows the three manufacturers working through one distributor, who contacts the three customers. This system requires only six contacts. In this way, intermediaries reduce the amount of work that must be done by both producers and consumers.

From the economic system's point of view, the role of marketing intermediaries is to convert the assortments of products made by producers into the assortments wanted by consumers. Producers make narrow assortments of products in large quantities, but consumers want broad assortments of products in small quantities. In the distribution channels, intermediaries buy the large quantities of many producers and break them down into the smaller quantities and broader assortments wanted by consumers. As such, intermediaries play an important role in matching supply and demand.

Caterpillar Logistics Services offer a curious example of a manufacturer that exploited its distribution prowess and extended the benefits of third-party distribution to companies outside its immediate business arena.

> The story starts in the US – homebase of construction machinery manufacturer Caterpillar. Caterpillar examined the skills it had built up over many decades of selling construction equipment and how it might gain 'leverage' from them. The logistics of distribution and product support are a key factor for success in selling hydraulic excavators and have been a source of competitive advantage for Caterpillar. Senior Caterpillar managers thought of providing similar services to companies outside construction equipment. Encouraged by the interest

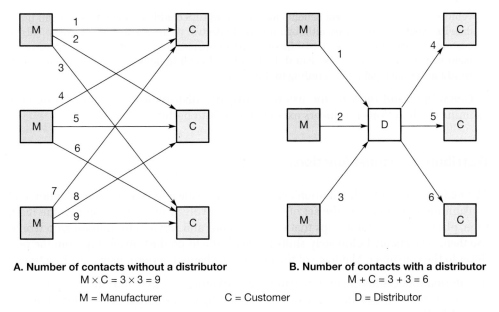

**A. Number of contacts without a distributor**

$M \times C = 3 \times 3 = 9$

M = Manufacturer          C = Customer

**B. Number of contacts with a distributor**

$M + C = 3 + 3 = 6$

D = Distributor

**Figure 21.1**  How a distributor reduces the number of channel transactions and raises economy of effort.

shown by potential users of the service and an agreement signed with Land Rover Parts of the UK in 1986, the company formed Caterpillar Logistics Services (CLS) in 1987 to distribute on behalf of other companies. By 1991, CLS was distributing lavatories, shower stalls and other equipment made by Florida-based Beauty Ware Plumbing Products, air compressors for Ohio-based Copeland, vehicle parts for Range Rover, Navistar and Iveco and sportswear for Puma. Many of these distribution contracts initially involved US distribution only, but, later, CLS won a contract to handle pan-European distribution of replacement parts for Chrysler in Europe. In the first five years of inception, CLS saw revenues rise at 30 per cent a year, with the value of product shipped running at about $500m. a year. CLS's expanding distribution business in Europe reflects distribution channel and logistics trends for the US and Europe that have important implications for global companies. For years, manufacturers used transport companies, freight forwarders and public warehouses to help turn a high fixed-cost business, if carried out in-house, into a lower risk activity and one where the client pays according to volume distributed. According to Steven Wunning, CLS vice-president, the company is offering an innovative service by entering long-term strategic alliances with its clients that give special performance guarantees by CLS and risk-sharing. Through warehousing services, transport management, systems support and other professional services, CLS helps the client to reduce costs as well as to improve service offered to clients' customers.

The alliance starts with CLS helping the client formulate a distribution strategy. Although this could take many months of detailed discussions and cost CLS several million dollars, the reward could be a contract lasting five years or more. In Europe third-party distribution is already well established in most countries. Wunning predicts that many more companies will seek to improve distribution performance through contracting out to firms like CLS as a means of differentiation by giving consistently better customer service than the competition. CLS also offers clients the benefits of reduced risk and less to worry about, particularly when entering a new market. Alan Simpson, managing director of Land Rover Parts, noted that management could concentrate on dealing with customers and suppliers without being distracted by the need to develop warehousing expertise. CLS handles the worldwide distribution of Land Rover Parts from a distribution centre at Leicester in the UK. It also distributes for Range Rover of North America. According to Simpson, 'We were able to launch Range Rover in the US with a fully cost-effective parts service from day one without a single vehicle being sold'. The cash benefits for a client of CLS could be immediate if it can liqui-date its existing warehouses, although it would take two or three years for improvements in customer service to show in actual financial performance. For Land Rover, the CLS arrange-ment had cost a fraction more than if the firm had done it in-house, a big investment which would never have paid off according to Simpson.[5]

Given the trend towards the use of third-party distribution channels, let us now examine the functions producers expect channels to perform.

## Distribution channel functions

The main function of a distribution channel is to provide a link between production and consumption. In doing so, the set of institutions involved in the channel fills the main time, place and possession gaps that separate goods and services from those who would use them. The channel ultimately shifts the legal title to product ownership from the pro-ducer to the consumer. Members of the marketing channel perform many key functions:

- *Information.* Gathering and distributing marketing research and intelligence infor-mation about actors and forces in the marketing environment needed for planning and facilitating exchange.
- *Promotion.* Developing and spreading persuasive communications about an offer.
- *Contact.* Finding and communicating with prospective buyers.
- *Matching.* Shaping and fitting the offer to the buyer's needs, including such activi-ties as manufacturing, grading, assembling and packaging.
- *Negotiation.* Reaching an agreement on price and other terms of the offer so that ownership or possession can be transferred.
- *Physical distribution.* Transporting and storing goods.
- *Financing.* Acquiring and using funds to cover the costs of the channel work.
- *Risk taking.* Assuming the risks of carrying out the channel work.

The first five functions help to complete transactions; the last three help fulfil the completed transactions.

The question is not *whether* these functions need to be performed, but rather *who* is to perform them. The producer can eliminate or substitute institutions in the chan-nel system, but, the functions cannot be eliminated. When channel members are eliminated, their functions are moved either forwards or backwards in the channel, only to be assumed by other members. In short, the producers can do without middle-men, but they cannot eliminate their functions.

Nonetheless, businesses must recognize that all the functions use up scarce resources and they can often be performed better through specialization. To the extent that the manufacturer performs these functions, its costs go up and its prices have to be higher. At the same time, when some of these functions are shifted to intermediaries, the produ-cer's costs and prices may be lower, but the intermediaries must charge more to cover the costs of their work. In dividing the work of the channel, the various functions should be assigned to the channel members who can perform them most efficiently and effectively to provide satisfactory assortments of goods to target consumers.

## Number of channel levels

Distribution channels can be described by the number of channel levels involved. Each layer of marketing intermediaries that performs some work in bringing the product and its ownership closer to the final buyer is a **channel level**. Because the producer and the final consumer both perform some work, they are part of every channel. We use the *number of intermediary levels* to indicate the *length* of a channel. Figure 21.2A shows several consumer distribution channels of different lengths.

Channel 1, called a **direct-marketing channel**, has no intermediary levels. It consists of a manufacturer selling directly to consumers, as in the case of a farmer selling farm produce at the farm gate. Other examples are the long-established home sales parties Tupperware uses to sell their kitchen products, Land's End's telephone selling and direct mail order distribution of clothes, and Singer, which sells its sewing machines through its own stores. Direct sales of consumer goods in some European countries has enjoyed record growth in recent years, and is one sector of the retail economy, for example, that has survived the recession. (In Chapter 22, we will examine the methods organizations use to market directly to consumers.)

The remaining channels in Figure 21.2A are *indirect*-marketing channels. Channel 2 contains one intermediary level. In consumer markets, this level is typically a retailer. For example, the makers of televisions, cameras, furniture, major appliances and many other products sell their goods directly to large retailers, which then sell the goods to final consumers. Channel 3 contains two intermediary levels, a wholesaler and retailer. This channel is often used by small manufacturers of food, drugs, hardware and other products. Channel 4 contains three intermediary levels. In the meat-packing industry, for example, jobbers usually come between wholesalers and retailers. The jobber buys from wholesalers and sells to smaller retailers who generally

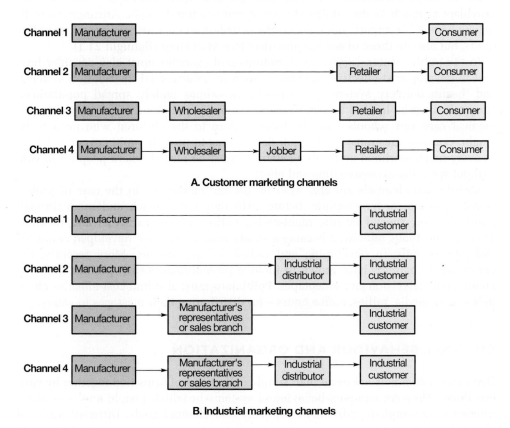

**A. Customer marketing channels**

**B. Industrial marketing channels**

**Figure 21.2** Consumer and industrial marketing channels.

are not served by larger wholesalers. Distribution channels with even more levels are sometimes found, but less often. From the producer's point of view, a greater number of levels means less control and greater channel complexity.

Figure 21.2B shows some common industrial or business distribution channels. The business marketer can use its own salesforce to sell directly to business customers. It can also sell to industrial distributors, who in turn sell to business customers. It can sell through manufacturers' representatives or its own sales branches to business customers, or it can use these representatives and branches to sell through industrial distributors. Thus business markets commonly include multilevel distribution channels.

In summary, channel institutions play an important role in making products or services available to customers. Between them, channel members ensure the transfer of several entities: the *physical product*, *ownership*, *money* or *payment*, *information* and *promotion* These transfers can even make channels with only one or a few levels very complex.

### Channels in the service sector

The concept of distribution channels is not limited to the distribution of physical goods. Producers of services and ideas also face the problem of making their output *available* to target populations. In the private sector, department stores, hotels, banks and other service providers take great care to place their outlets in locations convenient to target customers. Channel changes and their evolution affect service providers as much as they do producers of manufactured goods. Advances in technology have a big impact, not only on the distribution channel systems of manufacturers, but also on those of service providers (see Marketing Highlight 21.1).

In the public sector, service organizations and agencies must also consider how best to develop cost-effective channels – such as 'educational distribution systems' and 'health delivery systems' – to reach, sometimes widely spread populations. Hospitals must be located to serve various patient populations with comprehensive medical care and schools must be located close to the children who need to be taught. Communities must locate their fire stations to provide rapid coverage of fires in every neighbourhood and polling stations must be placed where people can vote without spending excessive time and effort.

Distribution channels are also used in 'person' marketing. In the case of professional entertainers, for example, before 1940 they could reach audiences through public houses, special events, night-clubs, radio, movies, carnivals and theatres. Then, in the 1950s television became a strong channel in most developed countries and subsequently in developing and industrializing nations. More recently, the entertainer's channels have grown to include promotional events, product endorsements, cable television and videotapes. Politicians must also find cost-effective channels – mass media, rallies, coffee hours – for distributing their messages to voters.

## CHANNEL BEHAVIOUR AND ORGANIZATION

Distribution channels are more than simple collections of firms tied together by various flows. They are complex behavioural systems in which people and companies interact to accomplish individual, company and channel goals. Different forms of channel systems exist.

Some channel systems consist only of informal interactions among loosely organized firms, while others consists of formal interactions guided by strong organizational structures. Moreover channel systems do not stand still – new types of intermediaries surface and whole new channel systems evolve. Here we look at channel behaviour and at how members organize to do the work of the channel.

## Channel behaviour

A distribution channel consists of dissimilar firms that have banded together for their common good. Each channel member is dependent on the others. For example, a Volvo dealer depends on the Swedish manufacturer, Volvo, to design cars that meet consumer needs. In turn, Volvo depends on the dealer to attract consumers, persuade them to buy Volvo cars, and service cars after the sale. The Volvo dealer also depends on the other dealers to provide good sales and service that will uphold the reputation of Volvo and its dealer body. In fact, the success of individual Volvo dealers depends on how well the entire Volvo distribution channel competes with the channels of other auto manufacturers, be it in Volvo's home or overseas markets.

Each channel member plays a role in the channel and specializes in performing one or more functions. For example, Philips' role is to produce hi-fi equipment that consumers will like and to create demand through national and worldwide advertising. The role of the specialist shops, department stores and other independent outlets that stock and sell Philips' products is to display these items in convenient locations, to answer buyers' questions, to close sales and to provide a good level of customer service. The channel will be most effective when each member is assigned the tasks it can do best.

Ideally, because the success of individual channel members depends on overall channel success, all channel firms should work together smoothly to secure healthy margins or profitable sales. They should understand and accept their roles, coordinate their goals and activities and cooperate to attain overall channel goals. By cooperating, they can more effectively sense, serve and satisfy the target market, thereby creating and benefiting individually from a 'win-win' situation.

Unfortunately, individual channel members rarely take such a broad view. They are usually more concerned with their own short-run goals and their dealings with those firms closest to them in the channel. Cooperating to achieve overall channel goals sometimes means compromising individual company goals. Although channel members are dependent on one another, they often act alone in their own short-term best interests. They often disagree on the roles each should play – that is, on who should do what and for what rewards. Such disagreements over goals and roles generate **channel conflict**. Conflict can occur at two levels.

*Horizontal conflict* is conflict among firms at the same level of the channel. For instance, dealers may complain about other dealers in the city who steal sales from them by being too aggressive in their pricing and advertising or by selling outside their assigned territories. Car dealers, consumer appliance outlets and or industrial equipment dealers who do not have sole distribution rights for the manufacturer's brand often encounter such conflict.

*Vertical conflict* is even more common and refers to conflicts between different levels of the same channel. For example, in the pharmaceutical industry, concentration of the distribution systems in some countries, such as the United States, results in enhanced negotiating power for channel intermediaries, particularly the big wholesalers. Drug companies have to work harder to manage their relationship with distributors and other vital channel partners and to minimize conflict (see Marketing Highlight 21.2).

Some conflict in the channel may, however, take the form of healthy competition, which can be good for the channel in that it stops channel members from becoming passive and it triggers innovation. Sometimes, conflict can damage the channel though. For the channel as a whole to perform well, each channel member's role must be clearly specified and channel conflict must be managed. Cooperation, role assignment and conflict management in the channel are attained through strong

---

## MARKETING HIGHLIGHT 21.1

### Elvis in cyberspace?

Technological advances are set to hit worldwide music distribution. Believe it or not?

### Behold, the digital jukebox...

Two cyber-buffs from California, Rob Lord and Jeff Patterson, used their computer science skills to develop a $20,000 computer system to reach out to fellow music fans. At the end of 1993, they launched their *digital jukebox*, the Internet Underground Music Archive (IUMA). IUMA uses the Internet – a global network of millions of computers – to send samples of alternative rock music everywhere, from Arizona to Australia. Each band of musicians pays it $20 to $75. Listeners tune in for free. All they have to do is access the Internet to download the music on to their computer sound cards before transferring it to an ordinary cassette.

Lord and Patterson's concept has since been copied by hundreds of other digital jukeboxes worldwide. It has attracted the attention of multinationals that dominate the $30.4bn global music industry. The big record companies cannot ignore digital diffusion any longer as the technology will eventually account for a significant chunk of music distribution.

### But, how soon will that be?

'We're working in the dark,' says Sara John, director of legal affairs for the British Phonographic Industry (BPI) in London. Record firms do not know how quickly it will take off or how to approach it. 'There's no doubt that at some stage digital diffusion will become a major part of the music market. My personal opinion is that it could happen very, very quickly,' asserts Ms John.

The music industry is unsure if digital diffusion is a golden opportunity to boost profits or a threat to their financial stability. If a compact disc sells for £12.99 in the United Kingdom, the artist earns 88p, the producer 44p, the publisher 44p and the manufacturer £1.05. The retailer, mostly to cover distribution costs, takes £3.25 and the record company £4.66, leaving £2.27 for VAT (value added tax). If a record company could deliver a compact disc directly to the consumer's home, it would save the whole of the £4.66 previously spent on distributing it to the record shop and the retailer's £3.25. Using direct distribution, it would be able to sell the same product for the same price much more profitably . The big global music companies – Sony, Time Warner, Matsushita, Bertelsmann, Thorn-EMI and Polygram – are, however, encouraged by such calculations to dabble in digital diffusion. Warner Bros, part of the Time Warner group, offers on-line access to some of their recordings through on-line services such as America Online and CompuServe. Matsushita's subsidiary, Geffen Records, also releases material on CompuServe. With Jasmine Multimedia, a small Californian software house, it even produced a CD-ROM game – Vid Grid – which was a visual jigsaw allowing the user to assemble videos from artistes including Red Hot Chilli Peppers, Aerosmith and Jimi Hendrix.

### The 'virtual record shop'...fact or fantasy?

Projects like Vid Grid are seen as 'experiments'. Sceptics say the current generation of on-line music services is not sophisticated enough for mass market use – it takes as long as fifteen minutes to down-load a three-minute song from IUMA on the Internet,

channel leadership. The channel will perform better if it includes a firm, agency or mechanism that has the power to assign roles and manage conflict.

In a large company, the formal organization structure assigns roles and provides needed leadership. But in a distribution channel made up of independent firms, leadership and power are not formally set. Such distribution channels have lacked the leadership needed to assign roles and manage conflict. In recent years, however, new types of channel organizations have appeared that provide stronger leadership and improved performance.

---

sound quality is reminiscent of the FM radio, not CD reproduction, and visuals are limited to black and white. However, some of the newer digital diffusers are delivering services by computer modem. Although distribution is more limited than the Internet's 25m. users, the technology makes the most of the vivid colours and sharp definition offered by computer graphics. Like it or not, as the Internet becomes progressively more efficient, and with the launch of recordable video-CDs, digital junkies will soon be able to transfer music to compact discs instead of cassettes. Furthermore, the eventual expansion of digital cable radio, now a fledgling medium in Europe and the United States, which transmits dozens of specialist music stations to the home on cable TV connections, offers another digital distribution system. The future envisages each home to have its own virtual record shop – the TV viewer orders an album by remote control via an in-built digital cable box, pays for it by credit card and records it on to a CD, rather than buying it from the intermediary – the retailer.

### But what about the risks to record companies?

Record companies could be marginalized by the technology. Without it, well-known artistes need record companies to gain access to their vast retail distribution systems. If digital diffusion technologies became the chief medium, artistes could bypass record companies and manage their own distribution. Also, if the technology were allowed to continue to develop in a fragmented form as an underground movement (the first wave of digital diffusers were effectively pirate operations!), then there would be a devastating impact on the industry's revenue.

### So if you can't beat 'em...

Rather than risk the proliferation of an underground movement, digital diffusers should, theoretically, be licensed to sell music by the appropriate industry authority (for example, the UK's Performing Right Society (PRS), and its equivalents in other countries). They should pay royalties to the authority and the record company. At the end of 1994, the PRS estimated that hundreds of on-line services had surfaced in the United Kingdom, and that it had been approached by only three operators and officially licensed only one, Cerberus. David Uwemedimo, head of legal affairs for PRS stressed that: 'We encourage new technology within the regulatory system. We want to find a fair way for these new services to pay for their music. We're still working on it.'

### Time's running out though!

BPI's recent research suggested that once consumers have access to on-line services like digital cable radio, expenditures on compact discs and cassettes decline dramatically. The law and the industry's thought processes are, arguably, moving too slowly – indeed, much too slowly compared with the pace of advance in digital diffusion technology. Elvis can be found in cyberspace! Ms John gives this warning: 'Record companies have historically made a lot of money from distribution and if they don't act quickly they could lose it.'

Source: The above account draws extensively from Alice Rawsthorn, 'Elvis found in cyberspace', *Financial Times* (21 November 1994), 15: see also Louise Kehoe, 'Mosaic: software sprat to catch an Internet mackerel', *Financial Times* (21 November 1994), 15.

## MARKETING HIGHLIGHT 21.2

### Wholesale drug buyers call the tune

The US market is a key market for global pharmaceutical firms. In recent years, many drug firms have faced increasing pressure to respond to changes in the US healthcare system, not least the downward pressure on costs and the growing threat from rising prominence of a new breed of distributors, known as *Pharmacy Benefit Managers* (PBMs), and their formularies – lists of recommended drugs they maintain, which doctors are steered towards when prescribing. The wholesale drug distributors in the United States, therefore, have a very powerful weapon in their armoury – if a drug the doctor prescribes is not included in its formulary, the doctor is likely to get a call from the distributor suggesting that he or she should switch to another (usually) cheaper drug that is included.

For example, Caremark, an independent distributor, claims that it manages to persuade three in five doctors to change their prescriptions under these circumstances. Manufacturers must increasingly align themselves with the big distributors if they are to defend and keep their lines of distribution open to prescribers. The task is not easy given the strength of the big distributors and their grip on drug sales in the United States: more than half of all Americans get their drugs through distribution companies, such as Medco, Diversified Pharmaceutical Services, McKesson and its subsidiary, PCS, and Caremark. Medco claims that it accounts for 38m. people (or 'lives' as they are known in the trade) under a variety of managed care arrangements. Diversified Pharmaceutical Services claims 44m. lives, PCS 45m. and Caremark 28m. They complete prescriptions for people cov-

ered under company health plans and other bulk programmes. They have also made it a priority to convert their customers to the formulary approach, using heavy price discounts as an inducement. Drug manufacturers must get their products on distributors' formularies. Those seeking to maximize returns on new drug sales in this market are finding the going tough under pressure, from both the bulk distributors and government quarters, to hold down prices.

Increasingly, the battle between drug manufacturer and distributor has resulted in a scramble for big distributors: Merck took over Medco for $6.7bn in 1993; Pfizer, Rhône-Poulenc Rorer and Bristol-Myers Squibb signed agreements with Caremark to have their products put on its formulary; Pfizer has also signed a similar deal with Value Health, another distributor; SmithKline Beecham has bought Diversified Pharmaceutical Services. If it is difficult to secure distributor cooperation, the alternative is to control it altogether. As we have seen, this is the main force behind the recent takeovers and alliances American and European drug manufacturers have set up with distributors in the United States. Control of distribution also enables the manufacturer to gain access to critical market and customer/patient information sitting in the databases of these distribution companies. Such information is vital to support product marketing and the development of new products for the market. If you can't beat 'em, join 'em – better still, own 'em!

Source:   Richard Waters, 'Drug industry seeks prescription for growth', *Financial Times* (11 May 1994), 32; see also Marcel Corstjens, *Marketing Strategy in the Pharmaceutical Industry* (London: Chapman & Hall, 1992), 229-31.

### Channel organization

Historically, distribution channels have been loose collections of independent companies, each showing little concern for overall channel performance. These *conventional distribution channels* have lacked strong leadership and have been troubled by damaging conflict and poor performance. However, over the last decade, new channel organizations have evolved to challenge conventional channels. A range of marketplace changes – evolving customers' needs, emergence of new competition, and developments and advances in technology – have led more innovative companies to exploit new mechanisms for delivering valued offerings to customers. Let us now look at the principal changes in channel organization, which continue to impact on businesses in the 1990s.

## Growth of vertical marketing systems

One of the biggest channel developments in recent years is the *vertical marketing system*, which has emerged to challenge conventional marketing channels. Figure 21.3 contrasts the two types of channel arrangement.

A **conventional distribution channel** consists of one or more independent producers, wholesalers and retailers. Each is a separate business seeking to maximize its own profits, even at the expense of profits for the system as a whole. No channel member has much control over the other members and no formal means exists for assigning roles and resolving channel conflict.

In contrast, a **vertical marketing system (VMS)** consists of producers, wholesalers and retailers acting as a unified system. One channel member owns the others or has contracts with them, or wields so much power that they all cooperate. The VMS can be dominated by the producer, wholesaler or retailer. Vertical marketing systems came into being to control channel behaviour and manage channel conflict. They achieve economies through size, bargaining power and elimination of duplicated services. As we saw in an earlier example of conflict between drug manufacturers and distribution companies in the US market, the former sought to increase control over the channel system through either acquiring a distributor (see corporate VMS below) or cooperative alliance arrangements (see contractual VMS below).

We now look more closely at the three main types of VMSs shown in Figure 21.4. Each type uses a different means for setting up leadership and power in the channel.

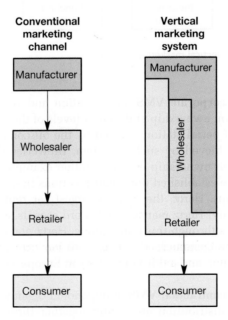

**Figure 21.3** A conventional marketing channel versus a vertical marketing system.

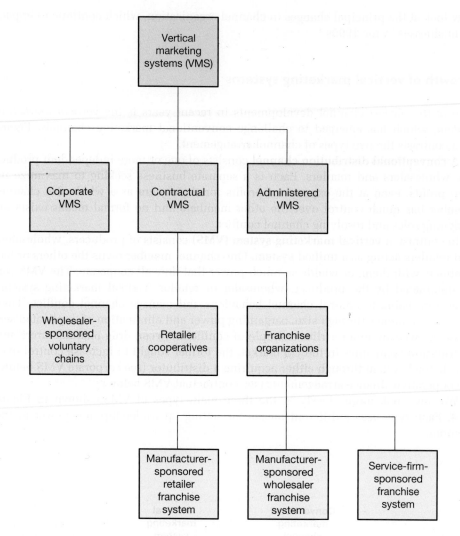

**Figure 21.4**  Main types of vertical marketing systems.

*Corporate VMS*    In a **corporate VMS**, coordination and conflict management are attained through common ownership at different levels of the channel. Petrol distribution through chains of petrol stations owned by the oil company is an example of delivery and control achieved by such a system. Breweries that sell beer through public houses under their ownership provide another example. In the car rental market, vehicle makers have established dominant positions in most of the world's leading vehicle rental groups. Hertz, the world's largest car rental company is jointly owned by Ford, Volvo and Hertz management. Ford sees its stake in Hertz as a vital means for retaining sales through this outlet alone. Hertz plays a key role for Ford as its biggest single private customer, with nearly 70 per cent of Hertz's vehicle purchases in the United States, and a third of its fleet in Europe, coming from Ford.[6]

*Contractual VMS*    In a **contractual VMS**, independent organizations at different levels of production and distribution are bound together through contacts to obtain more economies or sales impact than each could achieve alone. Coordination and conflict management are attained through the legal arrangements agreed amongst channel members. The contracts range from loosely structured agreements about the specification of goods and payment conditions to more detailed agreements about dealer responsibilites or a franchise contract.

Franchising has been a fast-growing retailing form in recent yeas. It is based on the concept of selling the right to sell the company's product or service. In **franchise organizations**, a channel member called a *franchiser* links several stages in the production–distribution process. Almost every kind of business has been franchised – from hotels and fast-food restaurants to dental and garden maintenance services, from wedding consultants and domestic services to funeral homes and fitness centres. Although the basic idea is an old one, some forms of franchising are quite new.

There are three forms of franchises. The first form is the *manufacturer-sponsored retailer franchise system*, as found in the automobile industry. BMW, for example, licenses dealers to sell its cars; the dealers are independent business-people who agree to meet various conditions of sales and service. Shell, the oil company, recently adopted a franchising system on many of its forecourts in Britain.

The second type of franchise is the *manufacturer-sponsored wholesaler franchise system*, as found in the soft-drink industry. Coca-Cola, for example, licenses bottlers (wholesalers) in various markets, who buy Coca-Cola syrup concentrate and then carbonate, bottle and sell the finished product to retailers in local markets. The third franchise form is the *service-firm-sponsored retailer franchise system*, in which a service firm licenses a system of retailers to bring its service to consumers. Examples are found in the fashion business (Benetton, Stefanel, The Body Shop); car rental business (Hertz, Avis); the fast food service business (McDonald's, Burger King); and the hotel business (Holiday Inn, Ramada Inn).

The fact that most consumers cannot tell the difference between contractual and corporate VMSs shows how successfully the contractual organizations compete with corporate chains. In Chapter 22, we will discuss VMSs in greater detail.

*Administered VMS*   In an **administered VMS**, leadership is assumed by one or a few dominant channel members. The system coordinates successive stages of production and distribution, not through common ownership or contractual ties, but through the size and power of one of the parties. Manufacturers of a top-selling brand can obtain strong trade cooperation and support from resellers. As dominant members, they exert power over the other members in the channel. For example, in the fast-moving consumer-goods market, companies like Unilever can command unusual cooperation from resellers regarding displays, shelf space, promotions and price policies. In the consumer electronics sector, Sony can wield a great deal of trade support for its top-selling brands. Large retailers like Marks & Spencer and Toys 'R' Us can exert strong influence on the manufacturers that supply the products they sell.

### Growth of horizontal marketing systems

Another channel development is the **horizontal marketing system**, in which two or more companies at one level join together to follow a new marketing opportunity. By working together, companies can combine their capital, production capabilities or marketing resources to accomplish more than any one company working alone. Companies might join forces with competitors or noncompetitors.[7] They might work with each other on a temporary or permanent basis or they may even create a separate company:

Nestlé and Coca-Cola formed a joint venture to market ready-to-drink coffee and tea worldwide. Coke provided worldwide experience in marketing and distributing beverages and Nestlé contributed two established brand names – Nescafé and Nestea.

Such channel arrangements work well globally. Because of its excellent coverage of international markets, Nestlé sells General Mills' Cheerios brand in markets outside North America. Seiko Watch's distribution partner in Japan, K. Hattori, markets Schick's razors and, as a result, Schick has the leading market share in Japan, despite Gillette's overall strength in many other markets.[8]

The number of such horizontal marketing systems has increased dramatically in recent years, so businesses must develop flexibility and management capabilities to enable them to capitalize on the growing opportunities presented by such marketing channel systems.

### Growth of hybrid marketing systems

In the past, many companies used a single channel to sell to a single market or market segment. Today, with the proliferation of customer segments and channel possibilities, more and more companies have adopted *multichannel distribution systems* – often called **hybrid marketing channels**. Such multichannel marketing occurs when a single firm sets up two or more marketing channels to reach one or more customer segments.

Figure 21.5 shows a hybrid channel system. In the figure, the producer sells directly to consumer segment 1 using direct-mail catalogues and telemarketing, and reaches consumer segment 2 through retailers. It sells indirectly to business segment 1 through distributors and dealers, and to business segment 2 through its own salesforce.

Sony maintains a wide distribution coverage by adopting a hybrid marketing system. Sony UK sells its consumer products through exclusive retail outlets such as the Sony Centres, through mass merchandisers like electrical chains and catalogue shops (e.g. Comet, Dixons and Argos), and using direct marketing channels, such as mail-order catalogues operated by direct marketers Grattan, Freemans and Kays.

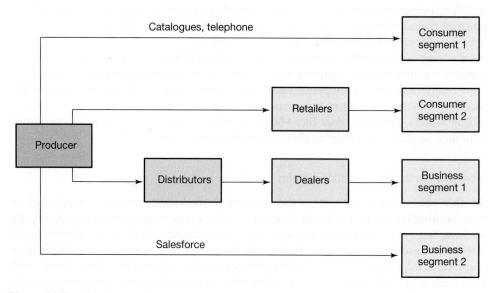

**Figure 21.5**   Hybrid marketing channel.

Hybrid channels offer many advantages to companies facing large and complex markets. With each new channel, the company expands its sales and market coverage and gains opportunities to tailor its products and services to the specific needs of diverse customer segments. But such hybrid channel systems are harder to control, and they generate conflict as more channels compete for customers and sales. The key to successfully managing hybrid channel systems is minimizing interchannel member conflict, while maximizing consumer demand through superior product quality and design and extensive communications to reinforce brand values and identity.

## CHANNEL DESIGN DECISIONS

We now look at several channel decisions facing manufacturers. In designing marketing channels, manufacturers struggle between what is ideal and what is practical. A new firm usually starts by selling in a limited market area – a few manufacturers' sales agents, a few wholesalers, some existing retailers, a few trucking companies and a few warehouses. Deciding on the *best* channels might not be a problem: the problem might simply be how to convince one or a few good intermediaries to handle the line.

If the new firm is successful, it might branch out to new markets. Again, the manufacturer will tend to work through the existing intermediaries, although this strategy might mean using hybrid marketing channels. In smaller markets, the firm might sell directly to retailers; in larger markets, it might sell through distributors. In one part of the country, it might grant exclusive franchises because that is the way merchants normally work; in another, it might sell through all outlets willing to handle the merchandise.

Thus channel systems often evolve to meet local opportunities and conditions. However, for maximum effectiveness, channel analysis and decision making should be more purposeful. Designing a channel system calls for:

- Analysing customer service needs.
- Defining the channel objectives and strategy.
- Identifying the main channel alternatives.
- Evaluating those alternatives.

### Analysing customer service needs

Like most marketing decisions, designing a channel begins with the customer. Marketing channels can be thought of as *customer value delivery systems* in which each channel member adds value for the customer. As noted earlier, the success of one company depends not just on its own actions, but on how well its entire channel competes with the channels of other companies. This idea is based on the notion that the unit of competition is not the individual company or organization in the channel, but the entire channel system or supply chain.[9] For example, Marks & Spencer imposes rigorous quality control on its suppliers to maintain its own quality reputation in food retailing. BMW imposes stringent operating requirements on its dealers, down to a level of detail which includes showroom display. Similarly, Toyota is just one link in a customer-value delivery system that includes thousands of dealers worldwide. Even if Toyota makes the best cars in the world, it will lose out to Ford,

General Motors, BMW or Nissan if these competitors have superior dealer networks. Similarly, the best Toyota dealer in the world cannot do well if Toyota supplies inferior cars. And Toyota cannot supply superior quality and reliable cars if its suppliers fail to maintain their own quality standards for parts and components that go into Toyota cars. The company has to design an integrated marketing channel system that will deliver superior value to its customers.

Thus designing the distribution channel starts with finding out what *values* consumers in various target segments want from the channel.[10] Customers generally expect suppliers' distribution systems to meet one or more of the following criteria: product availability and variety, rapid delivery, reliable delivery and dependability, convenient access to outlets, sales and after-sales service and support. Customer service is determined by the interaction of all these factors that affect the process of making the product or service available to the customer. Companies who recognize these needs must then build channel strategies that will serve them better than the competition. For example, the firm must identify whether consumers want to buy from nearby locations, or are willing to travel to more distant centralized locations. Would they rather buy over the phone or through the mail? Do they want immediate delivery or are they willing to wait? Do consumers value breadth of assortment or do they prefer specialization? Do consumers want many add-on services (delivery, credit, repairs, installation) or will they obtain these elsewhere? The more decentralized the channel, the faster the delivery, and the greater the assortment provided. Additionally, the more add-on services supplied, the greater the channel's service level.

Consider the distribution channel service needs of business computer-system buyers:

> The delivery of service might include such things as demonstration of the product before the sale or provision of long-term warranties and flexible financing. After the sale, there might be training programmes for using the equipment and a programme to install and repair it. Customers might appreciate 'loaners' while their equipment is being repaired or technical advice over a telephone hot line.[11]

For the individual buyer, seeking to buy a personal computer for the first time, channel service must be more sensitive to the consumer's relative ignorance of, 'shyness' with, and discomfort about, PC technology. Not only does the novice computer user need advice on what PC (the hardware) to buy, but also on the range of software to do the tasks he or she requires. This group of buyers also needs help on how to set up the equipment, load the software and learn to use the 'new toy'.

Providing the fastest delivery, the greatest assortment and the most comprehensive services may not be possible or practical. As in the case of servicing the PC buyer, providing a high level of personal service, in addition to warranties, maintenance and after-sales support, does not come cheap. A morning's training on a new graphics package can cost up to several hundred pounds. The company and its channel members may not have the resources or skills needed to provide all the desired services. Also, providing higher levels of service results, not only in higher costs for the channel, but also in higher prices for consumers. Realistically, the company must balance consumer service needs against the feasibility and costs of meeting these needs as well as customer price preferences. Fortunately for the PC consumer, self-help, in the form of a variety of specialist magazines – *What Micro*, *PC Novice's Handbook*, and so forth – is within reach. Also, these days, the direct sales channel is well established and most direct sales computer manufacturers provide reasonably priced basic, but powerful enough, PCs straight to one's door, with an on-site maintenance contact (for a reasonable fee) and lifetime telephone support for all those problems, large and small, that the standard user manual fails to answer.

Furthermore, in other product sectors, such as household, food and consumer packaged goods, customers also make trade-offs between service quality and other purchase dimensions, such as price. The success of off-price and discount retailing in recent years, as exemplified by the rise of discount retailers like Germany's Aldi and Lidl, the British Kwik Save and Superdrug and the Dutch Makro, shows that consumers are often willing to accept lower service levels if this means lower prices. Such discount operators are not just a European or US phenomenon (we will examine the growth in this type of retail channel in Chapter 22). Makro, for example, has expanded outside its key European markets and boasts a successful operation in the Thai market. In Japan, where consumers are noted for their obsession with and preparedness to pay for quality, no-frills discount houses, too, are gaining in popularity.

## Defining the channel objectives and strategy

Channel objectives should be stated in terms of the desired service level of target customers. Usually, a company can identify several segments wanting different levels of channel service. To secure a cost-effective channel system, the company should decide which segments to serve and the best channels to use in each case. In each segment, the company wants to minimize the total channel cost of supplying customers, while also meeting their service requirements.

The company's channel objectives are also influenced by the nature of its products, company policies, marketing intermediaries, competitors and the environment.

*Product characteristics* greatly affect channel design. For example, perishable products require more direct marketing to avoid delays and too much handling. Bulky products such as building materials or soft drinks, require channels that minimize shipping distance and the amount of handling.

*Company characteristics* also play an important role. For example, the company's size and financial situation determine which marketing functions it can handle itself and which it must give to intermediaries. Furthermore a company marketing strategy based on speedy customer delivery affects the functions that the company wants its intermediaries to perform, the number of its outlets, and the choice of its transportation methods.

The *characteristics of intermediaries* also influence channel design. The company must find intermediaries who are willing and able to perform the needed tasks. In general, intermediaries differ in their abilities to handle promotion, customer contact, storage and credit provision. For example, manufacturers' representatives who are hired by several different firms can contact customers at a low cost per customer because several clients share the total cost. However, the selling effort behind the product is less intense than if the company's own salesforce did the selling.

When designing its channels, a company must also consider its *competitors' channels*. In some cases, a company may want to compete in or near the same outlets that carry competitor"s products. Thus companies may want their brands to be displayed next to competing brands: in town or city centres, Burger King wants to locate near McDonald's; Pizzaland wants to be sited near Pizza Hut; Sony, Panasonic and Philips audio-video systems all compete for floor space in similar retail outlets; Nestlé and Mars confectionery brands want to be positioned side by side, apart from aggressively competing for shelf space, in the same grocery outlets.

In other cases, producers may avoid the channels used by competitors. Avon, for example, decided not to compete with other cosmetics makers for scarce positions in retail stores and, instead, set up a profitable door-to-door selling operation in the home and overseas markets.

Finally, *environmental factors*, such as economic conditions and legal constraints, affect channel design decisions. For example, in a depressed economy, producers want to distribute their goods in the most economical way, using shorter channels and dropping unneeded services that add to the final price of the goods. Legal regulations may also prevent channel arrangements that tend to lessen competition substantially or tend to create a monopoly. In countries where governments are actively encouraging free competition, such regulatory restrictions have helped to keep competitive channels open, as in the case of telecommunications in Britain, where both Mercury and the privatized BT exist in parallel as national suppliers of telephone services.

Having considered these factors, a channel strategy must be determined based on the target market segments and the differential advantage the firm needs to create in order to compete successfully in those segments. The channel or channels selected must have the knowledge and experience to serve the target segments effectively. The channels must also be able to reflect and support the manufacturer's differential advantage. The European construction machinery maker JCB recognized that its early problems in the French market were due to the inadequacies of its distribution outlet. It used manufacturers' agents to sell its equipment in France. These agents sold the products, but were not capable of providing the service facilities essential for competitive success in the market. JCB subsequently set up a company-owned full-service distribution network which was sufficiently competent to communicate the company's product advantages and provide the value-added services expected by customers.

## Identifying the main alternatives

The firm must make decisions about the *type(s)* and *number* of intermediaries to use and the *responsibilities* of each channel member.

### Types of intermediaries

A number of options exist. If the company decides to use direct marketing methods, the options range from direct response selling via advertisements in print media, radio or television, mail order and catalogues to telephone selling. The firm may consider the use of its own salesforce to sell direct to customers or to deploy another firm's salesforce, as Glaxo did with its best selling anti-ulcer drug, Zantac. Alternatively, a contract salesforce might be used. Or, middlemen could be employed to handle the firm's distribution.

Let us consider the options for a manufacturer of test equipment which has developed an audio device that detects poor mechanical connections in any machine with moving parts. Company executives think this product would have a market in all industries where electric, combustion, or steam engines are made or used. This market includes industries such as aviation, automobile, railroad, food canning, construction and oil. The company's current salesforce is small, and the problem is how best to reach these different industries. The following channel alternatives might emerge from management discussion:

- *Company salesforce.* Expand the company's direct salesforce. Assign salespeople to territories and have them contact all prospects in the area or develop separate company salesforces for different industries.
- *Manufacturer's agency.* Hire manufacturer's agents – independent firms whose salesforces handle related products from many companies – in different regions or industries to sell the new test equipment.
- *Industrial distributors.* Find distributors in the different regions or industries who will buy and carry the new line. Give them exclusive distribution, good margins, product training and promotional support.

### Number of marketing intermediaries

Companies must also decide on *channel breadth*: that is, how extensive their market coverage should be and, therefore, the number of channel members to use at each level. Three strategies are available: intensive distribution, exclusive distribution and selective distribution.

Producers of convenience products and common raw materials typically seek **intensive distribution** – a strategy whereby they stock their products in as many outlets as possible. These goods must be available where and when consumers want them. For example, sweets, chewing gum, disposable razors, soft drinks, batteries, camera film and other similar items are sold in myriads of outlets to provide maximum brand exposure and consumer convenience. Bic, Coca-Cola, Nestlé, Duracell, Fuji, Kodak and many consumer-goods companies distribute their products in this way.

Convenience goods are sold through every available outlet. Prestige goods are sold exclusively through a limited number of stores.

Photograph: Telegraph Colour Library

By contrast, some producers purposely limit the number of intermediaries handling their products. The extreme form of this practice is **exclusive distribution**, in which the producer gives only a limited number of dealers the exclusive rights to distribute its products in their territories. Exclusive distribution is often found in the distribution of luxury cars (e.g. Rolls-Royce, Lexus) and prestige clothes for men and women (e.g. Giorgio Armani, Hugo Boss, Yves St Laurent, Christian Dior). Rolls-Royce and Lexus dealers are few and far between – even large cities may have only one or two dealers. By granting exclusive distribution, the manufacturers gain strong distributor selling support and more control over dealer prices, promotion, credit and services. Exclusive distribution also enhances brand image and allows for higher mark-ups. The same logic can be applied to up-market designer-label clothes, the restricted distribution reinforcing the brands' prestigious image and expensive positioning.

Between intensive and exclusive distribution lies **selective distribution** – the use of more than one, but fewer than all of the intermediaries who are willing to carry a company's products. Many electronics and other small household appliance brands are distributed in this manner. For example, Philips-Whirlpool, Braun, Electrolux and Hoover sell their major appliances through dealer networks and selected large retailers. By using selective distribution, they do not have to spread their efforts over many outlets, including many marginal ones. They can develop good working relationships with selected channel members and expect a better-than-average selling effort. Selective distribution gives producers good market coverage with more control and less cost than does intensive distribution.

### Responsibilities of channel members

The producer and middlemen need to agree on the terms and responsibilities of each channel member. They should agree on price policies, conditions of sale, territorial rights, and specific services to be performed by each party. The producer should establish a list price and a fair set of discounts for intermediaries. It must define each channel member's territory, and it should be careful about where it places new resellers. Mutual services and duties need to be spelled out carefully, especially in franchise and exclusive distribution channels. For example, McDonald's provides franchisees with promotional support, a record-keeping system, training and general management assistance. In turn, franchisees must meet company standards for physical facilities, cooperate with new promotion programmes, provide requested information, and buy and supply specified food products.

## Evaluating the main alternatives

Suppose a company has identified several channel alternatives and wants to select the one that will best satisfy its long-run objectives. The firm must evaluate each alternative against economic, control and adaptive criteria. Consider the following situation:

> A furniture manufacturer wants to sell its line through retailers in the country. The manufacturer is trying to decide between two alternatives:
>
> 1. It could hire ten new sales representatives who would operate out of a sales office in the major or capital city. They would receive a basic salary plus a commission on their sales.
> 2. It could use a manufacturer's sales agency that has extensive contacts with retailers countrywide. The agency has thirty salespeople who would receive a commission based on their sales.

*Economic criteria*

Each channel alternative will produce a different level of sales and costs. The first step is to figure out what sales would be produced by a company salesforce compared to a sales agency. Most marketing managers believe that a company salesforce will sell more. Company salespeople sell only the company's products and are better trained to handle them. They sell more aggressively because their future depends on the company. And they are more successful because customers prefer to deal directly with the company.

On the other hand, the sales agency could possibly sell more than a company salesforce. First, the sales agency invariably has many more salespeople, not just ten. Second, the agency salesforce may be just as aggressive as a direct salesforce, depending on how much commission the line offers in relation to other lines carried. Third, some customers prefer dealing with agents who represent several manufacturers rather than with salespeople from one company. Fourth, the agency has many existing contacts, whereas a company salesforce would have to build them from scratch.

The next step is to estimate the costs of selling different volumes through each channel. The costs are shown in Figure 21.6. The fixed costs of using a sales agency are lower than those of setting up a company sales office. But costs rise faster through a sales agency because sales agents get a larger commission than company salespeople. There is one sales level $S_B$ at which selling costs are the same for the two chemicals. The company would prefer to use the sales agency at any sales volume below $S_B$, and the company sales branch at any volume higher than $S_B$. In general, sales agents tend to be used by smaller firms, or by larger firms in smaller territories where the sales volume is too low to warrant a company salesforce.

*Control and motivation criteria*

Next, evaluation must be broadened to consider control issues with the two channels. Using a sales agency poses more of a control problem. A sales agency is an independent business firm interested in maximizing its profits. The agent may be motivated to concentrate on the customers who buy the largest volume of goods from their entire mix of client companies rather than those most interested in a particular company's goods. And the agency's salesforce may not master the technical details of the company's product or handle its promotion materials effectively.

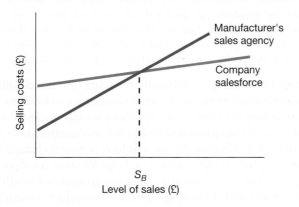

**Figure 21.6**  Breakeven cost: company salesforce versus manufacturer's sales agency.

*Adaptive criteria*

Each channel involves some long-term commitment and loss of flexibility. The producer must therefore assess the level of risks attached to selecting a channel system. A company using a sales agency may have to offer a five-year contract. During this period, other means of selling, such as a company salesforce, may become more effective, but the company cannot drop the sales agency. To be considered, a channel involving a long commitment should be greatly superior on economic or control grounds.

## Designing international distribution channels

International marketers face many additional complexities in designing their channels. Each country has its own unique distribution system that has evolved over time and changes very slowly. These channel systems can vary widely from country to country. The relative significance of different members or elements of a channel system – for example, the role of wholesalers versus retailers or shopkeepers – can vary significantly across countries. For instance, in food and drinks retailing, contract distributors play a far more important role in the delivery of goods from producer to retailer in the United Kingdom than in other EU countries like Germany, France, Spain or Italy. Also, multiple retailer dominance of the grocery market is more pervasive in the United Kingdom than the latter countries. Intercountry variations are partly due to history, tradition, legal conditions and economic reasons behind effectiveness and efficiency. Thus global marketers usually must adapt their channel strategies to the existing structures within each country. In some markets, the distribution system is complex and hard to penetrate, consisting of many layers and large numbers of intermediaries. Consider Japan:

> The Japanese distribution system stems from the early seventeenth century when cottage industries and a [quickly growing] urban population spawned a merchant class. ... Despite Japan's economic achievements, the distribution system has remained remarkably faithful to its antique pattern. ... [It] encompasses a wide range of wholesalers and other agents, brokers and retailers, differing more in number than in function from their European or American counterparts. There are myriad tiny retail shops. An even greater number of wholesalers supplies goods to them, layered tier upon tier, many more than most executives in other country markets would think necessary. For example, soap may move through three wholesalers plus a sales company after it leaves the manufacturer before it ever reaches the retail outlet. A steak goes from rancher to consumers in a process that often involves a dozen middle agents. ...The distribution network...reflects the traditionally close ties among many Japanese companies...[and places] much greater emphasis on personal relationships with users. ...Although [these channels appear] inefficient and cumbersome, they seem to serve the Japanese customer well. ... Lacking much storage space in their small homes, most Japanese homemakers shop several times a week and prefer convenient [and more personal] neighbourhood shops.[12]

Many Western firms have had great difficulty breaking into the closely knit, tradition-bound Japanese distribution network. Foreign companies have often found this a formidable barrier to setting up shop in Japan, though more recently, channel changes within the Japanese market have enabled fast-footed multinationals to secure a foothold in this unwieldy market. In Chapter 22, we will look at recent changes in Japan's Large-Scale Retail Store Law, for example, and how large Western retailers have succeeded in breaking into Japan's famously restrictive and overregulated retailing industry.

At the other extreme, distribution systems in developing countries may be scattered and inefficient or altogether lacking. For example, China and India are huge markets, each containing hundreds of millions of people. In reality, however, these markets are much smaller than the population numbers suggest. Because of inadequate distribution systems in both countries, most companies can profitably access only the small portion of the population that is located in each country's most affluent cities.[13]

In some Far Eastern markets such as Singapore, Malaysia, Thailand and Hong Kong, distribution systems are moderately developed and less unwieldy than that characterizing the Japanese market.

Thus international marketers face a wide range of channel alternatives. Designing efficient and effective channel systems between and within various country markets poses a difficult challenge.

## CHANNEL MANAGEMENT DECISIONS

Once the company has reviewed its channel alternatives and decided on the best channel design, it must be implement and manage the chosen channel. Channel management calls for selecting and motivating individual channel members and evaluating their performance over time.

### Selecting channel members

Producers vary in their ability to attract qualified marketing intermediaries. Some producers have no trouble signing up channel members. For example, Toyota had no trouble attracting new dealers for its Lexus line. In fact, it had to turn down many would-be resellers. In some cases, the promise of exclusive or selective distribution for a desirable product will draw plenty of applicants.

At the other extreme are producers who have to work hard to line up enough qualified intermediaries. When Reckitt & Coleman first launched their new 'green' detergent brand, Down to Earth, in the UK market in 1990, access was restricted to one supermarket chain – Tesco's. The Belgian firm Ecover managed to acquire sole rights for distribution in Asda stores, and in Sainsbury's, Safeway and the Co-op when, in 1986, it launched its radical 'green' detergents at the height of green consumerism in Britain. A rival green brand, Ark, was launched in 1989 and secured distribution in specialist retail outlets, but, since then, declining sales have meant an erosion of the brand to the extent that it is no longer able to secure distribution at all except through its mail-order network. Similarly, many small food and grocery producers who own marginal brands often have difficulty getting retailers to carry their products.

When selecting intermediaries, the company should determine what characteristics distinguish the better ones. It will want to evaluate the channel member's years in business, other lines carried, growth and profit record, cooperativeness and reputation. If the intermediaries are sales agents, the company will want to evaluate the number and character of other lines carried and the size and quality of the salesforce. If the intermediary is a retail store that wants exclusive or selective distribution, the company will want to evaluate the store's customers, location and future growth potential.

### Motivating channel members

Once selected, channel members must be continuously motivated to do their best. The company must sell not only *through* the intermediaries, but *to* them. Most producers see the problem as finding ways to gain intermediary cooperation. At times they offer *positive* motivators such as higher margins, special deals, premiums, cooperative advertising allowances, display allowances and sales contests. At other times they use *negative* motivators, such as threatening to reduce margins, to slow down delivery, or to end the relationship altogether. A producer using this approach usually has not done a good job of studying the needs, problems, strengths and weaknesses of its distributors.

More advanced companies try to forge long-term partnerships with their distributors. This involves building a planned, professionally managed, vertical marketing system that meets the needs of both the manufacturer *and* the distributors.[14] Manufacturer and distributor work together to create superior value for final consumers. They jointly plan merchandising goals and strategies, inventory levels and advertising and promotion plans. By working closely with its independent dealers the manufacturer increases its chances of successfully selling the company's products. In managing its channels, a company must convince distributors that they can make their money by being part of an advanced vertical marketing system.

## Evaluating and controlling channel members

The manufacturer must agree performance targets – sales quotas, average inventory levels, customer delivery time, treatment of damaged and lost goods, cooperation in company promotion and training programmes, and services to the customer – with channel members. The company must periodically monitor attainment of these targets by channel members and take remedial actions when deviations from agreed performance standards occur. Ideally, the producer should control, if not significantly influence, channel members to behave in a way that fulfils its goals and interests. However, the producer should aim to lead the channel in such a way as to enhance overall channel performance, thereby generating desired returns (e.g. sales, financial benefits) not just for itself, but also for channel members. That way, channels remain motivated to secure agreed performance goals. They also recognise that they are subordinate to the producer, whose power and control over the channel is subsequently maintained because of channel members' dependency on the producer. The company should recognize and reward intermediaries who are performing well. It may have to 'requalify' its intermediaries. Those who are performing poorly should be helped or, as a last resort, replaced. Finally, manufacturers need to be sensitive to their dealers. Those who treat their dealers lightly risk not only losing their support but also causing some legal problems. Sometimes, as the US brewery group, Anheuser-Busch, found, disputes with dealers can only be counterproductive, while also creating bottlenecks that frustrate the company's growth plans.

> Anheuser-Busch is keen to expand sales of its Budweiser brand in the Czech Republic. The brewery had distributed its product via Budêjovicky Budvar, the Czech Republic's most famous brewer in which the US company was trying to take a minority stake. In two related moves, Anheuser-Busch suspended negotiations on buying 34 per cent of Budvar, and halted the renewal of a moratorium on legal action in a dispute between the two companies on the use of the Budweiser trademark. Meanwhile, Anheuser-Busch also had to increase pressure on the Czech government to decide the future of Budvar, which the government was planning to privatise. Negotiations on making an investment in Budvar had started in 1990, and Anheuser-Busch was later, in 1994, named the sole foreign negotiating partner in Budvar's privatisation. Anheuser-Busch had to divorce the purchase of the stake in Budvar from a resolution of the trademark dispute, which was hampering the brewery's plans to

market Budweiser in other important European markets. Jack Purnell, chairman and chief executive of Anheuser-Busch International said he hoped that separation of the investment from the trademark dispute would advance progress in both issues. At the time of writing this, agreement between the Czech government and Anheuser-Busch had not been reached. So, while the government would eventually decide on how Budvar should be privatised, Anheuser-Busch pursued further negotiations on reaching a stand-alone trademark agreement. Budvar argued that the moratorium on legal action had already expired in September 1994, and was no longer accepted by many courts. Budvar, however, are still keen to link with Anheuser-Busch to help it expand its own sales of the Budweiser brand in current export markets – Germany and Austria – and to enter other European markets, particularly the UK. Anheuser-Busch, on the offensive, stressed that a new agreement would not be as comprehensive as the one offered to Budvar together with its proposal for a minority stake in the Czech brewery. The dispute continues.[15]

Remember, the key to profitable channel management lies in creating a win-win situation for all in the channel system – a symbiotic relationship rather than a coercive or confrontational one, among channel participants will almost always yield fruitful channel performance.

## PHYSICAL DISTRIBUTION AND LOGISTICS MANAGEMENT

In today's global marketplace, selling a product is sometimes easier than physically getting it to customers. Companies must decide on the best way to store, handle and move their products and services so that they are available to customers in the right assortments, at the right time and in the right place. Logistics effectiveness will have a significant impact on both customer satisfaction and company costs. A poor distribution system can destroy an otherwise good marketing effort. Here we consider the nature and importance of marketing logistics, goals of the logistics system, primary logistics functions, and the need for integrated logistics management.

### Nature and importance of physical distribution and marketing logistics

To some managers, physical distribution means only trucks and warehouses. But modern logistics is much more than this. **Physical distribution** – or marketing logistics – involves planning, implementing and controlling the physical flow of materials, final goods, and related information from points of origin to points of consumption to meet customer requirements at a profit.

Traditional physical distribution has typically started with products at the plant and tried to find low-cost solutions to get them to customers. However, today's marketers prefer *market logistics* thinking, which starts with the marketplace and works backwards to the factory. Logistics addresses not only the problem of outbound distribution (moving products from the factory to customers), but also the problem of inbound distribution (moving products and materials from suppliers to the factory). It involves the management of entire *supply chains*, value-added flows from suppliers to final users, as shown in Figure 21.7. Thus the logistics manager's task is to coordinate the whole channel physical distribution system – the activities of suppliers, purchasing agents, marketers, channel members, and customers. These activities include forecasting, purchasing, production planning, order processing, inventory management, warehousing and transportation planning.[16]

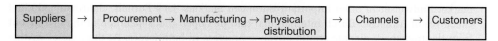

**Figure 21.7** Supply chain depicting value-added flows from suppliers to final users.

Companies today are placing greater emphasis on logistics for several reasons:

■ First, customer service and satisfaction have become the cornerstones of marketing strategy in many businesses, and distribution is an important customer service element. More and more, effective logistics is becoming a key to winning and keeping customers. Companies are finding that they can attract more customers by giving better service or lower prices through better physical distribution. On the other hand, companies may lose customers when they fail to supply the right products on time.

■ Second, logistics is a large cost element for most companies. Poor physical distribution decisions result in high costs. Even large companies sometimes make too little use of modern decision tools for coordinating inventory levels, transportation modes, and plant, warehouse and store locations. Improvements in physical distribution efficiency can yield tremendous cost savings for both the company and its customers.

■ Third, the explosion in product variety has created a need for improved logistics management. For example, in the early part of this century, the typical grocery store carried only two to three hundred items. The store manager could keep track of this inventory on about ten pages of notebook paper stuffed in a shirt pocket. Today, the average store carries a bewildering stock of thousands of items. Ordering, shipping, stocking and controlling such a variety of products presents a sizeable logistics challenge.

Finally, improvements in information technology have created opportunities for positive gains in distribution efficiency. The increased use of computers, electronic point-of-sale scanners, uniform product codes, satellite tracking, electronic data interchange (EDI) and electronic funds transfer (EFT) has allowed companies to create advanced systems for order processing, inventory control and handling, and transportation routing and scheduling. The benefits of recent and emerging technological advances accrue not only to manufacturers, but also to any member at any level of the channel. Take EDI, for example: it speeds up the sending of business information, such as invoices and orders. With the need for fast response time, a retailer connected up to its suppliers could ensure that the lead time between order and supply is shortened as far as is possible. The manufacturers or suppliers have up-to-date information on retailer stocking levels and needs and can respond faster than by using traditional manual methods. Consumers further down the line also gain, in that they can buy what they want at the right time and the right place. Indeed, in some industry sectors, such as retailing, certain companies are demanding EDI connections as a condition of trading.

## Goals of the logistics system

The starting point for designing a logistics system is to study the service needs of customers. Customers may want several distribution services from suppliers: fast and efficient order processing, speedy and flexible delivery, presorting and pretagging of merchandise, order-tracking information, a willingness to take back or replace defective goods.

Some companies state their logistics objective as providing maximum customer service at the least cost. Unfortunately, no logistics system can *both* maximize customer service *and* minimize distribution costs. Maximum customer service implies rapid delivery, large inventories, flexible assortments, liberal returns policies and a host of other services – all of which raise distribution costs. In contrast, minimum distribution cost implies slower delivery, small inventories and larger shipping lots – which represent a lower level of overall customer service.

Instead, the goal of the marketing logistics system should be to provide *a targeted level of customer service at the least cost.* A company must first research the importance of various distribution services to its customers, then set desired service levels for each segment. The company will normally want to offer at least the same level of service as its competitors. But the objective is to maximize *profits,* not sales. Therefore, the company must weigh the benefits of providing higher levels of service against the costs. Some companies offer less service than their competitors and charge a lower price. Other companies offer more service and charge higher prices to cover higher costs.

The company ultimately must set logistics objectives to guide its planning. For example, Coca-Cola's distribution standard is 'to put Coke within arm's length of desire'. Some companies go further and define standards for each service factor: for instance, to deliver at least 95 per cent of the dealer's order within two days of receipt, to fill the dealer's order with 99 per cent accuracy, to answer dealer questions on order status within three hours, and to ensure that damage to merchandise in transit does not exceed 1 per cent.

## Primary logistics functions

Given a set of logistics objectives, the company is ready to design a logistics system that will minimize the cost of attaining these objectives. The primary logistics functions include order processing, warehousing, inventory management and transportation.

### Order processing

The logistics process starts with the firm getting an order from the customer. Orders can be submitted in many ways – by mail or telephone, through salespeople, or via computer and electronic data interchange (EDI). In some cases, the suppliers might actually generate orders for their customers. Distribution outlets may select suppliers to manage their product stock replenishment. The outlets transmit daily records of product sales to the supplier, who analyses the sales information, comes up with an order and sends it back to the distributors through EDI. Once in the outlet's system, the order is treated as though they themselves created it. The success of such a system of order processing is based on trust between the supplier and the outlets who rely on the vendor to create the type of order that will best meet their inventory needs.

Once received, orders must be processed quickly and accurately. The order processing system prepares invoices and sends order information to those who need it. The appropriate warehouse receives instructions to pack and ship the ordered items.

Products out of stock are back-ordered. Shipped items are accompanied by shipping and billing documents, with copies going to various departments.

Both the company and its customers benefit when the order-processing steps are carried out efficiently. Ideally, salespeople send in their orders daily, often using on-line computers. The order department quickly processes these orders and the warehouse sends the goods out on time. Bills go out as soon as possible. Most companies now use computerized order-processing systems that speed up the order–shipping–billing cycle. Such modern computing systems enable firms to reduce distribution costs, while speeding up activities and increasing the level of service to customers.

### Warehousing

Every company must store its goods while they wait to be sold. A storage function is needed because production and consumption cycles rarely match. For example, a lawn mower manufacturer must produce all year long and store up their product for the heavy spring and summer buying season. The storage function overcomes differences in needed quantities and timing.

A company must decide on *how many* and *what types* of warehouses it needs, and *where* they will be located. The more warehouses the company uses, the more quickly goods can be delivered to customers. However, more locations mean higher warehousing costs. The company, therefore, must balance the level of customer service against distribution costs.

Some company stock is kept at or near the plant, with the rest located in warehouses around the country. The company might own private warehouses, rent space

Photograph shows the IBD warehouse at Magna Park, Lutterworth, Europe's largest dedicated distribution centre. The park has over 700,000 square metres (200 hectares) of which 350,000 square metres is already occupied.

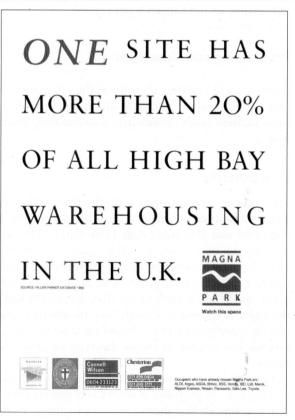

ONE SITE HAS MORE THAN 20% OF ALL HIGH BAY WAREHOUSING IN THE U.K.

in public warehouses, or both. Companies have more control over owned warehouses, but that ties up their capital and is less flexible if desired locations change. In contrast, public warehouses charge for the rented space and provide additional services (at a cost) for inspecting goods, packaging them, shipping them and invoicing them. By using public warehouses, companies also have a wide choice of locations and warehouse types.

Companies may use either *storage warehouses* or *distribution centres*. Storage warehouses store goods for moderate to long periods. **Distribution centres** are designed to move goods rather than just store them. They are large and highly automated warehouses designed to receive goods from various plants and suppliers, take orders, fill them efficiently, and deliver goods to customers as quickly as possible. In the European market, producers of industrial and consumer goods, while making trade-offs between customer service level and costs, are also beginning to match these needs against the feasibility of a pan-European distribution network that consistently provides high standards of service and flexibility. For example, British Steel, in the face of stiff competition in mainland European markets, set up regional distribution centres to be closer to customers, while also developing information-technology links between production plants, distribution operators and customers in attempts to improve service efficiency.[17]

Additionally, warehousing facilities and equipment technology have improved greatly in recent years. Older, multistoried warehouses with slow elevators and outdated materials-handling methods are facing competition from newer, single-storied *automated warehouses* with advanced materials-handling systems under the control of a central computer. In these warehouses, only a few employees are necessary. Computers read orders and direct lift trucks, electric hoists, or robots to gather goods, move them to loading docks and issue invoices. The modern high-tech warehouse, with high bay storage using narrow aisle trucks and more stacker cranes backed by multilevel picking or sorting systems, is a growing trend in Europe. Such warehouses have reduced worker injuries, labour costs, theft and breakage and have improved inventory control. Producers, however, do not necessarily have to make heavy capital investments to secure such high-tech warehousing – increasingly the advanced software and warehousing solutions are being provided by specialist distribution companies who are taking over large sections of firms' in-house warehousing and distribution functions.

Automated warehouses: this sophisticated Compaq computer distribution centre can ship any of 500 different types of Compaq computer and options within four hours of receiving an order.

## Inventory

Inventory levels also affect customer satisfaction. The basic problem is to maintain the delicate balance between carrying too much inventory and carrying too little. Carrying too much inventory results in higher-than-necessary inventory carrying costs and stock obsolescence. Carrying too little may result in stock-outs, costly emergency shipments or production and customer dissatisfaction. In making inventory decisions, management must balance the costs of carrying larger inventories against resulting sales and profits.

Inventory decisions involve knowing both *when* to order and *how much* to order. In deciding when to order, the company balances the risks of running out of stock against the costs of carrying too much. In deciding how much to order, the company needs to balance order-processing costs against inventory carrying costs. Larger average-order size means fewer orders and lower order-processing costs, but it also means larger inventory carrying costs.

During the past decade, many companies have greatly reduced their inventories and related costs through *just-in-time* (JIT) logistics systems. Through such systems, producers and retailers carry only small inventories of parts or merchandise, often only enough for a few days of operations. New stock arrives exactly when needed, rather than being stored in inventory until being used. JIT systems require accurate forecasting along with fast, frequent and flexible delivery, so that new supplies will be available when needed. However, these systems result in substantial savings in inventory carrying and handling costs. Advances in technology will continue to provide opportunities to secure faster stockturns and higher space utilization, and to support the use of JIT working practices. By keeping the flow in the pipeline – raw materials, work-in-progress, finished goods – to a minimum, manufacturers and suppliers alike can enhance logistics efficiency, while ensuring that customer service objectives are regularly met.

## Transportation

Marketers need to take an interest in their company's *transportation* decisions. The choice of transportation carriers affects the pricing of products, delivery performance and condition of the goods when they arrive – all of which will affect customer satisfaction.

In shipping goods to its warehouses, dealers and customers, the company can choose among five transportation modes: road, rail, water, pipeline and air.

*Road*   Highway developments in many developed, and increasingly industrializing, countries have sustained the popularity of trucks as a means of transporting cargo. Trucks are highly flexible in their routing and time schedules. They can move goods door to door, saving shippers the need to transfer goods from truck to rail and back again, with a loss of time and risk of theft or damage. Trucks are efficient for short hauls of high-value merchandise. In many cases, their rates are competitive with railway rates, and trucks can usually offer faster service.

In the EU, the bulk of goods traded is moved by road vehicles. The Conference of European Transport Ministers (CEMT) reported that transport volumes in the EU have risen by more than 50 per cent in the last twenty years. The bulk of this growth has been in road transport, which accounts for over 74 per cent of European freight transport.[18] Haulage rates for different cargo loads over different distances among EU member nations, do, however, vary – Greek domestic rates are the lowest, followed by UK rates; German haulage costs are the highest, with France and Italy close behind in the high end of the rate spectrum.[19] The gradual deregulation of the road transport market in the EU is expected to increase both intra-EU and international haulage competition, with a downward pressure on rates. Also, there will be greater freedom for international hauliers to transport goods between destinations within one country, thereby raising the efficiency in use of trucks. Those companies willing to invest in haulage planning and innovation are most likely to reap the potential benefits of road haulage deregulation and removal of restrictive practices in the EU.

*Rail*   Railroads are one of the most cost-effective modes for shipping large amounts of bulk products – coal, sand, minerals, farm and forest products – over long distances. In some countries, railroads have made a comeback as a transportation mechanism. In Europe, rail accounts for just over 17 per cent of total freight traffic. Recent developments, such as the Channel tunnel and its associated freight links, together with the EU's efforts to speed up the development of railfreight and combined road/rail transport services throughout Europe (not to mention the opening up of networks in eastern Europe) are, however, pushing rail transport much more firmly into the general distribution spotlight:

> Rail has been steadily losing share of traffic to roads over the last two decades. Many argue that rail's answer to its problems is the high-speed train and a vast, expanded European network. A European 'rail renaissance' will cost a staggering ecu 300bn. The importance given

Sophisticated distribution providers, operating in today's global markets, integrate transportation and computer-based technologies to ensure that they deliver the highest level of service to customers.

to railways is apparent from the European Commission's list of 2 dozen or more priority transport projects. Nine of them are high-speed rail links, including the Brenner rail tunnel through the Austrian Alps and the Fehnmarn Belt Baltic fixed link running between Denmark and Germany. However, real collaboration and standardisation among Europe's railways is indispensable for reinforcing rail's presence on main cross-border routes. While there is some evidence that Europe's new railways are attracting passengers back, the revitalisation of rail freight may take some time. There is optimism in the air as authorities and politicians alike agree that it is not a simple question of road versus rail – Europe must have both.[20]

Moreover, the introduction of new equipment to handle special categories of goods, the use of flatcars for carrying truck trailers by rail (that is, to piggyback trailers), and the provision of in-transit services such as the diversion of shipped goods to other destinations en route and the processing of goods en route are helping railways to service the transportation needs of producers and suppliers more effectively.

*Water*  In countries and economic regions favourably served by coastal and inland waterways, a large amount of goods can be moved by ships and barges. On the one hand, the cost of water transportation is very low for shipping bulky, low-value, nonperishable products such as sand, coal, grain, oil and metallic ores. Shipping also provides a safe, reliable, cheap and environmentally-friendly alternative. On the other hand, water transportation is the slowest transportation mode and is sometimes affected by the weather. Again, producers and suppliers have to make choice decisions based on trade-offs between speed, security and costs of transportation.

In the EU, waterways' share of freight transport volume has fallen from 13.5 per cent in 1970 to just over 8 per cent by the early 1990s. Waterways represent immense potential for freight transportation – a single coaster or ro-ro (roll on roll off) ship can carry the same cargo as dozens of trains or hundreds of trucks. Its full potential, however, cannot be realized without harmonization of European shipping and port policies, and the removal of existing restrictive and unnecessary legislations. The past recessionary climate had blighted the industry, but additionally, EU deregulation and differing pricing systems have added to waterways' problems – German operators, for example, have been set against traditional cheaper rivals in Holland, Belgium and France, not to mention increased competition from new operators in the east. Despite the problems, the EU and member governments are set on pushing ahead with ambitious plans to upgrade Europe's waterway network, with hopes pinned on a healthier waterway freight industry in the future.[21]

*Pipeline*  Pipelines are a specialized means of shipping raw commodities such as petroleum, natural gas and chemicals from sources to markets. Pipeline shipment of petroleum products costs less than rail shipment, but more than water shipment. Most pipelines are used by their owners to ship their own products.

*Air*  Although the use of air carriers tends to be restricted to low-bulk goods, they are becoming more important as a transportation mode. Air-freight rates are much higher than rail or truck rates, but air freight is ideal when speed is needed or distant markets have to be reached. Among the most frequently air-freighted products are perishables (fresh fish, cut flowers) and high-value, low-bulk items (technical instruments, jewellery). Companies find that air freight also reduces inventory levels, packaging costs and the number of warehouses needed.

## Choosing transportation modes

In choosing a transportation mode for a product, shippers consider as many as five criteria, as shown in Table 21.1. Thus, if a shipper needs speed, air and truck are the prime choices. If the goal is low cost, then water or pipeline might be best. Trucks appear to offer the most advantages.

Thanks to *containerization*, shippers are increasingly combining two or more modes of transportation. **Containerization** consists of putting goods in boxes or trailers that are easy to transfer between two transportation modes. *Piggyback* describes the use of rail and trucks; *fishyback*, water and trucks; *trainship* water and rail; and *airtruck*, air and trucks. Each combination offers advantages to the shipper. For example, not only is piggyback cheaper than trucking alone, but it also provides flexibility and convenience.

## International logistics

International logistics is a critical area for more and more global businesses whose inbound supply movements are shifting from domestic sources to global ones and outbound supplies undergo an equally international trade flow. Sophisticated computer-based technologies, such as computer-integrated logistics (CIL), are being used to enable international companies and logistics service providers to manage the supply chain and specific logistics functions.

International logistics place even greater demands on good integration of logistics operations and systems between supplier/manufacturer and others involved in moving supplies or goods along the supply chain across national borders. In the European market, increasing competitive pressures and the continuing drive for greater efficiency have forced distribution service providers, in the first instance, to focus more heavily on service quality improvement or risk losing out on invitations to bid for new business. Manufacturers and distribution operators alike have sought to set up pan-European distribution networks, although with mixed results.[22] To be effective, international logistics must be planned and coordinated to achieve desired cost advantages while meeting customer service needs.

| **TABLE 21.1** | *Ranking of transportation modes* | | | | |
|---|---|---|---|---|---|
| | Speed (door-to-door) delivery time | Dependability (meeting schedules on time) | Capability (ability to handle various products) | Availability (no. of geographic points served) | Cost (per ton-mile) |
| Rail | 3 | 4 | 2 | 2 | 3 |
| Water | 4 | 5 | 1 | 4 | 1 |
| Truck | 2 | 2 | 3 | 1 | 4 |
| Pipeline | 5 | 1 | 5 | 5 | 2 |
| Air | 1 | 3 | 4 | 3 | 5 |
| Note: 1 = highest rank. | | | | | |

Source: Carl M. Guelzo, *Introduction to Logistics Management* (Englewood Cliffs, NJ: Prentice Hall, 1986), 46.

## Integrated logistics management

Today, more and more companies are adopting the concept of **integrated logistics management**. This concept recognizes that providing better customer service and trimming distribution costs require *teamwork*, both inside the company and among all the marketing channel organizations. Inside the company, the various functional departments must work closely together to maximize the company's own logistics performance. Very importantly, the company must integrate its logistics system with those of its suppliers and customers to maximize the performance of the entire distribution system. Where firms recognize that particular logistics functions are not their area of core competency, they should have these activities carried out by specialists who would achieve greater effectiveness and efficiency. However, to extract maximum rewards from channel participation, channel and physical distribution decisions must remain customer-driven.

### Cross-functional teamwork inside the company

In most companies, responsibility for various logistics activities is assigned to many different functional units – marketing, sales, finance, manufacturing, purchasing. Too often, each function tries to optimize its own logistics performance without regard for the activities of the other functions. However, transportation, inventory, warehousing and order processing activities interact, often in an inverse way. For example, lower inventory levels reduce inventory carrying costs. But they may also reduce customer service and increase costs from stock-outs, backorders, special production runs and costly fast-freight shipments. Because distribution activities involve strong trade-offs, decisions by different functions must be coordinated to achieve superior overall logistics performance.

Thus the goal of integrated logistics management is to harmonize all of the company's distribution decisions. Close working relationships among functions can be achieved in several ways.

Some companies have created permanent logistics committees made up of managers responsible for different physical distribution activities. These committees meet often to set policies for improving overall logistics performance.

Companies can also create management positions that link the logistics activities of functional areas. Many companies have created 'supply managers' who manage the full supply chain activities for each of its product categories.[23] Some have a head of logistics with cross-functional authority. In fact, according to one logistics expert, three-quarters of all large wholesalers and retailers and a third of the big manufacturing companies, have senior logistics officers at top management level.[24]

> For example, the Rover Large Cars division, at Cowley, UK, has a senior logistics executive who controls the entire production of the hugely successful Rover 600 and revamped 800 series. According to Hilary Briggs, the logistics director, this literally means 'from digging of the iron ore to delivery to the customer'.[25]

The location of the logistics functions within the company is a secondary concern. The important thing is that the company coordinates its logistics and marketing activities to create high market satisfaction at a reasonable cost.

### Building channel partnerships

The members of a distribution channel are linked closely in delivering customer satisfaction and value. One company's distribution system is another company's supply system.

The success of each channel member depends on the performance of the entire supply chain. For example, a big supermarket can charge the lowest prices at retail only if its entire supply chain – consisting of thousands of merchandise suppliers, transport companies, warehouses and service providers – operates at maximum efficiency.

Companies must do more than improve their own logistics. They must also work with other channel members to improve whole-channel distribution. This would enable all involved to enhance total customer satisfaction. For example, it makes little sense for a clothing manufacturer to ship finished apparel to its own warehouses, then from these warehouses to a department store's warehouses, from which they are then shipped to the department store. If the two companies can work together, the apparel producer might be able to ship much of its merchandise directly to the department store, saving time, inventory and shipping costs for both.

Today, smart companies are coordinating their logistics strategies and building strong partnerships with suppliers and customers to improve customer service and reduce channel costs. Literature about the channels offers firm evidence that channel performance varies directly with channel cooperation.[26]

These channel partnerships can take many forms. Many companies have created *cross-functional, cross-company teams*. Other companies partner through *shared projects*. For example, many larger retailers are working closely with suppliers on in-store programmes. Some retailers even allow key suppliers to use their stores as a testing ground for new merchandising programmes. The suppliers spend time at the stores watching how their product sells and how customers relate to it. They then create programmes specially tailored to the store and its customers. In this way, both supplier and customer benefit from such partnerships.

Channel partnerships may also take the form of *information sharing* and *continuous inventory replenishment* systems. Companies manage their supply chains through information. Suppliers link up with customers through electronic data interchange (EDI) systems to share information and coordinate their logistics decisions. The recent success of America's big drug wholesalers or Pharmacy Benefit Managers has been, in part, due to their ability to supply such information services to retailers and bulk buyers of medicines. Benetton, the Italian company, has also gained competitive advantage through its management of total supply or throughput time. It uses direct feedback from its franchised outlets to monitor sales trends, links this information into its computer-aided design and manufacturing system and, making use of its highly flexible manufacturing processes, quickly produces (even small quantities) to order.[27]

Today, as a result of such partnerships, many companies have switched from *anticipatory-based distribution systems* to *response-based distribution systems*.[28] In anticipatory distribution, the company produces the amount of goods called for by a sales forecast. It builds and holds stock at various supply points such as the plant, distribution centres and retail outlets. Each supply point reorders automatically when its order point is reached. When sales are slower than expected, the company tries to reduce its inventories by offering discounts, rebates and promotions.

A response-based distribution system, in contrast, is *customer-triggered*. The producer continuously builds and replaces stock as orders arrive. It produces what is currently selling. For example, Japanese car makers take orders for cars, then produce and ship them within four days. Some large appliance manufacturers, such as Philips-Whirlpool, are moving to this system. And Benetton uses a *quick-response system* – it dyes its sweaters and garments in grey, so that these can be swiftly redyed in the new 'in' colours for the season, instead of trying to guess long in advance which colours people will want. Producing for order rather than for forecast substantially cuts down inventory costs and risks.

---

**MARKETING HIGHLIGHT 21.3**

## The attraction of logistics partnership

The trend towards globalization means that more and more multinational businesses have cut their number of factories in Europe and concentrated production in fewer countries. Many such companies have also subcontracted their transport and warehousing services to a single outside provider of logistics services.

A recent study carried out jointly by McKinsey, the management consultancy, and the Centre for European Logistics examined logistics alliances between fifty customer companies and twenty logistics specialists across five northern European countries. The study's main conclusion was that most of companies' outsourcing of logistics activities was excessively driven by cost reduction with insufficient focus on improving service quality to customers.

The study showed that logistics alliances were being set up rapidly in both industrial and consumer product sectors. So far, most involved the stocking, handling and transporting of finished goods. Less than 50 per cent of firms studied also developed alliances

for handling the inflow of goods, parts and materials. Two main motives for creating logistics alliances were highlighted by the study:

1. To specialize production across national borders.
2. To focus on the firm's core competences, such as production, product development, marketing and selling.

Thus it was deemed better to outsource logistics to a specialist provider.

The study showed that pioneers like the photocopier maker, Rank Xerox, and the Dutch transport company, Frans Maas, have maintained an evolving relationship for over ten years, with periodic increases in the scope and value added by the arrangement. It takes a great deal of time to build this level of relationship. Almost half the arrangements studied which involved international flows were taken by freight forwarders like Sweden's ASG and Germany's Kuehne & Nagel. If national alliances were included, the leaders

---

Partnerships in logistics are expected to grow in importance in the 1990s. However, the purpose of setting up alliances with external logistics partners must primarily be to improve service delivery to customers, whatever their level in the supply chain, and, consequently, enhance customer satisfaction. Too often, however, logistics alliances are focused too much on cost reduction and too little on achieving real improvements in service deliveries to customers (see Marketing Highlight 21.3)

## SUMMARY

*Distribution channel decisions* are among the most complex and challenging decisions facing the firm. Each channel system creates a different level of sales and costs. Once a distribution channel has been chosen, the firm usually must stick with it for a long time. The chosen channel strongly affects, and is affected by, the other elements in the marketing mix.

Each firm needs to identify alternative ways to reach its market. Available means vary from direct selling to using one, two, three or more intermediary *channel levels*. Marketing channels face continuous and sometimes dramatic change. Three of the most important trends are the growth of *vertical, horizontal* and *hybrid marketing systems*. These trends affect channel cooperation, conflict and competition.

*Channel design* begins with assessing customer channel-service needs and company channel objectives and constraints. The company then identifies the main channel alternatives in terms of the *types* of intermediaries, the *number* of intermedi-

were warehousing specialists, such as Nedlloyd's Districenters and NFC's Excel.

For the majority of logistics deals, the relationship would best be described as 'contract logistics', not mature alliances. Companies tended to choose logistic service providers on the basis of hard, competitive cost bidding, with only one in seven of the customer companies opting to negotiate with an existing service provider on a 'sole-source' basis. The excessive focus on cost cutting and the lamentably low emphasis given to service improvement was largely due to the fact that the main stimulus behind many of the alliances was corporate restructuring.

The McKinsey consultants stress that such cost-oriented thinking underlying alliance negotiations inhibits a successful outcome. Rather, customer companies should prioritize delivery service. If this can be improved, then arguably, cost reduction will occur through improved methods and the very cooperation between the alliance partners.

Furthermore, to set up successful logistics partnerships, companies must nurture their relationship with service providers. To flourish, there must be information sharing and a desire to explore means of extending the scope of the arrangement: for example, subcontracting management control of all or part of the company's inward and outward logistics, or supply chain.

Logistics alliances are a means of achieving competitive advantage in the supply chain. However, companies must balance cost pressures (efficiencies) against the pursuit of longer-run benefits like service delivery improvements and customer satisfaction. Ultimately, only by taking a more customer-driven approach will companies' logistics deals deliver.

Sources: Peter van Laarhoven and Graham Sharman, 'Logistics alliances: the European experience', *McKinsey Quarterly*, 1 (1994); Christopher Lorenz, 'A deal that aims to deliver', *Financial Times* (1 June 1994), 19.

aries and the *channel responsibilities* of each. Each channel alternative must be evaluated according to economic, control and adaptive criteria. Channel management calls for selecting qualified intermediaries and motivating them. Individual channel members must be evaluated periodically. Companies operating in different geographic markets can apply the key principles of channel management but must adapt approaches to the conditions in individual markets.

More business firms are now paying attention to *physical distribution* or *marketing logistics*. Logistics is an area of potentially high cost savings and improved customer satisfaction. Better logistics management can provide a significant source of competitive advantage for companies. Marketing logistics involves coordinating the activities of the entire *supply chain* to deliver maximum value to customers. No logistics system can both maximize customer service and minimize distribution costs. Instead, the goal of logistics management is to provide a targeted level of service at the least cost. The primary logistics functions include *order processing, warehousing, inventory management* and *transportation*.

The *integrated logistics concept* recognizes that improved logistics requires teamwork – in the form of close working relationships across functional areas inside the company, and across various organizations in the supply chain. Companies can achieve logistics harmony among functions by creating cross-functional logistics teams, with cross-functional authority. Channel partnerships can take the form of cross-company teams, shared projects and information-sharing systems. Through such partnerships, many companies have switched from *anticipatory-based distribution systems* to customer-triggered *response-based distribution systems*.

# ■ DISCUSSING THE ISSUES

1. Name a book club that has successfully marketed books by mail. Why do so few publishers sell books by mail themselves? How might a mail-order book club successfully compete against established retail booksellers?

2. Why is franchising such a fast-growing form of retail organization?

3. Why have horizontal marketing arrangements become more common in recent years? Suggest several pairs of companies that you think could have successful horizontal marketing programmes.

4. Describe the channel service needs of: (a) consumers buying a computer for home use; (b) retailers buying computers to resell to individual consumers; (c) purchasing agents buying computers for company use. What channels would a computer manufacturer design to satisfy these different needs?

5. Which distribution channel strategies – intensive, selective or exclusive – are used for the following products and why? (a) Piaget watches; (b) Lexus cars; (c) Yamaha motorcycles; (d) KitKat chocolate bars; (e) Häagen-Dazs ice-cream.

6. When planning desired inventory levels, what consequences of running out of stock need to be considered?

# ■ APPLYING THE CONCEPTS

1. Discount houses and so-called factory outlet centres have been increasing in popularity in recent years. If you have one of these outlets nearby, visit it and study the retailers. What sort of merchandise is sold in these stores? Do these stores compete with the retailers normally used by manufacturers? What are the pros and cons of operating through discount stores?

2. Go through a camera or computer magazine and pay special attention to large advertisements for mail-order retailers. Look for ads for brand-name products that use selective distribution, such as Nikon cameras or Compaq computers. Can you find an ad that is from an authorized dealer and one that appears not to be? How can you judge which channel is legitimate? Are there price differences between the legitimate and the unauthorized dealers? If so, are they what you would expect?

# ■ REFERENCES

1. Ian Roger, 'Sealed with innovation', *Financial Times* (3 August 1993), 10.
2. Report on distribution operations by retailers and manufacturers in the United Kingdom, compiled by Corporate Development Consultants Ltd (1988); see also 'Managing the European supply chain', NFC Contract Distribution Report (1989), 6.
3. Louis Stern and Adel I. El-Ansary, *Marketing Channels*, 4th edn (Englewood Cliffs, NJ: Prentice Hall, 1992), 3.
4. For alternative levels of definition of a channel of distribution, see Michael J. Baker, *Macmillan Dictionary of Marketing and Advertising*, 2nd edn. (London: Macmillan, 1990), 47–8.
5. Andrew Baxter, 'Caterpillar find uses for distribution skills', *Financial Times* (5 June 1991), 14.
6. Kevin Done, 'Ford to increase stake in Hertz to 54%', *Financial Times* (15 February, 1994), 23.
7. This has been called 'symbiotic marketing'. For further reading, see Lee Adler, 'Symbiotic marketing,' *Harvard Business Review* (Nov.–Dec. 1966), 59–71; P. 'Rajan' Varadarajan and Daniel Rajaratnam, 'Symbiotic marketing revisited', *Journal of Marketing* (January 1986), 7–17; and Gary Hamel, Yves L. Doz and C. D. Prahalad, 'Collaborate with your competitors and win', *Harvard Business Review* (Jan.–Feb. 1989), 133–9.
8. See Allan J. Magrath, 'Collaborative marketing comes of age again', *Sales & Marketing Management* (September 1991), 61–4; and Lois Therrien, 'Café au lait, à croissant and trix', *Business Week* (24 August 1992), 50–1.
9. See Martin Christopher, *Logistics and Supply Management: Strategies for reducing costs and improving services* (London: Pitman, 1992), 184–208; Colin Egan, 'Spread the word', *Marketing Business* (Dec.–Jan. 1991/92), 32–5.
10. See Louis W. Stern and Frederick D. Sturdivant, 'Customer-driven distribution systems', *Harvard Business Review* (July–Aug. 1987), 35.
11. Ibid.

12. Subhash C. Jain, *International Marketing Management*, 3rd edn (Boston: PWS-Kent Publishing, 1990), 489–91; see also Emily Thornton, 'Revolution in Japanese retailing', *Fortune* (7 February, 1994), 143–7.

13. See Philip Cateora, *International Marketing*, 7th edn (Homewood, IL: Irwin, 1990), 570–1.

14. See James A. Narus and James C. Anderson 'Turn your industrial distributors into partners', *Harvard Business Review* (Mar.–Apr. 1986), 66–71; and Marty Jacknis and Steve Kratz, 'The channel empowerment solution', *Sales & Marketing Management* (March 1993), 44–9.

15. Vincent Boland, 'Anheuser-Busch seeks decision on Czech brewer', *Financial Times* (13 October 1994), 34.

16. For further discussion on the role of logistics in cost reduction and service improvements, see Christopher, *Logistics and Supply Chain Management*, op. cit.

17 Michael Terry, 'Drive for greater efficiency', *Financial Times* (3 September 1992), IV.

18. Tom Todd, 'The new ground rules', *EuroBusiness* (May 1994), 43–4.

19. E. J. Gubbins and P. Hancox, 'Cabotage and the Single European Market', *European Business Review* (1990), 2, 14.

20. 'Rays of hope and prophesies of doom', *EuroBusiness* (May 1994), 46–7.

21. 'Taking arms against a sea of troubles' and 'Bright future, present problems', *Eurobusiness* (May 1994), 48–51 and 56–9 respectively.

22. Phillip Hastings, 'Efficiency and quality rule', *Financial Times* (3 September 1992), I.

23. Anderson Consulting, 'Managing logistics in the 1990s', in *id.*, *Logistics Perspectives* (Cleveland, OH: Anderson Consulting, July 1990), 1–6.

24. Shlomo Maital, 'The last frontier of cost reduction', *Across the Board*, **31**, 2 (February 1994), 51–2.

25. Richard Halstead, 'Rover's Miss Cool', *BusinessAge Magazine* (November 1994), 102–6.

26. See Narus and Anderson, 'Turn your distributors into partners', op. cit., 66–71; D. Shipley, 'What British distributors dislike about manufacturers', *Industrial Marketing Management*, **16** (1987), 153–62; P. Rossen and D. I. Ford, 'Manufacturer–overseas distributor relations and export performance', *Journal of International Business Studies*, **13** (1982), 57–72; D. A. Michie and S. D. Sibley, 'Channel member satisfaction: controversy resolved', *Journal of the Academy of Marketing Science*, **13** (1985), 188–205; S. D. Hunt, N. M. Ray and V. R. Wood, 'Behavioural dimensions of distribution: review and synthesis', *Journal of the Academy of Marketing Science*, **13** (1985), 1–24; R. F. Dwyer, 'Channel member satisfaction: laboratory insights', *Journal of Retailing*, **55** (1980), 61–78.

27. Martin Christopher, 'From logistics to competitive advantage', *Marketing Business* (August 1989), 20–1.

28. Based on an address by Professor Donald J. Bowersox at Michigan State University on 5 August 1992.

## CASE 21

### Freixenet *Cava*: bubbles down a new way

### Roberto Alvarez del Blanco and Jeff Rapaport*

The Spanish company Freixenet is the world's largest producer and exporter of *cava* (sparkling wines). In September 1985, management needed to decide a new distribution strategy for the US market. There was much concern and uncertainty regarding the decision. Freixenet had enjoyed spectacular growth from 1983 to 1985 and the management questioned the wisdom of implementing far-reaching changes so soon.

The Freixenet management team had two main responsibilities for the US market. These were the distribution system, and the development of strategies to market and advertise the brand. International wine and liquor producers that export to the American market typically choose one company, usu-

ally in New York, as a national importer. This distribution company buys the goods from the international supplier and then sells to a network of wholesalers located in each state or territory. The margin typically charged by these importers was 15 per cent of the US-landed price. Under this system, a brand manager employed by the import company usually heads the marketing of brands. He or she is responsible for the annual advertising and promotional budget allocated by the brand owner and the supplier.

### The company

Freixenet, SA is a family-run business located at Sant Sadurni d'Anoia in the Region del Cava (the sparkling wine region), about 35 kilometres south-east of

* University of California Berkeley Haas School of Business, USA.

Barcelona in Catalonia, Spain. Freixenet's annual sales in 1985 were about Pta 17,100 million,* 28 per cent of which are from exports. Freixenet's products sold in forty countries; it had commercial branches in Britain, Germany and the United States, and production facilities in Spain, Mexico and California.

### The product

*Cava*-type sparkling wine is produced by the 'Méthode Champenoise' where the second stage of the fermentation process occurs in the original bottle. Only sparkling wines produced by the *Méthode champenoise* in the Champagne region of France could bear the name 'champagne'. Wines produced outside the region can only use *méthode champenoise* on their label. However, a decision by the EU forbade the use of this description and established a transitional period of eight years.

Another method of producing sparkling wines is the *granvas* method (sometimes called the *cuve-close* method), in which the second stage of fermentation is in large tanks instead of the original bottle. It is faster and less expensive than the *champenoise* method but yields a lower quality wine. Freixenet produces five *cavas*: Carta Nevada, Cordon Negro, Brut Nature, Brut Barroco and Brut Rose. Each *cava* has a distinctive quality resulting from its production process.

### Expanding internationally

At the end of World War II Freixenet began significant international expansion. José Ferrer, president and general manager, travelled to various European countries searching for opportunities to sell his products. Fellow *cava* producers did not share his eagerness for international expansion. José Ferrer remembered: 'One day, at a "*cava* producers" meeting, a colleague … stated, "this business of exports is a joke. What you like is to travel. Forget this business – outside of Spain you won't sell a single bottle."'

The country initially targeted for export was the United Kingdom because of its high champagne consumption and need to import due to its lack of vineyards and local brands. Unfortunately, Freixenet met with difficulties resulting from a British bias towards French products and the poor image of Spanish products. José Ferrer explained:

> We believed it necessary to join forces with a British company to distribute our products because no one wanted to buy from a Spanish distributor. After two years, the British company became tired of losing money and was replaced by two other associates who also became tired of the business. At this point we took over the whole operation.

The new British company was named Direct Wine Supply. Freixenet's hopes for the British market were overinflated. In 1984, the Freixenet group sold only about 45,000 cases of its product in Britain (25,000 Freixenet and the remainder Freixenet's Castellblanch brand). These results were poor considering the eight years of work invested in developing the brand. José Ferrer further explained:

> The Direct Wine Supply was essentially a deadweight. We should have dropped them, but we haven't done it yet because we believe that in the end it will work out when we implement a more dynamic and creative management team instead of the conservative one which we had for eight years. If this doesn't work, we might sell the company to some of the 'admirers' who recognise our success domestically and internationally. If we do this, we can recoup the £200,000* to £300,000 that we have already invested.

The first phase of international expansion lasted over thirty years during which Direct Wine Supply (DWS) began to export to several European countries. In the United States, Freixenet hired a representative in New Jersey to import products and market them nationally. This distribution system, which employs only one import representative for the whole country, followed the system Freixenet used in Europe.

The second phase of international expansion began during the early 1980s with the establishment of two commercial branches, one in the United States and the other in Germany. Freixenet's exports to the United States had grown slowly during the 1960s and early 1970s. Management realized that one

*1 ecu = US$1.26 = Pta 161 (Spanish pesetas).

*1 ecu = US$1.26 = UK£0.83.

representative located on the east coast could not adequately cover the whole country because of diverse regional markets. In 1978, the company decided to hire a wine consultant to help the representative establish distribution to untapped states and to increase sales in states where distribution was already established. In 1980, the contract with this representative expired. Instead of renewing it, Freixenet opened a US branch in New Jersey called Freixenet USA, Inc. The new national distribution system emphasized decentralization by assigning roughly one import-distributor to each state. This structure allowed the company to establish a significantly more active presence in each market by having a more concentrated market focus through each distributor. Freixenet USA provided marketing support for these importer-distributors. Ramon Masia, the export manager of the Freixenet group of companies, described the work of Freixenet USA:

> The office helps the importer-distributors by solving problems related to advertising, shipments and internal logistics. It provides support for advertising in four ways. First, it negotiates national advertising contracts. Second, it co-ordinates these advertising campaigns with regional distributors. Third, it manages all of the co-operative advertising that Freixenet USA uses with direct distributors. Fourth, it develops point-of-sale materials. The office also manages stock between distributors and does follow up work for Freixenet, SA.

Twelve Americans currently work in the subsidiary. The annual cost of running this office, including personnel and regional agents' salaries, is approximately $600,000.* This amount does not include advertising and promotional expenses.

The third phase of international expansion began with setting up two production facilities: one in Mexico and one in the United States. The first bottles produced in Mexico would be available for sale in 1986. The operation included about 50 hectares of vineyards and a production plant with a one million bottle capacity. The total investment was Pta 500 million. This facility supplied the Mexican and Latin American market. The rationale for this investment in Mexico was that the Mexican market had been

*1 ecu = US$1.26.

closed to foreign sparkling wines for more than twenty years.

The American production facility, Freixenet Sonoma Champagne Caves, opened at the beginning of 1985. This facility was in the Carneros area of Napa Valley, just north of San Franciso. It consisted of 180 acres considered to have the best vineyards and had a one million bottle capacity. Completed in 1986, it required an initial investment of $6 million. The wine produced here would be a Californian *cava*, named Gloria Ferrer, in honour of José Ferrer's wife.

Export manager, Ramon Masia, headed the international Freixenet branch. He supervised the export managers of Castellblanch and Segura Viudas, as well as the managers for the US, German and British DWS commercial branches. The Mexican and US facilities were not under his management.

### Establishing joint ventures and subcontracting

Freixenet wished to explore new ways of expanding their business through joint-venture and subcontracting opportunities. They also bought two businesses from the well-known Spanish company, Rumasa, which included an immediately available idle production facility in Sant Sadurni d'Anoia. Freixenet used this plant to produce wine for an American company that owned the Paul Cheneau brand. José Ferrer described this subcontracting operation:

> They began to entrust its production to Freixenet, but they soon told us that they liked neither our product nor our price and they looked for other subcontractors. After a while, they came back to Freixenet under the same conditions.

In 1984 Freixenet was contacted by Domecq, a large Spanish producer of wines and brandies, who had nineteen sales representatives and distributors in the United States. Domecq's salesforce sold well-known Spanish and Mexican brands of wine and liqueurs. They soon discovered that they needed more products to sell and hoped to form a joint venture with Freixenet. The two companies created a new French brand name, 'Lembey', and equally shared marketing expenses and profits. Freixenet produced this *cava* in Sant Sadurni. The brand had a successful start in the United States and was forecast to achieve a sales volume of over 80,000 cases in 1985. José Ferrer commented on the joint ventures:

> The experience with 'Paul Cheneau' demonstrated the dangers of subcontracting. In a market with established surplus capacity, the subcontractor is totally at the mercy of his client who can constantly pressure him on prices. On the other hand, with a brand joint venture, the first year promotional expenses correspond to the second year price discount involved in subcontracting. The difference is that in a joint venture you own 50 per cent of the brand and if business has been good, this investment will have gained in value.

### International market for sparkling wines

In 1984, the world production of sparkling wines was about 120 million cases, an increase of 16.8 per cent from 1979. The main producers were France (25 per cent), Germany (17 per cent), USSR (17 per cent), Italy (13 per cent) and Spain (8 per cent). These six countries controlled 91 per cent of the total world production and the latter four countries showed a large increase in their production compared to 1979. The top sparkling-wine exporting countries were: France with 13 million cases a year, Italy with 10 million and Spain with 2.9 million. The top importing countries were: the United States with 7 million cases a year, Germany with 6.8 million and Britain with 2 million. The industrialized production methods (the 'cuve-close' and 'transfert' methods) accounted for most of the total production.

Germany's market was the largest with 28 million cases sold per year, followed by the United States with 17 million cases, France with 16 million cases and the USSR with 15 million cases. Germany also led with a per capita consumption of 5.5 bottles per year, followed by the United States' 3.7, France's 2.3 and USSR's 1.7.

### The US market for sparkling wines

The United States is one of the main world producers, consumers and importers of sparkling wines. Although per capita consumption is not high, it shows regular and rapid increases, especially in the large urban areas of California, the East Coast and

Texas. Between 1978 and 1982, annual per capita consumption increased from 1.75 to 2.69 bottles in the District of Columbia and from 1.31 to 1.77 in California. Between 1975 and 1984, consumption of sparkling wine increased from 7.1 million to almost 16.3 million cases. The top ten states accounted for almost three-quarters of the total consumption in the United States.

Sales by month reveal an interesting pattern. October was the top month in 1984, with 18.2 per cent of the year's sales. November and December had more than 12.0 per cent and May registered 10.1 per cent. February was the lowest sales month of the year with only 4.2 per cent. This data pattern shows a strong seasonality that is typical for this industry.

The US sparkling wine markets had four price segments. American preference is clearly for wines costing less than four dollars. Spanish and Italian wines dominated the four to nine dollar segment; Italian and Californian dominated the nine to fifteen dollar segment and French champagnes dominated the over fifteen dollar segment. The first two segments, those costing less than nine dollars, represented 86 per cent of market share.

American sales of sparkling wine increased noticeably between 1979 and 1984. Italian sparkling wines, especially Asti Spumante, took first place for imports in 1984 with 50.1 per cent of total sparkling wines. French champagnes follow with 24.5 per cent and Spanish *cavas* with 21.9 per cent. Total imported brands with the highest sales in 1984 were Freixenet, Tosti and Martini & Rossi.

### Freixenet marketing in the US

Starting in 1973, Freixenet's sales to the United States grew explosively. From 1980 onwards, Freixenet's average sales increased by over 50 per cent per year. For 1985, the US market should represent more than 70 per cent of Freixenet's exports. This figure included the sale of Freixenet brands and joint ventures, Paul Cheneau and Lembey.

Five types of distributors operated in the American market: nation-wide importers; regional importers; 'brokers' or brand-representatives; wholesale distributors; and retailers. Retail trade has three categories: retailers who specialize in wines and liquors; supermarkets and small retail shops; and 'clubs' patronized by wine connoisseurs. Two large distribution channels handled Freixenet's products in the United States. Approximately 75 per cent of sales were to supermarkets and liquor stores, known as 'off premises'. The other 25 per cent of sales were to restaurants, bars and hotels, known as 'on premises'.

According to a Freixenet executive, advertising was one of the principal components of Freixenet USA's marketing strategy. For 1985, Freixenet budgeted $4 million to promote its products to the American market and $1 million for the remainder of the export markets. Of the $4 million that would be invested in the United States, $1 million was for television commercials in the twelve main regional markets, $2 million for national magazine advertisements, $500,000 for cooperative advertising (the same amount being invested by the importers-distributors), $300,000 for public relations, $100,000 for a gigantic blimp that travels throughout the country, and $100,000 for the yearly importers' convention.

Other imported sparkling wines had smaller budgets. Among these, the most popular French champagne sold in the United States is Moët et Chandon, which had a $1 million budget for public relations involving social events and benefit projects and a $1 million budget for print and television advertising.

A key reason for success in the United States was the design of the Freixenet bottle. Ramon Masia explained:

> We did marketing research on Cordon Negro, the most popular sparkling wine sold in the US. The research indicated that Cordon Negro's black bottle exerts an immediate attraction for people. Americans perceive it as an indicator of high prestige and since it sells for only $6, they see it as a great bargain. Since the word Freixenet is difficult to pronounce, Americans ask for it by asking for the black bottle.

The president of Freixenet USA, Inc., Bill Kroesing, summarized some of the most important factors regarding the company's strategy:

> The success achieved in the US is due to the bottle, the promotion, the distribution system and the proper quality/price relationship. Regarding the latter factor, Freixenet has filled the void left by the French and the American producers.

Ramon Masia added:

> We realised that there were four markets for 'cava' in the US. The first market is for a sparkling wine with low quality and price, the second is for an average wine, the third is for a wine with high quality and price and the fourth is the super high quality market. American producers who, like Gallo, produce a low-quality 'granvas' wine, supply the low-price national segment. The higher price segment is controlled by California producers and the highest quality segment by French champagnes. There was no participant positioned for the middle segment and this is where we entered with 'Carta Nevada' and 'Cordon Negro' and we now dominate this segment of the market.

Low labour and material costs allowed the Spanish producers to be more price competitive than the French, Italians and Californians. The price of one kilo of grapes in the cava region was Pta 25 to 30. In contrast, a kilo of grapes in the Champagne region costs FFr 23.[*] In the US the prices of French champagnes fluctuated between $15 and $20, prices of Spanish *cavas* between $4 and $5 bottle and the Cordon Negro between $6 and $7 a bottle. Both use 750 ml. bottles. The American tariffs on Spanish *cava* imports were 15 to 20 per cent of the landed-price, varying from state to state. Of the total cost of Freixenet products, 60 per cent consisted of raw materials, labour and production. The remaining 40 per cent covered administration and marketing activities. Freixenet was not content with the budget's allocation.

Management felt that they were not getting a good return for their advertising dollar. Armando Gavidia, the vice-president for the north-east region of Freixenet USA, who had a big portion of the cooperative budget to invest, was not satisfied with the service he was getting from the advertising and public relations companies. He suggested to José Ferrer that Freixenet should create its own advertising and public relations company to service all the Freixenet brands in the US market. His reasoning was:

> Our advertising and public relations budgets are small for the big advertising and PR companies, so they assign junior account executives to our accounts who do not know the wine market and business. They also have a high personnel turnover

*I ecu = US$1.26 = FFr 6.47 (French francs).

rate. Whenever one of these people gets familiar with our company and the wine business, he or she jumps to another company and we have to start from scratch again and again. If we hire a couple of advertising managers we could create our own advertising 'shop'. The creative part will be handled by free-lancers. The media buying will be performed by one of the well-known media buying services and then we will assign our own people to create and maintain our own database for public relations. In this way, we will get the proper return for the money we allocate. Our people will be more con-cerned with the small brands, like Segura Viudas, and they will ensure that they get the service and attention each deserves to maximize each brand's potential.

## Entering the US high-price segment

Freixenet decided to launch the Gloria Ferrer brand in the US high-price segment. This positioned *cava* against the California producers. Even though the *cava* would not be available until 1986, Californian producers made a small amount sold in 1984. The Gloria Ferrer brand sold for $13 to $16 a bottle. José Ferrer explained the decision to produce a California *cava*:

> We expect that our distributors will be able to offer the whole range of products that the market requires and there is a large market for California *cava*. There are restaurants and bars that sell only California wines. This includes some California *cavas* which sell for higher prices than French *cavas*....We could have entered the lower price (under $4) seg-ment with 'Dubois', but we did not want to risk devaluing the image of Spanish champagne....We have set up own own vineyards and production facili-ties to promote and improve our image. This helps our sales efforts in the US. All of the prestigious wineries have their own vineyards in California.... Furthermore, producing in California protects us from any increases in the American import restric-tions from the EU.

Gloria Ferrer was sold through the same importers who distributed the *cava* brought from Spain. These distributors sold a wide range of products and some had separate salesforces to sell to 'off premises' and 'on premises' locations.

## The new distribution system

In September 1985, Freixenet USA needed to set up a new US distribution system. The new proposed structure employed no national 'agent', 'broker' or brand-assigned nominee. Freixenet would retain all rights of administrative coordination, marketing and advertising. This system also extended certain responsibilities to the primary US importers. These importers would not only be distributors, but would also be Freixenet's representatives in their respective marketing areas.

This new import-distribution system aimed to eliminate the 'national importer' and create one wholesaler per state acting as the direct importer, brand representative and wholesaler for his or her territory. The Freixenet USA office would assist the national network of direct importers by sending their orders to Spain and communicating with the winery regarding shipments and transport problems.

The Freixenet USA office would also handle the national marketing budget for advertising and public relations and assist the local importers in developing their regional and local advertising and promotional campaigns. This system also established a cooperative advertising budget in which Freixenet USA would match each local importer's investment. Armando Gavidia explained:

> With this new distribution structure, Freixenet will get more involvement with the brand from the importers and they will create their own local adver-tising and promotions. This will motivate these man-agers to achieve better results. The beauty is that this co-operative investment program will not cost Freixenet any extra money because it will be funded by the 15% profit margin that would have been paid to the national importer.

A new contract had an explicit description of the Freixenet primary importers' obligations and rights. If implemented, each primary importer would sign this contract. Under the terms of the contract the importers had a number of obligations:

1. Primary importer must have current licences to service its assigned territories.
2. Primary importer must solicit and distribute all brands throughout assigned territories.
3. Primary importer must order sufficient stock of

all basic items to ensure adequate inventory to service expected demand for a minimum of 90 days.

4. Cheques must be sent with each order.
5. Primary importer must give Freixenet immediate notice of its selection of wholesaler distributor(s). Importers must also notify Freixenet of any sales made by a distributor to wholesalers or retailers located outside the importer's assigned territory.
6. Primary importers must provide Freixenet with monthly depletion reports.
7. Primary importer must perform operational supervision of the distributor(s), including personal visits as necessary.
8. Primary importer must agree always to apply 'its very best' efforts on an equal basis to all of Freixenet SA's brands.
9. Primary importer must coordinate marketing and promotional programmes with the Freixenet USA Marketing Office and advertising with Freixenet's Advertising Agency.
10. The 'basic six' Freixenet sparkling wines must be inventoried and offered for sale by all distributors.
11. The primary importers' advertising and marketing must be in reasonable conformity with Freixenet's international and national programme and trademark protection interests. Product segmentation is an important part of this – this is why Carta Nevadas is available in two bottle sizes.
12. At least every six months, primary importer must provide a copy of its posting or price list and that of the distributor(s) for Freixenet brands to Freixenet USA and to all regional vice presidents.
13. Primary importers must not provide false or misleading information to Freixenet or the regional vice presidents. Freixenet must receive 60 days' notice of the planned or actual sale of the primary importer's company.

According to its proponents, this strategy would eliminate a layer of management and reduce costs significantly. With the savings, Freixenet would offer a 'managerial service performance allowance' to reimburse each importer as a brand representative and to pay for brand-management costs incurred by each importer/marketing representative.

Proponents of the new distribution system expected it to be well received by the national wholesale network. They believed that with this system, all importers would feel more involved with the brand than in the past. They would appreciate the allocation of the marketing budget according to their local market needs. The proponents believed that the importers would consider Freixenet's strategy a big improvement compared with the other brands' systems that used national importers. This was largely because the national brand managers in New York never really understood the local needs of each market. This was the key reason proponents expected everyone in the network to be pleased with this new strategic distribution design.

Proponents also hoped to have a National Importer Convention in Lanzarote, Spain in May 1986, and planned a special recognition ceremony for the following achievements: number one importer of the year, best promotion of the year, best local advertising of the year, and best on-premises promotion of the year (promotions related to restaurants and bars). During this convention, each importer would present and explain his or her accomplishments and results to the rest of the network. It would give each importer the chance to share different strategies and policies that were effective in different markets. Another important objective was to create a 'family' feeling among the distribution network members. Armando Gavidia explained:

> I expect that most of our distributors will become friends with each other and also will develop a very positive attitude towards the brand. This will create many positive feelings and generate loyalty to the company. This will help our future growth and increase the speed for expanding our market share in the USA.

However, critics of the plan had serious misgivings:

1. Freixenet did not currently have enough managers with adequate experience to implement the system.
2. The financial risk would be significantly greater because the company would have to ship to fifty different companies in the United States and the risk involved would be very difficult to assess.

852          *Place*
## CASE 21 (cont)

3. The money that would be saved by eliminating the importers would be spent in the organization of Freixenet USA.

4. The new system would not be well received by the wholesalers who are used to the 'old boy' network.

5. If the implementation of the new distribution strategy failed, it could permanently damage the US marketing operation.

### Questions

1. Contrast Freixenet's entry into the US and UK markets. What went wrong in the UK market?

2. Identify the different sorts of distribution and relationships Freixenet used in the US market. What are the advantages of each? How do Freixenet's control and investment change in each case?

3. Does the distribution system change with the segments they serve? Does the different only apply to the retailers used?

4. Is it wise for Freixenet to change its distribution system? What is the case for and against the existing and proposed distribution systems? How do Freixenet's relationship and controls change with the move from the existing to the proposed system?

## CHAPTER TWENTY TWO

# Placing products

## Retailing and wholesaling

## CHAPTER OBJECTIVES

After reading this chapter, you should be able to:

■ Explain the roles of retailers and wholesalers in the distribution channel.

■ Describe the main types of retailers and give examples of each.

■ Identify the main types of wholesalers and give examples of these.

■ Explain the marketing decisions facing retailers and wholesalers.

## CHAPTER PREVIEW

### IKEA

In just over four decades, IKEA, the privately owned Swedish furniture retailer, has grown from a single store in Sweden's backwoods to become one of the most successful international retailers in the world. The company's vast blue and yellow retail sheds selling about 11,000 stylish, low-cost, strangely named products, such as Orgryte sofas and Smedvik dining tables, are a feature of the international retailing landscape. Smart targeting, careful attention to customer needs and rock-bottom prices have made IKEA the world's largest home furnishings company.

1 ecu = US$1.26
= SKr 9.29
(Swedish kronor)

IKEA now runs more than 100 outlets in over twenty-five countries across the globe, taking over Skr 39bn a year in sales. It opened its first non-Scandinavian store in Switzerland in 1973. Since then, its vast warehouse stores (two to three football fields in size) have marched triumphantly across the globe. Its success formula was based on reinventing the furniture-retailing business. Traditionally, selling furniture was a fragmented affair, shared between department stores and small family-owned shops. All sold expensive products and delivered up to two or three months after a customer's order.

IKEA trims costs to a minimum while still offering service. It does this by using a global sourcing network stretching to about 2,300 suppliers in sixty-seven countries. IKEA suppliers get long-term contracts, technical advice and leased equipment in return for an exclusive contract and low prices. IKEA's designers also work closely with suppliers to reduce product costs from the outset. Other savings come from IKEA displaying its vast product range in cheap out-of-town stores. It sells most of its furniture as knocked-down kits for customers to take home and assemble themselves. The firm enjoys huge economies of scale from operating such huge stores, and from enormous production runs made possible by selling the same furniture all around the world. This enables IKEA to compete on quality while undercutting rival manufacturers by up to 30 per cent on price. According to Mr Ingvar Kamprad, IKEA's entrepreneurial owner, the firm's business philosophy is to 'offer a wide range of home furnishing items of good design and function, at prices so low, that the majority of people can afford to buy them'. However, IKEA offers consumers more than just quality merchandise at low cost. Each store provides a 'complete shopping destination' for value-seeking, car-borne consumers. Consumers browse through the store's comfortable display area, where signs and stickers on each item note its price, details of its construction, assembly instructions, its location in the adjacent warehouse – even which other pieces complement the item. Customers wrestle desired items from warehouse stacks, haul their choices away on large trolleys and pay at giant-sized checkout counters. There is a free supervised crèche and a reasonably priced Scandinavian restaurant for the hungry shopper.

IKEA is one of a new breed of retailers called 'category killers'. Other examples are Toys 'R' Us and Tower Records. Unlike warehouse clubs and other 'off-price' retailers, which offer the lowest prices but few choices within any given category, category killers offer an exhaustive selection in one line. Toys 'R' Us stocks 18,000 different toy items, also in football-field-size stores. Tower Records stores carry up to 75,000 titles – twenty-five times more than the average competitor. With such large assortments, category killers generate big sales that often allow them to charge prices as low as those of their discount competitors. As we can see, these retailers get their name from their marketing strategy: that is, to carry a huge selection of merchandise in a single product category at such good prices that you destroy the competition. Category killers are now striking in a wide range of industries, including furniture, toys, records, sporting goods, housewares and consumer electronics.

The category killers face a few problems, however. For example, IKEA has encountered occasional difficulty managing its huge inventory, sometimes overpromising or inconveniencing customers. The company's expansive stores also require large investments and huge markets. Some consumers find that they want more personal service than IKEA gives or that the savings are not worth the work required to find products in the huge store, haul them out and assemble them at home. Despite such problems, IKEA has gained worldwide prosperity beyond its founders' dreams. But success also brings untold difficulties. Its managers have continually to reinvent its success. For IKEA this is exacerbated by the fact that, to sustain its competitive position and growth, the firm has to venture into new geographic markets. As it strikes out beyond its home and familiar current markets, it often has to change the formula that had previously guaranteed success. It has to adapt to local market peculiarities, but without destroying the very things that created success in the first instance.

The lesson on adaptation, for IKEA and retailers venturing overseas, is clearly brought home in IKEA's invasion of the famously competitive US retail market, which has a well-deserved reputation as a 'graveyard' for foreign, especially Europe's, nonfood retailers. In 1985, IKEA opened a 15,700 square metre warehouse store outside Philadelphia. Initially, with the dollar buoyant at around SKr 8.6, it was easy to make money. Six new stores were opened in the next six years. By 1989, things had started to go wrong. In each new European country IKEA entered, it normally broke into profit after 2 to 3 years with its third or fourth store. In America, it was still losing money. Customers flocked to the stores but many left empty-handed: long queues, constant stock-outs and the rising cost of the imported Swedish-made furniture (the dollar's value had dropped to SKr 5.8 by 1991) threatened IKEA's delivery of its low-cost merchandise with a service difference! IKEA recognized that it had to do something if it were to hold its place in the world's most competitive retail market. Göran Carstedt, head of IKEA's North American operations in 1990 said: 'If you're going to be the world's best furnishing company you have to show you can succeed in America, because there's so much to learn here.'

IKEA had to adapt its retailing strategy in several ways. First, it had to revise its product policy – what is sold in Helsingborg could be sold the same way in Houston. Talking to the US consumer, Mr Anders Moberg, IKEA's chief executive, learnt that European products jarred with American tastes and, sometimes, physiques. Swedish beds were narrow and measured in centimetres. IKEA did not sell the matching bedroom suites Americans liked. Its kitchen cupboards were too narrow for the large dinner plates needed for pizza (believe it or not!). Its glasses were too small for a nation that often piles them high with ice (Mr Carstedt elicited that Americans were buying IKEA's flower vases as drinking glasses).

In response to these differing American needs, IKEA adapted. For example, it now offers king- and queen-sized beds denominated in inches and sold as part of complete suites. Similarly, the drawers in bedroom chests were made an inch or two deeper as Americans used these to store their sweaters: sales of drawers immediately increased by 30 to 40 per cent. IKEA has redesigned over a fifth of its products in the United States. It has also revised its supply strategy, with at least 45 per cent of the furniture sold in American stores being produced locally, compared with 15 per cent in 1990. As for the queues, IKEA has redesigned store layout and installed new cash registers in the American stores, thus increasing throughput by some 20 per cent. American consumers are also given a more generous returns policy than European customers – and a next-day delivery service!

IKEA's perseverance has paid off. The Swedish firm is going from strength to strength in America, having adapted but not destroyed its original formula. Since 1990, sales in America have tripled, and by mid-1993, IKEA at last made a profit. It now has fifteen stores in the United States, bringing in more than $480m. in annual sales. IKEA plans to open a further sixty stores around the country over the next twenty-five years. Meanwhile, IKEA's experience in America has persuaded it to remix its recipe elsewhere. China is the prime target, where the company plans to open up ten stores in the years to come. The bones of a supply network in China are already assembled. IKEA's Mr Carstedt intends to take the lessons learnt from his firm's invasion of the US retail market and apply these in Asia's potentially most lucrative market. After 'stars and stripes', IKEA's Mr Carstedt expects a 'red star' to join IKEA's already rather multicoloured galaxy.[1]

1 ecu = US$1.26

This chapter looks at *retailing* and *wholesaling*. In the first section, we look at the nature and importance of retailing, main types of store and nonstore retailers, the decisions retailers make, and the future of retailing. In the second section, we discuss these same topics as they relate to wholesalers.

## RETAILING

What is retailing? Department stores, supermarkets, the local florist and wine bar are examples of retailers, but so are the Novotel Hotel, a doctor seeing a patient and the door-to-door sales representative who tries to sell you an insurance policy or a window-cleaning service. **Retailing** includes all the activities involved in selling goods or services directly to final consumers for their personal, nonbusiness use. Retailing is an important channel activity as it provides ultimate consumers with goods and services. Many institutions – manufacturers, wholesalers and retailers – do retailing. But most retailing is done by **retailers**: business whose sales come *primarily* from selling to final consumers. Retailing covers a wide range of sectors, including food, beverages and grocery, clothes, footwear, household goods, electrical items, books/ stationery, hire and repair services, restaurants, hotels and catering, banking and financial services. Although most retailing occurs in retail stores, in recent years, transactions outside stores or nonstore retailing – selling by mail, telephone, door-to-door contact, vending machines and numerous electronic means – has grown tremendously. Because store retailing accounts for most of the retail business, we discuss it first. We then look at nonstore retailing.

## STORE RETAILING

Retail stores come in all shapes and sizes, and new retail types keep emerging. They can be classified by one or more of several characteristics: amount of service, product line, relative prices, control of outlets and type of store cluster. Table 22.1 shows these classifications and the corresponding retailer types.

| TABLE 22.1 | *Different ways to classify retail outlets* | | | |
|---|---|---|---|---|
| Amount of service | Product line sold | Relative price emphasis | Control of outlets | Type of cluster |
| Self-service | Speciality store | Open market | Corporate chain | International shopping |
| Limited | Department store | Discount store | Retailer cooperative | centre |
| service | Variety store | Category killer | Franchise organization | City and town- |
| Full service | Supermarket | Cash-and-carry | Merchandising | centre shopping zone |
| | Convenience store | store | conglomerate | Parades and |
| | Superstore, and | Catalogue | | neighbourhood |
| | hypermarket | showroom | | store |
| | Service business | | | The corner shop |
| | | | | Edge-of-town |
| | | | | and out-of-town |
| | | | | cluster |
| | | | | Sheltered complex |
| | | | | and shopping |
| | | | | mall |
| | | | | Retail park |

## Amount of service

Different products require different amounts of service and customer service preferences vary. We focus on three levels of service – self-service, limited service and full service – and the types of retailers that use them.

**Self-service retailers** have increased rapidly in big developed economies over the years. The reasons for their rising acceptance by consumers vary in different countries, but, in general, customers were willing to perform their own 'locate-compare-select' process to save money. Today, self-service is the basis of all discount operations and typically is used by sellers of grocery and convenience goods (such as supermarkets) and nationally branded, fast-moving shopping goods (e.g. discount stores).

**Limited-service retailers**, such as department stores, provide more sales assistance because they carry more shopping goods about which customers need information. They also offer additional services such as credit and merchandise return not usually offered by low-service stores. Their increased operating costs, however, result in higher prices.

In **full-service retailers**, such as speciality stores and first-class department stores, salespeople assist customers in every phase of the shopping process. Full-service stores usually carry more speciality goods and slower-moving items, such as cameras, jewellery and fashions, for which customers like to be 'waited on'. They provide more liberal return policies, various credit plans, free delivery, home servicing and extras such as lounges and restaurants. More services result in much higher operating costs, which are invariably passed along to customers as higher prices.

## Product line

Retailers can also be classified by the length and breadth of their product assortments. Among the most important types of retailers are: the speciality store, the department store, the variety store, the supermarket, the convenience store, the superstore and the service business.

### Speciality store

A **speciality store** carries a narrow product line with a deep assortment within that line. Examples include stores selling sporting goods, furniture, books, cosmetics, jewellery, electronics, flowers or toys. Speciality stores can be classified further by the narrowness of their product lines. There are single-line stores such as Esprit, or Benetton that sells a range of clothes for men and women, outfitters such as the Swedish Hennes & Mauritz, and The Body Shop that specializes in personal care products. The 012 Benetton and The Gap stores, that offer only clothes for children, are *limited-line stores*, and a shop such as Rohan that focuses on outdoor leisure garments, or a men's custom-made shirt store, is a *superspeciality store*.

Today, speciality stores are flourishing for several reasons. The increasing use of market segmentation, market targeting and product specialization has resulted in a greater need for specialist stores that focus on specific products and segments. Because of changing consumer lifestyles and the increasing number of two-income households, many consumers have greater incomes but less time to spend shopping. They are attracted to speciality stores that provide high-quality products, convenient locations, excellent service and quick entry and exit.

### Department store

A **department store** carries a wide variety of product lines – typically clothing and fashion accessories, cosmetics, home furnishings and household goods. Each line is operated as a separate department managed by specialist buyers or merchandisers. Examples of well-known department stores include House of Fraser stores such as Harrods and Debenhams, John Lewis and Harvey Nichols in Britain, Sogo, Takashimaya and Isetan (in Japan and South East Asia), Saks Fifth Avenue and Bloomingdale (in the United States), El Corte Ingles (in Spain), Galeries Lafayette (in France) and Karlstadt (in Germany).

Department stores are large (typically 20,000–25,000 square metres) and occupy prime sites in town and city central shopping centres. Up to the 1970s, department stores grew rapidly in many Western developed countries. However, over the 1970s and 1980s they began to lose ground to other types of retailers, including discount stores, speciality store chains and 'category killers' (we discuss these later). The department stores used to enjoy some competitive advantage from running credit accounts; the credit card boom put paid to that. And the nature of the department stores – stocking a little bit of everything – puts them at a disadvantage compared with specialized retailers ordering bulk when it comes to exerting leverage over suppliers. Furthermore, in large cities, the heavy traffic and poor parking facilities made town shopping less appealing and department stores started to lose trade to out-of-town retailers. Many stores closed, were taken over by, or merged, with others.

To combat these threats, surviving department stores refurbished their existing stores and improved merchandise quality and assortment. Some built new stores which were more conveniently sited within big shopping malls and covered shopping centres (e.g. Debenhams and Rackhams are sited in big malls such as the Shires in Leicester and Meadowhall in Sheffield). Many have added 'bargain basements' to meet the discount threat. Still others have remodelled their stores or set up 'boutiques' and other store formats that compete with speciality stores. In the 1990s, department stores must continue to invest in good management and service quality in order to compete successfully with more focused and flexible speciality stores on the one hand, and with more efficient, lower-priced discounters on the other.

Service remains the key differentiating factor. Many department stores fail to appreciate this and failure to provide service to demanding consumers results in customers going elsewhere to obtain the goods they seek. When it comes to service, most retailers could learn a lesson from Japan's Odakyu Department Store (see Marketing Highlight 22.1).

### Variety store

**Variety stores** tend to be low-cost, self-service stores. They specialize in a wider range of goods than specialist stores, but have a narrower range compared to department stores. Also, these are more basic in terms of the level of extra amenities offered. Woolworth, for example, sells a variety of products – compact discs, records, cassettes, household goods, children's clothes and confectionery – but, except for a cafe/restaurant, does not offer the extra facilities and services provided by a huge department store. However, some variety stores like Marks & Spencer, which sells clothing and accessories, food, cosmetics, household goods, home furnishing, and financial services, have not only focused on quality, but also differentiated themselves from the competition by providing extra services for customers, including store cards, special events and mail order.

### Supermarket

**Supermarkets** are large, low-cost, low-margin, high-volume, self-service stores that carry a wide variety of food, laundry and household products. Their growth in Europe has been phenomenal since the 1960s. More recently, these outlets have developed in affluent Asian markets. When supermarkets expanded, they squeezed out many of the small independent grocery retailers in the town or city centre, including the small corner shops in local residential areas, which could not match supermarkets' wider product assortment, shopping convenience and lower prices.

The first supermarkets introduced the concepts of self-service, customer turnstiles and checkout counters. Many of these supermarkets were located in town or city-centre high streets with ample car parking and, for a while, offered a good range and value-for-money to consumers. However, with town and city centres becoming increasingly congested and car-ownership rising fast in the 1980s, people were keen to shop outside towns and cities. Supermarkets also faced slower sales growth because of slower population growth and an increase in competition from convenience stores, discount stores and superstores. Many supermarkets also became increasingly conspicuous for their general ugliness and grubbiness. With competitive pressures intensifying in the 1980s, the big supermarket chains were forced to invest their way out of trouble. Thus supermarkets like Safeway, Tesco, and others in the United Kingdom, began to look for new ways to build their sales. Many started to close unprofitable high-street stores and built big edge-of-town stores. Most chains now operate fewer but larger stores including superstores – Asda, Sainsbury, Safeway and Tesco, for example, are now established grocery superstore retailers. They practise 'scrambled merchandising', carrying many nonfood items – beauty aids, household goods, toys, nonprescription medicines, electrical appliances, video cassettes, sporting goods, garden supplies – hoping to find high-margin lines to improve profits. Supermarkets are also improving their facilities and services to

## MARKETING HIGHLIGHT 22.1

### Now that's department store service

In the following account, a foreign visitor to Japan describes her amazing shopping experience with Odakyu Department Store.

'My husband and I bought one souvenir the last time we were in Tokyo – a Sony compact-disc player. The transaction took seven minutes at the Odakyu Department Store, including time to find the right department and to wait while the salesman filled out a second charge slip after misspelling my husband's name on the first.

'My in-laws, who were our hosts in the outlying city of Sagamihara, were eager to see their son's purchase, so he opened the box for them the next morning. But when he tried to demonstrate the player, it wouldn't work. We peered inside. It had no innards! My husband used the time until Odakyu would open at 10.00 a.m. to practice for the rare opportunity in that country to wax indignant. But at a minute to 10.00 a.m. he was pre-empted by the store ringing us.

'My mother-in-law took the call and had to hold the receiver away from her ear against the barrage of Japanese honorifics. Odakyu's vice president was on his way over with a new disc player. A taxi pulled up 50 minutes later and spilled out the vice president and a junior employee who was laden with packages and a clipboard. In the entrance hall the two men bowed vigorously. The younger man was still bobbing as he read from a log that recorded the progress of their efforts to rectify their mistake, beginning at 4.32

p.m. the day before, when the sales clerk alerted the store's security guards to [catch] my husband at the door. When that didn't work, the clerk turned to his supervisor, who turned to his supervisor, until a SWAT team leading all the way to the vice president was in place to work on the only clues – a name and an American Express card number. Remembering that the customer had asked him about using the disc player in the United States, the clerk called thirty-two hotels in and around Tokyo to ask if a Mr Kitasei was registered. When that turned up nothing, the Odakyu commandeered a staff member to stay until 9 p.m. to call American Express headquarters in New York. American Express gave him our New York telephone number. It was after 11.00 when he reached my parents, who were staying at our apartment. My mother gave him my in-laws' telephone number.

'The younger man looked up from his clipboard and gave us, in addition to the $280 disc player, a set of towels, a box of cakes and a Chopin disk. Three minutes after this exhausted pair had arrived, they were climbing back into the waiting cab. The vice president suddenly dashed back. He had forgotten to apologize for my husband having to wait while the salesman had rewritten the charge slip, but he hoped we understood that it had been the young man's first day.'

Source:   Reprinted from Hilary Hinds Kitasei, 'Japan's got us beat in the service department, too', *Wall Street Journal* (30 July 1985), 10.

attract more customers. Typical improvements are better locations, improved decor, longer store hours, cheque cashing, catering facilities, and baby changing and feeding facilities. Although consumers have always expected supermarkets to offer good prices, convenient locations and speedy checkout, today's, more sophisticated food buyer wants even more. Quality is critical and supermarkets must offer this to compete in the 1990s. Shoppers want subtly lit, clean stores, and they like fresh fruit, hot croissants and preprepared gourmet meals. They still expect to get their cheap baked beans, but would pay over the odds for high-quality fresh food. Many supermarkets, therefore, are 'moving up-market', providing 'from-scratch' bakeries that actually do their own baking, gourmet delicatessen counters and fresh seafood departments. Many are cutting costs, establishing more efficient and effective operations through rigid quality control, centralized distribution and electronic technologies, and lowering prices in order to compete more effectively with food discounters. In Europe particularly, grocery discounters such as the German Aldi, Normas, and Lidl, the Danish Netto and the French Carrefour have been expanding aggressively away from their home territory. All five, for example, have opened discount stores in the United Kingdom in the early 1990s, with Aldi planning a chain of 200 in this country. These discounters hit the supermarkets hard with their 'pile it high and sell it cheap' concept.[2] Supermarkets too have to compete with each other in their push for increased market shares. Those that strive to serve consumers' wants and deliver superior service quality are most likely to sustain their market position in the long run.

## Convenience store

**Convenience stores** are small stores that carry a limited line of high-turnover convenience goods – essential groceries, toiletries, cigarettes and newspapers. Examples include Happy Shopper, Spar, Mace and VG stores. These locate near residential areas and remain open for long hours, seven days a week. Convenience stores must charge high prices to make up for higher operating costs and lower sales volume. But they satisfy an important consumer need in a niche segment – shoppers in this segment use convenience stores for emergency or 'fill-in' purchases at off hours or when time is short, and they are willing to pay for the convenience of location and opening hours.

## Superstore and hypermarket

Superstores, discount sheds and hypermarkets are large-scale outlets – typically spanning several thousand square metres of retail space. These are well developed in many parts of Europe where they account for a sizeable share of total retail sales (see Table 22.2).

**TABLE 22.2** *Hypermarkets and superstores in Western Europe, latest available year*

| | Number of outlets | | % share of total retail sales |
|---|---|---|---|
| | Hypermarkets | Superstores | |
| France | 914 | 765 | 29.4 |
| United Kingdom | 746 | 1,701 | 17.6 |
| Netherlands | 40 | 339 | 14.0 |
| Germany | 892 | 1,164 | 11.3 |
| Norway | 25 | 175 | 10.0 |
| Switzerland | na | na | 10.0 |
| Spain | 116 | 39 | 7.7 |
| Denmark | 15 | – | 6.0 |
| Finland | 57 | – | 5.8 |
| Austria | 77 | 152 | 5.0 |
| Sweden | 67 | – | 3.7 |
| Belgium | 70 | 30 | 3.0 |
| Italy | 118 | na | 1.8 |
| Portugal | 25 | – | na |

Note: na = not available.
Source: *Euromonitor*.

**Superstores** typically occupy 2,000–4,000 square metres and sell everything from baked beans to fine wines, aspirins to ankle socks. They also offer a range of services such as dry cleaning, post-offices, film developing and photo finishing, cheque cashing, petrol forecourts and self-service car washing facilities. Most are located out-of-town, frequently in retail parks, with vast free car parks. As mentioned earlier, grocery retailers led the way in establishing purpose-built edge-of-town superstores in the late 1980s. In Britain, Sainsbury, Argyll (which owns Safeway), Asda and Tesco, between them, spent about £5bn on building superstores during 1988-91. In recent years, nongrocery retailers, such as the US Toys 'R' Us, the UK Specialist Computer Holdings (SCH) and IKEA have also opened superstores in out-of-town sites. SCH sells leading hardware and software brands such as IBM, Toshiba, Compaq, Apple, Microsoft, Lotus and Borland, and offers finance, training and maintenance packages. Analysts report that superstores will account for more than 40 per cent of computer sales by the mid-1990s.[3]

**Hypermarkets** are even bigger than superstores. A typical hypermarket occupies about 10,000 square metres of space, almost as big as six football fields. They combine supermarket, discount and warehouse retailing (see below). They carry more than just routinely purchased goods, for they also sell furniture, appliances, clothing and many other things. The hypermarket operates like a warehouse. Products in wire 'baskets' are stacked high on metal racks; forklifts move through aisles during selling hours to restock shelves. The store gives discounts to customers who carry their own heavy appliances and furniture out of the store. Examples are the French Carrefour and Casino, and Savacentre which is owned by the British Sainsbury.

Hypermarkets have been successful in world markets. For example, Carrefour, the large French retailer, successfully operates hundreds of these giant stores in Europe, South America and Asia. However, although Carrefour has experimented with hypermarkets in the United States it has met with little success. The main advantage of hypermarkets – their size – also can be a serious drawback for some consumers. Many people, especially older shoppers, balk at the amount of walking involved. And despite their size and volume of sales, most hypermarkets have only limited product variety. Thus many retailers have abandoned the idea of hypermarkets in favour of smaller, more shoppable, better-serviced stores.[4] Nonetheless, there is a continuing trend towards large-scale retail development, particularly in rapidly developing economies, such as Southeast Asia, Japan and South America.

### Service business

For some businesses, the 'product line' is actually a service. Service retailers include hotels, banks, airlines, colleges, hospitals, cinemas, theatres, health and fitness clubs, bowling alleys, restaurants, repair services, hairdressing shops and dry cleaners. Service retailers have been growing faster than product retailers in recent years. Banks look for new ways to distribute their services, including automatic tellers, direct deposit and telephone banking. Bowling alleys have been extending their services to include catering facilities.

## Relative prices

Retailers can also be classified according to the prices they charge. Most retailers charge regular prices and offer normal-quality goods and customer service. Some offer higher quality goods and service at higher prices. The retailers that feature low prices are open markets, discount stores, cash-and-carry warehouses and catalogue showrooms.

## Open markets

The traditional **open market**, perhaps one of the most established forms of retailing, is known for its low prices. Most towns have markets selling fresh agricultural produce, including fruits, vegetables, meat, fish and poultry, and a variety of household goods, clothes and haberdashery. Some markets have stalls that also sell toys, furnishings, books, compact discs/records/cassettes and a host of other products. These retail markets are typically situated in the town's main shopping centre or square, or in open areas or covered halls close to town centre shops. Open markets are not as convenient as modern-day supermarkets, particularly for consumers used to one-stop shopping, although they remain attractive because of their lower prices.

## Discount store

A **discount store** sells standard merchandise at lower prices by accepting lower margins selling higher volume. The use of occasional discounts or specials does not make a store a discount store. A true discount store *regularly* sells its merchandise at lower prices, offering national brands, not inferior goods. Examples are the German Lidl, Aldi and Norma, the Danish Netto, Britain's Kwik Save and Shoprite, and the French Carrefour's Ed, all of which are grocery retailers.

The early discount stores (e.g. Aldi) cut expenses by operating in warehouse-like facilities or discount-sheds in low-rent, heavily travelled districts. These discount-sheds were usually on one floor, had no extra amenities, not even window displays. They slashed prices, advertised widely and carried a reasonable width and depth of products. In recent years, facing intense competition from other high-street discounters and department stores, many discount retailers have 'traded up'. They have improved decor, added new lines and services, and opened edge-of-town or suburban branches, which has led to higher costs and prices, as in the case of the British Kwik Save, which has recently expanded its product range, invested in new displays and computerized checkouts and built larger edge-of-town stores to counter the threat of discounters like Aldi and Netto. Furthermore, to differentiate from the supermarkets and grocery superstores, like Sainsbury and Tesco, Kwik Save has stepped up advertising, particularly posters and illuminated displays, stressing its price advantage and 'no frills' approach.[5]

Some department stores have cut their prices to compete with discounters, blurring the distinction between many discount and low-cost department stores. Conversely, many department-store retailers have again upgraded their stores and services to set themselves apart from the improved discounters. Discounters, however, continue to be a threat, as European and US players, in a bid for continued growth, look set to battle it out in European and Asian markets (see Marketing Highlight 22.2)

## Category killers

**Category killers** are not just discounters, but are a new breed of exceptionally aggressive discounters. They are superstore outlets offering a wide range of branded products in a clearly defined category. Their predatory pricing strategy – pile them high, sell them cheaper than the competition – and ability to decimate much of the compe-

## Retailers come to terms with the global marketplace

Selling goods across shop counters is a knack worth over $5 trillion a year worldwide, but one that once proved difficult to transfer across national frontiers. In the past, many retailers have tried to go international. Some of the best were old-timers like America's original 'five-and-dime' store, F. W. Woolworth, and C&A, founded by the Dutch Brenninkmeyer family. Few, however, have succeeded. The list of failures is depressingly long, and includes many well-known names: for example Marks & Spencer's costly entry into the Canadian market; France's Printemps, whose joint venture in Japan almost went bankrupt; and Dixons, the UK electrical stores group, with its acquisition of the US Silo chain. Today, though, the picture is changing. A new generation of retailers increasingly train their sights on world markets, and have the ability to carry off international ventures.

For many retailers, internationalization has become a key issue for the 1990s. Large retailers are spreading out in all directions: east, west, north, south. Dutch retailer Ahold has bought eleven supermarkets in the Czech Republic; Germany's Obi, the do-it-yourself chain and part of the Tengelmann Group, look set to expand in Italy, Hungary and the Czech Republic. Carrefour has a discount chain, Ed, in the United Kingdom and a significant stake in the warehouse club, Costco, which opened in the United Kingdom in 1993. Indeed Ahold, Aldi and Tengelmann, Belgium's Delhaize and Carrefour are among those which have built up the proportion of sales coming from outside domestic markets to more than 30 per cent – 70 per cent in the case of Delhaize. Britain's Tesco acquired the 92-store Catteau chain of supermarkets in northern France in 1992, while Sainsbury, through acquisitions, has become the eleventh-largest grocer in the United States. Migros, the Swiss grocery retailer, until recently only active in Switzerland, now operates in France, Germany and Austria, where it is committed to taking a leading position. French fashion chains like Pimkie, Promod, Camieu and Naf Naf have made a substantial impact on the Belgian market; so has Marks & Spencer in French, Spanish and Far Eastern markets. To the list of those that can be considered global can be added Italy's Benetton, the Swedish IKEA and America's McDonald's and Toys 'R' Us.

The extent of cross-border retailing is highlighted by recent research conducted by the Oxford Institute of Retail Management (UK). The study reported that retailers made 530 international moves between 1991 and 1993, of which 381 or 72 per cent involved European firms expanding into other European countries. A further 676 moves were made in Europe by non-European retailers. The United Kingdom was the most popular country for international moves, followed by France. The move to Eastern European countries was also very popular, with the Czech republic, Slovakia, Poland and Hungary being the most favoured destinations outside the EU. Another recent study published by Corporate Intelligence, a retail research group, reinforced the quickening pace of internationalization by retailers – it reported that European retailers made 610 cross-border moves in the first four years of the 1990s, compared with 611 cross-border deals in the whole of the 1980s.

Also noteworthy is the dramatic increase in the number of US store groups operating in Europe – forty-five today, up fifteen from 1991. The UK market, in particular, has been targeted as a 'springboard' for retail attack. US retailers, specialists and discounters alike, such as TJ Maxx (clothing), Bath and Body Works (cosmetics and toiletries), Walt Disney and Time Warner (entertainment merchandise) Lands End and LL Bean (mail-order), Staples (superstore stationery), Sunglass Hut, Nevada Bob (sports goods), Pier 1 (crafts) and QVC (home shopping) are among some of those newly arrived with ambitious expansion plans.

Retailers with international ambitions are also emerging from eastern Asia. Japanese store groups, such as Sogo, Mitsukoshi, Takashimaya, Isetan and Yaohan, have spread across Japan, Singapore, Hong Kong and Thailand. Yaohan claims that it will have opened 170 department stores in China, Hong Kong and Macau by 1997. Hong Kong's Bossini and Giordano have spread to Malaysia, Taiwan and Singapore. Both are making the running in China. The Japanese retailers have more ambitious plans – they are coming to the West.

Similarly, Asia's rich countries are attracting Western retailers, who are scrambling to meet the increasingly sophisticated demands of newly prosperous consumers eager to buy products ranging from deodorants and frozen food to luxury accessories

US retail giant Wal-Mart comes to Hong Kong in the form of 'Value Clubs'.

and designer fashion brands. Leading retailers who have set up stores across the region include Carrefour, Galeries Lafayette, Makro, Marks & Spencer, IKEA, Toys 'R' Us, The Body Shop, K-Mart and Wal-Mart. Wal-Mart has opened several 'Value Clubs' – retail/wholesale cash-and-carry membership warehouse clubs – in Hong Kong, with the intention of learning about the Chinese consumer in preparation for its longer-term assault on the greatly underserved China market. The American giant is not alone here, as the Japanese Jusco, which also happens to be one of the world's largest retailers, has already successfully used the warehouse club format in Hong Kong.

Since 1990, deregulation of Japan's 'Large Scale Retail Law', which controlled planning consent for new stores and opening hours in order to protect small retailers from new high-street competitors, has removed local shopkeepers' power to veto a new supermarket or big store and allowed stores to stay open later. This has created new opportunities for superstore retailers who can now open stores with floor space of up to 1,000 square metres without the approval of the Ministry of International Trade and Industry. Retailing law reforms have also enabled foreign retailers to break the links between the manufacturers and the high street. Toys 'R' Us skipped over the intricate web of wholesalers to deal directly with one of its suppliers, Nintendo, the video game maker, and was thus able to undercut Japanese toy prices. Large supermarket chains with bulk purchasing power are also bypassing the traditional multilayered wholesale network that has kept prices high, and are procuring merchandise direct from manufacturers or producers. Stronger antitrust laws in Japan have overturned manufacturers' grip on retail prices. Large manufacturers had controlled retail prices and prevented discounting of their products by threatening to stop supplies. Now retailers can discount prices without fear of losing supply contracts. More importantly, the door is now more firmly open to superstores/discounters and leading retailers who are used to dealing directly with their suppliers – Marks & Spencer, The Gap, and others are expressing keen interest in Japan.

The wave of internationalization has been prompted by a combination of 'push' and 'pull' factors. The biggest 'push' factor is saturation of the domestic markets. While there is room for expansion at home, there is no need to look abroad, but that option is fast disappearing for retailers in developed EU member states, the United States and Japan.

The 'pull' factors include:

1. The falling barriers to entry into markets worldwide. The creation of a Single European Market has made Europe more attractive for US and Asian retailers, just as deregulation in Japan would make the market more accessible to foreign retailers.

2. Retailers' suppliers are becoming more international themselves. For example, Unilever are restructuring manufacturing operations on a pan-European basis, and adopting international marketing campaigns. This leads to the growing importance of internationally recognized brand names in consumer goods, electricals and consumer durables.

3. Increased foreign travel by consumers and the spread of cross-border mass media (e.g. satellite television) are creating similarities in consumer desires for certain wares. Marks & Spencer's European Division director, Alan Lambert says: 'Our best selling products are the same in London, Madrid or Hong Kong.'

The trend towards internationalization in retailing cannot be ignored. Those that do cross frontiers must consider and select the most appropriate target markets before determining the entry and marketing strategy for the international operation.

### Entry mode

Some have found *partnerships* and *joint ventures* with local retailers the best way to expand abroad. For example, Marks & Spencer formed a joint venture with local retailer Cortefiel in Spain, which helped to find sites, get to know the market, and deal with local authorities. Others, such as Benetton, Body Shop, and McDonald's, have tended to take the direct *franchising* path indirectly as a store within a store, as Harrods does inside Mitsukoshi's flagship store in Japan. In saturated markets such as the United States, Canada, the United Kingdom, France, Germany, the Netherlands and Australia, there is limited scope for winning market share through growth. The only retailers that can expect to do so are the ones that are highly *innovative* in one or more aspect of their business: store format, shopping environment, cus-

tition in their sector explains their name. The leading category killers operate in the large consumer durables market, such as furniture, hi-fi and office equipment, but, in the United States, category killers are already well established in toys, games, electrical/consumer electronics, office supplies, do-it-yourself (DIY), sports goods and computer products. Classic examples making an impact in Europe, the United States and Asia include the furniture giant, IKEA and Toys 'R' Us. The formula has also been successfully applied to the entertainment software market, as in the case of Virgin Megastore, which has a chain of stores sited in high-profile locations in large cities, and has captured a substantial share of the market for prerecorded music – its first outlet in Paris, for example, took an estimated 5 per cent of the entire French market.

Category killers' competitive advantage lies both in their size compared with smaller specialist operators in the sector, and in their range of products compared with other large mixed retailers. Their price advantage is generally based on scale

tomer service, product quality or choice, or operating systems and distribution methods. For others, *acquisition* of existing groups may be a better route, as in the case of Migros, which bought the chain of 112 Familia supermarkets in the western Austrian province of Vorarlberg from the Zumtobel group. Migros also formed two joint ventures with Konsum, Austria's largest supermarket chain, and so used a hybrid approach for entry into the Austrian market. In emerging markets, retailers that can be acquired are limited, but *organic growth* offers an exciting, if risky opportunity.

### Target markets

Retailing analysts identifies ten markets divided into: the 'tough three'; the 'torrid three'; and the 'formidable four':

- The 'tough three' – Italy, South Korea and Japan – are strong economies with large middle classes.

Local restrictions have limited foreign entry in the past, although with some of the entry barriers easing over the 1990s, these markets offer significant opportunities.

- The 'torrid three' – Mexico, Argentina and Turkey – are experiencing rapid if volatile economic growth, but with an underdeveloped retail sector. These offer even more promising growth prospects, but with a moderate degree of economic risk.
- The 'formidable four' – Brazil, China, Russia and India – have a poor retail infrastructure, but offer the most exciting prospects, given their rapidly growing middle classes hungry for consumer goods. These, however, offer the greatest economic and political risks.

Isetan in Volgograd or Migros in Shanghai may still be years away. Nonetheless, one of the world's biggest but most localized industries – retailing – is finally coming to terms with the global marketplace.

Sources: Neil Buckley, 'Retailers' global shopping spree', *Financial Times* (12 October 1994), 25; Clive Branson, 'Find what the customer likes before opening doors abroad', *The European* (18–24 March 1994), 22; Wilf Altman, 'Customers pick up rewards from cross-border retailing', *The European* (18–24 February 1994), 20; Neil Buckley and Ian Rodger, 'Sticking to the border', *Financial Times* (20 May 1993), 15; Richard Tomkins, 'A long walk for the shops', *Financial Times* (11 April 1994), 15; Richard Halstead, 'Let competition commence', *BusinessAge Magazine* (July 1994), 84–6; Bronwyn Cosgrave 'France fills the T-shirt gap', *The European-élan* (6–12 May 1994), 14; Neil Herndon, 'Wal-Mart goes to Hong Kong, looks at China', *Marketing News*, **28**, 24 (21 November 1994), 2; Guy de Jonquières, 'Temptations along the eastern aisle', *Financial Times* (6 April 1994), 19; Emiko Terazono, 'Cheap and cheerful', *Financial Times* (15 March 1994), 24; 'Japanese industry: inefficient structure', *Financial Times* (6 December 1994), IV; William Dawkins, 'Japanese industry: progress will be painfully slow', *Financial Times* (6 December 1994), VI, 'Asian retailing: teach me shopping', *The Economist* (18 December 1993) 78–9.

economies, bulk buying power and a rigorous attention to costs. In the case of Toys 'R' Us, for example, all its superstores are at least 4,000 square metres and it stocks every branded toy under the sun. It buys stocks internationally on a big scale, has cheap rented sites, well-controlled store designs and layouts, and selling in bulk keeps prices lower than smaller rivals.

It is important to note that this new generation of discounters are not dowdy shed-retailers – their best selling points are depth of products on offer and presentation of the store (Virgin Megastore offers consumers a more vibrant and exciting shopping environment than rival discounters like Our Price); in many cases price competition is no longer a key factor. This presents a formidable task to competitors who have none of the advantages of size, low costs, product depth/breadth.

Category killers have, in recent years, been one of the most dynamic growth sectors in retailing. Leading US and European category killers have been successful in penetrating overseas markets, with long-term growth potential predicted for the format as well as for its leading players (see Table 22.3). Importantly, the American market is near saturation, and Europe is now a focus for expansion for many more of those leading players – K Mart, T J Maxx, Blockbuster Video, Staples and Sports Authority, to name but a few.[6] (See Marketing Highlight 22.2.)

### Cash-and-carry stores

**Cash-and-carry** stores are large stores (around 3,000-4,000 square metres) selling an extensive assortment of goods, ranging from groceries to office furniture. The Dutch Makro is an example of this type of retailer. Across Europe it operates self-service warehouses that sell food, beverages, wines and spirits, confectionery, household goods, clothes and other assortments to a dual customer base – consumers and trade (resellers/retailers). The latter are mainly the small shopkeepers, local supermarkets, convenience stores and catering trade. Individual consumers (e.g. small business people, the self-employed and their staff, or anyone with a Makro card) can take advantage of bulk discounts when they shop at Makro. Discount bulk-retailing of this

| **TABLE 22.3** | *Forecast number of category killers in selected markets in the year 2000* | | | |
|---|---|---|---|---|
| | **Number of stores** | | | |
| | Toys and games | DIY | Electricals/consumer electronics/home furnishings | Office supplies |
| Australia | 20 | 41 | 29 | 25 |
| Austria | 5 | 8 | 6 | 6 |
| Belgium | 6 | 8 | 7 | 5 |
| Brazil | 20 | 30 | 25 | 20 |
| Canada | 45 | 40 | 35 | 35 |
| Denmark | 5 | 8 | 7 | 6 |
| France | 27 | 33 | 30 | 30 |
| Germany | 56 | 84 | 69 | 60 |
| Indonesia | 20 | – | – | – |
| Italy | 27 | 44 | 35 | 30 |
| Japan | 117 | 200 | 153 | 140 |
| Mexico | 30 | 45 | 40 | 40 |
| Netherlands | 14 | 17 | 15 | 15 |
| Norway | 4 | 4 | 4 | 4 |
| Philippines | 10 | – | – | – |
| Portugal | 3 | 3 | 3 | 3 |
| South Korea | 40 | – | – | – |
| Spain | 35 | 50 | 42 | 40 |
| Sweden | 4 | 6 | 5 | 5 |
| Switzerland | 5 | 5 | 5 | 5 |
| Taiwan | 15 | – | – | – |
| Thailand | 10 | – | – | – |
| United Kingdom | 45 | 60 | 55 | 55 |

Note: [1]Based on current category killer sectors.
Source: *Euromonitor*.

nature is no longer a Western phenomenon. Cash-and-carry operators like Makro have made inroads into Asia.

> Makro opened its cash-and-carry store (the size of about two football fields) in Bangkok, Thailand in 1989. It is heaped from floor to ceiling with discounted goods of every kind. Open from 6am to 10pm every day, it is packed with shoppers wheeling giant trolleys filled with an eclectic assortment of goods, ranging from office furniture and TV sets to soft drinks and live eels. It has been the trail-blazer in bulk discount retailing in Asia, with revenues of nearly £1.3bn in 1992. Makro succeeded in Thailand despite sceptics' fear that the Dutch firm would find it difficult to break the close ties between Thai manufacturers and distributors. By the end of 1993, it already had six stores in place in Thailand and spread to other parts of Asia, including Taiwan, Indonesia and Malaysia. Joint ventures in South Korea and China are next on the list. Makro's success in Thailand was helped by its alliance with Charoen Pokphand, a powerful local conglomerate, which opened doors to Thai manufacturers. Makro also was helped by demand from small shopkeepers, its main customers. These 'mom-and-pop' stores traditionally are captive customers for the big distribution companies, which dictate the assortment of goods to be sold. Makro gives these small buyers not just the chance to by-pass the traditional distributors and buy their own selection of merchandise, but to do so in bulk and at lower prices. Makro's success has attracted rivals, with Save-One, a joint-venture between four Thai firms, and defectors from Wal-Mart, the giant American discount retailer, following Makro with their own stores in Thailand. Others, like the 7-Eleven grocery chain, have also struck alliances, in this case with Charoen Pokphand, and now has 258 stores in Thailand, with plans to increase these to 1,000 by 1997.[7]

1 ecu = UK£0.83

**Warehouse clubs** (also known as *wholesale clubs* or *membership warehouses*) are another American style of trading that has crossed the Atlantic. In the United States, warehouse clubs sell huge volumes of a narrow range of goods – typically brand name grocery items, appliances, clothing and a hodge-podge of other goods – at rock-bottom prices from low-cost, edge-of-town warehouselike facilities to members who pay an annual membership fee. Members are mainly business customers, such as small retailers and caterers, who use the clubs as a wholesale outlet; the remainder are everyday shoppers drawn in by the cheap prices. The clubs have experienced explosive growth in the United States over the past decade, but now, saturation and the effective reactions by supermarkets, department stores and regular discounters, have led to consolidation in the industry and retailers in this sector are also looking for growth opportunities abroad.

Britain, in particular, is targeted as a springboard for their 'attack' on the affluent single market of northern and western Europe. One of the leading US warehouse-clubs, Costco, in which the French Carrefour has a 20 per cent stake, opened Britain's first warehouse-club, a hypermarket the size of two football fields, in Thurrock, Essex, in 1993.

Costco is sited on a huge retail park (see description below) accommodating thirty or so aircraft hangars, occupied by familiar and unfamiliar retail superstores – Allied, MFI, World of Leather, Do it All, B&Q, Toys 'R' Us, PC World, Shoe City, Carpet City and many others. Prices in the stores are 10 or 15 per cent cheaper than in other places. Membership of Costco is limited to those operating or owning a business, professionals and civil servants. Because its margins are so low, Costco relies on bulk buying and the annual £23.50 membership fee for profit. It selects its target customers carefully. According to Clive Vaughan of retail research company Verdict, 'Individuals are allowed to join provided they have an above-average income and stable employment. They're going for doctors and solicitors with Volvos and big houses to store things in. They're going for *Which?*-reading ABs looking for bargains. Lower social groups are catered for by discount supermarkets such as Kwik Save and Netto.'[8]

There is much debate as to whether the American warehouse-club formula will successfully take off in Europe, given the differences in costs, market structures, culture and consumer preferences between the US and European retailing industries. But, given the extraordinary popularity of this style of trading in the United States, it would not be wise for European and global retailers to discount the threat entirely or underestimate their customers' desire for bargains.

**Factory outlets** or mill shops are owned and operated by manufacturers and carry the manufacturer's surplus, discounted or irregular goods. They offer prices as low as 50 per cent below the usual retail prices on a wide variety of items. The concept is similar to the factory mill shops in which manufacturers' merchandise is heavily discounted.

### Catalogue showroom

A **catalogue showroom** sells a wide selection of high-mark-up, fast-moving, brand-name goods at discount prices. These include jewellery, power tools, cameras, luggage, small appliances, toys and sporting goods. Catalogue showrooms make their money by cutting costs and margins to provide low prices that will attract a higher volume of sales. Products on sale are all listed in catalogues, which are placed on counters in the store. Consumers fill in order forms for goods they want and pass these to sales assistants who complete the transaction. The customer collects the merchandise from the sales assistants or picks these up from a collection point in the store. Catalogue showrooms operate warehouses adjacent to the store, from which merchandise can be quickly despatched to the customer in the store. Only one of each item or only common goods are displayed in the catalogue showroom, which saves display and labour costs. Argos and Index are examples of catalogue retailers who operate on British high streets. Indeed, Argos developed this concept of shopping in Britain. It offers the consumer the benefits of convenience, low cost and product variety. Over the years, in response to greater competition from high-street retailers and discounters, Argos has broadened its lines, renovated its stores and added services to attract more customers. For example, it offers consumers extra security with its 10-day no-quibble returns policy; it has introduced a 24-hour telephone-ordering service and free delivery on certain purchases. Through innovative strategies, stores, such as Argos, are able to sustain their position in an increasingly competitive retail environment.

## Control of outlets

Most retail stores are independent. Other forms of ownership include the corporate chain, the voluntary chain and retailer cooperative, the franchise organization and the merchandising conglomerate.

### Corporate chain

The chain store is one of the most important retail developments of this century. **Chain stores** are two or more outlets that are commonly owned and controlled, employ central buying and merchandising, and sell similar lines of merchandise. Corporate chains appear in all types of retailing, but they are strongest in department stores (e.g. Britain's House of Frazer, Holland's Vendex International and C & A), variety stores (e.g. Woolworth, Marks & Spencer), food and grocery stores (e.g. Sainsbury,

Dansk Supermarket, Sweden's Ica, Kesco from Finland, Konsum in Austria), and clothing (e.g. the British Burton Group, the Swedish outfitters Hennes & Mauritz, the Dutch C & A). Corporate chains have many advantages over independents. Their size allows them to buy in large quantities at lower prices. They can afford to hire corporate-level specialists to deal with areas such as pricing, promotion, merchandising, inventory control and sales forecasting. Chains also gain promotional economies because their advertising costs are spread over many stores and over a large sales volume.

### Retailer cooperative

The great success of corporate chains encouraged many independent retailers to band together to benefit from the economies of group buying and merchandising. The **retailer cooperative** is a group of independent retailers that has set up a jointly owned central wholesale operation and conducts joint merchandising and promotion efforts. Examples include the Swiss Migros which is a federation of twelve cooperative societies and the United Kingdom's Co-operative Societies. These organizations give independents the buying and promotion economies they need to match the prices of corporate chains.

### Franchise organization

A **franchise** is a contractual association between a manufacturer, wholesaler or service organization (the franchisor) and independent businesspeople (the franchisees) who buy the right to own and operate one or more units in the franchise system. The idea of franchising goes back to the Middle Ages, where a king would grant the barons a franchise to collect taxes in return for them providing him with soldiers. The concept re-appeared in its more modern guise in the mid-nineteenth century when the American Singer Sewing Machine company franchised independent operators to sell and service its equipment. This was still really just a form of licensing the distribution of an existing product. It is one form of franchise system where the manufacturer authorizes the dealer to sell its branded product or service. Franchising can also be based on techniques or methods of doing business, or on the trade/brand name, goodwill or patent that the franchisor has developed, instead of a complete product. The format which is most popular today – where the franchisor sells to the franchisee the right to merchandise its product or service under its tradename or trademark – made its first appearance in the mid 1950s. It is also called 'business format' franchising. The franchisor typically provides a brand identity and start-up, marketing and accounting assistance as well as management know-how to the franchisee. In return, the franchisor gets some form of compensation, such as an initial fee and a continuing royalty payment, lease fees for equipment and a share of the profits. Franchising has been prominent in fast-food companies, petrol stations, video stores, health and fitness centres, car rentals, hairdressing salons, travel agencies and dozens of other product and service areas. Franchisors include many household names like The Body Shop, McDonald's, Kentucky Fried Chicken (KFC), Avis, Hertz, Europcar, Stefanel, Benetton, Holiday Inn and Shell (which recently switched from a licensing to a franchising system on many of its petrol forecourts).

Franchising offers a number of benefits to both the franchisor and franchisee. The main advantages for franchisors are:

■ the franchisor secures fast distribution for its products and services but does not incur the full costs of setting up and running its own operations. The system enables franchisors to expand a successful business more rapidly than by using its own capital.

- Franchisors are provided with a very highly motivated management as the franchisees are working for themselves rather than a salary.
- The contractual relationship ensures that franchisees operate to and maintain franchisors' standards.

The main advantages for franchisees are:

- They are buying into a proven system if selling an established brandname (e.g. McDonald's, Shell, Interflora).
- They can start a business with limited capital and benefit from the experience of the franchisor. This way they reduce the costs and risks of starting a new business.
- Franchisees also get the benefits of centralized purchasing power – since the franchisors will buy in bulk for the franchisees.
- They get instant expertise in operational issues such as advertising, promotions, accounts and legal matters, and can rely on franchisors' help should things go wrong.

Just how important such benefits are to both sides is apparent in Shell's decision to franchise many of its service stations. Traditionally, Shell, like most other oil companies, licensed sites. Licensees got a three-year licence to operate a service station, but it was up to them how they did so. The arrangement covered little more than the provision of Shell fuel to the service station and the basics of site operation, such as health and safety issues. In May 1990, Shell launched its SHARE (an acronym for standards, high quality and retailer excellence) programme, site operators were able to buy a 10-year franchise backed by a major package of business and marketing support. Promotional and merchandising support services are also given to Shell forecourt franchisees. In return, Shell is able to ensure that motorists get consistently high standards of service whichever Shell service station they go to. Shell gets standardisation of service levels – according to Shell's own research, this is what the customer wants. According to a Shell franchisee, being part of the Shell franchise system means that he is part of a Marks & Spencer-type operation. He adds, 'petrol retailing has been a pretty mucky, grotty industry for some while. We've got to serve the customer well and be seen as a high-street retailer rather than a service station. If you go into a Marks & Spencer, you know what you are going to get. Shell's aim is that if you go to a Shell Share site you'll know what to expect. It'll be clean, the people will be nice and there'll be a range of goods you know and which are reliable.'[9]

Franchise systems have several disadvantages:

- Franchisors invariably have to forfeit some control when operating through franchisees.
- The franchisees may not all perform exactly to franchisors' operating standards, and inconsistencies in service levels can tarnish the brand name.
- Franchisees may not always have a good deal in that they have to work extremely hard to meet sales and financial targets to make the business pay, and, though they have already paid their initial fee, have to meet continuing management services or royalty payments.

However, franchise systems offer retail business a quick route for expansion in both domestic and overseas markets. More and more companies are actively looking for franchise opportunities in new markets. For example, early ventures like The Body Shop, Stefanel, Benetton, Yves Rocher (French beauty products company) and Eurodollar International (British car rental firm), which have been expanding across

Europe in the 1980s, are now followed by newcomers. In recent years, for example, there has been an upsurge of interest, particularly among French retailers, in selling licences and franchising directly into the UK market – fashion firms such as Rodier and Jacadi, and designer garden furniture company Jardin en Plus, together with budget hotel operators like Climat, Balladins and Primevere, are all keen to franchise overseas. Franchising has grown rapidly in the last two decades. Given its importance and potential advantages, it is likely to remain a strong force in retailing in the 1990s.

### Merchandising conglomerate

**Merchandising conglomerates** are corporations that combine several different retailing forms under central ownership and share some distribution and management functions. For example, Sears operates over twenty speciality and department stores in the United Kingdom, including Selfridges (department store), Olympus Sports (sportswear), Adams Childrenswear, Miss Selfridge, Warehouse (clothing/fashion clothing), Zy (jewellery), Bertie, Roland Cartier, Saxone (footwear) and Freemans (mail order). In the United States, F. W. Woolworth, in addition to its variety stores, operates twenty-eight speciality chains, including Kinney Shoe Stores, Afterthoughts (costume jewellery and handbags), Face Fantasies (budget cosmetics), Herald Square Stationers, Frame Scene, Foot Locker (sports shoes), and Kids Mart. Diversified retailing, which provides superior management systems and economies that benefit all the separate retail operations, is likely to increase throughout the 1990s and beyond.

## Type of store cluster

Retail outlets tend to cluster together to increase their customer pulling power and to give consumers the convenience of one-stop shopping. We will examine the main types of store clusters next.

### International shopping centre

One type of store cluster is the **international shopping centre**. There is a familiar array of international shopping clusters which are found across the globe – for example, in London, Paris, New York, Rome, Milan, Florence, Zurich, Tokyo, Hong Kong, Singapore, and Sydney. On a global level, these have immense retail pulling power. The top national and international retailers will invariably be present. They act as **anchor stores** – key retailers which are the nucleus of a shopping cluster – whose presence invariably draw other retailers to the centre. Together they form the main attraction for millions of affluent, up-market shoppers coming in from all over the country and the world. The international shopping cluster is characterized by its enormous assortment of fashionable boutiques, speciality retailers and up-market department stores. The international shopping cities also are invariably centres of commerce, art, culture and/or fashion. Retailing therefore thrives in these large affluent global cities. Anchor stores are invariably the country's leading specialist and chain stores, together with international mass and specialist retailers that add lustre to the centre. They come with their array of international designer brands (e.g. Giorgio Armani, Gianni Versace, Yves St Laurent, Luis Vuitton, Bally, Bruno Magli,

Ferragamo Salvatorre, to name a few in clothings, accessories and footwear) and exclusive offerings. Global retailers such as The Body Shop, Laura Ashley, Benetton, The Gap, Virgin Megastore, Burger King, McDonald's and Pizza Hut are also familiar hallmarks of the global shopping centre.

### City and town centre shopping zones

**City-centre shopping zones** are traditionally the main form of store cluster, which still dominates in much of Europe. Every large city has a central shopping zone which contains most of the well-known retail chain stores, big department stores, speciality shops and super/megastores (e.g. Virgin Megastore, which sells audio-video tapes, CDs and multimedia entertainment products). Many large stores that sell consumer durable shopping goods (e.g. electrical appliances, electronics, watches and so forth) will anchor in these central shopping zones. A city centre shopping zone will also have civic/municipal buildings (e.g. town hall, law courts), legal offices, retail banks, cinemas/theatre and other amenities (e.g. library, post office), which form the hub of the city. City centre shops serve not just the 'locals' who actually live in the city, but also consumers who live in nearby towns and villages and travel into the city to do their shopping. In this way they may be called *regional shopping centres.*

**Town-centre shopping zones** tend to serve mainly consumers who live and/or work in the town. Unlike a city centre, the town centre stores form a *community shopping centre* that draws consumers from the local vicinity. A town centre store cluster typically has smaller independent stores – big department and super/megastores are seldom present – a limited number of fashion clothing, shoe and accessory shops, one or two small supermarkets or grocery retailers, variety shops, some professional offices and one or more high-street banks. Depending on the town's affluence, it could have more discounters or up-market speciality shops.

### Parades and neighbourhood store cluster

Another store cluster is the **parade** or **neighbourhood shopping centre**. This is a small cluster of several small independent shops, typically including a greengrocer, post office, fast-food take-away, video rental shop, a chemist, hardware store, self-service launderette, a barber/hairdresser and some other service or convenience stores. These stores are not located outside a town, but close to it, and tend to straddle the street which leads into or out of the town. They are close and convenient, serving residents living in the immediate neighbourhood adjoining the town.

### The corner shop

The **corner shop** is located within a residential area. It is a small shop owned and run by a local resident, and is often a convenience store or a CTN (confectioner, tobacconist and newsagent). These stores have traditionally served local residents who use them for emergency purchases. Sometimes, as in the case of a CTN, consumers' visits are habitual – the routine purchase of a Sunday paper, for example, or when the local resident goes to the store to have a chat with the proprietor and exchange the latest 'gossip'. The corner shop will continue to exist and fulfil a specific retailing function in a local neighbourhood, but this type of store remains a minor player in the fast changing retailing world.

Some European countries have undertaken ambitious expansion schemes for city centre shopping facilities despite the recession and the trend towards out-of-town developments. However, in some cities, retailers have seen turnover decline. In some instances, large retailers are moving out of town because of legislation which imposes tight controls on big city-centre developments, as in France. In Belgium and Holland, however, out-of-town retailing has been strictly controlled and city-centre shopping dominates. In Britain and Germany, there is also much pressure for retail development outside the big cities coming from the big retailers whose expansion schemes are being frustrated by city-centre legislation. Also, in many places, more and more consumers are deterred from shopping in city centres because of their heavy traffic and parking problems. These, together with increasing suburban development, have reduced the attractiveness of city and town centres for retailers, and encouraged a move out of town. Let us now examine recent out-of-town retail developments.

### Edge-of-town and out-of-town retail clusters

The development of **edge-of-town retail clusters** was led mainly by the hypermarkets, superstores and supermarkets. Typically also, car, electrical goods, furniture and fast-food retailers capitalized on the move to town peripheries over the late 1980s.

**Out-of-town retail clusters** are located well out of town. In fact the town is irrelevant, in terms of consumer traffic. The retail stores are situated in transport nodes which are very accessible by road from several regional locations, such as the intersection of main motorways. This is best illustrated by one of Britain's most successful out-of-town megamalls, Meadowhall, in Sheffield. This is situated just off the north–south M1 motorway and can readily be reached by travellers from the north, south, east and west of the country. Another – Brent Cross – is at the intersection of the A1 and M1 in north London. In the United States, the equivalents are Ala Moana shopping centre and the Altamonte Mall, the largest mall in central Florida. In the case of the latter, big department stores – for example, Sears, Maison Blanche, Jordan Marsh and Burdine's – anchor the mall with its 165 or so speciality shops. These malls are conveniently reached by car, there is ample car parking, and other amenities, such as restaurants and banks, are readily available. Many of these new retail clusters, in marked contrast to town and city centre clusters, offer a superior shopping environment and service to customers – they are safe and secure; heated/air-conditioned, so consumers can shop in comfort; there is enormous store choice and easy parking. In the United States, the move out of town has gone so far that it has caused irreversible decline in many towns and cities.

### Sheltered complexes and shopping mall clusters

In Europe, however, many governments, in anticipation of the damage out-of-town shopping does to city centres and city centre retailing, are taking steps to stop this happening. Rather than encourage the building of huge out-of-town malls and complexes, many town planners and retail business developers are encouraged to promote the concept of huge **sheltered shopping complexes** or 'mega-malls' into the towns and cities themselves. In fact the Canadians were among the first to put this formula into practice. The spectacular Eaton Centre, standing on one of Canada's best known roads, Yonge Street in Toronto, is an enormous city shopping complex which stretches for several blocks. It is enclosed by a gigantic glass and steel arched roof. Inside, with its natural lighting, trees, plants and fountains, it is reminiscent of London's

Shopping is Singaporeans' favourite pastime. Up-market shopping complexes are a ubiquitous sight in this city state.

Victorian Crystal Palace. There are shops and restaurants on three levels, with offices above.

Singapore gives another example of how downtown shopping complexes can be a viable modern retail cluster. Shopping arcades and malls are a ubiquitous sight in this city state. Locals and tourists alike seem to enjoy air-conditioned, multilevel, 'mini-cities' of shopping, featuring stores of all kinds, boutiques, snack bars, restaurants and, usually, a large department store or two. Centrepoint, Liang Court, Lucky Plaza, The Promenade, People's Park, Scotts, Shaw Centre, Tanglin Shopping Centre are just a few examples of the mini-shopping cities that line Singapore's half dozen or so main shopping roads. New complexes are still being built, such as Ngee Ann City, Singapore's largest shopping and office complex.[10] Moreover the complexes suit different tastes. Lucky Plaza is a bargainer's paradise. The Promenade, however, is a mecca of ritzy, up-market shops.

In Britain, there are similar attempts at town/city centre shopping revival: the Shires in Leicester and Victoria Centre in Nottingham are modern developments of the old Victorian arcades. These try to replicate the enclosed shopping centres built in the nineteenth century, such as the Burlington Arcade in London, and the famous Galleria in Milan. Another movement toward the regeneration of city centre retail sites is the refurbishment of old markets – for example, Covent Garden. This is a square that was originally part of a convent vegetable garden. It was laid out as a market in 1632 by Inigo Jones with a neoclassical arcade enclosing stalls in which fruit, vegetables and flowers were sold until 1974, when the stalls were moved to a site near Vauxhall Bridge. It now has its stalls again but these have moved rather more up-market.[11]

### Retail parks

The attraction of edge-of-town and out-of-town retail clusters is unlikely to decline in the 1990s. Their success has encouraged the construction of a new generation of **retail parks**. A retail park is an organized cluster of retailers which are located in edge-of-town and out-of-town locations. Typically, retailers such as Toys 'R' Us, Marks & Spencer, McDonald's, Pizza Hut or KFC, and one or two grocery, electrical or hardware superstores anchor the park to a few more large retail chains or discount warehouse operators. Retail parks are more organized than the early edge/out-of-town retail clusters. These have large car parking grounds, jointly provided by retailers on the site. Unlike the early generation of discount superstores and warehouses that built out- or at the edge-of-town, the new wave retail parks offer consumers many extra amenities and services (e.g. clean toilets, baby/crèche facilities, catering facilities, petrol forecourt services), in addition to convenient access, assortment range and, frequently, lower price. Retail parks are likely to remain an important group of retail cluster through the 1990s.

## NONSTORE RETAILING

Although most goods and services are sold through stores, nonstore retailing has been growing much faster than has store retailing. Traditional store retailers are facing increasing competition from nonstore retailers who sell through catalogues, direct mail, telephone, home TV shopping shows, on-line computer shopping services, home and office parties and other direct retailing approaches. Nonstore retailing includes direct marketing, direct selling and automatic vending.

## Direct marketing

**Direct marketing** uses various media to interact directly with carefully targeted consumers, generally calling for the consumer to make a direct response. Mass advertising typically reaches an unspecified number of people, most of whom are not in the market for a product or will not buy it until some future date. Direct advertising vehicles are used to obtain immediate orders directly from targeted consumers. Although direct marketing initially consisted mostly of direct mail and mail-order catalogues, it has taken on several additional, and, more exciting, forms in recent years, including telemarketing, direct radio, magazine and television advertising and on-line computer shopping. In the context of retailing, marketers should focus on direct response marketing, an umbrella term for all the various means of persuading consumers to buy products and services directly on the phone or through the post.

### Growth and benefits of direct marketing

Direct marketing in Europe has been growing in recent years and is poised for further growth in the 1990s. Even in the European Commission, once thought to be hostile to the technique, in its 'Panorama of EC Industry 93', reported that 'Barring an EC Directive limiting direct marketing, this activity should be the major promotion tool of the sector (advertising and marketing) within five years'.[12] All kinds of organizations use direct marketing: manufacturers, retailers, services companies, catalogue merchants and non-profit organizations, to name a few. Its growing use in consumer marketing is largely a response to the 'demassification' of mass markets, which has resulted in an ever-greater number of fragmented market segments with highly individualized needs and wants. Direct marketing allows sellers to focus efficiently on these minimarkets with offers that better match specific consumer needs.

Other trends have also fuelled the growth of direct marketing. The increasing number of women entering the workforce has decreased the time households have to shop. The higher costs of driving, the traffic congestion and parking headaches, the shortage of retail sales help and the longer lines at checkout counters have all promoted in-home shopping. The development of toll-free telephone numbers and the increased use of credit cards have made it easier for sellers to reach and transact with consumers away from the stores. Finally, the growth of computer power and communication technology have allowed marketers to build better customer databases and telecommunication channels with which to reach the best prospects for specific products.

Direct marketing has also grown rapidly in business-to-business marketing. It can help reduce the high costs of reaching business markets through the salesforce. Lower-cost media, such as telemarketing and direct mail, can be used to identify the best prospects and prime them before a sales representative makes an expensive call.

Consumers also derive many benefits from direct marketing. Instead of driving their cars through congested city streets to shop in crowded shopping malls, customers can use their telephones or computers to whizz along the information superhighway. Today's sophisticated communications networks carry voice, video and data over the fibreoptic telephone lines, linking buyers and sellers in convenient, exciting ways. People who buy through direct mail or by telephone say that such shopping is convenient, trouble-free and fun. It saves them time, and it introduces them to new lifestyles and a larger selection of merchandise. Consumers can compare products and prices from their armchairs by browsing through catalogues. They can order and receive products without having to leave their homes. Industrial customers can learn about and order products and services without tying up valuable time by meeting and listening to salespeople.

Sellers are another category to benefit from direct marketing, which allows them greater selectivity. A direct marketer can buy a mailing list containing the names of almost any group – millionaires, parents of newborn babies, left-handed people or recent university graduates. The direct marketing message can be personalized and customized. Eventually, according to one expert, 'We will store hundreds...of messages in memory. We will select 10 thousand families with 12 or 20 specific characteristics and send them very individualised laser-printed letters.'[13]

With direct marketing, the seller can build a continuous customer relationship, tailoring a steady stream of offers to a regular customer's specific needs and interests. Direct marketing can also be timed to reach prospects at just the right moment. Moreover, because it reaches more interested prospects at the best times, direct-marketing materials receive higher readership and response. Direct marketing also permits easy testing of specific messages and media, and because results are direct and immediate, it lends itself more readily to response measurement. Finally, direct marketing provides privacy – the direct marketer's offer and strategy are not visible to competitors.

Let us now address the main forms of direct marketing.

## Forms of direct marketing

The four main forms of direct marketing are direct mail and catalogue marketing, telemarketing, television marketing and on-line shopping. Most of these techniques were first developed in the United States, but have since been exported to Europe. The EU should see further growth in some forms of direct marketing – notably direct mail and telemarketing – although in practice, the impact of a unified Europe, since 1992, has been limited by the labyrinth of legislation across the continent, which means that certain direct response techniques are feasible in some countries but not others.

For example, telemarketing is widely practised in some countries but virtually illegal in Germany. Differences in postal systems, standards and rates for different countries pose problems for pan-European direct-mailing programmes. Direct mail is strong in countries with efficient and inexpensive postal systems (e.g. the UK, Sweden) and weak where the mail is slow and delivery unreliable (e.g. Spain, Italy). Until EU-wide uniformity of postal prices and standards is achieved, the growth of pan-European direct marketing will be restricted.[14] Even etiquette is a problem. The bright, brash American-style direct-mail methods used in the United Kingdom would be considered anything but courteous in France. On the other hand, the flowery phrases of a formal letter in France would definitely be *de trop* on the other side of the channel.

*Direct-mail and catalogue marketing* **Direct-mail marketing** involves mailings of letters, ads, samples, foldouts and other 'salespeople on wings' sent to prospects on mailing lists. The mailing lists are developed from customer lists or obtained from

Direct mail: Royal Mail International offers a unique direct marketing service – Direct Entry – for its international customers.

### With Direct Entry you can dress your mailings to suit your market.

Direct Entry from Royal Mail is an exciting new option for international direct marketeers. Ideal for targeted mailings or niche marketing, it could improve your current response rates.

Effective and simple to use, Direct Entry mailings look exactly like a local mailing from within the destination country. We advise you on preparing your mailing, then take care of everything else from collection to delivery.

We can even arrange the International Admail reply service to enhance the effect of Direct Entry. It further encourages prospects by enabling them to respond free of charge to a local reply address.

To find out more on how Direct Entry could improve your international marketing, send your business card to: Royal Mail, Dept. DEW1, 12 Fenton Way, BASILDON, Essex SS15 6TY or call us on 0800 269 242.

**Direct Entry**

**Royal Mail**
**International**

mailing-list houses that provide names of people fitting almost any description – the superwealthy, mobile-home owners, veterinarians, pet owners, the typical catalogue purchaser, and many, many others.

Direct mail is well suited to direct, one-on-one communication. It permits high target-market selectivity, can be personalized, is flexible and allows easy measurement of results (the firm can count the responses it gets and the value of those responses to the business). Whereas the cost per thousand people reached is higher than with mass media such as television or magazines, the people who are reached are much better prospects, since direct-mail marketers target individuals according to their personal suitability to receive particular offerings and promotions. Direct mail has proved very successful in promoting and selling books, magazine subscriptions, insurance and financial products. Increasingly, it is being used to sell novelty and gift items, clothing, gourmet foods, consumer packaged goods and industrial products. Direct mail is also used heavily by charities, such as Oxfam and Action Aid, which rely heavily on correspondence selling to persuade individuals to donate to their charity.

Within the EU, direct mail is worth over ecu 12bn. Direct mail in Europe represents around 60 per cent of Europe's total spend on direct marketing. Over the late 1980s and early 1990s, expenditure on direct mail has grown faster than that spent by organizations on other advertising media. With direct mail's unique ability to target individuals, its future seems bright. However, there are a number of barriers that must be overcome to assure direct mail's future: EU legislation that prejudices its use; differences in postal standards, systems and prices; 'cowboy' operators, whose indiscriminate mass-mailings earn direct-mail the 'junk-mail' tag. In the case of junk mail, the cowboys' efforts can effectively be strangled through compulsory observation of industry standards or a code of practice, and linkages with national and international regulatory authorities to expose these operators. Users of direct mail and the direct-mail industry, in general, agree that the way forward must be to seek balanced consumer protection with a mixture of statutory and self-regulatory controls.[15]

**Catalogue marketing** or correspondence sales involves selling through catalogues mailed to a select list of customers or made available in stores. Examples of mail-order catalogue operators include Freemans, GUS, Empire Stores, Otto Versand, La Redoute and Trois Suisses. Buying from a mail-order catalogue used to be popular among isolated populations or less affluent, older married women. The image of catalogue retailing, however, has been transformed by some retailers. Consider the following example:

Trois Suisses, the French mail-order giant, has distanced itself from the old-fashioned catalogue image. Its 1995 Spring/Summer catalogue featured nothing less than a pair of sensuous lips. Inside this catalogue, customers find a range of products by the leading textiles designers, Vivienne Westwood and Elizabeth de Senneville, as well as household articles designed by Starck and André Putman. The new style is a far cry from the first catalogue sent out when the company was founded in 1932. It was the first major catalogue to aim for the glossy high-fashion market when it featured the American model Cindy Crawford on a 1992 catalogue cover.

Some retailers, such as Laura Ashley, Marks & Spencer, Habitat and Hulsta also use catalogues for selling specific merchandise. Trois Suisses president, Emmanuel d'André, stresses that the 'traditional rural clientele is giving way to young working women who are busy and under pressure'. The catalogue's upmarket re-positioning reflects these changes. The company's recent market analysis suggests that over a quarter of the regular clients who place orders six or more times a year are women under the age of 24; the new catalogue has thus become a fashion and media event in France. Trois Suisses is described as an aggressive direct marketer – it sends out more than eight million catalogues a year and keeps its best clients in touch with follow-up literature every two weeks. Trois Suisses also operates in Belgium, the Netherlands, UK, Austria, Germany, Italy, Spain and Portugal. Its upmarket move is paying off. But this re-positioning is not the only reason for its success. The firm has streamlined operations and improved performance (staff spends on average not more than three and a half minutes on each order). It recently introduced a 24-hour delivery service on most items: order one day and receive the goods the next. Sales are processed in a three-storey depot in Croix, near Lille. One vast room is dedicated to the express sales section where each regular client is allotted a location within the section earmarked for his or her town. Over a kilometre of conveyor belts carry the items round the complex and out to the delivery vans.

Thanks also to mail-order, which has resisted the recession better than any other retail outlet, Trois Suisses has profited more than its competitors, with sales having grown from around FFr 11.2bn in 1992 to FFr 12.4bn in 1993, and up to FFr 14bn for the year ending February 1994.[16]

1 ecu = US$1.26 = FFr 6.47 (French francs)

Catalogues are also now being used by store retailers who see these as an additional medium for cultivating sales, as in the case of Habitat, Marks & Spencer, Laura Ashley and others.

Most consumers enjoy receiving catalogues and will sometimes even pay to get them. Many catalogue marketers are now even selling their catalogues at book stores and magazine stands. Advances in technology are enabling retailers and manufacturers to experiment with multiple forms of media – for example, videotapes, computer discs and CD-ROM – to deliver high-tech catalogue selling. The revolution has already begun in the United States – Royal Silk, a clothing company, sells a 35-minute video catalogue to its customers for $5.95. The tape contains a polished presentation of Royal Silk products, tells customers how to care for silk, and provides ordering information. Soloflex uses a video brochure to help sell its in-home exercise equipment. The 22-minute video shows an attractive couple demonstrating the exercises possible with the system. Soloflex claims that almost half of those who view the video brochure later place an order via telephone, compared with only a 10 per cent response from those receiving regular direct mail.[17]

Many business-to-business marketers also rely heavily on catalogues. Whether in the form of a simple brochure, three-ring binder, or book, or encoded on a videotape or computer disc, catalogues remain one of today's hardest-working sales tools. For some companies, in fact, catalogues have even taken the place of salespeople.

This award-winning direct response advertising campaign run by the Scottish Health Education Board, drew tremendous responses from smokers seeking counselling, showing what communication can achieve when advertisers get it right.

*Telemarketing*     **Telemarketing** uses the telephone to sell directly to consumers. It has become a primary direct-marketing tool. Marketers use *outbound* telephone marketing in a proactive way to sell directly to consumers and businesses. Calls may also be for research, testing, database building, appointment-making, as a follow-up to a previous contact, or as part of a motivation or customer-care programme. For example, Raleigh Bicycles uses telemarketing to generate and qualify sales leads and to manage specific accounts. Telemarketing helps the business to reduce the amount of personal selling needed for contacting its dealers – in the first year, salesforce travel costs were reduced 50 per cent and sales in a single quarter increased 34 per cent.[18]

Marketers use inbound free-phone or toll-free numbers to receive orders from customers. These calls are usually made in response to an ad in the press, on radio or television, in a door drop or direct mailing, in catalogues, or via a mixture of these media. Marketers also use the telphone in a reactive way for inbound calls involving customer enquiries and complaints.

The use of telemarketing has grown in recent years, particularly in the United States. One US study suggests the average household receives 19 telephone sales calls each year and makes 16 calls to place orders, and that during 1990, the American AT&T logged more than 7 billion 800-number calls.[19] Other marketers use 900 numbers to sell consumers information, entertainment, or the opportunity to voice an opinion. For example, for a charge, consumers can obtain weather forecasts from American Express (1-900-WEATHER – 75 cents a minute); pet care information from Quaker Oats (1-900-990-PETS – 95 cents a minute); advice on snoring and other sleep disorders from Somnus (1-900-USA-SLEEP – $2 for the first minute, then $1 a minute); or golf lessons from Golf Digest (1-900-454-3288 – 95 cents a minute). Altogether, the 900-number industry now generates $860 million in annual revenues.[20]

In the UK, the growth of inbound telemarketing may be linked to BT's introduction of the 0800 Linkline in 1985. Prospects, once converted to a customer, use the 0345 number which charges only a local rate. Over 6000 companies used these lines in 1989, with around 10,000 calls an hour passing through them, double the numbers a year earlier.[21] In Europe, telemarketing is more established in the Netherlands than in countries such as Germany which has the toughest telemarketing laws. For example, telemarketing in Germany is impossible because the consent of the prospects or consumers is needed before they can be contacted. If someone buys a shovel from a garden centre in winter, even if they gave their name and telephone number, the centre cannot telephone them in the spring with a special offer on bulbs because that would be illegal. Contrast the situation in Holland, where, for example, before the election, political parties are permitted to ring voters to gain their support.[22]

Not surprisingly, the rise in unsolicited telephone marketing annoys customers who object to 'junk phone calls' that pull them away from the dinner table or clog up their answering machines. Laws or self-regulatory measures have been introduced in different countries in response to complaints from irate customers. At the same time, consumers can appreciate many of the genuine and well-presented offers they receive by telephone. When properly designed and targeted, telemarketing does provide many benefits, including purchasing convenience and increased product and service information.[23]

*Television marketing*     **Television marketing** takes one of two main forms. The first is *direct-response advertising*. Direct marketers air television spots, typically 60 to 120 seconds long, that persuasively describe a product or service and give customers a free-phone number for ordering. Television viewers may encounter longer advertising programmes, or *infomercials*, for a single product. Infomercials are themed programmes which are broadcast on existing pan-European satellite stations such as NBC Super Channel and Eurosport. The infomercial industry is expanding, with companies such as Quantum International, the market leader in Europe, operating globally. Such direct-response advertising works well for magazines, books, small appliances, tapes, CDs and collectors' items. Direct-response television marketing has also been successfully used by charities and specific aid campaigners to persuade viewers to offer donations or volunteer services. The 'Live Aid' campaign that captured the imagination of millions of people across the globe, 'Children in Need', and many other international fund-raising events have used direct-response advertising to good effect.

*Home shopping channels*, another form of television direct marketing, are television programmes or entire channels dedicated to selling goods and services. US television home shopping broadcasters take the lead in this field.

> In the US, home shopping channels, such as the Quality Value Channel (QVC) and the Home Shopping Network (HSN), broadcast 24 hours a day. QVC's live shows run, not just 24 hours a day, but 364 days a year, and it processes over 130,000 phone-calls every day. On HSN, the programme's hosts offer bargain prices on products ranging from jewelry, lamps, collectible dolls and clothing to power tools and consumer electronics – usually obtained by the home shopping channel at close-out prices. The show is upbeat, with the hosts honking horns, blowing whistles and praising viewers for their good taste. Viewers call an 800 number to order goods. At the other end of the operation, 400 operators handle more than 1,200 incoming lines, entering orders directly into computer terminals. Orders are shipped within 48 hours.
>
> Sales through home shopping channels grew from $450 million in 1986 to an estimated $2 billion in 1994. More than half of all US homes have access to QVC, HSN or other home shopping channels such as Value Club of America, Home Shopping Mall, or TelShop. Sears, K mart, J. C. Penney, Spiegel and other major retailers are now looking into the home shopping industry. Many experts think that advances in two-way, interactive television will make video shopping one of the major forms of direct marketing by the end of the century.[24]

QVC has arrived in Europe, although prising open the UK market (its European bridgehead) has been an unprofitable venture. According to Barry Diller, QVC's president, the channel's main problem was not that viewers were not buying, but that it had too few subscribers. As part of the Sky Multi-Channels Package, QVC broadcasts in Britain via the BSkyB satellite, and not enough homes subscribe to Sky to make QVC profitable – only about 3 million homes have access to the channel, via BSkyB, instead of the 10 million it needs. Eight per cent of households with access to QVC programmes bought something from them – the same percentage as in the US. Another problem has been the fact that many of QVC UK's customers do not have a credit card, the simplest way to pay for goods over the phone, so hampers purchases. Another problem has been rivals like infomercials which have taken off in Europe. In the long term, access for customers via cable will be the key route to increasing its customer base. Meanwhile, QVC remains confident that it can turn the corner and that the UK will take to TV shopping. It aims to promote itself on other satellite and cable channels and to work with other retailers which add credibility to its operation. Peter Risdale, chief executive officer of QVC stresses that early losses are inevitable as 'We're here for the long haul, not a quick buck.'[25]

*On-line shopping*   **On-line computer shopping** is conducted through interactive on-line computer services – two-way systems that link consumers with sellers electronically. These services create computerized catalogues of products and services offered by producers, retailers, banks, travel organizations and others. Consumers use a home computer to hook into the system through cable or telephone lines. For example, a consumer wanting to buy a new compact-disc player could request a list of all brands in the computerized catalogue, compare the brands, then order one using a credit or charge card – all without leaving home.

Such on-line services are still in their infancy. In recent years, several large systems have failed because of a lack of subscribers or too little use. The on-line shopping services industry has its roots in the United States. Three currently successful systems in the US are CompuServe, Prodigy and America Online. Prodigy, developed through a partnership by IBM and Sears, offers in-home shopping services and much more. Through Prodigy, subscribers can order thousands of products and services electronically from dozens of large stores and catalogues. They can also do their banking with local banks; buy and sell investments through a discount brokerage service; make airline, hotel and car-rental reservations; play games, quizzes, and contests; check *Consumer Reports* ratings of various products; receive the latest sports scores and statistics; obtain weather forecasts; and exchange messages with other subscribers around the country.

Although relatively few consumers subscribe to such electronic systems at the moment, the number is expected to grow in future years. In fact, some experts predict that computers, televisions, and telephones will soon mutate into a single 'smart box', which users will manipulate to receive entertainment, information and direct access to 'video shopping malls'. By the turn of the century, they assert, all of us will enjoy the wonders of interactive, on-line shopping.[26] Already, cable TV shopping network operators and on-line shopping network companies are working at creating truly global on-line electronic shopping opportunities:

> For example, America's leading TV shopping company, Home Shopping Network (HSN), which acquired Internet Shopping Network (ISN), are set on creating the first large-scale-on-line electronic shopping mall, accessible to millions of personal computer users. HSN already provides services on Compuserve, the commercial on-line service. ISN, a Californian start-up company, has been selling goods over the Internet, a global network of computers with an estimated 25m–30m users. It offered some 20,000 computer-related products from nearly 1,000 companies. Through alliances with well-known retailers, brand-ed manufacturers and Internet service providers, HSN-ISN, however, seeks to become the pre-eminent electronic merchant in on-line inter-active retailing. HSN sees on-line shopping as the forerunner of inter-active television. There are many advantages for on-line users and operators: users can shop whenever they desire from the home or office, while providers avoid the expense of producing and mailing catalogues and escape the overhead costs of store facilities. The ISN is available at any time, from anywhere on the Internet. Users with Apple Macintosh, Windows or Unix-based computers, fitted with a modem and communications software, can connect to ISN. To order goods from ISN, users provide the service with delivery and billing information by telephone to avoid sending sensitive data over the Internet.
>
> Other future developments are on their way. Hewlett-Packard Co. and the Japanese NEC Corporation have designed TV set-top boxes (based on Microsoft software) that consumers can use to inter-act with their televisions. To date, such technologies have been tested by international companies such as Deutsche Telekom of Germany, Telstra Corp. of Australia and the American West Communications Inc.[27]

On-line or electronic shopping technology would give 'virtual' shopping malls a competitive edge on the real thing, with electronic 'intelligent assistants' travelling the data networks in search of information or products at the behest of their owner – the consumer. Many retailers see these developments as an opportunity to experiment in the brave new world of 'virtual' shopping before it becomes a twenty-first century mass consumer service on 'interactive TV'. Companies do acknowledge that though the on-line shopping world may not be just around the corner, there is no doubt that it is going to happen.

## Direct marketing databases

Successful direct marketing begins with a good customer database. The **marketing database** is an organized set of data about individual customers or prospects, including geographic, demographic, psychographic and buying behaviour data. The database can be used to locate good potential customers, tailor products and services to the special needs of targeted consumers, and maintain long-term customer relationships. Many companies are now building and using customer databases for targeting marketing communications and selling efforts at the individual customer. Data protection regulations in some countries may slow down growth in database marketing practices – for example, usage in the United States and United Kingdom is far more widespread, with data laws being much more open compared to the rest of Europe. But the international race is on to exploit database marketing and few businesses can afford to ignore this important vehicle for competitive success. As Tom Peters comments in *Thriving on Chaos*, 'A market has never bought things. Customers buy things. That's why database marketing's ability to target the individual customer in the crowded marketplace is so valuable.'[28]

Building a marketing database takes time and involves much cost, but, if operated effectively, can pay handsome dividends. For example, a home electronic appliance manufacturer may have a customer database containing each customer's demographic and psychographic characteristics, along with an appliance purchasing history. The firm's direct marketers use this database to assess how long specific customers have owned their current appliances and which past customers might be ready to purchase again. They can determine which customers need a new video-recorder, compact disc player, stereo receiver or something else to go with other recently purchased electronics products. Or they can identify the company's best past purchasers and send them gift certificates or other promotions to apply against their next purchases. Clearly, a rich-customer database allows the firm to build profitable new business by locating good prospects, anticipating customer needs, cross-selling products and services, and rewarding loyal customers.[29] The firm can maximize its overall marketing effectiveness through the use of such a database. BMW, for instance, has a database that helps it plan new initiatives, run marketing programmes and mount direct marketing campaigns in selected European markets.

Not only manufacturers, but also retailers can benefit from direct-marketing databases. A recent UK survey showed that retailers in the country were the biggest investors in software, data and hardware for their database, with many reporting spends of more than £250,000 to above £1 million.[30]

Companies must distinguish between *transactional-based* and *custom-built* marketing databases. Transactional databases are put in by an accounts department for the purpose of sending invoices/bills out and getting money back. By contrast, custom-built databases focus on what the firm's marketing people need to know to profitably serve and satisfy customers better than the competition can – for example, the most cost-effective way to reach target customers, the net worth of a transaction, customers' requirements and lifetime values, lapsed customers and why they departed, why competitors are making inroads and where.

## Integrated direct marketing

Many direct marketers use only a 'one-shot' effort to reach and sell a prospect, or a single vehicle in multiple stages to trigger purchases. For example, a magazine publisher might send a series of four direct-mail notices to a household to get a subscriber to renew before giving up. A more powerful approach is **integrated direct marketing**, which involves using multiple-vehicle, multiple-stage campaigns. Such campaigns can greatly improve response. Whereas a direct-mail piece alone might generate a 2 per cent response, adding a free-phone number can raise the response rate by 50 per cent. A well-designed outbound telemarketing effort might lift response by another 500 per cent. Suddenly a 2 per cent response has grown to 13 per cent or more by adding interactive marketing channels to a regular mailing.[31]

More elaborate integrated direct-marketing campaigns can be used. Consider the following multimedia, multistage marketing campaign:

| Paid ad with a response channel | $\rightarrow$ | Direct mail | $\rightarrow$ | Outbound telemarketing | $\rightarrow$ | Face-to-face sales call |
|---|---|---|---|---|---|---|

Here, the paid ad to target customers creates product awareness and stimulates inquiries. The company immediately sends direct mail to those who inquire. Within a few days, the company follows up with a phone call seeking an order. Some prospects will order by phone; others might request a face-to-face sales call. In such a campaign, the marketer seeks to improve response rates and profits by adding media and stages that contribute more to additional sales than to additional costs.

In the first of the following examples, by combining direct-marketing methods, a small (and relatively unknown) company improved sales and has made a mark trading in postal packed flowers:

> Flying Flowers is a UK flowers-by-post business. The 17-acre Jersey-based carnation nursery now offers a postal pack service to most northern European countries. Its strong sales have been achieved through direct response advertising and by mailing to an increasingly large customer database. The firm's progressive involvement with retail chains, mail order companies and credit card operators have also generated additional sales. It also recently became an Air Miles promoter – In a special Valentines and Mothers Day promotion, Air Miles members who get Flying Flowers to despatch a bouquet of flowers would get up to 35 Air Miles awards. All the consumer has to do is order by phone, quoting his/her membership number, credit card details, bouquet code and Air Miles promotion reference number. Easy! It is clear that Flying Flowers uses multiple non-store retailing channels, while also taking advantage of its expanding marketing database to maintain a consistent sales growth record.[32]

> The French mail-order giant, Trois Suisses, integrates its existing mail-order format with other direct retailing approaches. It takes orders by post, telephone and the French interactive information network, Minitel, which is installed in more than 3 million houses. It is linked with a shopping programme on the French RTL-TV and is taking the step into television shopping. Trois Suisses believes that the on-line revolution could strengthen its foothold in the new shopping environment of the future.[33]

## Direct selling

**Door-to-door retailing**, which started centuries ago with roving pedlars, has grown into a huge industry. Companies sell their products door to door, office to office or at home-sales parties. Direct selling became organized selling in the United States. Not surprisingly, US multinational corporations dominate direct selling worldwide. The pioneers in door-to-door selling are the Fuller Brush Company, vacuum cleaner companies like Electrolux, and book-selling companies, such as World Book and Southwestern. The image of door-to-door selling improved greatly when Avon Cosmetics entered the industry with its Avon representative – the homemaker's friend and beauty consultant. In the United Kingdom, Avon still leads in the field.

Electrolux also has a direct-sales business in Europe. Betterware plc, a British direct-selling household products company, has seen strong sales growth in recent years and expanded its operations into France. Others, notably Tupperware, the British Dee Group (clothes), Ladybird Books and Oriflame Cosmetics have also helped to popularize home selling, particularly sales parties or party plan, in which several friends and neighbours attend a party at a private home where products are demonstrated and sold. Tupperware pioneered party plan or selling directly to a group.

The US direct-selling businesses have been successful in other parts of Europe. Apart from France, where indigenous French companies dominate the world, US firms' sales have been growing. In Japan, the success of the US businesses has been extraordinary – Japan is the world's largest direct sales market with sales in 1992 estimated at over $20 billion.[34]

The advantages of door-to-door selling are consumer convenience and personal attention. But the high costs of hiring, training, paying and motivating the salesforce result in higher prices. Although some door-to-door companies are still thriving, door-to-door selling has a somewhat uncertain future. The increase in the number of single-person and working-couple households decreases the chances of finding a buyer at home. Home-party companies are having trouble finding nonworking women who want to sell products part-time. Besides, direct selling does have an image problem, which, although inaccurate, has stuck. And, with recent advances in interactive direct-marketing technology, the door-to-door salesperson may well be replaced in the future by the household telephone, television or home computer.

## Automatic vending

**Automatic vending** is not new – in 215BC Egyptians could buy sacrificial water from coin-operated dispensers. But this method of selling has increased in popularity in the last few decades. Today's automatic vending uses space-age and computer technology to sell a wide variety of convenience and impulse goods – cigarettes, beverages, confectionery, newspapers, foods and snacks, contraceptive devices, cosmetics, paperback books, T-shirts, audio tapes and video cassettes. Vending machines are found everywhere – in factories, offices, lobbies, retail stores, petrol stations, airports and train and bus terminals. Automatic teller machines provide bank customers with cheques, savings, withdrawals and fundtransfer services. Compared to store retailing, vending machines offer consumers greater convenience (24 hours, self-service) and fewer damaged goods. But the expensive equipment and labour required for automatic vending make it a costly channel, and prices of vended goods are often 15 to 20 per cent higher than those in retail stores. Customers must also put up with aggravating machine breakdowns, out-of-stock items, and the fact that merchandise cannot be returned.[35]

## RETAILER MARKETING DECISIONS

Retailers are searching for new marketing strategies to attract and hold customers. In the past, retailers attracted customers with unique products, more or better services than their competitors offered, or credit cards. Today, national and global brand manufacturers, in their drive for volume, have placed their branded goods everywhere. National brands are found not only in department stores, but also in mass-merchandise and off-price discount stores. Thus stores offer similar assortments, and, as a result, stores are looking more and more alike – they have become 'commoditized'. In any city, a shopper can find many stores but few different assortments.

Service differentiation among retailers has also eroded. Many department stores have trimmed their services, whereas discounters have increased theirs. Customers have become smarter and more price sensitive. They see no reason to pay more for identical brands, especially when service differences are shrinking. And because bank credit cards are now accepted at most stores, consumers no longer need credit from a particular store. For all these reasons, many retailers today are rethinking their marketing strategies.[36]

As shown in Figure 22.1, retailers face vital marketing decisions about their target markets and positioning, product assortment and services, price, promotion and place.

## Target market and positioning decisions

Retailers must first define their targets and then decide how they will position themselves in these markets:

- Should the store focus on up-market, mid-market, or down-market shoppers?
- Do target shoppers want variety, depth of assortment, convenience, or low prices?

Until they define and profile their markets, retailers cannot make consistent decisions about product assortment, services, pricing, advertising, store decor or any of the other decisions that must support their positions.

Too many retailers fail to define their target markets and positions clearly. They try to have 'something for everyone' and end up satisfying no market well. In contrast, successful retailers define their target markets well and position themselves strongly, as in the case of The Body Shop which, over the 1980s, secured a leadership position in the animal-friendly personal-care products segment. Retailers such as IKEA, Aldi, and Marks & Spencer clearly define their chief target markets in order to design effective marketing strategies. McDonald's Restaurants are not just any burger bar, but the fast-food place kids love to go to. As for the kids' parents and grandparents,

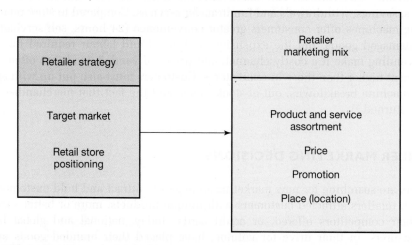

**Figure 22.1**  Retailer marketing decisions.

junk food is junk food anywhere, but…at least, Mac's has clean toilets. Hard Rock Café (the trendy, expensive bar where customers cannot place table bookings but have to queue for hours to get in), TGI's Friday (an American Diner for the smoothies and slightly more well-off!) and the Ritz are a few more cases of service retailers who have clear target markets and have created unique positionings that set them apart from their competition.

## Product assortment and services decisions

Retailers must decide on three main product variables: product assortment, services mix and store atmosphere.

The retailer's *product assortment* must match target shoppers' expectations. The retailer must determine both the product assortment's *width* and its *depth*. Thus a restaurant can offer a narrow and shallow assortment (small lunch counter), a narrow and deep assortment (delicatessen), a wide and shallow assortment (cafeteria), or a wide and deep assortment (large restaurant).

Another product assortment element is the *quality* of the goods: The customer is interested not only in the range of choice but also in the quality of the products available.

No matter what the store's product assortment and quality level, there always will be competitors with similar assortments and quality. Therefore, the retailer must search for other ways to *differentiate* itself from similar competitors. It can differentiate its products in several ways:

- First, it can offer merchandise that no other competitor carries, such as its own private brands or national brands on which it holds exclusive agreements. For example, Marks & Spencer offers its own exclusive St Michael's brand. Some boutiques in a shopping centre may get exclusive rights to carry a well-known designer's label.
- Second, the retailer can feature merchandising events or previews featuring new stocks or special sales items for store-card members or valued customers.
- Third, the retailer can differentiate itself by offering a highly targeted product assortment – Etam carries goods for larger-sized women; Long Tall Sally carries clothing and shoe items for the slim, tall woman; Mothercare focuses on maternity, baby and younger children's clothes and accessories, including nursery and feeding equipment.

Retailers must also decide on a *services mix* to offer customers. The old-fashioned grocery stores offered home delivery, credit and conversation – services that today's supermarkets ignore. Table 22.4 lists some typical services full-service retailers can offer. A superior services mix is one of the key tools of nonprice competition, allowing one retailer to set itself apart from another. Consider the following:

> Jeans are Jeans! Not quite so. The search for the perfect-fitting pair of jeans can turn into a lifetime crusade for some women. A new software programme is changing that. Sung Park, an ex-IBM software programmer and president of Custom Clothing Technology, has developed a way of making custom-fitting jeans by computer. The technology was launched in December 1994 in four US stores. These stores will sell ordinary Levi jeans as well as offer the custom-fitting service for consumers who want a perfect pair of jeans. Sales assistants measure women's waist, hips, rise – the distance from the front waistband, between the legs and up to the back waistband – and inside leg. The measurements are entered into a computer which identifies a prototype jean providing the closest match. Each store is stocked

**TABLE 22.4    *Typical retail services***

| Primary services | Supplemental services | |
|---|---|---|
| • Complaint handling | • Alterations | • Personal shopping |
| • Convenient store hours | • Baby strollers | • Product locator |
|   parking | • Bill payment | • Restaurant or snack counters |
| • Credit | • Bridal registries | • Shopping consultants |
| • Delivery | • Cheque cashing | • Shopping information |
| • Fitting rooms, rest rooms | • Children's play rooms | • Shows, displays and exhibits |
| • Installation  and assembly | • Demonstrations | • Special ordering |
| • Merchandise returns and | • Lost and found | • Wheelchairs |
|   adjustments | • Packaging and gift wrapping | |

with hundreds of prototypes. The customer tries on the prototype and after final adjustments the sales person sends the information by modem to the factory. Three weeks later, the customer can pick up the jeans at the store or have them mailed. The tailored jeans cost $10 above the normal price. By the end of January, Levi Strauss offered the product in seven other stores. Because sales staff have to be trained to use the computer programme, Levi Strauss expects it would take time before the new programme is widely available. Sung Park said he developed the programme after spending time in Hong Kong, where he could get a suit tailored in a day. He thought it would be wonderful if custom-tailoring were available in the US. He had to find the best applications for the technology. His female flatmates unanimously agreed that the piece of clothing they found most difficult to find a good fit in was JEANS! Sung Park has the exclusive contract with Levi Strauss for tailored jeans. Levi aims to expand the product to men's jeans and other women's clothes. Park, meanwhile, is talking to other clothing companies about custom-made bathing suits and men's suits.[37]

The *store's atmosphere* is another element in retailers' product arsenal. Atmosphere is important as it influences consumers' judgement about the store as well as their shopping experience. There are a number of elements that contribute to a store's atmosphere:

■ *The external characteristics of the store.* The store's exterior – the appearance of the front, window displays, the immediate and surrounding environment (i.e. the appearance of the street, car-park, other shops located next to it) – affect consumers' impression of the store even before they enter it.

■ *The internal characteristics of the store.* Interior store design is an important consideration as this determines a retail outlet's attractiveness to consumers. The layout, decor, colour, lighting and other sensory elements like sound and scent also contribute to a store's atmosphere – these give the store its 'feel'. Every store, for example, has a physical layout – arrangement of display shelves/departments/service units, width of aisles, location of payment counters – that affects how well shoppers can move around in it. A cluttered store impedes shoppers' mobility and reduces shopping efficiency. Aesthetically, a well-laid-out store is more pleasing and conducive to exploratory shopping than an overcrowded one. However, an empty store (e.g. an empty restaurant or bar) can deter customers from entering as it suggests inferior-quality merchandise, service or other reasons for its unpopularity. Retailers use one or more elements of interior-store design to generate an appropriate 'ambience' – a store may feel charming, plush, friendly, exciting or sombre.

The store must have a planned atmosphere that suits the target market, attracts their attention and moves customers to shop for goods or services in the store. A bank should be quiet, solid and peaceful; a night-club should be flashy, loud and vibrating; a boutique should exude luxury and exclusivity. Increasingly, retailers are working to create selling environments that meet the tastes of their target markets.

## Price decisions

A retailer's price policy is a crucial positioning factor and must be decided in relation to its target market, its product and service assortment and its competition. All retailers would like to charge high mark-ups and achieve high volume, but the two seldom go together. Most retailers seek *either* high mark-ups on lower volume (most speciality stores) *or* low mark-ups on higher volume (mass merchandisers and discount stores.

Retailers must also pay attention to pricing tactics. Most retailers will put low prices on some items to serve as 'traffic builders' or 'loss leaders'. On some occasions, they run storewide sales. On others, they plan mark-downs on slower-moving merchandise. For example, shoe retailers may expect to sell 50 per cent of their shoes at the normal mark-up, 25 per cent at a higher mark-up, and the remaining 25 per cent at cost.

## Promotion decisions

Retailers use the normal promotion tools – advertising, personal selling, sales promotion and public relations – to reach consumers. They advertise in newspapers, magazines, radio and television. Advertising may be supported by circulars and direct-mail pieces. Personal selling requires careful training of salespeople in how to greet customers, meet their needs and handle their complaints. Sales promotions may include in-store demonstrations, displays, contests and visiting celebrities. Public relations activities, such as press conferences and speeches, store openings, special events, newsletters, magazines and public service activities, are always available to retailers.

## Place decisions

Retailers often cite three critical factors in retailing success: *location*, *location* and *location*! A retailer's location is the key to its ability to attract customers. Location decisions are not easy or quick to reverse. Moreover the costs of building or leasing facilities have a significant impact on the retailer's profits. Thus site-location decisions are among the most important the retailer makes. Retailers must consider a number of factors when making site location decisions:

- *Type of retail location.* The retailer may locate in the town or city, or at the edge or out of town. The store may be placed in one or more retail clusters – that is, international city/town shopping centres, parade/neighbourhood shopping centre, retail park and so forth. It could be a free-standing unit situated well away from other retailers or part of an organized retail complex. Location choice affects retailers' costs. Take for example, the big shopping cities in the world. Hong Kong's Pedder Street, costing over $7,400 to rent per square metre per year is the most expensive anywhere in the world. Tokyo's Ginza is a close second, with a rent of just over $7,300 per square metre. Contrast these with America's most expensive – Manhattan's East 57th Street ($4,900 per square metre), Europe's most expensive street – Munich's fashionable Kaufingerstrasse (around $2,600 per square metre), and London's Oxford Street, where a square metre costs about $2,550. Lisbon's pretty Amoreiras have the cheapest rents at just over $800 per square metre a year.[38]

- *Site characteristics.* The general appearance, size and visibility of the site or the building, and accessibility for consumers and delivery vehicles, are important considerations. The presence of anchor stores can be an attractive feature for other smaller retailers as the former are a magnet that pulls customers to the shopping zone. Compatibility with nearby stores ensures that stores complement each other, thus further enhancing customer traffic.

- *Target customers' characteristics, location and shopping needs.* A boutique that sells expensive designer wear to up-market, discerning and fashion-conscious buyers will locate in an exclusive shopping zone, usually in the more fashionable part of a town or a city. A discount superstore that attracts middle- or down-market consumers will be found on a site more congruous with the store's image (e.g. edge-of-town, out-of-town or retail park). Retailers must consider customers' location, with most operators choosing sites with high pedestrian or vehicular traffic. Retailers, such as hypermarkets, supermarkets and furniture superstores, targeting car-borne customers, select sites that can provide ample car parking and good access for customers and delivery vans, just as service stations and convenience stores require locations with high vehicular (but, not congested) traffic. Retail banks, restaurants, fast-food outlets and many other retailers select sites based on high pedestrian traffic, availability of town parking and public transport.

- *Competitors' location.* Many retailers follow competition, as in the case of banks, building societies, estate agencies, restaurants, food, shoe, clothing and variety stores. Their main reasons for doing so are that complementarity and choice attract a larger number of buyers to the retail centre, so that each retailer benefits, while staying close to key competitors – which are the magnets or anchor stores – ensures that the retailer is aware of and keeps track of competitive developments all the time. On the other hand, some retailers may prefer to avoid competition by locating on secondary sites, as in the case of Kentucky Fried Chicken (KFC), or to benefit from being the sole trader in a particular area.

Location decisions are important and retailers must continually be aware of environmental trends that present new opportunities for creating a competitive advantage. Consider, for example, Cité Europe:

> Cité Europe is the $120m., 73,000-square metre retail complex in Calais built by Espace Expansion, a subsidiary of Arc Union, one of France's largest property companies. Calais, the main port in northern France, handles 4 million heavy goods and commercial vehicles a year and 3.7m. cars. On both sides of the Channel Tunnel, confidence runs high that the increased traffic generated by the tunnel, high speed rail-links and new motorways will assure this massive flow of vehicles and people, thus making Calais a natural location for retailers. Over 75% of the shops were pre-let ahead of Cité Europe's opening in March 1995. Benetton has taken a 215 square metre store, far larger than any of its usual units; Carrefour has an 18,000 square metre hypermarket and there are a further ten large units, ranging from 1,000 to 1,850 square metre, as well as standard, smaller sized shops. Toys 'R' Us, Darty, Tesco Vins, Go Sport, Camieu and Marrionnaud have all taken large stores. There is a 10,000 square metre food-court and a 12,000 square metre leisure complex, including a multiplex cinema. Cité Europe is a testing ground for new shopping concepts in Europe. If it works, major retailers cannot afford to ignore the revolution.[39]

Cité Europe: a testing ground for new shopping concepts in Europe.

## RETAILING TRENDS

Give or take individual country differences, a number of general trends affect the retailing industry worldwide. During the 1980s, retail sales in real terms grew in most European countries, the United States and Japan. Many retailers expanded their operations quickly, often using borrowed money. Towards the late 1980s and early 1990s, a combination of sluggish consumer spending – as recession hit harder in these countries – rising interest rates and overcapacity led to many casualties:

> A host of American department stores, including Bloomingdales and Bon Marché filed for bankruptcy; its most famous store, Sears Roebuck, had been reduced to offering every-day low prices; bankruptcy also hit the British specialty fashion retailer, Sock Shop International; Harvey Nicholls, a fashionable London department store was sold by its owner, Burton Group, to Dickson Poon, a Hong Kong entrepreneur who runs an international retailing and wholesaling company; Aquascutum and Daks-Simpson fashion groups were taken over by Japanese companies; banks came to the rescue of Germany's Co-op, having agreed to write off loans of $1 billion; Germany's two largest store groups, Karstadt and Hartie have merged; Benetton gave up its financial services business and sought to re-focus its efforts on its fashion business. In Japan, small shopkeepers were panicking as the Large-Scale Store Law which unfairly protected their trade was to be repealed.[40]

Most exposed to the retailing difficulties were stores that grew too fast and/or borrowed too much over the 1980s. However, as discussed earlier in this chapter, other retailers and retailing approaches – mail-order companies, discounters, warehouses, hypermarket chains and the large and out-of-town 'category killers' – have gained.[41]

Another trend that will have crucial implications for retailers is the increasing internationalization of the industry worldwide. For many domestic retailers, the opportunities for natural expansion in current and new markets in the home territory are drying up. Growth will have to come from winning share from competitors in existing markets. But, greater competition and new types of retailers make it harder to improve market shares. As such, more big retailers are now looking overseas for earnings growth. They must develop an awareness of international retailing developments and develop the skills for international retailing (see Marketing Highlight 22.2).

To be successful, then, retailers must adjust to a tougher trading climate in the 1990s. They must do several things well:

- First, they must choose target segments carefully and position themselves strongly.
- Second, retailers have to find new ways to boost sales. To do this, they must stress good value for money, respond to demographic trends and strive to deliver products that consumers want. Good service will also be paramount for success. The latter means more than just smiling sales staff; it means efficient stock control, quality assurance, logical store layouts and convenient access, including good opening hours to encourage the parsimonious shopper of the 1990s to spend more in the shops.
- Third, quickly rising costs will make more efficient operation and smarter buying essential to successful retailing. Controlling costs will be vital. As a result, retail technologies are growing in importance as competitive tools. Progressive retailers are using computers to produce better forecasts, reduce and control inventory costs, order electronically from suppliers, communicate between stores, and even sell to consumers within stores. They are adopting checkout scanning systems, in-store television, on-line transaction processing and electronic funds transfer – all this to slice time out of the supply process.

## Wheel of retailing

Many retailing innovations are partially explained by the **wheel of retailing** concept.[42] According to this concept, many new types of retailing forms begin as low-margin, low-price, low-status operations. They challenge established retailers that have become 'fat' by letting their costs and margins increase. The new retailers' success leads them to upgrade their facilities, carry higher-quality merchandise and offer more services. In turn, their costs increase, forcing them to increase their prices. Eventually, the new retailers become like the conventional retailers they replaced. The cycle begins again when still newer types of retailers evolve with lower costs and prices. The wheel of retailing concept seems to explain the initial success and later troubles of department stores, supermarkets and discount stores, and the recent success of off-price retailers.

New retail forms will continue to emerge to meet new consumer needs and new situations. But the life cycle of new retail forms is getting shorter. Department stores took about 100 years to reach the mature stage of the life cycle. More recent forms, such as catalogue showrooms and furniture warehouse stores, reached maturity in about ten years. In such an environment, seemingly solid retail positions can crumble quickly. For example, of the top ten discount retailers in 1962 (the year that the great American retail giants, Wal-Mart and K Mart, began), not one still exists today.

Thus retailers can no longer sit back with a successful formula. To remain successful, they must keep adapting and reshape their business accordingly.[43]

## The retailing accordion

The retailing accordion is a phenomenon worth noting. While the wheel of retailing explains the evolution and development of new types of retail stores, the concept of the **retailing accordion** refers to the intermittent changes in the width of merchandise offered by the retailer or the scope of a retailer's operations. Typically, retailers begin by selling a wide assortment of products. They are followed by retailers offering a narrower or more specialized range of products, who in turn are eventually superseded by broad line mass merchandisers. The theory suggests that retailers pass through a *general–specific–general cycle.*[44]

The theory adequately tapped the evolution of the American retail scene, where the nineteenth-century general stores gave way to the twentieth-century specialist retailers, who were then superseded by the postwar mass merchandisers.

Arguably, the accordion concept may be used to describe the more recent *specific–general–specific* cycle of retailing observed in some sectors. For instance, retailers often also begin by selling a narrow range or special type of goods. Take, for example, a grocery store that carries mainly food, drinks and convenience items. As sales expand, the store manager tends to add new merchandise, such as household goods, stationery, cosmetics and nonprescription drugs, to his or her portfolio. As it grows further, extra services and amenities – for example, delicatessen, fresh-fish-and-seafood counter, in-store bakery, credit card and cheque facilities – are added. This is the path reflected by large supermarkets in the United Kingdom, which started as narrow-line high-street grocery retailers, stretching out, over the 1980s, into broad-line superstores. More recently, as further growth in edge-of-town superstores is slowing down and out-of-town shopping centres are reaching saturation point, Britain's largest supermarkets are contemplating moving back into the high streets. Sainsbury and Tesco have recently developed small town-centre formats, Metro and Central respectively, which they claim are able to trade more profitably than they could ten years ago now that they have already secured increased buying power and efficiency.[45] Extension and contraction of product assortments are also a reflection of the tendency of businesses to diversify when existing markets are saturated, in order to achieve further growth. But, consistent with observations in other industries ranging from chemicals to communications, companies that overspread their resources and dilute their efforts must ultimately refocus their attention on core competencies to sustain and build core businesses.

## WHOLESALING

**Wholesaling** includes all activities involved in selling goods and services to those buying for resale or business use. A retail bakery is engaging in wholesaling when it sells pastry to the local hotel. We call **wholesalers** those firms engaged *primarily* in wholesaling activity. Wholesalers buy mostly from producers and sell mostly to retailers, industrial customers, other wholesalers and institutional buyers. Rarely does a wholesaler sell to ultimate consumers.

Why are wholesalers used at all? For example, why would a producer use wholesalers rather than sell directly to retailers or consumers? Quite simply, wholesalers are often better at performing one or more of the following channel functions:

- *Selling and promotion.* Wholesalers' salesforces help manufacturers reach any small customers at a low cost. The wholesaler has more contacts and is often more trusted by the buyer than the distant manufacturer.
- *Buying and assortment building.* Wholesalers can select items and build assortments needed by their customers, thereby saving the consumers much work.
- *Bulk-breaking.* Wholesalers save their customers money by buying in huge lots and breaking bulk (breaking large lots into small quantities).

- *Warehousing.* Wholesalers hold inventories, thereby reducing the inventory costs and risks of suppliers and customers.
- *Transportation.* Wholesalers can provide quicker delivery to buyers because they are closer than the producers.
- *Financing.* Wholesalers finance their customers by giving credit, and they finance their suppliers by ordering early and paying bills on time.
- *Risk bearing.* Wholesalers absorb risk by taking title and bearing the cost of theft, damage, spoilage and obsolescence.
- *Market information.* Wholesalers give information to suppliers and customers about competitors, new products, and price developments.
- *Management services and advice.* Wholesalers often help retailers train their sales-clerks, improve store layouts and displays, and set up accounting and inventory control systems.

Wholesalers therefore render important services to producers and resellers and, as such, play a key role within the marketing channel. The wholesaler is the intermediary linking producer and reseller.

## TYPES OF WHOLESALERS

Wholesalers are classified according to whether they take title to the merchandise they handle, the breadth and depth of their product/service lines and the range of services they offer. There are three main groups of wholesaling organizations (see Table 22.5): merchant wholesalers, brokers and agents, and manufacturers' sales branches and offices.

### Merchant wholesalers

**Merchant wholesalers** are independently owned businesses that take title to the merchandise they handle. They buy and resell products to industrial or retail customers. Merchant wholesalers include two broad types: full-service wholesalers and limited-service wholesalers.

**TABLE 22.5     *Classification of wholesalers***

| Merchant wholesalers | Brokers and agents | Manufacturers' and retailers' branches and offices |
|---|---|---|
| Full-service wholesalers<br>  Wholesale merchants<br>  Industrial distributors<br>Limited-service wholesalers<br>  Cash-and-carry wholesalers<br>  Truck wholesalers<br>  Drop shippers<br>  Rack jobbers<br>  Producers' cooperatives<br>  Mail-order wholesalers | Brokers<br>Agents | Sales branches and offices<br>Purchasing offices |

## Full-service wholesalers

**Full-service wholesalers** provide a full set of services, such as carrying stock, using a salesforce, offering credit, making deliveries and providing technical advice and management assistance. They are either wholesale merchants or industrial distributors.

*Wholesale merchants*   Wholesale merchants sell mostly to retailers and provide a full range of services. They vary in the width of their product line. *General merchandise wholesalers* carry several lines of goods – for example, hardware, cosmetics, detergents, nonperishable foods, household goods – to meet the needs of both general-merchandise retailers and single-line retailers. *Limited-line wholesalers* carry one or two lines of goods, but offer a greater depth of assortment. Examples are hardware wholesalers, drug wholesalers and clothing wholesalers. Some *speciality-line-wholesalers* carry only part of a line in great depth, such as health-food wholesalers, seafood wholesalers and automotive parts wholesalers. They offer customers deeper choice and greater product knowledge.

*Industrial distributors*   Industrial distributors are merchant wholesalers that sell to producers rather than to retailers. They provide inventory, credit, delivery, technical advice and other services. Like merchant wholesalers, they may handle a wide, limited or special line of products. Industrial distributors concentrate on lines such as maintenance and operating supplies, original-equipment goods (such as ball bearings and motors), or equipment (such as power tools and forklift trucks).

## Limited-service wholesalers

**Limited-service wholesalers** perform a limited number of functions and offer fewer services to their suppliers and customers. There are several types of limited-service wholesalers.

*Cash-and-carry wholesalers*   *Cash-and-carry wholesalers* have a limited line of fast-moving goods, such as groceries, toys, household goods, clothes, electrical supplies, office supplies and building materials. They sell to small retailers and industrial firms for cash and normally do not deliver. A small fish-store retailer, for example, normally drives at dawn to a cash-and-carry fish wholesalers and buys several crates of fish, pays on the spot, drives the merchandise back to the store and unloads it. Cash-and-carry wholesalers are important to some small retailers and industrial customers who are not served by the bigger wholesalers. They may not benefit from the services that full-service wholesalers can offer, but they do get lower-priced merchandise and immediate access to goods. Examples of cash-and-carry wholesalers include Booker, Landmark, Nurdin & Peacock and Makro, although, as mentioned earlier, Makro is a hybrid operator, servicing both consumers and small retailers.

*Truck wholesalers*   *Truck wholesalers* (also called *truck jobbers*) perform a selling and delivery function. They carry a limited line of goods (such as milk, bread or snack foods) that they sell for cash as they make their rounds of supermarkets, small groceries, hospitals, restaurants, factory cafeterias and hotels.

*Drop shippers*   *Drop shippers* operate in bulk industries such as coal, oil, chemicals, lumber and heavy equipment. They do not carry inventory or handle the product. They receive orders from retailers, industrial buyers or other wholesalers and then forward these to producers, who ship the goods directly to the customer. The drop shipper takes title and risk from the time the order is accepted to the time it is delivered to the customer. Because drop shippers do not carry inventory, their costs are lower and they can pass on some savings to customers.

*Rack jobbers*     *Rack jobbers* serve grocery and general merchandise retailers, mostly in the area of branded nonfood items, such as books, magazines, toys, stationery, housewares, health and beauty aids, and hardware items. These retailers do not want to order and maintain displays of hundreds of nonfood items. Rack jobbers send delivery trucks to stores and the delivery person sets up display racks for the merchandise. They price the goods, keep them fresh and keep inventory records. Rack jobbers sell on consignment – they retain title to the goods and bill the retailers only for the goods sold to consumers. Thus they provide services such as delivery, shelving, inventory and financing. They do little promotion because they carry many branded items that are already highly advertised.

*Producers' cooperatives*     *Producers' cooperatives*, owned by farmer-members, assemble farm produce to sell in local markets. Their profits are divided among members at the end of the year.

*Mail-order wholesalers*     *Mail-order wholesalers* use catalogues to sell to retail, industrial and institutional customers and give discounts for large orders. They handle products, such as jewellery, cosmetics, special foods, car parts, office supplies and other items. Their main customers are businesses located in small outlying areas. They have no salesforces to call on customers and provide very few services. The orders are filled and goods are sent to customers by mail, truck or other means.

## Brokers and agents

*Brokers* and *agents* differ from merchant wholesalers in two ways: they do not take title to goods, and they perform only a few functions. Their main function is to help in buying and selling, and for these services they earn a commission on the selling price. Like merchant wholesalers, they generally specialize by product line or customer type. Because they are specialists, they can offer valuable sales advice and expertise to clients.

### Broker

A **broker** brings buyers and sellers together and assists in negotiation. Brokers are employed temporarily and paid by the parties hiring them. They do not carry inventory, get involved in financing, or assume risk. The most familiar examples are food brokers, real estate brokers, insurance brokers and security brokers.

### Agent

**Agents** represent buyers or sellers on a more permanent basis. There are several types.

*Manufacturers' agents* (also called *manufacturers' representatives*) are the most common type of agent wholesaler. They represent two or more manufacturers of related lines. They have a formal agreement with each manufacturer, covering prices, territories, order-handling procedures, delivery, warranties and commission rates. They know each manufacturer's product line and use their wide contacts to sell the products. They do not, however, have much influence over prices and other marketing decisions, and provide limited, if any, technical, product or service support. Manufacturers' agents are used in lines such as apparel, furniture and electrical goods. Most manufacturers' agents are small businesses, with only a few employees who are skilled salespeople. They are hired by small producers who cannot afford to maintain their own field salesforces and by large producers who want to open new territories to sell in areas that cannot support a full-time salesperson. Manufacturers' agents therefore help producers to minimize selling costs for current and new products and market territories.

*Selling agents*    *Selling agents* contract to sell a producer's entire output – either the manufacturer is not interested in doing the selling or feels unqualified. The selling agent serves as a sales department and has much influence over prices, terms and conditions of sale, as well as packaging, product development, promotion and distribution policies. Unlike other agent wholesalers, the selling agent normally has no territory limits. Selling agents are found in product areas such as textiles, industrial machinery and equipment, coal and coke, chemicals and metals.

*Purchasing agents*    *Purchasing agents* generally have a long-term relationship with buyers. They make purchases for buyers and often receive, inspect, warehouse and ship goods to the buyers. One type of purchasing agent is a *resident buyer* in big clothing markets – purchasing specialists who look for apparel lines that can be carried by small retailers located in small cities. They know a great deal about their product lines, provide helpful market information to clients, and can also obtain the best goods and prices available.

*Commission merchants*    Commission merchants (or *houses*) are agents that take physical possession of products, grade, store and transport them, and negotiate sales with buyers in the market. They are normally not used on a long-term basis. They are used most often in agricultural marketing by farmers who do not want to sell their own output and who do not belong to cooperatives. Typically, the commission merchant will take a truckload of farm products to a central market, sell it for the best price, deduct expenses and a commission and pay the balance to the farmer. Commission merchants have more power than the small producer over prices and terms of sale. Not only do they obtain the best price possible in the market for the producer, but they may also offer planning and financial assistance.

## Manufacturers' sales branches and offices

The third main type of wholesaling is that done in **manufacturers' sales branches and offices** by sellers or buyers themselves rather than through independent wholesalers. Manufacturers often set up their own sales branches and offices to improve inventory control, selling and promotion. These are located in principal market centres where the big customers are found and where demand is high. *Sales branches* carry inventory and are found in industries such as lumber, electrical supplies and automotive equipment and parts.

*Sales offices* do not carry inventory and are most often found in the dry goods and notion industries. Many retailers also set up *purchasing offices* in principal market centres, usually in the big cities. These purchasing offices perform a role similar to that of brokers or agents, but are part of the buyer's organization.

## WHOLESALER MARKETING DECISIONS

Wholesalers have experienced mounting competitive pressures in recent years. They have faced new sources of competition, more demanding customers, new technologies and more direct-buying programmes on the part of large industrial, institutional and retail buyers. As a result, they have had to improve their strategic decisions on target markets and positioning and on the marketing mix – product assortments and services, price, promotion and place (see Figure 22.2).

### Target market and positioning decisions

Like retailers, wholesalers must define their target markets and position themselves effectively – they cannot serve everyone. They can choose a target group by size of customer (only large retailers), type of customer (convenience food stores only), need for service (customers who need credit), or other factors. Within the target group, they can identify the more profitable customers, design stronger offers and build better relationships with them. They can propose automatic reordering systems, set up management-training and advisory systems or even sponsor a voluntary chain. They can discourage less profitable customers by requiring larger orders or adding service charges to smaller ones.

### Marketing mix decisions

Like retailers, wholesalers must decide on product assortment and services, prices, promotion and place. The wholesaler's 'product' is the assortment of *products and services* that it offers. Wholesalers are under great pressure to carry a full line and to stock enough for immediate delivery. But this practice can damage profits. Wholesalers today are cutting down on the number of lines they carry, choosing to

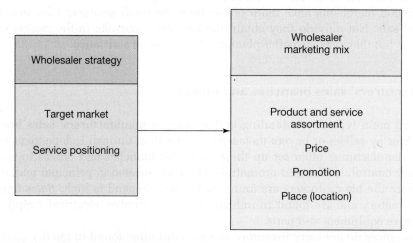

**Figure 22.2**  Wholesaler marketing decisions.

carry only the more profitable ones. Wholesalers are also rethinking which services count most in building strong customer relationships and which should be dropped or charged for. The key is to find the mix of services most valued by their target customers and for which they are prepared to pay.

*Price* is also an important wholesaler decision. Wholesalers usually mark up the cost of goods by a standard percentage, say, 20 per cent. Expenses may run at 17 per cent of the gross margin, leaving a profit margin of 3 per cent. In grocery wholesaling, the average profit margin is often less than 2 per cent. Wholesalers are trying new pricing approaches. They may cut their margin on some lines in order to win important new customers. They may ask suppliers for special price breaks when they can turn them into an increase in the supplier's sales.

Although *promotion* can be critical to wholesaler success, most wholesalers are not promotion-minded. Their use of trade advertising, sales promotion, personal selling and public relations is largely scattered and unplanned. Many are behind the times in personal selling – they still see selling as a single salesperson talking to a single customer, rather than as a team effort to sell, build and service important accounts. Wholesalers also need to adopt some of the nonpersonal promotion techniques used by retailers. They need to develop an overall promotion strategy and to make greater use of supplier promotion materials and programmes.

Finally, *place* is important to wholesalers who must choose their locations and facilities carefully. Wholesalers typically locate in low-rent, low-tax areas and tend to invest little money in their buildings, equipment and systems. As a result, their materials-handling and order-processing systems are often outdated. In recent years, however, large and progressive wholesalers have been reacting to rising costs by investing in automated warehouses and on-line ordering systems. Orders are fed from the retailer's system directly into the wholesaler's computer, and the items are picked up by mechanical devices and automatically taken to a shipping platform where they are assembled. Most large wholesalers employ computers to carry out accounting, billing, inventory control and forecasting. Modern wholesalers are adapting their services to the needs of target customers and finding cost-reducing methods of doing business.

## TRENDS IN WHOLESALING

Progressive wholesalers constantly watch for better ways to meet the changing needs of their suppliers and target customers. They recognize that, in the long run, their only reason for existence comes from increasing the efficiency and effectiveness of the entire marketing channel. To achieve this goal, they must constantly improve their services and reduce their costs.

One study predicts several developments in the wholesaling industry.[46] Consolidation will significantly reduce the number of wholesaling firms. The remaining wholesaling companies will grow larger, primarily through acquisition, merger and geographic expansion. Geographic expansion will require distributors to learn how to compete effectively over wider and more diverse areas. The increased use of computerized and automated systems will help wholesalers.

The distinction between large retailers and large wholesalers continues to blur. Many retailers now operate formats such as wholesale clubs and hypermarkets that perform many wholesale functions. In return, many large wholesalers are setting up their own retailing operations. A prime example of this type of *hybrid* operator is the Dutch cash-and-carry self-service wholesaler, Makro, which in one sense is a limited-service wholesaler, selling primarily to the trade – that is, to small shopkeepers/

# Pharmaceutical wholesalers: global trends

Pharmaceutical wholesalers, by nature and tradition, are local operators, with no single operator operating worldwide, in marked contrast to the pharmaceutical company which tends to be global. Generally, drug wholesalers worldwide tend to be fragmented, with few firms serving an entire national territory. The majority are family-owned firms and most of the large ones grew from small-sized operations. Globally, there are no standard channel structures and systems differ from country to country. However, many are affected by common operational and regulatory conditions. In countries where the wholesalers plays a dominant role in supply, the traditional channel system bears the following features and trends:

- Wholesalers tend to consolidate goods from all manufacturers and deliver them to a specific group of clients (primarily pharmacies, hospitals and other bulk buyers of medicines). Such clients usually have a one-stop-shop relationship with one wholesaler who serves their needs. In the principal developed economies, the majority of pharmaceutical products reach patients through the wholesaler–pharmacy route. On average, about 80 per cent of pharmaceutical products flow to retailers through wholesalers; however, the figures for individual countries vary as show in Table 1.

So long as the multiplicity of drug suppliers and retailers exists industry observers and analysts predict that the trend toward greater use of wholesalers will continue over the 1990s. Manufacturers continue to use wholesalers because of the high 'value-added' they contribute to the manufacturers' product, their provision of customer service, and their sophisticated level of operation and potential efficiencies. The number of drug wholesalers varies from country to country: for exam-

**Table 1  Percentage of drugs going through wholesalers**

| Country | Percentage |
|---|---|
| United States | 60 |
| Japan | 80 |
| United Kingdom | 72 |
| Germany | 80 |
| France | 82 |
| Belgium | 90 |
| Netherlands | 91 |
| Spain | 85 |
| Italy | 79 |
| Scandinavia | 100 |

ple, there is one, the state-owned distributor, operating in Norway; two in Sweden; three in Finland; from five to 280 in the other European countries; 180 in the United States; and over 7,000 in Japan.

- In most countries, the pharmaceuticals industry, as part of the healthcare industry, faces strong pressures to lower prices. Wholesalers in this industry will invariably be affected by these conditions. Wholesaler margins are already being squeezed due to pressure for cost containment by governments, private healthcare insurance programmes, and increased competition in many markets. The need to stock large assortments of goods and to provide high levels of service has reduced margins to lower than 5 per cent in most countries.
- Fortunately, increased automation and use of electronic data processing, invoicing and inventory control have helped wholesalers to reduce costs, with most of the savings being passed to customers.
- Consolidation and more of this is expected to occur in the drug wholesaling industry. This will

retailers. In another sense, Makro is also a large retailer given that many of the 'trade visitors' who purchase goods from its warehouse, are not resellers but individuals buying for personal consumption. Furthermore Makro stores do not fit the traditional notion of the frills-free 'pile 'em high, sell 'em cheap' shed operators. Their depots are neither dowdy nor devoid of amenities and services. Indeed, carefully controlled store designs and layouts, well-trained staff, customer service and ongoing customer-

result in fewer, but financially stronger, companies. A recent Economist Intelligence Unit (EIU) study reports that, with the exception of Italy, Japan and Spain, the drug wholesalers sector in countries is dominated by just two operators (e.g. the top two wholesalers have 45 per cent share of the market in Germany, 55 per cent in France, 65 per cent in Canada, 67 per cent in the United Kingdom, 41 per cent in the United States and 80 per cent in the Netherlands).

■ Diversification is increasingly pursued by wholesalers. The most pervasive form has been expansion into new geographic markets. Over recent years, many national wholesalers have attempted to 'Europeanize' their operations through acquisitions or alliances: CERP Rouen (France) acquired SA Defraene (Belgium) and three other Spanish wholesalers; ERP (France) and the Italian Alleanza have taken stakes in the Portuguese SIF; CERP Lorraine (France) now owns Leige Pharma and Promephar of Belgium, while the German Schulz have acquired France's Chafer and Brocaceph of the Netherlands. Tredimed was formed as a result of the alliance between OCP (France), AAH (UK) and GEHE (Germany); the PAG alliance includes Unichem (UK), OPG (Netherlands), Anzag and Egwa-Wiweda (both from Germany); FPN is formed by companies from thirteen countries, while Alliance Sante was formed by Italy's Alleanza FCA and France's IFP and ERPI. It may be that by the turn of the century drug wholesaling in Europe will be dominated by five or six large European organizations.

■ Vertical integration is also on wholesalers' agenda. Some have started up manufacturing or retailing operations. For example, the Dutch OPG runs Pharmachemie, which produces ethical drugs, SAN makes OTC (over-the-counter) medicines and operates the retail outlet Apoteck Extra. Unichem, in the United Kingdom, manufacturers own-label OTCs as well as running the Moss retail outlets.

More aggressive competition and the high pressure on drug wholesaler margins are forcing wholesale organizations to look for ways to reduce costs, while enhancing customer service. Many have sought to exploit technology to improve systems and streamline operations, hence much greater importance has been attached to automated logistics systems, computerization, and electronic order systems. Market information and intelligence have also become crucial concerns of the big wholesalers. Those that have lots of timely data, like the big distributors in the United States, are able to service key customers more effectively than others, while also using such assets to tie up one very important resource – the manufacturers who supply them with the merchandise.

The pharmaceutical industry worldwide is affected by the general trend towards higher cost and increasing competition and by the pressures of internationalization. Wholesalers dictate the critical flow of products from producer to end-user in this sector. In creating 'place' value, they play a dominant role. To sustain their position, they must respond by adapting to the state of continuous flux that has created new competition and fresh challenges for all in the industry.

Source: 'Wholesale changes', *SCRIP Magazine* (June 1992), 38–40; Barrie James, 'The global pharmaceutical industry in the 1990s: the challenge of changes', The Economist Intelligence Unit (November 1990); Richard Platford, 'Changing distribution channel strategy', Coopers & Lybrand (1992); William Goests, 'Wholesalers', International Federation of Pharmaceutical Wholesalers (1990); Peter O'Donnell, *Pharmaceutical Wholesaling World-Wide: A study of present practice and future issues* (London: PJO Publications 1986).

relationship building are hallmarks of the Makro operation. Makro's regular newsletter also keeps customers (trade members who own a Makro card) informed of store developments, promotions and other news.[47]

Wholesalers will continue to increase the services they provide to retailers – retail pricing, cooperative advertising, marketing and management information reports, accounting services and others. Rising costs on the other hand, and the demand for increased services on the other, will put the squeeze on wholesaler profits. Wholesalers who do not find efficient ways to deliver value to their customers will soon drop by the wayside.

Finally, facing slow growth in their domestic markets and the trend towards globalization, many large wholesalers are now going global, thus creating new challenges for the wholesaling industry worldwide. The above trends in wholesaling are evident in global industries, notably pharmaceuticals (see Marketing Highlight 22.3). To survive, players must learn to adapt to their changing environment. Like their customers – the resellers or retailers, whose success relies on their ability to capture and retain customers by offering better value than competition can – wholesalers must consistently add to that value-creation process if they are to retain the importance universally ascribed to the middleman. For both wholesaler and retailer, nothing happens until a sale takes place, until customers buy. And there are no long-term rewards unless these customers come back for more!

## SUMMARY

Retailing and wholesaling consist of many organizations bringing goods and services from the point of production to the point of use. *Retailing* includes all activities involved in selling goods or services directly to final consumers for their personal, nonbusiness use. Retailers can be classified as store retailers and nonstore retailers. *Store retailers* can be further classified by the *amount of service* they provide (self-service, limited service or full service); *product line sold* (speciality store, department store, supermarket, convenience store, superstore, hypermarket and service businesses); *relative prices* (discount store, category killers, cash-and-carry warehouse, warehouse club and catalogue showroom); *control of outlets* (corporate chains, voluntary chains and retailer cooperatives, franchise organizations and merchandising conglomerates); and *type of store cluster* (international shopping cities, city and town centre shopping zones, parade/neighbourhood shopping centre, the corner shop, edge-of-town and out-of-town shopping zones, organized retail parks, sheltered or covered shopping complexes).

Although most goods and services are sold through stores, nonstore retailing has been growing faster than has store retailing. Nonstore retailing consists of *direct marketing*, *direct selling* and *automatic vending*.

Each retailer must make decisions about its target markets, product assortment and services, price, promotion and place. Retailers need to choose target markets carefully and position themselves strongly. They need to be aware of retailing trends and their impact on the future of their industry.

*Wholesaling* includes all the activities involved in selling goods or services to those who are buying for the purpose of resale or for business use. Wholesalers perform many functions, including selling and promoting, buying and assortment building, bulk-breaking, warehousing, transporting, financing, risk bearing, supplying market information and providing management services and advice. Wholesalers fall into three groups. First, *merchant wholesalers* take possession of the goods. They include *full-service wholesalers* (whole merchants, industrial distributors) and *limited-service wholesalers* (cash-and-carry wholesalers, trucks wholesalers, drop shippers, rack jobbers, producers' cooperatives and mail-order wholesalers). Second, *agents* and *brokers* do not take possession of the goods but are paid a commission for facilitating buying and selling. Third, *manufacturers' sales branches and offices* are wholesaling operations conducted by nonwholesalers to bypass the wholesalers. Wholesaling is an important business activity. Progressive wholesalers must adapt their services to the needs of target customers and seek cost-reducing methods of doing business in an increasingly competitive and international environment.

## ■ DISCUSSING THE ISSUES

1. Which would do more to increase a convenience store's sales – an increase in the length or the breadth of its product assortment? Why?

2. Warehouse clubs that are restricted to registered or fee-paying members only, such as Makro and Costco, are growing rapidly. They offer a very broad line of products, often in institutional packaging, at very low prices. Some members buy for resale, others buy to supply a business and still others buy for personal use. Are these stores wholesalers or retailers? How can you make a distinction?

3. 'Category killers' and discounters provide tough price competition to other retailers. Will large retailers' growing power in channels of distribution affect manufacturers' willingness to sell to 'category killers' and other discounters? What policy should Sony have regarding selling to these retailers?

4. Postal rate increases make it more expensive to send direct mail, catalogue, and purchased products to consumers. How would you expect direct-mail and catalogue marketers to respond to an increase in postage rates?

5. A typical 'country store' in a village community sells a variety of food and nonfood items – snacks, staples, hardware and many other types of goods. What kinds of wholesalers do the owners of such stores use to obtain the items they sell? Are these the same suppliers that a supermarket uses?

6. Are there any fundamental differences between retailers, wholesalers and manufacturers in the types of marketing decisions they make? Give examples of the marketing decisions made by the three groups which show their similarities and differences.

## ■ APPLYING THE CONCEPTS

1. Collect all the catalogues that you have received in the mail recently.

   - Sort them by type of product line. Is there some pattern to the types of direct marketers that are targeting you?
   - Where do you think these catalogue companies got your name?
   - How do you think a company that was selling your name and address to a direct marketer would describe your buying habits?

2. Watch a satellite or cable television shopping channel, or tune in to a television shopping show.

   - How are these shows attempting to target buyers? Do they mix football studs and fine china in the same programme, or are they targeting more carefully?
   - How much of the merchandise shown appears to be close-outs? How can you tell?

## ■ REFERENCES

1. 'Furnishing the world', *The Economist* (19 November 1994), 101–2; John Thornhill, 'IKEA logs furniture sales of 2.7 times industry average', *Financial Times* (18 May 1992), 10; John Thornhill, 'IKEA's logic furnishes a market riddle', *Financial Times* (20 October 1992), 27; see also Bill Saporito, 'IKEA's got 'em lining up', *Fortune* (11 March 1991), 72; 'North America's top 100 furniture stores', *Furniture Today* (18 May 1992), 50; Laura Loro, 'IKEA', *Advertising Age* (4 July 1994), S2.

2. 'Grocery profits', *The Economist* (23 February, 1991), 33–4; Suzanne Bidlake 'Cut price Carrefour targets UK', *Marketing* (19 November 1992), 3; 'Norma and Carrefour invade UK', *Marketing Week* (22 January 1993), 6.

3. Andrew Adonis, 'Computer seller sets up UK "superstores"', *Financial Times* (2 August 1993), 15.

4. See Laurie M. Grossman, 'Hypermarkets: a sure-fire hit bombs', *Wall Street Journal* (25 June 1992), B1; Emily DeNitto, 'Hypermarkets seem to be a big flop in US', *Advertising Age* (4 October 1993), 20.

5. Guy de Jonquières, 'A spartan approach that beats the recession', *Financial Times* (26 November 1992), 26.

6. 'Killing off the competition', *Marketing Business* (April 1994), 11–14; *Category Killers: Prospects for the year 2000* (London: Euromonitor, 1994).

7. 'Retailing in Asia: Makro-economics', *The Economist* (25 September 1993), 100, 105; 'Asian retailing: teach me

shopping', *The Economist* (18 December 1993), 78–9.

8. John Thornhill, 'Silent enemy poised for attack', *Financial Times* (5 March 1992), 11; Alex Spillius, 'Invasion of the category killers', *Observer Life* (27 February 1994), 6–7; David Nicholson-Lord, 'Britain targeted as springboard for retail "attack"', *Independent* (31 January 1994), 5.

9. Malcolm Brown, 'Joint effort', *Marketing Business* (September 1992), 13–16.

10. Guy de Jonquières, 'Temptations along the eastern aisle', *Financial Times* (6 April 1994), 19.

11. Microsoft, *Encarta*, electronic multimedia encyclopaedia (Microsoft Corporation, 1993).

12. Anne Massey, 'Direct hit', *Marketing Business* (November 1994), 42–4; Alice Rawthorn, 'Profiting by the direct approach', *Financial Times* (27 September 1990), 10.

13. See Mary Lou Roberts and Paul D. Berger, *Direct Marketing Management* (Englewood Cliffs, NJ: Prentice Hall, 1989), 11–15.

14. Alena Hola, 'Can the EC deliver postal harmony?' *Marketing Business* (February 1994), 24–8.

15. Tony Coad, 'Distinguishing marks', *Marketing Business* (October 1992), 12–14.

16. Ian Harding, 'Trois Suisses change the image of mail-order', *The European* (2–8 December 1994), 28.

17. Richard L. Bencin, 'Telefocus: telemarketing gets synergized', *Sales & Marketing Management* (February 1992), 49–53: 50.

18. See Bill Kelley, 'Is there anything that can't be sold by phone?' *Sales & Marketing Management* (April 1989), 60–4; Rudy Oetting and Geri Gantman, 'Dial M for maximize', *Sales & Marketing Management* (June 1991), 100–6; Bencin, 'Telefocus', op. cit. 49–57; Martin Everett, 'Selling by telephone', *Sales and Marketing Management* (December 1993), 75–9.

19. Rudy Oetting, 'Telephone marketing: where we've been and where we should be going', *Direct Marketing* (February 1987), 98.

20. For more discussion, see Junu Bryan Kim, '800/900: king of the road in marketing value, usage', *Advertising Age* (17 February 1992), S1, S4.

21. A. Burnside, 'Calling the shots', *Marketing* (25 January, 1990).

22. Anne Massey, 'Ring my bell', *Marketing Business* (June 1992), 35–9.

23. Michael Stevens, *The Handbook of Telemarketing* (London: Kogan Page, 1992).

24. See Rebecca Piirto, 'The TV beast', *American Demographics* (May 1993), 34–42.

25. Torin Douglas, 'A case of sofa not so good', *Marketing Week* (30 September 1994), 17: David Short, 'QVC loses out in UK screen test', *The European* (9–15 September 1994), 21.

26. See Rebecca Piirto, 'Over the line', *American Demographics* (July 1992), 6; Evan J. Schwartz, 'Prodigy installs a new program', *Business Week* (14 September 1991), 96–100; Scott Donaton, 'In fast-changing world, a sense of urgency at Prodigy', *Advertising Age* (15 April 1993), S1.

27. 'Microsoft signs agreements to work on interactive TV', *AMA Marketing News* (5 December 1994), 9; Louise Kehoe, 'Home shopping to go on line with Internet', *Financial Times* (8 September 1994), 1, 24; Louise Kehoe, 'The armchair shopper', *Financial Times* (22–23 October 1994), 9.

28. Tom Peters, *Thriving on Chaos* (New York: Knopf, 1987).

29. See Joe Schwartz, 'Databases deliver the goods', *American Demographics* (September 1989), 23–5; Lynn G. Coleman, 'Data-base masters become king in the marketplace', *Marketing News* (18 February, 1991), 13, 18; Laura Loro, 'Data bases seen as driving force', *Advertising Age* (18 March 1991), 39; Gary Levin, 'Database draws fevered interest,' *Advertising Age* (8 June 1992), 31.

30. Dunn Humby Associates, *Use and Attitudes to Computers in Marketing*, vols 1 and 2 (London: Dunn Humby Associates, 1993); Louella Miles, 'Hoy data', *Marketing Business* (March 1993), 39–42.

31. See Ernan Roman, *Integrated Direct Marketing* (New York: McGraw-Hill, 1988), 108; and Mark Suchecki, 'Integrated marketing: making it pay', *Direct* (October 1993), 43.

32. Gary Evans, 'Valentine bloom for Flying Flowers', *Financial Times* (15 February 1994), 22; see also *Air Miles Members' Newsletter*, Air Miles Travel Promotions Ltd (winter 1995), 4.

33. Harding, 'Troiss Suisse', op. cit., 28.

34. Richard Berry, 'Doorstepping', *Marketing Business* (November 1992), 43–5.

35. See J. Taylor Buckley, 'Machines start new fast–food era', *USA Today* (19 July 1991), B1, B2; Laurie McLaughlin, 'Vending machines open to new ideas', *Advertising Age* (19 August 1991), 35.

36. For a fuller discussion, see Lawrence H. Wortzel, 'Retailing strategies for today's mature marketplace', *The Journal of Business Strategy* (spring 1987), 45–56.

37. 'The perfect pair of jeans', *Financial Times* (16 December 1994), 14.

38. These are 1991 seasonally adjusted figures taken from *The Economist* (16 July 1991), 117.

39. Clive Branson, 'Cité Europe shapes up in Calais', *The European* (18–24 November 1994), 26.

40. Clive Branson, 'Out-of-town shopping set to reach saturation', *The European* (29 July–4 Aug. 1994), 30; 'Tough on the streets', *The Economist* (24 February 1990), 81–2; John Thornhill, 'Burton sells Harvey Nicholls and Angus Foster' and 'Niche market success for Hong Kong businessman', *Financial Times* (16 August 1991), 1 and 15 respectively; Laura Zinn, 'Retailing: who will survive?' *Business Week* (26 November 1990), 134; see also Susan Caminiti, 'The new retailing champs', *Fortune* (24 September 1990), 85–100.

41. 'No frills, please', *The Economist* (20 July 1991), 31–2.

42. See Malcolm P. McNair and Eleanor G. May, 'The next revolution of the retailing wheel', *Harvard Business Review* (Sept.–Oct. 1978), 81–91; Eleanor G. May, 'A retail odyssey', *Journal of Retailing* (Fall 1989), 356–67; Stephen Brown, 'The wheel of retailing: past and future', *Journal of Retailing* (summer 1990), 143–37.

43. Bill Saporito, 'Is Wal-Mart unstoppable?', *Fortune* (6 May 1991), 50–9. For more on retailing trends, see Eleanor G. May, William Ress, and Walter J. Salmon, *Future Trends in Retailing* (Cambridge, MA: Marketing Science Institute, February 1985); Daniel Sweeney, 'Toward 2000', *Chain Store Age Executive* (January 1990), 27–39; Howard L. Green, 'New consumer realities for retailers', *Advertising Age* (25 April 1994), 4–5.

44. S. C. Hollander, 'Notes on the retail accordion', *Journal of Retailing*, **42**, 2 (1966), 24.

45. Neil Buckley, 'Still shopping as the margins drop', *Financial Times* (4 August 1994), 15; Clive Branson, 'Out-of-town shopping centres set to reach saturation point', *The European* (29 July– 4 Aug. 1994), 30.

46. See Arthur Andersen and Co., *Facing the Forces of Change: Beyond future trends in wholesale distribution* (Washington, DC: Distribution Research and Education Foundation, 1987), 7; see also Joseph Weber, 'It's "like somebody had shot the postman"', *Business Week* (13 January 1992), 82.

47. Various *Makro (UK) Newsletters* (Leeds: Makro Self-Service Wholesalers, 1994, 1995); for more details about the cash-and-carry sector, see *Cash and Carry Outlets* (Hampton, Middx: Key Note Publications, 1992).

## CASE 22

# Pieta luxury chocolates

Peter Abel, the young managing director of his family's firm, was pleased with the way he had revitalized the firm after he took over in 1985. Since formed in 1923, Pieta had sold its luxury Belgian chocolates through its own small shops. It had a high reputation within the trade and many devoted customers. It was the country's largest luxury chocolate manufacturer but, until Peter took over, the company had stagnated. In his opinion, Pieta's should be more like other leading family firms such as Cadbury, Ferrero and Mars.

When he took over he had launched the company into new ventures. Franchising had widened distribution to some small shops who now had corners devoted to Pieta's range. He felt these did not compete with Pieta's own shops because the franchisees were CTNs (confectionery, tobacco and news) shops where people made many impulse purchases. These contrasted with Pieta's shops which people visited to make purchases for a special occasion or as an indulgence. Other channels developed included own label to Britain's Marks & Spencer's, direct mailing for special occasions and exporting (see Exhibit 22.1).

There were some new Pieta shops and 20 per cent of the old ones were refurbished. The refurbishment rate was slower than he would have liked, for he knew that many of the shops were poorly located, cluttered and overcrowded. The well-sited shops often had queues trailing out of the their doors when they were busy, but most did not do so well. The company had not kept pace with changes in shopping and geodemographics. Most of Pieta's shops were on secondary sites in a declining industrial town.

However, the product range was now wider. The chocolate market was seasonal so the shops sold ice-creams to help summer sales. The outlets also carried a range of greetings cards and Pieta gift vouchers to make them more of a one-stop-shop. Soon he would be introducing countlines aimed at the mass market.

As a result of his efforts Peter was able to present a dynamic set of results to his family shareholders (see Exhibit 22.2). He was angry to find that some shareholders were not as supportive as they had been. Some worried about the company's reputation

## CASE 22 (cont)

**Exhibit 22.1**   Channel performance

| Year | Sales tonnage | | | | | Number of own shops |
|------|------|------|------|------|------|------|
| | Own shops | CTN Franchise | M & S own label | Direct mail | Export | |
| 1985 | 6,049 | 1 | 3 | 3 | 3 | 128 |
| 1986 | 7,203 | 92 | 255 | 136 | 11 | 130 |
| 1987 | 8,351 | 392 | 661 | 167 | 24 | 130 |
| 1988 | 9,933 | 1,002 | 636 | 172 | 149 | 132 |
| 1989 | 11,845 | 1,303 | 462 | 205 | 184 | 138 |
| 1990 | 14,753 | 1,259 | 868 | 205 | 167 | 148 |
| Gross margin (%) | 55 | 45 | 37 | 35 | 33 | |
| Net profit (%) | 6 | 14 | 7 | 3 | (6) | |

**Exhibit 22.2**   Company performance (BF m.)

| Year | Sales | Gross profit | Net profit | Net assets | Equity | Debt |
|------|------|------|------|------|------|------|
| 1980 | 2,262 | 1,285 | 282 | 1,218 | 809 | 409 |
| 1981 | 2,222 | 1,215 | 308 | 1,305 | 885 | 420 |
| 1982 | 2,783 | 1,568 | 387 | 1,503 | 1,043 | 460 |
| 1983 | 3,461 | 1,961 | 636 | 1,896 | 1,241 | 655 |
| 1984 | 4,270 | 2,405 | 723 | 2,373 | 1,488 | 885 |
| 1985 | 5,653 | 3,005 | 779 | 2,931 | 1,735 | 1,196 |
| 1986 | 7,091 | 4,066 | 951 | 3,425 | 2,002 | 1,423 |
| 1987 | 8,821 | 4,696 | 793 | 4,228 | 2,217 | 2,011 |
| 1988 | 10,887 | 5,803 | 975 | 4,749 | 2,661 | 2,088 |
| 1989 | 12,826 | 6,891 | 1,123 | 6,201 | 2,594 | 3,607 |
| 1990 | 15,551 | 9,064 | 1,372 | 7,515 | 3,113 | 4,402 |

1 ecu = US$1.26 = BF38.8 (Belgian francs).

**Exhibit 22.3**   Economic performance

| Year | Retail sales (index) | CTN sales (index) | Cost of living (index) | Cost of debt (%) | Cost of equity (%) |
|------|------|------|------|------|------|
| 1980 | 100 | 100 | 100 | 11 | 13 |
| 1981 | 108 | 107 | 109 | 9 | 12 |
| 1982 | 133 | 121 | 117 | 11 | 17 |
| 1983 | 151 | 131 | 128 | 14 | 18 |
| 1984 | 175 | 155 | 148 | 16 | 23 |
| 1985 | 208 | 191 | 184 | 17 | 28 |
| 1986 | 238 | 223 | 213 | 17 | 21 |
| 1987 | 271 | 257 | 251 | 12 | 20 |
| 1988 | 310 | 285 | 274 | 13 | 26 |
| 1989 | 345 | 297 | 311 | 16 | 23 |
| 1990 | 389 | 351 | 360 | 16 | 25 |

## CASE 22 (*cont*)

being spoilt by it becoming less exclusive. Others were anxious about the new injection of equity he was requesting. He thought it odd that the strategy they had supported and backed financially two years ago was now in question. He reminded them how well the firm had done despite the tough economic climate over the last few years (see Exhibit 22.3). The company was now more professional than it had ever been. He had just introduced a new tier of senior people to manage the day-to-day operations of the company. These were not family members but were bright, very well qualified and had broad experience within the industry. With them in place he would have more time to think about and initiate other ways of developing the company.

### Questions

1. Comment on Abel's expansion strategy and Pieta's performance since he took over.

2. Argue the case for further expansion wanted by Abel.

3. Practise the case of the shareholders against Abel. How is Abel's strategy endangering Pieta's future performance and brand image? What, if anything, has Abel been neglecting?

4. Track the changes in $C^3$ (capital cost covered) and EVA (economic value added) for Pieta over the last ten years. Marketing Highlight 16.4 shows how to do it.

5. Comment on the $C^3$ and EVA trends and compare them with the impression given by the growth in profits and sales. What strategies of Abel's explains the performance that the $C^3$ and EVA reveal? Should the trend be changed, and, if so, how could it be changed?

Source: From company records. All dates, figures and names have been changed for commercial reasons.

# GTE

## Competition comes calling

As he drove into the parking lot at the Smile gas station on Route 70 in Durham, North Carolina, Kevin Murphy thought about how the payphone business had changed. In 1983 he had joined General Telephone and Electronics (GTE) as a salaried sales consultant. Since then he had witnessed the impact of deregulation on the telephone industry and he had seen all kinds of competitive moves. He was now stopping to call on Jim Lewis, the manager of Smile Gas. Mr Lewis had a relative in the private payphone business. Eight months ago, Mr Lewis had agreed to have one of his relative's phones installed in the gas station and had asked GTE to remove its phone. However, his relative's company had gone out of business before installing its phone.

Many of Smile's customers want to make only one stop to buy gas or food and to use a phone. Now, when Mr Lewis's customers enquire about a payphone, he has to send them across the intersection to the Wilco gas station. Mr Lewis is angry about losing business to the competition and he decided to call GTE.

Like Mr Lewis's customers, you have probably used a payphone many times. They are everywhere, but have you ever really paid much attention to them? Probably you haven't. Unfortunately, neither has GTE. Now that is a real problem, given that GTE owns and operates 29,000 payphones in its franchised areas in nine south-eastern states.

However, because of dramatic changes in its marketing environment, GTE is now starting to pay attention to its public communications operation instead of taking it for granted as it has traditionally done. Other companies have noticed the payphone market. Virtually hundreds of small companies are racing to enter what promises to be a lucrative business, challenging the almost monopolistic grip GTE and other telephone companies have had on the payphone market.

## THE PUBLIC COMMUNICATIONS MARKET

Although payphones may seem out of date amid the rapid technological advances in the modern telecommunications world, the approximately 2 million US payphones generated $6.3bn in revenues in 1989. Callers deposited about 25 per cent of this amount as 'coins in the box'. The remaining 75 per cent consisted of credit card, collect and other operator-assisted calls. GTE receives 100 per cent of the cost of local calls (usually 25 cents each) made on its payphones, 100 per cent of the cost of long-distance calls made inside GTE's franchise area, and between 6 and 10 cents per

1 ecu = US$1.26

911

minute for long-distance calls going outside its area. In total, GTE's 29,000 pay-phones produced about $56m. in total revenues in 1989.

Telephone companies generally segment the public communications market based on the number of payphones installed at each location. Exhibit 8.1 presents the overall breakdown of US businesses by number of payphones per location and gives the chief attributes of each segment. The table shows that 90 per cent of all businesses have fewer than four payphones per location and that these businesses account for 40 per cent of the total number of payphones installed. In contrast, only 4 per cent of businesses have more than ten payphones, but these businesses account for 49 per cent of all payphones installed. Convenience stores, shopping centres and fast-food restaurants are the best locations. Generally, GTE wants to place its payphones in safe, well-lit locations with a lot of car or foot traffic. GTE budgets $1,500 to $2,000 to install an outside payphone booth; wall-mounted units cost slightly less. The booths are depreciated over a seven-year period. The company estimates that the variable cost of a phone is $35 per month and that a phone must generate at least $90 per month to break even.

Before 1984, the telephone companies enjoyed a monopoly in the payphone market. Only regulated telephone companies could install a payphone connected to their telephone networks. Although customers paid to use the phones, the phone companies subsidized their payphone operations from general revenues. GTE did not even account for payphones separately from its general telephone operations. If a business wanted a payphone installed, it would file a request with the local telephone company, such as GTE. GTE would evaluate the request based on the revenue potential of the location and on the company's obligation as a regulated monopoly to provide a public service. If the location looked profitable, GTE would install one or more *public* payphones. The phone cost the owner nothing, but GTE made no payments to the owner. If a location did not justify a public payphone, GTE could offer the customer a *semi-public* phone, for which the customer paid an installation fee and guaranteed GTE a fixed monthly revenue. In this process of receiving requests and evaluating locations, telephone companies did no 'marketing'. GTE either accepted requests or rejected them – in practice, it accepted only two out of every ten requests – and rarely searched for new places to install payphones.

## DEREGULATION STRIKES

However, in June 1984 everything changed. The Federal Communications Commission (FCC), as part of the general deregulation of the telecommunications industry, ruled

**Exhibit 8.1**  Payphone market segments (%)

|  | 0–4 pay phones per location | 5–9 pay phones per location | 10+ pay phones per location |
|---|---|---|---|
| Business | 90 | 6 | 4 |
| Payphones | 40 | 11 | 49 |
| *Revenue* | | | |
| Local | 53 | 47 | 26 |
| Coin | 8 | 7 | 16 |
| Noncoin | 49 | 46 | 58 |

that any person who bought a coin-operated telephone had the right to connect it to the local telephone network. This ruling created a new product and a new market: the customer-owned, coin-operated telephone (COCOT). Many entrepreneurs set up businesses to develop and run private payphone networks. These firms included everything from one-person businesses operated out of the back of a pick-up truck to People's Telephone, the largest independent operator, with 6,500 phones in fifteen states in 1989.

Another aspect of deregulation further spurred the development of the COCOT industry. With deregulation, AT&T lost its monopoly over long-distance service. Because of a rule stipulating 'equal access', local telephone companies had to furnish all long-distance carriers with the same access to their networks that they had previously given only to AT&T. The local telephone company could no longer automatically select AT&T to provide long-distance service to its customers. Each customer would select one of the new carriers (AT&T, MCI, Sprint) or an alternative operator service (AOS) to provide long-distance service. AOSs buy blocks of long-distance service at wholesale rates from the main carriers and then resell the service at higher rates (sometimes even higher than AT&T rates) to their customers. To attract the AOS business, the main carriers also began offering commissions to the AOSs. In turn, the AOSs began offering commissions to COCOTs who tied their payphone systems to the AOSs for long-distance service. These commissions provided revenues to the COCOT business, making it profitable and competitive. Until December 1988, these commissions also provided the COCOTs with a competitive advantage, because GTE and the other telephone companies had to use AT&T for their long-distance payphone service. AT&T paid them no commission.

Before deregulation, once GTE installed a phone, it had a customer for life. GTE did not require any contracts for public phones and it paid no commissions to the owner of payphone locations. GTE could take customers for granted – and it usually did. The COCOTs, however, entered the business with a vengeance. Taking advantage of their low overhead and the commissions, they began offering the location-owner a part of the coins in the box as a commission for allowing them to install a payphone. Further, they targeted established payphones. Because GTE had no contracts with location-owners, the COCOTs could suggest that the owner ask GTE to remove its phone. Then the COCOT would install a phone and pay the owner a commission, typically 20 to 30 per cent of the coins in the box. To most owners, a payphone is a payphone – they were glad to dump GTE to make some extra money. Some COCOTs even hired college students to go door-to-door, signing up businesses for new payphones and for removal of existing phones. COCOTs also targeted retail chains, which operated in many locations. Whereas GTE can provide payphone service only in its franchised areas, COCOTs operate over large areas and can offer chains the ability to handle much or all of their payphone service with one contract.

GTE responded by offering a commission of 30 per cent of the coins in the box over $60 a month and asking owners to agree to give 30 days' notice before removing a phone. However, these actions did not slow the loss of customers. GTE then introduced a second contract, which paid 15 to 20 per cent of all coins in the box in return for the customer signing a 3- to 5-year contract. The contract, however, allowed the owner to have the GTE phone removed if the owner paid the installation and removal costs, usually about $500 to $650.

Competitors responded to these moves in some cases by offering commissions of 30 to 50 per cent of *net* profits (payphone revenues less maintenance and collection costs), including revenue on long-distance calls. GTE argued that this higher percentage of net profit might often be less than its 15 to 20 per cent of gross. In some cases, competition had even offered to pay GTE's installation and removal costs for the location-owner to win the location.

## BACK AT SMILE GAS

Kevin Murphy agreed to install a new payphone at Smile Gas. He told Mr Lewis that he would receive 20 per cent of the coin-in-the-box revenue. Mr Lewis asked about a commission on long-distance calls. Kevin indicated that the FCC does not allow GTE to recommend long-distance carriers and that Mr Lewis would have to choose a carrier and negotiate with that carrier about commissions. When Mr Lewis also asked about maintenance and repair service for the phone, Kevin assured him that GTE provided 24-hour, around-the-clock service.

Kevin left the meeting with Mr Lewis to attend a sales meeting in GTE's Durham office. The ten sales consultants for GTE South were gathering for the first time ever to begin sales training and to help develop a new marketing strategy for GTE's public communications operations in the south-east. As he drove to the meeting, Kevin rehearsed the suggestions he wanted to make. Competitors' fierce moves had created trouble already and Kevin knew that analysts predicted only a 1.5 per cent annual market growth rate through 1994. This slow growth would fuel even more competitive challenges. GTE's market share in its franchised areas had already fallen from 100 to 85 per cent. Kevin knew GTE had to improve its payphone strategy to stop the erosion.

## QUESTIONS

1. What kind of service does GTE sell?
2. How do the characteristics of GTE's services affect its marketing efforts?
3. How should the concepts of internal and interactive marketing shape GTE's marketing strategy?
4. What changes should GTE make in its marketing strategy? Be sure to address each aspect of the marketing mix and the issues of managing differentiation, service quality and productivity.
5. The telecommunication industry's deregulation has caused the marketing situation GTE faces. Does deregulation promote economic efficiency? Does it help the consumer?

## NOTE

1. GTE Telephone Operations cooperated in the development of this case.

# Glossary

**Accessibility**   The degree to which a market segment can be reached and served.

**Accessory equipment**   Portable factory equipment and tools and office equipment that do not become part of the finished product.

**Acquisition**   A means of obtaining new products or services by buying a whole company, a patent or a license to produce someone else's product or market someone else's service.

**Actionability**   The degree to which effective programmes can be designed for attracting and serving a given market segment.

**Actual product**   A product's parts, quality level, features, design, brand name, packaging and other attributes that combine to deliver core product benefits.

**Adapted marketing mix**   An international marketing strategy for adjusting the marketing-mix elements to each international target market, bearing more costs but hoping for a larger market share and return.

**Administered VMS**   A vertical marketing system that coordinates successive stages of production and distribution, not through common ownership or contractual ties, but through the size and power of one of the parties.

**Adoption**   The decision by an individual to become a regular user of the product.

**Adoption process**   The mental process through which an individual passes from first hearing about an innovation to final adoption.

**Advertising**   Any paid form of nonpersonal presentation and promotion of ideas, goods, or services by an identified sponsor.

**Advertising objective**   A specific communication *task* to be accomplished with a specific *target* audience during a specific period of *time*.

**Advertising specialities**   Useful articles imprinted with an advertiser's name, given as gifts to consumers.

**Affordable method**   Setting the promotion budget at the level management thinks the company can afford.

**Age and life-cycle segmentation**   Dividing a market into different age and life-cycle groups.

**Agent**   A wholesaler who represents buyers or sellers on a relatively permanent basis, performs only a few functions, and does not take title to goods.

**Allowance**   (1) Reduction in price on damaged goods. (2) Promotional money paid by manufacturers to retailers in return for an agreement to feature the manufacturer's product in some way.

**Alternative evaluation**   The stage of the buyer decision process in which the consumer uses information to evaluate alternative brands in the choice set.

**Anchor stores**   Key retailers which form the nucleus of a shopping cluster. Their presence makes it all the more attractive for other retailers to set up shop in that shopping zone.

**Annual plan**   A short-term plan that describes the company's current situation, its objectives, the strategy, action programme and budgets for the year ahead and controls.

**Approach**   The step in the selling process in which the sales person meets and greets the buyer to get the relationship off to a good start.

**Aspirational group**   A group to which an individual wishes to belong.

**Atmospheres**   Designed environments that create or reinforce the buyer's leanings toward consumption of a product.

**Attitude**   A person's consistently favourable or unfavourable evaluations, feelings, and tendencies toward an object or idea.

**Augmented product**   Additional consumer services and benefits built around the core and actual products.

**Automatic vending**   Selling through vending machines.

**Available market**   The set of consumers who have interest, income, and access to a particular product or service.

**Balance sheet**   A financial statement that shows assets, liabilities, and net worth of a company at a given time.

**Barter transaction**   A marketing transaction in which goods or services are traded for other goods or services.

**Basing-point pricing**   A geographic pricing strategy in which the seller designates some city as a basing point and charges all customers the freight cost from that city to the customer location, regardless of the city from which the goods are actually shipped.

**Behavioural segmentation**   Dividing a market into groups based on consumer knowledge, attitude, use, or response to a product.

**Belief**   A descriptive thought that a person holds about something.

**Benchmarking**   The process of comparing the company's products and processes to those of competitors or leading firms in other industries to find ways to improve quality and performance.

**Benefit segmentation**   Dividing the market into groups according to the different benefits that consumers seek from the product.

**Brand**   A name, term, sign, symbol, or design, or a combination of these intended to identify the goods or services of one seller or group of sellers and to differentiate them from those of competitors.

**Brand equity**   The value of a brand, based on the extent to which it has high brand loyalty, name awareness, perceived quality, strong brand associations, and other assets such as patents, trademarks, and channel relationships.

**Brand extension**   Using a successful brand name to launch a new or modified product in a new category.

**Brand image**   The set of beliefs consumers hold about a particular brand.

**Breakeven pricing (target profit pricing)**   Setting price to break even on the costs of making and marketing a product; or setting price to make a target profit.

**Broker**   A wholesaler who does not take title to goods and whose function is to bring buyers and sellers together and assist in negotiation.

**Business analysis**   A review of the sales, costs, and profit projections for a new product to find out whether these factors satisfy the company's objectives.

**Business buying process**   The decision-making process by which business buyers establish the need for purchased products and services and identify, evaluate, and choose among alternative brands and suppliers.

**Business market**   All the organizations that buy goods and services to use in the production of other products and services or for the purpose of reselling or renting them to others at a profit.

**Business portfolio**   The collection of businesses and products that make up the company.

**Buyer**   The person who makes an actual purchase.

**Buyer-readiness states**   The stages consumers normally pass through on their way to purchase, including awareness, knowledge, liking, preference, conviction, and purchase.

**Buyers**   People in an organization's buying centre with formal authority to select the supplier and arrange terms of purchase.

**Buying centre**   All the individuals and units that participate in the business buying-decision process.

**By-products**   Items produced as a result of the main factory process, such as waste and reject items.

**By-product pricing**   Setting a price for by-products in order to make the main product's price more competitive.

**Capital items**   Industrial goods that partly enter the finished product, including installations and accessory equipment.

**Captive-product pricing**   Setting a price for products that must be used along with a main product, such as blades for a razor and film for a camera.

**Cash-and-carry retailers**   Large, 'no-frills' stores that sell an extensive assortment of goods, and noted particularly for their bulk discounts.

**Cash-and-carry wholesalers**   Wholesalers who stock a limited line of fast-moving goods – such as groceries, toys, household goods, clothes, electrical supplies and building materials – and who sell to small retailers and industrial firms for cash and normally do not provide a delivery service.

**Cash cows**   Low-growth, high-share businesses or products; established and successful units that generate cash the company uses to pay its bills and support other business units that need investment.

**Cash discount**   A price reduction to buyers who pay their bills promptly.

**Cash refund offers (rebates)**   Offers to refund part of the purchase price of a product to consumers who send a 'proof of purchase' to the manufacturer.

**Catalogue marketing**   Direct marketing through catalogues that are mailed to a select list of customers or made available in stores.

**Catalogue showroom**   A retail operation that sells a wide selection of high mark-up, fast-moving, brand-name goods at discount prices.

**Category killers**   A modern 'breed' of exceptionally aggressive 'off-price' retailers that offer branded merchandise in clearly defined product categories at heavily discounted prices.

**Causal research**   Marketing research to test hypotheses about cause-and-effect relationships.

**Chain stores**   Two or more outlets that are commonly owned and controlled, have central buying and merchandising, and sell similar lines of merchandise.

**Channel conflict**   Disagreement among marketing channel members on goals and roles – who should do what and for what rewards.

**Channel level**   A layer of middlemen that performs some work in bringing the product and its ownership closer to the final buyer.

**City-centre shopping zone (regional shopping centre)**   A store cluster situated in a city centre. Major retail chain stores, department stores, speciality shops and superstores form the anchor stores in the shopping centre. The stores attract shoppers from a wide region. Many travel in from outside the city.

**Closed-end questions**   Questions that include all the possible answers and allow subjects to make choices among them.

**Closing**   The step in the selling process in which the salesperson asks the customer for an order.

**Cognitive dissonance**   Buyer discomfort caused by postpurchase conflict.

**Commercialization**   Introducing a new product into the market.

**Company and individual brand strategy**   A branding approach which focuses on the company name and individual brand name.

**Comparison advertising (knocking copy)**   Advertising that compares one brand directly or indirectly to one or more other brands.

**Competitions, sweepstakes, lotteries, games**   Promotional events that give consumers the chance to win something – such as cash, trips, or goods – by luck or through extra effort.

**Competitive advantage**   An advantage over competitors gained by offering consumers greater value, either through lower prices or by providing more benefits that justify higher prices.

**Competitive-parity method**   Setting the promotion budget to match competitors' outlays.

**Competitive strategies**   Strategies that strongly position the company against competitors and that give the company the strongest possible strategic advantage.

**Competitor analysis**   The process of identifying key competitors; assessing their objectives, strategies, strengths and weaknesses, and reaction patterns; and selecting which competitors to attack or avoid.

**Competitor-centred company**   A company whose moves are mainly based on competitors' actions and reactions; it spends most of its time tracking competitors' moves and market shares and trying to find strategies to counter them.

**Complex buying behaviour**   Consumer buying behaviour in situations characterized by high consumer involvement in a purchase and significant perceived differences among brands.

**Concentrated marketing**   A market-coverage strategy in which a firm goes after a large share of one or a few submarkets.

**Concept testing**   Testing new product concepts with a group of target consumers to find out if the concepts have strong consumer appeal.

**Confused positioning**   A positioning error which leaves consumers with a confused image of the company, its product or a brand.

**Consumer buying behaviour**   The buying behaviour of final consumers – individuals and households who buy goods and services for personal consumption.

**Consumer franchise building promotions**   Sales promotions that promote the product's positioning and include a selling message along with the deal.

**Consumer goods**   Goods bought by final consumers for personal consumption.

**Consumer market**   All the individuals and households who buy or acquire goods and services for personal consumption.

**Consumer-oriented marketing**   A principle of enlightened marketing which holds that a company should view and organize its marketing activities from the consumers' point of view.

**Consumer promotion**   Sales promotion designed to stimulate consumer purchasing, including samples, coupons, rebates, prices-off, premiums, patronage rewards, displays, and contests and sweepstakes.

**Consumerism**   An organized movement of citizens and government agencies to improve the rights and power of buyers in relation to sellers.

**Containerization**   Putting the goods in boxes or trailers that are easy to transfer between two transportation modes. They are used in multimode systems commonly referred to as piggyback, fishyback, trainship, and airtruck.

**Continuity**   Scheduling ads evenly within a given period.

**Contract manufacturing**   A joint venture in which a company contracts with manufacturers in a foreign market to produce the product.

**Contractual VMS**   A vertical marketing system in which independent firms at different levels of production and distribution join together through contracts to obtain more economies or sales impact than they could achieve alone.

**Convenience goods**   Consumer goods that the customer usually buys frequently, immediately, and with a minimum of comparison and buying effort.

**Convenience store**   A small store located near a residential area that is open long hours seven days a week and carries a limited line of high-turnover convenience goods.

**Conventional distribution channel**   A channel consisting of one or more independent producers, wholesalers, and retailers, each a separate business seeking to maximize its own profits even at the expense of profits for the system as a whole.

**Copy testing**   Measuring the communication effect of an advertisement before or after it is printed or broadcast.

**Core product**   The problem-solving services or core benefits that consumers are really buying when they obtain a product.

**Core strategy**   The 'hub' of marketing strategy. It has two parts: the identification of a group of customers for whom the firm has a differential advantage; and then positioning itself in that market.

**Corner shop**   A small store, usually owned and managed by a person who lives in the local neighbourhood. It is typically a grocery store, a convenience store or a confectioner-tobacconist-newsagent (CTN). It serves the immediate neighbourhood.

**Corporate brand strategy**   A brand strategy whereby the firm makes its company name the dominant brand identity across all of its products.

**Corporate licensing**   A form of licensing whereby a firm rents a corporate trademark or logo made famous in one product or service category and uses it in a related category.

**Corporate VMS**   A vertical marketing system that combines successive stages of production and distribution under single ownership – channel leadership is established through common ownership.

**Cost of goods sold**   The direct costs allocated to goods sold. These include variable cost items such as raw materials and labour used in making a product.

**Cost-plus pricing**   Adding a standard mark-up to the cost of the product.

**Countertrade**   International trade involving the direct or indirect exchange of goods for other goods instead of cash. Forms include barter compensation (buyback), and counterpurchase.

**Coupons**   Certificates that give buyers a saving when they purchase a product.

**Critical success factors**   The strengths and weaknesses that most critically affect an organization's success. These are measured relative to competition.

**Cultural empathy**   An understanding of and true feeling for a culture.

**Cultural environment**   Institutions and other forces that affect society's basic values, perceptions, preferences, and behaviours.

**Cultural universals**   Cultural characteristics and attributes that are found in a wide range of cultures: that is, features that transcend national cultures.

**Culture**   The set of basic values, perceptions, wants, and behaviours learned by a member of society from family and other important institutions.

**Current marketing situation**   The section of a marketing plan that describes the target market and the company's position in it.

**Customer-centred company**   A company that focuses on customer developments in designing its marketing strategies and on delivering superior value to its target customers.

**Customer delivered value**   The difference between total customer value and total customer cost of a marketing offer – 'profit' to the customer.

**Customer lifetime value**   The amount by which revenues from a given customer over time will exceed the company's costs of attracting, selling, and servicing that customer.

**Customer salesforce structure**   A salesforce organization under which salespeople specialize in selling only to certain customers or industries.

**Customer value**   The consumer's assessment of the product's overall capacity to satisfy his or her needs.

**Customer value analysis**   Analysis conducted to determine what benefits target customers value and how they rate the relative value of various competitor's offers.

**Customer value delivery system**   The system made up of the value chains of the company and its suppliers, distributors, and ultimately customers who work together to deliver value to customers.

**Cycle**   The medium-term wavelike movement of sales resulting from changes in general economic and competitive activity.

**Decider**   The person who ultimately makes a buying decision or any part of it – whether to buy, what to buy, how to buy, or where to buy.

**Deciders**   People in the organization's buying centre who have formal or informal powers to select or approve the final suppliers.

**Decision-and-reward system**   Formal and informal operating procedures that guide planning, targeting, compensation and other activities.

**Decision-making unit (DMU)**   All the individuals who participate in, and influence, the consumer buying-decision process.

**Decline stage**   The product life-cycle stage at which a product's sales decline.

**Deficient products**   Products that have neither immediate appeal nor long-run benefits.

**Demand curve**   A curve that shows the number of units the market will buy in a given time period, at different prices that might be charged.

**Demands**   Human wants that are backed by buying power.

**Demographic segmentation**   Dividing the market into groups based on demographic variables such as age, sex, family size, family life cycle, income, occupation, education, religion, race and nationality.

**Demography**   The study of human populations in terms of size, density, location, age, sex, race, occupation, and other statistics.

**Department store**   A retail organization that carries a wide variety of product lines – typically clothing, home furnishings, and household goods; each line is operated as a separate department managed by specialist buyers or merchandisers.

**Derived demand**   Business demand that ultimately comes from (derives from) the demand for consumer goods.

**Descriptive research**   Marketing research to better describe marketing problems, situations, or markets, such as the market potential for a product or the demographics and attitudes of consumers.

**Desirable products**    Products that give both high immediate satisfaction and high long-run benefits.

**Differential advantage**    A sustainable internal or external strength an organization has over its competitors.

**Differentiated marketing**    A market-coverage strategy in which a firm decides to target several market segments and designs separate offers for each.

**Direct investment**    Entering a foreign market by developing foreign-based assembly or manufacturing facilities.

**Direct-mail marketing**    Direct marketing through single mailings that include letters, ads, samples, foldouts, and other 'salespeople on wings' sent to prospects on mailing lists.

**Direct marketing**    Marketing through various advertising media that interact directly with consumers, generally calling for the consumer to make a direct response.

**Direct-marketing channel**    A marketing channel that has no intermediary levels.

**Discount**    A straight reduction in price on purchases during a stated period of time.

**Discount store**    A retail institution that sells standard merchandise at lower prices by accepting lower margins and selling at higher volume.

**Dissonance-reducing buying behaviour**    Consumer buying behaviour in situations characterized by high involvement but few perceived differences among brands.

**Distribution centre**    A large, highly automated warehouse designed to receive goods from various plants and suppliers, take orders, fill them efficiently, and deliver goods to customers as quickly as possible.

**Distribution channel (marketing channel)**    A set of interdependent organizations involved in the process of making a product or service available for use or consumption by the consumer or industrial user.

**Diversification**    A strategy for the company growth by starting up or acquiring businesses outside the company's current products and markets.

**Dogs**    Low-growth, low-share businesses and products that may generate enough cash to maintain themselves but do not promise to be large sources of cash.

**Door-to-door retailing**    Selling door to door, office to office, or at home-sales parties.

**Durable goods**    Consumer goods that usually are used over an extended period of time and that normally survive many uses.

**Economic environment**    Factors that affect consumer buying power and spending patterns.

**Edge-of-town retail cluster**    A cluster of stores – typically supermarkets, superstores or hypermarkets – located at the edge of town. The cluster of retailers are not organized as a unit.

**Embargo**    A ban on the import of a certain product.

**Emotional appeals**    Message appeals that attempt to stir up negative or positive emotions that will motivate purchase; examples include fear, guilt, shame, love, humour, pride, and joy appeals.

**Emotional selling proposition (ESP)**    A nonfunctional attribute which has unique associations for consumers.

**Engel's laws**    Differences noted over a century ago by Ernst Engel in how people shift their spending across food, housing, transportation, health care, and other goods and services categories as family income rises.

**Enlightened marketing**    A marketing philosophy holding that a company's marketing should support the best long-run performance of the marketing system; its five principles include consumer-oriented marketing, innovative marketing, value marketing, sense-of-mission marketing, and societal marketing.

**Environmental management perspective**    A management perspective in which the firm takes aggressive actions to affect the publics and forces in its marketing environment rather than simply watching it and reacting to it.

**Environmentalism**    An organized movement of concerned citizens and government agencies to protect and improve people's living environment.

**Events**    Occurrences staged to communicate messages to target audiences; examples include news conferences and grand openings.

**Exchange**    The act of obtaining a desired object from someone by offering something in return.

**Exchange controls**    Government limits on the amount of its foreign exchange with other countries and on its exchange rate against other currencies.

**Exclusive distribution**    Giving a limited number of dealers the exclusive right to distribute the company's products in their territories.

**Experience curve (learning curve)**    The drop in the average per-unit production cost that comes with accumulated production experience.

**Experimental research**    The gathering of primary data by selecting matched groups of subjects, giving them different treatments, controlling related factors, and checking for differences in group responses.

**Exploratory research**    Marketing research to gather preliminary information that will help to better define problems and suggest hypotheses.

**Export department**    A form of international marketing organization that comprises a sales manager and a few assistants whose job is to organize the shipping out of the company's goods to foreign markets.

**Exporting**    Entering a foreign market by sending products and selling them through international marketing middlemen (indirect exporting) or through the company's own department, branch, or sales representatives or agents (direct exporting).

**External audit**    A detailed examination of the markets, competition, business and economic environment in which the organization operates.

**Factory outlets**    Off-price retailing operations that are owned and operated by manufacturers and that normally carry the manufacturer's surplus, discontinued, or irregular goods.

**Fads**    Fashions that enter quickly, are adopted with great zeal, peak early, and decline very fast.

**Family life cycle**    The stages through which families might pass as they mature over time.

**Fashion**    A currently accepted or popular style in a given field.

**Financial intermediaries**    Banks, credit companies, insurance companies, and other businesses that help finance transactions or insure against the risks associated with the buying and selling of goods.

**Fixed costs**    Costs that do not vary with production or sales level.

**FOB-origin pricing**    A geographic pricing strategy in which goods are placed free on board a carrier; the customer pays the freight from the factory to the destination.

**Focus group**    A small sample of typical consumers under the direction of a group leader who elicits their reaction to a stimulus such as an ad or product concept.

**Follow-up**    The last step in the selling process in which the salesperson follows up after the sale to ensure customer satisfaction and repeat business.

**Forecasting**    The art of estimating future demand by anticipating what buyers are likely to do under a given set of conditions.

**Fragmented industry**    An industry characterized by many opportunities to create competitive advantages, but each advantage is small.

**Franchise**    A contractual association between a manufacturer, wholesaler, or service organization (a franchiser) and independent businesspeople (franchisees) who buy the right to own and operate one or more units in the franchise system.

**Franchise organization**   A contractual vertical marketing system in which a channel member, called a franchiser, links several stages in the production–distribution process.

**Freight-absorption pricing**   A geographic pricing strategy in which the company absorbs all or part of the actual freight charges in order to get the business.

**Frequency**   The number of times the average person in the target market is exposed to an advertising message during a given period.

**Full-service retailers**   Retailers that provide a full range of services to shoppers.

**Full-service wholesalers**   Wholesalers that provide a full set of services such as carrying stock, using a salesforce, offering credit, making deliveries, and providing management assistance.

**Functional discount (trade discount)**   A price reduction offered by the seller to trade channel members who perform certain functions such as selling, storing and recordkeeping.

**Gatekeepers**   People in the organization's buying centre who control the flow of information to others.

**Gender segmentation**   Dividing a market into different groups based on sex.

**General need description**   The stage in the business buying process in which the company describes the general characteristics and quantity of a needed item.

**Geodemographics**   The study of the relationship between geographical location and demographics.

**Geographical pricing**   Pricing based on where customers are located.

**Geographic segmentation**   Dividing a market into different geographical units such as nations, states, regions, counties, cities, or neighbourhoods.

**Global firm**   A firm that, by operating in more than one country, gains R&D, production, marketing, and financial advantages in its costs and reputation that are not available to purely domestic competitors.

**Global industry**   An industry in which the strategic positions of competitors in given geographic or national markets are affected by their overall global positions.

**Global marketing**   Marketing which is concerned with integrating or standardizing marketing actions across different geographic markets.

**Global organization**   A form of international organization whereby top corporate management and staff plan worldwide manufacturing or operational facilities, marketing policies, financial flows and logistical systems. The global operating unit reports directly to the chief executive, not to an international divisional head.

**Going-rate pricing**   Setting price based largely on following competitors' prices rather than on company costs or demand.

**Government market**   Governmental units – national and local – that purchase or rent goods and services for carrying out the main functions of government.

**Gross margin**   The difference between the direct cost of products and what they are sold for.

**Gross sales**   The total amount charged to customers over a period.

**Growth-share matrix**   A portfolio-planning method that evaluates a company's strategic business units (SBUs) in terms of their market growth rate and relative market share. SBUs are classified as stars, cash cows, question marks, or dogs.

**Growth stage**   The product life-cycle stage at which a product's sales start climbing quickly.

**Habitual buying behaviour**   Consumer buying behaviour in situations characterized by low consumer involvement and few significant perceived brand differences.

**Handling objections**   The step in the selling process in which the salesperson seeks out, clarifies, and overcomes customer objections to buying.

**Horizontal marketing systems**   A channel arrangement in which two or more companies at one level join together to follow a new marketing opportunity.

**Human need**   A state of felt deprivation.

**Human want**   The form that a human need takes as shaped by culture and individual personality.

**Hybrid marketing channels**   Multichannel distribution, as when a single firms sets up two or more marketing channels to reach one or more customer segments. A variety of direct and indirect approaches are used to deliver the firm's goods to its customers.

**Hypermarkets**   Huge stores that combine supermarket, discount, and warehouse retailing; in addition to food, they carry furniture, appliances, clothing, and many other products.

**Idea generation**   The systematic search for new-product ideas.

**Idea screening**   Screening new-product ideas in order to spot good ideas and drop poor ones as soon as possible.

**Income segmentation**   Dividing a market into different income groups.

**Industrial goods**   Goods bought by individuals and organizations for further processing or for use in conducting a business.

**Industry**   A group of firms which offer a product or class of products that are close substitutes for each other. The set of all sellers of a product or service.

**Inelastic demand**   Total demand for a product that is not much affected by price changes, especially in the short run.

**Influencer**   A person whose views or advice carries some weight in making a final buying decision; they often help define specifications and also provide information for evaluating alternatives.

**Information search**   The stage of the buyer decision process in which the consumer is aroused to search for more information; the consumer may simply have heightened attention or may go into active information search.

**Informative advertising**   Advertising used to inform consumers about a new product or feature and to build primary demand.

**Initiator**   The person who first suggests or thinks of the idea of buying a particular product or service.

**Innovation**   An idea, product or technology that has been developed and marketed to customers who perceive it as novel or new. It is a process of identifying, creating and delivering new-product service values that did not exist before in the marketplace.

**Innovative marketing**   A principle of enlightened marketing which requires that a company seek real product and marketing improvements.

**Institutional market**   Schools, hospitals, nursing homes, prisons, and other institutions that provide goods and services to people in their care.

**Integrated direct marketing**   Direct marketing campaigns that use multiple vehicles and multiple stages to improve response rates and profits.

**Integrated logistics management**   A physical distribution concept that recognizes the need for a firm to integrate its logistics system with those of its suppliers and customers. The aim is to maximize the performance of the entire distribution system.

**Intensive distribution**   Stocking the product in as many outlets as possible.

**Interactive marketing**   Marketing by a service firm that recognizes that perceived service quality depends heavily on the quality of buyer–seller interaction.

**Internal audit**   An evaluation of the firm's entire value chain.

**Internal marketing**    Marketing by a service firm to train and effectively motivate its customer-contact employees and all the supporting service people to work as a team to provide customer satisfaction.

**Internal records information**    Information gathered from sources within the company to evaluate marketing performances and to detect marketing problems and opportunities.

**International division**    A form of international marketing organization in which the division handles all of the firm's international activities. Marketing, manufacturing, research, planning and specialist staff are organized into operating units according to geography or product groups or as an international subsidiary responsible for its own sales and profitability.

**International market**    Buyers in other countries, including consumers, producers, resellers and governments.

**International shopping centre**    Store cluster in the heart of an affluent and major international city. Examples include fashionable cities such as Paris, Tokyo, New York, Rome, Milan and London. The international shopping centre attracts shoppers from all over the country and the world.

**Introduction stage**    The product life-cycle stage when the new product is first distributed and made available for purchase.

**Invention**    A new technology or product which may or may not deliver benefits to customers.

**Joint ownership**    A joint venture in which a company joins investors in a foreign market to create a local business in which the company shares joint ownership and control.

**Joint venturing**    Entering foreign markets by joining with foreign companies to produce or market a product or service.

**Leading indicators**    Time series that change in the same direction but in advance of company sales.

**Learning**    Changes in an individual's behaviour arising from experience.

**Licensing**    A method of entering a foreign market in which the company enters into an agreement with a licensee in the foreign market, offering the right to use a manufacturing process, trademark, patent, trade secret, or other item of value for a fee or royalty.

**Lifestyle**    A person's pattern of living as expressed in his or her activities, interests, and opinions.

**Limited-service retailers**    Retailers that provide only a limited number of services to shoppers.

**Limited-service wholesalers**    Those who offer only limited services to their suppliers and customers.

**Line extension**    Using a successful brand name to introduce additional items in a given product category under the same brand name, such as new flavours, forms, colours, added ingredients or package sizes.

**Long-range plan**    A plan that describes the principal factors and forces affecting the organization during the next several years, including long-term objectives, the chief marketing strategies used to attain them and the resources required.

**Macroenvironment**    The larger societal forces that affect the whole microenvironment – demographic, economic, natural, technological, political, and cultural forces.

**Management contracting**    A joint venture in which the domestic firm supplies the management know-how to a foreign company that supplies the capital; the domestic firm exports management services rather than products.

**Manufacturer's brand** (or **national brand**)    A brand created and owned by the producer of a product or service.

**Manufacturers' sales branches and offices**   Wholesaling by sellers or buyers themselves rather than through independent wholesalers.

**Market**   The set of all actual and potential buyers of a product or service.

**Market-build-up method**   A method used mainly by business goods firms to estimate the market potential of a city, state or country based on determining all the potential buyers in the market and estimating their potential purchases.

**Market-centred company**   A company that bays balanced attention to both customers and competitors in designing its marketing strategies.

**Market challenger**   A runner-up firm in an industry that is fighting hard to increase its market share.

**Market development**   A strategy for company growth by identifying and developing new segments and markets for current company products.

**Market-factor index method**   A method used mainly by consumer goods firms to estimate the market potential for consumer goods.

**Market follower**   A runner-up firm in an industry that wants to hold its share without rocking the boat.

**Market leader**   The firm in an industry with the largest market share; it usually leads other firms in price changes, new product introductions, distribution coverage, and promotion spending.

**Market nicher**   A firm in an industry that serves small segments that the other firms overlook or ignore.

**Market penetration**   A strategy for increasing sales of current products to current market segments. This is achieved by winning over competitors' customers, acquiring a competitor, and/or by increasing product usage rate.

**Market-penetration pricing**   Setting a low price for a new product in order to attract large numbers of buyers and a large market share.

**Market positioning**   Arranging for a product to occupy a clear, distinctive, and desirable place relative to competing products in the minds of target consumers. Formulating competitive positioning for a product and a detailed marketing mix.

**Market segment**   A group of consumers who respond in a similar way to a given set of marketing stimuli.

**Market segmentation**   Dividing a market into distinct groups of buyers with different needs, characteristics, or behaviour who might require separate products or marketing mixes.

**Market-skimming pricing**   Setting a high price for a new product to skim maximum revenues layer by layer from the segments willing to pay the high price; the company makes fewer but more profitable sales.

**Market targeting**   The process of evaluating each market segment's attractiveness and selecting one or more segments to enter.

**Marketing**   A social and managerial process by which individuals and groups obtain what they need and want through creating and exchanging products and value with others.

**Marketing audit**   A comprehensive, systematic, independent, and periodic examination of a company's environment objectives, strategies, and activities to determine problem areas and opportunities and to recommend a plan of action to improve the company's marketing performance.

**Marketing budget**   A section of the marketing plan that shows projected revenues, costs, and profits.

**Marketing concept**   The marketing management philosophy which holds that achieving organizational goals depends on determining the needs and wants of target markets and delivering the desired satisfactions more effectively and efficiently than competitors do.

**Marketing control**  The process of measuring and evaluating the results of marketing strategies and plans, and taking corrective action to ensure that marketing objectives are attained.

**Marketing database**  An organized set of data about individual customers or prospects that can be used to generate and qualify customer leads, sell products and services, and maintain customer relationships.

**Marketing environment**  The actors and forces outside marketing that affect marketing management's ability to develop and maintain successful transactions with its target customers.

**Marketing implementation**  The process that turns marketing strategies and plans into marketing actions in order to accomplish strategic marketing objectives.

**Marketing information system (MIS)**  People, equipment, and procedures to gather, sort, analyse, evaluate and distribute needed, timely, and accurate information to marketing decision makers.

**Marketing intelligence**  Everyday information about developments in the marketing environment that helps managers prepare and adjust marketing plans.

**Marketing intermediaries**  Firms that help the company to promote, sell, and distribute its goods to final buyers; they include middlemen, physical distribution firms, marketing-service agencies, and financial intermediaries.

**Marketing management**  The analysis, planning, implementation, and control of programmes designed to create, build, and maintain beneficial exchanges with target buyers for the purpose of achieving organizational objectives.

**Marketing mix**  The set of controllable tactical marketing tools – product, price, place, and promotion – that the firm blends to produce the response it wants in the target market.

**Marketing process**  The process of (1) analysing marketing opportunities; (2), selecting target markets; (3) developing the marketing mix; and (4) managing the marketing effort.

**Marketing research**  The function that links the consumer, customer, and public to the marketer through information – information used to identify and define marketing opportunities and problems; to generate, refine and evaluate marketing actions; to monitor marketing performance; and to improve understanding of the marketing process.

**Marketing services agencies**  Marketing research firms, advertising agencies, media firms, marketing consulting firms, and other service providers that help a company to target and promote its products to the right markets.

**Marketing strategy**  The marketing logic by which the business unit hopes to achieve its marketing objectives.

**Marketing strategy statement**  A statement of the planned strategy for a new product that outlines the intended target market, the planned product positioning, and the sales, market share, and profit goals for the first few years.

**Markup/markdown**  The difference between selling price and cost as a percentage of selling price or cost.

**Materials and parts**  Industrial goods that enter the manufacturer's product completely; including raw materials and manufactured materials and parts.

**Maturity stage**  The stage in the product life cycle where sales growth slows or levels off.

**Measurability**  The degree to which the size, purchasing power and profits of a market segment can be measured.

**Media**  Nonpersonal communications channels including print media (newspapers, magazines, direct mail); broadcast media (radio, television); and display media (billboards, signs, posters).

**Media impact**   The qualitative value of an exposure through a given medium.

**Media vehicles**   Specific media within each general media type, such as specific magazines, television shows, or radio programmes.

**Membership groups**   Groups that have a direct influence on a person's behaviour and to which a person belongs.

**Merchandising conglomerates**   Corporations that combine several different retailing forms under central ownership and that share some distribution and management functions.

**Merchant wholesalers**   Independently owned businesses that take title to the merchandise they handle.

**Message source**   The company, the brand name, the salesperson of the brand, or the actor in the ad who endorses the product.

**Microenvironment**   The forces close to the company that affect its ability to serve its customers – the company, market channel firms, customer markets, competitors, and publics.

**Micromarketing**   A form of target marketing in which companies tailor their marketing programmes to the needs and wants of narrowly defined geographic, demographic, psychographic, or behavioural segments.

**Middlemen**   Distribution channel firms that help the company find customers or make sales to them, including wholesalers and retailers who buy and resell goods.

**Mission statement**   A statement of the organization's purpose – what it wants to accomplish in the larger environment.

**Modified rebuy**   A business buying situation in which the buyer wants to modify product specifications, prices, terms, or suppliers.

**Monetary transaction**   A marketing transaction in which goods or services are exchanged for money.

**Monopolistic competition**   A market in which many buyers and sellers trade over a range of prices rather than a single market price.

**Moral appeals**   Message appeals that are directed to the audience's sense of what is right and proper.

**Motive** (or drive)   A need that is sufficiently pressing to direct the person to seek satisfaction of the need.

**Multibrand strategy**   A strategy under which a seller develops two or more brands in the same product category.

**Natural environment**   Natural resources that are needed as inputs by marketers or that are affected by marketing activities.

**Need recognition**   The first stage of the buyer decision process in which the consumer recognizes a problem or need.

**Net profit**   The difference between the income from goods sold and all expenses incurred.

**New product**   A good, service, or idea that is perceived by some potential customers as new.

**New-product development**   The development of original products, product improvements, product modifications, and new brands through the firm's own R&D efforts.

**New task**   A business buying situation in which the buyer purchases a product or service for the first time.

**Nondurable goods**   Consumer goods that are normally consumed in one or a few uses.

**Nonpersonal communication channels**   Media that carry messages without personal contact or feedback, including media, atmospheres, and events.

**Nontariff trade barriers** Nonmonetary barriers to foreign products such as biases against a foreign company's bids or product standards that go against a foreign company's product features.

**Objective-and-task method** Developing the promotion budget by (1) defining specific objectives; (2) determining the tasks that must be performed to achieve these objectives; and (3) estimating the costs of performing these tasks. The sum of these costs is the proposed promotion budget.

**Observational research** The gathering of primary data by observing relevant people, actions, and situations.

**Occasion segmentation** Dividing the market into groups according to occasions when buyers get the idea to buy, actually make their purchase, or use the purchased item.

**Oligopolistic competition** A market in which there are a few sellers who are highly sensitive to each other's pricing and marketing strategies.

**On-line computer shopping** A form of direct marketing conducted through interactive on-line computer services, which provide two-way systems that link consumers with sellers electronically.

**Open-end questions** Questions that allow respondents to answer in their own words.

**Open market** An old and established form of retailing. It is popular because of its low prices. The market attracts vendors selling fresh agricultural products, housewares, clothings, haberdashery and many other products. The stalls are situated in an open square/area in the village or town or in covered halls.

**Operating control** Checking on-going performance against annual plans and taking corrective action.

**Operating statement** (or profit-and-loss statement or income statement). A financial statement that shows company sales, cost of goods sold, and expenses during a given period of time.

**Opinion leaders** People within a reference group who, because of special skills, knowledge, personality, or other characteristics, exert influence on others.

**Optional-product pricing** The pricing of optional or accessory products along with a main product.

**Order-routine specification** The stage of the business buying process in which the buyer writes the final order with the chosen suppliers(s), listing the technical specifications, quantity needed, expected time of delivery, return policies and warranties.

**Out-of-town retail cluster** A cluster of stores situated out-of-town, usually in a transport node, which is very accessible by road from several regional locations, such as the intersection of main highways/motorways. The cluster of retailers may not be organized as a unit.

**Overpositioning** A positioning error referring to too narrow a picture of the company, its product or a brand being communicated to target customers.

**Packaging** The activities of designing and producing the container or wrapper for a product.

**Packaging concept** What the package should *be* or *do* for the product.

**Parade (neighbourhood shopping centre)** Store cluster typically comprising small, independent speciality stores and convenience stores. It serves mainly residents living in the surrounding neighbourhood.

**Patronage rewards** Cash or other awards for the regular use of a certain company's products or services.

**Penetrated market** The set of consumers who have already bought a particular product or service.

**Percentage-of-sales method**   Setting the promotion budget at a certain percentage of current or forecasted sales or as a percentage of the sales price.

**Perception**   The process by which people select, organize, and interpret information to form a meaningful picture of the world.

**Perceptual maps**   A product positioning tool that uses multidimensional scaling of consumers' perceptions and preferences to portray the psychological distance between products and segments.

**Performance review**   The stage of the business buying process in which the buyer rates its satisfaction with suppliers, deciding whether to continue, modify or drop them.

**Personal communication channels**   Channels through which two or more people communicate directly with each other, including face to face, person to audience, over the telephone, or through the mail.

**Personal influence**   The effect of statements made by one person on another's attitude or probability of purchase.

**Personal selling**   Oral presentation in a conversation with one or more prospective purchasers for the purpose of making sales.

**Personality**   A person's distinguishing psychological characteristics that lead to relatively consistent and lasting responses to his or her own environment.

**Persuasive advertising**   Advertising used to build selective demand for a brand by persuading consumers that it offers the best quality for their money.

**Physical distribution**   (marketing logistics) The tasks involved in planning, implementing, and controlling the physical flow of materials and final goods from points of origin to points of use to meet the needs of customers at a profit.

**Physical distribution firms**   Warehouse, transportation, and other firms that help a company to stock and move goods from their points of origin to their destinations.

**Place**   All the company activities that make the product or service available to target customers.

**Planned obsolescence**   A strategy of causing products to become obsolete before they actually need replacement.

**Pleasing products**   Products that give high immediate satisfaction but may hurt consumers in the long run.

**Point-of-purchase (POP) promotions**   Displays and demonstrations that take place at the point of purchase or sale.

**Political environment**   Laws, government agencies, and pressure groups that influence and limit various organizations and individuals in a given society.

**Portfolio analysis**   A tool by which management identifies and evaluates the various businesses that make up the company.

**Postpurchase behaviour**   The stage of the buyer decision process in which consumers take further action after purchase based on their satisfaction or dissatisfaction.

**Potential market**   The set of consumers who profess some level of interest in a particular product or service.

**Preapproach**   The step in the selling process in which the salesperson learns as much as possible about a prospective customer before making a sales call.

**Premiums**   Goods offered either free or at low cost as an incentive to buy a product.

**Presentation**   The step in the selling process in which the salesperson tells the product 'story' to the buyer, showing how the product will make or save money for the buyer.

**Price**   The amount of money charged for a product or service, or the sum of the values that consumers exchange for the benefits of having or siung the product or service.

**Price elasticity** A measure of the sensitivity of demand to changes in price.

**Price packs** Reduced prices that are marked by the producer directly on the label or package.

**Primary data** Information collected for the specific purpose at hand.

**Primary demand** The level of total demand for all brands of a given product or service – for example, the total demand for motorcycles.

**Private brand** (or middleman, distributor, or store brand) A brand created and owned by a reseller of a product or service.

**Problem recognition** The first stage of the business buying process in which someone in the company recognizes a problem or need that can be met by acquiring a good or a service.

**Product** Anything that can be offered to a market for attention, acquisition, use, or consumption that might satisfy a want or need. It includes physical objects, services, persons, places, organizations, and ideas.

**Product adaptation** Adapting a product to meet local conditions or wants in foreign markets.

**Product-bundle pricing** Combining several products and offering the bundle at a reduced price.

**Product concept** The idea that consumers will favour products that offer the most quality, performance, and features and that the organization should therefore devote its energy to making continuous product improvements. A detailed version of the new-product idea stated in meaningful consumer terms.

**Product design** The process of designing a product's style and function: creating a product that is attractive; easy, safe, and inexpensive to use and service; and simple and economical to produce and distribute.

**Product development** A strategy for company growth by offering modified or new products to current market segments. Developing the product concept into a physical product in order to ensure that the product idea can be turned into a workable product.

**Product idea** An idea for a possible product that the company can see itself offering to the market.

**Product image** The way consumers perceive an actual or potential product.

**Product innovation charter (PIC)** A new product strategy statement formalizing management's reasons or rationale behind the firm's search for innovation opportunities, the product/market and technology to focus upon and the goals and objectives to be achieved.

**Product invention** Creating new products or services for foreign markets.

**Product life cycle (PLC)** The course of a product's sales and profits over its lifetime. It involves five distinct stages: product development, introduction, growth, maturity, and decline.

**Product line** A group of products that are closely related because they function in a similar manner, are sold to the same customer groups, are marketed through the same types of outlets, or fall within given price ranges.

**Product line filling** Increasing the product line by adding more items within the present range of the line.

**Product line pricing** Setting the price steps between various products in a product line based on cost differences between the products, customer evaluations of different features, and competitors' prices.

**Product line stretching** Increasing the product line by lengthening it beyond its current range.

**Product mix** (or **product assortment**) The set of all product lines and items that a particular seller offers for sale to buyers.

**Product position**    The way the product is defined by consumers on important attributes – the place the product occupies in consumers' minds relative to competing products.

**Product quality**    The ability of a product to perform its functions; it includes the product's overall durability, reliability, precision, ease of operation and repair, and other valued attributes.

**Product salesforce structure**    A salesforce organization under which salespeople specialize in selling only a portion of the company's products or lines.

**Product specification**    The stage of the business buying process in which the buying organization decides on and specifies the best technical product characteristics for a needed item.

**Product-support services**    Services that augment actual products.

**Production concept**    The philosophy that consumers will favour products that are available and highly affordable and that management should therefore focus on improving production and distribution efficiency.

**Promotion**    Activities that communicate the product or service and its merits to target customers and persuade them to buy.

**Promotion mix**    The specific mix of advertising, personal selling, sales promotion, and public relations a company uses to pursue its advertising and marketing objectives.

**Promotional allowance**    A payment or price reduction to reward dealers for participating in advertising and sales-support programmes.

**Promotional pricing**    Temporarily pricing products below the list price, and sometimes even below cost, to increase short-run sales.

**Proposal solicitation**    The stage of the business buying process in which the buyer invites qualified suppliers to submit proposals.

**Prospecting**    The step in the selling process in which the salesperson identifies qualified potential customers.

**Psychographics**    The technique of measuring lifestyles and developing lifestyle classifications; it involves measuring the chief AIO dimensions (activities, interests, opinions).

**Psychographic segmentation**    Dividing a market into different groups based on social class, lifestyle, or personality characteristics.

**Psychological pricing**    A pricing approach that considers the psychology of prices and not simply the economics; the price is used to say something about the product.

**Public**    Any group that has an actual or potential interest in or impact on an organization's ability to achieve its objectives.

**Public relations**    Building good relations with the company's various publics by obtaining favourable publicity, building up a good 'corporate image', and handling or heading off unfavourable rumours, stories, and events. Major PR tools include press relations, product publicity, corporate communications, lobbying and counselling.

**Publicity**    Activities to promote a company or its products by planting news about it in media not paid for by the sponsor.

**Pull strategy**    A promotion strategy that calls for spending a lot on advertising and consumer promotion to build up consumer demand. If the strategy is successful, consumers will ask their retailers for the product, the retailers will ask the wholesalers, and the wholesalers will ask the producers.

**Pulsing**    Scheduling ads unevenly, in bursts, over a certain time period.

**Purchase decision**    The stage of the buyer decision process in which the consumer actually buys the product.

**Pure competition**    A market in which many buyers and sellers trade in a uniform commodity – no single buyer or seller has much effect on the going market price.

**Pure monopoly**   A market in which there is a single seller – it may be a government monopoly, a private regulated monopoly, or a private nonregulated monopoly.

**Push strategy**   A promotion strategy that calls for using the salesforce and trade promotion to push the product through channels. The producer promotes the product to wholesalers, the wholesalers promote to retailers, and the retailers promote to consumers.

**Qualified available market**   The set of consumers who have interest, income, access, and qualifications for a particular product or service.

**Qualitative research**   Exploratory research used to uncover consumers' motivations, attitudes and behaviour. Focus group interviewing, elicitation interviews and repertory grid techniques are typical methods used in this type of research.

**Quality**   The totality of features and characteristics of a product or service that bear on its ability to satisfy stated or implied needs.

**Quantitative research**   Research which involves data collection by mail or personal interviews from a sufficient volume of customers to allow statistical analysis.

**Quantity discount**   A price reduction to buyers who buy large volumes.

**Quantity premium**   A surcharge paid by buyers who purchase high volumes of a product.

**Question marks**   Low-share business units in high-growth markets that require a lot of cash in order to hold their share or become stars.

**Quota**   A limit on the amount of goods that an importing country will accept in certain product categories; it is designed to conserve on foreign exchange and to protect local industry and employment.

**Range branding strategy**   A brand strategy whereby the firm develops separate product range names for different families of product.

**Rational appeals**   Message appeals that relate to the audience's self-interest and show that the product will produce the claimed benefits; examples include appeals of product quality, economy, value, or performance.

**Reach**   The percentage of people in the target market exposed to an ad campaign during a given period.

**Reference groups**   Groups that have a direct (face-to-face) or indirect influence on the person's attitudes or behaviour.

**Reference prices**   Prices that buyers carry in their minds and refer to when they look at a given product.

**Relationship marketing**   The process of creating, maintaining, and enhancing strong, value-laden relationships with customers and other stakeholders.

**Reminder advertising**   Advertising used to keep consumers thinking about a product.

**Reseller market**   The individuals and organizations who buy goods and services to resell at a profit.

**Retail park**   An organized cluster of retailers located either at the edge of town or out of town. The provision of car parks and other extra amenities is usually agreed and manned jointly by the retailers in the cluster.

**Retailer cooperatives**   Contractual vertical marketing systems in which retailers organize a new, jointly owned business to carry on wholesaling and possibly production.

**Retailers**   Businesses whose sales come *primarily* from retailing.

**Retailing**   All activities involved in selling goods or services directly to final consumers for their personal, nonbusiness use.

**Retailing accordion**   A phenomenon describing how the width of retailers' product assortment or operations shifts over time: there tends to be a general–specific–general cycle. However, it is possible that many retailing businesses evolve along a specific–general–specific cycle.

**Role**   The activities a person is expected to perform according to the people around him or her.

**Sales promotion**   Short-term incentives to encourage purchase or sales of a product or service.

**Sales quotas**   Standards set for salespeople, stating the amount they should sell and how sales should be divided among the company's products.

**Salesforce management**   The analysis, planning, implementation, and control of salesforce activities. It includes setting salesforce objectives; designing salesforce strategy; and recruiting, selecting, training, supervising, and evaluating the firm's salespeople.

**Salesforce promotion**   Sales promotion designed to motivate the salesforce and make salesforce selling efforts more effective, including bonuses, contests, and sales rallies.

**Salesperson**   An individual acting for a company by performing one or more of the following activities: prospecting, communicating, servicing, and information gathering.

**Salutary products**   Products that have low appeal but may benefit consumers in the long run.

**Sample**   A segment of the population selected for marketing research to represent the population as a whole.

**Samples**   Offers to consumers of a trial amount of a product.

**Sealed-bid pricing**   Setting price based on how the firm thinks competitors will price rather than on its own costs or demand – used when a company bids for jobs.

**Seasonal discount**   A price reduction to buyers who buy merchandise or services out of season.

**Seasonality**   The recurrent consistent pattern of sales movements within the year.

**Secondary data**   Information that already exists somewhere, having been collected for another purpose.

**Segmented pricing**   Pricing which allows for differences in customers, products and locations. The differences in prices are not based on differences in costs.

**Selective attention**   The tendency of people to screen out most of the information to which they are exposed.

**Selective demand**   The demand for a given brand of a product or service.

**Selective distortion**   The tendency of people to adapt information to personal meanings.

**Selective distribution**   The use of more than one, but less than all of the middlemen who are willing to carry the company's products.

**Selective retention**   The tendency of people to retain only part of the information to which they are exposed, usually information that supports their attitudes or beliefs.

**Self-concept**   Self-image, or the complex mental pictures people have of themselves.

**Self-service retailers**   Retailers that provide few or no services to shoppers; shoppers perform their own locate-compare-select process.

**Selling concept**   The idea that consumers will not buy enough of the organization's products unless the organization undertakes a large-scale selling and promotion effort.

**Selling process**   The steps that the salesperson follows when selling, which include prospecting and qualifying, preapproach, approach, presentation and demonstration, handling objections, closing, and follow-up.

**Sense-of-mission marketing**  A principle of enlightened marketing which holds that a company should define its mission in broad social terms rather than narrow product terms.

**Sequential product development**  A new-product development approach in which one company department works individually to complete its stage of the process before passing the new product along to the next department and stage.

**Served market (or target market)**  The part of the qualified available market the company decides to pursue.

**Service**  Any activity or benefit that one party can offer to another which is essentially intangible and does not result in the ownership of anything.

**Service inseparability**  A major characteristic of services – they are produced and consumed at the same time and cannot be separated from their providers, whether the providers are people or machines.

**Service intangibility**  A major characteristic of services – they cannot be seen, tasted, felt, heard, or smelled before they are bought.

**Service perishability**  A major characteristic of services – they cannot be stored for later sale or use.

**Service variability**  A major characteristic of services – their quality may vary greatly, depending on who provides them and when, where, and how.

**Services**  Activities, benefits, or satisfactions that are offered for sale.

**Sheltered shopping complex (shopping mall)**  A large store cluster housed within a sheltered or covered building. An indoor shopping area that has many storeys of stores and, in some countries, stretches across several blocks of buildings. The cluster consists of a broad mix of stores – general, speciality, small, large, independent and chain. Some even house large grocery and nonfood superstores within the complex.

**Shopping goods**  Consumer goods that the customer, in the process of selection and purchase, characteristically compares on such bases as suitability, quality, price, and style.

**Simultaneous product development**  An approach to developing new products in which various company departments work closely together, overlapping the steps in the product-development process to save time and increase effectiveness.

**Single-source data systems**  Electronic monitoring systems that link consumers' exposure to television advertising and promotion (measured using television metres) with what they buy in stores (measured using store checkout scanners).

**Slotting fees**  Payments demanded by retailers from producers before they will accept new products and find 'slots' for them on the shelves.

**Social classes**  Relatively permanent and ordered divisions in a society whose members share similar values, interests, and behaviours.

**Societal marketing**  A principle of enlightened marketing which holds that a company should make marketing decisions by considering consumers' wants, the company's requirements, consumers' long-run interests, and society's long-run interests.

**Societal marketing concept**  The idea that the organization should determine the needs, wants and interests of target markets and deliver the desired satisfactions more effectively and efficiently than competitors in a way that maintains or improves the consumer's and society's well-being.

**Speciality goods**  Consumer goods with unique characteristics or brand identification for which a significant group of buyers is willing to make a special purchase effort.

**Speciality store**  A retail store that carries a narrow product line with a deep assortment within that line.

**Specialized industry**   An industry where there are many opportunities for firms to create competitive advantages which are huge or give a high pay-off.

**Stalemate industry**   An industry that produces commodities and is characterized by a few opportunities to create competitive advantages, with each advantage being small.

**Standardized marketing mix**   An international marketing strategy for using basically the same product, advertising, distribution channels, and other elements of the marketing mix in all the company's international markets.

**Stars**   High-growth, high-share businesses or products that often require heavy investment to finance their rapid growth.

**Statistical demand analysis**   A set of statistical procedures used to discover the most important real factors affecting sales and their relative influence; the most commonly analysed factors are prices, income, population, and promotion.

**Status**   The general esteem given to a role by society.

**Straight product extension**   Marketing a product in a foreign market without any change.

**Straight rebuy**   A business buying situation in which the buyer routinely reorders something without any modifications.

**Strapline**   A slogan often used in conjunction with a brand's name, advertising and other promotions.

**Strategic business-planning grid**   A portfolio planning method that evaluates a company's strategic business units using indexes of industry attractiveness and the company's strength in the industry.

**Strategic business unit (SBU)**   A unit of the company that has a separate mission and objectives and that can be planned independently from other company businesses. An SBU can be a company division, a product line within a division, or sometimes a single product or brand.

**Strategic control**   Checking whether the company's basic strategy matches its opportunities and strengths.

**Strategic focus**   A strategic planning tool to help marketers identify ways of achieving sales and profit growth. Two routes – productivity increases and volume expansion – form the basis of analysis.

**Strategic group**   A group of firms in an industry following the same or a similar strategy.

**Strategic plan**   A plan that describes how a firm will adapt to take advantage of opportunities in its constantly changing environment, thereby maintaining a strategic fit between the firm's goals and capabilities and its changing market opportunities.

**Strategic planning**   The process of developing and maintaining a strategic fit between the organization's goals and capabilities and its changing marketing opportunities. It relies on developing a clear company mission, supporting objectives, a sound business portfolio, and coordinated functional strategies.

**Style**   A basic and distinctive mode of expression.

**Subculture**   A group of people with shared value systems based on common life experiences and situations.

**Substantiality**   The degree to which a market segment is sufficiently large or profitable.

**Supermarkets**   Large, low-cost, low-margin, high-volume, self-service stores that carry a wide variety of food, laundry, and household products.

**Superstore**   A store almost twice the size of a regular supermarket that carries a large assortment of routinely purchased food and nonfood items and offers such services as dry cleaning, post offices, film developing, photo finishing, cheque cashing, petrol forecourts, and self-service car-washing facilities.

**Supplier search**   The stage of the business buying process in which the buyer tries to find the best vendors.

**Supplier selection**   The stage of the business buying process in which the buyer reviews proposals and selects a supplier or suppliers.

**Suppliers**   Firms and individuals that provide the resources needed by the company and its competitors to produce goods and services.

**Supplies and services**   Industrial goods that do not enter the finished product at all.

**Survey research**   The gathering of primary data by asking people questions about their knowledge, attitudes, preferences, and buying behaviour.

**SWOT analysis**   A distillation of the findings of the internal and external audit which draws attention to the critical organizational strengths and weaknesses and the opportunities and threats facing the company.

**Systems buying**   Buying a packaged solution to a problem and without all the separate decisions involved.

**Target costing**   A technique to support pricing decision, which starts with deciding a target cost for a new product and working back to designing the product.

**Target market**   A set of buyers sharing common needs or characteristics that the company decides to serve.

**Target profit pricing**   See Breakeven pricing

**Tariff**   A tax levied by a government against certain imported products. Tariffs are designed to raise revenue or to protect domestic firms.

**Technological environment**   Forces that create new technologies, creating new product and market opportunities.

**Telemarketing**   Using the telephone to sell directly to consumers.

**Television marketing**   Direct marketing via television using direct-response advertising or home shopping channels.

**Territorial salesforce structure**   A salesforce organization that assigns each salesperson to an exclusive geographic territory in which that salesperson carries the company's full line.

**Test marketing**   The stage of new-product development where the product and marketing programme are tested in more realistic market settings.

**Time-series analysis**   Breaking down past sales into its trend, cycle, season, and erratic components, then recombining these components to produce a sales forecast.

**Total costs**   The sum of the fixed and variable costs for any given level of production.

**Total customer cost**   The total of all the monetary, time, energy, and psychic costs associated with a marketing offer.

**Total customer value**   The total of all of the product, services, personnel, and image values that a buyer receives from a marketing offer.

**Total market demand**   The total volume of a product or service that would be bought by a defined consumer group in a defined geographic area in a defined time period in a defined marketing environment under a defined level and mix of industry marketing effort.

**Town-centre shopping zone (community shopping centre)**   A store cluster in the town centre. Typically, smaller independent stores, variety stores, a limited number of chain stores and speciality retailers form the cluster. The stores attract mainly shoppers who work or live in or near the town.

**Trade-in allowance**   A price reduction given for turning in an old item when buying a new one.

**Trade (or retailer) promotion**   Sales promotion designed to gain reseller support and to improve reseller selling efforts, including discounts, allowances, free goods, cooperative advertising, push money, and conventions and trade shows.

**Transaction**   A trade between two parties that involves at least two things of value, agreed-upon conditions, a time of agreement, and a place of agreement.

**Trend**   The long-term, underlying pattern of sales growth or decline resulting from basic changes in population, capital formation and technology.

**Two-part pricing**   A strategy for pricing services in which price is broken into a fixed fee plus a variable usage rate.

**Underpositioning**   A positioning error referring to failure to position a company, its product or brand.

**Undifferentiated marketing**   A market-coverage strategy in which a firm decides to ignore market segment differences and go after the whole market with one offer.

**Uniform delivered pricing**   A geographic pricing strategy in which the company charges the same price plus freight to all customers, regardless of their location.

**Unique selling proposition (USP)**   The unique product benefit which a firm aggressively promotes in a consistent manner to its target market. The benefit usually reflects functional superiority: best quality, best services, lowest price, most advanced technology.

**Unsought goods**   Consumer goods that the consumer either does not know about or knows about but does not normally think of buying.

**User**   The person who consumes or uses a product or service.

**Users**   Members of the organization who will use the product or service; users often initiate the buying proposal and help define product specifications.

**Value analysis**   An approach to cost reduction in which components are studied carefully to determine if they can be redesigned, standardized, or made by less costly methods of production.

**Value-based pricing**   Setting price based on buyers' perceptions of product values rather than on cost.

**Value chain**   A major tool for identifying ways to create more customer value.

**Value marketing**   A principle of enlightened marketing which holds that a company should put most of its resources into value-building marketing investments.

**Value pricing**   Offering just the right combination of quality and good service at a fair price.

**Variable costs**   Costs that vary directly with the level of production.

**Variety-seeking buying behaviour**   Consumer buying behaviour in situations characterized by low consumer involvement but significant perceived brand differences.

**Variety store**   Self-service store that specializes in a wide range of merchandise. It offers a wider range than specialist stores but a narrower variety than department stores.

**Vertical marketing system (VMS)**   A distribution channel structure in which producers, wholesalers, and retailers act as a unified system. One channel member owns the others, has contracts with them, or has so much power that they all cooperate.

**Volume industry**   An industry characterized by few opportunities to create competitive advantages, but each advantage is huge and give a high pay-off.

**Warehouse club (wholesale club, membership warehouse)**   Off-price retailer that sells a limited selection of brand-name grocery items, appliances, clothing, and a hodgepodge of other goods at deep discounts to members who pay annual membership fees.

**Wheel of retailing**   A concept of retailing which states that new types of retailers usually begin as low-margin, low-price, low-status operations but later evolve into higher-priced, higher-service operations, eventually becoming like the conventional retailers they replaced.

**Wholesaler**   A firm engaged *primarily* in wholesaling activity.

**Wholesaling**   All activities involved in selling goods and services to those buying for resale or business use.

**Word-of-mouth influence**   Personal communication about a product between target buyers and neighbours, friends, family members, and associates.

**Workload approach**   An approach to setting salesforce size, whereby the company groups accounts into different size classes and then determines how many sales people are needed to call on them the desired number of times.

**Zone pricing**   A geographic pricing strategy in which the company sets up two or more zones. All customers within a zone pay the same total price; the more distant the zone, the higher the price.

# Subject index

ACE research 799
ACORN categories 361–3
acquisitions and mergers 48–9, 87
adoption process 297–300
advertising 686, 696–7, 701–2, 754
  agencies 716
  bad taste 696–7
  budget 718–20, 754
  comparison 717–18
  creating message 720–5
  and cultural differences 733–4
  errors with foreign cultures 185
  evaluation 730–2, 754
    copy testing 730–1
  execution styles 722–5
  expenditure by country 728
  informative 717
  objectives 716–18
  reach, frequency and impact
    725–6
  reminder 718
  teasers 696
  tone 724
  worldwide 732–8
    centralization/decentralization 735
    standardization 733–4
  see also media; promotions
Advertising Standards Authority (ASA)
  42, 696, 697, 717
agencies, marketing services 136
airline industry 208–10, 314, 315, 367,
  476–7, 760–1
Asia 145, 158, 167, 828–9
  demographic details 140–3
  fast food penetration 236
audit, marketing 78–9, 98–9, 100–1, 105
Austria 345–6
Automatic Interaction Detection (AID)
  376–7
automatic vending 887

baby milk 65–7
baking soda products 384–5
balance sheet 79
banking industry 601, 604
  virtual 673
barter transaction 9, 10, 182, 672–3
beliefs and attitudes of consumer 288
  see also culture
benchmarking 472, 474–5
Boston Consulting Group 83–4, 108, 401
bottled water industry 250–1
brand
  advantages of 560
  awareness 557
  decisions 555–69
  defined 556–7
  dilution 567
  equity 557–9
  extension 563
  image 293, 597
    differentiation 408–9
  licensing 561–2, 704–5
  line extensions 568
  loyalty 557, 704
  management system 102–4
  name selection 569
  nonbranding 559–60, 564–7
  portfolios 557
  preferences 557
  repositioning 568–9
  sponsor 561–2
  strategy options 562–3
  world's top 557–9
brand plan 97–102
  action programmes 101
  contents 97–8
  controls and implementation 102, 104–9
  executive summary 98
  marketing audit 98–9, 100–1
  marketing mix 99
  marketing strategy 99

  objectives and issues 99
  SWOT analysis 99
breakeven pricing 637–43
bribes 183
business buyer behaviour 315–28
  buying centre 317–19
  centralized purchasing 320–1
  environmental factors 319–20
  individual factors 321, 324
  influences on 319–25
  interpersonal factors 321
  just-in-time production 321, 324–5
  long-term contracts 321
  making decisions 325–8
  model of 315
  organization factors 320
  participants 317–19
  purchasing performance evaluation
    321
  stages of buying process 325–8
  types of decisions 316–17
  upgraded purchasing 320
business markets 136, 307–43
  characteristics of 310–15, 333
  decision process 313–14, 333
  institutional and government
    markets 329–32, 333
  market structure and demand 310–14
  nature of buying unit 312–13
  segmentation 369–71
business portfolio 83–8
buyback 181
buyers see business; consumer
  behaviour

Cambodia 186
capital items 550
car industry 499–503, 542–3
  acquisitions 48–9
  advertising 717
  environmentalism 51

international marketing 191
legislation 51
luxury/sports 422–3, 499, 632–3
market segmentation 359–60
pricing 632–3, 648–53
catalogue marketing 880–1
catalogue showroom 870
category killers 855, 858, 863, 866–8
Caux Round Table (CRT) ethics code 58
chain stores 870–1
challenger, market 96
China 186–7, 198, 782–4, 828
choice, maximization of 22
Citizen's Charter 603
cluster analysis 377–8
coffee/coffee creamers 345–7, 389–97
communication, effective 687–709
competition 137
    international 167
    monopolistic/oligopolistic 629–30
competitive advantage 401–5, 409,
        465–503
    and differentiation 479
    as market-centred company 495
    marketing strategy for 95–6
    selecting 421, 424–6
    types of industry 401, 404
    *see also* competitive strategies;
        competitor analysis;
        differentiation
competitive strategies 477–94, 495–6
    balancing customer orientations and
        494–5
    market-challenger strategies 480,
        487–90
    market-follower strategies 480, 490–1
    market-leader strategies 480–7
    market-nicher strategies 480, 491–4
competitor analysis 468–77, 495
    assessing strengths and weaknesses
        472
    attacking or avoiding 473, 476–7
    customer value analysis 473, 476
    designing intelligence system 477
    determining competitors' objectives
        471
    estimating reaction patterns 472–3
    identifying 469–70
    strategies 471–2
concept, product 519–21
confectionery industry 115–26, 429–34
conjunctive model of consumer choice
    295
consumer
    -oriented marketing 53–4
    concerns 37
    education and information 62
    freedom 61
    interest groups 153–4
    markets 136, 267–306
    protection 62
consumer behaviour 267–301
    buyer decision process 291–7, 300
        evaluation of alternatives 293–5

information research 292–3
    need recognition 292
    for new products 297–300
buyer-readiness states 689–91, 706–7
buying roles 275–6, 277–82
characteristics affecting 270–88, 300
complex buying behaviour 289–90
cultural factors 270–3
decision process 288–9
dissonance-reducing buying
        behaviour 290
habitual buying behaviour 290–1
models of 269–70
personal factors 276–82
psychological factors 282–8
purchase decision 295–6
social factors 273–6
survey of intentions 239, 247
types of buying decision behaviour
        289–91
variety-seeking buying behaviour 291
consumerism 49–51, 63, 153–4
Consumers' Association (UK) 42, 44–5
consumption, maximization of 21
contract manufacturing 189
control, marketing 102, 104–5, 109
    operating 104
    strategic 104–5
convenience goods 547–8
convenience store 861
core product 546
core strategy 400–1, 427
    differentiation 401–9
    *see also* competitive advantage;
        positioning; satisfaction;
        segmentation
corruption, political 330–1
cosmetic industry 203–7
cost leadership 74
counterpurchase 181
countertrade 171, 180–2
credit cards 604, 672
criticism of marketing 36–49
    cultural pollution 48
    deceptive practices 38–9
    excessive mark-ups 38
    false wants and materialism 46–7
    high advertising and promotion costs
        37–8
    high cost of distribution 37
    high prices 37
    high-pressure selling 39–41
    impact on other businesses 48–9
    planned obsolescence 43, 46
    political power of business 48
    poor service to disadvantaged
        consumers 46
    shoddy and unsafe products 42–3
    too few social goods 47–8
culture
    and business etiquette 182–5, 322–3
    and buyer behaviour 270–3, 300
        cultural shifts 271
    and consumer choices 182

cultural universals 193
differences 143–4, 355–7
    and advertising 733–4
    and brands 559
environment 155–9, 182–5
    beliefs and values 156–9
customer
    cost 439, 440
    -focused firms 438, 444
    four Cs 97
    markets 136–7
    retention 449–55
        relationship marketing 450–3,
            454–5, 460
    service 574, 580

databases, marketing 885
demand
    business markets 311, 312, 333
    defined 7–8
    forecasting 93, 237–43, 246–7
    measurement of 93, 231, 233–7, 247
    and pricing 629–34
    states 12–13
Demming prize 551
demographic environment 140–4
demographic segmentation 356, 357–8
Denmark 167, 170
department store 858–9, 860
designing products *see* innovation; new
        product
detergent market 351–3
differentiation 74, 401–9, 427
    and competitive advantage 167, 479
    image 408–9, 427
    personnel 407–8, 427
    product 405–6, 427
    retailing 889
    services 406–7, 427, 596–7, 605
    *see also* competitive advantage
digital diffusion 814–15
direct investment 190
direct line financial services 271, 405,
        658
direct marketing 877–86
direct purchasing 314
direct selling 886–7
discount store 863
disjunctive model of consumer choice
    295
distribution channels 807–8, 842, 845–52
    behaviour and organization 812–21
    conflict 813–15
    design decisions 821–9, 842
        analysing customer service needs
            821–3
        evaluating alternatives 826–8
        identifying alternatives 824–6
        objectives and strategy 823–4
    exclusive 826
    firms 135
    functions 810
    horizontal marketing systems 819–20
    hybrid marketing channels 820–1

distribution channels *continued*
  intensive 825
  international 828–9
  management decisions 829–31, 843
  nature of 808–12
  number of levels 810–12
  selective 826
  in service sector 812
  vertical marketing system 817–19
  *see also* logistics
diversification 91
dumping 197

e-money 673
Eastern Europe 146–7
education and information, consumer 62
electronic data interchange 832, 833
electronic funds transfer (EFT) 832
emotional selling proposition 424
enlightened marketing 53–6, 63
environment, marketing 129–64
  macroenvironment 140–59, 160
    cultural 155–9
    demographic 140–4
    economic 144–5
    natural 146–50
    political 152–5
    technological 151–2
  microenvironment 134–8, 160
    company 134–5
    suppliers 135
  responses to 159
environmentalism 51–2, 63, 146–50
  environmental industry 149, 150
ethics 26–7, 56–69, 154
  codes 58, 59
  and social responsibility 33–67
Euroconsumer 143–4
Europe/European Union 145, 178–9, 246
  car prices 648–53
  comparison advertising 717–18
  consumer expenditure by product
    146–7
  corporate intelligence 216, 217
  deceptive practices 38–9
  demographic details 140–4
  environmental policy 150
  as Fortress Europe 175, 177, 178
  hypermarkets and superstores 861
  and Japan 261–4
  lifestyle research 280–1, 799–800
  permitted sales promotions 744
  and pharmaceutical industry 154–5
  regulations 152, 153, 192
  technological research 152
  TQM 459
European Society for Opinion and
  Marketing Research (ESOMAR)
  245–6
exchange 9, 11
exchange controls 176
expectancy value model of consumer
  choice 294
exporting 188

express delivery industry 465–8
factor analysis 378
factory outlets 870
family and buyer behaviour 274–5, 277
ferry operators 676–80
FOB-origin pricing 665
focused companies 74–5
follower, market 96
fragrance market 427, 544–5
France 182, 183, 184, 330
  business etiquette 323
franchise organization 819, 871–3
free trade areas 176–7
funeral services 594–5
furniture retailing 853–6

gender and buyer behaviour 275
General Electric grid 85–7, 88, 108
Germany 150, 175, 192, 330, 331
  business behaviour 183–4, 322, 323
  Free Democratic Party 271
global firm 170
global marketplace 165–207
  *see also* international marketing
global organizations 170, 199–200
government markets 136, 329–31
grocery retailing 360
groups and buyer behaviour 273–4, 275, 300

harm, transactional 61
holiday destinations 411–14
hospitality, corporate 786–7
hypermarket 861–2

implementation of marketing plans 102,
  105–8, 109
  and company culture 107–8, 109
Independent Television Commission 42
India 181, 186, 828
Indonesia 323
industrial goods 549–51, 580
information, marketing 208–59
  developing information 211–31
    internal records 212–13
  distributing 243, 246
  Europe 245
  forecasting demand 237–43, 247
    expert opinion 239, 240
    information analysis 242–3
    leading indicators 241
    statistical demand analysis 242
    survey of buyers' intentions 239
    time-series analysis 241
  international 244–6
  marketing intelligence 213–14
  marketing research 214–15, 218–31
  measuring demand 231, 233–7, 247
    defining the market 231–3
    estimating actual sales and market
      shares 237, 238
    estimating area and market demand
      235–7
    estimating total market demand
      233–5

MIS (marketing information system)
  211, 212, 213–15, 218–31, 247
  *see also* research, marketing
innovation 61–2, 481, 511
  organizing for 529–31
  risks and returns 511–12
  *see also* new product
innovative marketing 54
institutional markets 136, 329
insurance, sales methods 40–1, 658
intelligence, marketing 213–14, 216–18, 247
intermediaries 135–6
international marketing 136, 166–201
  allocating resources 191–2
  analysis of opportunity 173–85
  assessing product potential 187
  business manners 322–3
  commitment 191
  constraints by host government 172
  cultural environment 182–5
  defining objectives and policies 186–7,
    201
  distribution channels 198
  economic environment 177, 180
  establishing market entry mode
    187–90, 201
  evaluation of operations 200
  global environment 174–85, 201
  indicators of market potential 187
  market segmentation 371–2
    geographic 372
    political and legal factors 372
  operational team and implementing
    strategy 199–200
  planning model 173
  politico-legal environment 180–2, 372
  price setting 197–8
  product strategies 195–6
  promotion strategies 196–7
  risks in 171–3
  services 601, 604–5
  standardization or adaptation 193–5
  strategic marketing plan 192–8
  technical issues 192
internationalization 23–6, 28, 166–71
  importance of 170
Ireland, confectionery 429–33
Italy 322, 323, 330

Japan 165–6, 169, 236, 330, 331, 828
  branding 555
  business etiquette 322, 323
  car marketing 499, 502
  corporate intelligence 214, 216
  dumping by 197
  ethics 58
  internationalization 167, 168–70, 174,
    175, 191, 261–4
  nontariff barriers 176
  personal selling to 782–4
  TQM 458
joint ventures 188–90
just-in-time logistics systems 836
just-in-time production 321, 324–5

labelling 571, 580
leader, market 96
learning and buyer behaviour 287–8
leasing 314–15
legal issues 51, 52, 53, 152–3
licensing 189, 561
life quality, maximisation of 22
lifestyle 277–82, 300
   segmentation 356, 358–9, 364–5
logistics, marketing 831–42, 843
   alliances 842–3
   integrated management 840–2, 843
   international 839
   inventory 836
   order processing 833–4
   transportation modes 836–9
   warehousing 834–5
loss leaders 664
loyalty, customer 441

Malaysia 282
management contracting 189
managers, marketing 134
market-challenger strategies 480, 487–90, 496
   attack strategies 488–90
market-follower strategies 480, 490–1, 496
market–leader strategies 480–7, 496
   defending position 483–6
   increasing market share 486–7
   more usage and users 481–3
market-nicher strategies 480, 491–4, 496
   specialist roles 493–4
market/s
   consumer 136, 267–306
   definitions 10–11, 231–3, 247, 353–4
   global 171–85
   *see also* segmentation; targeting
marketing
   challenges in 1990s 22–3
   concept 15–18, 28, 35–6
   defined 11–12, 18
   described 6–13
   landscape 27
   mix 6, 96–7, 99
   process 91–7
   system 20–2, 28
marketing audit (the) (TMA) 216, 217
marketing management 12–13, 28, 91–2, 457
   defined 13
   demand states 12–13
   market analysis, implementation and control 91–2
   philosophies 14–20
marketing strategy 92–5
   for competitive advantage 95–6
   demand measurement and forecasting 93
   differential advantage 94
   market segmentation 93–4
   market targeting 94–5
   positioning 95

target consumers 93
   *see also* strategic marketing
markups and markdowns 638–9
mass marketing 353, 387
materialism and marketing critics 46–7
media 411
   advantages/limitations by form 729
   available by country 726–7, 736–7
   buying and costs 737–8
   planning 730
   ratings 221
   segmentation of 373–4
   selecting 695–9, 725–30
   timing 730
merchandising conglomerate 873
micromarketing 354
microprocessor industry 312–13
middlemen 135
mission statement 73–7
mix, marketing 6, 96–7, 99
mobile phones 654–5, 659
monopolistic competition 629, 630
motivation and buyer behaviour 282–5, 286
mousetraps 112–14
music industry 814–15

natural environment 146–50
needs 3–32, 438–9
   and buying behaviour 283–4, 286, 292
   and public policy 61
Netherlands 139, 149
new product 511–39
   adoption process 297–300
   business analysis 522
   commercialization 527–8
   concept development and testing 519–21
   development process 514–31, 538
   idea generation 515–18
   idea rating process 519
   idea screening 518–19
   innovation charter 515
   marketing strategy development 521–2
   organizational structures 514
   pricing 656–8, 673
   reason for failures 512
   speeding up development 528
   strategy 515
   success factors 512–14
   test marketing 524–7
newspapers 373–4, 619–21
   positioning 411
nicher, market 96
non-profit organizations 4–5, 218
nontariff trade barriers 176, 178
on-line shopping 883–4
operating statement 79, 80–1
opinion leaders 273–4
organization of marketing 102–4
OTC drug market 583–5
overpositioning 424
own-label products 559–60, 564–7
packaging 569–71, 572–3, 580

international issues 579–80
party selling 274
payphones 911–14
perception and buyer behaviour 285–7
   perceptual maps 411–14, 416–19, 427
personal selling 686, 702
   international 781, 782–4, 788–95
   principles of 777–85
   relationship marketing 781, 785
   *see also* salesforce
personality and buyer behaviour 282, 365
pharmaceutical industry 151, 153, 816
   and EU 154–5
   patent protection 155
   R and D 155
   wholesaling trends 902–3
placing products *see* distribution
   channels; logistics; wholesaling
planning *see* strategic marketing
political environment 152–5
positioning 95, 354, 398–434
   communicating and delivering chosen position 426–7
   and competitive strategies 478–80
   and competitors 411–12, 416–18, 420
   defined 409–10
   perceptual maps 412–14, 416–19
   selecting competitive advantages 421, 424–6
   strategies 410–12, 414–15, 418–20, 421–7
   underpositioning, overpositioning and confused 424–5
postpurchase behaviour 296–7, 300
   cognitive dissonance 296
price/pricing 619–80, 654–80
   breakeven pricing 637–43
   by-product 660
   captive-product 659
   changes 668–73, 674
      of competitors 670–2
   competition based 644–5, 646
      going-rate 644
      sealed-bid 644–5
   and competitors 634
   consumer perceptions of price and value 630–1
   cost-based 636–43, 646
   discount and allowance 661–2
   economic conditions 635
   economic value added 640–2
   factors to consider 622–35
      costs 624–8
      market and demand 629–34, 646
      marketing objectives 622–3
      marketing-mix strategy 623–4
      organizational 628–9
   geographical 665–8
   international 197–8, 668
   and marketing mix 96
   markups and markdowns 638–9
   new products 656–8, 673
      market-penetration 656, 657–8
      market-skimming 656, 657

price/pricing *continued*
  optional-product 659
  price-adjustment strategies 660–8
  primary concerns 635–6, 645–6
  product line 658–9
  product-bundle 660
  promotional 663–4
  psychological 663
  segmented 662–3
  social concerns 635
  strategies 655–6
  value 643–4, 646, 664, 666–7
producer freedom 61
product
  actual 546, 580
  attributes 551–5, 580
    and buyer behaviour 293, 297–300
  augmented 546, 580
  brand decisions 555–69
  classifications 547–51
  concept 14–15, 28, 519–21
  consumer goods 547–9, 580
  convenience goods 547–9
  core 546, 580
  defined 8, 545–7
  design 554–5
  differentiation 405–6
  durable and non-durable 547
  individual product decisions 551–74
  industrial goods 549–51
  international 579–80
  ladder 410
  life-cycle strategies 531–8, 539
    decline 537–8
    growth 534–5
    introduction 533–4
    maturity 535–7
  and marketing mix 96
  mix 89, 578–9
  position 95
  societal classification 55–6, 57
  strategies for international markets
    195–6
  support services 571–4
  -variety marketing 353, 387
  *see also* innovation; new product;
    positioning
product line 580–1
  decisions 574–8, 580–1
  defined 574
  filling 577, 581
  modernization 577–8, 581
  stretching 575–7
production concept 14
profitability, customer 453–5
  customer lifetime value 453–4
promotions 685–713
  advertising, sales promotion and
    public relations 714–59
  budget 699–700, 708
  buyer-readiness states 689–91, 706–7
  for children 704–5
  choosing media 695–9, 709
    non-personal communication 698–9

    personal communication 695, 698
  choosing message 691–5, 709
    format 693–5
    structure 693
  collecting feedback 707–8, 709
  communication and promotion
    strategy 685–713
  determining response sought 689, 709
  emotional appeals 692–3
  identifying target audience 688–9
  industrial markets 703, 706
  international markets 196–7
  managing and coordinating 708–9
  and marketing mix 96
  mix 686–7, 701–7
    push versus pull strategy 703–6, 707
    type of product/market 703
  moral appeals 693
  personal selling and sales management
    760–95
  product life-cycle stage 707
  public relations 750–4
  sales promotion 738–50
  sponsorship 752–3
  *see also* advertising; sales
public interest groups 153–4
public policy 60–2, 63, 152–3
public relations 687, 702–3, 750–4, 755
publics, types of 137–8
purchase probability scale 239

quality 456–7, 458–9, 460, 551–4
  and services 597–600
quick response system 448
quotas 175

razors 304–6
reciprocity 314
regulation 152
  citizen and public action 49–52
relationship marketing 10, 450–3, 454–5,
  460
  personal selling 781, 785
research and development 135, 151–2,
  155
research, marketing 214–15, 218–31, 247
  defining objectives 215, 218
  expenditure on methods by country
    225
  experimental 222–3
  instruments 226–7, 230, 247
  interpreting and reporting 230–1
  mail and telephone questionnaires 223,
    225
  observational 221–2
  personal interviewing 224–6
  primary and secondary data 219–21,
    247
  sampling 226
  surveys 222
  types of questionnaires 228–9
  *see also* information, marketing
reseller markets 136
retailing 856–95, 904

accordion 894–5
classification 857
control of outlets 870–3
cooperative 871
internationalization 864–7, 893
marketing decisions 887–92, 904
  place 891–2
  price 891
  product assortment and services
    889–91
  promotion 891
  target market and positioning 888–9
product line 857–62
relative prices 862–70
store 856–77, 904
store clusters 873–7
trends 893–5
wheel of 894
rights of buyers and sellers 50

safety standards 152
sales promotion 687, 702, 738–50, 754–5
  developing programme 745–9
  in Europe 744, 746–7
  evaluating results 749–50
  objectives 741
  pretesting and implementing 749
  purpose of 739–41
  tools 738, 739, 741–5
salesforce 762–85
  automation 772–3
  compensation 766–7
  designing strategy 764–7
  evaluation 774–7
  management 762–3, 785
  motivating 773–4
  recruiting and selecting 767–8
  setting objectives 763–4
  size 766
  structure 764–6
  supervising 769–73
  training 768–9, 785
  use of time 770–1
satisfaction, customer 435–64
  customer delight 441
  defined 441–5
  delivering 445–8
  maximization of 21–2
  measurement of 442–4
    complaint and suggestions systems
      442
    ghost shopping 443
    lost customer analysis 443
    surveys 442–4
  and needs 438–9
  and repeat buying 296
  and value 8–9
Saudi Arabia 323
Scantrack service 213, 219, 220, 525
segmentation, market 93–4, 354–79, 387
  attitudes towards product 369
  Auromatic Interaction Detection (AID)
    376–7
  bases for 355–75

behavioural 356, 365–6
benefit 366–7
business markets 369–71
buyer-readiness stage 369
cluster analysis 377–8
conjoint analysis 379
demographic 356, 357–8
factor analysis 378
gender 359–60
geodemographics 361–3
geographic 355–7
income 360
international markets 371–2
lifestyle 356, 358–9, 364–5
loyalty status 367–9
multivariate 373–5
personality 365
psychographic 356, 363–4
pubs 408
requirements for effective 379
stages in development of 375–9
and targeting 351–97
usage rate 367
user status 367
ways of 376–7
*see also* targeting
selling
concept 15, 28
rights 50
sense-of-mission marketing 54–5
service/s 550, 586–609
defined 547
differentiation 406–7
inseparability 589–90, 605
intangibility 589, 605
interactive marketing 596, 605
international marketing 601, 604–5
lack of ownership 592–3, 605
managing productivity 600–1
marketing strategies 593–601
internal marketing 593, 596
nature and characteristics 588–93
perishability 591–2, 605
turning complaints to opportunities 602–4
variability 590–1, 605
setting *see* environment; global marketplace; information
shopping centres/malls 873–4, 875–7
shopping goods 548
Singapore 876
snack industry/market 429–33, 681–2
social class and buyer behaviour 272–3, 364
social marketing 4–5
social responsibility 26–7, 52–60, 154
and marketing ethics 33–67

societal marketing 18–20, 55–6
soft drinks industry 250–9, 505–6
perceptual maps 416–19
South Korea 167
Spain 330
sparkling wines case study 845–52
speciality goods 548
speciality store 858
strategic business units 83–7, 88
strategic marketing planning 68–113
annual plan 71, 108
business portfolio 83–8, 108
conflict between departments 73
developing growth strategies 88–91
from mission to strategic objectives 78
functional strategies 71–2
long-range plan 71, 108
marketing and other business functions 72
marketing process 91–7
marketing strategy 92–5
matrix approaches 83–8
mission 73–7
overview 70–1
product/market expansion grid 90
strategic audit 78–9, 98
external audit 78
internal audit 78
strategic focus 88–9
strategic plan 71, 73–7
SWOT analysis 71, 79–83, 99, 108
*see also* brand plan
supermarket 859–61
supplier 135
analysis 328
search and selection 326–7
SWOT analysis 71, 79–83, 99, 108
symbols 409, 597

Taiwan 167, 555
target costing 624
target profit pricing 637
targeting, market 94–5, 353–4, 380–7
concentrated marketing 384–5, 386–7
differentiated 383, 386
evaluating segments 380–1
and product variability 387
selecting segments 381
strategies 382–7
undifferentiated marketing 382–3
tariffs 175
technological environment 151–2
television marketing 882–3
test marketing 241, 524–7
Thailand 186
tobacco industry 33–5
toothpaste market 44, 45, 366, 470
total market demand 233–5

Total Quality Management *see* quality
trade barriers 175–7
transactional analysis 284
transactions 9–10

underpositioning 424
unique selling proposition 424
United Kingdom
business etiquette 323
cultural arrogance 194
government market 330
internationalization 191
United States 149, 167, 175, 330
bribes 183
business etiquette 322, 323
car imports 499, 502
corporate intelligence 216, 217
cultural values 158, 159
demographic details 141–4
FDA 33–4, 152
internationalization 169
as market 191
materialism 46–7
on-line shopping 884
personal selling to 782–4
Public Citizen group 153
purchasing power 145
spirits market 711–13
subcultures 272
tariffs 197
technological research 152
test marketing 525
top brands 558, 559
unsought goods 548–9

value, customer 8–9, 54, 89, 439–41
and competitor analysis 473, 476
value chain 78, 445–8
value delivery system 438, 448, 460
Values and Lifestyles typology 278–82
variety store 859
video game industry 402–3
vodka 711–13

wants 7–8, 12
warehouse clubs 869–70
watch market 541–3
wholesaling 895–904
brokers and agents 898–9
classification 896
manufacturers' sales branches 899–900
marketing mix decisions 900–1
merchant 896–8
target market and positioning 900
trends 901–4

Zambia 611–15

# Company/brand index

ABB industrial equipment 765
Absolut Vodka 711–13
Action Aid 369
Acuvue lenses 473
Advanced Micro Devices (AMD) 312, 313
AEG 335–43
Aerostructures Hamble 509–10
AGB 219, 221, 237
Air France 677
Airbus 450, 451, 488–9, 760–1
Airtours 360
Akzo Nobel 85
Alcatel 151, 691, 692
Aldi 360, 564, 623, 823, 861, 863, 888
Allen-Bradley Company 530–1
Allied Breweries 408
Allied-Lyons 752
American Express 7, 285, 367, 598
Amphitrion 30–2
Amstrad 491, 513
Anheuser-Busch 830–1
Aquafresh toothpaste 424
Argos 870
Arm & Hammer 384–5, 482–3
Asea Brown Boveri 73, 151, 200
AT&T 212–13, 425
Audi 56, 422, 499
Avis car rental 602, 717
Avon cosmetics 271, 886
Axel group 609

Ballygowan Spring Water Company
    250–9
Bang & Olufsen 75, 479, 797–801
Barratts housing 359
Bausch & Lomb 473, 515, 628
Beck's Bier 752
Beecham 424
Belgacom 442
Ben & Jerry's 482
Benetton 78, 697, 841

Bernard Matthew 365
Betamax 512
Betterware 887
Betty's Café Tea Rooms 492, 493
Bic razors 167, 304–6
Black & Decker 195, 558
BMW (Bayerische Motorenwerke) 49, 51,
    95, 171, 372, 422, 423, 486,
    499–503, 558, 576, 723, 821
Boddington's beer 478
Body Shop 6, 20, 702
Boeing 181, 314, 488–9, 518, 760–1
Bolswessanen 219
Bombardier Gax business jet 309, 314
Britcraft Aviation 788–95
British Aerospace 509–10
British Airways 49, 196, 421, 476–7,
    490, 592, 677–8
British and American Tobacco (BAT) 33–5
British Gas 602–3, 696
British Home Stores 685–6
British Leyland 500
British Rail 696–7
British Telecom 190, 458, 599, 692
Brittany Ferries 676–80
Brown & Williamson Tobacco
    33–5
Budweiser beer 830–1
Bulmer (H.P.) 569
Burger King 424–5
Butlins holiday camps 364

Cadbury 119, 121, 123–4, 125, 126, 144,
    429–34, 525
Calvin Klein cosmetics 426
Campbell soup 103, 195, 483, 558, 668
Canon 191, 490
Capital Barter Corporation 672
Caremark 816
Carlsberg lager 167, 170, 415, 717
Carrefour 861, 862, 863, 864

Castrol 398–401
Caterpillar Logistics Services 808–10
Cathay Pacific airline 286
Cellnet 654–5
Center Parcs 364
Cereal Partners Worldwide 219
Chanel 206
Chips & Technologies 312
Christian Salvesen 807
Chrysler 49, 531
Church & Dwight 384–5
Cité Europe 892–3
Citroën 423
Clinique 206
Club 18–30 359
Co-operative Bank 60
Coca-Cola 18–19, 24, 169, 353, 357, 484,
    506, 557, 558, 565, 566, 820, 833
    internationalization 144, 194–5, 198
    licensing 189, 819
    new Coke 427
    sponsorship 752
Coffee-Mate 389–97, 525
Colgate-Palmolive 103, 583, 584–5
    segmentation 366–7
Compaq Computers 94, 313, 624, 835
Compuserve 814, 884
Concorde aircraft 512
Costco 869
Cott 564
Courtauld Fibres 311
Cover Girl cosmetics 203–6
Crayola crayons 536–7
Crest toothpaste 451, 692, 723
Crusha milk drink 705
Custom Clothing Technology 889–90
CWS Funeral Services Group 594–5
Cyrix 312, 313

Daimler-Benz 151, 181
Dale Parsons Men's Wear 80–1

946

Damart 406
dan Technologies 443, 444, 658
Danone yoghurt 165–6
Dawn French Fashions 492–3
Dell computers 54, 443, 658, 667
Design to Distribution (D2D) 458
Deutsche Bundespost Telekom 190
DHL courier service 407, 465–8
Diesel Jeans & Workwear 757–9
DigiCash 673
Direct Line insurance 271, 405, 658
Disney 557, 558, 607–9
Dixons electrical retailers 290
Domino's Pizza 18, 76
Dun & Bradstreet 213, 214

Eastman Kodak *see* Kodak
Economos 805–6, 807
Ecover 386
EG&G 491
Electrolux 886, 887
Elida Gibbs 103–4, 723
Energis 635
Eramet 87
Esso 196
Estée Lauder 205, 206
EuroDisney 78, 331, 512, 607, 608–9
Eurostar 677–8

Federal Express 21–2, 454, 465–8
Feinschmecker Sauce 462–4
Ferrari 49, 424
Ferrero 106
Fiat 49, 51, 696
First Direct banking 271, 376–7
First Virtual Bank 673
Fisher-Price 724
Flora margarine 276, 717, 718
Flying Flowers 886
Ford Motor Company 14, 24–5, 48, 95,
    151, 168, 170, 474, 484, 518, 531
  and Hertz 818
Foseco 169
France Télécom 190, 657
Freixenet SA 845–52
Fuld and Company Inc. (FCI) 216

General Dynamics 59
General Electric 94, 456, 486, 576, 667
General Foods 364
General Mills 87
General Motors 27, 48, 95, 151, 360, 383,
    531
General Telephone and Electronics (GTE)
    911–14
GenPharm International 139
GFT clothes 200
Gillette 167, 193–4, 304–6, 359, 527, 565,
    768
Glen Dimplex 625
Golden Wonder 367
Goodyear 181, 332
Grand Metropolitan 557
Grand Peninsula 607, 608–9

Grundig 661
Gucci 197
Gulfstream 308

Häagen-Dazs 94, 193, 482, 692–3, 752
Hampton Inn 357
Harley Davidson 458
Healey & Baker 678
Heineken beer 186, 195, 450
Heinz 564, 735
  Weightwatchers 451
Helene Curtis 196
Hershey 558, 559
Hertz car hire 818
Hewlett-Packard 105, 106–7, 148, 443
Hitachi 151, 558
Holiday Inns 441, 483
Home Shopping Network 884
Honda 96, 168, 191, 197, 288, 365, 422,
    441, 443, 444, 554
  and Rover 499–500, 501–2
Hong Kong Bank 175
Hong Kong and Shanghai Bank 442
Hoover 745, 748, 826
Hornby toys 572
Hoverspeed 676
Hyatt hotels 567–8
Hyundai 717

I Can't Believe It's Not Butter 420, 421, 565
IBD warehouse 834
IBM 94, 195, 313, 491, 692, 714, 746
  salesforce 768–9
ICI chemicals 478
ICL 474
Ideal Standard 363
IKEA 16, 23–4, 26, 357, 362–3, 666,
    853–6, 866, 867, 888
Index 870
Intel 94, 312–13, 491, 657
International Mineral and Chemical
    Corporation 78
Internet 673
Internet Underground Music Archive 814
ISS (International Service System) 600
Istel 212–13

J. Feliu de la Peña, SA (JFP) 335–43
Jacobs biscuits 430, 705
Jacobs Kaffee Wien 345–7
Jaguar cars 95, 423
JCB machinery 190, 216, 772, 824
JetCo 308–9, 318
Joe Bloggs 758
Johnson Controls (US) 624
Johnson & Johnson 19–20, 54, 358, 415,
    477–8, 482, 535, 569, 746–7
  Tylenol 19, 584, 750
  Vistakon 473
Jusco 865

Kaliber beer 411–12
Kao company 518
Kawasaki 197

Kellogg Company 195, 196, 214, 219,
    367, 558, 564, 733, 738
Kemira Group 138
KFC fast food 236
Kinnaird Communications Group 770–1
Kirk Tyson International 216
Kisqua 250–9
KitKat 115–26, 430, 431
Kleinwort Benson 310
KLM airline 386, 445
Kodak 76–7, 332, 355, 366, 469, 481, 485,
    557, 558, 559
Kraft 85, 103, 482
Kronenbourg lager 144, 696
Kwik Save 360, 823, 863

Laker Airlines 49, 490
Lamborghini 180
Land Rover 18, 501, 809–10
Landor Associates 558–9
Learjet 307
Lego 358–9, 572–3
Leica cameras 458
Levi Strauss 59, 68–70, 448, 566, 758,
    889–90
Leyland Trucks 324
Lidl 823, 861
Life Stage vitamins 358
London International Group 481
L'Oréal cosmetics 204, 205, 426
Lufthansa 421, 586–7
LVMH 360

McCann-Erickson 506
McClan whisky 722
McDonald's Corporation 16–17, 195, 438,
    557, 558, 666, 687–8, 704, 888–9
  Charities 157
  franchising 189, 826
McGraw-Hill 706
Makro 823, 868–9, 901–3
Mapanza Breweries 611–15
Marks & Spencer 16, 78, 448, 570–1,
    603–4, 666, 752, 819, 821, 888
Marlboro 427
Marriott hotels 16, 453, 483, 567–8
Mars 119, 123, 124, 125, 381, 485
  Twix 430, 431
Martini 383, 386
Mary Kay Cosmetics 216, 274
Master Foods Austria 462–4
Matchbox toys 572
Matsushita 814
Max Factor 204–6
Mazda cars 191, 423, 632–3
MCI 190
Mercedes-Benz 89–91, 171, 372, 422–3,
    456–7, 499, 503, 557, 558
  and Swatch 543
Merck 816
Mercury, One-2-One 654–5
Michelin Tyre Company 82, 310, 483, 692
Microsoft 94, 491
Miller Brewing company 568

Milliken & Co. 407, 474
Minolta 197–8, 490
Mitsui & Company 261–4
Morgan (J.P.) 452
Motorola 458, 459, 474–5, 552–3
MTV 23, 25, 695

Nabisco 103
National Cash Register Company 196
NBC 558
Nestlé 65–7, 71, 87, 167, 194, 364–5, 368,
    485, 486, 564, 565, 566, 735, 820
    Gold Blend 290–1, 415
    Rowntree 115–26, 430, 431, 557
Netto 623, 861, 863
Nielsen 213, 219, 221, 237
Nike 415
Nintendo 402–3
Nissan cars 174, 191, 423, 499, 666
Nokia 105
Nordström 16
NutraSweet 549
Nutricia 139

Odakyu Department Store 859, 860
Office World 212, 667
Online, America 884
Orange cellular phones 654–5
Oshkosh Truck 386
Oxfam 369

P&O 360, 676–80
Paradiset 758, 759
Paramount Communications 86
Pargasa 357
Parker Pen Company 576, 631, 733
PCjr computer 512
Penn Racquet Sports 579
PepsiCo 10, 24, 181, 198, 320, 505–6,
    558, 565
    Taco Bell 666
Persil/Omo Power 42, 94, 129–33, 138,
    427, 527
Peugeot 191
Pfizer 816
Philip Morris 85, 87, 558, 559, 564, 565
Philips 27, 94, 151, 195, 357, 530, 558
    HOMESTEAD 523
    JIT production 325
    Laservision 425
Pieta chocolates 907–9
Pillsbury cake mix 518
Plantsbrook Group 595
Polaroid 169, 366
Polo mints 383
Porsche 267–9, 386–7, 423, 499, 558
Post-it notes 517
Procter & Gamble 16, 102, 103, 169,
    351–3, 451, 472, 488, 558, 559, 565
    cosmetics 203–7
    Pampers Phases 527–8
    product mix width 578–9
    and Unilever 129–33, 138
Procter & Gamble Europe 746

Prodigy 884
Protec-Data 217
Proton cars 648–53
Prudential Corporation 59

Qantas 208–10
Quaker Oats 87, 565

Rank Xerox *see* Xerox
RCA 27
Ready Brek 714–15
Reckitt & Coleman 56
Recycled Paper Products 386
Red Bull energy drink 414–15
Renault 51, 355
Revlon 204–6, 544–5, 546
Richardson Sheffield 53
Richer Sounds 442
Roberts radios 625–8
Rolex 415, 424
Rolls-Royce 94, 95, 423, 502, 503, 558
Rover Group 49, 168, 191, 422, 840
    and Honda 499–500, 501–2
    segmentation 360
Royal Dutch Shell 381
Royal Mail International 879
RSPCA 696
RTZ 381
Rubbermaid 435–7
Ryder trucks 314

Saab 95, 372, 422, 423
Saatchi & Saatchi 285
Saga Holidays 359
Sainsbury (J.) 564, 565, 566, 567, 623,
    863, 864
St Ivel Gold 717, 718
Sapona Foam Cleaners 43
Scholl 169
Sears Roebuck 54, 482–3
Seiko 95, 558
Shearson-Lehman Hutton 666
Shell Chemical company 772, 819
Shuttle, Le 677–9
Siemens 76, 77, 94
Signode Corporation 371
Sinclair C5 512
Singapore Airlines 75, 458, 722
Skoda 49, 324
SMH group 415
SmithKline Beecham 583–4, 816
Snapple 271
Solid State Logic 169
Sony 74, 76, 557, 558, 577, 819, 820
    MiniDisc 299–300
Spillers Foods 527, 528
SRI market research 752
Stanley hinges 630
Steelcase 424
Stena Sealink 676–80
Storehouse Group 685–6
Sun Alliance International 772–3
Sunkist 752
Superdrug 823

Swatch 368, 541–3

Tango drink 696
Teknek Electronics 169
Tesco 138, 623, 863, 864
Texas Instruments 14, 458
3D Systems Inc. 521
3M 74, 75, 105, 516–17
Tibigarden 609
TimeOut snack 429–34
*Times, The* 619–21
TNT courier service 407, 465–8
Tower Records 855
Toyota cars 16–17, 174, 191, 358, 422,
    423, 441, 499, 558, 821–2
    innovation 515
    JIT production 325
Toys 'R' Us 24, 26, 572, 666, 819, 855,
    865, 866
Trap-Ease 112–13
Trois Suisses 880–1, 886
Troll (JFP) 335–43
Trout & Ries 585
Tupperware 271, 887
Tussaud's group 607
Twix 430, 431
Tylenol 19, 584, 750

Uncle Ben's Rice 462–4
Unilever 10, 103, 192, 204, 368, 472, 488,
    558, 559, 565, 579, 704, 735
    Elida Gibbs 103–4
    Impulse 144
    Persil/Omo Power 42, 94, 129–33, 138,
        427, 527
    Walls 94, 485
Union Carbide 59
United Distillers 424
UPS 465–8

Van Den Bergh 420, 421, 565, 717, 718
Virgin 715
    Airlines 76, 490, 596
    Megastores 176, 866, 867
Vodaphone 654–5
Volkswagen 49, 51, 181, 314, 360, 558
    performance quality 456–7
    Skoda 324, 419
Volvo 27, 83, 95, 372, 423, 424, 499, 692,
    752, 818
Vosper Thornycroft 332

Wal-Mart 865
Walkers crisps 705
Warner Bros 814
Weightwatchers, Heinz 451
Whirlpool 442, 826, 841
Williams (J.D.) 493
Wonderbra 411–12

Xerox 106, 182, 321, 449, 458, 481

Young and Rubicam 364, 696
Yves Rocher 192, 746

# Name index

Aaker, David A. 111, 459, 498, 582
Abel, Peter 907–9
Abraham, Magid M. 756
Abrahams, Paul 64, 503, 585
Adler, Lee 844
Adlwarth, W. 162
Adonis, Andrew 905
Ahmed, Shami 758
Ajzen, Icek 303
Albrecht, Karl 30, 304, 306
Alden, Dana L. 249
Alden, Vernon R. 169
Aldersey-Williams, Hugh 582
Alderson, Matti 697
Alenroth, Pontus 711–13
Alexander, Jack 582
Alexander, Ralph 328
Alreck, Pamela L. 304
Alsem, Karel Jan 250
Alsop, Ronald 285
Altman, Wilf 867
Andersen, Arthur 907
Anderson, Erin 335
Anderson, James C. 334, 455, 845
Ansoff, H. Igor 111
Applebaum, Ullrich 756
Armistead, Colin 604
Armstrong, Larry 202, 633
Arnold, Stephen J. 303
Arthur, Iain 746, 747
Artzt, Edwin L. 130, 203–5, 206
Assael, Henry 289, 303
Atkins, Ralph 302, 675
Attir, Mustafa O. 249
Authers, John 41

Baker, Michael J. 29, 335, 844
Baldwin, Mike 429
Ballen, Kate 274
Band, William 461
Barbey, Peter 604

Barents, Brian 307
Barley, Peter 444
Barnett, F. William 250
Barnevik, Percy 200
Barol, Bill 162
Baron, Steve 379
Barr, Andy 509–10
Barth, Andreas 313
Bartimo, Jim 249
Barwise, T. P. 582
Batchelor, Charles 680
Bateson, John E. G. 606
Bauer, Raymond A. 303
Baxter, Andrew 647, 844
Beard, Christel 249
Beard, Mike 786
Bearden, William O. 275, 302
Beatty, Sharon E. 303
Beauchamp, Marc 110
Beck, Melinder 162
Beckham, J. Daniel 462
Belk, Russel W. 303
Bells, Paul 788
Bencin, Richard L. 906
Bennett, Margaret 403
Bennett, Peter D. 582, 710
Berelson, B. 711
Berger, Paul D. 906
Berman, Gary L. 302
Berrigan, John 370, 389
Berry, Jessica 459
Berry, Jonathan 675
Berry, Leonard L. 461, 606, 607
Berry, Richard 906
Bertrand, Kate 313, 389, 462
Bettman, James R. 302
Betts, Paul 334
Bhide, Amar 111
Bhoyrul, Anil 428, 675, 787
Bich, Marcel 305
Bidlake, Suzanne 905

Biong, Harald 461
Bishop, William S. 334
Björnström, Robert 711–13
Black, Conrad 620–1
Blackthorn, M. 285
Blackwell, David 498, 540, 667
Blackwell, Roger D. 302
Blanco, Roberto Alvarez del 845–52
Bloemer, José M. M. 249, 361
Bloom, Paul N. 64
Bock, Dieter 307
Boggis, David 334
Boland, Vincent 844
Bolgar, Andrew 335
Bolger, Andrew 428
Bonoma, Thomas V. 334, 335, 370, 389, 757
Boorstin, Daniel J. 420
Boström, Gert-Olof 389
Bounce, Christina 493
Bounds, Gregory 475
Boustani, Pari 303
Bowersox, Donald J. 845
Boyle, RoseMarie 17
Bragg, Arthur 10
Branch, Ben 498
Brandt, Richard 313, 403
Brandt, Willy 185
Branson, Clive 680, 867, 906, 907
Branson, Richard 76, 490, 496, 715
Brauhn, Joanna 499–503
Bredbury, Ole 609
Bremner, Brian 87, 162
Brierley, Sean 64, 161, 585, 747
Brierty, Edward G. 335
Britten, Samuel 673
Broman, Gunnar 711–12
Brown, Andrew 67, 498
Brown, Glen M. 757
Brown, James R. 334
Brown, Malcolm 335, 497, 906

Brown, Stephen 907
Brown, William P. 756
Bruce, Margaret 582
Buckley, J. Taylor 906
Buckley, Neil 30, 642, 647, 667, 673, 867, 907
Buderi, Robert 162
Buell, Barbara 107
Buetow, Richard 474
Bullen, Terry 389
Burdick, Richard K. 335
Burhenne, Wim 379
Burnett, John 756
Burns, Tom 680
Burns, Toni 609
Burnside, A. 906
Burrows, Peter 772–3
Burt, Tim 498, 647
Bussey, John 531
Butler, Chris 77, 680
Butter, David 679, 746
Button, Kate 217, 249
Buzzell, Robert D. 428, 462, 498, 756

Calonius, Erik 461, 497
Caminiti, Susan 907
Camp, Robert C. 475
Campanelli, Melissa 302
Cane, Alan 313, 675
Capon, Claire H. 582
Capp, Clive 458
Carnegie, Dale 777
Carstedt, Goran 855, 856
Carter, Meg 428
Caruso, Thomas E. 30, 461
Casey, Don 558–9
Cassino, Kip D. 250
Cateora, Philip R. 582, 675, 756, 757, 845
Cavanagh, Richard E. 498
Center, Allen H. 757
Cespedes, Frank V. 788
Chajet, Clive 584, 585
Chandran, Rajan 111, 498
Channon, Charles 388, 389
Charlton, John 58
Cheeseright, Paul 461
Cheong, Celine 461
Chirac, Jacques 607, 608
Chonko, Lawrence B. 65
Christiansen, Mike 537
Christie, Alix 331
Christopher, Martin 844, 845
Chu, Weyien 335
Churchill, David 250, 595
Churchill, Gilbert A., Jr. 249
Clancy, Kevin J. 540
Clark, Graham 604
Clark, Terry 607
Clemons, Erik K. 325
Clifford, Donald K. 498
Clutterbuck, David 217, 604
Coad, Tony 906
Cohen, Dorothy 582
Cohen, Joel B. 303

Cohen, Norma 41
Cohen, William A. 470
Coleman, Lynn G. 249, 906
Coleman, Richard P. 302
Coleman, Terry 240
Colley, Russell H. 756
Conway, Isabel 249
Cook, Jack 302
Cook, Victor J. 368
Cooke, Kieren 64
Cookson, Clive 498, 585
Coombes, Peter 385
Cooper, Arnold C. 498
Cooper, Neville 58
Cooper, Robert G. 540
Cordon, Carlos 325
Corstjens, Judith 724, 756
Corstjens, Marcel 756, 816
Cosier, Richard A. 65
Cosgrave, Bronwyn 429, 867
Cote, Kevin 30
Cowe, Roger 647
Cowles, Deborah, 334, 455
Cox, Donald F. 303
Cox, Jonathan M. 757
Craig, C. Samuel 187
Cramer, Stuart 302
Crawford, C. Merle 540
Crispell, Diane 162, 249
Cronin, Joseph, Jr. 607
Crosby, Lawrence A. 334, 455
Crosby, Philip 459
Cross, James 328
Culf, Andrew 647
Cullen, Brenda 250–9
Cundiff, Edward W. 302
Cunningham, Sarah 697
Cunningham, William and Isabella 756
Curry, David J. 302
Curtindale, Frieda 388
Cutler, Blayne 202
Cutlip, Scott M. 757
Czinkota, Michael R. 541, 607, 756

Dalgleish, Julie Gordon 29
Dalton, Dan R. 65
d'Andre, Emmanuel 880
Daniels, Kevin 497
David, Fred R. 111
Davidow, William H. 30, 582, 606
Davies, Hunter 759
Davies, Simon 503
Davis, Riccardo A. 385
Dawkins, William 867
Day, George S. 428, 498, 541
Day, Graham 500–1
de Chertony, Leslie 497
de Combray, Natalie 162
DeGeorge, Gail 162, 429
De Groot, G. 285
de Jonquières, Guy 111, 162, 203, 567, 867, 905, 906
de la Billiere, General Sir Peter 335
Dembkowski, Sabine 162

de Mooij, Marieke 281, 303, 388, 756
Deming, W. Edwards 458, 551
Dempsey, Judy 302
DeNitto, Emily 905
de Raad, Geert 459
Desanick, Robert L. 30
Deshpande, Rohit 111, 250
Deutschman, Alan 313
Deveny, Kathleen 207, 483, 559
Dewar, Robert 111
Diamantopoulos A. 647
Diamond, S. J. 582
Dichter, Ernest 302
Dickens, Martin 498
Dickson, Martin 517
Dickson, Tim 58
Diller, Barry 883
Dolley, Margaret 202
Donaldson, David 765–6
Donaton, Scott 906
Done, David 428
Done, Kevin 25, 203, 334, 543, 844
Donnelly, James H., Jr. 461
Doppelfeld, Volker 502
Douglas, Susan P. 187
Douglas, Torin 906
Doyle, Peter 64, 169, 203, 379, 413, 429, 756
Doyle, Stephen X. 788
Doz, Y. 653
Doz, Yves L. 844
Dreker, Angelika 382, 389
Dreyfack, Kenneth 162
Drucker, Peter 6, 22, 29, 72, 439
Dumaine, Brian 111, 217, 540, 647
Duncan, Tom 757
Dunn, R. 756
Dwyer, R. F. 845

Ebert, Ronald J. 65
Eccles, Terry 753
Eckstein, Alissa 757
Edwards, Michael 500
Egan, Colin 179, 261–4, 844
Ehrenberg, Andrew S. S. 389
Ehrengart, Bernd D. 800
Eiglier, Pierre 606
Eisenhammer, John 302
Ejiri, Koichiro 261
El-Ansary, Adel 844
Elliott, Jeremy 389
Emerson, Ralph Waldo 29, 111
Endicott, R. Craig 559
Engardio, Pete 582
Engel, Ernst 145
Engel, James F. 302
English, J. 363
Enis, Ben M. 316, 582
Eppright, David R. 710
Erickson, Gary M. 675
Eriksson, Joakim 711–13
Erramilli, M. K. 202
Erzel, Michael J. 275
Esiner, Michael 607, 608

Etzel, Michael 64, 302
Evans, Gary 906
Evans, Kenneth R. 334, 455
Evans, Philip 461
Evans, Richard 501
Everett, Martin 906
Evers, Myrlie 37
Exter, Thomas 162, 389

Fahey, Liam 169
Fallon, Ivan 647
Fannin, Rebecca 403, 633
Farber, Barry J. 334, 455, 582, 788
Faris, Charles W. 326, 335
Farmer, Richard N. 30
Farquhar, Peter H. 582
Farrell, Christopher 647
Farris, Paul W. 757
Fazey, Ian Hamilton 64
Feinstein, Selwyn 249
Feldman, Laurence P. 541
Feliu de la Peña, Miguel Tey 335–43
Fenwick, Ian 379
Fern, Edward F. 334
Ferrer, José 846, 847, 850
Festinger, Leon 304
Field, Nora E. 607
Field, Peter 388
Fine, Niame 217
Finkbeiner, Carl 370, 389
Fischer, Gus 619
Fishbein, Martin 303
Fisher, Anne B. 64, 162
Fisher, Christy 302
Fisher, D. 653
Fisher, Eileen 303
Fisher, George 76, 77
Fiske, John 303, 757, 759
Fitzgerald, Kate 403
Fitzgerald, Niall 130, 132, 133
Flax, Steven 217
Fletcher, Ian 680
Flint, Rod 120
Foltz, Kim 303
Ford, D. I. 845
Ford, Henry 14
Foster, Catherine 537
Fouke, Carol J. 302
Fox, Karen 29
Foxall, Gordon R. 303
Frank, Sergey 323, 784
Frankel, Carl 162
Fraser, Ian 675
Frazier, Gary L. 325
Freedman, Robert J. 788
Freeman, Laurie 388
French, Dawn 492–3
Freud, Sigmund 283
Frey, William H. 162
Friedman, Milton 28
Fry, Arthur 517
Fuld, Leonard 216, 249, 498
Futrell, Charles 30

Galbraith, J. K. 28
Gale, Bradley T. 428, 462, 498
Galen, Michele 217, 249, 498
Ganesh, G. K. 202
Gantman, Geri 906
Garfield, Charles 768
Garnett, Christopher 678, 679
Garvin, David A. 428, 459, 582
Gaski, John F. 64
Gatignon, Hubert 4
Gaudet, H. 711
Gault, Stanley 436
Gavidia, Armando 849, 850, 851
Geier, Phili 756
Georgano, Nick 423
Georgoff, David M. 250
Gerstner, Lou 313
Geyer, Hans 313
Ghemawat, Pankaj 498
Gibson, Marcus 498
Gillett, Charles 240
Gilligan, C. 756
Ginn, Steve 772
Giscard D'Estain, Olivier 58
Glancey, Jonathan 543
Glazer, Rashi 249
Glenn, Norval D. 64
Gluckman, Robert L. 303
Goading, Kenneth 111
Goests, William 903
Goldman, Debra 302
Goodfellow, Matthew 788
Gooding, Claire 788
Gooding, Kenneth 503
Gooskens, Roel 186
Gopalakrishna, Pradeep 756
Gouillart, Francis J. 627
Gourlay, Richard 325, 498
Graham, John L. 334
Graham, Robert 475, 498
Gray, Daniel H. 111
Green, Daniel 498
Green, Howard L. 907
Green, Nigel 493
Green, Robert T. 756
Greenbaum, Thomas L. 249
Greyser, Stephen A. 64
Griffin, John 475
Griffin, Michael 498
Griffin, Ricky E. 65
Griffith, Victoria 249
Griffiths, John 428, 503, 653
Gronroos, Christian 607
Grossman, Laurie M. 905
Grunewald, Joachim 183
Gubbins, E. J. 845
Guelzo, Carl M. 839
Gwynne, S. C. 633

Haahti, A. 429
Hagedorn, Homer F. 531
Hager, Bruce 217
Hahn, Carl 191
Haines, Daniel W. 111, 498

Haley, Russell J. 366
Halliburton, Chris 179, 756
Halstead, Richard 845, 867
Hamel, Gary 844
Hamermesh, Richard G. 111
Han, Julia Y. 582
Hanchler, Ingomar 183
Hancock, Jane 64
Hancox, P. 845
Hanmer-Lloyd, Stuart 162
Hanna, Sherman 277
Harbrecht, Douglas A. 64
Harding, Ian 335, 498, 906
Harper, Marion, Jr. 249
Hart, Christopher W. L. 607
Hart, Norman 413, 429
Harte, Susan 323
Hartley, Robert F. 67
Hartmann-Olesen, Anton 797–801
Harveson, Patrick 77
Harvey, Donald F. 107
Hastings, Phillip 497, 845
Hawkins, Chuck 334, 497
Hawkins, Del I. 223, 250
Hayek, Nicolas 541–3
Haywood, K. Michael 711
Head, Robert G. 788
Heilbrunn, Benoit 429–34
Helgadottir, Birna 429
Helgesson, Thomas 711–13, 757–9
Hemnes, Thomas M. S. 582
Henkoff, Ronald 162
Hernant, Mikael 249
Herndon, Neil 867
Herther, Karen 711
Heskett, James L. 111, 607
Higgins, Kevin T. 111, 541
Higham, Nick 756
Higler, Marye Tharp 302
Higson, C. J. 582
Hill, Julie Skur 30
Hill, Richard 328
Hilton, Andrew 179, 202
Hirshman, Elizabeth 303
Hitchins, R. E. 389
Hite, Robert 757
Hodgson, Howard 594–5
Hof, Robert D. 107, 313
Hofstede, Geert 303
Hola, Alena 906
Holberton, Simon 248, 303, 459, 461
Holbrook, Morris 303
Holden, Reed K. 643, 647, 675
Hollander, S. C. 907
Hollinger, Peggy 249
Holmes, M. 285
Holstein, William J. 203
Homer, Pamela 303
Homma, Norbert 281
Hong-Chun Tong 784
Hooley, Graham 111, 203, 302, 388, 413, 419, 428, 429, 498
Hopfenbeck, W. 65
Hornik, Jacob 249

Horton, Cleveland 302, 388
Houlder, Vanessa 459
Howard, Daniel J. 711
Howard, John A. 302, 303
Howard, Martin 389
Howard, R. 203
Hout, Thomas M. 429
Huey, John 162
Hughes, James W. 162
Hughes, Penny 334
Huldén, Eivor 498
Hume, Scott 17, 757
Hunerberg, Reinhard 179
Hunt, James B. 710
Hunt, Liz 540
Hunt, Shelby D. 65, 845
Huntington, Paul A. 647
Hyatt, Joshua 110

Iacocca, Lee 558
Ijiri, Yuji 582

Jack, Andrew 30
Jacknis, Marty 845
Jackson, Barbara Bund 455
Jackson, Donald W., Jr. 335
Jackson, Tony 161, 498, 647
Jacob, Rahul 202
Jacobs, Timothy 423
Jacobson, Robert 459, 498, 582
Jacquet, Susan 429
Jain, Subhash C. 246, 306, 389, 845
James, Barrie 903
Janes, Robert 757
Jatusripitak, Somkid 169
Jobber, David 249
Johansson, Johnny K. 675
John, Sara 814, 815
Johne, Axel 540
Johnson, Gerry 497
Johnson, Richard D. 461
Jolibert, Alain J. P. 249
Jones, Helen 161
Jones, John Philip 757
Jones, Mark 403
Jones, Michael H. 334
Juhl, Hans Jorn 647

Kabeta, Hapenga M. 611–15
Kahle, Lynn R. 303
Kaku, Ryuzaburo 58
Kamprad, Ingvar 854
Kanemaru, Shin 331
Kanuk, Leslie Lazar 302, 304, 388, 389, 710, 711
Kapferer, Jean-Noel 582, 756
Kardes, Frank R. 711
Karlsson, Sune 73
Kashani, Kamran 203
Ka-shing, Li 655
Kasper, Hans 249
Kassarjian, Harold H. 303
Kate, Nancy Ten 302
Kauper-Petschnika, Ingrid 463

Kawamoto, Kiyoshi 502
Kawamoto, Nobuhiko 502
Keegan, Warren 187, 202, 203
Keeler, Dan 497
Kefer, Peter 347
Kehoe, Louise 313, 815, 906
Keith, Janet E. 335
Keller, Kevin Lane 582
Kelley, Bill 667, 788, 906
Kelly, Alistair 458
Kelly, Kevin 517
Kennedy, John F. 49
Kerin, Roger A. 111
Kern, Richard 788
Kessler, David 33–4
Kiechel, Walter 87
Kim, Junu Bryan 906
Kinnear, Thomas C. 303
Kirk, Margaret O. 537
Kirkpatrick, David 647
Kistemaker, Cor 379
Kitasei, Hilary Hinds 860
Kivenko, Kenneth 462
Kleinschmidt, Elko J. 540
Klienman, Philip 249
Koeppel, Dan 585
Kohli, Ajay 335
Konrad, Walecia 162
Koren, Leonard 236
Kornakovich, Ron J. 334
Kotabe, Masaaki 541
Kotler, Philip 29, 250, 428, 461, 498, 541, 582, 756
Kotter, John P. 111
Kraar, Louis 203
Kratz, Steve 845
Kristenson, Kai 647
Kroc, Ray 16, 157
Kroesing, Bill 849
Kunkel, Paul 531
Kupfer, Andrew 203
Kurland, Mark A. 497

Laaksonen, Haari 567
Laforet, Sylvie 67, 115–26
Laker, Freddie 49, 490
Lambert, Alan 866
Lander, Nicholas 493
Landler, Mark 303, 429
Lane, Ronald 757
Langeard, Eric 606
Langford, Brian 679
Lanning, Michael J. 461
Lannon, Judie 756
Lapper, Richard 461
Laslett, Peter 142
Lauterborn, Robert 111
Lawrence, Jennifer 162, 207, 541
Lawson, R. 757
Lawton, Leigh 540
Lax, Jonathan 217
Lazarsfeld, P. F. 711
Leader, Charles 475
Lee, John Y. 647

Leeflang, Peter S. H. 250
Lefkowith, Edwin F. 607
Lehmann, Donald R. 335
Lemmink, Jos G. A. M. 249, 461
Lepisto, Lawrence 303
Lev, Michael 756
Leverick, Fiona 498
Levin, Gary 162, 756, 906
Levin, Irwin P. 461
Levitt, Theodore 29, 39, 64, 428, 546, 606
Levy, Sidney J. 285
Lewin, Tony 503
Lewis, Janny 582
Lewis, Jordan D. 30
Lewis, Tony 543
Lie, Leiv Gunner 429
Liesse, Julie 582
Light, Larry 207
Lighton, Nick 474
Likierman, J. A. 582
Lilien, Gary A. 756
Lilien, Gary L. 250
Lin, Lynn Y. S. 250
Lindeberg, Johan 758–9
Lindemann, Michael 64, 673
Linden, Fabian 162
Lipman, Joanne 582, 585
Little, John D. C. 756
Littler, Dale 498
Locander, William 475
Lodish, Leonard M. 756
Lopez de Arriotua, José Ignacio 217
Lorange, Peter 30
Lord, Rob 814
Lorenz, Andrew 503, 567
Lorenz, Christopher 87, 459, 582, 843
Loro, Laura 905, 906
Lovelock, Christopher H. 606
Lövgren, Arne 713
Lowe, Joe 285
Luchs, Bob 456, 462
Luderitz, Hagan 502
Lynch, Richard 648–53
Lynn, Matthew 503
Lyons, J. 757
Lysonski, Steven 675

McBurnie, Tony 217
McCarthy, E. Jerome 111
McCarthy, Michael J. 250
McCarthy, Terry 331
McConnell, Sara 302
McDonald, Hamish 248
McDonald, Richard and Maurice 16
MacDonald, Malcolm 110
Macdonald, Sandy 594
McFarlan, F. Warren 325
McIvor, Greg 111, 713
McKiernan, Peter 179, 261–4
McKnight, Gail 17
McLaughlin, Laurie 906
McLoughlin, Damien 429–34
McNair, Malcolm P. 907
McNeal, James U. 162

McWilliams, Gary 107
Mackay, Harvey B. 788
Mackenzie, Dorothy 64
Madigan, Kathleen 675
Magdalinos, Alkis S. 30–2, 162–4
Magiera, Marcy 110
Maglitta, Joseph 497
Magnet, Myron 64
Magnusson, Paul 202
Magrath, Allan J. 844
Mahajan, Vijay 111, 389
Maier, Jens 389
Main, Jeremy 217, 475, 541
Maital, Shlomo 497, 845
Makamoto, Michiyo 647
Mallet, Victor 10
Mallory, Maria 461
Mandese, Joe 10
Manoochehri, G. H. 325
Marchart, Horst 269
Maremont, Mark 202, 302, 389
Margry, Jacques 576
Marks, Reuben 584, 585
Marsh, Peter 41, 498, 582
Marshall, Cristy 461
Martin, Dennis 756
Masia, Ramon 847, 849
Maslow, Abraham 283–4, 286, 303
Massey, Anne 906
Mathews, Brian P. 647
Matthews, Virginia 493
May, Eleanor G. 907
May, Tony 647
Mayerhof, Helmut 805, 806
Mazur, Laura 302
Mead, Gary 582, 697
Meagher, James P. 385
Melcher, Richard A. 179
Menasco, Michael B. 302
Merriman, Walker 34
Mersh, Cath 249
Michie, D. A. 845
Miles, Louella 249, 697, 705, 753, 906
Miller, Annetta 162, 285, 303
Miller, Cyndee 10, 179, 202, 203
Miller, Peter 503
Milliken, John 474
Mills, John 40
Mindak, William A. 368
Miniard, Paul W. 302, 303
Miracle, Gordon 756
Mitchel, F. Kent 757
Mitchell, Alan 65, 667
Mitchell, Arnold 303
Mitchell, Russel 517, 541
Mitchell, V. W. 303
Miyazawa, Kiichi 331
Moberg, Anders 855
Mole, John 203
Monaghan, Thomas 76
Moncrief, William C., III 788
Monroe, Kent B. 675
Moore, Chris 18
Moore, Thomas 87

Moore, Timothy 303
Moore, William L. 541
Moorman, Christine 250
Moorthy, K. Sridhar 250
Morgan, Adam 388
Morgan, Bradford W. 667
Morgan, Fred W. 582
Morgan, J. C. and J. J. 784
Moriarty, Rowland T. 389, 788
Moriarty, Sandra 756
Morita, Akio 76
Morris, Eugene 302
Morrison, Bradley G. 29
Morrow, David J. 582
Moser, Penny 17
Moutinho, Luiz 250
Moynagh, Patrick 379
Much, Marilyn 207
Mulbacher, Hans 382, 389
Mulcahey, Mark 363
Murdick, Robert G. 250
Murdoch, Rupert 619, 620
Murphy, Claire 498, 567, 680, 697
Murphy, Patrick E. 277, 582
Murray, Keith B. 303

Nader, Ralph 48, 50, 64, 153
Nagle, Thomas P. 643, 647, 675
Nakamoto, Michiyo 169, 325, 423
Narus, James A. 334, 455, 845
Narver, John C. 111, 498
Nash, Laura 111
Nathan, Stephen 595
Neff, Robert 30
Neisbitt, John 211, 249
Nestlé, Henri 65, 66
Neuborne, Ellen 537
Newcombe, J. R. 203
Nicholson-Lord, David 162, 302, 906
Nicosia, Francesco M. 302
Nilsson, Malin 757–9
Nonaka, Ikujiro 531
Norgan, Susan 65, 756
Nulty, Peter 385
Nunn, Peter 423
Nycander, Curt 712
Nyström, Margareta 713

O'Donnell, Peter 155, 903
Oehme, Wulf 271
Oetting, Rudy 906
O'Halloran, David 475
Ohmae, Kenichi 203
Oliver, Joyce Anne 517
O'Neal, Charles R. 325
Oneal, Michael 203
Onkvist, Sak 541
Oram, Roderick 161, 680
O'Reilly, Brian 162
O'Reilly, Tony 620
O'Shaughnessy, John 335
Oster, Patrick 30
Osterhoff, Robert 475
O'Sullivan, Tim 567

O'Sullivan, Tom 45, 64, 161
Packshaw, Helen 685
Page, Albert L. 541
Paley, Norton 647
Parasuraman A. 461, 540, 607
Parés, Franscesc 335–43
Park, C. Whan 582
Park, Sung 889–90
Parkes, Christopher 111, 503
Parkhe, Arvind 111, 498
Parry, John 543, 675
Patey, Tony 77, 248, 606
Patty, C. Robert 757
Patterson, Jeff 814
Peattie, K. 65
Pechmann, Cornelia 711
Perelman, Ronald 204
Perry, Sir Michael 132
Persson, Per-Göran 249
Peston, Robert 334
Peters, Thomas J. 105, 106, 107, 111, 428,
    454, 885, 906
Peterson, Don 474
Peterson, Robert A. 249
Petro, Thomas M. 461
Pfeffer, Eckhard 313
Philips, Frederik 58
Phillips, Dianne 379
Phillips, Lynn W. 461
Piercy, Nigel F. 111
Pierson, Jean 760
Pieters, Rik 302
Piirto, Rebecca 285, 303, 906
Pile, Stephen 240
Pirate, Rebecca 249
Pläcking, Jocken 388
Platform, Richard 903
Plummer, Joseph T. 278, 303
Port, Otis 498, 541, 582
Porter, Michael E. 75, 78, 111, 389, 428,
    445–7, 461, 478, 497, 498
Potter, Stephen 582
Power, Christopher 162
Prahalad, C. D. 844
Price, Kevin 582
Priemer, Verena M. 345–7, 462–4
Pringle, Ian 400
Proctor, Paul 248

Quelch, John A. 757

Raia, Ernest 325, 553
Rajaratnam, Daniel 844
Rajendran, K. N. 675
Rambert, Yves 87
Randall, Julie 363
Rangan, V. Kasturi 389, 461
Rao, C. P. 202
Rapaport, Jeff 845–52
Rapoport, Carla 202
Rath, Gustav 29
Rawsthorn, Alice 388, 429, 609, 815, 906
Ray, N. M. 845
Read, Geoff 250

Read, Julie 331, 680
Reed, David 444, 475
Reeder, Betty H. 335
Reeder, Robert R. 335
Reese, Jennifer 541
Reeves, Rosser 421
Reichard, Clifton J. 335
Reicheld, Redrick F. 461
Reichheld, F. F. 389
Reinstein, F. 784
Reinstine, F. 203
Reitman, Valerie 207, 461
Reitzle, Wolfgang 402
Renart, Lluis G. 335–43
Ress, William 907
Reuyl, Jan C. 250
Reynolds, J. 30
Rice, Faye 64, 667, 756
Rich, Motoka 673
Riche, Martha Farnsworth 279
Ricks, David A. 185
Ridding, John 497, 609
Ries, Al 410–12, 429, 497, 582, 585
Rijkens, Rein 389, 756
Rink, David R. 541
Risdale, Peter 883
Ritter, Angelika 382, 389
Roach, John D. C. 498
Roach, Stephen S. 607
Roberto, Eduardo 29
Roberts, Mary Lou 906
Robertson, Thomas S. 303, 304
Robey, Bryant 162
Robinson, Patrick J. 326, 335
Robinson, S. J. Q. 389
Rocasalbas, Javier 342
Roddick, Gordon 20
Rodger, Ian 844, 867
Rodkin, Dennis 302
Roel, Raymond 403
Rogers, Everett M. 298, 304
Rogers, Ian 388
Roman, Ernan 906
Ronkainen, Ilkka A. 607, 756
Roos, Johan 30
Rose, Frank 304, 459, 582
Rossant, John 179
Rossen, P. 845
Rossman, Marlene L. 389
Rosso, Renzo 758, 759
Rotfeder, Jeffrey 249
Roth, Kendall 203
Rothery, Brian 179
Rothman, Andrea 788
Rothschild, Michael L. 711, 756
Roush, Gary B. 249
Rowell, Roland 64, 203
Rowland, Tiny 307
Roy, Robin 582
Rozen, Miriam 110
Rubython, Tom 675
Rudd, Roland 334
Ruddock, Allan 647
Ruekert, Robert W. 111

Russell, Cheryl 162
Russell, J. Thomas 757

Sakala, Samson 613–14
Sakkab, Nabil 129, 130
Salmon, Walter J. 907
Saminee, Saeed 203
Sammon, William L. 497
Sampson, Peter 285
Samualson, Robert J. 64
Saporito, Bill 30, 675, 905, 907
Sarda, Javier 335–43
Sasser, W. Earl, Jr. 461, 607
Saunders, John 111, 249, 388, 389, 428, 498
Sawyer, Alan G. 711
Schiffman, Leon G. 302, 304, 388, 389, 710, 711
Schiller, Zachary 207, 249, 461, 541, 675
Schisano, Roberto 475
Schlender, Brenton R. 110
Schlesinger, Leonard A. 607
Schlossberg, Howard 30, 169, 249, 498, 541
Schnebelt, Derrick C. 788
Schultz, Don 111
Schultz, Donald E. 756
Schuster, R. 64
Schutz, Peter 302
Schwartz, David A. 541
Schwartz, David J. 647
Schwartz, Evan J. 906
Schwartz, Joe 162, 389
Schwartzkopf, General H. Norman 335
Schweitzer, Louis 458
Scott, Tony 541
Sease, Douglas R. 531
Seligman, Daniel 711
Sellers, Patricia 162, 788
Selnes, Fred 461
Sequeira, Ian K. 757
Settle, Robert B. 304
Settler, Ulrich 342
Sewell, Charles 30
Shao, Maria 110, 203, 302
Shapiro, Benson P. 370, 389, 461
Sharkey, Betsy 388
Shaw, John J. 541
Shaw, Vivienne 203
Shawchuck, Norman 29
Sheffet, Mary Jane 303
Sherman, Stratford 667
Sheth, Jagdish N. 111, 302, 303
Shipley, D. 845
Short, David 64, 161, 162, 388, 429, 711, 756, 906
Shulman, Laurence E. 461
Shulman, Robert S. 540
Sibley, S. D. 845
Sidhva, Shiraz 428
Silver, Spencer 517
Simon, Bernard 334
Simonian, Haig 697
Simpson, Alan 809–10

Simpson, George 438
Sinclair, Upton 49
Sirgy, M. Joseph 303
Sjostrom, Anki 757–9
Skapinher, Mickael 609
Skapinker, Michael 388
Slater, Stanley F. 111, 498
Slingsby, Helen 249, 567, 647
Sloan, Pat 110, 162, 207, 582
Smit, Barbara 139, 161, 203
Smith, Adam 440
Smith, Alison 41
Smith, Andreas Whittam 647
Smith, Daniel C. 582
Smith, Fred 468
Smith, Lee 607
Smith, Randall 207
Smith, Whittam 620
Snelson, Patrician 540
Snoddy, Raymond 647
Snook, Hans 655
Snowden, Ros 403, 429
Soldow, Gary F. 497
Solo, Sally 444
Sookdeo, Ricardo 607
Southey, Caroline 595
Spaeth, Anthony 181
Sparks, John 67
Speed, Richard 498
Speer, Tibbett L. 302
Spekman, R. E. 325
Spendolini, Michael J. 475
Spethman, Betsey 111
Spillius, Alex 906
Spiro, Rosann L. 302
Spitalnic, Robert 497
Springett, Rod 573
Sriram, Ven 756
Stalk, George 461
Stalker, George 429
Stanton, William J. 30
Staples, William A. 277
Star, Steven H. 64
Staunton, George 236
Steele, Paul 320
Stelly, Philip, Jr. 429
Stern, Aimee L. 461
Stern, Gabriella 207
Stern, Lee 673
Stern, Louis 844
Stern, Louis W. 844
Stevens, Michael 906
Stevenson, Tom 303
Stipp, Horst H. 162
Stocker, Ernst 806
Stokes, Donald 500
Strang, Roger A. 757
Strauss, Gary 540, 667
Strazewski, Len 274
Street, Julie 429
Strong, Liam 248
Studemann, Frederick 183, 459
Sturdivant, Frederick D. 627, 844
Suchecki, Mark 906

Sullivan, Ruth 498
Sultan, Ralph G. M. 498
Summers, Diane 161, 335, 429, 697, 710, 771, 787
Sun, Zi 78
Sussman, Vic 274
Sutch, Peter 286
Sutton, Henry 713
Sviokla, John J. 461
Swan, John E. 541
Swartz, Gordon S. 389, 788
Swasy, Alecia 207, 582
Sweeney, Daniel 907
Swick, Eduard 183
Szathmary, Richard 757

Tabaksblat, Morris 132
Tait, Nikki 497
Takeuchi, Hirotake 531
Tanner, John F. 710
Tanzer, Andrew 236
Tatsumo, Sheridan M. 236
Taylor, Cathy 559
Taylor, James W. 498
Taylor, Robert 498
Taylor, Thayer C. 335, 788
Taylor, W. 203
Taylore, Steven A. 607
Tefft, Sheila 181
Tegnérlunden, Gustavsson 713
Tegnérlunden, Häggblom 713
Teinowitz, Ira 111
Teitalbaum, Richard S. 217
Teitzle, Wolfgang 502
Tellis, Gerard J. 675, 756
Terazono, Emiko 867
Terry, Michael 845
Thatcher, Margaret 500
Theobald, Stephanie 759
Therrien, Lois 459, 498, 553, 711, 844
Thomas, Gloria P. 497
Thomas, Hester 541
Thomas, Michael J. 388
Thomas, Robert J. 541
Thompson, Damion 67
Thompson, Thomas W. 461
Thornhill, John 905, 906, 907
Thornton, Emily 845
Thurman, Shannon 274
Ticer, Scott 334
Timmer, Jan 458
Todd, Tom 845
Tomkin, Richard 302
Tomkins, Richard 64, 444, 567, 867
Tonks, David 388
Toscani, Oliviero 697
Townsend, Bickley 388
Toy, Steward 179
Toynbee, Arnold 28
Toyne, Brian 203

Trachenberg, Jeffrey A. 207
Trapp, Raymond J. 671
Trapp, Roger 756
Treacy, Michael 461
Trout, Jack 410–12, 429, 582
Tsiantar, Dody 285, 303
Tull, Donald S. 223, 250
Tully, Shawn 179, 642, 788
Turnbull, Peter W. 335
Turner, Paul 249

Uelzhoffer, Jorg 281
Uncles, Mark 389
Upton, Bryon 53
Urry, Maggie 162
Uttal, Bro 30, 531, 582, 606
Uwemedimo, David 815

van de Krol, Ronald 161, 162
Van den Bulte, Christophe 111
van den Heuvel, R. R. 429
van Laarhoven, Peter 843
Vanhaeverbeke, Anne 752
Vann, John W. 303
van Waterschoot, Walter 111
Varadarajan, P. Rajan 111, 844
Vardiabasis, Demos 203
Vaughan, Clive 493, 869
Verchère, Ian 87, 248, 334, 497
Vidale, M. L. 720, 756
Viscusi, Gregory 675
von Hipple, Eric 541
Vriens, Marco 379
Vuursteen, Karel 186

Wachsman, David 712
Wade, D. P. 389
Wagner, Janet 277
Wald, Kurt 269
Waldhausen, Martin 51
Waldrop, Judith 162
Walker, Janina 497
Walker, Orville C., Jr. 111
Walker, Rob 449
Walleck, A. Steven 475
Waller, David 302, 747
Walsh, Vivien 582
Walters, Peter G. P. 203
Wanamaker, John 699
Waterman, Robert H. 105, 106, 107, 111
Waters, Richard 816
Weber, Joseph 203, 497, 907
Webster, Frederick E. Jr. 30, 111, 334, 335, 461
Wedel, Michel 379
Wee, Chow-Hou 461
Weinberg, Neil 423
Weir, Walter 303
Weisendanger, Betsy 475
Weitz, Barton 335

Welch, John F. Jr. 456, 667
Wells, William D. 303, 756
Welt, Leo G. B. 202
Wensley, Robin 389, 428, 498
Westlake, Michael 248
Wheatley, Malcolm 323
Wheelwright, G. 313
Whent, Gerry 654
Whinney, Peter 18
White, Joseph B. 667
White, Martin 467
Whitely, Richard C. 30
Whitman, David R. 65
Widrick, S. M. 675
Wiersema, Fred 461
Wiesendanger, Betsy 249
Wiggenhorn, William 553
Wilkinson, Endymion 236
Williams, Bridget 675
Wilson, Timothy L. 389
Wimmer, F. 162
Wind, Yoram 111, 326, 334, 335, 389
Winnington-Ingram, Rebecca 607, 608, 609
Winski, Joseph M. 162, 249, 302
Wittink, Dick R. 379
Wolfe, Alan 642
Wolfe, H. R. 720, 756
Wolpin, Stewart 403
Wong, Eugine 303
Wong, Veronica 111, 203
Wong, Wendy 678
Woo, Carolyn Y. 498
Wood, Van R. 65, 845
Wooley, Benjamin 521
Worcester, Robert 64, 285
Worthy, Ford S. 169
Wortzel, Lawrence H. 906
Wren, Bruce 29
Wroe, Martin 29
Wycoff, Joyce 334, 455, 582, 788

Yadav, Manjit S. 675
Yang, Dori Jones 203, 788
Yip, George S. 203
Young, John 443, 459
Yovovich, B. G. 553

Zaig, Tamar 249
Zaltman, Gerald 250
Zeithaml, Carl P. 162
Zeithaml, Valerie A. 162, 607
Zell, Anneli 757–9
Zellner, Wendy 217
Zemke, Ron 304, 606
Zetlin, Minda 627
Zinn, Laura 302, 907
Zotos, Yiorgos 675

# Copyright acknowledgements